BUSINESS CAREERS

Select from over 30 Web sites offering career opportunities in business and learn how to obtain information about companies that interest you.

STOCK MARKET GAME

Develop your investment skills by competing with your classmates to achieve the greatest gain in stock value.

READING ROOM

Click inside a map of the United States or the entire world to access your choice of local, national, or international business news.

International News

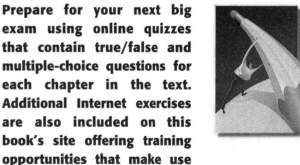

National News

ONLINE QUIZZING AND INTERNET EXERCISES

Prepare for your next big exam using online quizzes that contain true/false and multiple-choice questions for each chapter in the text. Additional Internet exercises are also included on this book's site offering training opportunities that make use of the Internet.

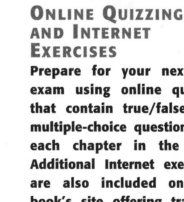

INTERNATIONAL BUSINESS

SIXTH EDITION

Harcourt College Publishers

Where Learning Comes to Life

TECHNOLOGY

Technology is changing the learning experience, by increasing the power of your textbook and other learning materials; by allowing you to access more information, more quickly; and by bringing a wider array of choices in your course and content information sources.

Harcourt College Publishers has developed the most comprehensive Web sites, e-books, and electronic learning materials on the market to help you use technology to achieve your goals.

PARTNERS IN LEARNING

Harcourt partners with other companies to make technology work for you and to supply the learning resources you want and need. More importantly, Harcourt and its partners provide avenues to help you reduce your research time of numerous information sources.

Harcourt College Publishers and its partners offer increased opportunities to enhance your learning resources and address your learning style. With quick access to chapter-specific Web sites and e-books . . . from interactive study materials to quizzing, testing, and career advice . . . Harcourt and its partners bring learning to life.

Harcourt's partnership with Digital:Convergence™ brings :CRQ™ technology and the :CueCat™ reader to you and allows Harcourt to provide you with a complete and dynamic list of resources designed to help you achieve your learning goals. You can download the free :CRQ software from www.crq.com. Visit any of the 7,100 RadioShack stores nationwide to obtain a free :CueCat reader. Just swipe the cue with the :CueCat reader to view a list of Harcourt's partners and Harcourt's print and electronic learning solutions.

http://www.harcourtcollege.com/partners

INTERNATIONAL BUSINESS

SIXTH EDITION

Michael R. Czinkota
Georgetown University

Ilkka A. Ronkainen
Georgetown University

Michael H. Moffett
The American Graduate School of International
Management (Thunderbird)

Harcourt College Publishers

Fort Worth Philadelphia San Diego New York Austin Orlando San Antonio
Toronto Montreal London Sydney Tokyo

Publisher	Mike Roche
Acquisitions Editor	Tracy Morse
Market Strategist	Beverly Dunn
Developmental Editor	Kerri Jones
Project Manager	Andrea Archer

ISBN: 0-03-033564-7
Library of Congress Catalog Card Number: 2001090570

Address for Domestic Orders
Harcourt College Publishers, 6277 Sea Harbor Drive, Orlando, FL 32887-6777
800-782-4479

Address for International Orders
International Customer Service
Harcourt, Inc., 6277 Sea Harbor Drive, Orlando, FL 32887-6777
407-345-3800
(fax) 407-345-4060
(e-mail) hbintl@harcourt.com

Address for Editorial Correspondence
Harcourt College Publishers, 301 Commerce Street, Suite 3700, Fort Worth, TX 76102

Web Site Address
http://www.harcourtcollege.com

Harcourt College Publishers will provide complimentary supplements or supplement packages to those adopters qualified under our adoption policy. Please contact your sales representative to learn how you qualify. If as an adopter or potential user you receive supplements you do not need, please return them to your sales representative or send them to: Attn: Returns Department, Troy Warehouse, 465 South Lincoln Drive, Troy, MO 63379.

Printed in the United States of America

1 2 3 4 5 6 7 8 9 0   048   9 8 7 6 5 4 3 2 1

Harcourt College Publishers

To all the Czinkotas: Ilona, Margaret, Ursula, Mihaly, Birgit, and Thomas—MRC

To Sirkka and Alpo Ronkainen—IAR

To Bennie Ruth and Hoy Moffett—MHM

The Harcourt College Publishers Series in Management

We are grateful for the leadership position the market has awarded to this book. We are keenly aware of the fact that best-selling status in the educational field also imposes an obligation to deliver cutting-edge innovations and improvements in terms of content as well as presentation. We honor your trust by doing our best to delight you through our presentation of conceptually sound, reality-based knowledge and by easing your task of teaching and learning about international business.

This textbook is unique in its approach to international business. Our direct corporate experience and advising of companies, both large and small, allows us to share with you the realities of the battle in the international marketplace. Due to our on-going policy work with both national and international organizations, we are able to give you a firsthand perspective of government activities in international business. Through our research leadership we can provide you with insights at the forefront of global thinking. As a result, this book offers you the perspective of the multinational corporation as well as that of the small international start-up firm. It lets you understand how and why governments intervene in markets and suggests alternatives for working with governments to achieve corporate goals. This book provides you with a strong theory base but also fully reflects the managerial concerns of those who work on the front lines in the business world. Finally, ongoing improvements in pedagogy, presentation, and writing continue to make this book fun to teach with and learn from.

Changes in the Sixth Edition

We have streamlined the text and worked hard to make it even more user friendly. The book now has twenty chapters. Important issues, such as investment flows, are now integrated early on into the text. Multinational corporate issues, together with cooperative modes of market development, are presented in the context of international business entry and strategic planning. Countertrade is covered in conjunction with multinational financial management. The specific changes in this edition are explained below.

Current Coverage

In preparing this edition, we have listened closely to our market in order to deliver an outstanding product. We start out by presenting the impact of international business on countries, corporations, and individuals. In-depth attention is paid to the role of culture, policies, and politics. The dimensions of ethics, social responsibility, and diversity are fully reflected through examples and vignettes.

We reflect more fully on some of the controversies in international business today, including the role of international institutions such as the World Trade Organization, the World Bank, and the International Monetary Fund. We also discuss why some groups are disenchanted with increased globalization. Also presented are some of the links between international business and development, such as payment for intellectual property rights, distribution of patented medication to poor countries, and development of genetically engineered foods. We address the issues of bribery and corruption and the benefit of international scrutiny, and we explain the increased use of arbitration procedures.

Use of Worldwide Examples

The global orientation of this book is reinforced by drawing on worldwide examples, trends, and data rather than just on U.S.-based information. For example, many of the data sets presented and sources recommended come from Europe and Asia.

We also ensure the reality and pragmatism of our content by always addressing the issue of "What does all this mean for firms in terms of implementing international business activities?" As an example, we explain how to use cultural variables for segmentation purposes in order to create new competitive tools.

Technology, Electronic Commerce, and the Internet

Harcourt has teamed with Digital: Convergence™ taking instructors and students beyond the book to obtain further up-to-date information on topics discussed in the text. This new technology connects to any home computer and, with the sweep of a bar code, gives students instant access to supporting web sites and online quizzing. In addition, web-based questions and research exercises at the end of each chapter permit immersion in ongoing international business issues and communicate the excitement of rapid change.

We have developed a strong focus on Internet-based research but also highlight the strengths and weaknesses of electronic data bases. We highlight, for example, that culture has a major effect on technology use and content expectations, and that search engines tend to pick only a small portion of actual work carried out and are still heavily biased toward English language publications. We also show how new technology can help even very small firms to reach out to international markets and compete successfully abroad.

Blending Current Theory and Application

Our theory section presents the latest thinking both from leading economists and business researchers. We also present the interdependence and linkages between the different theories so that the student gains an appreciation of the overall context of international business thought. All tables, figures, and maps were updated to present the most current information.

To link theory and practice, we present sixteen cases, eleven of which are new or updated. We draw case materials from firms around the world to offer truly global business scenarios, ranging from China and Russia to Iceland. The cases deal not only with established manufacturing industries, such as Harley Davidson, but also with online service by Hewlett Packard and the dot.com revolution. We present some of the controversy emanating from tobacco exports and from mad cow disease, and we also focus on the human dimension that is so highly important for expatriates. In addition to the cases specified here, there are many more cases available in Harcourt's Digital Library. Professors can choose any number of cases from the library, and even add their own content, to create a customized course-specific casebook that can be packaged with the text. Visit this book's web site for details (www.harcourtcollege.com/management/czinkota6e/).

Up-to-Date Coverage of EU, Asia, and Transition Economies

In Part 3 we have streamlined the discussion of the international monetary system, included the issues surrounding the introduction of the euro, and expanded the discussion of financial markets in order to reflect the financial turmoil in Asia. We provide in-depth coverage of the new developments in the European Union together with the changing roles of Mercosur and APEC. In discussing the latest changes in transition economies, we are, due to our direct involvement in founding three business learning institutions in Russia, able to highlight the human and leadership dimensions inherent in the change to a market economy.

Increased Coverage of Research

Part 4 has a greatly strengthened research chapter. An in-depth information appendix enhances the student's ability to conduct independent research, primarily by using web sites and other resources of the Internet. We devote a new section to the issue of data privacy, where we highlight best practices of firms and provide a comparison of the different approaches to privacy in Europe and in the United States.

We also focus on "born global" firms, which have a global orientation from their inception, and differentiate the levels of internationalization of the firm. We offer a new model of the internationalization process, reflecting the latest in research findings. We show how firms can receive export help from their governments and provide the Internet information for the leading export promotion organizations from around the globe. A new section highlights how leading-edge firms are developing "Export Complaint Management Systems" in order to stay close to their customers, adapt products quickly, and regain control of export channels.

Strengthened Strategy Orientation

Part 5 offers a strengthened strategy orientation. The chapter on strategic planning presents a framework for planning and market choice and offers a new context for formulating global strategy. An in-depth treatment of supply-chain management is offered to complement the logistics discussion. We deal with important implementation issues such as product tracking, electronic data interchange, early supplier involvement and mass customization. We also highlight the emergence of a new "post-mortem" stage in the product life cycle, during which firms will have to engage in the reverse distribution of the products they have sold many years ago. Global community relations are addressed, including insights on corporate preparations for crisis situations and the ability to transfer best practices. This section also offers the unique insights from a global delphi study conducted by the authors, the results of which are being used by several governments and corporations in structuring international trade strategies. Finally, a special section highlights the increasing role of women in international business leadership and offers extensive new information on international employment opportunities.

Special Features

Art and Photo Program

In order to inspire the student's imagination, many color photographs are presented in this edition. Throughout the text, concepts are visually depicted through tables, figures, and graphics. Artwork is designed to reiterate key concepts as well as to provide a pleasing format for student learning.

Organization

The text is divided into five parts. The first part introduces the impact of international business on countries, firms, and individuals. The second part focuses on the theoretical foundations of international trade and investment and the economic activity of the nation. Part 3 concentrates on the economic and financial environment together with economic integration and economies in transition. Part 4 is devoted to the preparation for international business and market entry. Part 5 covers strategic management issues.

Coverage

The text covers the international business activities of small and medium-sized firms that are new to the international arena as well as those of giant multinational corporations. It also provides thorough coverage of the policy aspects of international business, reflecting the concerns of the U.S. government, foreign governments, and international institutions.

The text consistently adopts a truly global approach. Attention is given to topics that are critical to the international manager yet so far have eluded other international texts. This coverage includes chapters on supply-chain management, international service trade, and doing business with newly emerging market economies under conditions of privatization.

Geography

To encourage the geographic literacy of students, color maps have been redesigned and updated. They provide the instructor with the means to visually demonstrate concepts such as political blocs, socioeconomic variables, and transportation routes. In addition, a unique appendix focuses specifically on the topic of geography and international business. A list of maps appears on page xxix.

Contemporary Realism

Each chapter offers a number of Global Perspectives that describe actual contemporary business situations. They are intended to serve as reinforcing examples, or mini-cases. As such, they will assist the instructor in stimulating class discussion and aid the student in understanding and absorbing the text material.

Research Emphasis

A special effort has been made to provide current research information. Apart from sharing the results of our own research, and that of our colleagues, we offer at the end of each chapter a list of relevant recommended readings. These materials will enable the instructor and the student to go beyond the text whenever time permits. We also offer information about web sites for research and exercise purposes so that the reader can go beyond the printed information.

Cases and Video Support

The text is followed by cases, many written especially for this book. Of a total of sixteen cases, three are also supported by video materials available to the instructor. Challenging questions accompany each case. They encourage in-depth discussion of the material covered in the chapters and allow students to apply the knowledge they have gained. Additional cases are available in Harcourt's Digital Library allowing professors to create a customized course-specific casebook that can be packaged with the text. Visit this book's web site for details (www.harcourtcollege.com/management/czinkota6e/).

Pedagogy

A textbook is about teaching, and we have made a major effort to strengthen the pedagogical value of this book.

- The listing of web sites allows the student to go directly to the source and receive up-to-the-minute information.

- The use of color makes it easier to differentiate sections and improves the presentation of graphs and figures.
- The design of maps specific to chapters adds a visual dimension to the verbal explanation.
- The Global Perspectives bring concrete examples from the business world into the classroom.
- The video support materials enable better and more efficient instruction.
- A glossary has been provided for the student's benefit. Each key term is bold-faced and defined in the text where it first appears. A complete glossary is provided at the end of the text.

Personal Support

Most important, we personally stand behind our product and we will work hard to delight you. Should you have any questions or comments on this book, you can contact us and provide us with your feedback.

Michael R. Czinkota	Ilkka A. Ronkainen	Michael H. Moffett
Czinkotm@msb.edu	Ronkaii@msb.edu	Moffettm@t-bird.edu

Comprehensive Learning Package

Instructor's Manual

The text is accompanied by an in-depth *Instructor's Manual,* devised to provide major assistance to the professor. The material in the manual includes the following:

Teaching Plans   Alternative teaching plans and syllabi are presented to accommodate the instructor's preferred course structure and varying time constraints. Time plans are developed for the course to be taught in a semester format, on a quarter basis, or as an executive seminar.

Discussion Guidelines   For each chapter, specific teaching objectives and guidelines are developed to help stimulate classroom discussion.

End-of-Chapter Questions   All questions for discussion are fully developed in the manual to accommodate different scenarios and experience horizons. Where appropriate, the relevant text section is referenced. In addition, each chapter includes two or more Internet-based questions offering the students the opportunity to explore the application of new technology to international business on their own.

Cases   Detailed answers are provided for all discussion questions that follow the cases that appear in the text. The manual also includes teaching notes for every video case.

Transparency Masters   The manual contains a substantial number of transparency masters that include figures from the text.

Test Bank

The greatly expanded test bank, consists of more than 1,500 short-answer questions, essay questions, true/false questions, and multiple choice questions. All the questions are also available on computer diskette.

Lecture Presentation Software

An asset to any instructor, the lectures in Microsoft PowerPoint provide outlines for every chapter, graphics of the illustrations from the text, and additional examples providing instructors with a number of learning opportunities for students.

Overhead Transparencies

A package of 100 transparency acetates, which feature text art and maps, is available. The acetates are accompanied by detailed teaching notes that include summaries of key concepts.

Companion Web Site

International Business's web site at **www.harcourtcollege.com** provides additional instructor and student resources. Students can access a resource library of articles with applications to text lessons, useful information on international business etiquette, student activities, and online quizzing. Additional supplementary materials are included on a password-protected site for instructors.

Harcourt College Publishers will provide complimentary supplements or supplement packages to those adopters qualified under our adoption policy. Please contact your sales representative to learn how you may qualify.

Acknowledgments

We are grateful to many reviewers for their imaginative comments and criticisms and for showing us how to get it even more right:

Kamal M. Abouzeid
Lynchburg College
Yaur Aharoni
Duke University
Zafar U. Ahmed
Minot State University
Riad Ajami
Rensselaer Polytechnic Institute
Joe Anderson
Northern Arizona University
Robert Aubey
University of Wisconsin–Madison
David Aviel
California State University
Marilynn Baker
University of North Carolina–Greenshoro
Bharat B. Bhalla
Fairfield University
Julius M. Blum
University of South Alabama
Sharon Browning
Northwest Missouri State University
Peggy E. Chaudhry
Villanova University
Ellen Cook
University of San Diego

Lauren DeGeorge
University of Central Florida
Luther Trey Denton
Georgia Southern University
Dharma deSilva
Wichita State University
Gary N. Dicer
The University of Tennessee
Peter Dowling
University of Tasmania
Derrick E. Dsouza
University of North Texas
Massoud Farahbaksh
Salem State College
Runar Framnes
Norwegian School of Management
Anne-Marie Francesco
Pace University–New York
Esra F. Gencturk
University of Texas–Austin
Debra Glassman
University of Washington–Seattle
Raul de Gouvea Neto
University of New Mexico
Antonio Grimaldi
Rutgers, The State University of New Jersey

John H. Hallaq
University of Idaho
Daniel Himarios
University of Texas at Arlington
Veronica Horton
Middle Tennessee State University
Basil J. Janavaras
Mankato State University
Michael Kublin
University of New Haven
Diana Lawson
University of Maine
Jan B. Luytjes
Florida International University
David McCalman
Indiana University–Bloomington
Tom Morris
University of San Diego
James Neelankavil
Hofstra University
Moonsong David Oh
California State University–Los Angeles
Sam C. Okoroafo
University of Toledo
Diane Parente
State University of New York–Fredonia
Mike W. Peng
Ohio State University
Jesus Ponce de Leon
Southern Illinois University–Carbondale
Jerry Ralston
University of Washington–Seattle

Peter V. Raven
Eastern Washington University
William Renforth
Florida International University
Martin E. Rosenfeldt
The University of North Texas
Tagi Sagafi-nejad
Loyola College
Rajib N. Sanyal
Trenton State College
Ulrike Schaede
University of California–Berkeley
John Stanbury
Indiana University–Kokomo
John Thanopoulos
University of Akron
Douglas Tseng
Portland State University
Betty Velthouse
University of Michigan–Flint
Heidi Vernon-Wortzel
Northeastern University
Steven C. Walters
Davenport College
James O. Watson
Millikin University
George H. Westacott
SUNY–Binghamton
Jerry Wheat
Indiana University Southeast
Tim Wilkinson
University of Akro
Kitty Y. H. Young
Chinese University of Hong Kong

Many thanks to those faculty members and students who helped us in sharpening our thinking by cheerfully providing challenging comments and questions. Several individuals had particular long-term impact on our thinking. These are Professor Bernard LaLonde, of the Ohio State University, a true academic mentor; the late Professor Robert Bartels, also of Ohio State; Professor Arthur Stonehill, of Oregon State University; Professor James H. Sood, of American University; Professor Arch G. Woodside, of Tulane University; Professor David Ricks, of University of Missouri, St. Louis; Professor Brian Toyne, of St. Mary's University; and Professor John Darling, of Mississippi State University. They are our academic ancestors.

Many colleagues, friends, and business associates graciously gave their time and knowledge to clarify concepts; provide us with ideas, comments, and suggestions; and deepen our understanding of issues. Without the direct links to business and policy that you have provided, this book could not offer its refreshing realism. In particular, we are grateful to Secretaries Malcolm Baldrige, C. William Verity, Clayton Yeutter, and William Brock for the opportunity to gain international business policy experience and to William Morris, Paul Freedenberg, H. P. Goldfield, and J. Michael Farrell for enabling its implementation. We also thank William Casselman, Lew Cramer of Summit Ventures, and Reijo Luostarinen of HSE.

Valuable research assistance was provided by Bridget McConnell, Jesse Nelson, and Anna Starikovsky, as well as Wyatt Cross White and Jian Gao, all of Georgetown University. We appreciate all of your work!

A very special word of thanks to the people at Harcourt College Publishers. Thanks to Michael Roche for not dealing with suppliers but collaborating with authors instead, and to Kerri Jones for her enthusiasm, creativity, and constructive feedback. Major assistance was also provided by the friendliness, expertise, and help of Michele Heinz and Brandi Nelson of Elm Street Publishing Services. Many thanks to Beverly Dunn, who creatively markets *International Business.*

Foremost, we are grateful to our families, who have had to tolerate late-night computer noises, weekend library absences, and curtailed vacations. The support and love of Ilona Vigh-Czinkota and Margaret Victoria Czinkota, Susan, Sanna, and Alex Ronkainen, Megan Murphy, Caitlin Kelly, and Sean Michael Moffett gave us the energy, stamina, and inspiration to write this book.

Michael R. Czinkota
Ilkka A. Ronkainen
Michael H. Moffett
August 2001

Michael R. Czinkota is on the faculty of marketing and international business of the Graduate School and the Robert Emmett McDonough School of Business at Georgetown University. He has held professorial appointments at universities in Asia, Australia, Europe, and the Americas.

Dr. Czinkota served in the U.S. government as Deputy Assistant Secretary of Commerce. He was responsible for macro trade analysis, support of international trade negotiations and retaliatory actions, and policy coordination for international finance, investment, and monetary affairs. He also served as head of the U.S. Delegation to the OECD Industry Committee in Paris and as senior trade advisor for Export Controls.

Dr. Czinkota's background includes eight years of private sector business experience as a partner in an export-import firm and in an advertising agency and seventeen years of research and teaching in the academic world. His research has been supported by the National Science Foundation, the National Commission of Jobs and Small Business, the Organization of American States, and the U.S. government. He was listed as one of the three most published contributors to international business research in the *Journal of International Business Studies* and has written several books including *Best Practices in International Business* (Harcourt) and *Trends in International Business* (Blackwell). He is also the author of the *STAT-USA/Internet Companion to International Business,* an official publication of the U.S. Department of Commerce.

Dr. Czinkota serves on the Global Advisory Board of the American Marketing Association, the Board of Governors of the Academy of Marketing Science, and the International Council of the American Management Association. He is on the editorial boards of *Journal of Business Research, Journal of the Academy of Marketing Science, International Marketing Review,* and *Asian Journal of Marketing.* For his work in international business and trade policy, he was named a Distinguished Fellow of the Academy of Marketing Science and a Fellow of the Chartered Institute of Marketing in the United Kingdom. He has also been awarded honorary degrees from the Universidad Pontificia Madre y Maestra in the Dominican Republic and the Universidad del Pacifico in Lima, Peru.

Dr. Czinkota serves on several corporate boards and has worked with corporations such as AT&T, IBM, GE, Nestlé, and US WEST. He serves as advisor to the United Nations' and World Trade Organization's Executive Forum on National Export Strategies.

Dr. Czinkota was born and raised in Germany and educated in Austria, Scotland, Spain, and the United States. He studied law and business administration at the University of Erlangen-Nürnberg and was awarded a two-year Fulbright Scholarship. He holds an MBA in international business and a Ph.D. in logistics from Ohio State University.

Ilkka A. Ronkainen is a member of the faculty of marketing and international business at the School of Business Administration at Georgetown University. From 1981 to 1986 he served as Associate Director and from 1986 to 1987 as Chairman of the National Center for Export-Import Studies.

Dr. Ronkainen serves as docent of international marketing at the Helsinki School of Economics. He was visiting professor at HSE during the 1987–1988 and 1991–1992 academic years and continues to teach in its Executive MBA, International MBA, and International BBA programs. Dr. Ronkainen holds a Ph.D. and a master's degree from the University of South Carolina as well as an M.S. (Economics) degree from the Helsinki School of Economics.

Dr. Ronkainen has published extensively in academic journals and the trade press. He is a co-author of *International Marketing*. He serves on the review boards of the *Journal of Business Research, International Marketing Review*, and *Journal of International Business Studies*. He served as the North American coordinator for the European Marketing Academy 1986–1990. He was a member of the board of the Washington International Trade Association from 1981 to 1986 and started the association's newsletter, Trade Trends.

Dr. Ronkainen has served as a consultant to a wide range of U.S. and international institutions. He has worked with entities such as IBM, the Rand Organization, and the Organization of American States. He maintains close relations with a number of Finnish companies and their internationalization and educational efforts.

Michael H. Moffett is currently Associate Professor of Finance and International Business at the American Graduate School of International Management (Thunderbird). Dr. Moffett has a B.A. in Economics from the University of Texas at Austin (1977), an M.S. in Resource Economics from Colorado State University (1979), and M.A. and Ph.D. in International Economics from the University of Colorado–Boulder (1985).

Dr. Moffett has lectured at a number of universities around the world, including the Aarhus School of Business (Denmark), the Helsinki School of Economics and Business Administration (Finland), the Norwegian School of Economics (Norway), and the University of Ljubljana (Slovenia). Dr. Moffett has also lectured at a number of universities in the United States, including Trinity College, Washington, DC, and the University of Colorado–Boulder. He is a former visiting research fellow at the Brookings Institution, and he recently completed a two-year visiting professorship in the Department of International Business at the University of Michigan–Ann Arbor.

Michael Moffett's research publications have appeared in a number of academic journals, including the *Journal of International Money and Finance*, the *Journal of Financial and Quantitative Analysis*, *Contemporary Policy Issues*, and the *Journal of International Financial Management and Accounting*. He is co-author of *Multinational Business Finance*, eighth edition, 1998, with David Eiteman and Arthur Stonehill, as well as co-editor with Arthur Stonehill of *Transnational Financial Management* for the United Nations Centre for Transnational Corporations, 1993. He is a continuing contributor to numerous collective works in the fields of international finance and international business, including the *Handbook of Modern Finance* and the *International Accounting and Finance Handbook*. Dr. Moffett has also consulted with a number of private firms both in the United States and Europe.

BRIEF CONTENTS

DETAILED CONTENTS

4   Politics and Laws   90

PART 2   Theoretical Foundations   115

5   The Theory of International Trade and Investment   116

6 The International Economic Activity of the Nation: The Balance of Payments 143

PART 3 The International Business Environment 163

7 International Financial Markets 164

PART 5   International Business Strategy and Operations   329

13   International Marketing   330

14   International Services   366

15   International Logistics and Supply-Chain Management   387

16   Multinational Financial Management   418

17   International Accounting and Taxation   451

18   International Human Resource Management   474

MAPS

PART I

The globalization of business brings new opportunities and threats to governments, firms, and individuals. The challenge is to compete successfully in the global marketplace as it exists today and develops tomorrow.

Part I sets the stage by introducing the effects of international business and demonstrating the need to participate in international activities. In order to do so, one needs to be able to manage conflicts between cultures. This in turn requires an understanding of cultural differences in language, religion, values, customs, and education, so that one can develop cross-cultural competence. A chapter on culture addresses these dimensions.

To achieve an understanding of the political and legal dimensions which affect international business, this section highlights the policy issues surrounding the corporate decision maker and discusses the effect of politics and laws on business, together with the agreements, treaties, and laws that govern the relationships between home and host countries.

THE

IMPACT

OF

INTERNATIONAL

BUSINESS

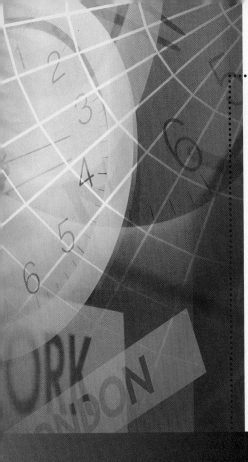

CHAPTER 1

The International Business Imperative

LEARNING OBJECTIVES

- To understand the history and impact of international business

- To learn the definition of international business

- To recognize the growth of global linkages today

- To understand the U.S. position in world trade and the impact international business has on the United States

- To appreciate the opportunities and challenges offered by international business

INTERNATIONAL BUSINESS: OPPORTUNITY AND CONFLICT

Globalization of business is seen by much of the world as creating wealth that benefits nations and individuals worldwide. Peter Woicke, a managing director of the World Bank, credits globalization with providing the essential ingredients of success to entrepreneurs and corporations in developing regions.

- A hydroelectric dam in Uganda constructed by a multinational power plant builder ensures that farmers, manufacturers, and service businesses have the reliable electricity they need.
- A banana grower in Ecuador gained markets in Russia and China, enabling him to expand into an integrated agribusiness. With his profits, this grower financed schools and helped protect a tropical rain forest.
- World Bank funding supported a network of entrepreneurs in South Africa and bank services upgrading in Latin America, making the formation of new businesses much easier.

"Globalization," Woicke concludes, "is what can help would-be industrialists change the labels of their countries from developing to developed."

Critics of business globalization, on the other hand, believe that it increases the wealth of corporations and investors at the expense of the poor, ignores human rights abuses and supports dictators, fails to relieve the massive debts of developing countries, and spoils the environment. They point to the growing number of people in poverty and note that one billion people live on less than the equivalent of $1 a day. In December 1999, 30,000 protestors demonstrated at the meeting of the World Trade Organization in the "Battle of Seattle." The next year, 8,000 protestors disrupted the September meeting of the International Monetary Fund (IMF) and World Bank in Prague. At the World Economic Forum in Davos, Switzerland, early in 2001, activists voiced their outrage at policy makers.

The World Bank, IMF, WTO, and other institutions believe it is simplistic to blame globalization for worsening poverty worldwide. The causes of poverty are numerous and complex, including war, disease (such as the African AIDS pandemic), corruption, illiteracy, and lawlessness. In fact, the percentage of people living in absolute poverty worldwide has actually declined. Furthermore, a joint study released in February 2001 by the United Nations, the Organization for Economic Cooperation and Development, the World Bank, and the IMF reports that the goal of reducing poverty by half from 1990 to 2015 is on schedule. ●

Sources: Paul Blustein, "A Quiet Round in Qatar?" *Washington Post,* January 30, 2001, p. E1; William Drozdiak, "Well-Guarded Elite Ponders World's Division," *Washington Post,* January 30, 2001; William Drozdiak and Steven Pearlstein, "Protesters Paralyze Prague," *Washington Post,* September 27, 2000, p. A6.

The Need for International Business

You are about to begin an exciting, important, and necessary task: the exploration of international business. International business is exciting because it combines the science and the art of business with many other disciplines, such as economics, anthropology, geography, history, language, jurisprudence, statistics, and demography. International business is important and necessary because economic isolationism has become impossible. Failure to become a part of the global market assures a nation of declining economic influence and a deteriorating standard of living for its citizens. Successful participation in international business, however, holds the promise of improved quality of life and a better society, even leading, some believe, to a more peaceful world.

On an individual level, most students of international business are likely to work for a multinational organization at one point in their careers. Manufacturing firms, as well as service companies such as banks, insurance, or consulting firms are going global. Artwork, films, and music are already widely exposed to the international market. Many of the future professional colleagues and competitors of today's students will come from around the world. In an era of open borders, niche marketing, instant communications, and virtually free ways of reaching millions of people, there emerges an unprecedented opportunity for individuals to enter the international business arena. Start-up firms can challenge the existing, long dominant large competition. Speed, creativity, and innovation have often become more important to international success than size. Understanding international business is therefore crucial in preparing for the opportunities, challenges, and requirements of a future career.

International business offers companies new markets. Since the 1950s, the growth of international trade and investment has been substantially larger than the growth of domestic economies. Technology continues to increase the reach and the ease of conducting international business, pointing to even larger growth potential in the future. A combination of domestic and international business, therefore, presents more opportunities for expansion, growth, and income than does domestic business alone. International business causes the flow of ideas, services, and capital across the world. As a result, innovations can be developed and disseminated more rapidly, human capital can be used better, and financing can take place more quickly. International business also offers consumers new choices. It can permit the acquisition of a wider variety of products, both in terms of quantity and quality, and do so at reduced prices through international competition. International business facilitates the mobility of factors of production—except land—and provides challenging employment opportunities to individuals with professional and entrepreneurial skills. At the same time, international business reallocates resources, makes preferential choices, and shifts activities on a global level. It also opens up markets to competition, which, in many instances has been unexpected and is difficult to cope with. As a result, international business activities do not benefit everyone to the same degree. Just like Janus, the two faced god of the Romans, international business can bring benefits and opportunity to some, while delivering drawbacks and problems to others. The international firm and its managers, as well as the consumers of international products and services, need to understand how to make globalization work for them, as well as think about how to ensure that these benefits are afforded to a wide variety of people and countries. Therefore, both as an opportunity and a challenge, international business is of vital concern to countries, companies, and individuals.

Protesters blocking traffic at the WTO's 1999 meeting in Seattle were met with tear gas as police opened up the streets.

A Definition of International Business

International business consists of transactions that are devised and carried out across national borders to satisfy the objectives of individuals, companies, and organizations. These transactions take on various forms, which are often interrelated. Primary types of international business are export-import trade and direct foreign investment. The latter is carried out in varied forms, including wholly owned subsidiaries and joint ventures. Additional types of international business are licensing, franchising, and management contracts.

As the definition indicates, and as for any kind of domestic business, "satisfaction" remains a key tenet of international business. The fact that the transactions are *across national borders* highlights the difference between domestic and international business. The international executive is subject to a new set of macroenvironmental factors, to different constraints, and to quite frequent conflicts resulting from different laws, cultures, and societies. The basic principles of business still apply, but their application, complexity, and intensity vary substantially.

The definition also focuses on international *transactions*. The use of this term recognizes that doing business internationally is an activity. Subject to constant change, international business is as much an art as a science. Yet success in the art of business depends on a firm grounding in its scientific aspects. Individual consumers, policymakers, and business executives with an understanding of both aspects will be able to incorporate international business considerations into their thinking and planning. They will be able to consider international issues and repercussions and make decisions related to questions such as these:

- How will our idea, good, or service fit into the international market?
- Should we enter the market through trade or through investment?
- Should I obtain my supplies domestically or from abroad?
- What product adjustments are necessary to be responsive to local conditions?
- What threats from global competition should be expected and how can these threats be counteracted?

When management integrates these issues into each decision, international markets can provide growth, profit, and needs satisfaction not available to those that limit their activities to the domestic marketplace. To aid in this decision process is the purpose of this book.

A Brief History

Ever since the first national borders were formed, international business has been conducted by nations and individuals. In many instances, international business itself has been a major force in shaping borders and changing world history.

As an example, international business played a vital role in the formation and decline of the Roman Empire, whose impact on thought, knowledge, and development can still be felt today. Although we read about the marching of the Roman legions, it  was not through military might that the empire came about. The Romans used the **Pax Romana,** or Roman peace, as a major stimulus. This ensured that merchants were able to travel safely and rapidly on roads built, maintained, and protected by the Roman legions and their affiliated troops. A second stimulus was the use of common coinage, which simplified business transactions and made them comparable throughout the empire. In addition, Rome developed a systematic law, central market locations through the founding of cities, and an effective communication system; all of these actions contributed to the functioning of the marketplace and a reduction of business uncertainty.

International business flourished within the empire, and the improved standard of living within the empire became apparent to those outside. Soon city-nations and tribes that were not part of the empire decided to join as allies. They agreed to pay tribute and taxes because the benefits were greater than the drawbacks.

Thus, the immense growth of the Roman Empire occurred mainly through the linkages of business. Of course, preserving this favorable environment required substantial effort. When pirates threatened the seaways, for example, Pompeius sent out a large fleet to subdue them. Once this was accomplished, the cost of international distribution within the empire dropped substantially because fewer shipments were lost at sea. Goods could be made available at lower prices, which in turn translated into larger demand and greater, more widely available benefits.

The fact that international business was one of the primary factors that held the empire together can also be seen in the decline of Rome. When "barbaric" tribes overran the empire, again it was not mainly through war and prolonged battles that Rome had lost ground. Rather, outside tribes were attacking an empire that was already substantially weakened at its foundations because of infighting and increasing decadence. The Roman peace was no longer enforced, the use and acceptance of the common coinage had declined, and communications no longer worked as well. Therefore, affiliation with the empire no longer offered the benefits of the past. Former allies, who no longer saw any benefits in their association with Rome, willingly cooperated with invaders rather than face prolonged battles.

Similar patterns also can be seen in later eras. The British Empire grew mainly through its effective international business policy, which provided for efficient transportation, intensive trade, and an insistence on open markets.[1] More recently, the United States developed a world leadership position largely due to its championship of market-based business transactions in the Western world; the broad flow of ideas, goods, and services across national borders; and an encouragement of international communication and transportation. One could say the period from 1945 to 1990 for Western countries, and since then, for the world, was characterized by a **Pax Americana,** an American peace.

The importance of international business has not always persisted, however. For example, in 1896, the Empress Dowager Tz'u-hsi, in order to finance the renovation of the summer palace, impounded government funds that had been designated for Chinese shipping and its navy. As a result, China's participation in world trade almost came to a halt. In the subsequent decades, China operated in almost total isolation, without any transfer of knowledge from the outside, without major inflow of goods, and without the innovation and productivity increases that result from exposure to international business.

Withholding the benefits of international business has also long been a tool of national policy. The use of economic coercion by nations or groups of nations, for example, can be traced back to the time of the Greek city-states and the Peloponnesian War. In the Napoleonic Wars, combatants used naval blockades to achieve their goal of "bringing about commercial ruin and shortage of food by dislocating trade."[2] Similarly, during the Civil War period in the United States, the North consistently pursued a strategy of denying international business opportunities to the South in order to deprive it of needed export revenues. More recently, the United Nations imposed a trade embargo against Iraq for its invasion and subsequent occupation of Kuwait in an attempt to ensure it had destroyed its chemical and biological weapons.

The importance of international business linkages was highlighted during the 1930s. At that time, the **Smoot-Hawley Act** raised import duties to reduce the volume of goods coming into the United States. The act was passed in the hope that it would restore domestic employment. The result, however, was retaliation by most trading partners. The ensuing worldwide depression and the collapse of the world financial system were instrumental in bringing about the events that led to World War II.

World trade and investment have assumed a heretofore unknown importance to the global community. In past centuries, trade was conducted internationally but not at the level or with the impact on nations, firms, and individuals that it has recently achieved. In the past 30 years alone, the volume of international trade in goods and services has expanded from $200 billion to more than $6.8 trillion.[3] As Figure 1.1 shows, the growth in the value of trade has greatly exceeded the level of overall world output growth.

FIGURE 1.1

Growth of World Output and Trade, 1987–2000

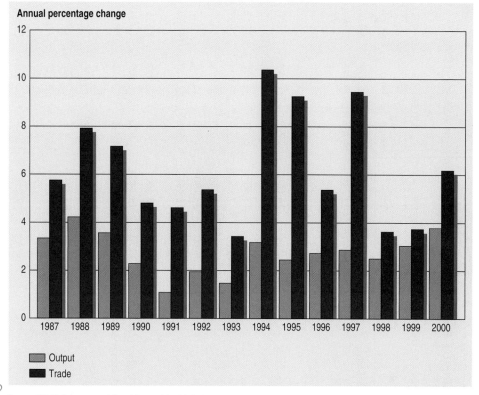

Annual percentage change

Sources: *World Economic and Social Survey*, New York: United Nations, 2000. http://www.unctad.org; WTO, www.wto.org; *International Financial Statistics Yearbook*, New York: IMF, 2001, www.imf.org.

During the same time, foreign direct investment mushroomed to more than $4.7 trillion by 2000. The sales of foreign affiliates of **multinational corporations** are now twice as high as global exports.[4] As Table 1.1 shows, many of these corporations have their origins in developing economies as well. Nonetheless, foreign direct investment is highly selective—in 1999 ten countries received 74 percent of foreign direct investment flows.[5] Individuals and firms have come to recognize that they are competing not only domestically but in a global marketplace. As a result, the international market has taken on a new dynamic, characterized by major change. Global Perspective 1.1 explains how this change offers both an opportunity and a threat.

Global Links Today

International business has forged a network of **global links** around the world that binds us all—countries, institutions, and individuals—much closer than ever before. These links tie together trade, financial markets, technology, and living standards in an unprecedented way. A freeze in Brazil and its effect on coffee production are felt around the world. The sudden decline in the Mexican peso affected financial markets in the United States and reverberated throughout Poland, Hungary, and the Czech Republic. The economic turmoil in Asia influenced stock markets, investments, and trade flows in all corners of the earth.

These linkages have also become more intense on an individual level. Communication has built new international bridges, be it through music or the watching of international programs transmitted by CNN (**www.cnn.com**). New products have attained international appeal and encouraged similar activities around the world—we wear blue jeans; we dance the same dances; we eat hamburgers, pizzas, and tacos.[6]

TABLE 1.1   The Top 25 Multinational Firms from Developing Economies, Ranked by Foreign Assets, 1998 (millions of dollars, number of employees)

RANKING BY Foreign Assets	Corporation	Home Country	Industry	ASSETS Foreign	ASSETS Total	SALES Foreign	SALES Total	EMPLOYMENT Foreign	EMPLOYMENT Total
1.	Petróleos de Venezuela S.A.	Venezuela	Petroleum expl./ref./distr.	$7,926	$48,816	$11,003	$25,659	6,026	50,821
2.	Daewoo Corporation	Republic of Korea	Trade	N/A	22,135	N/A	30,547	N/A	15,000
3.	Jardine Matheson Holdings, Limited	Hong Kong (China)/Bermuda	Diversified	5,954	9,565	7,921	11,230	N/A	160,000
4.	Cemex, S.A.	Mexico	Construction	5,639	10,460	2,334	4,315	9,745	19,761
5.	PETRONAS—Petroliam Nasional Berhad	Malaysia	Petroleum expl./ref./distr.	5,564	26,184	3,757	11,133	2,700	18,578
6.	Sappi Limited	South Africa	Pulp and paper	4,574	6,475	3,246	4,308	10,725	23,640
7.	Hutchison Whampoa, Limited	Hong Kong (China)	Diversified	N/A	13,389	2,191	6,639	20,845	39,860
8.	First Pacific Company Limited	Hong Kong (China)	Other	4,086	7,646	2,527	2,894	15,063	30,673
9.	Sunkyong Group	Republic of Korea	Diversified	3,851	36,944	12,029	38,274	2,400	29,000
10.	Petroleo Brasileiro S.A.—Petrobras	Brazil	Petroleum expl./ref./distr.	3,700	33,180	1,300	15,520	417	42,137
11.	New World Development Co., Limited	Hong Kong (China)	Construction	3,414	13,465	376	2,628	30	16,512
12.	China State Construction Engineering Corporation	China	Construction	3,290	7,300	1,950	5,890	5,535	239,102
13.	YPF Sociedad Anonima	Argentina	Petroleum expl./ref./distr.	3,278	13,146	880	5,500	1,754	9,486
14.	LG Electronics, Incorporated	Republic of Korea	Electronics and electrical equipment	3,127	12,824	4,841	12,213	27,819	60,753
15.	China National Chemicals Import & Export Corporation	China	Trade	3,000	4,950	7,920	13,800	510	8,415
16.	Keppel Corporation Limited	Singapore	Diversified	2,598	17,321	376	2,127	1,700	11,900
17.	Companhia Vale do Rio Doce	Brazil	Transportation	1,947	13,539	3,025	4,321	7,076	40,334
18.	Hyundai Engineering & Construction Co.	Republic of Korea	Construction	N/A	7,094	N/A	3,815	N/A	22,787
19.	Citic Pacific, Limited	Hong Kong (China)	Diversified	1,842	8,771	908	1,755	7,639	11,871
20.	Enersis, S.A.	Chile	Electric utilities or services	1,697	16,117	306	3,406	9,342	14,336
21.	Guangdong Investment Limited	Hong Kong (China)	Diversified	1,695	2,577	614	812	16,015	17,330
22.	San Miguel Corporation	Philippines	Food and beverages	1,676	3,552	287	1,811	4,338	15,923
23.	Samsung Electronics Co., Limited	Republic of Korea	Electronics and electrical equipment	N/A	17,213	N/A	16,640	N/A	42,154
24.	Shougang Group	China	Steel and Iron	1,610	6,990	830	4,270	1,548	212,027
25.	Barlow Limited	South Africa	Diversified equipment	1,574	2,624	1,734	3,769	N/A	27,804
				N/A	4,483	N/A	2,921	N/A	19,719

Source: UNCTAD/Erasmus University database, www.UNCTAD. org, February 8, 2001.

GLOBAL PERSPECTIVE 1.1

Free Trade Faced with New Obstacles

The whole notion of reducing trade barriers is in serious trouble. Some of the sources of this trouble include the slow growth of most of the world's economies, increased competition from developing countries, global excess capacity in most industries, and, as a result of all of these forces, the politically disruptive weakness of job markets around the world. A little-noted problem may also undermine further attempts to negotiate trade pacts and keep commerce as open as it is now. No one is in a dominant position to impose free trade.

Only twice in history has free trade had such a powerful advocate, according to Susan B. Stanton, an economist at A. Gary Shilling & Co. She first cites the mid-nineteenth century, when Britain took advantage of its industrial head start and began liberalizing its trade in a search for markets for its greatly increased production. After a while, other industrializing nations followed Britain's path to prosperity and negotiated liberal trade agreements.

After World War II, Ms. Stanton writes, "The U.S., like 19th century Britain, was in a unique position to push for liberal trade." It had vastly expanded its industrial base during the war years, and it bore the cost of free trade to help rebuild other nations' economies and fortify Cold War allies.

But in the 1970s, the Bretton Woods monetary agreement and stable currency rates collapsed. Oil shocks and surging inflation further rattled financial markets. As other industrial nations, notably Japan, grew stronger, international competition sharpened. The ending of the Soviet threat weakened the

Western alliance. And developing nations stepped up exports of manufactured goods. Now, the world's economies are facing this startling array of changes without a dominant nation able to uphold free trade.

"The sudden entry of three billion people from low-wage economies such as China, Mexico, and India into the global marketplace for goods, industries, and services is provoking new concerns among workers in the old industrial countries about their living standards," said David Hale, chief economist at Kemper Financial Companies. "Demographers project that practically all the growth in the world labor supply during the next half century will occur in developing nations." New technology will play a major role, too. The invasion of developing-world competitors into the marketplace will be facilitated by continuing improvements in worldwide communications. Almost across the board, technological change will keep wiping out old jobs while creating new ones.

Many people will blame the resulting turmoil in various industries and job markets on foreign competition. In fact, the European Union's increasing worldwide economic clout may have fueled recent trade skirmishes with the United States over bananas, beef, and airplane subsidies. When both parties have similar economic strength, neither may see the need to back down. If protectionism spreads, unchecked by a strong, persistent free trade champion, the growth of international trade could slow down in coming decades and the world's economies would pay a heavy price.

 Source: "At Daggers Drawn," *The Economist,* May 8, 1999, **www.economist.com**; Henry F. Meyers, "Free Trade Idea Needs a Dominant Champion," *The Wall Street Journal,* November 22, 1993, A1.

Large firms are expanding around the globe. They may become so well entrenched that they are thought of as local firms.

Transportation links let individuals from different countries see and meet each other with unprecedented ease. Common cultural pressures result in similar social phenomena and behavior—for example, more dual-income families are emerging around the world, which leads to more frequent, but also more stressful, shopping.[7]

International business has also brought a global reorientation in production strategies. Only a few decades ago, for example, it would have been thought impossible to produce parts for a car in more than one country, assemble it in another, and sell it in yet other countries around the world. Today, such global strategies, coupled with production and distribution sharing, are common. Consumers, union leaders, policymakers, and sometimes even the firms themselves are finding it increasingly difficult to define where a particular product was made, since subcomponents may come from many different nations. Firms are also linked to each other through global supply agreements and joint undertakings in research and development. Figure 1.2 gives an example of how such links result in a final consumer product.

In addition to the production of goods, service firms are increasingly part of the international scene. Consulting firms, insurance companies, software firms, and universities are participating to a growing degree in the international marketplace. Firms and governments are recognizing production's worldwide effects on the environment common to all. For example, high sulfur emissions in one area may cause acid rain in another. Pollution in one country may result in water contamination in another. Service activities can have cross-national impacts as well. For example, weaknesses in some

FIGURE 1.2

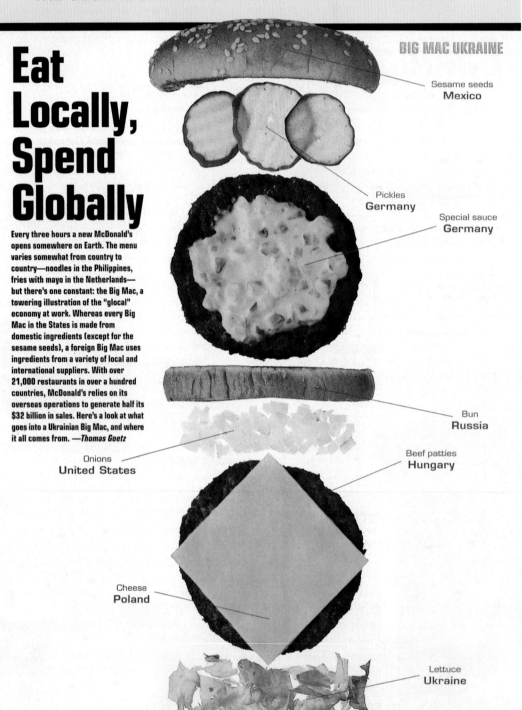

THE GLOBAL COMPONENTS OF A BIG MAC IN UKRAINE

BIG MAC UKRAINE

Eat Locally, Spend Globally

Every three hours a new McDonald's opens somewhere on Earth. The menu varies somewhat from country to country—noodles in the Philippines, fries with mayo in the Netherlands—but there's one constant: the Big Mac, a towering illustration of the "glocal" economy at work. Whereas every Big Mac in the States is made from domestic ingredients (except for the sesame seeds), a foreign Big Mac uses ingredients from a variety of local and international suppliers. With over 21,000 restaurants in over a hundred countries, McDonald's relies on its overseas operations to generate half its $32 billion in sales. Here's a look at what goes into a Ukrainian Big Mac, and where it all comes from. —*Thomas Goetz*

Sesame seeds
Mexico

Pickles
Germany

Special sauce
Germany

Bun
Russia

Beef patties
Hungary

Onions
United States

Cheese
Poland

Lettuce
Ukraine

currencies, due to problems in a country's banking sector, can quickly spill over and affect the currency values of other nations. The deregulation of some service industries, such as air transport or telephony can thoroughly affect the structure of these industries around the world.

All these changes have affected the international financial position of countries and the ownership of economic activities. For example, the United States, after having been a net creditor to the world for many decades, has been a world debtor since 1985. This means that the United States owes more to foreign institutions and individuals than they owe to U.S. entities. The shifts in financial flows have had major effects on international direct investment into plants as well. U.S. direct investment abroad in 1999 had a market value of more than $2.6 trillion; foreign direct investment in the United States had grown to $2.8 trillion.[8] One-third of the workers in the U.S. chemical industry toil for foreign owners.[9] Many U.S. office buildings are held by foreign landlords. The opening of plants abroad and in the United States increasingly takes the place of trade. All of these developments make us more and more dependent on one another.

This interdependence, however, is not stable. On an ongoing basis, realignments take place on both micro and macro levels that make past orientations at least partially obsolete. For example, for its first 200 years, the United States looked to Europe for markets and sources of supply. Despite the maintenance of this orientation by many individuals, firms, and policymakers, the reality of trade relationships has changed. U.S. two-way merchandise trade across the Pacific totalled $592 billion in 1999, $207 billion more than trade across the Atlantic.[10]

At the same time, entirely new areas for international business activities have opened up. The East-West juxtaposition had for more than 40 years effectively separated the "Western" economies from the centrally planned ones. The lifting of the Iron Curtain presents a new array of trading and investment partners.

Concurrently, an increasing regionalization is taking place around the world, resulting in the split up of countries in some areas of the world and the development of country and trading blocs in others. Over time, firms may find that the free flow of goods, services, and capital encounters new impediments as regions become more inward looking.

Not only is the environment changing, but the pace of change is accelerating. Atari's Pong was first introduced in the early 1980s; today, action games and movies are made with computerized humans. The first office computers emerged in the mid 1980s; today, home computers have become commonplace. E-mail was introduced to a mass market only in the 1990s; today, many college students hardly ever send personal notes using a stamp and an envelope.[11]

These changes and the speed with which they come about significantly affect countries, corporations, and individuals. For example, the relative participation of countries in world trade is shifting. Over the past decades, in a world of rapidly growing trade, the market share of Western Europe in trade has been declining. For the United States, the export share has declined while the import share has increased. Concurrent with these shifts, the global market shares of Japan, Southeast Asian countries, and China have increased.

The **composition of trade** has also been changing. For example, from the 1960s to the 1990s, the trade role of primary commodities has declined precipitously while the importance of manufactured goods has increased. This has meant that those countries and workers who had specialized in commodities such as *caoutchouc* (rubber plantations) or mining were likely to fall behind those who had embarked on strengthening their manufacturing sector. With sharply declining world market prices for their commodities and rising prices for manufactured goods, their producers were increasingly unable to catch up. More recently, there has been a shift from manufacturing to services—perhaps presaging a similar shift of trade composition for the future.

International Trade as a Percentage of Gross Domestic Product

Total Gross Domestic Product by Region
(in millions of US $)

United States
$9,962,650

Western Europe
$8,262,179

Japan
$4,759,519

China and India
$2,027,475

Latin America and Caribbean
$1,944,222

East Asia & Pacific
$1,475,369

Eastern Europe and Central Asia
$953,996

Middle East and North Africa
$823,154

Canada
$699,473

Sub-Saharan Africa
$317,787

South Asia
$133,926

Source: *2001 World Development Indicators*, The World Bank.

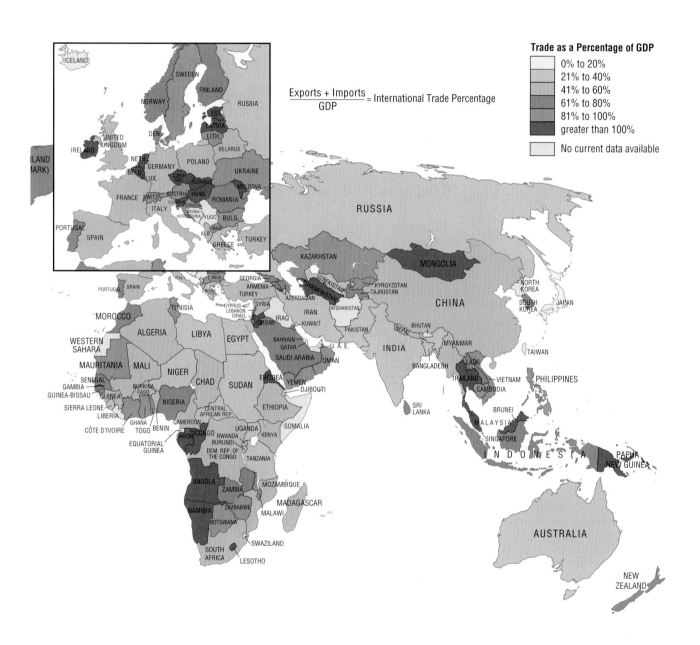

Trade as a Percentage of GDP

- 0% to 20%
- 21% to 40%
- 41% to 60%
- 61% to 80%
- 81% to 100%
- greater than 100%
- No current data available

$$\frac{\text{Exports + Imports}}{\text{GDP}} = \text{International Trade Percentage}$$

The Current U.S. International Trade Position

From a global perspective, the United States has gained in prominence as a market for the world but has lost some of its importance as a supplier to the world. In spite of the decline in the global market share of U.S. exports, the international activities of the United States have not been reduced. On the contrary, exports have grown rapidly and successfully. However, many new participants have entered the international market. In Europe, firms in countries with war-torn economies following World War II have reestablished themselves. In Asia, new competitors have aggressively obtained a share of the growing world trade. U.S. export growth was not able to keep pace with the total growth of world exports.

U.S. exports as a share of the GDP have grown substantially in recent years. However, this increase pales when compared with the international trade performance of other nations. Germany, for example, has consistently maintained an export share of more than 28 percent of GDP. Japan, in turn, which so often is maligned as the export problem child in the international trade arena, exports less than 10 percent of its GDP.[12] Table 1.2 shows the degree to which the United States comparatively "underparticipates" in international business on a per capita basis, particularly on the export side.

The Impact of International Business on the United States

Why should we worry about this underparticipation in trade? Why not simply concentrate on the large domestic market and get on with it? Why should it bother us that the largest portion of U.S. exports is attributed to only 2,500 companies? Why should it concern us that the U.S. Census Bureau estimates that less than 2 percent of all U.S. firms export?[13] Why should it be of concern that many U.S. e-tailers don't accept orders from outside their home market and 55 percent of U.S. web merchants will not even ship to Canada?[14]

U.S. international business outflows are important on the **macroeconomic level** in terms of balancing the trade account. Lack of U.S. export growth has resulted in long-term trade deficits. In 1983, imports of products into the United States exceeded exports by more than $70 billion. While in the ensuing years exports increased at a rapid rate, import growth also continued. As a result, in 2000, the U.S. merchandise trade deficit had risen to $448 billion.[15] Ongoing annual trade deficits in this range are un-

TABLE 1.2			
Exports and Imports per Capita for Selected Countries (US$)	Country	Exports per Capita	Imports per Capita
	Canada	$ 9,215	$ 8,013
	China	173	156
	France	6,455	5,953
	Germany	7,498	7,371
	India	50	61
	Japan	3,881	3,076
	Mexico	1,480	1,619
	Netherlands	16,020	14,793
	United Kingdom	6,226	6,750
	United States	3,878	5,217

Sources: **www.wto.org**, February 13, 2001; CIA, "The World Factbook, 2000," **www.cia.gov**, February 13, 2001; **www.stat.can**, March 20, 2001.

supportable in the long run. Such deficits add to the U.S. international debt, which must be serviced and eventually repaid. Exporting is not only good for the international trade picture but also a key factor in increasing employment. It has been estimated that $1 billion of exports supports the creation, on average, of 15,500 jobs.[16] Imports, in turn, bring a wider variety of products and services into a country. They exert competitive pressure for domestic firms to improve. Imports, therefore, expand the choices of consumers and improve their standard of living.

On the **microeconomic level,** participation in international business can help firms achieve economies of scale that cannot be achieved in domestic markets. Addressing a global market greatly adds to the number of potential customers. Increasing production lets firms ride the learning curve more quickly and therefore makes goods available more cheaply at home. Finally, and perhaps most important, international business permits firms to hone their competitive skills abroad by meeting the challenge of foreign products. By going abroad, firms can learn from their foreign competitors, challenge them on their ground, and translate the absorbed knowledge into productivity improvements back home. Firms that operate only in the domestic market are at risk of being surprised by the onslaught on foreign competition and thus seeing their domestic market share threatened. Research has shown that U.S. multinationals of all sizes and in all industries outperformed their strictly domestic counterparts—growing more than twice as fast in sales and earning significantly higher returns on equity and assets.[17] Workers also benefit. As Figure 1.3 shows, exporting firms of all sizes pay significantly higher wages than nonexporters.

The United States as a nation and as individuals must therefore seek more involvement in the global market. The degree to which Americans can successfully do business internationally will be indicative of their competitiveness and so help to determine their future standard of living.

As Global Perspective 1.2 shows, individual firms and entire industries are coming to recognize that in today's trade environment isolation is no longer possible. Both the willing and unwilling are becoming participants in global business affairs. Most

FIGURE 1.3

Average Plant Salary and Wages (per worker, dollars per hour)

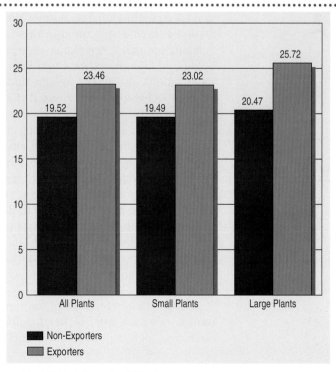

Source: Business America, Vol. 117, No. 9, September 1996, p. 9.

GLOBAL PERSPECTIVE 1.2

Competition, Incentives Spur Smaller U.S. Firms to Go Global

A report by the United Nations confirms what the U.S. business community is all too aware of: Small and medium-sized companies in the United States are far behind their counterparts in other countries in setting up operations abroad. For example, the head of the U.S. Export-Import Bank, James Harmon, noted the need for American businesses to increase investments in and sales to Africa; U.S. exports account for a mere 7 percent of total African imports. Harmon said small businesses should realize their potential to increase sales to Africa. As an incentive, the Ex-Im bank recently increased credits and loan guarantees to $400 million, from $49 million the previous year.

The bank now also backs loans in local currencies and limits volatility in the currency market. The scheme started in India. Up to $1 billion in rupee loans were made available to encourage Indian companies to buy from small and medium-sized U.S. firms.

Hopes are, however, that smaller firms within the United States will become more active internationally as globaliza-

tion accelerates. There are some encouraging signs. The large size of the U.S. marketplace was the main reason why so many smaller companies tended to stay home. Now even small and medium-sized U.S. companies are beginning to feel competition from less developed countries. In addition, more firms are finding it easier to manage foreign operations or a joint venture because "recent technological developments in communications, transportation, and financial services have enabled firms of all sizes to better exploit international opportunities."

The growth in exports by U.S. companies of all sizes may well accelerate the pace of direct investments as well, according to John Williams, chief global economist of Bankers Trust Company. Adds John Endean, vice president of the American Business Conference, "What we found with our members was that they start as exporters and move very quickly to rolling out direct investments to enhance or supplant their export strategy."

Source: Harry Dunphy, "Ex-Im Bank Backs Africa Investments," Associated Press, May 11, 1999; Fred R. Bleakley, "Smaller Firms in U.S. Avoid Business Abroad," *The Wall Street Journal,* August 24, 1993, A7, **www.cnnfn.com,** February 21, 2000.

U.S. firms are affected directly or indirectly by economic and political developments in the international marketplace. Firms that refuse to participate actively are relegated to reacting to the global economy. Consider how the industrial landscape in the United States has been restructured in the past decade as a result of international business.

Many industries experience the need for international adjustments. U.S. farmers, because of high prices, increased international competition, trade-restricting government actions, and unfair foreign trade practices, have lost world market share. U.S. firms in technologically advanced industries, such as semiconductor producers, saw the prices of their products and their sales volumes drop precipitously because of global competition. As a result of competition, many industries have adjusted, but with great pain. Examples abound in the steel, automotive, and textile sectors of the U.S. economy.

Still other U.S. industries never fully recognized what had happened and, therefore, in spite of attempts to adjust, have ceased to exist. VCRs are no longer produced domestically. Only a small percentage of motorcycles are manufactured in the United States. The shoe industry is in its death throes.

These developments demonstrate that it has become virtually impossible to disregard the powerful impact that international business has on all of us. Temporary isolation may be possible and delay tactics may work for a while, but the old adage applies: You can run, but you cannot hide. Participation in the world market has become truly imperative.

Global activities offer many additional opportunities to business firms. Market saturation can be delayed by lengthening or rejuvenating the life of products in other countries. Sourcing policies that once were inflexible have become variable because plants can be shifted from one country to another and suppliers can be found on every continent. Cooperative agreements can be formed that enable each party to bring its major strength to the table and emerge with better goods, services, and ideas than it could on its own. Consumers all over the world can select from among a greater variety of products at lower prices, which enables them to improve their choices and lifestyles.

All of these opportunities need careful exploration if they are to be realized. What is needed is an awareness of global developments, an understanding of their meaning, and a development of the capability to adjust to change. Judging by the global linkages found in today's market and the rapid changes taking place, a background in international business is highly desirable for business students seeking employment. **Globalization** is the watchword that "describes the need for companies and their employees, if they are to prosper, to treat the world as their stage."[18]

The Structure of the Book

This book is intended to enable you to become a better, more successful participant in the global business place. It is written for both those who want to attain more information about what is going on in international markets in order to be more well-rounded and better educated and for those who want to translate their knowledge into successful business transactions. The text melds theory and practice to balance conceptual understanding and knowledge of day-to-day realities. The book, therefore, addresses the international concerns of both beginning internationalists and multinational corporations.

The beginning international manager will need to know the answers to basic, yet important, questions: How can I find out whether demand for my product exists abroad? What must I do to get ready to market internationally? These issues are also relevant for managers in multinational corporations, but the questions they consider are often much more sophisticated. Of course, the resources available to address them are also much greater.

Throughout the book, public policy concerns are included in discussions of business activities. In this way, you are exposed to both macro and micro issues. Part 1 of the book introduces the importance of international business; discusses the interaction between international business and the nation-state; and addresses policy, political, legal, and cultural issues. Part 2 presents the theoretical dimensions of international trade and investment and explains the effect of international economic activities on a country. Part 3 covers the macroenvironment for international business and highlights the role of the international monetary system, economic integration, and economic development. Part 4 presents the research activities required to properly prepare for international business and lays out the options for market entry. Part 5 then addresses all the business management issues relevant to international business, using a strategic and applied perspective.

We hope that upon finishing the book, you will not only have completed another academic subject but also be well versed in the theoretical, policy, and strategic aspects of international business and therefore will be able to contribute to improved international competitiveness and a better global standard of living.

Summary

International business has been conducted ever since national borders were formed and has played a major role in shaping world history. Growing in importance over the past three decades, it has shaped an environment that, due to economic linkages, today presents us with a global marketplace.

In the past three decades, world trade has expanded from $200 billion to more than $6.8 trillion, while international direct investment has grown to $4.7 trillion. The growth of both has been far more rapid than the growth of most domestic economies. As a result, nations are much more affected by international business than in the past.

Global links have made possible investment strategies and business alternatives that offer tremendous opportunities. Yet these changes and the speed of change also can represent threats to nations, firms and individuals.

Over the past 30 years, the dominance of the U.S. international trade position has gradually eroded. New participants in international business compete fiercely for world market share. Individuals, corporations, and policymakers around the globe have awakened to the fact that international business is a major imperative and offers opportunities for future growth and prosperity. International business provides access to new customers, affords economies of scale, and permits the honing of competitive skills. Performing well in global markets is the key to improved standards of living, higher profits, and better wages. Knowledge about international business is therefore important to everyone, whether it is used to compete with foreign firms or simply to understand the world around us.

Key Terms and Concepts

Pax Romana	multinational corporation	composition of trade	microeconomic level
Pax Americana	global links	macroeconomic level	globalization
Smoot-Hawley Act			

Questions for Discussion

1. Will future expansion of international business be similar to that in the past?
2. Does increased international business mean increased risk?
3. Is it beneficial for nations to become dependent on one another?
4. Discuss the reasons for the increase in Chinese world trade market share.
5. With wages in some countries at one-tenth of U.S. wages, how can America compete?
6. Compare and contrast domestic and international business.
7. Why do more firms in other countries enter international markets than do firms in the United States?

Internet Exercise

1. Using World Trade Organization data (shown on the International Trade page of its web site, **www.wto.org**), determine the following information: (a) the fastest growing traders; (b) the top ten exporters and importers in world merchandise trade; and (c) the top ten exporters or importers of commercial services.

Recommended Readings

Czinkota, Michael R., and Masaaki Kotabe, eds. *Trends in International Business.* Oxford: Blackwell, 1998.

Czinkota, Michael R., and llkka A. Ronkainen. *Best Practices in International Business.* Ft. Worth, TX: Harcourt College Publishers, 2001.

Friedman, Thomas L. *The Lexus and the Olive Tree: Understanding Globalization.* New York: Farrar Straus & Giroux, 2000.

Kalb, Don, ed., Marco Van Der Land and Richard Staring, and Nico Wilterdink, ed. *The Ends of Globalization: Bringing Society Back In.* Lanham, MD: Rowman and Littlefield, 2000.

Mittelman, James H. *The Globalization Syndrome.* Princeton, NJ: Princeton University Press, 2000.

Morrison, Terri, Wayne A. Conoway, George A. Borden, and Hans Koehler. *Kiss, Bow, or Shake Hands: How to Do Business in 60 Countries.* Holbrook, MA: Adams Media Corporation, 1995.

Porter, Michael E. *The Competitive Advantage of Nations.* New York: The Free Press, 1990.

Porter, Michael, Jeffrey Sachs, Andrew Warner, and Klaus Schwab. *The Global Competitiveness Report 2000.* Oxford: Oxford Press, 2001.

Reich, Robert B. *The Future of Success.* Canada: Knopf Press, 2001.

Rodrik, Dani. *Has Globalization Gone Too Far?* Washington, DC: Institute for International Economics, 1997.

Notes

1. Paul R. Krugman, "What Do Undergraduates Need to Know about Trade?" AEA Papers and Proceedings, May 1993: 23–26.

2. Margaret P. Doxey, *Economic Sanctions and International Enforcement* (New York: Oxford University Press, 1980), 10.

3. World Trade Organization, "International Trade Statistics," **www.wto.org** February 13, 2001.

4. World Investment Report 2000, United Nations Conference on Trade and Development, New York, 2000, 1, 5.

5. World Investment Report 2000, United Nations Conference on Trade and Development, New York, 2000, 4.

6. Michael Marquardt and Angus Reynolds, *The Global Learning Organization* (Burr Ridge, IL.: Irwin, 1994), vi.

7. Eugene H. Fram and Riad Ajami, "Globalization of Markets and Shopping Stress: Cross-Country Comparisons," *Business Horizons,* January–February 1994, 17–23.

8. *Survey of Current Business* (U.S. Department of Commerce, Washington, D.C.), January 2001, D-57.

9. Manufacturers Alliance, *Globalization of the Economy: Implications of Foreign Investment in U.S. Manufacturing* (Arlington, VA: Manufacturers Alliance), 1997.

10. World Trade Organization, "International Trade Statistics," Geneva, 2001, 46.

11. Michael R. Czinkota and Sarah McCue, *The STAT-USA Companion to International Business,* Economics and Statistics Administration (U.S. Department of Commerce, Washington, D.C.), 2001, 16.

12. OECD, Quarterly National Accounts, Paris, **www.oecd.org**, 2001.

13. *Characteristics of Business Owners,* U.S. Bureau of the Census, Washington, DC, November 5, 1997.

14. Ian Putzger, "Online and International," *Journal of Commerce Week,* November 13–19, 2000, 27–28.

15. **www.STAT-USA.gov**, February 13, 2001.

16. *U.S. Jobs Supported by Exports of Goods and Services* (U.S. Department of Commerce, Washington, DC), June 17, 1996.

17. Charles Taylor and Witold Henisz, *U.S. Manufacturers in the Global Market Place,* Report 1058, The Conference Board, 1994.

18. "Management Education," *The Economist,* March 2, 1991, 7.

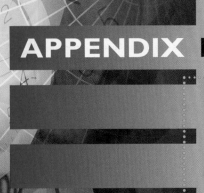

Geographic Perspectives on International Business

The dramatic changes in the world of business have made geography indispensable for the study of international business. Without significant attention to the study of geography, critical ideas and information about the world in which business occurs will be missing.

Just as the study of business has changed significantly in recent decades, so has the study of geography. Once considered by many to be simply a descriptive inventory that filled in blank spots on maps, geography has emerged as an analytic approach that uses scientific methods to answer important questions.

Geography focuses on answering "Where?" questions. Where are things located? What is their distribution across the surface of the earth? An old aphorism holds, "If you can map it, it's geography." That statement is true, because one uses maps to gather, store, analyze, and present information that answers "Where?" questions. But identifying where things are located is only the first phase of geographic inquiry. Once locations have been determined, "Why?" and "How?" questions can be asked. Why are things located where they are? How do different things relate to one another at a specific place? How do different places relate to each other? How have geographic patterns and relationships changed over time? These are the questions that take geography beyond mere description and make it a powerful approach for analyzing and explaining geographical aspects of a wide range of different kinds of problems faced by those engaged in international business.

Geography answers questions related to the location of different kinds of economic activity and the transactions that flow across national boundaries. It provides insights into the natural and human factors that influence patterns of production and consumption in different parts of the world. It explains why patterns of trade and exchange evolve over time. And because a geographic perspective emphasizes the analysis of processes that result in different geographic patterns, it provides a means for assessing how patterns might change in the future.

Geography has a rich tradition. Classical Greeks, medieval Arabs, enlightened European explorers, and twentieth-century scholars in the United States and elsewhere have organized geographic knowledge in many different ways. In recent decades, however, geography has become more familiar and more relevant to many people because emphasis has been placed on five fundamental themes as ways to structure geographic questions and to provide answers for those questions. Those themes are (1) location, (2) place, (3) interaction, (4) movement, and (5) region. The five themes are neither exclusive nor exhaustive. They complement other disciplinary approaches for organizing information, some of which are better suited to addressing specific kinds of questions. Other questions require insights related to two or more of the themes. Experience has shown, however, that the five themes provide a powerful means for introducing students to the geographic perspective. As a result, they provide the structure for this discussion.

Note: This appendix was contributed by Thomas J. Baerwald. Dr. Baerwald is deputy assistant director for the geosciences at the National Science Foundation in Arlington, Virginia. He is co-author of *Prentice Hall World Geography*—a best-selling geography textbook.

Location

For decades, people engaged in real estate development have said that the value of a place is a product of three factors: location, location, and location. This statement also highlights the importance of location for international business. Learning the location and characteristics of other places has always been important to those interested in conducting business outside their local areas. The drive to learn about other kinds of places, and especially their resources and potential as markets, has stimulated geographic exploration throughout history. Explorations of the Mediterranean by the Phoenicians; Marco Polo's journey to China; and voyages undertaken by Christopher Columbus, Vasco de Gama, Henry Hudson, and James Cook not only improved general knowledge of the world but also expanded business opportunities.

Assessing the role of location requires more than simply determining specific locations where certain activities take place. Latitude and longitude often are used to fix the exact location of features on the Earth's surface, but to simply describe a place's coordinates provides relatively little information about that place. Of much greater significance is its location relative to other features. The city of Singapore, for example, is between 1 and 2 degrees North latitude and is just west of 104 degrees East longitude. Its most pertinent locational characteristics, however, include its being at the southern tip of the Malay Peninsula near the eastern end of the Strait of Malacca, a critical shipping route connecting the Indian Ocean with the South China Sea. For nearly 150 years, this location made Singapore an important center for trade in the British Empire. After attaining independence in 1965, Singapore's leaders diversified its economy and complemented trade in its bustling port with numerous manufacturing plants that export products to nations around the world.

An understanding of how location influences business therefore is critical for the international business executive. Without clear knowledge of an enterprise's location relative to its suppliers, to its market, and to its competitors, an executive operates like the captain of a fog-bound vessel that has lost all navigational instruments and is heading for dangerous shoals.

Place

In addition to its location, each place has a diverse set of characteristics. Although many of those characteristics are present in other places, the ensemble makes each place unique. The characteristics of places—both natural and human—profoundly influence the ways that business executives in different places participate in international economic transactions.

Natural Features

Many of the characteristics of a place relate to its natural attributes. **Geologic characteristics** can be especially important, as the presence of critical minerals or energy resources may make a place a world-renowned supplier of valuable products. Gold and diamonds help make South Africa's economy the most prosperous on that continent. Rich deposits of iron ore in southern parts of the Amazon Basin have made Brazil the world's leading exporter of that commodity, while Chile remains a preeminent exporter of copper. Coal deposits provided the foundation for massive industrial development in the eastern United States, the Rhine River Basin of Europe, in western Russia, and in northeastern China. Because of abundant pools of petroleum beneath desert sands, standards of living in Saudi Arabia and nearby nations have risen rapidly to be among the highest in the world.

The geology of place also shapes its **terrain.** People traditionally have clustered in lower, flatter areas, because valleys and plains have permitted the agricultural development necessary to feed the local population and to generate surpluses that can be traded. Hilly and mountainous areas may support some people, but their population densities invariably are lower. Terrain also plays a critical role in focusing and inhibiting the movement of people and goods. Business leaders throughout the centuries have capitalized on this fact. Just as feudal masters sought control of mountain passes in order to collect tolls and other duties from traders who traversed an area, modern executives maintain stores and offer services near bridges and at other points where terrain focuses travel.

The terrain of a place is related to its **hydrology.** Rivers, lakes, and other bodies of water influence the kinds of economic activities that occur in a place. In general, abundant supplies of water boost economic development, because water is necessary for the sustenance of people and for both agricultural and industrial production. Locations like Los Angeles and Saudi Arabia have prospered despite having little local water, because other features offer advantages that more than exceed the additional costs incurred in delivering water supplies from elsewhere. While sufficient water must be available to meet local needs, overabundance of water may pose serious problems, such as in Bangladesh, where development has been inhibited by frequent flooding. The character of a place's water bodies also is important. Smooth-flowing streams and placid lakes can stimulate transportation within a place and connect it more easily with other places, while waterfalls and rapids can prevent navigation on streams. The rapid drop in elevation of such streams may boost their potential for hydroelectric power generation, however, thereby stimulating development of industries requiring considerable amounts of electricity. Large plants producing aluminum, for example, are found in the Tennessee and Columbia river valleys of the United States and in Quebec and British Columbia in Canada. These plants refine materials that originally were extracted elsewhere, especially bauxite and alumina from Caribbean nations like Jamaica and the Dominican Republic. Although the transport costs incurred in delivery of these materials to the plants is high, those costs are more than offset by the presence of abundant and inexpensive electricity.

Climate is another natural feature that has profound impact on economic activity within a place. Many activities are directly affected by climate. Locales blessed with pleasant climates, such as the Côte d'Azur of France, the Crimean Peninsula of Ukraine, Florida, and the "Gold Coast" of northeastern Australia, have become popular recreational havens, attracting tourists whose spending fuels the local economy. Agricultural production also is influenced by climate. The average daily and evening temperatures, the amount and timing of precipitation, the timing of frosts and freezing weather, and the variability of weather from one year to the next all influence the kinds of crops grown in an area. Plants producing bananas and sugar cane flourish in moist tropical areas, while cooler climates are more conductive for crops such as wheat and potatoes. Climate influences other industries, as well. The aircraft manufacturing industry in the United States developed largely in warmer, drier areas where conditions for test and delivery flights were most beneficial throughout the year. In a similar way, major rocket-launching facilities have been placed in locations where climatic conditions and trajectories are most favorable. As a result, the primary launch site of the European Space Agency is not in Europe at all but rather in the South American territory of French Guiana. Climate also affects the length of the work day and the length of economic seasons. For example, in some regions of the world, the construction industry can build only during a few months of the year because permafrost makes construction prohibitively expensive the rest of the year.

Variations in **soils** have a profound impact on agricultural production. The world's great grain-exporting regions, including the central United States, the Prairie Provinces of Canada, the "Fertile Triangle" stretching from central Ukraine through southern Russia into northern Kazakhstan, and the Pampas of northern Argentina, all have been blessed with mineral-rich soils made even more fertile by humus from natural grasslands that once dominated the landscape. Soils are less fertile in much of the Amazon Basin of Brazil and in central Africa, where heavy rains leave few nutrients in upper layers of the soil. As a result, few commercial crops are grown in those areas.

The **interplay between climate and soils** is especially evident in the production of wines. Hundreds of varieties of grapes have been bred to take advantage of the different physical characteristics of various places. The wines fermented from these grapes are shipped around the world to consumers, who differentiate among various wines based not only on the grapes but also on the places where they were grown and the conditions during which they matured.

Human Features

The physical features of a place provide natural resources and influence the types of economic activities in which people engage, but its human characteristics also are critical. The **population** of a place is important because farm production may require intensive labor to be successful, as is true in rice-growing areas of eastern Asia. The skills and qualifications of the population also play a role in determining how a place fits into global economic affairs. Although blessed with few mineral resources and a terrain and climate that limit agricultural production, the Swiss have emphasized high levels of education and training in order to maintain a labor force that manufactures sophisticated products for export around the world. In recent decades, Japan and smaller nations such as South Korea and Taiwan have increased the productivity of their workers to become major industrial exporters.

As people live in a place, they modify it, creating a **built environment** that can be as or more important than the natural environment in economic terms. The most pronounced areas of human activity and their associated structures are in cities. In nations around the world, cities have grown dramatically during the twentieth century. Much of the growth of cities has resulted from the migration of people from rural areas. This influx of new residents broadens the labor pool and creates vast new demand for goods and services. As urban populations have grown, residences and other facilities have replaced rural land uses. Executives seeking to conduct business in foreign cities need to be aware that the geographic patterns found in their home cities are not evident in many other nations. For example, in the United States, wealthier residents generally have moved outward and as they established their residences, stores and services followed. Residential patterns in the major cities of Latin America and other developing nations tend to be reversed, with the wealthy remaining close to the city center while poorer residents are consigned to the outskirts of town. A store location strategy that is successful in the United States therefore may fail miserably if transferred directly to another nation without knowledge of the different geographic patterns of that nation's cities.

Interaction

The international business professional seeking to take advantage of opportunities present in different places learns not to view each place separately. How a place functions depends not only on the presence and form of certain characteristics but also on interactions among those characteristics. Fortuitous combinations of features can spur a region's economic development. The presence of high-grade supplies of iron ore, coal, and limestone powered the growth of Germany's Ruhr Valley as one of Europe's foremost steel-producing regions, just as the proximity of the fertile Pampas and the deep channel of the Rio de la Plata combine to make Buenos Aires the leading economic center in southern South America.

Interactions among different features change over time within places, and as they do, so does that place's character and its economic activities. Human activities can have profound impacts on natural features. The courses of rivers and streams are changed, as dams are erected and meanders are straightened. Soil fertility can be improved through fertilization. Vegetation is changed, with naturally growing plants replaced by crops and other varieties that require careful management.

Many human modifications have been successful. For centuries, the Dutch have constructed dikes and drainage systems, slowly creating polders—land that once was covered by the North Sea but that now is used for agricultural production. But other human activities have had disastrous impacts on natural features. A large area in Ukraine and Belarus was rendered uninhabitable by radioactive materials leaked from the Chernobyl reactor in 1986. In countless other places around the globe, improper disposal of wastes has seriously harmed land and water resources. In some places, damage can be repaired, as has happened in rivers and lakes of the United States following the passage of measures to curb water pollution in the past four decades, but in other locales, restoration may be impossible.

Growing concerns about environmental quality have led many people in more economically advanced nations to call for changes in economic systems that harm the natural environment. Concerted efforts are under way, for example, to halt destruction of forests in the Amazon Basin, thereby preserving the vast array of different plant and animal species in the region and saving vegetation that can help moderate the world's climate. Cooperative ventures have been established to promote selective harvesting of nuts, hardwoods, and other products taken from natural forests. Furthermore, an increasing number of restaurants and grocers are refusing to purchase beef raised on pastures that are established by clearing forests.

Like so many other geographical relationships, the nature of human-environmental interaction changes over time. With technological advances, people have been able to modify and adapt to natural features in increasingly sophisticated ways. The development of air conditioning has permitted people to function more effectively in torrid tropical environments, thereby enabling the populations of cities such as Houston, Rio de Janeiro, and Jakarta to multiply many times over in recent decades. Owners of winter resorts now can generate snow artificially to ensure favorable conditions for skiers. Advanced irrigation systems now permit crops to be grown in places such as the southwestern United States, northern Africa, and Israel. The use of new technologies may cause serious problems over the long run, however. Extensive irrigation in large parts of the U.S. Great Plains has seriously depleted groundwater supplies. In central Asia, the diversion of river water to irrigate cotton fields in Kazakhstan and Uzbekistan has reduced the size of the Aral Sea by more than one-half since 1960. In future years, business leaders may need to factor into their decisions additional costs associated with the restoration of environmental quality after they have finished using a place's resources.

Movement

Whereas the theme of interaction encourages consideration of different characteristics within a place, movement provides a structure for considering how different places relate to each other. International business exists because movement permits the transportation of people and goods and communication of information and ideas among different places. No matter how much people in one place want something found elsewhere, they cannot have it unless transportation systems permit the good to be brought to them or allow them to move to the location of the good.

The location and character of transportation and communication systems long have had powerful influences on the economic standing of places. Especially significant have been places on which transportation routes have focused. Many ports have become prosperous cities because they channeled the movement of goods and people between ocean and inland waterways. New York became the largest city in North America because its harbor provided sheltered anchorage for ships crossing the Atlantic; the Hudson River provided access leading into the interior of the continent. In eastern Asia, Hong Kong grew under similar circumstances, as British traders used its splendid harbor as an exchange point for goods moving in and out of southern China.

Businesses also have succeeded at well-situated places along overland routes. The fabled oasis of Tombouctou has been an important trading center for centuries because it has one of the few dependable sources of water in the Sahara. Chicago's ascendancy as the premier city of the U.S. heartland came when its early leaders engineered its selection as the termination point for a dozen railroad lines converging from all directions. Not only did much of the rail traffic moving through the region have to pass through Chicago, but passengers and freight passing through the city had to be transferred from one line to another, a process that generated numerous jobs and added considerably to the wealth of many businesses in the city.

In addition to the business associated directly with the movement of people and goods, other forms of economic activity have become concentrated at critical points in the transportation network. Places where transfers from one mode of transportation to another were required often were chosen as sites for manufacturing activities. Buffalo was the most active flour-milling center in the United States for much of the twentieth century because it was the point where Great Lakes freighters carrying wheat from the northern Great Plains and Canadian prairies were unloaded. Rather than simply transfer the wheat into rail cars for shipment to the large urban markets of the northeastern United States, millers transformed the wheat into flour in Buffalo, thereby reducing the additional handling of the commodity.

Global patterns of resource refining also demonstrate the wisdom of careful selection of sites with respect to transportation systems. Some of the world's largest oil refineries are located in places like Bahrain and Houston, where pipelines bring oil to points where it is processed and loaded onto ships in the form of gasoline or other distillates for transport to other locales. Massive refinery complexes also have been built in the Tokyo and Nagoya areas of Japan and near Rotterdam in the Netherlands to process crude oil brought by giant tankers from the Middle East and other oil-exporting regions. For similar reasons, the largest new steel mills in the United States are near Baltimore and Philadelphia, where iron ore shipped from Canada and Brazil is processed. Some of the most active aluminum works in Europe are beside Norwegian fjords, where abundant local hydroelectric power is used to process imported alumina.

Favorable location along transportation lines is beneficial for a place. Conversely, an absence of good transportation severely limits the potential for firms to succeed in a specific place. Transportation patterns change over time, however, and so does their impact on places. Some places maintain themselves because their business leaders use their size and economic power to become critical nodes in newly evolving transportation networks. New Yorks's experience provides a good example of this process. New York became the United States's foremost business center in the early nineteenth century because it was ideally situated for water transportation. As railroad networks evolved later in that century, they sought New York connections in order to serve its massive market. During the twentieth century, a complex web of roadways and major airports reinforced New York's supremacy in the eastern United States. In similar ways, London, Moscow, and Tokyo reasserted themselves as transportation hubs for their nations through successive advances in transport technology.

Failure to adapt to changing transportation patterns can have deleterious impacts on a place. During the middle of the nineteenth century, business leaders in St. Louis discouraged railroad construction, seeking instead to maintain the supremacy of river transportation. Only after it became clear that railroads were the mode of preference did St. Louis officials seek to develop rail connections for the city, but by then it was too late; Chicago had ascended to a dominant position in the region. For about 30 years during the middle part of the twentieth century, airports at Gander, Newfoundland, Canada, and Shannon, Ireland, became important refueling points for trans-Atlantic flights. The development of planes that could travel nonstop for much longer distances returned those places to sleepy oblivion.

Continuing advances in transportation technology effectively have "shrunk" the world. Just a few centuries ago, travel across an ocean took harrowing months. As late as 1873, readers marveled when Jules Verne wrote of a hectic journey around the world in 80 days. Today's travelers can fly around the globe in less than 80 hours, and the speed and dependability of modern modes of transport have transformed the ways in which business is conducted. Modern manufacturers have transformed the notion of relationships among suppliers, manufacturers, and markets. Automobile manufacturers, for example, once maintained large stockpiles of parts in assembly plants that were located near the parts plants or close to the places where the cars would be sold. Contemporary auto assembly plants now are built in places where labor costs and worker productivity are favorable and where governments have offered attractive inducements. They keep relatively few parts on hand, calling on suppliers for rapid delivery of parts as they are needed when orders for new cars are received. This "just-in-time" system of production leaves manufacturers subject to disruptions caused by work stoppages at supply plants and to weather-related delays in the transportation system, but losses associated with these infrequent events are more than offset by reduced operating costs under normal conditions.

The role of advanced technology as a factor affecting international business is even more apparent with respect to advances in communications systems. Sophisticated forms of telecommunication that began more than 150 years ago with the telegraph have advanced through the telephone to facsimile transmissions and electronic mail networks. As a result, distance has practically ceased to be a consideration with respect to the transmission of information. Whereas information once moved only as rapidly as the person carrying the paper on which the information was written, data and ideas now can be sent instantaneously almost anywhere in the world.

These communication advances have had a staggering impact on the way that international business is conducted. They have fostered the growth of multinational corporations, which operate in diverse sites around the globe while maintaining effective links with headquarters and regional control centers. International financial operations also have been transformed because of communication advances. Money and stock markets in New York, London, Tokyo, and Frankfurt now are connected by computer systems that process transactions around the clock. As much as any other factor, the increasingly mobile forms of money have enabled modern business executives to engage in activities around the world.

Regions

In addition to considering places by themselves or how they relate to other places, regions provide alternative ways to organize groups of places in more meaningful ways. A region is a set of places that share certain characteristics. Many regions are defined by characteristics that all of the places in the group have in common. When economic characteristics are used, the delimited regions include places with similar kinds of economic activity. Agricultural regions include areas where certain farm products dominate. Corn is grown throughout the "Corn Belt" of the central United States, for example, although many farmers in the region also plant soybeans and many raise hogs. Regions where intensive industrial production is a prominent part of local economic activity include the manufacturing belts of the northeastern United States, southern Canada, northwestern Europe, and southern Japan.

Regions can also be defined by patterns of movement. Transportation or communication linkages among places may draw them together into configurations that differentiate them from other locales. Studies by economic geographers of the locational tendencies of modern high-technology industries have identified complex networks of firms that provide products and services to each other. Because of their linkages, these firms cluster together into well-defined regions. The "Silicon Valley" of northern California, the "Western Crescent" on the outskirts of London, and "Technopolis" of the Tokyo region all are distinguished as much by connections among firms as by the economic landscapes they have established.

Economic aspects of movement may help define functional regions by establishing areas where certain types of economic activity are more profitable than others. In the early nineteenth century, German landowner Johann Heinrich von Thünen demonstrated how different costs for transporting various agricultural goods to market helped to define regions where certain forms of farming would occur. Although theoretically simple, patterns predicted by von Thünen can still be found in the world today. Goods such as vegetables and dairy products that require more intensive production and are more expensive to ship are produced closer to markets, while less demanding goods and commodities that can be transported at lower costs come from more remote production areas. Advances in transportation have dramatically altered such regional patterns, however. Whereas a New York City native once enjoyed fresh vegetables and fruit only in the summer and early autumn when New Jersey, upstate New York, and New England producers brought their goods to market, New Yorkers today buy fresh produce year-round, with new shipments flown in daily from Florida, California, Chile, and even more remote locations during the colder months.

Governments have a strong impact on the conduct of business, and the formal borders of government jurisdictions often coincide with the functional boundaries of economic regions. The divisive character of these lines on the map has been altered in many parts of the world in recent decades, however. The formation of common markets and free trade areas in Western Europe and North America has dramatically changed the patterns and flows of economic activity, and similar kinds of formal restructuring of relationships among nations likely will continue in this century. As a result, business analysts increasingly need to consider regions that cross international boundaries.

Some of the most innovative views of regional organization essentially have ignored existing national boundaries. In 1981, Joel Garreau published a book titled *The Nine Nations of North America,* which subdivided the continent into a set of regions based on economic activities and cultural outlooks. Seven of Garreau's nine regions include territory in at least two nations. In the Southwest, "Mexamerica" recognized the bicultural heritage of Anglo and Hispanic groups and the increasingly close economic ties across the U.S.–Mexican border that were spurred by the *maquiladora* and other export-oriented programs. The evolution of this region as a distinctive collection of places has been accelerated by the passage of the North American Free Trade Agreement (NAFTA). Another cross-national region identified by Garreau is "The Islands," a collection of nations in the Caribbean for which Miami has become the functional "capital." Many business leaders seeking to tap into this rapidly growing area have become knowledgeable of the laws and customs of those nations. They

The New Superregions of Europe

Source: Darrell Delamaide. *The New Superregions of Europe.* New York: Dutton, 1994.

The Nine Nations of North America

Source: Joel Garreau. *The Nine Nations of North America.* New York: Houghton Mifflin, 1981.

often have done so by employing émigrés from those nations who may now be U.S. citizens but whose primary language is not English and whose outlook on the region is multinational.

In a similar vein, Darrell Delamaide's 1994 book entitled *The New Superregions of Europe* divides the continent into ten regions based on economic, cultural, and social affinities that have evolved over centuries. His vision of Europe challenges regional structures that persist from earlier times. Seen by many as a single region known as Eastern Europe, the formerly communist nations west of what once was the Soviet Union are seen by Delamaide as being part of five different "superregions": "The Baltic League," a group of nations clustered around the Baltic Sea; "Mitteleuropa," the economic heartland of northern Europe; "The Slavic Federation," a region dominated by Russia with a common Slavic heritage; "The Danube Basin," a melange of places along and near Europe's longest river; and "The Balkan Peninsula," a region characterized by political turmoil and less advanced economies.

Delamaide's book has been as controversial as Garreau's was a decade earlier. In both cases, however, the value of the ideas they presented was not measured in terms of the "accuracy" of the regional structures they presented, but rather by their ability to lead more people to take a geographic perspective of the modern world and how it functions. The regions defined by Garreau and Delamaide are not those described by traditional geographers, but they reflect the views of many business leaders who have learned to look across national boundaries in their search for opportunities. As business increasingly becomes international, the most successful entrepreneurs will be the ones who complement their business acumen with effective application of geographic information and principles.

References Cited

Darrell Delamaide. *The New Superregions of Europe.* New York: Dutton, a division of Penguin Books, 1994.

Joel Garreau. *The Nine Nations of North America.* New York: Houghton Mifflin Co., 1981.

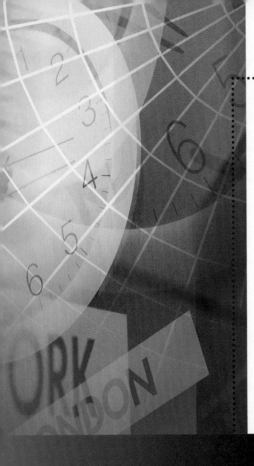

CHAPTER 2

Culture and International Business

LEARNING OBJECTIVES

- To define and demonstrate the effect of culture's various dimensions on international business

- To examine ways in which cultural knowledge can be acquired and individuals and organizations prepared for cross-cultural interaction

- To illustrate ways in which cultural risk poses a challenge to the effective conduct of business communications and transactions

- To suggest ways in which international businesses act as change agents in the diverse cultural environments in which they operate

Cultural diversity is everywhere. Managers both at home and abroad must plan strategies without assuming mutual understanding. People from different cultures share basic concepts but view them from different angles and perspectives, leading them to behave in ways that may seem irrational or even directly contradictory to what others consider appropriate. It is critical to remember that while all managers evaluate and criticize others' behavior, their own actions are also coming under scrutiny.

The significant prominence of the U.S. economy and the subsequent respect for the U.S. economic model has been accompanied by a corresponding fall-off in the efforts by U.S. companies and their managers to understand and respect other ways of conducting business. Misled by the sense that the world is becoming even more "American," and reassured by the increasingly universal ability of counterparts to speak English, many U.S. managers do not fully comprehend how cultural misunderstandings can sour relationships and sabotage deals. The following perceptions of U.S. managers' practices highlight the point.

Hans Riedel, Germany; Executive Vice President/Sales and Marketing, Porsche AG

We are coming from two different cultures, but we have to deal with each other. This starts with little things such as scheduling meetings on Thanksgiving. It does not show up in our [German] calendars or in our perceptions, but we should make it our business to know about this most important holiday. The same should go for Americans and German holidays.

Jaime Zevada, Mexico; Manager of Investor Relations, Bufete Industrial, S.A.

Time represents something else for an American than for a Mexican. If you have a meeting at 1:30, for a Mexican that could mean 1:45 or 2:00. It's a normal thing, everyone is late in Mexico, but it takes time for U.S. managers to understand this. In Mexico, we begin working at 9:00 or 9:30. We have breakfast meetings, with lots of food. Then we have a big lunch and siesta from 3:00 to 5:00. We are back at 5:00, then work until 9:00 or 10:00 at night. Similarly, the concept of law is different in Mexico. We try to tell our U.S. counterparts that here, when you handle relationships with the government, you invite their representatives for the weekend or you take them to dinner. To handle the union leader, it is the same thing. It is not written anywhere, but it is something you just do.

Maciej Kosinski, Poland; Founder and President, EMTV/Euromedia

Americans are intellectually open. If they do not understand where we are coming from, they are ready to listen. When we were working on the script for the Polish version of *Sesame Street,* we wanted to title one segment "Who is Afraid of the Black Beast?" The Americans were concerned, but for them it had racial connotations. But we explained that in Poland "The Black Beast" is a nursery rhyme, and it has nothing to do with race, which was accepted by the Americans. It is flexibility that Germans, for example, would never show. What does bother me, however, is the imperial tone that some of the big American companies adopt when they talk to us. It is always about how they know best and how we should learn from them. We are really allergic to that in Central Europe, because for many years we had Big Brother on our backs.

Hiroshi Tsujimura, Japan; Co-Chief Executive Officer, Nomura Securities International

Asians and Europeans are more interested in the long term while Americans are short term, meaning less than one year. If we have a project that is only going to be profitable in the long term, Americans are difficult to convince that it is worth doing. That affects what kind of deals get done with the Americans.

Kim Samuel-Johnson, Canada; Director, The Samuel Group

All Americans care about is size. Unless you are a huge company, with a well-known name, you are not worth their time. ●

Source: Courtney Fingar, "Table Manners," *Global Business,* (July 2000): 48–52; Stephan Herrera, "Damn Yankees," *Forbes* (March 10, 1997): 22–23; and Richard D. Lewis, *When Cultures Collide* (London: Nicholas Brealy Publishing, 1997): 2.

The ever-increasing level of world trade, opening of new markets, and intensifying competition have allowed—and sometimes forced—businesses to expand their operations. The challenge for managers is to handle the different values, attitudes, and behavior that govern human interaction. First, managers must ensure smooth interaction of the business with its different constituents, and second, they must assist others to implement programs within and across markets. It is no longer feasible to think of markets and operations in terms of domestic and international. Because the separation is no longer distinguishable, the necessity of culturally sensitive management and personnel is paramount.

As firms expand their operations across borders, they acquire new customers and new partners in new environments. Two distinct tasks become necessary: first, to understand cultural differences and the ways they manifest themselves and, second, to determine similarities across cultures and exploit them in strategy formulation. Success in new markets is very much a function of cultural adaptability: patience, flexibility, and appreciation of others' beliefs.[1] Recognition of different approaches may lead to establishing best practice; that is, a new way of doing things applicable throughout the firm. Ideally, this means that successful ideas can be transferred across borders for efficiency and adjusted to local conditions for effectiveness. Take the case of Nestlé. In one of his regular trips to company headquarters in Switzerland, the general manager of Nestlé Thailand was briefed on a summer coffee promotion from the Greek subsidiary, a cold coffee concoction called the Nescafe Shake. The Thai Group swiftly adopted and adapted the idea. It designed plastic containers to mix the drink and invented a dance, the Shake, to popularize the activity.[2]

Cultural competence must be recognized as a key management skill.[3] Cultural incompetence, or inflexibility, can easily jeopardize millions of dollars through wasted negotiations; lost purchases, sales, and contracts; and poor customer relations. Furthermore, the internal efficiency of a multinational corporation may be weakened if managers and workers are not "on the same wavelength." The tendency for U.S. managers is to be open and informal, but in some cultural settings that may be inappropriate. Similar hurdles are highlighted in the opening vignette. Cultural risk is just as real as commercial or political risk in the international business arena.

The intent of this chapter is to analyze the concept of culture and its various elements and then to provide suggestions for meeting the cultural challenge.

Culture Defined

Culture gives an individual an anchoring point, an identity, as well as codes of conduct. Of the more than 160 definitions of culture analyzed by Kroeber and Kluckhohn, some conceive of culture as separating humans from nonhumans, some define it as communicable knowledge, and some as the sum of historical achievements produced by man's social life.[4] All of the definitions have common elements: Culture is learned, shared, and transmitted from one generation to the next. Culture is primarily passed on from parents to their children but also transmitted by social organizations, special interest groups, the government, schools, and churches. Common ways of thinking and behaving that are developed are then reinforced through social pressure. Geert Hofstede calls this the "collective programming of the mind."[5] Culture is also multidimensional, consisting of a number of common elements that are interdependent. Changes occurring in one of the dimensions will affect the others as well.

For the purposes of this text, culture is defined as an *integrated system of learned behavior patterns that are characteristic of the members of any given society.* It includes everything that a group thinks, says, does, and makes—its customs, language, material artifacts, and shared systems of attitudes and feelings.[6] The definition, therefore, encompasses a wide variety of elements from the materialistic to the spiritual. Culture is inherently conservative, resisting change and fostering continuity. Every person is encultured into a particular culture, learning the "right way" of doing things. Problems may arise when a person encultured in one culture has to adjust to another one. The process of **acculturation**—adjusting and adapting to a specific culture other than one's own—is one of the keys to success in international operations.

Edward T. Hall, who has made some of the most valuable studies on the effects of culture on business, makes a distinction between high- and low-context cultures.[7] In **high-context cultures,** such as Japan and Saudi Arabia, context is at least as important as what is actually said. The speaker and the listener rely on a common understanding of the context. In **low-context cultures,** however, most of the information is contained explicitly in the words. North American cultures engage in low-context communications. Unless one is aware of this basic difference, messages and intentions can easily be misunderstood. As an example, performance appraisals are typically a human resources function. If performance appraisals are to be centrally guided or conducted in a multinational corporation, those involved must be acutely aware of cultural nuances. One of the interesting differences is that the U.S. system emphasizes the individual's development, whereas the Japanese system focuses on the group within which the individual works. In the United States, criticism is more direct and recorded formally, whereas in Japan it is more subtle and verbal. What is not being said can carry more meaning than what is said.

Few cultures today are as homogeneous as those of Japan and Saudi Arabia. Elsewhere intracultural differences based on nationality, religion, race, or geographic

Mutual awareness of cultural differences is essential in international business. Levels of formality vary greatly among cultures. In most situations, restraint equals respect.

areas have resulted in the emergence of distinct subcultures. The international manager's task is to distinguish relevant cross-cultural and intracultural differences and then to isolate potential opportunities and problems. Good examples are the Hispanic subculture in the United States and the Flemish and the Walloons in Belgium. On the other hand, borrowing and interaction among national cultures may narrow gaps between cultures. Here the international business entity acts as a **change agent** by introducing new products or ideas and practices. Although this may only shift consumption from one product brand to another, it may also lead to massive social change in the manner of consumption, the type of products consumed, and social organization. Consider, for example, that in the 1990s the international portion of McDonald's annual sales grew from 13 percent to 58 percent.[8] In markets such as Taiwan, one of the 119 countries on six continents entered, McDonald's and other fast food entities dramatically changed eating habits, especially of the younger generation.

The example of Kentucky Fried Chicken in India illustrates the difficulties marketers may have in entering culturally complex markets. Even though the company opened its outlets in two of India's most cosmopolitan cities (Bangalore and New Delhi), it found itself the target of protests by a wide range of opponents. KFC could have alleviated or eliminated some of the anti-Western passions by tailoring its activities to the local conditions. First, rather than opting for more direct control, KFC should have allied itself with local partners for advice and support. Second, KFC should have tried to appear more Indian rather than using high-profile advertising with Western ideas. Indians are ambivalent toward foreign culture, and its ideas may not always work well there. Finally, KFC should have planned for competition, which came from small restaurants with political clout at the local level.[9]

In bringing about change or in trying to cater to increasingly homogeneous demand across markets, the international business entity may be accused of "cultural imperialism," especially if the changes brought about are dramatic or if culture-specific adaptations are not made in management or marketing programs. Some countries, such as Brazil, Canada, France, and Indonesia, protect their "cultural industries" (such as music and motion pictures) through restrictive rules and subsidies. The WTO agreement that allows restrictions on exports of U.S. entertainment to Europe is justified by the Europeans as a cultural safety net intended to preserve national and regional identities.[10] This is highlighted in Global Perspective 2.1. In June 1998, Canada organized a meeting in Ottawa about U.S. cultural dominance. Nineteen countries attended, including Britain, Brazil, and Mexico; the United States was excluded. At issue were ways of exempting cultural goods from treaties lowering trade barriers, on the view that free trade threatened national cultures. The Ottawa meeting followed a similar gathering in Stockholm, sponsored by the United Nations, which resolved to press for special exemptions for cultural goods in the Multilateral Agreement on Investment.[11]

Even if a particular country is dominant in a cultural sector, such as the United States in movies and television programming, the commonly suggested solution of protectionism may not work. Although the European Union has a rule that 40 percent of the programming has to be domestic, anyone wanting a U.S. program can choose an appropriate channel or rent a video. Quotas will also result in behavior not intended by regulators. U.S. programming tends to be scheduled more during prime time, while the 60 percent of domestic programming may wind up being shown during less-attractive times. Furthermore, quotas may also lead to local productions designed to satisfy official mandates and capture subsidies that accompany them. Many emerging markets are following suit; in Cambodia, for example, local TV stations are requested by the Information Ministry to show local films three times a week.[12]

Popular culture is not only a U.S. bastion. In many areas, such as pop music and musicals, Europeans have had an equally dominant position worldwide. Furthermore, no market is only an exporter of culture. Given the ethnic diversity in the United States (as in many other country markets), programming from around the world is made available. Many of the greatest successes of cultural products in 1999–2001 in the

GLOBAL PERSPECTIVE 2.1

Culture Wars

Films made in the United States have continued to sweep the globe. According to the list of 1998's most successful movies put together by *Variety* magazine, U.S. films took the top 39 places; Britain's *The Full Monty* came in at number 40. As a consequence, British movies' market share fell to 14 percent of the home market, while the respective figures for French films were 27 percent in France and 10 percent for German films in Germany. The European Union's trade deficit with the United States in films and television is annually between $5 and $6 billion.

A number of developments seem to conspire to favor U.S. films. Multiplex cinemas have spread throughout Europe with attendance increasing dramatically. However, multiplexes tend to show more U.S. movies. Along with the multiplexes has come the return of the blockbuster, such as *Titanic* and *Star Wars: The Phantom Menace*. These movies are made with budgets beyond the Europeans' wildest dreams. At the same time, studios' spending on marketing has leapt. Marketing compaigns start typically six months before the release and spending has increased to an average of $3.2 million; up twofold from the mid-1990s. Finally, U.S. studios are becoming increasingly dependent on overseas revenues and are, therefore, keen on investing more in developing those markets. In 1998, foreign revenues were almost level with the domestic ones; 15 years earlier they were half as big.

The Europeans have found a powerful ally in Canada, which has long been concerned about being overly influenced by its closest neighbor. Of the films shown on Canadian screens, 96 percent are foreign, primarily American. In 2000, a Molson advertisement in which the spokesperson ("Joe Canada") extolled the virtues of being a Canadian ("I have a prime minister, not a president; I speak English and French, not American. . . . I believe in peace-keeping, not policing; diversity, not assimilation. . . . Canada is the second-largest land

mass, and the first nation of hockey, and the best part of North America") became a cult phenomenon.

A strong case can be made regarding the dominance of the United States. It does not make the most feature films, but its movies reach and are sought out by every market in the world. Movies made in India and Hong Kong, although numerous, seldom travel outside their regions. However, many arguments can also be made to negate the threat. The nature of U.S. films is increasingly not just "American." From its earliest days, Hollywood has been open to overseas talent and money. Some of the great figures—Chaplin and Hitchcock, for example—were imports. Today, two of the powerful studios (Columbia Tristar and Fox) are owned by media conglomerates from abroad (Japan's SONY and Australia's News Corporation).

Several of Hollywood's most successful movies have drawn from international resources. *Three Men and a Baby* was a remake of French comedy. *Total Recall* was made partly by French money, was directed by a Dutchman and starred an Austrian. *The English Patient* was directed by a Briton, shot in Italy, and starred French and British talent. The quest for new ideas and fresh talent has lead studios to develop subsidiaries in Europe: SONY's Bridge in London, Miramax in Berlin, and Warner Brothers both in Berlin and Paris.

One could conclude that it is less a matter of Hollywood corrupting the world than the world corrupting Hollywood. The more Hollywood becomes dependent on the world market, the more it produces generic blockbusters made to play from Pisa to Peoria to Penang. One could argue that since these films are more likely to be driven by special effects (that can be appreciated by people with a minimal grasp of English) rather than by dialogue and plot, and have subjects that anyone can identify with, there is something inherently objectionable in them. The movie goer is the final arbiter in this consumption situation as well.

Sources: "'Joe Canada' Crosses the Line," *The Washington Post*, January 17, 2001, A11; "Think Globally, Script Locally," *Fortune*, November 9, 1999, 156–160; "European Film Industry: Worrying Statistix," *The Economist*, February 6, 1999, 40–41; "If In Doubt, Bash the French," *The Economist*, December 12, 1998, 70–73; "Culture Wars," *The Economist*, September 12, 1998, 97–99; and "Does Canadian Culture Need This Much Protection?" *Business Week*, June 8, 1998.

United States were non-U.S.; e.g., in television programming, "Who Wants to Be a Millionaire?" is a British concept, as is the best-seller in children's literature, Harry Potter. In cartoons, Pokémon hails from Japan.

The Elements of Culture

The study of culture has led to generalizations that may apply to all cultures. Such characteristics are called **cultural universals,** which are manifestations of the total way of life of any group of people. These include such elements as bodily adornment, courtship rituals, etiquette, concept of family, gestures, joking, mealtime customs,

TABLE 2.1	• Language	• Manners and customs
Elements of Culture	Verbal	• Material elements
	Nonverbal	• Aesthetics
	• Religion	• Education
	• Values and attitudes	• Social institutions

music, personal names, status differentiation, and trade customs.[13] These activities occur across cultures, but they may be uniquely manifested in a particular society, bringing about cultural diversity. Common denominators can indeed be found across cultures, but cultures may vary dramatically in how they perform the same activities.[14]

Observation of the major cultural elements summarized in Table 2.1 suggests that these elements are both material (such as tools) and abstract (such as attitudes). The sensitivity and adaptation to these elements by an international firm depends on the firm's level of involvement in the market—for example, licensing versus direct investment—and the good or service marketed. Naturally, some goods and services or management practices require very little adjustment, while some have to be adapted dramatically.

Language

Language has been described as the mirror of culture. Language itself is multidimensional by nature. This is true not only of the spoken word but also of what can be called the nonverbal language of international business. Messages are conveyed by the words used, by how the words are spoken (for example, tone of voice), and through nonverbal means such as gestures, body position, and eye contact.

Very often mastery of the language is required before a person is accultured to a culture other than his or her own. Language mastery must go beyond technical competency, because every language has words and phrases that can be readily understood only in context. Such phrases are carriers of culture; they represent special ways a culture has developed to view some aspect of human existence.

Language capability serves four distinct roles in international business.[15] Language is important in information gathering and evaluation. Rather than rely completely on the opinions of others, the manager is able to see and hear personally what is going on. People are far more comfortable speaking their own language, and this should be treated as an advantage. The best intelligence on a market is gathered by becoming part of the market rather than observing it from the outside. For example, local managers of a multinational corporation should be the firm's primary source of political information to assess potential risk. Second, language provides access to local society. Although English may be widely spoken and may even be the official company language, speaking the local language may make a dramatic difference. Third, language capability is increasingly important in company communications, whether within the corporate family or with channel members. Imagine the difficulties encountered by a country manager who must communicate with employees through an interpreter. Finally, language provides more than the ability to communicate. It extends beyond mechanics to the interpretation of contexts.

The manager's command of the national language(s) in a market must be greater than simple word recognition. Consider, for example, how dramatically different English terms can be when used in the United Kingdom or the United States. In negotiations, for U.S. delegates, "tabling a proposal" means that they want to delay a decision, while their British counterparts understand the expression to mean that immediate action is to be taken. If the British promise something "by the end of the day," this does not mean within 24 hours, but rather when they have completed the job. Additionally, they may say that negotiations "bombed," meaning that they were a success, which to an American could convey exactly the opposite message. Other languages are not immune to this phenomenon either. Goodyear has identified five different terms for the word "tires" in the Spanish-speaking Americas: *cauchos* in Venezuela, *cubiertas* in Argentina, *gomas* in Puerto Rico, *neumaticos* in Chile, and *llantas* in most of the other countries in the region. The company has to adjust its communications messages accordingly.[16]

The two advertising campaigns presented in Figure 2.1 highlight the difficulties of transferring advertising campaigns across markets. Electrolux's theme for vacuum cleaners is taken literally in the United Kingdom, but in the United States, slang implications interfere with the intended message. With Lucky Goldstar, adaptation into Arabic was carried out without considering that Arabic reads from right to left. As a result, the creative concept in this execution was destroyed.

The role of language extends beyond that of a communication medium. Linguistic diversity often is an indicator of other types of diversity. In Quebec, the French language has always been a major consideration of most francophone governments, because it is one of the clear manifestations of the province's identity vis-à-vis the English-speaking provinces. The Charter of the French Language states that the rights of the francophone collectivity are: (1) the right of every person to have the civil administration, semipublic agencies, and business firms communicate with him or her in French; (2) the right of workers to carry on their activities in French; and (3) the right of consumers to be informed and served in French. The Bay, a major Quebec retailer, spends $8 million annually on translation. It has even changed its name to La Baie in appropriate areas. Similarly, in trying to battle English as the *lingua franca*, the French government has tried to ban the use of any foreign term or expression wherever an officially approved French equivalent (e.g., *mercatique*, not *un brain-storming* and *jeune-pousse*, not *un start-up*).[17] This applies also to web sites that bear the "fr" designation; they have to be in the French language.

FIGURE 2.1   Example of Ads That Transferred Poorly

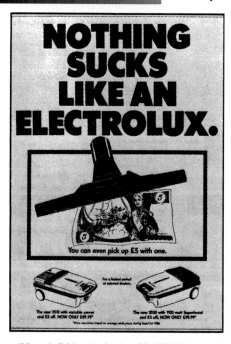

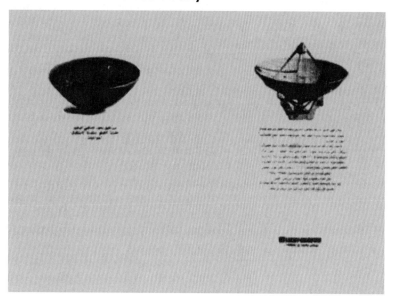

Sources: "Viewpoint," *Advertising Age*, June 29, 1987, 20; Mourad Boutros, "Lost in Translation," *M&M Europe*, September 1992, iv–v.

Despite the fact that English is encountered daily by those on the Internet, the "e" in e-business does not translate into English. In a survey, European users highlighted the need to bridge the language gap. One-third of the senior managers said they will not tolerate English online, while less than 20 percent of German middle managers and less than 50 percent of French ones believe they can use English well. Being forced to use nonlocalized content was perceived to have a negative impact on productivity among 75 percent of those surveyed.[18] A truly global portal works only if the online functions are provided in a multi-lingual and multi-culturalized format.

Dealing with language invariably requires local assistance. A good local advertising agency and a good local market research firm can prevent many problems. When translation is required, as when communicating with suppliers or customers, care should be taken in selecting the translator. The old saying, "If you want to kill a message, translate it," is true in that what needs to be conveyed is a feeling, which may require dramatically different terms than is achieved through a purely technical translation. In this context, translation software can generate a rough translation (it is 85 percent accurate) which then can be proofread and edited.[19] To make sure, the simplest method of control is **backtranslation**—translating a foreign language version back to the original language by a different person than the one who made the first translation. This approach may be able to detect only omissions and blunders, however. To assess the quality of the translation, a complete evaluation with testing of the message's impact is necessary.[20] A significant benefit of the Internet is accessibility to translation services worldwide to secure best quality and price.

Language has to also be understood in the historic context. Nokia launched an advertising campaign in Germany for the interchangeable covers for its portable phones using a theme "*Jedem das Seine*" ("to each his own"). The campaign was withdrawn after the American Jewish Congress pointed out that the same slogan was found on the entry portal to Buchenwald, a Nazi-era concentration camp.[21]

Nonverbal Language

Managers also must analyze and become familiar with the hidden language of foreign cultures.[22] Five key topics—time, space, material possessions, friendship patterns, and business agreements—offer a starting point from which managers can begin to acquire the understanding necessary to do business in foreign countries. In many parts of the world, time is flexible and not seen as a limited commodity; people come late to appointments or may not come at all. In Hong Kong, for example, it is futile to set exact meeting times, because getting from one place to another may take minutes or hours depending on the traffic situation. Showing indignation or impatience at such behavior would astonish an Arab, Latin American, or Asian. Understanding national and cultural differences in the concept of time is critical for an international business manager.

In some countries, extended social acquaintance and the establishment of appropriate personal rapport are essential to conducting business. The feeling is that one should know one's business partner on a personal level before transactions can occur. Therefore, rushing straight to business will not be rewarded, because deals are made on the basis of not only the best product or price but also the entity or person deemed most trustworthy. Contracts may be bound on handshakes, not lengthy and complex agreements—a fact that makes some, especially Western, businesspeople uneasy.

Individuals vary in the amount of space they want separating them from others. Arabs and Latin Americans like to stand close to people when they talk. If an American, who may not be comfortable at such close range, backs away from an Arab, this might incorrectly be taken as a negative reaction. Also, Westerners are often taken aback by the more physical nature of affection between Slavs—for example, being kissed squarely on the lips by a business partner, regardless of sex.

International body language must be included in the nonverbal language of international business. For example, an American manager may, after successful completion of negotiations, impulsively give a finger-and-thumb OK sign. In southern France, the manager would have indicated that the sale was worthless and, in Japan that a little bribe had been requested; the gesture would be grossly insulting to Brazilians. An interesting exercise is to compare and contrast the conversation styles of different nationalities. Northern Europeans are quite reserved in using their hands and maintain a good amount of personal space, whereas southern Europeans involve their bodies to a far greater degree in making a point.

Religion

In most cultures, people find in religion a reason for being and legitimacy in the belief that they are of a larger context. To define religion requires the inclusion of the supernatural and the existence of a higher power. Religion defines the ideals for life, which in turn are reflected in the values and attitudes of societies and individuals. Such values and attitudes shape the behavior and practices of institutions and members of cultures.

Religion has an impact on international business that is seen in a culture's values and attitudes toward entrepreneurship, consumption, and social organization. The impact will vary depending on the strength of the dominant religious tenets. While religion's impact may be quite indirect in Protestant Northern Europe, its impact in countries where Islamic fundamentalism is on the rise (such as Algeria) may be profound.

Religion provides the basis for transcultural similarities under shared beliefs and behavior. The impact of these similarities will be assessed in terms of the dominant religions of the world, Christianity, Islam, Hinduism, Buddhism, and Confucianism. Other religions may have smaller numbers of followers, such as in the case of Judaism with 14 million followers around the world, but their impact is still significant due to the centuries they have influenced world history. While some countries may officially have secularism, such as Marxism-Leninism as a state belief (for example, China, Vietnam, and Cuba), traditional religious beliefs still remain a powerful force in shaping behavior.

International managers must be aware of the differences not only among the major religions but also within them. The impact of these divisions may range from hostility, as in Sri Lanka, to barely perceptible historic suspicion, as in many European countries where Protestant and Catholic are the main divisions. With some religions, such as Hinduism, people may be divided into groups, which determines their status and to a large extent their ability to consume.

Christianity has the largest following among world religions, with more than 2 billion people.[23] While there are many subgroups within Christianity, the major division is between Catholicism and Protestantism. A prominent difference between the two is the attitude toward making money. While Catholicism has questioned it, the Protestant ethic has emphasized the importance of work and the accumulation of wealth for the glory of God. At the same time, frugality was emphasized and the residual accumulation of wealth from hard work formed the basis for investment. It has been proposed that the work ethic is responsible for the development of capitalism in the western world and the rise of predominantly Protestant countries into world economic leadership in the twentieth century.[24]

Major holidays are often tied to religion. Holidays are observed differently from one culture to the next, to the extent that the same holiday may have different connota-

Religions of the World: A Part of Culture

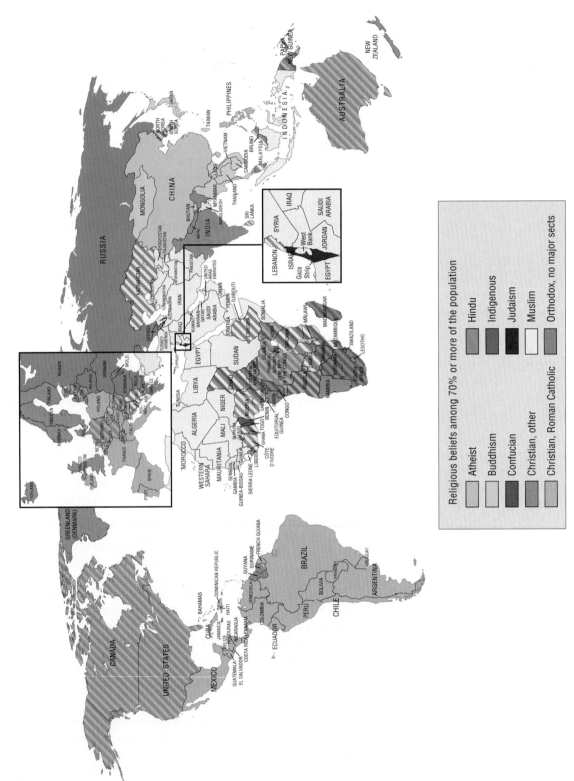

Religious beliefs among 70% or more of the population

- Atheist
- Buddhism
- Confucian
- Christian, other
- Christian, Roman Catholic
- Hindu
- Indigenous
- Judaism
- Muslim
- Orthodox, no major sects

Source: *The World Factbook 2000*

tions. Christian cultures observe Christmas and exchange gifts on either December 24 or December 25, with the exception of the Dutch, who exchange gifts on St. Nicholas Day, December 6. Tandy Corporation, in its first year in the Netherlands, targeted its major Christmas promotion for the third week of December with less than satisfactory results. The international manager must see to it that local holidays are taken into account in scheduling events ranging from fact-finding missions to marketing programs and in preparing local work schedules.

Islam, which reaches from the west coast of Africa to the Philippines and across a broad band that includes Tanzania, central Asia, western China, India, and Malaysia, has more than 1.2 billion followers.[25] Islam is also a significant minority religion in many parts of the world, including Europe. Islam has a pervasive role in the life of its followers, referred to as Muslims, through the Sharia (law of Islam). This is most obvious in the five stated daily periods of prayer, fasting during the holy month of Ramadan, and the pilgrimage to Mecca, Islam's holy city. While Islam is supportive of entrepreneurship, it nevertheless strongly discourages acts that may be interpreted as exploitation. Islam is also absent of discrimination, except against those outside the religion. Some have argued that Islam's basic fatalism (that is, nothing happens without the will of Allah) and traditionalism have deterred economic development in countries observing the religion.

The role of women in business is tied to religion, especially in the Middle East, where women do not function as they would in the West. This affects the conduct of business in various ways; for example, the firm may be limited in its use of female managers or personnel in these markets, and women's role as consumers and influencers in the consumption process may be different. Access to women in Islamic countries may only be possible through the use of female sales personnel, direct marketing, and women's specialty shops.[26] Religion impacts goods and services, as well. When beef or poultry is exported to an Islamic country, the animal must be killed in the "halal" method and certified appropriately. Recognition of religious restrictions on products (for example, alcoholic beverages) can reveal opportunities, as evidenced by successful launches of several nonalcoholic beverages in the Middle East. Other restrictions may call for innovative solutions. A challenge for the Swedish firm that had the primary responsibility for building a traffic system to Mecca was that non-Muslims are not allowed access to the city. The solution was to use closed-circuit television to supervise the work. Given that Islam considers interest payments usury, bankers and Muslim scholars have worked to create interest-free banking that relies on lease agreements, mutual funds, and other methods to avoid paying interest.[27]

Hinduism has 860 million followers, mainly in India, Nepal, Malaysia, Guyana, Suriname, and Sri Lanka. In addition to being a religion it is also a way of life predicated on the caste, or class to which one is born. While the caste system has produced social stability, its impact on business can be quite negative. For example, if it is difficult to rise above one's caste, individual effort is hampered. Problems in work force integration and coordination may become quite severe. Furthermore, the drive for business success may not be important if followers place value mostly on spiritual rather than materialistic achievement.

The family is an important element of Hindu society, with extended families being a norm. The extended family structure affects the purchasing power and consumption of Hindu families, and market researchers, in particular, must take this into account in assessing market potential and consumption patterns.

Buddhism, which extends its influence throughout Asia from Sri Lanka to Japan, has 360 million followers. Although it is an offspring of Hinduism, it has no caste system. Life is seen as filled with suffering, with achieving nirvana—a spiritual state marked by an absence of desire—as the solution. The emphasis in Buddhism is on spiritual achievement rather than worldly goods.

Confucianism has over 150 million followers throughout Asia, especially among the Chinese, and has been characterized as a code of conduct rather than a religion.

However, its teachings, which stress loyalty and relationships, have been broadly adopted. Loyalty to central authority and placing the good of a group before that of the individual may explain the economic success of Japan, South Korea, Singapore, and the Republic of China. It also has led to cultural misunderstandings: Western societies often perceive the subordination of the individual to the common good as a violation of human rights. The emphasis on relationships is very evident in developing business ties in Asia. Preparation may take years before understanding is reached and actual business transactions can take place.

Values and Attitudes

Values are shared beliefs or group norms that have been internalized by individuals.[28] Attitudes are evaluations of alternatives based on these values. Differences in cultural values affect the way planning is executed, decisions are made, strategy is implemented, and personnel are evaluated. Table 2.2 provides examples of how U.S. values differ from other values around the world and how this, in turn, affects management functions. These cultural values have to be accommodated or used in the management of business functions.

The more rooted values and attitudes are in central beliefs (such as religion), the more cautiously one has to move. Attitude toward change is basically positive in industrialized countries, as is one's ability to improve one's lot in life; in tradition-bound societies, however, change is viewed with suspicion—especially when it comes from a foreign entity.

The Japanese culture raises an almost invisible—yet often unscalable—wall against all *gaijin* (foreigners). Many middle-aged bureaucrats and company officials believe that buying foreign products is downright unpatriotic. The resistance is not so much to foreign products as to those who produce and market them. Similarly, foreign-based corporations have had difficulty hiring university graduates or midcareer personnel because of bias against foreign employers. Even under such adverse conditions, the race can be run and won through tenacity, patience, and drive.

Dealing in China and with the Chinese, the international manager will have to realize that making deals has more to do with cooperation than competition. The Chinese believe that one should build the relationship first and, if successful, transactions will follow. The relationship, or *guanxi*, is a set of favor exchanges to establish trust.[29]

Cultural differences themselves can be a selling point suggesting luxury, prestige, or status. Occasionally, U.S. firms successfully use American themes abroad that would not succeed at home. In Japan, Levi Strauss promoted its popular jeans with a television campaign featuring James Dean and Marilyn Monroe, who represent the epitome of Japanese youths' fantasy of freedom from a staid, traditional society. The commercials helped establish Levi's as *the* prestige jeans, and status-seeking Japanese youth were willing to pay 40 percent more for them than local brands. Their authentic Levi's, however, are designed and mostly made in Japan, where buyers like a tighter fit. Similarly, many global brands, such as Nike and Reebok, are able to charge premium prices for their products due to a loyal following.[30] At the same time, in the U.S. market, many companies have been successful emphasizing their foreign, imported image. For example, some of the best tuna from New England may make it to New York and Los Angeles via Tokyo as soon as it has been validated as top quality by the decision to ship it to Japan by air for sale at Tokyo's seafood market. There, it may be purchased by one of a selected few of sushi exporters who then supply premier expatriate sushi chefs in the world's leading cities.[31]

A manager must be careful not to assume that success in one market using the cultural extension ensures success somewhere else. For example, while the Disneyland

TABLE 2.2	Effect of Value Differences on Management Practice	
Value of U.S. Culture	Alternative Value	Management Functions Affected
The individual can influence the future (where there is a will there is a way).	Life follows a preordained course, and human action is determinated by the will of God.	Planning and scheduling
We must work hard to accomplish our objectives (Protestant ethic).	Hard work is not the only prerequisite for success. Wisdom, luck, and time are also required.	Motivation and reward system
Commitments should be honored (people will do what they say they will do).	A commitment may be superseded by a conflicting request or an agreement may only signify intention and have little or no relationship to the capacity of performance.	Negotiating and bargaining
One should effectively use one's time (time is money that can be saved or wasted).	Schedules are important but only in relation to other priorities.	Long- and short-range planning
A primary obligation of an employee is to the organization.	The individual employee has a primary obligation to his family and friends.	Loyalty, commitment, and motivation
The best qualified persons should be given the positions available.	Family considerations, friendship, and other considerations should determine employment practices.	Employment, promotions, recruiting, selection, and reward.
Intuitive aspects of decision making should be reduced, and efforts should be devoted to gathering relevant information.	Decisions are expressions of wisdom by the person in authority, and any questioning would imply a lack of confidence in his judgment.	Decision-making process
Data should be accurate.	Accurate data are not as highly valued.	Record keeping
Company information should be available to anyone who needs it within the organization.	Withholding information to gain or maintain power is acceptable.	Organization communication, managerial style
Each person is expected to have an opinion and to express it freely even if his views do not agree with his colleagues.	Deference is to be given to persons in power or authority, and to offer judgment that is not in support of the ideas of one's superiors is unthinkable.	Communications, organizational relations
A person is expected to do whatever is necessary to get the job done (one must be willing to get one's hands dirty).	Various kinds of work are accorded low or high status and some work may be below one's "dignity" or place in the organization.	Assignment of tasks, performance, and organizational effectiveness
Change is considered an improvement and a dynamic reality.	Tradition is revered, and the power of the ruling group is founded on the continuation of a stable structure.	Planning, morale, and organization development

Source: Adapted from Philip R. Harris and Robert T. Moran, *Managing Cultural Differences* (Houston, TX: Gulf Publishing, 1996), table 4.1.

concept worked well in Tokyo, it had a tougher time in Paris. One of the main reasons was that while the Japanese are fond of American pop culture, the Europeans are quite content with their own cultural heritage.[32]

Manners and Customs

Changes occurring in manners and customs must be carefully monitored, especially in cases that seem to indicate a narrowing of cultural differences among peoples.

GLOBAL PERSPECTIVE 2.2

Negotiating in Europe: Splitting the Many Differences

While the European Union is an economic dynamo with over 375 million people and economic power to match any other bloc, it is also a patchwork quilt of different languages and national customs, which makes it far less homogeneous than Japan, the United States, or even Asia as a whole. All of this can make negotiating in Europe a challenge. Businesspeople tend to be relatively reserved and quite formal (especially compared with their U.S. counterparts). One has to be prepared to wait for the work to begin and for an atmosphere of trust to be created. While any stereotyping of negotiators can be dangerous, broad characterizations do help negotiators as sensitization tools.

Even among Europeans, if two partners have not taken the trouble to get acquainted or complete their homework, the results can be disastrous. In one case, the Italian director of a construction company went to Germany to negotiate for a project. He began the discussion with a presentation of his company that vaunted its long history and its achievements. The German managers first looked startled, then they excused themselves and walked out the door, without even listening to the offer. The explanation: Germans typically do all the necessary background research before walking in the door. They thought the Italian manager was engaged in idle boasting about his company, and they found that offensive. Yet the Italian manager thought he was engaged in a vague preliminary to any real negotiations. Real negotiating, as far as he was concerned, would not start at least for another day.

The example also illustrates the stark differences between the business styles of the northern and southern Europeans. Northern Europe, with its Protestant tradition and indoor culture, tends to emphasize the technical, the numerical, the tested. Southern Europe, on the other hand, with its Catholic background and open-air lifestyle, tends to favor personal networks, social context, innovation, and flair. Meetings in the south are often longer, but the total decision process may be faster. Differences exist within regions as well. For example, in approaching negotiations, Nordics embrace win-win styles, while the British and Germans prefer position-based tactics in which the parties act as adversaries who stake out their positions and fight aggressively to defend them.

The French do not neatly fit into the north-south dichotomy: One study found that the style of French negotiators was the most aggressive of thirteen diverse cultures studied. In a way, the French still embrace the art of diplomatic negotiating invented in France in the fourteenth century. French managers will have carefully prepared for the negotiations, but they generally will begin with some light, logical sparring. Throughout the preliminary and middle stages of negotiating, the French manager will judge the partners carefully on their intellectual skills and their ability to reply quickly and with authority. As one French manager put it: "Sometimes I am impressed more by brilliant savvy than by a well-reasoned argument." Because the French education system stresses mathematics and logic, doing business is a highly intellectual process for French managers. The details come last in French negotiations, so the final stage can prove to be tricky. French managers tend to slip in little extras when finalizing, like executive bonuses. It is therefore important to insist on what one wants at this stage, even if days have been spent getting to this point.

Source: "Splitting the Difference," *Global Business*, July 2000, 50; John L. Graham, "Vis-à-vis International Business Negotiations," Chap. 7 *in International Business Negotiations*, ed. Jean-Claude D. Usunier and Pervez N. Ghauri (London, U.K.: Dryden Press, 1996); "Negotiating in Europe," *Hemispheres*, (July 1994): 43–47.

Phenomena such as McDonald's and Coke have met with success around the world, but this does not mean that the world is becoming westernized. Modernization and westernization are not at all the same, as can be seen in Saudi Arabia, for example.

Understanding manners and customs is especially important in negotiations, because interpretations based on one's own frame of reference may lead to a totally incorrect conclusion. Universal respect is needed in cross-cultural negotiation, as seen in Global Perspective 2.2. To negotiate effectively abroad, all types of communication should be read correctly. Americans often interpret inaction and silence as negative signs. As a result, Japanese executives tend to expect that their silence can get Americans to lower prices or sweeten a deal. Even a simple agreement may take days to negotiate in the Middle East because the Arab party may want to talk about unrelated issues or do something else for a while. The aggressive style of Russian negotiators and their usual last-minute change requests may cause astonishment and concern on the part of ill-prepared negotiators. Some of the potential ways in which negotiators may not be prepared include: (1) insufficient understanding of different ways of thinking;

(2) insufficient attention to the necessity to save face; (3) insufficient knowledge and appreciation of the host country—its history, culture, government, and image of foreigners; (4) insufficient recognition of the decision-making process and the role of personal relations and personalities; and (5) insufficient allocation of time for negotiations.[33]

One area where preparation and sensitivity are called for is in the area of gift giving. Table 2.3 provides examples of what and when to give. Gifts are an important part of relationship management during visits or recognizing partners during holidays. Care should be taken how the gift is wrapped; i.e., in appropriately-colored paper. If delivered in person, the actual giving has to be executed correctly; e.g., in China, by extending the gift to the recipient using both hands.[34]

Managers must be concerned with differences in the ways products are used. Usage differences have to be translated into product form and promotional decisions. General Foods' Tang is positioned as a breakfast drink in the United States; in France, where fruit juices and drinks are not usually consumed at breakfast, Tang is positioned as a refreshment. To shake powdered-soup domination in Argentina, Campbell markets its products as "the real soup," stressing its list of fresh ingredients. In Poland, where most soup consumed is homemade, Campbell promotes to mothers looking for convenience. The questions that the international manager has to ask are, "What are we selling?" "What are the benefits we are providing?" and "Who or what are we competing against?" Care should be taken not to assume cross-border similarities even if many of the indicators converge. For example, a jam producer noted that the Brazilian market seemed to hold significant potential because per capita jelly and jam consumption was one-tenth that of Argentina, clearly a difference not justified by obvious factors. However, Argentines consume jam at tea time, a custom that does not exist in Brazil. Furthermore, Argentina's climate and soil favor growing wheat, leading it to consume three times the bread Brazil does.[35]

Approaches that would not be considered in the United States or Europe might be recommended in other regions; for example, when Conrad Hotels (the international division of Hilton Hotels) experienced low initial occupancy rates at its Hong Kong facility, they brought in a *fung shui* man. These traditional "consultants" are foretellers of future events and the unknown through occult means, and are used extensively by Hong Kong businesses.[36] In Hilton's case, the *fung shui* man suggested a piece of sculpture be moved outside the hotel's lobby because one of the characters in the statue looked like it was trying to run out of the hotel. The hotel's occupancy rate boomed.

Meticulous research plays a major role in avoiding these types of problems. Concept tests determine the potential acceptance and proper understanding of a proposed

TABLE 2.3		When to Give and What in Gifts		
China	**India**	**Japan**	**Mexico**	**Saudi Arabia**
Chinese New Year (January or February)	*Hindu Diwali festival (October or November)*	*Oseibo (January 1)*	*Christmas/New Year*	*Id al-Fitr (December or January)*
✓ Modest gifts such as coffee table books, ties, pens	✓ Sweets, nuts, and fruit; elephant carvings; candleholders	✓ Scotch, brandy, Americana, round fruit such as melons	✓ Desk clocks, fine pens, gold lighters	✓ Fine compasses to determine direction for prayer, cashmere
✗ Clocks, anything from Taiwan	✗ Leather objects, snake images	✗ Gifts that come in sets of four or nine	✗ Sterling silver items, logo gifts, food baskets	✗ Pork and pigskin, liquor

✓ recommended
✗ to be avoided

Source: Kate Murphy, "Gifts Without Gaffes for Global Clients," *Business Week*, December 6, 1999, 153.

new product. **Focus groups,** each consisting of 8 to 12 consumers representative of the proposed target audience, can be interviewed and their responses used as disaster checks and to fine-tune research findings. The most sensitive products, such as consumer packaged goods, require consumer usage and attitude studies as well as retail distribution studies and audits to analyze the movement of the product to retailers and eventually to households.

Material Elements

Material culture refers to the results of technology and is directly related to how a society organizes its economic activity. It is manifested in the availability and adequacy of the basic economic, social, financial, and marketing infrastructure for the international business in a market. The basic **economic infrastructure** consists of transportation, energy, and communications systems. **Social infrastructure** refers to housing, health, and educational systems prevailing in the country of interest. **Financial** and **marketing infrastructures** provide the facilitating agencies for the international firm's operation in a given market—for example, banks and research firms. In some parts of the world, the international firm may have to be an integral partner in developing the various infrastructures before it can operate, whereas in others it may greatly benefit from their high level of sophistication.

The level of material culture can aid segmentation efforts if the degree of industrialization of the market is used as a basis. For companies selling industrial goods, such as General Electric, this can provide a convenient starting point. In developing countries, demand may be highest for basic energy-generating products. In fully developed markets, time-saving home appliances may be more in demand.

Technological advances have been the major cause of cultural change in many countries. Increasingly, consumers are seeking more diverse products as a way of satisfying their demand for a higher quality of life and more leisure time. For example, a 1999 Gallup survey in China found that 44 percent of the respondents were saving to buy electronic items and appliances, which was second only to saving for a rainy day.[37] With technological advancement comes also **cultural convergence.** Black and white television sets extensively penetrated U.S. households more than a decade before similar levels occurred in Europe and Japan. With color television, the lag was reduced to five years. With video cassette recorders, the difference was only three years, but this time the Europeans and Japanese led the way while the United States was concentrating on cable systems. With the compact disc, penetration rates were equal in only one year. Today, with MTV available by satellite across Europe and the use of the Internet increasing, no lag exists.[38]

Material culture—mainly the degree to which it exists and how it is esteemed—has an impact on business decisions. Many exporters do not understand the degree to which Americans are package conscious; for example, cans must be shiny and beautiful. In foreign markets, packaging problems may arise due to the lack of materials, different specifications when the material is available, and immense differences in quality and consistency of printing ink, especially in developing markets. Ownership levels of television sets, radios, and personal computers have an impact on the ability of media to reach target audiences.

Aesthetics

Each culture makes a clear statement concerning good taste, as expressed in the arts and in the particular symbolism of colors, form, and music. What is and what is not acceptable may vary dramatically even in otherwise highly similar markets. Sex, for example, is a big selling point in many countries. In an apparent attempt to preserve the purity of Japanese womanhood, however, advertisers frequently turn to blond, blue-eyed foreign models to make the point. In introducing the shower soap Fa from the European market to the North American market, Henkel extended its European advertising campaign to the new market. The main creative difference was to have the young woman in the waves don a bathing suit rather than be naked as in the German original.

Color is often used as a mechanism for brand identification, feature reinforcement, and differentiation. In international markets, colors have more symbolic value than in domestic markets. Black, for instance, is considered the color of mourning in the United States and Europe, whereas white has the same symbolic meaning in Japan and most of the Far East. A British bank was interested in expanding its operations to Singapore and wanted to use blue and green as its identification colors. A consulting firm was quick to tell the client that green is associated with death in that country. Although the bank insisted on its original choice of colors, the green was changed to an acceptable shade.[39]

With the global reach of World Wide Web, symbols used have to be tested for universal appropriateness. The e-mailbox with its red flag is baffling to users outside of the United States and Canada. Similarly, the trash can on the e-mail interface may look to some like the British-styled mailbox. A British software application used the owl as a help icon only to find that in some countries it was not a symbol of wisdom but of evil and insanity.[40]

International firms, such as McDonald's, have to take into consideration local tastes and concerns in designing their outlets. They may have a general policy of uniformity in building or office space design, but local tastes often warrant modifications. Respecting local cultural traditions may also generate goodwill toward the international marketer. For example, McDonald's painstakingly renovated a seventeenth-century building for their third outlet in Moscow.

Education

Education, either formal or informal, plays a major role in the passing on and sharing of culture. Educational levels of a culture can be assessed using literacy rates, enrollment in secondary education, or enrollment in higher education available from secondary data sources. International firms also need to know about the qualitative aspects of education, namely, varying emphases on particular skills and the overall level of the education provided. Japan and South Korea, for example, emphasize the sciences, especially engineering, to a greater degree than do Western countries.

Educational levels also affect various business functions. For example, a high level of illiteracy suggests the use of visual aids rather than printed manuals. Local recruiting for sales jobs is affected by the availability of suitably trained personnel. In some cases, international firms routinely send locally recruited personnel to headquarters for training.

The international manager may also need to overcome obstacles in recruiting a suitable sales force or support personnel. For example, the Japanese culture places a premium on loyalty, and employees consider themselves members of the corporate family. If a foreign firm decides to leave Japan, its employees may find themselves stranded in midcareer, unable to find their place in the Japanese business system. Therefore, university graduates are reluctant to join any but the largest and most well known of foreign firms.[41]

If technology is marketed, the product's sophistication will depend on the educational level of future users. Product adaptation decisions are often influenced by the extent to which targeted customers are able to use the good or service properly.

Social Institutions

Social institutions affect the ways people relate to each other. The family unit, which in Western industrialized countries consists of parents and children, in a number of cultures is extended to include grandparents and other relatives. This affects consumption patterns and must be taken into account, for example, when conducting market research.

The concept of kinship, or blood relations between individuals, is defined in a very broad way in societies such as those in sub-Saharan Africa. Family relations and a strong obligation to family are important factors to consider in human resource management in those regions. Understanding tribal politics in countries such as Nigeria may help the manager avoid unnecessary complications in executing business transactions.

The division of a particular population into classes is termed **social stratification.** Stratification ranges from the situation in northern Europe, where most people are members of the middle class, to highly stratified societies in which the higher strata control most of the buying power and decision-making positions.

An important part of the socialization process of consumers worldwide is **reference groups.** These groups provide the values and attitudes that influence behavior. Primary reference groups include the family and coworkers and other intimate acquaintances, and secondary groups are social organizations where less-continuous interaction takes place, such as professional associations and trade organizations. In addition to providing socialization, reference groups develop a person's concept of self, which is manifested, for example, through the choice of products used. Reference groups also provide a baseline for compliance with group norms, giving the individual the option of conforming to or avoiding certain behaviors.

Social organization also determines the roles of managers and subordinates and how they relate to one another. In some cultures, managers and subordinates are separated explicitly and implicitly by various boundaries ranging from social class differences to separate office facilities. In others, cooperation is elicited through equality. For example, Nissan USA has no privileged parking spaces and no private dining rooms, everyone wears the same type of white coveralls, and the president sits in the same room with a hundred other white-collar workers. Fitting an organizational culture to the larger context of a national culture has to be executed with care. Changes that are too dramatic may disrupt productivity or, at the minimum, arouse suspicion.

Although Western business has impersonal structures for channeling power and influence—primarily through reliance on laws and contracts—the Chinese emphasize personal relationships to obtain clout. Things can get done without this human political capital, or *guanxi,* only if one invests enormous personal energy, is willing to offend even trusted associates, and is prepared to see it all melt away at a moment's notice.[42] For the Chinese, contracts form a useful agenda and a symbol of progress, but obligations come from relationships. McDonald's found this out in Beijing, where it was evicted from a central building after only 2 years despite having a 20-year contract. The incomer had a strong *guanxi,* whereas McDonald's had not kept its in good repair.[43]

Sources of Cultural Knowledge

The concept of cultural knowledge is broad and multifaceted. Cultural knowledge can be defined by the way it is acquired. Objective or factual information is obtained from others through communication, research, and education. **Experiential knowledge,** on the other hand, can be acquired only by being involved in a culture other than one's own.[44] A summary of the types of knowledge needed by the international manager is provided in Table 2.4. Both factual and experiential information can be general or country-specific. In fact, the more a manager becomes involved in the international arena, the more he or she is able to develop a metaknowledge; that is, ground rules

TABLE 2.4

Types of International Information

Source of Information	TYPE OF INFORMATION	
	General	**Country Specific**
Objective	Examples: Impact of GDP Regional integration	Examples: Tariff barriers Government regulations
Experiential	Example: Corporate adjustment to internationalization	Examples: Product acceptance Program appropriateness

that apply whether in Kuala Lumpur, Malaysia, or Asunción, Paraguay. Market-specific knowledge does not necessarily travel well; the general variables on which the information is based do.

In a survey of managers on how to acquire international expertise, they ranked eight factors in terms of their importance, as shown in Table 2.5. The managers emphasized the experiential acquisition of knowledge. Written materials played an important but supplementary role, very often providing general or country-specific information before operational decisions were made. Interestingly, many of today's international managers have precareer experience in government, the Peace Corps, the armed forces, or missionary service. Although the survey emphasized travel, a one-time trip to London with a stay at a very large hotel and scheduled sightseeing tours does not significantly contribute to cultural knowledge. Travel that involves meetings with company personnel, intermediaries, facilitating agents, customers, and government officials, on the other hand, does contribute.

However, from the corporate point of view, global capability is developed in more painstaking ways: foreign assignments, networking across borders, and the use of multicountry, multicultural teams to develop strategies and programs. At Nestlé, for example, managers move around a region (such as Asia or Latin America) at four- or five-year intervals and may serve stints at headquarters for two to three years between such assignments. Such broad experience allows managers to pick up ideas and tools to be used in markets where they have not been used or where they have not been necessary before. In Thailand, where supermarkets are revolutionizing consumer-goods marketing, techniques perfected elsewhere in the Nestlé system are being put to effective use. The experiences then, in turn, are used to develop newly emerging markets in the same region, such as Vietnam.

Managers have a variety of sources and methods to extend their knowledge of specific cultures. Most of these sources deal with factual information that provides a necessary basis for market studies. Beyond the normal business literature and its anecdotal information, specific-country studies are published by the U.S. government, private

TABLE 2.5

Managers' Ranking of Factors Involved in Acquiring International Expertise

Factor	Considered Critical	Considered Important
1. Business travel	60.8%	92.0%
2. Assignments overseas	48.8	71.2
3. Reading/television	16.0	63.2
4. Training programs	6.4	28.8
5. Precareer activities	4.0	16.0
6. Graduate courses	2.4	15.2
7. Nonbusiness travel	0.8	12.8
8. Undergraduate courses	0.8	12.0

Source: Stephen J. Kobrin, *International Expertise in American Business* (New York: Institute of International Education, 1984), 38.

GLOBAL PERSPECTIVE 2.3

Knowing Local Culture Pays Off in Profits

Thousands of European and U.S. companies have entered or expanded their operations in the fastest-growing region in the world—Asia. In the 1990s, the region outpaced the growth of the world's twenty-four leading industrial economies by more than six times. A total of 400 million Asian consumers have disposable incomes at least equal to the rich-world average.

Few companies have had as much experience—or success—as the 3M Company. The maker of everything from heart-lung machines to Scotch tape, the company's revenues for 2000 from international sales from 200 countries reached 8 billion (52 percent of total), with a full third coming from the Asia-Pacific. At the root of the company's success are certain rules that allow it both to adjust to and exploit cultural differences.

- **Embrace Local Culture**—3M's plant near Bangkok, Thailand, is one example of how the company embraces local culture. A gleaming Buddhist shrine, wreathed in flowers, pays homage to the spirits Thais believe took care of the land prior to the plant's arrival. Showing sensitivity to local customs helps sales and builds employee morale, officials say. It helps the company understand the market and keeps it from inadvertently alienating people.
- **Employ Locals to Gain Cultural Knowledge**—The best way to understand a market is to have grown up in it. Of the 7,500 3M employees in Asia, fewer than 10 are Americans. (As a matter of fact, of the 34,000 3M employees in companies outside the United States, fewer than 300 are expatriates not residing in their home countries). The rest are locals who know the customs and buying habits of their compatriots. 3M also makes grants of up to $50,000 available to its Asian employees to study product innovations, making them equals with their U.S. counterparts.
- **Build Relationships**—3M executives started preparing for the Chinese market soon after President Nixon's historic visit in 1972. For ten years, company officials visited Beijing and invited Chinese leaders to 3M headquarters in St. Paul, Minnesota, building con-

tacts and trust along the way. Such efforts paid off when, in 1984, the government made 3M the first wholly owned foreign venture on Chinese soil. 3Mers call the process FIDO ("first in defeats other"), a credo built on patience and a long-term perspective.

- **Adapt Products to Local Markets**—Examples of how 3M adapts its products read like insightful lessons on culture. In the early 1990s, sales of 3M's famous Scotchbrite cleaning pads were languishing. Company technicians interviewed maids and housewives to determine why. The answer: Filipinos traditionally scrub floors by pushing a rough coconut shell around with their feet. 3M responded by making the pads brown and shaping them like a foot. In China, a big seller for 3M is a composite to fill tooth cavities. In the United States, dentists pack a soft material into the hole and blast it with a special beam of light, making it hard as enamel in five seconds. But in the People's Republic, dentists cannot afford the light. The solution is an air-drying composite that does the same thing in two minutes: it takes a little longer but is far less expensive.
- **Help Employees Understand You**—At any given time, more than 30 Asian technicians are in the United States, where they learn the latest product advances while gaining new insight into how the company works. At the same time, they are able to contribute by infusing their insight into company plans and operations.
- **Coordinate by Region**—When designers in Singapore discovered that consumers wanted to use 3M's Nomad household floor mats in their cars, they spread the word to their counterparts in Malaysia and Thailand. Today, the specially made car mats with easy-to-clean vinyl loops are big sellers across Southeast Asia. The company encourages its product managers from different Asian countries to hold regular meetings and share insights and strategies. The goal of this cross-pollination is to come up with regional programs and "Asianize" a product more quickly. In addition, joint endeavors support the effort to build cross-border esprit de corps especially when managers may have their own markets' interests primarily at heart.

Sources: "3M Operational Facts, Year-End 2000," available at **www.mmm.com**; Charlene Solomon, "Managing an Overseas Sales Force," *World Trade,* April 1999, S4–S6; John R. Engen "Far Eastern Front," *World Trade* (December 1994): 20–24; "A Survey of Asia," *The Economist* (October 30, 1993).

companies, and universities. The U.S. Department of Commerce's (**www.ita.doc.gov**) *Country Commercial Guides* cover more than 133 countries, while the Economist Intelligence Unit's (**www.eiu.com**) *Country Reports* cover 180 countries. *Culturegrams* (**www.culturegrams.com**), which detail the customs of people of 174 countries, are published by the Center for International and Area Studies at Brigham Young University. Many agencies—such as advertising agencies, banks, consulting firms, and transportation companies—provide background information on the markets they serve for their clients. These range from Runzheimer International's (**www.runzheimer.com**)

international reports on employee relocation and site selection for 44 countries, the Hong Kong and Shanghai Banking Corporation's (**www.hsbc.com**) *Business Profile Series* for 22 countries in the Asia-Pacific, to *World Trade* (**www.worldtrademag.com**) magazine's "Put Your Best Foot Forward" series, which covers Europe, Asia, Mexico/Canada, and Russia.

Blunders in foreign markets that could have been avoided with factual information are generally inexcusable. A manager who travels to Taipei without first obtaining a visa and is therefore turned back has no one else to blame. Other oversights may lead to more costly mistakes. For example, Brazilians are several inches shorter than the average American, but this was not taken into account when Sears erected American-height shelves that block Brazilian shoppers' view of the rest of the store.

International business success requires not only comprehensive fact finding and preparation but also an ability to understand and fully appreciate the nuances of different cultural traits and patterns. Gaining this **interpretive knowledge** requires "getting one's feet wet" over a sufficient length of time. Over the long run, culture can become a factor in the firm's overall success, as seen in Global Perspective 2.3.

Cultural Analysis

To try to understand and explain differences among and across cultures, researchers have developed checklists and models showing pertinent variables and their interaction. An example of such a model is provided in Figure 2.2. Developed by Sheth and

FIGURE 2.2   A Model of Cross-Cultural Behavior

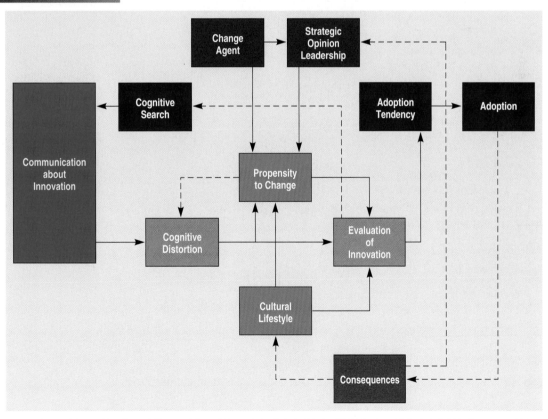

Source: Adapted by permission of the publisher from "A Theory of Cross-Cultural Buying Behavior," by Jagdish N. Sheth and S. Prakash Sethi, in *Consumer and Industrial Buyer Behavior*, eds. Arch G. Woodside, Jagdish N. Sheth, and Peter D. Bennett, 1977, 373. Copyright 1977 by Elsevier Science Publishing Co., Inc.

Sethi, this model is based on the premise that all international business activity should be viewed as innovation and as producing change.[45] After all, multinational corporations introduce management practices, as well as goods and services, from one country to others, where they are perceived to be new and different. Although many question the usefulness of such models, they do bring together all or most of the relevant variables on how consumers in different cultures may perceive, evaluate, and adopt new behaviors. However, any manager using such a tool should periodically cross-check its results against reality and experience.

The key variable of the model is propensity to change, which is a function of three constructs: (1) cultural lifestyle of individuals in terms of how deeply held their traditional beliefs and attitudes are, and also which elements of culture are dominant; (2) change agents (such as multinational corporations and their practices) and strategic-opinion leaders (for example, social elites); and (3) communication about the innovation from commercial sources, neutral sources (such as government), and social sources, such as friends and relatives.

It has been argued that differences in cultural lifestyle can be explained by four dimensions of culture.[46] The dimensions consist of: (1) individualism ("I" consciousness versus "we" consciousness); (2) power distance (levels of equality in society); (3) uncertainty avoidance (need for formal rules and regulations); and (4) masculinity (attitude toward achievement, roles of men and women). Figure 2.3 presents a summary of 12 countries' positions along these dimensions. A fifth dimension has also been added to distinguish cultural differences: long-term versus short-term orienta-

---

FIGURE 2.3   **Culture Dimension Scores for Twelve Countries (0 = low; 100 = high)**

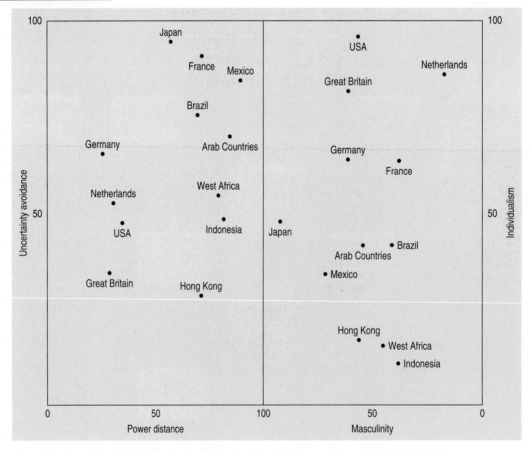

Source: Data for the figure derived from Geert Hofstede, "Management Scientists Are Human," *Management Science* 40, no. 1 (1994): 4–13.

TABLE 2.6		**Culture-Based Segmentation**				
			CULTURAL CHARACTERISTICS			
	Size (Million)	Power Distance	Uncertainty Avoidance	Individualism	Masculinity	Illustrative Marketing Implications
Cluster 1 Austria, Germany, Switzerland, Italy, Great Britain, Ireland	203	Small	Medium	Medium-High	High	Preference for "high-performance" products; use "successful-achiever" theme in advertising; desire for novelty, variety, and pleasure; fairly risk-averse market
Cluster 2 Belgium, France, Greece, Portugal, Spain, Turkey	182	Medium	Strong	Varied	Low-Medium	Appeal to consumer's status and power position, reduce perceived risk in product purchase and use, emphasize product functionality
Cluster 3 Denmark, Sweden, Finland, Netherlands, Norway	37	Small	Low	High	Low	Relatively weak resistance to new products, strong consumer desire for novelty and variety, high consumer regard for "environmentally friendly" marketers and socially conscious firms

Source: Sudhir H. Kale, "Grouping Euroconsumers: A Culture-Based Clustering Approach," *Journal of International Marketing* 3, 3 (1995): 42.

tion.[47] All of the high-scoring countries are Asian (e.g., China, Hong Kong, Taiwan, Japan, and South Korea), while most Western countries (such as the United States and Britain) have low scores. Some have argued that this cultural dimension may explain the Japanese marketing success based on market share (rather than short-term profit) motivation in market development.

Knowledge of similarities along these four dimensions allows us to cluster countries and regions and establish regional and national marketing or business programs.[48] An example is provided in Table 2.6, in which the European market is segmented along cultural lines for the development of marketing programs. Cluster 2, consisting of Southern Europe, displays the highest uncertainty avoidance and should therefore be targeted with risk-reducing marketing programs such as extended warranties and return privileges.[49] It is important to position the product as a continuous innovation that does not require radical changes in consumption patterns.[50] Since the United States highly regards individualism, promotional appeals should be relevant to individual empowerment. Also, in order to incorporate the lower power distance, messages should be informal and friendly. In opposite situations, marketing communications have to emphasize that the new product is socially accepted. However, if the product is imported it can sometimes utilize global or foreign cultural positioning. For example, in China, individualism is often used for imported products but almost never for domestic ones.[51]

Understanding the implications of the dimensions helps businesspeople prepare for international business encounters. For example, in negotiating in Germany one can expect a counterpart who is thorough, systematic, very well prepared, but also rather dogmatic and therefore less flexible and willing to compromise. Efficiency is emphasized. In Mexico, however, the counterpart may prefer to address problems on a personal and private basis rather than on a business level. This means more emphasis on socializing and conveying one's humanity, sincerity, loyalty, and friendship. Also, differences in the pace and business practices of a region have to be accepted. Boeing Airplane Company found in its annual study on world aviation safety that countries with both low individualism and substantial power distances had accident rates 2.6 times greater than those at the other end of the scale. The findings naturally have an impact on training and service operations of airlines.[52]

Communication about innovation takes place through the physical product itself (samples) or through experiencing a new company policy. If a new personnel practice, such as quality circles or flextime, is being investigated, results may be communicated in reports or through word of mouth by the participating employees. Communication content depends on the following factors: the good's or policy's relative advantage over existing alternatives; compatibility with established behavioral patterns; complexity, or the degree to which the good or process is perceived as difficult to understand and use; trialability, or the degree to which it may be experimented with without incurring major risk; and observability, which is the extent to which the consequences of the innovation are visible.

Before a good or policy is evaluated, information should be gathered about existing beliefs and circumstances. Distortion of data may occur as a result of selective attention, exposure, and retention. As examples, anything foreign may be seen in a negative light, another multinational company's efforts may have failed, or the government may discourage the proposed activity. Additional information may then be sought from any of the sources or from opinion leaders in the market.

Adoption tendency refers to the likelihood that the product or process will be accepted. Examples are advertising in the People's Republic of China and equity joint ventures with Western participants in Russia, both of them unheard of a decade ago. If an innovation clears the hurdles, it may be adopted and slowly diffused into the entire market. An international manager has two basic choices: to adapt company offerings and methods to those in the market or to try to change market conditions to fit company programs. In Japan, a number of Western companies have run into obstructions in the Japanese distribution system, where great value is placed on established relationships; everything is done on the basis of favoring the familiar and fearing the unfamiliar. In most cases, this problem is solved by joint ventures with a major Japanese entity that has established contacts. On occasion, when the company's approach is compatible with the central beliefs of a culture, the company may be able to change existing customs rather than adjust to them. Initially, Procter & Gamble's traditional hard-selling style in television commercials jolted most Japanese viewers accustomed to more subtle approaches. Now the ads are being imitated by Japanese competitors. However, this is not to be interpreted to mean that the Japanese will adapt to Western approaches. The emphasis in Japan is still on who speaks rather than on what is spoken. That is why, for example, Japan is a market where Procter & Gamble's company name is presented as well in the marketing communication for a brand, rather than only the product's brand name, which is customary in the United States and European markets.[53]

Although models such as the one in Figure 2.2 may aid in strategy planning by making sure that all variables and their interlinkages are considered, any analysis is incomplete without the basic recognition of cultural differences. Adjusting to differences requires putting one's own cultural values aside. James A. Lee proposes that the natural **self-reference criterion**—the unconscious reference to one's own cultural values—is the root of most international business problems.[54] However, recognizing and admitting this are often quite difficult. The following analytical approach is recommended to reduce the influence of cultural bias:

1. Define the problem or goal in terms of the domestic cultural traits, habits, or norms.
2. Define the problem or goal in terms of the foreign cultural traits, habits, or norms. Make no value judgments.
3. Isolate the self-reference criterion influence in the problem, and examine it carefully to see how it complicates the problem.
4. Redefine the problem without the self-reference criterion influence, and solve for the optimum-goal situation.

This approach can be applied to product introduction. If Kellogg Co. wants to introduce breakfast cereals into markets where breakfast is traditionally not eaten or where consumers drink very little milk, managers must consider very carefully how to instill the new habit. The traits, habits, and norms concerning the importance of breakfast are quite different in the United States, France, and Brazil, and they have to be outlined before the product can be introduced. In France, Kellogg's commercials are aimed as much at providing nutrition lessons as they are at promoting the product. In Brazil, the company advertised on a soap opera to gain entry into the market because Brazilians often emulate the characters of these television shows.

Analytical procedures require constant monitoring of changes caused by outside events as well as the changes caused by the business entity itself. Controlling **ethnocentrism**—the tendency to consider one's own culture superior to others—can be achieved only by acknowledging it and properly adjusting to its possible effects in managerial decision making. The international manager needs to be prepared and able to put that preparedness to effective use.[55]

The Training Challenge

International managers face a dilemma in terms of international and intercultural competence. The lack of adequate foreign language and international business skills have cost U.S. firms lost contracts, weak negotiations, and ineffectual management. A UNESCO study of 10- to 14-year-old students in nine countries placed Americans next to last in their comprehension of foreign cultures. Even when cultural awareness is high, there is room for improvement. For example, a survey of European executives found that a shortage of international managers was considered the single most important constraint on expansion abroad.[56] The increase in the overall international activity of firms has increased the need for cultural sensitivity training at all levels of the organization. Further, today's training must encompass not only outsiders to the firm but interaction within the corporate family as well. However inconsequential the degree of interaction may seem, it can still cause problems if proper understanding is lacking. Consider, for example, the date 11/12/01 on a telex; a European will interpret this as the 11th of December, an American as the 12th of November.

Some companies try to avoid the training problem by hiring only nationals or well-traveled Americans for their international operations. This makes sense for the management of overseas operations but will not solve the training need, especially if transfers to a culture unfamiliar to the manager are likely. International experience may not necessarily transfer from one market to another.

To foster cultural sensitivity and acceptance of new ways of doing things within the organization, management must institute internal education programs. The programs may include: (1) culture-specific information (data covering other countries, such as videopacks and culturegrams); (2) general cultural information (values, practices, and assumptions of countries other than one's own); and (3) self-specific information (identifying one's own cultural paradigm, including values, assumptions, and perceptions about others).[57] One study found that Japanese assigned to the United States get mainly language training as preparation for the task. In addition, many companies use mentoring, whereby an individual is assigned to someone who is experienced and who will spend time squiring and explaining. Talks given by returnees and by visiting lecturers hired specifically for the task round out the formal part of training.[58] At Samsung, several special interest groups were formed to focus on issues such as Japanese society and business practices, the Chinese economy, changes in Europe, and the U.S. economy. In addition, groups also explore cutting-edge business issues, such as new technology and marketing strategies. And for the past few years, Samsung has been sending the brightest junior employees abroad for a year.[59]

The objective of formal training programs is to foster the four critical characteristics of preparedness, sensitivity, patience, and flexibility in managers and other personnel. The programs vary dramatically in terms of their rigor, involvement, and, of course, cost.[60] A summary of the programs is provided in Figure 2.4.

Environmental briefings and cultural-orientation programs are types of **area studies** programs. The programs provide factual preparation for a manager to operate in, or work with people from, a particular country. Area studies should be a basic prerequisite for other types of training programs. Alone, area studies serve little practical purpose because they do not really get the manager's feet wet. Other, more involved, programs contribute context in which to put facts so that they can be properly understood.

The **cultural assimilator** is a program in which trainees must respond to scenarios of specific situations in a particular country. The programs have been developed for the Arab countries, Iran, Thailand, Central America, and Greece.[61] The results of the trainees' assimilator experience are evaluated by a panel of judges. This type of program has been used most frequently in cases of transfers abroad on short notice.

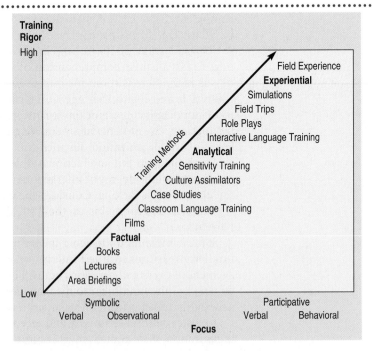

FIGURE 2.4

Cross-Cultural Training Methods

Source: J. Stewart Black and Mark Mendenhall, "A Practical but Theory-Based Framework for Selecting Cross-Cultural Training Methods," in *International Human Resource Management*, eds. Mark Mendenhall and Gary Oddou (Boston: PWS-Kent, 1991), 188.

GLOBAL PERSPECTIVE 2.4

Online Cultural Training

The Internet can play an important role in preparing marketing people for the international marketplace. While it cannot replace real-life interaction as an experiential tool, it does provide a number of benefits including comparisons between cultural ways of behaving and can provide an opportunity to develop the skills needed to interact successfully with people from other cultures.

Companies typically rely on the following elements in designing web-based training:

1. **Detailed Scenarios.** Much of the training material consists of a detailed, realistic story that is tied into elements of the learner's background; i.e., the session becomes more than a briefing; it becomes a narrated experience full of learning moments for participants. This is made possible by the ability of the web to store and circulate a lot of information instantaneously around the world.

2. **Gradual Delivery.** The ability to control the flow of information to the participant supports the learning process in a number of ways. First, the participant is allowed to fit the training into his/her schedule. Secondly, the real-life flow of information is mimicked and a higher degree of realism is achieved.

3. **Support.** A set of detailed materials is provided to the participants 24 hours a day. At any hour and at any location, participants can check their perceptions against the materials, reinforce learning from a dimly

recalled lesson, or seek feedback on an important point or issue.

4. **Relevant Exercises.** Participants can be provided topical exercises and activities the level of which can be adjusted depending upon how the participant has invested in the training.

5. **Online Discussions.** Sessions can be simulcast to hundreds of participants around the world. The lack of face-to-face interaction can be remedied by having discussion groups where participants can share their experiences with each other. The pooled learning experience is stronger than one with a solitary participant.

The following case highlights some of the points made:

Joe Schmed is a marketing representative for a pharmaceutical company. His company has just undertaken a joint venture with a pan-Asian pharmaceutical company based in Kuala Lumpur. In order to develop a successful sales plan, it was decided that over the next six months, Joe will travel to Southeast Asia at least eight times. The first trip will be in two weeks. However, Joe lacks the time to take two full days out of his schedule for a traditional training program. Additionally, since his undergraduate major was in Asian studies, Joe feels that his cultural understanding is quite adequate. Nevertheless, he would like to brush up on some of his knowledge and gain a better understanding of Asian business. Logging on, he enters a training course, completing parts of it as he finds time—on airplanes and after work, for example.

Source: Peter T. Burgi and Brant R. Dykehouse, "On-Line Cultural Training: The Next Phase," *International Insight*, Winter 2000, 7–10. See also http://www.runzheimer.com.

When more time is available, managers can be trained extensively in language. This may be required if an exotic language is involved. **Sensitivity training** focuses on enhancing a manager's flexibility in situations that are quite different from those at home. The approach is based on the assumption that understanding and accepting oneself is critical to understanding a person from another culture. While most of the methods discussed are best delivered in face-to-face settings, web-based training is becoming more popular as seen in Global Perspective 2.4.

Finally, training may involve **field experience,** which exposes a manager to a different cultural environment for a limited amount of time. Although the expense of placing and maintaining an expatriate is high (and, therefore, the cost of failure is high), field experience is rarely used in training. One field experience technique that has been suggested when the training process needs to be rigorous is the host-family surrogate. This technique places a trainee (and possibly his or her family) in a domestically located family of the nationality to which they are assigned.[62]

Regardless of the degree of training, preparation, and positive personal characteristics, a manager will always remain foreign. A manager should never rely on his or her own judgment when local managers can be consulted. In many instances, a manager should have an interpreter present at negotiations, especially if the manager is not completely bilingual. Overconfidence in one's language capabilities can create problems.

Summary

Culture is one of the most challenging elements of the international marketplace. This system of learned behavior patterns characteristic of the members of a given society is constantly shaped by a set of dynamic variables: language, religion, values and attitudes, manners and customs, aesthetics, technology, education, and social institutions. To cope with this system, an international manager needs both factual and interpretive knowledge of culture. To some extent, the factual knowledge can be learned; its interpretation comes only through experience.

The most complicated problems in dealing with the cultural environment stem from the fact that one cannot learn culture—one has to live it. Two schools of thought exist in the business world on how to deal with cultural diversity. One is that business is business the world around, following the model of Pepsi and McDonald's. In some cases, globalization is a fact of life; however, cultural differences are still far from converging.

The other school proposes that companies must tailor business approaches to individual cultures. Setting up policies and procedures in each country has been compared to an organ transplant; the critical question centers around acceptance or rejection. The major challenge to the international manager is to make sure that rejection is not a result of cultural myopia or even blindness.

The internationally successful companies all share an important quality: patience. They have not rushed into situations but rather built their operations carefully by following the most basic business principles. These principles are to know your adversary, know your audience, and know your customer.

Key Terms and Concepts

cultural risk	Christianity	social infrastructure	interpretive knowledge
acculturation	Islam	financial infrastructure	self-reference criterion
high-context cultures	Hinduism	marketing infrastructure	ethnocentrism
low-context cultures	Buddhism	cultural convergence	area studies
change agent	Confucianism	social stratification	cultural assimilator
cultural universals	focus groups	reference groups	sensitivity training
backtranslation	economic infrastructure	experiential knowledge	field experience

Questions for Discussion

1. Comment on the assumption, "If people are serious about doing business with you, they will speak English."
2. You are on your first business visit to Germany. You feel confident about your ability to speak the language (you studied German in school and have taken a refresher course), and you decide to use it. During introductions, you want to break the ice by asking "Wie geht's?" and insisting that everyone call you by your first name. Speculate as to the reaction.
3. Q: "What do you call a person who can speak two languages?"
   A: "Bilingual."
   Q: "How about three?"
   A: "Trilingual."
   Q: "Excellent. How about one?"
   A: "Hmmmm. . . . American!"
   Is this joke malicious, or is there something to be learned from it?
4. What can be learned about a culture from reading and attending to factual materials?
5. Provide examples of how the self-reference criterion might manifest itself.
6. Is any international business entity not a cultural imperialist? How else could one explain the phenomenon of multinational corporations?

Internet Exercises

1. Various companies, such as Windham International, are available to prepare and train international managers for the cultural challenge. Using Windham's web site (www.windhamworld.com), assess their role in helping the international manager.
2. Compare and contrast an international company's home pages for presentation and content; for example, Coca-Cola (at www.coca-cola.com) and its Japanese version (www.cocacola.co.jp). Are the differences cultural?

Recommended Readings

Axtell, Roger E. *Do's and Taboos Around the World*. New York: John Wiley & Sons, 1993.

Bache, Ellyn. *Culture Clash*. Yarmouth, ME: Intercultural Press, 1990.

Brislin, R. W., W. J. Lonner, and R. M. Thorndike. *Cross-Cultural Research Methods*. New York: Wiley, 1973.

Catlin, Linda, and Thomas White. *Cultural Sourcebook and Case Studies*. Cincinnati: South-Western, 1994.

Copeland, Lennie, and Lewis Griggs. *Going International: How to Make Friends and Deal Effectively in the Global Marketplace*. New York: Random House, 1990.

Fisher, Glen. *International Negotiation*. Yarmouth, ME: Intercultural Press, 1986.

Hall, Edward T., and Mildred Reed Hall. *Understanding Cultural Differences*. Yarmouth, ME: Intercultural Press, 1990.

Kenna, Peggy, and Sondra Lacy. *Business Japan: Understanding Japanese Business Culture*. Lincolnwood, IL: NTC, 1994.

Lewis, Richard D. *When Cultures Collide*. London: Nicholas Brealey Publishing, 1996.

Marx, Elizabeth. *Breaking Through Culture Shock: What You Need to Succeed in International Business*. London: Nicholas Brealey Publishing, 1999.

O'Hara-Devereaux, Mary, and Robert Johansen. *Global Work: Bridging Distance, Culture, and Time*. San Francisco: Jossey-Bass Publishers, 1994.

Parker, Barbara. *Globalization and Business Practice: Managing Across Boundaries*. London: Sage Publications, 1999.

Terpstra, Vern, and Keith David. *The Cultural Environment of International Business*. Cincinnati: South-Western, 1991.

Trompenaars, Fons, and Charles Hampden-Turner. *Riding the Waves of Culture*. New York: Irwin, 1998.

U.S. Department of Commerce. *International Business Practices*. Washington, DC: U.S. Government Printing Office, 1993.

Notes

1. "Rule No. 1: Don't Diss the Locals," *Business Week*, May 15, 1995, 8.
2. Carla Rapoport, "Nestlé's Brand-Building Machine," *Fortune*, September 19, 1994, 147–156.
3. Mary O'Hara-Devereaux and Robert Johansen, *Global Work: Bridging Distance, Culture, and Time* (San Francisco: Jossey-Bass Publishers, 1994), 11.
4. Alfred Kroeber and Clyde Kluckhohn, *Culture: A Critical Review of Concepts and Definitions* (New York: Random House, 1985), 11.
5. Geert Hofstede, "National Cultures Revisited," *Asia-Pacific Journal of Management* 1 (September 1984): 22–24.
6. Robert L. Kohls, *Survival Kit for Overseas Living* (Chicago: Intercultural Press, 1979), 3.
7. Edward T. Hall, *Beyond Culture* (Garden City, NY: Anchor Press, 1976), 15.
8. See http://www.mcdonalds.com.
9. Marita von Oldenborgh, "What's Next for India?" *International Business* (January 1996): 44–47; and Ravi Vijh, "Think Global, Act Indian," *Export Today* (June 1996): 27–28.
10. Michael T. Malloy, "America, Go Home," *The Wall Street Journal*, March 26, 1993, R7.
11. "Culture Wars," *The Economist*, September 12, 1998, 97–99.
12. "Information Minister Aims to Throw Cultural Vulgarians Out of the Game," *The Washington Post*, February 2, 1999, A16.
13. George P. Mundak, "The Common Denominator of Cultures," in *The Science of Man in the World*, ed. Ralph Linton (New York: Columbia University Press, 1945), 123–142.
14. Philip R. Harris and Robert T. Moran, *Managing Cultural Differences* (Houston: Gulf, 1996), 201.
15. David A. Ricks, *Big Business Blunders* (Homewood, IL.: Irwin, 1983), 4.
16. David A. Hanni, John K. Ryans, and Ivan R. Vernon, "Coordinating International Advertising: The Goodyear Case Revisited for Latin America," *Journal of International Marketing* 3, no. 2 (1995): 83–98.
17. "French Snared in Web of English," *The Washington Post*, September 27, 2000, A19; and "France: Mind Your Language," *The Economist*, March 23, 1996, 70–71.
18. Rory Cowan, "The *e* Does Not Stand for English," *Global Business*, March 2000, L/22.
19. Stephen P. Iverson, "The Art of Translation," *World Trade*, April 2000, 90–92.
20. Margareta Bowen, "Business Translation," *Jerome Quarterly* (August–September 1993): 5–9.
21. "Nokia Veti Pois Mainoskampanjansa," *Uutislehti 100*, June 15, 1998, 5.
22. Edward T. Hall, "The Silent Language of Overseas Business," *Harvard Business Review* 38 (May–June 1960): 87–96.
23. *Statistical Abstract of the United States* (Washington, DC: U.S. Government Printing Office, 1999): 870.
24. David McClelland, *The Achieving Society* (New York: Irvington, 1961): 90.
25. *World Almanac and the Book of Facts* (Mahwah, NJ: Funk & Wagnalls, 2001), 721.
26. Mushtaq Luqmami, Zahir A. Quaraeshi, and Linda Delene, "Marketing in Islamic Countries: A Viewpoint," *MSU Business Topics* 23 (Summer 1980): 17–24.
27. "Islamic Banking: Faith and Creativity," *New York Times*, April 8, 1994, D1, D6.
28. James F. Engel, Roger D. Blackwell, and Paul W. Miniard, *Consumer Behavior* (Ft. Worth, TX: Harcourt, 2001), 381.
29. Y.H. Wong and Ricky Yee-kwong, "Relationship Marketing in China: Guanxi, Favoritism and Adaptation," *Journal of Business Ethics* 22, no. 2 (1999): 107–118; and Tim Ambler,

"Reflections in China: Re-Orienting Images of Marketing," *Marketing Management* 4, no. 1 (1995): 23–30.

30. "Latest Sneakers Fly Off Tokyo Shelves Even at $1,300 a Pair," *The Washington Post,* November 7, 1996, A1, A10.

31. "How Sushi Went Global," *Foreign Policy,* November/December 2000, 54–63.

32. Earl P. Spencer, "EuroDisney—What Happened?" *Journal of International Marketing* 3, no. 3 (1995): 103–114.

33. Sergey Frank, "Global Negotiations: Vive Les Differences!" *Sales and Marketing Management* 144 (May 1992): 64–69.

34. See, for example, Terri Morrison, *Kiss, Bow, or Shake Hands: How to Do Business In Sixty Countries* (Holbrook, MA.: Adams Media, 1994) or Roger Axtell, *Do's and Taboos Around the World* (New York: John Wiley & Sons, 1993). For holiday observances, see http://www.religioustolerance.org/main_day.htm#cal and http://www.yahoo.com/society_and_culture/holidays_and_observances

35. James A. Gingrich, "Five Rules for Winning Emerging Market Consumers," *Strategy and Business* (second quarter, 1999): 68–76.

36. "Feng Shui Strikes Cord," available at http://www.cnnfn.com/1999/09/11/life/q_fengshui/; and "Fung Shui Man Orders Sculpture Out of Hotel," *South China Morning Post,* July 27, 1992, 4.

37. The results of the Gallup study are available at http://www.fortune.com/fortune/china/chart.html.

38. Kenichi Ohmae, "Managing in a Borderless World," *Harvard Business Review* 67 (May–June 1989): 152–161.

39. Joe Agnew, "Cultural Differences Probed to Create Product Identity," *Marketing News,* October 24, 1986, 22.

40. Greg Bathon, "Eat the Way Your Mama Taught You," *World Trade,* December 2000, 76–77.

41. Joseph A. McKinney, "Joint Ventures of United States Firms in Japan: A Survey," *Venture Japan* 1 (1988): 14–19.

42. Peter McGinnis, "Guanxi or Contract: A Way to Understand and Predict Conflict Between Chinese and Western Senior Managers in China-Based Joint Ventures," in *Multinational Business Management and Internationalization of Business Enterprises,* ed. Daniel E. McCarthy and Stanley J. Hille (Nanjing, China: Nanjing University Press, 1993), 354–351.

43. Tim Ambler, "Reflections in China: Re-Orienting Images of Marketing," *Marketing Management* 4 (summer 1995): 23–30.

44. James H. Sood and Patrick Adams, "Model of Management Learning Styles as a Predictor of Export Behavior and Performance," *Journal of Business Research* 12 (June 1984): 169–182.

45. Jagdish N. Sheth and S. Prakash Sethi, "A Theory of Cross-Cultural Buying Behavior," in *Consumer and Industrial Buying Behavior,* eds. Arch G. Woodside, Jagdish N. Sheth, and Peter D. Bennett (New York: Elsevier North-Holland, 1977), 369–386.

46. Geert Hofstede, *Culture's Consequences: International Differences in Work-Related Values* (Beverly Hills, CA.: Sage Publications, 1984), Chapter 1.

47. Geert Hofstede and Michael H. Bond, "The Confucius Connection: From Cultural Roots to Economic Growth," *Organizational Dynamics* 16 (spring 1988): 4–21.

48. Simcha Ronen and Oded Shenkar, "Clustering Countries on Attitudinal Dimensions: A Review and Synthesis," *Academy of Management Journal* 28 (September 1985): 440–452.

49. For applications of the framework, see Sudhir H. Kale, "Culture-Specific Marketing Communications," *International Marketing Review* 8, no. 2 (1991): 18–30; and Sudhir H. Kale, "Distribution Channel Relationships in Diverse Cultures," *International Marketing Review* 8, no. 3 (1991): 31–45.

50. Jan-Benedict Steenkamp and Frenkel ter Hofstede, "A Cross-National Investigation into the Individual and National Cultural Antecedents of Consumer Innovativeness," *Journal of Marketing* 63 (April 1999): 55–69.

51. Hong Cheng and John C. Schweitzer, "Cultural Values Reflected in Chinese and U.S. Television Commercials," *Journal of Advertising Research* 36 (May/June 1996): 27–45.

52. "Building a 'Cultural Index' to World Airline Safety," *The Washington Post,* August 21, 1994, A8.

53. "Exploring Differences in Japan, U.S. Culture," *Advertising Age International,* September 18, 1995, 1–8.

54. James A. Lee, "Cultural Analysis in Overseas Operations," *Harvard Business Review* 44 (March–April 1966): 106–114.

55. Peter D. Fitzpatrick and Alan S. Zimmerman, *Essentials of Export Marketing* (New York: American Management Organization, 1985), 16.

56. "Expansion Abroad: The New Direction for European Firms," *International Management* 41 (November 1986): 20–26.

57. W. Chan Kim and R. A. Mauborgne, "Cross-Cultural Strategies," *Journal of Business Strategy* 7 (Spring 1987): 28–37.

58. Mauricio Lorence, "Assignment USA: The Japanese Solution," *Sales and Marketing Management* 144 (October 1992): 60–66.

59. "Special Interest Group Operations" available at http://www.samsung.com; and "Sensitivity Kick," *The Wall Street Journal,* December 30, 1996, 1, 4.

60. Rosalie Tung, "Selection and Training of Personnel for Overseas Assignments," *Columbia Journal of World Business* 16 (Spring 1981): 68–78.

61. Harris and Moran, *Managing Cultural Differences,* 267–295.

62. Simcha Ronen, "Training the International Assignee," in *Training and Career Development,* ed. I. Goldstein (San Francisco: Jossey-Bass, 1989), 426–440.

CHAPTER 3

National Trade and Investment Policies

LEARNING OBJECTIVES

- To see how trade and investment policies have historically been a subset of domestic policies

- To examine how historical attitudes toward trade and investment policies are changing

- To see how global links in trade and investment have made policymakers less able to focus solely on domestic issues

- To understand that nations must cooperate closely in the future to maintain a viable global trade and investment environment

WOULD REGULATION HURT E-COMMERCE?

E-commerce is an increasing part of business. It is predicted that in the United States alone the value of business-to-business goods and services traded via the Internet will reach $183 billion in 2001 as compared to only $8 billion in 1997.

Some governments in Europe and Asia believe that regulation and state control will aid in the development of the Internet. State regulation, they claim, protects Internet consumers from fraud. By contrast, the United States' current view is that the e-commerce market should primarily police itself. As countries adopt an array of different rules and regulations, a system of consistency needs to be established. In Europe, the EU commission has proposed a system that favors the enforcement of the laws of the country where a transaction originated to solve cross-border disputes. However, European businesses seem to disagree. In a strong statement regarding the potential wealth-building that can be provided by a global e-commerce environment, Bertelsmann AG chairman Thomas Middelhoff said, "It can't happen if the digital realm is choked in an entanglement of local regulation."

While governments throughout the world support varying levels of regulation, an international group of executives has united to oppose Internet taxes and to oppose restrictions on data exports. This group, working together as the Global Business Dialogue on Electronic Commerce, has pushed for the adoption of a "seal of approval" for web sites that protect consumer privacy. They have also advocated third-party arbitration in solving e-commerce disputes. Following up a report from the Progressive Policy Institute, U.S. Senator Joseph Lieberman and Rep. Ellen Tauscher planned to caution any additional e-commerce regulation by their respective chambers.

It seems clear that some supervision is needed to assure fairness and privacy. What is unclear is the location of such supervision—domestic governments, international organizations such as the WTO, or a newly formed supranational group. ●

Sources: Victoria Shannon, "CEO's Lobby for E-commerce: Technology Chiefs Call for Restraint in Regulation of Internet," *The Washington Post*, September 14, 1999, E03; Woranuj Maneerungsee, "E-Commerce—Electronic Trade to Be Encouraged," *The Bangkok Post*, October 20, 1999, News 1; Chris Philips, "A More Sensible Approach to Legislating for e-Commerce Security Is Emerging," *New Media Age*, July 8, 1999, New Media Vision 8; Andy Sullivan, "Hands off e-Commerce, Democratic Lawmakers Say," Reuters, March 15, 2001; **www.gbd.org**.

This chapter discusses the policy actions taken by countries. All nations have international trade and investment policies. The policies may be publicly pronounced or kept secret, they may be disjointed or coordinated, or they may be applied consciously or determined by a laissez-faire attitude. Trade policy actions become evident when measures taken by governments affect the flow of trade and investment across national borders.

Rationale and Goals of Trade and Investment Policies

Government policies are designed to regulate, stimulate, direct, and protect national activities. The exercise of these policies is the result of **national sovereignty,** which provides a government with the right and burden to shape the environment of the country and its citizens. Because they are "border bound," governments focus mainly on domestic policies. Nevertheless, many policy actions have repercussions on other nations, firms, and individuals abroad and are therefore a component of a nation's trade and investment policy.

Government policy can be subdivided into two groups of policy actions that affect trade and investment. One affects trade and investment directly, the other indirectly. The domestic policy actions of most governments aim to increase the **standard of living** of the country's citizens, to improve the **quality of life,** to stimulate national development, and to achieve full employment. Clearly, all of these goals are closely intertwined. For example, an improved standard of living is likely to contribute to national development. Similarly, quality of life and standard of living are closely interlinked. Also, a high level of employment will play a major role in determining the standard of living. Yet all of these policy goals will also affect international trade and investment indirectly. For example, if foreign industries become more competitive and rapidly increase their exports, employment in the importing countries may suffer. Likewise, if a country accumulates large quantities of debt, which at some time must be repaid, the present and future standard of living will be threatened.

In more direct ways, a country may also pursue policies of increased development that mandate either technology transfer from abroad or the exclusion of foreign industries to the benefit of domestic infant firms. Also, government officials may believe that imports threaten the culture, health, or standards of the country's citizens and thus the quality of life. As a result, officials are likely to develop regulations to protect the citizens.

Nations also institute **foreign policy** measures designed with domestic concerns in mind but explicitly aimed to exercise influence abroad. One major goal of foreign policy may be national security. For example, nations may develop alliances, coalitions, and agreements to protect their borders or their spheres of interest. Similarly, nations may take measures to enhance their national security preparedness in case of international conflict. Governments also wish to improve trade and investment opportunities and to contribute to the security and safety of their own firms abroad.

Policy aims may be approached in various ways. For example, to develop new markets abroad and to increase their sphere of influence, nations may give foreign aid to other countries. This was the case when the United States generously awarded Marshall Plan funds for the reconstruction of Europe. Governments may also feel a need to restrict or encourage trade and investment flows in order to preserve or enhance the capability of industries that are important to national security.

Each country develops its own domestic policies, and therefore policy aims will vary from nation to nation. Inevitably, conflicts arise. For example, full employment policies in one country may directly affect employment policies in another. Similarly, the development aims of one country may reduce the development capability of another. Even when health issues are concerned, disputes may arise. One nation may argue that its regulations are in place to protect its citizens, whereas other nations may interpret the regulations as market barriers. An example of the latter situation is the celebrated hormone dispute between the United States and the European Union. U.S. cattle are treated with growth hormones. While the United States claims that these hormones are harmless to humans, many Europeans find them scary. Given the differences in perspectives, there is much room for conflict when it comes to trade policies, particularly when the United States wants to export more beef and the European Union attempts to restrict such beef imports.

Cattle in Europe are raised without hormones. Since 1989 hormone-fed beef has been banned in European countries, effectively restricting imports of U.S. beef. A WTO review of the hormones found the ban was not based on scientific evidence, but despite threats of sanctions, the ban has not been lifted.

The trade disagreement between the United States and Japan in the automotive sector is another example. While the U.S. claimed that Japanese firms prevent the importation and sale of U.S.-made auto parts, Japan's government blamed quality concerns and lack of effort by U.S. firms. Such disagreements can quickly escalate into major trade conflicts.

Differences among national policies have always existed and are likely to erupt into occasional conflict. Yet, the closer economic links among nations have made the emergence of such conflicts more frequent and the disagreements more severe. In recognition of this development, efforts have been made since 1945 to create a multilateral institutional arrangement that can help to resolve national conflicts, harmonize national policies, and facilitate increased international trade and investments.

Global Trade Regulation Since 1945

In 1945, the United States led in the belief that international trade and investment flows were a key to worldwide prosperity. Many months of international negotiations in London, Geneva, and Lake Success (New York) culminated on March 24, 1948, in Havana, Cuba, with the signing of the Havana Charter for the **International Trade Organization (ITO).** The charter represented a series of agreements among 53 countries. It was designed to cover international commercial policies, restrictive business practices, commodity agreements, employment and reconstruction, economic development and international investment, and a constitution for a new United Nations agency to administer the whole.[1]

Even though the International Trade Organization incorporated many farsighted notions, most nations refused to ratify its provisions. They feared the power and bureaucratic size of the new organization—and the consequent threats to national sovereignty. As a result, this most forward-looking approach to international trade and investment was never implemented. However, other organizations conceived at the time have made major contributions toward improving international business. An agreement was initiated for the purpose of reducing tariffs and therefore facilitating trade. In addition, international institutions such as the United Nations, the World Bank, and the International Monetary Fund were negotiated.

The **General Agreement on Tariffs and Trade (GATT)** has been called a "remarkable success story of a postwar international organization that was never intended to become one."[2] It started out in 1947 as a set of rules to ensure nondiscrimination, transparent procedures, the settlement of disputes, and the participation of the lesser-developed countries in international trade. To increase trade, GATT used tariff concessions, through which member countries agreed to limit the level of tariffs they would impose on imports from other GATT members. An important tool is the **Most-Favored Nation (MFN)** clause, which calls for each member country to grant every other member country the same most favorable treatment that it accords to any other country with respect to imports and exports.[3] MFN, in effect, provides for equal, rather than special, treatment.

The GATT was not originally intended to be an international organization. Rather, it was to be a multilateral treaty designed to operate under the International Trade Organization (ITO). However, because the ITO never came into being, the GATT became the governing body for settling international trade disputes. Gradually it evolved into an institution that sponsored various successful rounds of international trade negotiations with an initial focus on the reduction of prevailing high tariffs. Headquartered in Geneva, Switzerland, the GATT Secretariat conducted its work as instructed by the representatives of its member nations. Even though the GATT had no independent enforcement mechanism and relied entirely on moral suasion and on frequently wavering membership adherence to its rules, it achieved major progress for world trade.

Early in its history, the GATT accomplished the reduction of duties for trade in 50,000 products, amounting to two-thirds of the value of the trade among its participants. In subsequent years, special GATT negotiations such as the Kennedy Round, named after John F. Kennedy, and the Tokyo Round, named after the location where the negotiations were agreed upon, further reduced trade barriers and improved dispute-settlement mechanisms. The GATT also developed better provisions for dealing with subsidies and more explicit definitions of roles for import controls. Table 3.1 provides an overview of the different GATT rounds.

The latest GATT negotiations, called the Uruguay Round, were initiated in 1987. Even though tariffs still were addressed in these negotiations, their importance has been greatly diminished due to the success of earlier agreements. The main thrust of negotiations had become the sharpening of dispute-settlement rules and the integration of the trade and investment areas that were outside of the GATT. After many years of often contentious negotiations, a new accord was finally ratified in early 1995. The GATT was supplanted by a new institution, the **World Trade Organization (WTO)**,  which now administers international trade and investment accords (www.wto.org). These accords will gradually reduce governmental subsidies to industries and will convert nontariff barriers into more transparent tariff barriers. The textile and clothing industries eventually will be brought into the WTO regime, resulting in decreased subsidies and fewer market restrictions through the General Agreement on Trade in Services (GATS). An entire new set of rules was designed to govern the service area, and agreement also was reached on new rules to encourage international investment flows.

The GATT and now the WTO have made major contributions to improved trade and investment flows around the world. The success of the GATT and the resulting increase in welfare has refuted the old postulate that "the strong is most powerful alone". Nations have increasingly come to recognize that international trade and investment activities are important to their own economic well-being.

Nations also have come to accept that they must generate sufficient outgoing export and incoming investment activities to compensate for the inflow of imports and outgoing investment. In the medium and long term, the balance of payments must be maintained. For short periods of time, gold or capital transfers can be used to finance a deficit. Such financing, however, can continue only while gold and foreign assets last or while foreign countries will accept the IOUs of the deficit countries, permitting them to pile up foreign liabilities. This willingness, of course, will vary. Some countries, such as the United States, can run up deficits of hundreds of billions of dollars because of political stability, acceptable rates of return, and perceived economic security. Yet, over the long term, all nations are subject to the same economic rules.

TABLE 3.1		**Negotiations in the GATT**			
Round	**Dates**	**Numbers of Countries**	**Value of Trade Covered**	**Average Tariff Cut**	**Average Tariffs Afterward**
Geneva	1947	23	$10 billion	35%	n/a
Annecy	1949	33	Unavailable		n/a
Torquay	1950	34	Unavailable		n/a
Geneva	1956	22	$2.5 billion		n/a
Dillon	1960–1961	45	$4.9 billion		n/a
Kennedy	1962–1967	48	$40 billion	35%	8.7%
Tokyo	1973–1979	99	$155 billion	34%	4.7%
Uruguay	1986–1994	124	$300 billion	38%	3.9%

Sources: John H. Jackson *The World Trading System* (Cambridge, Mass.: MIT Press. 1989), and *The GATT: Uruguay Round Final Act Should Produce Overall U.S. Economic Gains.* U.S. General Accounting Office, Report to Congress, Washington, DC, July 1994, **www.gao.gov.**

Changes in the Global Policy Environment

Three major changes have occurred over time in the global policy environment: a reduction of domestic policy influence, a weakening of traditional international institutions, and a sharpening of the conflict between industrialized and developing nations. These three changes in turn have had a major effect on policy responses in the international trade and investment field.

Reduction of Domestic Policy Influences

The effects of growing global influences on a domestic economy have been significant. Policymakers have increasingly come to recognize that it is very difficult to isolate domestic economic activity from international market events. Again and again, domestic policy measures are vetoed or counteracted by the activities of global market forces. Decisions that were once clearly in the domestic purview now have to be revised due to influences from abroad. At the same time, the clash between the fixed geography of nations and the nonterritorial nature of many of today's problems and solutions continues to escalate. Nation-states may simply no longer be the natural problem-solving unit. Local government may be most appropriate to address some of the problems of individuals, while transnational or even global entities are required to deal with larger issues such as economics, resources, or the environment.[4]

Agricultural policies, for example—historically a domestic issue—have been thrust into the international realm. Any time a country or a group of nations such as the European Union contemplates changes in agricultural subsidies, quantity restrictions, or even quality regulations, international trade partners are quick to speak up against the resulting global effects of such changes. Global Perspective 3.1 shows how the fishing industry is influenced by global considerations. When countries contemplate specific industrial policies that encourage, for example, industrial innovation or collaboration, they often encounter major opposition from their trading partners, who believe that their own industries are jeopardized by such policies. Those reactions and the resulting constraints are the result of growing interdependencies among nations and a closer link between industries around the world. The following examples highlight the penetration of U.S. society by international trade considerations.

- One of every six American manufacturing jobs is in the export sector.[5]
- One of every three U.S. farm acres produces crops for export.[6]
- U.S. firms that export experience 20 percent faster employment growth and are 9 percent less likely to go out of business than are nonexporting firms.[7]
- Wages for U.S. jobs supported by merchandise exports are 20 percent higher than the national average.[8]
- Foreign central banks and private investors hold over 28 percent of the total number of outstanding U.S. Treasury securities.[9]

To some extent, the economic world as we knew it has been turned upside down. For example, trade flows used to determine **currency flows** and therefore the exchange rate. In the more recent past, currency flows have taken on a life of their own, increasing from an average daily trading volume of $18 billion in 1980 to almost $2 trillion in the late 1990s. As a result, they have begun to set the value of exchange rates independent of trade. These exchange rates in turn have now begun to determine the level of trade. Governments that want to counteract these developments with monetary policies find that currency flows outnumber trade flows by more than ten to one. Also, private sector financial flows vastly outnumber the financial flows that can be marshaled by governments, even when acting in concert. The interactions between global and domestic financial flows have severely limited the freedom for governmental action. For example, if the European Central Bank or the Federal Reserve of the United States changes interest rate levels, these changes will not only influence domestic ac-

GLOBAL PERSPECTIVE 3.1

Global Sushi Appetite Nets Profits for Fishers from Maine to Spain

A new supplier has entered Tokyo's sushi market—the New England fishing industry. How did the small companies in this industry end up sending their catch all the way around the world?

As early as the 1920s, Japanese culinary arts were introduced in popular U.S. magazines, but it took half a century for bluefin tuna to evolve from cat food to sushi, a prized delicacy. The splendors of raw fish were a hard sell until the 1970s, when health-conscious Americans began replacing red meat and potatoes with rice, vegetables, fish, and poultry. Sushi's appeal was further enhanced by Japan's emerging industrial prowess and its sophisticated design aesthetics as reflected in the dish. Skilled hands in Japan cut and trim fish for shipment to the finest sushi bars from London to Los Angeles.

Although people around the world have gained a taste for sushi, the Japanese remain the most voracious, increasing their annual consumption fivefold within only ten years. The Japanese fishing industry found it impossible to satisfy this demand. Not only had consumption increased, other countries increased their coastal water limits to 200 miles. Mounting environmental regulations also limited their access to fishing areas. To meet the demand for sushi, Japan needed new suppliers for all fish.

In the northern waters off New England, bluefin was traditionally pursued for sport by anglers battling for a prize catch. When prices for sushi-grade tuna climbed in the mid-

1980s, commercial fishers set sail for more profitable waters. Today, family fishing businesses can reel in thousands of dollars, depending on market conditions, for one top-grade "export fish." The price sometimes is determined by secret bids from individual buyers who come to pier-side auctions. Japanese representatives often purchase the best of the catch for air shipment to Tokyo.

Across the Atlantic in warmer Mediterranean waters, fishing conglomerates compete with the New England firms. Off the coast of Spain, bluefin is caught in miles of nets during spawning season and raised in "tuna farms." These operations illustrate the global flow of process, knowledge, and capital— Spanish sailors crew Japanese vessels financed by Japanese trading companies; the tuna are raised according to Australian aquaculture techniques; European drug companies supply vitamins fed to the tuna; Japanese computer models are used to monitor feeding schedules, weight goals, and target markets.

Tuna prices worldwide are set by Tokyo's Tsukiji market, the financial capital of the fishing industry. Worldwide markets ensure more price stability for fishing companies from Maine to the Mediterranean. For example, the U.S. taste for raw tuna kept bluefin fishers afloat when the Japanese economy began to sink in the early 1990s. Nevertheless, both small and large operations are vulnerable to factors at home and a world away: weather and nature, economic cycles, consumer demand, and pressure from environmental groups.

Source: Theodore C. Bestor, "How Sushi Went Global," *Foreign Policy,* November/December 2000, pp. 54–63.

---

tivities, but also trigger international flows of capital that may reduce, enhance, or even negate the domestic effects. Similarly, rapid technological change and vast advances in communication permit firms and countries to quickly emulate innovation and counteract carefully designed plans. As a result, governments are often powerless to implement effective policy measures, even when they know what to do.

Governments also find that domestic regulations often have major international repercussions. In the United States, for example, the breakup of AT&T resulted in significant changes in the purchasing practices of the newly formed Bell companies. Overnight, competitive bids became decisive in a process that previously was entirely with the firm. This change opened up the U.S. market to foreign suppliers of telecommunications equipment, with only limited commensurate market developments abroad for U.S. firms. Therefore, U.S. telecommunications firms found themselves suddenly under much greater competitive pressures than did their foreign counterparts.

Legislators around the world are continually confronted with such international links. In some countries, the implications are understood, and new legislation is devised with an understanding of its international consequences. In other nations, legislators often ignore the international repercussions and side effects of their actions. Yet, given the links among economies, this is an unwarranted and sometimes even dangerous view. It threatens to place firms at a competitive disadvantage in the international marketplace or may make it easier for foreign firms to compete in the domestic market.

Even when policymakers want to take decisive steps, they are often unable to do so. In the late 1980s, for example, the United States decided to impose **punitive tariffs** of

FIGURE 3.1

Japanese Products Can Drive the U.S. Economy

Source: Toyota Motor Company

100 percent on selected Japanese imports to retaliate for Japanese nonadherence to a previously reached semiconductor agreement. The initial goal was clear. Yet the task became increasingly difficult as the U.S. government developed a list of specific imports to be targeted. In many instances, the U.S. market was heavily dependent on the Japanese imports, which meant that U.S. manufactures and consumers would be severely affected by punitive tariffs. As Figure 3.1 shows, many Japanese products are actually produced or assembled in the United States. To halt the importing of components would throw Americans out of work.

Other targeted products were not actually produced in Japan. Rather, Japanese firms had opened plants in third countries, such as Mexico. Penalizing these product imports would therefore punish Mexican workers and affect Mexican employment, an undesirable result.

More and more products were eliminated from the list before it was published. In two days of hearings, additional links emerged. For example, law enforcement agencies testified that if certain fingerprinting equipment from Japan was sanctioned, law enforcement efforts would suffer significantly. Of the $1.8 billion worth of goods initially considered for the sanctions list, the government was barely able to scrape together $300 million worth. Figure 3.2 illustrates how far such links have progressed in the aircraft industry. With so many product components being sourced from different countries around the world, it becomes increasingly difficult to decide what constitutes a domestic product. In light of this uncertainty, policy actions against foreign products become more difficult as well.

Policymakers find themselves with increasing responsibilities, yet with fewer and less effective tools to carry them out. More segments of the domestic economy are vulnerable to international shifts at the same time that they are becoming less controllable. To regain some power to influence policies, some governments have sought to restrict the influence of world trade by erecting barriers, charging tariffs, and implementing import regulations. However, these measures too have been restrained by the existence of international agreements forged through institutions such as the WTO or bilateral negotiations. World trade has therefore changed many previously held notions about the sovereignty of nation-states and extraterritoriality. The same interdependence that made us all more affluent has also left us more vulnerable.

FIGURE 3.2   Who Builds the Boeing 777?

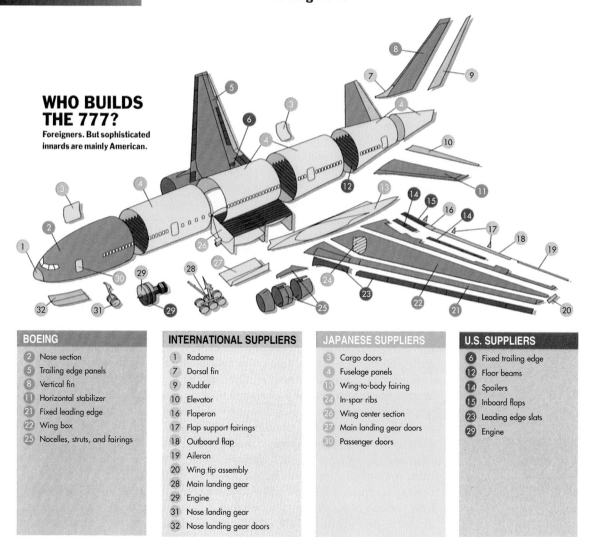

WHO BUILDS THE 777?
Foreigners. But sophisticated innards are mainly American.

BOEING	INTERNATIONAL SUPPLIERS	JAPANESE SUPPLIERS	U.S. SUPPLIERS
2 Nose section	1 Radome	3 Cargo doors	6 Fixed trailing edge
5 Trailing edge panels	7 Dorsal fin	4 Fuselage panels	12 Floor beams
8 Vertical fin	9 Rudder	13 Wing-to-body fairing	14 Spoilers
11 Horizontal stabilizer	10 Elevator	24 In-spar ribs	15 Inboard flaps
21 Fixed leading edge	16 Flaperon	26 Wing center section	23 Leading edge slats
22 Wing box	17 Flap support fairings	27 Main landing gear doors	29 Engine
25 Nocelles, struts, and fairings	18 Outboard flap	30 Passenger doors	
	19 Aileron		
	20 Wing tip assembly		
	28 Main landing gear		
	29 Engine		
	31 Nose landing gear		
	32 Nose landing gear doors		

Source: Boeing as appeared in *Fortune* (April 20, 1992): 140. 1992 Time Inc.

Weakening International Institutions

The intense links among nations and the new economic environment resulting from new market entrants and the encounter of different economic systems are weakening the traditional international institutions and are therefore affecting their roles.

The formation of the WTO (**www.wto.org**) has provided the former GATT with new impetus. However, the organization is confronted with many difficulties. One of them is the result of the organization's success. Historically, a key focus of the WTO's predecessor was on reducing tariffs. With tariff levels at an unprecedented low level, however, attention now has to rest with areas such as nontariff barriers, which are much more complex and indigenous to nations. As a consequence, any emerging dispute is likely to be more heatedly contested and more difficult to resolve. A second traditional focus rested with the right to establishment in countries. Given today's technology, however, the issue has changed. Increasingly, firms will clamor for the right to operations in a country without seeking to establish themselves there. For example, given the opportunities offered by telecommunications, one can envision a bank becoming active in a country without establishing a single office or branch.

Another key problem area results from the fact that many disagreements were set aside for the sake of concluding the negotiations. Disputes in such areas as agriculture or intellectual property rights protection continue to cause a series of trade conflicts among nations. If the WTO's dispute settlement mechanism is then applied to resolve the conflict, outcries in favor of national sovereignty may cause nations to withdraw from the agreement whenever a country loses in a dispute.

A final major weakness of the WTO may result from the desire of some of its members to introduce "social causes" into trade decisions. It is debated, for example, whether the WTO should also deal with issues such as labor laws, competition, and emigration freedoms. Other issues, such as freedom of religion, provision of health care, and the safety of animals are being raised as well. It will be very difficult to have the WTO remain a viable organization if too many nongermane issues are loaded onto the trade and investment mission. The 140 governments participating in the WTO have diverse perspectives, histories, relations, economies, and ambitions. Many of them fear that social causes can be used to devise new rules of protectionism against their exports. Then there is also the question of how much companies—which, after all, are the ones doing the trading and investing—should be burdened with concerns outside of their scope.

To be successful, the WTO needs to be able to focus on its core mission, which deals with international trade and investment. The addition of social causes may appear politically expedient, but will be a key cause for divisiveness and dissent, and thus will inhibit progress on further liberalization of trade and investment. Failure to achieve such progress would leave the WTO without teeth and would negate much of the progress achieved in the Uruguay Round negotiations. It might be best to leave the WTO free from such pressures and look to increased economic ties to cross-pollinate cultures, values, and ethics and to cause changes in the social arena.[10]

Similar problems have befallen international financial institutions. For example, although the **International Monetary Fund (www.imf.org)** has functioned well so far, it is currently under severe challenge by new substantial financial requirements. So far, the IMF has been able to smooth over the most difficult problems, but has not found ways to solve them. For example, in the 1995 peso crisis of Mexico, the IMF was able to provide some relief through a stand-by credit. Yet, given the financial needs of many other nations such as South Korea, Malaysia, Indonesia, Thailand, and Russia, the nations of central Europe, and many countries in Latin America, the IMF simply does not have enough funds to satisfy such needs. In cases of multiple financial crises, it then is unable to provide its traditional function of calming financial markets in turmoil.

Apart from its ability to provide funds, the IMF must also rethink its traditional rules of operations. For example, it is quite unclear whether stringent economic rules and benchmark performance measures are equally applicable to all countries seeking IMF assistance. New economic conditions that have not been experienced to date may require different types of approaches. The link between economic and political stability also may require different considerations, possibly substantially changing the IMF's mission.

Similarly, the **World Bank (www.worldbank.org)** successfully met its goal of aiding the reconstruction of Europe but has been less successful in furthering the economic goals of the developing world and the newly emerging market economies in the former Soviet bloc. Some even claim that instead of alleviating poverty, misguided bank policies may have created poverty.[11] Therefore, at the same time when domestic policy measures have become less effective, international institutions that could help to develop substitute international policy measures have been weakened by new challenges to their traditional missions and insufficient resources to meet such challenges.

Sharpening of the Conflict Between Industrialized and Developing Nations

In the 1960s and 1970s it was hoped that the developmental gap between industrialized nations and many countries in the less-developed world could gradually be closed. This goal was to be achieved with the transfer of technology and the infusion of major funds.

GLOBAL PERSPECTIVE 3.2

The Environmental Bargain

Ozone depletion, acid rain, and global warming make headlines daily. But different countries have different concerns. World leaders met in Rio de Janeiro for a United Nations–sponsored Earth Summit to discuss the health of the planet. At the meetings, the developing world voiced two essential concerns: their lack of money and technology. The industrialized nations in turn focused primarily on the environment wanting to do something about potential threats such as global warming.

The two viewpoints often clash. Maximo Kalaw, Jr., for Manila said, "The message is, if you cannot help us on debt, forget about the environmental conservation of our forests, because it is too much of a burden to handle." In essence, the developing countries are suggesting a straightforward bargain: If we get money, they say to the industrialized world, we will protect the environmental resources you claim to value so highly.

By contrast, the developed world sees a common responsibility of humanity that developing nations have to help fulfill. For example, the rosy periwinkle, a pink shrub found only in Madagascar, can be used to make drugs that have proved effective in fighting childhood leukemia and Hodgkin's disease. Plant genes found in Africa can also be used to improve varieties of wheat, corn, rice, and tomatoes. Therefore, it is important to maintain as much biodiversity as possible, a goal that requires the protection of natural resources. Some companies have already taken action to help. BankAmerica Corp., for example, forgave $6 million of its outstanding loans to Latin American countries in exchange for the debtor nations' promise to conserve ecologically critical rain forests.

In spite of the wide praise for such debt-for-nature swaps, many developing nations see them as a potential threat to their sovereignty. There is concern that these swaps are an attempt to somehow put areas of sovereign territory off limits to domestic control.

Meeting again five years after the Earth Summit, world leaders found themselves still stalemated over the same North-South divisions that created conflict in 1992. At the Earth Summit+5, many of the same opinions were voiced. Minister Msuya Waldi Mangachi of Tanzania, speaking for the "Group of 77" representing 132 developing countries, said that conflict occurred because "developing countries were expecting reaffirmation of commitments for financial support made at Rio, while developed-country partners came to fine tune [Rio's plan of action for environmental preservation] and add new areas".

The Kyoto agreement—a massive plan involving hundreds of nations—was developed in 1997 and calls for industrial nations to reduce emissions. No industrial country has ratified the protocol. In early 2001 the United States said strict and costly environmental rules were the last thing the U.S. energy industry needed. The U.S. Senate had also voted 95–0 against taking any action on climate change unless developing countries reduce heat-trapping "greenhouse" gases, which are mainly carbon dioxide from burning fossil fuels.

Is all hope for environmental preservation lost? Not yet. Governments are beginning to take notice of the value of their natural resources. By early 1999, 150 countries had established national councils on sustainable development (economic growth while protecting vital resources).

Almost ten years after the Rio de Janeiro conference, talks continue.

Sources: John Heilprin, "U.S. Won't Implement Climate Treaty," Associated Press, March, 27, 2001. "Deputy Secretary-General Stresses Determination to Implement Rio Agreements and to Achieve Truly Sustainable Development," United Nations press release, February 23, 1999, www.un.org; Eugene Robinson, "At the Earth Summit, South Aims to Send Bill North," *The Washington Post,* June 1, 1992, A1, A14; "Earth Summit Review Ends with Few Commitments," United Nations press release, July 1997. UN Division for Sustainable Development: www.un.org/dpcsd/dsd.

Even though the 1970s saw vast quantities of petrodollars available for recycling and major growth in borrowing by some developing nations, the results have not been as expected. Although several less-developed nations have gradually emerged as newly industrialized countries (NICs), even more nations are facing grim economic futures.

In Latin America, many nations are still saddled with enormous amounts of debt, rapidly increasing populations, and very fragile economies. The newly emerging democracies in central Europe and the former Soviet Union also face major debt and employment problems. In view of their shattered dreams, policymakers in these nations have become increasingly aggressive in their attempts to reshape the ground rules of the world trade and investment flows. Although many policymakers share the view that major changes are necessary to resolve the difficulties that exist, no clear-cut solutions have emerged.

Lately, an increase in environmental awareness has contributed to a further sharpening of the conflict. As Global Perspective 3.2 shows, developing countries may place

The Global Environment: A Source of Conflict
Between Developed and Less-Developed Nations

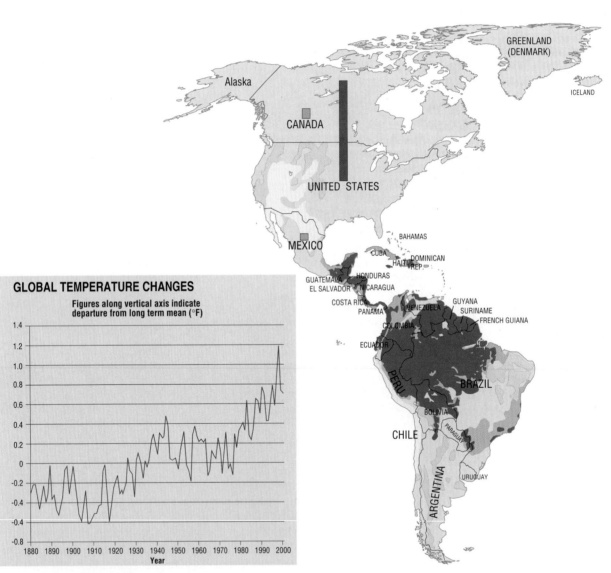

DESERTIFICATION

Areas with risk of desertification

Existing deserts

GLOBAL TEMPERATURE CHANGES

Figures along vertical axis indicate departure from long term mean (°F)

Sources: U.S. National Climatic Data Center, 2001; U.S. Department of Agriculture, 2001;
National Geographic Society, Biodiversity map supplement, Feb. 1999;
AAAS Atlas of Population and Environment, 2000; United Nations Environment Programme, 2001;
World Resources Institute, World Resources , 1998–1999;
Energy Information Administration, *International Energy Annual*, 1999.

RAINFOREST DESTRUCTION

Present distribution of forest area

Area originally forested

GREENHOUSE GAS EMISSIONS

Million metric tons of carbon equivalent

100–200

200–400

over 400

Color of bar indicates total emissions;
height of bar per capita level of emissions

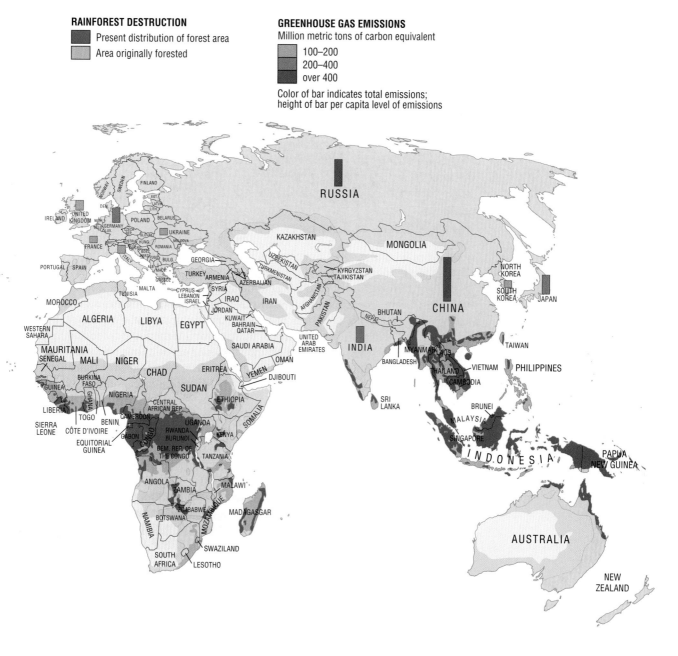

different emphasis on environmental protection. If they are to take measures that will assist the industrialized nations in their environmental goals, they expect to be assisted and rewarded in these efforts. Yet, many in the industrialized world view environmental issues as a "global obligation," rather than as a matter of choice, and are reluctant to pay.

Policy Responses to Changing Conditions

The word *policy* conjures up an image of well-coordinated set of governmental activities. Unfortunately, in the trade and investment sector, as in most of the domestic policy areas, this is rarely the case. Policymakers need to respond too often to short-term problems, need to worry too much about what is politically salable to multiple constituencies, and in some countries, are in office too short a time to formulate a guiding set of long-term strategies. All too often, because of public and media pressures, policymakers must be concerned with current events—such as monthly trade deficit numbers and investment flow figures—that may not be very meaningful in the larger picture. In such an environment, actions may lead to extraordinarily good tactical measures but fail to achieve long-term success.

Restrictions of Imports

In the United States, the Congress has increasingly focused on trade issues and provided the president with additional powers to affect trade. Unfortunately, apart from the consent to the NAFTA and WTO trade agreements, most of these new powers provide only for an increasing threat against foreign importers and investors, not for better conditions for U.S. exporters of goods, services, or capital. As a result, the power of the executive branch of government to improve international trade and investment opportunities for U.S. firms through international negotiations and the relaxation of rules, regulations, and laws has become increasingly restricted over time.

Worldwide, most countries maintain at least a surface-level conformity with international principles. However, many exert substantial restraints on free trade through import controls and barriers. Some of the more frequently encountered barriers are listed in Table 3.2. They are found particularly in countries that suffer from major trade deficits or major infrastructure problems, causing them to enter into voluntary restraint agreements with trading partners or to selectively apply trade-restricting measures such as tariffs, quotas, or nontariff barriers against trading partners.

Tariffs are taxes based primarily on the value of imported goods and services. **Quotas** are restrictions on the number of foreign products that can be imported. **Nontariff barriers** consist of a variety of measures such as testing, certification, or simply bureaucratic hurdles that have the effect of restricting imports. All of these measures tend to raise the price of imported goods. They therefore constitute a transfer of funds from the buyers (or, if absorbed by them, the sellers) of imports to the government, and—if accompanied by price increases of competing domestic products—to the domestic producers of such products.

Voluntary restraint agreements are designed to help domestic industries reorganize, restructure, and recapture production prominence. Even though officially voluntary, these agreements are usually implemented through severe threats against trading partners. Due to their "voluntary" nature, the agreements are not subject to any previously negotiated bilateral or multilateral trade accords.

When nations do not resort to the subtle mechanism of voluntary agreements to affect trade flows, they often impose tariffs and quotas. Many countries use **antidumping** laws to impose tariffs on imports. Antidumping laws are designed to help domestic industries that are injured by unfair competition from abroad due to products being "dumped" on them. Dumping may involve selling goods overseas at prices

TABLE 3.2

Trade Barriers

There are literally hundreds of ways to build a barrier. The following list provides just a few of the trade barriers that exporters face.

- Restrictive licensing
- Special import authorization
- Global quotas
- Voluntary export restraints
- Temporary prohibitions
- Advance import deposits
- Taxes on foreign exchange deals
- Preferential licensing applications
- Excise duties
- Licensing fees
- Statistical taxes
- Sales taxes
- Consumption taxes
- Discretionary licensing

- Licenses for selected purchases
- Country quotas
- Seasonal prohibitions
- Health and sanitary prohibitions
- Foreign exchange licensing
- Licenses subject to barter and countertrade
- Customs surcharges
- Stamp taxes
- Consular invoice fees
- Taxes on transport
- Service charges
- Value-added taxes
- Turnover taxes
- Internal taxes

Source: Mark Magnier, "Blockades to Food Exports Hide Behind Invisible Shields," *The Journal of Commerce* (September 18, 1989): 5A. Reprinted with permission.

lower than those in the exporter's home market or at a price below the cost of production or both. The growing use of antidumping measures by governments around the world complicates the pricing decisions of exporters. Large domestic firms, on the other hand, can use the antidumping process to obtain strategic shelter from foreign competitors.[12]

For example, in 1983 the International Trade Commission imposed a five-year tariff on Japanese heavy motorcycles imported into the United States. The 49.4 percent duty was granted at the request of Harley-Davidson, which could no longer compete with the heavily discounted bikes being imported by companies such as Honda and Kawasaki. The gradually declining tariff gave Harley-Davidson the time to enact new management strategies. Within four years, Harley-Davidson was back on its feet and again had the highest market share in the heavyweight class of bikes. In 1987, Harley-Davidson officials requested that the tariff be lifted a year early. As a result, the policy was labeled a success. However, at no time were the costs of these measures to U.S. consumers even considered.

The third major method by which imports have been restricted is nontariff barriers. These consist of buy-domestic campaigns, preferential treatment for domestic bidders compared with foreign bidders, national standards that are not comparable to international standards, and an emphasis on the design rather than the performance of products. Such nontariff barriers are often the most insidious obstacles to free trade, since they are difficult to detect, hard to quantify, and demands for their removal are often blocked by references to a nation's cultural and historic heritage.

One other way in which imports are sometimes reduced is by tightening market access and entry of foreign products through involved procedures and inspections. Probably the most famous are the measures implemented by France. In order to stop or at least reduce the importation of foreign video recorders, the French government ruled that all of them had to be sent to the customs station at Poitiers. This customhouse was located away from major transport routes, woefully understaffed, and open only a few days each week. In addition, the few customs agents at Poitiers insisted on opening each package separately to inspect the merchandise. Within a few weeks, imports of video recorders came to a halt. Members of the French government, however, were able to point to the fact that they had not restrained trade at all; rather, they had only made some insignificant changes in the procedures of domestic governmental actions.

The Effects of Import Restriction   Policymakers are faced with several problems when trying to administer import controls. First, most of the time such controls exact a huge price from domestic consumers. Import controls may mean that the most efficient sources of supply are not available. The result is either second-best products or higher costs for restricted supplies, which in turn cause customer service standards to drop and consumers to pay significantly higher prices. Even though these costs may be widely distributed among many consumers and are less obvious, the social cost of these controls may be damaging to the economy and subject to severe attack from individuals. However, these attacks are countered by pressure from protected groups that benefit from import restrictions. For example, while citizens of the European Union may be forced by import controls to pay an elevated price for all the agricultural products they consume, agricultural producers in the region benefit from higher incomes. Achieving a proper trade-off is often difficult, if not impossible, for the policymaker.

A second major problem resulting from import controls is the downstream change in the composition of imports that may result. For example, if the importation of copper ore is restricted, through either voluntary restraints or quotas, producing countries may opt to shift their production systems and produce copper wire instead, which they can export. As a result, initially narrowly defined protectionistic measures may snowball in order to protect one downstream industry after another.

Another major problem that confronts the policymaker is that of efficiency. Import controls designed to provide breathing room to a domestic industry so it can either grow or recapture its competitive position often do not work. Rather than improve the productivity of an industry, such controls may provide it with a level of safety and a cushion of increased income, subsequently causing it to lag behind in technological advancements.

One must also be aware of the corporate response to import restrictions. Corporations faced with such restrictions can encourage their governments to erect similar barriers to protect them at home. The result is a gradually escalating set of trade obstacles. In addition, corporations can make strategic use of such barriers by incorporating them into their business plans and exploiting them in order to gain market share. For example, some multinational corporations have pressed governments to initiate antidumping actions against their competitors when faced with low-priced imports. In such instances, corporations may substitute adroit handling of government relations for innovation and competitiveness.

Finally, corporations also can circumvent import restrictions by shifting their activities. For example, instead of conducting trade, corporations can shift to foreign direct investment. The result may be a drop in trade inflow, yet the domestic industry may still be under strong pressure from foreign firms. The investments of Japanese car producers in the United States serve as an example. However, due to the job-creation effects of such investment, such shifts may have been the driving desire on the part of the policymakers who implemented the import controls.

Restrictions of Exports

In addition to imposing restraints on imports, nations also control their exports. The reasons are short supply, national security and foreign policy purposes, or the desire to retain capital.

The United States, for example, regards trade as a privilege of the firm, granted by government, rather than a right or a necessity. As will be explained in more detail in

Chapter 4, U.S. legislation to control exports focuses on **national security** controls—that is, the control of weapons exports or high-technology exports that might adversely affect the safety on the nation. In addition, exports can be controlled for reasons of foreign policy and short supply. These controls restrict the international business opportunities of firms if a government believes that such a restriction would send a necessary foreign policy message to another country. Such action may be undertaken regardless of whether the message will have any impact or whether similar products can easily be supplied by companies in other nations. Although perhaps valuable as a tool of international relations, such policies may give a country's firms the reputation of being unreliable suppliers and may divert orders to firms in other nations.

Export Promotion

The desire to increase participation in international trade and investment flows has led nations to implement export promotion programs. These programs are designed primarily to help domestic firms enter and maintain their position in international markets and to match or counteract similar export promotion efforts by other nations.

Most governments supply some support to their firms participating or planning to participate in international trade. Typically, this support falls into one of four categories: export information and advice, production support, marketing support, or finance and guarantees. While such support is widespread and growing, its intensity varies by country. For example, the United States spends 3 cents per $1,000 of GDP on export promotion, compared with Germany's and Japan's expenditures of 5 cents, Great Britain's 7 cents, France's 18 cents, and Canada's 33 cents.[13]

U.S. Export Promotion   Given the deterioration of the U.S. trade balance, U.S. government trade policy is focusing on export programs to improve the international trade performance of U.S. firms. The Department of Commerce offers information services that provide data on foreign trade and market developments (**www. usatrade.gov**). The department's **Commercial Service** posts hundreds of professionals around the world to gather information and to assist business executives in their activities abroad.

In addition, a wide variety of federal and state agencies are now collaborating in order to coordinate their activities in support of exporters. As a result, a national network of export assistance centers has been created, capable of providing one-stop shops for exporters in search of export counseling and financial assistance. Also, an advocacy network helps U.S. companies win overseas contracts for large government purchases abroad.

Another area of activity by the U.S. government is export financing. The Export-Import Bank of the United States provides U.S. firms with long-term loans and loan guarantees so that they can bid on contracts where financing is a key issue. In response to actions by foreign competitors, the bank has, on occasion also resorted to offering mixed aid credits. The credits, which take the form of loans composed partially of commercial interest rates and partially of highly subsidized developmental aid interest rates, result in very low interest loans to exporters.

Tax legislation that inhibited the employment of Americans by U.S. firms abroad has also been altered. In the past, U.S. nationals living abroad were, with some minor exclusion, fully subject to U.S. federal taxation. The cost of living abroad can often be quite high—for example, rent for a small apartment can approach $5,000 per month—so this tax structure often imposed a significant burden on U.S. firms and citizens abroad. As a result, companies frequently were not able to send U.S. employees to their foreign subsidiaries. However, a revision of the tax code now allows a substantial amount of income (up to $78,000 in 2001) to remain tax-free.[14] More Americans can now be posted abroad. In their work they may specify the use of U.S. products, thus enhancing the competitive position of U.S. firms.

Any export promotion raises several questions. One concerns the justification of the expenditure of public funds for what is essentially an activity that should be driven by profits. It appears, however, that the start-up cost for international operations, particularly for smaller firms, may be sufficiently high to warrant some kind of government support.[15] A second question focuses on the capability of government to provide such support. Both for the selection and reach of firms as well as the distribution of support, government is not necessarily better equipped than the private sector to do a good job. A third issue concerns competitive export promotion. If countries provide such support to their firms, they may well distort the flow of trade. If other countries then increase their support of firms in order to counteract the effects, all that results is the same volume of trade activity, but at subsidized rates. It is therefore important to carefully evaluate export promotion activities as to their effectiveness and competitive impact. Perhaps such promotion is only beneficial when it addresses existing market gaps.

Import Promotion

Some countries have also developed import promotion measures. The measures are implemented primarily by nations that have accumulated and maintained large balance-of-trade surpluses. They hope to allay other nations' fears of continued imbalances and to gradually redirect trade flows.

Japan, for example, has completely refurbished the operations of the Japan External Trade Organization (JETRO) (**www.jetro.org**). This organization, which initially was formed to encourage Japanese exports, has now begun to focus on the promotion of imports to Japan. It organizes trade missions of foreign firms coming to Japan, hosts special exhibits and fairs within Japan, and provides assistance and encouragement to potential importers.

Investment Policies

The discussion of policy actions has focused thus far on merchandise trade. Similar actions are applicable to investment flows and, by extension, to international trade in services. In order to protect ownership, control, and development of domestic industries, many countries attempt to influence investment capital flows. Most frequently, investment-screening agencies decide on the merits of any particular foreign investment project. Canada, for example, has "Investment Canada" an agency that scrutinizes foreign investments.[16] So do most developing nations, where special government permission must be obtained for investment projects. This permission frequently carries with it certain conditions, such as levels of ownership permitted, levels of dividends that can be repatriated, numbers of jobs that must be created, or the extent to which management can be carried out by individuals from abroad. The United States restricts foreign investment in instances where national security or related concerns are at stake. Major foreign investments may be reviewed by the **Committee on Foreign Investments in the United States (CFIUS),** as shown in Global Perspective 3.3.

The Host-Country Perspective

The host government is caught in a love-hate relationship with foreign direct investment. On the one hand, the host country has to appreciate the various contributions, especially economic, that the foreign direct investment will make. On the other hand,

GLOBAL PERSPECTIVE 3.3

Foreign Purchases of U.S. Telecoms Prompt Security Concerns

Shattering geographical boundaries, telecommunications has exploded from simple voice communications to text, video, graphics, and audio using the Internet. Purchases of U.S. telecommunications equipment and technology by non-U.S. companies are considered sensitive in terms of international security because law enforcement methods, like wiretapping, depend on access to telephone networks. Proposed purchases by or mergers with non-U.S. companies are therefore carefully scrutinized by the Committee on Foreign Investments (CFIUS).

In a landmark review in mid-2000, CFIUS considered Nippon Telegraph & Telephone's proposed acquisition of Verio Inc., an Internet company based in Seattle, Washington. Verio hosted 400,000 web sites for small and mid-sized businesses. NTT is partly owned by the Japanese government. This case was the first time the Communications Assistance Law Enforcement Act of 1994, which provides law enforcement access to telephone networks, was applied to an Internet company. It also tested a regulation banning FCC licenses to companies with more than 25 percent ownership by a foreign government, unless the service could be shown to increase the public good.

Debate about the merger was divided along organization lines within CFIUS, comprised of representatives from the Justice Department, the Treasury Department, and the FBI among others. The Treasury Department accused the FBI of exaggerating the risks and acting as a roadblock to open markets and free trade. After 45 days of review and negotiations among CFIUS, Verio, and NTT, the purchase was approved. Later, the FCC waived the regulation against foreign government ownership of 25 percent and more.

The merger also provoked a backlash by 29 U.S. senators, who believed liberalizing the international telecommunication markets would leave the nation vulnerable. They sponsored a bill restricting the FCC's power to waive the cap on ownership by a foreign government, claiming non-U.S. ownership of U.S-based telecommunications companies jeopardizes sensitive information about the federal government and corporations and possibly compromises wiretapping.

In contrast to the nationalistic stance of the Senate group, the U.S. Trade Representatives supported recent World Trade Organization (WTO) accords to encourage multinational telecomm mergers. The new rules allow foreign companies to use holding companies to purchase telecommunications companies in other nations. This ownership is in direct conflict with FCC regulations, vividly illustrating the tensions between varying agencies and constituencies.

The NTT acqusition of Verio threw the doors open to other suitors of U.S. communications companies. Deutsche Telekom, with nearly 60 percent ownership by the German government, announced its intention to purchase VoiceStream Wireless in mid-2001. As part of ongoing negotiation, Deutsche Telekom is reducing its government ownership and has also agreed to ensure the confidentiality of authorized wiretapping by U.S. authorities.

Sources: "Telekom, U.S. Strike Accord," *AP Online,* January 17, 2001; Peter S. Goodman, "Telecom Mergers Come Calling on U.S." *Washington Post,* July 13, 2000, p. EI; Kris Hudson, "Purchase of Verio Likely to Be Delayed by Fed," *Denver Rocky Mountain News,* July 7, 2000, p. IB; Peter S. Goodman and David A. Vise, "Bid for U.S. Firm Closely Watched," *Washington Post,* August 12, 2000, p. EI.

fears of dominance, interference, and dependence are often voiced and acted on. The major positive and negative impacts are summarized in Table 3.3.

The Positive Impact   Foreign direct investment has contributed greatly to world development in the past 40 years. Said Lord Lever, a British businessman who served in the cabinets of Harold Wilson and James Callaghan, "Europe got twenty times more out of American investment after the war than the multinationals did; every country gains by productive investment."[17]

Capital flows are especially beneficial to countries with limited domestic sources and restricted opportunities to raise funds in the world's capital markets. In addition, foreign direct investment may attract local capital to a project for which local capital alone would not have sufficed.

The role of foreign direct investment has been seen as that of **technology transfer.**[18] Technology transfer includes the introduction of not only new hardware to the market but also the techniques and skills to operate it. In industries where the role of intellectual property is substantial, such as pharmaceuticals or software development, access to parent companies' research and development provides benefits that may be far greater than those gained through infusion of capital. This explains the interest

TABLE 3.3

Positive and Negative Impacts of Foreign Direct Investment on Host Countries

Positive Impact

1. Capital formation
2. Technology and management skills transfer
3. Regional and sectoral development
4. Internal competition and entrepreneurship
5. Favorable effect on balance of payments
6. Increased employment

Negative Impact

1. Industrial dominance
2. Technological dependence
3. Disturbance of economic plans
4. Cultural change
5. Interference by home government of multinational corporation

Sources: Jack N. Behrman, *National Interests and the Multinational Enterprise* (Englewood Cliffs. NJ: Prentice-Hall, 1970), Chapters 2 through 5; Jack N. Behrman, *Industrial Policies: International Restructuring and Transnationals* (Lexington, MA: Lexington Books, 1984), Chapter 5; and Christopher M. Korth, *International Business* (Englewood Cliffs, NJ: Prentice-Hall 1985), Chapters 12 and 13.

that many governments have expressed in having multinational corporations establish R&D facilities in their countries.

An integral part of technology transfer is managerial skills, which are the most significant labor component of foreign direct investment. With the growth of the service sector, many economies need skills rather than expatriate personnel to perform the tasks.

Foreign direct investment can be used effectively in developing a geographical region or a particular industry sector. Foreign direct investment is one of the most expedient ways in which unemployment can be reduced in chosen regions of a country. Furthermore, the costs of establishing an industry are often too prohibitive and the time needed too excessive for the domestic industry, even with governmental help, to try it on its own. In many developing countries, foreign direct investment may be a way to diversify the industrial base and thereby reduce the country's dependence on one or a few sectors.

At the company level, foreign direct investment may intensify competition and result in benefits to the economy as a whole as well as to consumers through increased productivity and possibly lower prices. Competition typically introduces new techniques, goods and services, and ideas to the markets. It may improve existing patterns of how business is done.

The major impact of foreign direct investment on the balance of payments is long term. Import substitution, export earnings, and subsidized imports of technology and management all assist the host nation on the trade account side of the balance of payments. Not only may a new production facility substantially decrease the need to import the type of products manufactured, but it may start earning export revenue as well. Several countries, such as Brazil, have imposed export requirements as a precondition for foreign direct investment. On the capital account side, foreign direct investment may have short-term impact in lowering a deficit as well as long-term impact in keeping capital at home that otherwise could have been invested or transferred abroad. However, measurement is difficult because significant portions of the flows may miss—or evade—the usual government reporting channels. In 1990, more than half of foreign investment was "unidentified," in that experts could not figure out what type it was or where it came from.[19]

Jobs are often the most obvious reason to cheer about foreign direct investment. Foreign companies directly employ three million Americans, or about 3 percent of the workforce, and indirectly create opportunities for millions more. The benefits reach far beyond mere employment. Salaries paid by multinational corporations are usually higher than those paid by domestic firms. The creation of jobs translates also into the training and development of a skilled work force. Consider, for example, the situation of many Caribbean states that are dependent on tourism for their well-being. In most cases, multinational hotel chains have been instrumental in establishing a pool of trained hospitality workers and managers.

All of the benefits discussed are indeed possible advantages of foreign direct investment. Their combined effect can lead to an overall enhancement in the standard of living in the market as well as an increase in the host country's access to the world market and its international competitiveness. It is equally possible, however, that the impact can be negative rather than positive.

The Negative Impact   Although some of the threats posed by multinational corporations and foreign direct investment in terms of stunted economic development, low levels of research and development, and poor treatment of local employees are exaggerated, in many countries some industrial sectors are dominated by foreign-owned entities. In Belgium, for example, oil refining (78 percent) and electrical engineering (87 percent) showed very high rates of foreign participation.[20]

Foreign direct investment most often is concentrated in technology-intensive industries. Therefore, research and development is another area of tension. Multinational corporations usually want to concentrate their R&D efforts, especially their basic research. With its technology transfer, the multinational corporation can assist the host country's economic development, but it may leave the host country dependent on flows of new and updated technology. Furthermore, the multinational firm may contribute to the **brain drain** by attracting scientists from host countries to its central research facility. Many countries have demanded and received research facilities on their soil, where they can better control results. Many countries are weary of the technological dominance of the United States and Japan and view it as a long-term threat. Western European nations, for example, are joining forces in basic research and development under the auspices of the so-called EUREKA project, which is a pan-European pooling of resources to develop new technologies with both governmental and private sector help.

The economic benefits of foreign direct investment are controversial as well. Capital inflows may be accompanied by outflows in a higher degree and over a longer term than is satisfactory to the host government. For example, hotels built in the Caribbean by multinational chains often were unable to find local suppliers and had to import supplies and thus spend much-needed foreign currency. Many officials also complain that the promised training of local personnel, especially for management positions, has never taken place. Rather than stimulate local competition and encourage entrepreneurship, multinationals with their often superior product offering and marketing skills have stifled competition. Many countries, including the United States, have found that multinational companies do not necessarily want to rely on local suppliers but rather bring along their own from their domestic market.

Governments also see multinationals as a disturbance to their economic planning. Decisions are made concerning their economy over which they have little or no control. Host countries do not look favorably on a multinational that may want to keep the import content of a product high, especially when local suppliers may be available.

Multinational companies are, by definition, change agents. They bring about change not only in the way business may be conducted but also, through the products and services they generate and the way they are marketed, cause change in the lifestyles of the consumers in the market. The extent to which this is welcomed or accepted varies by country. For example, the introduction of fast-food restaurants to Taiwan dramat-

ically altered eating patterns, especially of teenagers, who made these outlets extremely popular and profitable. Concern has been expressed about the apparent change in eating patterns and the higher relative cost of eating in such establishments.

The multinational corporation will also have an impact on business practices. Although multinationals usually pay a higher salary, they may also engage in practices that are alien to the local work force, such as greater flexibility in work rules. Older operators in Japan, for example, may be removed from production lines to make room for more productive employees. In another country where the Japanese firm establishes a plant, tradition and union rules may prevent this.[21]

Some host nations have expressed concern over the possibility of interference, economically and politically, by the home government of the multinational corporation; that is, they fear that the multinational may be used as an instrument of influence.[22] The United States has used U.S.-based corporations to extend its foreign policy in areas of capital flows, technology controls, and competition. Foreign direct investment regulations were introduced in the United States in the 1960s to diminish capital outflows from the country and thus to strengthen the country's balance-of-payment situation. If the actions of affiliates of U.S.-based companies are seen to have a negative impact on competition in the U.S. market, antitrust decrees may be used to change the situation.

Of course, the multinational firm is subject not only to the home government political and economic directions but also to those of the host government and other groups. Fixed investments by multinationals can be held hostage by a host country in trying to win concessions from other governments.

Countries engage in informal evaluation of foreign direct investment, both outbound and inbound. Canada, for example, uses the Foreign Investment Review Agency to determine whether foreign-owned companies are good corporate citizens. Sweden reviews outbound foreign direct investment in terms of its impact on the home country, especially employment.

The Home-Country Perspective

Most of the aspects of foreign direct investment that concern host countries apply to the home country as well. Foreign direct investment means addition to the home country's gross domestic product from profits, royalties, and fees remitted by affiliates. In many cases, intracompany transfers bring about additional export possibilities.[23] Many countries, in promoting foreign direct investment, see it as a means to stimulate economic growth—an end that would expand export markets and serve other goals, such as political motives, as well. Some countries, such as Japan, have tried to gain preferential access to raw materials by purchasing firms that owned the deposits. Other factors of production can be obtained through foreign direct investment as well. Companies today may not have the luxury of establishing R&D facilities wherever they choose but must locate them where human power is available. This explains, for example, why Northern Telecom, the Canadian telecommunications giant, has more than 500 of its roughly 2,000 R&D people based in the United States, mostly in California.

The major negative issue centers on employment. Many unions point not only to outright job loss but also to the effect on imports and exports. The most controversial have been investments in plants in developing countries that export back to the home countries. Multinationals such as electronics manufacturers, who have moved plants to southeast Asia and Mexico, have justified this as a necessary cost-cutting competitive measure.

Another critical issue is that of technological advantage. Some critics state that, by establishing plants abroad or forming joint ventures with foreign entities, the country may be giving away its competitive position in the world marketplace. This is es-

pecially true when the recipients may be able to avoid the time and expense involved in developing new technologies.

Restrictions on Investment

Many nations also restrict exports of capital, because **capital flight** is a major problem for them. Particularly in situations where countries lack necessary foreign exchange reserves, governments are likely to place restrictions on capital outflow. In essence, government claims to have higher priorities for capital than its citizens. They in turn, often believe that the return on investment or the safety of the capital is not sufficiently ensured in their own countries. The reason may be governmental measures or domestic economic factors, such as inflation. These holders of capital want to invest abroad. By doing so, however, they deprive their domestic economy of much-needed investment funds.

Once governments impose restrictions on the export of funds, the desire to transfer capital abroad only increases. Because companies and individuals are ingenious in their efforts to achieve capital flight, governments, particularly in developing countries, continue to suffer. In addition, few new outside investors will enter the country because they fear that dividends and profits will not be remitted easily.

Investment Promotion

Many countries also implement policy measures to attract foreign direct investment. These policies can be the result of the needs of poorer countries to attract additional foreign capital to fuel economic growth without taking out more loans that call for fixed schedules of repayment.[24] Industrialized nations also participate in these efforts since governments are under pressure to provide jobs for their citizens and have come to recognize that foreign direct investment can serve as a major means to increase employment and income. Global Perspective 3.4 reports on some of the investment promotion efforts undertaken in the EU. Increasingly, even state and local governments are participating in investment promotion. Some U.S. states, for example, are sending out "Invest in the USA" missions on a regular basis. Others have opened offices abroad to inform local businesses about the beneficial investment climate at home.

Incentives used by policymakers to facilitate such investments are mainly of three types: fiscal, financial, and nonfinancial. **Fiscal incentives** are specific tax measures designed to attract the foreign investor. They typically consist of special depreciation allowances, tax credits or rebates, special deductions for capital expenditures, tax holidays, and the reduction of tax burdens on the investor. **Financial incentives** offer special funding for the investor by providing, for example, land or building, loans, and loan guarantees. **Nonfinancial incentives** can consist of guaranteed government purchases; special protection from competition through tariffs, import quotas, and local content requirements; and investments in infrastructure facilities.

All of these incentives are designed primarily to attract more industry and therefore create more jobs. They may slightly alter the advantage of a region and therefore make it more palatable for the investor to choose to invest in that region. By themselves, they are unlikely to spur an investment decision if proper market conditions do not exist.

Investment promotion policies may succeed in luring new industries to a location and in creating new jobs, but they may also have several drawbacks. For example, when countries compete for foreign investment, several of them may offer more or less the same investment package. The slight advantage that the incentives of one country may have over another's package generally makes little difference in the investment site selected.[25] Moreover, investment policies aimed at attracting foreign direct investment may occasionally place established domestic firms at a disadvantage if they do not receive any support.

GLOBAL PERSPECTIVE 3.4

Courting Foreign Investors

European unemployment rates are double the U.S. level, placing pressure on European politicians to come up with innovative ways to create jobs. Increasingly European governments are turning to multinational corporations with incentives linked to the number of jobs the company will create by investing in the country. The more jobs a multinational manufacturer promises, the more subsidies the government will provide. European countries thus find themselves competing with each other for foreign investment.

Britain, the leader in this race with 10 percent of all foreign investment in the European Union, paid $48,600 for each of the 6,00 jobs created in 1996 when LG, a south Korean firm, invested in an electronics complex. According to Britain's Trade and Industry Ministry, more than 285,000 jobs were created or preserved through foreign investment from 1994 to 1997. The subsidized jobs in turn created nonsubsidized jobs through purchases from local suppliers and improved the quality of local sourcing.

As European firms themselves seek to lower operating costs by building plants abroad—including in Central and Eastern Europe—Germany, France, and Switzerland often have to play the foreign investment game with European companies. For example, France paid over $55,000 per job to get Mercedes-Benz's Swatch auto plant to locate in its eastern region of Lorraine.

To control competition among European countries, the European Union maintains strict rules covering incentives. For example, Ireland's low corporate tax rate of 10 percent, which lured a number of firms, was seen as unfair by the rest of Europe, and Irish officials raised it to 12.5 percent.

Individual U.S. states have investment agencies in Europe that court foreign investors, offering cash incentives for job creation in the United States. For every job Mercedes-Benz created at its Alabama factory, it reaped around $165,000 in state subsidies; at its Spartanburg, South Carolina plant, BMW received more than $100,000 per job. In 2000, Honda received $158 million in incentives for a plant that will generate 1,500 jobs.

American companies investing in Europe have also benefited from investment support. In 1995 Ford got a $104 million grant for a new Jaguar plant in Birmingham, U.K. The auto maker later threatened to close its assembly plant in Liverpool unless it received a government grant toward the cost of restructuring the plant for building a new model there.

When countries such as China and Mexico offer low-cost locations for production, industrialized nations feel compelled to counter with other kinds of incentives. By offering incentive packages, Curitiba, 250 miles from Sao Paolo, has become Brazil's second largest auto center. Manufacturers who invest in eastern Germany can obtain cash worth up to 50 percent of their capital investment. Changwon, South Korea, offers cheap loans and tax rebates to foreign manufacturers.

Governments use subsidies to induce investment not only from auto firms but, at even greater cost, from high-tech computer and electronics companies. With countries engaged in a bidding war for multinational investment, smaller nations face the prospect of being outspent by bigger competitors. Despite the high cost of the handouts, no country wants to miss the opportunity to gain job growth and modernized industry, especially when plagued by high unemployment.

Sources: Bruce Barnard, "A Buyer's Job Market," *The Journal of Commerce* (February 12, 1997): 1C, 23C; Weld Royal, "Money for Jobs," *Industry Week,* April 3, 2000.

Management of the Policy Relationship

Arguments for and against foreign direct investment are endless. Costs and benefits must be weighed. Only the multinational corporation itself can assess expected gains against perceived risks in its overseas commitments. At the same time, only the host and home countries can assess benefits realized against costs in terms of their national priorities. If these entities cannot agree on objectives because their most basic interests are in conflict, they cannot agree on the means either. In most cases, the relationship between the parties is not necessarily based on logic, fairness, or equity, but on the relative bargaining power of each.[26] Futhermore, political changes may cause rapid changes in host government–MNC relations.

The bargaining positions of the multinational corporation and the host country change over time. The course of these changes is summarized in Figure 3.3. The multinational wields its greatest power before the investment is actually made; in the negotiation period, it can require a number of incentives over a period of time. Whether or not the full cycle of events takes place depends on developments in the market as well as the continued bargaining strength of the multinational.

FIGURE 3.3

Bargaining Position of Multinational Corporation (MNC) and Host Country

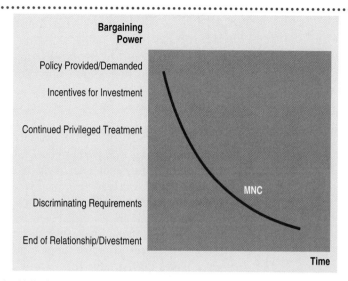

Sources: Christopher M. Korth, *International Business*, (Englewood Cliffs. NJ: Prentice-Hall, 1985), 350; and Thomas A. Poynter, "Managing Government Intervention: A Strategy for Defending the Subsidy." *Columbia Journal of World Business* 21 (winter 1986): 55–65.

The multinational corporation can maintain its bargaining strength by developing a local support system through local financing, procurement, and business contracts as well as by maintaining control over access to technology and markets. The first approach attempts to gain support from local market entities if discriminating actions by the government take place. The second approach aims to make the operation of the affiliate impossible without the contribution of the parent.

Host countries, on the other hand, try to enhance their role by instituting control policies and performance requirements. Governments attempt to prevent the integration of activities among affiliates and control by the parent. In this effort, they exclude or limit foreign participation in certain sectors of the economy and require local participation in the ownership and management of the entities established. The extent of this participation will vary by industry, depending on how much the investment is needed by the host economy. Performance requirements typically are programs aimed at established foreign investors in an economy. These often are such discriminatory policies as local content requirements, export requirements, limits on foreign payments (especially profit repatriation), and demands concerning the type of technology transferred or the sophistication and level of operation engaged in. In some cases, demands of this type have led to firms' packing their bags. For example, Coca-Cola left India when the government demanded access to what the firm considered to be confidential intellectual property. Only India's free-market reforms have brought Coca-Cola and many other investors back to the country. Cadbury Schweppes sold its plant in Kenya because price controls made its operation unprofitable.[27] On their part, governments can, as a last resort, expropriate the affiliate, especially if they believe that the benefits are greater than the cost.[28]

A Strategic Outlook for Trade and Investment Policies

All countries have international trade and investment policies. The importance and visibility of these policies have grown dramatically as international trade and investment flows have become more relevant to the well-being of most nations. Given the growing links among nations, it will be increasingly difficult to consider domestic policy without looking at international repercussions.

A U.S. Perspective

The U.S. need is for a positive trade policy rather than reactive, ad hoc responses to specific situations. **Protectionistic legislation** can be helpful, provided it is not enacted. Proposals in Congress, for example, can be quite useful as bargaining chips in international negotiations. If passed and signed into law, however, protectionistic legislation can result in the destruction of the international trade and investment framework.

It has been suggested that a variety of regulatory agencies could become involved in administering U.S. trade policy. Although such agencies could be useful from the standpoint of addressing narrowly defined grievances, they carry the danger that commercial policy will be determined by a new chorus of discordant voices. Shifting the power of setting trade and investment policy from the executive branch to agencies or even states could give the term *New Federalism* a quite unexpected meaning and might cause progress at the international negotiation level to grind to a halt. No U.S. negotiator can expect to retain the goodwill of foreign counterparts if he or she cannot place issues on the table that can be negotiated without constantly having to check back with various authorities.

In light of continuing large U.S. trade deficits, there is much disenchantment with past trade policies. The disappointment with past policy measures, particularly trade negotiations, is mainly the result of overblown expectations. Too often, the public has mistakenly expected successful trade negotiations to affect the domestic economy in a major way, even though the issue addressed or resolved was only of minor economic importance. Yet, in light of global changes, U.S. trade policy does need to change. Rather than treating trade policy as a strictly "foreign" phenomenon, it must be recognized that it is mainly domestic economic performance that determines global competitiveness. Therefore, trade policy must become more domestically oriented at the same time that domestic policy must become more international in vision. Such a new approach should pursue at least five key goals. First, the nation must improve the quality and amount of information government and business share to facilitate competitiveness. Second, policy must encourage collaboration among companies in such areas as goods and process technologies. Third, American industry collectively must overcome its export reluctance and its short-term financial orientation. Fourth, America must invest in its people, providing education and training suited to the competitive challenges of the next century.[29] Finally, the executive branch must be given authority by Congress to negotiate international agreements with a reasonable certainty that the negotiation outcome will not be subject to minute amendments. Therefore, the extension of **trade promotion authority,** which still gives Congress the right to accept or reject trade treaties and agreements, but reduces the amendment procedures, is very important. Such authority is instrumental if new, large-scale trade accords such as a Free Trade Agreement of the Americas are to succeed.

An International Perspective

From an international perspective, trade and investment negotiations must continue. In doing, so, trade and investment policy can take either a multilateral or bilateral approach. **Bilateral negotiations** are carried out mainly between two nations, while **multilateral negotiations** are carried out among a number of nations. The approach can also be broad, covering a wide variety of products, services, or investments, or it can be narrow in that it focuses on specific problems.

In order to address narrowly defined trade issues, bilateral negotiations and a specific approach seem quite appealing. Very specific problems can be discussed and resolved expediently. However, to be successful on a global scale, negotiations need to produce winners. Narrow-based bilateral negotiations require that there be, for each issue, a clearly identified winner and loser. Therefore, such negotiations have less chance for long-term success, because no one wants to be the loser. This points toward multilateral negotiations on a broad scale, where concessions can be traded off among countries, making it possible for all participants to emerge and declare themselves as winners. The difficulty lies in devising enough incentives to bring the appropriate and desirable partners to the bargaining table.

Policymakers must be willing to trade off short-term achievements for long-term goals. All too often, measures that would be beneficial in the long term are sacrificed to short-term expediency to avoid temporary pain and the resulting political cost. Given the increasing links among nations and their economies, however, such adjustments are inevitable. In the recent past, trade and investment volume continued to grow for everyone. Conflicts were minimized and adjustment possibilities were increased manyfold. As trade and investment policies must be implemented in an increasingly competitive environment, however, conflicts are likely to increase significantly. Thoughtful economic coordination will therefore be required among the leading trading nations. Such coordination will result to some degree in the loss of national sovereignty.

New mechanisms to evaluate restraint measure will also need to be designed. The beneficiaries of trade and investment restraints are usually clearly defined and have much to gain, whereas the losers are much less visible, which will make coalition building a key issue. The total cost of policy measures affecting trade and investment flows must be assessed, must be communicated, and must be taken into consideration before such measures are implemented.[30]

The affected parties need to be concerned and join forces. The voices of retailers, consumers, wholesalers, and manufacturers all need to be heard. Only then will policymakers be sufficiently responsive in setting policy objectives that increase opportunities for firms and choice for consumers.

Summary

Trade and investment policies historically have been a subset of domestic policies. Domestic policies in turn have aimed primarily at maintaining and improving the standard of living, the developmental level, and the employment level within a nation. Occasionally, foreign policy concerns also played a role. Increasingly, however, this view of trade and investment policies is undergoing change. While the view was appropriate for global developments that took place following World War II, changes in the current world environment require changes in policies.

Increasingly, the capability of policymakers simply to focus on domestic issues is reduced because of global links in trade and investment. In addition, traditional international institutions concerned with these policies have been weakened, and the developmental conflict among nations has been sharpened. As a result, there is a tendency by many nations to restrict imports either through tariff or nontariff barriers. Yet, all these actions have repercussions that negatively affect industries and consumers.

Nations also undertake efforts to promote exports through information and advice, production and marketing support, and financial assistance. While helpful to the individual firm, in the aggregate, such measures may only assist firms in efforts that the profit motive would encourage them to do anyway. Yet, for new entrants to the international market such assistance may be useful. Foreign direct investment restrictions are often debated in many countries. Frequently, nations become concerned about levels of foreign direct investment and the "selling out" of the patrimony. However, the bottom line is that although the restriction of investments may permit more domestic control over industries, it also denies access to foreign capital. This in turn can result in a tightening up of credit markets, higher interest rates, and less impetus for innovation. Governments also promote imports and foreign direct investment in order to receive needed products or to attract economic activity.

In the future, nations must cooperate closely. They must view domestic policymaking in the global context in order to maintain a viable and growing global trade and investment environment. Policies must be long term in order to ensure the well-being of nations and individuals.

Key Terms and Concepts

national sovereignty
standard of living
quality of life
foreign policy
International Trade
  Organization (ITO)
General Agreement on
  Tariffs and Trade (GATT)
Most-Favored Nation
  (MFN)

World Trade Organization
  (WTO)
currency flows
punitive tariffs
International Monetary
  Fund (IMF)
World Bank
tariffs
quotas
nontariff barriers

voluntary restraint
  agreements
antidumping
national security
Commerical Service
mixed aid credits
Committee on Foreign
  Investments in the
  United States (CFIUS)
technology transfer

brain drain
capital flight
fiscal incentives
financial incentives
nonfinancial incentives
protectionistic legislation
trade promotion authority
bilateral negotiations
multilateral negotiations

Questions for Discussion

1. Discuss the role of voluntary import restraints in international business.
2. What is meant by multilateral negotiations?
3. Discuss the impact of import restrictions on consumers.
4. Why would policymakers sacrifice major international progress for minor domestic policy gains?
5. Discuss the varying inputs to trade and investment restrictions by beneficiaries and by losers.
6. Why are policymakers often oriented to the short term?
7. Discuss the effect of foreign direct investment on trade.
8. Do investment promotion programs of state (or provincial) governments make sense from a national perspective?

9. The Bureau of Economic Analysis (**www.bea.doc.gov**) and Stat-USA (**www.stat-usa.gov**) provide a multitude of information about the current state of the U.S. economy. Go to the International Investment Tables (D-57) to find the current market value of direct investment abroad as well as the value of direct investment in the United States.
10. Check the U.S. Department of Commerce web site (**www.doc.gov**) to determine the assistance available to exporters. Which programs do you find most helpful to firms?

Internet Exercise

Go to the World Bank web site (**www.worldbank.org**) to obtain an overview of the bank's purpose and programs. Search for criticism of bank programs on other web sites and prepare a two-page report of the key issues accounting for the "World Bank Controversy."

Recommended Readings

Cavusgil, S. Tamer, and Michael R. Czinkota, eds. *International Perspectives on Trade Promotion and Assistance.* New York: Quorum, 1990.

Haar, Jerry, and Anthony T. Bryan, eds. *Canadian–Caribbean Relations in Transition: Trade, Sustainable Development and Security (International Political Economy Series).* New York: St. Martin's Press, 1999.

Hindley, Brian. *Antidumping Industrial Policy: Legalized Protectionism in the WTO and What To Do About It.* Washington, DC: AEI Press, 1996.

Howse, Robert, and Michael J. Trebilcock. *The Regulation of International Trade.* London: Routledge Press, 1999.

Hufbauer, Gary Clyde, and Kimberly Ann Elliott. *Measuring the Costs of Protection in the United States.* Washington, DC: Institute for International Economics, 1994.

Krugman, Paul R., and Maurice Obstfeld. *International Economics: Theory and Policy.* Cambridge: Addison-Wesley Publishing Company, 2000.

Mundo, Philip A. *National Politics in a Global Economy: The Domestic Sources of U.S. Trade Policy.* Washington, DC: Georgetown University Press, 1999.

Schott, Jeffrey J. *Prospects for Western Hemisphere Free Trade.* Washington, DC: Institute for International Economics, 2001.

Schott, Jeffrey J. *The WTO After Seattle.* Washington, DC: Institute for International Economics, 2000.

Special Issue on Export Promotion of *The International Trade Journal* vol. 11, no. 1 (spring 1997).

Notes

1. Michael R. Czinkota, "The World Trade Organization: Perspectives and Prospects," *Journal of International Marketing* 3, 1 (1995), 85–92.

2. Thomas R. Graham, "Global Trade: War and Peace," *Foreign Policy* 50 (spring 1983): 124–127.

3. Edwin L. Barber III, "Investment-Trade Nexus," in *U.S. International Policy,* ed. Gary Clyde Hufbauer (Washington, DC: The International Law Institute, 1982), 9–4.

4. Jessica T. Mathews, "Power Shift," *Foreign Affairs* (January/February 1997): 50–66.

5. Federal News Service (September 16, 1997).

6. *The Washington Post,* October 13, 1996.

7. J. David Richardson and Karin Rindal, *Why Exports Matter: More!* (Washington, DC: The Institute for International Economics and The Manufacturing Institute, February 1996).

8. Department of Commerce, Office of Trade and Economic Analysis, *Business America* (May 1997).

9. 1995 data, reported in *Investor's Business Daily* (December 30, 1996).

10. Michael R. Czinkota, "The World Trade Organization: Perspectives and Prospects," 85–92.

11. Chris Sewell, "The World Bank Controversy Explained," Medill News Service, (www.studentadvantage.com) February 8, 2001.

12. Michael R. Czinkota and Masaaki Kotabe, "A Marketing Perspective of the U.S. International Trade Commission's Antidumping Actions—An Empirical Inquiry," *Journal of World Business* 32, 2 (1997): 169–187.

13. U.S. Department of Commerce, *National Export Strategy* (Washington DC: U.S. Government Printing Office), October 1996.

14. *2000 U.S. Master Tax Guide,* (Chicago: CCH, Inc., 2000), 572.

15. Masaaki Kotabe and Michael R. Czinkota, "State Government Promotion of Manufacturing Exports: A Gap Analysis," *Journal of International Business Studies* (winter 1992): 637–658.

16. Investment Canada Act, http://investcan.ic.gc.ca, February 9, 2001.

17. Jaclyn Fierman, "The Selling Off of America," *Fortune,* December 22, 1986, 35.

18. Mark Casson, *Alternatives to the Multinational Enterprise,* London: Macmillan, 1979, 4.

19. Vivian Brownstein, "The Credit Crunch Myth," *Fortune* (December 17, 1990): 59–69.

20. Daniel van Den Bulcke, "Belgium," in *Multinational Enterprise, Economic Structure and International Competitiveness,* ed. John H. Dunning (Chichester, England: Wiley, 1985), 249–280.

21. "At Sanyo's Arkansas Plant the Magic Isn't Working," *Business Week* (July 14, 1986): 51–52.

22. Joseph S. Nye, "Multinational Corporations in World Politics," *Foreign Affairs* 53 (October 1974): 153–175.

23. Lawrence Franko, "Foreign Direct Investment in Less Developed Countries: Impact on Home Countries," *Journal of International Business Studies* 9 (winter 1978): 55–65.

24. Stephen Guisinger, "Attracting and Controlling Foreign Investment," *Economic Impact* (Washington, DC: United States Information Agency, 1987), 18.

25. Ibid., 20.

26. Peter P. Gabriel, "MNCs in the Third World: Is Conflict Unavoidable?" *Harvard Business Review* 50 (July–August 1972): 91–102.

27. Victor H. Frank, "Living with Price Control Abroad," *Harvard Business Review* 62 (March–April 1984): 137–142.

28. Thomas W. Shreeve, "Be Prepared for Political Charges Abroad," *Harvard Business Review* 62 (July–August 1984): 111–118.

29. Michael R. Czinkota and Masaaki Kotabe, "America's New World Trade Order," *Marketing Management* 1, 3 (1992): 46–54.

30. Michael R. Czinkota, ed., *Proceedings of the Conference on the Feasibility of a Protection Cost Index,* August 6, 1987 (Washington, DC: Department of Commerce, 1987), 7.

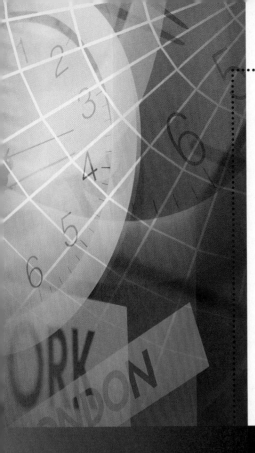

CHAPTER 4

Politics and Laws

LEARNING OBJECTIVES

- To understand the importance of the political and legal environments in both the home and host countries to the international business executive

- To learn how governments affect business through legislation and regulations

- To see how the political actions of countries expose firms to international risks

- To examine the differing laws regulating international trade found in different countries

- To understand how international political relations, agreements, and treaties can affect international business

BRIBES, GUNS, AND CIVIL WAR

Corporations often have long-standing business relationships with their customers and suppliers abroad. Culture, laws, and policies are familiar quantities, and the occasional trade disputes are quickly settled. Increasingly, however, a global economy means that companies transact business in emerging nations where the political and legal climates are not only unfamiliar, but also often unstable. It is difficult—if not impossible—for global corporations to maintain productive trade relationships when corruption, lawlessness, and political turmoil reign.

It doesn't take long for a traveler to Sierra Leone to see that the rules for an orderly exchange between buyers and sellers do not apply. Demands for bribes begin from the time the visitor disembarks at the airport—clearing immigration requires fifty cents, and ensuring a seat on the helicopter to the capital city adds a few under-the-table dollars to the cost. Cab rides are frequently interrupted by checkpoints, where "tolls" must be paid to troops armed with assault rifles. Throughout Sierra Leone, anyone with authority can name a price to grease the wheels of its otherwise paralytic bureaucracy.

Corrupt? Yes. But in a desperate situation Sierra Leoneans have turned to desperate measures. The country is torn apart from its decade-long civil war, which continues to erupt intermittently. With a population of about 5 million, Sierra Leone lost 50,000 people to war. Another 1.5 million have been displaced. The country ranks at the bottom of the world in income and life expectancy. Government workers are often unpaid for months and depend on bribes for their income.

Sierra Leone is not without resources. Before its civil war, it exported bauxite and rutile, and it continues to mine diamonds, although most are smuggled out of the country illegally. The black market diamond trade is estimated at as much as $100 million per year. In fact, Sierra Leone traces its civil strife to the exploitation of its natural wealth. Sierra Leone's rebel forces grew from a small loose band to 20,000 well-armed troops, financed by "conflict diamonds."

Business dealings with Sierra Leone are conducted with caution. Employees of U.S. firms who work or travel there face physical risks and the challenge to conduct ethical transactions. But hope is on the horizon. The United Nations and other international organizations are providing funds and resources to rebuild Sierra Leone's economy. Key to these efforts is halting the illegal diamond trade. The groundwork is being laid for the Strategic Resources Commission, which would provide a solid foundation for managing Sierra Leone's diamond wealth and using it to bring peace and raise the standard of living in Sierra Leone. ●

Sources: *The World Factbook 2000*, Central Intelligence Agency; "Africa's Diamonds: Precious, Perilous, Too," testimony of Deputy Assistant Secretary of State for African Affairs Howard F. Jeter, House of Representatives Committee on International Relations Subcommittee on Africa, May 9, 2000; Douglas Farah "Forget Sunblock, Visit Sierra Leone Armed with Cash," *The Washington Post*, April 10, 2000, p. A14.

Politics and laws play a critical role in international business. Even the best plans can go awry as a result of unexpected political or legal influences, and the failure to anticipate these factors can be the undoing of an otherwise successful business venture.

Of course, a single international political and legal environment does not exist. The business executive has to be aware of political and legal factors on a variety of levels. For example, while it is useful to understand the complexities of the host country's legal system, such knowledge may not protect against sanctions imposed by the home country. The firm, therefore, has to be aware of conflicting expectations and demands in the international arena.

This chapter will examine politics and laws from the manager's point of view. The two subjects are considered together because laws generally are the result of political decisions. The chapter discussion will break down the study of the international political and legal environment into three segments: the politics and laws of the home country; those of the host country; and the bilateral and multilateral agreements, treaties, and laws governing the relations among host and home countries.

The Home–Country Perspective

No manager can afford to ignore the rules and regulations of the country from which he or she conducts international business transactions. Many of the laws and regulations may not specifically address international business issues, yet they can have a major impact on a firm's opportunities abroad. Minimum-wage legislation, for example, has a bearing on the **international competitiveness** of a firm using production processes that are highly labor intensive. The cost of domestic safety regulations may significantly affect the pricing policies of firms. For example, U.S. legislation creating the Environmental Superfund requires payment by chemical firms based on their production volume, regardless of whether the production is sold domestically or exported. As a result, these firms are at a disadvantage internationally when exporting their commodity-type products. They are required to compete against firms that have a cost advantage because their home countries do not require payment into an environmental fund.

Other legal and regulatory measures, however, are clearly aimed at international business. Some may be designed to help firms in their international efforts. For example, governments may attempt to aid and protect the business efforts of domestic companies facing competition from abroad by setting standards for product content and quality.

The political environment in most countries tends to provide general support for the international business efforts of firms headquartered within the country. For example, a government may work to reduce trade barriers or to increase trade opportunities through bilateral and multilateral negotiations. Such actions will affect individual firms to the extent that they improve the international climate for free trade.

Often governments also have specific rules and regulations that restrict international business. Such regulations are frequently political in nature and are based on governmental objectives that override commercial concerns. The restrictions are particularly sensitive when they address activities outside the country. Such measures challenge the territorial sovereignty of other governments and raise the issue of **extraterritoriality**—meaning a nation's attempt to set policy outside its territorial limits. Yet actions implying such extraterritorial reach are common, because nations often argue that their citizens and products maintain their nationality wherever they may be, and they therefore continue to be subject to the rules and laws of their home country.

Three main areas of governmental activity are of major concern to the international business manager. They are embargoes or trade sanctions, export controls, and the regulation of international business behavior.

Embargoes and Sanctions

The terms **sanction** and **embargo** as used here refer to governmental actions that distort free flows of trade in goods, services, or ideas for decidedly adversarial and political, rather than economic, purposes. Sanctions tend to consist of specific coercive trade measures such as the cancellation of trade financing or the prohibition of high-technology trade, while embargoes are usually much broader in that they prohibit trade entirely. For example, the United States imposed sanctions against some countries by prohibiting the export of weapons to them, but it initiated an embargo against Cuba when all but humanitarian trade was banned. To understand sanctions and embargoes better, it is useful to examine the auspices and legal justifications under which they are imposed.

Trade embargoes have been used quite frequently and successfully in times of war or to address specific grievances. For example, in 1284, the Hansa, an association of north German merchants, believed that its members were suffering from several injustices by Norway. On learning that one of its ships had been attacked and pillaged by the Norwegians, the Hansa called an assembly of its members and resolved an economic blockade of Norway. The export of grain, flour, vegetables, and beer was prohibited on pain of fines and confiscation of the goods. The blockade was a complete success. Deprived of grain from Germany, the Norwegians were unable to obtain it from England or elsewhere. As a contemporary chronicler reports: "Then there broke out a famine so great that they were forced to make atonement." Norway was forced to pay indemnities for the financial losses that had been caused and to grant the Hansa extensive trade privileges.[1]

Over time, economic sanctions and embargoes have become a principal tool of the foreign policy for many countries. Often, they are imposed unilaterally in the hope of changing a country's government or at least changing its policies. Reasons for the impositions have varied, ranging from the upholding of human rights to attempts to promote nuclear nonproliferation or antiterrorism.

Iraq continues to live under a United Nation's trade embargo following Iraq's invasion of Kuwait. While devastating Iraq's economy, sanctions were not effective in curbing regional military confrontations during the 1990s.

After World War I, the League of Nations set a precedent for the legal justification of economic sanctions by subscribing to a covenant that contained penalties or sanctions for breaching its provisions. The members of the League of Nations did not intend to use military or economic measures separately, but the success of the blockades of World War I fostered the opinion that "the economic weapon, conceived not as an instrument of war but as a means of peaceful pressure, is the greatest discovery and most precious possession of the League."[2] The basic idea was that economic sanctions could force countries to behave peacefully in the international community.

The idea of multilateral use of economic sanctions was again incorporated into international law under the charter of the United Nations, but greater emphasis was placed on the enforcement process. Sanctions decided on are mandatory, even though each permanent member of the Security Council can veto efforts to impose them. The charter also allows for sanctions as enforcement actions by regional agencies, such as the Organization of American States, the Arab League, and the Organization of African Unity, but only with the Security Council's authorization.

The apparent strength of the United Nations' enforcement system was soon revealed to be flawed. Stalemates in the Security Council and vetoes by permanent members often led to a shift of discussions to the General Assembly, where sanctions are not enforceable. Also, concepts such as "peace" and "breach of peace" were seldom perceived in the same context by all members, and thus no systematic sanctioning policy developed under the United Nations.[3]

Another problem with sanctions is that frequently their unilateral imposition has not produced the desired result. Sanctions may make the obtaining of goods more difficult or expensive for the sanctioned country, yet their purported objective is almost never achieved. In order to work, sanctions need to be imposed multilaterally and affect goods that are vital to the sanctioned country—goals that are clear, yet difficult to implement. On rare occasions, however, global cooperation can be achieved. For example, when Iraq invaded Kuwait in August of 1990, virtually all members of the United Nations condemned this hostile action and joined a trade embargo against Iraq. Over time, however, the closed ranks began to weaken and, in spite of continued sanctions, trade flows resumed. Such developments are typical, since individual countries have different relationships with the country subject to the sanctions due to geographic or historic reasons, and therefore cannot or do not want to terminate trade relations.

Close multinational collaboration can strengthen the sanctioning mechanism of the United Nations greatly. Economic sanctions can extend political control over foreign companies operating abroad, with or without the support of their local government.[4] When one considers that sanctions may well be the middle ground between going to war or doing nothing, their effective functioning can represent a powerful arrow in the quiver of international policy measures.

Sanctions usually mean significant loss of business to firms. One estimate claims that the economic sanctions held in place by the United States annually cost the country some $20 billion in lost exports.[5] Due to these costs, the issue of compensating the domestic firms and industries affected by these sanctions needs to be considered. Yet, trying to impose sanctions slowly or making them less expensive to ease the burden on these firms undercuts their ultimate chance for success. The international business manager is often caught in this political web and loses business as a result. Frequently, firms try to anticipate sanctions based on their evaluations of the international political climate. Nevertheless, even when substantial precautions are taken, firms may still suffer substantial losses due to contract cancellations. However, the reputation of a supplier unable to fill a contractual obligation will be damaged much more seriously than that of an exporter who anticipates sanctions and realizes it cannot accept the offer in the first place.[6]

GLOBAL PERSPECTIVE 4.1

Weapons Controlled for Export Include Satellites, Firearms . . . and PCs?

Nations must ensure that trade promotion is carefully balanced with responsible foreign policy. Clearly, trade embargoes on U.S.-made arms to nations like Iran and Libya that support worldwide terrorism are necessary export controls. But what about supercomputer exports to India or Pakistan? Will they be used to advance the nations' economies or to speed development of nuclear weapons? In a delicate balancing act, U.S. export policy is swayed by U.S. producers, the national political climate, shifts in the geopolitical map, and rapid technology advances.

State Department charges against the Lockheed Martin Corporation, the nation's largest defense contractor, vividly illustrate the complexities of export controls. The Office of Defense Trade Controls (a branch of the State department) alleged that Lockheed Martin provided scientific evaluations of a satellite motor to Asiasat, a China-owned conglomerate, before the Department of Defense reviewed it for sensitive information.

Claiming innocence, Lockheed Martin countered that the report was edited before submission. Furthermore, since the communication satellite motor was a commercial rather than a defense technology, Lockheed claimed its license from the Commerce Department satisfied export requirements at the time. This is a prime example of how political shifts in the U.S. government can affect trade regulations. In 1994, regulatory control of satellite exports was handed from the State Department to the Commerce Department, but five years later that responsibility returned to the State Department.

While Lockheed Martins may be more subject to scrutiny, smaller companies are also on the radar screen of the Commerce Department's Bureau of Export Administration (BXA). Trijicon, Inc., was recently charged with the illegal export of optical sighting systems for firearms from 1994 to 1998 to Argentina and South Africa. BXA imposed a $64,000 civil penalty on Trijicon for its failure to obtain licenses.

Even more difficult to control is how foreign governments might use powerful computer chips and high-speed computers. While computers are widely used in business, academia, and entertainment, hardware ad software are key ingredients in sophisticated armaments. The issue is further complicated by increases in processing power. Until recently, computers with processing speeds greater than 2 billion operations per second had been subject to a ten-day waiting period before they could be exported to countries with nuclear programs. This was to allow federal agencies time to review the transaction. In early 2000, the level was increased to 6.5 billion operations per second before the export required government review—even though a Department of Energy study revealed that China and India could improve their nuclear weapons with computers functioning at only 4 billion operations per second.

To balance the interests of U.S. computer and chipmakers against national security concerns, the federal government has grouped countries into four tiers. Each tier has different specifications as to which computers may be exported from the United States under what conditions. In tier four, with countries such as Iraq and Libya, an embargo is in effect and no computers can be exported at all. At the other extreme, companies in Canada, western Europe, Mexico, and other countries in tier one can purchase any computer without U.S. federal review—as long as it is not re-exported.

Supporters of restrictions contend that precautions are necessary. Critics argue that foreign customers can easily obtain chips and computers elsewhere.

Sources: "Michigan Firm Settles Charges of Illegal Export," Bureau of Export Administration, September 29, 2000: Vernon Loeb, "Lockheed Aided China on Rocket Motor, U.S. Says," *Washington Post,* April 6, 2000, p. A1; Gary Milhollin, "With Looser Computer Controls, We're Selling Our Safety Short," *Washington Post,* March 12, 2000, p. B3.

Export Controls

Many nations have **export control systems,** which are designed to deny or at least delay the acquisition of strategically important goods by adversaries. The legal basis for export controls varies in nations. For example, in Germany, armament exports are covered in the so-called War Weapons list which is a part of the War Weapons Control Law. The exports of other goods are covered by the German Export List. **Dual use items,** which are goods useful for both military and civilian purposes, are then controlled by the Joint List of the European Union.[7] Global Perspective 4.1 discusses how U.S. decisions are made regarding export controls. In the United States, the export control system is based on the Export Administration Act and the Munitions Control

Act. These laws control all export of goods, services, and ideas from the United States. The determinants for controls are national security, foreign policy, short supply, and nuclear nonproliferation.

Export licenses are issued by the Department of Commerce, which administers the Export Administration Act.[8] In consultation with other government agencies—particularly the Departments of State, Defense, and Energy—the Commerce Department has drawn up a list of commodities whose export is considered particularly sensitive. In addition, a list of countries differentiates nations according to their political relationship with the United States. Finally, a list of individual firms that are considered to be unreliable trading partners because of past trade-diversion activities exists for each country.

After an export license application has been filed, specialists in the Department of Commerce match the commodity to be exported with the **critical commodities list,** a file containing information about products that are either particularly sensitive to national security or controlled for other purposes. The product is then matched with the country of destination and the recipient company. If no concerns regarding any of the three exist, an export license is issued. Control determinants and the steps in the decision process are summarized in Figure 4.1.

This process may sound overly cumbersome, but it does not apply in equal measure to all exports. Most international business activities can be carried out under NLR conditions, which stands for "no license required." NLR provides blanket permission to export to most trading partners, provided that neither the end-user nor the end-use is considered sensitive. It therefore pays to check out the denied persons list published by the U.S. government (**www.bxa.doc.gov/DPL**) to ensure that one's trading partner is not a prohibited trading partner. However, the process becomes more complicated and cumbersome when products incorporating high-level technologies and countries not friendly to the United States are involved. The exporter must then apply for an export license, which consists of written authorization to send a product abroad. However, even in most of these cases, license applications can be submitted via the Internet and licensing forms can be downloaded from it.

The international business repercussions of export controls are important. It is one thing to design an export control system that is effective and that restricts those international business activities subject to important national concerns. It is, however, quite another when controls lose their effectiveness and when one country's firms are placed at a competitive disadvantage with firms in other countries whose control systems are less extensive or even nonexistent.

A Changed Environment for Export Controls

Six major changes have fundamentally altered the parameters of the traditional export control regime.[9] The most important change has been the collapse of the Iron

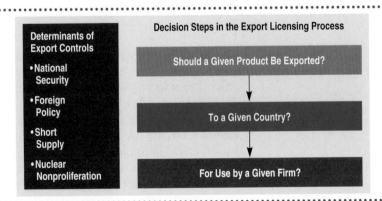

FIGURE 4.1

U.S. Export Control System

Curtain and the subsequent disappearance of the Soviet Union and the Eastern Bloc. As a result, both the focus and the principal objective of export controls have been altered. It makes little sense today to still speak of "Soviet adversaries," nor is the singular objective of maintaining the "strategic balance of power" still valid.

A second change derives directly from the first. Nowadays, the principal focus of export controls must rest on the Third World. Quite a number of countries from this region want chemical and nuclear weapons and the technology to make use of them. For example, a country such as Libya can do little with its poison gas shells without a suitable delivery system.[10] As a result, export controls have moved from a "strategic balance" to a "tactical balance" approach. Nevertheless, even though the political hot spots addressed may be less broad in terms of their geographic expanse, the peril emanating from regional disintegration and local conflict may be just as dangerous to the world community as earlier strategic concerns with the Soviet Union.[11]

A third major change consists of the loosening of mutual bonds among allied nations. For many years the United States, Western Europe, and Japan, together with emerging industrialized nations, held a generally similar strategic outlook. This outlook was driven by the common desire to reduce, or at least contain, the influence of the Soviet Union. However, with the disintegration of the Soviet Union in 1991, individual national interests that had been subsumed by the overall strategic objective gained in importance. As a consequence, differences in perspectives, attitudes, and outlooks can now lead to ever-growing conflicts among the major players in the trade field.

Major change has also resulted from the increased **foreign availability** of high technology products. In the past decade, the number of participants in the international trade field has grown rapidly. High technology products are available worldwide from many sources. The broad availability makes any denial of such products more difficult to enforce. If a nation does control the exports of widely available products, it imposes a major competitive burden on its firms.

The speed of change and the rapid dissemination of information and innovation around the world also has shifted. For example, the current life cycle of computer chips is only 18 months. More than 70 percent of the data processing industry's sales resulted from the sale of devices that did not exist two years earlier.[12] This enormous technical progress is accompanied by a radical change in computer architecture. Instead of having to replace a personal computer or a workstation with a new computer, it is possible now to simply exchange microprocessors or motherboards with new, more efficient ones. Furthermore, today's machines can be connected to more than one microprocessor and users can customize and update configurations almost at will. Export controls that used to be based largely on capacity criteria have become almost irrelevant because they can no longer fulfill the function assigned to them. A user simply acquires additional chips, from whomever, and uses expansion slots to enhance the capacity of his or her computer.

The question arises as to how much of the latest technology is required for a country to engage in "dangerous" activity. For example, nuclear weapons and sophisticated delivery systems were developed by the United States and the Soviet Union long before supercomputers became available. Therefore, it is reasonable to assert that researchers in countries working with equipment that is less than state of the art, or even obsolete, may well be able to achieve a threat capability that can result in major destruction and affect the world order.

From a control perspective, there is also the issue of equipment size. Due to their size, supercomputers and high technology items used to be fairly difficult to hide and any movement of such products was easily detectable. Nowadays, state-of-the-art technology has been miniaturized. Much leading-edge technological equipment is so small that it can fit into a briefcase, and most equipment is no larger than the luggage compartment of a car. Given these circumstances, it has become difficult, if not impossible, to closely supervise the transfer of such equipment.

Export Control Problems and Conflicts

There are several key export control problem areas for firms and policymakers. First is the continuing debate about what constitutes military-use products, civilian-use products, and **dual-use products.** Increasingly, goods are of a dual-use nature, typically commercial products that have potential military applications. The classic example is a pesticide factory that, some years later, is revealed to be a poison gas factory.[13] It is difficult enough to clearly define weapons. It is even more problematic to achieve consensus among nations regarding dual-use goods. For example, what about quite harmless screws if they are to be installed in rockets or telecommunications equipment used by the military? The problem becomes even greater with attempts to classify and list subcomponents and regulate their exportation. Individual country lists will lead to a distortion of competition if they deviate markedly from each other. The very task of drawing up any list is itself fraught with difficulty when it comes to components that are assembled. For example, the Patriot missile, which was deployed in the Persian Gulf War, consists, according to German law, only of simple parts whose individual export is permissible.

Even if governments were to agree on lists and continuously updated them, the resulting control aspects would be difficult to implement. Controlling the transfer of components within and among companies across economic areas such as NAFTA or the European Union (EU) would significantly slow down business. Even more importantly, to subject only the export of physical goods to surveillance is insufficient. The transfer of knowledge and technology is of equal or greater importance. Weapons-relevant information easily can be exported via books, periodicals, and disks, therefore their content also would have to be controlled. Foreigners would need to be prevented from gaining access to such sources during visits or from making use of data networks across borders. Attendance at conferences and symposia would have to be regulated, the flow of data across national borders would have to be controlled, and today's communication systems and highways such as the Internet would have to be scrutinized. All these concerns have lead to the emergence of controls of **deemed exports.** These controls address people rather than products in those instances where knowledge transfer could lead to a breach of export restrictions. Global Perspective 4.2 explains some of the issues surrounding the concept. More information is available

under **www.bxa.doc.gov/Deemed Exports.**

Conflicts also result from the desire of nations to safeguard their own economic interests. Due to different industrial structures, these interests vary between nations. For example, Germany, with a strong world market position in machine tools, motors, and chemical raw materials, will think differently about manufacturing equipment controls than a country such as the United States, which sees computers as an area of its competitive advantage.

These problems and conflicts seem to ensure that dissent and disagreement in the export control field are unlikely to decrease, but rather will multiply in the future. As long as regulations are not harmonized internationally, firms will need to be highly sensitive to different and perhaps rapidly changing export control regimens.

Regulating International Business Behavior

Home countries may implement special laws and regulations to ensure that the international business behavior of firms headquartered in them is conducted within moral and ethical boundaries considered appropriate. The definition of appropriateness may vary from country to country and from government to government. Therefore, the content, enforcement, and impact of such regulations on firms may vary substantially among nations. As a result, the international manager must walk a careful line, balancing the expectations held in different countries.

GLOBAL PERSPECTIVE 4.2

National Security Stalls High-Tech Industry

What does a U.S. company that exports sensitive technology to an unfriendly country have in common with a firm that hires a native of that country to work in the United States on the technology? Both face stiff penalties from the U.S. government if they fail to obtain an export license. Most export control rules govern the shipments of sensitive products to foreign countries, but the regulation of "deemed exports" controls the flow of technology to individuals. U.S. companies must obtain a license before a non-U.S. individual can work on technology that would require a license to export to the individual's home country. The reach of this regulation even extends to non-U.S. individuals attending universities or conferences in the United States. In effect, the United States treats foreign engineers and scientists as if they were foreign countries.

High-tech firms want this regulation abolished, calling it "bureaucratic overkill" and a "leftover from the Cold War." They claim the deemed export regulation stalls the hiring of specialists who are in demand. Obtaining a deemed export license from the State Department for military-related technologies takes twelve weeks, and a license for commercial technologies from the Bureau of Export Administration takes six weeks. The companies argue that the technologies are adequately safeguarded without the deemed export regulation and that separate regulations already require exporters to act if they know an illegal technology transfer will occur. Companies themselves guard their own technologies and require nondisclosure agreements from their employees.

Although the end of the Cold War was heralded as an opportunity for U.S. policymakers to make economic competitiveness a top priority, the State Department, Congress, and the Pentagon are concerned about threats of nuclear proliferation. The Los Alamos nuclear missile spy scandal was a major blow to industry's hope for abolishing or easing regulations. On the other hand that incident prompted a dialog about a policy that strives to protect everything rather than protecting true security secrets. Recent reviews by government agencies also revealed that industry compliance with deemed export policies is probably low, and the regulations need clarification.

The Bush administration may help improve the status of foreign nationals working for U.S. high tech firms. Only six weeks into the presidency, the Aerospace Industries Association (AIA) proposed sixteen legislative and regulatory reforms that would increase exports and U.S. jobs, among them a review of deemed export rules. Whatever the outcome, the debate over potential military application of commercial technology exports will endure as long at there are hostile nations. In the meantime, the U.S. government will continue to grapple with the conflict between its economic and security interests.

Sources: "AIA Announces New Reform Initiatives for Export Control," *US Newswire,* March 7, 2001; Jennifer Weeks, "When Too Much Is Classified, Too Little Is Secure," *Washington Post,* June 15, 2000, p. B3; "Interagency Review of the Export Licensing Process for Foreign National Visitors," Report No. D-2000-109, Departments of Commerce, Defense, Energy, and State, Offices of the Inspector General, March 24, 2000.

One major area in which nations attempt to govern international business activities involves **boycotts.** As an example, Arab nations developed a blacklist of companies that deal with Israel. Further, Arab customers frequently demand assurance that products they purchase are not manufactured in Israel and that the supplier company does not do any business with Israel. The goal of these actions clearly is to impose a boycott on business with Israel. U.S. political ties to Israel caused the U.S. government to adopt antiboycott laws to prevent U.S. firms from complying with the boycott. The laws include a provision to deny foreign income tax benefits to companies that comply with the boycott. They also require notifying the U.S. government if boycott requests are received. U.S. firms that comply with the boycott are subject to heavy fines and to denial of export privileges. See **www.bxa.** **doc.gov/AntiboycottCompliance.**

Caught in a web of governmental activity, firms may be forced either to lose business or to pay substantial fines. This is especially true if the firm's products are competitive yet not unique, so that the supplier can opt to purchase them elsewhere. The heightening of such conflict can sometimes force companies to search for new, and possibly risky ways to circumvent the law or to totally withdraw operations from a country.

Another area of regulatory activity affecting the international business efforts of firms is **antitrust laws.** These laws often apply to international operations as well as to domestic business. In many countries, antitrust agencies watch closely when a firm buys a company, engages in a joint venture with a foreign firm, or makes an agreement abroad with a competing firm in order to ensure that the action does not result in restraint of competition.

Given the increase in worldwide cooperation among companies, however, the wisdom of extending antitrust legislation to international activities is being questioned. Some limitations to these tough antitrust provisions were already implemented decades ago. For example, in the United States the **Webb-Pomerene Act** of 1918 excludes from antitrust prosecution firms cooperating to develop foreign markets. This law was passed as part of an effort to aid export efforts in the face of strong foreign competition by oligopolies and monopolies. The exclusion of international activities from antitrust regulation was further enhanced by the Export Trading Company Act of 1982, which ensures that cooperating firms are not exposed to the threat of treble damages. Further steps to loosen the application of antitrust laws to international business are under consideration because of increased competition from strategic alliances and global megacorporations.

Firms operating abroad are also affected by laws against **bribery** and **corruption.** In many countries, payments or favors are a way of life, and "a greasing of the wheels" is expected in return for government services. As a result, many companies doing business internationally routinely are forced to pay bribes or do favors for foreign officials in order to gain contracts. Even in the late 1990s, the British Chamber of Commerce reported that bribery and corruption was a problem for 14 percent of exporters.[14] In the 1970s, a major national debate erupted in the United States about these business practices, led by arguments that U.S. firms have an ethical and moral leadership obligation and that contracts won through bribes do not reflect competitive market activity. As a result, the **Foreign Corrupt Practices Act** was passed in 1977, making it a crime for U.S. executives of publicly traded firms to bribe a foreign official in order to obtain business.

A number of U.S. firms have complained about the act, arguing that it hinders their efforts to compete internationally against companies whose home countries have no such antibribery laws. The problem is one of ethics versus practical needs and, to some extent, of the amounts involved. For example, it may be hard to draw the line between providing a generous tip and paying a bribe in order to speed up a business transaction. Many business executives believe that the United States should not apply its moral principles to other societies and cultures in which bribery and corruption are endemic. To compete internationally, executives argue, they must be free to use the most common methods of competition in the host country.

On the other hand, applying different standards to executives and firms based on whether they do business abroad or domestically is difficult to do. Also, bribes may open the way for shoddy performance and loose moral standards among executives and employees and may result in a spreading of general unethical business practices. Unrestricted bribery could result in firms concentrating on how to bribe best rather than on how to best produce and market their products. Typically, international businesses that use bribery fall into three categories: those who bribe to counterbalance the poor quality of their products or their high price; those who bribe to create a market for their unneeded goods; and, in the bulk of cases, those who bribe to stay competitive with other firms that bribe.[15] In all three of these instances, the customer is served poorly, the prices increase, and the transaction does not reflect economic competitiveness.

The international manager must carefully distinguish between reasonable ways of doing business internationally—that is, complying with foreign expectations—and outright bribery and corruption. To assist the manager in this task, the 1988 Trade Act clarifies the applicability of the Foreign Corrupt Practices legislation. The revisions outline when a manager is expected to know about violation of the act, and they draw a distinction between the facilitation of routine governmental actions and governmental policy decisions. Routine actions concern issues such as the obtaining of permits and licenses, the processing of governmental papers (such as visas and work orders), the providing of mail and phone service, and the loading and unloading of cargo. Policy decisions refer mainly to situations in which the obtaining or retaining of a contract is at stake. While the facilitation of routine actions is not prohibited, the illegal influencing of policy decisions can result in the imposition of servere fines and penalties. The risks inherent in bribery have grown since 1999, when the Organization for Economic Cooperation and Development (OECD) adopted a treaty criminalizing the bribery of foreign public officials, moving well beyond its previous discussions, which only sought to outlaw the tax deductibility of improper payments. The Organization of American States (OAS) has also officially condemned bribery. Similarly, the World Trade Organization has decided to consider placing bribery rules on its agenda. In addition, nongovernmental organizations such as Transparency International are conducting widely publicized efforts to highlight corruption and bribery and even rank countries on a Corruption Perceptions Index (**www.transparency.de**).

These issues place managers in the position of having to choose between home-country regulations and foreign business practices. This choice is made even more difficult because diverging standards of behavior are applied to businesses in different countries. However, the gradually emerging consensus among international organizations may eventually level the playing field.

A final, major issue that is critical for international business managers is that of general standards of behavior and ethics. Increasingly, public concerns are raised about such issues as environmental protection, global warming, pollution, and moral behavior. However, these issues are not of the same importance in every country. What may be frowned upon or even illegal in one nation may be customary or at least acceptable in others. For example, the cutting down of the Brazilian rain forest may be acceptable to the government of Brazil, but scientists and concerned consumers may object vehemently because of the effect on global warming and other climatic changes. The export of U.S. tobacco products may be legal but results in accusations of exporting death to developing nations. China may use prison labor in producing products for export, but U.S. law prohibits the importation of such products. Mexico may permit the use of low safety standards for workers, but the buyers of Mexican products may object to the resulting dangers.

International firms must understand the conflicts and should assert leadership in implementing change. Not everything that is legally possible should be exploited for profit. By acting on existing, leading-edge knowledge and standards, firms will be able to benefit in the long term through consumer goodwill and the avoidance of later recriminations.

Host Country Political and Legal Environment

Politics and laws of a host country affect international business operations in a variety of ways. The good manager will understand these dimensions of the countries in which the firm operates so that he or she can work within existing parameters and can anticipate and plan for changes that may occur.

Political Action and Risk

Firms usually prefer to conduct business in a country with a stable and friendly government, but such governments are not always easy to find. Managers must therefore continually monitor the government, its policies, and its stability to determine the potential for political change that could adversely affect corporate operations.

There is **political risk** in every nation, but the range of risks varies widely from country to country. In general, political risk is lowest in countries that have a history of stability and consistency. Political risk tends to be highest in nations that do not have this sort of history. In a number of countries, however, consistency and stability that were apparent on the surface have been quickly swept away by major popular movements that drew on the bottled-up frustrations of the population. Three major types of political risk can be encountered: **ownership risk,** which exposes property and life; **operating risk,** which refers to interference with the ongoing operations of a firm; and **transfer risk,** which is mainly encountered when attempts are made to shift funds between countries. Firms can be exposed to political risk due to government actions or even actions outside the control of governments. The type of actions and their effects are classified in Figure 4.2.

A major political risk in many countries is that of conflict and violent change. A manager will want to think twice before conducting business in a country in which the likelihood of such change is high. To begin with, if conflict breaks out, violence directed toward the firm's property and employees is a strong possibility. Guerrilla warfare, civil disturbances, and **terrorism** often take an anti-industry bent, making companies and their employees potential targets. International corporations are often subject to major threats, even in countries that boast great political stability. Sometimes the sole fact that a firm is market oriented is sufficient to attract the wrath of terrorists. For example, in the spring of 1991, Detlev Rohwedder, chairman of the German Treuhand (the institution in charge of privatizing the state-owned firms of

FIGURE 4.2   Exposure to Political Risk

Contingencies May Include:	Loss May Be the Result of:	
	The actions of legitimate government authorities	Events caused by factors outside the control of government
The involuntary loss of control over specific assets without adequate compensation	• Total or partial expropriation • Forced divestiture • Confiscation • Cancellation or unfair calling of performance bonds	• War • Revolution • Terrorism • Strikes • Extortion
A reduction in the value of a stream of benefits expected from the foreign-controlled affiliate	• Nonapplicability of "national treatment" • Restriction in access to financial, labor, or material markets • Controls on prices, outputs, or activities • Currency and remittance restrictions • Value-added and export performance requirements	• Nationalistic buyers or suppliers • Threats and disruption to operations by hostile groups • Externally induced financial constraints • Externally imposed limits on imports or exports

Source: José de la Torre and David H. Neckar, "Forecasting Political Risks for International Operations," in H. Vernon-Wortzel and L. Wortzel. *Global Strategic Management: The Essentials,* 2nd ed. (New York: John Wiley and Sons, 1990), 195.

The Risk of Terrorist Activity: A Factor in International Business Decisions

International Terrorist Incidents Over Time, 1978-99

Year	Frequency
1978	530
1979	434
1980	499
1981	489
1982	487
1983	497
1984	565
1985	635
1986	612
1987	666
1988	605
1989	375
1990	437
1991	565
1992	363
1993	431
1994	322
1995	440
1996	296
1997	304
1998	274
1999	392

Source: *Patterns of Global Terrorism*, April 2000; U.S. Department of State

Number of Terrorist incidents

- Over 100
- 30 to 50
- 10 to 29
- 3 to 9
- 1 to 2
- None / no data

Type of Terrorist Activity

- Bombing or arson
- Civil war, unrest, or killing
- Kidnapping

Source: *Patterns of Global Terrorism*, April 2000; U.S. Department of State
www.state.gov/www/global/terrorism; January 31, 2001

Source: www.state.gov/global/terrorism; Jan. 31, 2001.

McDonald's franchises, both within and outside the United States, have been the targets of international terrorists around the world, from Canada to France to Moscow to Seattle.

the former East Germany), was assassinated at his home in Germany by the Red Army Faction because of his "representation of capitalism."

International terrorists have frequently targeted U.S. corporate facilities, operations, and personnel abroad for attack in order to strike a blow against the United States and capitalism. U.S. firms, by their nature, cannot have the elaborate security and restricted access of U.S. diplomatic offices and military bases. As a result, United States businesses are the primary target of terrorists worldwide, and remain the most vulnerable targets in the future.[16] Ironically enough, in many instances, the businesses attacked or burned are the franchisees of U.S. business concepts. Therefore, the ones suffering most from such attacks are the local owners and local employees. The methods used by terrorists against business facilities include bombing, arson, hijacking, and sabotage. To obtain funds, the terrorists resort to kidnapping executives, armed robbery, and extortion.[17]

In many countries, particularly in the developing world, **coups d'état** can result in drastic changes in government. The new government often will attack foreign firms as remnants of a Western-dominated colonial past, as has happened in Cuba, Nicaragua, and Iran. Even if such changes do not represent an immediate physical threat, they can lead to policy changes that may have drastic effect. The past few decades have seen coups in Ghana, Ethiopia, Iraq, and Iran, for example, that have seriously impeded the conduct of international business.

Less drastic, but still worrisome, are changes in government policies that are not caused by changes in the government itself. These occur when, for one reason or another, a government feels pressured to change its policies toward foreign businesses. The pressure may be the result of nationalist or religious factions or widespread anti-Western feeling.

A broad range of policy changes is possible as a result of political unrest. All of the changes can affect the company's international operations, but not all of them are equal in weight. Except for extreme cases, companies do not usually have to fear violence against their employees, although violence against company property is quite common. Also common are changes in policy that result from a new government or a strong new stance that is nationalist and opposed to foreign investment. The most drastic public steps resulting from such policy changes are usually expropriation and confiscation.

Expropriation is the transfer of ownership by the host government to a domestic entity with payment of compensation. Expropriation was an appealing action to many countries because it demonstrated their nationalism and transferred a certain amount of wealth and resources from foreign companies to the host country immediately. It did have costs to the host country, however, to the extent that it made other firms more hesitant to invest there. Expropriation does not relieve the host government of providing compensation to the former owners. However, these compensation negotiations are often protracted and frequently result in settlements that are unsatisfactory to the owners. For example, governments may offer compensation in the form of local, nontransferable currency or may base compensation on the book value of the firm. Even though firms that are expropriated may deplore the low levels of payment obtained, they frequently accept them in the absence of better alternatives.

The use of expropriation as a policy tool has sharply decreased over time. In the mid-1970s, more than 83 expropriations took place in a single year. By the turn of the century, the annual average had declined to fewer than 3. Apparently, governments have come to recognize that the damage they inflict on themselves through expropriation exceeds the benefits they receive.[18]

Confiscation is similar to expropriation in that it results in a transfer of ownership from the firm to the host country. It differs in that it does not involve compensation for the firm. Some industries are more vulnerable than others to confiscation and expropriation because of their importance to the host country's economy and their lack of ability to shift operations. For this reason, such sectors as mining, energy, public utilities, and banking have frequently been targets of such government actions.

Confiscation and expropriation constitute major political risk for foreign investors. Other government actions, however, are equally detrimental to foreign firms. Many countries are turning from confiscation and expropriation to more subtle forms of control, such as **domestication.** The goal of domestication is the same—that is, to gain control over foreign investment—but the method is different. Through domestication, the government demands transfer of ownership and management responsibility. It can impose **local content** regulations to ensure that a large share of the product is locally produced or demand that a larger share of the profit is retained in the country. Changes in labor laws, patent protection, and tax regulations are also used for purposes of domestication.

Domestication can have profound effects on an international business operation for a number of reasons. If a firm is forced to hire nationals as managers, poor cooperation and communication can result. If domestication is imposed within a very short time span, corporate operations overseas may have to be headed by poorly trained and inexperienced local managers. Domestic content requirements may force a firm to purchase its supplies and parts locally. This can result in increased costs, less efficiency, and lower-quality products. Export requirements imposed on companies may create havoc for their international distribution plans and force them to change or even shut down operations in third countries.

Finally, domestication usually will shield an industry within one country from foreign competition. As a result, inefficiencies will be allowed to thrive due to a lack of market discipline. This will affect the long-run international competitiveness of an operation abroad and may turn into a major problem when, years later, domestication is discontinued by the government.

If government action consists of weakening or not enforcing **intellectual property right** (IPR) protection, companies run the risk of losing their core competitive edge. Such steps may temporarily permit domestic firms to become quick imitators. Yet, in the longer term, they will not only discourage the ongoing transfer of technology and knowledge by multinational firms, but also reduce the incentive for local firms to invest in innovation and progress.

Poor IPR legislation and enforcement in the otherwise lucrative markets of Asia illustrate a clash between international business interests and developing nations' political and legal environments. Businesses attempting to enter the markets of China, Indonesia, Malaysia, Singapore, Taiwan, Thailand, and the Philippines face considerable risk in these countries, which have the world's worst records for copyright piracy and intellectual property infringements. But these newly industrialized countries argue that IPR laws discriminate against them because they impede the diffusion of technology and artificially inflate prices. They also point to the fact that industrialized nations such as the United States and Japan violated IPR laws during earlier stages of development. In fact, the United States became a signatory to the Berne Convention on copyrights only in 1989—around one hundred years after its introduction—and Japan disregarded IPR laws in adapting Western technologies during the 1950s. Furthermore, although newly industrialized nations are becoming increasingly aware that strong IPR protection will encourage technology transfer and foreign investment, the weak nature of these countries' court structures and the slow pace of legislation often fail to keep pace with the needs of their rapidly transforming economies.[19]

Due to successful international negotiations in the Uruguay Round, the World Trade Organization now has agreement on significant dimensions of the trade-related aspects of intellectual property rights (TRIPS) (**www.wto.org**). This agreement sets minimum standards of protection to be provided by each member country for copyrights, trademarks, geographical indications, industrial designs, patents, layout designs of integrated

circuits, and undisclosed information such as trade secrets and test data.[20] While not all-encompassing, these standards provide substantial assurances of protection, which after an implementation delay for the poorest countries, will apply to virtually all parts of the world.

One might ask why companies would choose to do business in risky markets. However, as with anything international (or any business for that matter), the issue is not whether there is any risk but rather the degree of risk that exists. Key links to risk are the dimension of reward. With appropriate rewards, many risks become more tolerable. For example, between 1991 and 1997, the average return on foreign direct investment in Africa was higher than in any other region, according to the UN Conference on Trade and Development. This is partly because the perceived risk of doing business in very poor countries is so great that firms tend to invest only in projects that promise quick profits. But it is also because there are good opportunities. For brave businessfolk, there may be rich returns in unexpected places.[21]

Economic Risk

Most businesses operating abroad face a number of other risks that are less dangerous, but probably more common, than the drastic ones already described. A host government's political situation or desires may lead it to impose economic regulations or laws to restrict or control the international activities of firms.

Nations that face a shortage of foreign currency will sometimes impose controls on the movement of capital into and out of the country. Such controls may make it difficult for a firm to remove its profits or investments from the host country. Sometimes **exchange controls** are also levied selectively against certain products or companies in an effort to reduce the importation of goods that are considered to be luxuries or to be sufficiently available through domestic production. Such regulations often affect the importation of parts, components, or supplies that are vital to production operations in the country. They may force a firm either to alter its production program or, worse yet, to shut down its entire plant. Prolonged negotiations with government officials may be necessary to reach a compromise on what constitutes a "valid" expenditure of foreign currency resources. Because the goals of government officials and corporate managers are often quite different, such compromises, even when they can be reached, may result in substantial damage to the international operations of the firm.

Countries may also use **tax policy** toward foreign investors in an effort to control multinational corporations and their capital. Tax increases may raise much-needed revenue for the host country, but they can severely damage the operations of foreign investors. This damage, in turn, will frequently result in decreased income for the host country in the long run. The raising of tax rates needs to be carefully differentiated from increased tax scrutiny of foreign investors. Many governments believe that multinational firms may be tempted to shift tax burdens to lower-tax countries by using artificial pricing schemes between subsidiaries. In such instances, governments are likely to take measures to obtain their fair contribution from multinational operations. In the United States, for example, increased focus on the taxation of multinational firms has resulted in various back-tax payments by foreign firms and the development of corporate pricing policies in collaboration with the Internal Revenue Service.[22]

The international executive also has to worry about **price controls.** In many countries, domestic political pressures can force governments to control the prices of imported products or services, particularly in sectors considered highly sensitive from a political perspective, such as food or health care. A foreign firm involved in these areas is vulnerable to price controls because the government can play on citizens' nationalistic tendencies to enforce the controls. Particularly in countries that suffer from high inflation, frequent devaluations, or sharply rising costs, the international executive may be forced to choose between shutting down the operation or continuing production at a loss in the hope of recouping profits when the government loosens or removes its price restrictions. Price controls can also be administered to prevent prices from being too low. As explained in more detail in Chapter 13, governments have enacted antidumping laws, which prevent foreign competitors from pricing their imports unfairly low in order to drive domestic competitors out of the market. Since dumping charges depend heavily on the definition of "fair" price, a firm can sometimes become the target of such accusations quite unexpectedly. Proving that no dumping took place can become quite onerous in terms of time, money, and information disclosure.

Managing the Risk

Managers face the risk of confiscation, expropriation, domestication, or other government interference whenever they conduct business overseas, but ways exist to lessen the risk. Obviously, if a new government comes into power and is dedicated to the removal of all foreign influences, there is little a firm can do. In less extreme cases, however, managers can take actions that will reduce the risk, provided they understand the root causes of the host country's policies.

Adverse governmental actions are usually the result of nationalism, the deterioration of political relations between home and host country, the desire for independence, or opposition to colonial remnants. If a host country's citizens feel exploited by foreign investors, government officials are more likely to take antiforeign action. To reduce the risk of government intervention, the international firm needs to demonstrate that it is concerned with the host country's society and that it considers itself an integral part of the host country, rather than simply an exploitative foreign corporation. Ways of doing this include intensive local hiring and training practices, better pay, contributions to charity, and societally useful investments. In addition, the company can form joint ventures with local partners to demonstrate that it is willing to share its gains with nationals. Although such actions will not guarantee freedom from political risk, they will certainly lessen the exposure.

Another action that can be taken by corporations to protect against political risk is the close monitoring of political developments. Increasingly, private sector firms offer such monitoring assistance, permitting the overseas corporation to discover potential trouble spots as early as possible and to react quickly to prevent major losses.

 Firms can also take out insurance to cover losses due to political and economic risk. Most industrialized countries offer insurance programs for their firms doing business abroad. In Germany, for example, Hermes Kreditanstalt (**www.hermes.de**) provides exporters with insurance. In the United States, the Overseas Private Investment Corporation (OPIC) (**www.opic.gov**) can cover three types of risk insurance: currency inconvertibility insurance, which covers the inability to convert profits, debt service, and other remittances from local currency into U.S. dollars; expropriation insurance, which covers the loss of an investment due to expropriation, nationalization, or confiscation by a foreign government; and political violence insurance, which covers the loss of assets or income due to war, revolution, insurrection, or politically motivated civil strife, terrorism, and sabotage. The cost of coverage varies by country and type of activity, but for manufacturers it averages $0.30 for $100 of coverage per year to protect against inconvertibility, $0.60 to protect against expropriation, and $1.05 to compensate for damage to business income and assets from political violence.[23] Usually the policies do not cover commercial risks and, in the event of a claim, cover only the actual loss—not lost profits. In the event of a major political upheaval, however, risk insurance can be critical to a firm's survival.

The discussion to this point has focused primarily on the political environment. Laws have been mentioned only as they appear to be the direct result of political change. However, the laws of host countries need to be considered on their own to some extent, for the basic system of law is important to the conduct of international business.

Legal Differences and Restraints

Countries differ in their laws as well as in their use of the law. For example, over the past decade the United States has become an increasingly litigious society in which institutions and individuals are quick to initiate lawsuits. Court battles are often protracted and costly, and even the threat of a court case can reduce business opportunities. In contrast, Japan's tradition tends to minimize the role of the law and of lawyers. On a per capita basis, Japan has only about 5 percent of the number of lawyers that the United States has.[24] Whether the number of lawyers is cause or effect, the Japanese tend not to litigate. Litigation in Japan means that the parties have failed to compromise, which is contrary to Japanese tradition and results in loss of face. A cultural predisposition therefore exists to settle conflicts outside the court system.

Over the millenia of civilization, many different laws and legal systems have emerged. King Hammurabi of Babylon codified a series of decisions by judges into a body of laws. Legal issues in many African tribes were settled through the verdicts of clansmen. A key legal perspective that survives today is that of **theocracy.** Examples are Hebrew law and Islamic law (the sharia) which are the result of the dictates of God, scripture, prophetic utterances and practices, and scholarly interpretations.[25] These legal systems have faith and belief as their key focus and are a mix of societal, legal, and spiritual guidelines.

While legal systems are important to society, from an international business perspective, the two major legal systems worldwide can be categorized into common law and code law. **Common law** is based on tradition and depends less on written statutes and codes than on precedent and custom. Common law originated in England and is the system of law in the United States. **Code law** on the other hand, is based on a comprehensive set of written statutes. Countries with code law try to spell out all possible legal rules explicitly. Code law is based on Roman law and is found in the majority of the nations of the world.

In general, countries with the code law system have much more rigid laws than those with the common law system. In the latter, courts adopt precedents and customs to fit cases, allowing a better idea of basic judgment likely to be rendered in new situations. The differences between code law and common law and their impact on international business, while wide in theory, are not as broad in practice. One reason is that many common-law countries, including the United States, have adopted commercial codes to govern the conduct of business.

Host countries may adopt a number of laws that affect the firm's ability to do business. Tariffs and quotas, for example, can affect the entry of goods. Special licenses for foreign goods may be required.

Other laws may restrict entrepreneurial activities. In Argentina, for example, pharmacies must be owned by the pharmacist. This legislation prevents an ambitious businessperson from hiring druggists and starting a pharmacy chain. Similarly, the law prevents the addition of a drug counter to an existing business such as a supermarket and thus the broadening of the product offering to consumers.

Specific legislation may also exist regulating what does and does not constitute deceptive advertising. Many countries prohibit specific claims that compare products to the competition, or they restrict the use of promotional devices. Even when no laws exist, regulations may hamper business operations. For example, in some countries, firms are required to join the local chamber of commerce or become a member of the national trade association. These institutions in turn may have internal sets of rules that specify standards for the conduct of business that may be quite confining.

Seemingly innocuous local regulations that may easily be overlooked can have a major impact on the international firm's success. For example, Japan had an intricate process regulating the building of new department stores or supermarkets. The government's desire to protect smaller merchants brought the opening of new, large stores to a virtual standstill. Since department stores and supermarkets serve as the major conduit for the sale of imported consumer products, the lack of new stores severely affected opportunities for market penetration of imported merchandise.[26] Only after intense pressure from the outside did the Japanese government decide to reconsider the regulations. Another example concerns the growing global controversy that surrounds the use of genetic technology. Governments increasingly devise new rules that affect trade in genetically modified products. Australia introduced a mandatory standard for foods produced using biotechnology, which prohibits the sale of such products unless the food has been assessed by the Australia New Zealand Food Authority.

Other laws may be designed to protect domestic industries and reduce imports. For example, Russia charges a 20 percent value-added tax on most imported goods, assesses high excise taxes on goods such as cigarettes, automobiles, and alcoholic beverages, and provides a burdensome import licensing regime for alcohol to depress Russian demand for imports.[27]

Finally, the interpretation and enforcement of laws and regulations may have a major effect on international business activities. For example, in deciding what product can be called a "Swiss" Army knife or "French" wine, the interpretation given by courts to the meaning of a name can affect consumer perceptions and sales of products.

The Influencing of Politics and Laws

To succeed in a market, the international manager needs much more than business know-how. He or she must also deal with the intricacies of national politics and laws. Although to fully understand another country's legal political system will rarely be possible, the good manager will be aware of its importance and will work with people who do understand how to operate within the system.

Many areas of politics and law are not immutable. Viewpoints can be modified or even reversed, and new laws can supersede old ones. Therefore, existing political and legal restraints do not always need to be accepted. To achieve change, however, some impetus for it—such as the clamors of a constituency—must occur. Otherwise, systemic inertia is likely to allow the status quo to prevail.

The international manager has various options. One is to simply ignore prevailing rules and expect to get away with it. Pursuing this option is a high-risk strategy because the possibility of objection and even prosecution exists. A second, traditional, option is to provide input to trade negotiators and expect any problem areas to be resolved in multilateral negotiations. The drawbacks to this option are, of course, the quite time-consuming process involved and the lack of control by the firm.

A third option involves the development of coalitions and constituencies that can motivate legislators and politicians to consider and ultimately implement change. This option can be pursued in various ways. One direction can be the recasting or redefinition of issues. Often, specific terminology leads to conditioned, though inappropriate responses. For example, in the United States, the trade status accorded to the People's Republic of China has been controversial for many years. The U.S. Congress had to decide annually whether or not to grant "Most Favored Nation" (MFN) status to China. The debate on this decision was always very contentious and acerbic, and often framed around the question as to why China deserved to be treated the "most favored way." Lost in the debate was often the fact that the term "most favored" was simply taken from WTO terminology, and only indicated that trade with China would be treated like that with any other country. Only in late 1999 was the terminology changed from MFN to NTR or "normal trade relations." Even though there was still considerable debate regarding China, at least the controversy about special treatment had been avoided.[28]

Lobbyists from other countries have a strong presence in Washington, D.C., where they work to influence legislation that will be favorable to their home countries.

Beyond terminology, firms can also highlight the direct links and their costs and benefits to legislators and politicians. For example, a manager can explain the employment and economic effects of certain laws and regulations and demonstrate the benefits of change. The picture can be enlarged by including indirect links. For example, suppliers, customers, and distributors can be asked to help explain to decision makers the benefit of change. In addition, the public at large can be involved through public statements or advertisements.

Developing such coalitions is not an easy task. Companies often seek assistance in effectively influencing the government decision-making process. Such assistance is particularly beneficial when narrow economic objectives or single-issue campaigns are involved. Typically, **lobbyists** provide this assistance. Usually, there are well-connected individuals and firms that can provide access to policymakers and legislators in order to communicate new and pertinent information.

Many U.S. firms have representatives in Washington, DC, as well as in state capitals and are quite successful at influencing domestic policies. Often, however, they are less adept at ensuring proper representation abroad even though, for example, the European Commission in Brussels wields far-reaching economic power. For example, a survey of U.S. international marketing executives found that knowledge and information about foreign trade and government officials was ranked lowest among critical international business information needs. This low ranking appears to reflect the fact that many U.S. firms are far less successful in their interactions with governments abroad and far less intensive in their lobbying efforts than are foreign entities in the United States.[29]

Many countries and companies have been effective in their lobbying in the United States. As an example, Brazil has retained nearly a dozen U.S. firms to cover and influence trade issues. Brazilian citrus exporters and computer manufacturers have hired U.S. legal and public relations firms to provide them with information on relevant U.S. legislative activity. The Banco do Brasil also successfully lobbied for the restructuring of Brazilian debt and favorable U.S. banking regulations.

Although representation of the firm's interests to government decision makers and legislators is entirely appropriate, the international manager must also consider any potential side effects. Major questions can be raised if such representation becomes very overt. Short-term gains may be far outweighed by long-term negative repercussions if the international firm is perceived as exerting too much political influence.

International Relations and Laws

In addition to understanding the politics and laws of both home and host countries, the international manager must also consider the overall international political and legal environment. This is important because policies and events occurring among countries can have a profound impact on firms trying to do business internationally.

International Politics

The effect of politics on international business is determined by both the bilateral political relations between home and host countries and by multilateral agreements governing the relations among groups of countries.

The government-to-government relationship can have a profound influence in a number of ways, particularly if it becomes hostile. Among numerous examples in recent years of the relationship between international politics and international business, perhaps the most notable involves U.S.–Iranian relations following the 1979

Iranian revolution. Although the internal political changes in the aftermath of that revolution certainly would have affected any foreign firm doing business in Iran, the deterioration in U.S.–Iranian political relations that resulted from the revolution had a significant additional impact on U.S. firms. Following the revolution, U.S. firms were injured not only by the physical damage caused by the violence, but also by the anti-American feelings of the Iranian people and their government. The resulting clashes between the two governments subsequently destroyed business relationships, regardless of corporate feelings or agreements on either side.

International political relations do not always have harmful effects. If bilateral political relations between countries improve, business can benefit. One example is the improvement in Western relations with Central Europe following the official end of the Cold War. The political warming opened the potentially lucrative former Eastern bloc markets to Western firms.

The overall international political environment has effects, whether good or bad, on international business. For this reason, the good manager will strive to remain aware of political currents and relations worldwide and will attempt to anticipate changes in the international political environment so that his or her firm can plan for them.

International Law

International law plays an important role in the conduct of international business. Although no enforceable body of international law exists, certain treaties and agreements are respected by a number of countries and profoundly influence international business operations. For example, the World Trade Organization (WTO) defines internationally acceptable economic practices for its member nations. Although it does not directly deal with individual firms, it does affect them indirectly by providing some predictability in the international environment.

The **Patent Cooperation Treaty** (**PCT**) provides procedures for filing one international application designating countries in which a patent is sought, which has the same effect as filing national applications in each of those countries. Similarly, the European Patent Office examines applications and issues national patents in any of its member countries. Other regional offices include the African Industrial Property Office (ARIPO), the French-speaking African Intellectual Property Organization (OAPI), and one in Saudi Arabia for six countries in the Gulf region.

International organizations such as the United Nations and the Organization for Economic Cooperation and Development have also undertaken efforts to develop codes and guidelines that affect international business. These include the Code on International Marketing of Breast-milk Substitutes, which was developed by the World Health Organization (WHO) (**www.who.org**), and the UN Code of Conduct for Transnational Corporations. Even though there are 34 such codes in existence, the lack of enforcement ability hampers their full implementation.

In addition to multilateral agreements, firms are affected by bilateral treaties and conventions between the countries in which they do business. For example, a number of countries have signed bilateral Treaties of Friendship, Commerce, and Navigation (FCN). The agreements generally define the rights of firms doing business in the host country. They normally guarantee that firms will be treated by the host country in the same manner in which domestic firms are treated. While these treaties provide for some sort of stability, they can also be canceled when relations worsen.

The international legal environment also affects the manager to the extent that firms must concern themselves with jurisdictional disputes. Because no single body of international law exists, firms usually are restricted by both home and host country laws. If a conflict occurs between contracting parties in two different countries, a question arises concerning which country's laws are to be used and in which court the dispute is to be settled. Sometimes the contract will contain a jurisdictional clause, which settles the matter with little problem. If the contract does not contain such a clause, however, the parties to the dispute have a few choices. They can settle the dispute by following the laws of the country in which the agreement was made, or they can resolve it by obeying the laws of the country in which the contract will have to be fulfilled. Which laws to use and in which location to settle the dispute are two different decisions. As a result, a dispute between a U.S. exporter and a French importer could be resolved in Paris but be based on New York State law. The importance of such provisions was highlighted by the lengthy jurisdictional disputes surrounding the Bhopal incident in India.

In cases of disagreement, the parties can choose either arbitration or litigation. Litigation is usually avoided for several reasons. It often involves extensive delays and is very costly. In addition, firms may fear discrimination in foreign countries. Therefore, companies tend to prefer conciliation and **arbitration,** because they result in much quicker decisions. Arbitration procedures are often spelled out in the original contract and usually provide for an intermediary who is judged to be impartial by both parties. Intermediaries can be representatives of chambers of commerce, trade associations, or third-country institutions. One key nongovernmental organization handling international commercial disputes is the International Court of Arbitration, founded in 1923 by the International Chamber of Commerce (**www.iccwbo.org**). Each year it handles arbitrations in some 48 different countries with arbitrators of some 57 different nationalities. Arbitration usually is faster and less expensive than litigation in the courts. In addition, the limited judicial recourse available against arbitral awards, as compared with court judgments, offers a clear advantage. Parties that use arbitration rather than litigation know that they will not have to face a prolonged and costly series of appeals. Finally, arbitration offers the parties the flexibility to set up a proceeding that can be conducted as quickly and economically as the circumstances allow. For example, a multimillion dollar ICC arbitration was completed in just over two months.[30]

Summary

The political and legal environment in the home and host countries and the laws and agreements governing relationships among nations are important to the international business executive. Compliance is mandatory in order to do business successfully abroad. To avoid the problems that can result from changes in the political and legal environment, it is essential to anticipate changes and to develop strategies for coping with them. Whenever possible, the manager must avoid being taken by surprise and letting events control business decisions.

Governments affect international business through legislation and regulations, which can support or hinder business transactions. An example is when export sanctions or embargoes are imposed to enhance foreign policy objectives. Similarly, export controls are used to preserve national security. Nations also regulate the international business behavior of firms by setting standards that relate to bribery and corruption, boycotts, and restraint of competition.

Through political actions such as expropriation, confiscation, or domestication, countries expose firms to international risk. Management therefore needs to be aware of the possibility of such risk and alert to new developments. Many private sector services are available to track international risk situations. In the event of a loss, firms may rely on insurance for political risk or they may seek redress in court. International legal action, however, may be quite slow and may compensate for only part of the loss.

Managers need to be aware that different countries have different laws. One clearly pronounced difference is between code law countries, where all possible legal rules are spelled out, and common law countries such as the United States, where the law is based on tradition, precedent, and custom.

Managers must also pay attention to international political relations, agreements, and treaties. Changes in relations or rules can mean major new opportunities and occasional threats to international business. Even though conflict in international business may sometimes lead to litigation, the manager needs to be aware of the alternative of arbitration, which may resolve the pending matter more quickly and at a lower cost.

Key Terms and Concepts

international competitiveness
extraterritoriality
sanction
embargo
export control system
dual-use items
export license
critical commodities list
foreign availability

dual-use products
deemed exports
boycott
antitrust laws
Webb-Pomerene Act
bribery
corruption
Foreign Corrupt Practices Act
political risk

ownership risk
operating risk
transfer risk
terrorism
coups d'état
expropriation
confiscation
domestication
local content
intellectual property rights

exchange controls
tax policy
price controls
theocracy
common law
code law
lobbyist
international law
Patent Cooperation Treaty
arbitration

Questions for Discussion

1. Discuss this potential dilemma: "High political risk requires companies to seek a quick payback on their investments. Striving for a quick payback, however, exposes firms to charges of exploitation and results in increased political risk."
2. Discuss this statement: "The national security that our export control laws seek to protect may be threatened by the resulting lack of international competitiveness of U.S. firms."
3. Discuss the advantages and disadvantages of common law and code law.
4. The United States has been described as a litigious society. How does frequent litigation affect international business?

5. After you hand your passport to the immigration officer in country X, he misplaces it. A small "donation" would certainly help him find it again. Should you give him the money? Is this a business expense to be charged to your company? Should it be tax deductible?
6. According to the anticorruption monitoring organization Transparency International, which countries have the highest levels of corruption? Which have the lowest levels? (Use the Corruption Perception Index found at **www.transparency.de.**) What problems might an exporter have in doing business in a country with high levels of corruption?

Internet Exercise

What are some of the countries suspected of nuclear proliferation by the United States? What types of exports might be barred from going to these countries? How would you go about obtaining a U.S. export license? What are some of the penalties that the U.S. government can impose on noncompliant exporters (see **www.bxa.doc.gov**)?

Recommended Readings

Arend, Anthony Clark. *Legal Rules and International Society.* New York: Oxford University Press, 1999.

Battling International Bribery, 2000 Report. Washington, DC: The World Bank Group, 2000.

Coplin, William D. and Michael K. O'Leary, eds. *Political Risk Yearbook.* Syracuse, NY: Political Risk Services, 2001.

Foreign Policy Report 2000. Washington, DC: U.S. Department of Commerce, Bureau of Export Administration, 2000.

A Global Forum on Fighting Corruption. Washington, DC: U.S. Department of State, Bureau for International Narcotics and Law Enforcement Affairs, September 1999.

Haass, Richard N., ed. *Economic Sanctions and American Diplomacy.* New York: Council on Foreign Relations Press, 1998.

Hirschhorn, Eric L. *The Export Control and Embargo Handbook.* Dobbs Ferry, NY: Oceana Publications, 2000.

Hufbauer, Gary Clyde, Jeffrey J. Schott, and Kimberly Ann Elliott. *Economic Sanctions Reconsidered:* History and Current Policy. Washington, DC: Institute for International Economics, 2001.

Maskus, Keith E. *Intellectual Property Rights in the Global Economy.* Washington, DC: Institute for International Economics, 2000.

Organization for Economic Cooperation and Development. *The European Union's Trade Policies and Their Economic Effects.* Paris: Organization for Economic Development, 2001.

Organization for Economic Cooperation and Development. *No Longer Business as Usual: Fighting Bribery and Corruption.* Paris: Organization for Economic Development, 2000.

Trade Information Center. *Export Programs: A Business Guide to Federal Export Assistance Programs.* Washington, DC: Trade Information Center, 2000.

Notes

1. Quoted in Philippe Dollinger, *The German Hansa* (Stanford, CA: Stanford University Press, 1970), 49.

2. Robin Renwick, *Economic Sanctions* (Cambridge, MA: Harvard University Press, 1981), 11.

3. Margaret P. Doxey, *Economic Sanctions and International Enforcement* (New York: Oxford University Press, 1980), 10.

4. George E. Shambaugh, *States, Firms, and Power: Successful Sanctions in United States Foreign Policy* (Albany, NY: State University of New York Press, 1999): 202.

5. Gary Clyde Hufbauer, Jeffrey J. Schott, and Kimberly Elliott, *Economic Sanctions Reconsidered: History and Current Policy,* 3d ed. (Washington, DC: Institute for International Economics, 2001).

6. G. Scott Erickson, "Export Controls: Marketing Implications of Public Policy Choices," *Journal of Public Policy and Marketing* 16, 1 (spring 1997): 83.

7. Michael R. Czinkota and Erwin Dichtl, "Export Controls and Global Changes," *der markt,* 35, 3, 1996: 148–155.

8. Robert M. Springer, Jr., "New Export Law an Aid to International Marketers," *Marketing News,* January 3, 1986, 10, 67.

9. This section has been adapted from: Michael R. Czinkota and Erwin Dichtl, "Export Controls: Providing Security in a Volatile Environment," *The International Executive* 37, 5 (1995): 485–497.

10. Erwin Dichtl, "Defacto Limits of Export Controls: The Need for International Harmonization," paper presented at the 2nd Annual CiMar Conference, Rio de Janeiro, August 1994.

11. Allen S. Krass, "The Second Nuclear Era: Nuclear Weapons in a Transformed World," in *World Security: Challenges for a New Century,* 2d ed., M. Klare and D. Thomas, eds. (St. Martin's Press, 1994), 85–105.

12. Paul Freedenberg, testimony before the Subcommittee on International Finance and Monetary Policy of the Committee on Banking, Housing, and Urban Affairs, United States Senate, Washington, DC, February 3, 1994, 2.

13. E. M. Hucko, *Aussenwirtschaftsrecht-Kriegswaffenkontrollrecht, Textsammlung mit Einführung,* 4th ed. (Cologne, 1993).

14. "Bribery a Problem with Overseas Customers," *Management Accounting* 75, 6 (June 1997): 61.

15. George Moody, *Grand Corruption: How Business Bribes Damage Developing Countries* (Oxford: World View Publishing, 1997): 23.

16. Michael G. Harvey, "A Survey of Corporate Programs for Managing Terrorist Threats," *Journal of International Business Studies* (Third Quarter 1993): 465–478.

17. Harvey J. Iglarsh, "Terrorism and Corporate Costs," *Terrorism* 10 (1987): 227–230.

18. Michael Minor, "LDCs, TNCs, and Expropriations in the 1980s," *The CYC Reporter* (spring 1988): 53.

19. Shengliang Deng, Pam Townsend, Maurice Robert, and Normand Quesnel, "A Guide to Intellectual Property Rights in Southeast Asia and China," *Business Horizons* (November–December 1996): 43–50.

20. TRIPS, a more detailed overview of the TRIPS agreement, **www.wto.org,** February 1, 2001.

21. "Risky Returns," *The Economist,* May 25, 2000, **www.economist.com.**

22. Paul Blustein, "Kawasaki to Pay Additional Taxes to U.S.," *The Washington Post,* December 11, 1992, D1.

23. **www.opic.gov,** Washington, DC: Overseas Private Investment Corporation, May 2, 2001.

24. Federal News Service, *Hearing of the House Judiciary Committee,* April 23, 1997.

25. Surya Prakash Sinha, *What Is Law? The Differing Theories of Jurisprudence* (New York: Paragon House, 1989).

26. Michael R. Czinkota and Jon Woronoff, *Unlocking Japan's Market* (Chicago: Probus Publishing, 1991).

27. *National Trade Estimate Report on Foreign Trade Barriers,* Washington, DC office of the United States Trade Representative, 2000, **www.ustr.gov.**

28. Michael R. Czinkota, "The Policy Gap in International Marketing," *Journal of International Marketing,* 8, 1, 2000: 99–111.

29. Michael R. Czinkota, "International Information Needs for U.S. Competitiveness," *Business Horizons* 34, 6 (November/December 1991): 86–91.

30. *International Court of Arbitration: 1999 Statistical Report* (Paris: International Chamber of Commerce, 2001).

PART 2

Part 2 provides theoretical background for international trade and investment activities. Classical concepts such as absolute and comparative advantage are explained. Key emphasis rests with modern-day theoretical developments that are presented in light of the realities of international business. In addition, the international economic activity of nations is discussed.

THEORETICAL FOUNDATIONS

CHAPTER 5

The Theory of International Trade and Investment

LEARNING OBJECTIVES

- To understand the traditional arguments of how and why international trade improves the welfare of all countries

- To review the history and compare the implications of trade theory from the original work of Adam Smith to the contemporary theories of Michael Porter

- To examine the criticisms of classical trade theory and examine alternative viewpoints of which business and economic forces determine trade patterns between countries

- To explore the similarities and distinctions between international trade and international investment

THE CHALLENGES AND OPPORTUNITIES OF e-COMMERCE

The World Trade Organization is facing up to the huge opportunities and challenges brought by the electronic commerce revolution. The WTO system is a series of agreements between governments. It involves a set of rules, freely negotiated and accepted by a consensus of the member governments, which limit governments' ability to interfere with trade. These rules apply in e-commerce as they do in other forms of trade. The work program on e-commerce now in progress at the WTO aims to provide answers to the following questions:

1. How do existing WTO programs impact e-commerce?
2. Are there any weaknesses or omissions in the law which need to be remedied?
3. Are there any new issues not covered by the WTO system on which members want to negotiate new disciplines?

There is a debate about whether some products, even in electronic form, should be classified and treated as goods. The point here is that if governments can agree that some digitized products—computer software, for example—should be classified as goods and that GATT rather than GATS (General Agreement on Trade in Services) obligations should apply to them, that is fine. But that must not be allowed to create doubt as to whether the electronic delivery of services is covered by GATS. Services are already supplied electronically in vast quantities. The only legal guarantees that such supply will continue to be permitted are in the market-access commitments WTO members have made under the GATS. ●

Source: Abstracted from "The Challenges and Opportunities of e-Commerce," by Mike Moore, *Business Credit,* New York, January 2001.

The debates, the costs, the benefits, and the dilemmas of international trade have in many ways not changed significantly from the time when Marco Polo crossed the barren wastelands of Eurasia to the time of the expansion of U.S. and Canadian firms across the Rio Grande into Mexico under the North American Free Trade Agreement. At the heart of the issue is what the gains—and the risks—are to the firm and the country as a result of a seller from one country servicing the needs of a buyer in a different country. If a Spanish firm wants to sell its product to the enormous market of mainland China, whether it produces at home and ships the product from Cadiz to Shanghai (international trade) or actually builds a factory in Shanghai (international investment), the goal is still the same: To sell a product for profit in the foreign market.

This chapter provides a directed path through centuries of thought on why and how trade and investment across borders occurs. Although theories and theorists come and go with time, a few basic questions have dominated this intellectual adventure:

- Why do countries trade?
- Do countries trade or do firms trade?

- Do the elements that give rise to the competitiveness of a firm, an industry, or a country as a whole, arise from some inherent endowment of the country itself, or do they change with time and circumstance?
- Once identified, can these sources of competitiveness be manipulated or managed by firms or governments to the benefit of the traders?

International trade is expected to improve the productivity of industry and the welfare of consumers. Let us learn how and why we still seek the exotic silks of the Far East.

The Age of Mercantilism

The evolution of trade into the form we see today reflects three events: the collapse of feudal society, the emergence of the mercantilist philosophy, and the life cycle of the colonial systems of the European nation-states. Feudal society was a state of **autarky,** a society that did not trade because all of its needs were met internally. The feudal estate was self-sufficient, although hardly "sufficient" in more modern terms, given the limits of providing entirely for oneself. Needs literally were only those of food and shelter, and all available human labor was devoted to the task of fulfilling those basic needs. As merchants began meeting in the marketplace, as travelers began exchanging goods from faraway places at the water's edge, the attractiveness of trade became evident.

In the centuries leading up to the Industrial Revolution, international commerce was largely conducted under the authority of governments. The goals of trade were, therefore, the goals of governments. As early as 1500 the benefits of trade were clearly established in Europe, as nation-states expanded their influence across the globe in the creation of colonial systems. To maintain and expand their control over these colonial possessions, the European nations needed fleets, armies, food, and all other resources the nations could muster. They needed wealth. Trade was therefore conducted to fill the governments' treasuries, at minimum expense to themselves but to the detriment of their captive trade partners. Although colonialism normally is associated with the exploitation of those captive societies, it went hand in hand with the evolving exchange of goods among the European countries themselves, **mercantilism.**

Mercantilism mixed exchange through trade with accumulation of wealth. Since government controlled the patterns of commerce, it identified strength with the accumulation of **specie** (gold and silver) and maintained a general policy of exports dominating imports. Trade across borders—exports—was considered preferable to domestic trade because exports would earn gold. Import duties, tariffs, subsidization of exports, and outright restriction on the importation of many goods were used to maximize the gains from exports over the costs of imports. Laws were passed making it illegal to take gold or silver out of the country, even if such specie was needed to purchase imports to produce their own goods for sale. This was one-way trade, the trade of greed and power.

The demise of mercantilism was inevitable given class structure and the distribution of society's product. As the Industrial Revolution introduced the benefits of mass production, lowering prices and increasing the supplies of goods to all, the exploitation of colonies and trading partners came to an end. However, governments still exercise considerable power and influence on the conduct of trade.

Classical Trade Theory

The question of why countries trade has proven difficult to answer. Since the second half of the eighteenth century, academicians have tried to understand not only the motivations and benefits of international trade, but also why some countries grow faster and wealthier than others through trade. Figure 5.1 provides an overview of the

FIGURE 5.1   **The Evolution of Trade Theory**

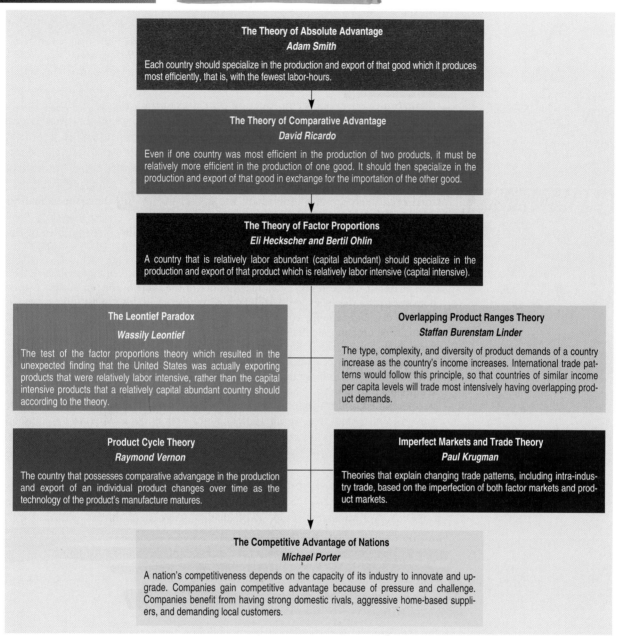

The Theory of Absolute Advantage
Adam Smith

Each country should specialize in the production and export of that good which it produces most efficiently, that is, with the fewest labor-hours.

The Theory of Comparative Advantage
David Ricardo

Even if one country was most efficient in the production of two products, it must be relatively more efficient in the production of one good. It should then specialize in the production and export of that good in exchange for the importation of the other good.

The Theory of Factor Proportions
Eli Heckscher and Bertil Ohlin

A country that is relatively labor abundant (capital abundant) should specialize in the production and export of that product which is relatively labor intensive (capital intensive).

The Leontief Paradox
Wassily Leontief

The test of the factor proportions theory which resulted in the unexpected finding that the United States was actually exporting products that were relatively labor intensive, rather than the capital intensive products that a relatively capital abundant country should according to the theory.

Overlapping Product Ranges Theory
Staffan Burenstam Linder

The type, complexity, and diversity of product demands of a country increase as the country's income increases. International trade patterns would follow this principle, so that countries of similar income per capita levels will trade most intensively having overlapping product demands.

Product Cycle Theory
Raymond Vernon

The country that possesses comparative advangage in the production and export of an individual product changes over time as the technology of the product's manufacture matures.

Imperfect Markets and Trade Theory
Paul Krugman

Theories that explain changing trade patterns, including intra-industry trade, based on the imperfection of both factor markets and product markets.

The Competitive Advantage of Nations
Michael Porter

A nation's competitiveness depends on the capacity of its industry to innovate and upgrade. Companies gain competitive advantage because of pressure and challenge. Companies benefit from having strong domestic rivals, aggressive home-based suppliers, and demanding local customers.

evolutionary path of trade theory since the fall of mercantilism. Although somewhat simplified, it shows the line of development of the major theories put forward over the past two centuries. It also serves as an early indication of the path of modern theory: the shifting focus from the country to the firm, from cost of production to the market as a whole, and from the perfect to the imperfect.

The Theory of Absolute Advantage

Generally considered the father of economics, Adam Smith published *The Wealth of Nations* in 1776 in London. In this book, Smith attempted to explain the process by which markets and production actually operate in society. Smith's two main areas of contribution, *absolute advantage* and the *division of labor* were fundamental to trade theory.

Production, the creation of a product for exchange, always requires the use of society's primary element of value, human labor. Smith noted that some countries, owing to the skills of their workers or the quality of their natural resources, could produce the same products as others with fewer labor-hours. He termed this efficiency **absolute advantage.**

Adam Smith observed the production processes of the early stages of the Industrial Revolution in England and recognized the fundamental changes that were occurring in production. In previous states of society, a worker performed all stages of a production process, with resulting output that was little more than sufficient for the worker's own needs. The factories of the industrializing world were, however, separating the production process into distinct stages, in which each stage would be performed exclusively by one individual, the **division of labor.** This specialization increased the production of workers and industries. Smith's pin factory analogy has long been considered the recognition of one of the most significant principles of the industrial age.

> To take an example, therefore, from a very trifling manufacture; but one in which the division of labour has been very often taken notice of the trade of the pin maker; a workman not educated to this business . . . could scarce, perhaps, with his utmost industry, make one pin in a day, and certainly could not make twenty. But in a way in which this business is now carried on, not only the whole work is a peculiar trade, but it is divided in to a number of branches, of which the greater part are likewise peculiar trades. One man draws out the wire, another straights it, a third cuts it, a fourth points it, a fifth grinds it at the top for receiving the head: to make the head requires two or three distinct operations; to put it on is a peculiar business . . . I have seen a small manufactory of this kind where ten men only were employed, and where some of them consequently performed two or three distinct operations. But though they were very poor, and therefore but indifferently accommodated with the necessary machine, they could, when they exerted themselves, make among them about twelve pounds of pins in a day. There are in a pound upwards of four thousand pins of a middling size.[1]

Adam Smith then extended his division of labor in the production process to a division of labor and specialized product across countries. Each country would specialize in a product for which it was uniquely suited. More would be produced for less. Thus, by each country, specializing in products for which it possessed absolute advantage, countries could produce more in total and exchange products—trade—for goods that were cheaper in price than those produced at home.

The Theory of Comparative Advantage

Although Smith's work was instrumental in the development of economic theories about trade and production, it did not answer some fundamental questions about trade. First, Smith's trade relied on a country possessing absolute advantage in production, but did not explain what gave rise to the production advantages. Second, if a country did not possess absolute advantage in any product, could it (or would it) trade?

David Ricardo, in his 1819 work entitled *On the Principles of Political Economy and Taxation,* sought to take the basic ideas set down by Smith a few steps further. Ricardo noted that even if a country possessed absolute advantage in the production of two products, it still must be relatively more efficient than the other country in one good's production than the other. Ricardo termed this the **comparative advantage.** Each country would then possess comparative advantage in the production of one of the two products, and both countries would then benefit by specializing completely in one product and trading for the other.

Country	Wheat	Cloth
England	2	4
France	4	2

TABLE 5.1

Absolute Advantage and Comparative Advantage*

- England has absolute advantage in the production of wheat. It requires fewer labor-hours (2 being less than 4) for England to produce one unit of wheat.
- France has absolute advantage in the production of cloth. It requires fewer labor-hours (2 being less than 4) for France to produce one unit of cloth.
- England has comparative advantage in the production of wheat. If England produces one unit of wheat, it is forgoing the production of 2/4 (0.50) of a unit of cloth. If France produces one unit of wheat, it is forgoing the production of 4/2 (2.00) of a unit of cloth. England therefore has the lower opportunity cost of producing wheat.
- France has comparative advantage in the production of cloth. If England produces one unit of cloth, it is forgoing the production of 4/2 (2.00) of a unit of wheat. If France produces one unit of cloth, it is forgoing the production of 2/4 (0.50) of a unit of wheat. France therefore has the lower opportunity cost of producing cloth.

*Labor-hours per unit of output.

A Numerical Example of Classical Trade

To fully understand the theories of absolute advantage and comparative advantage, consider the following example. Two countries, France and England, produce only two products, wheat and cloth (or beer and pizza, guns and butter, and so forth). The relative efficiency of each country in the production of the two products is measured by comparing the number of labor-hours needed to produce one unit of each product. Table 5.1 provides an efficiency comparison of the two countries.

England is obviously more efficient in the production of wheat. Whereas it takes France four labor-hours to produce one unit of wheat, it takes England only two hours to produce the same unit of wheat. France takes twice as many labor-hours to produce the same output. England has absolute advantage in the production of wheat. France needs two labor-hours to produce a unit of cloth that it takes England four labor-hours to produce. England therefore requires two more labor-hours than France to produce the same unit of cloth. France has absolute advantage in the production of cloth. The two countries are exactly opposite in relative efficiency of production.

David Ricardo took the logic of absolute advantages in production one step further to explain how countries could exploit their own advantages and gain from international trade. Comparative advantage, according to Ricardo, was based on what was given up or traded off in producing one product instead of the other. In this numerical example England needs only two-fourths as many labor-hours to produce a unit of wheat as France, while France needs only two-fourths as many labor-hours to produce a unit of cloth. England therefore has comparative advantage in the production of wheat, while France has comparative advantage in the production of cloth. A country cannot possess comparative advantage in the production of both products, so each country has an economic role to play in international trade.

National Production Possibilities

If the total labor-hours available for production within a nation were devoted to the full production of either product, wheat or cloth, the **production possibilities frontiers** of each country can be constructed. Assuming both countries possess the same

number of labor-hours, for example 100, the production possibilities frontiers for each country can be graphed, as in Figure 5.2. If England devotes all labor-hours (100) to the production of wheat (which requires 2 labor-hours per unit produced), it can produce a maximum of 50 units of wheat. If England devotes all labor to the production of cloth instead, the same 100 labor-hours can produce a maximum of 25 units of cloth (100 labor-hours/4 hours per unit of cloth). If England did not trade with any other country, it could only consume the products that it produced itself. England would therefore probably produce and consume some combination of wheat and cloth such as point A in Figure 5.2 (15 units of cloth, 20 units of wheat).

FIGURE 5.2   **Production Possibility Frontiers, Specialization of Production, and the Benefits of Trade**

England

1. Initially produces and consumes at point A.
2. England chooses to specialize in the production of wheat and shifts production from point A to point B.
3. England now exports the unwanted wheat (30 units) in exchange for imports of cloth (30 units) from France.
4. England is now consuming at point C, where it is consuming the same amount of wheat but 15 more units of cloth than at original point A.

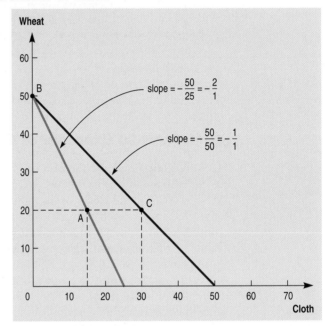

France

1. Initially produces and consumes at point D.
2. France chooses to specialize in the production of cloth and shifts production from point D to point E.
3. France now exports the unwanted cloth (30 units) in exchange for imports of wheat (30 units) from England.
4. France is now consuming at point F, where it is consuming the same amount of cloth but 15 more units of wheat than at original point D.

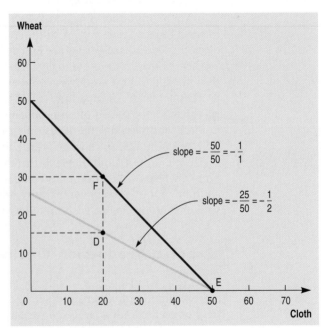

France's production possibilities frontier is constructed in the same way. If France devotes all 100 labor-hours to the production of wheat, it can produce a maximum of 25 units (100 labor-hours/4 hours per unit of wheat). If France devotes all 100 labor-hours to cloth, the same 100 labor-hours can produce a maximum of 50 units of cloth (100 labor-hours/2 hours per unit of cloth). If France did not trade with other countries, it would produce and consume at some point such as point D in Figure 5.2 (20 units of cloth, 15 units of wheat).

These frontiers depict what each country could produce in isolation—without trade (sometimes referred to as *autarky*). The slope of the production possibility frontier of a nation is a measure of how one product is traded off in production with the other (moving up the frontier, England is choosing to produce more wheat and less cloth). The slope of the frontier reflects the "trade-off" of producing one product over the other; the trade-offs represent prices, or **opportunity costs.** Opportunity cost is the forgone value of a factor of production in its next-best use. If England chooses to produce more units of wheat (in fact, produce only wheat), moving from point A to point B along the production possibilities frontier, it is giving up producing cloth to produce only wheat. The "cost" of the additional wheat is the loss of cloth. The slope of the production possibilities frontier is the ratio of product prices (opportunity costs). The slope of the production possibilities frontier for England is $-50/25$, or -2.00. The slope of the production possibilities frontier for France is flatter, $-25/50$, or -0.50.

The relative prices of products also provide an alternative way of seeing comparative advantage. The flatter slope of the French production possibilities frontier means that to produce more wheat (move up the frontier), France would have to give up the production of relatively more units of cloth than would England, with its steeper sloped production possibilities frontier.

The Gains from International Trade

Continuing with Figure 5.2, if England were originally not trading with France (the only other country) and it was producing at its own maximum possibilities (on the frontier and not inside the line), it would be producing at point A. Since it was not trading with another country, whatever it was producing it must also be consuming. So England could be said to be consuming at point A also. Therefore, without trade, you consume what you produce.

If, however, England recognized that it has comparative advantage in the production of wheat, it should move production from point A to point B. England should specialize completely in the product it produces best. It does not want to consume only wheat, however, so it would take the wheat it has produced and trade with France. For example, England may only want to consume 20 units of wheat, as it did at point A. It is now producing 50 units, and therefore has 30 units of wheat it can export to France. If England could export 30 units of wheat in exchange for imports of 30 units of cloth (a 1:1 ratio of prices), England would clearly be better off than before. The new consumption point would be point C, where it is consuming the same amount of wheat as point A, but is now consuming 30 units of cloth instead of just 15. More is better; England has benefited from international trade.

France, following the same principle of completely specializing in the product of its comparative production advantage, moves production from point D to point E, producing 50 units of cloth. If France now exported the unwanted cloth, for example 30 units, and exchanged the cloth with England for imports of 30 units of wheat (note that England's exports are France's imports), France too is better off as a result of international trade. Each country would do what it does best, exclusively, and then trade for the other product.

Current Account Balances as a Percentage of Gross Domestic Product

Legend:
- > −20%
- 0% to −20%
- > 0%
- No current data available

Source: *2001 World Development Indicators*, The World Bank.

But at what prices will the two countries trade? Since each country's production possibilities frontier has a different slope (different relative product prices), the two countries can determine a set of prices between the two domestic prices. In the above example, England's price ratio was $-2:1$, while France's domestic price was $-1:2$. Trading 30 units of wheat for 30 units of cloth is a price ratio of $-1:1$, a slope or set of prices between the two domestic price ratios. The dashed line in Figure 5.2 illustrates this set of trade prices.

Are both countries better off as a result of trade? Yes. The final step to understanding the benefits of classical trade is to note that the point where a country produces (point B for England and point E for France in Figure 5.2) and the point where it consumes are now different. This allows each country to consume beyond their own production possibilities frontier. Society's welfare, which is normally measured in its ability to consume more wheat, cloth, or any other goods or services, is increased through trade.

Concluding Points About Classical Trade Theory

Classical trade theory contributed much to the understanding of how production and trade operates in the world economy. Although like all economic theories they are often criticized for being unrealistic or out of date, the purpose of a theory is to simplify reality so that the basic elements of the logic can be seen. Several of these simplifications have continued to provide insight in understanding international business.

- **Division of Labor.** Adam Smith's explanation of how industrial societies can increase output using the same labor-hours as in preindustrial society is fundamental to our thinking even today. Smith extended this specialization of the efforts of a worker to the specialization of a nation.
- **Comparative Advantage.** David Ricardo's extension of Smith's work explained for the first time how countries that seemingly had no obvious reason for trade could individually specialize in producing what they did best and trade for products they did not produce.
- **Gains from Trade.** The theory of comparative advantage argued that nations could improve the welfare of their populations through international trade. A nation could actually achieve consumption levels beyond what it could produce by itself. To this day this is one of the fundamental principles underlying the arguments for all countries to strive to expand and "free" world trade.

Factor Proportions Trade Theory

Trade theory changed drastically in the first half of the twentieth century. The theory developed by the Swedish economist Eli Heckscher and later expanded by his former student Bertil Ohlin formed the theory of international trade that is still widely accepted today, **factor proportions theory.**

Factor Intensity in Production

The Heckscher-Ohlin theory considered two **factors of production,** labor and capital. Technology determines the way they combine to form a good. Different goods required different proportions of the two factors of production.

Figure 5.3 illustrates what it means to describe a good by its factor proportions. The production of one unit of good X requires 4 units of labor and 1 unit of capital. At the same time, to produce 1 unit of good Y requires 4 units of labor and 2 units of capital. Good X therefore requires more units of labor per unit of capital (4 to 1) relative to Y (4 to 2). X is therefore classified as a relatively labor-intensive product, and Y is relatively capital intensive. These **factor intensities,** or **proportions,** are truly rel-

FIGURE 5.3

FIGURE 5.3

Factor Proportions in Production

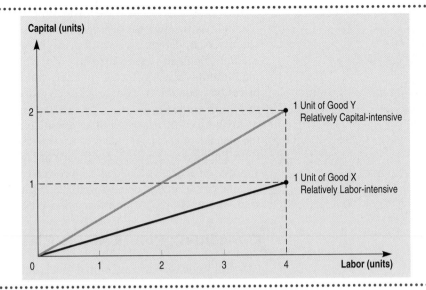

It is easy to see how the factor proportions of production differ substantially across goods. For example, the manufacturing of leather footwear is still a relatively labor-intensive process, even with the most sophisticated leather treatment and patterning machinery. Other goods, such as computer memory chips, however, although requiring some highly skilled labor, require massive quantities of capital for production. These large capital requirements include the enormous sums needed for research and development and the manufacturing facilities needed for clean production to ensure the extremely high quality demanded in the industry.

According to factor proportions theory, factor intensities depend on the state of technology—the current method of manufacturing a good. The theory assumed that the same technology of production would be used for the same goods in all countries. It is not, therefore, differences in the efficiency of production that will determine trade between countries as it did in classical theory. Classical theory implicitly assumed that technology or the productivity of labor is different across countries. Otherwise, there would be no logical explanation why one country requires more units of labor to produce a unit of output than another country. Factor proportions theory assumes no such productivity differences.

Factor Endowments, Factor Prices, and Comparative Advantage

If there is no difference in technology or productivity of factors across countries, what then determines comparative advantage in production and export? The answer is that factor prices determine cost differences. And these prices are determined by the endowments of labor and capital the country possesses. The theory assumes that labor and capital are immobile; factors cannot move across borders. Therefore, the country's endowment determines the relative costs of labor and capital as compared with other countries.

Using these assumptions, factor proportions theory stated that a country should specialize in the production and export of those products that use intensively its relatively abundant factor.

- A country that is relatively labor abundant should specialize in the production of relatively labor-intensive goods. It should then export those labor-intensive goods in exchange for capital-intensive goods.

GLOBAL PERSPECTIVE 5.1

Unintended 'Free-Riders': Biological Adversity

Bioinvasion is when weeds that do not normally grow in a region move in and smother the local flora. But not all problems associated with bioinvasion are confined to weeds. Residents of the southeastern United States, for example, are getting acquainted with the Formosan termite, whose colonies consume, on average, 1,000 pounds of wood in a year, compared with 7 pounds per year for native North American species. There is a seemingly unlimited number of other examples. Bioinvasion is a product of our global economy for two reasons. In the first place, some industries deploy exotics in the normal course of their business. Second, bioinvasion is a common by-product of many industries.

Source: Abstracted from "Biological Adversity," by Christopher Bright, *Harvard International Review,* Cambridge, Winter 2001.

- A country that is relatively capital abundant should specialize in the production of relatively capital-intensive goods. It should then export those capital-intensive goods in exchange for labor-intensive goods.

Assumptions of the Factor Proportions Theory

The increasing level of theoretical complexity of the factor proportions theory, as compared with the classical trade theory, increased the number of assumptions necessary for the theory to "hold." It is important to take a last look at the assumptions before proceeding further.

1. The theory assumes two countries, two products, and two factors of production, the so-called 2×2×2 assumption. Note that if both countries were producing all of the output they could and trading only between themselves (only two countries), both countries would have to have balances in trade!

2. The markets for the inputs and the outputs are perfectly competitive. The factors of production, labor, and capital were exchanged in markets that paid them only what they were worth. Similarly, the trade of the outputs (the international trade between the two countries) was competitive so that one country had no market power over the other.

3. Increasing production of a product experiences diminishing returns. This meant that as a country increasingly specialized in the production of one of the two outputs, it eventually would require more and more inputs per unit of output. For example there would no longer be the constant "labor-hours per unit of output" as assumed under the classical theory. Production possibilities frontiers would no longer be straight lines but concave. The result was that complete specialization would no longer occur under factor proportions theory.

4. Both countries were using identical technologies. Each product was produced in the same way in both countries. This meant the only way that a good could be produced more cheaply in one country than in the other was if the factors of production used (labor and capital) were cheaper.

Although a number of additional technical assumptions were necessary, these four highlight the very specialized set of conditions needed to explain international trade with factor proportions theory. Much of the trade theory developed since has focused on how trade changes when one or more of these assumptions is not found in the real world.

The Leontief Paradox

One of the most famous tests of any economic or business theory occurred in 1950, when economist Wassily Leontief tested whether the factor proportions theory could be used to explain the types of goods the United States imported and exported. Leontief's premise was the following.

> A widely shared view on the nature of the trade between the United States and the rest of the world is derived from what appears to be a common sense assumption that this country has a comparative advantage in the production of commodities which require for their manufacture large quantities of capital and relatively small amounts of labor. Our economic relationships with other countries are supposed to be based mainly on the export of such "capital intensive" goods in exchange for forgoing products which—if we were to make them at home—would require little capital but large quantities of American labor. Since the United States possesses a relatively large amount of capital—so goes this oft-repeated argument—and a comparatively small amount of labor, direct domestic production of such "labor intensive" products would be uneconomical; we can much more advantageously obtain them from abroad in exchange for our capital intensive products.[2]

Leontief first had to devise a method to determine the relative amounts of labor and capital in a good. His solution, known as **input-output analysis,** was an accomplishment on its own. Input-output analysis is a technique of decomposing a good into the values and quantities of the labor, capital, and other potential factors employed in the good's manufacture. Leontief then used this methodology to analyze the labor and capital content of all U.S. merchandise imports and exports. The hypothesis was relatively straightforward: U.S. exports should be relatively capital intensive (use more units of capital relative to labor) than U.S. imports. Leontief's results were, however, a bit of a shock.

Leontief found that the products that U.S. firms exported were relatively more labor intensive than the products the United States imported.[3] It seemed that if the factor proportions theory was true, the United States is a relatively labor-abundant country! Alternatively, the theory could be wrong. Neither interpretation of the results was acceptable to many in the field of international trade.

A variety of explanations and continuing studies have attempted to solve what has become known as the **Leontief Paradox.** At first, it was thought to have been simply a result of the specific year (1947) of the data. However, the same results were found with different years and data sets. Second, it was noted that Leontief did not really analyze the labor and capital contents of imports but rather the labor and capital contents of the domestic equivalents of these imports. It was possible that the United States was actually producing the products in a more capital-intensive fashion than were the countries from which it also imported the manufactured goods.[4] Finally, the debate turned to the need to distinguish different types of labor and capital. For example, several studies attempted to separate labor factors into skilled labor and unskilled labor. These studies have continued to show results more consistent with what the factor proportions theory would predict for country trade patterns.

Linder's Overlapping Product Ranges Theory

The difficulties in empirically validating the factor proportions theory led many in the 1960s and 1970s to search for new explanations of the determinants of trade between countries. The work of Staffan Burenstam Linder focused, not on the production or supply side, but instead on the preferences of consumers–the demand side. Linder acknowledged that in the natural resource–based industries, trade was indeed determined by relative costs of production and factor endowments.

However, Linder argued, trade in manufactured goods was dictated not by cost concerns but rather by the similarity in product demands across countries. Linder's was a significant departure from previous theory and was based on two principles:

1. As income, or more precisely per-capita income, rises, the complexity and quality level of the products demanded by the country's residents also rises. The total range of product sophistication demanded by a country's residents is largely determined by its level of income.

2. The entrepreneurs directing the firms that produce society's needs are more knowledgeable about their own domestic market than about foreign markets. An entrepreneur could not be expected to effectively serve a foreign market that is significantly different from the domestic market because competitiveness comes from experience. A logical pattern would be for an entrepreneur to gain success and market share at home first then expand to foreign markets that are similar in their demands or tastes.

International trade in manufactured goods would then be influenced by similarity of demands. The countries that would see the most intensive trade are those with similar per-capita income levels, for they would possess a greater likelihood of overlapping product demands.

So where does trade come in? According to Linder, the overlapping ranges of product sophistication represent the products that entrepreneurs would know well from their home markets and could therefore potentially export and compete with in foreign markets. For example, the United States and Canada have almost parallel sophistication ranges, implying they would have a lot of common ground, overlapping product ranges, for intensive international trade and competition. They are quite similar in their per-capita income levels. But Mexico and the United States, or Mexico and Canada, would not. Mexico has a significantly different product sophistication range as a result of a different per capita income level.

The overlapping product ranges described by Linder would today be termed **market segments.** Not only was Linder's work instrumental in extending trade theory beyond cost considerations, but it also found a place in the field of international marketing. As illustrated in the theories following the work of Linder, many of the questions that his work raised were the focus of considerable attention in the following decades.

International Investment and Product Cycle Theory

A very different path was taken by Raymond Vernon in 1966 concerning what is now termed **product cycle theory.** Diverging significantly from traditional approaches, Vernon focused on the product (rather than the country and the technology of its manufacture), not its factor proportions. Most striking was the appreciation of the role of information, knowledge, and the costs and power that go hand in hand with knowledge.

> . . . we abandon the powerful simplifying notion that knowledge is a universal free good, and introduce it as an independent variable in the decision to trade or to invest.

Using many of the same basic tools and assumptions of factor proportions theory, Vernon added two technology-based premises to the factor-cost emphasis of existing theory:

1. Technical innovations leading to new and profitable products require large quantities of capital and highly skilled labor. These factors of production are predominantly available in highly industrialized capital-intensive countries.

2. These same technical innovations, both the product itself and more importantly the methods for its manufacture, go through three stages of maturation as the

product becomes increasingly commercialized. As the manufacturing process becomes more standardized and low-skill labor-intensive, the comparative advantage in its production and export shifts across countries.

The Stages of the Product Cycle

Product cycle theory is both supply-side (cost of production) and demand-side (income levels of consumers) in its orientation. Each of these three stages that Vernon described combines differing elements of each.

Stage I: The New Product   Innovation requires highly skilled labor and large quantities of capital for research and development. The product will normally be most effectively designed and initially manufactured near the parent firm and therefore in a highly industrialized market due to the need for proximity to information and the need for communication among the many different skilled-labor components required.

In this development stage, the product is nonstandardized. The production process requires a high degree of flexibility (meaning continued use of highly skilled labor). Costs of production are therefore quite high. The innovator at this stage is a monopolist and therefore enjoys all of the benefits of monopoly power, including the high profit margins required to repay the high development costs and expensive production process. Price elasticity of demand at this stage is low; high-income consumers buy it regardless of cost.

Stage II: The Maturing Product   As production expands, its process becomes increasingly standardized. The need for flexibility in design and manufacturing declines, and therefore the demand for highly skilled labor declines. The innovating country increases its sales to other countries. Competitors with slight variations develop, putting downward pressure on prices and profit margins. Production costs are an increasing concern.

As competitors increase, as well as their pressures on price, the innovating firm faces critical decisions on how to maintain market share. Vernon argues that the firm faces a critical decision at this stage, either to lose market share to foreign-based manufacturers using lower-cost labor or to invest abroad to maintain its market share by exploiting the comparative advantages of factor costs in other countries. This is one of the first theoretical explanations of how trade and investment become increasingly intertwined.

Stage III: The Standardized Product   In this final stage, the product is completely standardized in its manufacture. Thus, with access to capital on world capital markets, the country of production is simply the one with the cheapest unskilled labor. Profit margins are thin, and competition is fierce. The product has largely run its course in terms of profitability for the innovating firm.

The country of comparative advantage has therefore shifted as the technology of the product's manufacture has matured. The same product shifts in its location of production. The country possessing the product during that stage enjoys the benefits of net trade surpluses. But such advantages are fleeting, according to Vernon. As knowledge and technology continually change, so does the country of that product's comparative advantage.

Trade Implications of the Product Cycle

Product cycle theory shows how specific products were first produced and exported from one country but, through product and competitive evolution, shifted their

GLOBAL PERSPECTIVE 5.2

When the Numbers Don't Add Up

The international trade statistics between countries, as reported by each, often do not match. As part of the continuing cooperation between the North American Free Trade Agreement (NAFTA) countries, the U.S. Department of Commerce recently concluded a study into the differences among the official trade statistics released by the United States, Mexico, and Canada in 1996 and 1997. The significance of these differences is compounded by the importance of trade among the three countries: 30 percent of all U.S. merchandise trade is with Canada and Mexico; 80 percent of Mexico's merchandise and service trade is with the United States and Canada.

The primary sources of the discrepancy in statistics include *geographic coverage, multicountry sourcing, indirect trade,*

nonfiling of U.S. exports, and *low-value transactions.* An example of *geographic coverage* is the fact that the United States considers Puerto Rico and the U.S. Virgin Islands as part of the United States for reporting purposes, while Mexico considers them separate countries. *Multicountry sourcing discrepancies,* in which a "single product" according to customs forms is actually a combination from several countries, is also a contributor. An example of *indirect trade* is a shipment of merchandise from Canada to Mexico via the United States. Canada may categorize these as exports to the United States, while Mexico may classify them as imports from Canada.

 For more details on the study of trade statistics discrepancies see **www.census.gov/ftp/pub/foreign-trade/.**

---

location of production and export to other countries over time. Figure 5.4 illustrates the trade patterns that Vernon visualized as resulting from the maturing stages of a specific product cycle. As the product and the market for the product mature and change, the countries of its production and export shift.

The product is initially designed and manufactured in the United States. In its early stages (from time t_0 to t_1), the United States is the only country producing and consuming the product. Production is highly capital-intensive and skilled-labor intensive at this time. At time t_1 the United States begins exporting the product to Other Advanced Countries, as Vernon classified them. These countries possess the income to purchase the product in its still New Product Stage, in which it was relatively high priced. These Other Advanced Countries also commerce their own production at time t_1 but continue to be net importers. A few exports, however, do find their way to the Less Developed Countries at this time as well.

As the product moves into the second stage, the Maturing Product Stage, production capability expands rapidly in the Other Advanced Countries. Competitive variations begin to appear as the basic technology of the product becomes more widely known, and the need for skilled labor in its production declines. These countries eventually also become net exporters of the product near the end of the stage (time t_3). At time t_2 the Less Developed Countries begin their own production, although they continue to be net importers. Meanwhile, the lower cost of production from these growing competitors turns the United States into a net importer by time t_4. The competitive advantage for production and export is clearly shifting across countries at this time.

The third and final stage, the Standardized Product Stage, sees the comparative advantage of production and export now shifting to the Less Developed Countries. The product is now a relatively mass-produced product that can be made with increasingly less-skilled labor. The United States continues to reduce domestic production and increase imports. The Other Advanced Countries continue to produce and export, although exports peak as the Less Developed Countries expand production and become net exporters themselves. The product has run its course or life cycle in reaching time t_5.

A final point: Note that throughout this product cycle, the countries of production, consumption, export, and import are identified by their labor and capital levels, not firms. Vernon noted that it could very well be the same firms that are moving production from the United States to Other Advanced Countries to Less Developed Coun-

FIGURE 5.4   **Trade Patterns and Product Cycle Theory**

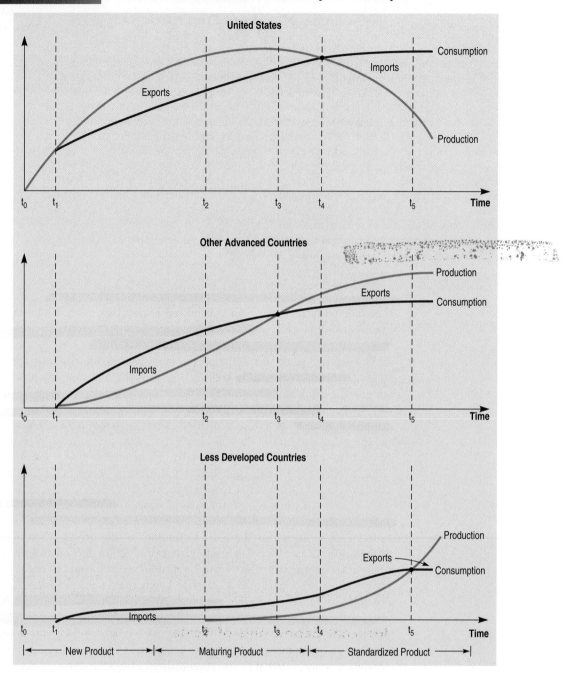

Source: Raymond Vernon, "International Investment and International Trade in the Product Cycle." *Quarterly Journal of Economics* (May 1966): 199.

tries. The shifting location of production was instrumental in the changing patterns of trade but not necessarily in the loss of market share, profitability, or competitiveness of the firms. The country of comparative advantage could change.

The Contributions of Product Cycle Theory

Although interesting in its own right for increasing emphasis on technology's impact on product costs, product cycle theory was most important because it explained international investment. Not only did the theory recognize the mobility of capital across countries (breaking the traditional assumption of factor immobility), it shifted the focus from the country to the product. This made it important to match the product by its maturity stage with its production location to examine competitiveness.

Product cycle theory has many limitations. It is obviously most appropriate for technology-based products. These are the products that are most likely to experience the changes in production process as they grow and mature. Other products, either resource-based (such as minerals and other commodities) or services (which employ capital but mostly in the form of human capital), are not so easily characterized by stages of maturity. And product cycle theory is most relevant to products that eventually fall victim to mass production and therefore cheap labor forces. But, all things considered, product cycle theory served to breach a wide gap between the trade theories of old and the intellectual challenges of a new, more globally competitive market in which capital, technology, information, and firms themselves were more mobile.

The New Trade Theory

Global trade developments in the 1980s and 1990s led to much criticism of the existing theories of trade. First, although there was rapid growth in trade, much of it was not explained by current theory. Secondly, the massive size of the merchandise trade deficit of the United States—and the associated decline of many U.S. firms in terms of international competitiveness—served as something of a country-sized lab experiment demonstrating what some critics termed the "bankruptcy of trade theory." Academics and policymakers alike looked for new explanations.

Two new contributions to trade theory were met with great interest. Paul Krugman, along with several colleagues, developed a theory of how trade is altered when markets are not perfectly competitive, or when production of specific products possess economies of scale. A second and very influential development was the growing work of Michael Porter, who examined the competitiveness of industries on a global basis, rather than relying on country-specific factors to determine competitiveness.

Economies of Scale and Imperfect Competition

Paul Krugman's theoretical developments once again focused on cost of production and how cost and price drive international trade. Using theoretical developments from microeconomics and market structure analysis, Krugman focused on two types of economics of scale, *internal economies of scale* and *external economies of scale*.[5]

Internal Economies of Scale
When the cost per unit of output depends on the size of an individual firm, the larger the firm the greater the scale benefits, and the lower the cost per unit. A firm possessing internal economies of scale could potentially monopolize an industry (creating an *imperfect market*), both domestically and internationally. If it produces more, lowering the cost per unit, it can lower the market price and sell more products, because it *sets* market prices.

The link between dominating a domestic industry and influencing international trade comes from taking this assumption of imperfect markets back to the original concept of comparative advantage. For this firm to expand sufficiently to enjoy its economies of scale, it must take resources away from other domestic industries in order to expand. A country then sees its own range of products in which it specializes narrowing, providing an opportunity for other countries to specialize in these so-called **abandoned product ranges.** Countries again search out and exploit comparative advantage.

A particularly powerful implication of internal economies of scale is that it provides an explanation of intra-industry trade, one area in which traditional trade theory had indeed seemed bankrupt. **Intra-industry trade** is when a country seemingly imports and exports the same product, an idea that is obviously inconsistent with any of the trade theories put forward in the past three centuries. According to Krugman, internal economies of scale may lead a firm to specialize in a narrow product line (to produce the volume necessary for economies of scale cost benefits); other firms in other countries may produce products that are similarly narrow, yet extremely similar: **product differentiation.** If consumers in either country wish to buy both products, they will be importing and exporting products that are, for all intents and purposes, the same.[6]

Intra-industry trade has been studied in detail in the past decade. Intra-industry trade is measured with the Grubel-Lloyd Index, the ratio of imports and exports of the same product occurring between two trading nations. It is calculated as follows:

$$\text{Intra-Industry Trade Index}_i = \frac{|X_i - M_i|}{(X_i + M_i)},$$

where i is the product category and $|X - M|$ is the absolute value of net exports of that product (exports − imports). For example, if Sweden imports 100 heavy machines for its forest products industry from Finland, and at the same time exports to Finland 80 of the same type of equipment, the intra-industry trade (IIT) index would be:

$$\text{IIT} = \frac{|80 - 100|}{(80 + 100)} = 1 - .1111 = .89.$$

The closer the index value to 1, the higher the level of intra-industry trade in that product category. The closer the index is to 0, the more one-way the trade between the countries exists, as traditional trade theory would predict.

Intra-industry trade is now thought to compose roughly 25 percent of global trade. And to its credit, intra-industry trade is increasingly viewed as having additive benefits to the fundamental benefits of comparative advantage. Intra-industry trade does allow some industrial segments in some countries to deepen their specialization while simultaneously allowing greater breadth of choices and commensurate benefits to consumers. Of course, one potentially disturbing characteristic of the growth in intra-industry trade is the potential for trade of all kinds to continue to expand in breadth and depth between the most industrialized countries (those producing the majority of the more complex manufactured goods) while those less industrialized nations do not see this added boost to trade growth.

External Economies of Scale   When the cost per unit of output depends on the size of an industry, not the size of the individual firm, the industry of that country may produce at lower costs than the same industry that is smaller in size in other countries. A country can potentially dominate world markets in a particular product, not because it has one massive firm producing enormous quantities (for example, Boeing), but rather because it has many small firms that interact to create a large, competitive, critical mass (for example, semiconductors in Penang, Malaysia). No one firm need be all that large, but several small firms in total may create such a competitive industry that firms in other countries cannot ever break into the industry on a competitive basis.[7]

Unlike internal economies of scale, external economies of scale may not necessarily lead to imperfect markets, but they may result in an industry maintaining its dominance in its field in world markets. This provides an explanation as to why all industries do not necessarily always move to the country with the lowest-cost energy, resources, or labor. What gives rise to this critical mass of small firms and their interrelationships is a much more complex question. The work of Michael Porter provides a partial explanation of how these critical masses are sustained.

The Competitive Advantage of Nations

The focus of early trade theory was on the country or nation and its inherent, natural, or endowment characteristics that might give rise to increasing competitiveness. As trade theory evolved, it shifted its focus to the industry and product level, leaving the national-level competitiveness question somewhat behind. Recently, many have turned their attention to the question of how countries, governments, and even private industry can alter the conditions within a country to aid the competitiveness of its firms.

The leader in this area of research has been Michael Porter of Harvard. As he states:

> National prosperity is created, not inherited. It does not grow out of a country's natural endowments, its labor pool, its interest rates, or its currency's values, as classical economics insists.
>
> A nation's competitiveness depends on the capacity of its industry to innovate and upgrade. Companies gain advantage against the world's best competitors because of pressure and challenge. They benefit from having strong domestic rivals, aggressive home-based suppliers, and demanding local customers.
>
> In a world of increasingly global competition, nations have become more, not less, important. As the basis of competition has shifted more and more to the creation and assimilation of knowledge, the role of the nation has grown. Competitive advantage is created and sustained through a highly localized process. Differences in national values, culture, economic structures, institutions, and histories all contribute to competitive success. There are striking differences in the patterns of competitiveness in every country; no nation can or will be competitive in every or even most industries. Ultimately, nations succeed in particular industries because their home environment is most forward-looking, dynamic, and challenging.[8]

Porter argued innovation is what drives and sustains competitiveness. A firm must avail itself of all dimensions of competition, which he categorized into four major components of "the diamond of national advantage":

1. **Factor Conditions:** The appropriateness of the nation's factors of production to compete successfully in a specific industry. Porter notes that although these factor conditions are very important in the determination of trade, they are not the only source of competitiveness as suggested by the classical, or factor proportions, theories of trade. Most importantly for Porter, it is the ability of a nation to continually create, upgrade, and deploy its factors (such as skilled labor) that is important, not the initial endowment.

2. **Demand Conditions:** The degree of health and competition the firm must face in its original home market. Firms that can survive and flourish in highly competitive and demanding local markets are much more likely to gain the competitive edge. Porter notes that it is the character of the market, not its size, that is paramount in promoting the continual competitiveness of the firm. And Porter translates *character* as demanding customers.

3. **Related and Supporting Industries:** The competitiveness of all related industries and suppliers to the firm. A firm that is operating within a mass of related firms and industries gains and maintains advantages through close working relationships, proximity to suppliers, and timeliness of product and information flows. The constant and close interaction is successful if it occurs not only in terms of physical proximity but also through the willingness of firms to work at it.

4. **Firm Strategy, Structure, and Rivalry:** The conditions in the home-nation that either hinder or aid in the firm's creation and sustaining of international competitiveness. Porter notes that no one managerial, ownership, or operational strategy is universally appropriate. It depends on the fit and flexibility of what works for that industry in that country at that time.

FIGURE 5.5

Determinants of National Competitive Advantage: Porter's Diamond

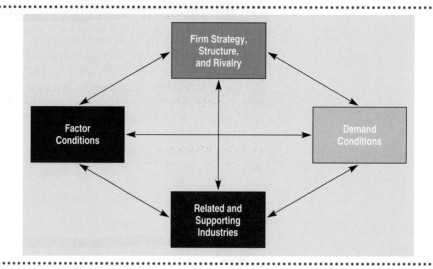

These four points, as illustrated in Figure 5.5, constitute what nations and firms must strive to "create and sustain through a highly localized process" to ensure their success.

Porter's emphasis on innovation as the source of competitiveness reflects an increased focus on the industry and product that we have seen in the past three decades. The acknowledgment that the nation is "more, not less, important" is to many eyes a welcome return to a positive role for government and even national-level private industry in encouraging international competitiveness. Including factor conditions as a cost component, demand conditions as a motivator of firm actions, and competitiveness all combine to include the elements of classical, factor proportions, product cycle, and imperfect competition theories in a pragmatic approach to the challenges that the global markets of the twenty-first century present to the firms of today.

The Theory of International Investment

Trade is the production of a good or service in one country and its sale to a buyer in another country. In fact, it is a firm (not a country) and a buyer (not a country) that are the subjects of trade, domestically or internationally. A firm is therefore attempting to access a market and its buyers. The producing firm wants to utilize its competitive advantage for growth and profit and can also reach this goal by international investment.[9]

Although this sounds easy enough, consider any of the following potholes on the road to investment success. Any of the following potholes may be avoided by producing within another country.

- Sales to some countries are difficult because of tariffs imposed on your good when it is entering. If you were producing within the country, your good would no longer be an import.
- Your good requires natural resources that are available only in certain areas of the world. It is therefore imperative that you have access to the natural resources. You can buy them from that country and bring them to your production process (import) or simply take the production to them.
- Competition is constantly pushing you to improve efficiency and decrease the costs of producing your good. You therefore may want to produce where it will be cheaper—cheaper capital, cheaper energy, cheaper natural resources, or cheaper

labor. Many of these factors are still not mobile, and therefore you will go to them instead of bringing them to you.

There are thousands of reasons why a firm may want to produce in another country, and not necessarily in the country that is cheapest for production or the country where the final good is sold.

The subject of international investment arises from one basic idea: the mobility of capital. Although many of the traditional trade theories assumed the immobility of the factors of production, it is the movement of capital that has allowed **foreign direct investments** across the globe. If there is a competitive advantage to be gained, capital can and will get there.

The Foreign Direct Investment Decision

Consider a firm that wants to exploit its competitive advantage by accessing foreign markets as illustrated in the decision-sequence tree of Figure 5.6.

The first choice is whether to exploit the existing competitive advantage in new foreign markets or to concentrate its resources in the development of new competitive advantages in the domestic market. Although many firms may choose to do both as

FIGURE 5.6   **The Direct Foreign Investment Decision Sequence**

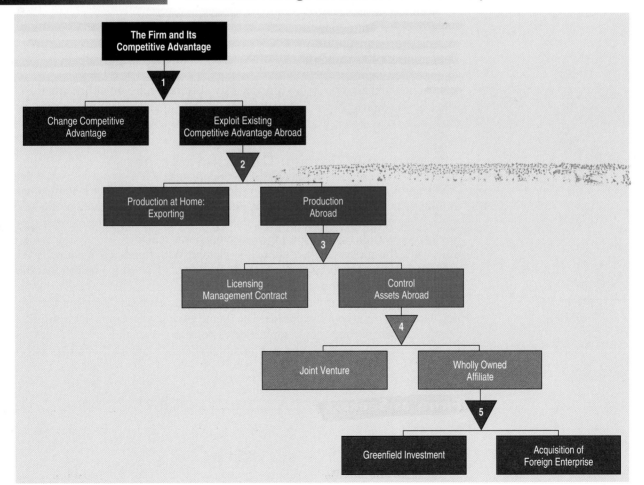

Source: Adapted from Gunter Dufey and R. Mirus, "Foreign Direct Investment: Theory and Strategic Considerations," unpublished, University of Michigan, May 1985.

resources will allow, more and more firms are choosing to go international as at least part of their expansion strategies.

Second, should the firm produce at home and export to the foreign markets, or produce abroad? The firm will choose the path that will allow it to access the resources and markets it needs to exploit its existing competitive advantage. But it will also consider two additional dimensions of each foreign investment decision: (1) the degree of control over assets, technology, information, and operations and (2) the magnitude of capital that the firm must risk. Each decision increases the firm's control at the cost of increased capital outlays.

After choosing to produce abroad, the firm must decide how. The distinctions among different kinds of foreign direct investment (branch 3 and downward in Figure 5.6), licensing agreements to greenfield construction (building a new facility from the ground up), vary by degrees of ownership. The licensing management contract is by far the simplest and cheapest way to produce abroad. Another firm is licensed to produce the product, but with your firm's technology and know-how. The question is whether the reduced capital investment of simply licensing the product to another manufacturer is worth the risk of loss of control over the product and technology.

The firm that wants direct control over the foreign production process next determines the degree of equity control: to own the firm outright, or as a joint investment with another firm. Trade-offs with joint ventures continue the debate over control of assets and other sources of the firm's original competitive advantage. Many countries try to ensure the continued growth of local firms and investors by requiring that foreign firms operate jointly with local firms.

The final decision branch between a "greenfield investment"—building a firm from the ground up—and the purchase of an existing firm, is often a question of cost. A greenfield investment is the most expensive of all foreign investment alternatives. The acquisition of an existing firm is often lower in initial cost but may also contain a number of customizing and adjustment costs that are not apparent at the initial purchase. The purchase of a going concern may also have substantial benefits if the existing business possesses substantial customer and supplier relationships that can be used by the new owner in the pursuit of its own business.

The Theory of Foreign Direct Investment

What motivates a firm to go beyond exporting or licensing? What benefits does the multinational firm expect to achieve by establishing a physical presence in other countries? These are the questions that the theory of foreign direct investment has sought to answer. As with trade theory, the questions have remained largely the same over time, while the answers have continued to change. With hundreds of countries, thousands of firms, and millions of products and services, there is no question that the answer to such an enormous question will likely get messy.

The following overview of investment theory has many similarities to the preceding discussion of international trade. The theme is a global business environment that attempts to satisfy increasingly sophisticated consumer demands, while the means of production, resources, skills, and technology needed become more complex and competitive.

Firms as Seekers

A firm that expands across borders may be seeking any of a number of specific sources of profit or opportunity.

    1. Seeking Resources: There is no question that much of the initial foreign direct investment of the eighteenth and nineteenth centuries was the result of firms seeking unique and valuable natural resources for their products. Whether it be the copper resources of Chile, the linseed oils of Indonesia, or the petroleum resources spanning the Middle East, firms establishing permanent presences around the world are seeking access to the resources at the core of their business.

2. **Seeking Factor Advantages:** The resources needed for production are often combined with other advantages that are inherent in the country of production. The same low-cost labor at the heart of classical trade theory provides incentives for firms to move production to countries possessing these factor advantages. As noted by Vernon's Product Cycle, the same firms may move their own production to locations of factor advantages as the products and markets mature.

3. **Seeking Knowledge:** Firms may attempt to acquire other firms in other countries for the technical or competitive skills they possess. Alternatively, companies may locate in and around centers of industrial enterprise unique to their specific industry, such as the footwear industry of Milan or the semiconductor industry of the Silicon Valley of California.

4. **Seeking Security:** Firms continue to move internationally as they seek political stability or security. For example, Mexico has experienced a significant increase in foreign direct investment as a result of the tacit support of the United States, Canada, and Mexico itself as reflected by the North American Free Trade Agreement.

5. **Seeking Markets:** Not the least of the motivations, the ability to gain and maintain access to markets is of paramount importance to multinational firms. Whether following the principles of Linder, in which firms learn from their domestic market and use that information to go international, or the principles of Porter, which emphasize the character of the domestic market as dictating international competitiveness, foreign market access is necessary.

Firms as Exploiters of Imperfections

Much of the investment theory developed in the past three decades has focused on the efforts of multinational firms to exploit the imperfections in factor and product markets created by governments. The work of Hymer, Kindleberger, and Caves noted that many of the policies of governments create imperfections. These market imperfections cover the entire range of supply and demand of the market: trade policy (tariffs and quotas), tax policies and incentives, preferential purchasing arrangements established by governments themselves, and financial restrictions on the access of foreign firms to domestic capital markets.

1. **Imperfections in Access:** Many of the world's developing countries have long sought to create domestic industry by restricting imports of competitive products in order to allow smaller, less competitive domestic firms to grow and prosper—so-called **import substitution policies.** Multinational firms have sought to maintain their access to these markets by establishing their own productive presence within the country, effectively bypassing the tariff restriction.

2. **Imperfections in Factor Mobility:** Other multinational firms have exploited the same sources of comparative advantage identified throughout this chapter—the low-cost resources or factors often located in less-developed countries or countries with restrictions on the mobility of labor and capital. However, combining the mobility of capital with the immobility of low-cost labor has characterized much of the foreign direct investment seen throughout the developing world over the past 50 years.

3. **Imperfections in Management:** The ability of multinational firms to successfully exploit or at least manage these imperfections still relies on their ability to gain an "advantage." Market advantages or powers are seen in international markets

as in domestic markets: cost advantages, economies of scale and scope, product differentiation, managerial or marketing technique and knowledge, financial resources and strength.

All these imperfections are the things of which competitive dreams are made. The multinational firm needs to find these in some form or another to justify the added complexities and costs of international investments.

Firms as Internalizers

The question that has plagued the field of foreign direct investment is, Why can't all of the advantages and imperfections mentioned be achieved through management contracts or licensing agreements (the choice available to the international investor at Step 3 in Figure 5.6)? Why is it necessary for *the firm itself* to establish a physical presence in the country? What pushes the multinational firm further down the investment decision tree?

The research of Buckley and Casson and Dunning has attempted to answer these questions by focusing on nontransferable sources of competitive advantage—proprietary information possessed by the firm and its people. Many advantages firms possess center around their hands-on knowledge of producing a good or providing a service. By establishing their own multinational operations they can internalize the production, thus keeping confidential the information that is at the core of the firm's competitiveness. **Internalization** is preferable to the use of arms-length arrangements such as management contracts or licensing agreements. They either do not allow the effective transmission of the knowledge or represent too serious a threat to the loss of the knowledge to allow the firm to successfully achieve the hoped-for benefits of international investment.

Summary

The theory of international trade has changed drastically from that first put forward by Adam Smith. The classical theories of Adam Smith and David Ricardo focused on the abilities of countries to produce goods more cheaply than other countries. The earliest production and trade theories saw labor as the major factor expense that went into any product. If a country could pay that labor less, and if that labor could produce more physically than labor in other countries, the country might obtain an absolute or comparative advantage in trade.

Subsequent theoretical development led to a more detailed understanding of production and its costs. Factors of production are now believed to include labor (skilled and unskilled), capital, natural resources, and other potentially significant commodities that are difficult to reproduce or replace, such as energy. Technology, once assumed to be the same across all countries, is now seen as one of the premier driving forces in determining who holds the competitive edge or advantage. International trade is now seen as a complex combination of thousands of products, technologies, and firms that are constantly innovating to either keep up with or get ahead of the competition.

Modern trade theory has looked beyond production cost to analyze how the demands of the marketplace alter who trades with whom and which firms survive domestically and internationally. The abilities of firms to adapt to foreign markets, both in the demands and the competitors that form the foreign markets, have required much of international trade and investment theory to search out new and innovative approaches to what determines success and failure.

Finally, as world economies grew and the magnitude of world trade increased, the simplistic ideas that guided international trade and investment theory have had to grow with them. The choices that many firms face today require them to directly move their capital, technology, and know-how to countries that possess other unique factors or market advantages that will help them keep pace with market demands. Even then, world business conditions constitute changing fortunes.

Key Terms and Concepts

autarky
mercantilism
specie
absolute advantage
division of labor
comparative advantage

production possibilities
   frontier
opportunity cost
factor proportions theory
factors of production
factor intensities

input-output analysis
Leontief Paradox
market segment
product cycle theory
abandoned product ranges
intra-industry trade

product differentiation
economies of scale
foreign direct investment
import substitution
internalization

Questions for Discussion

1. According to the theory of comparative advantage as explained by Ricardo, why is trade always possible between two countries, even when one is absolutely inefficient compared to the other?
2. The factor proportions theory of international trade assumes that all countries produce the same product the same way. Would international competition cause or prevent this from happening?
3. What, in your opinion, were the constructive impacts on trade theory resulting from the empirical research of Wassily Leontief?
4. Product cycle theory has always been a very "attractive theory" to many students. Why do you think that is?

5. If the product cycle theory were accepted for the basis of policymaking in the United States, what should the U.S. government do to help U.S. firms exploit the principles of the theory?
6. Many trade theorists argue that the primary contribution of Michael Porter has been to repopularize old ideas, in new, more applicable ways. To what degree do you think Porter's ideas are new or old?
7. How would you analyze the statement that "international investment is simply a modern extension of classical trade"?
8. How can a crisis in Asia impact jobs and profits in the United States?

Internet Exercises

1. The differences across multinational firms is striking. Using a sample of firms such as those listed here, pull from their individual web pages the proportions of their incomes that are earned outside their country of incorporation.

Walt Disney	http://www.disney.com/
Nestlé S.A.	http://www.nestle.com/html/home.html
Intel	http://www.intel.com/
Daimler-Benz	http://www.daimler-benz.com/index_e.htm
Mitsubishi Motors	http://www.mitsubishi-motors.com.jp/

Also note the way in which international business is now conducted via the Internet. Several of the above home

pages allow the user to choose the language of the presentation viewed. Others, like Daimler-Benz, report financial results in two different accounting frameworks, those used in Germany and the Generally Accepted Accounting Practices (GAAP) used in the United States.
2. There is no hotter topic in business today than corporate governance, the way in which firms are controlled by management and ownership across countries. Use the following sites to view recent research, current events and news items, and other information related to the relationships between a business and its stakeholders.

| Corporate Governance Net | http://www.corpgov.net/ |
| Corporate Governance Research | http://www.irrc.org/proxy/cgs.html |

Recommended Readings

Bhagwati, Jagdish, and Arvind Panagariya, eds. *The Economics of Preferential Trade Agreements*. Washington, DC: American Enterprise Institute, 1996.
Buckley, Peter J., and Mark Casson. *The Future of the Multinational Enterprise*. London: Macmillan, 1976.

Caves, Richard E. International Corporations: The Industrial Economics of Foreign Investment. *Economica* (February 1971): 1–27.
Dunning, John H. Trade Location of Economic Activity and the MNE: A Search for an Eclectic Approach. In *The Interna-*

tional Allocation of Economic Activity, edited by Bertil Ohlin, Per-Ove Hesselborn, and Per Magnus Wijkman. New York: Homes and Meier, 1977, 395–418.

Heckscher, Eli. The Effect of Foreign Trade on the Distribution of Income. In *Readings in International Trade,* edited by Howard S. Ellis and Lloyd A. Metzler. Philadelphia: The Blakiston Company, 1949.

Helpman, Elhaman, and Paul Krugman. *Market Structure and Foreign Trade.* Cambridge, MA: MIT Press, 1985.

Hymer, Stephen H. *The International Operations of National Firms: A Study of Direct Foreign. Investment.* Cambridge, MA: MIT Press, 1976.

Krugman, Paul R., and Maurice Obstfeld, *International Economics: Theory and Policy,* 5th ed., Addison-Wesley, 2000.

Linder, Staffan Burenstam. *An Essay on Trade and Transformation.* New York: John Wiley & Sons, 1961.

Maskus, Keith E., Deborah Battles, and Michael H. Moffett. Determinants of the Structure of U.S. Manufacturing Trade

with Japan and Korea, 1970–1984. In *The Internationalization of U.S. Markets,* edited by David B. Audretch and Michael P. Claudon. New York: New York University Press, 1989, 97–122.

Ohlin, Bertil. *Interregional and International Trade.* Boston: Harvard University Press, 1933.

Porter, Michael. "The Competitive Advantage of Nations." *Harvard Business Review* (March–April 1990).

Ricardo, David. *The Principles of Political Economy and Taxation.* Cambridge, United Kingdom: Cambridge University Press, 1981.

Smith, Adam. *The Wealth of Nations.* New York: The Modern Library, 1937.

Vernon, Raymond. International Investment and International Trade in the Product Cycle. *Quarterly Journal of Economics* (1966): 190–207.

Wells, Louis T., Jr., A Product Life Cycle for International Trade? *Journal of Marketing* 22 (July 1968): 1–6.

Notes

1. Adam Smith, *An Inquiry into the Nature and Causes of the Wealth of Nations* (New York: E.P. Dutton & Company, 1937), 4–5.

2. Wassily Leontief, "Domestic Production and Foreign Trade: the American Capital Position Re-Examined," *Proceedings of the American Philosophical Society,* 97, no. 4 (September 1953), as reprinted in Wassily Leontief, *Input-Output Economics* (New York: Oxford University Press, 1966), 69–70.

3. In Leontief's own words: "These figures show that an average million dollars' worth of our exports embodies considerably less capital and somewhat more labor than would be required to replace from domestic production an equivalent amount of our competitive imports. . . . The widely held opinion that—as compared with the rest of the world—the United States' economy is characterized by a relative surplus of capital and a relative shortage of labor proves to be wrong. As a matter of fact, the opposite is true." Leontief, 1953, 86.

4. If this were true, if would defy one of the basic assumptions of the factor proportions theory, that all products are manufactured with the same technology (and therefore same proportions of labor and capital) across countries. However, con-

tinuing studies have found this to be quite possible in our imperfect world.

5. For a detailed description of these theories see Elhanan Helpman and Paul Krugman, *Market Structure and Foreign Trade* (Cambridge: MIT Press, 1985).

6. This leads to the obvious debate as to what constitutes a "different product" and what is simply a cosmetic difference. The most obvious answer is found in the field of marketing: If the consumer believes the products are different, then they are different.

7. There are a variety of potential outcomes from external economies of scale. For additional details see Paul R. Krugman and Maurice Obstfeld, *International Economics: Theory and Policy,* 3rd ed. (Harper-Collins, 1994).

8. Michael E. Porter, "The Competitive Advantage of Nations," *Harvard Business Review* (March–April 1990): 73–74.

9. The term *international investment* will be used in this chapter to refer to all nonfinancial investment. International financial investment includes a number of forms beyond the concerns of this chapter, such as the purchase of bonds, stocks, or other securities issued outside the domestic economy.

CHAPTER 6

The International Economic Activity of the Nation: The Balance of Payments

LEARNING OBJECTIVES

- To understand the fundamental principles of how countries measure international business activity, the balance of payments

- To examine the similarities of the current and capital accounts of the balance of payments

- To understand the critical differences between trade in merchandise and services, and why international investment activity has recently been controversial in the United States

- To review the mechanical steps of how exchange rate changes are transmitted into altered trade prices and eventually trade volumes

- To understand how countries with different government policies toward international trade and investment, or different levels of economic development, differ in their balance of payments

"**S**ervices trade is the unsung hero of our trade balance," says Robert Litan, director, economic studies, at Washington's Brookings Institution. According to a University of Michigan forecast, U.S. service exports will hit $650 billion by 2010—about the same volume of current U.S. exports of farm and factory goods. Worldwide, cross-border sales of services are around $1.3 trillion, most booked by U.S. providers. Services sold by the number two exporter, Britain, total just $100 billion.

"Accounting for service-sector transactions is difficult enough at home, it's even more challenging when services cross borders," says Catherine Mann of the Institute for International Economics in Washington. Take packaged software, she says, whose delivery can be via CD-ROM in a box, loaded onto a computer, or downloaded via the Internet. As such, while overseas sales of software by U.S. companies topped $13 billion as long ago as 1995, the most recent data in the U.S. balance of payments, for 1998, show software exports of just $3 billion.

Another accounting anomaly: The more demand grows, the faster exports disappear. That's because as service providers increase sales abroad, they advance beyond the export stage to establish subsidiaries in-country. Consequently, sales to foreign customers are booked as domestic transactions between a branch of a U.S. multinational and a local buyer. Last year, more than $300 billion in such intracompany service exports went unreported in the U.S. trade balance, slightly more than the $250 billion in services officially exported from the United States. Combined, the two figures very nearly match all U.S. exports of merchandise. ●

Source: Abstracted from "Services May Lead U.S. to Trade Surplus," by Joel Millman, *Wall Street Journal*, December 4, 2000.

International business transactions occur in many different forms over the course of a year. The measurement of all international economic transactions between the residents of a country and foreign residents is called the **balance of payments (BOP).** Government policymakers need such measures of economic activity to evaluate the general competitiveness of domestic industry, to set exchange-rate or interest-rate policies or goals, and for many other purposes. Individuals and businesses use various BOP measures to gauge the growth and health of specific types of trade or financial transactions by country and regions of the world against the home country.

International transactions take many forms. Each of the following examples is an international economic transaction that is counted and captured in the U.S. balance of payments.

- U.S. imports of Honda automobiles, which are manufactured in Japan.
- A U.S.-based firm, Bechtel, is hired to manage the construction of a major water-treatment facility in the Middle East.

- The U.S. subsidiary of a French firm, Saint Gobain, pays profits (dividends) back to the parent firm in Paris.
- Daimler-Benz, the well-known German automobile manufacturer, purchases a small automotive parts manufacturer outside Chicago, Illinois.
- An American tourist purchases a hand-blown glass figurine in Venice, Italy.
- The U.S. government provides grant financing of military equipment for its NATO (North Atlantic Treaty Organization) military ally, Turkey.
- A Canadian dentist purchases a U.S. Treasury bill through an investment broker in Cleveland, Ohio.

These are just a small sample of the hundreds of thousands of international transactions that occur each year. The balance of payments provides a systematic method for the classification of all of these transactions. There is one rule of thumb that will always aid in the understanding of BOP accounting: Watch the direction of the movement of money.

The balance of payments is composed of a number of subaccounts that are watched quite closely by groups as diverse as investors on Wall Street, farmers in Iowa, politicians on Capitol Hill, and in boardrooms across America. These groups track and analyze the two major subaccounts, the **current account** and the **capital account,** on a continuing basis. Before describing these two subaccounts and the balance of payments as a whole, it is necessary to understand the rather unusual features of how balance of payments accounting is conducted.

Fundamentals of Balance of Payments Accounting

The balance of payments must balance. If it does not, something has either not been counted or counted properly. It is therefore improper to state that the BOP is in disequilibrium. It cannot be. The supply and demand for a country's currency may be imbalanced, but that is not the same thing. Subaccounts of the BOP, such as the merchandise trade balance, may be imbalanced, but the entire BOP of a single country is always balanced.

There are three main elements to the process of measuring international economic activity: (1) identifying what is and is not an international economic transaction; (2) understanding how the flow of goods, services, assets, and money creates debits and credits to the overall BOP; and (3) understanding the bookkeeping procedures for BOP accounting, called double entry.

Defining International Economic Transactions

Identifying international transactions is ordinarily not difficult. The export of merchandise, goods such as trucks, machinery, computers, telecommunications equipment, and so forth, is obviously an international transaction. Imports such as French wine, Japanese cameras, and German automobiles are also clearly international transactions. But this merchandise trade is only a portion of the thousands of different international transactions that occur in the United States or any other country each year.

Many other international transactions are not so obvious. The purchase of a glass figure in Venice, Italy, by an American tourist is classified as a U.S. merchandise import. In fact, all expenditures made by American tourists around the globe that are for goods or services (meals, hotel accommodations, and so forth) are recorded in the U.S. balance of payments as imports of travel services in the current account. The purchase of a U.S. Treasury bill by a foreign resident is an international financial transaction and is dutifully recorded in the capital account of the U.S. balance of payments.

The BOP as a Flow Statement

The BOP is often misunderstood because many people believe it to be a balance sheet, rather than a cash flow statement. By recording all international transactions over a period of time, it is tracking the continuing flow of purchases and payments between a country and all other countries. It does not add up the value of all assets and liabilities of a country like a balance sheet does for an individual firm.

There are two types of business transactions that dominate the balance of payments:

1. **Real Assets:** The exchange of goods (for example, automobiles, computers, watches, textiles) and services (for example, banking services, consulting services, travel services) for other goods and services (barter) or for the more common type of payment, money.
2. **Financial Assets:** The exchange of financial claims (for example, stocks, bonds, loans, purchases or sales of companies) in exchange for other financial claims or money.

Although assets can be separated as to whether they are real or financial, it is often easier to simply think of all assets as being goods that can be bought and sold. An American tourist's purchase of a handwoven area rug in a shop in Bangkok is not all that different from a Wall Street banker buying a British government bond for investment purposes.

BOP Accounting: Double-Entry Bookkeeping

The balance of payments employs an accounting technique called **double-entry bookkeeping.** Double-entry bookkeeping is the age-old method of accounting in which every transaction produces a debit and a credit of the same amount. Simultaneously. It has to. A debit is created whenever an asset is increased, a liability is decreased, or an expense is increased. Similarly, a credit is created whenever an asset is decreased, a liability is increased, or an expense is decreased.

An example clarifies this process. A U.S. retail store imports from Japan $2 million worth of consumer electronics. A negative entry is made in the merchandise-import subcategory of the current account in the amount of $2 million. Simultaneously, a positive entry of the same $2 million is made in the capital account for the transfer of a $2 million bank account to the Japanese manufacturer. Obviously, the result of hundreds of thousands of such transactions and entries should theoretically result in a perfect balance.

That said, it is now a problem of application, and a problem it is. The measurement of all international transactions in and out of a country over a year is a daunting task. Mistakes, errors, and statistical discrepancies will occur. The primary problem is that although double-entry bookkeeping is employed in theory, the individual transactions are recorded independently. Current and capital account entries are recorded independent of one another, not together as double-entry bookkeeping would prescribe. It must then be recognized that there will be serious discrepancies (to use a nice term for it) between debits and credits, and the possibility in total that the balance of payments may not balance!

The following section describes the various balance of payment accounts, their meanings, and their relationships, using the United States as the example. The chapter then concludes with a discussion—and a number of examples—of how different countries with different policies or levels of economic development may differ markedly in their balance of payment accounts.

The Accounts of the Balance of Payments

The balance of payments is composed of two primary subaccounts, the *Current Account* and the *Financial/Capital Account*. In addition, the *Official Reserves Account* tracks government currency transactions, and a fourth statistical subaccount, the *Net Errors and Omissions Account*, is produced to preserve the balance in the BOP. The international economic relationships between countries do, however, continue to evolve, as the recent revision of the major accounts within the BOP discussed below indicates.[2]

The Current Account

The *Current Account* includes all international economic transactions with income or payment flows occurring within the year, the *current* period. The *Current Account* consists of four subcategories:

1. **Goods Trade:** This is the export and import of goods. Merchandise trade is the oldest and most traditional form of international economic activity. Although many countries depend on imports of many goods (as they should according to the theory of comparative advantage), they also normally work to preserve either a balance of goods trade or even a surplus.

2. **Services Trade:** This is the export and import of services. Some common international services are financial services provided by banks to foreign importers and exporters, travel services of airlines, and construction services of domestic firms in other countries. For the major industrial countries, this subaccount has shown the fastest growth in the past decade.

3. **Income:** This category is predominantly *current income* associated with investments that were made in previous periods. If a U.S. firm created a subsidiary in South Korea to produce metal parts in a previous year, the proportion of net income that is paid back to the parent company in the current year (the dividend) constitutes current investment income. Additionally, wages and salaries paid to nonresident workers is also included in this category.

4. **Current Transfers:** Transfers are the financial settlements associated with the change in ownership of real resources or financial items. Any transfer between countries that is one-way, a gift, or a grant, is termed a *current transfer.* A common example of a current transfer would be funds provided by the United States government to aid in the development of a less-developed nation. Transfers associated with the transfer of fixed assets are included in a new separate account, the Capital Account, which now follows the Current Account. The contents of what previously had been called the capital account are now included within the *Financial Account.*

All countries possess some amount of trade, most of which is merchandise. Many smaller and less-developed countries have little in the way of service trade, or items that fall under the income or transfers subaccounts.

The Current Account is typically dominated by the first component described—the export and import of merchandise. For this reason, the *Balance on Trade* (BOT), which is so widely quoted in the business press in most countries, refers specifically to the balance of exports and imports of goods trade only. For a larger industrialized country, however, the BOT is somewhat misleading because service trade is not included; it may be opposite in sign on net, and it may actually be fairly large as well.

Table 6.1 summarizes the Current Account and its components for the United States for the 1996–1999 period. As illustrated, the U.S. goods trade balance has consistently been negative, but has been partially offset by the continuing surplus in services trade.

TABLE 6.1		1996	1997	1998	1999
The United States Current Account, 1996–1999 (billions of U.S. dollars)	Goods exports	614	682	672	687
	Goods imports	−803	−876	−917	−1030
	Goods trade balance (BOT)	−189	−195	−245	−343
	Services trade credits	238	255	261	270
	Services trade debits	−151	−167	−183	−191
	Services trade balance	87	89	78	78
	Income receipts	224	257	258	276
	Income payments	−205	−251	−265	−295
	Income balance	19	6	−6	−18
	Current transfers, credits	9	8	9	9
	Current transfers, debits	−49	−49	−53	−57
	Net transfers	−40	−41	−44	−48
	Current Account Balance	**−123**	**−141**	**−217**	**−331**

Source: Derived from International Monetary Fund's *Balance of Payments Statistics Yearbook 2000.*

Goods Trade   Figure 6.1 places the Current Account values of Table 6.1 in perspective over time by dividing the Current Account into its two major components: (1) goods trade and (2) services trade and **investment income.** The first and most striking message is the magnitude of the goods trade deficit in the 1990s (a continuation of a position created in the early 1980s). The balance on services and income,

FIGURE 6.1   U.S. Trade Balance & Balance on Services & Income, 1985–1999 (billions of U.S. dollars)

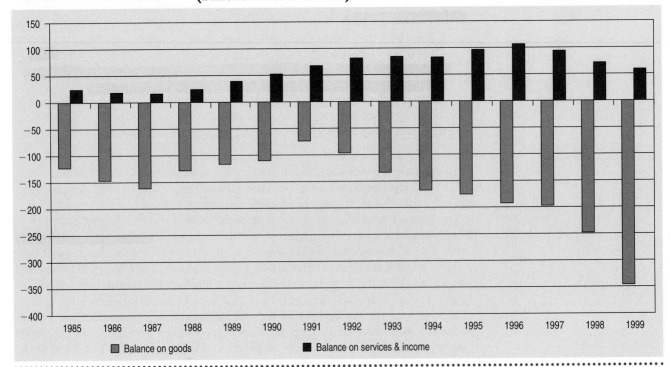

GLOBAL PERSPECTIVE 6.1

U.S. Exports to Asia: How Important are They?

The Asian economic crisis, which began in the summer of 1997, has had significant repercussions for all nations, regardless of whether they are within the region itself or not. For example, the United States exports significant amounts of goods to many of the countries in the Asian Pacific region. According to the United States International Trade Administration, the 1995 U.S. trade balance, export sales, and export rank for affected Asian countries was the following.

Country	1995 U.S. Bilateral Trade Balance	U.S. Exports to Each Country in 1995	Export Rank
Japan	(59,280)	583,865	2
Korea	1,230	25,413	5
Taiwan	(9,680)	19,295	7
Singapore	(3,246)	15,318	9
Hong Kong	3,926	14,220	11
China	(33,807)	11,748	13
Malaysia	(8,666)	8,818	17
Thailand	(4,949)	6,402	18
Philippines	(1,712)	5,294	23
Indonesia	(4,081)	3,356	29

Source: Data abstracted from United States Trade Representative. http://www.ustr.gov/reports/hte/1996/appendix.htm (January 1998).

although not large in comparison to net goods trade, has generally run a surplus over the past two decades.

The deficits in the BOT of the past decade have been an area of considerable concern for the United States. Merchandise trade is the original core of international trade. It has three major components: manufactured goods, agriculture, and fuels. The manufacturing of goods was the basis of the industrial revolution, and the focus of the theory of international trade described in the previous chapter. The U.S. goods trade deficit of the 1980s and 1990s was mainly caused by a decline in traditional manufacturing industries that have over history employed many of America's workers. Declines in the net trade balance in areas such as steel, automobiles, automotive parts, textiles, shoe manufacturing, and others caused massive economic and social disruption. The problems of dealing with these shifting trade balances will be discussed in detail in a later chapter.

The most encouraging news for U.S. manufacturing trade is the growth of exports in recent years. A number of factors contributed to the growth of U.S. exports, such as the weaker dollar (which made U.S.-manufactured goods cheaper in terms of the currencies of other countries), more rapid economic growth in Europe, and a substantial increase in agricultural exports. Understanding merchandise import and export performance is much like understanding the market for any single product. The demand factors that drive both imports and exports are income, the economic growth rate of the buyer, and price (the price of the product in the eyes of the consumer after passing through an exchange rate). For example, U.S. merchandise imports reflect the income level and growth of American consumers and industry. As income rises, so does the demand for imports.

Exports follow the same principles but in the reversed position. U.S. merchandise exports depend not on the incomes of U.S. residents, but on the incomes of the buyers of U.S. products in all other countries around the world. When these economies are growing, the demand for U.S. products will also rise. However, the recent economic crises in Asia now raise questions regarding U.S. export growth in the immediate future. Global Perspective 6.1 illustrates how significant Asia is to U.S. export growth.

The service component of the U.S. Current Account is one of mystery to many. As illustrated in both Table 6.1 and Figure 6.1, the U.S. has consistently achieved a surplus in services trade income. The major categories of services include travel and passenger fares, transportation services, expenditures by U.S. students abroad and foreign students pursuing studies in the United States, telecommunications services, and financial services.

The Capital and Financial Account

The *Capital and Financial Account* of the balance of payments measures all international economic transactions of financial assets. It is divided into two major components, the *Capital Account* and the *Financial Account*.

The Capital Account. The Capital Account is made up of transfers of financial assets and the acquisition and disposal of nonproduced/nonfinancial assets. The magnitude of capital transactions covered is of relatively minor amount, and will be included in principle in all of the following discussions of the financial account.

The Financial Account. The financial account consists of three components: *direct investment, portfolio investment,* and *other asset investment.* Financial assets can be classified in a number of different ways including the length of the life of the asset (its maturity) and by the nature of the ownership (public or private). The Financial Account, however, uses a third way. It is classified by the degree of control over the assets or operations the claim represents: *portfolio investment,* where the investor has no control, or *direct investment,* where the investor exerts some explicit degree of control over the assets. (The contents of the Financial Account are for all intents and purposes the same as those of the Capital Account under the IMF's BOP accounting framework used prior to 1996.)

Table 6.2 shows the major subcategories of the U.S. capital account balance from 1996–1999, *direct investment, portfolio investment,* and *other long-term and short-term capital.*

1. Direct Investment: This is the net balance of capital dispersed out of and into the United States for the purpose of exerting control over assets. For example, if

TABLE 6.2 **The United States Financial Account and Components, 1996–1999 (billions of U.S. dollars)**		1996	1997	1998	1999
	Direct Investment				
	Direct investment abroad	−92	−105	−146	−151
	Direct investment in the U.S.	87	106	186	276
	Net direct investment	−5	1	40	125
	Portfolio Investment				
	Assets, net	−150	−119	−136	−129
	Liabilities, net	368	386	269	342
	Net portfolio investment	218	267	133	214
	Other Investment				
	Other investment assets	−179	−264	−47	−159
	Other investment liabilities	117	265	27	136
	Net other investment	−61	1	−20	−24
	Net Financial Account Balance	151	269	154	315

Source: Derived from International Monetary Fund's *Balance of Payments Statistics Yearbook 2000.*

a U.S. firm either builds a new automotive parts facility in another country or actually purchases a company in another country, this would fall under *direct investment* in the U.S. balance of payments accounts. When the capital flows out of the U.S., it enters the balance of payments as a negative cash flow. If, however, foreign firms purchase firms in the U.S. (for example, Sony of Japan purchased Columbia Pictures in 1989) it is a capital inflow and enters the balance of payments positively. Whenever 10 percent or more of the voting shares in a U.S. company is held by foreign investors, the company is classified as the U.S. affiliate of a foreign company, and a *foreign direct investment.* Similarly, if U.S. investors hold 10 percent or more of the control in a company outside the United States, that company is considered the foreign affiliate of a U.S. company.

2. Portfolio Investment: This is net balance of capital that flows in and out of the United States, but does not reach the 10 percent ownership threshold of direct investment. If a U.S. resident purchases shares in a Japanese firm, but does not attain the 10 percent threshold, it is considered a *portfolio investment* (and in this case an outflow of capital). The purchase or sale of debt securities (like U.S. Treasury bills) across borders is also classified as *portfolio investment* because debt securities by definition do not provide the buyer with ownership or control.

3. Other Investment Assets/Liabilities: This final category consists of various short-term and long-term trade credits, cross-border loans from all types of financial institutions, currency deposits and bank deposits, and other accounts receivable and payable related to cross-border trade.

Direct Investment   Figure 6.2 shows how the major subaccounts of the U.S. capital account, *net direct investment, portfolio investment,* and *other investment* have changed since 1985.

FIGURE 6.2   **The United States Financial Account, 1985–1999 (billions of U.S. dollars)**

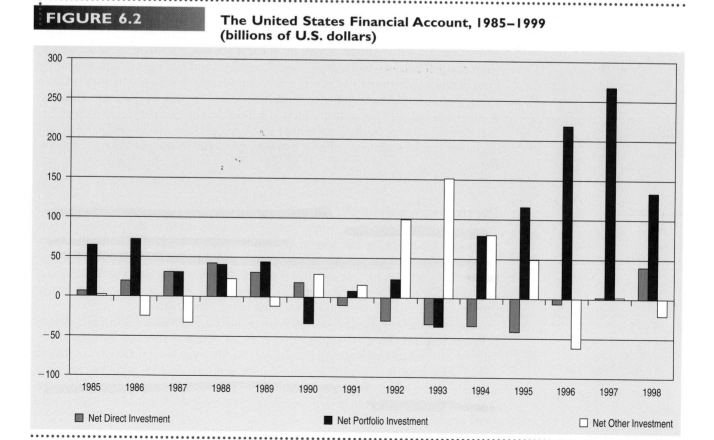

■ Net Direct Investment   ■ Net Portfolio Investment   □ Net Other Investment

The boom in foreign investment into the United States, or foreign resident purchases of assets in the U.S., during the 1980s was extremely controversial. The source of concern over foreign investment in any country, including the United States, focuses on two topics—**control** and **profit**. Most countries possess restrictions on what foreigners may own in their country. This is based on the premise that domestic land, assets, and industry in general should be held by residents of the country. For example, up until 1990 it was not possible for a foreign firm to own more than 20 percent of any company in Finland. This rule is the norm, rather than the exception. The United States has traditionally had few restrictions on what foreign residents or firms can own or control in the U.S.; most restrictions that remain today are related to national security concerns. As opposed to many of the traditional debates over whether international trade should be free or not, there is not the same consensus that international investment should necessarily be free. This is a question that is still very much a domestic political concern first, and an international economic issue second.

The second major source of concern over foreign direct investment is who receives the profits from the enterprise. Foreign companies owning firms in the United States will ultimately profit from the activities of the firms, or put another way, from the efforts of American workers. In spite of evidence that foreign firms in the United States reinvest most of the profits in the United States (in fact at a higher rate than domestic firms), the debate has continued on possible profit drains. Regardless of the actual choices made, workers of any nation feel the profits of their work should remain in the hands of their own citizens. Once again, this is in many ways a political and emotional concern rather than an economic one.

The choice of words used to describe foreign investment can also influence public opinion. If these massive capital inflows are described as "capital investments from all over the world showing their faith in the future of American industry," the net capital surplus is represented as decidedly positive. If, however, the net capital surplus is described as resulting in "the United States as the world's largest debtor nation," the negative connotation is obvious. Both are essentially spins on the economic principles at work. Capital, whether short-term or long-term, flows to where it believes it can earn the greatest return for the level of risk. Although in an accounting sense that is "international debt," when the majority of the capital inflow is in the form of direct investment and a long-term commitment to jobs, production, services, technological, and other competitive investments, the impact on the competitiveness of American industry (an industry located within the United States) is increased. The "net debtor" label is misleading in that it inappropriately invites comparison with large debt crisis conditions suffered by many countries in the past, like Mexico and Brazil.

Portfolio Investment   Portfolio investment is capital invested in activities that are purely profit-motivated (return), rather than ones made in the prospect of controlling or managing the investment. Investments that are purchases of debt securities, bonds, interest-bearing bank accounts, and the like are only intended to earn a return. They provide no vote or control over the party issuing the debt. Purchases of debt issued by the U.S. government (U.S. Treasury bills, notes, and bonds) by foreign investors constitute net portfolio investment in the United States.

As illustrated in Figure 6.2, portfolio investment has shown a much more volatile behavior than net direct investment over the past decade. Many U.S. debt securities, such as U.S. Treasury securities and corporate bonds, were in high demand in the late 1980s, while surging emerging markets in both debt and equities caused a reversal in direction in the 1990s. The motivating forces for portfolio investment flows are always the same, *return* and *risk*. This theoretical fact, however, does not make them any the more predictable.

FIGURE 6.3

Current and Financial/Capital Account Balances for Japan, the United States, and Germany, 1992–1999 (billions of U.S. dollars)

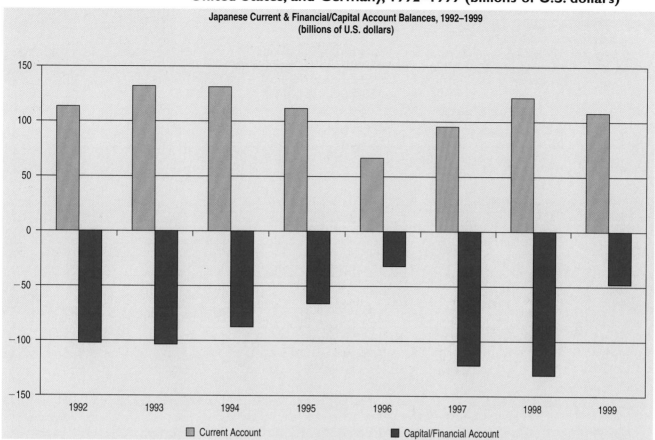

Japanese Current & Financial/Capital Account Balances, 1992–1999 (billions of U.S. dollars)

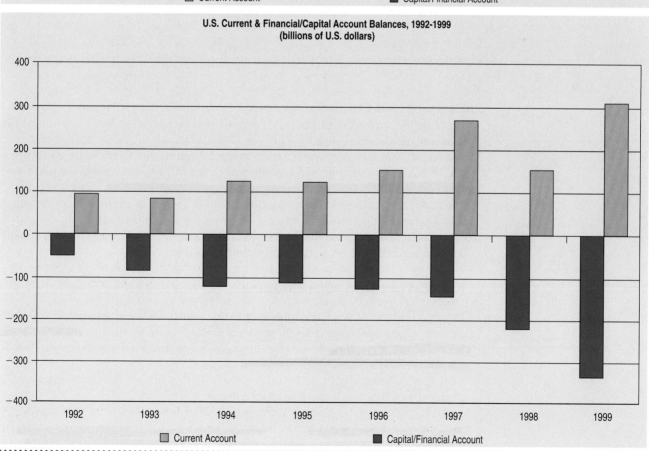

U.S. Current & Financial/Capital Account Balances, 1992–1999 (billions of U.S. dollars)

(Continued)

FIGURE 6.3   Continued

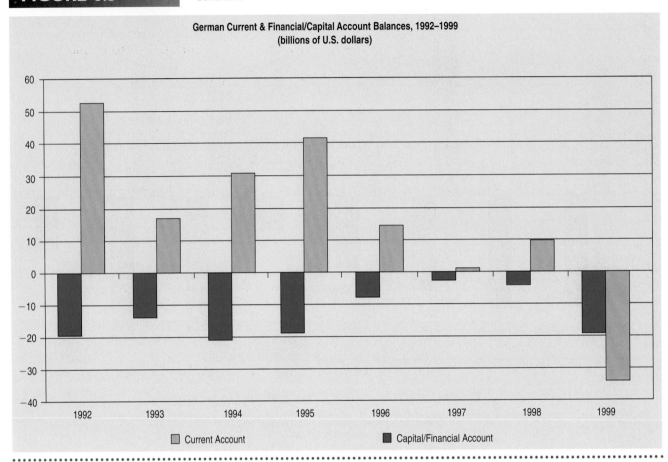

German Current & Financial/Capital Account Balances, 1992–1999
(billions of U.S. dollars)

☐ Current Account   ■ Capital/Financial Account

Current and Financial Account Balance Relationships   Figure 6.3 illustrates the current and financial account balances for Germany, Japan, and the United States over recent years. They are all presented on the same scale so that relative magnitudes are comparable across the three countries. What the figure shows is one of the basic economic and accounting relationships of the balance of payments: *the inverse relationship between the Current and Financial accounts.* This inverse relationship is not accidental. The methodology of the balance of payments, double-entry bookkeeping, requires that the current and financial accounts be offsetting. Countries experiencing large current account deficits "finance" these purchases through equally large surpluses in the financial account and vice versa.

Net Errors and Omissions

As noted before, because Current Account and Financial Account entries are collected and recorded separately, errors or statistical discrepancies will occur. The **net errors and omissions account** (this is the title used by the International Monetary Fund) makes sure that the BOP actually balances.

Official Reserves Account

The **official reserves account** is the total currency and metallic reserves held by official monetary authorities within the country. These reserves are normally com-

posed of the major currencies used in international trade and financial transactions (so-called "hard currencies" like the U.S. dollar, German mark, and Japanese yen) and gold.

The significance of official reserves depends generally on whether the country is operating under a **fixed exchange rate** regime or a **floating exchange rate** system. If a country's currency is fixed, this means that the government of the country officially declares that the currency is convertible into a fixed amount of some other currency. For example, for many years the South Korean won was fixed to the U.S. dollar at 484 won equal to 1 U.S. dollar. It is the government's responsibility to maintain this fixed rate (also called *parity rate*). If for some reason there is an excess supply of Korean won on the currency market, to prevent the value of the won from falling, the South Korean government must support the won's value by purchasing won on the open market (by spending its hard currency reserves, its *official reserves*) until the excess supply is eliminated. Under a floating rate system, the government possesses no such responsibility and the role of official reserves is diminished.

The Balance of Payments in Total

Table 6.3 provides the official balance of payments for the United States as presented by the International Monetary Fund (IMF), the multinational organization that collects these statistics for over 160 different countries around the globe. Now that the individual accounts and the relationships among the accounts have been discussed, Table 6.3 gives a comprehensive overview of how the individual accounts are combined to create some of the most useful summary measures for multinational business managers.

The current account (line A in Table 6.3), the capital account (line B), and the financial account (line C) combine to form the *basic balance (Total, Groups A Through C)*. This is one of the most frequently used summary measures of the BOP. It is used to describe the international economic activity of the nation as determined by market forces, not by government decisions (such as currency market intervention). The U.S. *basic balance* totaled a deficit of $20.3 billion in 1999. A second frequently used summary measure, the overall balance, also called the official settlements balance (*Total of Groups A Through D* in Table 6.3), was at a deficit of $8.7 billion in 1999.

The meaning of the balance of payments has changed over the past 30 years. As long as most of the major industrial countries were still operating under fixed exchange rates, the interpretation of the BOP was relatively straightforward. A surplus in the BOP implied that the demand for the country's currency exceeded the supply, and that the government should then allow the currency value to increase *(revalue)* or to intervene and accumulate additional foreign currency reserves in the Official Reserves Account. This would occur as the government sold its own currency in exchange for other currencies, thus building up its stores of hard currencies. A deficit in the BOP implied an excess supply of the country's currency on world markets, and the government would then either *devalue* the currency or expend its official reserves to support its value. But the transition to floating exchange rate regimes in the 1970s (described in the following chapter) changed the focus from the total BOP to its various subaccounts like the Current and Financial Account balances. These are the indicators of economic activities and currency repercussions to come. The recent crises in Mexico (1994) and Asia (1997) highlight the continuing changes in the role of the balance of payments. Global Perspective 6.2 describes India's recent initiative to solve a worsening balance of trade by attracting the offshore capital held by its own residents.

TABLE 6.3	**The United States Balance of Payments, Analytic Presentation, 1992–1999 (billions of U.S. dollars)**							
	1992	1993	1994	1995	1996	1997	1998	1999
A. Current Account	**−47.70**	**−82.69**	**−118.61**	**−109.46**	**−123.30**	**−140.55**	**−217.13**	**−331.48**
Goods: exports fob	442.13	458.73	504.45	577.69	613.96	681.65	672.29	686.66
Goods: imports fob	−536.45	−589.44	−668.59	−749.57	−803.33	−876.37	−917.19	−1,029.92
Balance on Goods	−94.32	−130.71	−164.14	−171.88	−189.37	−194.72	−244.90	−343.26
Services: credit	175.14	184.04	198.98	217.39	238.12	255.29	260.69	269.58
Service: debit	−116.47	−122.28	−131.88	−141.45	−150.85	−166.51	−182.68	−191.30
Balance on Goods and Services	−35.65	−68.95	−97.04	−95.94	−102.10	−105.94	−166.89	−264.98
Income: credit	132.05	134.16	165.44	211.50	223.81	257.35	258.45	276.17
Income: debit	−109.09	−110.26	−148.75	−190.96	−204.93	−251.16	−264.66	−294.65
Balance on Goods, Services, and Income	−12.69	−45.05	−80.35	−75.40	−83.22	−99.75	−173.10	−283.46
Current transfers: credit	7.56	5.93	6.48	7.68	8.89	8.47	9.33	9.41
Current transfers: debit	−42.57	−43.57	−44.74	−41.74	−48.97	−49.27	−53.36	−57.43
B. Capital Account	**0.61**	**−0.09**	**−0.46**	**0.37**	**0.69**	**0.35**	**0.64**	**−3.50**
Capital account: credit	0.61	0.37	0.31	0.67	0.69	0.35	0.64	0.49
Capital account: debit	0.00	−0.46	−0.77	−0.30	0.00	0.00	0.00	−3.99
Total, Groups A plus B	**−47.09**	**−82.78**	**−119.07**	**−109.09**	**−122.61**	**−140.20**	**−216.49**	**−334.98**
C. Financial Account	**92.35**	**82.87**	**124.60**	**123.04**	**151.11**	**269.04**	**153.59**	**314.64**
Direct investment	−28.44	−32.59	−34.05	−40.97	−5.38	1.02	40.27	124.64
Direct investment abroad	−48.26	−83.95	−80.17	−98.75	−91.88	−105.02	−146.05	−150.90
Direct investment in the United States	19.82	51.36	46.12	57.78	86.50	106.04	186.32	275.54
Portfolio investment assets	−49.17	−146.26	−60.31	−122.51	−149.83	−118.98	−136.00	−128.59
Equity securities	−32.40	−63.38	−48.10	−65.41	−82.85	−57.58	−101.24	−114.40
Debt securities	−16.77	−82.88	−12.21	−57.10	−66.98	−61.40	−34.76	−14.19
Portfolio investment liabilities	71.98	110.98	139.40	237.47	367.72	385.60	269.33	342.19
Equity securities	−5.61	20.93	0.89	16.56	11.13	67.85	41.95	98.07
Debt securities	77.59	90.05	138.51	220.91	356.59	317.75	227.38	244.12
Other investment assets	19.12	31.04	−40.91	−121.38	−178.88	−263.94	−46.60	−159.45
Monetary authorities	0.00	0.00	0.00	0.00	0.00	0.00	0.00	0.00
General government	−1.67	−0.35	−0.37	−0.98	−0.99	0.07	−0.42	2.75
Banks	21.18	30.62	−4.20	−75.11	−91.56	−141.12	−35.57	−69.86
Other sectors	−0.39	0.77	−36.34	−45.29	−86.33	−122.89	−10.61	−92.34
Other investment liabilities	78.86	119.70	120.47	170.43	117.48	265.34	26.59	135.85
Monetary authorities	30.31	68.00	9.60	46.72	56.88	−18.85	6.88	24.71
General government	2.82	1.31	2.77	0.9	0.52	−2.86	−3.48	−1.37
Banks	32.79	39.90	108.00	64.18	22.18	171.31	30.27	80.10
Other sectors	12.94	10.49	0.10	58.63	37.90	115.74	−7.08	32.41
Total, Groups A Through C	**45.26**	**0.09**	**5.53**	**13.95**	**28.50**	**128.84**	**−62.90**	**−20.34**
D. Net Errors and Omissions	**−49.19**	**1.28**	**−10.89**	**−4.22**	**−35.17**	**−127.83**	**69.65**	**11.63**
Total, Groups A Through D	**−3.93**	**1.37**	**−5.36**	**9.73**	**−6.67**	**1.01**	**6.75**	**−8.71**
E. Reserves and Related Items	**3.93**	**−1.38**	**5.35**	**−9.75**	**6.67**	**−1.01**	**−6.73**	**8.73**

Note: Totals may not match original source due to rounding.

Source: International Monetary Found, *Balance of Payments Statistics Yearbook 2000*, p. 917.

GLOBAL PERSPECTIVE 6.2

India Tries to Borrow Its Way Out of Trouble

India has hit on a not-so-novel idea to shield an economy made vulnerable by high international oil prices. The government has gotten State Bank of India, the country's largest bank, to sell five-year foreign currency deposits to expatriate Indians to help tackle a worsening balance of payments situation. SBI, whose largest owner is the Indian central bank, is expected to collect between $2 billion and $4 billion from the sale of India Millennium Deposits (IMD).

India's oil import bill is expected to double to about $18 billion this year. A widening trade deficit and a sell-off by foreign portfolio investors put the balance of payments in the red by about $1 billion in the quarter ended June, as compared with a surplus of $3.32 billion in the previous quarter. The rupee has lost around 6 percent of its value against the dollar since April.

Source: Abstracted from "India Tries to Borrow Its Way Out of Trouble," by Kala Rao, *Euromoney,* London, November 2000.

The Balance of Payments and Economic Crises

The sum of cross-border international economic activity—the balance of payments—can be used by international managers to forecast economic conditions and, in some cases, the likelihood of economic crises. The mechanics of international economic crisis often follow a similar path of development:

1. A country that experiences rapidly expanding current account deficits will simultaneously build financial account surpluses (the inverse relationship noted previously in this chapter).
2. The capital that flows into a country, giving rise to the financial account surplus, acts as the "financing" for the growing merchandise/services deficits—the constituent components of the current account deficit.
3. Some event, whether it be a report, a speech, an action by a government or business inside or outside the country, raises the question of the country's economic stability. Investors of many kinds, portfolio and direct investors in the country, fearing economic problems in the near future, withdraw capital from the country rapidly to avoid any exposure to this risk. This is prudent for the individual, but catastrophic for the whole if all individuals move similarly.
4. The rapid withdrawal of capital from the country, so-called "capital flight," results in the loss of the financial account surplus, creating a severe deficit in the country's overall balance of payments. This is typically accompanied by rapid currency depreciation (if a floating-rate currency) or currency devaluation (if a fixed-rate currency).

International debt and economic crises have occurred for as long as there have been international trade and commerce. And they will occur again. Each crisis has its own unique characteristics, but all follow the economic fundamentals described above (the one additional factor which differentiates many of the crises is whether inflation is a component). The recent Asian economic crisis was a devastating reminder of the tenuousness of international economic relationships.

The Asian Crisis

The roots of the Asian currency crisis extended from a fundamental change in the economics of the region—the transition of many Asian nations from net exporters to net importers. Starting as early as 1990 in Thailand, the rapidly expanding economies of the Far East began importing more than they exported, requiring major net capital inflows to support their currencies. As long as the capital continued to flow in—for manufacturing plants, dam projects, infrastructure development, and even real estate speculation—the pegged exchange rates of the region could be maintained. When the investment capital inflows stopped, however, crisis was inevitable.

The most visible roots of the crisis were the excesses in capital flows into Thailand in 1996 and early 1997. With rapid economic growth and rising profits forming the backdrop, Thai firms, banks, and finance companies had ready access to capital on the international markets, finding cheap U.S. dollar loans offshore. Thai banks continued to raise capital internationally, extending credit to a variety of domestic investments and enterprises beyond the level that the Thai economy could support. Capital flows into the Thai market hit record rates, pouring into investments of all kinds, including manufacturing, real estate, and even equity market margin-lending. As the investment "bubble" expanded, some participants raised questions about the economy's ability to repay the rising debt. The baht came under sudden and severe pressure.

Currency Collapse   The Thai government and central bank intervened in the foreign exchange markets directly (using up precious hard currency reserves) and indirectly (by raising interest rates to attempt to stop the continual out-flow). The Thai investment markets ground to a halt, causing massive currency losses and bank failures. On July 2, 1997, the Thai central bank, which had been expending massive amounts of its limited foreign exchange reserves to defend the baht's value, finally allowed the baht to float (or sink in this case). The baht fell 17 percent against the U.S. dollar and over 12 percent against the Japanese yen in a matter of hours. By November, the baht had fallen from Baht25/US$ to Baht40/US$, a fall of about 38 percent. As illustrated in Table 6.4, Thailand was not alone in creating massive current account deficits in the period leading up to 1997. In fact, with the rather special exceptions of China and Singapore, all of East Asia was in current account deficit beginning in 1994.

Within days, a number of neighboring Asian nations, some with and some without characteristics similar to Thailand, came under speculative attack by currency traders and capital markets. The Philippine peso, the Malaysian ringgit, and the Indonesian rupiah all fell within months, as shown in Figure 6.4. In late October, Taiwan caught the markets off balance with a surprise competitive devaluation of 15 percent. The Taiwanese devaluation seemed only to renew the momentum of the crisis. Although the Hong Kong dollar survived (at great expense to the central bank's foreign exchange reserves), the Korean won was not so lucky. In November the historically stable Korean won also fell victim, falling from Won900/US$ to more than Won1100/US$. By the end of November the Korean government was in the process of negotiating a US$50 billion bailout of its financial sector with the International Monetary Fund (IMF). The only currency which had not fallen besides the Hong Kong dollar was the Chinese renminbi, which was not freely convertible. Although the renminbi had not been devalued, there was rising speculation that the Chinese government would devalue it for competitive reasons. Figure 6.4 shows the change in exchange rates for four of these Asian economies.

Causal Complexities   The Asian economic crisis—for the crisis was more than just a currency collapse—had many roots besides the traditional balance of payments difficulties. The causes are different in each country, yet there are specific underlying similarities that allow comparison: corporate socialism, corporate governance, and banking stability and management.

Corporate Socialism   Although Western markets have long known the cold indifference of the free market, the countries of post–World War II Asia have largely known only the good. Because of the influence of government and politics in the business arena, even in the event of failure, government would not allow firms to fail, workers

TABLE 6.4   Current Account Balances of East Asian Countries, 1988–1999 (millions of U.S. dollars)

Country	1988	1989	1990	1991	1992	1993	1994	1995	1996	1997	1998	1999
Deficit Countries												
Indonesia	−1,397	−1,108	−2,988	−4,260	−2,780	−2,106	−2,792	−6,431	−7,663	−4,889	4,096	5,785
Korea	14,538	5,387	−1,745	−8,291	−3,944	990	−3,867	−8,507	−23,006	−8,167	40,365	24,477
Malaysia	1,867	315	−870	−4,183	−2,167	−2,991	−4,520	−8,644	−4,462	−5,935	9,529	12,606
Philippines	−390	−1,456	−2,695	−1,034	−1,000	−3,016	−2,950	−1,980	−3,953	−4,351	1,546	7,910
Thailand	−1,654	−2,498	−7,281	−7,571	−6,303	−6,364	−8,085	−13,554	−14,691	−3,021	14,243	12,428
Subtotal	**12,964**	**640**	**−15,579**	**−25,339**	**−16,194**	**−13,487**	**−22,214**	**−39,116**	**−53,775**	**−26,363**	**69,779**	**63,206**
Surplus Countries												
China	−3,802	−4,317	11,997	13,272	6,401	−11,609	6,908	1,618	7,243	36,963	31,472	15,667
Singapore	1,882	2,923	3,097	4,884	5,915	4,211	11,400	14,436	13,898	16,912	21,025	21,254
Subtotal	**−1,920**	**−1,394**	**15,094**	**18,156**	**12,316**	**7,398**	**18,308**	**16,054**	**21,141**	**53,875**	**52,497**	**36,921**

Asian Crisis

"Deficit Countries" are those with current account balances which were negative for the 1994 to 1997 period, leading up to the Asian Crisis.

"Surplus Countries" are those with current account balances which were positive for the 1994 to 1997 period. Hong Kong and Taiwan are not listed, as they are not individually reported by the IMF.

The Asian Crisis actually began with the devaluation of the Thai baht on July 1, 1997. However, given annual balance of payments statistics, it is shown here between the 1997 and 1998 calendar years.

Source: Data abstracted from the *Balance of Payments Statistics Yearbook 2000.* International Monetary Fund.

Comparative Daily Exchange Rates: Relative to U.S. Dollar Index

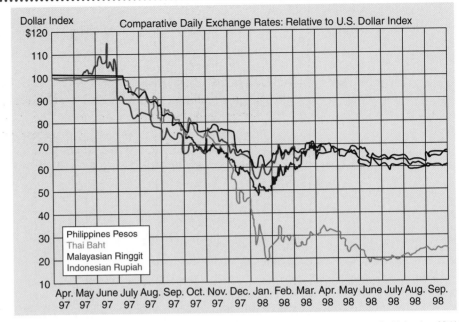

Source: Pacific Exchange Rate Service, **http://pacific.commerce.ubc.ca/xr** © 1999 by Prof. Werner Antweiler, University of British Columbia, Vancouver B.C., Canada. Time period shown in diagram: April 1, 1997 through September 30, 1998.

to lose their jobs, or banks to close. When the problems reached the size seen in 1997, the business liability exceeded the capacities of governments to bail business out. Practices that had persisted for decades without challenge, such as lifetime employment, were now no longer sustainable. The result was a painful lesson in the harshness of the marketplace.

Corporate Governance   An expression largely unused until the 1990s, corporate governance refers to the complex process of how a firm is managed and operated, who it is accountable to, and how it reacts to changing business conditions. There is little doubt that many firms operating within the Far Eastern business environments were often largely controlled by either families or groups related to the governing party or body of the country. The interests of stockholders and creditors were often secondary at best to the primary motivations of corporate management. Without focusing on "the bottom line," the bottom line deteriorated.

Banking Liquidity and Management   Banking is one of those sectors which has definitely fallen out of fashion in the past two decades. Bank regulatory structures and markets have been deregulated nearly without exception around the globe. The central role played by banks in the conduct of business, however, was largely ignored and underestimated. As firms across Asia collapsed, as government coffers were emptied, as speculative investments made by the banks themselves failed, banks closed. Without banks, the "plumbing" of business conduct was shut down. Firms could not obtain the necessary working capital financing they needed to manufacture their products or provide their services. This pivotal role of banking liquidity was the focus of the International Monetary Fund's bail-out efforts.

The Asian economic crisis had global impact. What started as a currency crisis quickly became a regionwide recession (or depression, depending on definitions).[3] The slowed economies of the region quickly caused major reductions in world demand for many products, commodities especially. World oil markets, copper markets, and agricultural products all saw severe price falls as demand fell. These price falls were immediately noticeable in declining earnings and growth prospects for other emerging economies.

The post-1997 period has been one of dramatic reversal for the countries of East Asia. As Table 6.4 illustrates, beginning in 1998, every nation within East Asia listed has run a current account surplus as a result of massive recession (imports fell voluntarily, as well as being restricted by governments), significant domestic currency devaluation (resulting in significantly lower purchasing power, hence the countries could no longer afford to purchase imports), and rising exports (as currency devaluation made their merchandise relatively cheaper for countries in other parts of the world to purchase). Unfortunately, the adjustment period has been one of massive unemployment, social disruption, and economic reconstruction with high human cost.

Summary

The balance of payments is the summary statement of all international transactions between one country and all other countries. The balance of payments is a flow statement, summarizing all the international transactions that occur across the geographic boundaries of the nation over a period of time, typically a year. Because of its use of double-entry bookkeeping, the BOP must always balance in theory, though in practice there are substantial imbalances as a result of statistical errors and misreporting of current account and capital account flows.

The two major subaccounts of the balance of payments, the current account and the capital account, summarize the current trade and international capital flows of the country.

Due to the double-entry bookkeeping method of accounting, the current account and capital account are always inverse on balance, one in surplus while the other experiences deficit. Although most nations strive for current account surpluses, it is not clear that a balance on current or capital account, or a surplus on current account, is either sustainable or desirable. The monitoring of the various subaccounts of a country's balance of payments activity is helpful to decision makers and policymakers at all levels of government and industry in detecting the underlying trends and movements of fundamental economic forces driving a country's international economic activity.

Key Terms and Concepts

balance of payments
current account
capital account
double-entry bookkeeping
goods trade
services trade

investment income
current transfers
direct investment account
portfolio investment
  account

control
profit
net errors and omissions
  account

official reserves account
fixed exchange rate
floating exchange rate

Questions for Discussion

1. Why must a country's balance of payments always be balanced in theory?
2. What is the difference between the merchandise trade balance (BOT) and the current account balance?
3. What is service trade?
4. Why is foreign direct investment so much more controversial than foreign portfolio investment? How did this relate to Mexico in the 1990s?
5. Should the fact that the United States may be the world's largest net debtor nation be a source of concern for government policymakers? Is the United States like Finland?

6. While the United States "suffered" a current account deficit and a capital account surplus in the 1980s, what were the respective balances of Japan doing?
7. What does it mean for the United States to be one of the world's largest indebted countries?
8. How do exchange rate changes alter trade so that the trade balance actually improves when the domestic currency depreciates?
9. How have trade balances in Asia contributed to the cause of the current Asian crisis?

Internet Exercises

1. The IMF, World Bank, and United Nations are only a few of the major world organizations that track, report, and aid international economic and financial development. Using these web sites and others that may be linked to them, briefly summarize the economic outlook for the developed and emerging nations of the world. For example, the full text of chapter 1 of the *World Economic Outlook* published annually by the World Bank is available through the IMF's web page.

International Monetary Fund	http://www.imf.org/
United Nations	http://www.unsystem.org/
The World Bank Group	http://www.worldbank.org/
Europa (EU) Homepage	http://europa.eu.int/
Bank for International Settlements	http://www.bis.org/

2. Current economic and financial statistics and commentaries are available via the IMF's web page under "What's New," "Fund Rates," and the "IMF Committee on Balance of Payments Statistics." For an in-depth examination of the IMF's ongoing initiative on the validity of these statistics, termed metadata, visit the IMF's Dissemination Standards Bulletin Board listed below.

International Monetary Fund	http://www.imf.org/
IMF's Dissemination Standards Bulletin Board	http://dsbb.imf.org/

3. Visit Moody's sovereign ceilings and foreign currency ratings service site on the web to evaluate what progress is being made in the nations of the Far East on recovering their perceived creditworthiness.

Moody's Sovereign Ceilings	http://www.moodys.com/repldata/ratings/ratsov.htm

Recommended Readings

Agenor, Pierre-Richard, Jagdeep S. Bhandari, and Robert P. Flood. Speculative Attacks and Models of Balance of Payments Crises. *International Monetary Fund Staff Papers*, 39, 2 (June 1992) 357–394.

Bergsten, C. Fred, ed. *International Adjustment and Financing: The Lessons of 1985–1991*. Washington, DC: Institute for International Economics, 1991.

Eiteman, David K., Arthur I. Stonehill, and Michael H. Moffett. *Multinational Business Finance*. 9th ed. Reading, MA: Addison Wesley Longman, 2001.

Evans, John S. *International Finance: A Markets Approach*. New York: Dryden Press, 1992.

Giddy, Ian H. *Global Financial Markets*. Lexington, MA: Elsevier, 1994.

Grabbe, J. Orlin. *International Financial Markets*. 2d ed. New York: Elsevier, 1991.

Handbook of International Trade and Development Statistics. New York: United Nations, 1989.

Husted, Steven, and Michael Melvin. *International Economics*. 4th ed. Reading, MA: Addison Wesley Longman, 1997.

IMF Balance of Payments Yearbook. Washington, DC: International Monetary Fund, annually.

Root, Franklin R. *International Trade and Investment*. 6th ed. Chicago: South-Western Publishing, 1990.

Notes

1. The official terminology used throughout this chapter, unless otherwise noted, is that of the International Monetary Fund (IMF). Since the IMF is the primary source of similar statistics for balance of payments and economic performance worldwide, it is more general than other terminology forms, such as that employed by the U.S. Department of Commerce.

2. All balance of payment data used in this chapter is drawn from the International Monetary Fund's *Balance of Payments Statistics Yearbook*. This source is used because the IMF presents the balance of payments statistics for all member countries on the same basis and in the same format, allowing comparison across countries.

3. The magnitude of the economic devastation in Asia is still largely unappreciated by Westerners. At a recent conference sponsored by the Milken Institute in Los Angeles, a speaker noted that the preoccupation with the economic problems of Indonesia was incomprehensible since "the total gross domestic product of Indonesia is roughly the size of North Carolina." The following speaker provided a rebuttal, noting that the last time he checked "North Carolina did not have a population of 220 million people."

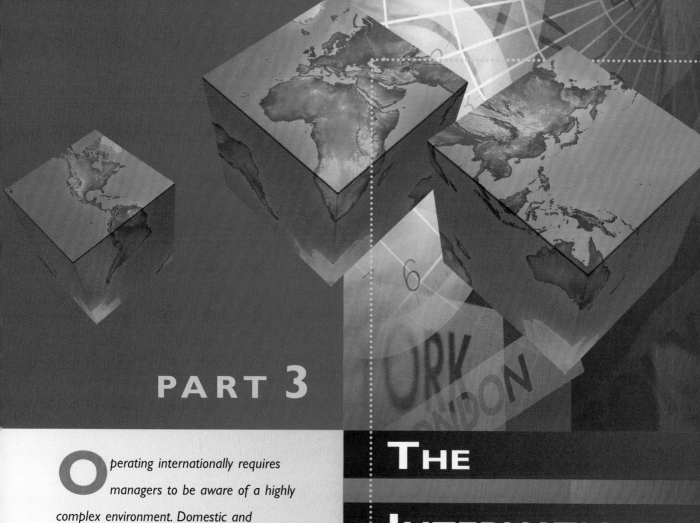

PART 3

Operating internationally requires managers to be aware of a highly complex environment. Domestic and international environmental factors and their interaction have to be recognized and understood. In addition, ongoing changes in these environments have to be appreciated.

Part 3 delineates the macroenvironmental factors and institutions affecting international business. It explains the workings of the international monetary system and financial markets and highlights the increasing trend toward economic integration around the world. This section concludes with a chapter on doing business in emerging markets. Particular focus rests on the new market orientation of nations whose economies used to be centrally planned, such as those of the former Soviet Union.

THE INTERNATIONAL BUSINESS ENVIRONMENT

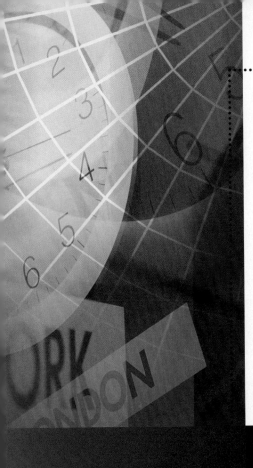

CHAPTER 7

International Financial Markets

LEARNING OBJECTIVES

- To understand how currencies are traded and quoted on world financial markets

- To examine the links between interest rates and exchange rates

- To understand the similarities and differences between domestic sources of capital and international sources of capital

- To examine how the needs of individual borrowers have changed the nature of the instruments traded on world financial markets in the past decade

- To understand how the debt crises of the 1980s and 1990s are linked to the international financial markets and exchange rates

ECUADOR BURIES SUCRE

QUITO, ECUADOR (Reuters)—Ecuadoreans waved goodbye to their national currency, the sucre, on Saturday, lamenting the loss of a national symbol but also optimistic the adoption of the U.S. dollar would usher in a new period of stability. While some held mock burials to protest the death of the 116-year old sucre, other Ecuadoreans praised the Andean country's dollarization as a way to bolster an economy on the verge of collapse last year.

"I think this is great. We finally have a stable currency," said Mercedes Gutierrez, one of the over a hundred people standing in line at a shopping mall to change their last sucres into dollars. "This will help the country grow." As of Sunday, the dollar will replace the sucre as Ecuador's main currency, capping the first phase of the shock move announced in January.

President Jamil Mahuad announced Ecuador's dollarization in January following the country's worst economic crisis in decades. The economy contracted 7.5 percent in 1999, inflation was Latin America's worst at over 60 percent and the sucre lost two-thirds of its value.

By scrapping the beleaguered sucre for a more stable greenback, Mahuad hoped inflation would stabilize and investment would flow back into the country—kick-starting the economy and creating jobs for the largely impoverished nation of 12.4 million people. Mahuad was eventually kicked out in a coup and replaced by his vice president.

So far, inflation has slowed after an initial jump in prices and the economy is expected to grow between 0.5 and 1 percent this year. But economists say dollarization is still a work in progress that must be backed up by a long list of reforms to guarantee a smooth flow of dollars into the country. Even other countries with similar monetary systems, like Argentina, which pegged its peso to the dollar in 1991, have had a tough time making the measure work.

Source: "Ecuador Buries Sucre, Bets on Dollar," by Carlos A. DeJuana, Reuters, September 9, 2000.

International financial markets serve as links between the financial markets of each individual country and as independent markets outside the jurisdiction of any one country. The market for currencies is the heart of this international financial market. International trade and investment are often denominated in a foreign currency, so the purchase of the currency precedes the purchase of goods, services, or assets.

This chapter provides a detailed guide to the structure and functions of the foreign currency markets, the international money markets, and the international securities markets. All firms striving to attain or preserve competitiveness will need to work with and within these international financial markets in the 2000s.

The Market for Currencies

The price of any one country's currency in terms of another country's currency is called a foreign currency exchange rate. For example, the exchange rate between the U.S. dollar (USD) and the German mark (deutschemark, or DEM) may be "1.5 marks per dollar," or simply abbreviated DEM 1.5000/USD. This is the same exchange rate as when stated USD 1.00 = DEM 1.50. Since most international business activities require at least one of the two parties to first purchase the country's currency before purchasing any good, service, or asset, a proper understanding of exchange rates and exchange rate markets is very important to the conduct of international business.

A word on symbols. As already noted, the letters USD and DEM are often used as the symbols for the U.S. dollar and the German mark. The field of international finance suffers, however, from a lack of agreement when it comes to currency abbreviations. This chapter will use the computer symbols used by the Telerate news service for the sake of consistency (although any other set would work just as well). As a practitioner of international finance, as with all fields, stay on your toes. Every market, every country, every firm, has its own set of symbols. For example, the symbol for the British pound sterling can be £ (the pound symbol), GBP (Great Britain pound), STG (sterling), or UKL (United Kingdom pound).

Exchange Rate Quotations and Terminology

The order in which the foreign exchange (FX) rate is stated is sometimes confusing to the uninitiated. For example, when the rate between the U.S. dollar and the German mark was stated above, a **direct quotation** on the German mark was used. This is simultaneously an **indirect quotation** on the U.S. dollar. The direct quote on any currency is the form when that currency is stated first; an indirect quotation refers to when the subject currency is stated second. Figure 7.1 illustrates both forms, direct and indirect quotations, for major world currencies for Friday, February 2, 2001.

Most of the quotations listed in Figure 7.1 are **spot rates.** A spot transaction is the exchange of currencies for immediate delivery. Although it is defined as immediate, in actual practice settlement actually occurs two business days following the agreed-upon exchange. The other time-related quotations listed in Figure 7.1 are the **forward rates.** Forward exchange rates are contracts that provide for two parties to exchange currencies on a future date at an agreed-upon exchange rate. Forwards are typically traded for the major volume currencies for maturities of 30, 90, 120, 180, and 360 days (from the present date). The forward, like the basic spot exchange, can be for any amount of currency. Forward contracts serve a variety of purposes, but their primary purpose is to allow a firm to lock in a future rate of exchange. This is a valuable tool in a world of continually changing exchange rates.

The quotations listed will also occasionally indicate if the rate is applicable to business trade (the commercial rate) or for financial asset purchases or sales (the financial rate). Countries that have government regulations regarding the exchange of their currency may post official rates, while the markets operating outside their jurisdiction will list a floating rate. In this case, any exchange of currency that is not under the control of its government is interpreted as a better indication of the currency's true market value.

Foreign exchange traders at banks can move millions of dollars, yen, or marks around the world with a few keystrokes on their networked computers. The deregulation of international capital flows contributes to faster, cheaper transactions in the currency markets.

Direct and Indirect Quotations

The Wall Street Journal quotations list the rates of exchange between major currencies, both in direct and indirect forms. The exchange rate for the German mark versus U.S. dollar, in the third column shown, is DEM 2.0900/USD. This is a direct quote

FIGURE 7.1

Exchange Rate and Cross Rate Tables

CURRENCY TRADING

EXCHANGE RATES

Friday; Febuary 2, 2001

The New York foreign exchange mid-range rates below apply to trading amoung banks in amounts of $1 million and more, as quoted at 4 p.m. Eastern time by Rueters and other sources. Retail transactions provide fewer units of foreign currency per dollar. Rates for the 12 Euro currency countries are derived from the latest dollar-euro rate using the exchange rates set 1/1/99.

COUNTRY	U.S. $ EQUIV. Fri	U.S. $ EQUIV. Thur	CURRENCY PER U.S. $ Fri	CURRENCY PER U.S. $ Fri
Argentina(Peso)	1,0005	1,0001	.9995	.9999
Australia(Dollar)	.5524	.5539	1.8104	1.8055
Austria(Schilling)	.06801	.06841	14.704	14.618
Bahrain(Tinar)	2.6525	2.6525	.3770	.3770
Belgium(Franc)	.0232	.0233	43.1074	42.8532
Brazil(Real)	.5025	.5025	1.9900	1.9900
Britian(Pound)	1.4696	1.4785	.6805	.6764
1-month forward	1.4694	1.4782	.6805	.6765
3-months forward	1.4685	1.4773	.6810	.6769
6-month forward	1.4672	1.4759	.6816	.6776
Canada(Dollar)	.6687	.6695	1.4955	1.4937
1-month forward	.6687	.6695	1.4954	1.4936
3-month forward	.6689	.6697	1.4951	1.4933
6-month forward	.6692	.6700	1.4944	1.4926
Chile(Peso)	.001774	.001778	563.85	562.55
China(Renminbi)	.1208	.1208	8.2774	8.2772
Columbia(Peso)	0004462	0004459	2241.25	2242.50
Czech.Rep.(Koruna)				
Commercial rate	.02691	.02701	37.156	37.026
Denmark(Krone)	.1253	.1261	7.9831	7.9295
Ecuador(US Dollar)	1.0000	1.0000	1.0000	1.0000
Finland(Markka)	.1574	.1583	6.3536	6.3162
France(Franc)	.1427	.1435	7.0096	6.9683
1-month forward	.1427	.1436	7.0054	6.9641
3-month forward	.1429	.1437	6.9983	6.9573
6-month forward	.1431	.1439	6.9898	6.9491
Germany(Mark)	.4785	.4813	2.0900	2.0777
1-month forward	.4788	.4816	2.0887	2.0764
3-month forward	.4792	.4821	2.0667	2.0744
6-month forward	.4798	.4826	2.0841	2.0720
Greece(Drachma)	.002746	.002763	364.13	361.98
Hong Kong(Dollar)	.1282	.1282	7.7991	7.7987
Hungary(Forint)	.003526	.003553	283.60	281.49
India(Rupee)	.02155	.02156	46.395	46.375
Indonesia(Rupiah)	.0001047	.0001148	9550.00	9540.00
Ireland(Punt)	1.1882	1.1953	.8416	.8366
Israel(Shekel)	.2413	.2415	4.1450	4.1400
Italy(Lira)	.0004833	.0004862	2069.11	2056.91

COUNTRY	U.S. $ EQUIV. Fri	U.S. $ EQUIV. Thur	CURRENCY PER U.S. $ Fri	CURRENCY PER U.S. $ Fri
Japan(Yen)	.008646	.008652	115.66	115.58
1-month forward	.008681	.008686	115.20	115.12
3-month forward	.008753	.008759	114.25	114.17
6-month forward	.008855	.008860	112.93	112.87
Jordan(Dinar)	1.4065	1.4085	.7110	.7100
Kuwait(Dinar)	3.2733	3.2733	.3055	.3055
Lebanon(Pound)	.0006634	.0006634	1507.50	1507.50
Malaysia(Ringgit)	.2631	.2632	3.8002	3.8000
Malta(Lira)	2.2894	2.2994	.4368	.4349
Mexico(Peso)				
Floating rate	.1023	.1022	9.7710	9.7805
Netherlands(Guilder)	.4246	.4272	2.3549	2.3410
New Zealand(Dollar)	.4460	.4467	2.2422	2.2386
Norway(Krone)	.1141	.1147	8.7673	8.7193
Pakistan(Rupee)	.01696	.01696	58.950	58950
Peru(New Sol)	.2832	.2833	3.5315	3.5293
Phillipines(Peso)	.02041	02035	49.000	49.150
Poland(Zolty)	.2456	.2480	4.0710	4.0325
Portugal(Escudo)	.004668	.004695	214.24	212.97
Russia(Rouble)	.03514	.03513	28.460	28.463
Saudi Arabia(Rlyan)	.2666	.2666	3.7506	3.7508
Singapore(Dollar)	.5754	.5758	1.7380	1.7367
Slovak Rep.(Koruna)	.02138	.02157	46.784	46.361
South Africa(Rand)	.1287	.1294	7.7700	7.72806
South Korea(Won)	.0008003	.0007959	1249.50	1256.50
Spain(Peseta)	.005624	.005658	177.80	176.75
Swedan(Krona)	.1051	.1058	9.5106	9.4510
Switzerland (Franc)	.6079	.6137	1.6449	1.6295
1-month forward	.6089	.6147	1.6423	1.6269
3-month forward	.6109	.6167	1.6369	1.6215
6-month forward	.6137	.6194	1.6295	1.6144
Taiwan(Dollar)	.03101	.03092	32.250	32.340
Thailand(Baht)	.02360	.02365	42.365	42.275
Turkey(Lira)	.00000148	.00000149	675375.00	672770.49
United Arab(Dirham)	.2723	.2723	3.6729	3.6729
Uruguay(Urug Peso)				
Financial	.07967	.07970	12.553	12.548
Venzuela(Bolivar)	.001427	.001427	701.00	700.75
SDR	1.3055	1.3055	.7660	.7660
Euro	.9358	.9414	10.686	1.0622

Special Drawing Rights (SDR) are based on exchange rates for the U.S., Germany, British, French, and Japanese currencies;Source:International Monotary fund.
a-Russian Central Bank rate. b-Government rate,d-Floating rate: trading band suspended on 4/11/00. e-Adopted U.S. dollar as of 9/11/00: Foreign Exchange rates are available from Readers Reference Service(413)592-3600

KEY CURRENCY CROSS RATES

Late New York Trading Fri, February 2, 2001

	DOLLAR	EURO	POUND	SFRANC	GUILDER	PESO	YEN	LIRA	D-MARK	FFRANC	CDNDIR
Canada	1.4955	1.3995	2.1978	0.9092	.63506	.15305	.01293	.00072	.71555	.21335	....
France	7.0096	6.5596	10.3013	4.2614	2.9766	.71739	.06061	.00339	3.3539	....	4.6871
Germany	2.0900	1.9558	3.0715	1.2706	.88751	.21390	.01807	.00101	....	.29816	1.3975
Italy	2069.1	1936.3	3040.8	1257.9	878.64	211.76	17.890	....	990.00	295.18	1383.6
Japan	115.66	108.23	169.97	70.314	49.115	11.837	....	.05590	55.340	16.500	77.339
Mexico	9.7710	9.1437	14.359	5.9402	4.1492	....	.08448	.00472	4.6751	1.3939	6.5336
Netherlands	2.3549	2.2037	3.4608	1.4316	....	.24101	.02036	.00114	1.1267	.33595	1.5747
Switzerland	1.6449	1.5393	2.4173	....	.69850	.16835	.01422	.00079	.78703	.23466	1.0999
U.K.	.68050	.6368	....	.4137	.28895	.06964	.00588	.00033	.32558	.09708	.45500
Euro	1.06860	....	1.5704	.64965	.45378	.10936	.00924	.00052	.51129	.15245	.71455
U.S.	....	.9358	1.4696	.60794	.42465	.10234	.00865	.00048	.47847	.14266	.66867

Source: Reuters

Source: The Wall Street Journal, February 5, 2001, p. C6.

on the German mark or indirect quote on the U.S. dollar. The inverse of this spot rate is listed in the first column, the indirect quote on the German mark or direct quote on the U.S. dollar, USD .4785/DEM. The two forms of the exchange rate are of course equal, one being the inverse of the other.[1]

$$\frac{1}{2.0900} = USD\ .4785/DEM$$

Luckily, world currency markets do follow some conventions to minimize confusion. With only a few exceptions, most currencies are quoted in direct quotes versus the U.S. dollar (DEM/USD, YEN/USD, FFR/USD), also known as **European terms.** The major exceptions are currencies at one time or another associated with the British Commonwealth, including the Australian dollar and, of course, the British pound sterling. These are customarily quoted as USD per pound sterling or USD per Australian dollar, known as **American terms.** Once again, it makes no real difference whether you quote U.S. dollars per Japanese yen or Japanese yen per U.S. dollar, as long as you know which is being used for the transaction.

Figure 7.2, the foreign currency quotations from the *Financial Times* of London, provides wider coverage of the world's currencies, including many of the lesser known and traded. These quotes are also for Friday, February 2, 2001, the same day as the quotes from *The Wall Street Journal* in Figure 7.1. However, even though the currency quotations are for the same day, they are not necessarily the same, reflecting the differences in the time zones, the local markets, and the banks surveyed for quotation purposes.

Cross Rates

Although it is common among exchange traders worldwide to quote currency values against the U.S. dollar, it is not necessary. Any currency's value can be stated in terms of any other currency. When the exchange rate for a currency is stated without using the U.S. dollar as a reference, it is referred to as a **cross rate.** For example, if the German mark and Japanese yen are both quoted versus the U.S. dollar, they would appear as DEM 2.0900/USD and YEN 115.58/USD. But if the YEN/DEM cross rate is needed, it is simply a matter of division:

$$\frac{\text{YEN } 115.58}{\text{DEM } 2.0900} = \text{YEN } 55.30/\text{DEM}$$

The YEN/DEM cross rate of 55.30 is the third leg of the triangle, which must be true if the first two exchange rates are known. If one of the exchange rates changes due to market forces, the others must adjust for the three exchange rates again to align. If they are out of alignment, it would be possible to make a profit simply by exchanging one currency for a second, the second for a third, and the third back to the first. This is known as **triangular arbitrage.** Besides the potential profitability of arbitrage that may occasionally occur, cross rates have become increasingly common in a world of rapidly expanding trade and investment.

Percentage Change Calculations

The quotation form is important when calculating the percentage change in an exchange rate. For example, if the spot rate between the Japanese yen and the U.S. dollar changed from YEN 125/USD to YEN 150/USD, the percentage change in the value of the Japanese yen is:

$$\frac{\text{YEN } 125/\text{USD} - \text{YEN } 150/\text{USD}}{\text{YEN } 150/\text{USD}} \times 100 = -16.67\%$$

The Japanese yen has declined in value versus the U.S. dollar by 16.67 percent. This is consistent with the intuition that it now requires more yen (150) to buy a dollar than it used to (125).

The same percentage change result can be achieved by using the inverted forms of the same spot rates (indirect quotes on the Japanese yen), if care is taken to also "in-

FIGURE 7.2 Guide to World Currencies

FT GUIDE TO WORLD CURRENCIES

The table below gives the latest available rates of exchange (rounded) against four key currencies on Friday, February 2, 2001. In some cases the rate is nominal. Market rates are the average of buying and selling rates except where they are shown to be otherwise. In some cases market rates have been calculated from those of foreign currencies to which they are tied.

		£ STG	US $	EURO €	YEN (X 100)
Afghanistan	(Afghani)	6976.09	4750.00	4433.41	4105.98
Albania	(Lek)	208.108	141.700	132.256	122.488
Algeria	(Diner)	109.400	74.4900	69.5257	64.3904
Andorra	(French Fr)	10.3217	7.0280	6.5596	6.0751
	(Sp Peseta)	261.813	178.268	166.386	154.097
Angola	(Readj Kwanza)	27.7964	18.9265	17.0297	15.7720
Antigua	(E Carib $)	3.9654	2.7000	2.5200	2.3339
Argentina	(Peso)	1.4680	0.9995	0.9329	0.8640
Armania	(Dram)	813.251o	553.740	518.551	480.252
Aruba	(Florin)	2.6289	1.7900	1.6707	1.5473
Australia	(A$)	2.6614	1.8121	1.6913	1.5664
Austria	(Schilling)	21.6522	14.7429	13.7603	12.7440
Azerbaijan	(Manat)	6683.83o	4551.00	4247.68	3933.96
Azores	(Port Escudo)	315.464	214.798	200.482	185.675
Bahamas	(Bahama $)	1.4687	1	0.9334	0.8644
Bahrain	(Dinar)	0.5537	0.3770	0.3519	0.3259
Balearic Is	(Sp Peseta)	261.813	178.268	166.386	154.097
Bangladesh	(Taka)(5)	79.4540	54.1000	50.4943	46.7649
Barbados	(Barb $)	2.9226	1.9900	1.8574	1.7202
Belarus	(Rouble)(4)	1828.47m	1245.00	1162.95	1077.06
Belgium	(Beig Fr)	63.4759	43.2206	40.3399	37.3605
Belize	(B $)	2.8933	1.9700	1.8387	1.7029
Benin	(CFA Fr)	1032.17	702.800	655.957	607.512
Bermuda	(Bermudian $)	1.4687	1	0.9334	0.8644
Bhutan	(Ngultrum)	68.1527	46.4050	43.3121	40.1132
Bolivia	(Boliviano)	9.4140	6.4100	5.9828	5.5409
Bosnia Herzagovina	(Marka)	3.0776	2.0955	1.9558	1.8114
Botswana	(Pula)	7.9796	5.4333	5.0712	4.6966
Brazil	(Real)	2.9233v	1.9905	1.8578	1.7206
Brunel	(Brunel $)	2.5536	1.7387	1.6228	1.5030
Bulgaria	(Lev)	3.0763	2.0946	1.9550	1.8106
Burkina Faso	(CFA Fr)	1032.17	702.800	655.957	607.512
Burma	(Kyat)	9.6432	6.5660	6.1284	5.6758
Burundi	(Burundi Fr)	1141.14	776.996	725.211	671.648
Cambodia	(Riel)	5632.28	3835.00	3579.40	3315.04
Cameroon	(CFA Fr)	1032.17	702.800	655.957	607.512
Canada	(Canadian $)	2.1943	1.4941	1.3945	1.2915
Canary Is	(Sp Peseta)	261.813	178.268	166.386	154.097
Cp. Verde	(CV Escudo)	170.364	116.000	108.959	100.912
Cayman Is	(CI $)	1.2043	0.8200	0.7653	0.7088
Cent. Afr. Rep	(CFA Fr)	1032.17	702.800	655.957	607.512
Chad	(CFA Fr)	1032.17	702.800	655.957	607.512
Chile	(Chilean Peso)	828.392	564.050	526.456	487.574
China	(Renminbi)	12.1566	8.2774	7.7258	7.1551
Colombia	(Col Peso)	3290.22	2240.30	2090.98	1936.55
Comoros	(Fr)	762.744	519.350	494.724	458.108
Congo	(CFA Fr)	1032.17	702.800	655.957	607.512
Congo (DemRep)	(Congo Fr)	6.6088	4.4999	4.2000	3.8898
Costa Rica	(Colon)	469.513	319.690	298.289	276.259
Cote d'Ivolre	(CFA Fr)	1032.17	702.800	655.957	607.512
Croatia	(Kuna)	12.1182	8.2512	7.7013	7.1325
Cuba	(Cuban Peso)	30.8417	21.0000	19.6004	18.1527
Cyprus	(Cyprus £)	0.9119	0.6209	0.5796	0.5367
Czech Rep	(Koruna)	54.7205	37.2590	34.7757	32.2073
Denmark	(Danish Krone)	11.7464	7.9981	7.4651	6.9137
Djibouti Rep	(Djib Fr)	252.608	172.000	150.643	139.517
Dominica	(E Carib $)	3.9654	2.7000	2.5200	2.3339
Dominican Rep	(D Peso)	23.7922	16.2000	15.0456	13.9344
Ecuador	(US $) (8)	1.4687	1.0000	23333.8	0.8644
Egypt	(Egyptian £)	5.6763	3.8650	3.6074	3.3410
El Salvador	(Colon)	12.8360	8.7400	8.1575	7.5550
Equat'l Guinea	(CFA Fr)	1032.17	702.800	655.957	607.512
Estonia	(Kroon)	24.6205	16.7640	15.6467	14.4911
Ethiopia	(Ethiopian Bkr)	12.1164	8.2500	7.6927	7.1245
Falkland Is	(Falk £)	1	0.6809	0.6355	0.5886
Faroe Is	(Danish Krone)	11.7464	7.9981	7.4651	6.9137
Fiji Is	(Fiji $)	3.1963	2.1764	2.0313	1.8813
Finland	(Markka)	9.3558	6.3703	5.9457	5.5066
France	(Fr)	10.3217	7.0280	6.5596	6.0751
Fr. Cty/Africa	(CFA Fr)	1032.17	702.800	655.957	607.512
Fr. Guiana	(Local Fr)	10.3217	7.0280	6.5596	6.0751
Fr. Pacific Is	(CFP Fr)	186.230	126.803	119.332	111.075
Gabon	(CFA Fr)	1032.17	702.800	655.957	607.512
Gambia	(Daiasl)	22.4338	15.2750	14.2570	13.2040
Georgia	(Larl)	2.9961	2.0400	1.8807	1.7418
Germany	(D-Mark)	3.0776	2.0955	1.9558	1.8114
Ghana	(Cedl)	10515.6	7160.00	6682.81	6189.22
Gibraltar	(Gib £)	1	0.6809	0.6355	0.5886
Greece	(Drachma)	536.179	365.083	340.750	315.584
Greenland	(Danish Krone)	11.7464	7.9981	7.4651	6.9137
Grenada	(E Carib $)	3.9654	2.7000	2.5200	2.3339
Guadeloupe	(French Fr)	10.3217	7.0280	6.5596	6.0751
Guam	(US $)	1.4687	1	0.9334	0.8644
Guatemala	(Quetzal)	11.5018	7.8315	7.3189	6.7783
Guinea	(Fr)	2724.35	1855.00	1731.36	1603.49
Guinea-Bissau	(CFA Fr)	1032.17	702.800	655.957	607.512
Guyana	(Guyanese $)	265.092	180.500	168.470	156.027
Haiti	(Gourde)	35.2476	24.0000	22.4004	20.7460
Honduras	(Lempira)	22.2941	15.1800	14.1496	13.1046
Hong Kong	(HK $)	11.4537	7.7988	7.2790	6.7414
Hungary	(Forint)	417.427	284.225	265.281	245.689
Iceland	(Icelandic Krona)	125.026	85.1300	79.4561	73.5878
India	(Indian Rupee)	68.1527	46.4050	43.3121	40.1132
Indonesia	(Ruplah)	14025.6	9550.00	8913.50	8255.18
Iran	(Rial)(7)	2566.47o	1747.50	1631.03	1510.57
Iraq	(Iraqi Dinar)	0.4588r	0.3124	0.2916	0.2700
Irish Rep	(Punt)	1.2393	0.8438	0.7876	0.7294
Israel	(Shekel)	6.0876	4.1450	3.8687	3.5830
Italy	(Lira)	3046.77	2074.54	1936.27	1793.26
Jamaica	(Jamaican $)	66.3830	45.2000	42.1408	39.0284
Japan	(Yen)	169.901	115.685	107.975	100
Jordan	(Jordanian Dinar)	1.0428	0.7100	0.6627	0.6137
Kazakhstan	(Tange)	213.204	145.170	135.494	125.487
Kenya	(Kenya Shilling)	114.702	78.1000	72.8947	67.5109
Kiribati	(Australian $)	2.6614	1.8121	1.6913	1.5664
Korea North	(Won)	3.2310	2.2000	2.0534	1.9017
Korea South	(Won)	1833.61	1248.50	1165.29	1079.22
Kuwait	(Kuwaiti Dinar)	0.4487	0.3055	0.2852	0.2641
Kyrgyzstan	(Som)	72.0332	49.0472	45.7238	42.3468
Laos	(New Kip)	11161.7	7600.00	7093.46	6569.56
Lalvia	(Lats)	0.9080	0.6183	0.5771	0.5344
Lebanon	(Lebanese £)	2213.99	1507.50	1407.03	1303.11
Lesotho	(Maluti)	11.4371	7.7875	7.2685	6.7316
Liberia	(Liberian $)	1.4687o	1	0.9334	0.8644
Libya	(Libyan Dinar)	0.7921	0.5393	0.5034	0.4662
Liechtanstein	(Swiss Fr)	2.4183	1.6466	1.5369	1.4233
Lithuania	(Litas)	5.8761	4.0010	3.7344	3.4585
Luxembourg	(Lux Fr)	63.4759	43.2206	40.3399	37.3605
Macao	(Pataca)	11.7375	7.9920	7.5013	6.9473
Macedonia	(Denar)	94.0598	64.0450	59.7764	55.3615
Madagascar	(MG Fr)	9264.25	6308.00	5880.11	5445.82
Madeira	(Port Escudo)	315.464	214.798	200.482	185.675
Malawi	(Kwacha)	117.125	79.7500	74.4348	68.9372
Malaysia	(Ringgit)	5.5809o	3.8000	3.5467	3.2848
	(Ringgit) (3)	5.5809	3.8000	3.5468	3.2848
Maldive Is	(Rufiya)	17.1979	11.7100	10.9855	10.1742
Mali Rep	(CFA Fr)	1032.17	702.800	655.957	607.512
Malta	(Maltese Lira)	0.6441	0.4385	0.4093	0.3790
Martinique	(Local Fr)	10.3217	7.0280	6.5596	6.0751
Mauritania	(Ouguiya)	367.339	250.120	233.450	216.208
Mauritius	(Maur Rupee)	41.1149	27.9950	26.1292	24.1993
Mexico	(Mexican Peso)	14.3260	9.7545	9.1044	8.4319
Moldova	(Lau)	18.7400	12.7600	11.9375	11.0559
Monaco	(French Fr)	10.3217	7.0280	6.5596	6.0751
Mongolia	(Tugrik)	1614.05	1099.00	1025.75	949.994
Montserrat	(E Carib $)	3.9654	2.7000	2.5200	2.3339
Morocco	(Dirtiam)	15.5920	10.6165	9.9089	9.1771
Mozambique	(Metical)	26729.5	18200.0	16987.0	15732.4
Namibia	(Dollar)	11.4371	7.7875	7.2685	6.7316
Nauru Is	(Australian $)	2.6614	1.8121	1.6913	1.5664
Nepal	(Nepalese Rupee)	108.915	74.1600	69.2023	64.0913
Netherlands	(Guilder)	3.4676	2.3611	2.2037	2.0410
N'nd Antilles	(A/Guilder)	2.6142	1.7800	1.6614	1.5387
New Zealand	(NZ $)	3.3055	2.2507	2.1008	1.9456
Nicaragua	(Gold Cordoba)	18.9456	12.9000	12.0402	11.1510
Niger Rep	(CFA Fr)	1032.17	702.800	655.957	607.512
Nigeria	(Naira)	163.094m	111.050	103.649	95.9934
Norway	(Nor. Krone)	12.9014	8.7845	8.1991	7.5935
Oman	(Rial Omani)	0.5654	0.3850	0.3594	0.3328
Pakistan	(Pak. Rupee)	86.9661	59.2150	55.268	51.1864
Panama	(Balboa)	1.4687	1	0.9334	0.8644
Papua New Guinea	(Kina)	4.5970	3.1301	2.9215	2.7057
Paraguay	(Guarani)	5294.48	3605.00	3364.73	3116.22
Peru	(New Sol)	5.1821	3.5285	3.2933	3.0501
Philippines	(Peso)	71.9639	49.0000	45.7342	42.3564
Pitcaim Is	(£ Sterling)	1	0.6809	0.6355	0.5886
	(NZ $)	3.3055	2.2507	2.1008	1.9456
Poland	(Zloty)	5.9187	4.0300	3.7614	3.4836
Portugal	(Escudo)	315.464	214.798	200.482	185.675
Puerto Rico	(US $)	1.4687	1	0.9334	0.8644
Qatar	(Riyal)	5.3470	3.6408	3.3981	3.1471
Reunion Is. de la	(F/Fr)	10.3217	7.0280	6.5596	6.0751
Romania	(Leu)	39058.7	26595.0	24822.4	22989.2
Russia	(Rouble)	41.7948m	28.4580	26.5613	24.5996
Rwanda	(Fr)	527.287	359.028	335.099	310.350
St Christopher	(E Carib $)	3.9654	2.7000	2.5200	2.3339
St Helena	(£)	1	0.6809	0.6355	0.5886
St Lucia	(E Carib $)	3.9654	2.7000	2.5200	2.3339
St Pierre & Miquelon	(F/Fr)	10.3217	7.0280	6.5596	6.0751
St Vincent	(E Carib $)	3.9654	2.7000	2.5200	2.3339
San Marino	(Italian Lira)	3046.77	2074.54	1936.27	1793.26
Sao Tome	(Dobra)	8872.12	6041.00	5638.37	5221.94
Saudi Arabia	(Riyal)	5.5077	3.7502	3.5002	3.2417
Senegal	(CFA Fr)	1032.17	702.800	655.957	607.512
Seychelles	(Rupee)	9.3421	6.3610	5.9968	5.5539
Sierra Leone	(Leone)	2990.17	2036.00	1827.50	1692.53
Singapore	($)	2.5536	1.7387	1.6228	1.5030
Slovakia	(Koruna)	68.8819	46.9015	43.7756	40.5424
Slovania	(Tolar)	339.214	230.970	215.576	199.654
Solomon Is	($)	7.5938	5.1706	4.8260	4.4696
Somall Rep	(Shilling)	3847.87	2620.00	2445.38	2264.77
South Africa	(Rand)	11.4371	7.7875	7.2685	6.7316
Spain	(Peseta)	261.813	178.268	166.386	154.097
Spanish Ports in N Africa	(Sp Peseta)	261.813	178.268	166.386	154.097
Sri Lanka	(Rupee)	129.69	88.2500	82.3682	76.2847
Sudan Rep	(Dinar)	379.940	258.700	241.458	223.625
Surinam	(Guilder)	1440.75	981.000	915.616	847.992
Swaziland	(Lilangeni)	11.4371	7.7875	7.2685	6.7316
Sweden	(Krona)	13.9985	9.5315	8.8962	8.2392
Switzerland	(Fr)	2.4183	1.6466	1.5369	1.4233
Syria	(£)	78.5728	53.5000	49.9342	46.2463
Taiwan	($)	47.4528	32.3105	30.1570	27.9297
Tanzania	(Shilling)	1194.01	813.000	758.814	702.771
Thailand	(Baht)	62.2194	42.3650	39.5414	36.6210
Togo Rep	(CFA Fr)	1032.17	702.800	655.957	607.512
Tonga Is	(Pa'anga)	2.6614	1.8121	1.6913	1.5664
Trinidad/Tobago	($)	9.1644	6.2400	5.8241	5.3940
Tunisia	(Dinar)	2.0276	1.3806	1.2886	1.1934
Turkey	(Lira)	993615.2	676550.0	631458.0	584820.8
Turks & Caicos	(US $)	1.4687	1	0.9334	0.8644
Tuvalu	(Australian $)	2.6614	1.8121	1.6913	1.5664
Uganda	(New Shilling)	2628.89	1790.00	1670.70	1547.31
Ukraine	(Hryvna)	7.9758	5.4307	5.0687	4.6944
U A E	(Dirham)	5.3941	3.6728	3.4280	3.1748
United Kingdom	(£)	1	0.6809	0.6355	0.5886
United States	(US $)	1.4687	1	0.9334	0.8644
Uruguay	(Peso Uruguayo)	18.4830	12.5850	11.7462	10.8787
Uzbekistan	(Sum) (1)	483.274o	329.060	305.952	283.356
Vanuatu	(Vatu)	208.813	142.180	132.704	122.903
Vatican	(Lira)	3046.77	2074.54	1936.27	1793.26
Venezuela	(Bolivar)	1029.54v	701.010	654.288	605.965
Vietnam	(Dong)	21358.6	14543.0	13573.7	12571.2
Virgin Is-British	(US $)	1.4887	1	0.9334	0.8644
Virgin Is-US	(US $)	1.4687	1	0.9334	0.8644
Western Samoa	(Taia)	4.9533	3.3727	3.1479	2.9154
Yemen (Rep of)	(Rial) (2)	244.384	166.400	155.309	143.839
Yugoslavia	(New Dinar)(9)	92.5067	62.9875	58.7894	54.4474
Zambia	(Kwacha)	5360.59	3650.00	3406.74	3155.12
Zimbabwe	($) (6)	80.9227	55.1000	51.4276	47.6293
Euro	(Euro)	1.5735	1.0714	1	0.9261
SDR	(SDR)	1.12920	0.768900	0.717600	0.664600

Abbrevlations: (a) Free rate; (m) market rate; (o) Official rate; (r) Principal rate (t) Tourist rate (u) Currency fixed against the US Dollar (v) Floating rate (1) Official rate shown for Uzbekistan Sum from Dec 12, 2000 (2) Yemeni Official rate replaces Parallel rate (3) Ringglt exchange rate for valuation of capital assets. (4) Belarus Rouble Market rate re-denominated on Jan 1 2000. (5) Bangladesh Taka devalued by 6% against the US Dollar on Aug 13th, 2000 (6) Zimbabwe Dollar devalued by 24% against the US Dollar on Aug 2nd, 2000. (7) Official rate shown for Iranian Real from Nov 19, 1999. (8) Ecuador has adopted the US Dollar (at approximately 25,000 Sucre per US$) as its official currency in response to it's recent economic crisis (9) Yugoslav New Dinar floated on 1/1/2001. Some data derived from THE WM/REUTERS CLOSING SPOT RATES & Bank of America, Economics Department, London Trading Center, Enquiries: 020 7634 4365. To obtainn a copy of this table by Fax from the Cityline service dial 0906 8437001. Calls are charged at 60p per minute at all times. FT Readers Enquiries: 0207873 4211.

Friday, February 2, 2001

Source: *The Financial Times*, February 8, 2001, p. 22.

GLOBAL PERSPECTIVE 7.1

Currenex

Currenex, Inc. is the first independent and open online global currency exchange, linking institutional buyers and sellers worldwide. Operational today, Currenex's Internet-based service, FX trades, provides banks, corporate treasury departments, institutional funds/asset managers, government agencies, international organizations, and central banks instant access to the $1.5 trillion daily globe foreign exchange market through multiple price discovery mechanisms on an open, impartial exchange.

FX trades is a real-time FX marketplace that provides secure and comprehensive FX trading from initiation and exe-

cution to settlement and reporting. As members in the Currenex exchange, CFOs, treasurers, and fund managers can approach currency transactions knowing that they are able to secure the most competitive bid while improving operational efficiencies, increasing productivity, and providing tight integration with back office operations.

Currenex has major multinational members including MasterCard International, Intel Corporation, as well as more than 25 global, market-making banks including ABN Amro, Barclays Capital, and Merrill Lynch.

Source: www.currenex.com

vert" the basic percentage change calculation. Using the inverse of YEN 125/USD (USD 0.0080/YEN) and the inverse of YEN 150/USD (USD 0.0067/YEN), the percentage change is still −16.67 percent:

$$\frac{\text{USD } 0.0067/\text{YEN} - \text{USD } 0.0080/\text{YEN}}{\text{USD } 0.0080/\text{YEN}} \times 100 = -16.67\%$$

If the percentage changes calculated are not identical, it is normally the result of rounding errors introduced when inverting the spot rates. Both methods are identical, however, when calculated properly.

Foreign Currency Market Structure

The market for foreign currencies is a worldwide market that is informal in structure. This means that it has no central place, pit, or floor like the floor of the New York Stock Exchange, where the trading takes place. The "market" is actually the thousands of telecommunications links among financial institutions around the globe, and it is open 24 hours a day. Someone, somewhere, is nearly always open for business. As described in Global Perspective 7.1, trading is also moving to the Internet.

For example, Table 7.1 reproduces a computer screen from one of the major international financial information news sources, Reuters. This is the spot exchange screen, called FXFX, which is available to all subscribers to the Reuters news network. The screen serves as a bulletin board, where all financial institutions wanting to buy or sell foreign currencies can post representative prices. Although the rates quoted on these computer screens are indicative of current prices, the buyer is still referred to the individual bank for the latest quotation due to the rapid movement of rates worldwide. There also are hundreds of banks operating in the markets at any moment that are not listed on the brief sample of Reuters FXFX page.[2] The speed with which this market moves, the multitude of players playing on a field that is open 24 hours a day, and the circumference of the earth with its time and day differences produce many dif-

TABLE 7.1			Typical Foreign Currency Quotations on a Reuters Screen				
13:07	CCY	Page	Name	*Reuters Spot Rates*	CCY	HI* Euro**	Lo FXFX
13.06	DEM	DGXX	DG BANK	FFT	1.8528/33 * DEM	1.8538	1.8440
13.06	GBP	AIBN	AL IRISH	N.Y.	1.7653/63 * GBP	1.7710	1.7630
13.06	CHF	CITX	CITIBANK	ZUR	1.5749/56 * CHF	1.5750	1.5665
13.06	JPY	CHNY	CHEMICAL	N.Y.	128.53/58 * JPY	128.70	128.23
13.07	FRF	MGFX	MORGAN	LDN	6.3030/60 * FRF	6.3080	6.2750
13.06	NLG	MGFX	MORGAN	LDN	2.0920/30 * NLG	2.0925	2.0815
13.00	ITL	MGFX	MORGAN	LDN	1356.45/6.58 * ITL	1356.45	1349.00
13.02	XEV	PRBX	PRIVAT	COP	1.1259/68 * XEV	1.1304	1.1255

Column 1: Time of entry of the latest quote to the nearest minute (British Standard time).

Column 2: Currency of quotation (bilateral with the U.S. dollar); quotes are currency per USD, except for the British pound sterling (dollars per unit of pound) and the European Currency Unit (dollars per unit of XEV). The currency symbols are as follows: DEM—German mark; GBP—British pound sterling; CFH—Swiss franc; JPY—Japanese yen; FRF—French franc; NGL—Netherlands guilder; ITL—Italian lira; XEV—European Currency Unit.

Column 3: Mnemonic of inputting bank. Allows the individual trader to dial up the correct page (by this mnemonic) where the trader could see the full set of spot and forward quotes for this and other currencies being offered by this bank.

Column 4: Name of the inputting bank.

Column 5: Branch location of that bank from which the quote has emanated (so that an inquiring trader can telephone the correct branch); FFT—Frankfurt; N.Y.—New York; ZUR—Zurich; LDN—London; COP—Copenhagen.

Column 6: Spot exchange rate quotation, bid quote, then offer quote.

Column 7: Recent high price for this specific quote.

Column 8: Recent low price for this specific quote.

Source: Adapted from C. A. E. Goodhart and L. Figliuoli, "Every Minute Counts in Financial Markets," *Journal of International Money and Finance,* 10, 1991, pp. 23–52.

ferent "single prices." Global Perspective 7.2 illustrates how trading occurs between traders themselves.

Market Size and Composition

Until recently there was little data on the actual volume of trading on world foreign currency markets. Starting in the spring of 1986, however, the Federal Reserve Bank of New York, along with other major industrial countries' central banks through the auspices of the Bank for International Settlements (BIS), started surveying the activity of currency trading every three years. Some of the principal results are shown in Table 7.2.

Growth in foreign currency trading has been nothing less than astronomical. The survey results for the month of April 1998 indicate that daily foreign currency trading on world markets exceeded $1,500,000,000,000 (a trillion with a *t*). In comparison, the annual (not daily) U.S. government budget deficit has never exceeded $300 billion, and the U.S. merchandise trade deficit has never topped $200 billion.

The majority of the world's trading in foreign currencies is still taking place in the cities where international financial activity is centered: London, New York, and Tokyo. A recent survey by the U.S. Federal Reserve of currency trading by financial institutions and independent brokers in New York reveals additional information of interest. Approximately 66 percent of currency trading occurs in the morning hours (Eastern Standard Time), with 29 percent between noon and 4 P.M., and the remaining 5 percent between 4 P.M. and 8 A.M. the next day.

GLOBAL PERSPECTIVE 7.2

The Linguistics of Currency Trading

"Yoshi, it's Maria in New York. May I have a price on twenty cable?"

"Sure, One seventy-five, twenty-thirty."

"Mine twenty."

"All right. At 1.7530, I sell you twenty million pounds."

"Done."

"What do you think about the Swiss franc? It's up 100 pips."

"I saw that. A few German banks have been buying steadily all day . . . ."

"Yoshi, it's Maria in New York. I am interested in either buying or selling 20 million British pounds."

"Sure. I will buy them from you at 1.7520 dollars to each pound or sell them to you at 1.7530 dollars to each pound."

"I'd like to buy them from you at 1.7530 dollars to each pound."

"All right. I sell you 20 million pounds at 1.7530 dollars per pound."

"The deal is confirmed at 1.7530."

"Is there any information you can share with me about the fact that the Swiss franc has risen one-one hundredth of a franc against the U.S. dollar in the past hour?"

"Yes, German banks have been buying Swiss francs all day, causing the price to rise a little . . . ."

Source: Adapted from *The Basics of Foreign Trade and Exchange*, by Adam Gonelli, The Federal Reserve Bank of New York, Public Information Department, 1993, p. 34.

Three reasons typically given for the enormous growth in foreign currency trading are:

1. **Deregulation of International Capital Flows:** It is easier than ever to move currencies and capital around the world without major governmental restrictions. Much of the deregulation that has characterized government policy over the past 10 to 15 years in the United States, Japan, and the now European Union has focused on financial deregulation.
2. **Gains in Technology and Transaction Cost Efficiency:** It is faster, easier, and cheaper to move millions of dollars, yen, or marks around the world than ever before. Technological advancements not only in the dissemination of information, but also in the conduct of exchange or trading, have added greatly to the ability of individuals working in these markets to conduct instanteous arbitrage (some would say speculation).
3. **The World Is a Risky Place:** Many argue that the financial markets have become increasingly volatile over recent years, with larger and faster swings in financial variables such as stock values and interest rates adding to the motivations for moving more capital at faster rates.

TABLE 7.2

Average Daily Turnover in Global Foreign Exchange and Over-the-Counter Derivatives Markets, April of Each Year (in billions of U.S. dollars)

	1989	1992	1994	1998
Spot currency trades	350	400	520	590
Forwards and swaps	240	420	670	900
Subtotal	590	820	1,190	1,500

Source: Bank for International Settlements, *Central Bank Survey of Foreign Exchange and Derivatives Market Activity in April 1998.* The BIS reports "[T]otal reported turnover net of local double counting" as $1,982 billion. From this number the BIS subtracts $540 billion as an "adjustment for cross-border double counting," and then adds $58 billion for "estimated gaps in reporting," to arrive at the $1,500 billion figure for 1998 above.

The Purpose of Exchange Rates

If countries are to trade, they must be able to exchange currencies. To buy wheat, or corn, or videocassette recorders, the buyer must first have the currency in which the product is sold. An American firm purchasing consumer electronic products manufactured in Japan must first exchange its U.S. dollars for Japanese yen, then purchase the products. And each country has its own currency.[3] The exchange of one country's currency for another should be a relatively simple transaction, but it's not.

What Is a Currency Worth?

At what rate should one currency be exchanged for another currency? For example, what should the exchange rate be between the U.S. dollar and the Japanese yen? The simplest answer is that the exchange rate should equalize purchasing power. For example, if the price of a move ticket in the United States is $6, the "correct" exchange rate would be one that exchanges $6 for the amount of Japanese yen it would take to purchase a movie ticket in Japan. If ticket prices are ¥540 (a common symbol for the yen is ¥) in Japan, then the exchange rate that would equalize purchasing power would be:

$$\frac{¥540}{\$6} = ¥90/\$.$$

Therefore, if the exchange rate between the two currencies is ¥90/$, she or he can purchase a ticket regardless of which country the movie goer is in. This is the theory of **purchasing power parity (PPP)**, generally considered the definition of what exchange rates ideally should be. The purchasing power parity exchange rate is simply the rate that equalizes the price of the identical product or service in two different currencies:

$$\text{Price in Japan} = \text{Exchange rate} \times \text{Price in U.S.}$$

If the price of the same product in each currency is $P^{¥}$ and $P^{\$}$, and the spot exchange rate between the Japanese yen and the U.S. dollar is $S^{¥/\$}$, the price in yen is simply the price in dollars multiplied by the spot exchange rate:

$$P^{¥} = S^{¥/\$} \times P^{\$}.$$

If this is rearranged (dividing both sides by $P^{\$}$), the spot exchange rate between the Japanese yen and the U.S. dollar is the ratio of the two product prices:

$$S^{¥/\$} = \frac{P^{¥}}{P^{\$}}.$$

These prices could be the price of just one good or service, such as the move ticket mentioned previously, or they could be price indices for each country that cover many different goods and services. Either form is an attempt to find comparable products in different countries (and currencies) in order to determine an exchange rate based on purchasing power parity. The question then is whether this logical approach to exchange rates actually works in practice.

The Law of One Price

The version of purchasing power parity that estimates the exchange rate between two currencies using just one good or service as a measure of the proper exchange for all goods and services is called the **Law of One Price.** To apply the theory to actual prices across countries, we need to select a product that is identical in quality and content in every country. To be truly theoretically correct, we would want such a product to

TABLE 7.3   The Golden-Arches Standard

	BIG MAC PRICES		Implied PPP* of the Dollar	Actual $ Exchange Rate 25/04/00	Under(−)/Over (+) Valuation Against the Dollar, %
	In Local Currency	In Dollars			
United States[†]	$2.51	2.51	–	–	–
Argentina	Peso2.50	2.50	1.00	1.00	0
Australia	A$2.59	1.54	1.03	1.68	−38
Brazil	Real2.95	1.65	1.18	1.79	−34
Britain	£1.90	3.00	1.32[‡]	1.58[‡]	+20
Canada	C$2.85	1.94	1.14	1.47	−23
Chile	Peso1,260	2.45	502	514	−2
China	Yuan9.90	1.20	3.94	8.28	−52
Czech Rep	Koruna54.37	1.39	21.7	39.1	−45
Denmark	DKr24.75	3.08	9.86	8.04	+23
Euro area	€2.56	2.37	0.98[§]	0.93[§]	−5
France	FFr18.50	2.62	7.37	7.07	+4
Germany	DM4.99	2.37	1.99	2.11	−6
Italy	Lire4,500	2.16	1,793	2,088	−14
Spain	Pta375	2.09	149	179	−17
Hong Kong	HK$10.20	1.31	4.06	7.79	−48
Hungary	Forint339	1.21	135	279	−52
Indonesia	Rupiah14,500	1.83	5,777	7,945	−27
Israel	Shekel14.5	3.58	5.78	4.05	+43
Japan	¥294	2.78	117	106	+11
Malaysia	M$4.52	1.19	1.80	3.80	−53
Mexico	Peso20.90	2.22	8.33	9.41	−11
New Zealand	NZ$3.40	1.69	1.35	2.01	−33
Poland	Zloty5.50	1.28	2.19	4.30	−49
Russia	Rouble39.50	1.39	15.7	28.5	−45
Singapore	S$3.20	1.88	1.27	1.70	−25
South Africa	Rand9.00	1.34	3.59	6.72	−47
South Korea	Won3,000	2.71	1,195	1,108	+8
Sweden	SKr24.00	2.71	9.56	8.84	+8
Switzerland	SFr5.90	3.48	2.35	1.70	+39
Taiwan	NT$70.00	2.29	27.9	30.6	−9
Thailand	Baht55.00	1.45	21.9	38.0	−42

*Purchasing-power parity: local price divided by price in United States

[†]Average of New York, Chicago, San Francisco, and Atlanta

[‡]Dollars per pound

[§]Dollars per euro

Sources: McDonald's; The Economist, April 29, 2000, p. 75.

be produced entirely domestically, so that there are no import factors in its construction.

Where would one find such a perfect product? McDonald's. Table 7.3 presents what *The Economist* magazine calls "the golden-arches standard." What it provides is a product that is essentially the same the world over and is produced and consumed entirely domestically.

The Big Mac Index compares the actual exchange rate with the exchange rate implied by the purchasing power parity measurement of comparing Big Mac prices across countries. For example, say the average price of a Big Mac in the United States on a given date is $2.51. On the same date, the price of a Big Mac in Canada, in Canadian dollars, is C$2.85. This then is used to calculate the PPP exchange rate as before:

$$\frac{\text{C\$2.85 per Big Mac}}{\text{\$2.51 per Big Mac}} = \text{C\$1.14/\$.}$$

The exchange rate between the Canadian dollar and the U.S. dollar should be C$1.14/$ according to a PPP comparison of Big Mac prices. The actual exchange rate on the date of comparison was C$1.47/$. This means that each U.S. dollar was actually worth 1.49 Canadian dollars, when the index indicates that each U.S. dollar should have been worth 1.14 Canadian dollars. Therefore, if one is to believe in the Big Mac index, the Canadian dollar was undervalued by 23 percent.

Monetary Systems of the Twentieth Century

The mixed fixed/floating exchange rate system operating today is only the latest stage of a continuing process of change. The systems that have preceded the present system varied between gold-based standards (**The Gold Standard**) and complex systems in which the U.S. dollar largely took the place of gold (**The Bretton Woods Agreement**). To understand why the dollar, the mark, and the yen are floating today, it is necessary to return to the (pardon the pun) *golden oldies.*

The Gold Standard

Although there is no recognized starting date, the gold standard as we call it today began sometime in the 1880s and extended up through the outbreak of the First World War. The gold standard was premised on three basic ideas:

1. A system of fixed rates of exchange existed between participating countries;
2. "Money" issued by member countries had to be backed by reserves of gold; and
3. Gold would act as an automatic adjustment, flowing in and out of countries, and automatically altering the gold reserves of that country if imbalances in trade or investment did occur.

Under the gold standard, each country's currency would be set in value per ounce of gold. For example, the U.S. dollar was defined as $20.67 per ounce, while the British pound sterling was defined as £4.2474 per ounce. Once each currency was defined versus gold, the determination of the exchange rate between the two currencies (or any two currencies) was simple:

$$\frac{\text{\$20.67/ounce of gold}}{\text{£4.2474/ounce of gold}} = \text{\$4.8665/£.}$$

The use of gold as the pillar of the system was a result of historical tradition, and not anything inherently unique to the metal gold itself. It was shiny, soft, rare, and generally acceptable for payment in all countries.

The Interwar Years, 1919–1939

The 1920s and 1930s were a tumultuous period for the international monetary system. The British pound sterling, the dominant currency prior to World War I, survived the war but was greatly weakened. The U.S. dollar returned to the gold standard in 1919, but gold convertibility was largely untested across countries throughout the 1920s, as world trade took long to recover from the destruction of the war. With the economic collapse and bank runs of the 1930s, the U.S. was forced to once again abandon gold convertibility.

The economic depression of the 1930s was worldwide. As all countries came under increasingly desperate economic conditions, many countries (including the United States) resorted to isolationist policies and protectionism. World trade slowed to a trickle, and with it the general need for currency exchange. It was not until the latter stages of the Second World War that international trade and commerce once again demanded a system for currency convertibility and stability.

The Bretton Woods Agreement, 1944–1971

The governments of 44 of the Allied Powers gathered together in Bretton Woods, New Hampshire, in 1944 to plan for the postwar international monetary system. The British delegation, headed by Lord John Maynard Keynes, the famous economist, and the U.S. delegation, headed by Secretary of the Treasury Henry Morgenthau, Jr., and director of the Treasury's monetary research department, Harry D. White, labored long and hard to reach an agreement. In the end, all parties agreed that a postwar system would be stable and sustainable only if it was able to provide sufficient liquidity to countries during periods of crisis. Any new system had to have facilities for the extension of credit for countries to defend their currency values.

After weeks of debate, the Bretton Woods Agreement was reached. The plan called for the following:

1. Fixed exchange rates between member countries, termed an "adjustable peg";
2. The establishment of a fund of gold and currencies available to members for stablization of their respective currencies (the **International Monetary Fund**); and
3. The establishment of a bank that would provide funding for long-term development projects (the **World Bank**).

Like the gold standard at the turn of the century, all participants were to establish par values of their currencies in terms of gold. Unlike the prior system, however, there was little if any convertibility of currencies for gold expected; convertibility was versus the U.S. dollar ("good as gold"). In fact, the only currency officially convertible to gold was the U.S. dollar (pegged at $35/ounce). It was this reliance on the value of the dollar and the reliance on the economic stability of the U.S. economy, in fact, which led to 25 years of relatively stable currency and to the system's eventual collapse.

One indicator of the success of the Bretton Woods system is the stability that it provided the major world currencies throughout the 1950s and 1960s (the long flat line in Figure 7.3). The U.S. dollar–British pound exchange rate enjoyed its longest period of stability at this time, and has certainly not experienced such either before or since.

Times of Crisis, 1971–1973

On August 15, 1971, President Richard M. Nixon of the United States announced that "I have instructed [Treasury] Secretary [John B.] Connally to suspend temporarily the convertibility of the dollar into gold or other assets." With this simple statement, President Nixon effectively ended the fixed exchange rates established at Bretton Woods, New Hampshire, more than 25 years earlier.

In the weeks and months following the August announcement, world currency markets devalued the dollar, although the United States had only ended gold convertibility, not officially declared the dollar's value to be less. In late 1971, the Group of Ten finance ministers met at the Smithsonian Institution in Washington, DC, to try to piece together a system to keep world markets operational. First, the dollar was offi-

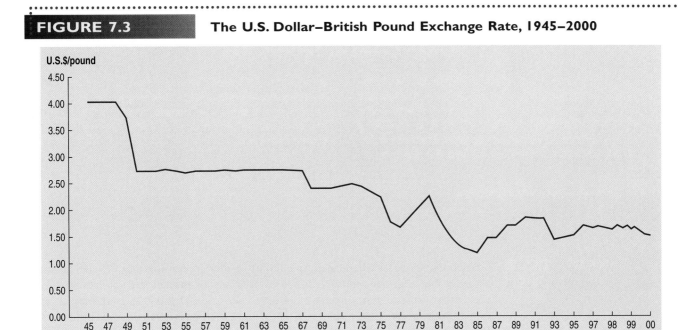

FIGURE 7.3   The U.S. Dollar–British Pound Exchange Rate, 1945–2000

cially devalued to $38/ounce of gold (as if anyone had access to gold convertibility). Secondly, all other major world currencies were revalued against the dollar (the dollar was relatively devalued), and all would now be allowed to vary from their fixed parity rates by plus/minus 2.25 percent from the previous 1.00 percent.

Without convertibility of at least one of the member currencies to gold, the system was doomed from the start. Within weeks, currencies were surpassing their allowed deviation limits; revaluations were occurring more frequently; and the international monetary system was not a "system," it was chaos. Finally, world currency trading nearly ground to a halt in March 1973. The world's currency markets closed for two weeks. When they reopened, major currencies (particularly the U.S. dollar) were simply allowed to float in value. In January 1976, the Group of Ten once again met, this time in Jamaica, and the Jamaica Agreement officially recognized what the markets had known for years—the world's currencies were no longer fixed in value.

Floating Exchange Rates, 1973–Present

Since March of 1973, the world's major currencies have floated in value versus each other. This flotation poses many problems for the conduct of international trade and commerce, problems that are themselves the subject of entire courses of study (*currency risk management* for one). The inability of a country, a country's government to be specific, to control the value of its currency on world markets has been a harsh reality for most.

Throughout the 1970s, if a government wished to alter the current value of its currency, or even slow or alter a trending change in the currency's value, the government would simply buy or sell its own currency in the market using its reserves of other major currencies. This process of **direct intervention** was effective as long as the depth of the government's reserve pockets kept up with the volume of trading on currency markets. For these countries—both then and today—the primary problem is maintaining adequate foreign exchange reserves.

By the 1980s, however, the world's currency markets were so large that the ability of a few governments (the United States, Japan, and Germany to name three) to move a market simply through direct intervention was over. The major tool now left was for

GLOBAL PERSPECTIVE 7.3

Foreign Currency Aptitude Test

If you think you are "savvy" when it comes to the fundamentals of foreign exchange rates and currency trading, take the Foreign Currency Aptitude Test. The test is offered online by the Chicago Mercantile Exchange (CME) in its continuing efforts to educate the general business public about the workings of the international currency markets and promote activity on the CME itself. The test consists of 16 questions surrounding the economic forces affecting currency values, the impacts of currency value changes on purchasing power, and the practices and procedures of how currencies are traded around the world.

 Go to: www.cme.com/market/cfot/quiz/.

government (at least when operating alone) to alter economic variables such as interest rates—to alter the *motivations* and *expectations* of market participants for capital movements and currency exchange. During periods of relative low inflation (a critical assumption), a country that wishes to strengthen its currency versus others might raise domestic interest rates to attract capital from abroad. Although relatively effective in many cases, the downside of this policy is that it raises interest rates for domestic consumers and investors alike, possibly slowing the domestic economy. The result is that governments today must often choose between an external economic policy action (raising interest rates to strengthen the currency) and a domestic economic policy action (lowering interest rates to stimulate economic activity).

There is, however, one other method of currency value management that has been selectively employed in the past 15 years, termed **coordinated intervention.** After the U.S. dollar had risen in value dramatically over the 1980 to 1985 period, the Group of Five or G5 nations (France, Japan, West Germany, United States, and United Kingdom) met at the Plaza Hotel in New York in September 1985 and agreed to a set of goals and policies, the **Plaza Agreement.** These goals were to be accomplished through coordinated intervention among the central banks of the major nations. By the Bank of Japan (Japan), the Bundesbank (Germany), and the Federal Reserve (United States) all simultaneously intervening in the currency markets, they hoped to reach the combined strength level necessary to push the dollar's value down. Their actions were met with some success in that instance, but there have been few occasions since then of coordinated intervention. Global Perspective 7.3 provides a "test" as to whether the lessons of currencies and economies are indeed understood.

The European Monetary System and the Euro

In the week following the suspension of dollar convertibility to gold in 1971, the finance ministers of a number of the major countries of western Europe discussed how they might maintain the fixed parities of their currencies independent of the U.S. dollar. By April 1972, they had concluded an agreement that was termed the "snake within the tunnel." The member countries agreed to fix parity rates between currencies with allowable trading bands of 2.25 percent variance. As a group they would allow themselves to vary by 4.5 percent versus the U.S. dollar. Although the effort was well intentioned, the various pressures and crises that rocked international economic order in the 1970s, such as the OPEC price shock of 1974, resulted in a relatively short life for the "snake."

In 1979 a much more formalized structure was put in place among many of the major members of the European Community. The **European Monetary System (EMS)** officially began operation in March 1979 and once again established a grid of fixed parity rates among member currencies. The EMS was a much more elaborate system for the management of exchange rates than its predecessor "snake." The EMS consisted of three different components that would work in concert to preserve fixed parities (also termed central rates).

First, all countries that were committing their currencies and their efforts to the preservation of fixed exchange rates entered the **Exchange-Rate Mechanism (ERM).** Although all the currencies of the countries of the European Union would be used in the calculation of important indices for management purposes, several countries chose not to be ERM participants. Participation in the ERM technically required that countries accept bilateral responsibility of maintaining the fixed rates.

The second element of the European Monetary System was the actual grid of bilateral exchange rates with their specified band limits. As under the Smithsonian Agreement and the former snake, member currencies were allowed to deviate ±2.25 percent from their parity rate. Some currencies, however, such as the Italian lira, were originally allowed larger bands (±10 percent variance) due to their more characteristic volatility.

The third and final element of the European Monetary System was the creation of the European Currency Unit (ECU). The ECU was a weighted average index of the currencies that are part of the EMS. Each currency was weighted by a value reflecting the relative size of that country's trade and gross domestic product. This allowed each currency to be defined in units per ECU.

Events and Performances of the EMS

The need for fixed exchange rates within Europe is clear. The countries of western Europe trade among themselves to a degree approaching interstate commerce in the United States. It is therefore critical to the economies and businesses of Europe that exchange rates be as stable as possible. Although it had its critics, the EMS generally was successful in providing exchange rate stability.

The Maastricht Treaty

In an attempt to maintain the momentum of European integration, the members of the European Union concluded the **Maastricht Treaty** in December 1991. The treaty, besides laying out long-term goals of harmonized social and welfare policies in the Union, specified a timetable for the adoption of a single currency to replace all individual currencies. This was a very ambitious move. The Maastricht Treaty called for the integration and coordination of economic and monetary policy so that few financial differences would exist by the time of currency unification in 1997. For a single currency to work, there could be only one monetary policy across all countries. Otherwise, different monetary policies would lead to different interest rates. Differences in interest rates often lead to large capital flows.

The first major hurdle for the single currency was the acceptance of the treaty. Denmark had been successful in gaining the right to conduct a popular vote of its citizens to determine whether the degree of integration described by Maastricht was indeed desirable. In May 1992, the Danes voted "nej" (no). The Irish and French immediately scheduled popular votes in their own countries. The Irish vote resulted in a relatively strong show of support, while the French vote conducted on September 20 was an extremely narrow yes vote. The French result was immediately dubbed "le petit oui."

The Euro

On December 31, 1998, the final fixed rates between the eleven participating currencies and the euro were put into place. On January 1, 1999, the **euro** was officially launched as a single currency for the European Union. This new currency will eventually replace all the individual currencies of the participating member states, resulting in a single, simple, efficient medium of exchange for all trade and investment activities.

"Why" Monetary Unification   According to the European Union, "Economic and Monetary Union (EMU) is a single currency area within the European Union single market in which people, goods, services, and capital move without restrictions." Beginning with the Treaty of Rome in 1957 and continuing with the Single European Act of 1987, the Maastricht Treaty of 1992, and the Treaty of Amsterdam of 1997 (draft), a core set of European countries has been working steadily toward integrating their individual countries into one larger, more efficient, domestic market. Even after the launch of the 1992 Single Europe program, however, a number of barriers to true openness remained. The use of different currencies was thought to still require both consumers and companies to treat the individual markets separately. And currency risk of cross-border commerce still persisted. The creation of a single currency is to move beyond these last vestiges of separated markets.

The growth of global markets and the increasing competitiveness of the Americas and Asia drove the members of the European Union in the 1980s and 1990s to take actions which would allow their people and their firms to compete globally. The reduction of barriers across all member countries to allow economies of scale (size and cost per unit) and scope (horizontal and vertical integration) was thought to be Europe's only hope to not be left behind in the new millennium. The economic potential of the EU is substantial. The successful implementation of a single, strong, and dependable currency for the conduct of "life" could well alter the traditional dominance of the U.S. dollar as the world's currency.

Fiscal Policy and Monetary Policy   The monetary policy for the EMU will be conducted by the newly formed European Central Bank (ECB), which according to its founding principles in the Maastricht Treaty, will have one singular responsibility: to safeguard the stability of the euro. Following the basic structures which were used in the establishment of the Federal Reserve System in the United States and the Bundesbank in Germany, the ECB is free of political pressures which have in history caused monetary authorities to yield to employment pressures by inflating economies. The ECB's independence will allow it to focus simply on the stability of the currency without falling victim to history's trap.

The ECB is headquartered in Frankfurt, and became operational in June of 1998. It became responsible for the entire monetary policy of the eleven participating states on January 1, 1999. It consists of a president whose term is eight years, assisted by a vice president and four executives from member states. The ECB's governing council sets interest rates in conjunction with the directors of the individual national central banks. These national central banks now—in conjunction with the ECB—form the European System of Central Banks (ESCB). The ECB will for the most part establish policy and the ESCB will be responsible for implementation, regulation, and enforcement. All things considered, however, the ECB will now set only one interest rate for the whole of the EU 11.

Fixing the Value of the Euro   The December 31, 1998, fixing of the rates of exchange between national currencies and the euro resulted in the conversion rates shown in Table 7.4. These are permanent fixes for these currencies. As illustrated, there are eleven EU member participants in the EMU. The British, as has been the case since the passage of the Maastricht Treaty, are skeptical of increasing EU infringement on their sovereignty, including the euro itself. Sweden, which has failed to see significant benefits from EU membership (although it is one of the newest members), is also skeptical of EMU participation. Denmark, like Britain and Sweden, has a strong political

TABLE 7.4

The Fixing of the Exchange Rates to the Euro (€)

Previous Currency	Symbol	Per Euro	
Belgian or Luxembourg francs	BEF/LUF	40.3399	1 euro = 40.3399 BEF or LUF
Deutschemarks	DEM	1.95583	1 euro = 1.95583 DEM
Spanish peseta	ESP	166.386	1 euro = 166.386 ESP
French francs	FRF	6.55957	1 euro = 6.55957 FRF
Irish punts	IEP	0.787564	1 euro = 0.787564 IEP
Italian lira	ITL	1936.27	1 euro = 1936.27 ITL
Netherlands guilders	NLG	2.20371	1 euro = 2.20371 NLG
Austrian shillings	ATS	13.7603	1 euro = 13.7603 ATS
Portuguese escudo	PTE	200.482	1 euro = 200.482 PTE
Finnish marks	FIM	5.94573	1 euro = 5.94573 FIM

element which is highly nationalistic, and has opted for now not to participate. The Greeks, however, were very much in favor of participation but could not currently qualify because of the size of their fiscal deficits and national debt, as well as inflation. It is believed, however, they will be able to reach the qualifying numbers relatively soon.

The European Union has been very careful to differentiate the euro from its predecessor the ecu (the European Currency Unit). The euro is actually money, whereas the ecu was an index of money. The ecu was never legal tender under European law, whereas the euro is already legal tender (although not yet available in coins or notes). The ecu's value was based upon the composition currencies of the European Union's participants in the European Monetary System, whereas the euro is a completely independent currency or money which is exchangeable into other currencies, but not dependent upon them for its value. The primary purpose for the ecu's existence was the construction of the exchange rate bands for the conduct of the Exchange Rate Mechanism (ERM) of the EMS. The euro is to replace all individual currencies.

On January 4, 1999, the euro began trading on world currency markets. Its introduction was a smooth one, with trading heavy and relatively stable. The euro's value has slid steadily since its introduction, however, primarily as a result of the robustness of the U.S. economy and U.S. dollar, and continuing sluggish economic sectors in the EMU countries. But all in all, it was a good start. Figure 7.4 illustrates the euro's value versus the U.S. dollar since its inception.

Under the present timetable, by January 1, 2002, the individual coins and notes of the national currencies will be gradually withdrawn from circulation and replaced with euro notes and coins. This would constitute the last remaining stage of monetary unification, and should not constitute major problems given current success.

The official abbreviation of the euro is EUR, and has been registered with the International Standards Organization (ISO), and is similar to the three-letter computer symbols used for the United States dollar, USD, and the British pound sterling, GBP. The official symbol of the euro is €, an E with two horizontal parallel lines across it. According to the European Commission, the symbol was inspired by the Greek letter epsilon, simultaneously referring to Greece's ancient role as the source of European civilization, as well as being the first letter in the word Europe.

Where the euro's value will go in the coming months and years is now a matter of markets. The fundamental factors which affect the supply and demand for any currency—inflation, monetary and fiscal policy, balance of payments—all will now drive the value of the euro. Many pundits believe the inherent strength and structure of the ECB will continue to provide a sound footing for the growth of EU business, and therefore the continued health of the euro's value on world currency markets. It is im-

FIGURE 7.4 Daily Exchange Rates: U.S. Dollars per Euro

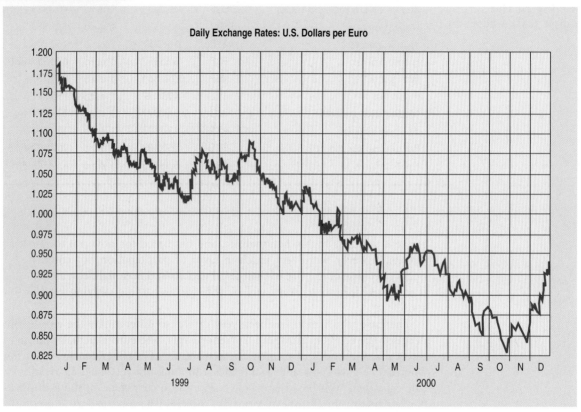

Daily Exchange Rates: U.S. Dollars per Euro

Source: © 2001 by Prof. Werner Antweiler, University of British Columbia, Vancouver, BC, Canada. Time period shown in diagram: 1/Jan/1999–31/Dec/2000.

portant to note, however, that the long-term goal of most exchange rate policies is stability, not *strength* or *weakness.*

International Money Markets

A money market traditionally is defined as a market for deposits, accounts, or securities that have maturities of one year or less. The international money markets, often termed the Eurocurrency markets, constitute an enormous financial market that is in many ways outside the jurisdiction and supervision of world financial and governmental authorities.

Eurocurrency Markets

A **Eurocurrency** is any foreign currency-denominated deposit or account at a financial institution outside the country of the currency's issuance. For example, U.S. dollars that are held on account in a bank in London are termed **Eurodollars.** Similarly, Japanese yen held on account in a Parisian financial institution would be classified as Euroyen. The *Euro* prefix does not mean these currencies or accounts are only European, as German marks on account in Singapore would also be classified as a Eurocurrency, a Euromark account.

Eurocurrency Interest Rates

What is the significance of these foreign currency-denominated accounts? Simply put, it is the purity of value that comes from no governmental interference or restrictions with their use. Eurocurrency accounts are not controlled or managed by governments (for example, the Bank of England has no control over Eurodollar accounts), therefore, the financial institutions pay no deposit insurance, hold no reserve requirements, and normally are not subject to any interest rate restrictions with respect to such accounts. Eurocurrencies are one of the purest indicators of what these currencies should yield in terms of interest. Sample Eurocurrency interest rates for 1995 are shown in Table 7.5.

There are hundreds of different major interest rates around the globe, but the international financial markets focus on a very few, the **interbank interest rates.** Interbank rates charged by banks to banks in the major international financial centers such as London, Frankfurt, Paris, New York, Tokyo, Singapore, and Hong Kong are generally regarded as "the interest rate" in the respective market. The interest rate that is used most often in international loan agreements is the Eurocurrency interest rate on U.S. dollars (Eurodollars) in London between banks: the London Interbank Offer Rate (LIBOR). Because it is a Eurocurrency rate, it floats freely without regard to governmental restrictions on reserves or deposit insurance or any other regulation or restriction that would add expense to transactions using this capital. The interbank rates for other currencies in other markets are often named similarly, PIBOR (Paris interbank offer rate), MIBOR (Madrid interbank offer rate), HIBOR (either Hong Kong or Helsinki interbank offer rate), SIBOR (Singapore interbank offer rate). While **LIBOR** is the offer rate—the cost of funds "offered" to those acquiring a loan—the equivalent deposit rate in the **Euromarkets** is LIBID, the London InterBank Bid Rate, the rate of interest other banks can earn on Eurocurrency deposits. Global Perspective 7.4 illustrates how low interest rates can get.

How do these international Eurocurrency and interbank interest rates differ from domestic rates? Answer: not by much. They generally move up and down in unison, by currency, but often differ by the percentage by which the restrictions alter the rates of interest in the domestic markets. For example, because the Euromarkets have no restrictions, the spread between the offer rate and the bid rate (the loan rate and the deposit rate) is substantially smaller than in domestic markets. This means the loan rates in international markets are a bit lower than domestic market loan rates, and deposit rates are a bit higher in the international markets than in domestic markets. This is, however, only a big-player market. Only well-known international firms, financial or nonfinancial, have access to the quantities of capital necessary to operate in the

TABLE 7.5 Exchange Rates and Eurocurrency Interest Rates	Exchange/Interest Rate	Maturity	U.S. Dollar (USD)	German Mark (DEM/USD)	Japanese Yen (JAP/USD)
	Spot Exchange Rate	—		1.5496	99.61%
	Eurocurrency Deposit Rate				
	London bid rates;	1 month	5.8750%	5.0625%	2.2813%
	percent per annum	3 months	6.3750%	5.1875%	2.3438%
		6 months	6.8750%	5.3750%	2.3438%
		12 months	7.6250%	5.7500%	2.5938%
	Forward Exchange Rate				
		1 month	—	1.5486	99.36
		3 months	—	1.5451	98.62
		6 months	—	1.5384	97.43
		12 months	—	1.5226	94.95

Source: Adpated from *Harris Bank Foreign Exchange Weekly Review,* Harris Trust and Savings Bank, Chicago, December 30, 1994.

GLOBAL PERSPECTIVE 7.4

Run on "Free" Money in Japan Cripples the Yen

There is a reason why the Japanese yen comes across as the weakling of the currency markets these days: Japan, with its struggling economy, frail stock market, and cheap funds has become a place to borrow, not invest. "Here in Japan you are in an extraordinary situation, and that extraordinary factor is that money is free," said Jesper Koll, an economist at J.P. Morgan Securities Asia Ltd. With rock-bottom interest rates essentially offset by inflation, he continued, money has become a free commodity. "As a result," he quickly added," it is flowing out of the country. Are we not now just witnessing the making of another bubble?"

So while some in the United States are preoccupied with how strong the dollar should be, here in Japan the headache is how weak the yen will get. Every few days, a Japanese official utters fretful remarks about the decline of the yen, which, in percentage terms, traveled twice as far against the dollar in January [1997] as it had moved on average each

month the previous year. Yet, Japanese officials might be relieved that investors have only recently acted on an increasingly legitimate reason for a weaker yen: the gap in interest rates between their country and the United States. People are pumping money out of Japan in search of higher yields, fueling the stock and bond markets in New York and overseas, several economists say. Investors come to Japan to raise funds, then convert their yen borrowings into dollars. When such activity turns into a flood, the value of the yen slides.

The role of interest rates becomes crucial. Japan's official discount rate, the interest rate the central bank charges commercial banks for overnight funds, stands at a record low 0.1 percent, and the rate for overnight funds secured with bonds has often hovered below that level. Factor in an inflation rate of 0.5 percent, and borrowed funds here are in theory not merely free, but offer a dividend.

Source: "Run on 'Free' Money in Japan Cripples the Yen," *International Herald Tribune,* February 22–23, 1997, 1.

Euromarkets. But as described in the following sections on international debt and equity markets, more and more firms are gaining access to the Euromarkets to take advantage of deregulated capital flows.

Linking Eurocurrency Interest Rates and Exchange Rates

Eurocurrency interest rates also play a large role in the foreign exchange markets themselves. They are, in fact, the interest rates used in the calculation of the forward rates we noted earlier. Recall that a forward rate is a contract for a specific amount of currency to be exchanged for another currency at a future date, usually 30, 60, 90, 180, or even 360 days in the future. Forward rates are calculated from the spot rate in effect on the day the contract is written along with the respective Eurocurrency interest rates for the two currencies.

For example, to calculate the 90-day forward rate, multiply the spot rate on that date by the ratio of the two Eurocurrency interest rates. Note that it is important to adjust the interest rates for the actual period of time needed, 90 days (3 months) of a 360-day financial year:

$$\text{90-Day Forward} = \text{Spot} \times \frac{1 + \left(i_{90}^{DEM} \times \frac{90}{360}\right)}{1 + \left(i_{90}^{USD} \times \frac{90}{360}\right)}$$

Now, plugging in the spot exchange rate of DEM 1.5496/USD and the two 90-day (3-month) Eurocurrency interest rates from Table 7.5 (5.1875 percent for the DEM and 6.3750 percent for the USD), the 90-day forward exchange rate is

$$\text{DEM 1.5496/USD} \times \frac{1 + \left(.051875 \times \frac{90}{360}\right)}{1 + \left(.06375 \times \frac{90}{360}\right)} = \text{DEM 1.5451/USD}$$

The forward rate of DEM 1.5451/USD is a "stronger rate" for the German mark than the current spot rate. This is because it takes 1.5496 marks to buy one dollar spot, but will only take 1.5451 marks to buy one dollar at the forward rate 90 days in the future. The German mark is said to be "**selling forward** at a premium," meaning that the forward rate for purchasing marks is more expensive than the spot rate.

Why is this the case? The reason is that the Eurocurrency interest rate on the German mark for 90 days is lower than the Eurocurrency interest rate on the U.S. dollar. If it were the other way around—if the German mark interest rate were higher than the U.S. dollar interest rate—the German mark would be "selling forward at a discount." The forward rates quoted in the foreign exchange markets, and used so frequently in international business, simply reflect the difference in interest rates between the two currencies.

Businesses frequently use forward exchange rate contracts to manage their exposure to currency risk. As Chapter 17 will detail, corporations use many other financial instruments and techniques beyond forward contracts to manage currency risk, but forwards are still the mainstay of industry.

International Capital Markets

Just as with the money markets, the international capital markets serve as links among the capital markets of individual countries, as well as constituting a separate market of their own—the capital that flows into the Euromarkets. Firms can now raise capital, debit or equity, fixed or floating interest rates, in any of a dozen currencies, for maturities ranging from one month to thirty years, in the international capital markets. Although the international capital markets traditionally have been dominated by debt instruments, international equity markets have shown considerable growth in recent years.

The international financial markets can be subdivided in a number of ways. The following sections describe the international debt and equity markets for securitized and nonsecuritized capital. This is capital that is separable and tradable, like a bond or a stock. *Nonsecuritized,* a fancy term for bank loans, was really the original source of international capital (as well as the international debt crisis).

Defining International Financing

The definition of what constitutes an international financial transaction is dependent on two fundamental characteristics: (1) whether the borrower is domestic or foreign, and (2) whether the borrower is raising capital denominated in the domestic currency or a foreign currency. These two characteristics form four categories of financial transactions, as illustrated in Figure 7.5

- **Category 1: Domestic Borrower/Domestic Currency.** This is a traditional domestic financial market activity. A borrower who is resident within the country raises capital from domestic financial institutions denominated in local currency. All countries with basic market economies have their own domestic financial markets, some large and some quite small. This is still by far the most common type of financial transaction.
- **Category 2: Foreign Borrower/Domestic Currency.** This is when a foreign borrower enters another country's financial market and raises capital denominated in the local currency. The international dimension of this transaction is based only on who the borrower is. Many borrowers, both public and private, increasingly go to the world's largest financial markets to raise capital for their enterprises. The ability of a foreign firm to raise capital in another country's financial market is sometimes limited by that government's restrictions on who can

FIGURE 7.5   Categorizing International Financial Transactions: Issuing Bonds in London

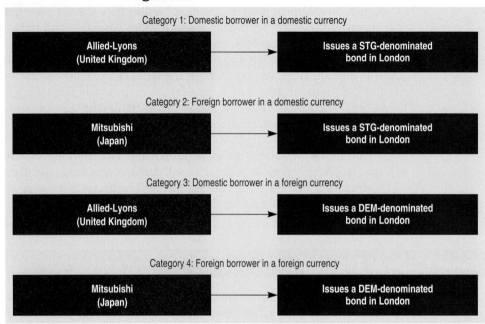

borrow, as well as the market's willingness to lend to foreign governments and companies that it may not know as well as domestic borrowers.

- **Category 3: Domestic Borrower/Foreign Currency.** Many borrowers in today's international markets need capital denominated in a foreign currency. A domestic firm may actually issue a bond to raise capital in its local market where it is known quite well, but raise the capital in the form of a foreign currency. This type of financial transaction occurs less often than the previous two types because it requires a local market in foreign currencies, a Eurocurrency market. A number of countries, such as the United States, highly restrict the amount and types of financial transactions in foreign currency. International financial centers such as London and Zurich have been the traditional centers of these types of transactions.

- **Category 4: Foreign Borrower/Foreign Currency.** This is the strictest form of the traditional Eurocurrency financial transaction, a foreign firm borrowing foreign currency. Once again, this type of activity may be restricted by which borrowers are allowed into a country's financial markets and which currencies are available. This type of financing dominates the activities of many banking institutions in the **offshore banking** market.

Using this classification system, it is possible to categorize any individual international financial transaction. For example, the distinction between an international bond and a Eurobond is simply that of a Category 2 transaction (foreign borrower in a domestic currency market) and a Category 3 or 4 transaction (foreign currency denominated in a single local market or many markets).

International Banking and Bank Lending

Banks have existed in different forms and roles since the Middle Ages. Bank loans have provided nearly all of the debt capital needed by industry since the start of the Industrial Revolution. Even in this age in which securitized debt instruments (bonds,

The Locations of the World's International Financial Centers (IFCs) and International Offshore Financial Centers (IOFCs)

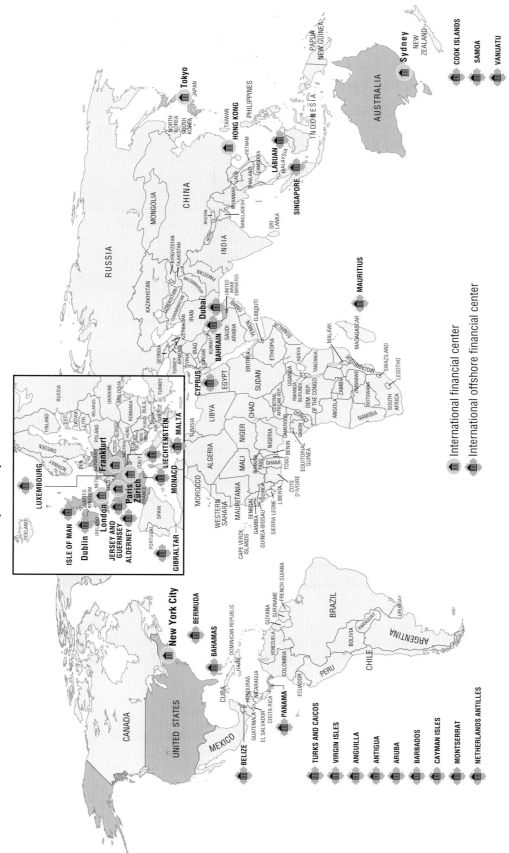

International financial center

International offshore financial center

Note: *International Financial Centers (IFCs)* are the traditional centers of international financial activity, and normally include the conduct of both domestic and international financial transactions. *International Offshore Financial Centers (IOFCs)* are centers of offshore financial activities only (no interaction is allowed with the domestic financial or business community), and normally exist because of specific tax laws and provisions which encourage their establishment and allow them special treatment.

Source: *Multinational Business Finance*, 7th Ed., Eiteman, Stonehill, and Moffett.

notes, and other types of tradable paper) are growing as sources of capital for firms worldwide, banks still perform a critical role by providing capital for medium-sized and smaller firms, which dominate all economies.

Structure of International Banking

Similar to the direct foreign investment decision sequence discussed in Chapter 5, banks can expand their cross-border activities in a variety of ways. Like all decisions involving exports and direct investment, increasing the level of international activity and capability normally requires placing more capital and knowledge at risk to be able to reap the greater benefits of expanding markets.

A bank that wants to conduct business with clients in other countries but does not want to open a banking operation in that country can do so through correspondent banks or representative offices. A **correspondent bank** is an unrelated bank (by ownership) based in the foreign country. By the nature of its business, it has knowledge of the local market and access to clients, capital, and information, which a foreign bank does not.

A second way that banks may gain access to foreign markets without actually opening a banking operation there is through representative offices. A **representative office** is basically a sales office for a bank. It provides information regarding the financial services of the bank, but cannot deliver the services itself. It cannot accept deposits or make loans. The foreign representative office of a U.S. bank will typically sell the bank's services to local firms that may need banking services for trade or other transactions in the United States.

If a bank wants to conduct banking business within the foreign country, it may open a branch banking office, a banking affiliate, or even a wholly owned banking subsidiary. A branch banking office is an extension of the parent bank and is not independently financed from the parent. The branch office is not independently incorporated, and therefore is commonly restricted in the types of banking activities that it may conduct. Branch banking is by far the most common form of international banking structure used by banks, particularly by banks based in the United States.

International Security Markets

Although banks continue to provide a large portion of the international financial needs of government and business, it is the international debt securities markets that have experienced the greatest growth in the past decade. The international security markets include bonds, equities, and private placements.

The International Bond Market

The **international bond** market provides the bulk of financing. The four categories of international debt financing discussed previously particularly apply to the international bond markets. Foreign borrowers have been using the large, well-developed capital markets of countries such as the United States and the United Kingdom for many years. These issues are classified generally as **foreign bonds** as opposed to Eurobonds. Each has gained its own pet name for foreign bonds issued in that market. For example, foreign bond issues in the United States are called Yankee bonds, in the United Kingdom Bulldogs, in the Netherlands Rembrandt bonds, and in Japan they are called Samurai bonds. When bonds are issued by foreign borrowers in these markets, they are subject to the same restrictions that apply to all domestic borrowers. If a Japanese firm issues a bond in the United States, it still must comply with all rules of the U.S. Securities and Exchange Commission, including the fact that they must be dollar-denominated.

Bonds that fall into Categories 3 and 4 are termed **Eurobonds.** The primary characteristic of these instruments is that they are denominated in a currency other than that of the country where they are sold. For example, many U.S. firms may issue Euro-yen bonds on world markets. These bonds are sold in international financial centers such as London or Frankfurt, but they are denominated in Japanese yen. Because these Eurobonds are scattered about the global markets, most are a type of bond known as a **bearer bond.** A bearer bond is owned officially by whoever is holding it, with no master registration list being held by government authorities who then track who is earning interest income from bond investments.[4] Bearer bonds have a series of small coupons that border the bond itself. On an annual basis, one of the coupons is cut or "clipped" from the bond and taken to a banking institution that is one of the listed paying agents. The bank will pay the holder of the coupon the interest payment due, and usually no official records of payment are kept.

International Equity Markets

Firms are financed with both debt and equity. Although the debt markets have been the center of activity in the international financial markets over the past three decades, there are signs that international equity capital is becoming more popular.

Again using the same categories of international financial activities, the Category 2 transaction of a foreign borrower in a domestic market in local currency is the predominant international equity activity. Foreign firms often issue new shares in foreign markets and list their stock on major stock exchanges such as those in New York, Tokyo, or London. The purpose of foreign issues and listings is to expand the investor base in the hope of gaining access to capital markets in which the demand for shares of equity ownership is strong.

A foreign firm that wants to list its shares on an exchange in the United States does so through American Depository Receipts. These are the receipts to bank accounts that hold shares of the foreign firm's stock in that firm's country. The equities are actually in a foreign currency, so by holding them in a bank account and listing the receipt on the account on the American exchange, the shares can be revalued in dollars and re-divided so that the price per share is more typical of that of the U.S. equity markets ($20 to $60 per share frequently being the desired range).

There was considerable growth in the 1990s in the Euro-equity markets. A Euro-equity issue is the simultaneous sale of a firm's shares in several different countries, with or without listing the shares on an exchange in that country. The sales take place through investment banks. Once issued, most Euro-equities are listed at least on the computer screen quoting system of the International Stock Exchange (ISE) in London, the SEAQ. As of late 1994, the Frankfurt stock exchange was the most globalized of major equity exchanges, with more than 45 percent of the firms listed on the exchange being foreign. At the same time, 18.8 percent of the firms on the London exchange were foreign, New York was a distant third with 7.6 percent foreign firms, with Tokyo was fourth with less than 6 percent.

Private Placements

One of the largest and largely unpublicized capital markets is the **private placement** market. A private placement is the sale of debt or equity to a large investor. The sale is normally a one-time-only transaction in which the buyer of the bond or stock purchases the investment and intends to hold it until maturity (if debt) or until repurchased by the firm (if equity). How does this differ from normal bond and stock sales? The answer is that the securities are not resold on a secondary market such as the domestic bond market or the New York or London stock exchanges. If the security was intended to be publicly traded, the issuing firm would have to meet a number of disclosure and registration requirements with the regulatory authorities. In the United States, this would be the Securities and Exchange Commission.

Historically, much of the volume of private placements of securities occurred in Europe, with a large volume being placed with large Swiss financial institutions and large private investors. But in recent years the market has grown substantially across all countries as the world's financial markets have grown and as large institutional investors (particularly pension funds and insurance firms) have gained control over increasing shares of investment capital.

Gaining Access to International Financial Markets

Although the international markets are large and growing, this does not mean they are for everyone. For many years, only the largest of the world's multinational firms could enter another country's capital markets and find acceptance. The reasons are information and reputation.

Financial markets are by definition risk-averse. This means they are very reluctant to make loans to or buy debt issued by firms that they know little about. Therefore, the ability to gain access to the international markets is dependent on a firm's reputation, its ability to educate the markets about what it does, how successful it has been, and its patience. The firm must in the end be willing to expend the resources and effort required to build a credit reputation in the international markets. If successful, the firm may enjoy the benefits of new, larger, and more diversified sources of the capital it needs.

The individual firm, whether it be a chili dog stand serving the international tastes of office workers at the United Nations Plaza or a major multinational firm such as Honda of Japan, is affected by exchange rates and international financial markets. Although the owner of the chili dog stand probably has more important and immediate problems than exchange rates to deal with, it is clear that firms such as Honda see the movements in these markets as critically important to their long-term competitiveness.

Summary

This chapter has spanned the breadth of the international financial markets from currencies to capital markets. The world's currency markets expanded threefold in only six years, and there is no reason to believe this growth will end. It is estimated that more than $1 trillion worth of currencies change hands daily, and the majority of it is either U.S. dollars, German marks, or Japanese yen. These are the world's major floating currencies.

But the world's financial markets are much more than currency exchanges. The rapid growth in the international financial markets—both on their own and as links between domestic markets—has resulted in the creation of a large and legitimate source of finance for the world's multinational firms. The recent expansion of market economics to more and more of the world's countries and economies sets the stage for further growth for the world's currency and capital markets, but also poses the potential for new external debt crises.

Key Terms and Concepts

direct quotation
indirect quotation
spot rates
forward rates
European terms
American terms
cross rates
triangular arbitrage
purchasing power parity
  (PPP)
Law of One Price

gold standard
Bretton Woods Agreement
International Monetary
  Fund
World Bank
direct intervention
coordinated intervention
Plaza Agreement
European Monetary
  System (EMS)

Exchange-Rate Mechanism
  (ERM)
Maastricht Treaty
euro
Eurocurrency
Eurodollars
interbank interest rates
LIBOR
Euromarkets

selling forward
offshore banking
correspondent bank
representative office
international bond
foreign bond
Eurobond
bearer bond
private placement

Questions for Discussion

1. How and where are currencies traded?
2. Does it matter whether a currency is quoted as DEM/USD or USD/DEM?
3. What is a forward rate? How do banks set forward rates?
4. What is a Eurocurrency?
5. What is a Eurocurrency interest rate? Is it different from LIBOR?
6. What makes a currency sell forward at a discount?
7. What is the difference between an international bond and a Eurobond?
8. How are the currencies of the Far East linked to the borrowing of private firms in the Far East?

9. Current economic and financial statistics and commentaries are available via the IMF's web page under "What's New," "Fund Rates," and the "IMF Committee on Balance of Payments Statistics." For an in-depth examination of the IMF's ongoing initiative on the validity of these statistics, termed *metadata*, visit the IMF's Dissemination Standards Bulletin Board listed below.

International Monetary Fund	http://www.imf.org/
IMF's Dissemination	
Standards Bulletin Board	http://dsbb.imf.org/

Internet Exercises

1. The IMF, World Bank, and United Nations are only a few of the major world organizations that track, report, and aid international economic and financial development. Using these web sites and others that may be linked to them, briefly summarize the economic outlook for the developed and emerging nations of the world. For example, the full text of chapter 1 of the *World Economic Outlook* published annually by the World Bank, is available through the IMF's web page.

International Monetary Fund	http://www.imf.org/
United Nations	http://www.unsystem.org/
The World Bank Group	http://www.worldbank.org/
Europa (EU) Homepage	http://europa.eu.int/
Bank for International Settlements	http://www.bis.org/

2. Current economic and financial statistics and commentaries are available via the IMF's web page under "What's

New," "fund Rates," and the "IMF Committee on Balance of Payments Statistics." For an in-depth examination of the IMF's ongoing initiative on the validity of these statistics, termed metadata, visit the IMF's Dissemination Standards Bulletin Board listed below.

International Monetary Fund	http://www.imf.org/
IMF's Dissemination	
Standards Bulletin Board	http://dsbb.imf.org/

3. Visit Moody's sovereign ceilings and foreign currency ratings service site on the web to evaluate what progress is being made in the nations of the Far East on recovering their perceived creditworthiness.

Moody's Sovereign Ceilings
  http://www.moodys.com/repldata/ratings/ratsov.htm/

4. American Depository Receipts (ADRs) now make up more than 10 percent of all equity trading on U.S. stock exchanges. As more companies based outside of the

United States list on U.S. markets, the need to understand the principal forces that drive ADR values increases with each trading day. Beginning with Deutsch Morgan Grenfell's detailed description of the ADR process and current ADR trading activity, prepare a briefing for senior management in your firm encouraging them to consider internationally diversifying the firm's liquid assest portfolio with ADRs.

Deutsche Morgan Grenfell
http://www.adr-dmg.com/adr-dmg/welcome.html

Recommended Readings

Bank for International Settlements. *Annual Report.* Basle, Switzerland, annually.

Black Wednesday: The Campaign for Sterling. *The Economist* (January 9, 1993): 52, 54.

Commission of the European Communities. The ECU and Its Role in the Process Towards Monetary Union. *European Economy* 48 (September 1991): 121–138.

Dewey, Davis Rich. *Financial History of the United States.* 2d ed. New York: Longmans, Green, and Company, 1903.

Driscoll, David D. *What Is the International Monetary Fund?* Washington, DC: External Relations Department, International Monetary Fund, November 1992.

Eiteman, David, Arthur Stonehill, and Michael H. Moffett. *Multinational Business Finance.* 9th ed. Reading, MA: Addison-Wesley, 2001.

Federal Reserve Bank of New York. *Summary of Results of the U.S. Foreign Exchange Market Turnover Survey,* April 1995.

The Financial Times. *FT Guide to World Currencies,* February 5, 2001.

Funabashi, Yuichi. *Managing the Dollar: From the Plaza to the Louvre.* Washington, DC: Institute of International Economics, 1988.

Giddy, Ian. *Global Financial Markets.* Lexington, MA: Heath, 1993.

Goodhart, C.A.E., and L. Figliuoli. "Every Minute Counts in Financial Markets." *Journal of International Money and Finance* 10 (1991): 23–52.

Grabbe, J. Orlin. *International Financial Markets.* 2d ed. New York: Elsevier, 1991.

International Monetary Fund. *International Financial Statistics.* Washington, DC, monthly.

Morgan Guaranty. *World Financial Markets,* New York, various issues.

The New Trade Strategy. *Business Week* (October 7, 1985): 90–93.

The Paris Pact May Not Buoy the Dollar for Long. *Business Week* (March 9, 1987): 40–41.

Rivalries Beset Monetary Pact. *Business Week* (July 15, 1944): 15–16.

Tran, Hung Q., Larry Anderson, and Ernst-Ludwing Drayss. Eurocapital Markets. Ch. 8 in *International Finance and Investing.* The Library of Investment Banking, edited by Robert Lawrence Kuhn. Homewood, IL: Dow Jones-Irwin, 1990, 129–160.

Treasury and Federal Reserve Foreign Exchange Operations. *Federal Reserve Bulletin* (October 1971): 783–814.

Ungerer, Horst, Jouko J. Hauvonen, Augusto Lopez-Claros, and Thomas Mayer. *The European Monetary System: Developments and Perspectives.* Washington, DC: International Monetary Fund, 1990.

Van Dormael, Armand. *Bretton Woods.* New York: Holmes & Meier, 1978.

The Wall Street Journal. Foreign Exchange Rates, February 5, 2001, C6.

Notes

1. Rounding errors are solved quite simply with exchange rates. With a few notable exceptions, all active trading takes place using direct quotations on foreign currencies versus the U.S. dollar (DEM 1.5152/USD, YEN 99.36/USD) and for a conventional number of decimal places. These are the base rates that are then used if needed for the calculation of the inverse indirect quotes on the foreign currencies.

2. A currency trader once remarked to the authors that the spot quotes listed on such a screen were no more and no less accurate to the "true price" than the sticker price on a showroom automobile. Of course, this may no longer be true since the introduction of the Saturn, which sells at sticker price only!

3. Actually, there are a few exceptions. Panama, for example, has used the U.S. dollar for many years.

4. Bearer bonds were issued by the U.S. government up until the early 1980s, when discontinued. Even though they were called bearer bonds, a list of bond registration numbers was still kept and recorded in order to tax investors holding the bearer instruments.

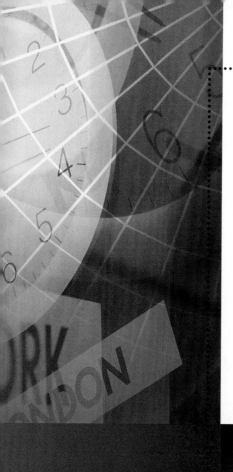

CHAPTER **8**

Economic Integration

LEARNING OBJECTIVES

- To review types of economic integration among countries

- To examine the costs and benefits of integrative arrangements

- To understand the structure of the European Union and its implications for firms within and outside Europe

- To explore the emergence of other integration agreements, especially in the Americas and Asia

Regional groupings based on economics became increasingly important in the last ten years. Thirty-two such groupings are estimated to be in existence: three in Europe, four in the Middle East, five in Asia, and ten each in Africa and the Americas. Trade within the three major blocs, the American, European, and Asian, has grown rapidly, while trading among these blocs or with outsiders is either declining or growing far more moderately.

Some of these groupings around the world have the superstructure of nation-states (such as the European Union), some (such as the ASEAN Free Trade Area) are multinational agreements that may be more political arrangements than cohesive trading blocs at present. Some arrangements are not trading blocs per se, but work to further them. The Free Trade Area of the Americas is a foreign policy initiative designed to further democracy in the region through incentives to capitalistic development and trade liberalization. The Andean Common Market and Mercosur have both indicated an intention to negotiate with the parties of the North American Free Trade Agreement (NAFTA) to create a hemispheric market. Regional economic integration in Asia has been driven more by market forces than by treaties and by a need to maintain balance in negotiations with Europe and North America. Broader formal agreements are in formative stages; for example, the Asia Pacific Economic Cooperation (APEC) initiated in 1989 would bring together partners from multiple continents and blocs. AFTA members are joined by such economic powerhouses as China, South Korea, Taiwan, and the United States.

NAFTA
North American Free Trade Agreement
Canada, Mexico, United States
GNP: $10.8 trillion; 406 million people

EEA
European Economic Area
Total of 19 European nations
GNP: $9 trillion; 386 million people

APEC

APEC

AFTA ASEAN Free Trade Area
Brunei, Indonesia, Laos, Malaysia, Myanmar, Philippines, Singapore, Thailand
GNP: $546 billion; 512 million people

FTAA
Free Trade Area of the Americas

MERCOSUR
Southern Cone Common Market
Argentina, Brazil, Paraguay, Uruguay
GNP: $1.3 trillion; 220 million people

Regional groupings are constantly being developed in multiple ways either internally, by adding new dimensions to the existing ones, or by creating new blocs. In 1995, informal proposals were made to create a new bloc between NAFTA and EU members called TAFTA, the Transatlantic Free Trade Area. Since the elimination of the Soviet Union in 1991, 12 former republics have tried to forge common economic policies, but thus far only Belarus, Kazakhstan, and Russia are signatories. By July, 2002, 12 EU countries will have adopted the euro as a common currency and eliminated their respective national currencies.

Companies are facing ever-intensifying competition and trading difficulties for sales inside a bloc. In the long term, firms encounter pressure to globalize and source locally. Actions of these global companies may also allay fears that regional blocs are nothing but protectionism on a grander scale. ●

Source: The World Factbook 2000 available at **www.cia.gov/cia/publications/factbook/index.html**; "The Euro: What You Need to Know," *The Wall Street Journal,* January 4, 1999, A5: A6; "World Trade Growth Slower in 1998 after Unusually Strong Growth in 1997," World Trade Organization press release, April 16, 1999, **www.wto.org**; "American Politics, Global Trade," *The Economist,* September 27, 1997, 23–26; Ilkka A. Ronkainen, "Trading Blocs: Opportunity or Demise for International Trade?" *Multinational Business Review* 1 (Spring 1993): 1–9; and Joseph L. Brand, "The New World Order," *Vital Speeches of the Day* 58 (December): 155–160.

The benefits of free trade and stable exchange rates are available only if nation-states are willing to give up some measure of independence and autonomy. This has resulted in increased economic integration around the world with agreements among countries to establish links through movement of goods, services, capital, and labor across borders. Some predict, however, that the regional **trading blocs** of the new economic world order will divide into a handful of protectionist super-states that, although liberalizing trade among members, may raise barriers to external trade.

Economic integration is best viewed as a spectrum. At one extreme we might envision a truly global economy in which all countries share a common currency and agree to a free flow of goods, services, and factors of production. At the other extreme would be a number of closed economies, each independent and self-sufficient. The various integrative agreements in effect today lie along the middle of this spectrum. The most striking example of successful integration is the historic economic unification that is taking place around the world today. These developments were discussed in the chapter's opening vignette. Some countries, however, give priority to maintaining economic self-sufficiency and independence. Their ranks have thinned considerably with countries such as Vietnam becoming heavily involved in international trade and investment as well as regional economic integration through membership in two blocs. Even North Korea is now considered as a possible future market by companies such as Coca-Cola.

This chapter will begin with an explanation of the various levels of economic integration. The level of integration defines the nature and degree of economic links among countries. The major arguments both for and against economic integration will be reviewed. Next, the European Union, the North American Free Trade Agreement, Asia Pacific Economic Cooperation, and other economic alliances will be discussed. Finally, possible strategic moves by international managers in response to integration are outlined.

Levels of Economic Integration

A trading bloc is a preferential economic arrangement among a group of countries. The forms it may take are shown in Table 8.1. From least to most integrative, they are the free trade area, the customs union, the common market, and the economic union.[1]

The Free Trade Area

The **free trade area** is the least restrictive and loosest from of economic integration among countries. In a free trade area, all barriers to trade among member countries are removed. Therefore, goods and services are freely traded among member countries in much the same way that they flow freely between, for example, South Carolina and New York. No discriminatory taxes, quotas, tariffs, or other trade barriers are allowed. Sometimes a free trade area is formed only for certain classes of goods and services. An agricultural free trade area, for example, implies the absence of restrictions on the trade of agricultural products only. The most notable feature of a free trade area is that each country continues to set its own policies in relation to nonmembers. In other words, each member is free to set any tariffs, quotas, or other restrictions that it chooses on trade with countries outside the free trade area. Among such free trade areas the most notable are the European Free Trade Area (EFTA) and the North American Free Trade Agreement (NAFTA). As an example of the freedom members have in terms of their policies towards nonmembers, Mexico has signed a number of bilateral free trade agreements with other blocs (the European Union) and nations (Chile) to both improve trade and to attract foreign direct investment.

The Customs Union

The **customs union** is one step further along the spectrum of economic integration. Like the members of a free trade area, members of a customs union dismantle barriers to trade in goods and services among themselves. In addition, however, the customs union establishes a common trade policy with respect to nonmembers. Typically, this takes the form of a common external tariff, where imports from nonmembers are subject to the same tariff when sold to any member country. Tariff revenues are then shared among members according to a prespecified formula. The Southern African Customs Union is the oldest and most successful example of economic integration in Africa.

The Common Market

Further still along the spectrum of economic integrations is the **common market.** Like the customs union, a common market has no barriers to trade among members and

TABLE 8.1 **Forms of International Economic Integration**	**Stage of Integration**	**Abolition of Tariffs and Quotas Among Members**	**Common Tariff and Quota System**	**Abolition of Restrictions on Factor Movements**	**Harmonization and Unification of Economic Policies and Institutions**
	Free trade area	Yes	No	No	No
	Customs union	Yes	Yes	No	No
	Common market	Yes	Yes	Yes	No
	Economic union	Yes	Yes	Yes	Yes

Source: Franklin R. Root, *International Trade and Investment,* Cincinnati, Ohio: South-Western Publishing Company, 1992, 254.

has a common external trade policy. In addition, however, factors of production are also mobile among members. Factors of production include labor, capital, and technology. Thus restrictions on immigration, emigration, and cross-border investment are abolished. The importance of **factor mobility** for economic growth cannot be overstated. When factors of production are freely mobile, then capital, labor, and technology may be employed in their most productive uses. To see the importance of factor mobility, imagine the state of the U.S. economy if unemployed steelworkers in Pittsburgh were prevented from migrating to the growing Sunbelt in search of better opportunities. Alternatively, imagine that savings in New York banks could not be invested in profitable opportunities in Chicago.

Despite the obvious benefits, members of a common market must be prepared to cooperate closely in monetary, fiscal, and employment policies. Furthermore, while a common market will enhance the productivity of members in the aggregate, it is by no means clear that individual member countries will always benefit. Because of these difficulties, the goals of common markets have proved to be elusive in many areas of the world, notably Central America and Asia. However, the objective of the **Single European Act** was to have a full common market in effect within the EU at the end of 1992. While many of the directives aimed at opening borders and markets were implemented on schedule, some sectors, such as automobiles and telecommunications, took longer to be liberalized.

The Economic Union

The creation of a true **economic union** requires integration of economic policies in addition to the free movement of goods, services, and factors of production across borders. Under an economic union, members would harmonize monetary policies, taxation, and government spending. In addition, a common currency would be used by all members. This could be accomplished de facto, or in effect, by a system of fixed exchange rates. Clearly, the formation of an economic union requires nations to surrender a large measure of their national sovereignty to supranational authorities in communitywide institutions such as the European Parliament. The ratification of the Maastricht Treaty by all of the then 12 member countries created the European Union, effective January 1, 1994. The treaty (jointly with the Treaty of Amsterdam which took effect in 1999) set the foundation for economic and monetary union (EMU) with the establishment of the Euro (€) as a common currency by January 1, 1999. A total of 12 of the EU countries are currently part of "Euroland" (Austria, Belgium, Finland, France, Germany, Greece, Holland, Ireland, Italy, Luxembourg, Portugal, and Spain). In addition, moves would be made toward a **political union** with common foreign and security policy, as well as judicial cooperation.[2]

Arguments Surrounding Economic Integration

A number of arguments surround economic integration. They center on (1) trade creation and diversion; (2) the effects of integration on import prices, competition, economies of scale, and factor productivity; and (3) the benefits of regionalism versus nationalism.

Trade Creation and Trade Diversion

Economist Jacob Viner first formalized the economic costs and benefits of economic integration.[3] Chapter 5 illustrated that the classical theory of trade predicts a win-win result for countries participating in free trade. The question is whether similar benefits accrue when free trade is limited to one group of countries. The case examined by

Viner was the customs union. The conclusion of Viner's analysis was that either negative or positive effects may result when a group of countries trade freely among themselves but maintain common barriers to trade with nonmembers.

Viner's arguments can be highlighted with a simple illustration. In 1986, Spain formally entered the European Union (EU) as a member. Prior to membership, Spain—like all nonmembers such as the United States, Canada, and Japan—traded with the EU and suffered the common external tariff. Imports of agricultural products from Spain or the United States had the same tariff applied to their products, for example, 20 percent. During this period, the United States was a lower-cost producer of wheat compared to Spain. U.S. exports to EU members may have cost $3.00 per bushel, plus a 20 percent tariff of $0.60, for a total of $3.60 per bushel. If Spain at the same time produced wheat at $3.20 per bushel, plus a 20 percent tariff of $0.64 for a total cost to EU customers of $3.84 per bushel, its wheat was more expensive and therefore less competitive.

But when Spain joined the EU as a member, its products were no longer subject to the common external tariffs; Spain had become a member of the "club" and therefore enjoyed its benefits. Spain was now the low-cost producer of wheat at $3.20 per bushel, compared to the price of $3.60 from the United States. Trade flows changed as a result. The increased export of wheat and other products by Spain to the EU as a result of its membership is termed **trade creation.** The elimination of the tariff literally created more trade between Spain and the EU. At the same time, because the United States was still outside of the EU, its products suffered the higher price as a result of tariff application. U.S. exports to the EU fell. When the source of trading competitiveness is shifted in this manner from one country to another, it is termed **trade diversion.**

Whereas trade creation is distinctly positive in moving toward freer trade, and therefore lower prices for consumers within the EU, the impact of trade diversion is negative. Trade diversion is inherently negative because the competitive advantage has shifted away from the lower-cost producer to the higher-cost producer. The benefits of Spain's membership are enjoyed by Spanish farmers (greater export sales) and EU consumers (lower prices). The two major costs are reduced tariff revenues collected and costs borne by the United States and its exports as a result of lost sales.

From the perspective of nonmembers such as the United States, the formation or expansion of a customs union is obviously negative. Most damaged will naturally be countries that may need to have trade to build their economies, such as the countries of the Third World. From the perspective of members of the customs union, the formation or expansion is only beneficial if the trade creation benefits exceed trade diversion costs. When Finland and Sweden joined the EU, the cost of an average food basket decreased by 10 percent. The only major item with a significant price increase was bananas due to the quota and tariff regime that the EU maintains in favor of its former colonies and against the major banana-producing nations in Latin America.

Reduced Import Prices

When a small country imposes a tariff on imports, the price of the goods will typically rise because sellers will increase prices to cover the cost of the tariff. This increase in price, in turn, will result in lower demand for the imported goods. If a bloc of countries imposes the tariff, however, the fall in demand for the imported goods will be substantial. The exporting country may then be forced to reduce the price of the goods. The possibility of lower prices for imports results from the greater market power of the bloc relative to that of a single country. The result may then be an improvement in the trade position of the bloc countries. Any gain in the trade position of bloc members, however, is offset by a deteriorating trade position for the exporting country. Again, unlike the win-win situation resulting from free trade, the scenario involving a trade bloc is instead win-lose.

Increased Competition and Economies of Scale

Integration increases market size and therefore may result in a lower degree of monopoly in the production of certain goods and services.[4] This is because a larger market will tend to increase the number of competing firms, resulting in greater efficiency and lower prices for consumers. Moreover, less energetic and productive economies may be spurred into action by competition from the more industrious bloc members.

Many industries, such as steel and automobiles, require large-scale production in order to obtain economies of scale in production. Therefore, certain industries may simply not be economically viable in smaller, trade-protected countries. However, the formation of a trading bloc enlarges the market so that large-scale production is justified. The lower per-unit costs resulting from scale economies may then be obtained. These lower production costs resulting from greater production for an enlarged market are called **internal economies of scale.** This is evident if the region adopts common standards, thus allowing not only for bigger markets for the companies but may enable them to become global powerhouses. Ericsson and Nokia both benefited from the EU adopting the GSM standard for wireless communication to build scale beyond their small domestic markets.

In a common market, **external economies of scale** may also be present. Because a common market allows factors of production to flow freely across borders, the firm may now have access to cheaper capital, more highly skilled labor, or superior technology. These factors will improve the quality of the firm's good or service or will lower costs or both.

Higher Factor Productivity

When factors of production are freely mobile, the wealth of the common market countries, in aggregate, will likely increase. The theory behind this contention is straightforward: factor mobility will lead to the movement of labor and capital from areas of low productivity to areas of high productivity. In addition to the economic gains from factor mobility, there are other benefits not so easily quantified. The free movement of labor fosters a higher level of communication across cultures. This, in turn, leads to a higher degree of cross-cultural understanding; as people move, their ideas, skills, and ethnicity move with them.

Again, however, factor mobility will not necessarily benefit each country in the common market. A poorer country, for example, may lose badly needed investment capital to a richer country, where opportunities are perceived to be more profitable. Another disadvantage of factor mobility that is often cited is the brain-drain phenomenon. A poorer country may lose its most talented workers when they are free to search out better opportunities. More-developed member countries worry that companies may leave for other member countries where costs of operation, such as social costs, are lower. Many multinationals, such as Philips and Goodyear, have shifted their Mercosur production to Brazil from Argentina to take advantage of lower costs and incentives provided by the Brazilian government.[5]

Regionalism versus Nationalism

Economists have composed elegant and compelling arguments in favor of the various levels of economic integration. It is difficult, however, to turn these arguments into reality in the face of intense nationalism. The biggest impediment to economic integration remains in the reluctance of nations to surrender a measure of their autonomy. Integration, by its very nature, requires the surrender of national power and self-determinism. An example of this can be seen in Global Perspective 8.1.

GLOBAL PERSPECTIVE 8.1

Integration Pains

Economic integration will not make everyone happy, despite promises of great benefits from the free flow of people, goods, services, and money. More developed countries, such as the United States and France, fear a hemorrhage of jobs as companies shift their operations to less prosperous regions with lower wages or fewer governmental controls.

Under NAFTA, cross-border controls on trucking were to be eliminated by the end of 1995, allowing commercial vehicles to move freely in four U.S. and six Mexican border states. But U.S. truckers, many of whom are members of the Teamsters Union, would have none of it. Mexican trucks were accused of being dirty, dangerous, and exceeding weight limits. President Clinton, eager for union support, delayed implementation of the agreement. The problem is that over 85 percent of the over $250 billion in U.S.-Mexican trade moves on trucks, and with no agreement, delays and red tape are common. The dispute has dragged on for years, hindering the flow of trade and upsetting business leaders on both sides of the border. In early 2001, the NAFTA Arbitration Panel ruled that Mexican trucks should be allowed on U.S. roads. At the same time,

free-trade foes who have lobbied against opening the border are ready to blame NAFTA for any accidents that involve Mexican trucks.

In Europe, politicians blame other member countries for job losses. U.S. vacuum cleaner maker Hoover decided to relocate its production facilities from France's Burgundy region to Scotland, axing 600 jobs in the process. The move has sparked controversy in France on whether the single European market will strip the country of jobs. France has accused Britain of "social dumping"—eroding workers' rights in a bid to attract foreign direct investment. As a part of the deal, Hoover's Scottish workers agreed to accept new working practices, including limits on strike action. Yet Hoover has done nothing wrong. To remain competitive in what is fast becoming a global business, the company believes it must concentrate vacuum cleaner production in Europe in a single plant. It also needs a flexible work force, which is a big competitive advantage in many industries. By shifting production bases, Hoover is estimated to cut costs by a quarter. Part of this savings will come from economies of scale, the rest from lower wages.

Source: "U.S. is Told to Let Mexican Trucks Enter," *The Wall Street Journal,* February 7, 2001, A2; Ben Fox, "Border Nations Near Deal on Trucking," *The Associated Press,* June 3, 1999; "The Trucks that Hold Back NAFTA," *The Economist* (December 13, 1997): 23–24; "A Singular Market," *The Economist* (October 22, 1994): 10–16; "French Say United Europe Promotes 'Job Poaching,'" *The Washington Post,* February 10, 1993; and "Labour Pains," *The Economist* (February 6, 1993): 71.

European Integration

Economic Integration in Europe from 1948 to the Mid-1980s

The period of the Great Depression from the late 1920s through World War II was characterized by isolationism, protectionism, and fierce nationalism. The economic chaos and political difficulties of the period resulted in no serious attempts at economic integration until the end of the war. From the devastation of the war, however, a spirit of cooperation gradually emerged in Europe.

The first step in this regional cooperative effort was the establishment of the Organization for European Economic Cooperation (OEEC) in 1948 to administer Marshall Plan aid from the United States. Although the objective of the OEEC was limited to economic reconstruction following the war, its success set the stage for more ambitious integration programs.

In 1952, six European countries (West Germany, France, Italy, Belgium, the Netherlands, and Luxembourg) joined in establishing the European Coal and Steel Community (ECSC). The objective of the ECSC was the formation of a common market in coal, steel, and iron ore for member countries. These basic industries were rapidly revitalized into competitive and efficient producers. The stage was again set for further cooperative efforts.

In 1957, the European Economic Community (EEC) was formally established by the **Treaty of Rome.** In 1967, ECSC and EEC as well as the European Atomic Energy

TABLE 8.2	1957	1993	1995	2004+	
Membership of the European Union	France	Great Britain (1973)	Austria (1995)	Czech Republic	Bulgaria
	West Germany	Ireland (1973)	Finland (1995)	Cyprus	Latvia
	Italy	Denmark (1973)	Sweden (1995)	Estonia	Lithuania
	Belgium	+ Greece (1981)		Hungary	Malta
	Netherlands	Spain (1986)		Poland	Romania
	Luxembourg	Portugal (1986)		Slovenia	Slovakia

Community (EURATOM) were merged to form the European Community (EC). Table 8.2 shows the founding members of the community in 1957, members who have joined since, as well as those invited to join early in the twenty-first century. The Treaty of Rome is a monumental document, composed of more than 200 articles. The main provisions of the treaty are summarized in Table 8.3. The document was (and is) quite ambitious. The cooperative spirit apparent throughout the treaty was based on the premise that the mobility of goods, services, labor, and capital—the "four freedoms" —was of paramount importance for the economic prosperity of the region. Founding members envisioned that the successful integration of the European economies would result in an economic power to rival that of the United States.

Some countries, however, were reluctant to embrace the ambitious integrative effort of the treaty. In 1960, a looser, less integrated philosophy was endorsed with the formation of the European Free Trade Association (EFTA) by eight countries: United Kingdom, Norway, Denmark, Sweden, Austria, Finland, Portugal, and Switzerland. Barriers to trade among member countries were dismantled, although each country maintained its own policies with nonmember states. Since that time EFTA has lost much of its original significance due to its members joining the European Union (Denmark and the United Kingdom in 1973, Portugal in 1986, and Austria, Finland, and Sweden in 1995). EFTA countries have cooperated with the EU through bilateral free trade agreements, and, since 1994, through the European Economic Area (EEA) arrangement, which allows for free movement of people, goods, services, and capital within the combined area of the EU and EFTA. Of the EFTA countries, Iceland and Liechtenstein (which joined the EEA only in May 1995) have decided not to apply for membership in the EU. Norway was to have joined in 1995, but after a referendum declined membership, as it did in 1973. Switzerland's decision to stay out of the EEA (mainly to keep the heaviest EU truck traffic from its roads) has hampered its negotiations for membership in the EU. In 2000, however, it entered into a series of bilateral agreements to liberalize its trading relations with the EU.[6]

A conflict that intensified throughout the 1980s was between the richer and more industrialized countries and the poorer countries of the Mediterranean region. The

TABLE 8.3	
Main Provisions of the Treaty of Rome	1. Formation of a free trade area: the gradual elimination of tariffs, and other barriers to trade among members
	2. Formation of a customs union: the creation of a uniform tariff schedule applicable to imports from the rest of the world
	3. Formation of a common market: the removal of barriers to the movement of labor, capital, and business enterprises
	4. The adoption of common agricultural policies
	5. The creation of an investment fund to channel capital from the more advanced to the less developed regions of the community

power of the bloc of poorer countries was strengthened in the 1980s when Greece, Spain, and Portugal became EU members. Many argue that the dismantling of barriers between the richer and poorer countries will benefit the poorer countries by spurring them to become competitive. However, it may also be argued that the richer countries have an unfair advantage and therefore should accord protection to the poorer members before all barriers are dismantled.

Another source of difficulty that intensified in the 1980s was the administration of the community's **common agricultural policy (CAP)**. Most industrialized countries, including the United States, Canada, and Japan, have adopted wide-scale government intervention and subsidization schemes for the agriculture industry. In the case of the EU, however, these policies have been implemented on a communitywide, rather than national, level. The CAP includes: (1) a price-support system whereby EU agriculture officials intervene in the market to keep farm product prices within a specified range; (2) direct subsidies to farmers; and (3) rebates to farmers who export or agree to store farm products rather than sell them within the community. The implementation of these policies absorbs about two-thirds of the annual EU budget.

The CAP has caused problems both within the EU and in relationships with nonmembers. Within the EU, the richer, more industrialized countries resent the extensive subsidization of the more agrarian economies. Outside trading partners, especially the United States, have repeatedly charged the EU with unfair trade practices in agriculture.

The European Union Since the Mid-1980s

By the mid-1980s, a sense of "Europessimism" permeated most discussions of European integration. Although the members remained committed in principle to the "four freedoms," literally hundreds of obstacles to the free movement of goods, services, people, and capital remained. For example, there were cumbersome border restrictions on trade in many goods, and although labor was theoretically mobile, the professional certifications granted in one country were often not recognized in others.

Growing dissatisfaction with the progress of integration, as well as threats of global competition from Japan and the United States, prompted the Europeans to take action. A policy paper published in 1985 (now known as the **1992 White Paper**) exhaustively identified the remaining barriers to the four freedoms and proposed means of dismantling them.[7] It listed 282 specific measures designed to make the four freedoms a reality.

The implementation of the White Paper proposals began formally in 1987 with the passage of the **Single European Act,** which stated that "the community shall adopt measures with the aim of progressively establishing the internal market over a period expiring on 31 December 1992." The Single European Act envisaged a true common market where goods, people, and money could move between Germany and France with the same ease that they move between Wisconsin and Illinois.

Progress toward the goal of free movement of goods has been achieved largely due to the move from a "common standards approach" to a "mutual recognition approach." Under the common standards approach, EU members were forced to negotiate the specifications for literally thousands of products, often unsuccessfully. For example, because of differences in tastes, agreement was never reached on specifications for beer, sausage, or mayonnaise. Under the mutual recognition approach, the laborious quest for common standards is in most cases no longer necessary. Instead, as long as a product meets legal and specification requirements in one member country, it may be freely exported to any other, and customers serve as final arbiters of success.

Less progress toward free movement of people in Europe has been made than toward free movement of goods. The primary difficulty is that EU members have been unable to agree on a common immigration policy. As long as this disagreement persists, travelers between countries must pass through border checkpoints. Some countries—notably Germany—have relatively lax immigration policies, while others—especially those with higher unemployment rates—favor strict controls on immigration. A second issue concerning the free movement of people is the acceptability of professional certifications across countries. In 1993, the largest EU member countries passed all of the professional worker directives. This means that workers' professional qualifications will be recognized throughout the EU, guaranteeing them equal treatment in terms of employment, working conditions, and social protection in the host country.

Attaining free movement of capital within the EU entails several measures. First, citizens will be free to trade in EU currencies without restrictions. Second, the regulations governing banks and other financial institutions will be harmonized. In addition, mergers and acquisitions will be regulated by the EU rather than by national governments. Finally, securities will be freely tradable across countries.

A key aspect of free trade in services is the right to compete fairly to obtain government contracts. Under the 1992 guidelines, a government should not give preference to its own citizens in awarding government contracts. However, little progress has been made in this regard. Open competition in public procurement has been calculated to save $10 billion a year. Yet the nonnational share of contracts has been 5 percent since 1992. Worse still, few unsuccessful bidders complain, for fear that they would be ignored in future bids.[8]

Project 1992 was always a part of a larger plan and a process more so than a deadline.[9] Many in the EU bureaucracy argued that the 1992 campaign required a commitment to **economic and monetary union** (**EMU**) and subsequently to political union. These sentiments were confirmed at the Maastricht summit in December 1991, which produced various recommendations to that effect. The ratification of the **Maastricht Treaty** in late 1993 by all of the 12 member countries of the EC created the **European Union** starting January 1, 1994. The treaty calls for a commitment to economic and monetary union and a move toward political union with common foreign and security policy.[10] (The European Monetary System, its history, and future are discussed in detail in Chapter 7.)

Despite the uncertainties about the future of the EU, new countries want to join. Most EFTA countries have joined or are EU applicants in spite of the fact that the EEA treaty gives them most of the benefits of a single market. They also want to have a say in the making of EU laws and regulations. Although no official and final timetable for final membership has been set, the EU invited the Czech Republic, Cyprus, Estonia, Hungary, Poland, and Slovenia to begin membership negotiations in March 1998. Five other central European countries (Bulgaria, Latvia, Lithuania, Romania, Slovakia) and Malta were given precandidate status.[11] The two-tier process was devised because some countries were deemed to have prepared their democratic institutions and economies better and faster than others. The optimistic expectation is that the new members will be able to take part in the elections for the European Parliament in 2004. Turkey's application has been hindered by its poor human rights record, its unresolved dispute with Greece over Cyprus, and internal problems with Kurdish separatists. In the meanwhile, these countries will enjoy preferential trade rights through association memberships with the EU. Access to EU markets is essential for growth in central Europe. The EU hopes, furthermore, that the promise of membership and access to its markets will result in greater political stability in the region.[12] The arrangement will also create investment opportunities for firms and cheaper goods for consumers in the EU.

Organization of the EU

The executive body of the EU is the European Commission, headquartered in Brussels. The commission may be likened to the executive branch of the U.S. government. It is

The European Union has several governing bodies, one of which is the EU Parliament. The Parliament has 626 members elected by popular vote in their home nations. The Parliament has power to veto membership applications and trade agreements with non-EU countries.

composed of 20 commissioners (two from each larger member country and one from each smaller member). The commissioners oversee more than 30 directorates-general (or departments), such as agriculture, transportation, and external relations. The commissioners are appointed by the member states, but according to the Treaty of Rome, their allegiance is to the community, not to their home country. The commission's staff in Brussels numbers over 15,000. Since the EU has 11 official languages, 20 percent of the staff are interpreters and translators.

The Council of Ministers has the final power to decide EU actions. There are a total of 87 votes in the council. The votes are allocated to the representatives of member countries on the basis of country size. For example, the U.K. has ten votes, while Luxembourg has two. Some of the most important provisions of the Single European Act expanded the ability of the council to pass legislation. The number of matters requiring unanimity was reduced, and countries' ability to veto legislation was weakened substantially. Most decisions are taken by qualified majority vote. The Presidency of the Council rotates among the member states every six months.

The Court of Justice is somewhat analogous to the judicial branch of the U.S. government. The court is composed of 15 judges and is based in Luxembourg. The court adjudicates matters related to the European Constitution, especially trade and business disputes. Judicial proceedings may be initiated by member countries, as well as by firms and individuals.

The European Parliament is composed of 626 members elected by popular vote in member countries for a five-year term. The Parliament started essentially as an advisory body with relatively little power. The fact that the only elected body of the EU had little policymaking power led many to charge that the EU suffers from a "democratic deficit." In other words, decisions are made bureaucratically rather than democratically. However, the Single European Act empowered the Parliament to veto EU membership applications as well as trade agreements with non-EU countries. The Maastricht and Amsterdam Treaties empowered the Parliament to veto legislation in certain policy areas and confer with the Council to settle differences in their respective drafts of legislation. Furthermore, the Parliament can question the Commission and Council, amend and reject the budget, and dismiss the entire Council.[13] The entities and the process of decision making are summarized in Figure 8.1. Not shown are the Court of Auditors (who are to ensure the sound financial management of the EU) and the European Central Bank which is responsible for monetary policy and the euro.

The future expansion of the EU will cause changes in the decision-making processes. The five big members will give up their second Commissioner in 2005, and new members will be able to name a Commissioner until the EU reaches 27 members. At that stage, a rotational system will take over. Within the Council, the number of votes will be reweighted to accommodate the new members. The European Parliament will be enlarged to 732 members.[14]

Implications of the Integrated European Market

Perhaps the most important implication of the four freedoms for Europe is the economic growth that is expected to result.[15] Several specific sources of increased growth have been identified. First, there will be gains from eliminating the transaction costs associated with border patrols, customs procedures, and so forth. Second, economic growth will be spurred by the economies of scale that will be achieved when production facilities become more concentrated. Third, there will be gains from more intense competition among EU companies. Firms that were monopolists in one country will now be subject to competition from firms in other EU countries. The introduction of

FIGURE 8.1   Organization and Decision Making of the EU

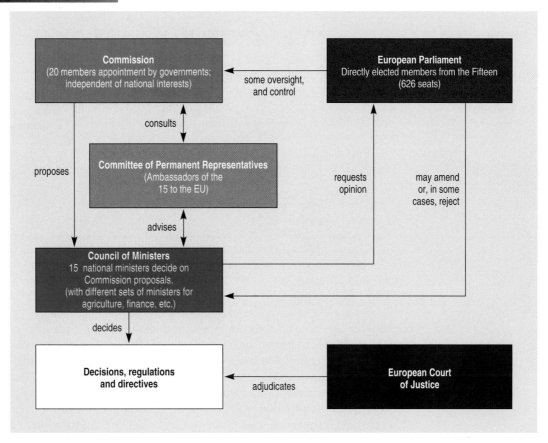

Source: Adapted from "My, How You've Grown," The Economist, January 25, 1992, 31–32.

the euro is expected to add to the efficiencies, especially in terms of consolidation of firms across industries and across countries. Furthermore, countries in Euroland will enjoy cheaper transaction costs, reduced currency risks, and consumers and businesses will enjoy price transparency and increased price-based competition. Corporate reactions to the euro will be discussed further in Chapter 13.

The proposals have important implications for firms within and outside Europe. There will be substantial benefits for those firms already operating in Europe. Those firms will gain because their operations in one country can now be freely expanded into others, and their products may be freely sold across borders. In a borderless Europe, firms will have access to many more millions of consumers. In addition, the free movement of capital will allow the firms to sell securities, raise capital, and recruit labor throughout Europe. Substantial economies of scale in production and marketing will also result. The extent of these economies of scale will depend on the ability of the managers to find panregional segments or to homogenize tastes across borders through their promotional activity.

For firms from nonmember countries, European integration presents various possibilities depending on the firm's position within the EU.[16] Table 8.4 provides four different scenarios with proposed courses of action. Well-established U.S.-based multinational marketers such as H.J. Heinz and Colgate-Palmolive will be able to take advantage of the new economies of scale. For example, 3M plants earlier turned

TABLE 8.4	Proposed Company Responses to European Markets	
Company Status	**Challenges**	**Response**
Established multinational in one market/multiple markets	Exploit opportunities from improved productivity	
	Meet challenge of competitors	Pan-European strategy
	Cater to customers/intermediaries doing same	
Firm with one European subsidiary	Competition	Expansion
	Loss of niche	Strategic alliances
		Rationalization
		Divestment
Exporter to Europe	Competition	European branch
	Access	Selective acquisition
		Strategic alliance
No interest in Europe	Competition at home	Entry
	Lost opportunity	

Source: Material drawn from John F. Magee, "1992 Moves Americans Must Make." *Harvard Business Review* 67 (May–June 1989): 78–84.

out different versions of the company's products for various markets. Now, the 3M plant in Wales, for example, makes videotapes and videocassettes for all of Europe.[17] Colgate-Palmolive has to watch out for competitors, such as Germany's Henkel, in the brutally competitive detergent market. At the same time, large-scale retailers, such as France's Carrefour and Germany's Aldi group, are undertaking their own efforts to exploit the situation with hypermarkets supplied by central warehouses with computerized inventories. Their procurement policies have to be met by companies such as Heinz. Many multinationals are developing pan-European strategies to exploit the emerging situation; that is, they are standardizing their products and processes to the greatest extent possible without compromising local input and implementation.

A company with a foothold in only one European market is faced with the danger of competitors who can use the strength of multiple markets. Furthermore, the elimination of barriers may do away with the company's competitive advantage. For example, more than half of the 45 major European food companies are in just one or two of the individual European markets and seriously lag behind broader-based U.S. and Swiss firms. Similarly, automakers PSA and Fiat are nowhere close to the cross-manufacturing presence of Ford and GM. The courses of action include expansion through acquisitions or mergers, formation of strategic alliances (for example, AT&T's joint venture with Spain's Telfónica to produce state-of-the-art microchips), rationalization by concentrating only on business segments in which the company can be a pan-European leader, and finally, divestment.

Exporters will need to worry about maintaining their competitive position and continued access to the market. Companies with a physical presence may be in a better position to assess and to take advantage of the developments. Some firms, such as Filament Fiber Technology Inc. of New Jersey, have established production units in Europe. Digital Microwave Corporation of California decided to defend its market share in Europe by joining two British communications companies and setting up a digital microwave radio and optical-fiber plant in Scotland.[18] In some industries, marketers do not see a reason either to be in Europe at all or to change from exporting to more involved modes of entry. Machinery and machine tools, for example, are in great demand in Europe, and marketers in these companies say they have little reason to manufacture there.

The term Fortress Europe has been used to describe the fears of many U.S. firms about a unified Europe. The concern is that while Europe dismantles internal barriers, it will raise external ones, making access to the European market difficult for U.S. and other non-EU firms. In a move designed to protect European farmers, for example, the EU has occasionally banned the import of certain agricultural goods from the United States. The EU has also called on members to limit the number of U.S. television programs broadcast in Europe. Finally, many U.S. firms are concerned about the relatively strict domestic content rules recently passes by the EU. These rules require certain products sold in Europe to be manufactured with European inputs. One effect of the perceived threat of Fortress Europe has been an increased direct investment in Europe by U.S. firms. Fears that the EU will erect barriers to U.S. exports and of the domestic content rules governing many goods have led many U.S. firms to initiate or expand European direct investment.

North American Economic Integration

Although the EU is undoubtedly the most successful and well-known integrative effort, integration efforts in North America, although only a few years old, have gained momentum and attention. What started as a trading pact between two close and economically well-developed allies has already been expanded conceptually to include Mexico, and long-term plans call for further additions. However, in North American integration the interest is purely economic; there are no constituencies for political integration.

U.S.–Canada Free Trade Agreement

After three failed tries this century, the United States and Canada signed a free trade agreement that went into effect January 1, 1989. The agreement created a $5 trillion continental economy.[19] The two countries had already had sectoral free trade arrangements; for example, one for automotive products had existed for over 20 years. Even before the agreement, however, the United States and Canada were already the world's largest trading partners, and there were relatively few trade barriers. The new arrangement eliminated duties selectively in three stages over the 1989–1999 period.[20] For example, the first round eliminated a 3.9 percent tariff on U.S. computers shipped to Canada as well as 4.9–22 percent duties on trade in whiskey, skates, furs, and unprocessed fish. The sensitive sectors, such as textiles, steel, and agricultural products, were not liberalized until the latter part of the transitionary period. Both countries see the free trade agreement as an important path to world competitiveness. Although there have been some dislocations, due to production consolidation, for example, the pact has created 750,000 jobs in the United States and 150,000 in Canada. It has also added as much as 1 percent in growth to both countries' economies. Trade between the United States and Canada exceeded $400 billion in 2000.

North American Free Trade Agreement

Negotiations on a North American Free Trade Agreement (NAFTA) began in 1991 to create the world's largest free market, with currently over 400 million consumers and a total output of over 10 trillion.[21] The pact marked a bold departure: never before had industrialized countries created such a massive free trade area with a developing country neighbor.

NAFTA opened North America to trade causing a flood of activity between the United States and Mexico. To deal with complaints about differences in environmental standards and worker protections between countries, the North American Agreement on Labor Cooperation and the Commission on Environmental Compliance were established.

Since Canada stands to gain very little from NAFTA (its trade with Mexico is 1 percent of its trade with the United States), much of the controversy has centered on the gains and losses for the United States and Mexico. Proponents have argued that the agreement will give U.S. firms access to a huge pool of relatively low-cost Mexican labor at a time when demographic trends are indicating labor shortages in many parts of the United States. At the same time, many new jobs will be created in Mexico. The agreement will give firms in both countries access to millions of additional consumers, and the liberalized trade flows will result in faster economic growth in both countries. Overall, the corporate view toward NAFTA is overwhelmingly positive.

Opposition to NAFTA has been on issues relating to labor and the environment. Unions in particular worried about job loss to Mexico given lower wages and work standards, some estimating that six million U.S. workers were vulnerable to job loss. A distinctive feature of NAFTA is the two side agreements that were worked out to correct perceived abuses in labor and in the environment in Mexico. The North American Agreement on Labor Cooperation (NAALC) was set up to hear complaints about worker abuse. Similarly, the Commission on Environmental Compliance was established to act as a public advocate on the environment. The side agreements have, however, had little impact, mainly because the mechanisms they created have almost no enforcement power.[22]

After a remarkable start in increased trade and investment, NAFTA suffered a serious setback due to significant devaluation of the Mexican peso in early 1995 and the subsequent impact on trade. Critics of NAFTA argued that too much was expected too fast of a country whose political system and economy were not ready for open markets. In response, advocates of NAFTA argued that there was nothing wrong with the Mexican real economy and that the peso crisis was a political one that would be overcome with time. As a matter of fact, with the help of the United States and the IMF, Mexico's economy started a strong recovery in 1996.

Trade between Canada, Mexico, and the United States has increased dramatically since NAFTA took effect, with total trade exceeding $650 billion in 2000.[23] Reforms have turned Mexico into an attractive market in its own right. Mexico's gross domestic product has been expanding by more than 3 percent every year since 1989, and exports to the United States have risen 20 percent a year to $138 billion in 2000. By institutionalizing the nation's turn to open markets, the free trade agreement has attracted considerable new foreign investment. The United States has benefited from Mexico's success. U.S. exports to Mexico are nearly double those to Japan at $112 billion in 2000. While the surplus of $1.3 billion in 1994 has turned to a deficit of $25 billion in 2000, these imports have helped in Mexico's growth and will, therefore, strengthen NAFTA in the long term. Furthermore, U.S. imports from Mexico have been shown to have much higher U.S. content than imports from other countries.[24] At present, cooperation between Mexico and the United States is taking new forms beyond trade and investment; for example, bi-national bodies have been established to tackle issues such as migration, border control, and drug trafficking.[25]

Among the U.S. industries to benefit are computers, autos, petrochemicals, and financial services. In 1990, Mexico opened its computer market by eliminating many burdensome licensing requirements and cutting the tariff from 50 percent to 20 percent. As a result, exports surged 23 percent in that year alone. IBM, which makes personal and mid-sized computers in Mexico, anticipates sales growth to about $1 billion from that country. In Mexico's growth toward a more advanced society, manufacturers of consumer goods will also stand to benefit. NAFTA has already had a major impact in the emergence of new retail chains, many established to handle new products from abroad.[26] The top 20 exports and imports between Mexico and the United States are in virtually the same industries, indicating intra-industry trade in complementary products. This is evidence of industry specialization and building of economies of scale for global competitiveness.[27]

Free trade does produce both winners and losers. Although opponents concede that the agreement is likely to spur economic growth, they point out that segments of the U.S. economy will be harmed by the agreement. Overall wages and employment for unskilled workers in the United States will fall because of Mexico's low-cost labor pool. U.S. companies have been moving operations to Mexico since the 1960s. The door was opened when Mexico liberalized export restrictions to allow for more so-called **maquiladoras,** over 3,600 plants that make goods and parts or process food for export back to the United States. The supply of labor is plentiful, the pay and benefits are low, and the work regulations are lax by U.S. standards. The average maquiladora wage ranges from $1.60 to $2.20 per hour, depending on other benefits.[28] The maquiladora industry has grown remarkably within NAFTA, constituting, $60 billion of Mexico's manufactured exports and employing 1.3 million people.[29] The investment mix within the industry is changing, however, with the arrival of Asian consumer-electronics producers, such as Philips, SONY, and Samsung.[30] In early 2001, a major change took place: tariff breaks formerly given on all imported parts, supplies, equipment, and machinery used by foreign maquiladora factories in Mexico now apply only to inputs from Canada, Mexico, and the United States. This will affect the Asian factories most since they still import a large amount of components from across the Pacific. Europeans are less affected because of Mexico's free trade agreement with the EU which will eliminate tariffs gradually by 2007.

A 1993 International Trade Commission assessment estimated that while NAFTA would create a net gain of 35,000 to 93,500 U.S. jobs by 1995, it would also cause U.S. companies to shed as many as 170,000 jobs.[31] Recent studies have put job gain or loss as almost a washout. The good news is that free trade has created higher skilled and better paying jobs in the United States as a result of growth in exports. As a matter of fact, jobs in exporting firms tend to pay 10 to 15 percent more than the jobs they replace. Losers have been U.S. manufacturers of auto parts, furniture, and household glass; sugar, peanut, and citrus growers; and seafood and vegetable producers. The fact that job losses have been in more heavily unionized sectors has made these losses politically charged. In most cases, high Mexican shipping and inventory costs will continue to make it more efficient for many U.S. industries to serve their home market from U.S. plants.

Countries dependent on trade with NAFTA countries are concerned that the agreement will divert trade and impose significant losses on their economies. Asia's continuing economic success depends largely on easy access to the North American markets, which account for more than 25 percent of annual export revenue for many Asian countries. Lower-cost producers in Asia are likely to lose some exports to the United States if they are subject to tariffs while Mexican firms are not and may, therefore, have to invest in NAFTA.[32] Similarly, many in the Caribbean and Central America fear that the apparel industries of their regions will be threatened, as would much-needed investments.

NAFTA may be the first step toward a hemispheric bloc, but nobody expects it to happen any time soon. It took more than three years of tough bargaining to reach an agreement between the United States and Canada, two countries with parallel economic, industrial, and social systems.[33] The challenges of expanding free trade throughout Latin America will be significant. However, many of Latin America's groupings are making provisions to join NAFTA and create a hemispheric trade regime.[34] As a first step, Chile was scheduled to join as a fourth member in 1997. However, Chile's membership has not materialized due to U.S. political maneuvering, which, in turn, has jeopardized economic integration in the Americas, as shown in Global Perspective 8.2. Overall, many U.S. companies fear that Latin Americans will move closer to the Europeans if free trade discussions do not progress. For example, both Mercosur and Mexico have signed free trade agreements with the EU.[35]

GLOBAL PERSPECTIVE 8.2

Lack of Negotiation Authority Leaves U.S. Behind

The United States has long regarded Latin America as its business backyard and NAFTA as the model for Western Hemispheric integration. However, this thinking and the goal of creating a free trade bloc covering the hemisphere by the year 2005 have run into considerable problems, some created by the United States and some by others.

The Clinton Administration failed to gain "fast track" negotiating authority from the U.S. Congress (that is, to broker deals that Congress could vote up or down but not amend). This was to be the major tool in extending NAFTA to the rest of Latin America and to boost U.S. exports, thereby eliminating local tariffs, which typically run from 10 to 13 percent. Without this authority, Latin Americans fear that any agreements negotiated could be turned down later or amended to have unacceptable terms by the U.S. Congress. "No fast track, no concrete negotiations," says Jose Botafogo, the Brazilian Foreign Ministry's subsecretary general of commerce. Rejecting the opinion that they are protectionist, the majority in the U.S. Congress argue that they want trade deals to include tough new requirements for U.S. trading partners to raise their labor and environmental standards. The alternative is that the U.S.'s standards might be dragged down.

The effects have been significant. Fed up with the wait to join NAFTA, Chile has moved closer to Europe and its own neighbors. It has joined MERCOSUR as an associate member, has free trade agreements with both Mexico (1992) and Canada (1996), and has begun formal talks on a separate trade deal with the EU. U.S. companies are reporting trade deals lost to their Canadian competitors who are free of Chile's average 11 percent tariffs. A number of U.S. companies have started shipping goods from plants in Canada and Mexico to Chile. Until 1997, Chrysler had been selling minivans in Chile that were made at its St. Louis, Missouri, plant. Now they've switched to importing those made at their plant in Ontario to capitalize on lower tariffs.

The failure to win fast track is likely to strengthen the hand of Mercosur, especially Brazil, in setting the terms of regional integration. A MERCOSUR-led move to hemispheric free trade could lead to slower efforts to remove barriers to U.S. exports and instead favor trade among South American nations. MERCOSUR's trade with the United States was $30 billion in 2000, while intra-bloc trade was $20 billion.

MERCOSUR's biggest trading partners, however, are the Europeans, who are expected to improve their positions dramatically as a result of U.S. inactivity. Their trade annually exceeds $40 billion. The EU and MERCOSUR want to build a trans-Atlantic free trade zone of 680 million by 2005. EU politicians are striving to make the European flavor of Latin America even stronger. Europeans have won many of the top privatization deals since the early 1990s when governments in South America started opening up their markets. Spain's Telefónica de Espána, for example, has spent $5 billion buying telephone companies in Brazil, Chile, Peru, and Argentina, where France Télécom and STET of Italy are active as well. France's Electricité de France and Lyonnaise des Eaux have taken over state-owned facilities. In Brazil, seven of the ten largest private companies are European-owned, while just two are controlled by U.S. interests. Europeans dominate huge sectors in the economy, from automakers Volkswagen and Fiat to French supermarket chain Carrefour to Anglo-Dutch personal-care products group Gesy-Lever.

United States' trading partners in Latin America are perceiving that the U.S. government is willing to subjugate its international obligations to domestic political concerns. If trade is increasingly being sacrificed for the ultimate purpose of gaining political votes, access to the U.S. market may lose some of its value as the ultimate prize. MERCOSUR, for example, is arguing that NAFTA is not the only game in the region. In response, U.S. corporations, which have been traditionally opposed to linking labor and environmental standards to trade, are willing to agree to such a link if it means that the Bush Administration can secure fast-track authority to negotiate trade agreements, especially with Latin American nations.

Source: "Firms Rethink Hostility to Linking Trade, Labor Rights," *The Wall Street Journal,* February 2, 2001, A12, "EU Aims to Raise Global Stature with Ties to Asia, Latin America," *The Wall Street Journal,* June 28, 2000, A16; Calvin Sims, "Latin America Fears Stagnation in Trade Talks with U.S.," *The New York Times,* April 19, 1998, www.nytimes.com; "Chile Takes Its Trade Elsewhere," *The Washington Post,* December 25, 1997, A29, A38; "In Backyard of the U.S., Europe Gains Ground In Trade, Diplomacy," *The Wall Street Journal,* September 18, 1997, A1, A8; "Is Europe Elbowing the U.S. Out of South America?" *Business Week,* August 4, 1997, 56; "Ah, Pan-American Free Trade," *The Economist,* March 1, 1997, 43; "Latin America Becomes USA's Lost Horizon," *Crossborder Monitor,* February 5, 1997.

Other Economic Alliances

The world's developing countries have perhaps the most to gain from successful integrative efforts. Because many of these countries are also quite small, economic growth is difficult to generate internally. Many of these countries have adopted policies of **import substitution** to foster economic growth. With an import substitution policy, new domestic industries produce goods that were formerly imported. Many of these industries, however, can be efficient producers only with a higher level of production than can be consumed by the domestic economy. Their success, therefore, depends on accessible export markets made possible by integrative efforts.

Integration in Latin America

Before the signing of the U.S.–Canada Free Trade Agreement, all of the major trading bloc activity in the Americas had taken place in Latin America. One of the longest-lived integrative efforts among developing countries was the Latin America Free Trade Association (LAFTA), formed in 1961. As the name suggests, the primary objective of LAFTA was the elimination of trade barriers. The 1961 agreement called for trade barriers to be gradually dismantled, leading to completely free trade by 1973. By 1969, however, it was clear that a pervasive protectionist ideology would keep LAFTA from meeting this objective, and the target date was extended to 1980. In the meantime, however, the global debt crisis, the energy crisis, and the collapse of the Bretton Woods system prevented the achievement of LAFTA objectives. Dissatisfied with LAFTA, the group made a new start as the Latin American Integration Association (LAIA) in 1980. The objective is a higher level of integration than that envisioned by LAFTA; however, the dismantling of trade barriers remains a necessary and elusive first step.

The Central American Common Market (CACM) was formed by the Treaty of Managua in 1960. The CACM has often been cited as a model integrative effort for other developing countries. By the end of the 1960s, the CACM had succeeded in eliminating restrictions on 80 percent of trade among members. A continuing source of difficulty, however, is that the benefits of integration have fallen disproportionately to the richer and more developed members. Political difficulties in the area have also hampered progress. However, the member countries renewed their commitment to integration in 1990.

Integration efforts in the Caribbean have focused on the Caribbean Community and Common Market formed in 1968. Caribbean nations (as well as Central American nations) have benefited from the **Caribbean Basin Initiative (CBI),** which, since 1983, has extended trade preferences and granted access to the markets of the United States. Under NAFTA the preferences are lost, which means that the countries have to cooperate more closely among each other. Mexico and CACM have already started planning for a free trade agreement. Legislation by the United States to extend unilaterally NAFTA benefits to CBI countries to protect them from investment and trade diversion was passed in 2000.[36]

None of the activity in Latin America has been hemispheric; the Central Americans have had their structures, the Caribbean nations theirs, and the South Americans had their own different forms. However, in a dramatic transformation, these nations are now looking for free trade as a salvation from stagnation, inflation and debt.[37] In response to the recent developments, Brazil, Argentina, Uruguay, and Paraguay set up a common market with completion by the end of 1994 called Mercosur (Mercado Comun del Sur).[38] Despite their own economic challenges and disagreements over trade policy, the Mercosur members and the two associate members, Bolivia and Chile, have agreed to economic-convergence targets similar to those of the EU as a precursor to the euro. These are in areas of inflation, public debt, and fiscal deficits. Bolivia, Colombia, Ecuador, Peru, and Venezuela have formed the Andean Common Market (ANCOM). Many Latin nations are realizing that if they do not unite, they will become in creasingly marginal in the global market. In approaching the EU with a free trade agreement, for example, Mercosur members want to diversity their trade relationships and reduce their dependence on U.S. trade.

The ultimate goal is a hemispheric free trade zone from Point Barrow, Alaska, to Patagonia. The first step to such a zone was taken in December 1994, when leaders of 34 countries in the Americas agreed to work toward the **Free Trade Area of the**

Americas (FTAA) by 2005. Ministerials held since have established working groups to gather data and make recommendations in preparation for the FTAA negotiations. The larger countries have agreed to consider giving smaller and less-developed countries more time to reduce tariffs, to open their economies to foreign investment, and to adopt effective laws in areas such as anti-trust, intellectual property rights, bank regulation, and prohibitions on corrupt business practices. At the same time, the less-developed countries have agreed to include labor and environmental standards in the negotiations.[39]

Changes in corporate behavior have been swift. Free-market reforms and economic revival have had companies ready to export and to invest in Latin America. For example, Brazil's opening of its computer market resulted in Hewlett-Packard establishing a joint venture to produce PCs. Companies are also changing their approaches with respect to Latin America. In the past, Kodak dealt with Latin America through 11 separate country organizations. It has since streamlined its operations to five "boundariless" companies organized along product lines and, taking advantage of trade openings, created centralized distribution, thereby making deliveries more efficient and decreasing inventory-carrying costs.[40]

Integration in Asia

The development in Asia has been quite different from that in Europe and in the Americas. While European and North American arrangements have been driven by political will, market forces may compel politicians in Asia to move toward formal integration. While Japan is the dominant force in the area and might seem the choice to take leadership in such an endeavor, neither the Japanese themselves nor the other nations want Japan to do it. The concept of a "Co-Prosperity Sphere" of 50 years ago has made nations wary of Japan's influence.[41] Also, in terms of economic and political distance, the potential member countries are far from each other, especially compared to the EU. However, Asian interest in regional integration is increasing for pragmatic reasons. First, European and American markets are significant for the Asian producers, and some type of organization or bloc may be needed to maintain leverage and balance against the two other blocs. Second, given that much of the growth in trade for the nations in the region is from intra-Asian trade, having a common understanding and policies will become necessary. A future arrangement will most likely use the frame of the most established arrangement in the region, the Association of Southeast Asian Nations (ASEAN). Before 1991, ASEAN had no real structures, and consensus was

reached through information consultations. In October 1991, ASEAN members (Brunei, Indonesia, Malaysia, Philippines, Singapore, Thailand, Vietnam and, since 1997, Cambodia, Myanmar, and Laos) announced the formation of a customs union called ASEAN Free Trade Area (AFTA), with completion expected by 2010. The Malaysians have pushed for the formation of the East Asia Economic Group (EAEG), which would add Hong Kong, Japan, South Korea, and Taiwan to the list. This proposal makes sense; without Japan and the rapidly industrializing countries of the region such as South Korea and Taiwan, the effect of the arrangement would be small. Japan's reaction has been generally negative toward all types of regionalization efforts, mainly because it has had the most to gain from free trade efforts. However, part of what has been driving regionalization has been Japan's reluctance to foster some of the elements that promote free trade, such as reciprocity.[42] Should the other trading blocs turn against Japan, its only resort may be to work toward a more formal trade arrangement in Pacific Asia.

Another formal proposal for cooperation would start building bridges between two emerging trade blocs. Some individuals have publicly called for a U.S.–Japan common market. Given the differences on all fronts between the two, the proposal may be quite unrealistic at this time. Negotiated trade liberalization will not open Japanese markets due to major institutional differences, as seen in many rounds of successful negotia-

GLOBAL PERSPECTIVE 8.3

In Support of Free Trade in Asia

General Motors—and all the major car makers—are driving into Asia. In the period of 2001–2010, vehicle sales in Asia are expected to grow by more than that of Europe and North America combined, making Asia the second largest automotive market with sales approaching 20 million per year. The world's largest industrial company has found the environmental challenges considerable despite the lure of substantial market potential made possible by the growing middle class. In addition to distribution challenges and aggressive competition from other manufacturers, both local and foreign, the most daunting ones are barriers to free trade. For example, in Indonesia, GM faces competition from a local model, the Timor, which costs substantially less due to government supports (that is, lower duties on imported components). Before President Suharto's resignation, the company was run by one of his sons.

To overcome distribution difficulties, GM will invest $450 million in a regional manufacturing facility in Rayong Province to build the specially designed and engineered Opel "Car for Asia" beginning early in the twenty-first century. The Thai facility is the culmination of GM's buildup in Asia that started in 1990 with the establishment of a regional office in Hong Kong and representative offices in Bangkok, Jakarta, Kuala Lumpur, and Beijing. In 1994, the GM's Asia headquarters was moved from Detroit to Singapore. Singapore provides coordination and support, but GM will tailor manufacturing, sales, and distribution to local requirements. It established GM China in 1994 as a separate entity, and in Japan it bought a 37.5 percent equity stake in Isuzu. The Asian economic crisis,

which hit Thailand especially hard, made GM scale down the investment in Thailand from $750 million and switch production from a $15,000 Astra to a considerably cheaper model.

The Asian market allows companies such as GM to test new strategies such as e-commerce because they still do not have a lot of bricks and mortar there. Retail operations are often controlled by the manufacturers (and not dealers who would object to real-time sales) and their factories are more flexible to allow build-to-order programs to operate.

To combat protectionism and further the cause of free trade, GM has developed a three-pronged strategy. The first approach focuses on executives working with government representatives from the United States, European Union, and Japan to dismantle what GM regards as the largest flaws. The company uses its clout as a major investor, but it can also call on support from industries that follow it into a new market, such as component manufacturers. On the second level, GM works within existing frameworks to balance the effects of nationalistic policies. In countries such as Indonesia and Malaysia, it develops company-specific plans to preserve avenues of sales even under challenging circumstances. Finally, GM is also pursuing its business strategy in Asia's free trade areas. Since it will be a long time before barriers are taken down in the Asia Pacific Economic Cooperation Forum (APEC), its immediate focus is on the ASEAN Free Trade Area (AFTA). GM is hopeful that the automotive sector will be a beneficiary of tariff reductions—provided that member governments can be persuaded that such cuts are in their best interests.

Source: "GM Tests E-Commerce Plans in Emerging Markets," *The Wall Street Journal,* October 25, 1999, B6, "YGM Press Conference," October 15, 1999, available at **http://www.generalmotors.com/company/news_events/speeches/991015.htm;** "U.S. Auto Makers Demonstrate Commitment to Thailand," U.S.–ASEAN Business Council press release, May 12, 1999, **www.us–asean.org;** "GM Delays Plans to Open Big Thai Plant," *The Wall Street Journal,* January 6, 1998, A2; and "GM Presses for Free Trade in Asia," *Crossborder Monitor,* January 15, 1997, 1, 9. See also: **http://www.GMBuyPower.com** and **www.gmautoworld.com.tw.**

tions but totally unsatisfactory results. The only solution for the U.S. government is to forge better cooperation between the government and the private sector to improve competitiveness.[43]

In 1989, Australia proposed the Asia Pacific Economic Cooperation (APEC) as an annual forum. The proposal called for ASEAN members to be joined by Australia, New Zealand, Japan, China, Hong Kong, Taiwan, South Korea, Canada, and the United States. It was initially modeled after the Organization for Economic Cooperation and Development (OECD), which is a center for research and high-level discussion. Since then, APEC's goals have become more ambitious. At present, APEC has 21 members with a combined GNP of $18 trillion, nearly 44 percent of global trade, and is the third largest economy of the world. The key objectives of APEC are to liberalize trade by 2020, to facilitate trade by harmonizing standards, and to build human capacities for realizing the region's ambitions. The trade-driven economies of the region have the world's largest pool of savings, the most advanced technologies, and fastest growing markets. Therefore, companies with interests in the region are observing and supporting APEC-related developments closely as shown in Global Perspective 8.3.

However, the future actions of the other two blocs will determine how quickly and in what manner the Asian bloc, whatever it is, will respond. Also, the stakes are the highest for the Asian nations since their traditional export markets have been in Europe and in North America and, in this sense, very dependent on free access.

Economic integration has also taken place on the Indian subcontinent. In 1985, seven nations of the region (India, Pakistan, Bangladesh, Sri Lanka, Nepal, Bhutan, and the Maldives) launched the South Asian Association for Regional Cooperation (SAARC). Cooperation is limited to relatively noncontroversial areas, such as agriculture and regional development. Elements such as the formation of a common market have not been included.

Integration in Africa and the Middle East

Africa's economic groupings range from currency unions among European nations and their former colonies to customs unions among neighboring states. In addition to wanting to liberalize trade among members, African countries want to gain better access to European and North American markets for farm and textile products. Given that most of the countries are too small to negotiate with the other blocs, alliances have been the solution. In 1975, 16 west African nations attempted to create a mega-market large enough to interest investors from the industrialized world and reduce hardship through economic integration. The objective of the Economic Community of West African States (ECOWAS) was to form a customs union and eventual common market. Although many of its objectives have not been reached, its combined population of 160 million represents the largest economic entirty in sub-Saharan Africa. Other entities in Africa include the Common Market for Eastern and Southern Africa (COMESA), the Economic Community of Central African States (CEEAC), the Southern African Customs Union, the Southern African Development Community (SADC), and some smaller, less globally oriented blocs such as the Economic Community of the Great Lakes Countries, the Mano River Union, and the East African Community (EAC). Most member countries are part of more than one block (for example, Tanzania is a member in both the EAC and SADC). The blocs, for the most part, have not been successful due to the small size of the members and lack of economic infrastructure to produce goods to be traded inside the blocs. Moreover, some of the blocs have been relatively inactive for substantial periods of time while their members endure internal political turmoil or even warfare amongst each other.[44]

Countries in the Arab world have made some progress in economic integration. The Arab Maghreb Union ties together Algeria, Libya, Mauritania, Morocco, and Tunisia in northern Africa. The Gulf Cooperation Council (GCC) is one of the most powerful, economically speaking, of any trade groups. The per-capita income of its six member states (Bahrain, Kuwait, Oman, Qatar, Saudi Arabia, and the United Arab Emirates) is in the ninetieth percentile in the world. The GCC was formed in 1980 mainly as a defensive measure due to the perceived threat from the Iran–Iraq war. Its aim is to achieve free trade arrangements with the EU and EFTA as well as bilateral trade agreements with western European nations.

A listing of the major regional trade agreements is provided in Table 8.5.

Economic Integration and the International Manager

Regional economic integration creates opportunities and challenges for the international manager. Economic integration may have an impact on a company's entry mode by favoring direct investment, since one of the basic rationales for integration is to generate favorable conditions for local production and inter-regional trade. By design, larger markets are created with potentially more opportunity. Harmonization efforts may result in standardized regulations, which can positively affect production and marketing efforts.

TABLE 8.5	**AFTA**	**ASEAN Free Trade Area**
Major Regional Trade Associations		Brunei, Cambodia, Indonesia, Laos, Malaysia, Myanmar, Philippines, Singapore, Thailand, Vietnam
	ANCOM	**Andean Common Market**
		Bolivia, Colombia, Ecuador, Peru, Venezuela
	APEC	**Asia Pacific Economic Cooperation**
		Australia, Brunei, Canada, Chile, China, Hong Kong, Indonesia, Japan, Malaysia, Mexico, New Zealand, Papua New Guinea, Peru, Philippines, Russia, Singapore, South Korea, Taiwan, Thailand, United States, Vietnam
	CACM	**Central American Common Market**
		Costa Rica, El Salvador, Guatemala, Honduras, Nicaragua, Panama
	CARICOM	**Caribbean Community**
		Antigua and Barbuda, Bahamas, Barbados, Belize, Dominica, Grenada, Guyana, Jamaica, Montserrat, St. Kitts-Nevis, St. Lucia, St. Vincent and the Grenadines, Suriname, Trinidad-Tobago
	ECOWAS	**Economic Community of West African States**
		Benin, Berkina Faso, Cape Verde, Gambia, Ghana, Guinea, Guinea-Bissau, Ivory Coast, Liberia, Mali, Mauritania, Niger, Nigeria, Senegal, Sierra Leone, Togo
	EU	**European Union**
		Austria, Belgium, Denmark, Finland, France, Germany, Greece, Ireland, Italy, Luxembourg, Netherlands, Portugal, Spain, Sweden, United Kingdom
	EFTA	**European Free Trade Association**
		Iceland, Liechtenstein, Norway, Switzerland
	GCC	**Gulf Cooperation Council**
		Bahrain, Kuwait, Oman, Qatar, Saudi Arabia, United Arab Emirates
	LAIA	**Latin American Integration Association**
		Argentina, Bolivia, Brazil, Chile, Colombia, Cuba, Ecuador, Mexico, Paraguay, Peru, Uruguay, Venezuela
	Mercosur	**Southern Common Market**
		Argentina, Brazil, Paraguay, Uruguay
	NAFTA	**North American Free Trade Agreement**
		Canada, Mexico, United States
	SAARC	**South Asian Association for Regional Cooperation**
		Bangladesh, Bhutan, India, Maldives, Nepal, Pakistan, Sri Lanka
	SACU	**Southern African Customs Union**
		Botswana, Lesotho, Namibia, South Africa, Swaziland

For information see http://www.aseansec.org; http://www.apec.org; http://www.caricom.org; http://www.eurunion.org; http://www.nafta.org.

The international manager must, however, make assessments and decisions regarding integrating markets from four points of view.[45] The first task is to create a vision of the outcome of the change. Change in the competitive landscape can be dramatic if scale opportunities can be exploited in relatively homogeneous demand conditions. This could be the case, for example, for industrial goods and consumer durables, such as cameras and watches, as well as for professional services. The

International Groupings

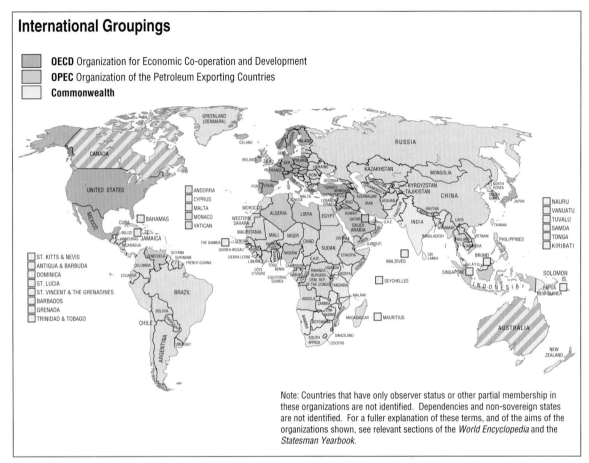

■ **OECD** Organization for Economic Co-operation and Development
▨ **OPEC** Organization of the Petroleum Exporting Countries
□ **Commonwealth**

Note: Countries that have only observer status or other partial membership in these organizations are not identified. Dependencies and non-sovereign states are not identified. For a fuller explanation of these terms, and of the aims of the organizations shown, see relevant sections of the *World Encyclopedia* and the *Statesman Yearbook*.

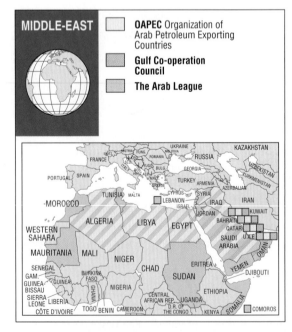

MIDDLE-EAST

□ **OAPEC** Organization of Arab Petroleum Exporting Countries
▨ **Gulf Co-operation Council**
▦ **The Arab League**

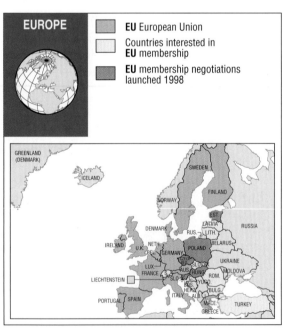

EUROPE

▨ **EU** European Union
□ Countries interested in **EU** membership
▦ **EU** membership negotiations launched 1998

Sources: *Statesman Yearbook* ; *The European Union: A Guide for Americans*, 2000, www.eurounion.org/infores/euguide/euguide.html; "Afrabet Soup," *The Economist*, February 10, 2001, p. 77, www.economist.com

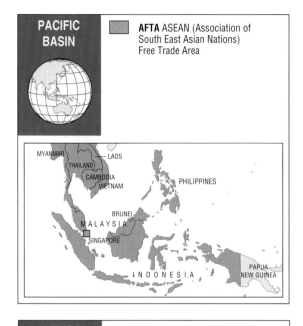

PACIFIC BASIN

AFTA ASEAN (Association of South East Asian Nations) Free Trade Area

MYANMAR
LAOS
THAILAND
CAMBODIA
VIETNAM
PHILIPPINES
BRUNEI
MALAYSIA
SINGAPORE
INDONESIA
PAPUA NEW GUINEA

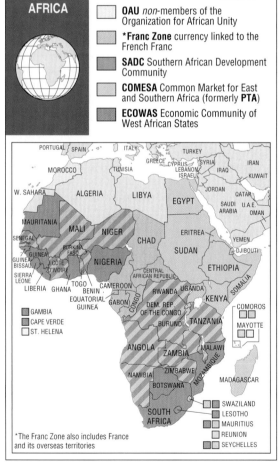

AFRICA

OAU *non*-members of the Organization for African Unity

***Franc Zone** currency linked to the French Franc

SADC Southern African Development Community

COMESA Common Market for East and Southern Africa (formerly **PTA**)

ECOWAS Economic Community of West African States

PORTUGAL SPAIN ITALY TURKEY
GREECE CYPRUS SYRIA IRAN
MOROCCO TUNISIA LEBANON IRAQ
ISRAEL KUWAIT
W. SAHARA ALGERIA LIBYA EGYPT JORDAN QATAR
SAUDI ARABIA U.A.E. OMAN
MAURITANIA MALI NIGER CHAD ERITREA YEMEN
SENEGAL BURKINA SUDAN DJIBOUTI
GUINEA FASO
GUINEA- CÔTE NIGERIA ETHIOPIA
BISSAU D'IVOIRE CENTRAL
SIERRA TOGO AFRICAN REPUBLIC SOMALIA
LEONE BENIN CAMEROON
LIBERIA GHANA RWANDA UGANDA
EQUATORIAL GABON CONGO DEM. REP. KENYA
GUINEA OF THE CONGO COMOROS
GAMBIA BURUNDI TANZANIA MAYOTTE
CAPE VERDE
ST. HELENA
ANGOLA MALAWI
ZAMBIA
NAMIBIA ZIMBABWE MOZAMBIQUE
BOTSWANA MADAGASCAR
SWAZILAND
SOUTH LESOTHO
AFRICA MAURITIUS
REUNION
*The Franc Zone also includes France SEYCHELLES
and its overseas territories

AMERICAS

NAFTA North American Free Trade Agreement

ANCOM Andean Common Market

MERCOSUR Southern Common Market

CARICOM Caribbean Community and Common Market

CACM Central American Common Market

GREENLAND (DENMARK)

CANADA

UNITED STATES

MEXICO
BAHAMAS
CUBA
HAITI
DOMINICAN REPUBLIC
BELIZE JAMAICA
GUATEMALA NICARAGUA
EL SALVADOR
HONDURAS VENEZUELA GUYANA
COSTA RICA SURINAME
PANAMA COLOMBIA FRENCH GUIANA
ECUADOR

PERU BRAZIL

BOLIVIA

CHILE PARAGUAY

ARGENTINA URUGUAY

ST. KITTS & NEVIS
ANTIGUA & BARBUDA
MONTSERRAT
DOMINICA
ST. LUCIA
ST. VINCENT & THE GRENADINES
BARBADOS
GRENADA
TRINIDAD & TOBAGO

international manager will have to take into consideration varying degrees of change readiness within the markets themselves; that is, governments and other stakeholders, such as labor unions, may oppose the liberalization of competition especially when national champions such as airlines, automobiles, energy, and telecommunications are concerned. However, with deregulation monopolies have had to transform into competitive industries. In Germany, for example, the price of long-distance calls has fallen 40 percent forcing the former monopolist, Deutsche Telekom, to streamline its operations and seek new business abroad. By fostering a single market for capital, the euro is pushing Europe closer to a homogeneous market in goods and services, thereby exerting additional pressure on prices.[46]

The international manager then will have to develop a strategic response to the new environment to maintain a sustainable long-term competitive advantage. Those companies already present in an integrating market should fill in gaps in goods and market portfolios through acquisitions or alliances to create a regional or global company. It is increasingly evident that even a regional presence is not sufficient and sights need to be set on a presence beyond that. In industries such as automobiles, mobile telephony, and retailing, blocs in the twenty-first century may be dominated by two or three giants leaving room only for niche players. Those with currently weak positions, or no presence at all, will have to create alliances for market entry and development with established firms. General Mills created Cereal Partners Worldwide with Nestlé to establish itself in Europe and to jointly develop new market opportunities in Asia. An additional option for the international manager is leaving the market altogether in response to the new competitive conditions or the level of investment needed to remain competitive. Bank of America sold its operations in Italy to Deutsche Bank once it determined the high cost of becoming a pan-European player.

Whatever the changes, they will call for company reorganization.[47] Structurally, authority will have to be more centralized so regional programs can be executed. In staffing, focus will have to be on individuals who understand the subtleties of consumer behavior across markets and therefore are able to evaluate the similarities and differences among cultures and markets. In developing systems for the planning and implementation of regional programs, adjustments will have to be made to incorporate views throughout the organization. If, for example, decisions on regional advertising campaigns are made at headquarters without consultation with country operations, resentment by the local staff will lead to less-than-optimal execution. The introduction of the euro will mean increased coordination in pricing as compared to the relative autonomy in price setting enjoyed by country organizations in the past. Companies may move corporate or divisional headquarters from the domestic market to be closer to the customer or centers of innovation. For example, after Procter & Gamble's reorganization, the fabric and home care business unit was headquartered in Brussels, Belgium.

Finally, economic integration will involve various powers and procedures, such as the EU's Commission and its directives. The international manager is not powerless to influence both of them; a passive approach may result in competitors gaining an advantage or a disadvantageous situation emerging for the company. For example, it was very important for the U.S. pharmaceutical industry to obtain tight patent protection as part of the NAFTA agreement and substantial time and money was spent on lobbying both the executive and legislative branches of the U.S. government in the effort to meet its goal. Often policymakers rely heavily on the knowledge and experience of the private sector in carrying out its own work. Influencing change will therefore mean providing policymakers with industry information such as test results. Lobbying will usually have to take place at multiple levels simultaneously; within the EU, this means the European Commission in Brussels, the European Parliament in Strasbourg, or the national governments within the EU. Managers with substantial resources have established their own lobbying offices in Brussels, while smaller companies get their voices heard through joint offices or their industry associations. In terms of lobbying, U.S. firms have been at an advantage given their experience in their home market; however, for many non-U.S. firms, lobbying is a new, yet necessary, skill to be acquired. At the same time, managers in two or more blocs can work together to produce more efficient trade through, for example, mutual recognition agreements (MRAs) on standards.[48]

Cartels and Commodity Price Agreements

An important characteristic that distinguishes developing countries from industrialized countries is the nature of their export earnings. While industrialized countries rely heavily on the export of manufactured goods, technology, and services, the developing countries rely chiefly on the export of primary products and raw materials— for example, copper, iron ore, and agricultural products. This distinction is important for several reasons. First, the level of price competition is higher among sellers of primary goods, because of the typically larger number of sellers and also because primary goods are homogeneous. This can be seen by comparing the sale of computers with, for example, copper. Only three of four countries are competitive forces in the computer market, whereas at least a dozen compete in the sale of copper. Furthermore, while goods differentiation and therefore brand loyalty are likely to exist in the market for computers, buyers of copper are likely to purchase on the basis of price alone. A second distinguishing factor is that supply variability will be greater in the market for primary goods because production often depends on uncontrollable factors such as weather. For these reasons, market prices of primary goods—and therefore developing country export earnings—are highly volatile.

Responses to this problem have included cartels and commodity price agreements. A **cartel** is an association of producers of a particular good. While a cartel may consist of an association of private firms, our interest is in the cartels formed by nations. The objective of a cartel is to suppress the market forces affecting its good in order to gain greater control over sales revenues. A cartel may accomplish this objective in several ways. First, members may engage in price fixing. This entails an agreement by producers to sell at a certain price, eliminating price competition among sellers. Second, the cartel may allocate sales territories among its members, again suppressing competition. A third tactic calls for members to agree to restrict production, and therefore supplies, resulting in artificially higher prices.

The most widely known cartel is the Organization of Petroleum Exporting Countries (OPEC). It consists of 11 oil-producing and exporting countries (Algeria, Indonesia, Iran, Iraq, Kuwait, Libya, Nigeria, Qatar, Saudi Arabia, United Arab Emirates, and Venezuela). OPEC became a significant force in the world economy in the 1970s. In 1973, the Arab members of OPEC were angered by U.S. support for Israel in the war in the Mideast. In response, the Arab members declared an embargo on the shipment of oil to the United States and quadrupled the price of oil—from approximately $3 to $12 per barrel. OPEC tactics included both price fixing and production quotas. Continued price increases brought the average price per barrel to nearly $35 by 1981. The cartel has experienced severe problems since, however. First, the demand for OPEC oil declined considerably as the result of conservation, efficiency (for example, while U.S. output has increased by 20 percent in the past years, oil consumption has increased only by 9 percent), the use of alternative sources, and increased oil production by nonmembers. Furthermore, the Asian financial crisis resulted in a downturn for oil for the last years of the twentieth century. OPEC's market share has declined from its 55 percent peak in 1974 to 40 percent at present.[49] All of these factors also contributed to sharp declines in the price of oil. Second, the cohesiveness among members diminished. Sales often occurred at less than the agreed-upon price, and production quotas were repeatedly violated. However, when low prices made it less profitable to explore for new reserves and resources, OPEC decided to cut back production in 1999 to coincide with Asia's economic rebound and increasing demand. To avoid damage to the global economy that a $40 per barrel price might bring, cooperation from OPEC in terms of production amounts is necessary.[50]

International **commodity price agreements** involve both buyers and sellers in an agreement to manage the price of a certain commodity. Often, the free market is allowed to determine the price of the commodity over a certain range. However, if demand and supply pressures cause the commodity's price to move outside that range, an elected or appointed manager will enter the market to buy or sell the commodity to bring the price back into the range. The manager controls the **buffer stock** of the commodity. If prices float downward, the manager purchases the commodity and adds to the buffer stock. Under upward pressure, the manager sells the commodity from the buffer stock. This system is somewhat analogous to a managed exchange rate system, in which authorities buy and sell to influence exchange rates. International commodity agreements are currently in effect for sugar, tin, rubber, cocoa, and coffee.

Summary

Economic integration involves agreements among countries to establish links through the movements of goods, services, and factors of production across borders. These links may be weak or strong depending on the level of integration. Levels of integration include the free trade area, customs union, common market, and full economic union.

The benefits derived from economic integration include trade creation, economies of scale, improved terms of trade, the reduction of monopoly power, and improved cross-cultural communication. However, a number of disadvantages may also exist. Most importantly, economic integration may work to the detriment of nonmembers by causing deteriorating terms of trade and trade diversion. In addition, no guarantee exists that all members will share the gains from integration. The biggest impediment to economic integration is nationalism. There is strong resistance to surrendering autonomy and self-determinism to cooperative agreements.

The most successful example of economic integration is the European Union. The EU has succeeded in eliminating most barriers to the free flow of goods, services, and factors of production. In addition, the EU has made progress toward the evolution of a common currency and central bank, which are fundamental requirements of an economic union. In the Americas, NAFTA is paving the way for a hemispheric trade bloc.

A number of regional economic alliances exist in Africa, Latin America, and Asia, but they have achieved only low levels of integration. Political difficulties, low levels of development, and problems with cohesiveness have impeded integrative progress among many developing countries. However, many nations in these areas are seeing economic integration as the only way to prosperity in the future.

International commodity price agreements and cartels represent attempts by producers of primary products to control sales revenues and export earnings. The former involves an agreement to buy or sell a commodity to influence prices. The latter is an agreement by suppliers to fix prices, set production quotas, or allocate sales territories. OPEC for example, has had inestimable influence on the global economy during the past 30 years.

Key Terms and Concepts

trading bloc
free trade area
customs union
common market
factor mobility
Single European Act
economic union
political union

trade creation
trade diversion
internal economies of scale
external economies of scale
Treaty of Rome
common agricultural
 policy (CAP)
1992 White Paper

Single European Act
economic and monetary
 union (EMU)
Maastricht Treaty
European Union
Fortress Europe
maquiladoras
import substitution

Caribbean Basin Initiative
 (CBI)
Free Trade Area of the
 Americas (FTAA)
cartel
commodity price
 agreement
buffer stock

Questions for Discussion

1. Explain the difference between a free-trade area and a customs union. Speculate why negotiations were held for a North American Free Trade Agreement rather than for a North American Common Market.
2. What problems might a member country of a common market be concerned about?
3. Construct an example of a customs union arrangement resulting in both trade creation and trade diversion.
4. Distinguish between external and internal economies of scale resulting from economic integration.

5. Are economic blocs (such as the EU and NAFTA) building blocs or stumbling blocs as far as worldwide free trade is concerned?
6. Suppose that you work for a medium-sized manufacturing firm in the Midwest. Approximately 20 percent of your sales are to European customers. What threats and opportunities does your firm face as a result of an integrated European market?

Internet Exercises

1. Compare and contrast two different points of view on expanding NAFTA by accessing the web sites of America Leads on Trade, an industry coalition promoting increased access to world markets (**http://www.fasttrack.org**), and the AFL-CIO, American Federation of Labor–Congress of Industrial Organizations (**http://www.aflcio.org**).

2. The euro will be either a source of competitive advantage or disadvantage for managers. Using "Euro case study: Siemens," available at **http://news.bbc.co.uk/hi/english/events/the_launch_of_emu**, assess the validity of the two points of view.

Recommended Readings

The Arthur Andersen North American Business Sourcebook. Chicago: Triumph Books, 1994.

Bannister, Rebecca R. *The NAFTA Success Story: More Than Just Trade.* Washington, DC: Progressive Policy Institute, 1997.

Business Guide to Mercosur. London: Economist Intelligence Unit, 1998.

Clement, Norris C., ed., *North American Economic Integration: Theory and Practice.* London: Edward Elgar Publications, 2000.

EC Commission. *Completing the Internal Market: White Paper from the Commission to the European Council.* Luxembourg: EC Commission, 1985.

The European Union: A Guide for Americans. Available at **www.eurunion.org/infores/euguide/Chapter1.htm**.

Fair, D.E., and C. de Boissieu, eds. *International Monetary and Financial Integration—The European Dimension.* Norwell, MA: Kluwer, 1987.

Ohmae, Kenishi. *The Borderless World: Power and Strategy in the Interlinked Economy.* New York: Harper Business, 1999.

Ryans, John K., Jr., and Pradeep A. Rau. *Marketing Strategies for the New Europe: A North American Perspective on 1992.* Chicago: American Marketing Association, 1990.

Schott, Jeffrey, *United States–Canada Free Trade: An Evaluation of the Agreement.* Washington, DC: Institute for International Economics, 1988.

Stoeckel, Andrew, David Pearce, and Gary Banks. *Western Trade Blocs.* Canberra, Australia: Centre for International Economics, 1990.

Sueo, Sekiguchi and Noda Makito, eds. *Road to ASEAN-10: Japanese Perspectives on Economic Integration.* Tokyo: Center for International Exchange, 2000.

Trade Liberalization: Western Hemisphere Trade Issues Confronting the United States Washington, DC: United States General Accounting Office, 1997.

United Nations. *From the Common Market to EC92: Integration in the European Community and Transnational Corporations.* New York: United Nations Publications, 1992.

Venables, Anthony, Richard E. Baldwin, and Daniel Cohen, eds. *Market Integration, Regionalism and the Global Economy.* Cambridge, England: Cambridge University Press, 1999.

Notes

1. The discussion of economic integration is based on the pioneering work by Bela Balassa, *The Theory of Economic Integration* (Homewood, IL: Richard D. Irwin, 1961).
2. "The Maths of Post-Maastricht Europe," *The Economist,* October 16, 1993, 51–52.

3. Jacob Viner, *The Customs Union Issue* (New York: Carnegie Endowment for International Peace, 1950).
4. J. Waelbroeck, "Measuring Degrees of Progress in Economic Integration," in *Economic Integration, Worldwide, Regional, Sectoral,* ed. F. Machlop (London: Macmillan, 1980).

5. "Argentina Cries Foul as Choice Employers Beat a Path Next Door," *The Wall Street Journal*, May 2, 2000, A1, A8.

6. "EU-Swiss Trade Opening Up," *World Trade*, September 2000, 20.

7. EC Commission, *Completing the Internal Market: White Paper from the Commission to the European Council* (Luxembourg: EC Commission, 1985).

8. "A Singular Market," *The Economist* (October 22, 1994): 10–16.

9. Various aspects of the 1992 Common Market are addressed in André Sapir and Alexis Jacquemin, eds., *The European Internal Market* (Oxford, England: Oxford University Press, 1990).

10. "The Maths of Post-Maastricht Europe," *The Economist* (October 16, 1993): 51–52.

11. "Ex-Communist Nations Receive Nod From EU," *The Washington Post*, December 14, 1997, A28.

12. "Will More Be Merrier?" *The Economist* (October 17, 1992): 75.

13. *The European Union: A Guide for Americans* (Washington, DC: Delegation of the European Commission to the United States, 2000), ch. 2.

14. Guenther Burghardt, "The Future of the European Union," speech given at the Johns Hopkins University School of Advanced International Studies, January 23, 2001.

15. Economic growth effects are discussed in Richard Baldwin, "The Growth Effects of 1992," *Economic Policy* (October 1989): 248–281; or Rudiger Dornbusch, "Europe 1992: Macroeconomic Implication," *Brookings Papers on Economic Activity* 2 (1989): 341–362.

16. John F. Magee, "1992: Moves Americans Must Make," *Harvard Business Review* 67(May–June 1989): 72–84.

17. Richard I. Kirkland, "Outsider's Guide to Europe in 1992," *Fortune* (October 24, 1988): 121–127.

18. "Should Small U.S. Exporters Take the Plunge?" *Business Week* (November 14, 1988): 64–68.

19. "Getting Ready for the Great American Shakeout," *Business Week* (April 4, 1988): 44–46.

20. "Summary of the U.S.–Canada Free Trade Agreement," *Export Today* 4 (November–December 1988): 57–61.

21. Raymond Ahearn, *Trade and the Americas* (Washington, DC: Congressional Research Service, 1997), 3–4.

22. "NAFTA's Do-Gooder Side Deals Disappoint," *The Wall Street Journal*, October 15, 1997, A19.

23. For annual trade information, see http://www.census.gov/foreign-trade/.

24. "U.S. Trade with Mexico During the Third NAFTA Year," *International Economic Review* (Washington, DC: International Trade Commission, April 1997): 11.

25. "Fox and Bush, for Richer, for Poorer," *The Economist*, February 3, 2001, 37–38.

26. "Mexico Retail Feels NAFTA Pinch," *Advertising Age*, January 17, 1994, I-4.

27. Sidney Weintraub, *NAFTA at Three: A Progress Report* (Washington, DC: Center for Strategic and International Studies, 1997), 17–18.

28. Jim Carlton, "The Lure of Cheap Labor," *The Wall Street Journal*, September 14, 1992, R16. Diane Lindquist, "Rules Change for Maquiladoras," *Industry Week*, January 15, 2001, 23–26.

29. "Mexico's NAFTA Trade Surge Led by Maquiladoras," *Crossborder Monitor* (July 23, 1997): 1–2; Lara L. Sowinski, "Maquiladoras," *World Trade*, September 2000, 88–92.

30. "Localizing Production," *Global Commerce* (August 20, 1997): 1.

31. "A Noose Around NAFTA," *Business Week* (February 22, 1993): 37.

32. Andrew Stoeckel, David Pearce, and Gary Banks, *Western Trade Blocs* (Canberra, Australia: Centre for International Economics, 1990).

33. "A Giant Step Closer to North America Inc." *Business Week* (December 5, 1988): 44–45.

34. "Next Stop South," *The Economist* (February 25, 1995): 29–30.

35. "Mexico, EU Sign Free-Trade Agreement," *The Wall Street Journal*, March 24, 2000, A15.

36. "Caribbean Parity Enters the Picture," *World Trade*, July 2000, 46.

37. Thomas Kamm, "Latin Links," *The Wall Street Journal*, September 24, 1992, R6.

38. "The World's Newest Trading Bloc," *Business Week* (May 4, 1992): 50–51; "Latin Lesson," *Far Eastern Economic Review*, January 4, 2001, 109.

39. "Free-Trade Zone for the Western Hemisphere Moves Forward," *The Washington Post*, November 5, 1999, E3.

40. "Ripping Down the Walls Across the Americas," *Business Week* (December 26, 1994): 78–80.

41. Emily Thornton, "Will Japan Rule a New Trade Bloc?" *Fortune* (October 5, 1992): 131–132.

42. Paul Krugman, "A Global Economy Is Not the Wave of the Future," *Financial Executive* 8 (March/April 1992): 10–13.

43. Michael R. Czinkota and Masaaki Kotabe, "America's New World Trade Order," *Marketing Management* 1 (summer 1992): 49–56.

44. "Afrabet Soup," *The Economist*, February 10, 2001, 77.

45. Eric Friberg, Risto Perttunen, Christian Caspar, and Dan Pittard, "The Challenges of Europe 1992," *The McKinsey Quarterly* 21, 2 (1988): 3–15.

46. "Lean, Mean, European," *The Economist*, April 29, 2000, 5–7.

47. Gianluigi Guido, "Implementing a Pan-European Marketing Strategy," *Long Range Planning* 24, 5 (1991): 23–33.

48. "TABD Uses Virtual Organization for Trade Lobbying," *Crossborder Monitor* (July 2, 1997): 1.

49. "OPEC's Joyride Was Great While It Lasted," *Business Week* (June 3, 1996): 52. See also www.opec.org.

50. "Are We Over a Barrel?" *Time*, December 18, 2000, B6–B11.

ern world as a whole to contribute to the democratization of the former Communist nations by searching for ways to bring them "the good life."

The Realities of Economic Change

Wendy's International operates four restaurants in Hungary.

For Western firms, the political and economic shifts converted a latent but closed market into a market offering very real and vast opportunities. Yet the shifts are only the beginning of a process. The announcement of an intention to change does not automatically result in change itself. For example, the abolition of a centrally planned economy does not create a market economy. Laws permitting the emergence of private sector entrepreneurs do not create entrepreneurship. The reduction of price controls does not immediately make goods available or affordable. Deeply ingrained systemic differences between the emerging democracies and Western firms continue. Highly prized, fully accepted fundamentals of the market economy, such as the reliance on competition, support of the profit motive, and the willingness to live with risk on a corporate and personal level, are not yet fully accepted. Major changes still need to take place. It is therefore useful to review the major economic and structural dimensions of the emerging democracies to identify major shortcomings and opportunities for international business.

Many transition economies face major **infrastructure shortages.** Transportation systems, particularly those leading to the West, are either nonexistent or in disrepair. Long-haul trucking is therefore an extremely expensive and difficult mode of transportation. Warehousing facilities are either lacking or very poor outside the major cities. A lack of refrigeration facilities places severe handicaps on transshipments of perishable products.[7] The housing stock is in need of major overhaul. Communication systems will take years to improve. Market intermediaries often do not exist. Payments and funds-transfer systems are inadequate. Infrastructure shortcomings will inhibit economic growth for years to come.

Capital shortages are also a major constraint. Catching up with the West in virtually all industrial areas requires major capital infusions. Even though major programs are being designed to attract hidden personal savings into the economies, transition economies must rely to a large degree on attracting capital from abroad. Continued domestic uncertainties and high demand for capital around the world make this difficult. In light of existing inefficiencies, corruption[8] and domestic uncertainties, it is then also a major task to ensure that the capital remains in the country rather than having capital flight remove incoming capital flows to safe havens abroad.

Firms doing business with the emerging democracies encounter interesting demand conditions. Buyers' preferences are often vague and undefined. Available market information is often inaccurate. For example, knowledge about pricing, advertising, research, and trading is very limited, and few institutions are able to accurately research demand and channel supply. As a result, it is quite difficult for corporations to respond to demand.

To the surprise of many investors, the emerging democracies have substantial knowledge resources to offer. For example, it is claimed that Russia and Central Europe possess about 35 to 40 percent of all researchers and engineers in the world.[9] At the same time, however, these nations suffer from the disadvantages imposed by a lack of management skills. In the past, management mainly consisted of skillful maneuvering within the allocation process. Central planning, for example, required firms to request tools seven years in advance; material requirements needed to be submitted two years in advance. Ordering was done haphazardly, since requested quantities were always reduced, and surplus allocations could always be traded with other firms. The driving mechanism for management was therefore not responsiveness to existing needs, but rather plan fulfillment through the development of a finely honed **allocation mentality,** which waits for instructions from above.

TABLE 9.1 **Russian Attitudes Toward Business Learning**	**Attitude** — **Dimension**

Attitude	Dimension
Pride	We are educated people, but our views are totally discounted.
Fear	This new order is more dangerous than the Cold War since it has no rules. This new international competition is coming in, and we are without shelter.
Suspicion	How do we know the market is good for us? Why should Americans tell Russians how to run their business?
Credibility	Schools are pushing courses like used carpets. Has training made people more successful?
Specificity	Expertise is only valuable in the context of Russia.
Compatibility	We understand the words but have no mental image of their meaning.
Complexity	Having fun during learning is not Russian. Complex ideas should be taught in a complex way.
Longevity	Will our learning truly make a difference?
Desire	We need to learn how to do civilized business. We must learn to care, break loose from old patterns.

Source: Michael R. Czinkota "Russia's Transition to a Market Economy: Learning about Business," *Journal of International Marketing* 5, 4 (1997): 73–93.

Commitment by managers and employees to their work is difficult to find. Many employees are still caught up in old work habits, which consisted of never having to work a full shift due to other commitments and obligations. The notion that "they pretend to pay us, and we pretend to work" is still very strong. The dismantling of the past policy of the "Iron Rice Bowl," which made layoffs virtually impossible, is further reducing rather than increasing such commitment.

The new environment also complicates managerial decision making. Even simple changes often require an almost unimaginable array of adjustments of licenses, taxes, definitions, and government rules.

To cope with all these challenges, transition economies need trained managers. Since no large supply of such individuals exists, much of the training must be newly developed. Simply applying established Western guidelines to such training is inappropriate due to the differences in the people to be trained and the society in which they live. Business learning in transition economies must focus on key business issues such as marketing, strategic planning, international business, and financial analysis. However, it must not just focus on the transmission of knowledge, but also aim to achieve behavioral change. Given the lack of market orientation in the previous business environment, managers must adapt their behavior in areas such as problem solving, decision making, the development of customer orientation, and team building. In addition, the attitudes held by managers toward business and Western teaching approaches must be taken into consideration. As Table 9.1 shows, these attitudes can be quite inhibiting to the acceptance of new knowledge.

Adjusting to Global Change

Both institutions and individuals tend to display some resistance to change. The resistance grows if the speed of change increases. It does not necessarily indicate a preference for the earlier conditions but rather a concern about the effects of adjustment and a fear of the unknown. In light of the major shifts that have occurred both politically and economically in central Europe and the former Soviet Union and the accompanying substantial dislocations, resistance should be expected. Deeply entrenched interests and traditions are not easily supplanted by the tender and shallow root of market-oriented thinking. The understanding of links and interactions cannot be expected to grow overnight. For example, greater financial latitude for firms also requires that inefficient firms be permitted to go into bankruptcy—a concept not cherished by many. The need for increased efficiency and productivity causes sharp reductions in employment—a painful step for the workers affected. The growing ranks of unemployed are swelled by the members of the military who have been brought home or demobilized. Concurrently, wage reforms threaten to relegate blue-collar workers, who were traditionally favored by the socialist system, to second-class status, while permitting the emergence of a new entrepreneurial class of the rich, an undesirable result for those not participating in the upswing. Retail price reforms endanger the safety net of larger population segments, and widespread price changes introduce inflation. It is difficult to accept a system where there are winners and losers, particularly for those on the losing side. As a result, an increase in ambivalence and uncertainty may well produce rapid shifts in economic and political thinking, which in turn may produce another set of unexpected results.

But it is not just in the emerging democracies that major changes have come about. The shifts experienced there also have major impact on the established market economies of the West. Take the reorientation of trade flows. With traditional and "forced" trade relationships vanishing and the need for income from abroad increasing, many more countries exert major efforts to become partners in global trade. They attempt to export much more of their domestic production. Many of the exports are in product categories such as agriculture, basic manufacturing, steel, aluminum, and textiles, which are precisely the economic sectors in which the industrialized nations are already experiencing surpluses. As a result, the threat of displacement is high for traditional producers in industrialized nations.

Due to domestic economic dislocations, the pressure is on Western governments to restrict the inflow of trade from the East. Giving in to such pressure, however, would be highly detrimental to the further development of these new market economies. The countries in transition need assistance in their journey. Providing them with open markets is the best form of assistance, much more valuable than the occasional transfer of aid funds. Rapid changes and substantial economic dislocation have caused many individuals and policymakers in the East to become suspicious and wary of Western business approaches. Unless Western governments and businesses are able to convincingly demonstrate how competition, variety, trade, and freedom of choice can improve the quality of life, the opportunity to transform postsocialist societies will be lost.[10] As Global Perspective 9.1 describes, the West must share the burden of global economic adjustment—a responsibility which has not diminished over the years, but rather has grown.

International Business Challenges and Opportunities

The pressure of change also presents vast opportunities for the expansion of international business activities. Large populations offer new potential consumer demand and production capability. Many opportunities arise out of the enthusiasm with which a market orientation is embraced in some nations. Companies that are able to tap into the desire for an improved standard of living can develop new demand on a large scale. Global Perspective 9.2 presents some of the opportunities in the automotive sector.

One major difficulty encountered is the frequent unavailability of convertible currency. Products, however necessary, often cannot be purchased by emerging market economies because no funds are available to pay for them. As a result, many of the countries resort to barter and countertrade. This places an additional burden on the

GLOBAL PERSPECTIVE 9.1

The Coresponsibility of the West

Eastern Europe has undergone almost incomprehensible change. The Czech Republic was deeply involved in the change and its president Vaclav Havel, has spoken very candidly about what has happened and what is at stake, for all the nations on Earth:

"The world used to be so simple: There was a single adversary who was more or less understandable, who was directed from a single center and whose sole aim in its final years was to maintain the status quo. At the same time, the existence of this adversary drew the West together as well, because faced with this global and clearly defined danger, it could always somehow agree on a common approach. All that has vanished. The world has suddenly become unusually complex and far less intelligible. The old order has collapsed, but no one has yet created a new one.

"... The 'postcommunist world' is constantly springing new surprises on the West: Nations hitherto unheard of are awakening and want countries of their own. Highly improbable people from God knows where are winning elections. It is not even clear whether the very people who four years ago so astonishingly roused themselves from their torpor and overthrew communism do not actually miss that system today. . . . How much easier it must have been for Western politicians when they were faced with a homogenous Soviet mass and didn't have to worry about distinguishing one nation from another.

". . . Now that the Cold War is over, the impression is that the headaches it caused are over. But the headaches are never over. . . . Our countries must deal with their own immense problems themselves. The 'non-postcommunist West,' however, should not look on as though it were a mere visitor at a zoo or the audience at a horror movie, on edge to know how it will turn out. It should perceive these processes at the very least as something that intrinsically concerns it, and that somehow decides its own fate, that demands its own active involvement and challenges it to make sacrifices in the interests of a bearable future for us all.

". . . To make my point briefly and simply: It seems to me that the fate of the so-called West is today being decided in the so-called East. If the West does not find a key to us, who were once violently separated from the West, it will ultimately lose the key to itself."

Source: Vaclav Havel, "A Call for Sacrifice: The Coresponsibility of the West." *Foreign Affairs* (March/April 1994): 2–7.

international manager, who must not only market products to the clients but must also market the products received in return to other consumers and institutions.

Problems also have arisen from the lack of protection some of the countries afford to intellectual property rights. Firms have complained about frequent illegal copying of films, books, and software, and about the counterfeiting of brand-name products. Unless importers can be assured that government safeguards will protect their property, trade and technology transfer will be severely inhibited.

Problems also can be encountered when attempting to source products from emerging market economies. Many firms have found that selling is not part of the economic culture in some of the countries. The few available descriptive materials are often poorly written and devoid of useful information. Obtaining additional information about a product may be difficult and time consuming.

The quality of the products obtained can also be a major problem. In spite of their great desire to participate in the global marketplace, many producers still tend to place primary emphasis on product performance and neglect, to a large extent, issues of style and product presentation. Therefore, the international manager needs to forge agreements that require the manufacturer to improve quality, provide for technical control, and ensure prompt delivery before sourcing products from emerging market economies.

Nevertheless, sufficient opportunities exist to make consideration of such international business activities worthwhile. Some transition economies have products that are unique in performance. While they were nontradable during a time of ideological conflict, they are becoming successful global products in an era of new trade relations. For example, research shows that Russian tractors can be sold successfully in the United

GLOBAL PERSPECTIVE 9.2

Carmakers Drive into Russia

In the showroom of a Moscow auto dealership, Volodya Dmitriev eyes the sleek design of a Skoda Felicia, a Volkswagen built in the Czech Republic. "It's a great car," he says. "Still . . . " He glances over at a Russian-made Lada, which starts at about half the $10,500 sticker price of the Volkswagen. The Russian leaves the dealership undecided, but Volkswagen and other foreign car dealers are boosting their efforts to lure car shoppers like Dmitriev back.

In Russia only 83 of every 1,000 people own their own car, less than half the ownership rate in Eastern Europe. Many who do are itching to trade in their Soviet clunkers for a car with superior foreign engineering. Car makers are happy to oblige to appeal to the annual Russian car buyers who spend $1.7 billion per year. General Motors agreed in February 2001 to form a joint venture to make a sport utility vehicle under the Chevy label with formerly state-owned Avto VAZ, Russia's leading auto maker. The $332 million project is being built at Avto VAZ's plant in Togliatti, at the base of the Ural mountains, and will produce roughly 75,000 vehicles. The car, to be called the Chevy Niva, is an updated version of Avto VAZ's Lada Niva, which is an all-wheel drive light sport utility vehicle. Production will begin in 2002.

The company hopes to price the Chevy Niva under $8,000 in Russia and considerably more than that when it is exported to western Europe. The new vehicle will initially be marketed to Russians and eventually be exported to western Europe. The Lada Niva has already made inroads in western Europe with a reputation for being affordable and reliable.

GM and Avto VAZ each hold a 41.5 percent stake, with the remaining 17 percent being provided by the London-based European Bank for Reconstruction and Development. David Herman, president of General Motors Russia, said having a Russian partner was essential. Making the huge investment to start from scratch to break into the Russian market didn't make sense in a market that has only 30,000 customers for cars priced at more than $10,000. New cars in Russia can sell for as little as $4,000.

U.S. Ford Motor Co. expects to launch its Focus model production at a plant near St. Petersburg in Russia's northwest, with $150 million invested in the project. The construction of the plant, a joint venture between Ford and several St Petersburg banks, started in 1999. Other major foreign car makers that have launched joint venture manufacturing in Russia include German luxury-car producer BMW and France's Renault. Italy's Fiat expects to start local production at a joint venture in 2002.

Foreign car makers still have difficult hurdles to overcome, though. In a region that often lacks the rule of law, many Russians feel that foreign-made cars will become targets of thieves and bribe-hungry traffic police. Consumer tastes are also very hard to predict in the new market economies. After his survey of the foreign models at the dealership, customer Akhmed Mirzoyev announces that he has decided on the Russian Lada. "I just needed something for running errands around town," he explains.

Sources: Carol Matlock, "Ready to Burn Rubber in Russia," *Business Week* (March 31, 1997); Hans Greimel, "GM joins venture in Russia," *The Globe and Mail.* February 28, 2001; "Ford to start production in Russia in October," *Reuters,* March 15, 2001; "BMW CEO Joachim Milberg: No Mergers Needed," *Business Week Online,* January 17, 2001.

States. A study found that many of the previously held negative attitudes about imports from the region have been modified by the improved political climate.[11] Many countries offer low labor costs and, in some instances, a great availability of labor. These nations can offer consumers in industrialized nations a variety of products at low costs once the labor force can perform at an international level.

Currently, most sourcing opportunities from Eastern Europe and the Commonwealth of Independent States are for industrial products, which reflects the past orientation of research and development expenditures. Over time, however, consumer products may play a larger role. As Global Perspective 9.3 explains, opportunities for international business can be found in many ways. There are also substantial opportunities for technology transfer. For example, the former Soviet training program for cosmonauts, which prepared space travelers for long periods of weightlessness, actually provides quite useful information for U.S. manufacturers of exercise equipment. Therefore, even if not interested in entering the emerging market economies, the international business executive would be wise to maintain relationship with them in order not to lose a potentially valuable source of supply.

GLOBAL PERSPECTIVE 9.3

Chinese Entrepreneur Fattens Geese for Foie Gras and Fat Profits

Vast markets once closed to international trade have opened their doors during the past two decades. Communist China's liberalized trade policy added more than a billion buyers and sellers to the global marketplace, and the disintegration of the Soviet Bloc added several hundred million more. These new buyers are a boon to producers worldwide, but the new sellers may be a bane to established producers who face unexpected competition.

Take foie gras, for centuries the delectable delicacy made from goose or duck livers, was made mainly in France. Even today, the country produces 80 percent of the world's 17,600 tons and 95 percent of the world's duck liver foie gras. In recent years, however, France has faced new and formidable competition. Hungary, a former Soviet Bloc nation, has become a formidable supplier. It not only exports duck liver, but it also produces and exports 1,250 tons of goose liver foie gras—twice as much as France. Moreover, Hungary's fowl liver prices are so highly competitive that angry French farmers raided stores of Hungarian duck liver in southwest France, destroying one and one-half tons.

Another nemesis looms on the foie gras horizon. China continues to capitalize on its vast natural resources and flex its abundant labor muscle in the global marketplace. Chen Xiuhong, an enterprising Chinese entrepreneur in southeast China, recognized that his region's wealth of tasty geese would be most valuable on gourmet tables. He and a partner are gearing up to produce as much as 1,000 tons of foie gras from goose livers each year, which could boost worldwide production by more than one-third.

The pair plan to spend nearly $25 million to convert a canned-foods factory acquired from the government into a state-of-the-art feeding and processing facility in Hepu, an impoverished region north of the Vietnamese border that is ripe for a large employer. Cheap labor is widely available, and skilled labor, which is instrumental to ensuring quality control, can be recruited from the Chinese government's ministries of agriculture and science and technology. What is more, it costs only $5.00 to raise a goose in Hepu, much less than in France. Animal rights activists, which have pressured U.S. and European foie gras producers to switch to kinder and more expensive production methods to feed the geese, have no clout in China.

If Hepu goose liver succeeds, the entrepreneurs estimate annual profits of $30 million or more. However, as with all bold business ventures, there are risks. 90 percent of the foie gras produced is consumed in France. Even if the Chinese liver passes culinary muster, it may fail in France simply because it's not French. French regulators who loyally protect their compatriots may also reject the Chinese foie gras.

However, the taste for this distinctively French delicacy may spread to other national palates and increase the market for all producers, as happened with Japanese sushi. Perhaps Hepu geese foie gras will even find a following among the Chinese. It would be ironic if this delicacy that commands as much as $100 per pound in the United States should find a market in a country that has derided capitalist greed for half a century. Nations that join the global trade fray are open not only to economic opportunity but also to cultural (and culinary) influences from their trading partners.

Sources: The World Factbook 2000, The Central Intelligence Agency; Clay Chandler, "A Golden Goose in Red China?" The Washington Post, August 1, 2000, p. E1.

State Enterprises and Privatization

One other area where the international business executive must deal with a period of transition is that of **state-owned enterprises.** These firms represent a formidable pool of international suppliers, customers, and competitors. Many of them are located in emerging market economies and are currently being converted into privately owned enterprises. This transition also presents new opportunities.

Reasons for the Existence of State-Owned Enterprises

A variety of economic and noneconomic factors has contributed to the existence of state-owned enterprises. Two primary ones are national security and economic security. Many countries believe that, for national security purposes, certain industrial sectors must be under state control. Typically, these sectors include telecommunications, airlines, banking, and energy.

Economic security reasons are primarily cited in countries that are heavily dependent on specific industries for their economic performance. This may be the case when countries are heavily commodity dependent. Governments frequently believe that, given such heavy national dependence on a particular industrial sector, government control is necessary to ensure national economic health.

Other reasons also contributed to the development of state-owned enterprises. On occasion, the sizable investment required for the development of an industry is too large to come from the private sector. Therefore, governments close the gap between national needs and private sector resources by developing these industries themselves. In addition, governments often decide to rescue failing private enterprises by placing them in government ownership. In doing so, they fulfill important policy objectives, such as the maintenance of employment, the development of depressed areas, or the increase of exports.

Some governments also maintain that state-owned firms may be better for the country than privately held companies because they may be more societally oriented and therefore contribute more to the greater good. This was particularly the case in areas such as telecommunications and transportation, where profit maximization, at least from a governmental perspective, was not always seen as the appropriate primary objective. Rather, social goals such as employment may be valued much higher than profits or rates of return.[12]

The Effect of State-Owned Enterprises on International Business

Three types of activities where the international manager is likely to encounter state-owned enterprises are market entry, the sourcing or marketing process, and international competition. On occasion, the very existence of a state-owned enterprise may inhibit or prohibit foreign market entry. For reasons of development and growth, governments frequently make market entry from the outside quite difficult so that the state-owned enterprise can perform according to plan. Even if market entry is permitted, the conditions under which a foreign firm can conduct business are often substantially less favorable than the conditions under which state-owned enterprises operate. Therefore, the international firm may be placed at a competitive disadvantage and may not be able to perform successfully even though economic factors would indicate success.

The international manager also faces a unique situation when sourcing from or marketing to state-owned enterprises. Even though the state-owned firm may appear to be simply another business partner, it is ultimately an extension of the government and its activities. This may mean that the state-owned enterprise conducts its transactions according to the overall foreign policy of the country rather than according to economic rationale. For example, political considerations can play a decisive role in purchasing decisions. Contracts may be concluded for noneconomic reasons rather than be based on product offering and performance. Contract conditions may depend on foreign policy outlook, prices may be altered to reflect government displeasure, and delivery performance may change to "send a signal." Exports and imports may be delayed or encouraged depending on the current needs of government.

Finally, the international firm also may encounter international competition from state-owned enterprises. Very often, the concentration of such firms is not in areas of comparative advantage, but rather in areas that at the time are most beneficial for the government owning the firm. Input costs often are much less important than policy objectives. Sometimes, state-owned enterprises may not even know the value of the products they buy and sell because prices in themselves have such a low priority. As a result, the international manager may be confronted with competition that is very tough to beat.

Privatization

Governments and citizens have increasingly recognized the drawbacks of government control of enterprises. Competition is restrained, which results in lower quality of goods and reduced innovation. Citizens are deprived of lower prices and of choice. The international competitiveness of state-controlled enterprises suffers, often resulting in the need for growing government subsidies. In addition, rather than focusing on business, many government-controlled corporations have become grazing grounds for political appointees or vote winners through job allocations. As a result, many government-owned enterprises excell only in losing money.[13]

It is possible to reduce the cost of governing by changing government's role and involvement in the economy. Through **privatization,** budgets can be reduced and more efficient—not fewer—services can be provided. Privatized goods and services are often more competitive and more innovative. Two decades of experience with privatization indicate that private enterprises almost invariable outperform state-run companies.[14] The conversion of government monopolies into market-driven activities also tends to attract foreign investment capital, bringing additional know-how and financing to enterprises. Finally, governments can use proceeds from privatization to fund other pressing domestic needs.

The methods of privatization vary from country to country. Some nations come up with a master plan for privatization, whereas others deal with it on a case-by-case basis. The Treuhandanstalt of Germany, for example, which was charged with disposing of most East German state property, aimed to sell firms but also to maximize the number of jobs retained. In other countries, ownership shares are distributed to citizens and employees. Some nations simply sell to the highest bidder in order to maximize the proceeds. For example, Mexico has used most of its privatization proceeds to amortize its internal debt, resulting in savings of nearly $1 billion a year in interest payments. As Figure 9.2 shows, governments have raised substantial amounts through privatization.

The purpose of most privatization programs is to improve productivity, profitability, and product quality and to shrink the size of government. As companies are exposed to market forces and competition, they are expected to produce better goods and services at lower costs. Privatization also intends to attract new capital

FIGURE 9.2

Trends in Global Privatization

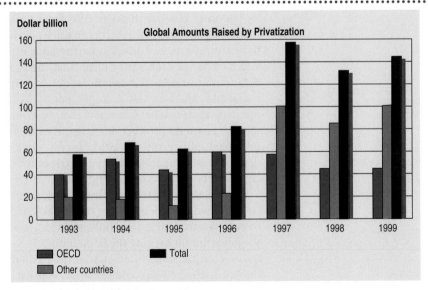

Source: Organization for Economic Cooperation and Development, *Financial Market Trends,* 76 (June 2000), **www.oecd.org**.

GLOBAL PERSPECTIVE 9.4

Privatization in Africa

The manager of the state-owned Tanzanian Brewery used to spend his mornings dealing with a long line of people outside his office. Most carried notes that read along these lines: "The bearer of this note is my friend. I am having a funeral at my brother's house this weekend. Please ensure that there is an adequate supply of beer." The note would usually be signed by a government minister or some other important official.

The Tanzanian Brewery was built with a capacity of 1.3 million liters of beer a day but produced only 400,000. It had a 25 percent share of the market but provided a bad-tasting product. A privatization drive by the Tanzanian government enabled South African Breweries to buy a 50 percent stake in the defunct state-run operation. After obtaining a five-year management contract, the South Africans cut the workforce, built a new brewery, improved the taste, and grabbed 75 percent of the market. Today, the government retains almost 30 percent of the ownership of the profitable and growing Tanzanian Brewery, and receives 59 percent of cash value added, in the form of excise duties, value added tax, customs duties, and dividends.

Tanzania has privatized more than half of its 250 companies, including cashew and tobacco farms, mines, a cigarette factory, and the brewery. But the most difficult part is ahead. The companies left to be privatized include decrepit state-run utilities that will be difficult to transfer to private hands because they are such unattractive investments. The problem is complicated by the government's desire to see a large portion of these companies in the hands of its citizens. The fact is that few people in Tanzania have the necessary capital to invest in these companies. Thus, instead of selling off companies out-

right, the government is retaining a share for later sale to the Tanzanians.

In theory the state has made strides to open up the country for business. In practice, investing in Tanzania is more like riding a roller coaster. Frequent power failures and shoddy telephone networks demonstrate the country's lack of investment in its infrastructure. Both foreign and local business people complain about the labyrinthlike tax system with over thirty different taxes from different authorities. Permits and licenses arrive late or not at all unless certain palms are greased. Firms working in difficult countries need to be resourceful. South African Breweries (SAB) has done well in several African markets that better-known brewers shun. When local infrastructure breaks down, SAB's managers improvise. In Mozambique, for example, when the water supply failed, SAB paid the local fire brigade to fetch water and hose it into the beer vats.

Clearly, privatization provides a mechanism for greater efficiency in emerging economies. Unfortunately, governments cannot simply wave a magic wand that makes privatization a reality. The task is overwhelming, especially in former socialist countries like Tanzania where an entrenched bureaucracy and other vested interests are an ingrained part of the society. Under the East Africa Community (EAC) Treaty signed in November 1999, Kenya, Tanzania, and Uganda agreed to form a common market, eliminate tariff barriers, and ease the movement of labor and capital. With a core market of over 81 million people, and valuable natural resources, their governments are reducing the size of their public sectors and hoping to attract growth in the private sector.

Sources: "Risky Returns," *The Economist,* May 18, 2000; South Africa Breweries, *Annual Report 2000,* **www.sab.co.za;** Focus on East Africa, **www.sei2000.com/eastafrica2000;** Dares Salam. "Private Sector Beer is Best." *The Economist* (November 2, 1996) p 46.

for these firms so that they can carry out necessary adjustments and improvements. Since local capital is often scarce, privatization efforts increasingly aim to attract foreign capital investment. Privatization, however, is no magic wand, as Global Perspective 9.4 shows. Its key benefits come from corporate adjustment, which is often quite painful.

The trend toward privatization offers unique opportunities for international managers. Existing firms, both large and small, can be acquired at low cost, often with governmental support through tax exemptions, investment grants, special depreciation allowances, and low-interest-rate credits. The purchase of such firms enables the international firm to expand operations without having to start from scratch. In addition, since wages are often low in the countries where privatization takes place, there is a major opportunity to build low-cost manufacturing and sourcing bases. Furthermore, the international firm can also act as a catalyst by accelerating the pace of transferring business skills and technology and by boosting trade prospects. In short, the very process of change offers new opportunities to the adept manager.

The Role of the Multinational Firm[*]

All problems aside, the market potential of transition and emerging economies is enormous. It is this promise that is paramount to understanding the developing role of multinational firms in transition economies. They enter because they see substantial profit potential. This potential, however, may not be attained quickly, and firms must time their entry and activity to pace themselves for the long race.

The experience to date in many transition economies has been mixed in terms of business success. Many of the newly formed purely domestic businesses have experienced relatively short life spans often characterized by rapid growth and significant profitability, albeit short lived in duration. The causes of failure typically are problems in general business management, the institution of new government regulations or taxes, or regulatory failures.

Multinational firms, however, have experienced higher rates of success in transition economies for a variety of reasons. First, foreign firms have had a tendency to enter—at least initially—service sectors that allowed high profit potential with minimal capital investments. This permits a first-stage entry of little capital at risk. Many of these service-sector market niches, such as insurance, Internet-based telecommunication services, security sales and brokerage services, and management consulting, to name a few, are "markets" that simply did not exist under the prior economic system.

As multinational firms gain experience and knowledge of the local markets, they may then increase the size of their capital investments, for example in the form of acquisitions or greenfield investments. The local market is then used as an export base to neighboring and other transition and emerging economies, taking advantage of long-standing links across countries for trade and commerce. At this point, the domestic market is not the focus of the firm's activity. With few exceptions, the profit potential is seen as cost-based access to other external markets.

This export orientation of the multinational firm is quite consistent with the economic policy goals of many economies. They are often sorely in need of export earnings. Having a multinational firm use their economic system as "base camp" for export-led development adds employment and infrastructure support. This is also one of the factors contributing to the special privileges accorded foreign multinationals by host governments such as preferential import duties, corporate tax breaks, and subsidized labor. In fact, many multinationals quickly find their access to local capital through the rapidly developing domestic financial sector to be easier than that of other domestic borrowers, since many domestic companies are effectively excluded from accessing necessary capital. This is in many ways an unfortunate result of the lower-risk profile of the multinational firm compared to recently established domestic enterprises. If not balanced by encouragement for domestic firms, this disadvantage may result in growing criticism of multinational firms and their impact on vulnerable economies. It can also lead to renewed nationalist pressures on governments and reduce the ability of multinational firms to expand their activities globally.

Finally, as multinational firms mature in transition or emerging economies, many find that the domestic market itself represents a legitimate market opportunity on a stand-alone basis. Although this is the commonly assumed goal of privatization, it is not always achieved. For example, as global firms expand their presence in an economy, thereby expanding their offerings in industrial and retail products and services, they may quickly become net importers of capital equipment and other necessary inputs for providing the high level of economic goods demanded by the populace. Due to simultaneous investments by many firms, they may also find many more competitors in this new market than they had expected.

---

*The authors gratefully acknowledge the valuable input of Professor Viktoria Dalko to this section.

Many economies now recognize that if they are to develop businesses that are **world-class competitors** and not just poor domestic copies of foreign firms, they must somehow tap the knowledge base already thriving within successful global firms. Frequently, multinational firms are invited to begin joint ventures only with domestic parties. This in itself is often difficult, given that these domestic businesses or entities rarely have significant capital to contribute, but rather bring to the table nonquantifiable contributions such as market savvy and emerging business networks.

For example, in the global telecommunications industry, access to capital is only one of the many needs for industrial development. The technical know-how of the world's key global players is also needed for the development of a first-class industry. Countries like Hungary, Indonesia, and Brazil have invited foreign companies in conjunction with domestic parties to form international joint ventures to bid for the rights to develop large segments or geographic areas within their borders. This requirement is intended to serve as a way of tapping the enormous technical and market knowledge base and commitment of established multinational firms. Without their cooperation, the ability to close the gap with the leading global competitors may be impossible.

Often the multinational firm is invited into an economy to bring capital and technical and market know-how to help improve existing second-class companies. For example, in the early 1990s, General Motors negotiated extensively with the Polish government on the establishment of a joint venture with one of the government-owned automobile manufacturers. GM would contribute capital and technology, while the Polish automobile manufacturer contributed its own existing asset base, workers already in place, and access to a potentially large market. The problem confronted by GM and so many other multinational firms in similar circumstances is that they view the contributions of their domestic partner to be less significant than the potential loss of technical and intellectual property, and the risks associated with maintaining the multinational firm's own reputation and quality standards. In addition, it is frequently more expensive to retool an existing manufacturing facility than it is to simply start fresh with a greenfield facility. These are difficult partnerships, and each and every one requires extended discussion, negotiation, and special "chemistry" for success.

Summary

Special concerns must be considered by the international manager when dealing with former centrally planned economies in transition. Although the emerging market economies offer vast opportunities for trade, business practices may be significantly different from those to which the executive is accustomed.

In the emerging market economies, the key to international business success will be an understanding of the fact that societies in transition require special adaptation of business skills and time to complete the transformation. Due to their growing degree of industrialization, other economies are also becoming part of the world trade and investment picture. It must be recognized that these global changes will, in turn, precipitate adjustments in industrialized nations, particularly in the trade sector. Adapting early to these changes can offer new opportunities to the international firm.

Often the international manager is also faced with state-owned enterprises that have been formed in noncommunist nations for reasons of national or economic security. These firms may inhibit foreign market entry, and they frequently reflect in their transactions the overall domestic and foreign policy of the country rather than any economic rationale. The current global trend toward privatization offers new opportunities to the international firm, either through investment or by offering business skills and knowledge to assist in the success of privatization.

Key Terms and Concepts

central plan
perestroika
glasnost

infrastructure shortages
allocation mentality

state-owned enterprise
privatization

world-class competitors

Questions for Discussion

1. Planning is necessary, yet central planning is inefficient. Why?
2. Discuss the observation that "Russian products do what they are supposed to do—but only that."
3. How can and should the West help eastern European countries?
4. How can central European managers be trained to be market oriented?
5. Where do you see the greatest potential in future trade between emerging market economies and industrialized nations?

6. What are the benefits of privatization?
7. Why do most transition economy governments require foreign multinationals to enter business via joint ventures with existing domestic firms?
8. Why do foreign multinationals often have advantaged access to capital in emerging economies over purely domestic companies?

Internet Exercises

1. Identify the key programs and information services offered to exporters operating in the former Soviet Union through the U.S. Department of Commerce. (Refer to Commerce's Business Information Service for the Newly Independent States, BISNIS, http://www.ita.doc.gov.)

2. What role does the European Bank for Reconstruction and Development play in transforming the formerly communist economies of Eastern Europe and the Soviet Union? (Refer to the web site, www.ebrd.com.)

Recommended Readings

Basanes, Federico, Evamaria Uribe, and Robert Willig. *Can Privatization Deliver?* Infrastructure for Latin America, Inter-American Development Bank, 1999.

Burstein, Daniel, and Arne De Keijzer. *Big Dragon: The Future of China—What It Means for Business, the Economy, and the Global Order.* New York: Touchstone Books, 1999.

Lieberman, Ira W., ed. and Christopher Kirkness. *Privatization and Emerging Equity Markets.* Washington, DC: World Bank, 1998.

Marber, Peter. *From Third World to World Class: The Future of Emerging Markets in the Global Economy.* New York: Perseus Press, 2000.

Nellis, John R. *Time to Rethink Privatization in Transition Economies?* Washington, DC: World Bank, 1999.

Oi, Jean C., and Andrew George Walder. *Property Rights and Economic Reform in China,* Palo Alto: Calif. Calite Stanford University Press, 1999.

Peng, Michael W. *Business Strategies in Transition Economies.* Thousand Oaks, CA: Sage, 2000.

Puffer, Sheila M., Daniel J. McCarthy, and Alexander I. Naumov. *The Russian Capitalist Experiment: From State-Owned Organization to Entrepreneurships.* Abington: Edward Elger Pub., 2000.

Notes

1. For further explanation on these definitions, see Michael W. Peng, *Business Strategies in Transition Economies* (Thousand Oaks, CA: Sage Publications, 2000), 8–10.
2. Richard M. Hammer, "Dramatic Winds of Change," *Price Waterhouse Review* 33 (1989): 23–27.
3. Peter G. Lauter and Paul M. Dickie, "Multinational Corporations in Eastern European Socialist Economies," *Journal of Marketing* 25 (Fall 1975): 40–46.
4. Eugene Theroux and Arthur L. George, *Joint Ventures in the Soviet Union: Law and Practice,* rev. ed. (Washington, DC: Baker & McKenzie, 1989), 1.
5. *The World Factbook 1994* (Washington, DC: Central Intelligence Agency, 1994).

6. Thomas Pickering, "Russia and America at Mid-Transition," *SAIS Review* (winter/spring 1995): 81–92.
7. Harry G. Broadman, "Reducing Structural Dominance and Entry Barriers in Russian Industry," *Russian Enterprise Reform: Policies to Further the Transition,* World Bank Discussion Paper No. 400 (Washington, DC: The World Bank, 1999), 15–34.
8. Thomas Wolf and Emine Guergen, *Improving Governance and Fighting Corruption in the Baltic and CIS Countries* (Washington, DC: International Monetary Fund, 2000).
9. Mihaly Simai, *East-West Cooperation at the End of the 1980s: Global Issues, Foreign Direct Investments, and Debts* (Budapest: Hungarian Scientific Council for World Economy, 1989), 21.

10. Michael R. Czinkota, Helmut Gaisbauer, and Reiner Springer, "A Perspective of Marketing in Central and Eastern Europe," *The International Executive* 39, 6 (November/December 1997): 831–848.

11. Johny K. Johansson, Ilkka A. Ronkainen, and Michael R. Czinkota, "Negative Country of Origin Effects: The Case of the New Russia," *Journal of International Business Studies* 25, 1 (1994): 157–176.

12. Kiran Karande, Mahesh N. Shankarmahesh, and C.P. Rao, "Marketing to Public- and Private-Sector Companies in Emerging Countries: A Study of Indian Purchasing Managers," *Journal of International Marketing* 2, 3 (1999): 64.

13. "European Privatization: Two Half Revolutions," *The Economist* (January 22, 1994): 55, 58.

14. Oleh Havrylyshyn and Donal McGettigan, *Privatization in Transition Countries* (Washington, DC: International Monetary Fund, 1999).

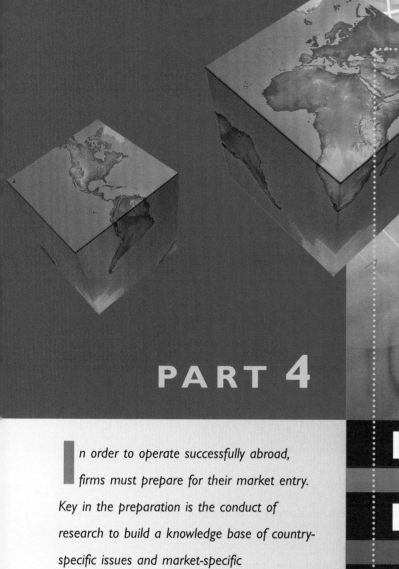

PART 4

I n order to operate successfully abroad, firms must prepare for their market entry. Key in the preparation is the conduct of research to build a knowledge base of country-specific issues and market-specific opportunities and concerns.

Once such a base is established, the company can enter international markets, initially through exporting and international intermediaries. Over time, expansion can occur through foreign direct investment and lead to the formation of the multinational corporation.

INTERNATIONAL BUSINESS PREPARATION AND MARKET ENTRY

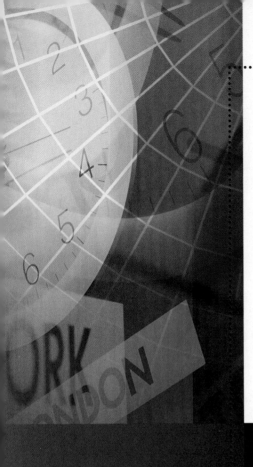

CHAPTER 10

International Business Research

With the expanding economic and political union occurring within Europe, official information resources are becoming more centralized. A short sampling of government sources of information helpful to international managers targeting the EU are reviewed below.

EUROPA

Located at **http:/europa.eu.int,** Europa is the main server that provides access to bibliographic, legal, and statistical databases offered by the European Commission. Many databases are available on Europa including IDEA, SCADplus, CELEX, and ECLAS. IDEA, also called the who's who in the EU, is an electronic directory of the various European Union institutions. Searches can be conducted by organization, by individual names, or by hierarchical ranking. SCADplus is a bibliographic database of official legislative documents that provides background on EU policies. CELEX gives access to EU law, covering treaties, acts, legislation, and resolutions. ECLAS is the online catalog of the Central Library of the Commission.

EUROSTAT

The Statistical Office of the European Communities (EUROSTAT) is located at **http:/europa.eu.int/en/comm/eurostat/serven/part6/6som.htm.** It offers a wide selection of electronic information on the key economic indicators and news releases on economic developments, as well as software for graphics using COMEXT mapping and graphing capabilities. This material is also available at **www.statesa.gov.**

EUROPARL

http:/www.europarl.eu.int offers free and timely information regarding the European Parliament. It is the documentary database of the European Parliament. Its files cover the status of legislation in progress; citations for sessions documents, debates, resolutions and opinions; bibliographic references to studies done by Parliament; and a catalog of the Parliament's library. ●

Source: Online information on the European Union accessed at **www.europa.eu.int,** January 22, 2001.

The single most important cause for failure in international business is insufficient preparation and information. The failure of managers to comprehend cultural disparities, the failure to remember that customers differ from country to country, and the lack of investigation into whether or not a market exists prior to market entry has made international business a high-risk activity.[1] International business research is therefore instrumental to international business success since it permits the firm to take into account different environments, attitudes, and market conditions. Fortunately, such research has become less complicated. As the opening vignette shows, information from around the globe can be obtained quite easily.

This chapter discusses data collection and provides a comprehensive overview of how to obtain general screening information on international markets, to evaluate business potential, and to assess current or potential opportunities and problems. Data sources that are low cost and that take little time to accumulate—in short, secondary data—are considered first. The balance of the chapter is devoted to more sophisticated forms of international research, including primary data collection and the development of an information system.

International and Domestic Research

The tools and techniques of international research are the same as those of domestic research. The difference is in the environment to which the tools are applied. The environment determines how well the tools, techniques, and concepts work. Although the objectives of research may be the same, the execution of international research may differ substantially from that of domestic research. The four primary reasons for this difference are new parameters, new environmental factors, an increase in the number of factors involved, and a broader definition of competition.

New Parameters

In crossing national borders, a firm encounters parameters not found in domestic business. Examples include duties, foreign currencies and changes in their value, different modes of transportation, and international documentation. New parameters also emerge because of differing modes of operating internationally. For example, the firm can export, it can license its products, it can engage in a joint venture, or it can carry out foreign direct investment. The firm that has done business only domestically will have had little or no experience with the requirements and conditions of these types of operations. Managers must therefore obtain information in order to make good business decisions.

New Environmental Factors

When going international, a firm is exposed to an unfamiliar environment. Many of the domestic assumptions on which the firm and its activities were founded may not hold true internationally. Management needs to learn the culture of the host country, understand its political systems and level of stability, and comprehend the existing differences in societal structures and language. In addition, it must understand pertinent legal issues in order to avoid violating local laws. The technological level of the society must also be incorporated in the business plan. In short, all the assumptions that were formulated over the years based on domestic business activities must now be reevaluated. This crucial point is often neglected because most managers are born in the environment of their domestic operations and only subconsciously learn to understand the constraints and opportunities of their business activities. The situation is analogous to learning one's native language. Being born to a language makes speaking it seem easy. Only when attempting to learn a foreign language does one begin to appreciate the structure of language and the need for grammatical rules.

The Number of Factors Involved

Environmental relationships need to be relearned whenever a firm enters a new international market. The number of changing dimensions increases geometrically. Coordination of the interaction among the dimensions becomes increasingly difficult because of their sheer number. Such coordination, however, is crucial to the international success of the firm for two reasons. First, in order to exercise some central control over its international operations, a firm must be able to compare results and activities across countries. Otherwise, any plans made by headquarters may be inappropriate. Second, the firm must be able to learn from its international operations and must find ways to apply the new lessons learned to different markets. Without coordination, such learning cannot take place in a systematic way. The international research process can help in this undertaking.

Broader Definition of Competition

The international market exposes the firm to a much greater variety of competition than that found in the home market. For example, a firm may find that ketchup competes against soy sauce. Similarly, firms that offer labor-saving devices domestically may suddenly be exposed to competition from cheap manual labor. As a result, the firms must determine the breadth of the competition, track competitive activities, and evaluate their actual and potential impact on company operations.

Recognizing the Need for International Research

Many firms do little research before they enter a foreign market. Often, decisions concerning entry and expansion in overseas markets and selection and appointment of distributors are made after a cursory, subjective assessment of the situation. The research done is often less rigorous, less formal, and less quantitative than for domestic activities.

A major reason why managers are reluctant to engage in international research is their lack of sensitivity to differences in culture, consumer tastes, and market demands. Often managers assume that their methods are both best and acceptable to all others. Fortunately, this is not true. What a boring place the world would be if it were!

A second reason is a limited appreciation for the different environments abroad. Often firms are not prepared to accept that labor rules, distribution systems, the availability of media, or advertising regulations may be entirely different from those in the home market. Due to pressure to satisfy short-term financial goals, managers are unwilling to spend money to find out about the differences.

A third reason is lack of familiarity with national and international data sources and inability to use international data once they are obtained. As a result, the cost of conducting international research is perceived to be prohibitively high and therefore not a worthwhile investment relative to the benefits to be gained.[2] However, the Internet makes international research much easier and much less expensive. Data which are hard to find now become accessible at a click of a mouse, as the opening vignette has shown. As the availability of the Internet grows around the world, so does the availability of research information.

Finally, firms often build their international business activities gradually, frequently based on unsolicited orders. Over time, actual business experience in a country or with a specific firm may then be used as a substitute for organized research.

Despite the reservations firms have, research is as important internationally as it is domestically. Firms must learn where the opportunities are, what customers want, why they want it, and how they satisfy their needs and wants so that the firm can serve them efficiently. Firms must obtain information about the local infrastructure, labor market, and tax rules before making a plant location decision. Doing business abroad without the benefit of research places firms, their assets, and their entire international future at risk.

Research allows management to identify and develop international strategies. The task includes the identification, evaluation, and comparison of potential foreign business opportunities and the subsequent target market selection. In addition, research is necessary for the development of a business plan that identifies all the requirements necessary for market entry, market penetration, and expansion. On a continuing basis, research provides the feedback needed to fine-tune various business activities. Finally, research can provide management with the intelligence to help anticipate events, take appropriate action, and adequately prepare for global changes.

Determining Research Objectives

As a starting point for research, research objectives must be determined. They will vary depending on the views of management, the corporate mission of the firm, the firm's level of internationalization, and its competitive situation.

Going International—Exporting

A frequent objective of international research is that of **foreign market opportunity analysis.** When a firm launches its international activities, it will usually find the world to be uncharted territory. Fortunately, information can be accumulated to provide basic guidelines. The aim is not to conduct a painstaking and detailed analysis of the world on a market-by-market basis, but instead to utilize a broad-brush approach. Accomplished quickly and at low cost, this approach will narrow the possibilities for international business activities.

Such an approach should begin with a cursory analysis of general variables of a country, including total and per capita GNP, mortality rates, and population figures. Although these factors in themselves will not provide any detailed information, they will enable the researcher to determine whether corporate objectives might be met in the market. For example, high-priced consumer products are unlikely to be successful in the People's Republic of China, as their price may be equal to a significant proportion of the customer's annual salary, the customer benefit may be minimal, and the government is likely to prohibit their importation. Similarly, the offering of computer software services may be of little value in a country where there is very limited use of computers. Such a cursory evaluation will help reduce the number of markets to be considered to a more manageable number—for example, from 225 to 25.

As a next step, the researcher will require information on each individual country for a preliminary evaluation. Information typically desired will highlight the fastest growing markets, the largest markets for a particular category of product or service, demand trends, and business restrictions. Although precise and detailed information on individual products may not be obtainable, information is available for general product categories or service industries. Again, this overview will be cursory but will serve to quickly evaluate markets and further reduce their number.

At this stage, the researcher must select appropriate markets for in-depth evaluation. The focus will now be on opportunities for a specific type of service, product, or brand, and will include an assessment as to whether demand already exists or can be stimulated. Even though aggregate industry data may have been obtained previ-

FIGURE 10.1

A Sequential Process of Researching Foreign Market Potentials

Source: S. Tamer Cavusgil, "Guidelines for Export Market Research," *Business Horizons* 28 (November–December 1985): 29. Copyright 1985 by the Foundation for the School of Business at Indiana University. Reprinted by permission.

ously, this general information is insufficient to make company-specific decisions. For example, the demand for sports equipment should not be confused with the potential demand for a specific brand. The research now should identify demand and supply patterns and evaluate any regulations and standards. Finally, a **competitive assessment** needs to be made, matching markets to corporate strengths and providing an analysis of the best potential for specific offerings. A summary of the various stages in the determination of market potential is provided in Figure 10.1.

Going International—Importing

When importing, the major focus shifts from supplying to sourcing. Management must identify markets that produce supplies or materials desired or that have the potential to do so. Foreign firms must be evaluated in terms of their capabilities and competitive standing.

Just as management would want to have some details on a domestic supplier, the importer needs to know, for example, about the reliability of a foreign supplier, the consistency of its product or service quality, and the length of delivery time. Information obtained through the subsidiary office of a bank or an embassy can prove very helpful. Information from business rating services and recommendations from current customers are also very useful in evaluating the potential business partner.

In addition, foreign government rules must be scrutinized as to whether exportation is possible. As examples, India may set limits on the cobra handbags it allows to be exported, and laws protecting a nations's cultural heritage may prevent the exportation of pre-Columbian artifacts from Latin American countries.

The international manager must also analyze domestic restrictions and legislation that may prohibit the importation of certain goods into the home country. Even though a market may exist at home for foreign umbrella handles, for example, quotas may restrict their importation to protect domestic industries. Similarly, even though domestic demand may exist for ivory, its importation may be illegal because of legislation enacted to protect wildlife worldwide.

Market Expansion

Research objectives include obtaining more detailed information for business expansion or monitoring the political climate so that the firm successfully can maintain its international operation. Information may be needed to enable the international manager to evaluate new business partners or assess the impact of a technological breakthrough on future business operations. The better defined the research objective is, the better the researcher will be able to determine information requirements and thus conserve the time and financial resources of the firm.

Conducting Secondary Research

Identifying Sources of Data

Typically, the information requirements of firms will cover both macro information about countries and trade, as well as micro information specific to the firm's activities. Table 10.1 provides an overview of the types of information that, according to a survey of executives, are most crucial for international business. If each firm had to go out and collect all the information needed on-site in the country under scrutiny, the task would be unwieldy and far too expensive. On many occasions, however, firms can make use of **secondary data,** that is, information that already has been collected by some other organization. A wide variety of sources present secondary data. The principal ones are governments, international institutions, service organizations, trade associations, directories, and other firms. This section provides a brief review of major data sources. Details on selected monitors of international issues are presented in Appendix 10A at the end of the chapter.

Governments   Most countries have a wide array of national and international trade data available. Typically, the information provided by governments addresses either macro and micro issues or offers specific data services. Macro information includes data on population trends, general trade flows among countries, and world agriculture production. Micro information includes materials on specific industries in a country, their growth prospects, and the extent and direction to which they are traded.

Unfortunately, the data are often published only in their home countries and in their native languages. The publications mainly present numerical data, however, and so the translation task is relatively easy. In addition, the information sources are often available at embassies and consulates, whose missions include the enhancement of trade activities. The commercial counselor or commercial attaché can provide the information as can government-sponsored web sites. The user should be cautioned, however, that the printed information is often dated and that the industry categories used abroad may not be compatible with industry categories used at home. Increasingly,

TABLE 10.1 **Critical International Information**	**Macro Data** • Tariff information • U.S. export/import data • Nontariff measures • Foreign export/import data • Data on government trade policy	**Micro Data** • Local laws and regulations • Size of market • Local standards and specifications • Distribution system • Competitive activity

Source: Michael R. Czinkota, "International Information Needs for U.S. Competitiveness," *Business Horizons* 34, 6 (November–December 1991): 86–91.

government data are available on the Internet—often well before they are released in printed form. Closer collaboration between governmental statistical agencies also makes the data more accurate and reliable, since it is now much easier to compare data such as bilateral exports and imports to each other.

While many of the current data are available at no charge, governments often charge a fee for the use of data libraries. Given the depth of information such data can provide, the cost usually is a worthwhile expenditure for firms in light of the insights into trade patterns and reduction in risk they can achieve.

International Organizations International organizations often provide useful data for the researcher. The *Statistical Yearbook* produced by the United Nations (UN) contains international trade data on products and provides information on exports and imports by country. However, because of the time needed for world-wide data collection, the information is often quite dated. Additional information is compiled and made available by specialized substructures of the United Nations. Some of these are the United Nations Conference on Trade and Development (**www.UNCTAD.org**), which concentrates primarily on international issues surrounding developing nations, such as debt and market access, the United Nations Center on Transnational Corporations and the International Trade Centre (**www. intracen.org**). The *World Atlas* published by the World Bank (**www.worldbank.org**) provides useful general data on population, growth trends, and GNP figures. The World Trade Organization (**www.wto.org**) and the Organization for Economic Co-operation and Development (OECD) (**www.oecd.org**) also publish quarterly and annual trade data on its member countries. Organizations such as the International Monetary Fund (**www.imf.org**) and the World Bank publish summary economic data and occasional staff papers that evaluate region- or country-specific issues in depth.

Service Organizations A wide variety of service organizations that provide information include banks, accounting firms, freight forwarders, airlines, international trade consultants, research firms, and publishing houses located around the world. Frequently they are able to provide information on business practices, legislative or regulatory requirements, and political stability, as well as trade and financial data.

Gatorade markets its products around the globe by diversifying the flavors it offers. While the flavor Cool Blue is popular in both the Middle East and Asia, Green Apple and Red Orange are popular only in the Middle East.

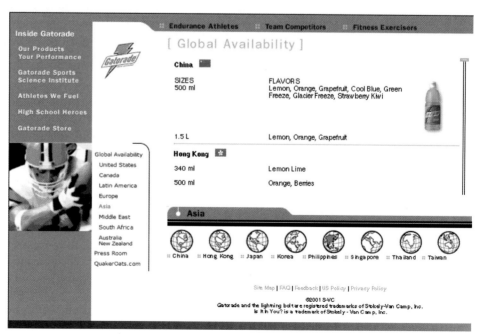

Trade Associations   Associations such as world trade clubs and domestic and international chambers of commerce (such as the American Chamber of Commerce abroad) can provide good information on local markets. Often files are maintained on international trade flows and trends affecting international managers. Valuable information can also be obtained from industry associations. These groups, formed to represent entire industry segments, often collect a wide variety of data from their members that are then published in an aggregate form. Most of these associations represent the viewpoints of their member firms to the government, so they usually have one or more publicly listed representatives in the capital. The information provided is often quite general, however, because of the wide variety of clientele served.

Directories and Newsletters   A large number of industry directories are available on local, national, and international levels. The directories primarily serve to identify firms and to provide very general background information, such as the name of the chief executive officer, the level of capitalization of the firm, the location, the address and telephone number, and some description of the firm's products. A host of newsletters discuss specific international business issues, such as international trade finance, legislative activities, countertrade, international payment flows, and customs news. Usually these newsletters cater to narrow audiences but can provide important information to the firm interested in a specific area.

Electronic Information Services   When information is needed, managers often cannot spend a lot of time, energy, or money finding, sifting through, and categorizing it. Consider laboring through every copy of a trade publication to find out the latest news on how environmental concerns are affecting marketing decisions in Mexico. With electronic information services, search results can be obtained within minutes. International online computer database services, numbering in the thousands, can be purchased to supply information external to the firm, such as exchange rates, international news, and import restrictions. Most database hosts do not charge any sign-up fee and request payment only for actual use. The selection of initial database hosts depends on the choice of relevant databases, taking into account their product and market limitations, language used, and geographical location. A large number of databases, developed by analysts who systematically sift through a wide range of periodicals, reports, and books in different languages, provide information on given products and markets. Many of the main news agencies now have information available through online databases, providing information on events that affect certain markets. Some databases cover extensive lists of companies in given countries and the products they buy and sell. Figure 10.2 provides an example.

Compact Disk/Read-Only Memory (CD-ROM) technology allows for massive amounts of information (the equivalent of 300 books of 1,000 pages each, or 1,500 floppy disks) to be stored on a single 12-centimeter plastic disk. Increasingly, the technology is used for storing and distributing large volumes of information, such as statistical databases. Typically, the user pays no user fees but instead invests in a CD-ROM "reader" and purchases the actual CDs.

An online service widely used in the United States is the National Trade Data Bank (NTDB), offered by the U.S. Department of Commerce's Economics and Statistics Administration. The NTDB includes more than 100,000 documents, including full-text market research reports, domestic and foreign economic data, import and export statistics, trade information and country studies, all compiled from 26 government agencies.[3] The NTDB can also provide profiles of screened businesses that are interested in importing U.S. products. An example of the structure of Country Commercial Guide, shown in Appendix 10B of this chapter, demonstrates how useful these materials can be.

Using data services for research means that professionals do not have to leave their offices, going from library to library to locate the facts they need. Many online services have late-breaking information available within 24 hours to the user. These tech-

niques of research are cost-effective as well. Stocking a company's library with all the books needed to have the same amount of data that is available online or with CD-ROM would be too expensive and space-consuming.

In spite of the ease of access to data on the Internet, it must be remembered that search engines only cover a portion of international publications. Also, they are heavily biased towards English language publications. As a result, sole reliance on electronic information may let the researcher lose out on valuable input.[4] Electronic databases should therefore be seen as only one important dimension of research scrutiny. A listing of selected databases useful for international business is presented in Appendix 10A of this chapter.

Selection of Secondary Data

Just because secondary information has been found to exist does not mean that it must be used. Even though one key advantage of secondary data over primary research is that they are available relatively quickly and inexpensively, the researcher should still assess the effort and benefit of using them. Secondary data should be evaluated regarding the quality of their source, their recency, and their relevance to the task at hand. Clearly, since the information was collected without the current research requirements in mind, there may well be difficulties in coverage, categorization, and comparability. For example, an "engineer" in one country may differ substantially in terms of training and responsibilities from a person in another country holding the same title. It is therefore important to be careful when getting ready to interpret and analyze data.

Interpretation and Analysis of Secondary Data

Once secondary data have been obtained, the researcher must creatively convert them into information. Secondary data were originally collected to serve another purpose than the one in which the researcher is currently interested. Therefore, they can often be used only as **proxy information** in order to arrive at conclusions that address the research objectives. For example, the market penetration of video recorders may be used as a proxy variable for the potential demand for DVD-players. Similarly, in an industrial setting, information about plans for new port facilities may be useful in determining future container requirements.

The researcher must often use creative inferences, and such creativity brings risks. Therefore, once interpretation and analysis have taken place, a consistency check must be conducted. The researcher should always cross-check the results with other possible sources of information or with experts. Yet, if properly implemented, such creativity can open up one's eyes to new market potential, as Global Perspective 10.1 shows.

Data Privacy

The attitude of society toward obtaining and using both secondary and primary data must be taken into account. Many societies are increasingly sensitive to the issue of **data privacy,** and the concern has grown exponentially as a result of e-business. Readily accessible databases may contain information valuable to marketers, but they may also be considered privileged by individuals who have provided the data.

In 1998, the European Union passed a directive that introduced high standards for data privacy to ensure the free flow of data throughout the 15 member states. More importantly, the directive also required member states to block transmission of data to non-EU countries if these countries do not have domestic legislation that provide for a level of protection judged as adequate by the European Union. These laws restrict access to lifestyle information and its use for segmentation purposes. It is particularly difficult for direct marketers to obtain international access to voter rolls, birth records, or mortgage information.[5] There are key differences between the European and the U.S. perspective on data privacy. The EU law permits companies to collect personal data only if the individuals consent to the collection, know how the data will be used, and have access to databases to correct or erase their information. The U.S. approach strictly safeguards data collected by banks and government agencies. However, it also recognizes that most personal data, such as age or zip code are collected because someone is trying to sell something. Consumers who are annoyed by such data requests or sales pitches can only refuse to provide the information, throw out the junk mail, or hang up on telemarketers.

In order to avoid a costly conflict over data privacy between the U.S. and EU, a compromise was negotiated in 2000, where the United States agreed to set up a "safe harbor"—in essence, a list maintained by the Department of Commerce of companies that voluntarily adopt EU-style safeguards of their customers' private information. Com-

GLOBAL PERSPECTIVE 10.1

Epiphany Helps Find the CRM of the Crop

When Hewlett-Packard introduced its new oscilloscope, "We expected all our top customers would jump all over it," said Hewlett-Packard marketing director Lane Michel. What Hewlett-Packard didn't realize, however, was that these customers—from all around the world—didn't even know about the product. Their names and addresses were buried in several different databases, and the marketing department couldn't identify them. Despite marketing's pleas, overworked programmers had not been able to write a program to pull this information from the databases.

A new type of software known as customer-relations management software, offered by Epiphany, saved the day. In a matter of weeks Michel was able to identify the missing customers, segment their global market, and send marketing materials to them, resulting in dramatic increases in sales of the new oscilloscope.

Customer-relations management software (CRM), offered by firms such as Epiphany and Siebel Systems, allows a business to store and sort information about its customers, in-

cluding their demographics, preferences, and purchase histories. More efficient marketing strategies and delivery methods, for both buyer and seller, are the goals of the software. Epiphany's technology uses a web browser to design and search algorithms, so even non-techie staff are comfortable using it to extract corporate data on customer behavior and analyzing them for patterns.

The technology follows on the heels of data warehousing software, which didn't offer the pinpoint searches firms needed in searches through massive stores of data about customers around the world. With CRM technology, marketers can sift through databases using precise search tools to get the information they need. Businesses are expected to spend up to $15 billion annually on implementing CRM technology. The international $1 million price tag that an individual firm might spend for it is usually seen as well spent when lower marketing costs and higher revenues result. It's important for a multinational firm to be able to reach its international customers.

Sources: Theresa Forsman, "The Promise, and the Perils, of Customer-Relations Management Software," *Business Week,* October 30, 2000; Julie Pitta, "Garbage In, Gold Out," *Forbes,* April 5, 1999, pp. 124–125.

panies on the list will receive unrestricted EU data flow.[6] Yet, by early 2001, only 12 companies had signed up for the list, leaving the potential for conflict wide open.[7]

Conducting Primary Research

Even though secondary data are useful to the researcher, on many occasions primary information will be required. **Primary data** are obtained by a firm to fill specific information needs. Although the research may not be conducted by the company with the need, the work must be carried out for a specific research purpose in order to qualify as primary research. Typically, primary research intends to answer such clear-cut questions as:

- What is the sales potential for our measuring equipment in Malaysia?
- How much does the typical Greek consumer spend on fast food?
- What effect will our new type of packaging have on our green consumers in Norway?
- What service standards do industrial customers expect in Japan?

The researcher must have a clear idea of what the population under study should be and where it is located before deciding on the country or region to investigate. Conducting research in an entire country may not be necessary if, for example, only urban centers are to be penetrated. Multiple regions of a country need to be investigated, however, if a lack of homogeneity exists because of different economic, geographic, or behavioral factors. One source reports of the failure of a firm in Indonesia due to insufficient geographic dispersion of its research. The firm conducted its study only in large Indonesian cities during the height of tourism season, but projected the results to the entire population. When the company set up large production and distribution facilities to meet the expected demand, it realized only limited sales to city tourists.[8]

The discussion presented here will focus mainly on the research-specific issues. Application dimensions such as market choice and market analysis will be covered in Chapter 13.

Industrial versus Consumer Sources of Data

The researcher must decide whether research is to be conducted in the consumer or the industrial product area, which in turn determines the size of the universe and respondent accessibility. Consumers usually are a very large group, whereas the total population of industrial users may be limited. Cooperation by respondents may also vary. In the industrial setting, differentiation between users and decision makers may be important because their personalities, their outlooks, and their evaluative criteria may differ widely. Determining the proper focus of the research is therefore of major importance to its successful completion.

Determining the Research Technique

Selection of the research technique depends on a variety of factors. First, the objectivity of the data sought must be determined. Standardized techniques are more useful in the collection of objective data than of subjective data. **Unstructured data** will require more open-ended questions and more time than structured data. Whether the data are to be collected in the real world or in a controlled environment must be determined. Finally, it must be decided whether to collect historical facts or information about future developments. This is particularly important for consumer research, because firms frequently want to determine the future intentions of consumers about buying a certain product.

Once the desired data structure is determined, the researcher must choose a research technique. As in domestic research, the types available are interviews, focus groups, observation, surveys, and experimentation. Each one provides a different depth of information and has its own unique strengths and weaknesses.

Interviews Interviews with knowledgeable people can be of great value for the corporation that wants international information. Bias from the individual may slant the findings, so the intent should be to obtain not a wide variety of data, but rather in-depth information. When specific answers are sought to very narrow questions, interviews can be particularly useful.

Focus Groups Focus groups are a useful research tool resulting in interactive interviews. A group of knowledgeable people is gathered for a limited period of time (two to four hours). Usually, seven to ten participants is the ideal size for a focus group. A specific topic is introduced and thoroughly discussed by all group members. Because of the interaction, hidden issues are sometimes raised that would not have been detected in an individual interview. The skill of the group leader in stimulating discussion is crucial to the success of a focus group as illustrated in Global Perspective 10.2. Focus groups, like in-depth interviews, do not provide statistically significant information; however, they can be helpful in providing information about perceptions, emotions, and attitudinal factors. In addition, once individuals have been gathered, focus groups are a highly efficient means of rapidly accumulating a substantial amount of information.

GLOBAL PERSPECTIVE 10.2

It's a Car, an SUV, It's PT Cruiser!

Early in the new millennium, the new boldly styled PT Cruiser (PT for personal transportation) started turning heads in the United States and Europe. With its chunky lines reminiscent of 1920s gangster cars and 1940s hotrods, the PT Cruiser wasn't for the automotive faint of heart. While many loved DaimlerChrysler AG's new introduction, others hated it. But because of the unconventional focus groups it had used for market research, DaimlerChrysler was prepared for this strong consumer response in its markets around the world.

In the mid-1990s, DaimlerChrysler called on G. Clotaire Rapaille, a medical anthropologist, to jump-start the development of an automobile that would be both functional and appealing. Rapaille was the creator of "archetype research," a market-research process he had developed based on his work with autistic children to help them learn to talk. He believed that remembering something required an association with an emotion, and that this concept could be applied to consumers, who would be able to remember a car by the memories it evoked.

Once prototypes were ready, Rapaille and members of the PT Cruiser team led a series of three-hour focus groups in major U.S. and European cities. The members were selected to represent an entire culture rather than a specific demographic segment.

In the first hour, Rapaille asked the team to describe the purpose of the ideal vehicle to an alien, which responded with the term "toylike." In the second hour, participants composed word collages to describe the ideal vehicle. Members of the U.S. focus groups found hatchbacks unappealing, noting concerns about rear-end collisions and outsiders looking in. Parisian focus group members were comfortable with a hatchback design but complained that the car wasn't as functional as it appeared to be. In the final hour, the focus group members relaxed on the floor in a dimly lit room, listened to soothing music, and wrote stories after seeing the PT Cruiser prototype. The stories evolved from a toy theme in the earlier sessions to the safety of the car's interior contrasted with the dangers lurking outside.

Rapaille learned that consumers wanted the PT Cruiser to be large and safe, and to be more like a sports utility vehicle than a car or van. Designers therefore gave the car heftier fenders and a smaller rear window to make the hatch look stronger. To further increase the vehicle's utility, they also added removable seats and a laptop computer tray that was formed by folding down a front passenger seat. These changes satisfied the focus groups and also produced a highly stylized vehicle that, although it deliberately lacked universal appeal, met the different cultural needs of the global market it targeted.

This thorough, although unorthodox, market research paid off. In 2000, more than 250,000 people asked DaimlerChrysler to send them information about the 2001 model after seeing it at car shows around the world. By the end of 2000 the company had a six-month backlog of orders. Clearly, the insights on individual as well as cultural attitudes gained in focus groups helped accelerate the vehicle's successful introduction.

Sources: Jeffrey Ball, "How Does It Make You Feel?" *Wall Street Journal*, May 18, 1999, p. B1; Johnny Diaz, "PT Cruisers Bring Happy Flashbacks for Baby Boomers," *Knight-Ridder/Tribune News Service*, December 29, 2000.

When planning international research using focus groups, the researcher must be aware of the importance of language and culture in the interaction process. Major differences may exist already in preparing for the focus group. In some countries, participants can simply be asked to show up at a later date at a location where they will join the focus group. In other countries, participants have to be brought into the group immediately because commitments made for a future date have little meaning. In some nations, providing a payment to participants is sufficient motivation for them to open up in discussion. In other countries, one first needs to host a luncheon or dinner for the group so that members get to know each other and are willing to interact.

Once the focus group is started, the researcher must remember that not all societies encourage frank and open exchange and disagreement among individuals. Status consciousness may result in the opinion of one participant being reflected by all others. Disagreement may be seen as impolite, or certain topics may be taboo. Unless a native focus group leader is used, it also is possible to completely misread the interactions among group participants and to miss out on nuances and constraints participants feel when commenting in the group situation. One of this book's authors, for example, used the term *group discussion* in a focus group with Russian executives, only to learn that the translated meaning of the term was *political indoctrination session.*[9]

Observation   **Observation** requires the researcher to play the role of a nonparticipating observer of activity and behavior. In an international setting, observation can be extremely useful in shedding light on practices not previously encountered or understood. This aspect is especially valuable to the researcher who has no knowledge of a particular market or market situation. It can help in understanding phenomena that would have been difficult to assess with other techniques. For example, Toyota sent a group of its engineers and designers to southern California to nonchalantly observe how women get into and operate their cars. They found that women with long fingernails have trouble opening the door and operating various knobs on the dashboard. Toyota engineers and designers were able to comprehend the women's plight and redesign some of their automobile exteriors and interiors, producing more desirable cars.[10]

All the research instruments discussed so far are useful primarily for the gathering of **qualitative information.** The intent is not to amass data or to search for statistical significance, but rather to obtain a better understanding of given situations, behavioral patterns, or underlying dimensions. The researcher using these instruments must be cautioned that even frequent repetition of the measurements will not lead to a statistically valid result. However, statistical validity often may not be the major focus of corporate research. Rather, it may be the better understanding, description, and prediction of events that have an impact on decision making. When **quantitative data** are desired, surveys and experimentation are more appropriate research instruments.

Surveys   Survey research is useful in quantifying concepts. **Surveys** are usually conducted via questionnaires that are administered personally, by mail, or by telephone. Use of the survey technique presupposes that the population under study is accessible and able to comprehend and respond to the question posed through the chosen medium. Particularly for mail and telephone surveys, a major precondition is the feasibility of using the postal system or the widespread availability of telephones. Obviously, this is not a given in all countries. In many nations only limited records about dwellings, their location, and their occupants are available. In Venezuela, for example, most houses are not numbered but rather are given individual names such as Casa Rosa or El Retiro. In some countries, street maps are not even available. As a result, reaching respondents by mail is virtually impossible. In other countries, obtaining a correct address may be easy, but the postal system may not function well.

Telephone surveys may also be inappropriate if telephone ownership is rare. In such instances, any information obtained would be highly biased even if the researcher randomized the calls. In some cases, inadequate telephone networks and systems, frequent line congestion, and a lack of telephone directories may also prevent the researcher from conducting surveys.

Since surveys deal with people who in an international setting display major differences in culture, preference, education, and attitude, just to mention a few factors, the use of the survey technique must be carefully examined. For example, in some regions of the world, recipients of letters may be illiterate. Others may be very literate, but totally unaccustomed to some of the standard research scaling techniques used in the United States and therefore may be unable to respond to the instrument. Survey respondents in different countries may have different extreme response styles. If members of one culture are much more likely than those of another culture to agree very much or very little with a question, for example, then the researcher must adjust the findings in order to make them comparable to each other.[11] Other recipients of a survey may be reluctant to respond in writing, particularly when sensitive questions are asked. This sensitivity, of course, also varies by country. In some nations, any ques-

FIGURE 10.3

The Funny Faces Scale

Very Happy   Happy   Not Happy But   Unhappy   Very Unhappy
                                Also Not Unhappy

Source: C. K. Corder, "Problems and Pitfalls in Conducting Marketing Research in Africa," *Marketing Expansion in a Shrinking World,* ed. Betsy Gelb. Proceedings of American Marketing Association Business Conference (Chicago: AMA, 1978), pp. 86–90.

tions about income, even in categorical form, are considered highly proprietary; in others the purchasing behavior of individuals is not readily divulged.

The researcher needs to understand such constraints and prepare a survey that is responsive to them. For example, surveys can incorporate drawings or even cartoons to communicate better. Personal administration or collaboration with locally accepted intermediaries may improve the response rate. Indirect questions may need to substitute for direct ones in sensitive areas. Questions may have to be reworded to ensure proper communication. Figure 10.3 provides an example of a rating scale developed by researchers to work with a diverse population with relatively little education. In its use, however, it was found that the same scale aroused negative reactions among better-educated respondents, who considered the scale childish and insulting to their intelligence.

In spite of all the potential difficulties, the survey technique remains a useful one because it allows the researcher to rapidly accumulate a large quantity of data amenable to statistical analysis. With constantly expanding technological capabilities, international researchers will be able to use this technique even more in the future.

Experimentation   Experimental techniques determine the effect of an intervening variable and help establish precise cause-and-effect relationships. However, **experimentation** is difficult to implement in international research. The researcher faces the task of designing an experiment in which most variables are held constant or are comparable across cultures. For example, an experiment to determine a causal effect within the distribution system of one country may be very difficult to transfer to another country because the distribution system may be quite different. For this reason, experimental techniques are only rarely used, even though their potential value to the international researcher is recognized.

The International Information System

Many organizations have data needs that go beyond specific international research projects. Most of the time, daily decisions must be made for which there is neither time nor money for special research. An **information system** can provide the decision maker with basic data for most ongoing decisions. Defined as "the systematic and continuous gathering, analysis, and reporting of data for decision-making purposes,"[12] such a system serves as a mechanism to coordinate the flow of information to corporate managers.

To be useful to the decision maker, the system must have certain attributes. First of all, the information must be *relevant.* The data gathered must have meaning for the manager's decision-making process. Only rarely can corporations afford to spend large amounts of money on information that is simply "nice to know." Any information system will have to continuously address the balance to be struck between the expense of the research design and process and the value of the information to ongoing business activities. Second, the information must be *timely.* Managers derive little benefit if decision information needed today does not become available until a month from now. To be of use to the international decision maker, the system must therefore feed from a variety of international sources and be updated frequently. For multinational corporations, this means a real-time link between international subsidiaries and a broad-based ongoing data input operation. Third, information must be *flexible*—that is, it must be available in the form needed by management. An information system must therefore permit manipulation of the format and combination of the data. Fourth, information contained in the system must be *accurate.* This is especially important in international research because information quickly becomes outdated as a result of major environmental changes. Fifth, the system's information bank must be reasonably *exhaustive.* Factors that may influence a particular decision must be appropriately represented in the information system because of the interrelationships among variables. This means that the information system must be based on a wide variety of factors. Sixth, the collection and processing of data must be *consistent.* This is to hold down project cost and turnaround time, while ensuring that data can be compared regionally. This can be achieved by centralizing the management under one manager who oversees the system's design, processing, and analysis.[13] Finally, to be useful to managers, the system must be *convenient* to use. Systems that are cumbersome and time-consuming to reach and to use will not be used enough to justify corporate expenditures to build and maintain them.

One area where international firms are gradually increasing the use of information system technology is in the export field. In order to stay close to their customers, proactive firms are developing **export complaint systems.** These systems allow customers to contact the original supplier of a product in order to inquire about products, to make suggestions, or to present complaints. Firms are finding that about 5 percent of their customers abroad are dissatisfied with the product. By establishing direct contact via e-mail, a toll-free telephone number, or a web site, firms do not need to rely on the filtered feed-back from channel intermediaries abroad and can learn directly about product failures, channel problems, or other causes of customer dissatisfaction. The development of such an export complaint system requires substantial resources, intensive planning, and a high degree of cultural sensitivity. Customers abroad must be informed of how to complain, and their cost of complaining must be minimized, for example, by offering an interactive web site. The response to complaints must also be tailored to the culture of the complainant. For example, to some customers, the speed of reply matters most, while to others the thoughtfulness of the reply is of key concern. As a result, substantial resources must be invested into personnel training so the system works in harmony with customer expectations. Most important, however, is a firm's ability to aggregate and analyze complaints and to make use of them internally. Complaints are often the symptom for underlying structural problems of a product or a process. If used properly, an export complaint system can become a rich source of information for product improvement and innovation.

To build an information system, corporations use the internal data that are available from divisions such as accounting and finance and also from various subsidiaries. In addition, many organizations put mechanisms in place to enrich the basic data flow to information systems. Three such mechanisms are environmental scanning, Delphi studies, and scenario building.

Environmental Scanning   Any changes in the business environment, whether domestic or foreign, may have serious repercussions on the activities of the firm. Corporations therefore understand the necessity for tracking new developments. Although this can be done implicitly in the domestic environment, the remoteness of international markets requires a continuous information flow. For this purpose, some large multinational organizations have formed environmental scanning groups.

Environmental scanning activities provide continuous information on political, social, and economic affairs internationally; on changes of attitudes of public institutions and private citizens; and on possible upcoming alterations. Environmental scanning models can be used for a variety of purposes, such as the development of long-term strategies, getting managers to broaden their horizons, or structuring action plans. Obviously, the precision required for environmental scanning varies with its purpose. The more immediate and precise the application will be within the corporation, the greater the need for detailed information. On the other hand, heightened precision may reduce the usefulness of environmental scanning in strategic planning, which is long term.

Environmental scanning can be performed in various ways. One consists of obtaining factual input on a wide variety of demographic, social, and economic characteristics of foreign countries. Frequently, managers believe that factual data alone are insufficient for their information needs. Particularly when forecasting future developments, other methods are used to capture underlying dimensions of social change. One significant method is that of **content analysis.** A wide array of newspapers, magazines, and other publications are scanned worldwide in order to pinpoint over time the gradual evolution of new views or trends. Corporations also use the technique of media analysis to pinpoint upcoming changes in their line of business. For example, the Alaskan oil spill by the Exxon *Valdez* and the rash of oil spills that followed resulted in entirely new international concern about environmental protection and safety, reaching far beyond the actual incidents and participants.

With the current heightened awareness of environmental and ethical issues such as pollution, preservation of natural resources, and animal testing, firms are increasingly looking for new opportunities to expand their operations while remaining within changing moral and environmental boundaries.

Environmental scanning is conducted by a variety of groups within and outside the corporation. Quite frequently, small corporate staffs are created at headquarters to coordinate the information flow. In addition, subsidiary staff can be used to provide occasional intelligence reports. Groups of volunteers are also formed to gather and analyze information worldwide and feed their individual analyses back to corporate headquarters, where the "big picture" can then be constructed. Rapidly growing use of the Internet also allows firms to find out about new developments in their fields of interest and permits them to gather information through bulletin boards and discussion groups. For example, some firms use search engines to comb through thousands of newsgroups for any mention of a particular product or application. If they find frequent references, they can investigate further to see what customers are saying.[14]

Finally, it should be kept in mind that internationally there may be a fine line between tracking and obtaining information and the misappropriation of corporate secrets. With growing frequency, governments and firms claim that their trade secrets are being obtained and abused by foreign competitors. The perceived threat from economic espionage has led to legislation[15] and accusations of government spying networks trying to undermine the commercial interests of companies.[16] Information gatherers must be sensitive to these issues in order to avoid conflict.

Delphi Studies   To enrich the information obtained from factual data, corporations and governments frequently resort to the use of creative and highly qualitative data-gathering methods. One approach is through **Delphi studies.** These studies are particularly useful in the international environment because they are "a means for aggregating the judgments of a number of . . . experts . . . who cannot come together physically."[17] This type of research clearly aims at qualitative measures by seeking a consensus from those who know, rather than average responses from many people with only limited knowledge.

Typically, Delphi studies are carried out with groups of about 30 well-chosen participants who possess expertise in an area of concern, such as future developments of the international trade environment. The participants are asked to identify the major issues in the given area of concern. They are also requested to rank order their statements according to importance and explain the rationale behind the order. The aggregated information and comments are then sent to all participants in the Delphi group. Group members are encouraged to agree or disagree with the various rank orders and the comments. This allows statements to be challenged. In another round, the participants respond to the challenges. Several rounds of challenges and responses result in a reasonably coherent consensus.

The Delphi technique is particularly valuable because it uses mail, facsimile, or electronic communication to bridge large distances and therefore makes experts quite accessible at a reasonable cost. It avoids the drawback of ordinary mail investigations, which lack interaction among participants. Several rounds may be required, however, so substantial time may elapse before the information is obtained. Also, a major effort must be expended in selecting the appropriate participants and in motivating them to participate in the exercise with enthusiasm and continuity. When carried out on a regular basis, Delphi studies can provide crucial augmentation of the factual data available for the information system. For example, a large portion of this book's last chapter was written based on an extensive Delphi study carried out by the authors.

Scenario Building   The information obtained through environmental scanning or Delphi studies can then be used to conduct a scenario analysis. One approach involves the development of a series of plausible scenarios that are constructed from trends observed in the environment. Another method consists of formally reviewing assumptions built into existing business plans and positions.[18] Subsequently, some of these key assumptions such as economic growth rates, import penetration, population growth, and political stability, can be varied. By projecting variations for medium- to long-term periods, completely new environmental conditions can emerge. The conditions can then be analyzed for their potential domestic and international impact on corporate strategy.

The identification of crucial variables and the degree of variation are of major importance in **scenario building.** Scenario builders also need to recognize the nonlinearity of factors. To simply extrapolate from currently existing situations is insufficient, since extraneous factors often enter the picture with significant impact. The possibility of **joint occurrences** must be recognized as well, because changes may not come about in isolated fashion but instead may spread over wide regions. For example, given large technological advances, the possibility of wholesale obsolescence of current technology must be considered. Quantum leaps in computer development and new generations of computers may render obsolete the entire technological investment of a corporation.

For scenarios to be useful, management must analyze and respond to them by formulating contingency plans. Such planning will broaden horizons and may prepare managers for unexpected situations. Through the anticipation of possible problems, managers hone their response capability and in turn shorten response times to actual problems.

The development of an international information system is of major importance to the multinational corporation. It aids the ongoing decision process and becomes a vital tool in performing the strategic planning task. Only by observing global trends and changes will the firm be able to maintain and improve its competitive position. Much of the data available are quantitative in nature, but researchers must also pay attention to qualitative dimensions. Quantitative analysis will continue to improve as the ability to collect, store, analyze, and retrieve data increases as a result of computer development. Nevertheless, the qualitative dimension will remain a major component for corporate research and planning activities.

Summary

Constraints of time, resources, and expertise are the major inhibitors to international research. Nevertheless, firms need to carry out planned and organized research in order to explore foreign market opportunities and challenges successfully. Such research must be linked closely to the decision-making process.

International research differs from domestic research in that the environment—which determines how well tools, techniques, and concepts apply—is different abroad. In addition, the international manager must deal with duties, exchange rates, and international documentation; a greater number of interacting factors; and a much broader definition of the concept of competition.

When the firm is uninformed about international differences in consumer tastes and preferences or about foreign market environments, the need for international research is particularly great. Research objectives need to be determined based on the corporate mission, the level of international expertise, and the business plan. These objectives will enable the research to identify the information requirements.

Given the scarcity of resources, companies beginning their international effort must rely on data that have already been collected. These secondary data are available from sources such as governments, international organizations, or electronic information services. It is important to respect privacy laws and preferences when making use of secondary data.

To fulfill specific information requirements, the researcher may need to collect primary data. An appropriate research technique must be selected to collect the information. Sensitivity to different international environments and cultures will aid the researcher in deciding whether to use interviews, focus groups, observation, surveys, or experimentation as data-collection techniques.

To provide ongoing information to management, an information system is useful. Such a system will provide for the continuous gathering, analysis, and reporting of data for decision-making purposes. Data gathered through environmental scanning, Delphi studies, or scenario building enable management to prepare for the future and hone its decision-making abilities.

Key Terms and Concepts

foreign market opportunity analysis	primary data	qualitative data	environmental scanning
competitive assessment	unstructured data	surveys	content analysis
secondary data	interviews	experimentation	Delphi studies
proxy information	focus groups	information system	scenario building
data privacy	observation	export complaint systems	joint occurrence
	qualitative information		

Questions for Discussion

1. What is the difference between domestic and international research?
2. You are employed by National Engineering, a firm that designs subways. Because you have had a course in international business, your boss asks you to spend the next week exploring international possibilities for the company. How will you go about this task?
3. Discuss the possible shortcomings of secondary data.
4. Why should a firm collect primary data in its international research?
5. Of all the OECD countries, which one(s) derives the largest share of its GDP from the services sector? from agriculture? from industry? (these figures can be downloaded from the OECD in Figures on the site **www.oecd.org**).

6. What are the top ten trading partners for the United States? What was the U.S.'s top commodity import from France? What was the U.S.'s top commodity export to Japan (use the U.S. Foreign Trade Highlights tables on the Department of Commerce's International Trade Administration site, **www.ita.doc.gov**)?
7. What are some of the products and services the World Bank offers to firms doing business in the developing world (refer to the World Bank's web page "Doing Business with the Bank," through **www.worldbank.org**)?
8. To which group of countries are NAFTA members most likely to export (use the Inter-American Development Bank's exports tables under the "Research and Statistics" database section of its web page, **www.iadb.org**)?

Internet Exercise

1. Show macro, aggregate changes in international markets by listing the total value of three commodities exported from your country to five other countries for the last four years. For each of the countries, provide a one paragraph statement in which you identify positive or negative trends. Give your opinion on whether or not these trends are relevant or reflect the reality of today's international business environment. What are the dangers of relying on perceived trends? You are encouraged to conduct research on products from your hometown or region.

Recommended Readings

Craig, C. Samuel, and Susan P. Douglas. *International Marketing Research: Concepts and Methods,* 2d ed. New York: John Wiley & Sons, 1999.

Churchill, Gilbert A., Jr. *Basic Marketing Research. Methodology* 4th ed. Fort Worth, TX: Harcourt, 2001.

Czinkota, Michael R., and Sarah McCue, *The STAT-USA Companion to International Business.* Washington, DC: U.S. Department of Commerce, 2001.

Directory of Online Databases. Santa Monica, CA: Cuadra Associates, published annually.

GreenBook 2000–2001, Worldwide Directory of Marketing Research Companies and Services. New York: American Marketing Association, 2001.

Zuckerman, Amy. *International Standards Desk Reference: Your Passport to World Markets, ISO 9000, CE Mark, QS-9000, SSM, ISO 14000, Q 9000, American, European, and Global Standards Systems.* New York: American Management Association, 1997.

Notes

1. David A. Ricks, *Blunders in International Business,* 3d ed. (Malden, MA: Blackwell, 2000.)
2. C. Samuel Craig and Susan P. Douglas, *International Marketing Research,* 2d ed. (New York: John Wiley & Sons, 1999).
3. "National Trade Data Bank," Government Documents Department: Lauinger Library, Georgetown University, 2001.
4. Michael R. Czinkota, "International Information Cross-Fertilization in Marketing: An Empirical Assessment," *European Journal of Marketing* 34, 11/12 (2000): 1305–1314.
5. Charles A. Prescott, "The New International Marketing Challenge: Privacy," *Target Marketing* 22 (no. 4, 1999): 28.
6. "Data Privacy Deal," *The Journal of Commerce,* March 28, 2000.
7. "Privacy: Safe Harbor Is a Lonely Harbor," *National Journal's Technology Daily,* January 5, 2001.
8. Ricks, *Blunders in International Business.*
9. Michael R. Czinkota, "Russia's Transition to a Market Economy: Learning About Business," *Journal of International Marketing* 5, 4 (fall 1997): 73–93.
10. Michael R. Czinkota and Masaaki Kotabe, "Product Development the Japanese Way," in M. Czinkota and M. Kotabe, *Trends in International Business: Critical Perspectives* (Oxford: Blackwell Publishers, 1998), 153–158.
11. Irvine Clarke III, "Global Marketing Research: Is Extreme Response Style Influencing Your Results?" *Journal of International Consumer Marketing,* 12, 4 (2000): 91–111.
12. Thomas C. Kinnear and James R. Taylor, *Marketing Research: An Applied Approach,* 5th ed. (New York: McGraw-Hill, 1996.
13. Joseph Marinelli and Anastasia Schleck, "Collecting, Processing Data for Marketing Research Worldwide," *Marketing News* 31, 17 (August 18, 1997): 12, 14.
14. David A. Andelman, "Betting on the Net," *Sales and Marketing Management* (June 1995): 47–59.
15. Barry R. Shapiro, "Economic Espionage," *Marketing Management* (spring 1998): 56–58.
16. Peter Clarke, "The Echelon Questions," *Electronic Engineering Times,* March 6, 2000: 36.
17. Andrel Delbecq, Andrew H. Van de Ven, and David H. Gustafson, *Group Techniques for Program Planning* (Glenview, IL: Scott Foresman, 1975), 83.
18. William H. Davidson, "The Role of Global Scanning in Business Planning," *Organizational Dynamics* (Winter 1991): 5–16.

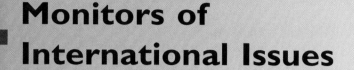

APPENDIX 10A

Monitors of International Issues

European Union

- **EUROPA**
  The umbrella server for all institutions
  www.europa.eu.int

- **ISPO (Information Society Project Office)**
  Information on telecommunications and information market developments
  Information Society
  European Commission
  Directorate General Information Society
  BU 24 O/74
  Rue de la Loi 200
  B-1049 Brussels
  www.ispo.cec.be

- **CORDIS**
  Information on EU research programs
  www.cordis.lu

- **EUROPARL**
  Information on the European Parliament's activities
  www.europarl.eu.int

- **Delegation of the European Commission to the U.S.**
  Press releases, EURECOM: Economic and Financial News, EU-US relations, information on EU policies and Delegation programs
  European Union
  Delegation of the European Commission to the United States

2300 M Street, NW
Washington, DC 20037
www.eurunion.org

- **Citizens Europe**
  Covers rights of citizens of EU member states
  citizens.eu.int

- **EUDOR (European Union Document Repository)**
  Bibliographic database
  www.eudor.com

- **Euro**
  The Single Currency
  euro.eu.int

- **European Agency for the Evaluation of Medicinal Products**
  Information on drug approval procedures and documents of the Committee for Proprietary Medicinal Products and the Committee for Veterinary Medicinal Products
  www.eudra.org/emea.html

- **European Central Bank**
  Kaiserstrasse 29
  D-60311 Frankfurt am Main
  Germany
  Postal:
  Postfach 160319
  D-60066 Frankfurt am Main
  Germany
  www.ecb.int

- **European Centre for the Development of Vocational Training**

Under construction with information on the Centre and contact information
Cedefop
Europe 123
GR-57001 Thessaloniki
(Pylea)
Mailing Address:
PO Box 22427
Thessaloniki
GR-55102 Thessaloniki
www.cedefop.gr

- **European Environment Agency**
  Information on the mission, products and services, and organizations and staff of the EEA
  www.eea.dk

- **European Investment Bank**
  Press releases and information on borrowing and loan operations, staff, and publications
  100, boulevard Konrad Adenauer
  L-2950 Luxembourg
  www.eib.org

- **European Union Internet Resources**
  Main Library, 2nd Floor
  The Library
  University of California
  Berkeley, CA 94720-6000
  http://lib.berkeley.edu/GSSI/eu/html

- **Office for Harmonization in the Internal Market**

Guidelines, application forms and other information to registering an EU trademark
oami.eu.int

- **Council of the European Union**
Information and news from the Council with sections covering Common Foreign and Security Policy (CFSP) and Justice and Home Affairs Under Construction
ue.eu.int

- **Court of Justice**
Overview, press releases, publications, and full-text proceedings of the court
europa.eu.int/ci/en/index.htm

- **Court of Auditors**
Information notes, annual reports, and other publications
www.eca.eu.int

- **European Community Information Service**
200 Rue de la Loi
1049 Brussels, Belgium
and
2100 M Street NW, 7th Floor
Washington, DC 20037

- **European Bank for Reconstruction and Development**
One Exchange Square
London EC2A 2JN
United Kingdom
www.ebrd.com

- **European Union**
200 Rue de la Loi
1049 Brussels, Belgium
and
2100 M Street NW 7th Floor
Washington, DC 20037
www.eurunion.org

United Nations

www.un.org

- **Conference of Trade and Development**
Palais des Nations
1211 Geneva 10
Switzerland
www.unctad.org

- **Department of Economic and Social Affairs**
1 United Nations Plaza
New York, NY 10017
www.un.org/ecosocdev/

- **Industrial Development Organization**
1660 L Street NW
Washington, DC 20036
and
Post Office Box 300
Vienna International Center
A-1400 Vienna, Austria
www.unido.org

- **International Trade Centre**
UNCTAD/WTO
54–56 Rue de Mountbrillant
CH-1202 Geneva
Switzerland
www.intracen.org

- **UN Publications**
Room 1194
1 United Nations Plaza
New York, NY 10017
www.un.org/pubs/

- **Statistical Yearbook**
1 United Nations Plaza
New York, NY 10017
www.un.org/Pubs/

- **Yearbook of International Trade Statistics**
United Nations Publishing Division
1 United Nations Plaza
Room DC2-0853
New York, NY 10017
www.un.org/Pubs/

U.S. Government

- **Agency for International Development**
Office of Business Relations
Washington, DC 20523
www.info.usaid.gov

- **Customs Service**
1300 Pennsylvania Ave. NW
Room 6.3D
Washington, DC 20229
www.customs.ustreas.gov

- **Department of Agriculture**
12th Street and Jefferson Drive SW
Washington, DC 20250
www.usda.gov

- **Department of Commerce**
Herbert C. Hoover Building
14th Street and Constitution Avenue NW
Washington, DC 20230
www.doc.gov

- **Department of State**
2201 C Street NW
Washington, DC 20520
www.state.gov

- **Department of the Treasury**
15th Street and Pennsylvania Avenue NW
Washington, DC 20220
www.ustreas.gov

- **Federal Trade Commission**
6th Street and Pennsylvania Avenue NW
Washington, DC 20580
www.ftc.gov

- **International Trade Commission**
500 E Street NW
Washington, DC 20436
www.usitc.gov

- **Small Business Administration**
409 Third Street SW
Washington, DC 20416
www.sbaonline.sba.gov

- **Trade Information Center**
International Trade Administration
U.S. Department of Commerce
Washington, D.C. 20230
www.ita.doc.gov/td/tic/

- **U.S. Trade and Development Agency**
1621 North Kent Street
Rosslyn, VA 22209
www.tda.gov

- **World Trade Centers Association**
1 World Trade Center, Suite 7701
New York, NY 10048
www.wtca.org

- **Council of Economic Advisers—
www.whitehouse.gov/gov/wh/eop/cea**

- **Department of Defense—
www.dtic.dla.mil**

- Department of Energy—
  www.osti. gov

- Department of Interior—
  www.doi. gov

- Department of Labor—
  www.dol.gov

- Department of Transportation—
  www.dot.gov

- Environmental Protection
  Agency—**www.epa.gov**

- National Trade Data Bank—
  www.stat-usa.gov

- National Economic Council—
  **www.whitehouse.gov/gov/
  wh/eop/nec**

- Office of the U.S. Trade Representative—**www.ustr.gov**

- Office of Management and
  Budget—**www.whitehouse.
  gov/gov/wh/eo/p/omb**

- Overseas Private Investment
  Corporation—**www.opic.gov**

Selected Organizations

- **American Bankers Association**
  1120 Connecticut Avenue NW
  Washington, DC 20036
  www.aba.com

- **American Bar Association**
  750 N. Lake Shore Drive
  Chicago, IL 60611
  and
  1800 M Street NW
  Washington, DC 20036
  **www.abanet.org/intlaw/
  home.html**

- **American Management Association**
  440 First Street NW
  Washington, DC 20001
  www.amanet.org

- **American Marketing Association**
  311 S. Wacker Drive, Suite 5800
  Chicago, IL 60606
  www.ama.org

- **American Petroleum Institute**
  1220 L Street NW

Washington, DC 20005
www.api.org

- **Asia-Pacific Economic Cooperation Secretariat**
  438 Alexandra Road
  #41-00, Alexandra Road
  Singapore 119958
  www.apecsec.org.sg

- **Asian Development Bank**
  2330 Roxas Boulevard
  Pasay City, Philippines
  www.asiandevbank.org

- **Association of South East Asian
  Nations (ASEAN)**
  Publication Office
  c/o The ASEAN Secretariat
  70A, Jalan Sisingamangaraja
  Jakarta 11210
  Indonesia
  www.asean.or.id

- **Canadian Market Data**
  www.strategis.ic.gc.ca

- **Chamber of Commerce of the
  United States**
  1615 H Street NW
  Washington, DC 20062
  www.uschamber.org

- **Commission of the European
  Communities to the United
  States**
  2100 M Street NW
  Suite 707
  Washington, DC 20037
  www.eurunion.org

- **Conference Board**
  845 Third Avenue
  New York, NY 10022
  and
  1755 Massachusetts Avenue
  NW Suite 312
  Washington, DC 20036
  www.conference-board.org

- **Deutsche Bundesbank**
  Wilhelm-Epstein-Str. 14
  P.O.B. 10 06 02
  D-60006 Frankfurt am Main
  www.bundesbank.de

- **Electronic Industries Association**
  2001 Pennsylvania Avenue NW
  Washington, DC 20004
  www.eia.org

- **The Emerging Markets Directory**
  http://www.emdirectory.com

- **Export-Import Bank of the
  United States**
  811 Vermont Avenue NW
  Washington, DC 20571
  www.exim.gov

- **Federal Reserve Bank of New
  York**
  33 Liberty Street
  New York, NY 10045
  www.ny.frb.org

- **The Federation of International
  Trade Associations**
  11800 Sunrise Valley Drive,
  Suite 210
  Reston, VA 20191
  www.fita.org

- **Inter-American Development Bank**
  1300 New York Avenue NW
  Washington, DC 20577
  www.iadb.org

- **International Bank for Reconstruction and Development
  (World Bank)**
  1818 H Street NW
  Washington, DC 20433
  www.worldbank.org

- **International Monetary Fund**
  700 19th Street NW
  Washington, DC 20431
  www.imf.org

- **International Chamber of
  Commerce**
  38, Cours Albert ler
  7800 Paris, France
  www.iccwbo.org

- **International Telecommunication
  Union**
  Place des Nations
  Ch-1211 Geneva 20
  Switzerland
  www.itu.int

- **International Trade Law
  Monitor**
  http://lexmercatoria.org

- **Michigan State University Center
  for International Business
  Education and Research**
  www.ciber.bus.msu.edu/busres

- **Marketing Research Society**
111 E. Wacker Drive, Suite 600
Chicago, IL 60601

- **National Association of Manufacturers**
1331 Pennsylvania Avenue
Suite 1500
Washington, DC 20004
www.nam.org

- **National Federation of Independent Business**
600 Maryland Avenue SW
Suite 700
Washington, DC 20024
www.nfib.org

- **Organization for Economic Cooperation and Development**
2 rue Andre Pascal
75775 Paris Cedex Ko, France
and
2001 L Street NW, Suite 700
Washington, DC 20036
www.oecd.org

- **Organization of American States**
17th and Constitution Avenue NW
Washington, DC 20006
www.oas.org

- **Society for International Development**
1401 New York Avenue NW
Suite 1100
Washington, DC 20005
www.aed.org/sid

- **Transparency International**
Otto-Suhr-Allee 97-99
D-10585 Berlin
Germany
www.transparency.de

Indexes to Literature

- **Business Periodical Index**
H.W. Wilson Co.
950 University Avenue
Bronx, NY 10452

- **New York Times Index**
University Microfilms
International
300 N. Zeeb Road
Ann Arbor, MI 48106
www.nytimes.com

- **Public Affairs Information Service Bulletin**
11 W. 40th Street
New York, NY 10018
www.pais.internet

- **Reader's Guide to Periodical Literature**
H.W. Wilson Co.
950 University Avenue
Bronx, NY 10452
www.tulane.edu/~horn/rdg.html

- **Wall Street Journal Index**
University Microfilms
International
300 N. Zeeb Road
Ann Arbor, MI 48106
www.wsj.com

Directories

- **American Register of Exporters and Importers**
38 Park Row
New York, NY 10038

- **Arabian Year Book**
Dar Al-Seuassam Est. Box 42480
Shuwahk, Kuwait

- **Directories of American Firms Operating in Foreign Countries**
World Trade Academy Press
Uniworld Business Publications Inc.
50 E. 42nd Street
New York, NY 10017

- **The Directory of International Sources of Business Information**
Pitman
128 Long Acre
London WC2E 9AN, England

- **Encyclopedia of Associations**
Gale Research Co.
Book Tower
Detroit, MI 48226

- **Polk's World Bank Directory**
R.C. Polk & Co.
2001 Elm Hill Pike
P.O. Box 1340
Nashville, TN 37202

- **Verified Directory of Manufacturer's Representatives**
MacRae's Blue Book Inc.
817 Broadway
New York, NY 10003

- **World Guide to Trade Associations**
K.G. Saur & Co.
175 Fifth Avenue
New York, NY 10010

Encyclopedias, Handbooks, and Miscellaneous

- **A Basic Guide to Exporting**
U.S. Government Printing Office
Superintendent of Documents
Washington, DC 20402

- **Doing Business In . . . Series**
Price Waterhouse
1251 Avenue of the Americas
New York, NY 10020

- **Economic Survey of Europe**
United Nations Publishing
Division
1 United Nations Plaza
Room DC2-0853
New York, NY 10017

- **Economic Survey of Latin America**
United Nations Publishing
Division
1 United Nations Plaza
Room DC2-0853
New York, NY 10017

- **Encyclopedia Americana, International Edition**
Grolier Inc.
Danbury, CT 06816

- **Encyclopedia of Business Information Sources**
Gale Research Co.
Book Tower
Detroit, MI 48226

- **Europa Year Book**
Europa Publications Ltd.
18 Bedford Square
London WCIB 3JN, England

- **Export Administration Regulations**
U.S. Government Printing Office
Superintendent of Documents
Washington, DC 20402

- **Exporters' Encyclopedia—World Marketing Guide**
Dun's Marketing Services
49 Old Bloomfield Rd.
Mountain Lake, NJ 07046

- **Export-Import Bank of the United States Annual Report**
U.S. Government Printing Office
Superintendent of Documents
Washington, DC 20402

- **Exporting for the Small Business**
U.S. Government Printing Office
Superintendent of Documents
Washington, DC 20402

- **Exporting to the United States**
U.S. Government Printing Office
Superintendent of Documents
Washington, DC 20402

- **Export Shipping Manual**
U.S. Government Printing Office
Superintendent of Documents
Washington, DC 20402

- **Forign Business Practices: Materials on Practical Aspects of Exporting, International Licensing, and Investing**
U.S. Government Printing Office
Superintendent of Documents
Washington, DC 20402

- **A Guide to Financing Exports**
U.S. Government Printing Office
Superintendent of Documents
Washington, DC 20402

- **Handbook of Marketing Research**
McGraw-Hill Book Co.
1221 Avenue of the Americas
New York, NY 10020

Periodic Reports, Newspapers, Magazines

- **Advertising Age**
Crain Communications Inc.
740 N. Rush Street
Chicago, IL 60611
www.adage.com

- **Advertising World**
Directories International Inc.
150 Fifth Avenue, Suite 610
New York, NY 10011
http://advertising.utexas.edu/world/

- **Arab Report and Record**
84 Chancery Lane
London WC2A 1DL, England

- **Barron's**
University Microfilms International
300 N. Zeeb Road
Ann Arbor, MI 48106
www.barrons.com

- **Business America**
U.S. Department of Commerce
14th Street and Constitution Avenue NW
Washington, DC 20230
www.doc.gov

- **Business International**
Business International Corp.
One Dag Hammarskjold Plaza
New York, NY 10017

- **Business Week**
McGraw-Hill Publications Co.
1221 Avenue of the Americas
New York, NY 10020
www.businessweek.com

- **Commodity Trade Statistics**
United Nations Publications
1 United Nations Plaza
Room DC2-0853
New York, NY 10017

- **Conference Board Record**
Conference Board Inc.
845 Third Avenue
New York, NY 10022
www.conference-board.org

- **Customs Bulletin**
U.S. Customs Service
1301 Constitution Avenue NW
Washington, DC 20229

- **The Economist**
Economist Newspaper Ltd.
25 St. James Street
London SWIA 1HG, England
www.economist.com

- **Europe Magazine**
2100 M Street NW Suite 707
Washington, DC 20037
www.eurunion.org/magazine/home.htm

- **The Financial Times**
Bracken House
10 Cannon Street
London EC4P 4BY, England
www.ft-se.co.uk

- **Forbes**
Forbes, Inc.
60 Fifth Avenue
New York, NY 10011
www.forbes.com

- **Fortune**
Time, Inc.
Time & Life Building
1271 Avenue of the Americas
New York, NY 10020
www.pathfinder.com/fortune

- **Global Trade**
North American Publishing Co.
401 N. Broad Street
Philadelphia, PA 19108

- **Industrial Marketing**
Crain Communications, Inc.
740 N. Rush Street
Chicago, IL 60611

- **International Financial Statistics**
International Monetary Fund
Publications Unit
700 19th Street NW
Washington, DC 20431
www.imf.com

- **Investor's Business Daily**
Box 25970
Los Angeles, CA 90025
Journal of Commerce
110 Wall Street
New York, NY 10005
www.investors.com

- **Journal of Commerce**
100 Wall Street
New York, NY 10005
www.joc.com

- **Sales and Marketing Management**
Bill Communications Inc.
633 Third Avenue
New York, NY 10017

- **Wall Street Journal**
  Dow Jones & Company
  200 Liberty Street
  New York, NY 10281
  www.wsj.com

- **World Agriculture Situation**
  U.S. Department of Agriculture
  Economics Management Staff
  www.econ.ag.gov

- **Pergamon Press Inc.**
  Journals Division
  Maxwell House
  Fairview Park
  Elmsford, NY 10523

- **World Trade Center Association
  (WTCA) Directory**
  World Trade Centers
  Association
  1 World Trade Center
  New York, NY 10048

- **International Encyclopedia of the
  Social Sciences**
  Macmillan and the Free Press
  866 Third Avenue
  New York, NY 10022

- **Marketing and Communications
  Media Dictionary**
  Media Horizons Inc.
  50 W. 25th Street
  New York, NY 10010
  www.horizons-media.com

- **Market Share Reports**
  U.S. Government Printing Office
  Superintendent of Documents
  Washington, DC 20402
  www.access.gpo.gov

- **Media Guide International:
  Business/Professional
  Publications**
  Directories International Inc.
  150 Fifth Avenue, Suite 610
  New York, NY 10011
  www.clubi.ie/bdi/index.html

- **Overseas Business Reports**
  U.S Government Printing Office
  Superintendent of Documents
  Washington, DC 20402
  www.access.gpo.gov

- **Sales and Marketing Management**
  **www.salesandmarketing.com/
  smmnew/**

- **Trade Finance**
  U.S. Department of Commerce
  International Trade
  Administration
  Washington, DC 20230
  www.doc.gov

- **World Economic Conditions in
  Relation to Agricultural Trade**
  U.S. Government Printing Office
  Superintendent of Documents
  Washington, DC 20402
  www.access.gpo.gov

Selected Trade Databases

News agencies
Comline-Japan Newswire
Dow Jones News
Nikkei Shimbun News
Database Omninews
Lexis-Nexis
Reuters Monitor
UPI

Trade Publication References with Bibliographic Keywords

Agris
Biocommerce Abstracts & Directory
Findex
Frost (short) Sullivan Market
Research Reports
Marketing Surveys Index
McCarthy Press Cuttings Service
Paperchern
PTS F & S Indexes
Trade and Industry Index

Trade Publication References with Summaries

ABI/Inform
Arab Information Bank
Asia-Pacific
BFAI
Biobusiness

CAB Abstracts
Chemical Business Newsbase
Chemical Industry Notes
Caffeeline
Delphes
InfoSouth Latin American Information System
Management Contents
NTIS Bibliographic Data Base
Paperchem
PIRA Abstract
PSTA
PTS Marketing & Advertising
Reference Service
PTS PromtRapra Abstracts
Textline
Trade & Industry ASAP
World Textiles

Full Text of Trade Publications

Datamonitor Market Reports
Dow Jones News
Euromonitor Market Direction
Federal News Service
Financial Times Business Report File
Financial Times Fulltext
Globefish
ICC Key Notes Market Research
Investext
McCarthy Press Cuttings Service
PTS Promt
Textline
Trade & Industry ASAP

Statistics

Agrostat (diskette only)
ARI Network/CNS
Arab Information Bank
Comext/Eurostat
Comtrade
FAKT-German Statistics
Globefish
IMF Data
OECD Data
Piers Imports
PTS Forecasts
PTS Time Series
Reuters Monitor
STATUSA.gov
Trade Statistics

Tradstat World Trade Statistics
TRAINS(CD-ROM being
   developed)
US I/E Maritime Bills of Lading
US Imports for Consumption
World Bank Statistics

Price Information

ARI Network/CNS
Chemical Business Newsbase
COLEACP
Commodity Options
Commodities 2000
Market News Service of ITC
Nikkei Shimbun News Database
Reuters Monitor
UPI
US Wholesale Prices

Company Registers

ABC Europe Production Europe
Biocommerce Abstracts & Directory
CD-Export (CD-ROM only)
Company Intelligence
D&B Duns Market Identifiers
   (U.S.A.)
D&B European Marketing File
D&B Eastern Europe
Dun's Electronic Business
   Directory
Firmexport/Firmimport
Hoppenstedt Austria

Hoppenstedt Germany
Hoppenstedt Benelux
Huco-Hungarian Companies
ICC Directory of Companies
Kompass Asia/Pacific
Kompass Europe (EKOD)
Mexican Exporters/Importers
Piers Imports
Polu-Polish Companies
SDOE
Thomas Register
TRAINS (CD-ROM being
   developed)
UK Importers
UK Importers (DECTA)
US Directory of Importers
US I/E Maritime Bills of Lading
World Trade Center Network

Trade Opportunities, Tenders

Business
Federal News Service
Huntech-Hungarian Technique
Scan-a-Bid
Tenders Electronic Daily
World Trade Center Network

Tariffs and Trade Regulations

Celex
ECLAS

Justis Eastern Europe
   (CD-ROM only)
Scad
Spearhead
Spicer's Centre for Europe
TRAINS(CD-ROM being
   developed)
US Code of Federal
   Regulations
US Federal Register
US Harmonized Tariff
   Schedule

Standards

BSI Standardline
Noriane/Perinorm
NTIS Bibliographic Data Base
Standards Infodisk ILI
   (CD-ROM only)

Shipping Information

Piers Imports
Tradstat World Trade Statistics
US I/E-Maritime Bills of Lading

Others

Fairbase
Ibiscus

The Structure of a Country Commercial Guide

Country Commercial Guide for Austria

Table of Contents

H. Prohibited Imports
I. Warranty and Non-Warranty Repairs
J. Export Controls
K. Standards
L. Free Trade Zones/Warehouses
M. Membership in Free Trade Agreements
N. Customs Contact Information

Chapter VII   Investment Climate
    A. Host Country Policies and Practices
        1. Openness to Foreign Investment
        2. Conversion and Transfer Policies
        3. Expropriation and Compensation
        4. Dispute Settlement
        5. Performance Requirements/Incentives
        6. Right to Private Ownership and Establishment
        7. Protection of Property Rights
        8. Transparency of the Regulatory System
        9. Efficient Capital Markets and Portfolio Investment
        10. Political Violence
        11. Corruption
    B. Bilateral Investment Agreements
    C. OPIC and Other Investment Insurance Programs
    D. Labor
    E. Foreign Trade Zones/Free Ports
    F. List of Major Foreign Investors

Chapter VIII   Trade and Project Financing
    A. Synopsis of Banking System
    B. Foreign Exchange Controls Affecting Trading
    C. General Financing Ability
    D. How to Finance Exports/Methods of Payment
    E. Types of Available Export Financing and Insurance
    F. Project Financing Available
    G. List of Banks with Correspondent U.S. Banking Arrangements

Chapter IX   Business Travel
    A. Business Customs
    B. Travel Advisory and Visas
    C. Holidays
    D. Business Infrastructure

Chapter X   Appendices
    Appendix A. Country Data
    Appendix B. Domestic Economy
    Appendix C. Trade
    Appendix D. Foreign Direct Investment
    Appendix E. U.S. & Austrian Contacts
        1. Austrian Government Agencies
        2. Austrian Trade Associations/Chambers of Commerce
        3. Austrian Market Research Firms
        4. Austrian Commercial Banks
        5. The Commercial Service
        6. U.S. Based Multipliers
        7. Washington-Based U.S. Government Contacts
    Appendix F. Market Research

      1. Foreign Agriculture Service
        a. Commodity Reports/Market Briefs
      2. Department of Commerce Industry Subsector Analyses
Appendix G. Trade Event Schedule
      1. Scheduled Agricultural/Food Trade Events
      2. Scheduled Trade Events of the Commercial Service Vienna

Source: U.S. Department of Commerce, The Commercial Service, Washington, DC, 2000.

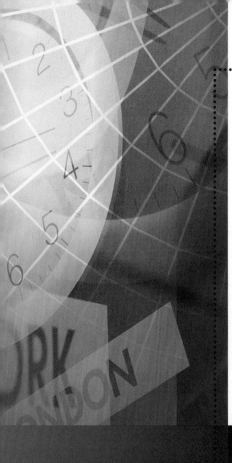

CHAPTER 11

International Business Entry and Development

LEARNING OBJECTIVES

- To learn how firms gradually progress through an internationalization process

- To understand the strategic effects of internationalization on the firm

- To study the various modes of entering the international market

- To understand the role and functions of international intermediaries

- To learn about the opportunities and challenges of cooperative modes of market development

The creation of more than 750 e-commerce exchanges has given small and medium-sized business owners a place at the global trade table. With just a few keystrokes on their personal computers, they can sell their products or source components anywhere in the world.

One of the first systems, Unibex (Universal Business Exchange), was launched in the mid-1990s by a group including AT&T, Dun & Bradstreet, General Electric, Microsoft, and the U.S. Chamber of Commerce. The Unibex software allows companies to stay anonymous as they sign in and submit requests for goods or services using an array of categories, including location, product type, payment, and shipping terms. Customers then receive bids from businesses hoping to land contracts. Once a bid is chosen, identities of the businesses are revealed and negotiations may begin on a more secure electronic mail network. In addition, Unibex users can transmit documents, such as confidentiality agreements, contracts, and purchase orders. Users also have access to Dun & Bradstreet's vast international database of company information and references to check out each other's profiles. After a deal is completed, Unibex enables users to locate freight forwarders, bankers, accountants, or customs brokers.

The system was designed to benefit smaller companies, capitalizing on increasing exports and rapid integration of computers and technology to offer corporation-sized advantages and web presence. For example, it offers consulting services to help companies develop their markets, as well as tools for building web sites, virtual trade booths, online catalogs and auctions.

Unibex has also integrated an aggregate purchasing function into its system, enabling smaller manufacturers to obtain volume discounts. Buyers can save more than 30 percent on steel, metal, raw materials, plastics, and more. "This is a unique combination of products that could only happen online," says Tom Orlowski, vice president of information systems for The National Association of Manufacturers.

Online exchanges may leap over geographic borders, but language remains a barrier. The assumption has been that English is the global business language. Even in Western Europe, however, less than 30 percent of users speak some English. Many vendors offer real-time translation software; Unibex can provide a basic translation of the terms of a deal from English into Spanish, French, or any of ten other languages. Even the best machines, although twice as fast as a human, are only 90 percent accurate. Moreover, machines can't produce the right tone, such as formality for the Japanese and informality for the United States. Many firms therefore use a combination of machines and translators. This enables buyers and sellers who speak different languages to strike satisfactory deals, suggesting a bright future for e-commerce exchanges. ●

Sources: Marcia MacLeod, "Language Barriers," *Supply Management,* July 13, 2000, 37; "Seller Beware," *The Economist,* March 4, 2000; www.unibex.com.

International business holds out the promise of large new market areas, yet firms cannot simply jump into the international marketplace and expect to be successful. They must adjust to needs and opportunities abroad, have quality products, understand their customers, and do their homework. They must also understand the vagaries of international markets. The rapid globalization of markets, however, reduces the time available to adjust to new market realities.

This chapter is concerned with firms preparing to enter international markets and companies expanding their current international activities. Initial emphasis is placed on export activities with a focus on the role of management in starting up international operations and a description of the basic stimuli for international activities. Entry modes for the international arena are highlighted, and the problems and benefits of each mode are discussed. The role of facilitators and intermediaries in international business is described. Finally, alternatives that involve a local presence by the firm are presented.

The Role of Management

Management dynamism and commitment are crucial to a firm's first steps toward international operations. Managers of firms with a strong international performance typically are active, aggressive, and display a high degree of international orientation.[1] Such an orientation is indicated by substantial global awareness and cultural sensitivity.[2] Conversely, the managers of firms that are unsuccessful or inactive internationally usually exhibit a lack of determination or devotion to international business. The issue of **managerial commitment** is a critical one because foreign market penetration requires a vast amount of market development activity, sensitivity toward foreign environments, research, and innovation. Regardless of what the firm produces or where it does business internationally, managerial commitment is crucial for enduring stagnation and sometimes even setbacks and failure.[3] To obtain such a commitment, it is important to involve all levels of management early on in the international planning process and to impress on all players that the effort will only succeed with a commitment that is companywide.[4]

Initiating international business activities takes the firm in an entirely new direction, quite different from adding a product line or hiring a few more people. Going international means that a fundamental strategic change is taking place. The decision to export usually comes from the highest levels of management, typically the owner, president, chairman, or vice president of marketing.[5]

The carrying out of the decision—that is, the implementation of international business transactions—is then the primary responsibility of marketing personnel. It is important to establish an organizational structure in which someone has the specific responsibility for international activities. Without such a responsibility center, the focus necessary for success can easily be lost. Such a center need not be large. For example, just one person assigned part time to international activities can begin exploring and entering international markets.

The first step in developing international commitment is to become aware of international business opportunities. Management must then determine the degree and timing of the firm's internationalization. For instance, a German corporation that expands its operation into Austria, Switzerland, Belgium, and the Netherlands is less international than a German corporation that launches operations in Japan and Brazil. Moreover, if a German-based corporation already has activities in the United States, setting up a business in Canada does not increase its degree of internationalization as much as if Canada was the first "bridgehead" in North America.[6] Management must decide the timing of when to start the internationalization process and how quickly it should progress. For example, market entry might be desirable as soon as possible because clients are waiting for the product or because competitors are expected to enter the market shortly. In addition, it may be desirable to either enter a market abroad selectively or to achieve full market coverage from the outset. Decisions on these timing issues will determine the speed with which management must mobilize and motivate the people involved in the process.[7] It must be kept in mind that a firmwide international orientation does not develop overnight, but rather needs time to grow. Internationalization is a matter of learning, of acquiring experiential knowledge. A firm must learn about foreign markets and institutions, but also about its own internal resources in order to know what it is capable of when exposed to new and unfamiliar conditions.[8] Planning and execution of an export venture must be incorporated into the firm's strategic management process. A firm that sets no strategic goals for its export venture is less likely to make the venture a long-term success.[9] As markets around the world become more linked and more competitive, the importance of developing and following a strategy becomes increasingly key to making things better.[10]

Management is often much too preoccupied with short-term, immediate problems to engage in sophisticated long-run planning. As a result, many firms are simply not interested in international business. Yet certain situations may lead a manager to discover and understand the value of going international and to decide to pursue international business activities. One trigger factor can be international travel, during which new business opportunities are discovered. Alternatively, the receipt of information can lead management to believe that international business opportunities exist. **Unsolicited orders** from abroad are an example. Research in Scotland has shown that two-thirds of small exporting firms started to do so because of unsolicited approaches from buyers or third parties. Management's entrepreneurial spirit manifested itself by following through on the lead.[11] Nonetheless, while such management by serendipity may be useful in a start-up phase, it is no substitute for effective planning when it comes to setting the long-term strategic corporate direction.

Managers who have lived abroad and have learned foreign languages or are particularly interested in foreign cultures are more likely to investigate whether international business opportunities would be appropriate for their firms. Countries or regions with high levels of immigration may, over time, benefit from greater export success due to more ties, better information, and greater international business sensitivity by their new residents.

New management or new employees can also introduce an international orientation. For example, managers entering a firm may already have had some international business experience and may use this experience to further the business activities of their new employer.

Motivations to Go Abroad

Normally, management will consider international activities only when stimulated to do so. A variety of motivations can push and pull individuals and firms along the international path. An overview of the major motivations that have been found to make firms go international is provided in Table 11.1. Proactive motivations represent stimuli for firm-initiated strategic change. Reactive motivations describe stimuli that result in a firm's response and adaptation to changes imposed by the outside environment. In other words, firms with proactive motivations go international because they want to; those with reactive motivations have to go international.

	Proactive	Reactive
TABLE 11.1	Profit advantage	Competitive pressures
Major Motivations to Firms	Unique products	Overproduction
	Technological advantage	Declining domestic sales
	Exclusive information	Excess capacity
	Tax benefit	Saturated domestic markets
	Economies of scale	Proximity to customers and ports

Proactive Motivations

Profits are the major proactive motivation for international business. Management may perceive international sales as a potential source of higher profit margins or of more added-on profits. Of course, the profitability expected when planning to go international is often quite different from the profitability actually obtained. Particularly in international start-up operations, initial profitability may be quite low due to the cost of getting ready for going international, and the losses resulting from early mistakes.[12] The gap between expectation and reality may be especially large when the firm has not previously engaged in international business. Even with thorough planning, unexpected influences can change the profit picture substantially. Shifts in exchange rates, for example, may drastically affect profit forecasts.

Unique products or a technological advantage can be another major stimulus. A firm may produce goods or services that are not widely available from international competitors. Again, real and perceived advantages must be differentiated. Many firms believe that they offer unique products or services, even though this may not be the case internationally. If products or technologies are unique, however, they certainly can provide a competitive edge. What needs to be considered is how long such an advantage will last. The length of time is a function of the product, its technology, and the creativity of competitors. In the past, a firm with a competitive edge could often count on being the sole supplier to foreign markets for years to come. This type of advantage has shrunk dramatically because of competing technologies and the frequent lack of international patent protection.

Special knowledge about foreign customers or market situations may be another proactive stimulus. Such knowledge may result from particular insights by a firm, special contacts an individual may have, in-depth research, or simply from being in the right place at the right time (for example, recognizing a good business situation during a vacation trip). Although such exclusivity can serve well as an initial stimulus for international business, it will rarely provide prolonged motivation because competitors can be expected to catch up with the information advantage. Only if firms build up international information advantage as an ongoing process, through, for example, broad market scanning or special analytical capabilities, can prolonged corporate strategy be based on this motivation.

Tax benefits can also play a major motivating role. Many governments use preferential tax treatment to encourage exports. As a result of such tax benefits, firms either can offer their product at a lower cost in foreign markets or can accumulate a higher profit.

A final major proactive motivation involves economies of scale. International activities may enable the firm to increase its output and therefore rise more rapidly on the learning curve. The Boston Consulting Group has shown that the doubling of output can reduce production costs up to 30 percent. Increased production for international markets can therefore help to reduce the cost of production for domestic sales and make the firm more competitive domestically as well.[13]

Nike's international success is a result of the company's efforts to connect the brand to consumers emotionally, culturally, and with local relevance. In June 2000, Nike joined "Global Compact," a UN project which supports human rights and environmental standards in business. Nike's involvement lends credence to the project, since its annual sales in Asia are more than $995 million.

Reactive Motivations

Reactive motivations influence firms to respond to environmental changes and pressures rather than blaze new trails. Competitive pressures are one example. A company may worry about losing domestic market share to competing firms that have benefited from the economies of scale gained through international business activities. Further, it may fear losing foreign markets permanently to competitors that have decided to focus on these markets. Since market share usually is most easily retained by firms that initially obtain it, some companies may enter the international market head over heels. Quick entry, however, may result in equally quick withdrawal once the firm recognizes that its preparation has been inadequate.

Similarly, overproduction may represent a reactive motivation. During downturns in the domestic business cycle, foreign markets can provide an ideal outlet for excess inventories. International business expansion motivated by overproduction usually does not represent full commitment by management, but rather than attempts to blaze trails. As soon as domestic demand returns to previous levels, international business activities are curtailed or even terminated. Firms that have used such a strategy once may encounter difficulties when trying to employ it again because many international customers are not interested in temporary or sporadic business relationships.

Declining domestic sales, whether measured in sales volume or market share, have a similar motivating effect. Goods marketed domestically may be at the declining stage of their product life cycle. Instead of attempting to push back the life cycle process domestically, or in addition to such an effort, firms may opt to prolong the product life cycle by expanding the market. Such efforts often meet with success, particularly with high-technology products which are outmoded by the latest innovation. Such "just-dated" technology may enable vast progress in manufacturing or services industries and, most importantly, may make such progress affordable. For example, a hospital without any imaging equipment may be much better off acquiring a "just-dated" MRI machine, rather than waiting for enough funding to purchase the latest state of the art equipment.

Excess capacity can also be a powerful motivator. If equipment for production is not fully utilized, firms may see expansion abroad as an ideal way to achieve broader distribution of fixed costs. Alternatively, if all fixed costs are assigned to domestic production, the firm can penetrate foreign markets with a pricing scheme that focuses mainly on variable cost. Yet such a view is feasible only for market entry. A market-penetration strategy based on variable cost alone is unrealistic because, in the long run, fixed costs have to be recovered to replace production equipment.

The reactive motivation of a saturated domestic market has similar results to that of declining domestic sales. Again, firms in this situation can use the international market to prolong the life of their good and even of their organization.

A final major reactive motivation is that of proximity to customers and ports. Physical and psychological closeness to the international market can often play a major role in the international business activities of the firm. For example, a firm established near a border may not even perceive itself as going abroad if it does business in the neighboring country. Except for some firms close to the Canadian or Mexican border, however, this factor is much less prevalent in the United States than in many other nations. Most European firms automatically go abroad simply because their neighbors are so close.

In general, firms that are most successful in international business are usually motivated by proactive—that is, firm internal—factors. Proactive firms are also frequently more service oriented than reactive firms. Further, proactive firms tend to be more marketing and strategy oriented than reactive firms, which have as their major concern operational issues. The clearest differentiation between the two types of firms can probably be made after the fact by determining how they initially entered international markets. Proactive firms are more likely to have solicited their first international order, whereas reactive firms frequently begin international activities after receiving an unsolicited order from abroad.

Strategic Effects of Going International

Going international presents the firm with new environments, entirely new ways of doing business, and a host of new problems. The problems have a wide range. They can consist of strategic considerations, such as service delivery and compliance with government regulations. In addition, the firm has to focus on start-up issues, such as how to find and effectively communicate with customers and operational matters, such as information flows and the mechanics of carrying out an international business transaction. This involves a variety of new documents, including commercial invoices, bills of lading, consular invoices, inspection certificates, and shipper's export declarations. The paperwork is necessary to comply with various domestic, international, or foreign regulations. The regulations may be designed to control international business activities, to streamline the individual transaction, or, as in the case of the shipper's export declaration, to compile trade statistics.

The firm needs to determine its preparedness for internationalization by assessing its internal strengths and weaknesses. This preparedness has to be evaluated in the context of the globalization of the industry within which the firm operates, since this context will affect the competitive position and strategic options available to the firm.[14] Unusual things can happen to both risk and profit. Management's perception of risk exposure grows in light of the gradual development of expertise, the many concerns about engaging in a new activity, and uncertainty about the new environment it is about to enter. Domestically, the firm has gradually learned about the market and therefore managed to decrease its risk. In the course of international expansion, the firm now encounters new and unfamiliar factors, exposing it to increased risk. At the same time, because of the investment needs required by a serious international effort, immediate profit performance may slip. In the longer term, increasing familiarity with international markets and the diversification benefits of serving multiple markets will decrease the firm's risk below the previous "domestic only" level and increase profitability as well. In the short term, however, managers may face an unusual, and perhaps unacceptable, situation: rising risk accompanied by decreasing profitability. In light of this reality, which is depicted in Figure 11.1, many executives are tempted to either not initiate international activities or to discontinue them.[15]

FIGURE 11.1

Profit and Risk During Early Internationalization

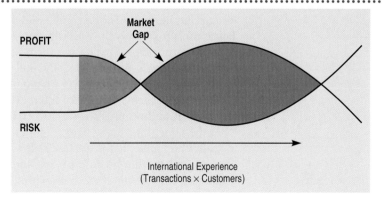

Source: Michael R. Czinkota, "A National Export Development Policy for New and Growing Businesses," *Journal of International Marketing* 2, 1 (1994): 95.

Understanding the changes in risk and profitability can help management overcome the seemingly prohibitive cost of going international, since the negative developments may only be short term. Yet, success does require the firm to be a risk taker, and firms must realize that satisfactory international performance will take time.[16] Satisfactory performance can be achieved in three ways: effectiveness, efficiency, and competitive strength. Effectiveness is characterized by the acquisition of market share abroad and by increased sales. Efficiency is manifested later by rising profitability. Competitive strength refers to the firm's position compared to other firms in the industry, and, due to the benefits of international experience, is likely to grow. The international executive must appreciate the time and performance dimensions associated with going abroad in order to overcome short-term setbacks for the sake of long-term success.

Entry and Development Strategies

Here we will present the most typical international entry and expansion strategies. These are exporting and importing, licensing, and franchising. Other key ways to expand is through a local presence either via interfirm cooperation or foreign direct investment. These can take on many forms such as contractual agreements, equity participation and joint ventures, or direct investment conducted by the firms alone.

Exporting and Importing

Firms can be involved in exporting and importing in an indirect or direct way. **Indirect involvement** means that the firm participates in international business through an intermediary and does not deal with foreign customers or firms. **Direct involvement** means that the firm works with foreign customers or markets with the opportunity to develop a relationship. The end result of exporting and importing is similar whether the activities are direct or indirect. In both cases, goods and services either go abroad or come to the domestic market from abroad, and goods may have to be adapted to suit the targeted market. However, the different approaches have varying degrees of impact on the knowledge and experience levels of firms. The less direct the involvement of the firm, the less likely is the internal development of a storehouse of information and expertise on how to do business abroad, information that the firm can draw on later for further international expansion. Therefore, while indirect activities represent a form of international market entry, they may not result in growing management commitment to international markets or increased capabilities in serving them.

Many firms are indirect exporters and importers, often without their knowledge. As an example, merchandise can be sold to a domestic firm that in turn sells it abroad. This is most frequently the case when smaller suppliers deliver products to large multinational corporations, which use them as input to their foreign sales. Foreign buyers may also purchase products locally and then send them immediately to their home country. While indirect exports may be the result of unwitting participation, some firms also choose this method of international entry as a strategic alternative that conserves effort and resources while still taking advantage of foreign opportunities.

At the same time, many firms that perceive themselves as buying domestically may in reality buy imported products. They may have long-standing relations with a domestic supplier who, because of cost and competitive pressures, has begun to source products from abroad rather than to produce them domestically. In this case, the buyer firm has become an indirect importer.

Firms that opt to export or import directly have more opportunities ahead of them. They learn more quickly the competitive advantages of their products and can therefore expand more rapidly. They also have the ability to control their international activities better and can forge relationships with their trading partners, which can lead to further international growth and success.

However, the firms also are faced with obstacles. These hurdles include indentifying and targeting foreign suppliers and/or customers and finding retail space, all of which are processes that can be very costly and time-consuming. Some firms are overcoming such barriers through the use of mail-order catalogs or electronic commerce ("storeless" distribution networks). In Japan, for example, "high-cost rents, crowded shelves, and an intricate distribution system have made launching new products via conventional methods an increasingly difficult and expensive proposition. Direct marketing via e-commerce eliminates the need for high-priced shop space."[17]

As a firm and its managers gather experience with exporting, they move through different levels of commitment, ranging from awareness, over-interest, trial, evaluation, and finally, adaptation of an international outlook as part of corporate strategy. Of course, not all firms will progress with equal speed through all these levels. Some will do so very rapidly, perhaps encouraged by success with an electronic commerce approach and move on to other forms of international involvement such as foreign direct investment. Others may withdraw from exporting, due to disappointing experiences or as part of a strategic resource allocation decision.[18]

International Intermediaries

Both direct and indirect importers and exporters frequently make use of intermediaries who can assist with troublesome yet important details such as documentation, financing, and transportation. The intermediaries also can identify foreign suppliers and customers and help the firm with long- or short-term market penetration efforts. Major types of international intermediaries are export management companies and trading companies. Together with export facilitators, the intermediaries can bring the global market to the domestic firm's doorstep and help overcome financial and time constraints. Table 11.2 shows those areas in which intermediaries have been found to be particularly helpful.

It is the responsibility of the firm's management to decide how to use the intermediaries. Options range from using their help for initial market entry to developing a long-term strategic collaboration. It is the degree of corporate involvement in and control of the international effort that determines whether the firm operates as an indirect or direct internationalist.

Export Management Companies

Firms that specialize in performing international business services as commission representatives or as distributors are known as **export management companies (EMCs)**. Most EMCs are quite small. Many were formed by one or two principals with experience in international business or in a particular geographic area. Their expertise enables them to offer specialized services to domestic corporations.

TABLE 11.2

How a Trade Intermediary Can Offer Assistance

1. Knows foreign market competitive conditions
2. Has personal contacts with potential foreign buyers
3. Evaluates credit risk associated with foreign buyers
4. Has sales staff to call on current foreign customers in person
5. Assumes responsibility for physical delivery of product to foreign buyer

Source: Richard M. Castaldi, Alex F. De Noble, and Jeffrey Kantor, "The Intermediary Service Requirements of Canadian and American Exporters," *International Marketing Review* 9, 2 (1992): 21–40.

EMCs have two primary forms of operation: they take title to goods and operate internationally on their own account, or they perform services as agents. They often serve a variety of clients, thus their mode of operation may vary from client to client and from transaction to transaction. An EMC may act as an agent for one client and as a distributor for another. It may even act as both for the same client on different occasions.

When working as an **agent,** the EMC is primarily responsible for developing foreign business and sales strategies and establishing contacts abroad. Because the EMC does not share in the profits from a sale, it depends heavily on a high sales volume, on which it charges commission. The EMC may therefore be tempted to take on as many products and as many clients as possible to obtain a high sales volume. As a result, the EMC may spread itself too thin and may be unable to adequately represent all the clients and products it carries. The risk is particularly great with small EMCs.

EMCs that have specific expertise in selecting markets because of language capabilities, previous exposure, or specialized contacts appear to be the ones most successful and useful in aiding client firms in their international business efforts. For example, they can cooperate with firms that are already successful in international business but have been unable to penetrate a specific region. By sticking to their area of expertise and representing only a limited number of clients, such agents can provide quite valuable services.

When operating as a **distributor,** the EMC purchases products from the domestic firm, takes title, and assumes the trading risk. Selling in its own name, it has the opportunity to reap greater profits than when acting as an agent. The potential for greater profit is appropriate, because the EMC has drastically reduced the risk for the domestic firm while increasing its own risk. The burden of the merchandise acquired provides a major motivation to complete an international sale successfully. The domestic firm selling to the EMC is in the comfortable position of having sold its merchandise and received its money without having to deal with the complexities of the international market. On the other hand, it is less likely to gather much international business expertise.

Compensation of EMCs

The mechanism of an EMC may be very useful to the domestic firm if such activities produce additional sales abroad. However, certain services must be performed that demand resources for which someone must pay. As an example, a firm must incur market development expenses to enter foreign markets. At the very least, product availability must be communicated, goods must be shown abroad, visits must be arranged, or contacts must be established. Even though it may often not be discussed, the funding for these activities must be found.

One possibility is a fee charged to the manufacturer by the EMC for market development, sometimes in the form of a retainer and often on an annual basis. The retainers vary and are dependent on the number of products represented and the difficulty of foreign market penetration. Frequently, manufacturers are also expected to pay all or part of the direct expenses associated with foreign market penetration. These expenses may involve the production and translation of promotional product brochures, the cost of attending trade shows, the provision of product samples, or trade advertising.

Alternatively, the EMC may demand a price break for international sales. In one way or another, the firm that uses an EMC must pay the EMC for the international business effort. Otherwise, despite promises, the EMC may simply add the firm and product in name only to its product offering and do nothing to achieve international success.

Power Conflicts Between EMCs and Clients

The EMC faces the continuous problem of retaining a client once foreign market penetration is achieved. Many firms use an EMC's services mainly to test the international arena, with the clear desire to become a direct participant once successful operations have been established.

Of course, this is particularly true if foreign demand turns out to be strong and profit levels are high. The conflict between the EMC and its clients, with one side wanting to retain market power by not sharing too much international business information, and the other side wanting to obtain that power, often results in short-term relationships and a lack of cooperation. Since international business development is based on long-term efforts, this conflict frequently leads to a lack of success.

For the concept of an export management company to work, both parties must fully recognize the delegation of responsibilities, the costs associated with those activities, and the need for information sharing, cooperation, and mutual reliance. Use of an EMC should be viewed just like a domestic channel commitment, requiring a thorough investigation of the intermediary and the advisability of relying on its efforts, a willingness to cooperate on a relationship rather than on a transaction basis, and a willingness to properly reward its efforts. The EMC in turn must adopt a flexible approach to managing the export relationship. As access to the Internet is making customers increasingly sophisticated and world-wise, export management companies must ensure that they continue to deliver true value added. They must acquire, develop, and deploy resources such as new knowledge about foreign markets or about export processes in order to lower their client firm's export-related transaction costs and therefore remain a useful intermediary.[19] By doing so, the EMC lets the client know that the cost is worth the service and thereby reduces the desire for circumvention.

Trading Companies

Another major intermediary is the trading company. The concept was originated by the European trading houses such as the Fuggers of Augsburg. Later on, monarchs chartered traders to form corporate bodies that enjoyed exclusive trading rights and protection by the naval forces in exchange for tax payments. Examples of such early trading companies are the Oost-Indische Compagnie of the Netherlands, formed in 1602, followed shortly by the British East India Company and La Compagnie des Indes chartered by France.[20] Today, the most famous trading companies are the **sogoshosha** of Japan. Names such as Mitsubishi, Mitsui, and C. Itoh have become household words around the world. The nine trading company giants of Japan act as intermediaries for about one-third of the country's exports and two-fifths of its imports.[21] The general trading companies play a unique role in world commerce by importing, exporting, countertrading, investing, and manufacturing. Their vast size allows them to benefit from economies of scale and perform their operations at high rates of return, even though their profit margins are less than 2 percent.

Four major reasons have been given for the success of the Japanese sogoshosha. First, by concentrating on obtaining and disseminating information about market opportunities and by investing huge funds in the development of information systems, the firms have the mechanisms and organizations in place to gather, evaluate, and translate market information into business opportunities. Second, economies of scale permit the firms to take advantage of their vast transaction volume to obtain preferential treatment by, for example, negotiating transportation rates or even opening up new transportation routes and distribution systems. Third, the firms serve large internal markets, not only in Japan but also around the world, and can benefit from opportunities for countertrade. Finally, sogoshosha have access to vast quantities of capital, both within Japan and in the international capital markets. They can therefore carry out transactions that are too large or risky to be palatable or feasible for other firms.[22] In spite of changing trading patterns, these giants continue to succeed by shifting their strategy to expand their domestic activities in Japan, entering more newly developing markets, increasing their trading activities among third countries, and forming joint ventures with non-Japanese firms. Global Perspective 11.1 explains some of the new business activities of the sogoshosha.

GLOBAL PERSPECTIVE 11.1

Japanese Trading Companies Develop New Ventures

When Japan rebuilt itself in the wake of World War II, its immense trading companies provided big business with badly needed trade conduits. As Japan's economy restructures once again, trading companies serve as providers of badly needed capital to international business ventures.

Japanese trading companies have wasted no time in launching their own venture capital units. The trading companies' new role has benefited small businesses. Take start-ups like CareNetInc., a cable broadcasting company that will feature programs and televised conferences for Japan's medical community. When Japanese banks dismissed the idea as too risky, CareNet's founders turned to Hitoshi Suga, president of the venture capital arm of trading giant Mitsui & Co. A few weeks later, Mr. Suga invested 30 million yen ($237,500) in the enterprise.

Since Japanese banks have been weighed down in debt, trading companies have evolved as one of the few credible sources of financing for local start-ups. "The times are changing," says Mitsuo Kurobe, a managing director of Salomon Brothers Japan. "I've been involved in many start-ups in need of financing, and the trading companies are easily spending tens of millions of dollars on them."

Throughout Japan's history, trading companies have led the economy through new and unexplored waters. At the turn of the century, trading companies were the foundation upon which many of Japan's big businesses were based when the country modernized. They established the overseas distribution channels that served as conduits for the country's export machine after World War II. They also ushered in many of the speculative investments that fueled Japan's economy in the 1980's.

However, technological changes combined with the economic slowdown of the early '90s began to eliminate many of the costly middleman functions upon which the Japanese trading companies had thrived. The sales of Japan's major trading companies have been stagnant for much of this decade because manufacturers are beginning to replace traditional distribution channels with their own sales networks.

"Taking a product and distributing it is no longer adequate," says Hiro Satake, president of Itochu Techno-Science Corp. "The information revolution has made many products accessible without middlemen, so we've been forced to find niches." Japanese trading companies appear to have found such a niche in venture capital.

Source: Alexandra Harney, "Sobering Up the Morning After," *Financial Times,* September 13, 2000; Steve Glain, "Japan's Trading Giants Spark Venture Capital," *The Wall Street Journal,* May 15, 1997, A18.

Expansion of Trading Companies   For many decades, the emergence of trading companies was commonly believed to be a Japan-specific phenomenon. Japanese cultural factors were cited as the reason that such intermediaries could operate successfully only from that country. In the last few decades, however, many other governments have established trading companies. In countries so diverse as Korea, Brazil, and Turkey, trading companies are now handling large portions of national exports.[23] The reason these firms have become so large is due, in good measure, to special and preferential government incentives, rather than market forces alone. Therefore, they may be vulnerable to changes in government policies.

In the United States, trading companies in which firms could cooperate internationally were initially permitted through the Webb-Pomerene associations established in 1918. While in the 1930s these collaborative ventures accounted for about 12 percent of U.S. exports, their share had dropped to less than 1 percent by the 1990s. Another governmental approach to export trade facilitation resulted in the implementation in 1982 of **export trading company** (**ETC**) legislation designed to improve the export performance of small and medium-sized firms. To improve export performance, bank participation in trading companies was permitted, and the antitrust threat to joint export efforts was reduced through precertification of planned activities by the U.S. Department of Commerce. Businesses were encouraged to join together to export or offer export services.

Permitting banks to participate in ETCs was intended to allow ETCs better access to capital and therefore permit more trading transactions and easier receipt of title to goods. The relaxation of antitrust provisions in turn was meant to enable firms to form joint ventures more easily. The cost of developing and penetrating international markets would then be shared, with the proportional share being, for many small and medium-sized firms, much easier to bear. As an example, in case a warehouse is needed in order to secure foreign market penetration, one firm alone does not have to bear all the costs. A consortium of firms can jointly rent a foreign warehouse. Similarly, each firm need not station a service technician abroad at substantial cost. Joint funding of a service center by several firms makes the cost less prohibitive for each one. The trading company concept also offers a one-stop shopping center for both the firm and its foreign customers. The firm can be assured that all international functions will be performed efficiently by the trading company, and at the same time, the foreign customer will have to deal with few individual firms.

Although ETCs seem to offer major benefits to many U.S. firms that want to go abroad, they have not been very extensively used. By 2001 only 181 individual ETC certificates had been issued by the U.S. Department of Commerce. Since some of the certificates covered all the members of trade associations, more than 5,000 companies were part of an ETC.[24]

Private Sector Facilitators

Facilitators are entities outside the firm that assist in the process of going international by supplying knowledge and information but not participating in the transaction. Such facilitators can come both from the private and the public sector.

Major encouragement and assistance can result from the statements and actions of other firms in the same industry. Information that would be considered proprietary if it involved domestic operations is often freely shared by competing firms when it concerns international business. The information not only has source credibility but is viewed with a certain amount of fear, because a too-successful competitor may eventually infringe on the firm's domestic business.

A second influential group of private sector facilitators is distributors. Often a firm's distributors are engaged, through some of their business activities, in international business. To increase their international distribution volume, they encourage purely domestic firms to participate in the international market. This is true not only for exports but also for imports. For example, a major customer of a manufacturing firm may find that materials available from abroad, if used in the domestic production process, would make the product available at lower cost. In such instances, the customer may approach the supplier and strongly encourage foreign sourcing.

Banks and other service firms, such as accounting and consulting firms, can serve as major facilitators by alerting their clients to international opportunities. While these service providers historically follow their major multinational clients abroad, increasingly they are establishing a foreign presence on their own. Frequently, they work with domestic clients on expanding market reach in the hope that their service will be used for any international transaction that results. Given the extensive information network of many service providers—banks, for example, often have a wide variety of correspondence relationships—the role of these facilitators can be major. Like a mother hen, they can take firms under their wings and be pathfinders in foreign markets.

Chambers of commerce and other business associations that interact with firms can frequently heighten their interest in international business. Yet, in most instances, such organizations function mainly as secondary intermediaries, because true change is brought about by the presence and encouragement of other managers.

Public Sector Facilitators

Government efforts can also facilitate the international efforts of firms. In the United States, for example, the Department of Commerce provides major export assistance, as do other federal organizations such as the Small Business Administration and the

Export-Import Bank. Most countries maintain similar export support organizations. Table 11.3 provides the names of selected export promotion agencies from around the globe, together with their web addresses. Employees of these organizations typically visit firms and attempt to analyze their international business opportunities. Through rapid access to government resources, these individuals can provide data, research reports, counseling, and financing information to firms. Government organizations can also sponsor meetings that bring interested parties together and alert them to new business opportunities abroad. Key governmental facilitation also occurs when firms are abroad. By receiving information and assistance from their embassies, many business ventures abroad can be made easier.

Increasingly, organizations at the state and local level also are active in encouraging firms to participate in international business. Many states and provinces have formed agencies for economic development that provide information, display products abroad, conduct trade missions, and sometimes even offer financing. Similar services can also be offered by state and local port authorities and by some of the larger cities. State and local authorities can be a major factor in facilitating international activities because of their closeness to firms.

Educational institutions such as universities and community colleges can also be major international business facilitators. They can act as trade information clearing houses, facilitate networking opportunities, provide client counseling and technical assistance, and develop trade education programs.[25] They can also develop course projects that are useful to firms interested in international business. For example, students may visit a firm and examine its potential in the international market as a course requirement. With the skill and supervision of faculty members to help the students de-

TABLE 11.3

Selected Export Promotion Agencies Around the Globe

Australia: Australian Trade Commission
http://www.austrade.gov.au
Canada: Export Development Corporation
http://www.edc.ca/
France: Centre Français du Commerce Extérieur
http://www.cfce.fr/
Germany: Federal Office of Foreign Trade Information (BfAI)
http://www.bfai.com
India: India Trade Promotion Organisation (ITPO)
http://economictimes.com/etonline/itpo
Japan: Japan External Trade Organization (JETRO)
http://www.jetro.go.jp
Malta: Malta External Trade Corporation Ltd.
http://metco.com.mt
Singapore: Trade Development Board
http://www.gov.sg/mti/tdbl.html
South Korea: Trade-Investment Promotion Agency (KOTRA)
http://www.kotra.or.kr/
United Kingdom: Overseas Trade Services
http://www.dti.gov.uk/ots/
United Nations/World Trade Organization: International Trade Centre
http://www.intracen.org
United States: Export-Import Bank
http://www.exim.gov
International Trade Administration
http://www.ita.doc.gov
Foreign Agricultural Service
http://www.fas.usda.gov

velop the final report, such projects can be useful to firms with scarce resources, while they expose students to real-world problems.

Licensing and Franchising

Licensing and franchising are two forms of international market entry and expansion beyond exporting. They are strategies that can be used by themselves or in conjunction with export activities.

Under a **licensing agreement,** one firm permits another to use its intellectual property for compensation designated as **royalty.** The recipient firm is the licensee. The property licensed might include patents, trademarks, copyrights, technology, technical know-how, or specific business skills. For example, a firm that has developed a bag-in-the-box packaging process for milk can permit other firms abroad to use the same process. Licensing therefore can also be called the export of intangibles.

Assessment of Licensing

Licensing has intuitive appeal to many would-be international managers. As an entry strategy, it requires neither capital investment nor detailed involvement with foreign customers. By generating royalty income, licensing provides an opportunity to exploit research and development already conducted. After initial costs, the licensor can reap benefits until the end of the license contract period. Licensing also reduces the risk of expropriation because the licensee is a local company that can provide leverage against government action.

Licensing may help to avoid host-country regulations applicable to equity ventures. Licensing also may provide a means by which foreign markets can be tested without major involvement of capital or management time. Similarly, licensing can be used as a strategy to preempt a market before the entry of competition, especially if the licensor's resources permit full-scale involvement only in selected markets.

A special form of licensing is **trademark licensing,** which has become a substantial source of worldwide revenue for companies that can trade on well-known names and characters. Trademark licensing permits the names or logos of designers, literary characters, sports teams, or movie stars to appear on clothing, games, foods and beverages, gift and novelties, toys, and home furnishings. Licensors can make millions of dollars with little effort, while licensees can produce a brand or product that consumers will recognize immediately. Trademark licensing is possible, however, only if the trademark name conveys instant recognition.

Licensing is not without disadvantages, as illustrated in Global Perspective 11.2. It is a very limited form of foreign market participation and does not in any way guarantee a basis for future expansion. As a matter of fact, quite the opposite may take place. In exchange for the royalty, the licensor may create its own competitor not only in the market for which the agreement was made but for third-country markets as well.

Licensing has also come under criticism from many governments and supranational organizations. They have alleged that licensing provides a mechanism for corporations in industrialized countries to capitalize on older technology. These accusations have been made even though licensing offers a foreign entity the opportunity for immediate market entry with a proven concept. It therefore eliminates the risk of R&D failure, the cost of designing around the licensor's patents, or the fear of patent-infringement litigation.

Franchising is the granting of the right by a parent company (the franchisor) to another, independent entity (the franchisee) to do business in a prescribed manner. The right can take the form of selling the franchisor's products, using its name, production, and marketing techniques, or using its general business approach.[26] Usually

Franchising is one way to expand into international markets. An example is this Dunkin' Donuts franchise in Thailand.

GLOBAL PERSPECTIVE 11.2

International Licensing Requires Adaptation

Many branded items, even those that are quintessential to U.S. pop culture, have traveled well to Europe and beyond. Some brands' identities successfully transcend culture—Peanuts, The Simpsons, and Pink Panther products are as available and almost as popular in London and Paris as they are in Philadelphia and Phoenix.

At first glance, it appears that rights owners of entertainment properties, sports teams, or consumer brands can quickly and easily profit through international licensing. It sounds simple: the owner lets a retailer or manufacturer take its product identity to new markets around the world and reaps a royalty. Upon closer inspection, corporations have discovered that capturing the global consumer is a fine art requiring appreciation of and adaptation to the distinctive culture, aesthetics, and religions of the targeted territory.

While economic policies forged by members of the European Union have joined nations together in a single entity for trading purposes, there are still substantial cultural differences from country to country. Usually, core U.S. licensed categories, such as apparel, toys, and publishing, translate well across Europe, and certain products have even more appeal outside the United States. For example, licensed food and confectionery, typically not big U.S. sellers, are popular in Europe. Twenty-two European food licensing partners were signed for the Sony movie Godzilla compared with only eight U.S. partners.

How can firms ensure that their brands will be successful in other countries? Their licensing campaigns must be preceded by marketing plans that take cultural nuances in styling, packaging, and point of sale into account. Attention to detail makes or breaks a brand outside its national borders of origin. French consumers, for example, prefer smaller logos on apparel than their U.S. counterparts do. In Spain, using the colors of the Spanish flag (red and yellow) in packaging will be perceived as an affront to Spanish patriotism. Purple will not boost a brand's image in Greece, where it is considered the color of mourning.

Sometimes a state's religious beliefs present obstacles, which can be insurmountable to a licensee. "Goosebumps" is a spooky TV show for children that could not be aired in many Muslim states because it featured images of skeletons and ghosts. Similarly, the lovable pig hero in the movie *Babe* could not appear in Turkish books, movies, or television productions because the pig is considered an unclean animal by Muslims.

Rights owners who are willing to meet the challenge of adapting a brand identity to satisfy consumers in different cultures, however, can find significant opportunities in worldwide licensing.

Sources: Kirk Bloomgarden, "Branching Out," *Marketing Business,* April 2000, p. 12; Central Intelligence Agency, *The World Factbook,* 2000.

franchising involves a combination of many of those elements. The major forms of franchising are manufacturer-retailer systems (such as car dealerships), manufacturer-wholesaler systems (such as soft drink companies), and service-firm retailer systems (such as lodging services and fast-food outlets).

Typically, to be successful in international franchising, the firm must be able to offer unique products or unique selling propositions. If such uniqueness can be offered, growth can be rapid and sustained. With its uniqueness, a franchise must offer a high degree of standardization. In most cases, standardization does not require 100 percent uniformity, but rather, international recognizability. Concurrent with this recognizability, the franchisor can and should adapt to local circumstances. Food franchisors, for example, will vary the products and product lines offered depending on local market conditions and tastes.

The reasons for international expansion of franchise systems are market potential, financial gain, and saturated domestic markets. Global market demand is also very high for franchises. From a franchisee's perspective, the franchise is beneficial because it reduces risk by implementing a proven concept. There are also major benefits from a governmental perspective. The source country does not see a replacement of exports or an export of jobs. The recipient country sees franchising as requiring little outflow of foreign exchange, since the bulk of the profits generated remains within the country.[27]

Even though franchising has been growing rapidly, problems are often encountered in international markets. A major problem is foreign government intervention. In the

Philippines, for example, government restrictions on franchising and royalties hindered ComputerLand's Manila store from offering a broader range of services, leading to a separation between the company and its franchisee. Selection and training of franchisees represents another problem area. Many franchise systems have run into difficulty by expanding too quickly and granting franchises to unqualified entities. Although the local franchisee knows the market best, the franchisor still needs to understand the market for product adaptation and operational purposes. The franchisor, in order to remain viable in the long term, needs to coordinate the efforts of individual franchisees—for example, to share ideas and engage in joint undertakings, such as cooperative advertising.

Local Presence

Interfirm Cooperation

The world is too large and the competition too strong for even the largest companies to do everything independently. Technologies are converging and markets are becoming integrated, thus making the costs and risks of both goods and market development ever greater. Partly as a reaction to and partly to exploit the developments, management in multinational corporations has become more pragmatic about what it takes to be successful in global markets. The result has been the formation of **strategic alliances** with suppliers, customers, competitors, and companies in other industries to achieve multiple goals.

A strategic alliance (or partnership) is an informal or formal arrangement between two or more companies with a common business objective. It is something more than the traditional customer-vendor relationship but something less than an outright acquisition. The alliances can take forms ranging from informal cooperation to joint ownership of worldwide operations. For example, Texas Instruments has reported agreements with companies such as IBM, Hyundai, Fujitsu, Alcatel, and L. M. Ericsson using such terms as "joint development agreement," "cooperative technical effort," "joint program for development," "alternative sourcing agreement," and "design/exchange agreement for cooperative product development and exchange of technical data."[28]

Reasons for Interfirm Cooperation   Strategic alliances are being used for many different purposes by the partners involved. Market development is one common focus. Penetrating foreign markets is a primary objective of many companies. In Japan, Motorola is sharing chip designs and manufacturing facilities with Toshiba to gain greater access to the Japanese market. Some alliances are aimed at defending home markets. With no orders coming in for nuclear power plants, Bechtel Group has teamed up with Germany's Siemens to service existing U.S. plants. Another focus is the spreading of the cost and risk inherent in production and development efforts. America Movil has joined forces with SBC Communications and Bell Canada International to share the burden of investments in buying wireless licenses, developing technology, and building networks. America Movil has key holdings in eight Latin American countries' wireless operations with ownership shares ranging from 7 to 81 percent.[29] The costs of developing new jet engines are so vast that they force aerospace companies into collaboration. One such consortium was formed by United Technologies' Pratt & Whitney division, Britain's Rolls-Royce, Motoren-und-Turbinen Union from Germany, Fiat of Italy, and Japanese Aero Engines (made up of Ishikawajima Heavy Industries and Kawasaki Heavy Industries).[30] Some alliances are formed to block and co-opt competitors.[31] For example, Caterpillar formed a heavy equipment joint venture with Mitsubishi in Japan to strike back at its main global rival, Komatsu, in its home market.

In the case of new technologies, companies have joined forces to win over markets to their operating standard. Toshiba and AOL/Time-Warner jointly developed the DVD (double-sided, digital videodisc) to compete against another format developed by Sony and Philips in an effort to establish the world standard for interactive compact disks.[32]

The most successful alliances are those that match the complementary strengths of partners to satisfy a joint objective. Often the partners have different product, geographic, or functional strengths that the partners build on, rather than use to fill gaps.[33] Some of the major alliances created on this basis are provided in Figure 11.2.

Types of Interfirm Cooperation

Each form of alliance is distinct in terms of the amount of commitment required and the degree of control each partner has. The equity alliances—minority ownership, joint ventures, and consortia—feature the most extensive commitment and shared control. The types of strategic alliances are summarized in Figure 11.3, using the extent of equity involved and the number of partners in the endeavor as defining characteristics. More detailed discussion of the various alliances follows.

Informal Cooperation

In informal cooperative deals, partners work together without a binding agreement. This arrangement often takes the form of visits to exchange information about new products, processes, and technologies or may take the more formal form of the exchange of personnel for limited amounts of time. Often such partners are of no real threat in each other's markets and are of modest size in comparison to the competition, making collaboration necessary.[34] The relationships are based on mutual trust and friendship, and may lead to more formal arrangements, such as contractual agreements or joint projects.

Contractual Agreements

Strategic alliance partners may join forces for joint R&D, joint marketing, or joint production. Similarly, their joint efforts might include **licensing,** cross-licensing, or **cross-marketing activities.** Nestlé and General Mills

---

FIGURE 11.2   **Complementary Strengths Create Value**

Partner *Strength...*	+ Partner *Strength...*	= Joint Objective
Pepsico *marketing clout for canned beverages*	**Lipton** *recognized tea brand and customer franchise*	*To sell canned iced tea beverages jointly*
Philips *consumer electronics innovation and leadership*	**Levi Strauss** *fashion design and distribution*	*Outdoor wear with integrated electronic equipment for fashion-conscious consumers*
Ford *automotive design and distribution*	**Qualcomm** *digital wireless communication*	*Phone, Internet, safety, navigation, and entertainment services for vehicles*
KFC *established brand and store format, and operations skills*	**Mitsubishi** *real estate and site-selection skills in Japan*	*To establish a KFC chain in Japan*
Siemens *presence in range of telecommunications markets worldwide and cable-manufacturing technology*	**Corning** *technological strength in optical fibers and glass*	*To create a fiber-optic-cable business*
Ericsson *technological strength in public telecommunications networks*	**Hewlett-Packard** *computers, software, and access to electronics-channels*	*To create and market network management systems*

Source: "Portable Technology Takes the Next Step: Electronics You Can Wear," *The Wall Street Journal,* August 22, 2000, B1, B4; "Qualcomm, Ford to Start Telematic Unit," *The Wall Street Journal,* July 31, 2000, A3, A14; Joel Bleeke and David Ernst, "Is Your Strategic Alliance Really a Sale?" *Harvard Business Review* 73 (January–February 1995): 97–105. See also 97–105; and Melanie Wells, "Coca-Cola Proclaims Nestea Time for CAA," *Advertising Age,* January 30, 1995, 2. See also http://www.pepsico.com; http://www.lipton.com; http://www.kfc.com; http://www.siecor.com; http://www.ericsson.com; and http://www.hp.com.

FIGURE 11.3

Forms of Interfirm Cooperation

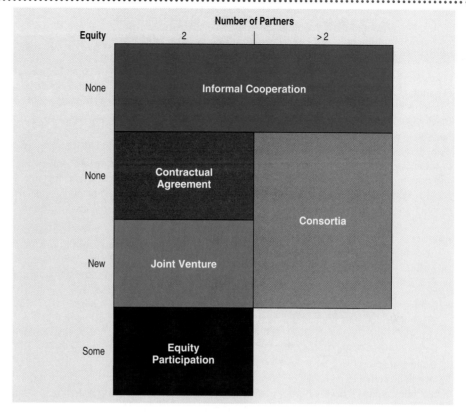

Source: Adapted with permission from Bernard L. Simonin, *Transfer of Knowledge of International Strategic Alliances: A Structural Approach,* unpublished dissertation, the University of Michigan, Ann Arbor, 1991.

signed an agreement whereby Honey Nut Cheerios and Golden Grahams were made in General Mills's U.S. plants, shipped in bulk to Europe for packaging at a Nestlé plant, and then marketed in France, Spain, and Portugal by Nestlé.[35] This arrangement—complementary marketing (also known as piggybacking)—allows firms to reach objectives that they cannot reach efficiently by themselves.[36] The alliance between General Mills and Nestlé evolved into a joint venture, Cereal Partners Worldwide, which markets both companies' products in Europe and Asia. Firms also can have a reciprocal arrangement whereby each partner provides the other access to its market. The New York Yankees and Manchester United sell each others' licensed products and develop joint sponsorship programs. International airlines have started to share hubs, coordinate schedules, and simplify ticketing. Alliances such as Star (joining airlines such as United and Lufthansa), Oneworld (British Airways and American Airlines), and Sky Team (Delta and Air France) provide worldwide coverage for their customers both in the travel and shipping communities.

Contractual agreements also exist for outsourcing. For example, General Motors buys cars and components from South Korea's Daewoo, and Siemens buys computers from Fujitsu. As corporations look for ways to simultaneously grow and maintain their competitive advantage, outsourcing has become a powerful new tool for achieving those goals. **Contract manufacturing** allows the corporation to separate the physical production of goods from the research and development and marketing stages, especially if the latter are the core competencies of the firm. Such contracting is popular in the footwear and garment industries as seen in Global Perspective 11.3. Benefits of such contracting are to improve company focus on higher value-added activities, to gain access to world-class capabilities, and to reduce operating costs. Contract manufacturing has been criticized because of the pressure it puts on the contractors to cut

GLOBAL PERSPECTIVE 11.3

Outsourcing: Just Do It!?

Nike, the footwear company based in Beaverton, Oregon, is expanding in international markets in both sales and production. While international sales currently account for one-third of Nike's total turnover, most of its footwear is produced by subcontractors outside the United States. Nike's own people focus on the services part of the production process, including design, product development, marketing, and distribution. For example, through its "Futures" inventory control system, Nike knows exactly what it needs to order early enough to plan production accordingly. This avoids excess inventory and assures better prices from its subcontractors.

To achieve both stability and flexibility in its supplier relationships, Nike has three distinct groups of subcontractors in its network:

- Developed partners, the most important group, participate in joint product development and concentrate on the production of the newest designs. Traditionally, they have been located in the People's Republic of China and Republic of China but, given rising labor costs, some of the more labor-intensive activities have been moved out. The developed partners typically have worked exclusively for Nike on a minimum monthly order basis.
- The second group of Nike's suppliers are called developing sources and offer low labor costs and the opportunity for Nike to diversify assembly sites. Currently, they are located in the People's Republic of China, Indonesia, and Thailand. Nearly all are exclusive suppliers to Nike and as such

receive considerable assistance from the company with a view of upgrading their production. They will be the next generation of developed partners for Nike.

- The third group, volume producers, are large-scale factories serving a number of other independent buyers. They generally manufacture a specific product for Nike, but they are not involved in any new product because of fears they could leak proprietary information to competitors. Orders from Nike for suppliers in this group fluctuate, with variations of 50 percent between monthly orders.

Nike's outsourcing activity over time follows a geographic pattern, as does its overall market participation. As a matter of fact, a "Nike index" has been developed by Jardine Fleming to track a country's economic development. Development starts when Nike products' manufacturing starts there (e.g., Indonesia in 1989, Vietnam in 1996). The second stage is reached when labor starts flowing from basic industries, such as footwear, to more advanced ones, such as automobiles and electronics (Hong Kong in 1985, South Korea in 1990). An economy is fully developed when a country is developed as a major market (Japan in 1984, Singapore in 1991, and South Korea in 1994).

Outsourcing has been the focus of concern. After widely publicized incidents of overwork and underpay of Asian workers, Nike has reexamined its practices. For example, it recently raised the wages of its Indonesian workers. But it will take a prolonged effort to reverse the negative publicity of the past years.

Sources: "Nike Raising Overseas Wages," CNN Financial Network, March 23, 1999, **cnnfn.com**; Bill Saporito, "Taking a Look Inside Nike's Factories," *Time*, March 30, 1998, **cgi.pathfinder.com/time/magazine**; Transparency International, **www.transparency.de**; "Pangs of Conscience," *Business Week* (July 29, 1996), 46–47; "Can Nike Just Do It?" *Business Week*, April 18, 1994, 86–90; and United Nations, *World Investment Report 1994: An Executive Summary* (New York: United Nations, 1994), 15. See also **www.nikeworkers.com** and **www.nike.com**.

prices and, thereby, labor costs. However, such work does provide many companies, especially in developing countries, the opportunity to gain the necessary experience in product design and manufacturing technology to allow them to function in world markets. Some have even voiced concerns that the experience eventually may make them competitors of their former developed-country partners.

In some parts of the world and in certain industries, governments insist on complete or majority ownership of firms, which has caused multinational companies to turn to an alternative method of enlarging their overseas business.[37] The alternative is a **management contract,** in which the firm sells its expertise in running a company while avoiding the risk or benefit of ownership. Depending on the extensiveness of the contract, it may even permit some measure of control. As an example, the manufacturing process may have to be relinquished to local firms, yet international distribution may be required for the product. A management contract could serve to maintain a strong hold on the operation by ensuring that all distribution channels remain firmly controlled.

Management contracts may be more than a defensive measure. Although they are used to protect existing investment interests when a firm has been partly expropriated by the local government, an increasing number of companies are using them as a profitable opportunity to sell valuable skills and resources. For example, companies in the service sector, such as hospitality management and power generation, often have independent entities with the sole task of seeking out opportunities and operating management contracts.[38]

Often a management contract is the critical element in the success of a project. For example, financial institutions may gain confidence in a project because of the existence of a management contract and may sometimes even make it a precondition for funding.[39]

One specialized form of management contract is the **turnkey operation.** Here, the arrangement permits a client to acquire a complete international system, together with skills sufficient to allow unassisted maintenance and operation of the system following its completion.[40] The client need not search for individual contractors or subcontractors or deal with scheduling conflicts or with difficulties in assigning responsibilities or blame. Instead, a package arrangement permits the accumulation of responsibility in one entity, thus greatly easing the negotiation and supervision requirements and subsequent accountability. When the project is running, the system will be totally owned, controlled, and operated by the customer. Companies such as AES are part of consortia building electric power facilities around the world, operating them, and, in some cases, even owning parts of them.

Management contracts have clear benefits for the client. They provide organizational skills not available locally, expertise that is immediately available rather than built up, and management assistance in the form of support services that would be difficult and costly to replicate locally. For example, hotels managed by the Sheraton Corporation have access to Sheraton's worldwide reservation system. Management contracts today typically involve training locals to take over the operation after a given period.

Similar advantages exist for the supplier. The risk of participating in an international venture is substantially lowered, while significant amounts of control are still exercised. Existing know-how that has been built up through substantial investment can be commercialized, and frequently the impact of fluctuations in business volume can be reduced by making use of experienced personnel who otherwise would have to be laid off. In industrialized countries such as the United States, with economies that are increasingly service based, accumulated service knowledge and comparative advantage should be used internationally. Management contracts permit firms to do so.

Equity Participation   Many multinational corporations have acquired minority ownerships in companies that have strategic importance for them to ensure supplier ability and build formal and informal working relationships. An example of this is Ford Motor Company's 33.4 percent share of Mazda. The partners continue operating as distinctly separate entities, but each enjoys the strengths the other partner provides. For example, thanks to Mazda, Ford has excellent support in the design and manufacture of subcompact cars, while Mazda has improved access to the global marketplace. The recipient of the investment will benefit as well. DaimlerChrysler's acquisition of a 34 percent stake in Mitsubishi is to help make Mitsubishi profitable but also to enhance its competitiveness through sharing of designs, engineering, and parts.[41] Equity ownership in an innovator may give the investing company first access to any new technology developed. Geoworks is a leading company developing operating systems specifically for smart phones. Through its 7 percent ownership, Nokia is given priority when new systems become available.[42]

Another significant reason for equity ownership is market entry and support of global operations. Telefonica de Espana has acquired varying stakes in Latin American telecommunications systems—a market that is the fastest growing region of the world after Asia.[43]

Joint Ventures A joint venture can be defined as the participation of two or more companies in an enterprise in which each party contributes assets, has some equity, and shares risk.[44] The venture is also considered long term. The reasons for establishing a joint venture can be divided into three groups: (1) government suasion or legislation; (2) one partner's needs for other partners' skills; and (3) one partner's needs for other partners' attributes or assets.[45] Equality of the partners is not necessary. In some joint ventures, each partners' contributions—typically consisting of funds, technology, plant, or labor—also vary.

The key to a joint venture is the sharing of a common business objective, which makes the arrangement more than a customer-vendor relationship but less than an outright acquisition. The partners' rationales for entering into the arrangement may vary. An example is New United Motor Manufacturing Inc. (NUMMI), the joint venture between Toyota and GM. Toyota needed direct access to the U.S. market, while GM benefited from the technology and management approaches provided by its Japanese partner.

Joint ventures may be the only way in which a firm can profitably participate in a particular market. For example, India restricts equity participation in local operations by foreigners to 40 percent. Other entry modes may limit the scale of operation substantially; for example, exports may be restricted because of tariff barriers. Many Western firms are using joint ventures to gain access to eastern and central European markets.

Joint ventures are valuable when the pooling of resources results in a better outcome for each partner than if each were to conduct its activities individually. This is particularly true when each partner has a specialized advantage in areas that benefit the venture. For example, a firm may have new technology yet lack sufficient capital to carry out foreign direct investment on its own. Through a joint venture, the technology can be used more quickly and market penetration achieved more easily. Similarly, one of the partners may have a distribution system already established or have better access to local suppliers, either of which permits a greater volume of sales in a shorter period of time.

Joint ventures also permit better relationships with local government and other organizations such as labor unions. Government-related reasons are the main rationale for joint ventures to take place in less-developed countries four times more frequently than in developed countries.[46] Particularly if the local partner is the government, or the local partner is politically influential, the new venture may be eligible for tax incentives, grants, and government support. Negotiations for certifications or licenses may be easier because authorities may not perceive themselves as dealing with a foreign firm. Relationships between the local partner and the local financial establishment may enable the joint venture to tap local capital markets. The greater experience (and therefore greater familiarity) with the local culture and environment of the local partner may enable the joint venture to benefit from greater insights into changing market conditions and needs.

A final major commercial reason to participate in joint ventures is the desire to minimize the risk of exposing long-term investment capital, while at the same time maximizing the leverage on the capital that is invested.[47] Economic and political conditions in many countries are increasingly volatile. At the same time, corporations tend to shorten their investment planning time span more and more. This financial rationale therefore takes on more importance.

Seven out of ten joint ventures have been found to fall short of expectations and/or are disbanded.[48] The reasons typically relate to conflicts of interest, problems with disclosure of sensitive information, and disagreement over how profits are to be shared in general, to lack of communication before, during, and after formation of the venture. In some cases, managers have been more interested in the launching of the venture than the actual running of the enterprise. Many of the problems stem from a lack of careful consideration in advance of how to manage the new endeavor. A partnership works on the basis of trust and commitment or not at all. Actually, if either or both partners insist on voting on critical matters, the venture has already failed.

Typical disagreements cover the whole range of business decisions, including strategy, management style, accounting and control, marketing policies and strategies, research and development, and personnel. The joint venture may, for example, identify a particular market as a target only to find that one of the partners already has individual plans for it. U.S. partners have frequently complained that their Japanese counterparts do not send their most competent personnel to the joint venture; instead, because of their lifetime employment practice, they get rid of less competent managers by sending them to the new entities.

Similarly, the issue of profit accumulation and distribution may cause discontent. If one partner supplies the joint venture with a good, the partner will prefer that any profits accumulate at headquarters and accrue 100 percent to one firm rather than at the joint venture, where profits are divided according to equity participation. Such a decision may not be greeted with enthusiasm by the other partner. Further, once profits are accumulated, their distribution may lead to dispute. For example, one partner may insist on a high payout of dividends because of financial needs, whereas the other may prefer the reinvestment of profits into a growing operation.

Consortia   A new drug can cost $500 million to develop and bring to market; a mainframe computer or a telecommunications switch can require $1 billion. Some $7 billion goes into creating a generation of computer chips. To combat the high costs and risks of research and development, research consortia have emerged in the United States, Japan, and Europe. For example, Ericsson, Matsushita, Motorola, Nokia, and Psion have formed Symbian to develop technologies for third-generation wireless communication. Since the passage of the **Joint Research and Development Act** of 1984 (which allows both domestic and foreign firms to participate in joint basic research efforts without the fear of antitrust action), well over 100 consortia have been registered in the United States. The consortia pool their resources for research into technologies ranging from artificial intelligence to those needed to overtake the Japanese lead in semiconductor manufacturing. (The major consortia in those fields are MCC and Sematech.) In the automotive sector, Chrysler, GM, and Ford formed CAR (Consortium for Automotive Research) for basic development work on issues such as safety and powering cars in the future. The European Union has five mega-projects to develop new technologies registered under the names EUREKA, ESPRIT, BRITE, RACE, and COMET. The Japanese consortia have worked on producing the world's highest-capacity memory chip and advanced computer technologies. On the manufacturing side, the formation of Airbus Industries secured European production of commercial jets. The consortium, backed by France's Aerospatiale, German's Messerschmitt Boklow Blohm, British Aerospace, and Spain's Construcciones Aeronauticas, has become a prime global competitor especially in the development of megaliners.[49]

Managerial Considerations   The first requirement of interfirm cooperation is to find the right partner. Partners should have an orientation and goals in common and should bring complementary and relevant benefits to the endeavor. The venture makes little sense if the expertise of both partners is in the same area; for example, if both have production expertise but neither has distribution know-how. Patience should be exercised; a deal should not be rushed into, nor should the partners expect immediate results. Learning should be paramount in the endeavor while at the same time, partners must try not to give away core secrets to each other.[50]

Second, the more formal the arrangement, the greater care that needs to be taken in negotiating the agreement. In joint venture negotiations, for example, extensive visions must be made for contingencies. The points to be explored should include, depending on the partner and the venture: (1) clear definition of the venture and its duration; (2) ownership, control, and management; (3) financial structure and policies; (4) taxation and fiscal obligation; (5) employment and training; (6) production; (7) government assistance; (8) transfer of technology; (9) marketing arrangements; (10) environmental protection; (11) record keeping and inspection; and (12) settlement of disputes.[51] The issues have to be addressed before the formation of the venture; otherwise, they eventually will surface as points of contention. A joint venture agreement, although comparable to a marriage agreement, should contain the elements of a divorce contract. In case the joint venture cannot be maintained to the satisfaction of partners, plans must exist for the dissolution of the agreement and for the allocation of profits and costs. Typically, however, one of the partners buys out the other partner(s) when partners decide to part ways.

A strategic alliance, by definition, also means a joining of two corporate cultures, which can often be quite different. To meet this challenge, partners must have frequent communication and interaction at three levels of the organization: the top management, operational leaders, and workforce levels. Trust and relinquishing control are difficult not only at the top but also at levels where the future of the venture is determined. A dominant partner may determine the corporate culture, but even then the other partners should be consulted. The development of specific alliance managers may be advised to forge the net of relationships both within and between alliance partners and, therefore, to support the formal alliance structure.[52]

Strategic alliances operate in a dynamic business environment and must therefore adjust to changing market conditions. The agreement between partners should provide for changes in the original concept so that the venture can flourish and grow. The trick is to have a prior understanding as to which party will take care of which pains and problems so that a common goal is reached.

Government attitudes and policies have to be part of the environmental considerations of corporate decision makers. While some alliances may be seen as a threat to the long-term economic security of a nation, such as the cancelled equity investment by Taiwan Aerospace in McDonnel-Douglas's commercial airframe operation, in some cases links with foreign operators may be encouraged. For example, the U.S. government urged major U.S. airlines to form alliances with foreign carriers to gain access to emerging world markets, partly in response to the failure to achieve free access to all markets for U.S. airlines through so-called "open-skies" agreements.[53]

Full Ownership

For some firms, the foreign direct investment decision is, initially at least, considered in the context of 100 percent ownership. The reason may have an ethnocentric basis; that is, management may believe that no outside entity should have an impact on corporate decision making. Alternatively, it may be based on financial concerns. For example, the management of IBM held the belief in the early 1990s that by relinquishing a portion of its ownership abroad, it would be setting a precedent for shared control with local partners that would cost more than that which could possibly be gained.[54] In some cases, IBM withdrew operations from countries rather than agree to government demands for local ownership.

In order to make a rational decision about the extent of ownership, management must evaluate the extent to which total control is important to the success of its international marketing activities. Often full ownership may be a desirable, but not a necessary, prerequisite for international success. At other times it may be essential, particularly when strong links exist within the corporation. Interdependencies between and among local operations and headquarters may be so strong that nothing short of total coordination will result in an acceptable benefit to the firm as a whole.[55]

Increasingly, however, the international environment is hostile to full ownership by multinational firms. Government action through outright legal restrictions or discriminatory actions is making the option less attractive. The choice is either to abide by existing restraints and accept a reduction in control or to lose the opportunity to operate in the country. In addition to formal action by the government, the general conditions in the market may make it advisable for the firm to join forces with local entities, with them being in charge of government relations.

A Comprehensive View of International Expansion

The central driver of internationalization is the level of managerial commitment. This commitment will grow gradually from an awareness of international potential to the adaptation of international business as a strategic business direction. It will be influenced by the information, experience, and perception of management, which in turn is shaped by motivations, concerns, and the activities of change agents.

Management's commitment and its view of the capabilities of the firm will then trigger various international business activities, which can range from indirect exporting and importing to more direct involvement in the global market. Eventually, the firm may then expand further through measures such as joint ventures, strategic alliances, or foreign direct investment. The latter activities are discussed in the next chapter.

All of the developments, processes, and factors involved in the overall process of going international are linked to each other. A comprehensive view of these links is presented schematically in Figure 11.4.

FIGURE 11.4   A Comprehensive Model of International Market Entry and Development

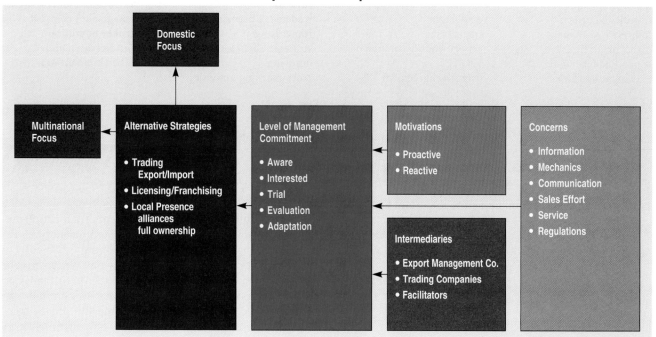

Summary

Firms do not become experienced in international business overnight, but rather progress gradually through an internationalization process. The process is triggered by different motivations to go abroad. The motivations can be proactive or reactive. Proactive motivations are initiated by aggressive management, whereas reactive motivations are the defensive response of management to environmental changes and pressures. Firms that are primarily stimulated by proactive motivations are more likely to enter international business and succeed.

In going abroad, firms encounter multiple problems and challenges, which range from a lack of information to mechanics and documentation. In order to gain assistance in its initial international experience, the firm can make use of either intermediaries or facilitators. Intermediaries are outside companies that actively participate in an international transaction. They are export management companies or trading companies. In order for these intermediaries to perform international business functions properly, however, they must be compensated. This will result in a reduction of profits.

International facilitators do not participate in international business transactions, but they contribute knowledge and information. Increasingly, facilitating roles are played by private sector groups, such as industry associations, banks, accountants, or consultants, and by universities and federal, state, and local government authorities.

Apart from exporting and importing, alternatives for international business entry are licensing, franchising, and local presence. The basic advantage of licensing is that it does not involve capital investment or knowledge of foreign markets. Its major disadvantage is that licensing agreements typically have time limits, are often proscribed by foreign governments, and may result in creating a competitor. The use of franchising as a means of expansion into foreign markets has increased dramatically. Franchisors must learn to strike a balance between, on the one hand, adapting to local environments and, on the other, standardizing to the degree necessary to maintain international recognizability.

Full ownership is becoming more unlikely in many markets as well as industries, and the firm has to look at alternative approaches. The main alternative is interfirm cooperation, in which the firm joins forces with other business entities, possibly even a foreign government. In some cases, when the firm may not want to make a direct investment, it will offer its management expertise for sale in the form of management contracts.

Key Terms and Concepts

managerial commitment	agent	royalty	contract manufacturing
unsolicited order	distributor	trademark licensing	management contract
indirect involvement	sogoshosha	franchising	turnkey operation
direct involvement	export trading company	strategic alliances	Joint Research and
export management	(ETC)	licensing	Development Act
companies (EMCs)	licensing agreement	cross-marking activities	

Questions for Discussion

1. Why is management commitment so important to export success?
2. Explain the benefits that international sales can have for domestic business activities.
3. Comment on the stance that "licensing is really not a form of international involvement because it requires no substantial additional effort on the part of the licensor."
4. What is the purpose of export intermediaries?
5. How can an export intermediary avoid circumvention by a client or customer?
6. The rate of expropriation has been ten times greater for a joint venture with the host government than for a 100 percent U.S.-owned subsidiary, according to a study on expropriation since 1960. Is this not contrary to logic?
7. Comment on the observation that "a joint venture may be a combination of Leonardo da Vinci's brain and Carl Lewis's legs; one wants to fly, the other insists on running."
8. Why would an internationalizing company opt for a management contract over other modes of operation? Relate your answer especially to the case of hospitality companies such as Hyatt, Marriott, and Sheraton.

Internet Exercises

1. What forms of export assistance are offered by the Small Business Administration and the Export-Import Bank (consult their web sites at **www.sba.gov** and **www.exim.gov.**)?
2. Prepare a one-page memo to a foreign company introducing your product or service. Include a contact listing of ten businesses in foreign countries looking to import your particular product. Include the company name, address, and other contact information along with special requirements of the company you note from their posting of an offer to buy. Cite the sources from which you prepared your list.

Sample sources of trade leads:
http://www.tradematch.com/uk/portail/index.asp
http://www.tradecompass.com/iebb
http://www.itrade.com
http://tradenet.org/
http://www.expogudie.com/shows/shows.htm
http://www.mnileads.com

3. Working conditions in subcontract factories have come under criticism for wages and working conditions. Using Nike's response (see **http://www.nikebiz.comlabor/indexes.html**), assess the type of criticisms heard and the ability of a company to address them.

Recommended Readings

Craighead's International Business, Travel and Relocation Guide to 81 Countries 2000–01, Detroit: Gale, 2001.

Davis, Warnock. *Partner Risk: Managing the Downside of Strategic Alliances.* West Lafayette, IN: Purdue University Press, 2000.

Hufbauer, Gary C., and Rita M. Rodriguez. *The Ex-Im Bank in the 21st Century: A New Approach?* Washington, DC: Institute for International Economics, 2001.

Lendrum, Tony. *The Strategic Partnering Handbook: The Practitioners' Guide to Partnerships and Alliances.* New York: McGraw-Hill, 2001.

Lewis, Howard, and J. David Richardson. *Why Global Integration Matters Most.* Washington, DC: Institute for International Economics, 2001.

McCue, Sarah. *Trade Secrets: The Export Answer Book.* Detroit: Small Business Development Center, Wayne State University, 1998.

Nelson, Carl A. *Import/Export: How to Get Started in International Trade.* New York: McGraw-Hill, 2000.

Noonan, Chris. *Cim Handbook of Export Marketing.* Boston: Butterworth-Heineman, 2000.

Pan, Yigang, and David Tse. "The Hierarchical Model of Market Entry Modes," *Journal of International Business Studies.* 31, 4, 2000, 535–554.

Rigsbee, Edwin R. *Developing Strategic Alliances.* New York: Crisp Publications, 2000.

Woznick, Alexandra, and Edward G. Hinkelman. *A Basic Guide to Exporting* 3d ed. Novato, CA: World Trade Press, 2000.

Yan, Aimin, and Yadong Luo, *International Joint Ventures: Theory and Practices,* Armonk, NY: M.E. Sharpe, 2001.

Notes

1. Hartmut Holzmüller and Barbara Stöttinger, "Structural Modeling of Success Factors in Exporting: Cross-Validation and Further Development of an Export Performance Model," *Journal of International Marketing* 4, 2 (1996): 29–55.
2. Brendan J. Gray, "Profiling Managers to Improve Export Promotion Targeting," *Journal of International Business Studies* 28, 2 (1997): 387–420.
3. Anthony C. Koh and James Chow, "An Empirical Investigation of the Variations in Success Factors in Exporting by Country Characteristics," *Midwest Review of International Business Research,* ed. Tom Sharkey, Vol. VII (Toledo, 1993).
4. S. Tamer Cavusgil, "Preparing for Export Marketing," *International Trade Forum* 2 (1993): 16–30.
5. Michael R. Czinkota, *Export Development Strategies* (New York: Praeger, 1982): 10.
6. Michael Kutschker and Iris Bäuerle, "Three Plus One: Multidimensional Strategy of Internationalization," *Management International Review* 37, 2 (1997): 103–125.
7. Michael Kutschker, Iris Bäuerle, and Stefan Schmid, "International Evolution, International Episodes, and International Epochs—Implications for Managing Internationalization," *Management International Review,* Special Issue 2 (1997): 101–124.
8. Kent Eriksson, Jan Johanson, Anders Majkgard, and D. Deo Sharma, "Experiential Knowledge and Cost in the Internationalization Process," *Journal of International Business Studies* 28, 2 (1997): 337–360.
9. S. Tamer Cavusgil and Shaoming Zou, "Marketing Strategy-Performance Relationship: An Investigation of the Empirical Link in Export Marketing Ventures," *Journal of Marketing* 58, 1 (1994): 1–21.

10. Michael W. Peng, *Business Strategies in Transition Economies* (Thousand Oaks: Sage Publications, 2000): 283–284.

11. Andrew McAuley, "Entrepreneurial Instant Exporters in the Scottish Arts and Crafts Sector," *Journal of International Marketing* 7, 4 (1999): 67–82.

12. Masaaki Kotabe and Michael R. Czinkota, "State Government Promotion of Manufacturing Exports: A Gap Analysis," *Journal of International Business Studies* (winter 1992): 637–658.

13. Michael R. Czinkota and Michael L. Ursic, "An Experience Curve Explanation of Export Expansion," in *International Marketing Strategy* (Fort Worth: Dryden Press, 1994): 133–141.

14. Carl Arthur Solberg, "A Framework for Analysis of Strategy Development in Globalizing Markets," *Journal of International Marketing* 5, 1 (1997): 9–30.

15. Michael R. Czinkota, "A National Export Development Policy for New and Growing Businesses," *Journal of International Marketing* 2, 1 (1994): 91–101.

16. Van Miller, Tom Becker, and Charles Crespy, "Contrasting Export Strategies: A Discriminant Analysis Study of Excellent Exporters," *The International Trade Journal* 7, 3 (1993): 321–340.

17. Michael R. Czinkota and Masaaki Kotabe, "Entering the Japanese Market: A Reassessment of Foreign Firms' Entry and Distribution Strategies," *Industrial Marketing Management*, 29, 2000, 483–491.

18. Pieter Pauwels and Paul Matthyssens, "A Strategy Process Perspective on Export Withdrawal," *Journal of International Marketing* 7, 4 (1999): 10–37.

19. Michael W. Peng and Anne Y. Ilinitch, "Export Intermediary Firms: A Note on Export Development Research," *Journal of International Business Studies* 3, 1998: 609–620.

20. Dong-Sung Cho, *The General Trading Company: Concept and Strategy* (Lexington, MA: Lexington Books, 1987): 2.

21. Lee Smith, "Does the World's Biggest Company Have a Future?" *Fortune* (August 7, 1995): 125.

22. Yoshi Tsurumi, *Sogoshosha: Engines of Export-Based Growth* (Montreal: The Institute for Research on Public Policy, 1980).

23. Atilla Dicle and Ulku Dicle, "Effects of Government Export Policies on Turkish Export Trading Companies," *International Marketing Review* 9, 3 (1992): 62–76.

24. Vanessa Bachman, Office of Export Trading Companies, U.S. Department of Commerce, Washington, DC, February 27, 2001.

25. Nancy Lloyd Pfahl, "Using a Partnership Strategy to Establish an International Trade Assistance Program," *Economic Development Review* (Winter 1994): 51–59.

26. Donald W. Hackett, "The International Expansion of U.S. Franchise Systems," in *Multinational Product Management*, ed. Warren J. Keegan and Charles S. Mayer (Chicago: American Marketing Association, 1979): 61–81.

27. Nizamettin Aydin and Madhav Kacker, "International Outlook of U.S.-Based Franchisers," *International Marketing Review* 7 (1990): 43–53.

28. Thomas Gross and John Neuman, "Strategic Alliances Vital in Global Marketing," *Marketing News* (June 19, 1989): 1–2. See also **www.ti.com**.

29. Telmex Spinoff Begins with NYSE Debut," *The Wall Street Journal*, February 7, 2001, A1, A22.

30. "MD-90 Airliner Unveiled by McDonnell Douglas," *The Washington Post*, February 14, 1993, A4.

31. Jordan D. Lewis, *Partnerships for Profit: Structuring and Managing Strategic Alliances* (New York: The Free Press, 1990), 85–87.

32. "Video Warfare: How Toshiba Took the High Ground," *Business Week* (February 20, 1995): 64–65; and Nikhil Hutheesing, "Betamax Versus VHS All Over Again?" *Forbes* (January 3, 1994): 88–89.

33. Joel Bleeke and David Ernst. "Is Your Strategic Alliance Really a Sale?" *Harvard Business Review* 73 (January–February 1995): 97–105.

34. Gary Hamel, Yves L. Doz, and C. K. Prahalad, "Collaborate with Your Competitors—and Win," *Harvard Business Review* 67 (January–February 1989): 133–139.

35. Richard Gibson, "Cereal Venture Is Planning Honey of a Battle in Europe," *Wall Street Journal*, November 14, 1990, B1, B8.

36. Vern Terpstra and Chwo-Ming J. Yu, "Piggy-backing: A Quick Road to Internationalization," *International Marketing Review* 7, (1990): 52–63.

37. Lawrence S. Welch and Anubis Pacifico, "Management Contracts: A Role in Internationalization?" *International Marketing Review* 7, (1990): 64–74.

38. Richard Ellison, "An Alternative to Direct Investment Abroad," *International Management* 31 (June 1976): 25–27.

39. Michael Z. Brooke, *Selling Management Services Contracts in International Business* (London: Holt, Rinehart and Winston, 1985), 7.

40. Richard W. Wright and Colin S. Russel, "Joint Ventures in Developing Countries: Realities and Responses," *Columbia Journal of World Business* 10 (spring 1975): 74–80.

41. "Riding Together," *Business Week*, February 26, 2001, 48–49.

42. "Nokia ja Amerikkalainen Geoworks Laajentavat Yhteistyotaan," *Helsingin Sanomat*, July 24, 1997, A16. See also **http://www.geoworks.com**.

43. "Spain's Phone Giant has Latin America Buzzing," *Business Week* (September 12, 1994): 92.

44. Kathryn Rudie Harrigan, "Joint Ventures and Global Strategies," *Columbia Journal of World Business* 19 (summer 1984): 7–16.

45. J. Peter Killing, *Strategies for Joint Venture Success* (New York: Praeger, 1983), 11–12.

46. Paul W. Beamish, "The Characteristics of Joint Ventures in Developed and Developing Countries," *Columbia Journal of World Business* 20 (Fall 1985), 13–19.

47. Charles Oman, *New Forms of International Investment in Developing Countries* (Paris: Organization for Economic Co-operation and Development, 1984), 79.

48. Yankelovich, Skelly and White, Inc., *Collaborative Ventures: A Pragmatic Approach to Business Expansion in the Eighties* (New York: Coopers and Lybrand, 1984), 10.

49. "How to Build a Really, Really, Really Big Plane," *Fortune*, March 5, 2001, 144–152; "Giving 'Em Away," *Business Week*, March 5, 2001, 52–53.

50. Jeremy Main, "Making Global Alliances Work," *Fortune* (December 17, 1990): 121–126.

51. United Nations, *Guidelines for Foreign Direct Investment* (New York: United Nations, 1975), 65–76.

52. Robert E. Spekman, Lynn A. Isabella, Thomas C. MacAvoy, and Theodore Forbes III, "Creating Strategic Alliances Which Endure," *Long Range Planning* 29, 3, 1996: 346–357.

53. "Airlines Urged to Link with Foreign Carriers," *The Washington Post,* November 2, 1994, F1, F3.

54. Dennis J. Encarnation and Sushil Vachani, "Foreign Ownership: When Hosts Change the Rules," *Harvard Business Review* 63 (September–October 1985): 152–160.

55. Richard H. Holton, "Making International Joint Ventures Work" (Paper presented at the seminar on the Management of Headquarters/Subsidiary Relationships in Transnational Corporations, Stockholm School of Economics, June 2–4, 1980), 4.

CHAPTER 12

Strategic Planning in International Business

LEARNING OBJECTIVES

- To outline the process of strategic planning in the context of the global marketplace

- To examine both the external and internal factors that determine the conditions for development of strategy and resource allocation

- To illustrate how best to utilize the environmental conditions within the competitive challenges and resources of the firm to develop effective programs

- To suggest how to achieve a balance between local and regional/global priorities and concerns in the implementation of strategy

THE GLOBAL APPLIANCE MAKERS

The $11 billion home appliance market is undergoing major consolidation and globalization. Many U.S.-based manufacturers are faced in their home markets with increased competition from foreign companies, such as the world's largest appliance maker, Electrolux, and newcomers such as China's Haier and Kelon. In addition, industry fundamentals in the United States are rather gloomy: stagnating sales, rising raw material prices, and price wars. On the other hand, markets abroad are full of opportunities. The European market, for example, is growing quite fast, and the breakdown of barriers within the European Union has made establishing business there even more attractive. Market potential is significant as well: While 65 percent of U.S. homes have dryers, only 18 percent of Europeans have them. Markets in Latin America, Asia, and Africa are showing similar trends as well; for example, only 15 percent of Brazil's households own microwave ovens compared with 91 percent in the United States. However, expansion was slowed down considerably by the currency crises of 1997–1999.

To take advantage of this growth, appliance makers have formed strategic alliances and made acquisitions. General Electric entered into a joint venture with Britain's General Electric PLC, and in its strategic shift to move the company's "center of gravity" from the industrialized world to Asia and Latin America, joint ventures were established in India with Godrej and in Mexico with Mabe. A strictly North American manufacturer before 1989, Whirlpool purchased the appliance business of Dutch giant, Philips. Whirlpool's move gave it ten plants on the European continent and some popular appliance lines, which is a major asset in a region characterized by loyalty to domestic brands. Today, Whirlpool is third in European market share after Electrolux and Bosch-Siemens. The company ranks first in the Americas, and in the mid 1990s it expanded into central and eastern Europe, as well as South Africa. Whirlpool's advantage in Brazil, for example, is that its 40 years of operating in Brazil have earned it strong loyalty (which it lacks in Asia). In the past five years, Whirlpool has expanded its operations in Eastern and Central Europe as well as South Africa, thus extending Whirlpool's total reach to 170 countries worldwide.

Product differences present global marketers with a considerable challenge. The British favor front-loading washing machines, while the French swear by top-loaders. The French prefer to cook their food at high temperatures, causing grease to splatter onto oven walls, which calls for self-cleaning ovens. This feature is in less demand in Germany, where lower temperatures are traditionally used. Manufacturers are hoping that European integration will bring about cost savings and product standardization. The danger to be avoided is the development of compromise products and programs that in the end appeal to no one. Care has to be taken also in promotional approaches. Whirlpool uses a worldwide advertising campaign to differentiate itself from competition. The campaign features a drying diva, an ice queen, and air-purifier angel, and a washing machine goddess. The women float on clouds, water, and in space, and introduce the company's products with the line "Just Imagine." The campaign started in Europe and before extending it to the Americas, Whirlpool and its advertising agency Publicis, conducted focus group research with women to test their reaction to the goddesses. Joint ventures also present their share of challenges to the global marketers. For example, in Whirlpool's Shanghai facility teams of American, Italian, and Chinese technicians must work through three translators to set up production.

Although opportunities do exist, competition is keen. Margins have suffered as manufacturers (more than 300 in Europe alone) scrape for business. The major players have decided to compete in all the major markets of the world. "Becoming a global appliance player is clearly the best use of our management expertise and well-established brand line-up," Whirlpool executives have said. Whirlpool's long-term goal is to leverage its global manufacturing and brand assets strategically across the world.

Not everyone has succeeded, however. In its move toward globalization, Maytag acquired Chicago Pacific Corporation, best known for its Hoover appliances. The products have a strong presence in the United Kingdom and Australia but not on the European continent, where Maytag ended up essentially trying to introduce new products to new markets. After six years, Maytag sold its European operations to an Italian manufacturer at a loss of $135 million in 1995. In early 2000, Maytag entered into an alliance with Sanyo Electric Company to develop and market home appliances for the Japanese and Pacific Rim markets. At the same time it has approached other appliance makers to gauge their interest in exploring a possible acquisition of Maytag. Of the possible suitors, Electrolux offers the best fit. Electrolux is under competitive pressure from Whirlpool in Europe and is looking to build a presence in North America. Also of interest are Maytag's commercial business in laundromats, restaurants, and hotels, with its washers and dryers, industrial cooking equipment, and vacuum cleaners.

The most recent entrants into the global home appliance market are China's Haier and Kelon, both mainly in refrigerators and air conditioners—industries in which China's technology is up to world standards. Their biggest challenge is to establish their brand names as household words and to penetrate mass merchandising channels. ●

Sources: "Whirlpool in Europe," Whirlpool Corporation web site, accessed June 16, 1999, **www.whirlpoolcorp.com**; "Maytag Discusses Acquisition with Three Firms," *The Wall Street Journal*, August 25, 2000, B4; "Whirlpool Conjures Up Appliance Divas," *The Wall Street Journal*, April 27, 2000, B14; "Maytag's Share Price Falls on Earnings Warning," *The Wall Street Journal*, February 15, 2000, B8; "Chinese Brands Out of the Shadows," *The Economist*, August 28, 1999, 78–81; "Whirlpool in the Wringer," *Business Week*, December 14, 1998, 83–84; "Did Whirlpool Spin Too Far Too Fast?" *Business Week*, June 24, 1996, 134–136; Regina Fazio Maruca, "The Right Way to Go Global: An Interview with Whirlpool CEO David Whitwam," *The Harvard Business Review* 72 (March–April 1994): 134–145; "Whirlpool Hangs Its Rivals Out to Dry," *USA Today*, December 10, 1993, 3B; "GE's Brave New World," *Business Week*, November 8, 1993, 64–69; and "Can Maytag Clean Up Around the World?" *Business Week*, January 30, 1989, 86–87.

Source: **www.whirlpoolcorp.com.**

Globalization

The transformations in the world marketplace have been extensive and, in many cases, rapid. Local industries operating in protected national economies are challenged by integrated global markets contested by global players. National borders are becoming increasingly irrelevant as liberalization and privatization take place. This has then led to such phenomena as the growing scale and mobility of the world's capital markets and many companies' ability to leverage knowledge and talent across borders.[1] Even the biggest companies in the biggest home markets cannot survive by taking their situation as a given if they are in global industries such as automobiles, banking, consumer electronics, entertainment, pharmaceuticals, publishing, travel services, or home appliances. Rather than seeking to maximize their share of the pie in home markets, they have to seek to maximize the size of the pie by having a presence in all of the major markets of the world.[2] These changes and subsequent corporate action for the appliance industry are highlighted in the opening vignette for the chapter.

Globalization reflects a business orientation based on the belief that the world is becoming more homogeneous and that distinctions between national markets are not only fading but, for some products, will eventually disappear. As a result, companies need to globalize their international strategy by formulating it across markets to take advantage of underlying market, cost, environmental, and competitive factors.

As shown in Figure 12.1, globalization can be seen as a result of a process that culminates a process of international market entry and expansion. Before globalization, companies utilize to a great extent a country-by-country **multidomestic strategy** with each country organization operated as a profit center. Each national entity markets a range of different products and services targeted to different customer segments, utilizing different strategies with little or no coordination of operations between countries.

However, as national markets become increasingly similar and scale economies become increasingly important, the inefficiencies of duplicating product and program development and manufacture in each country become more apparent and the pressure to leverage resources and coordinate activities across borders gains urgency.

FIGURE 12.1

Evolution of Global Strategy

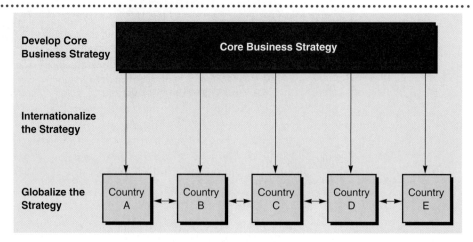

Source: Reprinted from "Global Strategy . . . In a World of Nations?" by George S. Yip, *Sloan Management Review* 31 (Fall 1989): 30, by permission of the publisher. Copyright 1989 by the Sloan Management Review Association. All rights reserved.

Globalization Drivers[3]

Both external and internal factors will create the favorable conditions for development of strategy and resource allocation on a global basis. These factors can be divided into market, cost, environmental, and competitive factors.

Market Factors   The world customer identified by Ernst Dichter more than 30 years ago has gained new meaning today.[4] For example, Kenichi Ohmae has identified a new group of consumers emerging in the triad of North America, Europe, and the Far East whom marketers can treat as a single market with the same spending habits.[5] Approximately 600 million in number, these consumers have similar educational backgrounds, income levels, lifestyles, use of leisure time, and aspirations. One reason given for the similarities in their demand is a level of purchasing power (ten times greater than that of LDCs or NICs) that translates into higher diffusion rates for certain products. Another reason is that developed infrastructures—diffusion of telecommunications and an abundance of paved roads—lead to attractive markets for other products. Products can be designed to meet similar demand conditions throughout the triad. These similarities also enhance the transferability of other program elements.

At the same time, channels of distribution are becoming more global; that is, a growing number of retailers are now showing great flexibility in their strategies for entering new geographic markets.[6] Some are already world powers (e.g., Benetton and McDonald's), whereas others are pursuing aggressive growth (e.g., Toys 'Я' Us and IKEA). Also noteworthy are cross-border retail alliances, which expand the presence of retailers to new markets quite rapidly.

Technology is changing the landscape of markets as well. In the area of personal financial services, for instance, 95 percent of the $300 billion market is currently captured by nationally based competitors. By 2005, this market is likely to double in size and is going to be accessible to global competitors via transplants or electronic distribution.

Cost Factors   Avoiding cost inefficiencies and duplication of effort are two of the most powerful globalization drivers. A single-country approach may not be large enough for the local business to achieve all possible economies of scale and scope as well as synergies, especially given the dramatic changes in the marketplace. Take, for example, pharmaceuticals. In the 1970s, developing a new drug cost about $16 million and took four years. The drug could be produced in Britain or the United States and eventually exported. Now, developing a drug costs from $250 to $500 million and takes as long as 12 years, with competitive efforts close behind. Only a global product for a global market can support that much risk.[7] Size has become a major asset, which partly explains the many mergers and acquisitions in industries such as aerospace, pharmaceuticals, and telecommunications. The paper industry underwent major regional consolidation between 1998 and 2000, as shown in Table 12.1. International Paper Company won Champion International in a tense bidding contest with Finland's UPM-Kymmene to protect its home market position. As a result, UPM immediately targeted Sappi Ltd., a South African magazine-paper maker with significant North American operations and two U.S.-based paper makers, Mead and Bowater.[8] In the heavily contested consumer goods sectors, launching a new brand may cost as much as $100 million, meaning that companies such as Unilever and Procter & Gamble are not necessarily going to spend precious resources on one-country projects.

In many cases, expanded market participation and activity concentration can accelerate the accumulation of learning and experience. General Electric's philosophy is to be first or second in the world in a business or to get out. This can be seen, for example, in its global effort to develop premium computed tomography (CT), a diagnostic scanning system. GE swapped its consumer electronics business with the French

TABLE 12.1	Consolidation in the Paper Industry 1998–2000		
Acquirer	**Target**	**Value**	**Date Announced**
Stora Enso (Finland)	**Consolidated Papers** (United States)	$3.9 billion	2/22/00
Int'l Paper (United States)	**Champion Int'l** (United States)	$7.3 billion	5/12/00
Abitibi-Consol. (Canada)	**Donohue** (Canada)	$4.0 billion	2/11/00
Weyerhaeuser (United States)	**MacMillan Bloedel** (Canada)	$2.3 billion	6/21/99
Int'l Paper (United States)	**Union Camp** (United States)	$5.9 billion	11/24/98
Stora (Sweden)*	**Enso** (Finland)*	Undisclosed	6/2/98

*Merger of equals

Source: "International Paper Has Its Work Cut Out For It," *The Wall Street Journal,*" May 15, 2000, A4; and "Stora Enso to Buy Consolidated Papers," *The Wall Street Journal,* February 23, 2000, A3, A8. See also, **http://www. storaenso.com; www.internationalpaper.com; www.upm-kymmene.com; www.abicon.com;** and **www. weyerhaeuser.com.**

Thomson for Thomson's diagnostic imaging business. At the same time, GE established GE Medical Systems Asia in Tokyo, anchored on Yokogawa Medical Systems, which is 75 percent owned by GE.

Environmental Factors As shown earlier in this text, government barriers have fallen dramatically in the last years to further facilitate the globalization of markets and the activities of companies within them. For example, the forces pushing toward a pan-European market are very powerful: The increasing wealth and mobility of European consumers (favored by the relaxed immigration controls), the accelerating flow of information across borders, the introduction of new products where local preferences are not well established, and the publicity surrounding the integration process itself all promote globalization.[9] Also, the resulting removal of physical, fiscal, and technical barriers is indicative of the changes that are taking place around the world on a greater scale.

At the same time, rapid technological evolution is contributing to the process. For example, Ford Motor Company is able to accomplish its globalization efforts by using new communications methods, such as teleconferencing intranet and CAD/CAM links, as well as travel, to manage the complex task of meshing car companies on different continents.[10] Newly emerging markets will benefit from advanced communications by being able to leapfrog stages of economic development. Places that until recently were incommunicado in China, Vietnam, Hungary, or Brazil are rapidly acquiring state-of-the-art telecommunications that will let them foster both internal and external development.[11]

A new group of global players is taking advantage of today's more open trading regions and newer technologies. **Mininationals,** or newer companies with sales between $200 million and $1 billion, are able to serve the world from a handful of manufacturing bases, compared with having to build a plant in every country as the established multinational corporations once had to do. Their smaller bureaucracies have also allowed these mininationals to move swiftly to seize new markets and develop new products—a key to global success.[12] This phenomenon is highlighted in Global Perspective 12.1.

Competitive Factors Many industries are already dominated by global competitors that are trying to take advantage of the three sets of factors mentioned earlier. To remain competitive, a company may have to be the first to do something or to be able to match or preempt competitors' moves. Products are now introduced, upgraded, and distributed at rates unimaginable a decade ago. Without a global network, carefully researched ideas may be picked off by other global players. This is what

GLOBAL PERSPECTIVE 12.1

Mininationals Create Global Markets

Exports account for 95 percent of Cochlear's $60 million sales after a real annual compounded rate of 25 percent throughout the 1990s. Cochlear is a company specializing in the production of implants for the profoundly deaf. Based in Australia, it maintains a global technological lead through its strong links with hospitals and research units around the world and through its collaborative research with a network of institutions around the world. Cochlear's global market share is 65 percent.

Cochlear is a prime example of small to medium-sized firms that are remaking the global corporation. The term *mininational* has been coined to reflect their smaller size compared with the traditional multinationals. Sheer size is no longer a buffer against competition in markets where customers are demanding specialized and customized products. With the advent of electronic process technology, mininationals are able to compete on price and quality—often with greater flexibility. By taking advantage of today's more open trading regions, they can serve the world from a handful of manufacturing bases, sparing them from the necessity of building a plant in every country. Developments in information technology have enabled mininationals to both access data throughout most of the world and to run inexpensive and responsive sales and service operations across languages and time zones.

The smaller bureaucracies of the mininationals allow them to move swiftly in seizing new markets and developing new products, typically in focused markets. In many cases, these new markets have been developed by the mininationals themselves. For example, Symbol Technologies Inc. of Holtsville, New York, invented the field of handheld laser scanners and now dominates this field. In a field that did not even exist in 1988, Cisco Systems Inc. of San Jose, California, grew from a mininational into a multinational corporation, with over 38,854 employees in more than 225 offices in 75 countries. Through its partnerships, Cisco operates in a total of 115 countries. Cisco provides computer networking systems and rode the wave of the Internet boom. Other mininationals continue to focus on their core products and services, growing and excelling at what they do best.

The lessons from these new generation global players are to: (1) keep focused and concentrate on being number one or number two in a technology niche; (2) stay lean by having small headquarters to save on costs and to accelerate decision making; (3) take ideas and technologies to and from wherever they can be found; (4) take advantage of employees regardless of nationality to globalize thinking; and (5) solve customers' problems by involving them rather than pushing on them standardized solutions. As a result of being flexible, they are able to weather storms, such as the Asian crisis, better by changing emphases in the geographical operations.

Sources: Cochlear Annual Report 2000 at **www.cochlear.com**; "Corporate Profile," *Cisco Systems 2000 Annual Report* at **www.cisco.com**; "Turning Small into an Advantage" *Business Week,* July 13, 1998, 42–44; Michael W. Rennie, "Born Global," *The McKinsey Quarterly* (number 4, 1993): 45–52; "Mininationals Are Making Maximum Impact," *Business Week,* September 6, 1993, 66–69.

Procter & Gamble and Unilever did to Kao's Attack concentrated detergent, which they mimicked and introduced into the United States and Europe before Kao could react.

With the triad markets often both flat in terms of growth and fiercely competitive, many global marketers are looking for new markets and for new product categories for growth. Nestlé, for example, is setting its sights on consumer markets in fast-growing Asia, especially China, and has diversified into pharmaceuticals by acquiring Alcon and by becoming a major shareholder in the world's number one cosmetics company, the French L'Oreal.[13]

Market presence may be necessary to execute global strategies and to prevent others from having undue advantage in unchallenged markets. Caterpillar faced mounting global competition from Komatsu but found out that strengthening its products and operations was not enough to meet the challenge. Although Japan was a small part of the world market, as a secure home base (no serious competitors), it generated 80 percent of Komatsu's cash flow. To put a check on its major global competitor's market share and cash flow, Caterpillar formed a heavy-equipment joint venture with Matsushita to serve the Japanese market.[14] Similarly, when Unilever tried to acquire Richardson-Vicks in the United States, Procter & Gamble saw this as a threat to its home market position and outbid its archrival for the company.

FIGURE 12.2   The Global Landscape

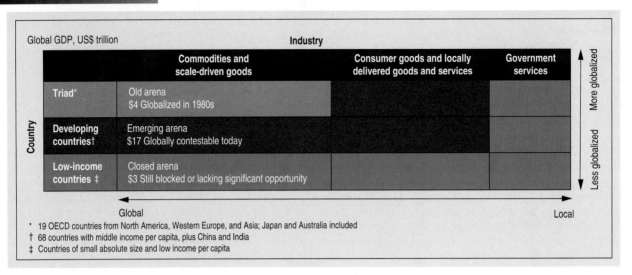

Source: Jane Fraser and Jeremy Oppenheim, "What's New About Globalization?" *The McKinsey Quarterly* 2 (1997), 173.

The Outcome   The four globalization drivers have affected countries and sectors differently. While some industries are truly globally contested, such as paper and pulp and soft drinks, some sectors, such as government services, are still quite closed and will open up as a decades-long evolution. Commodities and manufactured goods are already in globalized state, while many consumer goods are accelerating toward more globalization. Similarly, the leading trading nations of the world display far more openness than low-income countries, thus advancing the state of globalization in general. The expansion of the global trade arena is summarized in Figure 12.2. The size of markets estimated to be global by the turn of the century is well over $21 billion, boosted by new sectors and markets becoming available.

It should also be noted that leading companies by their very actions drive the globalization process. There is no structural reason why soft drinks should be at a more advanced stage of globalization while beer and spirits remain more local except for the opportunistic behavior of Coca-Cola. Similarly, Nike and Reebok have driven their business in a global direction by creating global brands, a global customer segment, and a global supply chain. By creating a single online trading exchange for all of their parts and suppliers, General Motors, Ford, and DaimlerChrysler created a worldwide market of $240 billion in automotive components.[15]

The Strategic Planning Process

Given the opportunities and challenges provided by the new realities of the marketplace, decision makers have to engage in strategic planning to match markets with products and other corporate resources more effectively and efficiently to strengthen the company's long-term competitive advantage. While the process has been summarized as a sequence of steps in Figure 12.3, many of the stages can occur in parallel. Furthermore, feedback as a result of evaluation and control may restart the process at any stage.

FIGURE 12.3

**Global Strategy
Formulation**

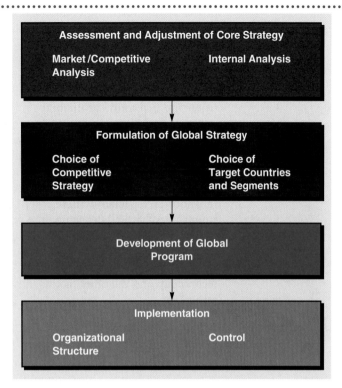

The authors appreciate the contributions of Robert M. Grant in the preparation of this figure.

Understanding and Adjusting the Core Strategy

The planning process has to start with a clear definition of the business for which strategy is to be developed. Generally, the strategic business unit (SBU) is the unit around which decisions are based. In practice, SBUs represent groupings based on product-market similarities based on: (1) needs or wants to be met; (2) end-user customers to be targeted; or (3) the good or service used to meet the needs of specific customers. For a global company such as Black & Decker, the options may be to define the business to be analyzed as the home improvement business, the do-it-yourself business, or the power tool business. Ideally, each of these SBUs should have primary responsibility and authority in managing its basic business functions.

This phase of the planning process requires the participation of executives from different functions, especially marketing, production, finance, logistics, and procurement. Geographic representation should be from the major markets or regions as well as from the smaller, yet emerging, markets. With appropriate members, the committee can focus on product and markets as well as competitors whom they face in different markets, whether they are global, regional, or purely local. Heading this effort should be an executive with highest level experience in regional or global markets. For example, one global firm called on the president of its European operations to come back to headquarters to head the global planning effort. This effort calls for commitment by the company itself both in calling on the best talent to participate in the planning effort and later in implementing their proposals.

Market and Competitive Analysis   Planning on a country-by-country basis can result in spotty worldwide market performance. The starting point for global strategic planning is to understand the underlying forces that determine business success are common to the different countries in which the firm competes. Planning processes that focus simultaneously across a broad range of markets provide global marketers with tools to help balance risks, resource requirements, competitive economies of scale, and profitability to gain stronger long-term positions.[16] On the demand side this requires an understanding of the common features of customer requirements and choice factors. In terms of competition, the key is to understand the structure of the global industry in order to identify the forces that will drive competition and determine profitability.[17]

For Ford Motor Company, strategy begins not with individual national markets, but with understanding trends and sources of profit in the global automobile market. What are the trends in world demand? What are the underlying trends in lifestyles and transportation patterns that will shape customer expectations and preferences with respect to safety, economy, design, and performance? What is the emerging structure of the industry, especially with regard to consolidation among both auto makers and their suppliers? What will determine the intensity of competition among the different auto makers? The level of excess capacity (currently about 40 percent in the worldwide auto industry) is likely to be a key influence.[18] If competition is likely to intensify, which companies will emerge the winners? An understanding of scale economies, state of technology, and the other factors that determine cost efficiency is likely to be critically important.

Internal Analysis   Organizational resources have to be used as a reality check for any strategic choice in that they determine a company's capacity for establishing and sustaining competitive advantage within global markets. Industrial giants with deep pockets may be able to establish a presence in any market they wish, while more thinly capitalized companies may have to move cautiously. Human resources may also present a challenge for market expansion. A survey of multinational corporations revealed that good marketing managers, skilled technicians, and production managers were especially difficult to find. This difficulty is further compounded when the search is for people with cross-cultural experience to run future regional operations.[19]

At this stage it is imperative that the company assess its own readiness for the moves necessary. This means a rigorous assessment of organizational commitment to global or regional expansion, as well as an assessment of the good's readiness to face the competitive environment. In many cases this has meant painful decisions to focus on certain industries and leave others. For example, Nokia, one of the world's largest manufacturer of cellular phones, started its rise in the industry when a decision was made at the company in 1992 to focus on digital cellular phones and to sell off dozens of other product lines. By focusing its efforts on this line, the company was able to bring new products to market quickly, build scale economies into its manufacturing, and concentrate on its customers, thereby communicating a commitment to their needs.[20]

Formulating Global Marketing Strategy

The first step in the formulation of global strategy is the choice of competitive strategy to be employed followed by the choice of country markets to be entered or to be penetrated further.

Choice of Competitive Strategy   In dealing with the global markets, the manager has three general choices of strategies, as shown in Figure 12.4: (1) cost leadership; (2) differentiation, and (3) focus.[21] A focus strategy is defined by its emphasis on a single industry segment within which the orientation may be either toward low cost or differentiation. Any one of these strategies can be pursued on a global or regional basis, or the manager may decide to mix and match strategies as a function of market or product dimensions.

In pursuing **cost leadership,** the company offers an identical product or service at a lower cost than competition. This often means investment in scale economies and

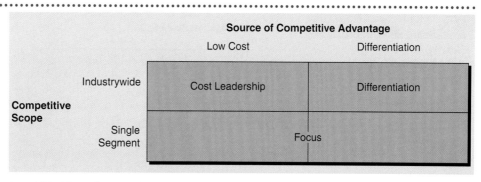

FIGURE 12.4

Competitive Strategies

Source: Michael Porter, Competitive Advantage (New York: The Free Press, 1987), ch. 1.

strict control of costs, such as overheads, research and development, and logistics. **Differentiation,** whether it is industrywide or focused on a single segment, takes advantage of the manager's real or perceived uniqueness on elements such as design or after-sales service. It should be noted, however, that a low-price, low-cost strategy does not imply a commodity situation.[22] Although Japanese, U.S., and European technical standards differ, mobile phone manufacturers like Motorola and Nokia design their phones to be as similar as possible to hold down manufacturing costs. As a result, they can all be made on the same production line, allowing the manufacturers to shift rapidly from one model to another to meet changes in demand and customer requirements. In the case of IKEA, the low-price approach is associated with clear positioning and a unique brand image focused on a clearly defined target audience of "young people of all ages." Similarly, companies that opt for high differentiation cannot forget the monitoring of costs. One common denominator of consumers around the world is their quest for value for their money. With the availability of information increasing and levels of education improving, customers are poised to demand even more of their suppliers.

Most global companies combine high differentiation with cost containment to enter markets and to expand their market shares. Flexible manufacturing systems using mostly standard components and total quality management reducing the occurrence of defects are allowing companies to customize an increasing amount of their production, while at the same time saving on costs. Global activities will in themselves permit the exploitation of scale economies not only in production but also in marketing activities, such as promotion.

Country-Market Choice A global strategy does not imply that a company should serve the entire globe. Critical choices relate to the allocation of a company's resources among different countries and segments. The usual approach is first to start with regions and further split the analysis by country. Many managers use multiple levels of regional groupings to follow the organizational structure of the company, e.g., splitting Europe into northern, central, and southern regions, which display similarities in demographic and behavioral traits. An important consideration is that data may be more readily available if existing structures and frameworks are used.[23]

Various **portfolio models** have been proposed as tools for this analysis. They typically involve two measures—internal strength and external attractiveness.[24] As indicators of internal strength, the following variables have been used: relative market share, product fit, contribution margin, and market presence, which would incorporate the level of support by constituents as well as resources allocated by the company itself. Country attractiveness has been measured using market size, market growth rate, number and type of competitors, governmental regulation, as well as economic and political stability. An example of such a matrix is provided in Figure 12.5.

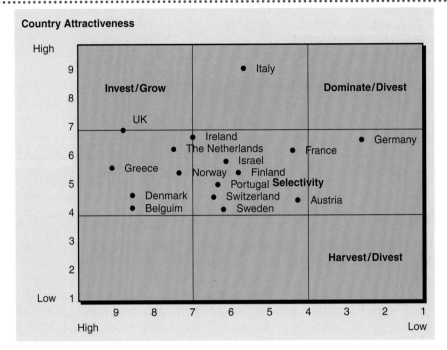

Source: Gilbert D. Harrell and Richard O. Kiefer, "Multinational Market Portfolios in Global Strategy Development," *International Marketing Review* 10 (1993): 60–72.

The 3 × 3 matrix on country attractiveness and company strength is applied to the European markets. Markets in the invest/grow position will require continued commitment by management in research and development, investment in facilities, and the training of personnel at the country level. In cases of relative weakness in growing markets, the company's position may have to be strengthened (through acquisitions or strategic alliances) or a decision to divest may be necessary.[25] For example, Procter & Gamble decided to pull out of the disposable diaper markets in Australia and New Zealand due to well-entrenched competition, international currency fluctuations, and importation of products from distant production facilities into the markets.[26] Furthermore, it is critical that those involved in the planning endeavor consider potential competitors and their impact on the markets should they enter. In Europe, many industrial giants are entering the telecommunications market, most of them without any previous experience in the industry. Some of these newcomers are joining forces with foreign telecommunications entities thereby facilitating their new market development. For example, German steel maker Thyssen teamed up with energy conglomerate Veba and U.S. BellSouth to exploit Germany's need for digital cellular networks.[27]

Portfolios should also be used to assess market, product, and business interlinkages. This effort should utilize increasing market similarities through corporate adjustments by setting up appropriate strategic business units and the coordination of programs. The presentation in Figure 12.6 shows a market-product-business portfolio for a global food company, such as Nestlé. The interconnections are formed by common target markets served, sharing of research and development objectives, use of similar technologies, and the benefits that can be drawn from sharing common marketing experience. The example suggests possibilities within regions and between regions: frozen food both in Europe and the United States, and ice cream throughout the three mega-markets.

Finally, the portfolio assessment also needs to be put into a larger context. The Korean market and the Korean automakers may not independently warrant urgent

FIGURE 12.6

Example of Strategic
Interconnectedness
Matrix

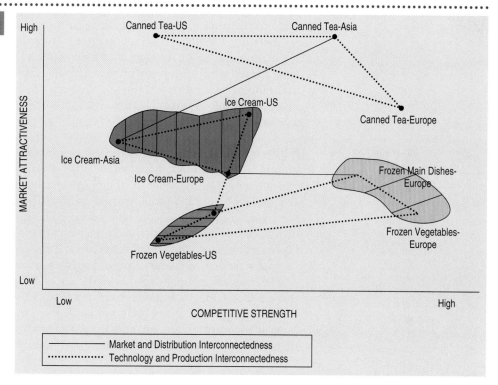

Source: Adapted from Susan P. Douglas and C. Samual Craig, "Global Portfolio Planning and Market Interconnectedness," *Journal of International Marketing* 4, 1 (1996): 93–110.

action on the part of the leading companies. However, as a part of the global strategic setting in the auto industry, both the market and its companies become critically important. Asia is expected to account for 70 percent of the growth in the world auto market between 2000 and 2004. Korea, along with China and Japan, is one of the three most important vehicle markets in Asia and can be considered an ideal platform for exporting to other parts of the continent. While Korean automakers, such as Daewoo Motor Company and Samsung Motors are heavily in debt, acquiring them would bring about the aforementioned benefits. Both Ford and GM want to acquire Daewoo to attain the top-producer position in the world. Renault, which wants to acquire Samsung, sees synergistic benefits in that Samsung relies heavily on technology from Nissan, acquired by Renault earlier. There are also other indirect benefits; whoever acquires Daewoo will gain the number one spot in Poland, long deemed crucial for tapping growth in Eastern Europe.[28] In choosing country markets, a company must make decisions beyond those relating to market attractiveness and company position. A market expansion policy will determine the allocation of resources among various markets. The basic alternatives are concentration on a small number of markets and diversification, which is characterized by growth in a relatively large number of markets.

The conventional wisdom of globalization requires a presence in all of the major triad markets of the world. In some cases, markets may not be attractive in their own right but may have some other significance, such as being the home market of the most demanding customers, thereby aiding in product development, or being the home market of a significant competitor (a preemptive rationale). For example, Procter & Gamble "rolled" its Charmin bath tissue into European markets in 2000 to counter an upsurge in European paper products sales by its global rival Kimberly-Clark.[29] European PC makers, such as Germany's Maxdata and Britain's Tiny both are taking aim at the U.S. market based on the premise that if they can compete with the big multinationals (Dell, Compaq, Hewlett-Packard, and Gateway) at home, there is no reason why they cannot be competitive in North America as well.[30]

Therefore, for global companies, three factors should determine country selection: (1) the stand-alone attractiveness of a market (e.g., China in consumer products due to its size); (2) global strategic importance (e.g., Finland in shipbuilding due to its lead in technological development in vessel design); and (3) possible synergies (e.g., entry into Latvia and Lithuania after success in the Estonian market given market similarities).

Segmentation   Effective use of segmentation, that is, the recognition that groups within markets differ sufficiently to warrant individual approaches, allows global companies to take advantage of the benefits of standardization (such as economies of scale and consistency in positioning) while addressing the unique needs and expectations of a specific target group. This approach means looking at markets on a global or regional basis, thereby ignoring the political boundaries that define markets in many cases. The identification and cultivation of such intermarket segments is necessary for any standardization of programs to work.[31]

The emergence of segments that span across markets is already evident in the world marketplace. Global companies have successfully targeted the teenage segment, which is converging as a result of common tastes in sports and music fueled by their computer literacy, travels abroad, and, in many countries, financial independence.[32] Furthermore, a media revolution is creating a common fabric of attitudes and tastes among teenagers. Today satellite TV and global network concepts such as MTV are both helping create this segment and providing global companies an access to the teen audience around the world. For example, Reebok used a global ad campaign to launch its Instapump line of sneakers in the United States, Germany, Japan, and 137 other countries. Given that teenagers around the world are concerned with social issues, particularly environmentalism, Reebok has introduced a new ecological climbing shoe made from recycled and environmentally sensitive materials. Despite the convergence, global companies still have to make adjustments in some of the program elements for maximum impact. For example, while Levi's jeans are globally accepted by the teenage segment, European teens reacted negatively to the urban realism of Levi's U.S. ads. Levi's converted its ads in Europe, drawing on a mythical America.[33] Similarly, two other distinct segments have been detected to be ready for a panregional approach, especially in Europe.[34] These include trendsetters who are wealthier and better educated and tend to value independence, refuse consumer stereotypes, and appreciate exclusive products. The second one includes Europe's businesspeople who are well-to-do, regularly travel abroad, and have a taste for luxury goods.

The greatest challenge for the global company is the choice of an appropriate base for the segmentation effort. The objective is to arrive at a grouping or groupings that are substantial enough to merit the segmentation effort (for example, there are nearly 230 million teenagers in the Americas, Europe, and the Asia-Pacific with the teenagers of the Americas spending nearly $60 billion of their own money yearly) and are reachable as well by the marketing effort (for example, the majority of MTV's audience consists of teenagers).

The possible bases for segmentation are summarized in Figure 12.7. Managers have traditionally used environmental bases for segmentation. However, using geographic proximity, political system characteristics, economic standing, or cultural traits as stand-alone bases may not provide relevant data for decision making. Using a combination of them, however, may produce more meaningful results. One of the segments pursued by global companies around the world is the middle-class family. Defining the composition of this global middle class is tricky, given the varying levels of development among nations in Latin America and Asia. However, some experts estimate that 23 percent of the world population enjoy middle-class lives.[35] Using household income alone may be quite a poor gauge of class. Income figures ignore vast differ-

FIGURE 12.7

Bases for Global Market Segmentation

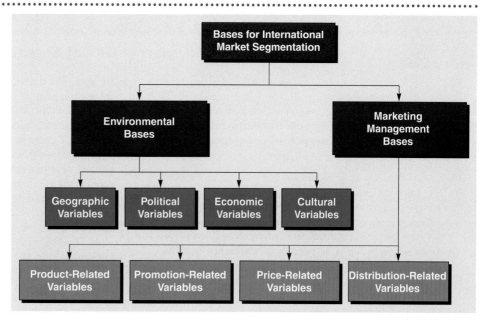

Source: Imad B. Baalbaki and Naresh K. Malhotra, "Marketing Management Bases for International Market Segmentation: An Alternate Look at the Standardization/Customization Debate," *International Marketing Review* 10, 1 (1993): 19–44.

ences in international purchasing power. Chinese consumers, for example, spend less than 5 percent of their total outlays on rent, transportation, and health, while a typical U.S. household spends 45 to 50 percent. Additionally, income distinctions do not reflect education or values—two increasingly important barometers of middle-class status. A global segmentation effort using cultural values is presented in Global Perspective 12.2.

It has also been proposed that markets that reflect a high degree of homogeneity with respect to marketing mix variables could be grouped into segments and thereby targeted with a largely standardized strategy.[36] Whether bases related to product, promotion, pricing, or distribution are used, their influence should be related to environmentally based variables. Product-related bases include the degree to which products are culture-based, which stage of the life cycle they occupy, consumption patterns, attitudes toward product attributes (such as country of origin), as well as consumption infrastructure (for example, telephone lines for modems). The growth of microwave sales, for example, has been surprising in low-income countries; however, microwaves have become status symbols and buying them more of an emotional issue. Many consumers in these markets also want to make sure they get the same product as available in developed markets, thereby eliminating the need in many cases to develop market-specific products. Adjustments will have to be made, however. Noticing that for reasons of status and space, many Asian consumers put their refrigerators in their living rooms, Whirlpool makes refrigerators available in striking colors such as red and blue.

With promotional variables, the consumers' values and norms may necessitate local solutions rather than opting for a regional approach. Similar influences may be exerted by the availability, or lack, of media vehicles or government regulations affecting promotional campaigns. On the pricing side, dimensions such as customers' price sensitivity may lead the manager to go after segments that insist on high quality despite high price in markets where overall purchasing power may be low to ensure global or regional uniformity in the marketing approach. Affordability is a major issue for customers, whose buying power may fall short for at least the time being. Offering only one option may exclude potential customers of the future who are not yet part

GLOBAL PERSPECTIVE 12.2

The International Marketplace—Global Segments Based on Values

The 1997 Roper Reports Worldwide Global Consumer Survey provided interview results of 1,000 people in 35 countries. As part of their responses, they ranked 56 values by the importance they hold as guiding principles in their lives. Among adults, six global values segments were identified.

Strivers—The largest group, Strivers, are slightly more likely to be men than women, and they place more emphasis on material and professional goals than do other groups. One in three people in developing Asia is a Striver, as is about one-fourth of the population in Russia and developed Asia.

Devouts—This group is 22 percent of adults. For devouts, which includes more women than men, tradition and duty are very important. Devouts are most common in Asia and in Middle Eastern and African countries. They are least common in developed Asia and Europe.

Altruists—This group is 18 percent of adults, with a slightly larger portion of females. Altruists are interested in social issues and the welfare of society. With a median age of 44, this group is older. More Altruists live in Latin America and Russia than in other countries.

Intimates—Intimates, with 15 percent of the population, value close personal relationships and family above all else. They are almost as likely to be men as women. One in four Europeans and North Americans qualify, compared with just 7 percent of developing Asia.

Fun Seekers—Although found in disproportionate numbers in developed Asia, this group accounts for 12 percent of the global population. Not surprisingly, Fun Seekers are the youngest group, with a female to male ratio of 54:46.

Creatives—This group is the smallest at 10 percent worldwide. Their hallmark trait is a strong interest in education, knowledge, and technology. Creatives are more common in Latin America and Europe. Along with Intimates, this group has the most balanced gender mix.

A country-by-country analysis revealed that Great Britain leads the world in wanting to protect the family, Brazil had the most Fun Seekers, Saudi Arabia ranked first in faith, the Netherlands had the highest percentage worldwide in esteeming honesty, and Korea was the front runner in valuing health and fitness.

Source: Tom Miller, "Global Segments from 'Strivers' to 'Creatives', "*Marketing News,* July 20, 1998, 11.

---

of a targeted segment. Companies like Procter & Gamble and Gillette offer an array of products at different price points to attract customers and to keep them as they move up the income scale.[37] As distribution systems converge, for example, with the increase of global chains, markets can also be segmented by outlet types that reach environmentally defined groups. For example, toy manufacturers may look at markets not only in terms of numbers of children but by how effectively and efficiently they can be reached by global chains such as Toys 'Я' Us, as opposed to purely local outlets.

Global Program Development

Decisions need to be made regarding how best to utilize the conditions set by globalization drivers within the framework of competitive challenges and the resources of the firm. Decisions will have to be made in four areas: (1) the degree of standardization in the product offering; (2) the marketing program beyond the product variable; (3) location and extent of value-adding activities; and (4) competitive moves to be made.

Product Offering   Globalization is not equal to standardization except in the case of the core product or the technology used to produce the product. The components used in a personal computer may to a large extent be standard, with the localization needed only in terms of the peripherals; for example, IBM produces 20 different keyboards for Europe alone. Product standardization may result in significant cost savings upstream. For example, Stanley Works' compromise between French preferences for handsaws with plastic handles and "soft teeth" and British preferences for wooden handles and "hard teeth"—to produce a plastic-handled saw with "hard teeth"—allowed consolidation for production and resulted in substantial economies of scale. At Whirlpool, use of common platforms allow European and American appliances to share technology and suppliers to lower cost and to streamline production. Many of the same components are used for products that eventually are marketed to segments looking for top-of-the-line or no-frills versions.[38] Similar differences in customer expectations have Bestfoods selling 15 versions of minestrone soup in Europe.

Marketing Approach   Nowhere is the need for the local touch as critical as in the execution of the marketing program. Uniformity is sought especially in elements that are strategic (e.g., positioning) in nature, whereas care is taken to localize necessary tactical elements (e.g., distribution). This approach has been called **glocalization.** For example, Unilever achieved great success with a fabric softener that used a common positioning, advertising theme, and symbol (a teddy bear) but differing brand names (e.g., Snuggle, Cajoline, Kuschel-weich, Mimosin, and Yumos) and bottle sizes. Gillette Co. scored a huge success with its Sensor shaver when it was rolled out in the United States, Europe, and Japan with a common approach based on the premise that men everywhere want the same thing in a shave. Although the language of its TV commercials varied, the theme ("the best a man can get") and most of the footage were the same. A comparison of the marketing mix elements of two global marketers is given in Table 12.2. Notice that adaptation is present even at Coca-Cola, which is acknowledged to be one of the world's most global companies.

Location of Value-Added Activities   Globalization strives at cost reductions by pooling production or other activities or exploiting factor costs or capabilities within a system. Rather than duplicating activities in multiple, or even all, country organizations, a firm concentrates its activities. For example, Texas Instruments has designated a single design center and manufacturing organization for each type of memory chip. To reduce high costs and to be close to markets, it placed two of its four new $250-million memory chip plants in Taiwan and Japan. To reduce high R&D costs, it has entered into a strategic alliance with Hitachi. Many global companies have established R&D centers next to key production facilities so that concurrent engineering can take place every day on the factory floor. To enhance the global exchange of ideas, the centers have joint projects and are in real-time contact with each other.

TABLE 12.2

Globalization of the Marketing Mix

Marketing Mix Elements	ADAPTATION		STANDARDIZATION	
	Full	Partial	Partial	Full
Product			N	C
Brand name			N	C
Product positioning		N		C
Packaging			C/N	
Advertising theme		N		C
Pricing		N	C	
Advertising copy	N			C
Distribution	N	C		
Sales promotion	N	C		
Customer service	N	C		

Key: C = Coca-Cola; N = Nestlé.

Source: John A. Quelch and Edward J. Hoff, "Customizing Global Marketing," *Harvard Business Review*, May–June 1986 (Boston: Harvard Business School Publishing Division), 61. Reprinted by permission of Harvard Business Review. Copyright © 1986 by the President and Fellows of Harvard College; all rights reserved.

The quest for cost savings and improved transportation methods has allowed some companies to concentrate customer service activities rather than having them present in all country markets. For example, Sony used to have repair centers in all of the Scandinavian countries and Finland; today, all service and maintenance activities are actually performed in a regional center in Stockholm, Sweden.

Competitive Moves   A company with regional or global presence will not have to respond to competitive moves only in the market where it is being attacked. A competitor may be attacked in its profit sanctuary to drain its resources, or its position in its home market may be challenged.[39] When Fuji began cutting into Kodak's market share in the United States, Kodak responded by drastically increasing its penetration in Japan and created a new subsidiary to deal strictly with that market. In addition, Kodak solicited the support of the U.S. government to gain more access to Japanese distribution systems that Kodak felt were unfairly blocked from them.

Cross-subsidization, or the use of resources accumulated in one part of the world to fight a competitive battle in another, may be the competitive advantage needed for the long term.[40] One major market lost may mean losses in others, resulting in a domino effect. Jockeying for overall global leadership may result in competitive action in any part of the world. This has manifested itself in the form of "wars" between major global players in industries such as soft drinks, automotive tires, computers, and wireless phones. The opening of new markets often signals a new battle, as happened in the 1990s in Russia, in Mexico after the signing of the North American Free Trade Agreement, and in Vietnam after the normalization of relations with the United States.[41] Given their multiple bases of operation, global companies may defend against a competitive attack in one country by countering in another country or, if the competitors operate in multiple businesses, countering in a different product category altogether. In the wireless phone category, the winners in the future will be those who can better attack less-mature markets with cheaper phones, while providing Internet-based devices elsewhere.[42]

The example of Nokia, a leading manufacturer of wireless telephones in the world, highlights globalization as a strategy. The company's focus is on wireless telecommunications (manufactured in Finland, Germany, and South Korea). The objective is to be a volume manufacturer, that is, to provide products for all major systems through a presence in all major markets. A global product range with customized variation for different distribution channels assures local acceptance.[43]

Implementing Global Programs

The successful global companies of the future will be those that can achieve a balance between the local and the regional/global concerns. Companies that have tried the global concept have often run into problems with local differences. Especially early on, global programs were seen as standardized efforts dictated to the country organizations by headquarters. For example, when Coca-Cola reentered the Indian market in 1993, it invested most heavily in its Coke brand, using its typical global positioning, and had its market leadership slip to Pepsi. Recognizing the mistake, Coke reemphasized a popular local cola brand (Thums Up) and refocused the Coke brand advertising to be more relevant to the local Indian consumer.[44]

Challenges   Pitfalls that handicap global programs and contribute to their suboptimal performance include market-related reasons, such as insufficient research and a tendency to overstandardize, as well as internal reasons, such as inflexibility in planning and implementation.

If a product is to be launched on a broader scale without formal research as to regional or local differences, the result may be failure. An example of this is Lego A/S, the Danish toy manufacturer, which decided to transfer sales promotional tactics successful in the U.S. market unaltered to other markets, such as Japan. This promotion included approaches such as "bonus packs" and gift promotions. However, Japanese consumers considered these promotions wasteful, expensive, and not very appealing.[45] Similarly, AT&T has had its problems abroad because its models are largely reworked U.S. models. Even after spending $100 million in adapting its most powerful switch for European markets, its success was limited because phone companies there prefer smaller switches.[46] Often, the necessary research is conducted only after a product or a program has failed.

Globalization by design requires a balance between sensitivity to local needs and deployment of technologies and concepts globally. This means that neither headquarters nor independent country managers can alone call the shots. If country organizations are not part of the planning process, or if adoption is forced on them by headquarters, local resistance in the form of the **not-invented-here syndrome (NIH)** may lead to the demise of the global program or, worse still, to an overall decline in morale. Subsidiary resistance may stem from resistance to any idea originating from the outside or from valid concerns about the applicability of a concept to that particular market. Without local commitment, no global program will survive.

Localizing Global Moves

The successful global companies of the twenty-first century will be those that can achieve a balance between country managers and global product managers at headquarters. This balance may be achieved by a series of actions to improve a company's ability to develop and implement global strategy. These actions relate to management processes, organization structures, and overall corporate culture, all of which should ensure cross-fertilization within the firm.[47]

Management Processes   In the multidomestic approach, country organizations had very little need to exchange ideas. Globalization, however, requires transfer of information not only between headquarters and country organizations but also between the country organizations themselves. By facilitating the flow of information, ideas are exchanged and organizational values strengthened. Information exchange can be achieved through periodic meetings of marketing managers or through worldwide conferences to allow employees to discuss their issues and local approaches to solving them. IBM, for example, has a Worldwide Opportunity Council that sponsors fellowships for employees to listen to business cases from around the world and develop global platforms or solutions. IBM has found that some country organizations find it easier to accept input of other country organizations than that coming directly from headquarters. The approach used at Levi Strauss & Co. is described in Global Perspective 12.3.

Part of the preparation for becoming global has to be personnel interchange. Many companies encourage (or even require) midlevel managers to gain experience abroad during the early or middle stages of their careers. The more experience people have in working with others from different nationalities—getting to know other markets and surroundings—the better a company's global philosophy, strategy, and actions will be integrated locally.

The role of headquarters staff should be that of coordination and leveraging the resources of the corporation. For example, this may mean activities focused on combining good ideas that come from different parts of the company to be fed into global planning. Many global companies also employ world-class staffs whose role should be to consult subsidiaries by upgrading their technical skills and to focus their attention not only on local issues but also on those with global impact.

GLOBAL PERSPECTIVE 12.3

It's Not All in the Jeans

Twice a year, Levi Strauss & Co. calls together managers from its worldwide operations for a meeting of the minds. In sessions that could be described as a cross between the United Nations general assembly and MTV, the participants brainstorm and exchange ideas on what seems to work in their respective markets, regionally or globally. If a marketing manager finds an advertising campaign appealing, he or she is encouraged to take it back home to sell more Levi's blue jeans.

All told, Levi's approach epitomizes a slogan that is becoming popular among companies around the world: Think globally, act locally. Levi's has deftly capitalized on the Levi's name abroad by promoting it as an enshrined piece of Americana, and consumers have responded by paying top dollar for the product. An Indonesian commercial shows Levi's-clad teenagers cruising around Dubuque, Iowa, in 1960s convertibles. In Japan, James Dean serves as a centerpiece in virtually all Levi's advertising. Overseas, Levi's products have been positioned as upscale, which has meant highly satisfactory profit margins. To protect the image, Levi's has avoided the use of mass merchants and discounters in its distribution efforts.

Levi's success turns on its ability to fashion a global strategy that does not stifle local initiative. It is a delicate balancing act, one that often means giving foreign managers the freedom needed to adjust their tactics to meet the changing tastes of their home markets. In Brazil, Levi's prospers by letting local managers call the shots on distribution. For instance, Levi's penetrated the huge, fragmented Brazilian market by launching a chain of 400 Levi's Only stores, some of them in tiny rural towns. Levi's is also sensitive to local tastes in Brazil, where it developed

the Feminina line of jeans exclusively for women, who prefer ultratight jeans. What Levi's learns in one market can often be adopted in another. The Dockers line of chino pants and casual wear originated in the company's Argentine unit and was applied to loosely cut pants by Levi's Japanese subsidiary. The company's U.S. operation adopted both in 1986, and the line now generates significant North American revenues.

From a high of 31 percent of the market in 1990, Levi Strauss' share fell to 17 percent the first six months of 1998. With increasing global competition and an aging world population, Levi's has targeted other product lines for growth, not just its blue jeans. In addition to its Dockers brand, which achieved record sales in 1998, Levi's launched a dress pant line, Slates, in 1996. Slates has become the number-one selling dress pant in the United States, capitalizing on the casual dress trend in offices.

The company has also launched a reorganization to focus on consumer needs. Although Levi Strauss has had a presence on the World Wide Web for several years, it recently revamped its site with consumer-friendly features, such as a virtual dressing room, custom-tailored blue jeans ordering, and virtual salespeople who offer tips on matching outfits. "Our single-minded goal is to make it easier to shop and buy our products," says Jay Thomas, director of digital marketing.

Levi's continues to focus on global sales with its three divisions: Levi Strauss, the Americas (the United States, Canada, Mexico, and Latin America); Levi Strauss Europe, Middle East, Africa; and Levi Strauss Asia Pacific. The Americas division contributed 69 percent of sales; Europe, Middle East, Africa, 22 percent; and Asia Pacific, 8 percent of $4.6 billion total sales for 2000.

Source: "Levi Strauss & Co. Fiscal 2000 Financial Results," at **www.levistrauss.com**; Alice Z. Cuneo, "Levi Strauss Begins 1st Online Sales Effort," *Advertising Age*, November 23, 1998, p. 18; "For Levi's a Flattering Fit Overseas," *Business Week*, November 5, 1990, 76–77.

Globalization calls for the centralization of decision-making authority far beyond that of the multidomestic approach. Once a strategy has been jointly developed, headquarters may want to permit local managers to develop their own programs within specified parameters and subject to approval rather than forcing them to adhere strictly to the formulated strategy. For example, Colgate Palmolive allows local units to use their own approaches, but only if they can prove they can beat the global "benchmark" version. With a properly managed approval process, effective control can be exerted without unduly dampening a country manager's creativity.

Overall, the best approach against the emergence of the NIH syndrome is utilizing various motivational policies such as: (1) ensuring that local managers participate in the development of strategies and programs; (2) encouraging local managers to generate ideas for possible regional or global use; (3) maintaining a product portfolio that includes local as well as regional and global brands; and (4) allowing local managers control over their budgets so that they can respond to local customer needs and counter global competition (rather than depleting budgets by forcing them to participate only in uniform campaigns).[48] Acknowledging this local potential, global companies can pick up successful brands in one country and make them cross-border stars. Since Nestlé acquired British candy maker Rowntree Mackintosh, it has increased its exports by 60 percent and made formerly local brands, such as After Eight Dinner mints, pan-European hits. When an innovation or a product is deemed to have global potential, rolling it out in other regions or worldwide becomes an important consideration.

Organization Structures   Various organization structures have emerged to support the globalization effort. Some companies have established global or regional product managers and their support groups at headquarters. Their task is to develop long-term strategies for product categories on a worldwide basis and to act as the support system for the country organizations. This matrix structure focused on customers, which has replaced the traditional country-by-country approach, is considered more effective in today's global marketplace according to companies that have adopted it.

Whenever a product group has global potential, firms such as Procter & Gamble, 3M, and Henkel create strategic-planning units to work on the programs. These units, such as 3M's EMATs (European Marketing Action Teams) consist of members from the country organizations that market the products, managers from both global and regional headquarters, as well as technical specialists.

To deal with the globalization of customers, companies such as Hewlett-Packard and DHL are extending national account management programs across countries, typically for the most important customers.[49] AT&T, for example, distinguishes between international and global customers and provides the global customers with special services including a single point of contact for domestic and international operations and consistent worldwide service. Executing **global account management** programs builds relationships not only with important customers but also allows for the development of internal systems and interaction.

Corporate Culture   Whirlpool's corporate profile states the following: "Beyond selling products around the world, being a global home-appliance company means identifying and respecting genuine national and regional differences in customer expectations, but also recognizing and responding to similarities in product development, engineering, purchasing, manufacturing, marketing and sales, distribution, and other areas. Companies which exploit the efficiencies from these similarities will outperform others in terms of market share, cost, quality, productivity, innovation, and return to shareholders."[50]

In truly global companies, very little decision making occurs that does not support the goal of treating the world as a single market. Planning for and execution of programs take place on a worldwide basis.

Examples of manifestations of the global commitment are a global identity that favors no specific country (especially the "home country" of the company). The management features several nationalities, and whenever teams are assembled, people from various country organizations get represented. The management development system has to be transparent, allowing nonnational executives an equal chance for the fast track to top management.[51]

In determining the optimal combination of products and product lines to be marketed, a firm should consider choices for individual markets as well as transfer of products and brands from one region or market to another. This will often result in a particular country organization marketing product lines and goods that are a combination of global, regional, and national brands.

Decisions on specific targeting may result in the choice of a narrowly defined segment in the countries chosen. This is a likely strategy of specialized products to clearly definable markets, for example, ocean-capable sailing boats. Catering to multiple segments in various markets is typical of consumer-oriented companies that have sufficient resources for broad coverage.

Summary

Globalization has become one of the most important strategy issues for managers in the past ten years. Many forces, both external and internal, are driving companies to globalize by expanding and coordinating their participation in foreign markets. The approach is not standardization, however. Managers may indeed occasionally be able to take identical concepts and approaches around the world, but most often, they must be customized to local tastes. Internally, companies must make sure that country organizations around the world are ready to launch global products and programs as if they had been developed only for their markets.

Managers need to engage in strategic planning to better adjust to the realities of the new marketplace. Understanding the firm's core strategy (i.e., what business they are really in) starts the process, and this assessment may lead to adjustments in what business the company may want to be in. In formulating global strategy for the chosen business, the decision makers have to assess and make choices about markets and competitive strategy to be used in penetrating them. This may result in the choice of one particular segment across markets or the exploitation of multiple segments in which the company has a competitive advantage. In manipulating and implementing programs for maximum effect in the chosen markets, the old adage, "think globally, act locally," becomes a critical guiding principle both as far as customers are concerned and in terms of country organization motivation.

Key Terms and Concepts

globalization
multidomestic strategy
mininationals
cost leadership

differentiation
portfolio models
glocalization
cross-subsidization

not-invented-here
  syndrome (NIH)

global account
  management

Questions for Discussion

1. What is the danger in oversimplifying the globalization approach? Would you agree with the statement that "if something is working in a big way in one market, you better assume it will work in all markets"?
2. What are the critical ways in which globalization and standardization differ?
3. In addition to teenagers as a global segment, are there possibly other groups with similar traits and behaviors that have emerged worldwide?

4. Why is the assessment of internal resources critical as early as possible in developing a global strategic plan?
5. Outline the basic reasons why a company does not necessarily have to be large and have years of experience to succeed in the global marketplace.
6. What are the basic reasons why country operations would not embrace a new regional or global plan (i.e., why the not-invented-here syndrome might emerge)?

Internet Exercises

1. Using the material available at their web site (**http://www. unilever.com**), suggest ways in which Unilever's business groups can take advantage of global and regional strategies due to interconnections in production and marketing.

2. Bestfoods is one of the largest food companies in the world with operations in more than 60 countries and products sold in 110 countries in the world. Based on the brand information given (**http://www.bestfoods.com/brands.htm**), what benefits does a company derive from having a global presence?

Recommended Readings

Davidson, William H. *Global Strategic Management.* New York: Wiley, 1982.

The Economist Intelligence Unit. *151 Checklists for Global Management.* New York: The Economist Intelligence Unit, 1993.

Feist, William R., James A. Heely, Min H. Lau, and Roy L. Nersesian. *Managing a Global Enterprise.* Westport, CT: Quorum, 1999.

Foster, Richard. *Innovation: The Attacker's Advantage.* New York: Summit Books, 1986.

Grant, Robert M., and Kent E. Neuport. *Cases in Contemporary Strategy Analysis.* Oxford, England: Blackwell, 1999.

Humes, Samuel. *Managing the Multinational: Confronting the Global-Local Dilemma.* London: Prentice-Hall International (U.K.) Ltd, 1993.

Kanter, Rosabeth Moss. *World Class.* New York: Simon & Schuster, 1995.

Kaynak, Erdener, ed. *The Global Business.* Binghamton, NY: Haworth Press, 1992.

Kotabe, Masaaki. *Global Sourcing Strategy: R&D, Manufacturing, and Marketing Interfaces.* Greenwich, CT: Greenwood Publishing Group, 1992.

Makridakis, Spyros G. *Forecasting, Planning, and Strategy for the 21st Century.* New York: Free Press, 1990.

Prahalad, C. K., and Yves L. Doz. *The Multinational Mission: Balancing Local and Global Vision.* New York: Free Press, 1987.

Rosensweig, Jeffrey. *Winning the Global Game: A Strategy for Linking People and Profits.* New York: Free Press, 1998.

Yip, George. *Total Global Strategy.* Englewood Cliffs, NJ: Prentice-Hall, 1992.

Notes

1. Global Business Policy Council, *Globalization Ledger,* Washington, DC: A.T. Kearney, April 2000, 3; and "What's New About Globalization?" *The McKinsey Quarterly* 2 (1997): 168–179.

2. Jeremey Main, "How to Go Global—and Why," *Fortune* (August 28, 1989): 70–76.

3. The section draws heavily from George S. Yip, "Global Strategy . . . In a World of Nations?" *Sloan Management Review* 31 (fall 1989): 29–41; Susan P. Douglas and C. Samuel Craig, "Evolution of Global Marketing Strategy: Scale, Scope, and Synergy," *Columbia Journal of World Business* 24 (Fall 1989): 47–58; and George S. Yip, Pierre M. Loewe, and Michael Y. Yoshino, "How to Take Your Company to the Global Market," *Columbia, Journal of World Business* 23 (winter 1988): 28–40.

4. Ernst Dichter, "The World Customer," *Harvard Business Review* 40 (July–August 1962): 113–122.

5. Kenichi Ohmae, *Triad Power—The Coming Shape of Global Competition* (New York: Free Press, 1985), 22–27.

6. Denise Incandela, Kathleen McLaughlin, and Christiana Smith Shi, "Retailers to the World," *The McKinsey Quarterly,* 35, 3(1999): 84–97.

7. "Vital Statistic: Disputed Cost of Creating a Drug," *The Wall Street Journal,* November 9, 1993, B1.

8. "Paper Prices Are Driving Flurry of Industry Mergers," *The Wall Street Journal,* May 10, 2000, B4; and "Finnish Paper Concern to Buy Champion," *The Wall Street Journal,* February 18, 2000, A3, A6.

9. Gianluigi Guido, "Implementing a Pan-European Marketing Strategy," *Long Range Planning* 24 (1991): 23–33.

10. Suzy Wetlaufer, "Driving Change: An Interview with Ford Motor Company's Jacques Nasser," *Harvard Business Review* 77 (March–April, 1999): 76–88.

11. Pete Engardio, "Third World Leapfrog," *Business Week/The Information Leapfrog 1994,* 47–49.

12. "Mininationals Are Making Maximum Impact," *Business Week* (September 1993): 66–69.

13. Nestlé: A Giant in a Hurry," *Business Week* (March 22, 1993): 50–54; and http://www.nestle.com.

14. Jordan D. Lewis, *Partnerships for Profit* (New York: Free Press, 1990), 86.

15. "3 Big Carmakers to Create Net Site for Buying Parts," *The Washington Post,* February 26, 2000, E1, E8.

16. Gilbert D. Harrell and Richard O. Kiefer, "Multinational Market Portfolios in Global Strategy Development," *International Marketing Review* 10, 1 (1993): 60–72.

17. Michael E. Porter, *Competitive Strategy* (New York: Free press, 1990), ch. 1.

18. "Europe's Car Makers Expect Tidy Profits," *The Wall Street Journal,* January 27, 2000, A16.

19. Lori Ioannou, "It's a Small World After All," *International Business* (February 1994): 82–88.

20. "Grabbing Markets from the Giants," *Business Week/21st Century Capitalism* (1994), 156.

21. Michael Porter, *Competitive Advantage* (New York: The Free press, 1987), ch. 1.

22. Robert M. Grant, *Contemporary Strategy Analysis: Concepts, Techniques, Applications* (Oxford, England: Blackwell, 1995), 203–205.

23. George S. Yip, *Total Global Strategy: Managing for Worldwide Competitive Advantage* (Englewood Cliffs, NJ: Prentice-Hall, 1992), 242–246.

24. The models referred to are GE/McKinsey, Shell International, and A. D. Little portfolio models.

25. Yoram Wind and Susan P. Douglas, "International Portfolio Analysis and Strategy: Challenge of the '80s," *Journal of International Business Studies* 12 (Fall 1981): 69–82.

26. "P&G Puts Nappies to Rest in Australia," *Advertising Age* (September 19, 1994): I-31.

27. "A Feeding Frenzy in European Telecom," *Business Week* (November 21, 1994): 119–122.

28. "Will Renault Go for Broke in Asia?" *Business Week,* February 28, 2000, and "Ford, GM Square Off Over Daewoo Motor: The Question is Why?" *The Wall Street Journal,* February 14, 2000, A1, A13.

29. "Tissue Titans Target Globally with Key Brands," *Advertising Age,* December 20, 1999, 4.

30. Richard Tomlinson, "Europe's New Computer Game," *Fortune,* February 21, 2000, 219–224.

31. Saeed Samiee and Kendall Roth, "The Influence of Global Marketing Standardization on Performance," *Journal of Marketing* 56 (April 1992): 1–17.

32. Shawn Tully, "Teens: The Most Global Market of All," *Fortune* (May 16, 1994): 90–97.

33. "The Euroteens (and How Not to Sell to Them)," *Business Week* (April 11, 1994): 84.

34. S. Vandermerwe and M. L'Huillier, "Euro-Consumers in 1992," *Business Horizons* 32 (January–February 1989): 34–40.

35. "Getting and Spending," *Business Week/21st Century Capitalism* (1994), 178–185.

36. Imad B. Baalbaki and Naresh K. Malhotra, "Marketing Management Bases for International Market Segmentation: An Alternate Look at the Standardization/Customization Debate," *International Marketing Review* 10, 1 (1993): 19–44.

37. Rahul Jacob, "The Big Rise," *Fortune* (May 30, 1994): 74–90.

38. "Call It Worldpool," *Business Week* (November 28, 1994): 98–99.

39. W. Chan Kim and R. A. Mauborgne, "Becoming an Effective Global Competitor," *Journal of Business Strategy* 8 (January–February 1988): 33–37.

40. Gary Hamel and C. K. Prahalad, "Do You Really Have a Global Strategy?" *Harvard Business Review* 63 (July–August 1985): 75–82.

41. "A Mexican War Heats Up for Cola Giants," *The Wall Street Journal*, April 20, 1993. B1.

42. "Nokia Widens Lead in Wireless Market While Motorola, Ericsson Fall Back," *The Wall Street Journal*, February 8, 2000, B8.

43. This example is courtesy of Jouko Hayrynen, vice president, exports, Nokia Mobile Phones Ltd.

44. James A. Gingrich, "Five Rules for Winning Emerging Market Consumers," *Strategy and Business* (Second Quarter, 1999): 19–33.

45. Kamran Kashani, "Beware the Pitfalls of Global Marketing," *Harvard Business Review* 67 (September–October 1989): 91–98.

46. "AT&T Slowly Gets Its Global Wires Uncrossed," *Business Week* (February 11, 1991): 82–83.

47. John A. Quelch and Edward J. Hoff, "Customizing Global Marketing," *Harvard Business Review* 64 (May–June 1986): 59–68; Yip, Loewe, and Yoshino, "Take Your Company to the Global Market."

48. Quelch and Hoff, "Customizing Global Marketing."

49. George S. Yip and Tammy L. Madsen, "Global Account Management: The New Frontier in Relationship Marketing," *International Marketing Review* 13, 3 (1996): 24–42.

50. Available **http://www.whirlpoolcorp.com/whr/ics/story/today.html**.

51. "Globalization Starts with Company's Own View of Itself," *Business International* (June 10, 1991): 197–198.

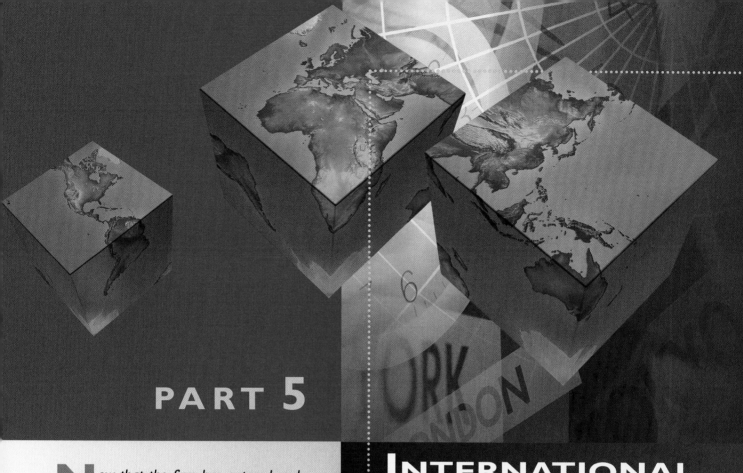

PART 5

Now that the firm has entered and established itself in international markets, it is important to devise and implement strategies which will help provide a competitively advantageous position. Part 5 starts with strategic planning and then focuses on important overarching dimensions such as services, logistics, and countertrade—as well as on the traditional functional areas of marketing, finance, accounting, taxation, human resources, and management.

Each one of the chapters in Part 5 is structured to differentiate between smaller firms and multinational corporations (MNCs). At the beginning of Part 5, low cost and low resource approaches are presented for firms with little international experience. Subsequent chapters assume a globally oriented perspective with a major focus on MNCs. Part 5 concludes with a chapter covering the newest developments, knowledge, and speculations about international business as well as information about professional and employment options in the international business field.

INTERNATIONAL BUSINESS STRATEGY AND OPERATIONS

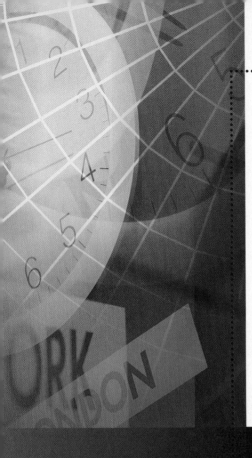

CHAPTER 13

International Marketing

LEARNING OBJECTIVES

- To suggest how markets for international expansion can be selected, their demand assessed, and appropriate strategies for their development devised

- To describe how environmental differences generate new challenges for the international marketing manager

- To compare and contrast the merits of standardization versus localization strategies for country markets and of regional versus global marketing efforts

- To discuss market-specific and global challenges facing the marketing functions: product, price, distribution, and promotion within both the traditional and e-business dimensions

ANATOMY OF A GLOBAL PRODUCT LAUNCH

By the end of the 1980s, with disposable razors taking up 50 percent of the market, executives at Gillette, the $10.1 billion Boston-based consumer products marketer, decided to break out of what they saw as a dead-end strategy. With disposables, the razor had become a commodity, and the buying decision was based solely on price and convenience. Gillette needed a differentiator, a product upon which the brand could be elevated and market share substantially increased. Rather than compete on the existing playing field, the decision was made to create a new category, the shaving system, and take control of it.

In 1990, after ten years of research and development, Gillette introduced its Sensor twin-bladed shaving system. The design not only produced a markedly better shave but also brought the company out of the disposable dilemma and back into an indisputable leadership position. The next step was to see if three blades could do a better job than two. In order to ensure that consumers did not simply scoff at three blades as a marketing gimmick, the result and the communication about it had to be demonstrably better.

A group, code-named the 225 Task Force, worked for five full years in concert with R&D to produce and orchestrate the introduction of a new product, Mach3. They concentrated as much on developing a great new brand as developing a great new product. The five years were characterized by ceaseless product improvement, constant product testing around the world, and, eventually, creation of a marketing strategy to not only press the new value propositions but also substantiate the claims. The marketing strategy was to look at the world as one market and be based on the following premises:

- Because the product would probably take off immediately, manufacturing had to ensure that it had enough capacity to avoid shortages at the outset.
- To facilitate smooth global introduction, all packaging, point of sale, and other promotional material had to be the same, simply translated into 30 languages for other geographics. The company purposefully kept the number of words on the front of the package to a minimum to avoid the need for design alterations.
- All marketing and advertising was based on a single campaign that was released in every market, again with minor local adjustments and translations. The European introduction was delayed by two months to September 1st from the North American July 1st to accommodate Europeans on holiday.
- Pricing needed a built-in elasticity, but by carefully testing the concept with consumers, Gillette fixed a profitable price point based on the expected number of blades per user per year.

By 1999, Mach3 became the type of success its developers and marketers had planned for. Market share varied from 13 to 16 percent in all of the markets in which it had been launched. The success was underscored by the introduction of copycats, especially British retailer Asda's Tri-Flex, retailing for $1.00 on the average less than Mach3.

In 2000, Gillette announced the launch of a new system, Gillette for Women Venus, backed by a similar global marketing push to that of Mach3. The campaign broke in April, 2001, including TV, print, outdoor, and Internet with a theme "Reveal the goddess in you." Europe and North America were slated for the initial rollout. Gillette spent $300 million to bring Venus to market with extensive worldwide consumer testing. ●

Product Development Summary for MACH3

Patents	35 patent protections on MACH3 and manufacturing processes
Development time	Ten years
R&D costs	$200 million
Capital investments	$550 million
Advertising and marketing	$300 million
Launch dates	North America and Israel—July 1, 1998; Europe—September 1998; Worldwide—1999
Retail price	Razor, two cartridges and organizer: $6.49–$6.99 Four-pack cartridges: $6.29–$6.79

Source: "No New CEO, But Gillette Does Have a New Product," *Advertising Age,* November 6, 2000, 25; "Gillette Unveils Major Global Product Launch," *Marketing Week,* October 26, 2000, 5; Glenn Rifkin, "MACH3: Anatomy of Gillette's Latest Global Launch," *Strategy & Business* 2 (1999): 34–41; "Gillette Flays Asda Over 'Inferior' Tri-Flex Razor," *Marketing Week,* June 10, 1999, 9; Hamantha S. B. Herath and Chan S. Park, "Economic Analysis of R&D Projects: An Options Approach," *The Engineering Economist* 44, 1, (1999): 1–35; **http://www.gillette.com; http://www.mach3.com.**

Marketing is the process of planning and executing the conception, pricing, promotion, and distribution of ideas, goods, and services to create exchanges that satisfy individual and organizational objectives.[1] The concepts of satisfaction and exchange are at the core of marketing. For an exchange to take place, two or more parties have to come together physically or electronically and they must communicate and deliver things of perceived value. Customers should be perceived as information seekers who evaluate marketers' offerings in terms of their own drives and needs. When the offering is consistent with their needs, they tend to choose the good or service; if it is not, other alternatives are chosen. A key task of the marketer is to recognize the ever-changing nature of needs and wants. Marketing techniques apply not only to goods but to ideas and services as well. Further, well over 50 percent of all marketing activities are business marketing—directed at other businesses, governmental entities, and various types of institutions.

The marketing manager's task is to plan and execute programs that will ensure a long-term competitive advantage for the company. This task has two integral parts: (1) the determining of specific target markets and (2) marketing management, which consists of manipulating marketing mix elements to best satisfy the needs of the individual target markets. Regardless of geographic markets, the basic tasks do not vary; they have been called the technical universals of marketing.[2]

This chapter will focus on the formulation of marketing strategy for international operations. The first section describes target market selection and how to identify pertinent characteristics of the various markets. The balance of the chapter is devoted to adjusting the elements of the marketing program to a particular market for maximum effectiveness and efficiency, while attempting to exploit global and regional similarities, as highlighted in the opening vignette.

Target Market Selection

The process of target market selection involves narrowing down potential country markets to a feasible number of countries and market segments within them. Rather than try to appeal to everyone, firms best utilize their resources by: (1) identifying potential markets for entry and (2) expanding selectively over time to those deemed attractive.

Identification and Screening

The National Trade Data Bank includes reports such as International Marketing Insight *and* Best Market Reports *that are of use throughout the stages of market choice* (**www.stat-usa.gov/tradtest.nsf**).

A four-stage process for screening and analyzing foreign markets is presented in Figure 13.1. It begins with very general criteria and ends with product-specific market analyses. The data and the methods needed for decision making change from secondary to primary as the steps are taken in sequence. Although presented here as a screening process for choosing target markets, the process is also applicable to change of entry mode or even divestment.

If markets were similar in their characteristics, the international marketer could enter any one of the potential markets. However, differences among markets exist in three dimensions: physical, psychic, and economic.[3] Physical distance is the geographic distance between home and target countries; its impact has decreased as a result of recent technological developments. Psychic, or cultural, distance refers to differences in language, tradition, and customs between two countries. Economic distance translates into the target's ability to pay. Generally, the greater the overall distance—or

FIGURE 13.1

The Screening Process in Target Market Choice

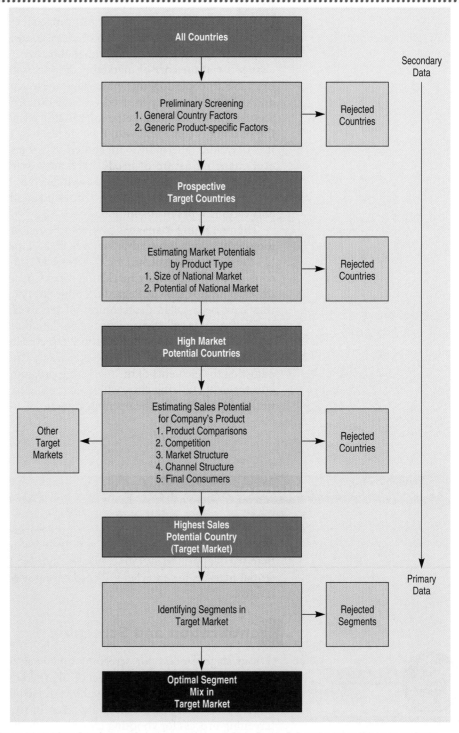

Source: Adapted from *Entry Strategies for International Markets,* p. 56, by Franklin R. Root (Lexington, MA: Lexington Books, D.C. Heath & Co., Copyright 1994, D. C. Heath & Co.).

difference—between the two countries, the less knowledge the marketer has about the target market. The amount of information that is available varies dramatically. For example, although the marketer can easily learn about the economic environment from secondary sources, invaluable interpretive information may not be available until the firm actually operates in the market. In the early stages of the assessment, international marketers can be assisted by numerous online and CD-ROM-based data sources as shown in Chapter 10.

The four stages in the screening process are: preliminary screening, estimation of market potential, estimation of sales potential, and identification of segments. Each stage should be given careful attention. The first stage, for example, should not merely reduce the number of alternatives to a manageable few for the sake of reduction, even though the expense of analyzing markets in depth is great. Unless care is taken, attractive alternatives may be eliminated.

*Services such as Tradeport provide frameworks to assist in rating of potential markets using environmental data (**www.tradeport.org/ts/ planning/marketlist.html**).*

Preliminary Screening   The preliminary screening process must rely chiefly on secondary data for country-specific factors as well as product- and industry-specific factors. Country-specific factors typically include those that would indicate the market's overall buying power; for example, population, gross national product in total and per capita, total exports and imports, and production of cement, electricity, and steel.[4] Product-specific factors narrow the analysis to the firm's specific areas of operation. A company such as Motorola, manufacturing for the automotive aftermarket, is interested in the number of passenger cars, trucks, and buses in use. The statistical analyses must be accompanied by qualitative assessments of the impact of cultural elements and the overall climate for foreign firms and products. A market that satisfies the levels set becomes a prospective target country.

Estimating Market Potential   Total market potential is the sales, in physical or monetary units, that might be available to all firms in an industry during a given period under a given level of industry marketing effort and given environmental conditions.[5] The international marketer needs to assess the size of existing markets and forecast the size of future markets. A number of techniques, both quantitative and qualitative are available for this task.

Income elasticity of demand is the relationship between demand and economic progress. The share of income spent on necessities reflects the level of development of the market as well as monies left for other purchases. When consumption per capita of a product category is mapped against GNP per capita, it reflects a diminishing rate in consumption as incomes rise. For the majority of goods, consumption rises most quickly between $3,000 and $10,000 per capita bringing in new consumers to the market while those who are already in the market may be trading into higher-value substitutes.[6] This points out the attractiveness of emerging markets in spite of their volatility.

If the data are available for product-specific analysis, the simplest way to establish a market-size estimate is to conduct a **market audit,** which adds together local production and imports with exports deducted from the total. However, in many cases, data may not exist, be current, or be appropriate. In such cases, market potentials may have to be estimated by methods such as **analogy.** This approach is based on the use of proxy variables that have been shown (either through research or intuition) to correlate with the demand for the product in question. The market size for a product (such as video games) in country A is estimated by comparing a ratio for an available indicator (e.g., PC ownership) for country A and country B, and using this ratio in conjunction with market data available on videogames for country B. In some cases, a time lag in demand patterns may be seen, thus requiring a **longitudinal analysis.** For example, the use of wireless communication in Southern Europe is suggested to lag Northern Europe by two years and that wireless telephony use overall is tied to the state of the economy (for example, GNP per capita). Therefore, to estimate wireless use in Southern Europe, the following formula could be used:

$$WC_{SE}^{2002} = GNP_{SE}^{2002} * (WC_{NE}^{2000}/GNP_{NE}^{2000})$$

Income Distribution: A Factor in Evaluating Market Potential

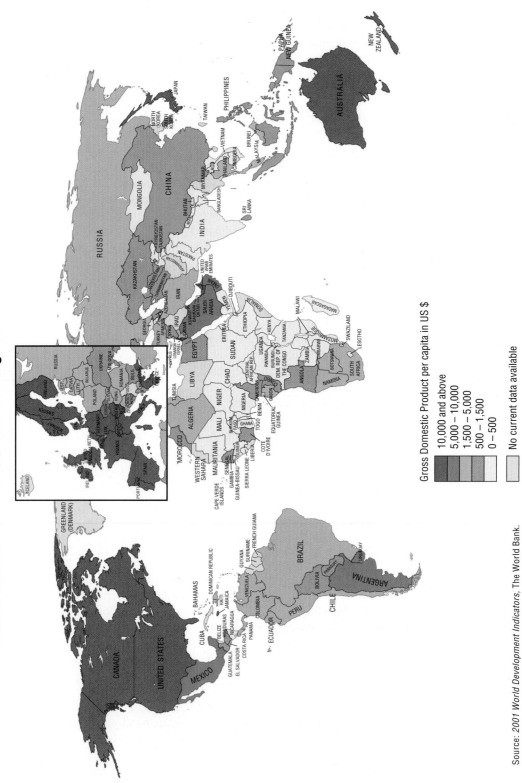

Gross Domestic Product per capita in US $

10,000 and above
5,000 – 10,000
1,500 – 5,000
500 – 1,500
0 – 500

No current data available

Source: *2001 World Development Indicators*, The World Bank.

Despite the valuable insight generated through the techniques, caution should be used in interpreting the results. All of the quantitative techniques are based on historical data that may be obsolete or inapplicable because of differences in cultural and geographic traits of the market. Further, with today's technological developments, lags between markets are no longer at a level that would make all of the measurements valid. Moreover, the measurements look at a market as an aggregate; that is, no regional differences are taken into account. In industrialized countries, the richest 10 percent of the population consumes 20 percent of all goods and services, whereas the respective figure for the developing countries may be as high as 50 percent.[7] Therefore, even in the developing countries with low GNP figures, segments exist with buying power rivaled only in the richest developed countries.

In addition to these quantitative techniques that rely on secondary data, international marketers can use various survey techniques. They are especially useful when marketing new technologies. A survey of end-user interest and responses may provide a relatively clear picture of the possibilities in a new market.

Comparing figures for market potential with actual sales will provide the international marketer with further understanding of his or her firm's chances in the market. If the difference between potential and reality is substantial, the reasons can be evaluated using **gap analysis.** The differences can be the result of usage, distribution, or product line gaps.[8] If the firm is already in the market, part of the difference between its sales and the market potential can be explained through the competitive gap. Usage gaps indicate that not all potential users are using the product or that those using it are not using as much as they could, which suggests mainly a promotional task. Distribution gaps indicate coverage problems, which may be vertical (concentrating only on urban markets) or horizontal (if the product is only available at large-scale international retailers and not local ones). Product line gaps typically suggest latent demand. An emerging trend in which Japanese consumers want to acquire an American look will help drive sales for companies like Ralph Lauren, L. L. Bean, and Northeastern Log Homes.

Estimating Sales Potential Even when the international marketer has gained an understanding of markets with the greatest overall promise, the firm's own possibilities in those markets are still not known. Sales potential is the share of the market potential that the firm can reasonably expect to get over the longer term. To arrive at an estimate, the marketer needs to collect product- and market-specific data. The data will have to do with:

1. Competition—strength, likely reaction to entry
2. Market—strength of barriers
3. Consumers—ability and willingness to buy
4. Product—degree of relative advantage, compatibility, complexity, trialability, and communicability
5. Channel structure—access to retail level

In studying the Russian market for entry, GM found that it would have to charge at least $15,000 for cars assembled there. The fact that nine out of ten new cars sold in Russia cost under $10,000 made the plan not feasible. However, the same research found that consumers would be willing to pay $1,000 to $1,500 more for a locally made car if it was called a Chevrolet. GM signed an agreement to put its logo on a vehicle developed by Russian automaker Avtovaz and selling it for only about $7,500.[9] The marketer's questions can never be fully answered until the firm has made a commitment to enter the market and is operational. The mode of entry has special significance in determining the firm's sales potential.

Identifying Segments   Within the markets selected, individuals and organizations will vary in their wants, resources, geographical locations, buying attitudes, and buying practices. Initially, the firm may cater to one or only a few segments and later expand to others, especially if the product is innovative. Segmentation is indicated when segments are indeed different enough to warrant individualized attention, are large enough for profit potential, and can be reached through the methods that the international marketer wants to use. For example, a European or U.S. entity in China may choose to offer the same product in China as it does at home and do so only through the western retailers such as Wal-Mart. This will mean that it focuses only on the urban consumers who are well-to-do.

Once the process is complete for a market or group of markets, the international marketer may begin it again for another one. When growth potential is no longer in market development, the firm may opt for market penetration.

Concentration versus Diversification

Choosing a market expansion policy involves the allocation of effort among various markets. The major alternatives are **concentration** on a small number of markets or **diversification,** which is characterized by growth in a relatively large number of markets in the early stages of international market expansion.[10]

Expansion Alternatives   Either concentration or diversification is applicable to market segments or to total markets, depending on the resource commitment the international marketer is willing and able to make. One option is a dual-concentration strategy, in which efforts are focused on a few segments in a limited number of countries. Another is a dual-diversification strategy, in which entry is to most segments in most available markets. The first is a likely strategy for small firms or firms that market specialized products to clearly definable markets, for example, ocean-capable sailing boats. The second is typical for large consumer-oriented companies that have sufficient resources for broad coverage. Market concentration/segment diversification opts for a limited number of markets but for wide coverage within them, putting emphasis on company acceptance. Market diversification/segment concentration usually involves the identification of a segment, possibly worldwide, to which the company can market without major changes in its marketing mix.

Factors Affecting Expansion Strategy   Expansion strategy is determined by the factors relating to market, mix, and company that are listed in Table 13.1. In most cases, the factors are interrelated.

Market-Related Factors   These factors are the ones that were influential in determining the attractiveness of the market in the first place. In the choice of expansion strategy, demand for the firm's products is a critical factor. With high and stable growth rates in certain markets, the firm will most likely opt for a concentration strategy. If the demand is strong worldwide, diversification may be attractive.

A forecast of the sales response function can be used to predict sales at various levels of marketing expenditure. Two general response functions exist: concave and S curve. When the function is concave, sales will increase at a decreasing rate because of competition and a lowering adoption rate. The function might involve a unique, innovative product or marketing program. An S-curve function assumes that a viable market share can be achieved only through sizable marketing efforts. This is typical for new entrants to well-established markets.

The uniqueness of the firm's offering with respect to competition is also a factor in the expansion strategy. If lead time over competition is considerable, the decision to

TABLE 13.1

Factors Affecting the
Choice Between
Concentration and
Diversification
Strategies

Factor	Diversification	Concentration
Market growth rate	Low	High
Sales stability	Low	High
Sales response function	Concave	S curve
Competitive lead time	Short	Long
Spillover effects	High	Low
Need for product adaptation	Low	High
Need for communication adaption	Low	High
Economies of scale in distribution	Low	High
Extent of constraints	Low	High
Program control requirements	Low	High

Source: Igal Ayal and Jehiel Zif, "Marketing Expansion Strategies in Multinational Marketing," *Journal of Marketing* 43
(Spring 1979): 89.

diversify may not seem urgent. However, complacency can be a mistake in today's competitive environment; competitors can rush new products into the market in a matter of days.

In many product categories marketers will be, knowingly or unknowingly, affected by spillover effects. Consider, for example, the impact that satellite channels have had on advertising in Europe, where ads for a product now reach most of the European market. Where geographic (and psychic) distances are short, spillover is likely, and marketers are most likely to diversify.

Government constraints—or the threat of them—can be a powerful motivator in a firm's expansion. While government barriers may naturally prevent new-market entry, marketers may seek access through using new entry modes, adjusting marketing programs, or getting into a market before entry barriers are erected.

Mix-Related Factors   These factors relate to the degree to which marketing mix elements—primarily product, promotion, and distribution—can be standardized. The more that standardization is possible, the more diversification is indicated. Overall savings through economies of scale can then be utilized in marketing efforts.

Depending on the good, each market will have its own challenges. Whether constraints are apparent (such as tariffs) or hidden (such as tests or standards), they will complicate all of the other factors. Nevertheless, regional integration has allowed many marketers to diversify their efforts.

Company-Related Factors   These include the objectives set by the company for its international operations and the policies it adopts in those markets. As an example, the firm may require—either by stated policy or because of its goods—extensive interaction with intermediaries and clients. When this is the case, the firm's efforts will likely be concentrated because of resource constraints.

The opportunity to take advantage of diversification is available for all types of companies, not only the large ones. The identification of unique worldwide segments for which a customized marketing mix is provided has proven to be successful for many small and medium-sized companies. For example, Symbol Technologies invented the hand-held laser scanner and now dominates the field worldwide. Cisco Systems claims 50 percent of the world market for gear that connects networks of computers, a field not in existence ten years ago.[11] The expansion of web portals to new markets is the focus of Global Perspective 13.1.

GLOBAL PERSPECTIVE 13.1

Bringing the New Economy to New Markets

With the U.S. market crowded with competitors, Yahoo!, Excite, Lycos, and America Online are expediting their plans to establish their brands in Asia, Europe, and Latin America before local competitors can create dominant positions of their own. With the non-U.S. share of users increasing, the fastest growth can be secured abroad.

The battle in Europe is the hottest among the portals that serve as starting points for web surfers looking for news, shopping, and search services. One significant reason for the growth is falling costs. At present, Internet users pay telephone charges on top of Internet access fees to use the web. Increasingly, however, operators are offering free monthly access and phone charges are dropping across the board.

Yahoo! and Lycos both operate about two dozen foreign sites, most with native-language news, shopping links, and other content custom-tailored to the local population. AOL has 12 international ventures, followed by Excite with 9. Lycos's German site features tips on brewing beer at home, and a program for calculating auto speeding fines. Yahoo's Singapore site offers real-time information on haze and smog in Southeast Asia.

The top U.S. players face tough domestic competitors that often have a better sense of the local culture and Internet styles. In many countries, the dominant telephone companies offer portals, giving them a significant competitive advantage with customers who are automatically sent to their home pages when they log on. Germany's leading portal, T-online, is run by Deutsche Telekom, while the leading French portal, Wanadoo, is run by France Telecom.

The danger for U.S. portals is that they might be viewed as "digital colonialists" trying to flex their muscles around the world. In Brazil, AOL was accused by its local competitor,

Universo Online, of using a misleading slogan: "We're the biggest because we're the best." The operation has also been hurt because 500 of the 5 million AOL's installation disks were either mistakenly loaded with music or some of the good disks altered the user's hard disks. Local newspapers, some owned by the parent of Universo Online, publicized the incidents.

Market challenges may lead to a desire to form partnerships with local outfits that would also help in understanding the local culture. Joint venture partners often front much of the capital needed to get the service off the ground, while AOL, for example, provides its technology and established brand name. In regional expansion, care has to be taken in choosing a partner that can provide support across countries. AOL ran into difficulties in Brazil because its Latin American partner was from Venezuela and had its relationships and influence built mostly in Spanish-speaking countries. In some cases, partners may be chosen for their influence in the local market; in Japan, Lycos teams up with Sumitomo, an ultra-traditional trading company with a 250-year history, while in Korea it teamed up with Mirae, a machinery and electronics company.

If a portal is late to a market, such as Lycos for the China market, the only approach is to differentiate. Not only are the leading U.S. portals well established in China (as seen in the chart on the opposite page), but local players, such as sina.com and sohu.com, are similar to their overseas rivals and they promise to know best where locals eat, shop, trade, or get news. One area where Lycos hopes to distinguish itself is wireless Internet. In China, mobile-phone penetration stands at 3 percent, while PCs are only owned by 1 percent of the population.

Marketing Management

After target markets are selected, the next step is the determination of marketing efforts at appropriate levels. A key question in international marketing concerns the extent to which the elements of the marketing mix—product, price, place, and distribution—should be standardized. The marketer also faces the specific challenges of adjusting each of the mix elements in the international marketplace.

Standardization versus Adaptation

The international marketer must first decide what modifications in the mix policy are needed or warranted. Three basic alternatives in approaching international markets are available:

1. Make no special provisions for the international marketplace but, rather, identify potential target markets and then choose products that can easily be marketed with little or no modification.

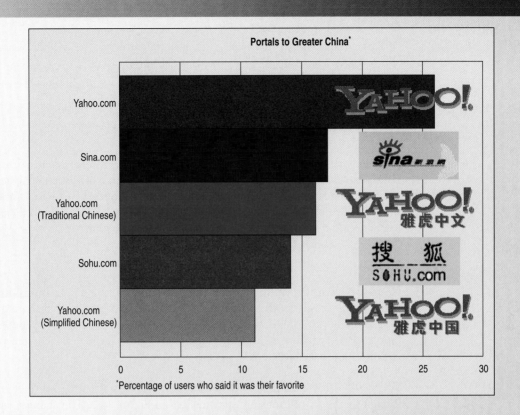

Portals to Greater China*

*Percentage of users who said it was their favorite

Source: "Yahoo Japan Learns from Parent's Achievements and Errors," *The Wall Street Journal,* December 11, 2000, A28; "The Word at Yahoo! Yikes!" *Business Week,* October 30, 2000, 63; "Yahoo! Makes Grass-Roots Push in Asia," *The Wall Street Journal,* August 1, 2000, B9; "AOL's Big Assault on Latin America Hits Snags in Brazil," *The Wall Street Journal,* July 11, 2000, A1, A16; "Lycos Belatedly Scales Great Wall," *The Wall Street Journal,* May 23, 2000, A21; "For U.S. Internet Portals, the Next Big Battleground Is Overseas," *The Wall Street Journal,* March 23, 2000, B1, B4; and "Shopping Around the Web," *The Economist,* February 26, 2000, S-54. See also: **http://www.yahoo.com; www.excite.com; www.lycos.com; www.aol.com.**

2. Adapt to local conditions in each and every target market (the multidomestic approach).
3. Incorporate differences into a regional or global strategy that will allow for local differences in implementation (globalization approach).

In today's environment, standardization usually means cross-national strategies rather than a policy of viewing foreign markets as secondary and therefore not important enough to have products adapted for them. Ideally, the international marketer should think globally and act locally, focusing on neither extreme: full standardization or full localization. Global thinking requires flexibility in exploiting good ideas and products on a worldwide basis regardless of their origin. Factors that encourage standardization or adaptation are summarized in Table 13.2.

Factors Affecting Adaptation   Even when marketing programs are based on highly standardized ideas and strategies, they depend on three sets of variables: (1) the market(s) targeted; (2) the product and its characteristics; and (3) company characteristics, including factors such as resources and policy.

TABLE 13.2

Standardization versus Adaptation

Factors Encouraging Standardization	Factors Encouraging Adaptation
• Economies in product R & D	• Differing use conditions
• Economies of scale in production	• Government and regulatory influences
• Economies in marketing	• Differing buyer behavior patterns
• Control of marketing programs	• Local initiative and motivation in implementation
• "Shrinking" of the world marketplace	• Adherence to the marketing concept

Questions of adaptation have no easy answers. Marketers in many firms rely on decision-support systems to aid in program adaptation, while others consider every situation independently. All goods must, of course, conform to environmental conditions over which the marketer has no control. Further, the international marketer may use adaptation to enhance its competitiveness in the marketplace.

Product Policy

Goods or services form the core of the firm's international operations. Its success depends on how well goods satisfy needs and wants and how well they are differentiated from those of the competition. This section focuses on product and product-line adaptation to foreign markets as well as product counterfeiting as a current problem facing international marketers.

Factors in Product Adaptation
Factors affecting product adaptation to foreign market conditions are summarized in Figure 13.2. The changes vary from minor ones, such as translation of a user's manual, to major ones, such as a more economical version of the product. Many of the factors have an impact on product selection as well as product adaptation for a given market.

FIGURE 13.2   Factors Affecting Product Adaptation Decisions

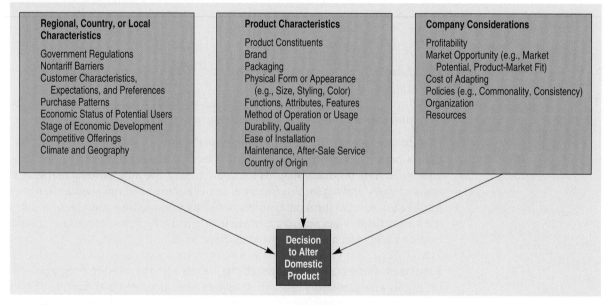

Source: Adapted from V. Yorio, *Adapting Products for Export* (New York: The Conference Board, 1983), 7.

A detailed examination of 174 consumer packaged goods destined for developing countries showed that, on the average, 4.1 changes per product were made in terms of brand name, packaging, measurement units, labeling, constituents, product features, and usage instructions. Only one out of ten products was transferred without modification. Some of the changes were mandatory, some discretionary.[12]

Regional, Country, or Local Characteristics   Typically, the market environment mandates the majority of product modifications. However, the most stringent requirements often result from government regulations. Some of the requirements may serve no purpose other than a political one (such as protection of domestic industry or response to political pressures). Because of the sovereignty of nations, individual firms must comply, but they can influence the situation either by lobbying directly or through industry associations to have the issue raised during trade negotiations. Government regulations may be spelled out, but firms need to be ever vigilant for changes and exceptions. The member countries of the European Economic Area are imposing standards in more than 10,000 product categories ranging from toys to tractor seats. While companies such as Murray Manufacturing have had to change their products to comply with the standards (in Murray's case, making its lawnmowers quieter), they will be able to produce one European product in the future. Overall, U.S. producers may be forced to improve quality of all their products because some product rules require adoption of an overall system approved by the International Standards Organization (ISO).[13] By 1999, more than 272,000 ISO 9000 certificates (relating to product and process quality) had been issued worldwide, 33,500 of those in North America.[14]

Product decisions made by marketers of consumer products are especially affected by local behavior, tastes, attitudes, and traditions—all reflecting the marketer's need to gain the customer's approval. A knowledge of cultural and psychological differences may be the key to success. For example, Brazilians rarely eat breakfast or they eat it at home; therefore, Dunkin' Donuts markets doughnuts as snacks, as dessert, and for parties. To further appeal to Brazilians, doughnuts are made with local fruit fillings such as papaya and guava. Chinese and Western consumers share similar standards when it comes to evaluating brand names. Both appreciate a brand name that is catchy, memorable, distinct, and says something indicative of the product. But, because of cultural and linguistic factors, Chinese consumers expect more in terms of how the names are spelled, written, and styled, and whether they are considered lucky. PepsiCo, Inc., introducted Cheetos in the Chinese market under a Chinese name, *qi duo*, roughly pronounced "chee-do," that translates as "many surprises."[15]

Often no concrete product changes are needed, only a change in the product's **positioning.** Positioning is the perception by consumers of the firm's brand in relation to competitors' brands; that is, the mental image a brand, or the company as a whole, evokes. Coca-Cola took a risk in marketing Diet Coke in Japan because the population is not overweight by Western standards. Further, Japanese women do not like to drink anything clearly labeled as a diet product. The company changed the name to Coke Light and subtly shifted the promotional theme from "weight loss" to "figure maintenance."

Nontariff barriers include product standards, testing or approval procedures, subsidies for local products, and bureaucratic red tape. The nontariff barriers affecting product adjustments usually concern elements outside the core product. For example, France requires the use of the French language "in any offer, presentation, advertisement, written or spoken, instructions for use, specification or guarantee terms for goods or services, as well as for invoices and receipts." Because nontariff barriers are usually in place to keep foreign products out or to protect domestic producers, getting around them may be the single toughest problem for the international marketer.

The monitoring of competitors' product features, as well as determining what has to be done to meet and beat them, is critical to product-adaptation decisions. Competitive offerings may provide a baseline against which resources can be measured—

for example, they may help to determine what it takes to reach a critical market share in a given competitive situation. American Hospital Supply, a Chicago-based producer of medical equipment, adjusts its product in a preemptive way by making products that are hard to duplicate. As a result, the firm increased sales and earnings in Japan about 40 percent a year over a ten-year period.

Management must take into account the stage of economic development of the overseas market. As a country's economy advances, buyers are in a better position to buy and to demand more sophisticated products and product versions. On the other hand, the situation in some developing markets may require **backward innovation;** that is, the market may require a drastically simplified version of the firm's product because of lack of purchasing power or of usage conditions. Economic conditions may shift rapidly, thus warranting change in the product or the product line. During the Asian currency crisis, McDonald's replaced French fries with rice in its Indonesian restaurants due to cost considerations. With the collapse of the local rupiah, potatoes, the only ingredient McDonald's imports to Indonesia, quintupled in price. In addition, a new rice and egg dish was introduced to maintain as many customers as possible.[16]

Product Characteristics Product characteristics are the inherent features of the product offering, whether actual or perceived. The inherent characteristics of products, and the benefits they provide to consumers in the various markets in which they are marketed, make certain products good candidates for standardization—and others not.

The international marketer has to make sure that products do not contain ingredients that might violate legal requirements or religious or social customs. DEP Corporation, a Los Angeles manufacturer with $19 million in annual sales of hair and skin products, takes particular pains to make sure that no Japan-bound products contain formaldehyde, an ingredient commonly used in the United States, but illegal in Japan. Where religion or custom determines consumption, ingredients may have to be replaced for the product to be acceptable. In Islamic countries, for example, vegetable shortening has to be substituted for animal fats. In deference to Hindu and Muslim beliefs, McDonald's "Maharaja Mac" is made with mutton in India.

Packaging is an area where firms generally do make modifications.[17] Due to the longer time that products spend in channels of distribution, international companies, especially those marketing food products, have used more expensive packaging materials and/or more expensive transportation modes for export shipments. Food processors have solved the problem by using airtight, reclosable containers that seal out moisture and other contaminants.

The promotional aspect of packaging relates primarily to labeling. The major adjustments concern legally required bilinguality, as in Canada (French and English), Belgium (French and Flemish), and Finland (Finnish and Swedish). Other governmental requirements include more informative labeling of products for consumer protection and education. Inadequate identification, failure to use the required languages, or inadequate or incorrect descriptions printed on the labels may all cause problems. Increasingly, environmental concerns are having an impact on packaging decisions. On the one hand, governments want to reduce the amount of packaging waste by encouraging marketers to adopt the four environmentally correct Rs: redesign, reduce, reuse, and recycle.[18] On the other hand, many markets have sizable segments of consumers who are concerned enough about protecting the environment to change their consumption patterns, which has resulted in product modifications such as the introduction of recyclable yogurt containers from marketers such as Dany and Danone in Europe.

Brand names convey the image of the good or service. Offhand, brands may seem to be one of the most standardizable items in the product offering. However, the establishment of worldwide brands is difficult; how can a marketer establish world brands when the firm sells 800 products in more than 200 countries, most of them under different names? This is the situation of Gillette. A typical example is Silkience hair conditioner, which is sold as Soyance in France, Sientel in Italy, and Silkience in Germany. Standardizing the name to reap promotional benefits is difficult because names have become established in each market, and the action would lead to objections from local managers or even government. In response, marketers have standardized all other possible elements of brand aesthetics, such as color, symbols, and packaging.

The product offered in the dometic market may not be operable in the foreign market. One of the major differences faced by appliance manufacturers is electrical power systems. In some cases, variations may exist within a country, such as Brazil. Some companies have adjusted their products to operate in different systems; for example, VCR equipment can be adjusted to record and play back on different color systems.

When a product that is sold internationally requires repairs, parts, or service, the problems of obtaining, training, and holding a sophisticated engineering or repair staff are not easy to solve. If the product breaks down and the repair arrangements are not up to standard, the product image will suffer. In some cases, products abroad may not even be used for their intended purpose and thus may require not only modifications in product configuration but also in service frequency. For instance, snowplows exported from the United States are used to remove sand from driveways in Saudi Arabia.

The country of origin of a product, typically communicated by the phrase "made in (country)," has considerable influence on quality perceptions. The perception of products manufactured in certain countries is affected by a built-in positive or negative assumption about quality. One study of machine tool buyers found that the United States and Germany were rated higher than Japan, with Brazil rated below all three of them.[19] These types of findings indicate that steps must be taken by the international marketer to overcome or at least neutralize biases. The issue is especially important to developing countries that need to increase exports, and for importers who source products from countries different from where they are sold.[20]

Company Considerations   Company policy will often determine the presence and degree of adaptation. Discussions of product adaptation often end with the question, "Is it worth it?" The answer depends on the company's ability to control costs, to correctly estimate market potential, and, finally, to secure profitability. The decision to adapt should be preceded by a thorough analysis of the market. Formal market research with primary data collection and/or testing is warranted. From the financial standpoint, some companies have specific return-on-investment levels (for example, 25 percent) to be satisfied before adaptation. Others let the requirement vary as a function of the market considered and also the time in the market—that is, profitability may be initially compromised for proper market entry.

Most companies aim for consistency in their market efforts. This means that all products must fit in terms of quality, price, and user perceptions. Consistency may be difficult to attain, for example, in the area of warranties. Warranties can be uniform only if use conditions do not vary drastically and if the company is able to deliver equally on its promise anywhere it has a presence.

Product Line Management   International marketers' product lines consist of local, regional, and global brands. In a given market, an exporter's product line, typically shorter than domestically, concentrates on the most profitable products. Product lines may vary dramatically from one market to another depending on the extent of the firm's operations. Some firms at first cater only to a particular market segment, then eventually expand to cover an entire market. For example, Japanese auto manufacturers moved into the highly profitable luxury car segment after establishing a strong position in the world small-car segment.

The domestic market is not the only source of new-product ideas for the international marketer, nor is it the only place where they are developed.[21] Some products may be developed elsewhere for worldwide consumption because of an advantage in skills. Colgate-Palmolive has set up **centers of excellence** around the world; in hair care, they are located in Paris, France, and Bangkok, Thailand. Ford Europe was assigned the task to develop the Ford Focus, which was then introduced to North America a year later.

Sensitivity to local requirements and tastes also has to be reflected in the company's product line. In Brazil, Levi Strauss developed a line of jeans exclusively for women there, who prefer ultratight jeans. However, what is learned in one market can often be adopted in another. Levi's line of chino pants and casual wear originated in the company's Argentine unit and was applied to loosely cut pants by its Japanese subsidiary. The company's U.S. operation adopted both in 1986, and the line became global in the 1990s.[22] This sensitivity also has to exist in how products are developed. With the Ford Focus, the Europeans maintained an overall leadership role but key responsibilities were divided. The U.S. side took over automatic transmissions, with Europe handling the manual version.[23]

Product Counterfeiting   About $200 billion in domestic and export sales are estimated to be lost by U.S. companies annually because of product counterfeiting and trademark patent infringement of consumer and industrial products.[24] The hardest hit are software, entertainment, and pharmaceutical sectors. Counterfeit goods are any goods bearing an unauthorized representation of a trademark, patented invention, or copyrighted work that is legally protected in the country where it is marketed.

The practice of product counterfeiting has spread to high technology and services from the traditionally counterfeited products: high-visibility, strong brand name consumer goods. In addition, a new dimension has emerged to complicate the situation. Previously, the only concern was whether a firm's product was being counterfeited; now, management has to worry about whether raw materials and components purchased for production are themselves real.[25]

Four types of action that can be taken against counterfeiting are legislative action, bilateral and multilateral negotiations, joint private sector action, and measures taken by individual firms. Governments have enacted special legislation and set country-specific negotiation objectives for reciprocity and retaliatory options for intellectual property protection.

In today's environment, firms are taking more aggressive steps to protect themselves. Victimized firms are not only losing sales but also goodwill in the longer term if customers, believing they are getting the real product, unknowingly end up with a copy of inferior quality. In addition to the normal measures of registering trademarks and copyrights, firms are taking steps in product development to prevent the copying of trademarked goods. For example, new authentication materials in labeling are virtually impossible to duplicate. Jointly, companies have formed organizations to lobby for legislation and to act as information clearinghouses.

The Business Software Alliance (www.bsa.org) is an international organization representing leading software and e-commerce developers in 65 countries around the world.

Pricing Policy

Pricing is the only element in the marketing mix that is revenue generating; all of the others are costs. It should therefore be used as an active instrument of strategy in the major areas of marketing decision making. Pricing in the international environment is more complicated than in the domestic market, however, because of such factors as government influence, different currencies, and additional costs. International pricing situations can be divided into four general categories: export pricing, foreign market pricing, price coordination, and intracompany, or transfer, pricing.

Export Pricing   Three general price-setting strategies in international marketing are a standard worldwide price; dual pricing, which differentiates between domestic and export prices; and market-differentiated pricing.[26] The first two are cost-oriented pricing methods that are relatively simple to establish, are easy to understand, and cover all of the necessary costs. **Standard worldwide pricing** is based on average unit costs of fixed, variable, and export-related costs.

In **dual pricing,** domestic and export prices are differentiated, and two approaches are available: the **cost-plus method** and the **marginal cost method.** The cost-plus strategy involves the actual costs, that is, a full allocation of domestic and foreign costs to the product. Although this type of pricing ensures margins, the final price may put the product beyond the reach of the customer. As a result, some exporters resort to flexible cost-plus strategy, wherein discounts are provided when necessary as a result of customer type, intensity of competition, or size of order. The marginal cost method considers the direct costs of producing and selling for export as the floor beneath which prices cannot be set. Fixed costs for plants, R&D, domestic overhead, and domestic marketing costs are disregarded. An exporter can thus lower export prices to be competitive in markets that otherwise might have been considered beyond access.

On the other hand, **market-differentiated pricing** is based on a demand-oriented strategy and is thus more consistent with the marketing concept. This method also allows consideration of competitive forces in setting export price. The major problem is the exporter's perennial dilemma: lack of information. Therefore, in most cases, marginal costs provide a basis for competitive comparisons, on which the export price is set.

In preparing a quotation, the exporter must be careful to take into account unique export-related costs and, if possible, include them. They are in addition to the normal costs shared with the domestic side. They include:

1. The cost incurred in modifying the good for foreign markets.
2. Operational costs of the export operation. Examples are personnel, market research, additional shipping and insurance costs, communications costs with foreign customers, and overseas promotional costs.
3. Costs incurred in entering foreign markets. These include tariffs and taxes; risks associated with a buyer in a different market (mainly commercial credit risks and political risks); and dealing in other than the exporter's domestic currency—that is, foreign exchange risk.

The combined effect of both clear-cut and hidden costs results in export prices far in excess of domestic prices. This is called **price escalation.** Dollar-based prices may also become expensive to local buyers in the case of currency devaluation. For example, during the Asian currency turmoil, many companies in Indonesia, Malaysia, South Korea, and Thailand scaled down their buying. The exporter has many alternatives under these circumstances, such as stretching out payment terms, cutting prices, or bringing scaled-down, more affordable products to the affected markets.[27]

Inexpensive imports often trigger accusations of **dumping**—that is, selling goods overseas for less than in the exporter's home market, at a price below the cost of production, or both. Dumping ranges from predatory to unintentional. Predatory dumping is the tactic of a foreign firm that intentionally sells at a loss in another country to increase its market share at the expense of domestic producers. This amounts to an international price war. Unintentional dumping is the result of time lags between the date of sales transactions, shipment, and arrival. Prices, including exchange rates, can change in such a way that the final sales price is below the cost of production or below the price prevailing in the exporter's home market.

In the United States, domestic producers may petition the government to impose antidumping duties on imports alleged to be dumped. The remedy is a duty equal to the dumping margin. International agreements and U.S. law provide for countervailing duties. They may be imposed on imports that are found to be subsidized by foreign governments. They are designed to offset the advantages imports would otherwise receive from the subsidy.

Foreign Market Pricing Pricing within the individual markets in which the firm operates is determined by: (1) corporate objectives; (2) costs; (3) customer behavior and market conditions; (4) market structure; and (5) environmental constraints. All of these factors vary from country to country, and pricing policies of the multinational corporation must vary as well. Despite arguments in favor of uniform pricing in multinational markets, price discrimination is an essential characteristic of the pricing policies of firms conducting business in differing markets. In a study of 42 U.S.-based multinational corporations, the major problem areas they reported in making pricing decisions were meeting competition, cost, lack of competitive information, distribution and channel factors, and governmental barriers.[28]

Studies have shown that non-U.S. based companies allow their U.S. subsidiaries considerable freedom in pricing due to the size and unique features of the market. Further, it has been argued that these subsidiaries control the North American market and that distances create a natural barrier against arbitrage practices (i.e., customers going for the lowest price) that would be more likely to emerge in Europe. However, many argue that price coordination has to be worldwide as a result of increasing levels of economic integration efforts around the world.

Price Coordination The issue of standard worldwide pricing may be mostly a theoretical one because of the influence of environments. If standardization is sought for, it relates more to price levels and the use of pricing as a positioning tool.

Calls for price coordination have increased especially after the introduction of the euro in 12 EU countries. The single currency will make prices completely transparent for all buyers. If discrepancies are not justifiable due to market differences such as consumption preferences, competition, or government interference, cross-border purchases will occur. The simplest solution would be to have one euro-based price throughout the market. However, given significant differences up to 500 percent, that solution would lead to significant losses in sales and/or profits, as a single price would likely be closer to the lower-priced countries' level. The recommended approach is a pricing corridor that considers existing country-specific prices while optimizing the profits at a pan-European level.[29] Such a corridor defines the maximum and minimum prices that a country organization can charge—enough to allow flexibility as a result of differences in price elasticities and competition, but not enough to attract people to engage in cross-border shopping that starts at price differences of 20 percent or higher.[30] This approach moves pricing authority away from country managers to regional management and requires changes in management systems and incentive structures.

Significant price gaps lead to the emergence of **gray markets**/parallel importation. The term refers to brand-name imports that enter a country legally but outside regular, authorized distribution channels. The gray market is fueled by companies that sell goods in foreign markets at prices that are far lower than prices charged to, for example, U.S. distributors, and by one strong currency, such as the dollar or the yen. The gray market in the United States has flourished in cars, watches, and even baby powder, cameras, and chewing gum. The retail value of gray markets in the United States has been estimated at $6 billion to $10 billion. This phenomenon not only harms the company financially but also may harm its reputation, because authorized distributors often refuse to honor warranties on items bought through the gray market. Cars bought through the gray market in the United States, for example, may not pass EPA inspections and thus may cause major expense to the unsuspecting buyer.[31]

The proponents of gray marketing argue for their right to "free trade" by pointing to manufacturers who are both overproducing and overpricing in some markets. The main beneficiaries are consumers, who benefit from lower prices, and discount distributors, who now have access to the good. Companies can combat gray marketing through strategic interference. For example, companies can make sure authorized dealers do not engage in transshipments. Companies can also promote the deficiencies in gray-marketed goods which may not carry a full warranties or after-sales service.

Transfer Pricing   Transfer, or intracompany, pricing is the pricing of sales to members of the corporate family. The overall competitive and financial position of the firm forms the basis of any pricing policy. In this, transfer pricing plays a key role. Intracorporate sales can easily change consolidated global results because they often are one of the most important ongoing decision areas in a company.

Four main transfer-pricing possibilities have merged over time: (1) transfer at direct cost; (2) transfer at direct cost plus additional expenses; (3) transfer at a price derived from end-market prices; and (4) transfer at an **arm's length price,** or the price that unrelated parties would have reached on the same transaction. Doing business overseas requires coping with complexities of environmental peculiarities, the effect of which can be alleviated by manipulating transfer prices. Factors that call for adjustments include taxes, import duties, inflationary tendencies, unstable governments, and other regulations.[32] For example, high transfer prices on goods shipped to a subsidiary and low ones on goods imported from it will result in minimizing the tax liability of a subsidiary operating in a country with a high income tax. Tax liability thus results not only from the absolute tax rate but also from differences in how income is computed. On the other hand, a higher transfer price may have an effect on the import duty, especially if it is assessed on an ad valorem basis. Exceeding a certain threshold may boost the duty substantially and thus have a negative impact on the subsidiary's posture.

Quite often the multinational corporation is put in a difficult position. U.S. authorities may think the transfer price is too low, whereas the foreign entity (especially a less-developed country) may perceive it to be too high. In a survey of 400 multinational companies, respondents facing transfer pricing disputes were able to defend their profit to local tax authorities in only half of the inquiries.[33]

In the host environments, the concern of the multinational corporation is to maintain its status as a good corporate citizen. Many corporations, in drafting multinational codes of conduct, have specified that intracorporate pricing will follow the arm's length principle. Multinationals have also been found to closely abide by tax regulations governing transfer pricing.[34] The OECD has issued transfer pricing guidelines including methodology and documentation scenarios to assist in the compliance process.

Distribution Policy

Channels of distribution provide the essential links that connect producers and customers. The channel decision is the longest term of the marketing mix decisions in that it cannot be readily changed. In addition, it involves relinquishing some of the control the firm has over the marketing of its products. The two factors make choosing the right channel structure a crucial decision. Properly structured and staffed, the distribution system will function more as one rather than as a collection of often quite different units.

Channel Design   The term *channel design* refers to the length and width of the channel employed. **Channel design** is determined by factors that can be summarized as the 11 Cs: customer, culture, competition, company, character, capital, cost, coverage, control, continuity, and communication. While there are no standard answers to channel design, the international marketer can use the 11 Cs as a checklist to determine the proper approach to reach target audiences before selecting channel members to fill the roles. The first three factors are givens in that the company must adjust its approach to the existing structures. The other eight are controllable to a certain extent by the marketer.

The demographic and psychographic characteristics of targeted *customers* will form the basis for channel-design decisions. Answers to questions such as what customers need as well as why, when, and how they buy are used to determine ways in which products should be made available to generate a competitive advantage.

Anheuser-Busch's success in Japan began, for example, when Suntory, one of the country's largest liquor distillers, acquired the importing rights. One important aspect of Suntory's marketing plan was to stress distribution of Budweiser in discos, pubs, and other night spots where Japan's affluent, well-traveled youth gather. Young people in Japan are influenced by American culture and adapt more readily to new products than do older Japanese. Taking advantage of this fact, Suntory concentrated its efforts on one generation. The result was that on-premise sales led to major off-premise (retail outlet) sales as well.

Customer characteristics may cause one product to be distributed through two different types of channels. All sales of Caterpillar's earthmoving equipment are handled by independent dealers, except for sales to the U.S. government and the People's Republic of China, which are direct.

The marketer must analyze existing channel structures, or what might be called the distribution *culture* of a market. For example, the general nature of the Japanese distribution system presents one of the major reasons for the apparent failure of foreign companies to penetrate the market.[35] In most cases, the international marketer must adjust to existing structures. In Finland, for example, 92 percent of all distribution of nondurable consumer goods is through four wholesale chains. In the United Kingdom, major retail chains control markets. Without their support, no significant penetration of the market is possible.

Foreign legislation affecting distributors and agents is an essential part of the distribution culture of a market. For example, legislation may require foreign companies to be represented only by firms that are 100 percent locally owned. Some countries have prohibited the use of dealers so as to protect consumers from abuses in which intermediaries have engaged.

Channels used by *competitors* form another basis for plans. First, channels utilized by the competition may make up the only distribution system that is accepted both by the trade and by consumers. In this case, the international marketer's task is to use the structure more effectively and efficiently as Wal-Mart has been able to do in Europe. An alternate strategy is to use a totally different distribution approach from the competition and hope to develop a competitive advantage in that manner as IKEA has been able to do with its use of supermarketing concepts in furniture retail. A new approach will have to be carefully analyzed and tested against the cultural, political, and legal environments in which it is to be introduced. In some cases, all feasible channels may be blocked by domestic competitors through contractual agreements or other means.

No channel of distribution can be properly selected unless it meets the requirements set by overall *company objectives* for market share and profitability. Sometimes management may simply want to use a particular channel of distribution, even though no sound business basis exists for the decision. Some management goals may have conflicting results. When investment in the restaurant business in Asia and Latin America has been liberalized, a number of U.S. fast-food chains will typically rush in to capitalize on the development. The companies have attempted to establish mass sales as soon as possible by opening numerous restaurants in the busiest sections of several cities. Unfortunately, control has proven to be quite difficult because of the sheer number of openings over a relatively short period of time.

The *character* of the good will have an impact on the design of the channel. Generally, the more specialized, expensive, bulky, or perishable the product and the more it may require after-sale service, the more likely the channel is to be relatively short. Staple items, such as soap, tend to have longer channels, while services have short channels. The type of channel chosen has to match the overall positioning of the product in the market. Changes in overall market conditions, such as currency fluctuations, may require changes in distribution as well. An increase in the value of the dollar may cause a repositioning of the marketed product as a luxury item, necessitating an appropriate channel (such as an upscale department store) for its distribution.

The term *capital* is used to describe the financial requirements in setting up a channel system. The international marketer's financial strength will determine the type of channel and the basis on which channel relationships will be built. The stronger the marketer's finances, the more able the firm is to establish channels it either owns or controls. Intermediaries' requirements for beginning inventories, selling on a consignment basis, preferential loans, and need for training will all have an impact on the type of approach chosen by the international marketer.

Closely related to the capital dimension is *cost*—that is, the expenditure incurred in maintaining a channel once it is established. Costs will naturally vary over the life cycle of the relationship as well as over the life cycle of the product marketed. An example of the costs involved is promotional monies spent by a distributor for the marketer's product. Costs may also be incurred in protecting the company's distributors against adverse market conditions. A number of U.S. manufacturers helped their distributors maintain competitive prices through subsidies when the exchange rate for the U.S. dollar caused pricing problems.

The term *coverage* is used to describe both the number of areas in which the marketer's products are represented and the quality of that representation. Coverage, therefore, is two dimensional in that both horizontal and vertical coverage need to be considered in channel design. The number of areas to be covered depends on the dispersion of demand in the market and also the time elapsed since the product's introduction to the market. A company typically enters a market with one local distributor, but, as volume expands, the distribution base often has to be adjusted.

The use of intermediaries will automatically lead to loss of some *control* over the marketing of the firm's products. The looser the relationship is between the marketer and the intermediaries, the less control can be exerted. The longer the channel, the more difficult it becomes for the marketer to have a final say over pricing, promotion, and the types of outlets in which the product will be made available.

Nurturing *continuity* rests heavily on the marketer because foreign distributors may have a more short-term view of the relationship. For example, Japanese wholesalers believe that it is important for manufacturers to follow up initial success with continuous improvement of the product. If such improvements are not forthcoming, competitors are likely to enter the market with similar, but lower-priced, products and the wholesalers of the imported product will turn to the Japanese suppliers.[36]

Communication provides the exchange of information that is essential to the functioning of the channel. Proper communication will perform important roles for the international marketer. It will help convey the marketer's goals to the distributors, help solve conflict situations, and aid in the overall marketing of the product. Communication is a two-way process that does not permit the marketer to dictate to intermediaries. Sometimes the planned program may not work because of a lack of communication. Prices may not be competitive; promotional materials may be obsolete or inaccurate and not well received overall.

Selection and Screening of Intermediaries Once the basic design of the channel has been determined, the international marketer must begin a search to fill the defined roles with the best available candidates. Choices will have to be made within the framework of the company's overall philosophy on distributors versus agents, as well as whether the company will use an indirect or direct approach to foreign markets.

Firms that have successful international distribution attest to the importance of finding top representatives. For companies such as Loctite, whose adhesives require high levels of technical selling skills, only the best distributors in a given market will do. The undertaking should be held in the same regard as recruiting and hiring within the company because "an ineffective foreign distributor can set you back years; it is almost better to have no distributor than a bad one in a major market."[37]

Various sources exist to assist the marketer in locating intermediary candidates. One of the easiest and most economical ways is to use the service of governmental agencies. The U.S. Department of Commerce has various services that can assist firms in identifying suitable representatives abroad; some have been designed specifically for that purpose. A number of private sources are also available to the international marketer. Trade directories, such as those by Dun & Bradstreet, usually list foreign representatives geographically and by product classification. Telephone directories, especially the yellow page sections or editions, can provide distributor lists. Although not detailed, the listings will give addresses and an indication of the products sold. The firm can solicit the support of some of its facilitating agencies, such as banks, advertising agencies, shipping lines, and airlines. The marketer can take an even more direct approach by buying advertising space to solicit representation. The advertisements typically indicate the type of support the marketer will be able to give to its distributor.

Intermediaries can be screened on their performance and professionalism. An intermediary's performance can be evaluated on the basis of financial standing and sales as well as the likely fit it would provide in terms of its existing product lines and coverage. Professionalism can be assessed through reputation and overall standing in the business community.

International Company Profiles

Why take business risks when you don't have to?

Take the gamble out of exporting to new customers abroad by using a U.S. Department of Commerce International Company Profile (ICP). These thorough background checks on your potential clients will reduce your risk and allow you to enter new business relationships with confidence.

Commercial specialists in U.S. embassies and consulates abroad will conduct an investigation for you and deliver the results in 30 to 45 days, at a very reasonable cost. Reports include up-to-date information on your potential clients, such as:

- bank and trade references
- principals, key officers and managers
- product lines
- number of employees
- financial data
- sales volume
- reputation
- market outlook

An International Company Profile may also include information on:

- subsidiary/parent relationships
- recent news items about the firm
- the firms' U.S. customers
- operational problems
- activities of prominent owners
- branch locations

The commercial specialists abroad who conduct your research will also give you their recommendation on whether you should enter a business relationship with the subject firm, and, if so, on what basis. Your request is held in strict confidence–the subject firm does not know who ordered the report.

Due to our in-country contacts and worldwide network of commercial professionals, International Company Profiles often provide information not available from other investigative services. And your ICP will qualify as one of the reports required for you to obtain foreign credit insurance coverage. (International Company Profiles may not be available in countries with well developed commercial credit reporting agencies.)

For more information on International Company Profiles, contact the U.S. Department of Commerce office nearest you.

Source: The Commercial Service (**www.ita.doc.gov/uscs**).

TABLE 13.3 — Managing Relations with Overseas Distributors

High Export Performance Inhibitors →	Bring →	Remedy Lies In
Separate ownership	• Divided loyalties • Seller-buyer atmosphere • Unclear future intentions	Offering good incentives, helpful support schemes, discussing plans frankly, and interacting in a mutually beneficial way
Geographic and cultural separation	• Communication blocks • Negative attitudes toward foreigners • Physical distribution strains	Making judicious use of two-way visits, establishing a well-managed communication program
Different rules of law	• Vertical trading restrictions • Dismissal difficulties	Complying fully with the law, drafting a strong distributor agreement

Source: Philip J. Rosson, "Source Factors in Manufacture—Overseas Distributor Relationships in International Marketing," in International Marketing Management, ed. Erdener Kaynak (New York: Praeger, 1984), 95.

Managing the Channel Relationship A channel relationship can be likened to a marriage in that it brings together two independent entities that have shared goals. For the relationship to work, each party has to be open about its expectations and openly communicate changes perceived in the other's behavior that might be contrary to the agreement. A framework for managing channel relationships is provided in Table 13.3.

The complicating factors that separate the two parties fall into three categories: ownership, geographic and cultural distance, and different rules of law. Rather than lament their existence, both parties must take strong action to remedy them. Often the first major step is for both parties to acknowledge that differences exist.

E-Commerce As shown in Table 13.4, **e-commerce,** the ability to offer goods and services over the web, is expected to grow at a compound annual rate of 100 percent in the next five years around the world. While the United States accounts for the majority of e-commerce activity, the non-U.S. portion is expected to double in the next five years with Western Europe providing the area with most significant growth. A survey by KPMG Management Consulting in Europe shows that more than one-third of the 500 European-based large and medium-sized companies reported Internet sales in 1998. The same group states that those sales represent about 2 percent of their total sales, a figure they expect will jump to 12 percent in three years and 20 percent in five years.[38]

Many companies willing to enter e-commerce will not have to do it on their own. Hub sites (also known as virtual malls or digital intermediaries) will bring together buyers, sellers, distributors, and transaction payment processors in one single marketplace, making convenience the key attraction. The share of such hubs in retail e-commerce increased from 15 percent in 1998 to 26 percent in 1999 with entities such as Compare.net (**www.compare.net**), Priceline.com (**www.priceline.com**), eBay (**www. ebay. com**), and VerticalNet (**www.verticalnet.com**) leading the way.[39]

TABLE 13.4 — Worldwide E-Commerce Revenue by Region

Region	1998	2003	Compound Annual Growth
United States	37.25	707.92	80%
Western Europe	5.61	430.37	138
Japan	1.98	44.94	87
Asia/Pacific	0.69	27.51	109
Rest of world	1.41	53.02	107

Source: International Data Corporation, "The Globalization of e-Commerce," August 1999.

It should be noted that as soon as customers have the ability to access a company through the Internet, the company itself must be prepared to provide 24-hour order taking and customer service, have the regulatory and customs-handling expertise to deliver internationally, and have an in-depth understanding of marketing environments for the further development of the business relationship.[40] The instantaneous interactivity users experience will also be translated into an expectation of expedient delivery of answers and products ordered. Many people living outside the United States who purchase online expect U.S.-style service. However, in many cases, these shoppers may find that shipping is not even available outside of the United States.

The challenges faced in terms of response and delivery capabilities can be overcome through outsourcing services or by building international distribution networks. Air express carriers such as DHL, FedEX, and UPS offer full-service packages that leverage their own Internet infrastructure with customs clearance and e-mail shipment notification. If a company needs help in order fulfillment and customer support, logistics centers offer warehousing and inventory management services as well as same-day delivery from in-country stocks. DHL, for example, has 7 express logistics centers and 45 strategic parts centers worldwide, with key centers in Bahrain for the Middle East, Brussels for Europe, and Singapore for Asia-Pacific. Some companies elect to build their own international distribution networks. Both QVC, a televised shopping service, and Amazon.com, an online retailer of books, have distribution centers in Britain and Germany to take advantage of the European Internet audience and to fulfill more quickly and cheaply the orders generated by their web sites.

Transactions and the information they provide of the buyer allow for more customization and service by region, market, or even by individual customer. One of the largest online sellers, Dell Computer, builds for its corporate customers with more than 400 employees a Premier Page that is linked to the customer's intranet, allowing approved employees to configure PCs, pay for them, and track their delivery status. Premier Pages also provide access to instant technical support and Dell sales representatives. Presently there are 5,000 companies with such service and $5 million of Dell PCs are ordered every day.[41]

Although English has long been perceived as the *lingua franca* of the web, the share of non-English speakers worldwide increased to 60 percent of all the users in 1999. It has also been shown that web users are three times more likely to buy when the offering is made in their own language.[42] However, not even the largest of firms can serve all markets with a full line of their products. Getting a web site translated and running is an expensive proposition, and, if done correctly, time-consuming as well. If the site is well developed, it will naturally lead to expectations that order fulfillment will be of equal caliber. Therefore, any World Wide Web strategy has to be tied closely to the company's overall growth strategy in world markets.

A number of hurdles and uncertainties are keeping companies out of global markets or from exploiting them to their full potential. Some argue that the World Wide Web does not live up to its name, since it is mostly a tool for the United States and Europe. Yet, as Internet penetration levels increase in the near future due to technological advances, improvements in many countries' web infrastructures, and customer acceptance, e-business will become truly global. As a matter of fact, in some cases, emerging markets may provide a chance to try out new approaches because the markets and the marketers in them are not burdened by history as seen in the Global Perspective 13.2.

The marketer has to be sensitive to the governmental role in e-commerce. No real consensus exists on the taxation of e-commerce, especially in the case of cross-border transactions. While the United States and the EU have agreed not to impose new taxes on sales through the Internet, there is no uniformity in the international taxation of transactions.[43] Other governments believe, however, that they have something to gain by levying new e-taxes. Until more firm legal precedents are established, international marketers should be aware of their potential tax liabilities and prepare for their im-

GLOBAL PERSPECTIVE 13.2

E-Commerce in Emerging Markets

General Motors is testing electronic commerce strategies in overseas markets such as Taiwan, where it already sells 10 percent of its vehicles through the Internet and began to build cars to order starting in 2000. "Emerging markets are a lab for us," said Mark Hogan who heads the new E-GM unit. "We do not have a lot of bricks and mortar in these markets, so they provide perfect conditions for us to learn from." The company hopes to sell about 30 percent of units in the next several years.

Although the United States has the greatest potential for online buying due to large customer base, channel culture reasons prevent the company from realizing it. The U.S. retail system consists of 20,000 dealers protected in many cases by state franchise laws that stand in the way of Internet sales. Additionally, automakers' production facilities cannot accommodate real-time Internet orders.

However, in many of the emerging markets, especially in Asia and Latin America, both GM and Ford have factories that are more flexible and will allow for build-to-order programs at a much faster pace. Furthermore, and more importantly, automakers do not have existing retail systems that would need to be over-

hauled. In some cases, as with GM in Taiwan, GM owns a significant share of the retail operations. Ford is experimenting with its Internet ideas in markets such as the Philippines where it has set up an e-commerce system that links consumers, dealers, the manufacturer, and suppliers to create a seamless e-business.

In addition to being able to buy cars online, Taiwanese customers can make service appointments through the GM web site. The company will come to the owner's house or office, pick up the car and return it within hours or overnight after completing the service.

Source: "GM Tests E-Commerce Plans in Emerging Markets," *The Wall Street Journal,* October 25, 1999, B6. See also **http://www.gm.com, www. GMBuyPower.com,** and **www.gmautoworld.com.tw.**

position, especially if they are considering substantial e-commerce investments. One of the likely scenarios is an e-commerce tax system that closely resembles sales taxes at physical retail outlets. Vendors will be made responsible for the collection of sales taxes and forwarding them to the governments concerned, most likely digitally. Another proposal involves the bit-tax—a variation of the Internet access tax.[44]

In addition, any product traded will still be subject to government regulations. For example, Virtual Vineyards has to worry about country-specific alcohol regulations, while software makers such as Softwareland.com Inc. have to comply with U.S. software export regulations. Dell Computer was fined $50,000 by the U.S. Department of Commerce for shipping computers online to Iran, a country on the sanctions list due to its sponsorship of terrorism.[45]

Governments will also have to come to terms with issues related to security, privacy, and access to the Internet.[46] The private sector argues for the highest possible ability to safeguard its databases, to protect cross-border transmission of confidential information, and to conduct secure financial transactions using global networks. This would require an unrestricted market for encryption products that interoperate globally. However, some governments, and especially the United States, fear that too good of an encryption will enable criminals and terrorist organizations to avoid detection and tracking. Therefore, a strong argument is made in favor of limiting the extent of encryption. Privacy issues have grown exponentially as a result of e-business. In 1998, the European Union passed a directive that introduces high standards of data privacy to ensure the free flow of data throughout the 15 member states. Each individual has the right to review personal data, correct them, and limit their use. But, and more importantly, the directive also requires member states to block transmission of data to countries, including the United States, if those countries' domestic legislation does not provide an adequate level of protection. The issue between the United States and the EU will most likely be settled by companies, such as IBM, adopting global privacy policies for managing information online and getting certified by groups such as the Better Business Bureau or Trust-E that are implementing privacy labeling systems that tell users when a site adheres to their privacy guidelines.[47] A 2001 study conducted by Consumers International found that Internet users' privacy was better protected in the United States than Europe.[48]

For industries such as music and motion pictures, the Internet is both an opportunity and a threat. The web provides a new efficient method of distribution and customization of products. At the same time, it can be a channel for intellectual property violation through unauthorized posting on web sites where they can be downloaded.[49] In addition, the music industry is concerned about a shift in the balance of economic power: if artists can deliver their works directly to customers via technologies such as MP3, what will be the role of labels and distributors?

Promotional Policy

The international marketer must choose a proper combination of the various promotional tools—advertising, personal selling, sales promotion, and publicity—to create images among the intended target audience. The choice will depend on the target audience, company objectives, the product or service marketed, the resources available for the endeavor, and the availability of promotional tools in a particular market. Increasingly, the focus is not a product or service but the company's image, as shown in Global Perspective 13.3.

Advertising   The key decision-making areas in advertising are: (1) media strategy; (2) the promotional message; and (3) the organization of the promotional program.

Media strategy is applied to the selection of media vehicles and the development of a media schedule. Worldwide media spending, which totaled $300 billion in 1999, varies dramatically around the world. In absolute terms, the United States spends the most, followed by Japan, the United Kingdom, Germany, France, and Brazil. The mature U.S. market anticipates slower growth in the future, but European integration and the development of the Pacific Rim's consumer markets are likely to fuel major growth.[50] The major spenders were Procter & Gamble ($4.7 billion), Unilever ($3.4 billion), General Motors ($3.2 billion), Ford ($2.2 billion), and Nestlé ($1.8 billion). While P&G spent 36 percent of its budget in the United States, Unilever's spending there was only 20 percent.[51]

Media spending varies also by market. Countries devoting the highest percentage to television were Peru (84 percent) and Mexico (73 percent). In some countries, the highest percentage is devoted to print: Kuwait (91) and Norway (77). Radio accounts for more than 20 percent in only a few countries, such as Trinidad and Tobago, and Nepal. Outdoor advertising accounted for 48 percent of Bolivia's media spending but only 3 percent of Germany's. Cinema advertising is important in India and Nigeria.[52]

Media regulations will also vary. Some regulations include limits on the amount of time available for advertisements; in Italy, for example, the state channels allow a maximum of 12 percent of advertising per hour and 4 percent over a week, and

GLOBAL PERSPECTIVE 13.3

Nurturing a Global Image

Corporate advertising can play a vital role in providing constituents with reassurances of quality and promises of trusted service. It is typically focused to support the company in several areas, such as product support, employment recommendation, crisis support, joint venture consideration, and stock purchase.

Several global marketers have used global image advertising to achieve particular objectives. Nokia is the world's largest company in the cellular business. However, many customers are not aware of Nokia to the extent that they are of its competitors such as Motorola. Nokia has, therefore, engaged in a number of corporate efforts, one of which is the title sponsorship of the Sugar Bowl in the United States. The sponsorship costs Nokia approximately $2.5 million annually. Worldwide, it sponsors the FIS Snowboard World Cup. ABB, the global engineering and technology company, wants to be better known among its constituents and launched a major global campaign under the theme "Brain Power." Similarly, the German chemical company BASF has wanted to increase constituent awareness of its far-flung operations: It has 100 companies under its umbrella producing in 39 countries and markets these goods in over 170. Its campaign theme, "We don't make a lot of the products you buy. We make a lot of the products you buy better," is intended to increase its brand equity and subsequently the behavior of important stakeholders.

In some cases corporations may look to reposition themselves. As a bloated, government-owned company, British Airways was generally regarded as "Bloody Awful." Upon privatization, the company needed to quickly improve its image among stakeholders. A series of corporate image campaigns since 1983 have helped change the airline into one of the most positively regarded in the industry. The renaming of companies must also be communicated to the constituents. Andersen Consulting changed its name in 2001 to Accenture and introduced a new theme line, "Now it Gets Interesting," to accentuate its expertise and strategic insight. The advertising program was launched across 46 countries, featuring Super Bowl commercials, building wraps, a customized magazine insert, as well as television, newspaper, magazine, and airport executions.

Some consider crises to be as sure as death and taxes. A solid corporate image and the ability of customers to get the company's point of view are tasks for image campaigns. Companies such as Exxon-Mobil Corporation have regularly engaged in extending the corporate view to dispel myths or misconceptions. In 2000, for example, the ads focused on climate change, unilateral trade sanctions, and international anticorruption efforts. It has also focused on its investments in developing countries, especially ones in the public eye (e.g., Indonesia). The message argues that rather than cut and run from these country markets, the company can do more good to work in them. Microsoft has engaged in a similar campaign of "essays on technology and its impact on society." Its campaign in March 2000 argued for the granting to China of Permanent Normal Trade Relations status to ensure continued access to Chinese markets.

Some marketers have elected to engage in promoting social causes as part of their image advertising. Probably the most controversial in this category are advertisements from Benetton, which while focusing on promoting harmony and understanding among people have sparked discussion about the appropriateness the message delivery.

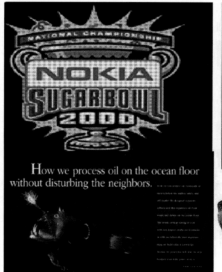

Source: "China, Trade and Technology," The Washington Post, March 6, 2000, A17; "Nokia in Brief," Nokia web site, accessed June 17, 1999, www.nokia.com; BASF corporation home page, accessed June 17, 1999, www.basf.com; "Growing from the Top," Marketing Management (Winter/Spring 1996): 10–19; and Rahul Jacob, "Corporate Campaigns Attract Bigger Slices of Advertising Pie," Advertising Age International, March 8, 1999, 2; "Nokia Fumbles, But Don't Count It Out," Fortune, February 19, 1996, 86–88; http://www.nokia.com, www.basf.com, www.british-airways.com, www.exxonmobil.com, www.benetton.com, www.abb.com, and www.accenture.com.

commercial stations allow 18 percent per hour and 15 percent per week. Furthermore, the leading Italian stations do not guarantee audience delivery when spots are bought. Strict separation between programs and commercials is almost a universal requirement, preventing U.S.-style sponsored programs. Restrictions on items such as comparative claims and gender stereotypes are prevalent; for example, Germany prohibits the use of superlatives such as "best."

Global media vehicles have been developed that have target audiences on at least three continents and for which the media buying takes place through a centralized office. These media have traditionally been publications that, in addition to the worldwide edition, have provided advertisers the option of using regional editions. For example, *Time* provides 133 editions, enabling advertising to reach a particular country, a continent, or the world. Other global publications include *The International Herald Tribune, The Wall Street Journal,* and *National Geographic.* The Internet provides the international marketer with an additional global medium. U.S. marketers have been slow to react to its potential because their domestic market is so dominant. They have also been reluctant to adapt their web sites but are willing to repeat what happened in the United States in these regions. One simple way of getting started is to choose a few key languages for the web site. For example, Gillette decided to add German and Japanese to its Mach3 web site after studying the number of Internet users in the countries.[53] If the marketer elects to have a global site and region-specific sites (e.g., organized by country), the look should be similar, especially in terms of the level of sophistication of the global site. Another method is to join forces with Internet service providers. For example, Unilever has expanded its sponsorship of the Microsoft online network in the United States to France, Germany, and the United Kingdom.[54] With the agreement, Unilever will provide banner ads, links, and sponsorship to MSN sites, particularly Women Central. Premier sponsorship on the MSN sites will include logo placement at the top right corner of the web pages. The projection is that the Internet may have a 5 percent market share by 2002, with ad spending reaching nearly $17 billion ($12.5 in North America, $2.2 in Europe, and $1.2 in the Asia-Pacific).[55] The level may reach $33 billion by 2004 as other markets increase their volume as well. In addition to PCs, wireless phones and interactive TV will become delivery mechanisms.

In broadcast media, panregional radio stations have been joined in Europe by television as a result of satellite technology. By the end of the 1990s, approximately half of the households in Europe had access to additional television broadcasts either through cable or direct satellite, and television will no longer be restricted by national boundaries. As a result, marketers need to make sure that advertising works not only within markets but across countries as well. The launch of STAR TV has increased the use of regional advertising in Asia.

Developing the **promotional message** is referred to as creative strategy. The marketer must determine what the consumer is really buying—that is, the consumer's motivations. They will vary, depending on:

1. The diffusion of the product, service, or concept into the market. For example, to enter China with online sales may be difficult with only 1 percent of the population and 10 percent of the urban population having a PC.
2. The criteria on which the consumer will evaluate the product. For example, in traditional societies, the time-saving qualities of a product may not be the best ones to feature, as Campbell Soup learned in Italy, Brazil, and Poland where preparers felt inadequate if they did not make soups from scratch.
3. The product's positioning. For example, Parker Pen's upscale image around the world may not be profitable enough in a market that is more or less a commodity business. The solution is to create an image for a commodity product and make the public pay for it—for example, the positioning of Perrier in the United States as a premium mineral water.

Source: **www.start.com.**

The ideal situation in developing message strategy is to have a world brand—a product that is manufactured, packaged, and positioned the same around the world. However, a number of factors will force companies to abandon identical campaigns in favor of recognizable campaigns. The factors are culture, of which language is the main manifestation, economic development, and lifestyles. Consider, for example, the campaign for Marriott International presented in Figure 13.3. While the ads share common graphic elements, two distinct approaches are evident. The top set of advertisements from the United States and Saudi Arabia are an example of a relatively standard approach, given the similarity in target audiences (i.e., the business traveler) and in the competitive conditions in the markets. The second set features ads for Latin America and German-speaking Europe. While the Latin advertisement stresses

FIGURE 13.3   Global Advertising Campaign Approaches

Courtesy: Marriott International http://www.marriott.com.

comfort, the German version focuses on results. While most of Marriott's ads have the theme ("When you're comfortable you can do anything") translated, the German version keeps the original English-language theme.

Many multinational corporations are staffed and equipped to perform the full range of promotional activities. In most cases, however, they rely on the outside expertise of advertising agencies and other promotions-related companies such as media-buying companies and specialty marketing firms. In a study of 40 multinational marketers, 32.5 percent are using a single agency worldwide, 20 percent are using two, 5 percent are using three, 10 percent are using four, and 32.5 percent are using more than four agencies. Of the marketers using only one or two agencies, McCann-Erickson was the most popular with 17 percent of the companies.[56] Local agencies will survive, however, because of governmental regulations. In Peru, for example, a law mandates that any commercial aired on Peruvian television must be 100 percent nationally produced. Local agencies tend to forge ties with foreign ad agencies for better coverage and customer service, and thus become part of the general globalization effort. Marketers are choosing specialized interactive shops over full-service agencies for Internet advertising. However, a major weakness with the interactive agencies is their lack of international experience.

Personal Selling   Although advertising is often equated with the promotional effort, in many cases promotional efforts consist of personal selling. In the early stages of internationalization, exporters rely heavily on personal contact. The marketing of industrial goods, especially of high-priced items, requires strong personal selling efforts. In some cases, personal selling may be truly international; for example, Boeing or Northrop Grumman salespeople engage in sales efforts around the world. However, in most cases, personal selling takes place at the local level. The best interests of any company in the industrial area lie in establishing a solid base of dealerships staffed by local people. Personal selling efforts can be developed in the same fashion as advertising. For the multinational company, the primary goal again is the enhancement and standardization of personal selling efforts, especially if the product offering is standardized.

As an example, Eastman Kodak has developed a line-of-business approach to allow for standardized strategy throughout a region.[57] In Europe, one person is placed in charge of the entire copier-duplicator program in each country. That person is responsible for all sales and service teams within the country. Typically, each customer is served by three representatives, each with a different responsibility. Sales representatives maintain ultimate responsibility for the account; they conduct demonstrations, analyze customer requirements, determine the right type of equipment for each installation, and obtain orders. Service representatives install and maintain the equipment and retrofit new-product improvements to existing equipment. Customer service representatives are the liaison between sales and service. They provide operator training on a continuing basis and handle routine questions and complaints. Each team is positioned to respond to any European customer within four hours.

Sales Promotion   Sales promotion has been used as the catchall term for promotion that is not advertising, personal selling, or publicity. Sales promotion directed at consumers involves such activities as couponing, sampling, premiums, consumer education and demonstration activities, cents-off packages, point-of-purchase materials, and direct mail. The success in Latin America of Tang, General Foods's presweetened powder juice substitute, is for the most part traceable to successful sales promotion efforts. One promotion involved trading Tang pouches for free popsicles from Kibon (General Foods's Brazilian subsidiary). Kibon also placed coupons for free groceries in Tang pouches. In Puerto Rico, General Foods ran Tang sweepstakes. In Argentina, in-store sampling featured Tang poured from Tang pitchers by girls in orange Tang dresses. Decorative Tang pitchers were a hit throughout Latin America.

For sales promotion to work, the campaigns planned by manufacturers or their agencies have to gain the support of the local retailer population. As an example, retailers must redeem coupons presented by consumers and forward them to the manufacturer or to the company handling the promotion. A. C. Nielsen tried to introduce cents-off coupons in Chile and ran into trouble with the nation's supermarket union, which notified its members that it opposed the project and recommended that coupons not be accepted. The main complaint was that an intermediary, such as Nielsen, would unnecessarily raise costs and thus the prices to be charged to consumers. Also, some critics felt that coupons would limit individual negotiations, because Chileans often bargain for their purchases.

Sales promotion directed at intermediaries, also known as trade promotion, includes activities such as trade shows and exhibits, trade discounts, and cooperative advertising. For example, attendance at an appropriate trade show is one of the best ways to make contacts with government officials and decision makers, work with present intermediaries, or attract new ones.

Public Relations   Public relations is the marketing communications function charged with executing programs to earn public understanding and acceptance, which means both internal and external communication. Internal communication is important, especially in multinational companies, to create an appropriate corporate culture. External campaigns can be achieved through the use of corporate symbols, corporate advertising, customer relations programs, the generation of publicity, as well as getting a company's view to the public via the Internet. Some material on the firm is produced for special audiences to assist in personal selling.

A significant part of public relations activity focuses on portraying multinational corporations as good citizens of their host markets. IBM's policy of good corporate citizenship means accepting responsibility as a participant in community and national affairs and striving to be among the most admired companies in host countries. In Thailand, for example, IBM provides equipment and personnel to universities and donates money to the nation's wildlife fund and environmental protection agency.[58]

Public relations activity includes anticipating and countering criticism. The criticisms range from general ones against all multinational corporations to specific complaints. They may be based on a market, for example, a company's presence in China. They may concern a product, for example, Nestlé's practices in advertising and promoting infant formula in developing countries where infant mortality is unacceptably high. They may center on the company's conduct in a given situation, for example, Union Carbide's perceived lack of response in the Bhopal industrial diaster. If not addressed, such criticisms can lead to more significant problems, such as an internationally orchestrated boycott of products. The six-year boycott of Nestlé did not so much harm earnings as it harmed image and employee morale.

Summary

The task of the international marketer is to seek new opportunities in the world marketplace and satisfy emerging needs through creative management of the firm's good, pricing, distribution, and promotional policies. By its very nature, marketing is the most sensitive of business functions to environmental effects and influences.

The analysis of target markets is the first of the international marketer's challenges. Potential and existing markets need to be evaluated and priorities established for each, ranging from rejection to a temporary holding position to entry. Decisions at the level of the overall marketing effort must be made with respect to the selected markets, and a plan for future expansion must be formulated. The closer that potential target markets are in terms of their geographical, cultural, and economic distance, the more attractive they typically are to the international marketer.

A critical decision in international marketing concerns the degree to which the overall marketing program should be standardized or localized. The ideal is to standardize as much as possible without compromising the basic task of marketing: satisfying the needs and wants of the target market. Many multinational marketers are adopting globalization strategies that involve the standardization of good ideas, while leaving the implementation to local entities.

The technical side of marketing management is universal, but environments require adaptation within all of the mix elements. The degree of adaptation will vary by market, good, or service marketed, and overall company objectives.

Key Terms and Concepts

income elasticity of
  demand
market audit
analogy
longitudinal analysis
gap analysis
concentration

diversification
positioning
backward innovation
center of excellence
standard worldwide
  pricing
dual pricing

cost-plus method
marginal cost method
market-differentiated
  pricing
price escalation
dumping

gray markets
arm's length price
channel design
e-commerce
media strategy
promotional message

Questions for Discussion

1. Many rational reasons exist for rejecting a particular market in the early stages of screening. Such decisions are made by humans, thus some irrational reasons must exist as well. Suggest some.
2. If, indeed, the three dimensions of distance are valid, to which countries would U.S. companies initially expand? Consider the interrelationships of the distance concepts.
3. Is globalization ever a serious possibility, or is the regional

approach the closest the international marketer can ever hope to get to standardization?
4. What are the possible exporter reactions to extreme foreign exchange rate fluctuations?
5. Argue for and against gray marketing.
6. What courses of action are open to an international marketer who finds all attractive intermediaries already under contract to competitors?

Internet Exercises

The software industry is the hardest hit by piracy. Using the web site of the Business Software Alliance (www.bsa.org), assess how this problem is being tackled. Many traditionalists do not foresee that virtual trade shows will become a major threat to the actual shows themselves.

Their view is that nothing can replace the actual seeing and touching of a product in person. Visit the E-Expo USA site (www.e-expousa.doc.gov) and develop arguments for and/or against this view.

Recommended Readings

Czinkota, Michael R., and Ilkka A. Ronkainen. *Global Marketing Imperative: Positioning Your Company for the New World of Business.* Lincolnwood, IL: NTC, 1995.

Czinkota, Michael R., and Ilkka A. Ronkainen. *International Marketing.* Ft. Worth, TX: Harcourt, 2001.

Czinkota, Michael R., and Jon Woronoff. *Unlocking Japan's Market.* Chicago: Probus Publishers, 1991.

Douglas, Susan P., and C. Samuel Craig, *International Marketing Research.* New York: John Wiley, 1999.

Leo Burnett. *Worldwide Advertising and Media Fact Book.* Chicago, IL: Triumph Books, 1994.

Monye, Sylvester O., ed. *The Handbook of International Marketing Communications.* Cambridge, MA: Blackwell Publishers, 2000.

Reedy, Joel, Shauna Schullo, and Kenneth Zimmerman. *Electronic Marketing.* Fort Worth, TX: The Dryden Press, 2000.

Ries, Laura, and Al Ries. *The 22 Immutable Laws of Branding: How to Build a Product or Service into a World-Class Brand.* New York: Harper Collins, 1999.

Schuster, Camille P., and Michael J. Copeland. *Global Business: Planning for Sales and Negotiations.* Fort Worth, TX: The Dryden Press, 1997.

U.S. Department of Commerce. *A Basic Guide to Exporting.* Washington, DC: U.S. Government Printing Office, 1996.

Yip, George S. *Total Global Strategy.* Englewood Cliffs, NJ: Prentice-Hall, 1992.

Notes

1. "AMA Board Approves New Marketing Definition," *Marketing News* (March 1, 1985): 1.

2. Robert Bartels, "Are Domestic and International Marketing Dissimilar?" *Journal of Marketing* 36 (July 1968): 56–61.

3. Reijo Luostarinen and Lawrence Welch, *Internationalization of the Firm* (Helsinki, Finland: The Helsinki School of Economics, 1990), ch.1.

4. For one of the best summaries, see Country Monitor, *Indicators of Market Size for 117 Countries* (New York: EIU), 2001.

5. Philip Kotler, *Marketing Management: Analysis, Planning and Control* (Englewood Cliffs, NJ: Prentice-Hall, 1999), 234.

6. James A. Gingrich, "Five Rules for Winning Emerging Market Consumers," *Strategy and Business* (second quarter, 1999): 68–76.

7. The World Bank, *World Development Indicators* (Washington, DC, 2000), 85.

8. J. A. Weber, "Comparing Growth Opportunities in the International Marketplace," *Management International Review* 19 (winter 1979): 47–54.

9. "How the Chevy Name Landed on SUV Using Russian Technology," *The Wall Street Journal*, February 20, 2001, A1, A8.

10. Igal Ayal and Jehiel Zif, "Marketing Expansion Strategies in Multinational Marketing," *Journal of Marketing* 43 (spring 1979): 84–94.

11. Michael Rennie, "Born Global," *The McKinsey Quarterly* 4 (1993): 45–52.

12. John S. Hill and Richard R. Still, "Adapting Products to LDC Tastes," *Harvard Business Review* 62 (March–April 1984): 92–101.

13. Davis Goodman, "Thinking Export? Think ISO 9000," *Export Today*, August 1998, 48–49.

14. *ISO Survey 1999*, available at www.iso.ch.

15. "The Puff, the Magic, the Dragon," *The Washington Post*, September 2, 1994, B1, B3; and "Big Names Draw Fine Line on Logo Imagery," *South China Morning Post*, July 7, 1994, 3.

16. "Holding the Fries—At the Border," *Business Week*, December 14, 1998, 8.

17. Bruce Seifert and John Ford, "Are Exporting Firms Modifying Their Product, Pricing and Promotion Policies?" *International Marketing Review* 6, 6 (1989): 53–68.

18. Barry Lynn, "Germany: the Packaging Environment," *Export Today* 11 (July, 1995): 58–64.

19. Phillip D. White and Edward W. Cundiff, "Assessing the Quality of Industrial Products," *Journal of Marketing* 42 (January 1978): 80–86.

20. Johny K. Johansson, Ilkka A. Ronkainen, and Michael R. Czinkota, "Negative Country-of-Origin Effects: The Case of the New Russia," *Journal of International Studies* 25, 1 (1994): 1–21.

21. Ilkka A. Ronkainen, "Product Development in the Multinational Firm," *International Marketing Review* 1 (winter 1983): 24–30.

22. "For Levi's, a Flattering Fit Overseas," *Business Week* (November 5, 1990): 76–77.

23. Erin Strout, "Reinventing a Company," *Sales and Marketing Management* 152 (February 2000): 86–92.

24. International Anti-Counterfeiting Coalition, available at **www.iacc.org**.

25. Michael G. Harvey and Ilkka A. Ronkainen, "International Counterfeiters: Marketing Success Without the Cost or Risk," *Columbia Journal of World Business* 20 (fall 1985): 37–46. For worldwide piracy information, see **http://www.iipa.com**.

26. S. Tamer Cavusgil, "Unraveling the Mystique of Export Pricing," *Business Horizons* 31 (May–June 1988): 54–63.

27. "Asian Flu Gives Medical-Equipment Firms a Headache," *The Wall Street Journal*, December 15, 1997, B4.

28. James C. Baker and John K. Ryans, "Some Aspects of International Pricing: A Neglected Area of Management Policy," *Management Decisions* (summer 1973): 177–182.

29. "Even After Shift to Euro, One Price Won't Fit All," *The Wall Street Journal Europe*, December 28, 1998, 1.

30. Stephen A. Butscher, "Maximizing Profits in Euroland," *Journal of Commerce*, May 5, 1999, 5.

31. Ilkka A. Ronkainen and Linda Van de Gucht, "Making a Case for Gray Markets," *Journal of Commerce*, January 6, 1987, 13A.

32. James Shulman, "When the Price is Wrong—By Design," *Columbia Journal of World Business* 4 (May–June 1967): 69–76.

33. "Multinationals Lose Half of Transfer Price Spats," *The Journal of Commerce* (September 4, 1997): 2A.

34. Mohammad F. Al-Eryani, Pervaiz Alam, and Syed H. Akhter, "Transfer Pricing Determinants of U.S. Multinationals," *Journal of International Business Studies* 21 (fall 1990): 409–425.

35. Gregory L. Miles, "Unmasking Japan's Distributors," *International Business* (April 1994): 38–42.

36. Michael R. Czinkota, "Distribution of Consumer Products in Japan," *International Marketing Review* 2 (Autumn 1985): 39–51.

37. "How to Evaluate Foreign Distributors: A *BI* Checklist," *Business International* (May 10, 1985): 145–149.

38. Miles Maguire, "Spinning the Web," *Export Today*, January 1998, 28–32.

39. Rolf Rykken, "Opening the Gate," *Export Today*, February 1999, 35–42.

40. Nick Wreden, "Internet Opens Market Abroad," *Information Week*, November 16, 1998, 46–48.

41. Eryn Brown, "Nine Ways to Win on the Web," *Fortune*, May 24, 1999, 112–125.

42. Hope Katz Gibbs, "Taking Global Local," *Global Business*, December 1999, 44–50.

43. Richard Prem, "Plan Your e-Commerce Tax Strategy," *e-Business Advisor*, April 1999, 36.

44. Erika Morphy, "The Geography of e-Commerce," *Global Business*, November 1999, 26–33.

45. Nick Wreden, "Internet Opens Markets Abroad," *Information Week*, November 16, 1998, 46–48.

46. Lou Gerstner, "A Policy of Restraint," *Think Leadership,* March 1999, 1–3.

47. Elizabeth De Bony, "EU, U.S. Plug Away at Data Privacy Abroad," *Industry Standard,* December 10, 1998, 45–46.

48. "Europe Lags Behind U.S. on Web Privacy," *The Wall Street Journal,* February 20, 2001, B11.

49. Jodi Mardesich, "How the Internet Hits Big Music," *Fortune,* May 10, 1999, 96–102.

50. Julie S. Hill, "Euro, Pacific Spending Spree, *Advertising Age* (April 10, 1989): 4, 55. See also the following web site: http://www.zenithmedia.com.

51. "Top Global Marketers," *Advertising Age International* (November 8, 1999): 1-11.

52. Compiled from Leo Burnett, *Worldwide Advertising and Media Fact Book* (Chicago: Triumph Books, 1994).

53. "The Internet," *Advertising Age International,* June 1999, 42.

54. "Unilever, Microsoft in European Net Deal," *The Wall Street Journal,* February 2, 2000, B8.

55. http://www.forrester.com.

56. "U.S. Multinationals," *Advertising Age International,* June 1999, 39.

57. Joseph A. Lawton, "Kodak Penetrates the European Copier Market with Customized Marketing Strategy and Product Changes," *Marketing News* (August 3, 1984): 1, 6.

58. "IBM Promotes Education," *Business Latin America* (May 24, 1993): 6–7.

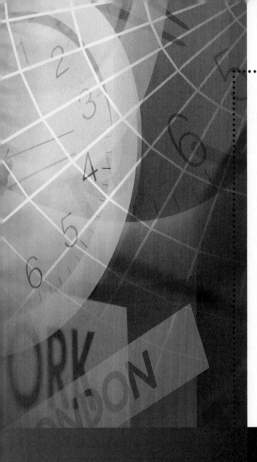

CHAPTER 14

International Services

LEARNING OBJECTIVES

- To examine the increasingly important role of services in international business

- To understand why international trade in services is more complex than international trade in goods

- To appreciate the heightened sensitivity required for international service success

- To learn that stand-alone services are becoming more important to world trade

- To examine the competitive advantage of firms in the service sector

When the World Bank surveyed 150 prominent U.S. and European hardware and software manufacturers, India's programmers were ranked first out of eight countries for both on-site and offshore software development, ahead of Ireland, Israel, Mexico, and Singapore. In fact, one in four software engineers in the world is of Indian origin. With average annual programmer salaries of about $3,000, quality software production in India costs much less than what it would cost in the United States. No wonder two out of five Fortune 500 corporations have outsourced their information technology (IT) needs to India, attracted to the highly skilled, but low-wage labor force.

British Airways scans every ticket it sells—35 million a year—and transmits the files to India, where they are reconciled with billing information sent by travel agents. General Electric has more than 1,000 people processing loans and performing accounting tasks in New Delhi. They also call calling customers who are late with payments. Ten thousand miles from the corporate home offices, Indian IT professionals are maintaining information for U.S. firms. Not only is India's work force English speaking and college educated, it's also available at a low price; a medical transcriber in India, for example, will do the job for about $4,000 a year against the $30,000 paid to a U.S.–based transcriber.

But IT in India is not just export oriented. Tata Consultancy Services (TCS), the leading software maker in India, sold in just one year 11,000 copies of a $140 accounting program for personal computers. This shows that the world's second most populous nation is developing its own viable domestic software market. Such a development is putting India in a position to compete in global software markets and software design as well.

India's software industry grew by 58 percent in one year. This growth is helping the hundreds of local software houses to hone their development and marketing skills at home so they can sell abroad. India's annual software exports are now running at $3 billion, up from just $100 million at the beginning of the 1990s and may reach $35 billion by the end of this decade. Although it is only a fraction of the $250 billion global software market, the exports are growing about 50 percent per year. With such growth figures, India's over 2.5 million computer and software professionals are finding opportunities to advance their careers without relocating abroad. ●

Sources: Khozem Merchant, "India: Gaining Membership to the Global Club," *Financial Times,* November 6, 2000; "Software Industry in India," India Times Online, accessed June 17, 1999, **india-times.com;** "TCS Profile." TCS web site, accessed June 17, 1999, **www.tcs.com;** John Zubrzycki, "Mastering Software Helps India Youths Snag Foreign Jobs," *The Christian Science Monitor,* November 13, 1997, p. 1; "Country Buzz," *Computers Today* (May 1, 1997): 14–33.

I nternational services are a major component of world trade. This chapter will highlight international business dimensions that are specific to services. A definition of services will be provided, and trade in services and in goods will be differentiated. The role of services in the world economy will then be explained. The chapter will discuss the opportunities and new problems that have arisen because of increasing service trade, with particular focus on the worldwide transformations of industries as a result of profound changes in the environment and in technology. The strategic responses to the transformations by both governments and firms will be explained. Finally, the chapter will outline the initial steps that firms need to undertake to offer services internationally and will look at the future of international service trade.

Differences Between Services and Products

We rarely contemplate or analyze the precise role of services in our lives. Services often accompany goods, but they are also, by themselves, an increasingly important part of the economy. One author has contrasted services and products by stating that "a good is an object, a device, a thing; a service is a deed, a performance, an effort."[1] That definition, although quite general, captures the essence of the difference between goods and services. Services tend to be more intangible, personalized, and custom-made than goods. Services also are typically using a different approach to customer satisfaction. It has been stated that "service firms do not have products in the form of preproduced solutions to customer's problems; they have processes as solutions to such problems."[2] Services are the fastest growing sector in world trade and as this chapter's opening vignette shows, employment in the services sector is becoming increasingly global. These major differences add dimensions to services that are not present in goods.

Link Between Services and Goods

Services may complement goods; at other times, goods may complement services. The offering of goods that are in need of substantial technological support and maintenance may be useless if no proper assurance for service can be provided. For this reason, the initial contract of sale often includes the service dimension. This practice is frequent in aircraft sales. When an aircraft is purchased, the buyer contracts not only for the physical good—namely, the plane—but often for the training of personnel, maintenance service, and the promise of continuous technological updates. Similarly, the sale of computer hardware depends on the availability of proper servicing and software. In an international setting, the proper service support can often be crucial. Particularly for newly opening markets or for goods new to market, providing the good alone may be insufficient. The buyer wants to be convinced that proper service backup will be offered for the good before making a commitment.

The link between goods and services often brings a new dimension to international business efforts. A foreign buyer, for example, may want to purchase helicopters and contract for service support over a period of ten years. If the sale involves a U.S. firm, both the helicopter and the service sale will require an export license. Such licenses, however, are issued only for an immediate sale. Therefore, over the ten years, the seller will have to apply for an export license each time service is to be provided. The issuance of a license is often dependent on the political climate, therefore, the buyer and the seller are haunted by uncertainty. As a result, sales may go to firms in countries that can unconditionally guarantee the long-term supply of support services.

Services can be just as dependent on goods. For example, an airline that prides itself on providing an efficient reservation system and excellent linkups with rental cars and hotel reservations could not survive if it were not for its airplanes. As a result,

FIGURE 14.1

Tangible and Intangible Offerings of Airlines

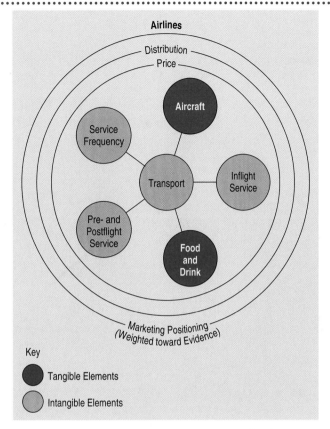

Airlines

Distribution

Price

Aircraft

Service Frequency

Transport

Inflight Service

Pre- and Postflight Service

Food and Drink

Marketing Positioning (Weighted toward Evidence)

Key

Tangible Elements

Intangible Elements

Source: G. Lynn Shostack, "Breaking Free from Product Marketing," in *Services Marketing: Text, Cases, and Readings,* ed. Christopher H. Lovelock (Englewood Cliffs, NJ: Prentice-Hall, Inc., 1984), 40.

many offerings in the marketplace consist of a combination of goods and services. A graphic illustration of the tangible and intangible elements in the market offering of an airline is provided in Figure 14.1.

The simple knowledge that services and goods interact, however, is not enough. Successful managers must recognize that different customer groups will frequently view the service-good combination differently. The type of use and the usage conditions will affect evaluations of the market offering. For example, the intangible dimension of "on-time arrival" by airlines may be valued differently by college students than by business executives. Similarly, a twenty-minute delay will be judged differently by a passenger arriving at his or her final destination than by one who has just missed an overseas connection. As a result, adjustment possibilities in both the service and the goods areas emerge that can be used as a strategic tool to stimulate demand and increase profitability. As Figure 14.2 shows, service and goods elements may vary substantially in any market offering. The manager must identify the role of each and adjust all of them to meet the desires of the target customer group. By rating the offerings on a scale ranging from dominant tangibility to dominant intangibility, the manager can compare offerings and also generate information for subsequent market positioning strategies.

Stand-Alone Services

Services do not have to come in unison with goods. They can compete against goods and become an alternative offering. For example, rather than buy an in-house

FIGURE 14.2

Scale of Dominance Between Goods and Services

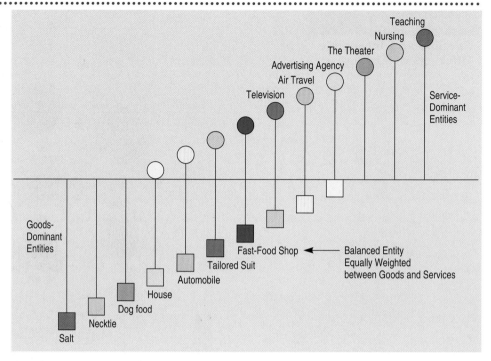

Source: Reprinted with permission from *Marketing of Services*, eds. J. Donnelly and W. George; G. Lynn Shostack, "How to Design a Service," 1981, p. 222, published by the American Marketing Association, Chicago, IL 60606.

computer, the business executive can contract computing work to a local or foreign service firm. Similarly, the purchase of a car (a good) can be converted into the purchase of a service by leasing the car from an agency. Services therefore can transform the ownership of a good into its possession or use. This transformation can greatly affect business issues such as distribution, payment structure and flows, and even recycling.

Services by themselves can satisfy needs and wants of customers. Entertainment services such as movies or music offer leisure time enjoyment. Insurance services can protect people from financial ruin in case of a calamity.

Services may also compete against one another. As an example, a store may have the option of offering full service to customers or of converting to the self-service format. The store may provide only checkout services, with customers engaging in other activities such as selection, transportation, and sometimes even packaging and pricing.

Services differ from goods most strongly in their **intangibility.** They are frequently consumed rather than possessed. Though the intangibility of services is a primary differentiating criterion, it is not always present. For example, publishing services ultimately result in a tangible good—namely, a book or a computer disk. Similarly, construction services eventually result in a building, a subway, or a bridge. Even in those instances, however, the intangible component that leads to the final good is of major concern to both the producer of the service and the recipient of the ultimate output, because it brings with it major considerations that are nontraditional to goods.

Another major difference concerns the storing of services. Due to their nature, services are difficult to inventory. If they are not used, the "brown around the edges" syndrome tends to result in high **perishability.** Unused capacity in the form of an empty seat on an airplane, for example, becomes nonsalable quickly. Once the plane has taken off, selling an empty seat is virtually impossible—except for an in-flight upgrade from coach to first class—and the capacity cannot be stored for future use. The difficulty of inventorying services makes it troublesome to provide service back-up for peak demand. To maintain **service capacity** constantly at levels necessary to satisfy peak demand would be very expensive. The business manager must therefore attempt to smooth out demand levels in order to optimize overall use of capacity.

For the services offering, the time of production is usually very close to or even simultaneous with the time of consumption. This often means close **customer involvement** in the production of services. Customers frequently either service themselves or cooperate in the delivery of services. As a result, the service provider may need to be physically present when the service is delivered. This physical presence creates both problems and opportunities, and introduces a new constraint that is seldom present in the marketing of goods. For example, close interaction with the customer requires a much greater understanding of and emphasis on the cultural dimension of each market. A good service delivered in a culturally unacceptable fashion is doomed to failure. Even in a domestic setting, international exposure can make a service culturally controversial, as Table 14.1 shows. A common pattern of internationalization for service businesses is therefore to develop stand-alone business systems in each country.[3]

The close interaction with customers also points to the fact that services often are custom-made. This contradicts the desire of the firm to standardize its offering; yet at the same time, it offers the service provider an opportunity to differentiate the service. The concomitant problem is that, in order to fulfill customer expectations, **service consistency** is required. For anything offered online, however, consistency is difficult to maintain over the long run. Therefore, the human element in the service offering takes on a much greater role than in the offering of goods. Errors may enter the system, and unpredictable individual influences may affect the outcome of the service delivery. The issue of quality control affects the provider as well as the recipient of services because efforts to increase control through uniform service may sometimes be perceived by customers as the limiting of options. Since research has shown that the relative importance of the serviced quality dimensions varies from one culture to another,[4] one single approach to service quality may therefore have a negative market effect.

Buyers have more difficulty observing and evaluating services than goods. This is particularly true when the shopper tries to choose intelligently among service providers. Even when sellers of services are willing and able to provide more **market**

TABLE 14.1 **Examples of Cultural Service Gaps**	**Manifestations of the Service Provider Performance Gap**	**Example: Japanese Guests in a German Restaurant**
	Provider's physical environment gap	Customers cannot read the menu or they mix up the restrooms because they cannot read the signs
	Provider's personnel gap	Customers feel uneasy because waiter maintains eye contact while taking the order
	Provider's system gap	Customers are irritated because they are neither greeted at the door nor seated
	Provider's co-customer gap	Customer feels uneasy because other guests greet them with a handshake when joining their table

Source: Bernd Stauss and Paul Mang, "'Culture Shocks' in Inter-cultural Service Encounters?" *Journal of Services Marketing,* 13, 4/5, 1999, 329–346.

transparency, the buyer's problem is complicated: Customers receiving the same service may use it differently. Since production lines cannot be established to deliver an identical service each time, and the quality of a service cannot be tightly controlled, the problem of **service heterogeneity** emerges,[5] meaning that services may never be the same from one delivery to another. For example, the counseling by a teacher, even if it is provided on the same day by the same person, may vary substantially depending on the student. But over time, even for the same student, the counseling may change. As a result, service offerings are not directly comparable, which makes quality measurements quite challenging. Therefore, service quality may vary for each delivery. Nonetheless, maintaining service quality is vitally important, since the reputation of the service provider plays an overwhelming role in the customer's choice process.

Services often require entirely new forms of distribution. Traditional channels frequently are multitiered and long and therefore slow. They often cannot be used at all because of the perishability of services. A weather news service, for example, either reaches its audience quickly or rapidly loses value. As a result, direct delivery and short distribution channels are required for international services. When they do not exist, service providers need to be distribution innovators to reach their market.

Increasingly, many services are "footloose," in that they are not tied to any specific location. Advances in technology make it possible for firms to separate production and consumption of services. As a result, labor-intensive service performance can be moved anywhere around the world where qualified, low-cost labor is plentiful. As communication technology further improves, services such as teaching, medical diagnosis, or bank account management can originate from any point in the world and reach customers around the globe.

The unique dimensions of services exist in both international and domestic settings, but their impact has greater importance for the international manager. For example, the perishability of a service, which may be a mere obstacle in domestic business, may become a major barrier internationally because of the longer distances involved. Similarly, quality control for international services may be much more difficult because of different service uses, changing expectations, and varying national regulations.

Services are delivered directly to the user and are therefore frequently much more sensitive to cultural factors than are products. Their influence on the individual abroad may be welcomed or greeted with hostility. For example, countries that place a strong emphasis on cultural identity have set barriers inhibiting market penetration by foreign films. France is leading a major effort within the European Union, for instance, to cap the volume of U.S.-produced films to obtain more playing time for French movies.

The Role of Services in the U.S. Economy

Since the Industrial Revolution, the United States has seen itself as a primary international competitor in the production of goods. In the past few decades, however, the U.S. economy has increasingly become a service economy, as Figure 14.3 shows. The service sector now produces 77 percent of the GNP and employs 79 percent of the workforce.[6] The major segments that comprise the service sector are communications, transportation, public utilities, finance, insurance and real estate, wholesale and retail businesses, government, and "services" (a diverse category including business services, personal services, and professional and health services). The service sector accounts for most of the growth in total nonfarm employment.

FIGURE 14.3

Employment in Industrial Sectors as a Percentage of the Total Labor Force

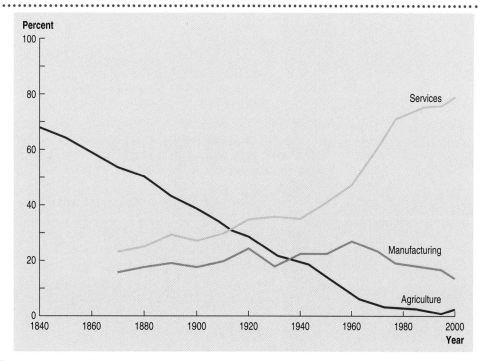

Sources: "Employment Situation Summary," U.S. Department of Labor, **http://stats.bls.gov**, January 25, 2001; J. B. Quinn, "The Impacts of Technology on the Service Sector," *Technology and Global Industry: Companies and Nations in the World Economy* (Washington, DC: National Academy of Sciences, 1987).

Only a limited segment of the total range of U.S. services is sold internationally. Federal, state, and local government employees, for example, sell few of their services to foreigners. U.S. laundries and restaurants only occasionally service foreign tourists. Many service industries that do sell abroad often have at their disposal large organizations, specialized technology, or advanced professional expertise. Strength in these characteristics has enabled the United States to become the world's largest exporter of services. Total U.S. services exported grew from $14 billion in 1970 to more than $295 billion in 2000.[7]

Global service trade has had very beneficial results for many U.S. firms. Most of the large management consulting firms derive more than half of their revenue from international sources. The largest advertising agencies serve customers around the globe, some of them in 107 countries. As Table 14.2 shows, 11 of the largest 20 law firms in the world are headquartered in the United States, but up to 80 percent of their lawyers reside outside their home country. These facts demonstrate that many service firms have become truly international and formidable in size. As a result, service employment has become global, as Global Perspective 14.1 demonstrates.

However, dramatic global growth is not confined to U.S. firms. The import of services into the United States is also increasing dramatically. In 2000, the United States imported more than $215 billion worth of services. Competition in global services is rising rapidly at all levels. Hong Kong, Singapore, and Western Europe are increasingly active in service industries such as banking, insurance, and advertising. Years ago, U.S. construction firms could count on a virtual monopoly on large-scale construction projects. Today, firms from South Korea, Italy, and other countries are taking a major share of the international construction business.

TABLE 14.2 World's Largest Law Firms

Rank/Firm	Headquarters	Web site	Lawyers	Lawyers Outside Home Country	Countries Where Firm has Offices
1. Baker & McKenzie	Chicago	bakerinfo.com	2,732	80%	35
2. Clifford Chance	London	cliffordchance.com	2,029	65%	19
3. Eversheds	London	eversheds.com	1,652	3%	7
4. Skadden, Arps, Slate, Meagher & Flom	New York	skadden.com	1,467	9%	12
5. Allen & Overy	London	allenovery.com	1,460	47%	20
6. Jones, Day, Reavis & Pogue	Cleveland	jonesday.com	1,411	11%	12
7. Freshfields	London	freshfields.com	1,397	59%	8
8. Linklaters	London	linklaters.com	1,360	49%	22
9. Morgan, Lewis & Bockius	Philadelphia	morganlewis.com	1,116	4%	5
10. White & Case	New York	whitecase.com	1,030	47%	24
11. Latham & Watkins	Los Angeles	lw.com	1,007	4%	6
12. DLA	London	dla.com	993	3%	3
13. Mayer, Brown & Platt	Chicago	mayerbrown.com	950	5%	4
14. Holland & Knight	Tampa	hklaw.com	900	1%	2
15. Lovells	London	lovells.com	897	45%	18
16. Sidley & Austin	Chicago	sidley.com	890	9%	6
17. Shearman & Sterling	New York	shearman.com	865	31%	10
18. Mallesons Stephan Jaques	Sydney	msj.com.au	860	2%	4
19. Akin, Grump, Strauss, Hauer & Feld	Dallas & DC	akingump.com	854	4%	4
20. Blake Dawson Waldron	Sydney	bdw.com.au	814	3%	4

Source: "Global 50 Rankings: Most Lawyers," www.2000Law.com.

374

GLOBAL PERSPECTIVE 14.1

White-Collar Jobs Go Overseas

For years, workers in industrialized countries have complained about losing manufacturing jobs overseas to countries that pay lower wages than in the United States or Europe. Now Americans are discovering that U.S. companies are also taking advantage of lower wage white-collar workers abroad for service jobs that used to be done in their offices. Instead of paying someone down the hall for jobs like data entry, some U.S. firms are hiring workers thousands of miles away.

With the advent of high-speed modems and low-cost satellite and fiber-optic communications, service workers in foreign countries can sometimes deliver faster results than their American counterparts. The quality of the work sent overseas also compares favorably with the services available in the United States.

As the U.S. Bureau of Labor Statistics has noted, overseas workers are performing jobs for which there is not a large enough qualified labor supply in the United States. Overseas information services jobs originally were mostly low-skilled data entry positions—processing insurance claims, credit card applications, and direct-mail responses. But today those overseas jobs are increasingly found in areas requiring more skills and education.

Almost half of U.S. firms' 1.6 million information technology positions will go unfilled. Since there are no U.S. workers, one in ten southern California software firms depends on skilled workers in foreign countries. Nearly a third of Microsoft's 34,000 employees work abroad in countries from England to Israel to China. Much smaller firms are also going overseas for skilled help. One firm has Israeli programmers at work in Israel or in the U.S., and an entertainment firm in Newport Beach, California, uses Russian programmers to develop its Internet site. Unable to pay the $90,000 starting salary for U.S. programmers, the company found highly skilled Russian programmers eager to earn $18,000 annually in Russia.

Although the number of service sector jobs sent overseas still remains relatively small, the practice has sparked governments in several countries to form special development corporations to help attract U.S. service jobs. Barbados, Ireland, Jamaica, the Philippines, St. Kitts, and St. Lucia have all entered the business. For many of these countries, the payoff is substantial: Barbados's largest single private employer is American Airlines' Caribbean Data Services, which has hired 1,100 people there to enter data about airline tickets.

Sources: Marc Ballon, "U.S. High-Tech Jobs Going Abroad," *Los Angeles Times,* April 24, 2000, p. C1; Mike Mills, "In the Modem World, White-Collar Jobs Go Overseas," *The Washington Post,* September 17, 1996: A1, A7.

The Role of Global Services in the World Economy

The rise of the service sector is a global phenomenon. Services are also rapidly moving to the forefront in many other nations as well, accounting for 65 percent of GDP in Argentina, 64 percent in Mexico, 65 percent in South Africa, and over 50 percent in Thailand.[8] Even in the least developed countries, services typically contribute at least 45 percent of GDP. With growth rates higher than other sectors, such as agriculture and manufacturing, services are instrumental in job creation in these countries.[9] In addition, service exports are very important to developing and transitional economies. On average, 20 percent of developing and transitional economy exports are service exports, accounting for more than 29 percent of the world's total services exports.

The economies of developing countries have traditionally first established a strong agricultural and then a manufacturing sector to meet basic needs such as food and shelter before venturing into the services sector. Some countries, such as Mexico, Singapore, Hong Kong, Bermuda, and the Bahamas, are steering away from the traditional economic development pattern and are concentrating on developing strong service sectors.[10] The reasons vary from a lack of natural resources with which to develop agricultural and/or manufacturing sectors to recognition of the strong demand for services and the ability to provide them through tourism and a willing, skilled, and inexpensive labor force. As a result, it is anticipated that services trade will continue to grow. However, as more countries enter the sector, the global services business will become more competitive.

Global Transformations in the Services Sector

Two major factors, environmental and technological change, account for the dramatic rise in services trade. One key environmental change has been the reduction of **government regulation** of service industries. In the early 1980s, many governments adopted the view that reduced government interference in the marketplace would enhance competition. As a result, new players have entered the marketplace. Some service sectors have benefited and others have suffered from this withdrawal of government intervention. Regulatory changes were initially thought to have primarily domestic effects, but they have rapidly spread internationally. For example, the 1984 **deregulation** of the U.S. telecommunication giant AT&T gave rise to competition not only in the United States. Japan's telecommunication monopoly, NT&T, was deregulated in 1985 and European deregulation followed in the mid-1990s.

Similarly, deregulatory efforts in the transportation sector have had international repercussions. New air carriers have entered the market to compete against established trunk carriers and have done so successfully by pricing their services differently, both nationally and internationally. Obviously, a British airline can count only to a limited extent on government support to remain competitive with new, low-priced fares offered by other carriers from abroad also serving the British market. The deregulatory movement has fostered new competition and new competitive practices. Many of these changes resulted in lower prices, stimulating demand and leading to a rise in the volume of international services trade.

Another major environmental change has been the decreased regulation of service industries by their service groups. For example, business practices in fields such as health care, law, and accounting are becoming increasingly competitive and aggressive. New economic realities require firms in these industries to search for new ways to attract market share and expand their markets. International markets are one frequently untapped possibility for market expansion and have therefore become a prime target for such firms.

Technological advancement is the second major change that has taken place. Increasingly, progress in technology is offering new ways of doing business and is permitting businesses to expand their horizons internationally. Through computerization, for instance, service exchanges that previously would have been prohibitively expensive are now feasible. As an example, Ford Motor Company uses one major computer system to carry out new car designs simultaneously in the United States and in Europe. This practice not only lowers expenditures on hardware and permits better utilization of existing equipment but also allows design teams based in different countries to interact closely and produce a car that can be successful in multiple markets. Of course, this development could take place only after advances in data transmission procedures. Technology has also sharply reduced the **cost of communication.** Fiberoptic cables have made the cost of international links trivial. A minute on a transatlantic cable laid 40 years ago cost $2.44, but now the same amount of time costs barely more than one cent. Although that figure does not allow for billing, marketing, and local network access costs, it does illustrate the revolution in the economics of international calls.[11]

Another result of technological advancement is that service industry expansion is not confined to those services that are labor intensive and therefore better performed in areas of the world where labor possesses a comparative advantage. Rather, technology-intensive services are becoming the sunrise industries of the next century. Increasingly, firms in a variety of industries can use technology to offer a presence without having to be there physically. Banks, for example, can offer their services through automatic teller machines or telephone and Internet banking. Consultants can advise via videoconferences and teachers can teach the world through multime-

Istanbul, Turkey, at the crossroads of Europe and Asia, is served by a Motorola digital cellular telephone system. Motorola has contracts worldwide for GSM systems (Global System for Mobile Communications).

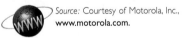

Source: Courtesy of Motorola, Inc., www.motorola.com.

dia classrooms. Physicians can advise and even perform operations in a distant country if proper computer links can drive roboticized medical equipment.

Due to the growth of corporate web sites, some firms—particularly in the service sector—can quickly become unplanned participants in the international market. For example, potential customers from abroad can visit a web site and require the firm to deliver internationally as well. Of course the firm can choose to ignore foreign interests and lose out on new markets. Alternatively, it can find itself unexpectedly an international service provider. Specialty retailing such as book stores and fitness equipment are examples of services that in this way have become international.[12]

Many service providers have the opportunity to become truly global players. To them, the traditional international market barrier of distance no longer matters. Knowledge, the core of many service activities, can offer a global reach without requiring a local presence. Service providers therefore may have only a minor need for local establishment, since they can operate without premises. You don't have to be there to do business! The effect of such a shift in service activities will be major. Insurance and bank palaces in the downtowns of the world may soon become obsolete. Talented service providers will see the demand for their performance increase, while less capable ones will suffer from increased competition. Most importantly, consumers and society will have a much broader range and quality of service choices available, often at a lower cost.

Problems in International Service Trade

Together with the increase in the importance of service trade, new problems have emerged in the service sector. Many of these problems have been characterized as affecting mainly the negotiations between nations, but they are of sufficient importance to firms engaged in international activities to merit a brief review.

Data Collection Problems

The data collected on service trade are often sketchy. Service transactions are often invisible statistically as well as physically. For example, the trip abroad of a consultant for business purposes may be hard to track and measure. The interaction of variables such as citizenship, residency, location of the transaction, and who or what (if anything) crosses national boundaries further contributes to the complexity of services transactions. Imagine that an Irish citizen working for a Canadian financial consulting firm headquartered in Sweden advises an Israeli citizen living in India on the management of funds deposited in a Swiss bank. Determining the export and import dimensions of such a services transaction is not easy.[13]

The fact that governments have precise data on the number of trucks exported down to the last bolt but little information on reinsurance flows reflects past governmental inattention to services. Consequently, estimates of services trade vary widely. Total actual volume of services trade may actually be much larger than the amount shown by official statistics.

When considering the dimension of the problem of data collection on services in industrialized countries, with their sophisticated data gathering and information systems, it is easy to imagine how many more problems are encountered in countries lacking such elaborate systems and unwilling to allocate funds for them. Insufficient knowledge and information have led to a lack of transparency, making it difficult for nations either to gauge or to influence services trade. As a result, regulations are often put into place without precise information as to their repercussions on actual trade performance.

Services as a Portion of Gross Domestic Product

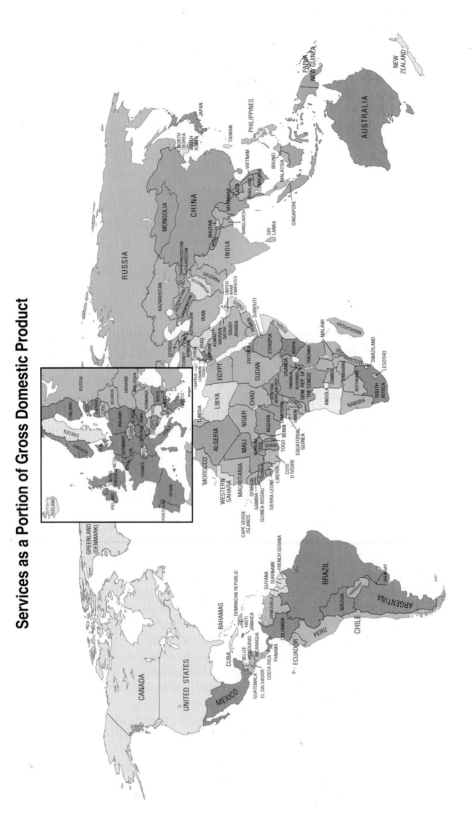

Services as a percent of GDP

- 61% to 85%
- 41% to 60%
- 21% to 40%
- 0% to 20%
- No current data available

Source: *2001 World Development Indicators*, The World Bank.

Global Regulations of Services

Global obstacles to service trade can be categorized into two major types: barriers to entry and problems in performing services abroad.

Barriers to entry are often explained by reference to **"national security"** and **"economic security."** For example, the impact of banking on domestic economic activity is given as a reason why banking should be carried out only by nationals or indeed should be operated entirely under government control. Sometimes the protection of service users is cited, particularly of bank depositors and insurance policyholders. Another justification used for barriers is the **infant-industry** argument: "With sufficient time to develop on our own, we can compete in world markets." Often, however, this argument is used simply to prolong the ample licensing profits generated by restricted entry. Yet, defining a barrier to services is not always easy. For example, Taiwan gives an extensive written examination to prospective accountants (as do most countries) to ensure that licensed accountants are qualified to practice. Naturally, the examination is given in Chinese. The fact that few German accountants, for example, read and write Chinese and hence are unable to pass the examination does not necessarily constitute a barrier to trade in accountancy services.[14]

Service companies also encounter difficulties once they have achieved access to the local market. One reason is that rules and regulations based on tradition may inhibit innovation. A more important reason is that governments pursue social objectives through national regulations. The distinction between **discriminatory** and **nondiscriminatory regulations** is of primary importance here. Regulations that impose larger operating costs on foreign service providers than on the local competitors, that provide subsidies to local firms only, or that deny competitive opportunities to foreign suppliers are a proper cause for international concern. The problem of discrimination becomes even more acute when foreign firms face competition from government-owned or government-controlled enterprises. On the other hand, nondiscriminatory regulations may be inconvenient and may hamper business operations, but they offer less cause for international criticism. Yet, such national regulations can be key inhibitors for service innovations. For example, in Japan, pharmaceuticals cannot be sold outside of a licensed pharmacy. Similarly, travel arrangements can only be made within a registered travel office and banking can only be done during banking hours. As a result, innovations offered by today's communications technology cannot be brought to bear in these industries.[15]

All of these regulations make it difficult for international services to penetrate world markets. At the governmental level, services frequently are not recognized as a major facet of world trade or are viewed with suspicion because of a lack of understanding, and barriers to entry often result. To make progress in tearing them down, much educational work needs to be done.

In a major breakthrough in the Uruguay Round, the major GATT participants agreed to conduct services trade negotiations parallel with goods negotiations. The negotiations resulted in 1995 in the forging of a **General Agreement on Trade in Services (GATS)** as part of the World Trade Organization, the first multilateral, legally enforceable agreement covering trade and investment in the services sector. Similar to earlier agreements in the goods sector, GATS provides for most-favored-nation treatment, national treatment, transparency in rule making, and the free flow of payments and transfers. Market-access provisions restrict the ability of governments to limit competition and new-market entry. In addition, sectoral agreements were made for the movement of personnel, telecommunications, and aviation. However, in several sectors, such as entertainment, no agreement was obtained. In addition, many provisions, due to their newness, are very narrow. Therefore, future negotiations have been agreed upon, which, at five-year intervals, will attempt to improve free trade in services.

Corporate Involvement in International Service Trade

Services and E-Commerce

Electronic commerce has opened up new horizons for global services reach, and has drastically reduced the meaning of distance. For example, when geographic obstacles make the establishment of retail outlets cumbersome and expensive, firms can approach their customers via the World Wide Web. Government regulations which might be prohibitive to a transfer of goods may not have any effect on the international marketing of services. Also, regardless of size, companies are finding it increasingly easy to appeal to a global marketplace. The Internet can help service firms in developing and transitional economies overcome two of the biggest barriers they face: gaining credibility in international markets and saving on travel costs. Little known firms can become instantly "visible" on the Internet. Even a small firm can develop a polished and sophisticated web presence and promotion strategy. Customers are less concerned about geographic location if they feel the firm is electronically accessible. An increasing number of service providers have never met their foreign customers except "virtually" online.[16] A quantitative assessment conducted by the World Trade Organization indicated that the share of value added that potentially lends itself to electronic commerce represents about 30 percent of GDP, most importantly distribution, finance, and business services.[17]

Nonetheless, several notes of caution must be kept in mind. First, the introduction of the Internet has occurred at different rates in different countries. There are still many businesses and consumers who do not have access to electronic business media. Unless they are to be excluded from a company's focus, more traditional ways of reaching them must be considered. Also, firms need to prepare their Internet presence for global visitors. For example, the language of the Internet is English—at least as far as large corporations are concerned. Yet, many of the visitors coming to web sites either may not have English as their first language or may not speak English at all. Companies respond differently to such visitor language capabilities. For example, one study determined that 70 percent of non-American companies with a web site offered more than their local language on their sites, while only 14 percent of American companies offered non-English language content.[18] Many companies also do not permit any interaction on their web sites, thus missing out on feedback from visitors. Some web sites are so culture bound that they often leave their visitors bewildered and disappointed due to the cultural assumptions made. However, over time, increasing understanding of doing business in the global marketplace will enable companies to be more refined in their approach to their customers.

Typical International Services

Although many firms are active in the international service arena, others do not perceive their existing competitive advantage. Numerous services that are efficiently performed in the home market may have great potential for internationalization.

Financial institutions can offer some functions very competitively internationally in the field of banking services. U.S. banks possess advantages in fields such as mergers and acquisitions, securities sales, and asset management. Banks in Europe and Japan are boosting their leadership through large assets and capital bases.

Construction, design, and **engineering services** also have great international potential. Providers of these services can achieve economies of scale not only for machinery and material but also in areas such as personnel management and the overall management of projects. Particularly for international projects that are large scale and long term, the experience advantage weighs heavily in favor of international firms.

Insurance services can be sold internationally by firms knowledgeable about underwriting, risk evaluation, and operations. Firms offering legal and accounting services can aid their clients abroad through support activities; they can also help firms and countries improve business and governmental operations. Knowledge of computer operations, data manipulations, data transmission, and data analysis is insufficiently exploited internationally by many small and medium-sized firms.

Similarly, **communication services** have substantial future international opportunities. For example, firms experienced in the areas of videotext, home banking, and home shopping can find international success, particularly where geographic obstacles make the establishment of retail outlets cumbersome and expensive. Alternatively, global communication services, as shown in Figure 14.4, can greatly expand the reach of corporations.

Many institutions in the educational and corporate sectors have developed expertise in **teaching services.** They are very knowledgeable in training and motivation as well as in the teaching of operational, managerial, and theoretical issues, yet have largely concentrated their work in their domestic markets. It is time to take education global! Too much good and important knowledge is not made available to broad audiences. More knowledge must be communicated, be it through distance learning, study and teaching abroad, or attracting foreign students into the domestic market. The latter option can spur a service industry in itself, as Global Perspective 14.2 shows.

Management **consulting services** can be provided by firms and individuals to the many countries and corporations in need of them. Of particular value is management expertise in areas where many developing economies need most help, such as transportation and logistics. Major opportunities also exist for industries that deal with societal problems. For example, firms that develop environmentally safe products or produce pollution-control equipment can find new markets, as nations around the world increase their awareness of and concern about the environment and tighten their laws. Similarly, advances in health care or new knowledge in combating AIDS offer major opportunities for global service success.

FIGURE 14.4

An Advertisement for an International Communications Service

Source: Courtesy of AT&T.

A Global Services Industry: Finding Basketball Players

Tall kids in countries around the world are finding golden opportunities on American basketball courts. The number of foreign players on U.S. college and professional basketball teams has recently jumped from 144 to 243 in a four-year period, and American recruiters can't seem to get enough of the foreign imports. Hakeem Olajuwon, an NBA star from Nigeria, has achieved the status of folk hero among many fans around the globe. Many credit his success with the current rush to recruit players from abroad.

Stiff competition for the tallest players has even led to recruiting foreign players at younger levels of the sport; high schools commonly use foreign exchange programs to fortify their teams with international talent. High school coaches are linked with foreign players through middlemen, like the Nigerian lawyer, Toyin Sonoiki, who spent $500,000 to send nine players to U.S. schools.

The role of middlemen is crucial in obtaining visas for the students. Another Nigerian lawyer, Lloyd Ukwu, lives in Washington, DC, and recruits on business trips back home. He started helping young Nigerians obtain U.S. visas in 1988. After meeting some players on a trip to Nigeria, he asked an assistant basketball coach at American University to write invitations for eight Nigerian players to visit the United States, and these letters were influential in helping them win visas. Word spread about Ukwu's recruiting efforts, and soon other universities were using his services.

The internationalization of the sport has changed the jobs of many American coaches and recruiters. For years, college recruiting has used tip sheets to describe U.S. high school players, but now there is one recruiting service that gives the scoop on foreign players as well. Dale Mock, a Georgia elementary school physical-education teacher, runs International Scouting Service, a five-year-old enterprise. His tip sheets give subscribers the details about foreign players and contact information for $300 a year. Although he hasn't yet quit his day job, his subscriber list is up to 100, from a start of only 20 his first year. Dale Brown, Louisiana State's former coach, described the internationalization of the recruiting scene: "In the 1960s, I would go to the European championships, to the Asian games and all the rest—and I was the only American. Now, so many Americans are there it's like being in Grand Central Station."

Source: Marc Fisher and Ken Denlinger, "The Market for Imports is Booming," *The Washington Post,* March 28, 1997, C1.

Tourism also represents a major service export. Every time foreign citizens come to a country and spend their funds, the Current Account effect is that of an export. Measured in current dollars, worldwide tourism receipts have tripled in the past ten years to $455 billion, making this particular service one of the most important ones in the world.[19]

An attractive international service mix might also be achieved by pairing the strengths of different partners. For example, information technology from one country can be combined with the financial resources of other countries. The strengths of the partners can then be used to offer maximum benefits to the international community.

Combining international advantages in services may ultimately result in the development of an even more drastic comparative lead. For example, the United States has an international head start in such areas as high technology, information gathering, information processing, information analysis, and teaching. Ultimately, the major thrust of U.S. international services might not be to provide these service components individually but rather to ensure that, based on a combination of competitive resources, better decisions are made. If better decision making is transferable to a wide variety of international situations, this in itself might become the overriding future comparative advantage of the United States in the international market.

Management consulting services can be provided by firms to institutions and corporations around the globe. Of particular value is management expertise in areas where firms possess global leadership, be it in manufacturing or process activities. For example, companies with highly refined transportation or logistics activities can sell their management experience abroad.

For many firms, participation in the Internet will offer the most attractive starting point in marketing their services internationally. The set up of a web site will allow visitors from any place in the globe to come see the offering. Of course, the most im-

portant problem will be how to communicate the existence of one's site and how to entice visitors to come. For that, often very traditional advertising and communication approaches need to be used. In some countries, for example, one can find rolling billboards announcing web sites and their benefits. Overall, however, one needs to keep in mind that not everywhere do firms and individuals have access to or make use of the new e-commerce opportunities.

Starting to Offer Services Internationally

For services that are delivered mainly in support of or in conjunction with goods, the most sensible approach for the international novice is to follow the path of the good. For years, many large accounting and banking firms have done this by determining where their major multinational clients have set up new operations and then following them. Smaller service providers who supply manufacturing firms can determine where the manufacturing firms are operating internationally. Ideally, of course, it would be possible to follow clusters of manufacturers abroad to obtain economies of scale internationally while simultaneously looking for entirely new client groups.

Service providers whose activities are independent from goods need a different strategy. These individuals and firms must search for market situations abroad that are similar to the domestic market. Such a search should be concentrated in their area of expertise. For example, a design firm learning about construction projects abroad can investigate the possibility of rendering its design services. Similarly, a management consultant learning about the plans of a country or firm to computerize its operations can explore the possibility of overseeing a smooth transition from manual to computerized activities. What is required is the understanding that similar problems are likely to occur in similar situations.

Another opportunity consists of identifying and understanding points of transition abroad. If, for example, new transportation services are introduced in a country, an expert in containerization may wish to consider whether to offer his or her service to improve the efficiency of the new system.

Leads for international service opportunities can also be gained by staying informed about international projects sponsored by domestic organizations such as the U.S. Agency for International Development or the Trade and Development Agency, as well as international organizations such as the United Nations, the International Finance Corporation, or the World Bank. Frequently, such projects are in need of support through services. Overall, the international service provider needs to search for similar situations, similar problems, or scenarios requiring similar solutions to formulate an effective international expansion strategy.

Strategic Indications

To be successful in the international service offering, the manager must first determine the nature and the aim of the services-offering core—that is, whether the service will be aimed at people or at things and whether the service act in itself will result in tangible or intangible actions. Figure 14.5 provides examples of such a classification strategy that will help the manager to better determine the position of the services effort.

During this determination, the manager must consider other tactical variables that have an impact on the preparation of the service offering. For example, in conducting research for services, the measurement of capacity and delivery efficiency often remains highly qualitative rather than quantitative. In communication and promotional efforts, the intangibility of the service reduces the manager's ability to provide samples. This makes communicating the service offered much more difficult than communicating an offer for a good. Brochures or catalogs explaining services often must show a proxy for the service to provide the prospective customer with tangible clues. A

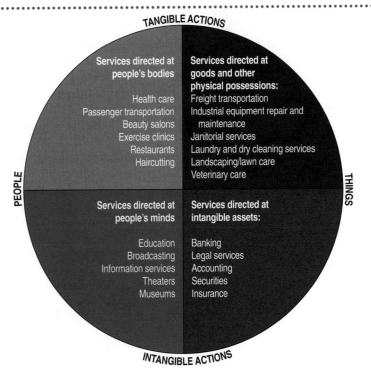

FIGURE 14.5

Different Types of Services

TANGIBLE ACTIONS

Services directed at people's bodies

Health care
Passenger transportation
Beauty salons
Exercise clinics
Restaurants
Haircutting

Services directed at goods and other physical possessions:

Freight transportation
Industrial equipment repair and maintenance
Janitorial services
Laundry and dry cleaning services
Landscaping/lawn care
Veterinary care

PEOPLE

THINGS

Services directed at people's minds

Education
Broadcasting
Information services
Theaters
Museums

Services directed at intangible assets:

Banking
Legal services
Accounting
Securities
Insurance

INTANGIBLE ACTIONS

Source: Christopher H. Lovelock, *Services Marketing,* 3d ed. (Upper Saddle River, NJ: Prentice-Hall, Inc., 1996), 29.

cleaning service, for instance, can show a picture of an individual removing trash or cleaning a window. However, the picture will not fully communicate the performance of the service. Service exporters have three ways to gain credibility abroad: (1) providing objective verification of their capabilities—perhaps through focusing on the company's professional license or certification by international organizations; (2) providing personal guarantees of performance, including referrals and testimonials by satisfied customers; and (3) cultivating a professional image through public appearances at international trade events or conferences and promotional materials such as a web site.[20] Due to the different needs and requirements of individual consumers, the manager must also pay attention to the two-way flow of communication. In the service area, mass communication often must be supported by intimate one-on-one follow-up.

The role of personnel deserves special consideration in international service delivery. The customer interface is intense, therefore, proper provisions need to be made for training of personnel both domestically and internationally. Major emphasis must be placed on appearance. Most of the time the person delivering the service—rather than the service itself—will communicate the spirit, value, and attitudes of the service corporation. Since the service person is both the producer as well as the marketer of the service, recruitment and training techniques must focus on dimensions such as customer relationship management and image projection as well as competence in the design and delivery of the service.[21]

This close interaction with the consumer will also have organizational implications. While tight control over personnel may be desired, the individual interaction that is required points toward the need for an international decentralization of service delivery. This, in turn, requires delegation of large amounts of responsibility to individuals and service "subsidiaries" and requires a great deal of trust in all organizational units. This trust, of course, can be greatly enhanced through proper methods of training and supervision. Sole ownership also helps strengthen this trust. Research has shown that service firms, in their international expansion, tend to greatly prefer the establishment of full-control ventures. Only when costs escalate and the company-specific advantage diminishes will service firms seek out shared-control ventures.[22]

The areas of pricing and financing require special attention. Because services cannot be stored, much greater responsiveness to demand fluctuation must exist, and therefore greater pricing flexibility must be maintained. At the same time, flexibility is countered by the desire to provide transparency for both the seller and the buyer of services in order to foster an ongoing relationship. The intangibility of services also makes financing more difficult. Frequently, even financial institutions with large amounts of international experience are less willing to provide financial support for international services than for products. The reasons are that the value of services is more difficult to assess, service performance is more difficult to monitor, and services are difficult to repossess. Therefore, customer complaints and difficulties in receiving payments are much more troublesome for a lender to evaluate in the area of services than for goods.

Finally, the distribution implications of international services must be considered. Usually, short and direct channels are required. Within these channels, closeness to the customer is of overriding importance to understand what the customer really wants, to trace the use of the service, and to aid the customer in obtaining a truly tailor-made service.

Summary

Services are taking on an increasing importance in international trade. They need to be considered separately from trade in merchandise because they no longer simply complement goods. Often, goods complement services or are in competition with them. Service attributes such as their intangibility, their perishability, their custom design, and their cultural sensitivity frequently make international trade in services more complex than trade in goods.

Services play an increasing role in the global economy. International growth and competition in this sector have begun to outstrip that of merchandise trade and are likely to intensify in the future. Even though services are un-

likely to replace production, the sector will account for the shaping of new competitive advantages internationally, particularly in light of new facilitating technologies which encourage electronic commerce.

The many service firms now operating only domestically need to investigate the possibility of going global. Historical patterns of service providers following manufacturers abroad have become partially obsolete as standalone services become more important to world trade. Management must therefore assess its vulnerability to service competition from abroad and explore opportunities to provide its services internationally.

Key Terms and Concepts

intangibility	service heterogeneity	infant industry	engineering services
perishability	government regulation	discriminatory and	insurance services
service capacity	deregulation	nondiscriminatory	communication services
customer involvement	cost of communication	regulations	teaching services
service consistency	national security	General Agreement on	consulting services
market transparency	economic security	Trade in Services (GATS)	tourism

Questions for Discussion

1. How has the Internet affected your services purchases? Have any of your purchases been international?
2. Discuss the major reasons for the growth of international services.

3. How does the international sale of services differ from the sale of goods?
4. What are some of the international business implications of service intangibility?

5. What are some ways for a firm to expand its services internationally?

6. How can a firm in a developing country participate in the international services boom?

7. Which services would you expect to migrate abroad in the next decade? Why?

Internet Exercises

1. Find the most current data on the five leading export and import countries for commercial services. The information is available on the World Trade Organization site www.wto.org—click the statistics button.

2. What are the key U.S. services exports and imports? What is the current services trade balance? (www.bea.doc.gov)

Recommended Readings

Bateson, John E.G. *Managing Services Marketing,* 4th ed. Fort Worth, TX: Dryden Press, 1999.

Business Guide to the World Trading System. Geneva: International Trade Centre UNCTAD/WTO and London: Commonwealth Secretariat, 1999.

Kurtz, David L., and Kenneth Clow, *Services Marketing.* New York: J. Wiley & Sons, 1998.

Lovelock, Christopher H. *Principles of Services Marketing and Management.* Upper Saddle River, NJ: Prentice Hall, 1999.

Meyer, Anton, and Frank Dornach. *The German Customer Barometer.* Munich: FMG-Verlag, 2001, Annual.

Notes

1. Leonard L. Berry, "Services Marketing Is Different," in *Services Marketing,* ed. Christopher H. Lovelock (Englewood Cliffs, NJ: Prentice-Hall, 1984), 30.

2. Christian Grönroos, "Marketing Services: The Case of a Missing Product," *Journal of Business & Industrial Marketing,* 13, 4/5 (1998): 322–338.

3. *Winning in the World Market* (Washington, DC: American Business Conference, November 1987), 17.

4. Olivier Furrer, Ben Shaw-Ching Liu, and D. Sudharshan, "The Relationships Between Culture and Service Quality Perceptions: Basis for Cross-cultural Market Segmentation and Resource Allocation," *Journal of Service Research* 2, 4 (2000): 355–371.

5. Pierre Berthon, Leyland Pitt, Constantine S. Katsikeas, and Jean Paul Berthon, "Virtual Services Go International: International Services in the Marketspace," *Journal of International Marketing* 7, 3 (1999): 84–106.

6. www.sitrends.org, February 28, 2001.

7. http://www.census.gov/indicator/www/ustrade.html, February 26, 2001.

8. Joseph P. Quinlan, "International Economics Trade in Global Services," www.uscsi.org, March 22, 2000.

9. International Trade Centre web page, www.intracen.org/servicexport, February 28, 2001.

10. Allen Sinai and Zaharo Sofianou, "Service Sectors in Developing Countries: Some Exceptions to the Rule," *The Service Economy,* July 1990, 13.

11. "Down with Distance," *The Economist* (September 13, 1997): 21.

12. Christian Grönroos, "Internationalization Strategies for Services," *Journal of Services Marketing* 13, 4/5 (1999): 290–297.

13. Terry Clark, Daniel Rajaratnam, and Timothy Smith, "Toward a Theory of International Services: Marketing Intangibles in a World of Nations," *Journal of International Marketing* 4, 2 (1996): 9–28.

14. Dorothy I. Riddle, *Key LDCs: Trade in Services,* American Graduate School of International Studies, Glendale, AZ, March 1987, 346–347.

15. Masao Yukawa, *The Information Superhighway and Multimedia: Dreams and Realities in Japan,* American Chamber of Commerce in Japan, Tokyo, October 12, 1994.

16. Dorothy Riddle, "Using the Internet for Service Exporting: Tips for Service Firms," *International Trade Forum,* March 1, 1999, 19–23.

17. Rosa Perez-Esteve and Ludger Schuknecht, "A Quantitative Assessment of Electronic Commerce," World Trade Organization, Staff Working Paper ERAD 99-01, September 1999.

18. Michael R. Czinkota, "Global Giants Slow to Join Net Revolution," *The Journal of Commerce,* November 5, 1999, 9.

19. Global Tourist Arrivals and Receipts, World Tourism Organization, www.hotelbenchmark.com/tourism/tourism_receipts.htm, February 26, 2001.

20. Dorothy I. Riddle, "Gaining Credibility Abroad as a Service Exporter," *International Trade Forum* 1 (1997): 4–7.

21. Paul G. Patterson and Muris Cicic, "A Typology of Service Firms in International Markets: An Empirical Investigation," *Journal of International Marketing* 3, 4 (1995): 57–83.

22. M. Krishna Erramilli and C. P. Rao, "Service Firms' International Entry-Mode Choice: A Modified Transaction-Cost Analysis Approach," *Journal of Marketing* 57 (July 1993): 19–38.

CHAPTER 15

International Logistics and Supply-Chain Management

LEARNING OBJECTIVES

- To understand the escalating importance of international logistics and supply-chain management as crucial tools for competitiveness

- To learn about materials management and physical distribution

- To learn why international logistics is more complex than domestic logistics

- To see how the transportation infrastructure in host countries often dictates the options open to the international manager

- To learn why inventory management is crucial for international success

Firms are redesigning their supply-chain strategies to meet new industry challenges. For example, increasing competition in Asia and consolidation among chemical companies' customers are fueling supply-chain reconfigurations. The changes mean big savings for chemical companies—60 to 80 percent of their cost structure is tied up in the supply chain. In other words, a 10 percent reduction in supply-chain expenses can lead to a 40 to 50 percent improvement in before-tax profits.

The U.S. chemical industry is particularly sensitive to the economics of supply chains; two-thirds of all U.S. chemical exports are sent to the foreign affiliates of U.S. companies. Chemicals are the largest single U.S. export group, ranging from fertilizers to plastics. But U.S. chemical exports are facing increasing competition from new operations in Malaysia, Singapore, South Korea, and Taiwan.

One U.S. firm, ARCO Chemical Co., decided to reorganize its supply chain in order to meet the challenges of global competition. Separate units in the nine countries where it operated had previously controlled different functions of its global supply chain. Adopting a new strategy, ARCO consolidated control of the supply chain under one organization responsible for purchasing raw materials, customer support, and logistics. The company's spokeswoman, Sallie Anderson, stated that "by putting these activities into one organization and redesigning the processes we will achieve significant working capital savings and more efficiency." In fact, the streamlined supply-chain management is part of a cost-cutting program that plans to cut $150 million from the annual $750 million budget for structural costs.

Firms are also able to use electronic data interchange—EDI—technology to streamline the supply chain. Eastman Kodak, for example, ships its products around the world to and from international ports. Rather than use thousands of different software systems, the firm now uses SAP software to schedule, track, and trace the cargo from point to point and to coordinate its delivery with its customers' needs, all in the quickest and best way possible.

A study by consulting firm A.T. Kearney confirmed the importance of supply-chain management in producing high earnings in the chemical industry; the four companies given the highest markes for supply-chain management also had earnings that were 5 to 7 percent higher than the other companies reviewed. Other important factors contributed to industry success, including smooth integration of suppliers and customers and the successful use of information technology. U.S. chemical companies that want to thrive in a globalized market will have to develop well-run supply chains to avoid prematurely expanding production capacity, a practice that contributes to boom and bust cycles. A.T. Kearney's vice president for chemical practice, Michael Eckstut, offered some advice for firms trying to reduce costs and stay competitive: "If you have a very efficient supply chain with good forecasting, tight scheduling and distribution, you can get by with less capacity." ●

Source: Arthur Gottschalk, "Chemical Firms Redesigning Supply-Chain Strategies," *The Journal of Commerce,* July 8, 1997, 1A, 6A; Michael Fabey, "Shipping by Numbers," *Traffic World,* September 11, 2000, 31–32.

For the international firm, customer locations and sourcing opportunities are widely dispersed. The firm can attain a strategically advantageous position only if it is able to successfully manage complex international networks, consisting of its vendors, suppliers, other third parties, and its customers. Neglect of links within and outside of the firm brings not only higher costs but also the risk of eventual non-competitiveness, due to diminished market share, more expensive supplies, or lower profits. As discussed in the opening vignette, effective international logistics and supply-chain management can produce higher earnings and greater corporate efficiency, which are the cornerstones of corporate competitiveness.

This chapter will focus on international logistics and supply-chain management. Primary areas of concentration will be the links between the firm, its suppliers, and its customers, as well as transportation, inventory, packaging, and storage issues. The logistics management problems and opportunities that are peculiar to international business will also be highlighted.

International Logistics Defined

International logistics is the design and management of a system that controls the flow of materials into, through, and out of the international corporation. It encompasses the total movement concept by covering the entire range of operations concerned with goods movement, including therefore both exports and imports simultaneously. By taking a systems approach, the firm explicitly recognizes the links among the traditionally separate logistics components within and outside of a corporation. By incorporating the interaction with outside organizations and individuals such as suppliers and customers, the firm is enabled to build on jointness of purpose by all partners in the areas of performance, quality, and timing. As a result of implementing these systems considerations successfully, the firm can develop just-in-time (JIT) delivery for lower inventory cost, electronic data interchange (EDI) for more efficient order processing, and early supplier involvement (ESI) for better planning of goods development and movement. In addition, the use of such a systems approach allows a firm to concentrate on its core competencies and to form outsourcing alliances with other companies. For example, a firm can choose to focus on manufacturing and leave all aspects of order filling and delivery to an outside provider. By working closely with customers such as retailers, firms can also develop efficient customer response (ECR) systems, which can track sales activity on the retail level. As a result, manufacturers can precisely coordinate production in response to actual shelf replenishment needs, rather than based on forecasts.

Two major phases in the movement of materials are of logistical importance. The first phase is **materials management,** or the timely movement of raw materials, parts, and supplies into and through the firm. The second phase is **physical distribution,** which involves the movement of the firm's finished product to its customers. In both phases, movement is seen within the context of the entire process. Stationary periods (storage and inventory) are therefore included. The basic goal of logistics management is the effective coordination of both phases and their various components to result in maximum cost effectiveness while maintaining service goals and requirements.

Key to business logistics are three major concepts: (1) the systems concept; (2) the total cost concept; and (3) the trade-off concept. The **systems concept** is based on the notion that materials-flow activities within and outside of the firm are so extensive and complex that they can be considered only in the context of their interaction. Instead of each corporate function, supplier, and customer operating with the goal of individual optimization, the systems concept stipulates that some components may have to work suboptimally to maximize the benefits of the system as a whole. The systems concept intends to provide the firm, its suppliers, and its customers, both domestic and foreign, with the benefits of synergism expected from the coordinated application of size.

In order for the systems concept to work, information flows and partnership trust are instrumental. Logistics capability is highly information dependent, since information availability influences not only the network planning process but also the day-to-day decisions that affect performance.[1] Long-term partnership and trust are required in order to forge closer links between firms and managers. An abuse of power is the fastest way to build barriers to such links.[2]

A logical outgrowth of the systems concept is the development of the **total cost concept.** To evaluate and optimize logistical activities, cost is used as a basis for measurement. The purpose of the total cost concept is to minimize the firm's overall logistics cost by implementing the systems concept appropriately.

Implementation of the total cost concept requires that the members of the system understand the sources of costs. To develop such understanding, a system of activity-based costing has been developed, which is a technique designed to more accurately assign the indirect and direct resources of an organization to the activities performed based on consumption.[3] In the international arena, the total cost concept must also incorporate the consideration of total after-tax profit, by taking the impact of national tax policies on the logistics function into account. The objective is to maximize after-tax profits rather than minimizing total cost. Tax variations in the international arena often have major consequences, therefore, the focus can be quite important.[4]

The **trade-off concept,** finally, recognizes the links within logistics systems that result from the interaction of their components. For example, locating a warehouse near the customer may reduce the cost of transportation. However, additional costs are associated with new warehouses. Similarly, a reduction of inventories will save money but may increase the need for costly emergency shipments. Managers can maximize performance of logistics systems only by formulating decisions based on the recognition and analysis of such trade-offs. A trade-off of costs may go against one's immediate interests. Consider a manufacturer building several different goods. The goods all use one or both of two parts, A and B, which the manufacturer buys in roughly equal amounts. Most of the goods produced use both parts. The unit cost of part A is $7, of part B, $10. Part B has more capabilities than part A; in fact, B can replace A. If the manufacturer doubles its purchases of part B, it qualifies for a discounted $8 unit price. For products that incorporate both parts, substituting B for A makes sense to qualify for the discount, since the total parts cost is $17 using A and B, but only $16 using Bs only. Part B should therefore become a standard part for the manufacturer. But departments building products that only use part A may be reluctant to accept the substitute part B because, even discounted, the cost of B exceeds that of A. Use of the trade-off concept will solve the problem.[5]

Supply-Chain Management

The integration of these three concepts has resulted in the new paradigm of **supply-chain management,** where a series of value-adding activities connect a company's supply side with its demand side. This approach views the supply chain of the entire extended enterprise, beginning with the supplier's suppliers and ending with consumers or end users. The perspective encompasses the entire product and information and funds flow that form one cohesive link to acquire, purchase, convert/manufacture, assemble, and distribute goods and services to the ultimate consumers. The implementation effects of such supply-chain management systems can be major. Efficient supply-chain design can increase customer satisfaction and save money at the same time.[6] For example, it has permitted Wal-Mart, the largest U.S. retailer, to reduce inventories by 90 percent, has saved the company hundreds of millions of dollars in inventory holding costs, and allows it to offer low prices to its customers.[7] On an industry-wide basis, research by Coopers and Lybrand has indicated that the use of such tools in the structuring of supplier relations could reduce operating costs of the European grocery industry by $27 billion per year, with savings equivalent to a 5.7 percent reduction in price.[8] Companies such as GE and Pitney Bowes have implemented web-based sourcing and payables systems. GE's Trading Process Network (**www.tpnregister.com**) allows GE Lighting's 25 production facilities and other buying facilities around the world to quickly find and purchase products from approved suppliers electronically. The electronic catalog information reflects the pricing and contract terms GE has negotiated with each of the suppliers and also ties in with GE's inventory and accounts payable systems. The result has been the virtual elimination of paper and mailing costs, a reduction in cycle time from 14 days to 1 day, 50 percent staff reduction, and 20 percent overall savings in the procurement process. Pitney Bowes' suppliers need only Internet access and a standard web browser to be electronically linked to the manufacturer's supply system to see how many of their products are on hand and to indicate how many will be needed in the future. The site, VendorSite (**www.aplgroup.com**), even includes data that small suppliers can use for production planning.

These developments open up supplier relationships for smaller companies and those outside of the buyer's domestic market; however, the supplier's capability of providing satisfying goods and services will play the most critical role in securing long-term contracts. In addition, the physical delivery of goods often can be old-fashioned and slow. Nevertheless, the use of such strategic tools will be crucial for international managers to develop and maintain key competitive advantages. An overview of the international supply chain is shown in Figure 15.1.

FIGURE 15.1   **The International Supply Chain**

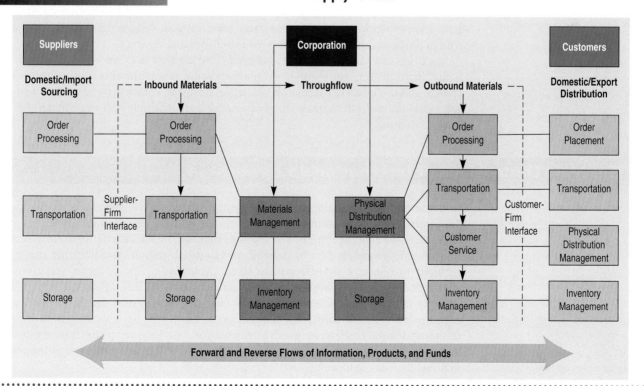

The Impact of International Logistics

Logistics costs comprise between 10 and 30 percent of the total landed cost of an international order.[9] International firms already have achieved many of the cost reductions that are possible in financing and production, and are now using international logistics as a competitive tool. The environment facing logistics managers in the next ten years will be dynamic and explosive. Technological advances and progress in communication systems and information-processing capabilities are particularly significant in the design and management of logistics systems.

For example, close collaboration with suppliers is required to develop a just-in-time inventory system, which in turn may be crucial to maintaining manufacturing costs at globally competitive levels. Yet, without electronic data interchange, such collaborations or alliances are severely handicapped. While most industrialized countries can offer the technological infrastructure for such computer-to-computer exchange of business information, the application of such a system in the global environment may be severely restricted. It may not be just the lack of technology that forms the key obstacle to modern logistics management, but rather the entire business infrastructure, ranging from ways of doing business in fields such as accounting and inventory tracking, to the willingness of businesses to collaborate with each other. A contrast between the United States and Russia is useful here.

In the United States, 40 percent of shipments are under a just-in-time/quick response regime. For the U.S. economy, the total cost of distribution is close to 10 percent of GNP.[10] By contrast, Russia only now is beginning to learn about the rhythm of demand and the need to bring supply in line. The country is battling space constraints, poor lines of supply, nonexistent distribution and service centers, limited rolling stock, and inadequate transportation systems. Producers are uninformed about issues such as inventory carrying costs, store assortment efficiencies, and replenishment techniques. The need for information development and exchange systems, for integrated supplier–distributor alliances, and for efficient communication systems is only poorly understood. As a result, distribution costs remain at well above 30 percent of GNP, holding back the domestic economy and severely restricting its international competitiveness. Unless substantial improvements are made, major participation by Russian producers in world trade will be severely handicapped,[11] since the high logistics and transaction costs make any transaction expensive and slow.

Logistics and supply-chain management increasingly are the key dimensions by which firms distinguish themselves internationally. Given the speed of technological change and the efficiency demands placed on business, competitiveness, international sales growth, and international business success increasingly will depend on the logistics function.[12]

The New Dimensions of International Logistics

In domestic operations, logistics decisions are guided by the experience of the manager, possible industry comparisons, an intimate knowledge of trends, and discovered heuristics—or rules of thumb. The logistics manager in the international firm, on the other hand, frequently has to depend on educated guesses to determine the steps required to obtain a desired service level. Variations in locale mean variations in environment. Lack of familiarity with such variations leads to uncertainty in the decision-making process. By applying decision rules based only on the environment encountered at home, the firm will be unable to adapt well to new circumstances, and the result will be inadequate profit performance. The long-term survival of international activities depends on an understanding of the differences inherent in the international logistics field.

International Transportation Issues

Transportation determines how and when goods will be received. Global Perspective 15.1 details some of the problems that can be encountered in the transportation process. The transportation issue can be divided into three components: infrastructure, the availability of modes, and the choice of modes among the given alternatives.

Transportation Infrastructure In industrialized countries, firms can count on an established transportation network. Around the globe, however, major infrastructural variations will be encountered. Some countries may have excellent inbound and outbound transportation systems but weak internal transportation links. This is particularly true in former colonies, where the original transportation systems were designed to maximize the extractive potential of the countries. In such instances, shipping to the market may be easy, but distribution within the market may represent a very difficult and time-consuming task. Infrastructure problems can also be found in countries where most transportation networks were established between major ports and cities in past centuries. The areas lying outside the major transportation networks will encounter problems in bringing their goods to market.

New routes of commerce have also opened up, particularly between the former East and West political blocs. Yet, without the proper infrastructure the opening of markets is mainly accompanied by major new bottlenecks. On the part of the firm, it is crucial to have wide market access to be able to appeal to sufficient customers. The firm's **logistics platform,** which is determined by a location's ease and convenience of market reach under favorable cost circumstances, is a key component of a firm's competitive position. Since different countries and regions may offer alternative logistics platforms, the firm must recognize that such alternatives can be the difference between success and failure.

The logistics manager must therefore learn about existing and planned infrastructures abroad and at home and factor them into the firm's strategy. In some countries, for example, railroads may be an excellent transportation mode, far surpassing the performance of trucking, while in others the use of railroads for freight distribution may be a gamble at best. The future routing of pipelines must be determined before any major commitments are made to a particular location if the product is amenable to pipeline transportation. The transportation methods used to carry cargo to seaports or airports must be investigated. Mistakes in the evaluation of transportation options can prove to be very costly. One researcher reported the case of a food processing firm that built a pineapple cannery at the delta of a river in Mexico. Since the pineapple plantation was located upstream, the company planned to float the ripe fruit down to the cannery on barges. To its dismay, however, the firm soon discovered that at harvest time the river current was far too strong for barge traffic. Since no other feasible alternative method of transportation existed, the plant was closed and the new equipment was sold for a fraction of its original cost.[13]

Extreme variations also exist in the frequency of transportation services. For example, a particular port may not be visited by a ship for weeks or even months. Sometimes only carriers with particular characteristics, such as small size, will serve a given location.

All of these infrastructural concerns must be taken into account in the planning of the firm's location and transportation framework. The opportunity of a highly competitive logistics platform may be decisive for the firm's investment decision, since it forms a key component of the cost advantages sought by multinational corporations. If a location loses its logistics benefits, due to, for example, a deterioration of the railroad system, a firm may well decide to move on to another, more favorable locale. Business strategist Michael Porter addressed the importance of infrastructure as a determinant of national competitive advantage and highlighted the capability of

GLOBAL PERSPECTIVE 15.1

Late, Lost, and Damaged Goods

No shipper would want to win Roberts Express "Shipments from Hell" contest. "Winners" have nightmare tales of late, lost, broken, or even burned shipments, demonstrating just about everything that could possibly go wrong in transit. Judges from *Industry Week* and *Transportation and Distribution* magazines gave the top award to a shipment of auto parts that needed to be at an assembly plant in a few hours, since the factory operated on a just-in-time basis. But a misunderstanding over the chartered plane's arrival time and the time the parts needed to arrive kept the freight on the ground for hours. The entire production line was forced to shut down, costing thousands of dollars a minute. Then a thunderstorm delayed the plane's take-off by another half-hour, adding more dollars to the cost of the late shipment.

In another "Shipment from Hell," attention to detail could have averted a sticky disaster. A Danish company arranged to send a shipment by rail from New York to Washington State, but forgot to mention that the cargo needed refrigeration. After a week's journey in a railcar, the shipment of imported margarine was a gooey yellow mess. Instances of damaged or destroyed goods abound in the contest. One "winner" found its custom-made products at the bottom of Houston

Harbor. Another company's millon-dollar computer system was smashed as it rolled off the delivery truck. In an ironic twist on the damaged goods problem, one shipment was found burned and melted inside a forty-foot ocean container. It turned out the goods were firefighting equipment, sprinklers, and valves.

One contest "winner" had to bring in the police to retrieve a lost shipment. A medical supply house handed over a $90,000 surgical kit to a courier who signed for it and then lost it. The company eventually reported the kit stolen so that police could search the courier's offices. They found that the kit had been there all along.

The stories behind the "Shipments from Hell" illustrate that a host of bizarre circumstances can turn an ordinary shipment into a comedy of errors. Other notable shipping calamities included a shipment held hostage, another sent with stowaway black widow spiders, and several that were frozen or melted along the way.

While strange shipments continue, the contest has not. Roberts Express's parent company, Caliber System Inc., was acquired by FedEx in 1998, which renamed Roberts Express as FedEx Custom Critical in 2000.

 Source: **http://customcritical.fedex.com**; Gregory S. Johnson, "Damaged Goods: Hard-luck Tales of '97," *The Journal of Commerce,* January 9, 1998, IA.

governmental efforts to influence this critical issue.[14] Governments must keep the transportation dimension in mind when attempting to attract new industries or trying to retain existing firms.

Availability of Modes   International transportation frequently requires ocean or airfreight modes, which many corporations only rarely use domestically. In addition, combinations such as **land bridges** or **sea bridges** may permit the transfer of freight among various modes of transportation, resulting in **intermodal movements.** The international logistics manager must understand the specific properties of the different modes to be able to use them intelligently.

Ocean Shipping   Water transportation is a key mode for international freight movement. Three types of vessels operating in **ocean shipping** can be distinguished by their service: liner service, bulk service, and tramp or charter service. **Liner service** offers regularly scheduled passage on established routes. **Bulk service** mainly provides contractual services for individual voyages or for prolonged periods of time. **Tramp service** is available for irregular routes and scheduled only on demand.

In addition to the services offered by ocean carriers, the type of cargo a vessel can carry is also important. Most common are conventional (break bulk) cargo vessels, container ships, and roll-on-roll-off vessels. Conventional cargo vessels are useful for oversized and unusual cargoes but may be less efficient in their port operations. **Container ships** carry standardized containers that greatly facilitate the loading and unloading of cargo and intermodal transfers. As a result, the time the ship has to spend in port is reduced as are the port charges. **Roll-on-roll-off (RORO)** vessels are essentially oceangoing ferries. Trucks can drive onto built-in ramps and roll off at the destination. Another vessel similar to the RORO vessel is the LASH (lighter aboard ship) vessel. LASH vessels consist of barges stored on the ship and lowered at the point of destination. The individual barges can then operate on inland waterways, a feature that is particularly useful in shallow water.

The availability of a certain type of vessel, however, does not automatically mean that it can be used. The greatest constraint in international ocean shipping is the lack of ports and port services. For example, modern container ships cannot serve some ports because the local equipment cannot handle the resulting traffic. The problem is often found in developing countries, where local authorities lack the funds to develop facilities. In some instances, nations may purposely limit the development of **ports** to impede the inflow of imports. Increasingly, however, governments have begun to recognize the importance of an appropriate port facility structure and are developing such facilities in spite of the large investments necessary.

Air Shipping **Airfreight** is available to and from most countries. This includes the developing world, where it is often a matter of national prestige to operate a national airline. The tremendous growth in international airfreight is shown in Figure 15.2. The total volume of airfreight in relation to total shipping volume in international business remains quite small. It accounts for less than 1 percent of the total volume of international shipments, although it often represents more than 20 percent of the value shipped by industrialized countries.[15] Clearly, high-value items are more likely to be shipped by air, particularly if they have a high **density,** that is, a high weight-to-volume ratio.

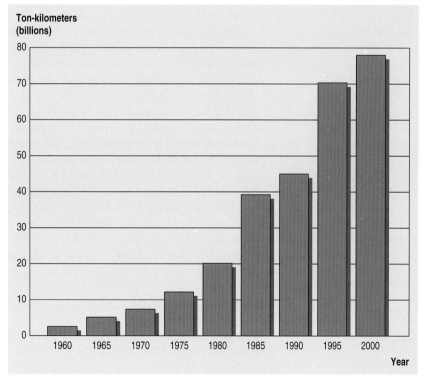

FIGURE 15.2
International Airfreight, 1960–2000

Based on data supplied by member states of the International Civil Aviation Organization (ICAO). As the number of member states increased from 116 in 1970 to 150 in 1983, there is some upward bias in the data, particularly from 1970 on, when data for the USSR were included for the first time.

Sources: *Civil Aviation Statistics of the World* (Montreal: ICAO), **(www.icao.org.)** Michael Kayal, "World Air Cargo Seen Growing 7.5% a Year to 2001," *The Journal of Commerce,* December 30, 1997, 10A.

FIGURE 15.3

Loading a Train on a Plane
Shipping by airfreight has really taken off in the past 20 years. Even large and heavy items, such as this locomotive, are shipped to their destination by air.

Source: Printed in the *Journal of Commerce,* August 29,1994.

Over the years, airlines have made major efforts to increase the volume of airfreight. Many of these activities have concentrated on developing better, more efficient ground facilities, automating air waybills, introducing airfreight containers, and providing and marketing a wide variety of special services to shippers. In addition, some airfreight companies and ports have specialized and become partners in the international logistics effort.

Changes have also taken place within the aircraft. As an example, 40 years ago, the holds of large propeller aircraft could take only about 10 tons of cargo. Today's jumbo jets can load up to 105 metric tons of cargo with an available space of 636 cubic meters,[16] hold more than 92 tons, and can therefore transport bulky products, such as locomotives, as shown in Figure 15.3. In addition, aircraft manufacturers have responded to industry demands by developing both jumbo cargo planes and combination passenger and cargo aircraft. The latter carry passengers in one section of the main deck and freight in another. These hybrids can be used by carriers on routes that would be uneconomical for passengers or freight alone.

From the shipper's perspective, the products involved must be appropriate for air shipment in terms of their size. In addition, the market situation for any given product must be evaluated. Airfreight may be needed if a product is perishable or if, for other reasons, it requires a short transit time. The level of customer service needs and expectations can also play a decisive role. For example, the shipment of an industrial product that is vital to the ongoing operations of a customer may be much more urgent than the shipment of packaged consumer products.

Selecting a Mode of Transport

The international logistics manager must make the appropriate selection from the available modes of transportation. The decision will be heavily influenced by the needs of the firm and its customers. The manager must consider the performance of each mode on four dimensions: transit time, predictability, cost, and noneconomic factors.

Transit Time   The period between departure and arrival of the carrier varies significantly between ocean freight and airfreight. For example, the 45-day **transit time** of an ocean shipment can be reduced to 24 hours if the firm chooses airfreight. The length of transit time can have a major impact on the overall operations of the firm. As an example, a short transit time may reduce or even eliminate the need for an overseas depot. Also, inventories can be significantly reduced if they are replenished frequently. As a result, capital can be freed up and used to finance other corporate opportunities. Transit time can also play a major role in emergency situations. For example, if the shipper is about to miss an important delivery date because of production delays, a shipment normally made by ocean freight can be made by air.

Perishable products require shorter transit times. Transporting them rapidly prolongs the shelf life in the foreign market. As shown in Figure 15.4, air delivery may be the only way to enter foreign markets successfully with products that have a short life

FIGURE 15.4

An Advertisement for Cut Flowers

How to ship tulips by air and come up smelling like a rose.

Cut flowers are almost as ephemeral as dreams. Beautiful, fragile, fragrant, they have a life span of mere days under the best of circumstances. So the challenge of shipping tulips from a field in Holland to a table in Ohio, still in their glorious prime, is a major one.

That's why so many tulip growers in Holland choose The New York & New Jersey Air Cargo Center through which to ship their flowers. Last year, more than $55 million worth of tulips were shipped through our airports.

The Dutch shippers know that time, coordination and connections are of the essence. They know that our Federal inspectors and import brokers are available when needed to meet their shipments as they arrive and to help expedite the flowers through the airport and on their way to market. And, they know we have the best air and surface connections to protect their flowers' freshness in transport and to meet tight delivery schedules.

We really care about the life of your product. We want you to come up smelling like a rose, whatever you ship.

Whether it's tulips or tubas, if it's going through the NY/NJ Air Cargo System, we'll get it there fast, fresh and—if it began that way—still fragrant.

For more information on air cargo services at the New York/New Jersey Airports, write to:

Manager, Air Cargo Market Development
Port Authority of New York and New Jersey
One World Trade Center, Suite 64N
New York, NY 10048

NEW YORK/NEW JERSEY AIRPORTS
Kennedy Newark LaGuardia

THE PORT AUTHORITY OF NY & NJ

Source: Courtesy of Customer and Marketing Services Division, Aviation Department, Port Authority of New York and New Jersey.

span. International sales of cut flowers have reached their current volume only as a result of airfreight.

The interaction among selling price, market distance, and form of transportation is not new. Centuries ago, Johann von Thünen, a noted German economist, developed models for the market reach of agricultural products that incorporated these factors. These models informed farmers as to what product could be raised profitably at different distances from its market. Yet, given the forms of transportation available today, the factors no longer pose the rigid constraints experienced by von Thünen, but rather offer new opportunities in international business.

At all times, the logistics manager must understand the interactions between different components of the logistics process and their effect on transit times. Unless a smooth flow throughout the supply chain can be assured, bottlenecks will deny any timing benefits from specific improvements. For example, Levi Strauss, the blue jeans manufacturer, offers customers in some of its stores the chance to be measured by a body scanner. Less than an hour after such measurement, a Levi factory has begun to cut the jeans of their choice. Unfortunately, it then takes ten days to get the finished jean to the customer.[17]

Predictability   Providers of both ocean freight and airfreight service wrestle with the issue of reliability. Both modes are subject to the vagaries of nature, which may impose delays. Yet, because **reliability** is a relative measure, the delay of one day for airfreight tends to be seen as much more severe and "unreliable" than the same delay for ocean freight. However, delays tend to be shorter in absolute time for air shipments. As a result, arrival time via air is more predictable. This attribute has a major influence on corporate strategy. For example, because of the higher predictability of airfreight, inventory safety stock can be kept at lower levels. Greater predictability also can serve as a useful sales tool, since it permits more precise delivery promises to customers. If inadequate port facilities exist, airfreight may again be the better alternative. Unloading operations for oceangoing vessels are more cumbersome and time-consuming than for planes. Merchandise shipped via air is likely to suffer less loss and damage from exposure of the cargo to movement. Therefore, once the merchandise arrives, it is more likely to be ready for immediate delivery—a fact that also enhances predictability.

An important aspect of predictability is also the capability of a shipper to track goods at any point during the shipment. **Tracking** becomes particularly important as corporations increasingly obtain products from and send them to multiple locations around the world. Being able to coordinate the smooth flow of a multitude of interdependent shipments can make a vast difference in a corporation's performance.[18] Tracking allows the shipper to check on the functioning of the supply chain and to take remedial action if problems occur. Cargo also can be redirected if sudden demand surges so require. However, such enhanced corporate response to the predictability issue is only possible if an appropriate information system is developed by the shipper and the carrier, and easily accessible to the user.

Cost of Transportation   International transportation services are usually priced on the basis of both cost of the service provided and value of the service to the shipper. Due to the high value of the products shipped by air, airfreight is often priced according to the value of the service. In this instance, of course, price becomes a function of market demand and the monopolistic power of the carrier.

The manager must decide whether the clearly higher cost of airfreight can be justified. In part, this will depend on the cargo's properties. The physical density and the value of the cargo will affect the decision. Bulky products may be too expensive to ship by air, whereas very compact products may be more appropriate for airfreight transportation. High-priced items can absorb transportation costs more easily than low-priced goods because the cost of transportation as a percentage of total product cost will be lower. As a result, sending diamonds by airfreight is easier to justify than sending coal. Alternatively, a shipper can decide to mix modes of transportation in order to reduce overall cost and time delays. For example, part of the shipment route can be covered by air, while another portion can be covered by truck or ship.

Most important, however, are the supply-chain considerations of the firm. The manager must determine how important it is for merchandise to arrive on time which, for example, will be different for standard garments versus high fashion dresses. The effect of transportation cost on price and the need for product availability abroad must also be considered. Simply comparing transportation modes on the basis of price alone is insufficient. The manager must factor in all corporate, supplier, and customer activities that are affected by the modal choice and explore the full implications of each alternative. For example, some firms may want to use airfreight as a new tool for aggressive market expansion. Airfreight may also be considered a good way to begin operations in new markets without making sizable investments for warehouses and distribution centers. The final selection of a mode will be the result of the importance of different modal dimensions to the markets under consideration. A useful overall comparison of different modes of transportation is provided in Table 15.1.

Noneconomic Factors   The transportation sector, nationally and internationally, both benefits and suffers from government involvement. Even though transportation carriers are one prime target in the sweep of privatization around the globe, many carriers are still owned or heavily subsidized by governments. As a result, governmental pressure is exerted on shippers to use national carriers, even if more economical alternatives exist. Such **preferential policies** are most often enforced when government cargo is being transported. Restrictions are not limited to developing countries. For example, in the United States, the federal government requires that all travelers on government business use national flag carriers when available.

For balance of payments reasons, international quota systems of transportation have been proposed. The United Nations Conference on Trade and Development (UNCTAD), for example, has recommended that 40 percent of the traffic between two nations be allocated to vessels of the exporting country, 40 percent to vessels of the importing country, and 20 percent to third-country vessels. However, stiff international competition among carriers and the price sensitivity of customers frequently render such proposals ineffective, particularly for trade between industrialized countries.

TABLE 15.1		MODE OF TRANSPORTATION				
Evaluating Transportation Choices	**Characteristics of Mode**	**Air**	**Pipeline**	**Highway**	**Rail**	**Water**
	Speed (1=fastest)	1	4	2	3	5
	Cost (1=highest)	1	4	2	3	5
	Loss and Damage (1=least)	3	1	4	5	2
	Frequency[1] (1=best)	3	1	2	4	5
	Dependability (1=best)	5	1	2	3	4
	Capacity[2] (1=best)	4	5	3	2	1
	Availablity (1=best)	3	5	1	2	4

[1]Frequency: number of times mode is available during a given time period.
[2]Capacity: ability of mode to handle large or heavy goods.

Source: Ronald H. Ballou, *Business Logistics Management,* 4th ed. (Upper Saddle River, NJ: Prentice-Hall, 1998), p. 146.

Although many justifications are possible for such national policies, ranging from prestige to national security, they distort the economic choices of the international corporation. Yet, these policies are a reflection of the international environment within which the firm must operate. Proper adaptation is necessary.

Export Documentation

A firm must deal with numerous forms and documents when exporting to ensure that all goods meet local and foreign laws and regulations.

A **bill of lading** is a contract between the exporter and the carrier indicating that the carrier has accepted responsibility for the goods and will provide transportation in return for payment. The bill of lading can also be used as a receipt and to prove ownership of the merchandise. There are two types of bills, negotiable and nonnegotiable. **Straight bills of lading** are nonnegotiable and are typically used in prepaid transactions. The goods are delivered to a specific individual or company. **Shipper's order** bills of lading are negotiable; they can be bought, sold, or traded while the goods are still in transit and are used for letter of credit transactions. The customer usually needs the original or a copy of the bill of lading as proof of ownership to take possession of the goods.

A **commercial invoice** is a bill for the goods stating basic information about the transaction, including a description of the merchandise, total cost of the goods sold, addresses of the shipper and seller, and delivery and payment terms. The buyer needs the invoice to prove ownership and to arrange payment. Some governments use the commercial invoice to assess customs duties.

Other export documents that may be required include export licenses, consular invoices (used to control and identify goods, they are obtained from the country to which the goods are being shipped), certificates of origin, inspection certification, dock and/or warehouse receipts, destination control statements (serve to notify the carrier and all foreign parties that the item may only be exported to certain destinations), insurance certificates, shipper's export declarations (used to control exports and compile trade statistics), and export packaging lists.[19]

The documentation required depends on the merchandise in the shipment and its destination. The number of documents required can be quite cumbersome and costly, creating a deterrent to trade. For example, before the introduction of document simplification, it was estimated that the border-related red tape and controls within the then-European Community cost European companies $9.2 billion in extra administrative costs and delays annually.[20] To eliminate the barriers posed by all this required documentation, the EC introduced the Single Administrative Document (SAD) in 1988. The SAD led to the elimination of nearly 200 customs forms required of truckers throughout the EC when traveling from one member country to another.

To ensure that all documentation required is accurately completed and to minimize potential problems, firms just entering the international market should consider using **freight forwarders,** who specialize in handling export documentation. Freight forwarders increasingly choose to differentiate themselves through the development of sophisticated information management systems, particularly with electronic data interchange (EDI). In fact, over half of freight forwarders currently use EDI.[21] Adoption of new technology by such intermediaries will be quite rapid, in light of the growing competitive pressures explained in Global Perspective 15.2.

Terms of Shipment and Sale

The responsibilities of the buyer and the seller should be spelled out as they relate to what is and what is not included in the price quotation and when ownership of goods passes from seller to buyer. **Incoterms** are the internationally accepted standard definitions for terms of sale set by the International Chamber of Commerce (ICC) since

GLOBAL PERSPECTIVE 15.2

Shop, Ship, and Track on the World Wide Web

By opening new market horizons worldwide, the Web has given retailers access to customers around the globe. While online shopping has not replaced printed catalogs and telephone call centers, it has extended the marketer's reach and has provided another valuable sales channel. An online shopper in Tokyo orders a rugged jacket from L.L. Bean with a few clicks of a mouse. The purchase is shipped from the company's Freeport, Maine, warehouse by FedEx and delivered to the customer's door within 72 hours. During its shipment, the shopper and L.L. Bean can track its movements. Bob Olive, Bean's senior logistics manager, reported that overseas sales "are growing briskly." The company web site's extensive customer service pages are available in English, Japanese, French, German, and Spanish.

The fulfillment logistics for orders typically remains the same, however, whether the orders are telephoned, faxed, mailed or placed online. After penetrating the Japanese market in the 1990s, Bean developed a $200 million business there and has smoothed out the logistics challenges of international orders. For example, Bean's in-house fulfillment center in Freeport processes domestic and international orders using product bar codes. The company's address label software is flexible enough for addresses anywhere in the world, including Japan's complex address system. All international packages are shipped within 24 hours. Orders placed at the Tokyo call center can even be shipped the same day, so Bean's Japanese customers may receive their purchases in as little as three days.

Key to the global success of direct retailers is reliable international shipping. Through companies like FedEx, the largest express transportation company, 90 percent of the world's GNP can be reached within 48 hours. FedEx continues to expand its services and networks to accommodate the growing flow of goods across national borders. The 1995 opening of its Asia-Pacific Hub in the Philippines allowed overnight intra-Asian deliveries as well as upgraded services on FedEx's own aircraft.

FedEx offers much more than timely worldwide delivery of small packages for consumers and documents for businesses. Increasingly, FedEx is handling larger packages, like component and product delivery to manufacturers and distributors. As small and medium-sized businesses become global trade players, they also need support services. "We have introduced a supply-chain management system and offer delivery services in Korea through twice-daily flight services to Korea by using our own aircraft," said Chung Myung Soo, senior manager of Pri-Ex, a Korean FedEx licensee. With FedEx, commercial customers can benefit from door-to-door service, customs clearance, and savings, in time, storage, and labor. Access to international shipment information, critical to businesses, is available both on the FedEx site and with its Super Tracker software.

While allowing firms and customers to focus on the details, such as package tracking and order status, the Internet has also opened up vast new markets across the globe to companies of all sizes. Through online sales and efficient express shipping, companies can quickly reach across continents to customers anywhere in the world.

Sources: Ken Cottrill, "Almost Business as Usual," *Traffic World,* June 19, 2000, p. 181; "FedEx Presents a Unique Total Logistics Solution," *Business Korea,* September 1999, p. 47; L.L. Bean, **www.llbean.com**, accessed April 6, 2001.

1936.[22] The Incoterms 2000 went into effect on January 1, 2000, with significant revisions to better reflect changing transportation technologies and the increased use of electronic communications.[23] Although the same terms may be used in domestic transactions, they gain new meaning in the international arena. The terms are grouped into four categories, starting with the term whereby the seller makes the goods available to the buyer only at the seller's own premises (the "E"-terms), followed by the group whereby the seller is called upon to deliver the goods to a carrier appointed by the buyer (the "F"-terms). Next are the "C"-terms, whereby the seller has to contract for carriage but without assuming the risk of loss or damage to the goods or additional costs after the dispatch, and finally the "D"-terms, whereby the seller has to bear all costs and risks to bring the goods to the destination determined by the buyer. The most common of the Incoterms used in international marketing are summarized in Figure 15.5.

Prices quoted **ex-works (EXW)** apply only at the point of origin, and the seller agrees to place the goods at the disposal of the buyer at the specified place on the date or within the fixed period. All other charges are for the account of the buyer.

FIGURE 15.5

Selected Trade Terms

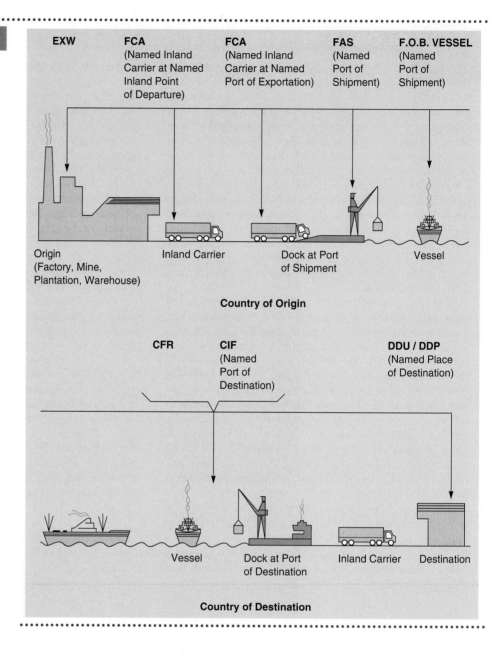

One of the new Incoterms is **free carrier (FCA),** which replaced a variety of FOB terms for all modes of transportation except vessel. FCA (named inland point) applies only at a designated inland shipping point. The seller is responsible for loading goods into the means of transportation; the buyer is responsible for all subsequent expenses. If a port of exportation is named, the costs of transporting the goods to the named port are included in the price.

Free alongside ship (FAS) at a named U.S. port of export means that the exporter quotes a price for the goods, including charges for delivery of the goods alongside a vessel at the port. The seller handles the cost of unloading and wharfage; loading, ocean transportation, and insurance are left to the buyer.

Free on board (FOB) applies only to vessel shipments. The seller quotes a price covering all expenses up to, and including, delivery of goods on an overseas vessel provided by or for the buyer.

Under **cost and freight (CFR)** to a named overseas port of import, the seller quotes a price for the goods, including the cost of transportation to the named port of debarkation. The cost of insurance and the choice of insurer are left to the buyer.

With **cost, insurance, and freight (CIF)** to a named overseas port of import, the seller quotes a price including insurance, all transportation, and miscellaneous charges to the point of debarkation from the vessel. If other than waterway transport is used, the terms are **CPT** (carriage paid to) or **CIP** (carriage and insurance paid to).

With **delivered duty paid (DDP),** the seller delivers the goods, with import duties paid, including inland transportation from import point to the buyer's premises. With **delivered duty unpaid (DDU),** only the destination customs duty and taxes are paid by the consignee. Ex-works signifies the maximum obligation for the buyer; delivered duty paid puts the maximum burden on the seller.

Careful determination and clear understanding of terms used, and their acceptance by the parties involved, are vital if subsequent misunderstandings and disputes are to be avoided not only between the parties but also within the marketer's own organization.[24]

These terms are also powerful competitive tools. The exporter should therefore learn what importers usually prefer in the particular market and what the specific transaction may require. An inexperienced importer may be discouraged from further action by a quote such as ex-plant Jessup, Maryland, whereas CIF Helsinki will enable the Finnish importer to handle the remaining costs because they are incurred in a familiar environment.

Increasingly, exporters are quoting more inclusive terms. The benefits of taking charge of the transportation on either a CIF or DDP basis include the following: (1) exporters can offer foreign buyers an easy-to-understand "delivered cost" for the deal; (2) by getting discounts on volume purchases for transportation services, exporters cut shipping costs and can offer lower overall prices to prospective buyers; (3) control of product quality and service is extended to transport, enabling the exporter to ensure that goods arrive to the buyer in good condition; and (4) administrative procedures are cut for both the exporter and the buyer.[25]

When taking control of transportation costs, however, the exporter must know well in advance what impact the additional costs will have on the bottom line. If the approach is implemented incorrectly, exporters can be faced with volatile shipping rates, unexpected import duties, and restive customers. Most exporters do not want to go beyond the CIF quotation because of uncontrollables and unknowns in the destination country. Whatever terms are chosen, the program should be agreed to by the exporter and the buyer(s) rather than imposed solely by the exporter.

International Inventory Issues

Inventories tie up a major portion of corporate funds. Capital used for inventory is not available for other corporate opportunities. Annual **inventory carrying costs** (the expense of maintaining inventories) though heavily influenced by the cost of capital and industry-specific conditions, can account for 15 percent or more of the value of the inventories themselves.[26] Therefore, proper inventory policies should be of major concern to the international logistician. In addition, **just-in-time inventory** policies, which minimize the volume of inventory by making it available only when it is needed, are increasingly required by multinational manufacturers and distributors engaging in supply-chain management. They choose suppliers on the basis of their delivery and inventory performance and their ability to integrate themselves into the supply chain. Proper inventory management may therefore become a determining variable in obtaining a sale.

The purpose of establishing **inventory** systems—to maintain product movement in the delivery pipeline and to have a cushion to absorb demand fluctuations—is the same for domestic and international operations. The international environment, however, includes unique factors such as currency exchange rates, greater distances, and duties. At the same time, international operations provide the corporation with an opportunity to explore alternatives not available in a domestic setting, such as new sourcing or location alternatives. In international operations, the firm can make use of currency fluctuation by placing varying degrees of emphasis on inventory operations, depending on the stability of the currency of a specific country. Entire operations can be shifted to different nations to take advantage of new opportunities. International inventory management can therefore be much more flexible in its response to environmental changes.

In deciding the level of inventory to be maintained, the international manager must consider three factors: the order cycle time, desired customer service levels, and use of inventories as a strategic tool.

Order Cycle Time

The total time that passes between the placement of an order and the receipt of the merchandise is referred to as **order cycle time.** Two dimensions are of major importance to inventory management: the length of the total order cycle and its consistency. In international business, the order cycle is frequently longer than in domestic business. It comprises the time involved in order transmission, order filling, packing and preparation for shipment, and transportation. Order transmission time varies greatly internationally depending on the method of communication. Supply-chain driven firms use electronic data interchange (EDI) rather than facsimile, telex, telephone, or mail.

EDI is the direct transfer of information technology between computers of trading partners.[27] The usual paperwork the partners send each other, such as purchase orders and confirmations, bills of lading, invoices, and shipment notices, are formatted into standard messages and transmitted via a direct link network or a third party network. EDI can save a large part of the processing and administrative costs associated with traditional ways of exchanging information.[28]

The order-filling time may also increase because lack of familiarity with a foreign market makes the anticipation of new orders more difficult. Packing and shipment preparation require more detailed attention. Finally, of course, transportation time increases with the distances involved. Larger inventories may have to be maintained both domestically and internationally to bridge the time gaps.

Consistency, the second dimension of order cycle time, is also more difficult to maintain in international business. Depending on the choice of transportation mode, delivery times may vary considerably from shipment to shipment. The variation requires the maintenance of larger safety stocks to be able to fill demand in periods when delays occur.

Customer Service Levels

The level of **customer service** denotes the responsiveness that inventory policies permit for any given situation. A customer service level of 100 percent would be defined as the ability to fill all orders within a set time—for example, three days. If, within the same three days, only 70 percent of the orders can be filled, the customer service level is 70 percent. The choice of customer service level for the firm has a major impact on the inventories needed. In highly industrialized nations, firms frequently are expected to adhere to very high levels of customer service. For example, in the European Union, actual performance measures for on-time delivery are 92 percent, for order accuracy 93 percent, and for damage-free delivery 95 percent.[29] Corporations are often tempted to design international customer service standards to similar levels.

Yet, service levels should not be oriented primarily around cost or customary domestic standards. Rather, the level chosen for use internationally should be based on expectations encountered in each market. The expectations are dependent on past performance, product desirability, customer sophistication, and the competitive status of the firm.

Because high customer service levels are costly, the goal should not be the highest customer service level possible, but rather an acceptable level. Different customers have different priorities. Some will be prepared to pay a premium for speed, some may put a higher value on flexibility, and another group may see low cost as the most important issue. Flexibility and speed are expensive, so it is wasteful to supply them to customers who do not value them highly.[30] If, for example, foreign customers expect to receive their merchandise within 30 days, for the international corporation to promise delivery within 10 or 15 days does not make sense. Indeed, such delivery may result in storage problems. In addition, the higher prices associated with higher customer service levels may reduce the competitiveness of a firm's product. By contrast, in a business to business setting, sometimes even a four-hour delay in the delivery of a crucial component may be unacceptable, since the result may be a shutdown of the production process.

In such instances, strategically placed depots in a region must ensure that near instantaneous response becomes possible. For example, Storage Technologies, a maker of storage devices for mainframe computers, keeps parts at seven of its European subsidiary offices so that in an emergency it can reach any continental customer within four hours.[31]

Inventory as a Strategic Tool

Inventories can be used by the international corporation as a strategic tool in dealing with currency valuation changes or to hedge against inflation. By increasing inventories before an imminent devaluation of a currency instead of holding cash, the corporation may reduce its exposure to devaluation losses. Similarly, in the case of high inflation, large inventories can provide an important inflation hedge. In such circumstances, the international inventory manager must balance the cost of maintaining high levels of inventories with the benefits accruing from hedging against inflation or devaluation. Many countries, for example, charge a property tax on stored goods. If the increase in tax payments outweighs the hedging benefits to the corporation, it would be unwise to increase inventories before a devaluation.

International Packaging Issues

Packaging is instrumental in getting the merchandise to the ultimate destination in a safe, maintainable, and presentable condition. Packaging that is adequate for domestic shipping may be inadequate for international transportation because the shipment will be subject to the motions of the vessel on which it is carried. Added stress in international shipping also arises from the transfer of goods among different modes of transportation. Figure 15.6 provides examples of some sources of stress in intermodal movement that are most frequently found in international transportation.

The responsibility for appropriate packaging rests with the shipper of goods. The U.S. Carriage of Goods by Sea Act of 1936 states: "Neither the carrier nor the ship shall be responsible for loss or damage arising or resulting from insufficiency of packing." The shipper must therefore ensure that the goods are prepared appropriately for international shipping. This is important because it has been found that "the losses that occur as a result of breakage, pilferage, and theft exceed the losses caused by major maritime casualties, which include fires, sinkings, and collision of vessels. Thus the largest of these losses is a preventable loss."[32]

Packaging decisions must also take into account differences in environmental conditions—for example, climate. When the ultimate destination is very humid or particularly cold, special provisions must be made to prevent damage to the product. The task becomes even more challenging when one considers that, in the course of long-distance transportation, dramatic changes in climate can take place. Still famous is the

FIGURE 15.6   **Stresses in Intermodal Movement**

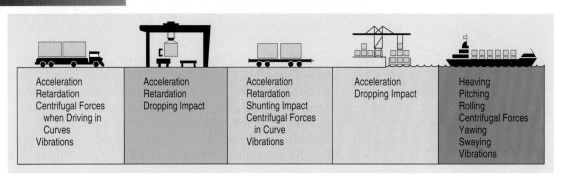

Acceleration Retardation Centrifugal Forces when Driving in Curves Vibrations	Acceleration Retardation Dropping Impact	Acceleration Retardation Shunting Impact Centrifugal Forces in Curve Vibrations	Acceleration Dropping Impact	Heaving Pitching Rolling Centrifugal Forces Yawing Swaying Vibrations

Note: Each transportation mode exerts a different set of stresses and strains on containerized cargoes. The most commonly overlooked are those associated with ocean transport.

Source: David Greenfield, "Perfect Packing for Export," from *Handling and Shipping Management*, September 1980 (Cleveland, Ohio: Penton Publishing), 47.

case of a firm in Taiwan that shipped drinking glasses to the Middle East. The company used wooden crates and padded the glasses with hay. Most of the glasses, however, were broken by the time they reached their destination. As the crates traveled into the drier Middle East, the moisture content of the hay dropped. By the time the crates were delivered, the thin straw offered almost no protection.[33]

The weight of packaging must also be considered, particularly when airfreight is used, as the cost of shipping is often based on weight. At the same time, packaging material must be sufficiently strong to permit stacking in international transportation. Another consideration is that, in some countries, duties are assessed according to the gross weight of shipments, which includes the weight of packaging. Obviously, the heavier the packaging, the higher the duty will be.

The shipper must pay sufficient attention to instructions provided by the customer for packaging. For example, requests by the customer that the weight of any one package should not exceed a certain limit or that specific package dimensions should be adhered to, usually are made for a reason. Often they reflect limitations in transportation or handling facilities at the point of destination.

Although the packaging of a product is often used as a form of display abroad, international packaging can rarely serve the dual purpose of protection and display. Therefore double packaging may be necessary. The display package is for future use at the point of destination; another package surrounds it for protective purposes.

One solution to the packaging problem in international logistics has been the development of intermodal containers—large metal boxes that fit on trucks, ships, railroad cars, and airplanes and ease the frequent transfer of goods in international shipments. Developed in different forms for both sea and air transportation, containers also offer better utilization of carrier space because of standardization of size. The shipper therefore may benefit from lower transportation rates. In addition, containers can offer greater safety from pilferage and damage. Of course, at the same time, the use of containers allows thieves to abscond with an entire shipment rather than just parts of it. On some routes in Russia, for example, theft and pilferage of cargo are so common that liability insurers will not insure container haulers in the region.[34] Container technology has greatly improved over the years. As Global Perspective 15.3 shows, specialized containers can greatly expand the trading range of products.

Container traffic is heavily dependent on the existence of appropriate handling facilities, both domestically and internationally. In addition, the quality of inland trans-

GLOBAL PERSPECTIVE 15.3

Keeping Exported Produce Fresh

From the outside, the intermodal steel container may not appear to be a very exciting piece of transportation equipment, but inside, some of them incorporate advanced technology that maintains the condition and value of the cargo. Such is the case of Sea-Land Service's "Fresh Mist" humidity-controlled refrigerated containers, designed to prevent dehydration of fresh produce during long ocean voyages. It does this by maintaining the moisture inside a refrigerated container at optimal levels, which keeps the produce fresh longer. The fresh produce arrives heavier and better looking, with a longer shelf-life and commands a higher price in overseas markets.

Inside the container, sophisticated microprocessor technology atomizes water into minute particles and injects them into the air stream—maintaining optimal humidity levels without damage to the product packaging.

Humidity Requirements and Shelf Life for Selected Fruits and Vegetables

Fresh Fruits and Vegetables	Percent Water Content	Expected Shelf Life	Optimum Humidity
Artichoke	83.7	2–3 weeks	90–95%
Asparagus	93.0	2–3 weeks	90–95%
Broccoli	89.9	10–14 days	90–95%
Cabbage (early)	92.4	3–6 weeks	95–100%
Celery	93.7	2–3 months	90–95%
Grapes	81.9	8–26 weeks	90–95%
Green onions	89.4	2–3 weeks	95–100%
Leeks	85.4	2–3 months	95–100%
Lettuce	94.8	2–3 weeks	90–95%

Source: Sea-Land Service, Inc., July 1997.

portation must be considered. If transportation for containers is not available and the merchandise must be removed, the expected cost reductions may not materialize.

In some countries, rules for the handling of containers may be designed to maintain employment. For example, U.S. union rules obligate shippers to withhold containers from firms that do not employ members of the International Longshoremen's Association for the loading or unloading of containers within a fifty-mile radius of Atlantic or Gulf ports. Such restrictions can result in an onerous cost burden.

Overall, cost attention must be paid to international packaging. The customer who ordered and paid for the merchandise expects it to arrive on time and in good condition. Even with replacements and insurance, the customer will not be satisfied if there are delays. Dissatisfaction will usually translate directly into lost sales.

International Storage Issues

Although international logistics is discussed as a movement or flow of goods, a stationary period is involved when merchandise becomes inventory stored in warehouses. Heated arguments can arise within a firm over the need for and utility of warehousing internationally. On the one hand, customers expect quick responses to orders and rapid delivery. Accommodating the customer's expectations would require locating many distribution centers around the world. On the other hand, warehouse space is expensive. In addition, the larger volume of inventory increases the inventory carrying cost. Fewer warehouses allow for consolidation of transportation and therefore lower transportation rates to the warehouse. However, if the warehouses are located far from customers, the cost of outgoing transportation increases. The international

Trade and Travel Networks

Civilization depends on trade for growth and travel makes this possible. Shipping is the most important method of world transport but economic progress and mobility are constantly being improved by the development of new routes and new methods of transport.

Road and Rail

Integrated road and rail networks are the basis of industrial society. Containerization and the extension of modern highway systems have increased flexibility and reduced the emphasis on railways transporting freight.

Roads

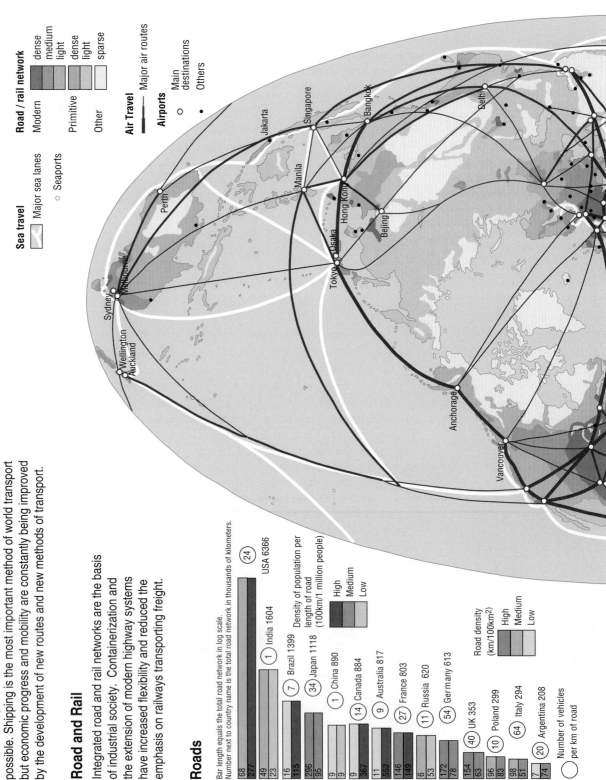

Sea travel
Major sea lanes
○ Seaports

Road / rail network
Modern: dense, medium, light
Primitive: dense, light
Other: sparse

Air Travel
Major air routes

Airports
○ Main destinations
• Others

Bar length equals the total road network in log scale.
Number next to country name is the total road network in thousands of kilometers.

(24) USA 6366 — 68 / 277
(1) India 1604 — 49 / 23
(7) Brazil 1399 — 16 / 115
(34) Japan 1118 — 296 / 95
(1) China 890 — 9 / 9
(14) Canada 884 — 9 / 367
(9) Australia 817 — 11 / 552
(27) France 803 — 146 / 149
(11) Russia 620 — 6 / 53
(54) Germany 613 — 172 / 78
(40) UK 353 — 154 / 63
(10) Poland 299 — 96 / 83
(64) Italy 294 — 98 / 51
(20) Argentina 208 — 7 / 74

Density of population per length of road (100km/1 million people)
High
Medium
Low

Road density (km/100km²)
High
Medium
Low

◯ Number of vehicles per km of road

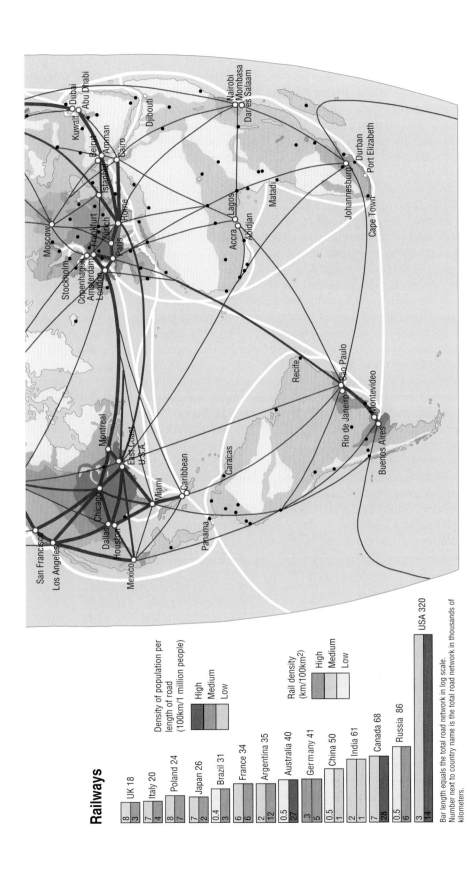

Railways

UK 18
Italy 20
Poland 24
Japan 26
Brazil 31
France 34
Argentina 35
Australia 40
Germany 41
China 50
India 61
Canada 68
Russia 86
USA 320

Density of population per length of road (100km/1 million people)
High
Medium
Low

Rail density (km/100km²)
High
Medium
Low

Bar length equals the total road network in log scale. Number next to country name is the total road network in thousands of kilometers.

Journey Time

The Suez Canal cuts 3600 nautical miles off the London–Singapore route, while the Concorde halves the London–New York journey time.

Air and Sea Routes

A complex network of primary air routes centered on the Northern Hemisphere provides rapid transit across the world for mass travel, mail, and urgent freight.

Ships also follow these principal routes, plying the oceans between major ports and transporting the commodities of world trade in bulk.

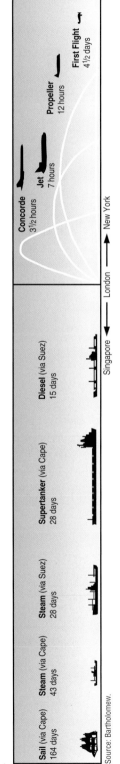

Concorde 3½ hours
Jet 7 hours
Propeller 12 hours
First Flight 4½ days

New York — London — Singapore

Sail (via Cape) 164 days
Steam (via Cape) 43 days
Steam (via Suez) 28 days
Supertanker (via Cape) 28 days
Diesel (via Suez) 15 days

Source: Bartholomew.

logistician must consider the tradeoffs between service and cost to the supply chain in order to determine the appropriate levels of warehousing.

Storage Facilities

The **location decision** addresses how many distribution centers to have and where to locate them. The availability of facilities abroad will differ from the domestic situation. For example, while public storage is widely available in some countries, such facilities may be scarce or entirely lacking in others. Also, the standards and quality of facilities can vary widely. As a result, the storage decision of the firm is often accompanied by the need for large-scale, long-term investments. Despite the high cost, international storage facilities should be established if they support the overall logistics effort. In many markets, adequate storage facilities are imperative to satisfy customer demands and to compete successfully. For example, since the establishment of a warehouse connotes a visible presence, in doing so a firm can convince local distributors and customers of its commitment to remain in the market for the long term.

Once the decision is made to use storage facilities abroad, the warehouse conditions must be carefully analyzed. As an example, in some countries warehouses have low ceilings. Packaging developed for the high stacking of products is therefore unnecessary or even counterproductive. In other countries, automated warehousing is available. Proper bar coding of products and the use of package dimensions acceptable to the warehousing system are basic requirements. In contrast, in warehouses still stocked manually, weight limitations will be of major concern. And, if no forklift trucks are available, palletized delivery is of little use.

To optimize the logistics system, the logistician should analyze international product sales and then rank order products according to warehousing needs. Products that are most sensitive to delivery time might be classified as "A" products. "A" products would be stocked in all distribution centers, and safety stock levels would be kept high. Alternatively, the storage of products can be more selective, if quick delivery by air can be guaranteed. Products for which immediate delivery is not urgent could be classified as "B" products. They would be stored only at selected distribution centers around the world. Finally, products for which there is little demand would be stocked only at headquarters. Should an urgent need for delivery arise, airfreight could again assure rapid shipment. Classifying products enables the international logistician to substantially reduce total international warehousing requirements and still maintain acceptable service levels.

Special Trade Zones

Areas where foreign goods may be held or processed and then reexported without incurring duties are called **foreign trade zones.** The zones can be found at major ports of entry and also at inland locations near major production facilities. For example, Kansas City, Missouri, has one of the largest foreign trade zones in the United States.

The existence of trade zones can be quite useful to the international firm. For example, in some countries, the benefits derived from lower labor costs may be offset by high duties and tariffs. As a result, location of manufacturing and storage facilities in these countries may prove uneconomical. Foreign trade zones are designed to exclude the impact of duties from the location decision. This is done by exempting merchandise in the foreign trade zone from duty payment. The international firm can therefore import merchandise; store it in the foreign trade zone; and process, alter, test, or demonstrate it—all without paying duties. If the merchandise is subsequently shipped abroad (that is, reexported), no duty payments are ever due. Duty payments become due only if the merchandise is shipped into the country from the foreign trade zone.

Trade zones can also be useful as transshipment points to reduce logistics cost and redesign marketing approaches. For example, Audiovox was shipping small quantities of car alarms from a Taiwanese contract manufacturer directly to distributors in Chile. The shipments were costly and the marketing strategy of requiring high minimum orders stopped distributors from buying. The firm resolved the dilemma by using a Miami trade zone to ship the alarms from Taiwan and consolidate the goods with other shipments to Chile. The savings in freight costs allowed the Chilean distributors to order whatever quantity they wanted and allowed the company to quote lower prices. As a result, sales improved markedly.[35]

All parties to the arrangement benefit from foreign trade zones. The government maintaining the trade zone achieves increased employment and investment. The firm using the trade zone obtains a spearhead in the foreign market without incurring all of the costs customarily associated with such an activity. As a result, goods can be reassembled, and large shipments can be broken down into smaller units. Also, goods can be repackaged when packaging weight becomes part of the duty assessment. Finally, goods can be given domestic "made-in" status if assembled in the foreign trade zone. Thus, duties may be payable only on the imported materials and component parts rather than on the labor that is used to finish the product.

In addition to foreign trade zones, governments also have established export processing zones and special economic areas. The common dimensions for all the zones are that special rules apply to them when compared with other regions of the country, and that the purpose of these special rules lies in the government's desire to stimulate the economy, particularly the export side of international trade.

Export processing zones usually provide tax- and duty-free treatment for production facilities whose output is destined abroad. The **maquiladoras** of Mexico are one example of a program that permits firms to take advantage of sharp differentials in labor costs. Firms can carry out the labor-intensive part of their operations in Mexico, while sourcing raw materials or component parts from other nations.

One country that has used trade zones very successfully for its own economic development is China. Through the creation of **special economic zones,** in which there are no tariffs, substantial tax incentives, and low prices for land and labor, the government has attracted many foreign investors bringing in billions of dollars. The investors have brought new equipment, technology, and managerial know-how and have increased local economic prosperity substantially. The job generation effect has been so strong that the central Chinese government has expressed concern about the overheating of the economy and the inequities between regions with and without trade zones.[36]

For the logistician, the decision whether to use such zones mainly is framed by the overall benefit for the supply-chain system. Clearly, additional transport and retransport are required, warehousing facilities need to be constructed, and material handling frequency will increase. However, the costs may well be balanced by the preferential government treatment or by lower labor costs.

Management of International Logistics

The very purpose of a multinational firm is to benefit from system synergism and a persuasive argument can be made for the coordination of international logistics at corporate headquarters. Without coordination, subsidiaries will tend to optimize their individual efficiency but jeopardize the efficiency of the overall performance of the supply chain.

Centralized Logistics Management

A significant characteristic of the centralized approach to international logistics is the existence of headquarters staff that retains decision-making power over logistics activities affecting international subsidiaries. If headquarters exerts control, it must also take the primary responsibility for its decisions. Clearly, ill will may arise if local managers are appraised and rewarded on the basis of a performance they do not control. This may be particularly problematic if headquarters staff suffers from a lack of information or expertise.

To avoid internal problems, both headquarters staff and local management should report to one person. This person, whether the vice president for international logistics or the president of the firm, can then become the final arbiter to decide the firm's priorities. Of course, the individual should also be in charge of determining appropriate rewards for managers, both at headquarters and abroad, so that corporate decisions that alter a manager's performance level will not affect the manager's appraisal and evaluation. Further, the individual can contribute an objective view when inevitable conflicts arise in international logistics coordination. The internationally centralized decision-making process leads to an overall supply-chain management perspective that can dramatically improve profitability.

Decentralized Logistics Management

An alternative to the centralized international logistics system is decentralization. The main rationale for such decentralization is the fact that dealing with markets on a global scale can quickly lead to problems of coordination. Particularly when the firm serves many international markets that are diverse in nature, total centralization might leave the firm unresponsive to local adaptation needs.

If each subsidiary is made a profit center in itself, each one carries the full responsibility for its performance, which can lead to greater local management satisfaction and to better adaptation to local market conditions. Yet often such decentralization deprives the logistics function of the benefits of coordination. For example, while headquarters, referring to its large volume of overall international shipments, may be able to extract bottom rates from transportation firms, individual subsidiaries by themselves may not have similar bargaining power. The same argument applies also to the sourcing situation, where the coordination of shipments by the purchasing firm may be much more cost-effective than individual shipments from many small suppliers around the world.

Once products are within a specific market, however, increased input from local logistics operations should be expected and encouraged. At the very least, local managers should be able to provide input into the logistics decisions generated by headquarters. Ideally, within a frequent planning cycle, local managers can identify the logistics benefits and constraints existing in their particular market and communicate them to headquarters. Headquarters can then either adjust its international logistics strategy accordingly or explain to the manager why system optimization requires actions different from the ones recommended. Such a justification process will help greatly in reducing the potential for animosity between local and headquarters operations.

Outsourcing Logistics Services

A third option, used by some corporations, is the systematic outsourcing of logistics capabilities. By collaborating with transportation firms, private warehouses, or other specialists, corporate resources can be concentrated on the firm's core product.

Many firms whose core competency does not include logistics find it more efficient to use the services of companies specializing in international shipping. This is usually true for smaller shipping volumes, for example in cases when smaller import-export firms or smaller shipments are involved. Such firms prefer to outsource at least some of the international logistics functions, rather than detracting from staff resources and time. Some logistical services providers carve specific niches in the transnational shipping market, specializing for example in consumer goods forwarding. The resulting lower costs and better service make such third parties the preferred choice for many firms. On the other hand, when hazardous or other strictly regulated materials are involved, some firms may choose to retain control over handling and storing activities, in view of possible liability issues.[37]

Going even further, **one-stop logistics** allows shippers to buy all the transportation modes and functional services from a single carrier,[38] instead of going through the pain of choosing different third parties for each service. One-stop logistics ensures a more efficient global movement of goods via different transportation modes. Specialized companies provide EDI tracking services and take care of cumbersome customs procedures; they also offer distribution services, such as warehousing and inventory management. Finally, third parties may even take some of the international shipper's logistical functions. This rapidly growing trend provides benefits to both carriers and shippers.[39] The latter enjoy better service and simplified control procedures, and claims settlement. On the other hand, one-stop logistics can help carriers achieve economies of scale and remain competitive in a very dynamic market. The proliferation of one-stop logistics practices is facilitated by the wider acceptance of EDI and the growing importance of quality criteria versus cost criteria in shipping decisions.

While the cost savings and specialization benefits of such a strategy seem clear, one must also consider the loss of control for the firm, its suppliers, and its customers that may result from such outsourcing. Yet, contract logistics does not and should not require the handing over of control. Rather, it offers concentration on one's specialization—a division of labor. The control and responsibility toward the supply chain remain with the firm, even though operations may move to a highly trained outside organization.

Logistics and the Environment

The logistician plays an increasingly important role in allowing the firm to operate in an environmentally conscious way. Environmental laws, expectations, and self-imposed goals set by firms are difficult to adhere to without a logistics orientation that systematically takes such concerns into account. Since laws and regulations differ across the world, the firm's efforts need to be responsive to a wide variety of requirements. One new logistics orientation that has grown in importance due to environmental concerns is the development of **reverse distribution** systems. Such systems are instrumental in ensuring that the firm not only delivers the product to the market, but also can retrieve it from the market for subsequent use, recycling, or disposal. To a growing degree the ability to develop such reverse logistics is a key determinant for market acceptance and profitability.

Society also recognizes that retrieval should not be restricted to short-term consumer goods, such as bottles. Rather, it may be even more important to devise systems that enable the retrieval and disposal of long-term capital goods, such as cars, refrigerators, air conditioners, and industrial goods, with the least possible burden on the environment. In Germany, for example, car manufacturers are required to take back their used vehicles for dismantling and recycling purposes. Global Perspective 15.4 presents some of the major issues connected to the design of a reverse logistics system.

Managers are often faced with the trade-offs between environmental concerns and logistical efficiency. Companies increasingly need to learn how to simultaneously achieve environmental and economic goals. Esprit, the apparel maker, and The Body

GLOBAL PERSPECTIVE 15.4

Reverse Logistics Management is Crucial

Reverse Logistics—the handling and disposition of returned products and use of related materials and information—is a new way for firms in a wide array of industries to improve customer service and increase revenue.

According to the Reverse Logistics Executive Council, U.S. firms pay more than an estimated $35 billion annually for handling, transportation, and processing of returned products. This does not include disposition management, administration time, and the cost of converting unproductive returns into productive assets. Monitoring this operation can help firms increase efficiency significantly.

Reverse logistics planning involves better gatekeeping of returns; quick disposition of those products; sound financial, warehouse, and transportation management; and well-defined recycling, refurbishment, and other return reuse features. It combines relevant software, policies, practices, systems, and training with commitment and dedication. Further complicating matters is the fact that each product has its own life cycle, and each return may require different treatment, depending on whether the product is defective, damaged, recyclable, or repackageable.

Despite the challenges, some firms are managing reverse logistics admirably. Even though returns can be as high as 50 percent for goods sold online, Office Depot Online, a division of the large office-supply retailer, is recording returns of under 10 percent. To reduce the number of returns, Office

Depot tries to ensure that customers don't order the wrong thing by mistake. When customers order laser printer toner cartridges, for example, they're automatically asked their printer's brand name to prevent mix-ups. Online shoppers are also allowed to review the list of products they purchased earlier, which reduces unnecessary duplication.

New York-based cosmetics company Estee Lauder is a champion of return management. At the heart of Lauder's reverse logistics operation is its proprietary software system. Since the system has been up and running, the company has been able to reduce production and inventory levels, shave $500,000 from annual labor costs, and write off far fewer destroyed products. The system automates the previously time-intensive process of sorting through returns. When Lauder receives returns, it scans package bar codes to determine the products' expiration date and condition. Based on this information, it can consolidate the items and immediately scrap damaged or expired ones.

Reverse logistics goes beyond keeping track of returns. It also encompasses disposing of them. Many firms are taking innovative approaches to reduce scrap and even produce surprising revenues. While all these reverse logistics activities are impressive, contributing to trimmed costs and enhanced revenues, the ultimate benefit of effectively managing reverse logistics is the information generated about product returns and related materials that can be shared within the company.

Source: Harvey Meyer, "Many Happy Returns," *Journal of Business Strategy* 20, July–August 1999, 27–31; http://www.officedepot.com; http://www.esteelauder.com.

Shop, the well-known British cosmetics producer, screen their suppliers for environmental and social responsibility practices. The significance of this trend is reaffirmed in the new set of rules issued by the International Organization of Standardization. ISO-14000 specifically targets international environmental practices by evaluating companies both at the organization level (management systems, environmental performance, and environmental auditing) and product level (life-cycle assessment, labeling, and product standards).[40]

From the perspective of materials management and physical distribution, environmental practices are those that bring about fewer shipments, less handling, and more direct movement. Such practices are to be weighted against optimal efficiency routines, including just-in-time inventory and quantity discount purchasing.

On the transportation side, logistics managers will need to expand their involvement in carrier and routing selection. For example, shippers of oil or other potentially hazardous materials increasingly will need to ensure that the carriers used have excellent safety records and use only double-hulled ships. Society may even expect corporate involvement in choosing the route that the shipment will travel, preferring routes that are far from ecologically important and sensitive zones. Firms will need to assert leadership in such consideration of the environment to provide society with a better quality of life.

Summary

As competitiveness is becoming increasingly dependent on efficiency, international logistics and supply-chain management are becoming of major importance.

International logistics is concerned with the flow of materials into, through, and out of the international corporation and therefore includes materials management as well as physical distribution. The logistician must recognize the total systems demands on the firm, its suppliers, and customers to develop trade-offs between various logistics components. By taking a supply-chain perspective, the manager can develop logistics systems that are supplier and customer focused and highly efficient. Implementation of such a system requires close collaboration between all members of the supply chain.

International logistics differs from domestic activities in that it deals with greater distances, new variables, and greater complexity because of national differences. One major factor to consider is transportation. The international manager needs to understand transportation infrastructures in other countries and modes of transportation such as ocean shipping and airfreight. The choice among these modes will depend on the customer's demands and the firm's transit time, predictability, and cost requirements. In addition, noneconomic factors such as government regulations weigh heavily in this decision.

Inventory management is another major consideration. Inventories abroad are expensive to maintain yet often crucial for international success. The logistician must evaluate requirements for order cycle times and customer service levels to develop an international inventory policy that can also serve as a strategic management tool.

International packaging is important because it ensures arrival of the merchandise at the ultimate destination in safe condition. In developing packaging, environmental conditions such as climate and handling conditions must be considered.

The logistics manager must also deal with international storage issues and determine where to locate inventories. International warehouse space will have to be leased or purchased and decisions will have to be made about utilizing foreign trade zones.

International logistics management is increasing in importance. Implementing the logistics function with an overall supply-chain perspective that is responsive to environmental demands will increasingly be a requirement for successful global competitiveness.

Key Terms and Concepts

materials management	container ships	freight forwarders	delivery duty unpaid
physical distribution	roll-on-roll-off (RORO)	Incoterms	(DDU)
systems concept	ports	ex-works (EXW)	inventory carrying costs
total cost concept	airfreight	free carrier (FCA)	just-in-time inventory
trade-off concept	density	free alongside ship (FAS)	inventory
supply-chain management	transit time	free on board (FOB)	order cycle time
logistics platform	reliability	cost and freight (CFR)	customer service
land bridges	tracking	cost, insurance, and	location decision
sea bridges	preferential policies	freight (CIF)	foreign trade zones
intermodal movements	bill of lading	carriage paid to (CPT)	maquiladora
ocean shipping	straight bill of lading	carriage and insurance	special economic zones
liner service	shipper's order	paid to (CIP)	one-stop logistics
bulk service	commercial invoice	delivery duty paid (DDP)	reverse distribution
tramp service			

Questions for Discussion

1. Explain the key aspects of supply-chain management.
2. Contrast the use of ocean shipping and airfreight.
3. Explain the meaning and impact of transit time in international logistics.
4. How and why do governments interfere in "rational" freight carrier selection?
5. How can an international firm reduce its order cycle time?
6. Why should customer service levels differ internationally? Is it, for example, ethical to offer a lower customer service level in developing countries than in industrialized countries?
7. What role can the international logistician play in improving the environmental friendliness of the firm?

Internet Exercises

1. What types of information are available to the exporter on The Transport Web? Go to **www.transportweb.com**, and give examples of transportation links that an exporter would find helpful and explain why.

2. Use an online database to select a freight forwarder. (Refer to **www.freightnet.com** or **http://forwarders.com**, directories of freight forwarders.)

Recommended Readings

Bowersox, Donald J., David L. Closs, and Theodore P. Stank. *21st Century Logistics: Making Supply Chain Integration a Reality.* Michigan: Michigan State University Press, 1999.

Harvard Business Review on Managing the Value Chain. Boston: Harvard Business School Press, 2000.

Kotabe, Masaaki. *Global Sourcing Strategy: R&D, Manufacturing and Marketing Interfaces.* New York: Quorum Books, 1992.

LaLonde, Bernard J., and James L. Ginter, *Supply Chain Management Bibliography.* Columbus, OH: The Supply Chain Management Research Group, Spring 1996.

Poirier, Charles C. *Advanced Supply Chain Management: How to Build a Sustained Competitive Advantage.* San Francisco: Berrett-Koehler, 1999.

Pollock, Daniel. *Precipice.* Oak Brook, IL: Council of Logistics Management, 1997.

Schary, Philip B., and Tage Skjott-Larsen. *Managing the Global Supply Chain.* Copenhagen: Copenhagen Studies in Economics and Management, 1998.

Simchi-Levi, David, Philip Kaminsky, and Edith Simchi-Levi. *Designing and Managing the Supply Chain: Concepts, Strategies, and Cases (Book and CD-ROM).* New York: Irwin/McGraw-Hill, 1999.

Stock, James R., and Douglas M. Lambert. *Strategic Logistics Management.* New York: McGraw-Hill, 2001.

Notes

1. Stanley E. Fawcett, Linda L. Stanley, and Sheldon R. Smith, "Developing a Logistics Capability to Improve the Performance of International Operations," *Journal of Business Logistics* 18, 2 (1997): 101–127.

2. Patrick M. Byrne and Stephen V. Young, "UK Companies Look at Supply Chain Issues," *Transportation and Distribution* (February 1995): 50–56.

3. Bernard LaLonde and James Gitner, "Activity-Based Costing: Best Practices," *Paper # 606*, The Supply Chain Management Research Group, The Ohio State University, September 1996.

4. Paul T. Nelson and Gadi Toledano, "Challenges for International Logistics Management," *Journal of Business Logistics* 1, 2 (1979): 7.

5. Toshiro Hiromoto, "Another Hidden Edge: Japanese Management Accounting," in *Trends in International Business: Critical Perspectives*, ed. M. Czinkota and M. Kotabe (Oxford, Blackwell Publishers, 1998), 217–222.

6. Tom Davis, "Effective Supply Chain Management," *Sloan Management Review* (Summer 1993): 35–45.

7. Perry A. Trunick, "CLM: Breakthrough of Champions, Council of Logistics Management's 1994 Conference," *Transportation and Distribution* (December 1994).

8. Coopers and Lybrand, "The Value Chain Analysis," *Efficient Consumer Response Europe* (London, 1995).

9. Richard T. Hise, "The Implications of Time-Based Competition on International Logistics Strategies," *Business Horizons* (September/October 1995): 39–45.

10. Charles C. Poirier and Stephen E. Reiter, *Supply Chain Optimization: Building the Strongest Total Business Network* (San Francisco: Berrett-Koehler Publishers, 1996).

11. Michael R. Czinkota, "Global Neighbors, Poor Relations," in *Trends in International Business*, ed. M. Czinkota and M. Kotabe Oxford: Blackwell 1998: 20–27.

12. James H. Perry, "Emerging Economic and Technological Futures: Implications for Design and Management of Logistics Systems in the 1990s," *Journal of Business Logistics* 12 (1991): 1–16.

13. David A. Ricks, *Blunders in International Business*, 3d ed. (Cambridge: Blackwell Publishers, 2000).

14. Michael E. Porter, *The Competitive Advantage of Nations* (New York: The Free Press, 1990).

15. Gunnar K. Sletmo and Jacques Picard, "International Distribution Policies and the Role of Air Freight," *Journal of Business Logistics* 6, 1 (1984): 35–52.

16. Ian Putzger, "Pricing: Based on Volume or Weight?" *The Journal of Commerce* (February 15, 2000): 10.

17. "Survey E-Management," *The Economist* (November 11, 2000): 36.

18. Peter Buxbaum, "Timberland's New Spin on Global Logistics," *Distribution* (May 1994): 32–36.

19. U.S. Department of Commerce, *A Basic Guide to Exporting* (Washington, DC: U.S. Government Printing Office, 1992).

20. Julie Wolf, "Help for Distribution in Europe," *Northeast International Business*, January 1989, 52.

21. Paul R. Murphy and James M. Daley, "International Freight Forwarder Perspectives on Electronic Data Interchange and Information Management Issues," *Journal of Business Logistics* 17, 1 (1996): 65, 77.

22. *International Trade Procedures* (Philadelphia: CoreStates Bank, 1995), 49.

23. International Chambers of Commerce, *Incoterms 2000* (Paris: ICC Publishing, 2000).

24. Kevin Maloney, "Incoterms: Clarity at the Profit Margin," *Export Today* 6 (November–December 1990): 45–46.

25. "How Exporters Efficiently Penetrate Foreign Markets," *International Business*, December 1993, 48.

26. James R. Stock and Douglas M. Lambert, *Strategic Logistics Management*, 4th ed. (New York: McGraw-Hill, 2001): 195.

27. Huan Neng Chiu, "The Integrated Logistics Management System: A Framework and Case Study," *International Journal of Physical Distribution and Logistics Management* 6 (1995): 4–22.

28. L. Solis, "Is It Time for EDI?" *Global Trade and Transportation* 5 (1993): 30.

29. Patrick M. Byrne, Johan C. Aurik, and Jan Van der Oord, "New Priorities for Logistics Services in Europe," *Transportation and Distribution* (February 1994): 43–48.

30. Bernard LaLonde, Kee-Hian Tan, and Michael Standing, "Forget Supply Chains, Think of Value Flows," *Transformation*, Gemini Consulting, 3 (summer 1994): 24–31.

31. Gregory L. Miles, "Have Spares, Will Travel," *International Business* (December 1994): 26–27.

32. Charles A. Taft, *Management of Physical Distribution and Transportation*, 7th ed. (Homewood, IL: Irwin, 1984): 324.

33. Ricks, *Blunders in International Business*, 2000.

34. Elizabeth Canna, "Russian Supply Chains," *American Shipper* (June 1994): 49–53.

35. Marita von Oldenborgh, "Power Logistics," *International Business* (October 1994): 32–34.

36. Li Rongxia, "Free Trade Zones in China," *Beijing Review* (August 2–8, 1993): 14–21.

37. Kant Rao and Richard R. Young, "Factors Influencing Outsourcing of Logistics Functions," *International Journal of Physical Distribution and Logistics Management* 6 (1994): 11–19.

38. B.J. LaLonde, "Whatever Happened to One-Stop Transportation Shopping?" *Transport Topics* 13 (1991): 1.

39. Janjaap Semeijn and David B. Vellenga, "International Logistics and One-Stop Shopping," *International Journal of Physical Distribution and Logistics Management* 10 (1995): 26–44.

40. Haw-Jan Wu and Steven C. Dunn, "Environmentally Responsible Logistics Systems," *International Journal of Physical Distribution and Logistics Management* 2 (1995): 20–38.

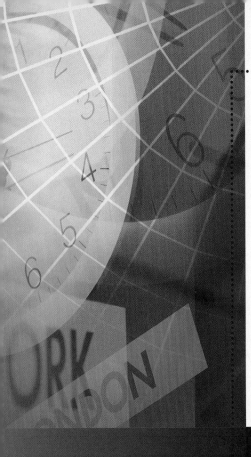

CHAPTER 16

Multinational Financial Management

LEARNING OBJECTIVES

- To understand how value is measured and managed across the multiple units of the multinational firm

- To understand how international business and investment activity alters and adds to the traditional financial management activities of the firm

- To understand the three primary currency exposures that confront the multinational firm

- To examine how exchange rate changes alter the value of the firm, and how management can manage or hedge these exposures

CHANGING VALUES: SATISFYING SHAREHOLDERS

Ulrich Hartmann, the chief executive of industrial giant Veba AG, is doing something unheard of in Germany: He's worrying about shareholder value. He has laid off thousands of workers, fired longtime managers, and closed divisions that date back to Veba's beginnings—all in the name of investors. "Our commitment," he said in the previous year's annual report, "is to create value for you, our shareholders."

The developments at Veba, Germany's fourth-largest company in revenue terms, underscore a trend catching hold in German boardrooms. Mr. Hartmann believes the trend will pick up in Germany if only, he says, because the pursuit of shareholder value is in everyone's interest. "Satisfying the shareholders is the best way to make sure that other stakeholders are served as well," he says. "It does no good when all the jobs are at sick companies."

But the German public—used to a fabled "German model" of management that advocates describe as "capitalism with a human face"—remains deeply suspicious of the alternative way of doing business. "A number of people are left behind," says Norbert Wieczorek, a member of Germany's lower house of parliament and an economic expert with the opposition Social Democratic Party. "That's not the German way."

Mr. Hartmann is one of a new breed of German managers who are enthusiastically embracing the shareholder-value concept. Others are Juergen Dormann at Hoescht AG and Juergen Schrempp at Daimler-Benz AG. During a recent interview, a secretary interrupted the conversation to notify Mr. Schrempp of Daimler's opening stock price. "A year ago, no one in the company knew what the stock price was," he says. Now, he adds, the company keeps stockholders in mind with everything it does.

Driving companies to change are ever-growing capital requirements. Unable to raise enough money in Germany, companies are turning to foreigners. Nearly half the shares of drug companies Hoechst, Bayer AG, and Schering AG are owned by non-Germans, who want more than just a dividend check. "There is no German or French or American capital market anymore," says Veba's Mr. Hartmann. "It is a global capital market, and we all have to play by the same rules." ●

Source: "Changing Values: Satisfying Shareholders Is a Hot New Concept at Some German Firms," Greg Steinmetz, *The Wall Street Journal,* Wednesday March 6, 1996, A1, A10.

What exactly is *management* of the multinational firm attempting to achieve? The **maximization of shareholder value** is, of course, the ultimate goal, and given the good graces of the marketplace, that is indeed what is eventually achieved. But internally, within the virtual walls of the multinational firm, what exactly is management trying to maximize or minimize in pursuit of this goal? This chapter discusses first how the global firm trades off complex goals in order to preserve and create shareholder value, and secondly, how the financial management activities of the firm are expanded and differ from domestic management.

Global Financial Goals

The multinational firm, because it is a conglomeration of many firms operating in a multitude of economic environments, must determine for itself the proper balance between three primary financial objectives:

1. Maximization of consolidated, after-tax, income
2. Minimization of the firm's effective global tax burden
3. Correct positioning of the firm's income, cash flows, and available funds

These goals are frequently inconsistent, in that the pursuit of one goal may result in a less desirable outcome in regard to another goal. Management must make decisions about the proper trade-offs between goals about the future (which is why people are employed as managers, not computers).

Genus Corporation

A sample firm aids in illustrating how the various components of the multinational firm fit together, and how financial management must make decisions regarding trade-offs. Genus Corporation is a U.S.-based manufacturer and distributor of extremity-stimulus medical supplies.[1] The firm's corporate headquarters and original manufacturing plant are in New Orleans, Louisiana.

Genus currently has three wholly owned foreign subsidiaries located in Brazil, Germany, and China. In addition to the parent company selling goods in the domestic (U.S.) market and exporting goods to Mexico and Canada, each of the foreign subsidiaries purchases subassemblies (transfers) from the parent company. The subsidiaries then add value in the form of specific attributes and requirements for the local-country market, and distribute and sell the goods in the local market (Brazil, Germany, and China).

The three countries where Genus has incorporated subsidiaries pose very different challenges for the financial management of the firm. These challenges are outlined in Figure 16.1.

FIGURE 16.1

Genus Corporation and Foreign Subsidiaries

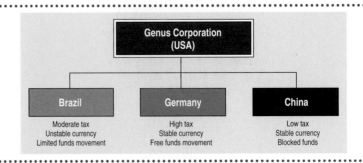

Tax Management   Genus, like all firms in all countries, would prefer to pay less taxes rather than more. Whereas profits are taxed at relatively low to moderate rates in China and Brazil, Germany's income tax rate is relatively high (though currently equal to that in the United States). If Genus could "rearrange" its profits among its units, it would prefer to make more of its profits in China and Brazil, given the lower tax burden placed upon profits in those countries.

Currency Management   Ultimately, for valuation purposes, the most important attribute of any of the three country currencies is its ability to maintain its value versus the U.S. dollar, the reporting currency of the parent company. The German mark (Deutschemark) is considered one of the world's three primary currencies, and although it occasionally suffers wide swings in value versus the dollar, has maintained its value well over time. The Chinese renminbi (or yuan as it is sometimes called) is not freely convertible into other currencies without governmental approval, and its value is therefore highly controlled and maintained. The Brazilian real, however, is of particular worry. In previous years the value of the Brazilian currency has been known to fall dramatically, wiping out the value of profits generated in Brazil when converted to any other currency, like the dollar. As opposed to what tax management would recommend, Genus would prefer to "rearrange" its profits into Germany and Deutschemarks for currency management purposes.

Funds Flow Management   The ability to move funds with relative ease and timeliness in a multinational firm is extremely important. For Genus, the German subsidiary experiences no problems with funds movements, as the German financial system is highly developed and open. Although Brazil possesses a number of bureaucratic requirements for justifying the movement of funds in and out of the country, it is still relatively open for moving funds cross-border. Genus's problems lie in China. The Chinese government makes it nearly impossible for foreign corporations to move funds out of China with any frequency, although bringing capital into China is not a problem. For funds management purposes, Genus would like to "rearrange" its profits and cash flows to minimize having funds blocked up in China.

The challenge to financial management of the global firm is management's ability to find the right trade-off between these often conflicting goals and risks.

Multinational Management

A number of helpful reminders about multinational companies aid in describing the financial management issues confronting Genus:

- The primary goal of the firm, domestic or multinational, is the maximization of consolidated profits, after tax.
- *Consolidated profits* are the profits of all the individual units of the firm originating in many different currencies as expressed in the currency of the parent company, in this case, the U.S. dollar. Consolidated profits are *not* limited to those earnings that have been brought back to the parent company (repatriated), and in fact these profits may never be removed from the country in which they were earned.
- Each of the incorporated units of the firm (the U.S. parent company and the three foreign subsidiaries) has its own set of traditional financial statements: statement of income, balance sheet, and statement of cash flows. These financial statements are expressed in the local currency of the unit for tax and reporting purposes to the local government.

Table 16.1 provides an overview of the current year's profits before and after tax on both the individual unit level and on the consolidated level, in both local currency and U.S. dollar value.

TABLE 16.1 — Genus Corporation's Consolidated Gross Profits (in 000s)

Unit (currency symbol)	Gross Profit (local currency)	Income Tax Rate (percent)	Taxes Payable (local currency)	Profit After Tax (local currency)	Exchange Rate (fc/US$)	Gross Profit (US$)
U.S. Parent company (US$)	4,500	35%	1,575	2,925	_____	$2,925
Brazilian subsidiary (R$)	6,250	25%	1,563	4,688	1.1500	$4,076
German subsidiary (DEM)	4,500	35%	1,575	2,925	1.7000	$1,721
Chinese subsidiary (RMB)	2,500	30%	750	1,750	8.5000	$ 206
Consolidated Profits after tax (000s)						$8,928
Shares outstanding						10,000,000
Earnings per share (EPS)						$ 0.89

Notes:
1. Each individual unit of the company maintains its books in local currency as required by host governments.
2. fc is foreign currency.
3. Each individual unit's profits are translated into U.S. dollars using the average exchange rate for the period (year).
4. U.S. parent company's sales are derived from both sales to unrelated parties in the United States, Mexico (exports), and Canada (exports), as well as intra-firm sales (transfers) to the three individual foreign subsidiaries.
5. Tax calculations assume all profits are derived from the active conduct of merchandise trade, and all profits are retained in the individual units (no dividend distributions from subsidiaries to parent).

- The owners of Genus, its shareholders, track the firm's financial performance on the basis of its earnings per share (EPS). EPS is simply the consolidated profits of the firm, in U.S. dollars, divided by the total number of shares outstanding:

$$EPS = \frac{\text{Consolidated profits after tax}}{\text{Shares outstanding}} = \frac{US\$8,928,000}{10,000,000} = US\$0.89/\text{share}$$

- Each affiliate is located within a country's borders and is therefore subject to all laws and regulations applying to business activities within that country. These laws and regulations include specific practices as they apply to corporate income and tax rates, currency of denomination of operating and financial cash flows, and conditions under which capital and cash flows may move into and out of the country.

Multinational financial management is not a separate set of issues from domestic or traditional financial management, but the additional levels of risk and complexity introduced by the conduct of business across borders. Business across borders introduces different laws, different methods, different markets, different interest rates, and most of all, different currencies.

The many dimensions of multinational financial management are most easily explained in the context of a firm's financial decision-making process in evaluating a potential foreign investment. Such an evaluation includes:

- Capital budgeting, which is the process of evaluating the financial feasibility of an individual investment, whether it be the purchase of a stock, real estate, or a firm
- Capital structure, which is the determination of the relative quantities of debt capital and equity capital that will constitute the funding of the investment
- Raising long-term capital, which is the acquisition of equity or debt for the investment; it requires the selection of the exact form of capital, its maturity, its reward or repayment structure, its currency of denomination, and its source

- Working capital and cash flow management, which is the management of operating and financial cash flows passing in and out of a specific investment project

Multinational financial management means that all the above financial activities will be complicated by the differences in markets, laws, and especially currencies. This is the field of financial risk management. Firms may intentionally borrow foreign currencies, buy forward contracts, or price their products in different currencies to manage their cash flows that are denominated in foreign currencies.

Changes in interest and exchange rates will affect each of the above steps in the international investment process. All firms, no matter how "domestic" they may seem in structure, are influenced by exchange rate changes. The financial managers of a firm that has any dimension of international activity, imports or exports, foreign subsidiaries or affiliates, must pay special attention to these issues if the firm is to succeed in its international endeavors. The discussion begins with the difficulties of simply getting paid for international sales, import/export financing.

Import/Export Trade Financing

Unlike most domestic business, international business often occurs between two parties that do not know each other very well. Yet, in order to conduct business, a large degree of financial trust must exist. This financial trust is basically the trust that the buyer of a product will actually pay for it on or after delivery. For example, if a furniture manufacturer in South Carolina receives an order from a distributor located in Cleveland, Ohio, the furniture maker will ordinarily fill the order, ship the furniture, and await payment. Payment terms are usually 30 to 60 days. This is trade on an "open account basis." The furniture manufacturer has placed a considerable amount of financial trust in the buyer but normally is paid with little problem.

Internationally, however, financial trust is pushed to its limit. An order from a foreign buyer may constitute a degree of credit risk (the risk of not being repaid) that the producer (the exporter) cannot afford to take. The exporter needs some guarantee that the importer will pay for the goods. Other factors that tend to intensify this problem include the increased lag times necessary for international shipments and the potential risks of payments in different currencies. For this reason, arrangements that provide guarantees for exports are important to countries and companies wanting to expand international sales. This can be accomplished through a sequence of documents surrounding the letter of credit.

Trade Financing Using a Letter of Credit (L/C)

A lumber manufacturer in the Pacific Northwest of the United States, Vanport, receives a large order from a Japanese construction company, Endaka, for a shipment of old-growth pine lumber. Vanport has not worked with Endaka before and therefore seeks some assurance that payment for the lumber will actually be made. Vanport ordinarily does not require any assurance of the buyer's ability to pay (sometimes a small down payment or deposit is made as a sign of good faith), but an international sale of this size is too large a risk. If Endaka could not or would not pay, the cost of returning the lumber products to the United States would be prohibitive. Figure 16.2 illustrates the following sequence of events that will complete the transaction.

1. Endaka Construction (JAP) requests a letter of credit (L/C) to be issued by its bank, Yokohama Bank.
2. Yokohama Bank will determine whether Endaka is financially sound and capable of making the payments as required. This is a very important step because Yokohama Bank simply wants to guarantee the payment, not make the payment.

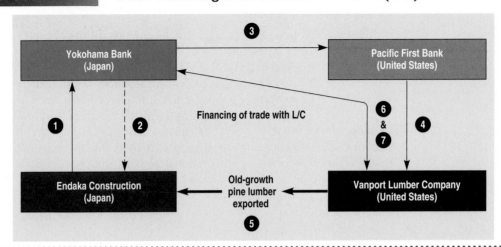

FIGURE 16.2   Trade Financing with a Letter of Credit (L/C)

3. Yokohama Bank, once satisfied with Endaka's application, issues the L/C to a representative in the United States or to the exporter's bank, Pacific First Bank. The L/C guarantees payment for the merchandise if the goods are shipped as stipulated in accompanying documents. Customary documents include the commercial invoice, customs clearance and invoice, the packing list, certification of insurance, and a bill of lading.

4. The exporter's bank, Pacific First, assures Vanport that payment will be made after evaluating the letter of credit. At this point the credit standing of Yokohama Bank has been substituted for the credit standing of the importer itself, Endaka Construction.

5. When the lumber order is ready, it is loaded onboard the shipper (called a common carrier). When the exporter signs a contract with a shipper, the signed contract serves as the receipt that the common carrier has received the goods, and it is termed the **bill of lading.**

6. Vanport draws a **draft** against Yokohama Bank for payment. The draft is the document used in international trade to effect payment and explicitly requests payment for the merchandise, which is now shown to be shipped and insured consistent with all requirements of the previously issued L/C. (If the draft is issued to the bank issuing the L/C, Yokohama Bank, it is termed a **bank draft.** If the draft is issued against the importer, Endaka Construction, it is a **trade draft.**) The draft, L/C, and other appropriate documents are presented to Pacific First Bank for payment.

7. If Pacific First Bank (US) had **confirmed** the letter of credit from Yokohama Bank, it would immediately pay Vanport for the lumber and then collect from the issuing bank, Yokohama. If Pacific First Bank had not confirmed the letter of credit, it only passes the documents to Yokohama Bank for payment (to Vanport). The confirmed, as opposed to unconfirmed, letter of credit obviously speeds up payment to the exporter.

Regardless, with the letter of credit as the financial assurance, the exporter or the exporter's bank is collecting payment from the importer's bank, not from the importer itself. It is up to the specific arrangements between the importer (Endaka) and the importer's bank (Yokohama) to arrange the final settlement at that end of the purchase.

If the trade relationship continues over time, both parties will gain faith and confidence in the other. With this strengthening of financial trust, the trade financing relationship will loosen. Sustained buyer-seller relations across borders eventually end up operating on an open account basis similar to domestic commerce.

International Capital Budgeting

Any investment, whether it be the purchase of stock, the acquisition of real estate, or the construction of a manufacturing facility in another country, is financially justified if the present value of expected cash inflows is greater than the present value of expected cash outflows, in other words, if it has a positive **net present value (NPV).** The construction of a **capital budget** is the process of projecting the net operating cash flows of the potential investment to determine if it is indeed a good investment.

Capital Budget Components and Decision Criteria

All capital budgets are only as good as the accuracy of the cost and revenue assumptions. Adequately anticipating all of the incremental expenses that the individual project imposes on the firm is critical to a proper analysis.

A capital budget is composed of three primary cash flow components:

1. **Initial Expenses and Capital Outlays:** The initial capital outlays are normally the largest net cash outflow occurring over the life of a proposed investment. Because the cash flows occur up front, they have a substantial impact on the net present value of the project.
2. **Operating Cash Flows:** The operating cash flows are the net cash flows the project is expected to yield once production is under way. The primary positive net cash flows of the project are realized in this stage; net operating cash flows will determine the success or failure of the proposed investment.
3. **Terminal Cash Flows:** The final component of the capital budget is composed of the salvage value or resale value of the project at its end. The terminal value will include whatever working capital balances can be recaptured once the project is no longer in operation (at least by this owner).

The financial decision criterion for an individual investment is whether the net present value of the project is positive or negative.[2] The net cash flows in the future are discounted by the average cost of capital for the firm (the average of debt and equity costs). The purpose of discounting is to capture the fact that the firm has acquired investment capital at a cost (interest). The same capital could have been used for other projects of other investments. It is therefore necessary to discount the future cash flows to account for this foregone income of the capital, its opportunity cost. If NPV is positive, then the project is an acceptable investment. If the project's NPV is negative, then the cash flows expected to result from the investment are insufficient to provide an acceptable rate of return, and the project should be rejected.

A Proposed Project Evaluation

The capital budget for a manufacturing plant in Singapore serves as a basic example. ACME, a U.S. manufacturer of household consumer products, is considering the construction of a plant in Singapore in 1999. It would cost US$1,660,000 to build and would be ready for operation on January 1, 2000. ACME would operate the plant for three years and then would sell the plant to the Singapore government.

To analyze the proposed investment, ACME must estimate what the sales revenues would be per year, the costs of production, the overhead expenses of operating the plant per year, the depreciation allowances for the new plant and equipment, and the Singapore tax rate on corporate income. The estimation of all net operating cash flows is very important to the analysis of the project. Often the entire acceptability of a foreign investment may depend on the sales forecast for the foreign project.

But ACME needs U.S. dollars, not Singapore dollars. The only way the stockholders of ACME would be willing to undertake the investment is if it would be profitable in terms of their own currency, the U.S. dollar. This is the primary theoretical

Although projects may be similar, the capital budgeting process must include an assessment of the higher risks associated with international projects, such as Mobil Corporation's expanded oil production platforms in the British sector of the North Sea.

Source: © Larry Lee 1992.

distinction between a domestic capital budget and a multinational capital budget. The evaluation of the project in the viewpoint of the parent will focus on whatever cash flows, either operational or financial, will find their way back to the parent firm in U.S. dollars.

ACME must therefore forecast the movement of the Singapore dollar (S$) over the four-year period as well. The spot rate on January 1, 1999 is S$1.6600/US$. ACME concludes that the rate of inflation will be roughly 5 percent higher per year in Singapore than in the United States. If the theory of purchasing power parity holds, as described in Chapter 7, it should take roughly 5 percent more Singapore dollars to buy a U.S. dollar per year. Using this assumption, ACME forecasts the exchange rate from 1999 to 2002.

After considerable study and analysis, ACME estimates that the net cash flows of the Singapore project, in Singapore dollars, would be those on line 1 in Table 16.2. Line 2 lists the expected exchange rate between Singapore dollars and U.S. dollars over the four-year period, assuming it takes 5 percent more Singapore dollars per U.S. dollar each year (the Singapore dollar is therefore expected to depreciate versus the U.S. dollar). Combining the net cash flow forecast in Singapore dollars with the expected exchange rates, ACME can now calculate the net cash flow per year in U.S. dollars. ACME notes that although the initial expense is sizable, S$1,660,000 or US$1,000,000, the project produces positive net cash flows in its very first year of operations (2000) of US$172,117, and remains positive every year after.

ACME estimates that its cost of capital, both debt and equity combined (the weighted average cost of capital), is about 16 percent per year. Using this as the rate of discount, the discount factor for each of the future years is found. Finally, the net cash flow in U.S. dollars multiplied by the present value factor yields the present values of each net cash flow. The net present value of the Singapore project is a negative US$107,919; ACME may now decide not to proceed with the project since it is financially unacceptable.

Risks in International Investments

How is the ACME capital budget different from a similar project constructed in Bangor, Maine? It is riskier, at least from the standpoint of cross-border risk. The higher risk of an international investment arises from the different countries, their laws, regulations, potential for interference with the normal operations of the investment project, and obviously currencies, all of which are unique to international investment.

The risk of international investment is considered greater because the proposed investment will be within the jurisdiction of a different government. Governments have

TABLE 16.2

Multinational Capital Budget: Singapore Manufacturing Facility

Line #	Description	1999	2000	2001	2002
1	Net cash flow in S$	(1,660,000)	300,000	600,000	1,500,000
2	Exchange rate, S$/US$	1.6600	1.7430	1.8302	1.9217
3	Net cash flow in US$	(1,000,000)	172,117	327,833	780,559
4	Present value factor	1.0000	0.8621	0.7432	0.6407
5	Present value in US$	(1,000,000)	148,377	243,633	500,071
6	Net present value in US$	(107,919)			
7	Net present value in S$	5,505			

Notes:

a. The spot exchange rate of S$1.6600/US$ is assumed to change by 5 percent per year, $1.6600 \times 1.05 = 1.7430$.

b. The present value factor assumes a weighted average cost of capital, the discount rate, of 16 percent. The present value factor then is found using the standard formula of $1/(1 + .16)^t$, where t is the number of years in the future (1, 2, or 3).

Inflation Rates and Interest Rates Around the World

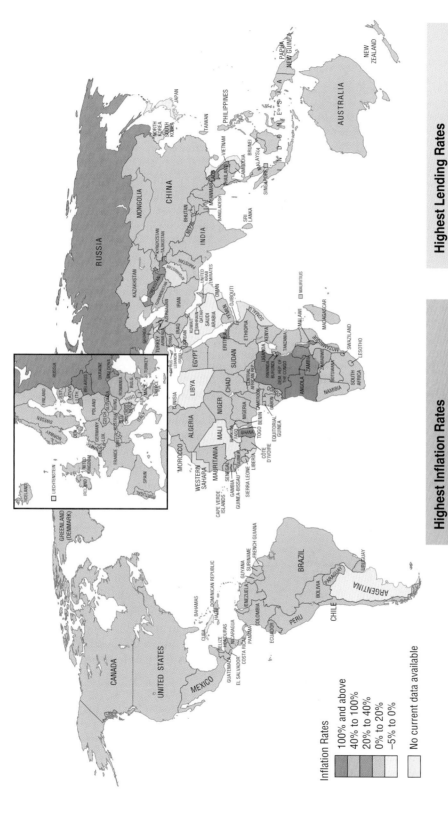

Inflation Rates

- 100% and above
- 40% to 100%
- 20% to 40%
- 0% to 20%
- −5% to 0%
- No current data available

Highest Inflation Rates

Dem. Rep. of Congo	555.7	Tajikistan	34.0
Angola	325.0	Burundi	31.9
Belarus	169.0	Moldova	31.3
Ecuador	96.2	Malawi	29.6
Zimbabwe	55.9	Ukraine	28.2
Turkey	54.9	Laos	27.1
Romania	45.7	Uzbekistan	25.4
		Ghana	25.0

Highest Lending Rates

Dem. Rep. of Congo	119.2	Uruguay	47.9
Angola	74.9	Belarus	45.6
Ecuador	58.6	Zambia	35.1
Kyrgystan	55.4	Russia	34.3
Zimbabwe	50.0	Armenia	33.4
Ukraine	49.5	Mongolia	32.2
Malawi	48.2	Moldova	30.1
		Bolivia	30.0

Sources: *2001 World Development Indicators*, The World Bank; International Monetary Fund, www.imf.org/external/pubs/ft/weo/2001/01/data/index

the ability to pass new laws, including the potential nationalization of the entire project. The typical problems that may arise from operating in a different country are changes in foreign tax laws, restrictions placed on when or how much in profits may be repatriated to the parent company, and other types of restrictions that hinder the free movement of merchandise and capital among the proposed project, the parent, and any other country relevant to its material inputs or sales.

The other major distinction between a domestic investment and a foreign investment is that the viewpoint or perspective of the parent and the project are no longer the same. The two perspectives differ because the parent only values cash flows it derives from the project. So, for example, in Table 16.2 the project generates sufficient net cash flows in Singapore dollars that the project is acceptable from the project's viewpoint, but not from the parent's viewpoint. Assuming the same 16 percent discount rate, the NPV in Singapore dollars is +S$5,505, while the NPV to the U.S. parent was −US$107,919 as noted previously. But what if the exchange rate were not to change at all—remain *fixed* for the 1999–2002 period? The NPV would then be positive from both viewpoints (project NPV remains +S$5,505, parent's NPV is now US$3,316). Or what if the Singapore government were to restrict the payment of dividends back to the U.S. parent firm, or somehow prohibit the Singapore subsidiary from exchanging Singapore dollars for U.S. dollars (capital controls)? Without cash flows in U.S. dollars, the parent would have no way of justifying the investment. And all of this could occur while the project itself is sufficiently profitable when measured in local currency (Singapore dollars). This split between project and parent viewpoint is a critical difference in international investment analysis.

Capital Structure: International Dimensions

The choice of how to fund the firm is called capital structure. Capital is needed to open a factory, build an amusement park, or even start a hot dog stand. If capital is provided by owners of the firm, it is called equity. If capital is obtained by borrowing from others, such as commercial banking institutions, it is termed debt. Debt must be repaid with interest over some specified schedule. Equity capital, however, is kept in the firm. Owners are risking their own capital in the enterprise; they are entitled to a proportion of the profits.

The Capital Structure of the Firm

The trade-offs between debt and equity are easily seen by looking at extreme examples of capital structures. If a firm had no debt, all capital would have to come from the owners. This may limit the size of the firm, as the owners do not have bottomless pockets. The primary benefit is that all net operating revenues are kept. There are no principal or interest payments to make. A firm with a large debt (highly leveraged), however, would have the capital of others with which to work. The scale of the firm could be larger, and all net profits would still accrue to the equity holders alone. The primary disadvantage of debt is the increasing expense of making principal and interest payments. At the extreme, this could prove to be an ever-increasing proportion of net cash flows.

Any firm's ability to grow and expand is dependent on its ability to acquire additional capital as it grows. The net profits generated over previous periods may be valuable but are rarely enough to provide needed capital expansion. Firms therefore need access to capital markets, both debt and equity. Chapter 7 provided an overview of the major debt and equity markets available internationally, but it is important to remember that the firm must have *access* to the markets to enjoy their fruits.

TABLE 16.3 **Financing Alternatives for Foreign Affiliates**	**Foreign Affiliate Can Raise Equity Capital:**	**Foreign Affiliate Can Raise Debt Capital:**
	1. From the parent	1. From the parent
	2. From a joint-venture partner in the parent's country, a joint-venture partner in the host country, or a share issue in the host country	2. From a bank loan or bond issue in the host country or the parent firm's home country
	3. From a third-country market such as a share issue in the Euro-equity market	3. From a third-country bank loan, bond issue, Euro-syndicated credit, or Euro-bond issue

The Capital Structure of Foreign Subsidiaries

The choice of what proportions of debt and equity to use in international investments is usually dictated by either the debt-equity structure of the parent or the debt-equity structure of competitive firms in the host country. The parent firm sees equity investment as capital at risk; therefore, it would usually prefer to provide as little equity capital as possible. Although funding the foreign subsidiary primarily with debt would still put the parent's capital at risk, debt service provides a strict schedule for cash flow repatriation to the lender. Equity capital's return, dividends from profits, depends on managerial discretion. It is this discretion, the proportion of profits returned to the parent versus profits retained and reinvested in the project or firm, that often leads to conflict between host-country authorities and the multinational firm.

The sources of debt for a foreign subsidiary theoretically are quite large, but in reality they often are quite limited. The alternatives listed in Table 16.3 are often radically reduced in practice because many countries have relatively small capital markets. These countries often either officially restrict the borrowing by foreign-owned firms in their countries or simply do not have affordable capital available for the foreign firm's use. The parent firm is then often forced to provide not only the equity but also a large proportion of the debt to its foreign subsidiaries.

The larger firms internationally will often have their own financial subsidiaries, companies purely for the purpose of acquiring the capital needed for the entire company's continuing growth needs. These financial subsidiaries will often be the actual unit extending the debt or equity capital to the foreign project or subsidiary. The hope is that, with time and success, the foreign investment will grow sufficiently to establish its own credit standing and acquire more and more of its capital needs from the local markets in which it operates.

International Working Capital and Cash Flow Management

Working capital management is the financing of short-term or current assets, but the term is used here to describe all short-term financing and financial management of the firm. Even a small multinational firm will have a number of different cash flows moving throughout its system at one time. The maintenance of proper liquidity, the monitoring of payments, and the acquisition of additional capital when needed—all of these require a great degree of organization and planning in international operations.

Operating Cash Flows and Financing Cash Flows

Firms possess both operating cash flows and financing cash flows. **Operating cash flows** arise from the everyday business activities of the firm such as paying for materials or resources (accounts payable) or receiving payments for items sold (accounts receivable). In addition to the direct cost and revenue cash flows from operations, there are a number of indirect cash flows. The indirect cash flows are primarily license fees paid to the owners of particular technological processes and royalties to the holders of patents of copyrights.

Financing cash flows arise from the funding activities of the firm. The servicing of existing funding sources, interest on existing debt, and dividend payments to share-holders constitute potentially large and frequent cash flows. Periodic additions to debt or equity through new bank loans, new bond issuances, or supplemental stock sales may also add to the volume of financing cash flows in the multinational firm.

A Sample Cash Flow Mapping

Figure 16.3 provides an overview of how operational and financial cash flows may ap-pear for a U.S.-based multinational firm. In addition to having some export sales in Canada, it may import some materials from Mexico. The firm has gained access to several different European markets by first selling its product to its German subsidiary, which then provides the final touches necessary for sales in Germany, France, and Switzerland. Sales and purchases by the parent with Canada and Mexico give rise to a continuing series of accounts receivables and accounts payable, which may be de-nominated in Canadian dollars, Mexican pesos, or U.S. dollars.

Intrafirm Cash Flows and Transfer Prices

Cash flows between the U.S. parent and the German subsidiary will be both opera-tional and financial in nature. The sale of the major product line to the German sub-sidiary creates intrafirm account receivables and payables. The payments may be de-nominated in either U.S. dollars or German marks. The intrafirm sales may, in fact, be two-way if the German subsidiary is actually producing a form of the product not made in the United States but needed there.

One of the most difficult pricing decisions many multinational firms must make concerns the price at which they sell their products to their own subsidiaries and af-filiates. These prices, called **transfer prices,** theoretically are equivalent to what the same product would cost if purchased on the open market. However, it is often impossible to find such a product on the open market; it may be unique to the firm and its product line. The result is a price that is set internally and may result in the subsidiary being more or less profitable. This, in turn, has impacts on taxes paid in host countries. Global Perspective 16.1 illustrates what happens when governments

FIGURE 16.3

Operating and Financing Cash Flows of a U.S.-Based Multinational Firm

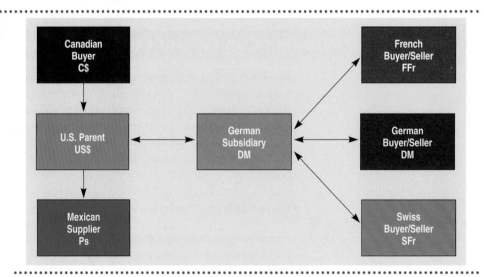

GLOBAL PERSPECTIVE 16.1

Swiss Unit Pays Penalty for Transfer Pricing Abuse

Tax authorities believe that Nippon Roche K.K. failed to declare taxable income totalling ¥14 billion between 1992 and 1995, according to sources familiar with the case. The income in question was allegedly transferred to the company's Swiss parent firm, Roche Holding Ltd., through a practice known as transfer pricing, in which a subsidiary pays artificially inflated prices for goods purchased from its overseas parent to cut taxable income in the host country, they said.

The sources said Nippon Roche allegedly manipulated prices of raw materials for cancer drugs and other medicine purchased from F. Hoffman-La Roche Ltd., a drug company under Roche Holding. Nippon Roche could be ordered to pay an additional ¥3.8. billion in taxes for failing to declare ¥4.5 billion in taxable income between 1989 and 1991. Under an agreement with Swiss tax authorities earlier this year, Japanese tax authorities settled on a figure of some ¥5.5 billion for the amount of undeclared income transferred to the parent firm to avoid double taxation.

Source: "Swiss Unit Faces Hefty Penalty for Tax Evasion," Japan Times, November 10, 1996.

and firms do not agree on transfer prices. (See Chapter 15 for a more detailed discussion of transfer pricing.)

The foreign subsidiary may also be using techniques, machinery, or processes that are owned or patented by the parent firm and so must pay royalties and license fees. The cash flows are usually calculated as a percentage of the sales price in Germany. Many multinational firms also spread the overhead and management expenses incurred at the parent over their foreign affiliates and subsidiaries that are using the parent's administrative services.

There are also a number of financing cash flows between the U.S. parent and the German subsidiary. If the subsidiary is partially financed by loans extended by the parent, the subsidiary needs to make regular payments to the parent. If the German subsidiary is successful in its operations and generates a profit, then dividends will be paid back to the parent. If, at some point, the German subsidiary needs more capital than what it can retain from its own profits, it may need additional debt or equity capital (from any of the potential sources listed in Table 16.3). These obviously would add to the potential financial cash flow volume.

The subsidiary, in turn, is dependent on its sales in Germany (German mark revenues), France (French franc revenues), and Switzerland (Swiss franc revenues) to generate the needed cash flows for paying everyone else. This "map" of operating and financing cash flows does not even attempt to describe the frequency of the various foreign currency cash flows, or to assign the responsibility for managing the currency risks. The management of cash flows in a larger multinational firm, one with possibly 10 or 20 subsidiaries, is obviously complex. The proper management of the cash flows is, however, critical to the success of the multinational business.

Cash Flow Management

The structure of the firm dictates how cash flows and financial resources can be managed. The trend in the past decade has been for the increasing centralization of most financial and treasury operations. The centralized treasury often is responsible for both funding operations and cash flow management. The centralized treasury often may enjoy significant economies of scale, offering more services and expertise to the various units of the firm worldwide than the individual units themselves could support. However, regardless of whether the firm follows a centralized or decentralized approach, there are a number of operating structures that help the multinational firm manage its cash flows.

Netting Figure 16.4 expands our firm to two European subsidiaries, one in Germany and one in France. The figure illustrates how many of the cash flows between units of a multinational firm are two-way and may result in unneeded transfer costs and transaction expenses. Coordination between units simply requires planning and budgeting of intrafirm cash flows so that two-way flows are "netted" against one another, with only one smaller cash flow as opposed to two having to be undertaken.

Netting can occur between each subsidiary and the parent, and between the subsidiaries themselves (it is often forgotten that many of the activities in a multinational firm occur between subsidiaries, and not just between individual subsidiaries and the parent). Netting is particularly helpful if the two-way flow is in two different currencies, as each would be suffering currency exchange charges for intrafirm transfers.

Cash Pooling A large firm with a number of units operating both within an individual country and across countries may be able to economize on the amount of firm assets needed in cash if one central pool is used for **cash pooling.** With one pool of capital and up-to-date information on the cash flows in and out of the various units, the firm spends much less in terms of foregone interest on cash balances, which are held in safekeeping against unforeseen cash flow shortfalls.

For example, for the firm described in Figure 16.4, the parent and German and French subsidiaries may be able to consolidate all cash management and resources in one place—for example, New York (associated with the U.S. parent). One cash manager for all units would be in a better position for planning intercompany payments, including controlling the currency exposures of the individual units. A single large pool also may allow the firm to negotiate better financial service rates with banking institutions for cash-clearing purposes. In the event that the cash manager would need to be closer to the individual units (both proximity and time zone), the two European units could combine to run cash from one or the other for both.

Leads and Lags The timing of payments between units of a multinational is somewhat flexible. Again, this allows the management of payments between the French and German subsidiaries and between the parent and the subsidiaries to be much more flexible, allowing the firm not only to position cash flows where they are needed most, but also to help manage currency risk. A foreign subsidiary that is expecting its local currency to fall in value relative to the U.S. dollar may try to speed up or **lead** its payments to the parent. Similarly, if the local currency is expected to rise versus the dollar, the subsidiary may want to wait, or **lag,** payments until exchange rates are more favorable.

Reinvoicing Multinational firms with a variety of manufacturing and distribution subsidiaries scattered over a number of countries within a region may often find it more economical to have one office or subsidiary taking ownership of all invoices and payments between units.

FIGURE 16.4 **Netting and Cash Pooling of Cash Flows in the Multinational Firm**

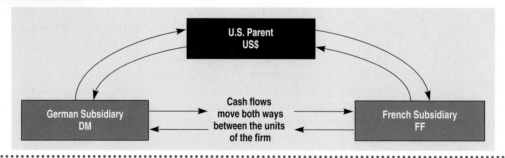

FIGURE 16.5   **Establishing a Reinvoicing Center in the Multinational Firm**

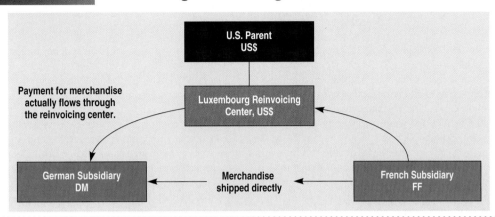

For example, Figure 16.5 illustrates how our sample firm could be restructured to incorporate a **reinvoicing** center. The site for the reinvoicing center in this case is Luxembourg, a country that is known to have low taxes and few restrictions on income earned from international business operations. The Luxembourg subsidiary buys from one unit and sells to a second unit, therefore taking ownership of the goods and reinvoicing the sale to the next unit. Once ownership is taken, the sale/purchase can be redenominated in a different currency, netted against other payments, hedged against specific currency exposures, or repriced in accordance with potential tax benefits of the reinvoicing center's host country.

Internal Banks   Some multinational firms have found that their financial resources and needs are becoming either too large or too sophisticated for the financial services that are available in many of their local subsidiary markets. One solution to this has been the establishment of an **internal bank** within the firm. The internal bank actually buys and sells payables and receivables from the various units, which frees the units of the firm from struggling for continual working capital financing and lets them focus on their primary business activities.

All of these structures and management techniques often are combined in different ways to fit the needs of the individual multinational firm. Some techniques are encouraged or prohibited by laws and regulations (for example, many countries limit the ability to lead and lag payments), depending on the host-country's government and stage of capital market liberalization. Multinational cash flow management requires flexibility in thinking—artistry in some cases—as much as technique on the part of managers.

Foreign Exchange Exposure

Companies today know the risks of international operations. They are aware of the substantial risks to balance sheet values and annual earnings that interest rates and exchange rates may inflict on any firm at any time. Financial managers, international treasurers, and financial officers of all kinds are expected to protect the firm from such risks. Firms have, in varying degrees, three types of foreign currency exposure:

1. **Transaction exposure:** This is the risk associated with a contractual payment of foreign currency. For example, a U.S. firm that exports products to France will receive a guaranteed (by contract) payment in French francs in the future. Firms that buy or sell internationally have **transaction exposure** if any of the cash flows are denominated in foreign currency.

GLOBAL PERSPECTIVE 16.2

Business Won't Hedge the Euro Away

The euro was not kind to large U.S. multinationals this year. As the currency plummeted from $1.04 last January to a low of about 82 cents in October, many companies watched helplessly as the dollar value of their European earnings headed south. McDonald's Corp., for instance, reported that the euro's fall could slash its full-year earnings by as much as 7 cents a share, or about 5 percent.

Such damage wasn't preordained. Coca-Cola Co., with 20 percent of its sales coming from Europe, didn't lose a penny. Reason: It hedged its foreign earnings by buying options that have a guaranteed currency exchange rate. Many other companies, though, were not so smart—or lucky. Should investors take them to task for failing to hedge successfully?

The short answer is no. Hedging is an expensive, inexact science—far more complex than it might appear at first glance. A company that spends large sums on hedging—by using forward contracts, swaps, or options to get fixed rates—is essentially betting on a currency's move. The euro's 20 percent plunge this year is an unusually large move, and most companies didn't foresee a need to hedge against it. Moreover, exchange rates also go up. It clearly wouldn't make sense to criticize a company that benefited from a windfall 20 percent gain because a currency went up.

No matter how well a company hedges, its earnings will sometimes get hit. But investors who buy shares of multinationals shouldn't complain. They would be smarter to hedge their own bets.

Source: "Business Won't Hedge the Euro Away," *Business Week,* Debra Sparks, December 4, 2000.

2. **Economic exposure:** This is the risk to the firm that its long-term cash flows will be affected, positively or negatively, by unexpected future exchange rate changes. Although many firms that consider themselves to be purely domestic may not realize it, all firms have some degree of **economic exposure.**

3. **Translation exposure:** This risk arises from the legal requirement that all firms consolidate their financial statements (balance sheets and income statements) of all worldwide operations annually. Therefore, any firm with operations outside its home country, operations that will be either earning foreign currency or valued in foreign currency, has **translation exposure.**

Transaction exposure and economic exposure are "true exposures" in the financial sense. This means they both present potential threats to the value of a firm's cash flows over time. The third exposure, translation, is a problem that arises from accounting. Under the present accounting principles in practice across most of the world's industrialized countries, translation exposure is not the problem it once was. For the most part, few real cash resources should be devoted to a purely accounting-based event. As illustrated by Global Perspective 16.2, hedging the currency risks of a multinational company is a controversial issue for management today.

Transaction Exposure

Transaction exposure is the most commonly observed type of exchange rate risk. Only two conditions are necessary for a transaction exposure to exist: (1) a cash flow that is denominated in a foreign currency and (2) the cash flow will occur at a future date. Any contract, agreement, purchase, or sale that is denominated in a foreign currency that will be settled in the future constitutes a transaction exposure.

The risk of a transaction exposure is that the exchange rate might change between the present date and the settlement date. The change may be for the better or for the worse. For example, suppose that an American firm signs a contract to purchase heavy rolled-steel pipe from a South Korean steel producer for 21,000,000 Korean won. The payment is due in 30 days upon delivery. The 30-day account payable, so typical of international trade and commerce, is a transaction exposure for the U.S. firm. If the spot exchange rate on the date the contract is signed is Won 700/$, the U.S. firm would expect to pay

$$\frac{\text{Won } 21,000,000}{\text{Won } 700/\$} = \$30,000$$

But the firm is not assured of what the exchange rate will be in 30 days. If the spot rate at the end of 30 days is Won 720/$, the U.S. firm would actually pay less. The payment would then be $29,167. If, however, the exchange rate changed in the opposite direction, for example to Won 650/$, the payment could just as easily increase to $32,308. This type of price risk, transaction exposure, is a major problem for international commerce.

Transaction Exposure Management

Management of transaction exposures usually is accomplished by either **natural hedging** or **contractual hedging.** Natural hedging is the term used to describe how a firm might arrange to have foreign currency cash flows coming in and going out at roughly the same times and same amounts. This is referred to as natural hedging because the management or hedging of the exposure is accomplished by matching offsetting foreign currency cash flows and, therefore, does not require the firm to undertake unusual financial contracts or activities to manage the exposure. For example, a Canadian firm that generates a significant portion of its total sales in U.S. dollars may acquire U.S. dollar debt. The U.S. dollar earnings from sales could then be used to service the dollar debt as needed. In this way, regardless of whether the C$/US$ exchange rate goes up or down, the firm would be naturally hedged against the movement. If the U.S. dollar went up in value against the Canadian dollar, the U.S. dollars needed for debt service would be generated automatically by the export sales to the United States. U.S. dollar inflows would match U.S. dollar cash outflows.

Contractual hedging is when the firm uses financial contracts to hedge the transaction exposure. The most common foreign currency contractual hedge is the **forward contract,** although other financial instruments and derivatives, such as currency futures and options, are also used. The forward contract (see Chapter 7) would allow the firm to be assured a fixed rate of exchange between the desired two currencies at the precise future date. The forward contract would also be for the exact amount of the exposure.

A **hedge** is an asset or a position whose value moves in the equal but opposite direction of the exposure. This means that if an exposure experienced a loss in value of $50, the hedge asset would offset the loss with a gain in value of $50. The total value of the position would not change. This would be termed a perfect hedge.

But perfect hedges are hard to find, and many people would not use them if they were readily available. Why? The presence of a perfect hedge eliminates all downside risk, but also eliminates all upside potential. Many businesses accept this two-sided risk as part of doing business. However, it is generally best to accept risk in the line of business, not in the cash-payment process of settling the business.

Risk Management versus Speculation

The distinction between managing currency cash flows and speculating with currency cash flows is sometimes lost among those responsible for the safe-keeping of the firm's treasury. If the previous description of currency hedging is followed closely (the selection of assets or positions only to counteract potential losses on existing exposures), few problems should arise. Problems arise when currency positions or financial instruments are purchased (or sold) with the expectation that a specific currency movement will result in a profit, termed speculation.

There are a number of major multinational firms that treat their international treasury centers as "service centers," but rarely do they consider financial management a "profit center." One of the most visible examples of what can go wrong when currency speculation is undertaken for corporate profit occurred in Great Britain in 1991. A large British food conglomerate, Allied-Lyons, suffered losses of £158 million ($268 million) on currency speculation after members of its international treasury staff suffered losses on currency positions at the start of the Persian Gulf War and then doubled-up on their positions in the following weeks in an attempt to recover previous losses. They lost even more.[3] As shown by Global Perspective 16.3, companies use currency hedging carefully—to aid management.

Transaction Exposure Case: Lufthansa (1985)

In January 1985, the German airline Lufthansa purchased 20 Boeing 737 jet aircraft. The jets would be delivered to Lufthansa in one year, in January 1986. Upon delivery of the aircraft, Lufthansa would pay Boeing (U.S.) $500 million. This constituted a huge transaction exposure for Lufthansa. (Note that the exposure falls on Lufthansa not Boeing. If the purchase agreement had been stated in deutschemarks, the transaction exposure would have been transferred to Boeing.)

The Exposure The spot exchange rate in January 1985, when Lufthansa signed the agreement, was DM 3.2/$. The expected cost of the aircraft to Lufthansa was then

$$\$500,000,000 \times DM3.2/\$ = DM1,600,000,000.$$

Figure 16.6 illustrates how the expected total cost of $500 million changes to Lufthansa with the spot exchange rate. If the deutschemark continued to fall against the U.S. dollar as it had been doing for more than four years, the cost to Lufthansa of the Boeing jets could skyrocket easily to more than DM 2 billion.

But the most important word here is expected. There was no guarantee that the spot exchange rate in effect in January of the following year would be DM 3.2/$. The U.S. dollar had been appreciating against the deutschemark for more than four years at this point. Senior management of Lufthansa was afraid the appreciating dollar trend might continue. For example, if the U.S. dollar appreciated over the coming year from DM 3.2/$ to DM 3.4/$, the cost of the aircraft purchased from Boeing would rise by DM 100 million. Figure 16.7 shows how the DM/$ exchange rate had continued to trend upward for several years. By looking at graphics such as this, it was hard to believe that the U.S. dollar would do anything but continue to rise. It takes the truly brave to buck the trend.

But at the same time many senior members of Lufthansa's management believed that the U.S. dollar had risen as far as it would go. They argued that the dollar would fall over the coming year against the deutschemark (see Figure 16.7). If, for example,

FIGURE 16.6   **Lufthansa's Transaction Exposure: Alternatives for Managing the Purchase of $500 Million in Boeing 737s**

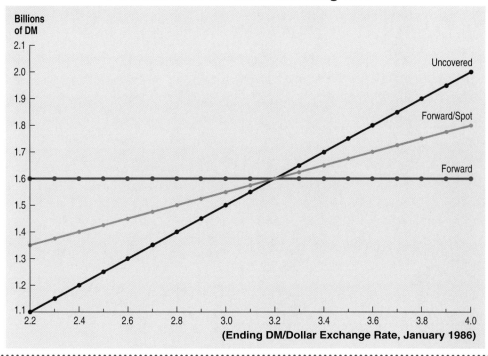

(Ending DM/Dollar Exchange Rate, January 1986)

the spot rate fell to DM 3.0/$ by January 1986, Lufthansa would pay only DM 1,500 million, a savings of DM 100 million. This was true currency risk in every sense of the word.

The Management Strategy   After much debate, Lufthansa's management decided to use forward contracts to hedge one-half of the $500 million exposure. This was obviously a compromise. First, because the exposure was a single large foreign currency payment, to occur one time only, natural hedging was not a realistic alternative. Second, although management believed the dollar would fall, the risk was too large to ignore. It was thought that by covering one-half of the exposure, Lufthansa would be protected against the U.S. dollar appreciating, yet still allow Lufthansa some opportunity to benefit from a fall in the dollar. Lufthansa signed a one-year forward contract (sold $250 million forward) at a forward rate of DM 3.2/$. The remaining $250 million owed Boeing was left unhedged.

The Outcome   By January 1986, the U.S. dollar not only fell, it plummeted versus the deutschemark. The spot rate fell from DM 3.2/$ in January 1985 to DM 2.3/$ in January 1986. Lufthansa had therefore benefited from leaving half the transaction exposure uncovered. But this meant that the half that was covered with forward contracts "cost" the firm DM 225 million!

The total cost to Lufthansa of delivering $250 million at the forward rate of DM 3.2/$ and $250 million at the ending spot rate of DM 2.3/$ was

[$250,000,000 × DM3.2/$] + [$250,000,000 × DM2.3/$] = DM 1,375,000,000.

Although this was DM 225 million less than the expected purchase price when the contract was signed in January 1985, Lufthansa's management was heavily criticized

FIGURE 16.7   **The DM/$ Spot Exchange Rate: Where Was It Headed?**

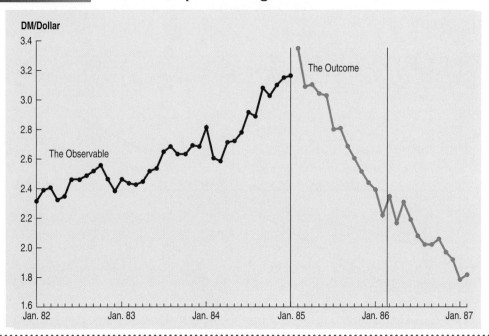

for covering any of the exposure. If the entire transaction exposure had been un-covered, the final cost would have been only DM 1,150 million. The critics, of course, had perfect hindsight.

Currency Risk Sharing

Firms that import and export on a continuing basis have constant transaction expo-sures. If a firm is interested in maintaining a good business relationship with one of its suppliers, it must work with that supplier to assure it that it will not force all cur-rency risk or exposure off on the other party on a continual basis. Exchange rate move-ments are inherently random; therefore some type of risk-sharing arrangement may prove useful.

If Ford (U.S.) imports automotive parts from Mazda (Japan) every month, year af-ter year, major swings in exchange rates can benefit one party at the expense of the other. One solution would be for Ford and Mazda to agree that all purchases by Ford will be made in Japanese yen as long as the spot rate on the payment date is between ¥120/$ and ¥130/$. If the exchange rate is between these values on the payment dates, Ford agrees to accept whatever transaction exposure exists (because it is paying in a foreign currency). If, however, the exchange rate falls outside of this range on the pay-ment date, Ford and Mazda will "share" the difference. If the spot rate on settlement date is ¥110/$, the Japanese yen would have appreciated versus the dollar, causing Ford's costs of purchasing automotive parts to rise. Since this rate falls outside the contractual range, Mazda would agree to accept a total payment in Japanese yen that would result from a "shared" difference of ¥10. Thus, Ford's total payment in Japanese yen would be calculated using an exchange rate of ¥115/$.

Risk-sharing agreements like these have been in use for nearly 50 years on world markets. They became something of a rarity during the 1950s and 1960s, when ex-change rates were relatively stable (under the Bretton Woods Agreement). But with the return to floating exchange rates in the 1970s, firms with long-term customer-supplier relationships across borders returned to some old ways of keeping old friends. And sometimes old ways work very well.

Economic Exposure

Economic exposure, also called operating exposure, is the change in the value of a firm arising from unexpected changes in exchange rates. Economic exposure emphasizes that there is a limit to a firm's ability to predict either cash flows or exchange rate changes in the medium to long term. All firms, either directly or indirectly, have economic exposure.

It is customary to think of only firms that actively trade internationally as having any type of currency exposure (such as Lufthansa described previously). But actually all firms that operate in economies affected by international financial events, such as exchange rate changes, are affected. A barber in Ottumwa, Iowa, seemingly isolated from exchange rate chaos, still is affected when the dollar rises as it did in the early 1980s. If U.S. products become increasingly expensive to foreign buyers, American manufacturers such as John Deere & Co. in Iowa are forced to cut back production and lay off workers, and businesses of all types decline—even the business of barbers. The impacts are real, and they affect all firms, domestic and international alike.

How exposed is an individual firm in terms of economic exposure? It is impossible to say. Measuring economic exposure is subjective, and for the most part it is dependent on the degree of internationalization present in the firm's cost and revenue structure, as well as potential changes over the long run. But simply because it is difficult to measure does not mean that management cannot take some steps to prepare the firm for the unexpected.

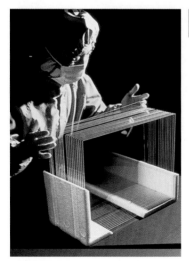

Companies are establishing manufacturing operations in countries around the world. As part of its global strategy, Corning Incorporated aims to be insulated against market fluctuations in any one particular country. This is a Japanese worker at the Corning Japan K.K. plant in Shizuoka, Japan.

Source: Courtesy of Corning Inc.

Impact of Economic Exposure

The impacts of economic exposure are as diverse as are firms in their international structure. Take the case of a U.S. corporation with a successful British subsidiary. The British subsidiary manufactured and then distributed the firm's products in Great Britain, Germany, and France. The profits of the British subsidiary are paid out annually to the American parent corporation. What would be the impact on the profitability of the British subsidiary and the entire U.S. firm if the British pound suddenly fell in value against all other major currencies (as it did in September and October 1992)?

If the British firm had been facing competition in Germany, France, and its own home market from firms from those other two continental countries, it would now be more competitive. If the British pound is cheaper, so are the products sold internationally by British-based firms. The British subsidiary of the American firm would, in all likelihood, see rising profits from increased sales.

But what of the value of the British subsidiary to the U.S. parent corporations? The same fall in the British pound that allowed the British subsidiary to gain profits would also result in substantially fewer U.S. dollars when the British pound earnings are converted to U.S. dollars at the end of the year. It seems that it is nearly impossible to win in this situation. Actually, from the perspective of economic exposure management, the fact that the firm's total value, subsidiary and parent together, is roughly a wash as a result of the exchange rate change is desirable. Sound financial management assumes that a firm will profit and bear risk in its line of business, not in the process of settling payments on business already completed.

Economic Exposure Management

Management of economic exposure is being prepared for the unexpected. A firm such as Hewlett Packard (HP), which is highly dependent on its ability to remain cost competitive in markets both at home and abroad, may choose to take actions now that would allow it to passively withstand any sudden unexpected rise of the dollar. This could be accomplished through diversification: diversification of operations and diversification of financing.

Diversification of operations would allow the firm to be desensitized to the impacts of any one pair of exchange rate changes. For example, a multinational firm such as Hewlett Packard may produce the same product in manufacturing facilities in Singapore, the United States, Puerto Rico, and Europe. If a sudden and prolonged rise in the dollar made production in the United States prohibitively expensive and uncompetitive, HP is already positioned to shift production to a relatively cheaper currency environment. Although firms rarely diversify production location for the sole purpose of currency diversification, it is a substantial additional benefit from such global expansion.

Diversification of financing serves to hedge economic exposure much in the same way as it did with transaction exposures. A firm with debt denominated in many different currencies is sensitive to many different interest rates. If one country or currency experiences rapidly rising inflation rates and interest rates, a firm with diversified debt will not be subject to the full impact of such movements. Purely domestic firms, however, are actually somewhat captive to the local conditions and are unable to ride out such interest rate storms as easily.

It should be noted that, in both cases, diversification is a passive solution to the exposure problem. This means that without knowing when or where or what the problem may be, the firm that simply spreads its operations and financial structure out over a variety of countries and currencies is prepared.

Translation Exposure

Translation or accounting exposure results from the conversion or translation of foreign currency denominated financial statements of foreign subsidiaries and affiliates into the home currency of the parent. This is necessary to prepare consolidated financial statements for all firms as country-law requires. The purpose is to have all operations worldwide stated in the same currency terms for comparison purposes. Management often uses the translated statements to judge the performance of foreign affiliates and their personnel on the same currency terms as the parent itself.

The problem, however, arises from the translation of balance sheets in foreign currencies into the domestic currency. Which assets and liabilities are to be translated at current exchange rates (at the current balance sheet date) versus historical rates (those in effect on the date of the initial investment)? Or should all assets and liabilities be translated at the same rate? The answer is somewhere in between, and the process of translation is dictated by financial accounting standards.

The Current Rate Method

At present in the United States, the proper method for translating foreign financial statements is given in Financial Accounting Standards Board statement No. 52 (FASB 52). According to FASB 52, if a foreign subsidiary is operating in a foreign currency functional environment,[4] most assets, liabilities, and income statement items of foreign affiliates are translated using current exchange rates (the exchange rate in effect on the balance sheet date). For this reason, it is often referred to as the current rate method. Table 16.4 provides an example of how this translation process might work.

A U.S. firm, Moab, established a Canadian subsidiary. The subsidiary, Moab-Can, is wholly owned and operated by Moab. The balance sheet of Moab-Can on December 31, 1998, is shown in Canadian dollars in Column (1) of Table 16.4. To construct a consolidated financial statement, all Moab-Can's assets and liabilities must be translated into U.S. dollars at the end-of-year exchange rate. This rate is C$1.20/$. All assets and liabilities are translated at the current rate except for equity capital, which is translated at the exchange rate in effect at the time of the Canadian subsidiary's establishment, C$1.10/$. The exchange rates used to translate each individual asset and liability of the Canadian subsidiary are listed in Column (2).

The U.S.-dollar value of all translated assets and liabilities is shown in Column (3). An imbalance results because all assets and liabilities, except equity capital, were translated at the current rate. A new account must be created for the translated balance sheet to balance. The new account, the **cumulative translation adjustment (CTA)** takes on a gain or loss value necessary to maintain a balanced translation. Moab-Can in this case suffers a CTA loss of US$36,000.

What does this translation loss mean to the company? The CTA account is an accounting construction. It is created to produce a consolidated balance sheet. Neither the Canadian subsidiary nor the U.S. parent experiences any cash flow impact as a result of the translation gain or loss.

The CTA account remains a "paper fiction" until the time the Canadian subsidiary is either sold or liquidated. On the sale or liquidation of the Canadian subsidiary, the CTA gains or losses attributed to Moab-Can must be realized by the parent company.[5]

Translation Exposure Management

Translation exposure under FASB 52 results in no cash flow impacts under normal circumstances. Although consolidated accounting does result in CTA translation losses or gains on the parent's consolidated balance sheet, the accounting entries are not ordinarily realized. Unless liquidation or sale of the subsidiary is anticipated, neither the subsidiary nor the parent firm should expend real resources on the management of an accounting convention.

TABLE 16.4

Translation of Foreign Affiliate's Balance Sheet: Canadian Subsidiary of a U.S. Firm

	(1) Canadian Dollars (thousands)	(2) Current Rate C$/$	(3) U.S. Dollars (thousands)
Assets			
Cash	120	1.20	100
Accounts payable	240	1.20	200
Inventory	120	1.20	100
Net plant and equipment	480	1.20	400
Total	C$ 960		$ 800
Liabilities and Net Worth			
Accounts payable	120	1.20	100
Short-term debt	120	1.20	100
Long-term debt	240	1.20	200
Equity capital	480	1.10	436
Cumulative Translation Adjustment			(36)
Total	C$ 960		$ 800

Interest Rate and Currency Swaps

One of the most significant developments in international finance in the past 20 years was the development of the interest rate and currency swap market. Although markets of all kinds (goods, services, labor, and capital) have continued to open up across the world in the past two decades, there are still "paper walls" between many capital markets. Firms operating in their home markets are both helped and hindered; they are well known in their own capital markets but still may not be recognized in other potentially larger capital markets. The interest rate and currency swap markets have allowed firms to arbitrage the differences between markets, using their comparative advantage of borrowing in their home market and swapping for interest rates or currencies that are not as readily accessible.

Interest Rate Swaps

Firms that are considered to be better borrowers in financial markets borrow at lower rates. The lower rates may be lower fixed rates or lower spreads over floating rate bases. In fact, lower quality borrowers often are limited in their choices to floating rates in many markets. The **interest rate swap,** often called the "plain vanilla swap," allows one firm to use its good credit standing to borrow capital at low fixed rates and exchange its interest payments with a slightly lower credit-rated borrower who has debt service payments at floating rates. Each borrower ends up making net interest payments at rates below those it could have achieved on its own.

If Firm Alpha is considered an extremely sound borrower, it can borrow capital at lower interest rates, probably fixed rates, than a second firm, Zeta. Zeta, although profitable and sound, is simply not rated as highly as a borrower in the eyes of the financial markets, and it must borrow at higher rates, often only at floating rates. If each firm were to borrow where it is "well received," using its comparative advantages, they may then swap or exchange their debt service payments. Alpha, which has taken on fixed rate debt service payments, will exchange these payments for Zeta's floating rate payments. Both companies end up paying less interest in the form that they desired by negotiating rates between themselves that are better than what the markets had offered directly.

FIGURE 16.8   **Sample Currency Swap: Arbitrage Between the U.S. Dollar and Swedish Krona Debt Markets**

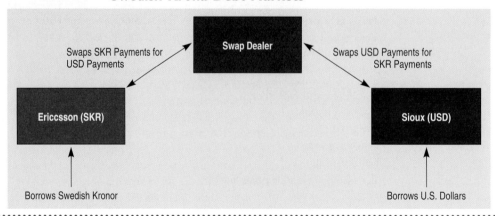

GLOBAL PERSPECTIVE 16.4

2000 Mid-Year Swap Market Survey

Global OTC derivatives use grew by 3 percent in the first half of 2000, revealed the semi-annual market survey sponsored by the International Swaps & Derivatives Association (ISDA). But among the top ten reporting institutions, volume was up 10 percent to $33.48 trillion.

Measured in national principal outstanding amounts, the survey tracks market growth in interest rate swaps, interest rate options, and currency swaps, as reported by member organizations. For the six months ending June 30, 2000, these totaled $60.366 trillion, compared with $58.265 trillion at the end of 1999. For the period ending June 30, 1999, the total stood at $52.711 trillion.

"These figures reflect the continuing appeal of OTC derivatives as a risk management mechanism, and demonstrate that consolidation among institutions has not slowed

the growth of product use," said Thomas K. Montag, vice-chairman of ISDA and chair of the Association's Market Survey Committee. Mr. Montag is a managing director and global head of derivatives trading at Goldman Sachs, based in Tokyo. "While the rate of growth at the top ten firms outstrips the headline figure, the results also show an increasing number of smaller member firms participating in these markets."

The survey, which is compiled twice yearly by Arthur Andersen, is performed on a confidential basis and produces a single headline statistic. This is complemented by the more comprehensive survey produced quarterly by the Bank for International Settlements. Outstandings in the ISDA survey represent notional volumes of 100 member institutions, of which 78 were also participants in the previous semiannual survey.

Source: **www.isda.org** (February, 2001).

Currency Swaps

The **currency swap** is the equivalent of the interest rate swap, only the currency of denomination of the debt is different. Many international and multinational firms need capital denominated in different currencies for international investments or even for the purpose of risk management (for natural hedging, as described previously). Foreign firms often find themselves at a disadvantage, however, when trying to enter new markets. The interest rates available to them in the necessary currencies simply may not be affordable.

Figure 16.8 illustrates how a currency swap arrangement would work for a Swedish firm desiring U.S. dollar debt, and a U.S. firm desiring Swedish krona debt. The mechanics of the swap are actually quite simple. The Swedish firm, Ericcsson, borrows capital in its home market, where it is well known and can obtain capital at attractive interest rates. The U.S. firm, Sioux, also acquires local debt in its own advantaged-access market. Then, working through a swap dealer, each firm exchanges the debt service payment schedule on its own debt for the debt service payment schedule of the other firm's debt. The principal amounts borrowed must be equal at current exchange rates for the swap to be made. The U.S. firm, Sioux, now agrees to make interest payments in Swedish kronor, and the Swedish firm, Ericcsson, agrees to make U.S. dollar interest payments. The two firms have swapped payment schedules.

But what of the risk of nonpayment? If one of the swap parties does not make its agreed-upon payments, who is responsible for meeting the obligations of the original debt agreement? The answer is that the initial borrower is responsible for covering any shortfall or nonpayment by the swap party. This risk, termed counterparty risk, is an increasing concern in the interest rate and currency swap markets as more and more firms utilize the markets to manage their debt structures. Global Perspective 16.4 reports recent survey data on the size and activity of the international swap markets.

Countertrade

General Motors exchanged automobiles for a trainload of strawberries. Control Data swapped a computer for a package of Polish furniture, Hungarian carpet backing, and Russian greeting cards. Uzbekistan, one of the new countries of the former Soviet Union, is offering crude venom of vipers, toads, scorpions, black widows, and tarantulas, as well as growth-controlling substances from snakes and lizards, in countertrade.[6] These are all examples of countertrade activities carried out around the world. As noted in Global Perspective 16.5, countertrade is growing in volume as well as in complexity.

A Definition of Countertrade

Countertrade is a sale that encompasses more than an exchange of goods, services, or ideas for money. In the international market, countertrade transactions "are those transactions that have as a basic characteristic a linkage, legal or otherwise, between exports and imports of goods or services in addition to, or in place of, financial settlements."[7] Historically, countertrade was mainly conducted in the form of **barter,** which is a direct exchange of goods of approximately equal value between parties, with no money involved. Such transactions were the very essence of business at times during which no money—that is, no common medium of exchange—existed or was available. Over time, money emerged as a convenient medium that unlinked transactions from individual parties and their joint timing and therefore permitted greater flexibility in trading activities. Repeatedly, however, we can see returns to the barter system as a result of environmental circumstances. For example, because of the tight financial constraints of both students and the institution, Georgetown University during its initial years of operation after 1789 charged part of its tuition in foodstuffs and required students to participate in the construction of university buildings. During periods of high inflation in Europe in the 1920s, goods such as bread, meat, and gold were seen as much more useful and secure than paper money, which decreased in real value by the minute. In the late 1940s, American cigarettes were an acceptable medium of exchange in most European countries, much more so than any particular currency except for the dollar.

Countertrade transactions have therefore always arisen when economic circumstances made it more acceptable to exchange goods directly rather than to use money as an intermediary. Conditions that encourage such business activities are lack of money, lack of value of or faith in money, lack of acceptability of money as an exchange medium, or greater ease of transaction by using goods.

Increasingly, countries and companies are deciding that, sometimes, countertrade transactions are more beneficial to them than transactions based on financial exchange alone. One reason is that the world debt crisis has made ordinary trade financing very risky. Many countries, particularly in the developing world, simply cannot obtain the trade credit or financial assistance necessary to pay for desired imports. Heavily indebted countries, faced with the possibility of not being able to afford imports at all, hasten to use countertrade to maintain at least some product inflow. However, it should be recognized that countertrade does not reduce commercial risk. Countertrade transactions will therefore be encouraged by stability and economic progress. Research has shown that countertrade appears to increase with a country's creditworthiness, since good credit encourages traders to participate in unconventional trading practices.[8]

The use of countertrade permits the covert reduction of prices and therefore allows the circumvention of price and exchange controls.[9] Particularly in commodity mar-

GLOBAL PERSPECTIVE 16.5

The Booming Business of Countertrade

Many Fortune 500 companies are now turning to barter or countertrade arrangements to clear their warehouses of everything from corporate jets to boxer shorts and dinner mints. With today's faster product cycles, increasingly rapid introduction of new technologies, and shorter business cycles, companies are anxious to get rid of older or obsolete merchandise without flooding established markets. Fueled by these developments in the business world, the practice of barter has grown tenfold over the past 20 years.

Barter allows companies to become more flexible and quicker in the face of international competition. Rather than selling old inventory for only 20 cents on the dollar in cash, firms can gain 80 cents or more by bartering. Big deals are increasingly found in corporate barter. In fact, North American companies traded $7.6 billion in goods and services in 1996, up from $980 million two decades earlier, according to the Corporate Barter Council.

The deals have become increasingly complex and geographically dispersed. Some examples of recent countertrade arrangements include the following:

- IBM's Mexico subsidiary exchanged 2,600 outmoded computers worth $1.7 million for $1 million worth of Volkswagen vehicles, plus $250,000 in trucking services and a quarter million worth of express-mail shipments.
- A cruise line used a barter company to trade $1 million worth of empty cabins for $1 million in trade credits. The cruise company used the credits, along with $3 million in cash, for a $4 million advertising campaign.
- A dental-care manufacturer exchanged 200,000 extra toothbrushes packaged in bulk for advertising worth twice the amount of the toothbrushes. A barter company repackaged the toothbrushes to be sold as a travel kit through a regional chain store.
- Volvo Cars of North America sold autos to the Siberian police force when it had no currency for the deal. A barter company accepted oil as payment for the vehicles, and used the gains from its sale to provide Volvo with advertising credits equal to the value of the cars. ●

Source: Paula L. Green, "The Booming Barter Business," *The Journal of Commerce* (April 1, 1997), 1A, 5A.

kets with cartel arrangements, such as oil or agriculture, this benefit may be very useful to a producer. For example, by using oil as a countertraded product for industrial equipment, a surreptitious discount (by using a higher price for the acquired products) may expand market share.

Another reason for the increase in countertrade is that many countries are again responding favorably to the notion of bilateralism. Thinking along the lines of "you scratch my back and I'll scratch yours," they prefer to exchange goods with countries that are their major business partners.

Countertrade is also often viewed by firms and nations alike as an excellent mechanism to gain entry into new markets. When a producer believes that marketing is not its strong suit, the producer often hopes that the party receiving the goods will serve as a new distributor, opening up new international marketing channels and ultimately expanding the original market. For example, countertrade transactions agreed to between the Japanese firm NEC and the government of Egypt have resulted in a major increase of Japanese tourism to Egypt.[10]

Because countertrade is highly sought after in many large markets such as China, the former Eastern bloc countries, as well as South America, engaging in such transactions can provide major growth opportunities for firms. In increasingly competitive world markets, countertrade can be a good way to attract new buyers. By providing countertrade services, the seller is in effect differentiating its product from those of its competitors.[11]

Countertrade also can provide stability for long-term sales. For example, if a firm is tied to a countertrade agreement, it will need to source the product from a particular supplier, whether or not it wants to do so. This stability is often valued very highly because it eliminates, or at least reduces, vast swings in demand and thus allows for better planning. Countertrade, therefore, can serve as a major mechanism to shift risk from the producer to another party. In that sense, one can argue that countertrade offers a substitute for missing forward markets.[12] Finally, under certain conditions, countertrade can ensure the quality of an international transaction. In instances where the seller of technology is paid in output produced by the technology delivered, the seller's revenue depends on the success of the technology transfer and maintenance services in production. Therefore, the seller is more likely to be concerned about providing services, maintenance, and general technology transfer.[13]

In spite of all the apparent benefits of countertrade, there are strong economic arguments against the activity. The arguments are based mainly on efficiency grounds. As Samuelson stated, "Instead of there being a double coincidence of wants, there is likely to be a want of coincidence; so that, unless a hungry tailor happens to find an undraped farmer, who has both food and a desire for a pair of pants, neither can make a trade."[14] Clearly, countertrade ensures that instead of balances being settled on a multilateral basis, with surpluses from one country being balanced by deficits with another, accounts must now be settled on a country-by-country or even transaction-by-transaction basis. Trade then results only from the ability of two parties or countries to purchase specified goods from one another rather than from competition. As a result, uncompetitive goods may be traded. In consequence, the ability of countries and their industries to adjust structurally to more efficient production may be restricted. Countertrade can therefore be seen as eroding the quality and efficiency of production and as lowering world consumption.

These economic arguments notwithstanding, however, countries and companies increasingly see countertrade as an alternative that may be flawed but worthwhile to undertake, since some trade is preferable to no trade. As the accompanying map shows, both industrialized and developing countries exchange a wide variety of goods via countertrade. And as Table 16.5 shows, countertrade knows few limits across goods.

TABLE 16.5 — A Sample of Barter Agreements

COUNTRY A	COUNTRY B	EXPORTED COMMODITY A	EXPORTED COMMODITY B
Hungary	Ukraine	• Foodstuffs • Canned foods • Pharmaceuticals	• Timber
Austria	Ukraine	• Power station emissions control equipment	• 800 megakilowatts/year for 15 years
U.S. (Chrysler)	Jamaica	• 200 pickup trucks	• Equivalent value in iron ore
Ukraine	Czech Republic	• Iron ore	• Mining equipment
U.S. (Pierre Cardin)	China	• Technical advice	• Silks and cashmeres
U.K. (Raleigh Bicycle)	CIS	• Training CIS scientists in mountain bike production	• Titanium for 30,000 bike frames per year
Indonesia	Uzbekistan	• Indian tea • Vietnamese rice • Miscellaneous Indonesian products	• 50,000 tons of cotton/year for three years
Zaire	Italy	• Scrap iron	• 12 locomotives
China	Russia	• 212 railway trucks of mango juice	• Passenger jet
Morocco	Romania	• Citrus products	• Several large ports/small harbors

Sources: American Countertrade Association, December 1996; Aspy P. Palia and Oded Shenkar, "Countertrade Practices in China," *Industrial Marketing Management*, 1991; 58. http://www.i-trade.com.

Preferred Items for Export in Countertrade Transactions

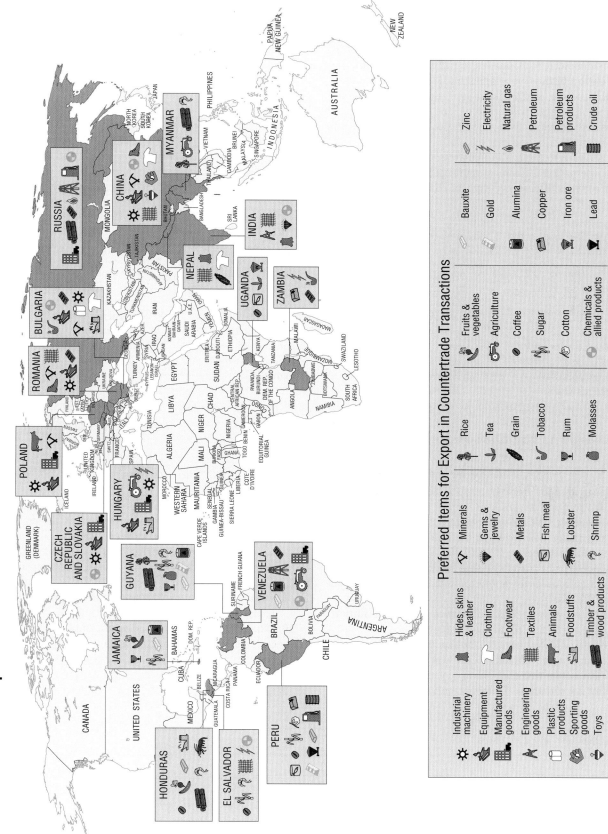

Source: *The World Factbook 2000*

Summary

Multinational financial management is both complex and critical to the multinational firm. All traditional functional areas of financial management are affected by the internationalization of the firm. Capital budgeting, firm financing, capital structure, and working capital and cash flow management, all traditional functions, are made more difficult by business activities that cross borders and oceans, not to mention currencies and markets.

In addition to the traditional areas of financial management, international financial management must deal with the three types of currency exposure: (1) transaction exposure; (2) economic exposure; and (3) translation exposure. Each type of currency risk confronts a firm with serious choices regarding its exposure analysis and its degree of willingness to manage the inherent risks.

This chapter described not only the basic types of risk, but also outlined a number of the basic strategies employed in the management of the exposures. Some of the solutions available today have only arisen with the development of new types of international financial markets and instruments, such as the currency swap. Others, such as currency risk-sharing agreements, are as old as exchange rates themselves.

Key Terms and Concepts

maximization of
  shareholder value
bill of lading
bank draft
trade draft
net present value (NPV)
capital budget
working capital
  management

operating cash flows
financing cash flows
transfer prices
netting
cash pooling
lead
lag
reinvoicing

internal bank
transaction exposure
economic exposure
translation exposure
natural hedging
contractual hedging
forward contract
hedge

cumulative translation
  adjustment (CTA)
interest rate swap
currency swap
barter
counterpurchase
buy-back

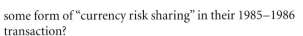

Questions for Discussion

1. Why is it important to identify the cash flows of a foreign investment from the perspective of the parent rather than from just the project?
2. Is currency risk unique to international firms? Is currency risk good or bad for the potential profitability of the multinational?
3. Which type of currency risk is the least important to the multinational firm? Should resources be spent to manage this risk?
4. Are firms with no direct international business (imports and exports) subject to economic exposure?
5. What would you have recommended that Lufthansa do to manage its transaction exposure if you had been the airline's chief financial officer in January 1985?
6. Why do you think Lufthansa and Boeing did not use some form of "currency risk sharing" in their 1985–1986 transaction?
7. Which type of firm do you believe is more "naturally hedged" against exchange rate exposure, the purely domestic firm (the barber) or the multinational firm (subsidiaries all over the world)?
8. Why have the currency and interest rate swap markets grown so rapidly in the past decade?
9. What are some of the causes for the resurgence of countertrade?
10. What forms of countertrade exist and how do they differ? What are their relative advantages and drawbacks?
11. How consistent is countertrade with the international trade framework?

Internet Exercises

1. Although major currencies like the U.S. dollar and the Japanese yen dominate the headlines, there are nearly as many currencies as countries in the world. Many of these currencies are traded in extremely thin and highly regulated markets, making their convertibility suspect. Finding quotations for these currencies is sometimes very difficult. Using some of the web pages listed below, see how many African currency quotes you can find. See Emerging Markets at http://emgmkts.com/.
2. JP Morgan calculates and maintains indices of many of the world's major currencies' values relative to baskets of other major currencies. Like those published by the In-

ternational Monetary Fund, these indices serve as more fundamental and general indicators of relative currency value. Look at JP Morgan Currency Indices at http://ipmorgan.com/MarketDataInd/Forex/CurrIndex.html.

3. The single unobservable variable in currency option pricing is the volatility, since volatility inputs are expected standard deviation of the daily spot rate for the coming period of the option's maturity. Using the following web sites, pick one currency volatility and research how its value has changed in recent periods over historical periods. See Philadelphia Stock Exchange at http://www.phlx.com/.

4. Using the following major periodicals as starting points, find a current example of a firm with a substantial op-

erating exposure problem. To aid in your search, you might focus on businesses having major operations in countries with recent currency crises, either through devaluation or major home currency appreciation. Sources are *Financial Times* at http://www.ft.com/; *The Economist* at http://www.economist.com/; *The Wall Street Journal* at http://www.wsj.com/.

5. In the World Trade Organization's Agreement on Government Procurement, how are *offsets* defined and what stance is taken toward them (refer to the government procurement page on the web site www.wto.org)?

Recommended Readings

Brealey, Richard A., and Stewart C. Myers. *Principles of Corporate Finance.* 5th ed. New York: McGraw-Hill, 1996.

Countertrade and Offsets. A newsletter published by DP Publications Co., Fairfax Station, VA.

Directory of Organizations Providing Countertrade Services 1996–97. 7th ed. Fairfax Station, VA: DP Publications Co., 1996.

Eaker, Mark R., Frank J. Fabozzi, and Dwight Grant. *International Corporate Finance.* Fort Worth, TX: The Dryden Press, 1996.

Eiteman, David K., Arthur I. Stonehill, and Michael H. Moffett. *Multinational Business Finance.* 8th ed. Reading, MA: Addison-Wesley Longman, 1998.

Eun, Cheol S., and Bruce G. Resnick. *International Financial Management.* Boston, MA: Irwin McGraw-Hill, 1998.

Giddy, Ian H., *Global Financial Markets.* Lexington, MA: Elsevier, 1994.

International Buy-Back Contracts. New York: United Nations, 1991.

Jacque, Laurent L. *Management and Control of Foreign Exchange Risk.* Boston, MA: Kluwer Academic Publishers, 1996.

Madura, Jeff. *International Financial Management.* 5th ed. Cincinnati, OH: Southwestern Publishing, 1998.

Martin, Stephen, ed. *The Economics of Offsets: Defence Procurement and Countertrade.* Amsterdam: Harwood Academic Publishers, 1996.

Mohring, Wolfgang. *Gegengeschaefte: Analyse einer Handelsform.* Frankfurt: M.P. Lang, 1991.

"Offsets," *Business America* 117, 9. Washington, DC: U.S. Department of Commerce, September, 1996.

Offsets in Defense Trade. Bureau of Export Administration, U.S. Department of Commerce, Washington, DC, May, 1996.

Shapiro, Alan C. *Foundations of Multinational Financial Management.* 3d ed. Upper Saddle River, NJ: Prentice Hall, 1998.

Smith, Clifford W., Charles W. Smithson, and D. Sykes Wilford. *Managing Financial Risk.* The Institutional Investor Series in Finance. New York: Harper Business, 1990.

UNCITRAL Legal Guide on International Countertrade Transactions. New York: United Nations, 1993.

Verzariu, Pompiliu, and Paula Mitchell, *A Guide on Countertrade Practices in the Newly Independent States of the Former Soviet Union.* Washington, DC: U.S. Department of Commerce, 1995.

Notes

1. Extremity-stimulus medical appliances are electrically charged sheaths that are fit over the hands, feet, or other extremities of the human subject where increased blood flow and nerve tissue regeneration is desired. This is a fictional product.

2. There are, of course, other traditional decision criteria used in capital budgeting, such as the internal rate of return, modified internal rate of return, payback period, and so forth. For the sake of simplicity, NPV is used throughout the analysis in this chapter. Under most conditions, NPV is also the most consistent criterion for selecting good projects, as well as selecting among projects.

3. A note of particular irony in this case was that the chief currency trader for Allied-Lyons had authored an article in the British trade journal *The Treasurer* only a few months before. The article had described the proper methods and strategies for careful corporate foreign currency risk management. He had concluded with the caution to never confuse "good luck with skillful trading."

4. The distinction as to what the "functional currency" of a foreign subsidiary or affiliate operation is depends on a number of factors, including the currency that dominates expenses and revenues. If the foreign subsidiary's dominant currency is the local currency, the current rate method of

translation is used. If, however, the functional currency of the foreign subsidiary is identified as the currency of the parent, the U.S. dollar in the example, the temporal method of translation is used. The temporal method is the procedure that was used in the United States from 1975 to 1981 under FASB 8.

5. Prior to the passage of FASB 52, FASB 8 had been the primary directive on translation in the United States. FASB 8, often termed the monetary/nonmonetary method, differed from FASB 52 in two important ways. First, it applied historical exchange rates to several of the long-term asset categories, usually resulting in a lower net exposed asset position. Second, all translation gains and losses were passed through the parent's consolidated income for the current period. This resulted in volatile swings in the critical earnings per share (EPS) reported by multinational firms. Although this was still only an accounting convention, the volatility introduced to EPS caused much concern among firms.

6. *Trade Finance,* May 1992, 13.

7. "Current Activities of International Organizations in the Field of Barter and Barter-Like Transactions," *Report of the Secretary General,* United Nations, General Assembly, 1984, 4.

8. Jean-François Hennart and Erin Anderson, "Countertrade and the Minimization of Transaction Costs: An Empirical Examination," *The Journal of Law, Economics, and Organization,* September 2, 1993, 307.

9. Jean-François Hennart, "Some Empirical Dimensions of Countertrade," *Journal of International Business Studies* 21, 2 (Second Quarter, 1990): 243–270.

10. Abla M. Abdel-Latif and Jeffrey B. Nugent, "Countertrade as Trade Creation and Trade Diversion," *Contemporary Economic Policy* 12 (January 1994): 1–10.

11. Jong H. Park, "Is Countertrade Merely a Passing Phenomenon? Some Public Policy Implications," in *Proceedings of the 1988 Conference,* ed. R. King (Charleston, SC: Academy of International Business, Southeast Region, 1988), 67–71.

12. Hennart, "Some Empirical Dimensions of Countertrade."

13. Rolf Mirus and Bernard Yeung, "Why Countertrade? An Economic Perspective," *The International Trade Journal* 7, 4 (1993): 409–433.

14. Paul Samuelson, *Economics,* 11th ed. (New York: McGraw Hill, 1980), 260.

CHAPTER 17

International Accounting and Taxation

LEARNING OBJECTIVES

- To understand how accounting practices differ across countries, and how these differences may alter the competitiveness of firms in international markets

- To isolate which accounting practices are likely to constitute much of the competitiveness debate in the coming decade

- To examine the two basic philosophies of international taxation as practiced by governments, and how they in turn deal with foreign firms in their home markets and domestic firms in foreign markets

- To understand how the degree of ownership and control of a foreign enterprise alters the taxable income of a foreign enterprise in the eyes of U.S. tax authorities

- To understand the problems faced by many U.S.-based multinational firms in paying taxes both in foreign countries and in the United States

WORLDWIDE ACCOUNTING STANDARDS

The International Accounting Standards Committee, which is pursuing the ambitious yet politically difficult goal of creating a single set of accounting principles to be used around the world, announced the board members who will be devising those standards.

The committee hopes that governments worldwide ultimately will permit companies to raise capital in their respective countries by complying with the standards to be set by the newly formed International Accounting Standards Board, rather than limiting access to only those companies that comply with their own country's accounting standards.

That goal, should it be attained, is likely many years away. But the idea is that investors will be more willing to invest in certain nations if their companies' financial reports are more transparent and reliable. In addition, many companies long have complained of the expense involved with presenting their financial statements in multiple ways to satisfy different standards.

The effort—bankrolled in part by the financial services and accounting industries—has received praise from departing Securities and Exchange Commission Chairman Arthur Levitt, as well as the U.S. Financial Accounting Standards Board. One big hurdle will be reaching consensus on a number of contentious issues, such as the proper way to account for stock-based compensation, which is treated differently in the United States than in most other countries. ●

Source: Abstracted from "Accounting Board Is Formed to Create One Set of Standards for Use Worldwide," *Wall Street Journal,* January 26, 2001, by Jonathan Weil.

The methods used in the measurement of company operations, accounting principles, and practices, vary across countries. The methods have a very large impact on how firms operate, how they compare against domestic and international competitors, and how governments view their respective place in society. Accounting principles are, however, moving toward more standardization across countries.

Taxation and accounting are fundamentally related. The principles by which a firm measures its sales and expenses, its assets and liabilities, all go into the formulation of profits, which are subject to taxation. The tax policies of more and more governments, in conjunction with accounting principles, are also becoming increasingly similar. Many of the tax issues of specific interest to officials, such as the avoidance of taxes in high-tax countries or the shielding of income from taxation by holding profits in so-called tax havens, are slowly being eliminated by increasing cooperation between governments. Like the old expression of "death and taxes," they are today, more than ever, inevitable.

This chapter provides an overview of the major differences between accounting practices and corporate taxation philosophies among major industrial countries. Although the average business manager cannot be expected to have a detailed understanding (or recall) of the multitudes of tax laws and accounting principles across countries, a basic understanding of many of these issues aids in the understanding of why "certain things are done certain ways" in international business.

Accounting Diversity

The fact that accounting principles differ across countries is not, by itself, a problem. The primary problem is that real economic decisions by lenders, investors, or government policymakers may be distorted by the differences. Table 17.1 provides a simple example of the potential problems that may arise if two identical firms were operating in similar or dissimilar economic and accounting environments.

First, if two identical firms (in terms of structure, products, and strategies) are operating in similar economic situations and are subject to similar accounting treatment (cell A), a comparison of their performance will be logical in practice and easily interpreted. The results of a competitive comparison or even an accounting audit (measurement and monitoring of their accounting practices) will lead to results that make sense. The two same firms operating in dissimilar economic situations will, when subject to the same accounting treatment, potentially look very different. And it may be that they should appear different if they are operating in totally different environments.

For example, one airline may depreciate its aircraft over five years, while another airline may depreciate over ten years. Is this justified? It is if the two identical air carriers are in fundamentally different economic situations. If the first airline flies predominantly short commuter routes, which require thousands of takeoffs and landings, and the second airline flies only long intercontinental flights, which require far fewer takeoffs and landings, the first may be justified in depreciating its fixed assets much faster. The airline with more frequent takeoffs and landings will wear out its aircraft more quickly, which is what the accounting principle of depreciation is attempting to capture.[1] The economic situations are different.

The most blatantly obvious mismatch of economic environments and accounting treatments is probably that of cell C. Two identical firms operating within the same economic environment that receive different accounting treatment are not comparable. The same firms, if placed in the same environment, would appear differently, with one potentially gaining competitive advantage over the other simply because of accounting treatment.

Finally, cell D offers the mismatch of different environments and different accounting treatments. Although logical in premise, the results are most likely incomparable in outcome. Identical firms in differing economic environments require differing approaches to financial measurement. But the fact that the results of financial comparison may not be usable is not an error; it is simply a fact of the differing markets in which the firms operate. As firms expand internationally, as markets expand

TABLE 17.1	**ECONOMIC SITUATION OF TWO IDENTICAL FIRMS**		
Accounting Diversity and Economic Environments	**Accounting Treatment**	**Similar**	**Dissimilar**
	Similar	Logical practice A Results are comparable	May/may not be logical B Results may/may not be comparable
	Dissimilar	Illogical practice C Results are not comparable	Logical practice D Results may not be comparable

Source: "International Accounting Diversity and Capital Market Decisions," Frederick D.S. Choi and Richard Levich, in *The Handbook of International Accounting,* Frederick D.S. Choi, ed., 1992.

across borders, as businesses diversify across currencies, cultures, and economies, the movement toward cell A continues from market forces rather than from government intention.

Principal Accounting Differences Across Countries

International **accounting diversity** can lead to any of the following problems in international business conducted with the use of financial statements: (1) poor or improper business decision making; (2) hinder the ability of a firm or enterprise to raise capital in different or foreign markets; and (3) hinder or prevent a firm from monitoring competitive factors across firms, industries, and countries.

Origins of Differences

Accounting standards and practices are in many ways no different from any other legislative or regulatory statutes in their origins. Laws reflect the people, places, and events of their time (see Global Perspective 17.1). Most accounting practices and laws are linked to the objectives of the parties who will use the financial information, including investors, lenders, and governments.

Classification Systems

There are several ways to classify and group national accounting systems and practices. Figure 17.1 illustrates one such classification based on a statistically based clustering of practices across countries by C.W. Nobes. The systems are first subdivided into micro-based (characteristics of the firms and industries) and macro-uniform (following fundamental government or economic factors per country). The micro-based national accounting systems are then broken down into those that follow a theoretical principle or pragmatic concerns. The latter category includes the national accounting systems of countries as diverse as the United States, Canada, Japan, the United Kingdom, and Mexico.

The macro-uniform systems, according to Nobes, are primarily used in European countries. The continental Europeans are typified by accounting systems that are formulated in secondary importance to legal organizational forms (Germany), for the apportionment and application of national tax laws (France, Spain, Italy), or the more pure forms of government and economic models (Sweden). An alternative approach to those in the European classification would be those used in Sweden and Germany, which have pushed their firms to adopt more widespread uniform standards. However, as with all classification systems, the subtle differences across countries can quickly make such classifications useless in practice. As the following sections will illustrate, slight differences can also yield significant competitive advantages or disadvantages to companies organized and measured under different financial reporting systems.

Principal Differences: The Issues

The resulting impact of accounting differences is to separate or segment international markets for investors and firms alike. Communicating the financial results of a foreign company operating in a foreign country and foreign currency is often a task that must be undertaken completely separately from the accounting duties of the firm. As long as significant accounting practices differ across countries, markets will continue to be segmented (and accountants may be required to be interpreters and marketers as much as bookkeepers).

GLOBAL PERSPECTIVE 17.1

The Father of Accounting: Luca Pacioli Who?

Doctors have Hippocrates and philosophers have Plato. But who is the father of accounting? Knowing that accountants have long had inferiority complexes, two Seattle University professors have decided that the profession should have a father and that he should be Luca Pacioli.

But their anointing of the Renaissance scholar occasions an identity crisis. Hardly anyone—accountants included—has ever heard of Pacioli (pronounced pot-CHEE-oh-lee).

Five centuries ago, Pacioli published "*Summa de Arithmetica, Geometria, Proportioni et Proportionalita*." It contained a slender tract for merchants on double-entry bookkeeping, which had been in wide use in Venice for years. Due to that, some accounting historians including Professors Weis and Tinius credit Pacioli with codifying accounting principles for the first time. That would seem to establish paternity.

Professor Vangermeersch, of the University of Rhode Island, says the origins of double-entry bookkeeping are open to question. "If you're crediting people of past centuries for contributions to accounting, you should include Leonardo of Pisa, who brought Arabic numerals to the West; James Pelle, who initiated journal-entry systems; and Emile Garcke and J.M. Fells, who applied accounting to factory use," he said. All the men have another thing in common, he added: They are just as obscure as Luca Pacioli.

Even in literature, says Vangermeersch, the only famous accountant was Daniel Defoe, who wrote *Robinson Crusoe*. Unfortunately, Defoe was a terrible businessman and failed in a series of ventures, the professor observed. "Even as a dissenter and pamphleteer, he was tarred and feathered by the public."

Source: Abstracted from "Father of Accounting Is a Bit of a Stranger to His Own Progeny," *The Wall Street Journal*, January 29, 1993, A1, A6. Reprinted by permission of The Wall Street Journal, © 1993 Dow Jones & Company, Inc. All Rights Reserved Worldwide.

FIGURE 17.1   Nobes Classification of National Accounting Systems

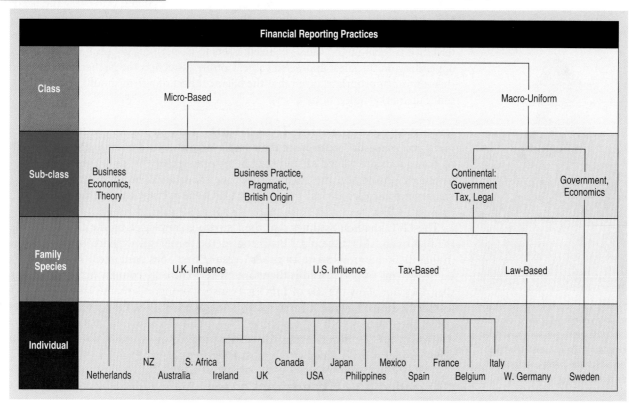

Source: C.W. Nobes, "International Classification of Accounting Systems," unpublished paper, April 1980. Table C, as cited in *International Accounting*, 2d ed., Frederick D.S. Choi and Gerhard G. Mueller, Englewood Cliffs, NJ: Prentice-Hall, 1992, p. 34.

Table 17.2 provides an overview of nine major areas of significant differences in accounting practices across countries.[2] There are, of course, many more hundreds of differences, but the nine serve to highlight some of the fundamental philosophical differences across countries. Accounting differences are real and persistent, and there is still substantial question of competitive advantages and informational deficiencies that may result from these continuing differences across countries.

Accounting for Research and Development Expenses

Are research and development expenses capitalized or expensed as costs are incurred? Those who argue that there is no certainty that the R&D expenditures will lead to benefits in future periods would require immediate recognition of all expenses as in typical conservative practice. Alternatively, if R&D expenditures do lead to future benefits and revenues, the matching of expenses and revenues would be better served if the R&D expenditures were capitalized, and expenses therefore spread out over the future benefit periods.

Accounting for Fixed Assets

How are fixed assets (land, buildings, machinery, equipment) to be expensed and carried? The assets constitute large outlays of capital, result in assets that are held by the firm for many years, and yield benefits for many future years. All countries require companies to capitalize these fixed assets, so that they are depreciated over their future economic lives (once again spreading the costs out over periods roughly matching the revenue-earning useful life). There are, however, significant differences in depreciation methods used (straight-line, sum-of-years-digits, accelerated methods of cost recovery, and so forth), resulting in very different expensing schedules across countries.

The primary issue related to the accounting of fixed assets is whether they are to be carried on company financial statements at historical cost or current value. The conservative approach, used for example, in the United States, is to carry the fixed assets at historical cost and to allow analysts to use their own methods and additional financial statement notes to ascertain current values of individual fixed assets. The alternative is to allow the values of fixed assets to be periodically revalued up or down, depending on the latest appraised value. Countries such as the Netherlands argue that this is more appropriate, given that the balance sheet of a firm should present the present fair market value of all assets.

Inventory Accounting Treatment

How are inventories to be valued? For many companies inventories are their single largest asset. Therefore, the reconciliation of how goods are valued as sold (on the income statement) and valued as carried in inventory unsold (on the balance sheet) is important. The three typical inventory-valuation principles are last-in-first-out, **LIFO,** the **average cost method,** and first-in-first-out, **FIFO.**

The LIFO method assumes that the last goods purchased by the firm (last-in) are the first ones sold (first-out). This is considered conservative by accounting standards in that the remaining inventory goods were the first ones purchased. The resulting expenses of cost of goods sold is therefore higher. The only country listed in Table 17.2 that does not allow the use of LIFO is France, although Germany only allows its use in specific cases, making it rarely used. The use of FIFO is thought to be more consistent theoretically with the matching of costs and revenues of actual inventory flows. The use of FIFO is generally regarded as creating a more accurately measured balance sheet, as inventory is stated at the most recent prices.

Capitalizing or Expensing Leases

Are financing leases to be capitalized? The recent growth in popularity of leasing for its financial and tax flexibility has created a substantial amount of accounting discussion across countries. The primary question is whether a leased item should actually be carried on the balance sheet of

Differences in depreciation methods used in accounting for fixed assets result in different expensing schedules across countries. The issue is quite complex for the many international firms participating in the Three Gorges project, which proposes to build the largest hydroelectric project in the history of the world on China's Yangtze River.

TABLE 17.2 Summary of Principal Accounting Differences Around the World

Accounting Principle	United States	Japan	United Kingdom	France	Germany	Netherlands	Switzerland	Canada	Italy	Brazil
1. Capitalization of R&D costs	Not allowed	Allowed in certain cases	Allowed in certain cases	Allowed in certain cases	Not allowed	Allowed in certain cases	Allowed in certain cases	Allowed in certain cases	Allowed in certain cases	Allowed in certain cases
2. Fixed asset revaluations stated at amount in excess of cost	Not allowed	Not allowed	Allowed	Allowed	Not allowed	Allowed in certain cases	Not allowed	Not allowed	Allowed in certain cases	Allowed
3. Inventory valuation using LIFO	Allowed	Allowed	Allowed but rarely done	Not allowed	Allowed in certain cases	Allowed	Allowed	Allowed	Allowed	Allowed but rarely done
4. Finance leases capitalized	Required	Allowed in certain cases	Required	Not allowed	Allowed in certain cases	Required	Allowed	Required	Not allowed	Not allowed
5. Pension expense accrued during period of service	Required	Allowed	Required	Allowed	Required	Required	Allowed	Required	Allowed	Allowed
6. Book and tax timing differences on balance sheet as deferred tax	Required	Allowed in certain cases	Allowed	Allowed in certain cases	Allowed but rarely done	Required	Allowed	Allowed	Allowed but rarely done	Allowed
7. Current rate method of currency translation	Required	Allowed in certain cases	Required	Allowed	Allowed	Required	Required	Allowed in certain cases	Required	Required
8. Pooling method used for mergers	Required in certain cases	Allowed in certain cases	Allowed in certain cases	Not allowed	Allowed in certain cases	Allowed but rarely done	Allowed but rarely done	Allowed but rarely done	Not allowed	Allowed but rarely done
9. Equity method used for 20–50% ownership	Required	Required	Required	Allowed in certain cases	Allowed	Required	Required	Required	Allowed	Required

Source: Adapted from "A Summary of Accounting Principle Differences Around the World," Phillip R. Peller and Frank J. Schwitter, 1991, p. 4.3.

457

the firm at all, since a lease is essentially the purchase of an asset only for a specified period of time. If not carried on the books, should the lease payments be expenses paid as if they were a rent payment?

Some argue that the lease results in the transfer of all risks and benefits of ownership to the firm (from the lessor to the lessee) and the lease contract should be accounted for as the purchase of an asset. This would be a capital lease, and if the lessee borrowed money in order to acquire the asset, the lease payments of principal and interest should be accounted for in the same manner as the purchase of any other capital asset.

The alternative is that the lessee has simply acquired the rental use of the services of the asset for a specified period of time, and payments on this **operating lease** should be treated only as rent. In this case the asset would remain on the books of the lessor.

Pension Plan Accounting A private pension plan is the promise by an employer to provide a continuing income stream to employees after their retirement from the firm. The critical accounting question is whether the pension promise should be expensed and carried at the time the employee is working for the firm (providing a service to the firm that will not be fully paid for by the firm until all pension payments are completed) or expensed only as pension payments are made after retirement.

The primary problem with expensing the pension as the services are provided is that the firm does not know the exact amount or timing of the eventual pension payments. If it is assumed that these eventual pension payments can be reasonably approximated, the conservative approach is to account for the expenses as employee services are provided and to carry the **pension liabilities** on the books of the firm. In some countries, if it is believed that these pension liabilities cannot be accurately estimated, they will be expensed only as they are incurred on payment.

Accounting for Income Taxes All countries require the payment of income taxes on earnings. However, the definition and timing of earnings can constitute a problem. In many countries, the definition of earnings for financial accounting purposes differs from earnings for tax purposes. The question then focuses on whether the tax effect should be recognized during the period in which the item appears on the income statement or during the period in which the item appears on the tax return.

If the expense is recognized during the period in which the item appears on the income statement, the tax gives rise to an associated asset or liability referred to as deferred tax. Some countries do not suffer the debate of whether the deferred tax should actually appear on the balance sheet of the firm by having all financial reporting follow tax rules.

Foreign Currency Translation As discussed in Chapter 16, corporations that operate in more than one country and one currency must periodically *translate* and *consolidate* all financial statements for home-country reporting purposes. The primary issues in foreign currency translation are which exchange rates should be used in the translation of currencies (historical or current rates) and how gains or losses resulting from the translation should be handled in the consolidation. The critical handling issue is whether the gains or losses are recognized in current income or carried on the consolidated balance sheet as an item under equity capital.

Figure 17.2 provides a simple decision tree approach to translation of foreign affiliates for U.S. corporations. The mechanical details of the translation of foreign affiliate balance sheets are covered in Chapter 16.

Accounting for Mergers and Acquisitions This is a relatively new issue in international accounting, given the sudden and rapid growth of merger and acquisition activity beginning in the United States and the United Kingdom in the 1980s. The primary accounting question is whether the assets and liabilities acquired should

FIGURE 17.2

United States Translation Procedure Flow Chart

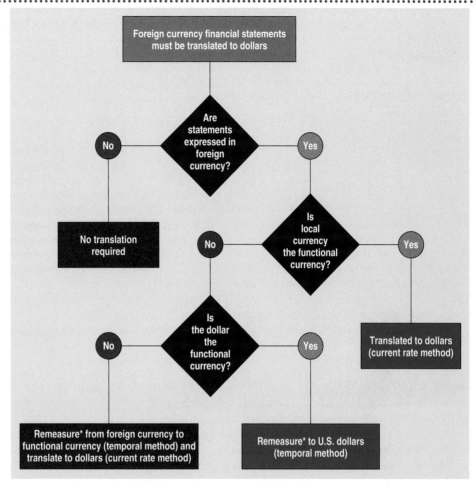

*The term *remeasure* means to translate so as to change the unit of measure from a foreign currency to the functional currency.

Source: Frederick D.S. Choi and Gerhard G. Mueller, *International Accounting,* 2d ed. (Englewood Cliffs, NJ: Prentice-Hall, 1992) p. 169.

be carried at their original historic value or at the value at acquisition. In certain cases, however, it is believed that the shareholders of the acquired company end up owning shares of the acquirer, and accountants argue that their assets and liabilities should not be revalued, but simply merged or pooled.

A second accounting issue of some concern is that often in the case of acquisitions, the price paid exceeds the fair value of the assets acquired. This is termed "goodwill" and constitutes a significant accounting problem Many accountants argue that this is a true value that is purchased, and would not have been paid for if it did not exist. Even if goodwill is accepted as a legitimate economic value, the question remains as to how it is to be carried on the firm's balance sheet.

In other countries, accountants do not believe that goodwill is a real asset and therefore should not be carried on the books of the firm. In this case, such as in the United Kingdom, the firm is allowed to write off the entire amount against equity in the year of acquisition. It is also argued that this gives British firms a distinct advantage in their ability to make acquisitions and not suffer income statement dilution impacts in the years following as the asset is amortized in the countries that capitalize goodwill. This is a classic example of the potential competitive benefits of a similar activity receiving dissimilar accounting treatment discussed at the beginning of this chapter and presented in Table 17.1.

GLOBAL PERSPECTIVE 17.2

Russia's Taxing Accounting Rules

CEOs don't like uncertainty. Moreover, boards of directors don't have much patience with financial statements that don't clearly present the financial health of an enterprise. All of which makes doing business in Russia a unique challenge, where the traditional focus has not been on profit, but on control.

This focus is well stated in Pulitzer Prizewinner Thomas L. Friedman's recent book, *The Lexus and the Olive Tree.* He writes: "The purpose of the Soviet economy was not to meet the demand of consumers, but to reinforce the control of the central government. . . . At a Soviet company that made bed frames, the managers were paid by the central government not according to how many bed frames they sold, but on the basis of how much steel they consumed. The number of bed frames sold is a measure of consumer

satisfaction. The amount of steel produced and used is a measure of state power. In the Cold War, the Soviet Union was only interested in the latter."

As a result, reports BISNIS, the section at the U.S. Department of Commerce that is the primary resource center for U.S. companies exploring business opportunities in Russia, "Russian accounting regulations (RARs) were drafted and used for tax calculation and bookkeeping purposes and not designed for use by potential investors as measurement of a company's financial performance. With the increased interest of Western investment, however, the need for understandable, comparable, transparent, detailed, and reliable financial statements has become apparent and the Government of the Russian Federation has taken steps to promote accounting reforms."

Source: Adapted from "Russia's Taxing Accounting Rules," *World Trade,* October 2000, by Scott T. Robertson.

Consolidation of Equity Securities Holdings When one company purchases and holds an investment in another company, the question arises as to how to account for the holdings. There are two major methods of consolidation of equity holdings, the equity method and the consolidation method. The equity method requires that the holder list the security holdings as a line item on the firm's balance sheet. This is generally required when the firm holds substantial interest in the other firm, typically 20 to 50 percent of outstanding voting shares, such that it can exert substantial influence over the other firm but not necessarily dictate management or policy.

The second method of equity holdings, the consolidation method, requires the addition of all of the investee's individual assets and liabilities to the company's assets and liabilities. A minority interest is then subtracted out for all assets for the percentage of the net asset not owned. When an investor has controlling interest in the other firm, most countries require the use of the consolidation method. The remaining accounting debates focus on whether the individual assets and liabilities should be consolidated when the subsidiaries are very dissimilar, even if controlling interest is held. Countries such as Italy and the United Kingdom believe that consolidation of dissimilar firms results in misleading information regarding the true financial status of the firms.

The Process of Accounting Standardization

One of the best indications as to the degree of success that has been achieved in international accounting standards is that there is still some conflict over the terminology of harmonization, standardization, or promulgation of uniform standards, as shown in Global Perspectives 17.2 and 17.3. As early as 1966, an Accountants International Study Group was formed by professional institutes in Canada, the United States, and the United Kingdom to begin the study of significant accounting differences across countries. They were primarily only to aid in the understanding of foreign practices, not to form guidelines for more consistent or harmonious policies.

GLOBAL PERSPECTIVE 17.3

How Green Is My Balance Sheet?

When it comes to environmental accounting, many companies have yet to come clean. Those that publish green accounts usually offer a few charts (printed, of course, on recycled and unbleached paper) showing trends in their output of waste. But the gases and gunk are measured in kilos or tonnes, not pounds or dollars. Few companies convert such data into figures that can appear in financial accounts (which are usually printed on recycled, chlorine-bleached paper).

The task is easier in America than elsewhere, if only because U.S. accounting rules force companies to include detailed data on known environmental liabilities in their accounts. But in Europe, where no such rules exist, information is much more patchy. Some firms, such as British Coal and Thorn EMI, publish figures on environmental liabilities. But Roger Adams, of Britain's Chartered Association of Certified Accountants, wishes that more would follow their lead. For the past four years, his institute has run a competition for the best corporate environmental accounts in Britain; this year, it is inviting entries from companies in other parts of Europe, too.

It might help if companies had a blueprint to follow. In fact, there are several different guidelines on corporate environmental reporting, including ones from the International Chamber of Commerce and from Japan's employers' association. Most favor reporting a firm's energy consumption and impact on the environment, but none tell green bean-counters how to translate this into monetary values in firms' accounts.

A few have tried anyway. One is BSO/Origin, a Dutch information-technology firm in which Philips, an electronics firm, has a 40 percent stake. It has recently published its fourth annual attempt to value the natural resources it uses and the environmental damage it does. In 1993, its environmental costs totalled 3.7m guilders ($2m), from which the company subtracted 450,000 guilders of "environmental expenditure"—taxes on fuel and waste collection—to arrive at a total of 3.3m guilders of "net value extracted." Eckhart Wintzen, BSO's president, wishes that companies were taxed on this figure. BSO/Origin's big shareholders, a less environmentally sensitive bunch, disagree.

Source: Abstracted from "How Green Is My Balance Sheet?" The Economist, September 3, 1994, 75.

The establishment of the International Accounting Standards Committee (IASC) in 1973 was the first strong movement toward the establishment of international accounting standards. In the latter half of the 1970s, other international institutions such as the United Nations, the Organization for Economic Cooperation and Development (OECD), and the European Union also began forming study groups and analyzing specific issues of confusion, such as corporate organization and varying degrees of disclosure required across countries.[3] The efforts of the European Union to harmonize standards between countries, not standardize, is particularly important in understanding how accounting principles and practices may be reformed to allow individual country differences but at the same time minimize the economic distortions.

Two other recent developments concerning international standardization merit special note. In 1985, the General Electric Company became the first major U.S. corporation to acknowledge that the accounting principles underlying its 1984 financial statements "are generally accepted in the United States and are consistent with standards issued by the International Accounting Standards Committee."[4] Second, the Financial Accounting Standards Board (FASB), the organization in the United States charged with setting most standards for corporate accounting practices, committed itself to the full consideration of "an international perspective" to all its work in the future.

International Taxation

Governments alone have the power to tax. Each government wants to tax all companies within its jurisdiction without placing burdens on domestic or foreign companies that would restrain trade. Each country will state its jurisdictional approach formally in the tax treaties that it signs with other countries. One of the primary purposes of tax treaties is to establish the bounds of each country's jurisdiction to prevent dou-

GLOBAL PERSPECTIVE 17.4

Offshore Centres' Regulation Under Fire

The European Commission's chief fraud-fighter yesterday accused the Channel Islands and the Isle of Man of having "lax regulation even by offshore standards," making them an ideal location for hiding illegal activities. The secrecy afforded by Switzerland was also a problem for its European Union neighbors and a "boon to fraudsters," Mr. Per Brix Knudesen, director of the Commission's antifraud coordination unit, told an International Financial Fraud Convention in London. His remarks were publicly challenged by Ms. Jannine Birtwistle, head of compliance at Credit Suisse (Guernsey) and a former regulator on the island. She said Guernsey's regulation had been favourably assessed by the Financial Action Task Force set up by the G7.

But Mr. Knudsen's attack on offshore centres was echoed by Mr. John Moscow, deputy chief of investigations for the New York district attorney's office. After outlining a case involving the Cook Islands, a New Zealand protectorate, Mr.

Moscow said: "There are jurisdictions which wish to earn their living protecting crooks." Mr. Knudsen, a Dane, said illicit entry of goods into the EU was alone costing member countries' treasuries Ecu5bn–Ecu6bn ($6.3bn–$7.6bn) in lost revenue each year. Smugglers potential profit per lorry or container-load ranged from Ecu1m for cigarettes to Ecu100,000 for agricultural produce. The Commission unit was also focusing on fraud in the public sector.

He said: "None of this is exclusive to the European Union. This is a truly worldwide phenomenon." Money acquired illicitly was then hidden in "phantom entities in safe havens and offshore centres." Existing arrangements for international judicial co-operation were "old-fashioned and bureaucratic," Mr. Knudsen said. These needed to be simplified and streamlined, and national law enforcement agencies should integrate their efforts and introduce more specialization.

Source: Adapted from "Offshore Centres' Regulation Under Fire," *Financial Times,* Wednesday December 4, 1996, p. 2.

ble taxation of international income. Global Perspective 17.4 shows the effect of taxes on one firm by its own government.

Tax Jurisdictions

Nations usually follow one of two basic approaches to international taxation: a residential approach or a territorial or source approach. The residential approach to international taxation taxes the international income of its residents without regard to where the income is earned. The territorial approach to transnational income taxes all parties, regardless of country of residency, within its territorial jurisdiction.

Most countries in practice must combine the two approaches to tax foreign and domestic firms equally. For example, the United States and Japan both apply the residential approach to their own resident corporations and the territorial approach to income earned by nonresidents within their territorial jurisdictions. Other countries, such as Germany, apply the territorial approach to dividends paid to domestic firms from their foreign subsidiaries; such dividends are assumed taxed abroad and are exempt from further taxation.

Within the territorial jurisdiction of tax authorities, a foreign corporation is typically defined as any business that earns income within the host country's borders but is incorporated under the laws of another country. The foreign corporation usually must surpass some minimum level of activity (gross income) before the host country assumes primary tax jurisdiction. However, if the foreign corporation owns income-producing assets or a permanent establishment, the threshold is automatically surpassed. As illustrated by Global Perspective 17.4, it is not always easy to capture income.

Tax Types

Taxes are generally classified as direct and indirect. **Direct taxes** are calculated on actual income, either individual or firm income. **Indirect taxes,** such as sales taxes, sev-

Accounting practices for the costs of environmental contamination treatment and restoration, such as Amoco Corporation's reclamation of the dunes of Coatham Sands, Great Britain, is an evolving issue in international business.

erance taxes, tariffs, and value-added taxes, are applied to purchase prices, material costs, quantities of natural resources mined, and so forth. Although most countries still rely on income taxes as the primary method of raising revenue, tax structures vary widely across countries.

The **value-added tax (VAT)** is the primary revenue source for the European Union. A value-added tax is applied to the amount of product value added by the production process. The tax is calculated as a percentage of the product price less the cost of materials and inputs used in its manufacture, which have been taxed previously. Through this process, tax revenues are collected literally on the value added by that specific stage of the production process. Under the existing General Agreement on Tariffs and Trade (GATT), the legal framework under which international trade operates, value-added taxes may be levied on imports into a country or group of countries (such as the European Union) in order to treat foreign producers entering the domestic markets equally with firms within the country paying the VAT. Similarly, the VAT may be refunded on export sales or sales to tourists who purchase products for consumption outside the country or community. For example, an American tourist leaving London may collect a refund on all value-added taxes paid on goods purchased within the United Kingdom. The refunding usually requires documentation of the actual purchase price and the amount of tax paid.

Income Categories and Taxation

There are three primary methods used for the transfer of funds across tax jurisdictions: royalties, interest, and dividends. Royalties are under license for the use of intangible assets such as patents, designs, trademarks, techniques, or copyrights. Interest is the payment for the use of capital lent for the financing of normal business activity. Dividends are income paid or deemed paid to the shareholders of the corporation from the residual earnings of operations. When a corporation declares the percentage of residual earnings that is to go to shareholders, the dividend is declared and distributed.

Taxation of corporate income differs substantially across countries. Table 17.3 provides a summary comparison for Japan, Germany, and the United States. In some countries, for example the United States and Japan, there is one **corporate income tax** rate applied to all residual earnings, regardless of what is retained versus what is distributed as dividends. In other countries, for example Germany, separate tax rates apply to **distributed** and **undistributed earnings.** (Note that Germany lists a specific corporate income tax rate for the branches of foreign corporations operating within Germany.)

Royalty and interest payments to nonresidents are normally subject to **withholding taxes.** Corporate profits are typically double taxed in most countries, through corporate and personal taxes. Corporate income is first taxed at the business level with corporate taxes, then a second time when the income of distributed earnings is taxed through personal income taxes. Withholding tax rates also differ by the degree of ownership that the corporation possesses in the foreign corporation. Minor ownership is termed portfolio, while major or controlling influence is categorized as substantial holdings. In the case of dividends, interest, or royalties paid to nonresidents, governments routinely apply withholding taxes to their payment in the reasonable expectation that the nonresidents will not report and declare such income with the host-country tax authorities. Withholding taxes are specified by income category in all bilateral tax treaties. Notice in Table 17.3 the differentials in withholding taxes across countries by bilateral tax treaties. The U.S. tax treaty with Germany results in a 0 percent withholding of interest or royalty payments earned by German corporations operating in the United States.

TABLE 17.3

Comparison of Corporate Tax Rates: Japan, Germany, and the United States

Taxable Income Category	Japan	Germany	United States
Corporate income tax rates:			
Profits distributed to stockholders	37.5%	30%	35%
Undistributed profits	37.5%	45%	35%
Branches of foreign corporations	37.5%	42%	35%
Withholding taxes on dividends (portfolio):			
with Japan	—	15%	15%
with Germany	15%	—	15%
with United States	15%	5%	—
Withholding taxes on dividends (substantial holdings):[a]			
with Japan	—	25%	10%
with Germany	10%	—	5%
with United States	10%	10%	—
Withholding taxes on interest:			
with Japan	—	10%	10%
with Germany	10%	—	0%
with United States	10%	0%	—
Withholding taxes on royalties:			
with Japan	—	10%	10%
with Germany	10%	—	0%
with United States	10%	0%	—

[a]"Substantial holdings" for the United States apply only to intercorporate dividends. In Germany and Japan, "substantial holdings" apply to corporate shareholders of greater than 25 percent.

Source: *Corporate Taxes: A Worldwide Summary*, Price Waterhouse Coopers, 1999.

U.S. Taxation of Foreign Operations

The United States exercises its rights to tax U.S. residents' incomes regardless of where the income is earned. The two major categories for U.S. taxation of foreign-source income are foreign branches of U.S. corporations and foreign subsidiaries of U.S. corporations.

Taxation of Foreign Branches of U.S. Corporations

The income of a foreign branch of a U.S. corporation is treated the same as if the income was derived from sources within the United States. Since a foreign branch is an extension of the U.S. corporation and not independently capitalized and established, its profits are taxed with those of the parent whether actually remitted to the parent or not. Similarly, losses suffered by foreign branches of U.S. corporations are also fully and immediately deductible against U.S. taxable income.

As always, however, the U.S. tax authorities want to prevent double taxation. The United States grants primary tax authority to the country in which the income is derived. If taxes are paid by the foreign branch to host-country tax authorities, the tax payments may be claimed as a tax credit toward U.S. tax liabilities on the same income.

Taxation of Foreign Subsidiaries of U.S. Corporations

Just as the United States taxes corporations from other countries operating within its borders, foreign countries tax the operations of U.S. corporations within their jurisdictions. Corporations operating in more than one country are therefore subject to

double taxation. Double taxation could hinder the ability of U.S. corporations to operate and compete effectively abroad. The U.S. tax code removes the burden by reducing the U.S. taxes due on the foreign-source income by the amount of foreign taxes deemed paid.

The calculation of the foreign income taxes deemed paid and the additional U.S. taxes due, if any, involves the interaction of the following four components.

- **Degree of Ownership and Control.** The degree of ownership and control of the foreign corporation has a significant impact on the calculation of U.S. taxes payable on the foreign-source income. There are three basic ownership ranges applicable to taxation: (1) less than 10 percent; (2) 10 to 50 percent; and (3) more than 50 percent. Figure 17.3 illustrates the three ownership classes under U.S. tax law. If the U.S. corporation owns more than 50 percent of the voting shares in the foreign corporation, the foreign corporation is classified as a Controlled Foreign Corporation (CFC).[5]

- **Proportion of Income Distributed.** The proportion of after-tax income that is distributed as profits to stockholders as dividends is also important to the calculation of U.S. tax liability. Income that is retained by the foreign corporation and not distributed to shareholders, U.S. or other, will have the result, in certain cases, of reducing the U.S. tax liability on the foreign corporation's income.

- **Active versus Passive Income.** If a foreign subsidiary generates income through its own actions or activities (e.g., producing a product, selling a product, providing a service), the income is classified as *active*. If, however, the foreign subsidiary or affiliate earns income through its ownership in another firm, or by acting as a creditor to another firm and earning interest income, the income is classified as *passive*. It is quite common for a foreign subsidiary to have both active and passive income. Each is then treated separately for tax purposes.

- **Relative Corporate Income Taxes.** Whether foreign corporate income taxes are higher or lower than similar U.S. corporate income taxes will largely determine whether the U.S. shareholders will owe additional taxes in the United States on the foreign-source income, or whether the foreign tax credit will completely cover U.S. tax liabilities. If withholding taxes were applied to dividends paid to nonresidents (the U.S. corporation owner), this also would affect the U.S. tax liability.

FIGURE 17.3   **Classification of U.S. Ownership of Foreign Corporations for Tax Uses**

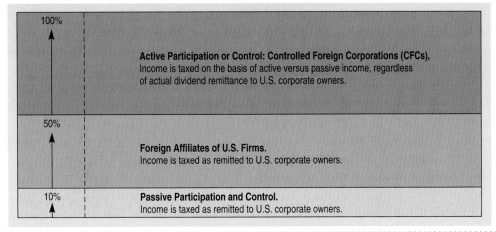

Corporate Tax Rates Around the World

Corporate Tax Rates

- 41% – 60%
- 36% – 40%
- 31% – 35%
- 1% – 30%
- 0%
- No current data available

Source: *2001 World Development Indicators*, The World Bank.

Calculation of U.S. Taxes on Foreign-Source Earnings

Table 17.4 illustrates the complete calculation of foreign taxes, U.S. tax credits, additional U.S. taxes due on foreign income, and total worldwide tax burdens for four different potential cases. Each of the four cases is structured to highlight the different combinations of the three components, relative corporate income taxes (lines a, b, and c), degree of control or ownership of the U.S. corporation in the foreign corporation (line d), and the proportion of available income distributed to stockholders as dividends (line e).

Case 1: Foreign Affiliate of a U.S. Corporation in a High-Tax Environment
This is a very common case. A U.S. corporation earns income in the form of distributed earnings (100 percent payout of available earnings to stockholders) from a foreign corporation in which it holds substantial interest (more than 10 percent) but does not control (less than 50 percent). The foreign corporate income tax rate (40 percent) is higher than the U.S. rate (35 percent). The foreign corporation has total taxable income of $2,000 (thousands of dollars), pays a 40 percent corporate income tax in the host country of $800, and distributes the entire after-tax income to stockholders. Total distributed earnings are therefore $1,200.

TABLE 17.4	U.S. Taxation of Foreign-Source Income (thousands of U.S. dollars)			
	Case 1	Case 2	Case 3	Case 4
Baseline Values				
a. Foreign corporate income tax rate	40%	20%	20%	20%
b. U.S. corporate income tax rate	35%	35%	35%	35%
c. Foreign dividend withholding tax rate	10%	10%	10%	10%
d. Proportional ownership held by U.S. corporation in foreign corporation	30%	30%	30%	100%
e. Payout rate (proportion of after-tax income declared as dividends)	100%	100%	50%	100%
Foreign Affiliate Tax Computation				
1. Taxable income of foreign affiliate	$2,000	$2,000	$2,000	$2,000
2. Foreign corporate income taxes (@ rate a above)	(800)	(400)	(400)	(400)
3. Net income available for profit distribution	$1,200	$1,600	$1,600	$1,600
4. Retained earnings (1 − rate e above × line 3)	—	—	800	—
5. Distributed earnings (rate e above × line 3)	$1,200	$1,600	$800	$1,600
6. Distributed earnings to U.S. corporation (rate d × line 5)	$360	$480	$240	$1,600
7. Withholding taxes on dividends to nonresidents (rate c × line 6)	(36)	(48)	(24)	(160)
8. Remittance of foreign income to U.S. corporation	$324	$432	$216	$1,440
U.S. Corporate Tax Computation on Foreign-Source Income				
9. Grossed-up U.S. income (rate d × rate e × line 1)	$600	$600	$300	$2,000
10. Tentative (theoretical) U.S. tax liability (rate b × line 9)	−210	−210	−105	−700
11. Foreign tax credit (rate d × rate e × line 2 + line 7)	276	168	84	560
12. Additional U.S. taxes due on foreign-source income (line 10 + line 11; if 11 > 10, U.S. tax liability is 0)	0	−42	−21	−140
13. After-tax dividends received by U.S. corporation (line 8 + line 12)	$324	$390	$195	$1,300
Worldwide Tax Burden				
14. Total worldwide taxes paid (line 10 or line 11, whichever is greater)	276	210	105	700
15. Effective tax rate on foreign income (line 14/line 9)	46.0%	35.0%	35.0%	35.0%

Note: When proportional ownership of the foreign corporation exceeds 50 percent, U.S. tax authorities classify it as a Controlled Foreign Corporation (CFC) and all passive income earned is taxed regardless of the payout rate or actual remittance to the U.S. corporation.

The foreign country imposes a 10 percent withholding tax on dividends paid to nonresidents. The U.S. corporation therefore receives its proportion of earnings (its 30 percent ownership entitles it to 30 percent of all dividends paid out) less the amount of the withholding taxes, $360 − $36, or $324. This is the net cash remittance actually received by the U.S. corporation on foreign earnings.

The calculation of U.S. taxes on foreign-source income requires first that the income be "grossed up," or reinflated to the amount of income the U.S. corporation has rights to prior to taxation by the foreign government. This is simply the percentage of ownership (30 percent) times the payout rate (100 percent) times the gross taxable income of the foreign affiliate ($2,000), or $600. A theoretical or **"tentative U.S. tax"** is calculated on this income to estimate U.S. tax payments that would be due on this income if it had been earned in the United States (or simply not taxed at all in the foreign country). U.S. taxes of 35 percent yield a tentative tax liability of $210.

Since taxes were paid abroad, however, U.S. tax law allows U.S. tax liabilities to be reduced by the amount of the **foreign tax credit.** The foreign tax credit is the proportion of foreign taxes deemed paid attributable to its ownership (30) percent ownership times the 100 percent payout rate of the foreign taxes paid, $800, plus the amount of withholding taxes imposed on the distributed dividends to the U.S. corporation, $36). The total foreign tax credit is then $240 + $36, or $276. Since the foreign tax credit exceeds the total tentative U.S. tax liability, no additional taxes are due the U.S. tax authorities on this foreign-source income. Special note should be made that the foreign tax credit may exceed the U.S. tax liabilities, but any excess cannot be applied toward other U.S. tax liabilities in the current period (it can be carried forward or back against this foreign-source income, however).

Finally, an additional calculation allows the estimation of the total taxes paid, both abroad and in the United States, on this income. In this first case, the $276 of total tax on gross income of $600 is an **effective tax rate** of 46 percent.

Case 2: Foreign Affiliate of a U.S. Corporation in a Low-Tax Environment
This case is exactly the same as the previous example, with the sole exception that the foreign tax rate (20 percent) is lower than the U.S. corporate tax rate (35 percent). All earnings, tax calculations, and dividends distributions are the same as before.

With lower foreign corporate income taxes, there is obviously more profit to be distributed, more income to the U.S. corporation's 30 percent share, and more withholding taxes to be paid on the larger dividends distributed. Yet the grossed-up income of the foreign-source income is the same as in the previous case, because grossed-up income is proportional ownership and distribution in the absence of taxes.

With lower foreign taxes, the foreign tax credit is significantly lower and is no longer sufficient to cover fully the tentative U.S. tax liability. The U.S. corporation will have an additional $42 due in taxes on the foreign-source income. After-tax dividends in total are still higher, however, rising to $390 from $324. Total worldwide taxes paid are now significantly less, $210 rather than $276.

Cases 1 and 2 point out the single most significant feature of the U.S. tax code's impact on foreign operations of U.S. corporations: The effective tax rate may be higher on foreign-source income but will never drop lower than the basic corporate income tax rate in effect in the United States (35 percent).

Case 3: Foreign Affiliate of a U.S. Corporation in a Low-Tax Environment, 50 Percent Payout
The third case changes only one of the baseline values of the previous case, the proportion of income available for dividends that is paid out to stockholders. All distributed earnings and withholding taxes are therefore half what they were previously, as is grossed-up income and the additional U.S. tax liability (because the foreign tax credit has also been cut in half).

This third case illustrates that a reduced income distribution by the foreign subsidiary does reduce income received and taxes due in the United States on the foreign income. The effective tax rate is again at the minimum achievable, the rate of taxation that would be in effect if the income had been earned within the United States. As will be shown in the fourth and final case, this third case's results rely partially on the fact that the foreign corporation is only an affiliate (less than 50 percent ownership) of the U.S. corporation and is not controlled by the U.S. corporation.

Case 4: Foreign Subsidiary of a U.S. Corporation Is a CFC in a Low-Tax Environment

This final case highlights one of the critical components of U.S. taxation of foreign subsidiary earnings: If the foreign corporation is effectively controlled by the U.S. corporation, as indicated by its greater than 50 percent ownership, and all income is passive income, U.S. tax authorities calculate U.S. tax liabilities on the foreign income as if the entire income available for distribution to shareholders were remitted to the U.S. parent, regardless of what the actual payout rate is.

This tax policy, a result of the 1962 tax reform act, is referred to as Subpart F income. Subpart F income taxation is a reflection of the control component; it is assumed that the U.S. corporation exercises sufficient control over the management of the foreign subsidiary to determine the payout rate. If the subsidiary has chosen not to pay out all passive earnings, it is taken as a choice of the U.S. corporation and is deemed to be an effort at postponing U.S. tax liabilities on the income.

The 1962 tax act was largely aimed at eliminating the abuses of foreign affiliates of U.S. corporations paying dividends and other passive income flows out to subsidiaries in various tax havens (such as Bermuda, the Bahamas, Panama, Luxembourg, and the Cayman Islands), and not remitting the income back to the U.S. corporation. By placing the passive income in the tax havens, they effectively were postponing and evading taxation by the U.S. government.

Concluding Remarks Regarding U.S. Taxation of Foreign Income

The previous series of sample tax calculations highlights the interplay of ownership, distribution, and relative tax rates between countries in determining the tax liabilities of income earned by U.S. interests abroad. In many ways, the case with the most long-term strategic significance was the first, the high-tax foreign environment. U.S. corporate income tax rates are among the lowest in the world. The usual result is the accumulation of substantial foreign tax credits by U.S. corporate interests, credits that increasingly cannot be applied to U.S. tax liabilities. The result is, as in Case 1, an effective tax rate that is significantly higher than if the income had been generated in the United States.

Recent accounting and tax rule changes may actually result in worsening this effective tax rate and excess foreign tax credit problem for U.S. corporations. Recent rule changes now require U.S. corporations to spread increasing amounts of parent-supplied overhead expenses to their foreign affiliates and subsidiaries, charging them for services provided. This results in increased costs for the foreign subsidiaries, reducing their profitability, reducing their taxable gross income, and subsequently reducing the foreign taxes, and tax credits, deemed paid. This is likely to increase the proportion of total taxes that are paid in the United States on the foreign-source income. Unfortunately, many of the overhead distributions are not recognized as a legitimate expense by many other governments (differing accounting practices in action), and the foreign units are paying a charge to the U.S. corporation that they are unable to expense against their local earnings. Recent concerns over the use of intrafirm sales (so-called transfer prices; see Chapter 15) to manipulate the profitability of foreign firms operating in the United States also has added fuel to the fires of governments and their individual shares of the world "tax pie." With that, the subject of accounting and taxation of international operations has completed a full circle.

Summary

Accounting practices differ substantially across countries. The efforts of a number of international associates and agencies in the past two decades have, however, led to increasing cooperation and agreement among national accounting authorities. Real accounting differences remain, and many of these differences still contribute to the advantaged competitive position of some countries' firms over international competitors.

International taxation is a subject close to the pocketbook of every multinational firm. Although the tax policies of most countries are theoretically designed to not change or influence financial and business decision making by firms, they often do.

The taxation of the foreign operations of U.S. multinational firms involves the elaborate process of crediting U.S. corporations for taxes paid to foreign governments. The combined influence of different corporate tax rates across countries, the degree of ownership and control a multinational may have or exercise in a foreign affiliate, and the proportion of profits distributed to stockholders at home and abroad combine to determine the size of the parent's tax bill. As governments worldwide search for new ways to close their fiscal deficits and tax shortfalls, the pressures on international taxation and the reporting of foreign-source income will only increase.

Key Terms and Concepts

accounting diversity	operating lease	value-added tax (VAT)	withholding taxes
LIFO	pension liabilities	corporate income tax	"tentative U.S. tax"
average cost method	direct taxes	distributed earnings	foreign tax credit
FIFO	indirect taxes	undistributed earnings	effective tax rate

Questions for Discussion

1. Do you think all firms, in all economic environments, should operate under the same set of accounting principles?
2. What is the nature of the purported benefit that accounting principles provide British firms over American firms in the competition for mergers and acquisitions?
3. Why do most U.S. corporations prefer the current rate method of translation over the temporal method? How does each method affect reported earnings per share per period?
4. Name two major indications that progress is being made toward standardizing accounting principles across countries.
5. What is the distinction between harmonizing accounting rules and standardizing accounting procedures and practices across countries?
6. Why are foreign subsidiaries in which U.S. corporations hold more than 50 percent voting power classified and treated differently for U.S. tax purposes?
7. Why do the U.S. tax authorities want U.S. corporations to charge their foreign subsidiaries for general and administrative services? What does this mean for the creation of excess foreign tax credits by U.S. corporations with foreign operations?
8. What would be the tax implications of combining Cases 1 and 4 in the U.S. taxation of foreign-source income, a U.S. Controlled Foreign Corporation (CFC) that is operating in a high-tax environment?
9. Why does countertrade pose special problems for accountants?

Internet Exercises

1. In order to analyze an individual firm's operating exposure more carefully, it is necessary to have more detailed information available than is in the normal annual report. Choose a specific firm with substantial international operations, for example Coca-Cola or PepsiCo, and search the Security and Exchange Commission's Edgar

Files for more detailed financial reports of their international operations. Search SEC EDGAR Archives at http://www.sec.gov/cgi-bin/srch-edgar.

2. The Financial Accounting Standards Board promulgates standard practices for the reporting of financial results by companies in the United States. It also, however, often leads the way in the development of new practices and emerging issues around the world. One major such issue today is the valuation and reporting of financial derivatives and derivative agreements by firms. Use the FASB's home page and the web pages of several of the major accounting firms and other interest groups around the world

to see current proposed accounting standards and the current state of reaction to the proposed standards. Use the web sites of FASB home page at http://raw.rutgers.edu/raw/fasb/ and Treasury Management Association at http://www.tma.org/.

3. Using Nestlé's web page, check Current Press Releases for more recent financial results, including what the company reports as the primary currencies and average exchange rates used for translation of international financial results during the most recent period. See Nestlé: The World Food Company at http://www.nestle.com/press/current/.

Recommended Readings

Alhashim, Dhia D., and Jeffrey S. Arpan. *International Dimensions of Accounting.* 3d ed. Boston: PWS-Kent Publishing Company, 1992.

Arpan, Jeffrey S., and Lee H. Radebaugh. *International Accounting and Multinational Enterprises..* New York: John Wiley & Sons, 1985.

BenDaniel, David J., and Arthur H. Rosenbloom. *The Handbook of International Mergers and Acquisitions.* Englewood Cliffs, NJ: Prentice-Hall, 1990.

Bodner, Paul M. "International Taxation." In *The Handbook of International Accounting.* ed. Frederick D.S. Choi. New York: John Wiley & Sons, 1992.

Choi, Frederick D.S., ed. *The Handbook of International Accounting.* 2d ed. New York: John Wiley & Sons, 1997.

Choi, Frederick D.S., and Richard Levich. "International Accounting Diversity and Capital Market Decisions." In *The Handbook of International Accounting.* ed. Frederick D.S. Choi. New York: John Wiley & Sons, 1992.

Choi, Frederick D.S., and Gerhard G. Mueller. *International Accounting.* 2d ed. Englewood Cliffs, NJ: Prentice-Hall, 1992.

Coopers & Lybrand, *International Accounting Summaries.* 2d ed. New York: John Wiley & Sons, 1993.

Eiteman, David K., Arthur I. Stonehill, and Michael H. Moffett. *Multinational Business Finance.* 9th ed. Reading, MA: Addison-Wesley Publishing, 2001.

Goeltz, Richard K. "International Accounting Harmonization: The Impossible (and Unnecessary?) Dream," *Accounting Horizons* (March 1991): 85–88.

Haskins, M., K. Ferris, and T. Selling. *International Financial Reporting and Analysis.* Burr Ridge, IL: R. D. Irwin, 1995.

Hosseini, Ahmad, and Raj Aggarwal. "Evaluating Foreign Affiliates: The Impact of Alternative Foreign Currency Translation Methods." *International Journal of Accounting* (fall 1983): 65–87.

Neuhausen, Benjamin. "Consolidated Financial Statements and Joint Venture Accounting." In *The Handbook of International Accounting.* ed. Frederick D.S. Choi. New York: John Wiley & Sons, 1992.

Nobes, Christopher, and Robert Parker. *Comparative International Accounting.* 3d ed. London: Prentice-Hall International, Ltd., 1991.

Price Waterhouse. *Corporate Taxes: A Worldwide Summary.* 1997 International ed. New York, 1997.

Notes

1. This example is borrowed from "International Accounting Diversity and Capital Market Decisions," by Choi and Levich, 1992.

2. This table and the following associated discussion draws heavily on the excellent study of this subject by Philip R. Peller and Frank J. Schwitter of Arthur Andersen & Company, "A Summary of Accounting Principle Differences Around the World," in *The Handbook of International Accounting,* ed. Frederick D.S. Choi, 1992, Chapter 4.

3. Disclosure has continued to be one of the largest sources of frustration between countries. The disclosure requirements of the Securities and Exchange Commission (SEC) in the

United States for firms—foreign or domestic—in order to issue publicly traded securities are some of the strictest in the world. Many experts in the field have long been convinced that the depth of U.S. disclosure requirements has prevented many foreign firms from issuing securities in the United States. The SEC's approval of Rule 144A, selective secondary market trading of private placements, is an attempt to alleviate some of the pressure on foreign firms from U.S. disclosure.

4. Frederick D.S. Choi and Gerhard G. Mueller, *International Accounting,* 2d ed. (Englewood Cliffs, NJ: Prentice-Hall, 1992), 262.

5. A. U.S. shareholder is a U.S. person (a citizen or resident of the United States, domestic partnership, domestic corporation, or any nonforeign trust or estate) owning 10 percent or more of the voting power of a controlled foreign corporation. A controlled foreign corporation (CFC) is any foreign corporation in which U.S. shareholders, including corporate parents, own more than 50 percent of the combined voting power or total value. The percentages are calculated on a constructive ownership basis, in which an individual is considered to own shares registered in the name of other family members, members of a trust, or any other related group.

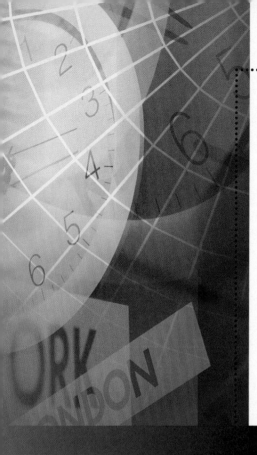

CHAPTER 18

International Human Resource Management*

LEARNING OBJECTIVES

- To describe the challenges of managing managers and labor personnel both in individual international markets and in worldwide operations

- To examine the sources, qualifications, and compensation of international managers

- To assess the effects of culture on managers and management policies

- To illustrate the different roles of labor in international markets, especially that of labor participation in management

*This chapter was contributed by Susan C. Ronkainen.

Many corporate decision makers have realized that human resources play at least as significant a role as advanced technology and economies of scale do when it comes to competing successfully in the new global world order. A full 29 percent of *Fortune 500* firms surveyed had nowhere near enough global leaders; 56 percent said they had fewer than needed; and two-thirds said that the global leaders in their companies had less capability than needed.

According to a survey of 1,200 midsize U.S. multinationals with annual sales of $1 billion or less conducted by *International Business* magazine, senior executives seek managers who are culturally diverse but responsive to the direction of headquarters. Most U.S.-based companies try to fill senior positions abroad with locals (see accompanying chart), using expatriates only for such specific projects as technology transfer. However, the same companies send their U.S. middle managers the clear message that overseas operations are so important to corporate welfare that solid international experience is needed for advancement.

While major markets in Europe and Asia possess deeper pools of managerial talent than ever before, many of these nationals prefer to work for domestic rather than foreign firms. In particularly short supply are marketing managers—49 percent of the surveyed companies say marketing is the hardest slot to fill (see accompanying chart). It is especially hard to find people who have the cross-cultural experience to make good regional managers.

Very few global leaders are born that way, that is, with an international childhood, a command of several languages, and an education from an institution with an international focus. In most cases, they have to be trained and nurtured carefully. To make a business global, its leaders have to be able to: (1) see the world's challenges and opportunities; (2) think with an international mindset; (3) act with fresh, global-centric behaviors; and (4) mobilize a world-class team and company.

To achieve this, companies are using various approaches. For example, Molex, a manufacturer based in Illinois with 47 manufacturing plants in 21 countries, concentrates on filling its human resource management positions with host-country nationals. Malou Roth, vice president of human resources, training, and development, explains that the company follows this practice not only so the managers can speak to employees in their own language and understand local legal requirements but also so the managers will know what current U.S. human resource practices will—and won't—work in their cultures.

Colgate-Palmolive promotes global leadership by hiring entry-level marketing candidates who have lived or worked abroad, speak more than one language or can demonstrate an existing aptitude for global business. Black & Decker has a team-based performance appraisal and feedback system, with members from around the world. Korea's Sunkyong uses both classroom and action-learning projects that emphasize exposure to people throughout the company. NetFRAME Systems Inc., a maker of networking computers, gathers its expatriate and non-U.S. managers at its California headquarters every quarter to encourage joint planning and problem solving on a global basis. Nortel manages each phase of its international transfers through candidate pools, informed self-selection, predeparture training, support mechanisms, repatriation debefriefing for employees and families, and disseminating repatriates' international skills and knowledge throughout the company.

Companies that spend time and money creating and training global talent naturally want to retain it as long as possible. Loctite Corp., maker of industrial adhesives, offers global opportunity, professional challenge, and a competitive compensation package to keep its rising stars. Of the three approaches, claims the company, compensation is the least important to the managers. ●

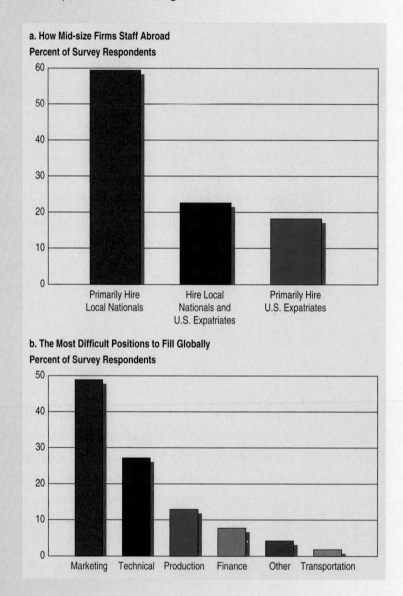

a. How Mid-size Firms Staff Abroad
Percent of Survey Respondents

b. The Most Difficult Positions to Fill Globally
Percent of Survey Respondents

Sources: "Distractions Make Global Manager a Difficult Role," *The Wall Street Journal,* November 21, 2000, B1, B18; "Whither Global Leaders?" *HR Magazine,* May 2000, 83–88; Hal B. Gregersen, Allen J. Morrison, and J. Stewart Black, "Developing Global Leaders for the Global Frontier," *Sloan Management Review* 40, fall 1998, 31–40; Shari Caudron, "World-Class Execs," *Industry Week,* December 1, 1997, www.Industryweek.com; "Globe Trotter: If It's 5:30, This Must Be Tel-Aviv," *Business Week,* October 17, 1994; Lori Ioannou, "It's a Small World After All," *International Business,* February 1994, 82–88; Shawn Tully, "The Hunt for the Global Manager," *Fortune,* May 21, 1990, 140–144. www.netframe.com; www.loctite.com; www.molex.com; www.blackanddecker.com; www.colgate.com; www.nortelnetworks.com; www.sunkyong.com.

Organizations have two general human resource objectives.[1] The first is the recruitment and retention of a workforce made up of the best people available for the jobs to be done. The recruiter in international operations will need to keep in mind both cross-cultural and cross-national differences in productivity and expectations when selecting employees. Once they are hired, the firm's best interest lies in maintaining a stable and experienced workforce.

The second objective is to increase the effectiveness of the workforce. This depends to a great extent on achieving the first objective. Competent managers or workers are likely to perform at a more effective level if proper attention is given to factors that motivate them.

To attain the two major objectives, the activities and skills needed include:

1. Personnel planning and staffing, the assessment of personnel needs, and recruitment
2. Personnel training to achieve a perfect fit between the employee and the assignment
3. Compensation of employees according to their effectiveness
4. An understanding of labor-management relations in terms of how the two groups view each other and how their respective power positions are established

All of this means that human resource management must become a basic element of a company's expansion strategy. In a study of 76 European and U.S. firms, a full 98 percent of the respondents had developed or were in the process of developing global human resource strategy. However, the majority reported that they had only moderate involvement in their company's overall business strategy. The task is, therefore, to establish human resources as not only a tactical element to fill needed positions but one whose programs affect overall business results.[2]

This chapter will examine the management of human resources in international business from two points of view, first that of manager and then that of labor.

Managing Managers

The importance of the quality of the workforce in international business cannot be overemphasized, regardless of the stage of internationalization of the firm. Those in early stages of internationalization focus on understanding cultural differences, while those more advanced are determined to manage and balance cultural diversity and eventually to integrate differences within the overall corporate culture. As seen in the chapter's opening vignette, international business systems are complex and dynamic and require competent people to develop and direct them.

Early Stages of Internationalization

The marketing or sales manager of the firm typically is responsible for beginning export activities. As foreign sales increase, an export manager will be appointed and given the responsibility for developing and maintaining customers, interacting with the firm's intermediaries, and planning for overall market expansion. The export manager also must champion the international effort within the company because the general attitude among employees may be to view the domestic market as more important. Another critical function is the supervision of export transactions, particularly documentation. The requirements are quite different for international transactions than for domestic ones, and sales or profits may be lost if documentation is not properly handled. The first task of the new export manager, in fact, often is to hire a staff to handle paperwork that typically had previously been done by a facilitating agent, such as a freight forwarder.

The firm starting international operations will usually hire an export manager from outside rather than promote from within. The reason is that knowledge of the product or industry is less important than international experience. The cost of learning through experience to manage an export department is simply too great from the firm's standpoint. Further, the inexperienced manager would be put in the position of having to demonstrate his or her effectiveness almost at once.

The manager who is hired will have obtained experience through Foreign Service duty or with another corporation. In the early stages, a highly entrepreneurial spirit with a heavy dose of trader mentality is required. Even then, management should not expect the new export department to earn a profit for the first few years.

Advanced Stages of Internationalization

As the firm progresses from exporting to an international division to foreign direct involvement, human resources-planning activities will initially focus on need vis-à-vis various markets and functions. Existing personnel can be assessed and plans made to recruit, select, and train employees for positions that cannot be filled internally. The four major categories of overseas assignments are: (1) CEO, to oversee and direct the entire operation; (2) functional head, to establish and maintain departments and ensure their proper performance; (3) troubleshooters, who are utilized for their special expertise in analyzing, and thereby preventing or solving, particular problems; and (4) white- or blue-collar workers.[3] Many technology companies have had to respond to shortages in skilled employees by globalized recruitment using web sites or by hiring headhunters in places such as China and India. For example, 60 percent of Nokia's worldwide workforce are non-Finns while that share was only half in the late 1990s.[4]

One of the major sources of competitive advantage of global corporations is their ability to attract talent around the world. The corporations need systematic management-development systems, with the objective of creating and carefully allocating management personnel. An example of this is provided in Figure 18.1. Increasingly, plans call for international experience as a prerequisite for advancement; for example, at Ford, the goal is to have 100 percent of the top managers with international work experience with the company.[5]

FIGURE 18.1   **An Example of an International Management Development System**

Tenure Years 0	1-2	3-5	5-10	10+	
Recruit worldwide	Foster international exposure and training	Apply companywide international screening for talent identification and promotion	Create opportunities to gain substantial international experience	Promote to top level	High caliber top management group of truly international spirit
Recruit internationally from best local resources to build broad base of young talent	Early international short-term assignments outside home country / International assignments as career-acceleration device / English as company language	Systematic international identification of talent / Cross-country and cross-business-unit career path planning	International experience as business-unit manager outside home country / Reward and facilitate long-term mobility	Substantial international experience (3–5 years) as prerequisite for promotion to top level	International culture / Continuing international job rotation

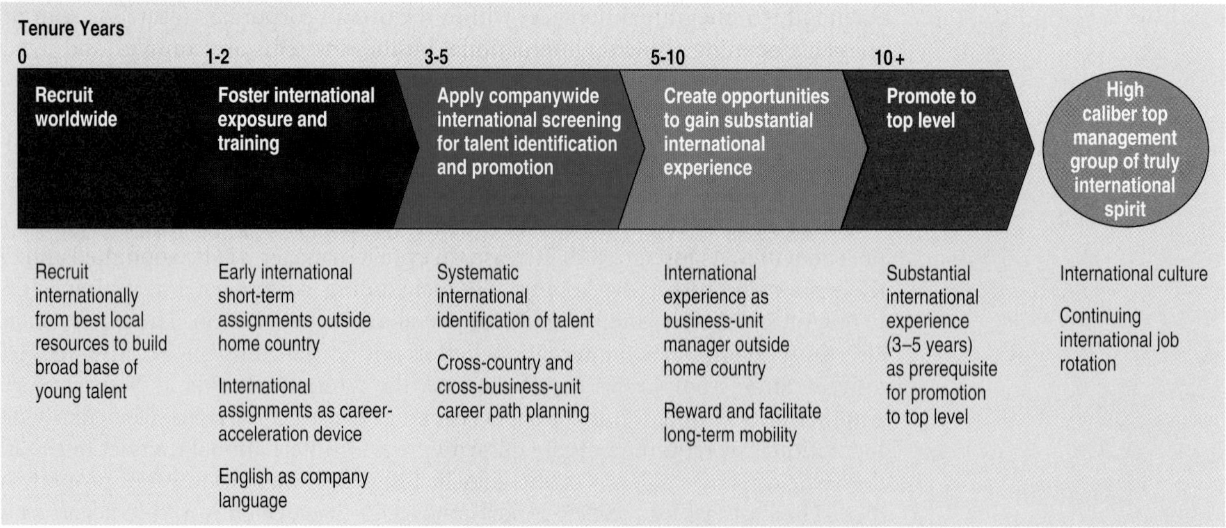

Source: Ingo Theuerkauf, "Reshaping the Global Organization," *McKinsey Quarterly* 3 (1991): 103–119.

In global corporations, there is no such thing as a universal global manager, but a network of global specialists in four general groups of managers has to work together.[6] Global business (product) managers have the task to further the company's global-scale efficiency and competitiveness. Country managers have to be sensitive and responsive to local market needs and demands but, at the same time, be aware of global implications. Functional managers have to make sure that the corporation's capabilities in technical, manufacturing, marketing, human resource, and financial expertise are linked and can benefit from each other. Corporate executives at headquarters have to manage interactions among the three groups of managers as well as identify and develop the talent to fill the positions.

As an example of this planning, a management review of human resources is conducted twice a year with each general manager of Heineken operating companies, which are located in such countries as Canada, France, Ireland, and Spain. The meeting is attended by the general manager, the personnel manager, the regional coordinating director in whose region the operating company is located, and the corporate director of management development. Special attention is given to managers "in the fast lane," the extent to which they are mobile, what might be done to foster their development, and where they fit into succession planning.[7] Of course, any gaps must be filled by recruitment efforts.

Companies should show clear career paths for managers assigned overseas and develop the systems and the organization for promotion.[8] This approach serves to eliminate many of the perceived problems and thus motivates managers to seek out foreign assignments. Furthermore, when jobs open up, the company can quickly determine who is able and willing to take them. Foreign assignments can occur at various stages of the manager's tenure. In the early stages, assignments may be short-term, such as a membership in an international task force or six to twelve months at headquarters in a staff function. Later, an individual may serve as a business-unit manager overseas. Many companies use cross-postings to other countries or across product lines to further an individual's acculturation to the corporation.[9] A period in a head office department or a subsidiary will not only provide an understanding of different national cultures and attitudes but also improve an individual's "know-who" and therefore establish unity and common sense of purpose necessary for the proper implementation of global programs.

Interfirm Cooperative Ventures

Global competition is forging new cooperative ties between firms from different countries, thereby adding a new management challenge for the firms involved. Although many of the reasons cited for these alliances (described in Chapter 11) are competitive and strategic, the human resource function is critical to their implementation. As a matter of fact, some of the basic reasons so many of these ventures fail relate to human resource management; for example, managers from disparate venture partners cannot work together, or managers within the venture cannot work with the owners' managers.[10] As more ventures are created in newly emerging markets, the challenge of finding skilled local managers is paramount. If such talent is secured, developing loyalty to the company may be difficult.[11]

While the ingredients for success of the human resource function will differ with the type of cooperative venture, two basic types of tasks are needed.[12] The first task is to assign and motivate people in appropriate ways so that the venture will fulfill its set strategic tasks. This requires particular attention to such issues as job skills and compatibility of communication and other work styles. For example, some cooperative ventures have failed due to one of the partners' assigning relatively weak management resources to the venture or due to managers' finding themselves with conflicting loyalties to the parent organization and the cooperative venture organization. The second task is the strategic management of the human resources, that is, the appropriate use of managerial capabilities not only in the cooperative venture but in other later contexts, possibly back in the parent organization. An individual manager needs to see that an assignment in a cooperative venture is part of his or her overall career development.

Sources for Management Recruitment

The location and the nationality of candidates for a particular job are the key issues in recruitment. A decision will have to be made to recruit from within the company or, in the case of larger corporations, within other product or regional groups, or to rely on external talent. Similarly, decisions will have to be made whether to hire or promote locally or use **expatriates;** that is, home-country nationals or third-country nationals (citizens of countries other than the home or host country). Typically, 70 percent of expatriates are posted in subsidiaries, while the remaining 30 percent have assignments in their company's headquarter's country (i.e., they are inpatriates).[13] The major advantages and disadvantages of expatriates are summarized in Table 18.1. In general, the choice process between expatriates and locals is driven by: (1) the avail-

TABLE 18.1

The Major Advantages and Disadvantages of Expatriates

The advantages of appointing a national of the headquarters country in an overseas post are that the expat:

1. Knows the company's products and culture.	5. Will protect and promote the interests of headquarters in international joint ventures and acquisitions and other situations requiring tight financial control.
2. Relates easily and efficiently to corporate headquarters; speaks the verbal and cultural language.	
3. Has technical or business skills not available locally.	6. Is unlikely to steal proprietary knowledge and set up competing businesses.
4. May have special transferable capabilities, for example, opening operations in emerging markets.	7. Does not put the country ahead of the company (unless he or she "goes native").
	8. Fits the company's need to develop future leaders and general managers with international experience.

The disadvantages of appointing an expat include:

1. High costs—covering relocation, housing, education, hardship allowance—often exceeding 200 percent of the home-country base.	6. Difficulty in finding experienced managers willing to move because of spouse's career, child's schooling or life-style and security concerns (for example, in Middle Eastern countries).
2. Black-outs; 25 percent of expats have to be called home easily.	
3. Brown-outs: another 30 percent to 50 percent stay but underperform, leading to lost sales, low staff morale and a decline in local goodwill.	7. Expat's concern about negative out-of-sight, out-of-mind impact on career development.
4. Prolonged start-up and wind-down time: in a typical three-year assignment the first year is spent unpacking and the third year is spent packing and positioning for the next move.	8. Re-entry problems: a high percentage of expats leave their companies after overseas assignments because jobs with similar breadth of responsibility are either not available or not offered.
5. A shortsighted focus: expats with a three-year assignment tend to focus on the next career rather than on building the local company.	9. Division of senior managers to overseas markets is difficult especially for smaller companies that do not yet have a lock on their domestic markets.

Source: John A. Quelch and Helen Bloom, "Ten Steps to a Global Human Resources Strategy," *Strategy and Business* (First Quarter, 1999): 18–29.

ability and quality of the talent pool; (2) corporate policies and their cost; as well as (3) environmental constraints on the legal, cultural, or economic front. Many countries still resist letting jobs go to foreigners, but under pressure from employers in areas such as engineering and programming, the resistance is fading.[14] In the new economy in which the physical location of work may not matter, the choice of becoming an expatriate may be the employee's. A new breed of telecommuters live countries or even continents apart from their companies' home offices.[15]

The recruitment approach changes over the internationalization process of the firm. During the export stage, outside expertise is sought at first, but the firm then begins to develop its own personnel for international operations. With expanded and more involved foreign operations, the firm's reliance on home-country personnel will be reduced as host-country nationals are prepared for management positions. The use of home-country and third-country nationals may be directed at special assignments, such as transfer of technology or expertise. The use of expatriates will continue as a matter of corporate policy to internationalize management and to foster the infusion of particular corporate culture into operations around the world.

When international operations are expanded, a management development dilemma may result. Through internal recruitment, young managers will be offered interesting new opportunities. However, some senior managers may object to the constant drain of young talent from their units. Selective recruitment from the outside will help to maintain a desirable combination of inside talent and fresh blood. Furthermore, with dynamic market changes or new markets and new business development, outside recruitment may be the only available approach. Even in Japan, the taboo against hiring executives from other companies is breaking down. The practice of hiring from the top universities can no longer be depended on to provide the right people in all circumstances.[16]

Currently, most managers in subsidiaries are host-country nationals. The reasons include an increase in availability of local talent, corporate relations in the particular market, and the economies realized by not having to maintain a corps of managers overseas. Local managers are generally more familiar with environmental conditions and how they should be interpreted. By employing local management, the multinational is responding to host-country demands for increased localization and providing advancement as an incentive to local managers. In this respect, however, localization can be carried too far. If the firm does not subscribe to a global philosophy, the manager's development is tied to the local operation or to a particular level of management in that operation. This has been an issue of contention, especially with Japanese employers in the United States. As a result, managers who outgrow the local operation may have nowhere to go except to another company.[17] Although the Japanese continue to express frustration in what they perceive to be disloyalty and opportunism on the part of U.S. employees, they are starting to change their practices so that they can retain talented U.S. nationals.[18]

Local managers, if not properly trained and indoctrinated, may see things differently from the way they are viewed at headquarters. As a result, both control and the overall coordination of programs may be jeopardized. For the corporation to work effectively, of course, employees must first of all understand each other. Most corporations have adopted a common corporate language, with English as the **lingua franca;** that is, the language habitually used among people of diverse speech to facilitate communication. At Olivetti, all top-level meetings are conducted in English.[19] In some companies, two languages are officially in use; for example, at Nestlé both English and French are corporate languages. A second goal is to avoid overemphasis on localization, which would prevent the development of an internationalized group of managers with a proper understanding of the impact of the environment on operations. To develop language skills and promote an international outlook in their management pools, multinational corporations are increasingly recruiting among foreign students at business schools in the United States, western Europe, and the Far East. When these

In Tokyo, Merck representative Satomi Tomihari confers with Yasumasa Nakamura, M.D. Tomihari is one of twenty-five women recruited by Merck affiliate, Banyu Pharmaceutical, Ltd.

Source: Griffiths, photographer for Magnum Photo, Courtesy of Merck & Co., Inc.

young managers return home, following an initial assignment at corporate headquarters, they will have a command of the basic philosophies of multinational operations.

Cultural differences that shape managerial attitudes must be considered when developing multinational management programs. For example, British managers place more emphasis than most other nationals on individual achievement and autonomy. French managers, however, value competent supervision, sound company policies, fringe benefits, security, and comfortable working conditions.[20]

The decision as to whether to use home-country nationals in a particular operation depends on such factors as the type of industry, the life-cycle stage of the product, the availability of managers from other sources, and the functional areas involved. The number of home-country managers is typically higher in the service sector than in the industrial sector, and overseas assignments may be quite short term. For example, many international hotel chains have established management contracts in the People's Republic of China with the understanding that home-country managers will train local successors within three to five years. In the start-up phase of an endeavor, headquarters involvement is generally substantial. This applies to all functions, including personnel. Especially if no significant pool of local managers is available or their competence levels are not satisfactory, home-country nationals may be used. For control and communication reasons, some companies always maintain a home-country national as manager in certain functional areas, such as accounting or finance.

The number of home-country nationals in an overseas operation rarely rises above 10 percent of the work force and is typically only 1 percent. The reasons are both internal and external. In addition to the substantial cost of transfer, a manager may not fully adjust to foreign working and living conditions. Good corporate citizenship today requires multinational companies to develop the host country's workforce at the management level. Legal impediments to manager transfers may exist, or other difficulties may be encountered. Many U.S.-based hotel corporations, for example, have complained about delays in obtaining visas to the United States not only for managers but also for management trainees.

The use of third-country nationals is most often seen in large multinational companies that have adopted a global philosophy. The practice of some companies, such as Philips, is to employ third-country nationals as managing directors in subsidiaries. An advantage is that third-country nationals may contribute to the firm's overall international expertise. However, many third-country nationals are career international managers, and they may become targets for raids by competitors looking for high levels of talent. They may be a considerable asset in regional expansion; for example, established subsidiary managers in Singapore might be used to start up a subsidiary in Malaysia. On the other hand, some transfers may be inadvisable for cultural or historical reasons, with transfers between Turkey and Greece as an example.

The ability to recruit for international assignments is determined by the value an individual company places on international operations and the experience gained in working in them. Based on a survey of 1,500 senior executives around the world, U.S. executives still place less emphasis on international dimensions than their Japanese, western European, and Latin American counterparts. While most executives agree that an international outlook is essential for future executives, 70 percent of foreign executives think that experience outside one's home country is important, compared with only 35 percent of U.S. executives, and foreign language capability was seen as important by only 19 percent of U.S. respondents, compared with 64 percent of non-U.S. executives.[21]

In an era of regional integration, many companies are facing a severe shortage of managers who can think and operate regionally or even globally. Very few companies—even those characterizing themselves as global—have systematically developed international managers by rotating young executives through a series of assignments in different parts of the world.[22] To help find the best cross-border talent, executive search firms such as A. T. Kearney and Heidrick & Struggles can be used.

Selection Criteria for Overseas Assignments

The traits that have been suggested as necessary for the international manager range from the ideal to the real. One characterization describes "a flexible personality, with broad intellectual horizons, attitudinal values of cultural empathy, general friendliness, patience and prudence, impeccable educational and professional (or technical) credentials—all topped off with immaculate health, creative resourcefulness, and respect of peers. If the family is equally well endowed, all the better."[23] In addition to flexibility and adaptability, they have to be able to take action where there is no precedent. Traits typically mentioned in the choosing of managers for overseas assignments are listed in Table 18.2. Their relative importance may vary dramatically, of course, depending on the firm situation, as well as where the choice is being made. The United States is particularly good at business literacy, while Latin Americans have developed the ability to cope with complex social relations.[24]

Competence Factors An expatriate manager usually has far more responsibility than a manager in a comparable domestic position and must be far more self-sufficient in making decisions and conducting daily business. To be selected in the first place, the manager's technical competence level has to be superior to that of local candidates'; otherwise, the firm would in most cases have chosen a local person. The manager's ability to do the job in the technical sense is one of the main determinants of ultimate success or failure in an overseas assignment.[25] However, management skills will not transfer from one culture to another without some degree of adaptation. This means that, regardless of the level of technical skills, the new environment still requires the ability to adapt the skills to local conditions. Technical competence must also be accompanied by the ability to lead subordinates in any situation or under any conditions.

Especially in global-minded enterprises, managers are selected for overseas assignments on the basis of solid experience and past performance. Many firms use the foreign tour as a step toward top management. By sending abroad internally recruited, experienced managers, the firm also ensures the continuation of corporate culture—a set of shared values, norms, and beliefs and an emphasis on a particular facet of performance. Two examples are IBM's concern with customer service and 3M's concentration on innovation.[26]

The role of **factual cultural knowledge** in the selection process has been widely debated. **Area expertise** includes a knowledge of the basic systems in the region or market for which the manager will be responsible—such as the roles of various ministries in international business, the significance of holidays, and the general way of doing business. None of these variables is as important as language, although language skill is not always highly ranked by firms themselves.[27] A manager who does not know the language of the country may get by with the help of associates and interpreters but is not in a position to assess the situation fully. Of the Japanese representing their

TABLE 18.2 Criteria for Selecting Managers for Overseas Assignment	Competence	Adaptability	Personal Characteristics
	Technical knowledge	Interest in overseas work	Age
	Leadership ability	Relational abilities	Education
	Experience, past performance	Cultural empathy	Sex
	Area expertise	Appreciation of new management styles	Health
	Language	Appreciation of environmental constraints	Marital relations
		Adaptability of family	Social acceptability

companies in the United States, for example, almost all speak English. As a matter of fact, some Japanese companies, such as Honda, have deployed some of their most talented executives to U.S. operations.[28] Of the Americans representing U.S. companies in Japan, however, few speak Japanese well.[29] Some companies place language skills or aptitude in a larger context; they see a strong correlation between language skill and adaptability. Another reason to look for language competence in managers considered for assignments overseas is that all managers spend most of their time communicating.

Adaptability Factors   The manager's own motivation to a great extent determines the viability of an overseas assignment and consequently its success. The manager's interest in the foreign culture must go well beyond that of the average tourist if he or she is to understand what an assignment abroad involves. In most cases, the manager will need counseling and training to comprehend the true nature of the undertaking.

Adaptability means a positive and flexible attitude toward change. The manager assigned overseas must progress from factual knowledge of culture to **interpretive cultural knowledge,** trying as much as possible to become part of the new scene, which may be quite different from the one at home. The work habits of middle-level managers may be more lax, productivity and attention to detail less, and overall environmental restrictions far greater. The manager on a foreign assignment is part of a multicultural team, in which both internal and external interactions determine the future of the firm's operations. For example, a manager from the United States may be used to an informal, democratic type of leadership that may not be applicable in countries such as Mexico or Japan, where employees expect more authoritarian leadership.[30]

Adaptability does not depend solely on the manager. Firms look carefully at the family situation because a foreign assignment often puts more strain on other family members than on the manager. As an example, a U.S. engineering firm had problems in Italy that were traced to the inability of one executive's wife to adapt. She complained to other wives, who began to feel that they too suffered hardships and then complained to their husbands. Morale became so low that the company, after missing important deadlines, replaced most of the Americans on the job.[31] As a response, networks intended for expatriate spouses have been developed on corporate intranets to allow for exchange of advice and ideas.[32]

The characteristics of the family as a whole are important. Screeners look for family cohesiveness and check for marital instability or for behavioral difficulties in children. Abroad, the need to work together as a family often makes strong marriages stronger and causes the downfall of weak ones. Further, commitments or interests beyond the nuclear family affect the adjustment of family members to a new environment. Some firms use earlier transfers within the home country as an indicator of how a family will handle transfer abroad. With the dramatic increase in two-career households, foreign assignments may call for one of the spouses to sacrifice a career or, at best, to put it on hold. Increasingly transferees are requesting for spouse reemployment assistance.[33] As a result, corporations are forming a consortia to try to tackle this problem. Members of the group interview accompanying spouses and try to find them positions with other member companies.[34]

Personal Characteristics   Despite all of the efforts made by multinational companies to recruit the best person available, demographics still play a role in the selection process. Due to either a minimum age requirement or the level of experience needed, many foreign assignments go to managers in their mid-30s or older. Normally, companies do not recruit candidates from graduating classes for immediate assignment overseas. They want their international people first to become experienced and familiar with the corporate culture, and this can best be done at the headquarters location.

Although the number of women in overseas assignments is only 12 percent according to one count, women are as interested as men are in the assignments.[35] Corporate hiring practices may be based on the myth that women will not be accepted in

GLOBAL PERSPECTIVE 18.1

Women and the Global Corporate Ladder

There is growing evidence to suggest that women are making greater strides on the international front than ever before. The 1999 Global Relocation Survey, conducted by Windham International and the National Foreign Trade Council, provides various measures of this trend. A full 13 percent of American corporate expatriates are women, up from 10 percent in 1993. *Fortune* magazine summarized it by stating, "The best reason for believing that more women will be in charge before long is that in a ferociously competitive global economy, no company can afford to waste valuable brainpower simply because it's wearing a skirt."

Some argue that the numbers are relatively small due to commonly held myths about women in international business. The first is that women do not want to be international managers, and the second is that foreigners' prejudice against them renders them ineffective, whether they are nationals or not.

In a study of more than 1,000 graduating MBAs from schools in North America and Europe, females and males displayed equal interest in pursuing international careers. (As a matter of fact, in a 2000 survey of 1,000 male and female managers, only 8 percent of female managers surveyed said they would never relocate overseas, compared to 17 percent of the men.) They also agreed that firms offer fewer opportunities to women pursuing international careers than to those pursuing domestic ones. Women expatriate managers agree that convincing superiors to let them go called for patience and persistence.

Expatriate women have generally reported numerous professional advantages to being female. Being highly visible (both internally and externally) has often been quoted as an advantage given that many women expatriates are "firsts" for their companies. Foreign clients are curious about them, want to meet them, and remember them after the first encounter. Emanuel Monogenis, a managing partner at the international search firm of Heidrick & Struggles, observed, "My clients now see women as equals in top global searches. In fact, more and more executives are saying they prefer women because they feel they are willing to work harder and take less for granted than male counterparts. Many also believe women have more of a sensibility and insight into human behavior and relationships than their male counterparts, and this is highly valued in culturally diverse workforces."

No person will be chosen for an assignment abroad without having the necessary technical and professional qualifications. The most successful approach for female managers is to be persistent in "educating" one's employer and constituents around the world to be open to the possibility of sending women abroad and granting them the same status and support accorded to male peers. One female expatriate summarized her experiences in this way, "Although I am viewed as a foreigner, I still have to cope with some chauvinism, but after I prove I have a brain, it is business as usual."

Sources: "Stay-at-Home Careers?" *Global Business,* January 2001, 62; 1999 Global Relocation Trends Survey Report, New York: Windham International, April 6, 1999, **www.windhamint.com;** Lori Ioannou, "Women's Global Career Ladder," *International Business,* December 1994, 57–60; Nancy J. Adler and Dafna N. Izraeli, eds., *Competitive Frontiers: Women Managers in a Global Economy* (Cambridge, Mass.: Blackwell Business, 1994): Chapters 1 and 2; Diana Kunde, "Management Opportunities for Women Brighten," *The Washington Post,* December 19, 1993, H2; and Anne B. Fisher, "When Will Women Get to the Top?" *Fortune,* September 21, 1992, 44–56; **www.heidrick.com.**

the host countries. Many of the relatively few women managers report being treated as foreign business people and not singled out as women. These issues are highlighted in Global Perspective 18.1.

In the selection process, firms are concerned about the health of the people they may send abroad. Some assignments are in host countries with dramatically different environmental conditions from the home country, and they may aggravate existing health problems. Moreover, if the candidate selected is not properly prepared, foreign assignments may increase stress levels and contribute to the development of peptic ulcers, colitis, or other problems.

When candidates are screened, being married is usually considered a plus. Marriage brings stability and an inherent support system, provided family relations are in order. It may also facilitate adaptation to the local culture by increasing the number of social functions to which the manager is invited.

Social acceptability varies from one culture to another and can be a function of any of the other personal characteristics. Background, religion, race, and sex usually become critical only in extreme cases in which a host environment would clearly reject a candidate based on one or more of these variables. The Arab boycott of the state of Israel, for example, puts constraints on the use of managers of Jewish and Arab origin.

Women cannot negotiate contracts in many Middle Eastern countries. This would hold true even if the woman were president of the company.

The Selection and Orientation Challenge   Due to the cost of transferring a manager overseas, many firms go beyond standard selection procedures and use **adaptability screening** as an integral part of the process. During the screening phase, the method most often used involves interviewing the candidate and the family. The interviews are conducted by senior executives, human relations specialists within the firm, or outside firms. Interviewers ask the candidate and the family to consider the personal issues involved in the transfer; for example, what each will miss the most. In some cases, candidates themselves will refuse an assignment. In others, the firm will withhold the assignment on the basis of interviews that clearly show a degree of risk.

The candidate selected will participate in an **orientation program** on internal and external aspects of the assignment. Internal aspects include issues such as compensation and reporting. External aspects are concerned with what to expect at the destination in terms of customs and culture. The extent and level of the programs will vary; for example, in a survey of 120 U.S. companies, 42 percent reported having no cultural preparation training for their executives. As shown in Figure 18.2, most programs offered extend the orientation to the spouse or the entire family. If the company is still in the export stage, the emphasis in this training will be on interpersonal skills and local culture. With expatriates, the focus will be on both training and interacting with host-country nationals. Actual methods vary from area studies to sensitivity training. For a discussion of these methods, see Chapter 2.

The attrition rate in overseas assignments averages 40 percent among companies with neither adaptability screening nor orientation programs, 25 percent among companies with cultural orientation programs, and 5 to 10 percent among companies that use both kinds of programs. Considering the cost of a transfer, catching even one potentially disastrous situation pays for the program for a full year. Most companies have no program at all, however, and others provide them for higher level management positions only. Companies that have the lowest failure rates typically employ a four-tiered approach to expatriate use: (1) clearly stated criteria; (2) rigorous procedures to determine the suitability of an individual across the criteria; (3) appropriate orientation; and (4) constant evaluation of the effectiveness of the procedures.[36]

In this context, it is also important to make the length of the overseas appointment make sense for the individual, the family, and the company. Three-year assignments are typical; however, in some cases when culture gaps are significant (as is in the case of western and eastern countries), it may be prudent to have longer tours.

FIGURE 18.2

Companies Offering Cultural Training

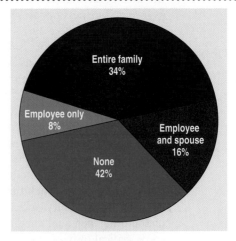

Source: Lori Ioannou, "Cultivating the New Expatriate Executive," *International Business* (July 1994): 46.

It is important that the expatriate and his or her family feel the support continuing during their tour. A significant share of the dissatisfaction expressed pertains to perceived lack of support during the international experience, especially in cases of dual-career households.[37]

Culture Shock

The effectiveness of orientation procedures can be measured only after managers are overseas and exposed to security and socio-political tensions, health, housing, education, social network and leisure activities, language, availability of products and services, and climate. **Culture shock** is the term used for the pronounced reactions to the psychological disorientation that is experienced in varying degrees when spending an extended period of time in a new environment.[38]

Of the locations around the world, those perceived to be the most pleasant have included Hong Kong, Rome, Buenos Aires, Dubai, and Prague. The most difficult to live in include Karachi, Tiranë, Lagos, Saigon, and Moscow.[39]

Causes and Remedies   Culture shock and its severity may be a function of the individual's lack of adaptability but may equally be a result of the firm's lack of understanding of the situation into which the manager was sent. Often goals set for a subsidiary or a project may be unrealistic or the means by which they are to be reached may be totally inadequate. All of these lead to external manifestations of culture shock, such as bitterness and even physical illness. In extreme cases, they can lead to hostility toward anything in the host environment.

The culture-shock cycle for an overseas assignment is presented in Figure 18.3. Four distinct stages of adjustment exist during a foreign assignment. The length of the stages is highly individual. The four stages are:

1. **Initial Euphoria:** Enjoying the novelty, largely from the perspective of a spectator
2. **Irritation and Hostility:** Experiencing cultural differences, such as the concept of time, through increased participation
3. **Adjustment:** Adapting to the situation, which in some cases leads to biculturalism and even accusations from corporate headquarters of "going native"
4. **Reentry:** Returning home to face a possibly changed home environment

FIGURE 18.3

Culture Shock Cycle for an Overseas Assignment

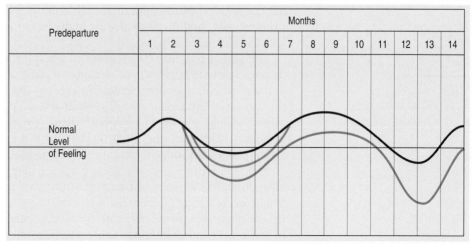

Note: Lines indicate the extreme severity with which culture shock may attack.

Source: L. Robert Kohls, *Survival Kit for Overseas Living* (Yarmouth, ME: Intercultural Press, 1984), 68.

The manager may fare better at the second stage than other members of the family, especially if their opportunities for work and other activities are severely restricted. The fourth stage may actually cause a reverse culture shock when the adjustment phase has been highly successful and the return home is not desired.

Firms themselves must take responsibility for easing one of the causes of culture shock: isolation. By maintaining contact with the manager beyond business-related communication, some of the shock may be alleviated. Exxon/Mobil, for example, assigns each expatriate a contact person at headquarters to share general information. This helps top management to keep tabs on the manager's progress especially in terms of management succession.

Terrorism: Tangible Culture Shock International terrorists have frequently targeted corporate facilities, operations, and personnel for attack, (as seen in Chapter 4). Corporate reactions have ranged from letting terrorism have little effect on operations to abandoning certain markets. Some companies try to protect their managers in various ways by fortifying their homes and using local-sounding names to do business in troubled parts of the world.[40] Of course, insurance is available to cover key executives; the cost ranges from a few thousand dollars to hundreds of thousands a year depending on the extent and location of the company's operations. Leading insurers include American International Underwriters, Chubb & Son, and Lloyd's of London.[41] The threat of terrorist activity may have an effect on the company's operations beyond the immediate geographic area of concern. Travel may be banned or restricted in times or areas threatened.

Repatriation

Returning home may evoke mixed feelings on the part of the expatriate and the family. Their concerns are both professional and personal. Even in two years, dramatic changes may have occurred not only at home but also in the way the individual and the family perceive the foreign environment. At worst, reverse culture shock may emerge.

The most important professional issue is finding a proper place in the corporate hierarchy. If no provisions have been made, a returning manager may be caught in a holding pattern for an intolerable length of time. For this reason, Dow Chemical, for example, provides each manager embarking on an overseas assignment with a letter that promises a job at least equal in responsibility upon return. Furthermore, because of their isolation, assignments abroad mean greater autonomy and authority than similar domestic positions. Both financially and psychologically, many expatriates find the overseas position difficult to give up. Many executive perks, such as club memberships, will not be funded at home.

The family, too, may be reluctant to give up their special status. In India, for example, expatriate families have servants for most of the tasks they perform themselves at home. Many longer-term expatriates are shocked by increases in the prices of housing and education at home. For the many managers who want to stay abroad, this may mean a change of company or even career—from employee to independent business person. According to one study, 20 percent of the employees who complete overseas assignments want to leave the company upon their return.[42]

This alternative is not an attractive one for the company, which stands to lose valuable individuals who could become members of an international corps of managers. Therefore, planning for repatriation is necessary.[43] A four-step process can be used for this purpose. The first step involves an assessment of foreign assignments in terms of environmental constraints and corporate objectives, making sure that the latter are realistically defined. The second stage is preparation of the individual for an overseas assignment, which should include a clear understanding of when and how repatriation takes place. During the actual tour, the manager should be kept abreast of developments at headquarters, especially in terms of career paths. Finally, during the actual reentry, the manager should receive intensive organizational reorientation, reasonable professional adjustment time, and counseling for the entire family on matters of, for example, finance. A program of this type allows the expatriate to feel a close bond with headquarters regardless of geographical distance.

Compensation

A Japanese executive's salary in cash is quite modest by U.S. standards, but he is comfortable in the knowledge that the company will take care of him. Compensation is paternalistic; for example, a manager with two children in college and a sizable mortgage would be paid more than a childless manager in a comparable job. As this example suggests, Japanese compensation issues go beyond salary comparisons. They include exchange rates, local taxes, and what the money will buy in different countries. Many compensation packages include elements other than cash.

A firm's expatriate compensation program has to be effective in: (1) providing an incentive to leave the home country on a foreign assignment; (2) maintaining a given standard of living; (3) taking into consideration career and family needs; and (4) facilitating reentry into the home country.[44] To achieve these objectives, firms pay a high premium beyond base salaries to induce managers to accept overseas assignments. The costs to the firm are 2 to 2.5 times the cost of maintaining a manager in a comparable position at home. For example, the average compensation package of a U.S. manager in Hong Kong is $225,500 (base salary is 47 percent of this figure) and for the British manager $170,500 (57 percent). U.S. firms traditionally offer their employees more high-value perks, such as bigger apartments.[45]

The compensation of the manager overseas can be divided into two general categories: (1) base salary and salary-related allowances and (2) nonsalary-related allowances. Although incentives to leave home are justifiable in both categories, they create administrative complications for the personnel department in tying them to packages at home and elsewhere. As the number of transfers increases, firms develop general policies for compensating the manager rather than negotiate individually on every aspect of the arrangement.

Base Salary and Salary-Related Allowances

A manager's **base salary** depends on qualifications, responsibilities, and duties, just as it would for a domestic position. Furthermore, criteria applying to merit increases, promotions, and other increases are administered as they are domestically. Equity and comparability with domestic positions are important, especially in ensuring that repatriation will not cause cuts in base pay.[46] For administrative and control purposes, the compensation and benefits function in multinational corporations is most often centralized.[47]

The cost of living varies considerably around the world, as can be seen in Global Perspective 18.2. The purpose of the **cost of living allowance (COLA)** is to enable the manager to maintain as closely as possible the same standard of living that he or she would have at home. COLA is calculated by determining a percentage of base salary that would be spent on goods and services at the foreign location. (Figures around 50 percent are typical.) The ratios will naturally vary as a function of income and family size. COLA tables for various U.S. cities (of which Washington, DC, is the most often used) and locations worldwide are available through the U.S. State Department Allowances Staff and various consulting firms, such as Business International Corporation. Fluctuating exchange rates will of course have an effect on the COLA as well, and changes will call for reviews of the allowance. As an example, assume that living in Helsinki costs the manager 49 percent more than living in Washington, DC. The

GLOBAL PERSPECTIVE 18.2

How Far Will Your Salary Go?

Living cost comparisons for Americans residing in foreign areas are developed four times a year by the U.S. Department of State Allowances Staff. For each post, two measures are computed: (1) a government index to establish post allowances for U.S. government employees and (2) a local index for use by private organizations. The government index takes into consideration prices of goods imported to posts and price advantages available only to U.S. government employees.

The local index is used by many business firms and private organizations to determine the cost of living allowance for their American employees assigned abroad. Local index measures for 12 key areas around the world are shown in the accompanying table. Maximum housing allowances, calculated separately, are also given.

The reports are issued four times annually under the title *U.S. Department of State Indexes of Living Costs Abroad, Quarters Allowances, and Hardship Differentials* by the U.S. Department of Labor.

	COST OF LIVING INDEX[a] (WASHINGTON, DC = 100)		MAXIMUM ANNUAL HOUSING ALLOWANCE[b]		
Location	Survey Date	Index	Effective Date	Family of 2	Family of 3–4
Buenos Aires, Argentina	Jan. 2000	140	NA	NA	NA
Canberra, Australia	Jan. 2000	121	October 1998	$17,600	$19,360
Brussels, Belgium	Nov. 1999	138	July 1999	$30,300	$33,330
Rio de Janeiro, Brazil	Nov. 1999	107	NA	NA	NA
Paris, France	Apr. 1999	153	February 1999	$49,300	$54,230
Frankfurt, Germany	Mar. 1999	141	July 1999	$25,700	$28,270
Hong Kong	Oct. 1999	143	NA	NA	NA
Tokyo, Japan	Jan. 2000	211	January 1999	$78,600	$86,460
Mexico City	Jul. 1999	111	June 1995	$37,500	$41,250
The Hague, Netherlands	Feb. 1999	139	June 1997	$33,600	$36,960
Geneva, Switzerland	Jan. 1999	196	June 1999	$47,900	$52,690
London, U.K.	Jun. 1999	165	July 1999	$51,200	$56,320

[a]Excluding housing and education.

[b]For a family of three to four members with an annual income of $62,000 and over. Allowances are computed and paid in U.S. dollars.

NA = not available.

http://www.state.gov.

manager's monthly pay is $10,000, and for his family of four, the disposable income is $5,375 (53.75 percent). Further assume that the dollar weakens from €1.08 to €1.00. The COLA would be:

$$\$5,375 \times 149/100 \times 1.08/1.00 = \$8,649$$

Similarly, if the local currency depreciated, the COLA would be less. When the cost of living is less than in the United States, no COLA is determined.

The **foreign service premium** is actually a bribe to encourage a manager to leave familiar conditions and adapt to new surroundings. Although the methods of paying the premium vary, as do its percentages, most firms pay it as a percentage of the base salary. The percentages range from 10 to 25 percent of base salary. One variation of the straightforward percentage is a sliding scale by amount—15 percent of the first $20,000, then 10 percent, and sometimes a ceiling beyond which a premium is not paid. Another variation is by duration, with the percentages decreasing with every year the manager spends abroad. Despite the controversial nature of foreign service premiums paid at some locations, they are a generally accepted competitive practice.

The environments in which a manager will work and the family will live vary dramatically. For example, consider being assigned to London or Brisbane versus Dar es Salaam or Port Moresby or even Bogota or Buenos Aires. Some locations may require little, if any, adjustment. Some call for major adaptation because of climatic differences; political instability; inadequacies in housing, education, shopping, or recreation; or overall isolation. For example, a family assigned to Beijing may find that schooling is difficult to arrange, with the result that younger children go to school in Tokyo and the older ones in the United States. To compensate for this type of expense and adjustment, firms pay **hardship allowances.** The allowances are based on U.S. State Department Foreign Post Differentials. The percentages vary from zero (for example, the manager in Helsinki) to 50 percent (as in Monrovia). The higher allowances typically include a danger pay extra added to any hardship allowance.[48]

Housing costs and related expenses are typically the largest expenditure in the expatriate manager's budget. Firms usually provide a **housing allowance** commensurate with the manager's salary level and position. When the expatriate is the country manager for the firm, the housing allowance will provide for suitable quarters in which to receive business associates. In most cases, firms set a range within which the manager must find housing. For common utilities, firms either provide an allowance or pay the costs outright.

One of the major determinants of the manager's lifestyle abroad is taxes. A U.S. manager earning $100,000 in Canada would pay nearly $40,000 in taxes—in excess of $10,000 more than in the United States. For this reason, 90 percent of U.S. multinational corporations have **tax-equalization** plans. When a manager's overseas taxes are higher than at home, the firm will make up the difference. However, in countries with a lower rate of taxation, the company simply keeps the difference. The firms' rationalization is that it does not make any sense for the manager in Hong Kong to make more money than the person who happened to land in Singapore. Tax equalization is usually handled by accounting firms that make the needed calculations and prepare the proper forms. Managers can exclude a portion of their expatriate salary from U.S. tax; in 2001 the amount was $78,000, with the figure increasing annually by $2,000.[49] Starting in 2008, the exclusion will be indexed for inflation.

Nonsalary-Related Allowances   Other types of allowances are made available to ease the transition into the period of service abroad. Typical allowances during the transition stage include: (1) a relocation allowance to compensate for the additional expense of a move, such as purchase of electric converters; (2) a mobility allowance as an incentive to managers to go overseas, usually paid in a lump sum and as a substitute for the foreign service premium (some companies pay 50 percent at transfer, 50 percent at repatriation); (3) allowances related to housing, such as home sale or rental protection, shipment and storage of household goods, or provision of household furnishings in overseas locations; (4) automobile protection in terms of covering possible losses on the sale of a car or cars at transfer and having to buy others overseas, usually at a higher cost; (5) travel expenses, using economy-class transportation except for long flights (for example, from Washington to Taipei); and (6) temporary living expenses, which may become substantial if housing is not immediately available—as for the expatriate family that had to spend a year at a hotel in Beijing, for example. Companies are also increasingly providing support to make up for income lost by the accompanying spouse.

Education for children is one of the major concerns of expatriate families. Free public schooling may not be available and the private alternatives expensive. In many cases, children may have to go to school in a different country. Firms will typically reimburse for such expenses in the form of an **education allowance.** In the case of college education, firms reimburse for one round-trip airfare every year, leaving tuition expenses to the family.

Finally, firms provide support for medical expenses, especially to provide medical services at a level comparable to the expatriate's home country. In some cases, this means traveling to another country for care; for example, from Malaysia to Singapore, where the medical system is the most advanced in southeast Asia. Other health-related allowances are in place to allow the expatriate to leave the challenging location periodically for rest and relaxation. Some expatriates in Mexico City get $300 to $500 per family member each month to cover a getaway from the pollution of the city.[50] Leaves from hardship posts such as Port Moresby are routine.

Other issues should be covered by a clearly stated policy. Home leave is provided every year, typically after 11 months overseas, although some companies require a longer period. Home leaves are usually accompanied by consultation and training sessions at headquarters. At some posts, club memberships are necessary because: (1) the status of the manager requires them and (2) they provide family members with access to the type of recreation they are used to in the home environment. Because they are extremely expensive—for example, a "mandatory" golf club membership in Tokyo might cost thousands of dollars—the firm's assistance is needed. Benefits and allowances are extended to "significant others" in 24 percent of the companies. Of these, 85 percent recognize nonmarried opposite-sex partners, 84 percent recognize same-sex partners.

Method of Payment   The method of payment, especially in terms of currency, is determined by a number of factors. The most common method is to pay part of the salary in the local currency and part in the currency of the manager's home country. Host-country regulations, ranging for taxation to the availability of foreign currency, will influence the decision. Firms themselves look at the situation from the accounting and administrative point of view and would like, in most cases, to pay in local currencies to avoid burdening the subsidiary. The expatriate naturally will want to have some of the compensation in his or her own currency for various reasons; for example, if exchange controls are in effect, to get savings out of the country upon repatriation may be very difficult.

Compensation of Host-Country Nationals   The compensation packages paid to local managers—cash, benefits, and privileges—are largely determined as a function of internal equity and external competitiveness. Internal equity may be complicated because of cultural differences in compensation; for example, in Japan a year-end bonus of an additional month's salary is common. On the other hand, some incentive programs to increase productivity may be unknown to some nationals. Furthermore, in many countries, the state provides benefits that may be provided by the firm elsewhere. Since the firm and its employees contribute to the programs by law, the services need not be duplicated.

External competitiveness depends on the market price of trained individuals and their attraction to the firm. External competitiveness is best assessed through surveys of compensation and benefits levels for a particular market. The firm must keep its local managers informed of the survey results to help them realize the value of their compensation packages.

Managing Labor Personnel

None of the firm's objectives can be realized without a labor force, which can become one of the firm's major assets or one of its major problems depending on the relationship that is established. Because of local patterns and legislation, headquarters' role in shaping the relations is mainly advisory, limited to setting the overall tone for the

UPS, the world's largest package distribution company, transports more than 3.1 billion parcels and documents annually. To transport packages most efficiently, UPS has developed an elaborate network of "hubs" or central sorting facilities located throughout the world.

interaction. However, many of the practices adopted in one market or region may easily come under discussion in another, making it necessary for multinational corporations to set general policies concerning labor relations. Often multinational corporations have been instrumental in bringing about changes in the overall work environment in a country. And as decisions are made where to locate and how to streamline operations, education and training become important criteria for both countries and companies.

At many companies, educational programs are a means of leveraging valuable company resources. Eastman Kodak has established eight training centers of excellence with functional specializations (for example, technical training and general business education). In China, AT&T has provided customized technical training to the government workers who will run the AT&T-supplied telecommunications networks.[51]

Labor strategy can be viewed from three perspectives: (1) the participation of labor in the affairs of the firm, especially as it affects performance and well-being; (2) the role and impact of unions in the relationship; and (3) specific human resource policies in terms of recruitment, training, and compensation.

Labor Participation in Management

Over the past quarter century, many changes have occurred in the traditional labor-management relationship as a result of dramatic changes in the economic environment and the actions of both firms and the labor force. The role of the worker is changing both at the level of the job performed and in terms of participation in the decision-making process. To enhance workers' role in decision making, various techniques have emerged: self-management, codetermination, minority board membership, and works councils. In striving for improvements in quality of work life, programs that have been initiated include flextime, quality circles, and work-flow reorganization. Furthermore, employee ownership has moved into the mainstream.

Labor Participation in Decision Making   The degree to which workers around the world can participate in corporate decision making varies considerably. Rights of information, consultation, and codetermination develop on three levels:

1. The shop-floor level, or direct involvement; for example, the right to be consulted in advance concerning transfers.
2. The management level, or through representative bodies; for example, works council participation in setting of new policies or changing of existing ones.
3. The board level: for example, labor membership on the board of directors.[52]

The extent of worker participation in decision making in 11 countries is summarized in Table 18.3. Yugoslavia, before its breakup, had the highest amount of worker participation in any country; **self-management** was standard through workers' councils, which decided all major issues including the choice of managing director and supervisory board.[53]

In some countries, employees are represented on the supervisory boards to facilitate communication between management and labor by giving labor a clearer picture of the financial limits of management and by providing management with a new awareness of labor's point of view. The process is called **codetermination.** In Germany, companies have a two-tiered management system with a supervisory board and the board of managers, which actually runs the firm. In a firm with 20,000 employees, for example, labor would have ten of the twenty supervisory board slots divided in the following way: three places for union officials and the balance to be elected from the workforce. At least one member must be a white-collar employee and one a managerial employee.[54] The supervisory board is legally responsible for the managing board. In some countries, labor has **minority participation.** In the Netherlands, for example, works councils can nominate (not appoint) board members and can veto the

	Direct Involvement of Workers[a]	Involvement of Representative Bodies[a]	Board Representation Standing[b]	Overall Standing[c]
Germany	3	1	1	A
Sweden	4	2	1	A
Norway	1	10	1	B
Netherlands	9	4	2	C
France	7	3	2	C
Belgium	5	6	3	D
Finland	2	9	3	D
Denmark	8	7	1	D
Israel	11	5	3	D
Italy	6	8	3	E
Great Britain	10	11	3	E

TABLE 18.3

Degree of Worker Involvement in Decision Making of Firms

[a]Involvement is rated on an 11-point scale, where 1 stands for the greatest degree of involvement and 11 for almost no involvement.

[b]All cases without any kind of board participation are coded 3; the right to appoint two or more members, 1; the in-between category, 2.

[c]Rankings are from high (A) to low (E).

Source: Adapted from Industrial Democracy in Europe International Research Group, *Industrial Democracy in Europe* (Oxford, England: Clarendon Press, 1981), 291.

appointment of new members appointed by others. In other countries, such as the United States, codetermination has been opposed by unions as an undesirable means of cooperation, especially when management–labor relations are confrontational.

A tradition in labor relations, especially in Britain, is **works councils.** They provide labor a say in corporate decision making through a representative body, which may consist entirely of workers or of a combination of managers and workers. The councils participate in decisions on overall working conditions, training, transfers, work allocation, and compensation. In some countries, such as Finland and Belgium, workers' rights to direct involvement, especially as it involves their positions, are quite strong. The European Union's works council directive will ultimately require over 1,000 multinational companies, both European and non-European, to negotiate works council agreements. The agreements will provide for at least one meeting per year to improving dialogue between workers and management.[55]

The countries described are unique in the world. In many countries and regions, workers have few, if any, of these rights. The result is long-term potential for labor strife in those countries and possible negative publicity elsewhere. Over a ten-year period from 1989 to 1998, the most working days lost occurred in Iceland, followed by Spain, Greece, Canada, Turkey, and Italy. In 1998, the most strike-prone country was Denmark, where workers sought a sixth week of paid holiday through strikes.[56]

In addition to labor groups and the media, investors and shareholders also are scrutinizing multinationals' track records on labor practices. As a result, a company investing in foreign countries should hold to international standards of safety and health, not simply local standards. This can be achieved, for example, through the use of modern equipment and training. Local labor also should be paid adequately. This increases the price of labor, yet ensures the best available talent and helps avoid charges of exploitation.[57] Companies subcontracting work to local or joint-venture factories need to evaluate industrial relations throughout the system not only to avoid lost production due to disruptions such as strikes, but to ensure that no exploitation exists at the facilities. Several large firms, such as Nike and Reebok, require subcontractors to sign

Labor Force - by Occupation

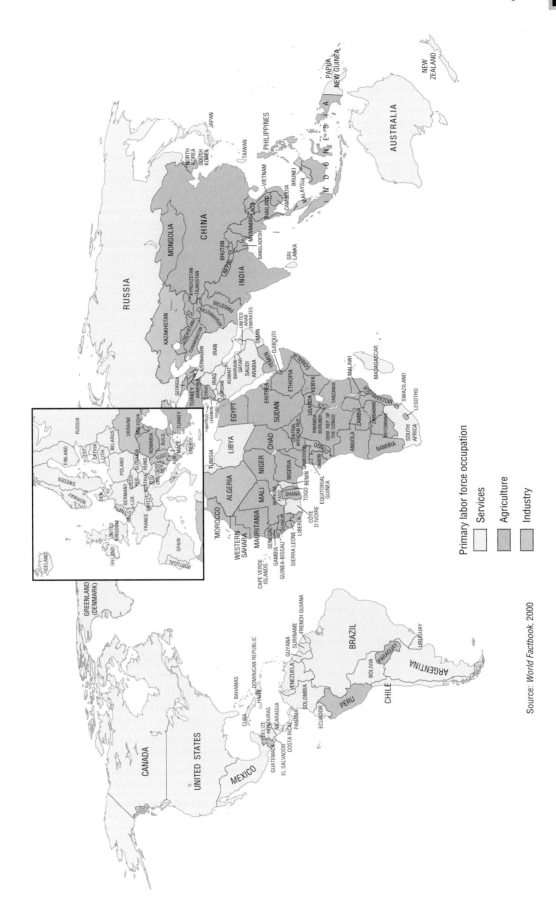

Primary labor force occupation

Services

Agriculture

Industry

Source: *World Factbook*, 2000

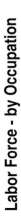

agreements saying they will abide by minimum wage standards.[58] While companies have been long opposed linking free trade to labor standards, the business community is rethinking its strategy mainly to get trade negotiations moving.[59]

Improvement of Quality of Work Life   The term **quality of work life** has come to encompass various efforts in the areas of personal and professional development. Its two clear objectives are to increase productivity and to increase the satisfaction of employees. Of course, programs leading to increased participation in corporate decision making are part of the programs; however, this section concentrates on individual job-related programs: work redesign, team building, and work scheduling.[60]

By adding both horizontal and vertical dimensions to the work, **work redesign programs** attack undesirable features of jobs. Horizontally, task complexity is added by incorporating work stages normally done before and after the stage being redesigned. Vertically, each employee is given more responsibility for making the decisions that affect how the work is done.[61] Japanese car manufacturers have changed some of the work routines in their plants in the United States. For example, at Honda's unit in Marysville, Ohio, workers reacted favorably to the responsibilities they had been given, such as inspecting their own work and instructing others.[62] On the other hand, work redesign may have significant costs attached, including wage increases, facility change costs, and training costs.

Closely related to work redesign are efforts aimed at **team building.** For example, in car plants, work is organized so that groups are responsible for a particular, identifiable portion of the car, such as interiors. Each group has its own areas in which to pace itself and to organize the work. The group must take responsibility for the work, including inspections, whether it is performed individually or in groups. The group is informed about its performance through a computer system. The team-building effort includes job rotation to enable workers to understand all facets of their jobs. Another approach to team building makes use of **quality circles,** in which groups of workers regularly meet to discuss issues relating to their productivity. Pioneered in Japan, quality circles began to appear in U.S. industry in the mid-1970s.

Flexibility in **work scheduling** has led to changes in when and how long workers are at the workplace. **Flextime** allows workers to determine their starting and ending hours in a given workday; for example, they might arrive between 7:00 and 9:30 A.M. and leave between 3:00 and 5:30 P.M. The idea spread from Germany, to the European Union and to other countries such as Switzerland, Japan, New Zealand, and the United States. Some 40 percent of the Dutch working population holds flex or part-time positions.[63] Despite its advantages in reducing absenteeism, flextime is not applicable to industries using assembly lines. Flexible work scheduling has also led to compressed workweeks—for example, the four-day week—and job sharing, which allows a position to be filled by more than one person.

Firms around the world also have other programs for personal and professional development, such as career counseling and health counseling. All of them are dependent on various factors external and internal to the firm. Of the external factors, the most important are the overall characteristics of the economy and the labor force. Internally, either the programs must fit into existing organizational structures or management must be inclined toward change. In many cases, labor unions have been one of the major resisting forces. Their view is that firms are trying to prevent workers from organizing by allowing them to participate in decision making and management.

The Role of Labor Unions

When two of the world's largest producers of electrotechnology, Swedish Asea and Switzerland's Brown Boveri, merged to remain internationally competitive in a market dominated by a few companies such as General Electric, Siemens, Hitachi, and

Toshiba, not everyone reacted positively to the alliance. For tax reasons, headquarters would not be located in Sweden, and this caused the four main Swedish labor unions to oppose the merger. They demanded that the Swedish government exercise its right to veto the undertaking because Swedish workers would no longer have a say in their company's affairs if it were headquartered elsewhere. Furthermore, Swedes objected to Brown Boveri's four subsidiaries in South Africa.[64]

The incident is an example of the role labor unions play in the operation of a multinational corporation. It also points up the concerns of local labor unions when they must deal with organizations directed from outside their national borders.

The role of labor unions varies from country to country, often because of local traditions in management–labor relations. The variations include the extent of union power in negotiations and the activities of unions in general. In Europe, especially in the northern European countries, collective bargaining takes place between an employers' association and an umbrella organization of unions, on either a national or a regional basis, establishing the conditions for an entire industry. On the other end of the spectrum, negotiations in Japan are on the company level, and the role of larger-scale unions is usually consultative. Another striking difference emerges in terms of the objectives of unions and the means by which they attempt to attain them. In the United Kingdom, for example, union activity tends to be politically motivated and identified with political ideology. In the United States, the emphasis has always been on improving workers' overall quality of life.

Internationalization of business has created a number of challenges for labor unions. The main concerns that have been voiced are: (1) the power of the firm to move production from one country to another if attractive terms are not reached in a particular market; (2) the availability of data, especially financial information, to support unions' bargaining positions; (3) insufficient attention to local issues and problems while focusing on global optimization; and (4) difficulty in being heard by those who eventually make the decisions.[65] This has been countered by new activism to secure core labor standards as fundamental human rights, including freedom of association and the right to organize and bargain collectively.[66]

Although the concerns are valid, all of the problems anticipated may not develop. For example, transferring production from one country to another in the short term may be impossible, and labor strife in the long term may well influence such moves. To maintain participation in corporate decision making, unions are taking action individually and across national boundaries as seen in Global Perspective 18.3. Individual unions refer to contracts signed elsewhere when setting the agenda for their own negotiations. Supranational organizations such as the International Trade Secretariats and industry-specific organizations such as the International Metal Workers' Federation exchange information and discuss bargaining tactics. The goal is also to coordinate bargaining with multinational corporations across national boundaries. The International Labor Organization, a specialized agency of the United Nations, has an information bank on multinational corporations' policies concerning wage structures, benefits packages, and overall working conditions.

The relations between companies and unions can be cooperative as well. Alliances between labor and management have emerged to continue providing well-paying factory jobs in the United States in face of global competition. For example, the Amalgamated Clothing and Textile Workers Union of America and Xerox have worked jointly to boost quality and cut costs to keep their jobs from going to Mexico, where wage rates are less than $2 an hour.[67]

Human Resource Policies

The objectives of a human resource policy pertaining to workers are the same as for management: to anticipate the demand for various skills and to have in place programs that will ensure the availability of employees when needed. For workers, however, the

GLOBAL PERSPECTIVE 18.3

Global Unions versus Global Companies

The United States is perceived by European companies from the labor point of view as more flexible and less costly. However, when these companies attempt to challenge U.S. unions by downsizing the workforce to increase profitability, they meet resistance not only from the U.S. unions but from the international federations of trade unions. Conflict arises when there are different understandings of the role of labor unions.

Trelleborg, a Swedish metal and mining conglomerate with operations in eight European countries, expanded into the United States with the purchase of a plant in Copperhill, Tennessee, in 1991 after the owner went bankrupt. The plant was managed under Trelleborg's subsidiary, Boliden Intertrade Inc. The unions at Copperhill deferred over $5 million in wages to help keep the plant alive in the early 1990s. But labor-management relations deteriorated during contract negotiations in 1996, when Trelleborg insisted on sweeping changes in work rules. Boliden executives recognized that there would be a considerable loss of jobs, but saw no other way to regain competitiveness.

The workers saw the changes as a direct assault on their seniority system and a threat to worker safety, and went to strike after their contract expired. The company responded by hiring replacement workers and a squad of security guards. Two weeks later, the company said it had received a petition

from its new employees indicating they did not want a union. Unions, on their part, demanded that Boliden withdraw its letter of derecognition and remove the replacement workers.

U.S. unions represent 16 percent of the public- and private-sector workforce, but in Sweden the unionization rate is over 80 percent. Although strikes are relatively rare in Sweden, replacing workers during a walkout is virtually unheard of. Swedish workers also have the right to shut down a company during a strike by stopping delivery trucks and other services, all actions that are banned in the United States.

Union activity was not limited to local moves in Tennessee. Metal, the powerful Swedish labor union representing Swedish workers in the industry, was recruited to pressure the parent company in Sweden. The International Federation of Chemical, Energy, Mine, and General Workers' Unions launched a campaign to pressure Trelleborg to rehire the Copperhill strikers. U.S. and Canadian unions warned institutional investors and pension fund managers that an investment in Boliden could be risky. They made their warnings as Trelleborg executives were visiting North America to raise $900 million in an initial public offering on the Toronto Stock Exchange.

Two months into the crisis, Trelleborg announced it would sell its U.S. subsidiary.

Source: Jay Mazur, "Labor's New Internationalism," *Foreign Affairs* 79 (January/February 2000): 79–93; Tim Schorrock, "Firm to Sell U.S. Unit at Center of Labor Flap," *The Journal of Commerce* (June 3, 1997): 3A; Joan Campbell, *The European Labor Unions* (Greenwood, CT: Greenwood Press, 1994), 429; and Tom DeVos, *U.S. Multinationals and Worker Participation in Management* (Westport, CT: Quorum Books, 1981), 195; http://www.trellgroup.se.

firm faces the problem on a larger scale and does not have, in most cases, an expatriate alternative. This means that, among other things, when technology is transferred for a plant, it has to be adapted to the local workforce.

Although most countries have legislation and restrictions concerning the hiring of expatriates, many of them—for example some of the EU countries and some oil-rich Middle Eastern countries—have offset labor shortages by importing large numbers of workers from countries such as Turkey and Jordan. The EU by design allows free movement of labor. A mixture of backgrounds in the available labor pool can put a strain on personnel development. As an example, the firm may incur considerable expense to provide language training to employees. In Sweden, a certain minimum amount of language training must be provided for all "guest workers" at the firm's expense.

Bringing a local labor force to the level of competency desired by the firm may also call for changes. As an example, managers at Honda's plant in Ohio encountered a number of problems: Labor costs were originally 50 percent higher and productivity 10 percent lower than in Japan. Automobiles produced there cost $500 more than the same models made in Japan and then delivered to the United States. Before Honda began to produce the Accord in the United States, it flew 200 workers representing all areas of the factory to Japan to learn to build Hondas the Sayama way and then to teach their coworkers the skills.

Compensation of the work force is a controversial issue. Payroll expenses must be controlled for the firm to remain competitive; on the other hand, the firm must attract in appropriate numbers the type of workers it needs. The compensation packages of U.S.-based multinational companies have come under criticism, especially when their level of compensation is lower in developing countries than in the United States. Criticism has occurred even when the salaries or wages paid were substantially higher than the local average.[68]

Comparisons of compensation packages are difficult because of differences in the packages that are shaped by culture, legislation, collective bargaining, taxation, and individual characteristics of the job. In northern Europe, for example, new fathers can accompany their wives on a two-week paternity leave at the employer's expense.

These differences in compensation and benefits may come to a head in merger and acquisition situations. When Ford Motor acquired Volvo, planned changes included moving to a three-shift, round-the-clock production schedule just like in the United States as compared to the two shifts in Sweden. Some of the differences may not be changeable, however. Night-shift workers get paid the same as day-shift workers although they work only 30 hours a week because of a government-mandated allocation. Some benefits, such as a fitness center which costs the company annually over $600,000 to maintain may come under scrutiny by the new owners.[69]

Summary

A business organization is the sum of its human resources. To recruit and retain a pool of effective people for each of its operations requires: (1) personnel planning and staffing; (2) training activities; (3) compensation decisions; and (4) attention to labor–management relations.

Firms attract international managers from a number of sources, both internal and external. In the earlier stages of internationalization, recruitment must be external. Later, an internal pool often provides candidates for transfer. The decision then becomes whether to use home-country, host-country, or third-country nationals. If expatriate managers are used, selection policies should focus on competence, adaptability, and personal traits. Policies should also be set for the compensation and career progression of candidates selected for out-of-country assignments. At the same time,

the firm must be attentive to the needs of local managers for training and development.

Labor can no longer be considered as simply services to be bought. Increasingly, workers are taking an active role in the decision making of the firm and in issues related to their own welfare. Various programs are causing dramatic organizational change, not only by enhancing the position of workers but by increasing the productivity of the work force as well. Workers employed by the firm usually are local, as are the unions that represent them. Their primary concerns in working for a multinational firm are job security and benefits. Unions therefore are cooperating across national boundaries to equalize benefits for workers employed by the same firm in different countries.

Key Terms and Concepts

expatriate
lingua franca
factual cultural knowledge
area expertise
interpretive cultural
    knowledge
adaptability screening

orientation program
culture shock
base salary
cost of living allowance
    (COLA)
foreign service premium
hardship allowance

housing allowance
tax equalization
education allowance
self-management
codetermination
minority participation
works councils

quality of work life
work redesign programs
team building
quality circles
work scheduling
flextime

Questions for Discussion

1. Is a "supranational executive corps," consisting of cosmopolitan individuals of multiple nationalities who would be an asset wherever utilized, a possibility for any corporation?

2. Comment on this statement by Lee Iacocca: "If a guy wants to be a chief executive 25 or 50 years from now, he will have to be well rounded. There will be no more of 'Is he a good lawyer, is he a good marketing guy, is he a good

finance guy?' His education and his experience will make him a total entrepreneur in a world that has really turned into one huge market. He better speak Japanese or German, he better understand the history of both of those countries and how they got to where they are, and he better know their economics pretty cold."

3. What additional benefit is brought into the expatriate selection and training process by adaptability screening?

4. A manager with a current base salary of $100,000 is being assigned to Lagos, Nigeria. Assuming that you are that manager, develop a compensation and benefits package for yourself in terms of both salary-related and nonsalary-related items.

5. What accounts for the success of Japanese companies with both American unions and the more ferocious British unions? In terms of the changes that have come about, are there winners or losers among management and workers? Could both have gained?

6. Develop general policies that the multinational corporation should follow in dealing (or choosing not to deal) with a local labor union.

Internet Exercises

1. Paguro. net (available at **www.paguro.net**) is a network that puts expatriates, and especially their family members) in touch with each other. What benefits can be gained from an individual or corporate membership to such a service?

2. Using the Homebuyer's Fair web site (**http://www.homefair.com**), compare the cost of living in your home city versus Vienna, Austria; Brussels, Belgium; Shanghai, China; Bogota, Colombia; and New Delhi, India. What accounts for the differences present?

Recommended Readings

Adler, Nancy J., and Dafna N. Izraeli, eds. *Competitive Frontiers: Women Managers in a Global Economy.* Cambridge, MA: Blackwell Business, 1994.

Austin, James. *Managing in Developing Countries.* New York: Free Press, 1990.

Black, J. Stewart, Hal B. Gregsen, Mark E. Mendenhall, Torsten M. Kuhlmann, and Gunther K. Stahl. *Developing Global Business Leaders: Policies, Resources, and Innovation.* New York: Quorum Books, 2000.

Casse, Pierre. *Training for the Multicultural Manager.* Washington, DC: SIETAR, 1987.

Deresky, Helen. *International Management: Managing Across Borders and Cultures.* Reading, MA: Addison-Wesley, 1997.

Harris, Philip, and Robert T. Moran. *Managing Cultural Differences.* Houston, TX: Gulf, 1996.

Hodgetts, Richard, and Fred Luthans. *International Management.* New York: McGraw-Hill, 2000.

Holley, William H., and Kenneth M. Jennings. *The Labor Relations Process.* Fort Worth, TX: Dryden Press, 1997.

Lane, Henry W., Joseph J. DiStephano, and Martha L. Maznevski. *International Management Behavior.* Cambridge, MA: Blackwell Publishers, 2000.

Lewis, Tom, and Robert Jungman, eds. *On Being Foreign: Culture Shock in Short Fiction.* Yarmouth, ME: Intercultural Press, 1986.

Marquardt, Michael J., and Dean W. Engel. *Global Resource Development.* Englewood Cliffs, NJ: Prentice-Hall, 1993.

Pucik, Vladimir, Noel M. Tichy, and Carole K. Barnett. *Globalizing Management: Creating and Leading the Competitive Organization.* New York: John Wiley, 1992.

Slomp, Hans. *Between Bargaining and Politics.* Westport, CT: Praeger, 1998.

Stroh, Linda, *Globalizing People Through International Assignments.* Reading, MA: Addison-Wesley, 1999.

Notes

1. Herbert G. Heneman and Donald P. Schwab, "Overview of the Personnel/Human Resource Function," in *Perspectives on Personnel/Human Resource Management.* ed. Herbert G. Heneman and Donald P. Schwab (Homewood, IL: Irwin, 1986), 3–11.

2. "Of Tactics and Strategy," *Global Business,* March 2000, 64; **www.arthurandesen.com.**

3. Richard D. Hays, "Expatriate Selection: Insuring Success and Avoiding Failure," *Journal of International Business Studies* 5 (summer 1974): 25–37.

4. "India's Technology Whizzes Find Passage to Nokia," *The Wall Street Journal,* August 1, 2000, B1; B12; and "Nokia's Secret Code," *Fortune,* May 1, 2000, 161–174.

5. "Ford's Brave New World," *The Washington Post,* October 16, 1994, H1, H4.

6. Christopher A. Bartlett and Sumantra Ghoshal, "What Is a Global Manager?" *Harvard Business Review* 70 (September–October 1992): 124–132.

7. Jan van Rosmalen, "Internationalising Heineken: Human Resource Policy in a Growing International Company," *In-*

ternational Management Development (summer 1985): 11–13.

8. John A. Quelch and Helen Bloom, "Ten Steps to a Global Human Resources Strategy," *Strategy and Business* (first quarter, 1999): 18–29.

9. Floris Majlers, "Inside Unilever: The Evolving Transnational Company," *Harvard Business Review* 70 (September–October 1992): 46–52.

10. Randall S. Schuler, Susan E. Jackson, Peter J. Dowling, and Denice E. Welch, "The Formation of an International Joint Venture: Davidson Instrument Panel," in *International Human Resource Management*, ed. Mark Mendenhall and Gary Oddou (Boston: PWS–Kent, 1991), 83–96.

11. "Company & Industry: Ukraine," *Crossborder Monitor* (October 23, 1996): 4; and "Middle Managers In Vietnam," *Business Asia* (May 8, 1995): 3–4.

12. Peter Lorange, "Human Resource Management in Multinational Cooperative Ventures," *Human Resources Management* 25 (winter 1986): 133–148.

13. *1999 Global Relocation Trends Survey Report* (New York: Windham International, 2000); available on **http://www.windhamworld.com**.

14. "People Who Need People," *The Wall Street Journal*, September 25, 2000, R8.

15. "For 'Extreme Telecommuters,' Remote Work Means Really Remote," *The Wall Street Journal*, January 31, 2001, B1, B7.

16. Carla Rapoport, "The Switch Is On in Japan," *Fortune* (May 21, 1990): 144.

17. Anders Edström and Peter Lorange, "Matching Strategy and Human Resources in Multinational Corporations," *Journal of International Business Studies* 16 (fall 1985): 125–137.

18. Elizabeth Klein, "The U.S./Japanese HR Culture Clash," *Personnel Journal* 71 (November 1992): 30–38.

19. "How Business Is Creating Europe Inc.," *Business Week* (September 7, 1987): 40–41.

20. Rabindra Kanungo and Richard W. Wright, "A Cross-Cultural Comparative Study of Managerial Job Attitudes," *Journal of International Business Studies* 14 (fall 1983): 115–129.

21. Lester B. Korn, "How the Next CEO Will Be Different," *Fortune* (May 22, 1990): 157–161.

22. "The Elusive Euromanager," *The Economist* (November 7, 1993): 83.

23. Jean E. Heller, "Criteria for Selecting an International Manager," *Personnel* (May–June 1980): 18–22.

24. Robert Rosen, *Global Literacies: Lessons on Business Leadership and National Cultures* (New York: Simon & Schuster, 2000).

25. Richard D. Hays, "Ascribed Behavioral Determinants of Success-Failure Among U.S. Expatriate Managers," *Journal of International Business Studies* 2 (summer 1971): 40–46.

26. Richard Pascale, "Fitting New Employees into the Corporate Culture," *Fortune* (May 28, 1984): 28–40.

27. *Compensating International Executives* (New York: Business International, 1970), 35.

28. Joel Bleeke and David Ernst, *Collaborating to Compete* (New York: John Wiley & Sons, 1993), 179.

29. Lennie Copeland, "Training Americans to Do Business Overseas," *Training* (July 1984): 22–33.

30. Lee Smith, "Japan's Autocratic Managers," *Fortune* (January 7, 1985): 14–23.

31. "Gauging a Family's Suitability for a Stint Overseas," *Business Week* (April 16, 1979): 127–130.

32. "Have Wife, Will Travel," *The Economist,* December 16, 2000, 70.

33. *Runzheimer Reports on Relocation,* Rochester, WI: Runzheimer International, 1997, at **http//www.runzheimer.com**.

34. "Global Managing," *The Wall Street Journal Europe,* January 10–11, 1992, 1, 20.

35. Nancy J. Adler, "Expecting International Success: Female Managers Overseas," *Columbia Journal of World Business* 19 (fall 1984): 79–85.

36. Rosalie Tung, "Selection and Training of Personnel for Overseas Assignments," *Columbia Journal of World Business* 16 (spring 1981): 68–78.

37. Michael G. Harvey, "Dual-Career Expatriates: Expectations, Adjustment and Satisfaction with International Relocation," *Journal of International Business Studies* 28, 3 (1997): 627–658.

38. L. Robert Kohls, *Survival Kit for Overseas Living* (Yarmouth, ME: Intercultural Press, 1979), 62–68.

39. "Polar Opposites," *Global Business,* August 2000, 24.

40. Michael G. Harvey, "A Survey of Corporate Programs for Managing Terrorist Threats," *Journal of International Business Studies* 24, 3 (1993): 465–478.

41. Mary Helen Frederick, "Keeping Safe," *International Business* (October, 1992): 68–69.

42. Nancy J. Adler, *International Dimensions of Organizational Behavior* (Boston: PWS–Kent, 1990), Chapter 4.

43. Michael G. Harvey, "The Other Side of Foreign Assignments: Dealing with the Repatriation Dilemma," *Columbia Journal of World Business* 16 (spring 1981): 79–85.

44. Raymond J. Stone, "Compensation: Pay and Perks for Overseas Executives," *Personnel Journal* (January 1986): 64–69.

45. Karen E. Thuemer, "Asia Adds Up," *Global Business,* June 2000, 51–55.

46. *1987 Professional Development Seminar: International Compensation* (Phoenix, AZ: American Compensation Association, 1987), module 1.

47. Brian Toyne and Robert J. Kuhne, "The Management of the International Executive Compensation and Benefits Process," *Journal of International Business Studies* 14 (winter 1983): 37–49.

48. U.S. Department of State, *Indexes of Living Costs Abroad, Quarters Allowances, and Hardship Differentials,* January 2000, Table 3.

49. Courtesy of Thomas B. Cooke, Esq.

50. "Mexico Is Perk Paradise for U.S. Middle Managers," *The Wall Street Journal,* May 23, 2000, B1, B18.

51. "The Winds of Change Blow Everywhere," *Business Week* (October 17, 1994): 87–88; and "School Days at Work: Firms See Training as Key to Empowerment," *Crossborder Monitor* (August 3, 1994): 1, 7.

52. Industrial Democracy in Europe International Research Group, *Industrial Democracy in Europe* (Oxford, England: Clarendon Press, 1981), Chapter 14.

53. Osmo A. Wiio, *Yritysdemokratia ja Muuttuva Yhteiskunta* (Tapiola, Finland: Weilin + Goos, 1970), Chapter 13.

54. E. B. Hoffman, "The German Way of Industrial Relations—Could We, Should We, Import It?" *Across the Board* (October 1977): 38–47.

55. "EU Works Councils Get Underway," *Crossborder Monitor* (October 16, 1996): 4.

56. "Labour Disputes," *The Economist*, April 22, 2000, 96.

57. "MNCs Under Fire to Link Trade with Global Labor Rights," *Crossborder Monitor* (May 25, 1994): 1.

58. "Labor Strife in Indonesia Spotlights Development Challenge," *Crossborder Monitor* (May 25, 1994): 7.

59. "Firms Rethink Hostility to Linking Trade, Labor Rights," *The Wall Street Journal*, February 2, 2001, A12.

60. Herman Gadon, "Making Sense of Quality of Work Life Programs," *Business Horizons* 27 (January–February 1984): 42–46.

61. Antone Alber, "The Costs of Job Enrichment," *Business Horizons* 22 (February 1984): 60–72.

62. Faye Rice, "America's New No. 4 Automaker—Honda," *Fortune* (October 28, 1985): 26–29.

63. "Hour by Hour," *Global Business*, November 2000, 25.

64. "Asean Ammattiliitot Vaativat Suuryhtyman Paapaikkaa Ruotsiin," *Helsingin Sanomat*, September 16, 1987, 34.

65. S. B. Prasad and Y. Kirshna Shetty, *An Introduction to Multinational Management* (Englewood Cliffs, NJ: Prentice-Hall, 1976), Appendix 8-A.

66. Jay Mazur, "Labor's New Internationalism," *Foreign Affairs*, January/February 2000, 79–93.

67. "Cooperation Worth Copying?" *The Washington Post*, December 13, 1992, H1, H6.

68. Oliver Williams, "Who Cast the First Stone?" *Harvard Business Review* 62 (September–October 1984): 151–160.

69. "Detroit Meets a 'Worker Paradise,'" *The Wall Street Journal*, March 3, 1999, B1; B4.

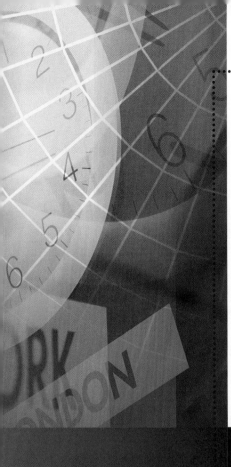

CHAPTER 19

Organization, Implementation, and Control of International Operations

LEARNING OBJECTIVES

- To describe alternative organizational structures for international operations

- To highlight factors affecting decisions about the structure of international organizations

- To indicate roles for country organizations in the development of strategy and implementation of programs

- To outline the need for and challenges of controls in international operations

Globalization is at the heart of Procter&Gamble's restructuring of its organization, code-named Organization 2005. Organization 2005 recognizes that there is a big difference between selling products in 140 countries around the world and truly planning and managing lines of business on a global basis.

There are five key elements to Organization 2005:

- **Global Business Units.** P&G is moving from four business units based on geographic regions to seven GBUs based on product lines. This will drive greater innovation and speed by centering strategy and profit responsibility globally on brands, rather than on geographics.

- **Market Development Organizations.** The company is establishing eight MDO regions that will tailor global programs to local markets and develop marketing strategies to build P&G's entire business based on superior local consumer and customer knowledge.

- **Global Business Services.** GBS brings together business activities such as accounting, human-resource systems, order management, and information technology into a single global organization to provide these services to all P&G business units at best-in-class quality, cost, and speed. They will be in the following locations: Americas (Cincinnati, United States, and San Jose, Costa Rica); Europe, Middle East, Africa (Newcastle, United Kingdom; Brussels, Belgium; and Prague, the Czech Republic); Asia (Kobe, Japan; Manila, Philippines; Guangzhou, China; and Singapore).

- **Corporate Functions.** P&G has redefined the role of corporate staff. Most have moved into new business units, with the remaining staff refocused on developing cutting-edge new knowledge and serving corporate needs. For example, the company decentralized its 3,600-person IT department so that 97 percent of them now work in P&G's individual product, market, and business teams, or are part of GBS, which supports shared services such as infrastructure to P&G units. The remaining 3 percent are still in corporate IT. In addition, 54 "change agents" have been assigned to work across the seven GBUs to lead cultural and business change by helping teams work together more effectively through greater use of IT, in particular, real-time collaboration tools.

- **Culture.** Changes to P&G's culture should create an environment that produces bolder, mind-stretching goals and plans, bigger innovations, and greater speed. For example, the reward system has been redesigned to better link executive compensation with new business goals and results.

The New Procter&Gamble

Global Business Units	Market Development Organizations	Global Business Services	Corporate Functions
• Baby Care	• North America	• Global Enabling Team	• Customer Business Development
• Beauty Care	• Latin America	• Regional Leadership Team	• Finance Resources
• Fabric & Home Care	• Western Europe	• Global Process Owners	• IT
• Feminine Protection	• Central & Eastern Europe		• Legal
• Food & Beverage	• ASEAN/India/Australia		• Market Research/Gov't Relations
• Health Care & Corporate Ventures	• Northeast Asia		• Product Supply
• Tissue & Towel	• Greater China		• Public Affairs
	• Middle East/Africa General Export		• R&D

Source: Procter&Gamble

Source: www.febreze.com

Source: www.pg.com

Source: www.swiffer.com

A good example of the increased use of collaborative technology is a product called Swiffer, a dust sweeper with disposal cloths electrostatically charged to attract dust and dirt. Swiffer, which was introduced to the market in August 1999, represents collaboration among multiple P&G product groups, including paper and chemicals. Swiffer took just 18 months from test market to global availability. In the past, when a product was introduced, it might have taken years for it to be available worldwide, the reason being that management in each region was responsible for the product's launch in his or her geography, including everything from test marketing to getting products onto retailers' shelves. Collaborative technologies, including chat rooms on the company's intranet, are transforming the company's conservative culture to one that encourages employees to be candid, test boundaries, and take chances.

Not all has gone well with the planned changes, however. The major overlooked factor was the personal upheaval that would be created. More than half of the executives at various levels are in new jobs. Physical transfers were significant as well; e.g., about 1,000 people were moved to Geneva from around Europe and another 200 to Singapore from different Asian locations. Furthermore, the changed reporting structures raised concerns as well. Food and beverages managers, who are mostly in Cincinnati, report to a president in Caracas, Venezuela, while everyone in laundry and household cleaners reports to Brussels. Personnel transferred from MDOs suddenly had no brands to manage and had to think across borders. The change from a U.S.-centric company to a globally thinking one was a substantial demand in a short period of time and the timetable of the process has subsequently been reevaluated. ●

Sources: Jack Neff, "Does P&G Still Matter?" *Advertising Age,* September 25, 2000, 48–56; "Rallying the Troops at P&G," *The Wall Street Journal,* August 31, 2000, B1, B4; P&G Jump-Starts Corporate Change," *Internetweek,* November 1, 1999, 30; "All Around the World," *Traffic World,* October 11, 1999, 22–24; "Organization 2005 Drive for Accelerated Growth Enters Next Phase," P&G News Releases, June 9, 1999, 1–5; and "Procter & Gamble Moves Forward with Reorganization," *Chemical Market Reporter,* February 1, 1999, 12.

As companies evolve from purely domestic to multinational, their organizational structure and control systems must change to reflect new strategies. With growth comes diversity in terms of products and services, geographic markets, and people in the company itself, bringing along a set of challenges for the company. Two critical issues are basic to all of these challenges: (1) the type of organization that provides the best framework for developing worldwide strategies while at the same time maintaining flexibility in implementation with respect to individual markets and operations, and (2) the type and degree of control to be exercised from headquarters to maximize total effort. Organizational structures, organizations' abilities to implement strategies, and control systems have to be adjusted as market conditions change, as seen in the chapter's opening vignette.

This chapter will focus on the advantages and disadvantages of various organizational structures, as well as their appropriateness at different stages of internationalization. A determining factor is where decision-making authority within the organizational structure will be placed. The roles of the different entities that make up the organization need to be defined, including how to achieve collaboration among the units for the benefit of the entire network. The chapter will also outline the need for devising a control system to oversee the international operations of the company, emphasizing the additional control instruments needed beyond those used in domestic business and the control strategies of multinational corporations. The appropriateness and eventual cost of the various control approaches will vary as the firm expands its international operations. The overall objective of the chapter is to study the intraorganizational relationships critical to the firm's attempt to optimize its competitiveness.

Organizational Structure

The basic functions of an organization are to provide: (1) a route and locus of decision making and coordination, and (2) a system for reporting and communications. Authority and communication networks are typically depicted in the organizational chart.

Organizational Designs

The basic configurations of international organizations correspond to those of purely domestic ones; the greater the degree of internalization, the more complex the structures can become. The types of structures that companies use to manage foreign activities can be divided into three categories, based on the degree of internationalization:

1. Little or no formal organizational recognition of international activities of the firm. This category ranges from domestic operations handling an occasional international transaction on an ad hoc basis to firms with separate export departments.
2. International division. Firms in this category recognize the ever-growing importance of the international involvement.
3. Global organizations. These can be structured by product, area, function, process, or customer, but ignore the traditional domestic-international split.

Hybrid structures may exist as well, in which one market may be structured by product, another by areas. Matrix organizations have merged in large multinational corporations to combine product-specific, regional, and functional expertise. As worldwide competition has increased dramatically in many industries, the latest organizational response is networked global organizations in which heavy flows of hardware, software, and personnel take place between strategically interdependent units to establish greater global integration. The ability to identify and disseminate best practices throughout the organization is an important competitive advantage for global companies. For example, a U.S. automaker found that in the face of distinctive challenges presented by the local environment, Brazilian engineers developed superior seals, which the company then incorporated in all its models worldwide.[1]

Little or No Formal Organization   In the very early stages of international involvement, domestic operations assume responsibility for international activities. The role of international activities in the sales and profits of the corporation is initially so minor that no organizational adjustment takes place. No consolidation of information or authority over international sales is undertaken or is necessary. Transactions are conducted on a case-by-case basis, either by the resident expert or quite often with the help of facilitating agents, such as freight forwarders.

As demand from the international marketplace grows and interest within the firm expands, the organizational structure will reflect it. As shown in Figure 19.1, an export department appears as a separate entity. This may be an outside export management company—that is, an independent company that becomes the de facto export department of the firm. This is an indirect approach to international involvement in that very little experience is accumulated within the firm itself. Alternatively, a firm may establish its own export department, hiring a few seasoned individuals to take responsibility for international activities. Organizationally, the department may be a sub-department of marketing (alternative b in Figure 19.1) or may have equal ranking with the various functional departments (alternative a). The choice will depend on the importance assigned to overseas activities by the firm. The export department is the first real step toward internationalizing the organizational structures. It should be a full-fledged marketing organization and not merely a sales organization; i.e., it should have the resources for market research and market-development activities (such as trade show participation).

Licensing as an international entry mode may be assigned to the R&D function despite its importance to the overall international strategy of the firm. A formal liaison among the export, marketing, production, and R&D functions has to be formed for the maximum utilization of licensing.[2] If licensing indeed becomes a major activity for the firm, a separate manager should be appointed.

The more the firm becomes involved in foreign markets, the more quickly the export department structure will become obsolete. For example, the firm may undertake

FIGURE 19.1   **The Export Department Structure**

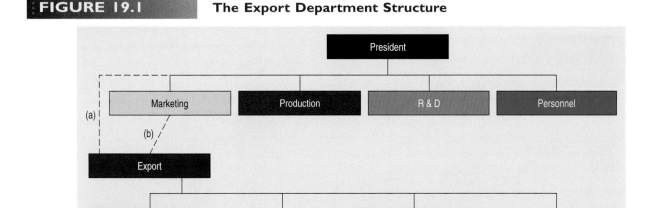

joint ventures or direct foreign investment, which require those involved to have functional experience. The firm therefore typically establishes an international division.

Some firms that acquire foreign production facilities pass through an additional stage in which foreign subsidiaries report directly to the president or to a manager specifically assigned the duty.[3] However, the amount of coordination and control that are required quickly establish the need for a more formal international organization in the firm.

The International Division   The international division centralizes in one entity, with or without separate incorporation, all of the responsibility for international activities, as illustrated in Figure 19.2. The approach aims to eliminate a possible bias against international operations that may exist if domestic divisions are allowed to serve international customers independently. In some cases, international markets have been treated as secondary to domestic markets. The international division concentrates international expertise, information flows concerning foreign market opportunities, and authority over international activities. However, manufacturing and other related functions remain with the domestic divisions to take advantage of economies of scale.

To avoid putting the international division at a disadvantage in competing for products, personnel, and corporate services, coordination between domestic and international operations is necessary. Coordination can be achieved through a joint staff or by requiring domestic and international divisions to interact in strategic planning and to submit the plans to headquarters. Further, many corporations require and encourage frequent interaction between domestic and international personnel to discuss common problems in areas such as product planning. Coordination is also important because domestic operations are typically organized along product or functional lines, whereas international divisions are geographically oriented.

International divisions best serve firms with few products that do not vary significantly in terms of their environmental sensitivity and with international sales and profits that are still quite insignificant compared with those of the domestic divisions.[4] Companies may outgrow their international divisions as their sales outside of the domestic market grow in significance, diversity, and complexity. European companies have traditionally used international divisions far less than their U.S. counterparts due to the relatively small size of their domestic markets. Philips, Nestlé, or Nokia, for example, would have never grown to their current prominence by relying on their home

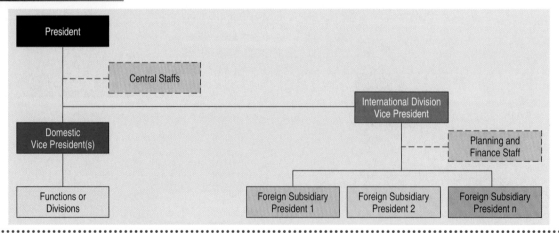

FIGURE 19.2   **The International Division Structure**

markets alone. While international divisions were popular among U.S. companies in the 1970s and 1980s, globalization of markets and the increased share of overseas sales have made international divisions less suitable in favor of global structures.[5] For example, Loctite, a leading marketer of sealants, adhesives and coatings, moved from an international division to a global structure by which the company is managed by market channel (e.g., industrial automotive and electronics industry) to enable Loctite employees to synergize efforts and expertise worldwide.[6]

Global Organizational Structures   Global structures have grown out of competitive necessity. In many industries, competition is on a global basis, with a result that companies must have a high degree of reactive capability.

Six basic types of global structures are available:

1. Global product structure, in which product divisions are responsible for all manufacture and marketing worldwide
2. Global area structure, in which geographic divisions are responsible for all manufacture and marketing in their respective areas
3. Global functional structures, in which functional areas (such as production, marketing, finance, and personnel) are responsible for the worldwide operations of their own functional area
4. Global customer structures, in which operations are structured based on distinct worldwide customer groups
5. Mixed—or hybrid—structures, which may combine the other alternatives
6. Matrix structures, in which operations have reporting responsibility to more than one group (typically, product, functions, or area)

Product Structure   The **product structure** is the form most often used by multinational corporations.[7] The approach gives worldwide responsibility to strategic business units for the marketing of their product lines, as shown in Figure 19.3. Most

FIGURE 19.3   **The Global Product Structure**

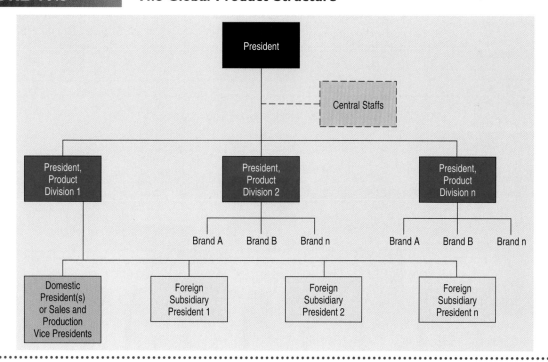

consumer-product firms use some form of this approach, mainly because of the diversity of their products. One of the major benefits of the approach is improved cost efficiency through centralization of manufacturing facilities. This is crucial in industries in which competitive position is determined by world market share, which in turn is often determined by the degree to which manufacturing is rationalized.[8] Adaptation to this approach may cause problems because it is usually accompanied by consolidation of operations and plant closings. A good example is Black & Decker, which rationalized many of its operations in its worldwide competitive effort against Makita, the Japanese power tool manufacturer. Similarly, Goodyear reorganized itself into a single global organization with a complete business-team approach for tires and general products. The move was largely prompted by tightening worldwide competition.[9] In a similar move, Ford merged its large and culturally distinct European and North American auto operations by vehicle platform type to make more efficient use of its engineering and product development resources against rapidly globalizing rivals.[10] The Ford Focus, Ford's compact car introduced in 1999, was designed by one team of engineers for worldwide markets.

Other benefits of the product structure are the ability to balance the functional inputs needed for a product and the ability to react quickly to product-specific problems in the marketplace. Even smaller brands receive individual attention. Product-specific attention is important because products vary in terms of the adaptation they need for different foreign markets. All in all, the product approach is ideally suited to the development of a global strategic focus in response to global competition.

At the same time, the product structure fragments international expertise within the firm because a central pool of international experience no longer exists. The structure assumes that managers will have adequate regional experience or advice to allow them to make balanced decisions. Coordination of activities among the various product groups operating in the same markets is crucial to avoid unnecessary duplication of basic tasks. For some of these tasks, such as market research, special staff functions may be created and then filled by the product divisions when needed. If they lack an appreciation for the international dimension, product managers may focus their attention only on the larger markets or only on the domestic, and fail to take the long-term view.

Area Structure   The second most used approach is the **area structure,** illustrated in Figure 19.4. Such firms are organized on the basis of geographical areas; for example, operations may be divided into those dealing with North America, the Far East, Latin

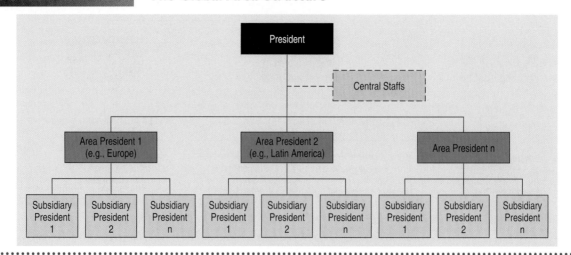

FIGURE 19.4   **The Global Area Structure**

GLOBAL PERSPECTIVE 19.1

Restructuring for Global Competitiveness

As regions continue their drive toward single economic markets, companies are positioning themselves to capitalize on the opportunities such developments are providing. 3M is responding in two of its key markets, Europe and the Americas, by bold organizational moves. In Europe, the formation of European Business Centers (EBCs) is focused on reaching the pan-European marketplace more efficiently. Each of the EBCs (e.g., Malakoff in France for dental products or Diegem, Belgium, for electro products) operates along product rather than geographic lines, and each is responsible for the business functions throughout Europe.

3M's North American Operational Plan centers on organizational restructuring based on three concepts: simplification, linkage, and empowerment. The plan was fully implemented in the United States and Canada in 1992 with Mexico added in 1994. Before the restructuring, Mexico was treated "as a far-off, foreign country." Now 3M manages by area rather than by country. Key goals of the operational plan are:

- Eliminate the role of 3M International Operations in cross-border activities within North America. All business units in Canada and Mexico will deal directly with 3M's divisions in the United States.
- Redefine management functions. General sales and marketing managers in Canada and Mexico will have a new title—business manager—and will serve as the key link between local customers and the corresponding U.S. general managers. The business managers will also be members of 3M U.S.'s planning, pricing, and operating committees; participate in the early stages of the global business planning; and execute the global strategy in Canada and Mexico.
- Coordinate functions and share resources among the three countries, especially in marketing, advertising, and sales. New-product launches will be synchronized throughout North America, with standardized sizing

and part numbers wherever possible. Distribution strategies and agreements will be coordinated. Sales literature, packaging, and labeling will be uniform and written in the appropriate local language.
- Establish North American tactical teams. Members from these groups, drawn from all three countries, will work on projects such as market research, new-product development, and competitor monitoring.
- Set up centers of excellence. To maximize efficiency and to avoid duplication of effort, each country will specialize in the function or process that it does best and eliminate those that can be performed better elsewhere. These centers may be built around manufacturing of a product or product line, market niches, customer service, or technical skills.
- Modify performance-measurement criteria. North American performance will be gauged by North American—not U.S., Canadian, or Mexican—market share, earnings growth, and income.

At 3M Canada, major changes have taken place. Layers of management have been trimmed, communication and coordination greatly enhanced, and the requirement to go through the international division removed. Incorporating Mexico into the plan presents some unique challenges, however. For 3M U.S. headquarters, meeting or communicating electronically with Canadian counterparts is far easier than doing the same with Mexico. Language and cultural barriers also present potential challenges. Given that only products are free to cross borders—not people—sales personnel cannot solicit business across borders, and direct cross-border reporting may not be possible.

The company is also concentrating on expanding its presence in emerging markets: Latin America, the Asia Pacific region, and Africa. More than half its revenues were generated from international sales in 2000.

Sources: 3M 2000 Annual Report, pp. 1–3, 15; "3M Restructuring for NAFTA," *Business Latin America* (July 19, 1993): 6–7; **www.mmm.com**.

America, and Europe. Ideally, no special preference is given to the region in which the headquarters is located—for example, North America or Europe. Central staffs are responsible for providing coordination support for worldwide planning and control activities performed at headquarters.

Regional integration is playing a major role in area structuring; for example, many multinational corporations have located their European headquarters in Brussels, where the EU has its headquarters. In some U.S. companies, North American integration led to the development of a North American division, which replaced the U.S. operation as the power center of the company. Organizational changes made at 3M as a result of economic integration are recounted in Global Perspective 19.1. The driver of structural choices may also be cultural similarity, such as in the case of Asia, or historic connections between countries, such as in the case of combining Europe with the Middle East and Africa.

The area approach follows the marketing concept most closely because individual areas and markets are given concentrated attention. If market conditions with respect to product acceptance and operating conditions vary dramatically, the area approach is the one to choose. Companies opting for this alternative typically have relatively narrow product lines with similar end uses and end users. However, expertise is needed in adapting the product and its marketing to local market conditions. Once again, to avoid duplication of effort in product management and in functional areas, staff specialists—for product categories, for example—may be used.

Without appropriate coordination from the staff, essential information and experience may not be transferred from one regional entity to another. Also, if the company expands its product lines and if end markets begin to diversify, the area structure may become inappropriate.

Some managers may feel that going into a global product structure may be too much, too quickly, and opt, therefore, to have a regional organization for planning and reporting purposes. The objective may also be to keep profit or sales centers of similar size at similar levels in the corporate hierarchy. If a group of countries has small sales as compared with other country operations, they may be consolidated into a region. The benefit of a regional operation and regional headquarters would be the more efficient coordination of programs across the region (as opposed to globally), a more sensitized management to country-market operations in the region, and the ability to have the region's voice heard more clearly at global headquarters (as compared to what an individual, especially smaller, country operation could achieve).[11]

Functional Structure   Of all the approaches, the **functional structure** is the simplest from the administrative viewpoint because it emphasizes the basic tasks of the firm—for example, manufacturing, sales, and research and development. The approach, illustrated in Figure 19.5, works best when both products and customers are relatively few and similar in nature. Coordination is typically the key problem, therefore, staff functions have been created to interact between the functional areas. Otherwise, the company's marketing and regional expertise may not be exploited to the fullest extent possible.

FIGURE 19.5   **The Global Function Structure**

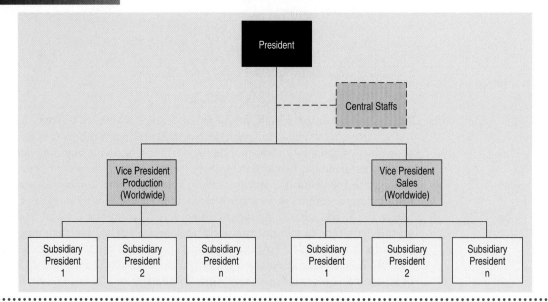

A variation of the functional approach is one that uses processes as a basis for structure. The **process structure** is common in the energy and mining industries, where one corporate entity may be in charge of exploration worldwide and another may be responsible for the actual mining operations.

Customer Structure   Firms may also organize their operations using the **customer structure,** especially if the customer groups they serve are dramatically different—for example, consumers and businesses and governments. Catering to such diverse groups may require concentrating specialists in particular divisions. The product may be the same, but the buying processes of the various customer groups may differ. Governmental buying is characterized by bidding, in which price plays a larger role than when businesses are the buyers.

Mixed Structure   In some cases, mixed, or hybrid, organizations exist. A **mixed structure** combines two or more organizational dimensions simultaneously. It permits adequate attention to product, area, or functional needs as is needed by the company. The approach may only be a result of a transitional period after a merger or an acquisition, or it may come about due to unique market characteristics or product line. It may also provide a useful structure before the implementation of a worldwide matrix structure.[12]

Naturally, organizational structures are never as clear-cut and simple as presented here. Whatever the basic format, product, functional, and area inputs are needed. Alternatives could include an initial product structure that would subsequently have regional groupings or an initial regional structure with subsequent product groupings. However, in the long term, coordination and control across such structures become tedious.

Matrix Structure   Many multinational corporations, in an attempt to facilitate planning for, organizing, and controlling interdependent businesses, critical resources, strategies, and geographic regions, have adopted the **matrix structure.**[13] Eastman Kodak shifted from a functional organization to a matrix system based on business units. Business is driven by a worldwide business unit (for example, photographic products or commercial and information systems) and implemented by a geographic unit (for example, Europe or Latin America). The geographical units, as well as their country subsidiaries, serve as the "glue" between autonomous product operations.[14]

Organizational matrices integrate the various approaches already discussed, as the Philips example in Figure 19.6 illustrates. The seven product divisions (which are then divided into sixty product groups) have rationalized manufacturing to provide products for continentwide markets rather than lines of products for individual markets.[15] Philips has three general types of country organizations. In "key" markets, such as the United States, France, and Japan, product divisions manage their own marketing as well as manufacturing. In "local business" countries, such as Nigeria and Peru, the organizations function as importers from product divisions, and if manufacturing occurs, it is purely for the local market. In "large" markets, such as Brazil, Spain, and Taiwan, a hybrid arrangement is used, depending on the size and situation. The product divisions and the national subsidiaries interact in a matrixlike configuration, with the product divisions responsible for the globalization dimension and the national subsidiaries responsible for local representation and coordination of common areas of interest, such as recruiting.

Matrices vary in terms of their number of dimensions. For example, Dow Chemical's three-dimensional matrix consists of five geographic areas, three major functions (marketing, manufacturing, and research), and more than 70 products. The matrix approach helps cut through enormous organizational complexities in making business managers, functional managers, and strategy managers cooperate. However, the matrix requires sensitive, well-trained middle managers who can cope with problems

FIGURE 19.6   **The Global Matrix Structure at Philips**

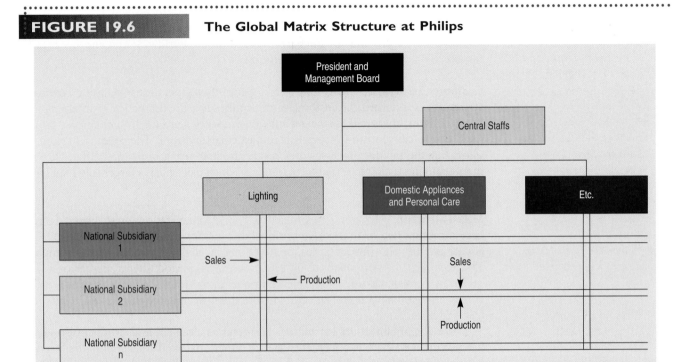

that arise from reporting to two bosses—for example, a product-line manager and an area manager. For example, every management unit may have a multidimensional reporting relationship, which may cross functional, regional, or operational lines. On a regional basis, group managers in Europe for example, report administratively to a vice president of operations for Europe, but report functionally to group vice presidents at global headquarters.

Most companies have found the matrix arrangement problematic.[16] The dual reporting channel easily causes conflict, complex issues are forced into a two-dimensional decision framework, and even minor issues may have to be solved through committee discussion. Ideally, managers should solve the problems themselves through formal and informal communication; however, physical and psychic distance often make that impossible. The matrix structure, with its inherent complexity, may actually increase the reaction time of a company, a potentially serious problem when competitive conditions require quick responses. As a result, the authority has started to shift in many organizations from area to product, although the matrix still may officially be used.

Evolution of Organizational Structures   Companies have been shown to develop new structures in a pattern of stages as their products diversify and share of foreign sales increases.[17] At the first stage of autonomous subsidiaries reporting directly to top management, the establishment of an international division follows. As product diversity and the importance of the foreign marketplace increase, companies develop global structures to coordinate subsidiary operations and to rationalize worldwide production. As multinational corporations have been faced with simultaneous pressures to adapt to local market conditions and to rationalize production and globalize competitive reactions, many have opted for the matrix structure.[18] The matrix structure probably allows a corporation to best meet the challenges of global markets

FIGURE 19.7

Evolution of International Structures

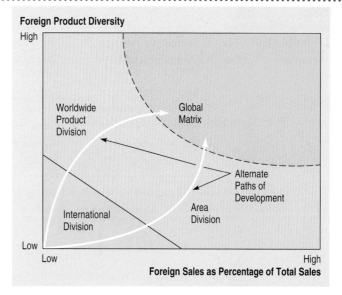

Source: From Christopher A. Bartlett, "Building and Managing the Transnational: The New Organizational Challenge," in *Competition in Global Industries,* ed. Michael E. Porter (Boston: Harvard Business School Press, 1986), 368.

(to be global and local, big and small, decentralized with centralized reporting) by allowing the optimizing of businesses globally and maximizing performance in every country of operation.[19] The evolutionary process is summarized in Figure 19.7.

Implementation

Organizational structures provide the frameworks for carrying out decision-making processes. However, for that decision making to be effective, a series of organizational initiatives are needed to develop strategy to its full potential, that is, to secure implementation both at the national level and across markets.[20]

Locus of Decision Making

Organizational structures themselves do not indicate where the authority for decision making and control rests within the organization nor will it reveal the level of coordination between the units. The different levels of coordination between country units are summarized in Table 19.1. Once a suitable structure is found, it has to be made to work.

If subsidiaries are granted a high degree of autonomy, the system is called **decentralization.** In decentralized systems, controls are relatively loose and simple, and the flows between headquarters and subsidiaries are mainly financial; that is, each subsidiary operates as a profit center. On the other hand, if controls are tight and the strategic decision making is concentrated at headquarters, the system is described as **centralization.** Firms are typically neither completely centralized nor decentralized; for example, some functions of the firm—such as finance—lend themselves to more centralized decision making; others—such as promotional decisions—do so far less. Research and development in organizations is typically centralized, especially in cases of basic research work. Some companies have, partly due to governmental pressures, added R&D functions on a regional or local basis. In many cases, however, variations

TABLE 19.1

Levels of Coordination

Level	Description
5. Central control	No national structures
4. Central direction	Central functional heads have line authority over national functions
3. Central coordination	Central staff functions in coordinating role
2. Coordinating mechanisms	Formal committees and systems
1. Informal cooperation	Functional meetings: exchange of information
0. National autonomy	No coordination between decentralized units, which may even compete in export markets

Level 5 = highest; Level 0 = lowest. Most commonly found levels are 1–4.

Source: Norman Blackwell, Jean-Pierre Bizet, Peter Child, and David Hensley, "Creating European Organizations that Work," *The McKinsey Quarterly* 27, 2 (1991): 376.

are product and market based; for example, Corning Incorporated's TV tube marketing strategy requires global decision making for pricing and local decision making for service and delivery.

The basic advantage of allowing maximum flexibility at the country-market level is that subsidiary management knows its market and can react to changes more quickly. Problems of motivation and acceptance are avoided when decision makers are also the implementors of the strategy. On the other hand, many multinationals faced with global competitive threats and opportunities have adopted global strategy formulation, which by definition requires a higher degree of centralization. What has emerged as a result can be called **coordinated decentralization.** This means that overall corporate strategy is provided from headquarters, while subsidiaries are free to implement it within the range agreed on in consultation between headquarters and the subsidiaries.

However, companies moving into this new mode may face significant challenges. Among these systemic difficulties are a lack of widespread commitment to dismantling traditional national structures, driven by an inadequate understanding of the larger, global forces at work. Power barriers from perceived threats to the personal roles of national managers, especially if their tasks are under the threat of being consolidated into regional organizations, can lead to proposals being challenged without valid reason. Finally, some organizationally initiatives (such as multicultural teams or corporate chat rooms) may be jeopardized by the fact the people do not have the necessary skills (e.g., language ability) or that an infrastructure (e.g., intranet) may not exist in an appropriate format.[21]

One particular case is of special interest. Organizationally, the forces of globalization are changing the country manager's role significantly. With profit-and-loss responsibility, oversight of multiple functions, and the benefit of distance from headquarters, country managers enjoyed considerable decision-making autonomy as well as entrepreneurial initiative when country operations were largely stand-alone. Today, however, many companies have to emphasize global and regional priorities, which means that the power has to shift at least to some extent from the country manager to worldwide strategic business unit and product-line managers. Many of the local decisions are now subordinated to global strategic moves. Therefore, the future country manager will have to wear many hats in balancing the needs of the operation for which the manager is directly responsible with those of the entire region or strategic business unit.[22] To emphasize the importance of the global/regional dimension in the country manager's portfolio, many companies have tied the country manager's compensation to how the company performs globally or regionally, not just in the market for which the manager is responsible.

Factors Affecting Structure and Decision Making

The organizational structure and locus of decision making in a multinational corporation are determined by a number of factors, such as: (1) its degree of involvement in international operations; (2) the products the firm markets; (3) the size and importance of the firm's markets; and (4) the human resource capability of the firm.[23]

The effect of the degree of involvement on structure and decision making was discussed earlier in the chapter. With low degrees of involvement, subsidiaries can enjoy high degrees of autonomy as long as they meet their profit targets. The same situation can occur even with the most globally oriented companies, but within a different framework. Consider, for example, Philips USA which generates 20 percent of the company's worldwide sales. Even more important it serves as a market that is on the leading edge of digital media development. Therefore, it enjoys independent status in terms of local policy setting and managerial practices but is still, nevertheless, within the parent company's planning and control system.

The firm's country of origin and the political history of the area can also affect organizational structure and decision making. For example, Swiss-based Nestlé, with only 3 to 4 percent of its sales from its small domestic market, has traditionally had a highly decentralized organization. Moreover, European history for the past 80 years—particularly the two world wars—has often forced subsidiaries of European-based companies to act independently to survive.

The type and variety of products marketed will affect organizational decisions. Companies that market consumer products typically have product organizations with high degrees of decentralization, allowing for maximum local flexibility. On the other hand, companies that market technologically sophisticated products—such as GE, which markets turbines—display centralized organizations with worldwide product responsibilities. Even within matrix organizations, one of the dimensions may be granted more say in decisions; for example, at Dow Chemical, geographical managers have been granted more authority than other managers.

Going global has recently meant transferring world headquarters of important business units abroad. For example, Philips has moved headquarters of several of its global business units to the United States, including its Digital Video Group, Optimal Storage, and Flat Panel Display activities to Silicon Valley.

The human factor in any organization is critical. Managers at both headquarters and the country organizations must bridge the physical and cultural distances separating them. If country organizations have competent managers who rarely need to consult headquarters about their challenges, they may be granted high degrees of autonomy. In the case of global organizations, local management must understand overall corporate goals in that decisions that meet the long-term objectives may not be optimal for the individual local market.

The Networked Global Organization

No international structure is ideal and some have challenged the wisdom of even looking for one. They have recommended attention to new processes that would, in a given structure, help to develop new perspectives and attitudes that reflect and respond to the complex, opposing demands of global integration and local responsiveness.[24] The question thus changes from which structural alternative is best to how the different perspectives of various corporate entities can better be taken into account when making decisions. In structural terms, nothing may change. As a matter of fact, Philips has not changed its basic matrix structure, yet major changes have occurred in internal relations. The basic change was from a decentralized federation model to a networked global organization, the effects of which are depicted in Figure 19.8. The term **glocal** has been coined to describe this approach.[25]

FIGURE 19.8   **The Networked Global Organization**

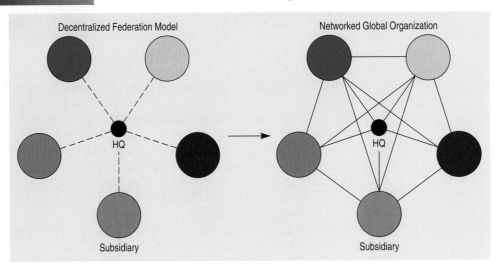

Source: Thomas Gross, Ernie Turner, and Lars Cederholm, "Building Teams for Global Operations," *Management Review,* June 1987 (New York: American Management Association), 34.

Companies that have adopted the approach have incorporated the following three dimensions into their organizations: (1) the development and communication of a clear corporate vision; (2) the effective management of human resource tools to broaden individual perspectives and develop identification with corporate goals; and (3) the integration of individual thinking and activities into the broad corporate agenda.[26] The first dimension relates to a clear and consistent long-term corporate mission that guides individuals wherever they work in the organization. Examples of this are Johnson & Johnson's corporate credo of customer focus and NEC's C&C (computers and communications). The second relates both to the development of global managers who can find opportunities in spite of environmental challenges as well as creating a global perspective among country managers. The last dimension relates to the development of a cooperative mind-set among country organizations to ensure effective implementation of global strategies. Managers may believe that global strategies are intrusions on their operations if they do not have an understanding of the corporate vision, if they have not contributed to the global corporate agenda, or if they are not given direct responsibility for its implementation. Defensive, territorial attitudes can lead to the emergence of the "not-invented-here" syndrome, that is, country organizations objecting to or rejecting an otherwise sound strategy.

The network avoids the problems of effort duplication, inefficiency and resistance to ideas developed elsewhere by giving subsidiaries the latitude, encouragement, and tools to pursue local business development within the framework of the global strategy. Headquarters considers each unit a source of ideas, skills, capabilities, and knowledge that can be utilized for the benefit of the entire organization. This means that subsidiaries must be upgraded from mere implementors and adaptors to contributors and partners in the development and execution of worldwide strategies. Efficient plants may be converted into international production centers, innovative R&D units converted into centers of excellence (and thus role models), and leading subsidiary groups given the leadership role in developing new strategies for the entire corporation.

Promoting Internal Cooperation

The global business entity in today's environment can only be successful if is able to move intellectual capital within the organization; i.e., take ideas and move them around faster and faster.[27]

One of the tools is teaching. For example, at Ford Motor Company, teaching takes three distinct forms as shown in Table 19.2. Ford's approach is similarly undertaken at many leading global companies. The focus is on teachable points of view; i.e., is an explanation of what a person knows and believes about what it takes to succeed in his or her business.[28] For example, GE's Jack Welch coined the term "boundarylessness" to describe to which means that people can act without regard to status or functional loyalty and can look for better ideas from anywhere. Top leadership of GE spends considerable time at GE training centers interacting with up-and-comers from all over the company. Each training class is given a real, current company problem to solve, and the reports can be career makers (or breakers). A number of benefits arise from this approach. A powerful teachable point of view can reach the entire company within a reasonable period by having students become teachers themselves. At PepsiCo, the CEO passed his teachable point to 110 executives who then passed it to 20,000 people within 18 months. Secondly, participants in teaching situations are encouraged to maintain the international networks they develop during the sessions. It should be noted that teachers do not necessarily need to be only top managers. When General Electric launched a massive effort to embrace e-commerce, many managers found that they knew little about the Internet. Following a London-based manager's idea to have a Internet mentor, GE encourages all managers to have one for a period of time for training each week.[29]

TABLE 19.2	Teaching Programs at Ford Motor Co.		
Program	**Participants**	**Teachers**	**Components**
Capstone	24 senior executives at a time	Jacques Nasser and his leadership team	• Conducted once a year • About 20 days of teaching and discussion • Teams given six months to solve major strategic challenges • 360-degree feedback • Community service
Business Leadership Initiative	All Ford salaried employees— 55,000 to date	The participants' managers	• Three days of teaching and discussion • Teams assigned to 100-day projects • Community service • 360-degree feedback • Participants make videos that contrast the old and the new Ford
Executive Partnering	Promising young managers— 12 so far	Nasser and his leadership team	• Participants spend eight weeks shadowing seven senior executives
Let's Chat about the Business	Everyone who receives e-mail at Ford—about 100,000 employees	Nasser	• Weekly e-mails describing Ford's new approach to business

Source: Suzy Wetlaufer, "Driving Change: An Interview with Ford Motor Company's Jacques Nasser," *Harvard Business Review* 77 (March–April 1999): 76–88.

Another method to promote internal cooperation for global strategy implementation is the use of international teams or councils. In the case of a new product or program an international team of managers may be assembled to develop strategy. While final direction may come from headquarters, it has been informed of local conditions, and implementation of the strategy is enhanced since local-country managers were involved in its development. The approach has worked even in cases involving seemingly impossible market differences. Both Procter & Gamble and Henkel have successfully introduced pan-European brands for which strategy was developed by European teams. These teams consisted of country managers and staff personnel to smooth eventual implementation and to avoid unnecessarily long and disruptive discussions about the fit of a new product to individual markets. On a broader and longer-term basis, companies use councils to share best practice; e.g., an idea that may have saved money or time, or a process that is more efficient than existing ones. Most professionals at the leading global companies are members of multiple councils. While technology has made such teamwork possible wherever the individual participants may be, relying only on technology may not bring about the desired results; "high-tech" approaches inherently mean "low touch," at the expense of results. Human relationships are still paramount.[30] A common purpose is what binds team members to a particular task which can only be achieved through trust, achievable through face-to-face meetings. At the start of its 777 project, Boeing brought members of the design team from a dozen different countries to Everett, Washington, giving them the opportunity to work together for up to 18 months. Beyond learning to function effectively within the company's project management system, they also shared experiences which, in turn, engendered a level of trust between individuals that later enabled them to overcome obstacles raised by physical separation. The result was a design and launch in 40 percent faster time than with comparable projects.

The term *network* also implies two-way communications between headquarters and subsidiaries and between subsidiaries themselves. While this communication can take the form of newsletters or regular and periodic meetings of appropriate personnel, new technologies are allowing businesses to link far-flung entities and eliminate the traditional barriers of time and distance. **Intranets** integrate a company's information assets into a single accessible system using Internet-based technologies such as e-mail, news groups, and the World Wide Web. In effect, the formation of **virtual teams** becomes a reality. For example, employees at Levi Strauss & Co. can join an electronic discussion group with colleagues around the world, watch the latest Levi's commercials, or comment on latest business programs or plans.[31] "Let's Chat About the Business" e-mails go out at Ford every Friday at 5 P.M. to about 100,000 employees to share information throughout the company and encourage dialogue. In many companies, the annual videotaped greeting from management has been replaced by regular and frequent e-mails (called e-briefs at GE). The benefits of intranet are: (1) increased productivity in that there is no longer a time lag between an idea and the information needed to assess and implement it; (2) enhanced knowledge capital, which is constantly updated and upgraded; (3) facilitated teamwork enabling online communication at insignificant expense; and (4) incorporation of best practice at a moment's notice by allowing managers and functional-area personnel to make to-the-minute decisions anywhere in the world.

As can be seen from the discussion, the networked approach is not a structural adaptation but a procedural one, calling for a change in management mentality. It requires adjustment mainly in the coordination and control functions of the firm. And while there is still considerable disagreement as to which of the approaches work, some measures have been shown to correlate with success as seen in Global Perspective 19.2. Of the many initiatives developed to enhance the workings of a networked global organization, such as cross-border task forces and establishment of centers of excellence, the most significant was the use of electronic networking capabilities.[32]

GLOBAL PERSPECTIVE 19.2

Characteristics of Success

A survey of chief executive officers of 43 leading U.S. consumer companies by McKinsey & Co. sheds light on organizational features that distinguish internationally successful companies. Companies were classified as more or less successful compared to their specific industry average, using international sales and profit growth over a five-year period as the most important indicators of success.

The survey results indicate 11 distinctive traits that are correlated with high performance in international markets. The following are moves that companies can make to enhance prospects for international success:

- Take a different approach to international decision making.
- Differentiate treatment of international subsidiaries.
- Let product managers in subsidiaries report to the country general manager.
- Have a worldwide management development program.

- Make international experience a condition for promotion to top management.
- Have a more multinational management group.
- Support international managers with global electronic networking capabilities.
- Manage cross-border acquisitions particularly well.
- Have overseas R & D centers.
- Remain open to organizational change and continuous self-renewal.

In general, successful companies coordinate their international decision making globally, with more central direction than less successful competitors, as seen in the accompanying exhibit. The difference is most marked in brand positioning, designing packaging, and setting prices. The one notable exception is an increasing tendency to decentralize product development.

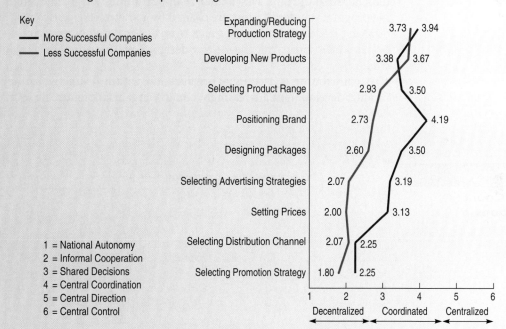

Key
— More Successful Companies
— Less Successful Companies

1 = National Autonomy
2 = Informal Cooperation
3 = Shared Decisions
4 = Central Coordination
5 = Central Direction
6 = Central Control

	More Successful	Less Successful
Expanding/Reducing Production Strategy	3.73	3.94
Developing New Products	3.38	3.67
Selecting Product Range	2.93	3.50
Positioning Brand	2.73	4.19
Designing Packages	2.60	3.50
Selecting Advertising Strategies	2.07	3.19
Setting Prices	2.00	3.13
Selecting Distribution Channel	2.07	2.25
Selecting Promotion Strategy	1.80	2.25

1   2   3   4   5   6
Decentralized   Coordinated   Centralized

Source: Ingo Theuerkauf, David Ernst, and Amir Mahini, "Think Local, Organize. . . ?" *International Marketing Review* 13, (1996): 7–12.

Further adjustment in organizational approaches is required as businesses face new challenges such as emerging markets, global accounts, and the digitization of business.[33] Emerging markets present the company with unique challenges such as product counterfeiters and informal competitors who ignore local labor and tax laws. How these issues are addressed may require organizational rethinking. Colgate-Palmolive, for example, grouped its geographies under two different organizations: one responsible for mature, developed economies and the other for high-growth, emerging markets.[34] Global account managers need to have skills and the empowerment to work across functional areas and borders to deliver quality service to the company's largest clients. Finally, digital business, such as business-to-business and business-to-consumer Internet-based activities, need to brought into the mainstay of the businesses activities and structures and not seen as a separate activity.

The Role of Country Organizations

Country organizations should be treated as a source of supply as much as a source of demand. Quite often, however, headquarters managers see their role as the coordinators of key decisions and controllers of resources and perceive subsidiaries as implementors and adaptors of global strategy in their respective local markets. Furthermore, they may see all country organizations as the same. This view severely limits utilization of the firm's resources and deprives country managers of the opportunity to exercise their creativity.[35]

The role that a particular country organization can play naturally depends on that market's overall strategic importance as well as its organizational competence. Using these criteria, four different roles emerge, as shown in Figure 19.9.

The role of a **strategic leader** can be played by a highly competent national subsidiary located in a strategically critical market. Such a country organization serves as a partner of headquarters in developing and implementing strategy. Procter & Gamble's Eurobrand teams, which analyze opportunities for greater product and marketing program standardization, are chaired by a brand manager from a "lead country."[36] Strategic leader countries may take over major development projects; for example, Nissan's new sports car, the Z, was designed by the company's La Jolla, California, studio.[37]

A **contributor** is a country organization with a distinctive competence, such as product development. Increasingly, country organizations are the source of new prod-

FIGURE 19.9

Roles for Country Organizations

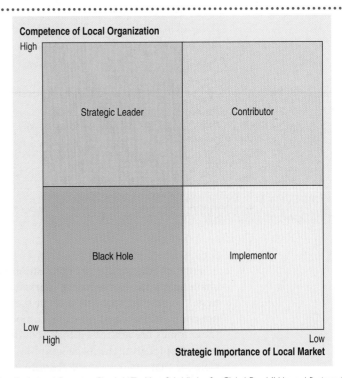

Source: Christopher Bartlett and Sumantra Ghoshal, "Tap Your Subsidiaries for Global Reach," *Harvard Business Review* 64, November–December 1986 (Boston: Harvard Business School Publishing Division), 87–94.

ucts. These range from IBM's recent breakthrough in superconductivity research, generated in its Zurich lab, to low-end innovations such as Procter & Gamble's liquid Tide, made with a fabric-softening compound developed in Europe.[38] Similarly, country organizations may be designated as worldwide centers of excellence for a particular product category, such as ABB Strömberg in Finland for electric drives, a category for which it is a recognized world leader.[39] For products or technologies with multiple applications, leadership may be divided among different country operations. For example, DuPont delegates responsibility for each different application of Lycra to managers in a country where the application is strongest; i.e., Brazil for swimwear and France for fashion. The global brand manager for Lycra ensures that those applications come together in an overall strategy.[40]

Implementors provide the critical mass for the global effort. These country organizations may exist in smaller, less-developed countries in which there is less corporate commitment for market development. Although most entities are given this role, it should not be slighted, since the implementors provide the opportunity to capture economies of scale and scope that are the basis of a global strategy.

The **black hole** situation is one in which the international company has a low-competence country organization—or no organization at all—in a highly strategic market. In strategically important markets such as the European Union, a local presence is necessary to maintain the company's global position and, in some cases, to protect others. One of the major ways of remedying the black hole situation is to enter into strategic alliances. For example, AT&T, which had long restricted itself to its domestic market, needed to go global fast. Some of the alliances it formed were with Philips in telecommunications and Olivetti in computers and office automation.[41] In some cases, firms may use their presence in a major market as an observation post to keep up with developments before a major thrust for entry is executed.

Depending on the role of the country organization, its relationship with headquarters will vary from loose control based mostly on support to tighter control to ensure that strategies get implemented appropriately. Yet, in each of these cases, it is imperative that country organizations have enough operating independence to cater to local needs and to provide motivation to country managers. For example, an implementor's ideas concerning the development of a regional or global strategy or program should be heard. Country organization initiative is the principal means by which global companies can tap into new opportunities in markets around the world.[42] For example, customers' unmet demands in a given market may result not only in the launch of a local product but subsequently in its roll-out regionally or even globally. Furthermore, in executing global strategies, country-specific buy-in is best secured through involvement of these organizations at the critical points in strategy development. Strategy formulators should make sure that appropriate implementation can be achieved at the country level.

Controls

The function of the organizational structure is to provide a framework in which objectives can be met. A set of instruments and processes is needed, however, to influence the performance of organizational members so as to meet the goals. Controls focus on means to verify and correct actions that differ from established plans. Compliance needs to be secured from subordinates through different means of coordinating specialized and interdependent parts of the organization.[43] Within an organization, control serves as an integrating mechanism. Controls are designed to reduce uncertainty, increase predictability, and ensure that behaviors originating in separate parts of the organization are compatible and in support of common organizational goals despite physical, psychic, and temporal distances.[44]

The critical issue here is the same as with organizational structure: What is the ideal amount of control? On the one hand, headquarters needs controls to ensure that international activities contribute the greatest benefit to the overall organization. On the other hand, they should not be construed as a code of laws and subsequently allowed to stifle local initiative.

This section will focus on the design and functions of control instruments available for international business operations, along with an assessment of their appropriateness. Emphasis will be placed on the degree of formality of controls used by firms.

Types of Controls

Most organizations display some administrative flexibility, as demonstrated by variations in how they apply management directives, corporate objectives, or measurement systems. A distinction should be made, however, between variations that have emerged by design and those that are the result of autonomy. The first are the result of a management decision, whereas the second typically have grown without central direction and are based on emerging practices. In both instances, some type of control will be exercised. Controls that result from headquarters initiative rather than those that are the consequences of tolerated practices will be discussed here. Firms that wait for self-emerging controls often experience rapid international growth but subsequent problems in product-line performance, program coordination, and strategic planning.[45]

Whatever the system, it is important in today's competitive environment to have internal benchmarking. This relates to organizational learning and sharing of best practices throughout the corporate system to avoid the costs of reinventing solutions that have already been discovered. A description of the knowledge transfer is provided in Global Perspective 19.3. Three critical features are necessary in sharing best practice. First, there needs to be a device for organizational memory. For example, at Xerox, contributors to solutions can send their ideas to an electronic library where they are indexed and provided to potential adopters in the corporate family. Second, best practice must be updated and adjusted to new situations. For example, best practice adopted by a company's China office will be modified and customized, and this learning should then become part of the database. Finally, best practice must be legitimized. This calls for a shared understanding that exchanging knowledge across units is organizationally valued and that these systems are important mechanisms for knowledge exchange. Use can be encouraged by including an assessment in employee performance evaluations of how effectively employees share information with colleagues and utilize the databases.

In the design of the control systems, a major decision concerns the object of control. Two major objects are typically identified: output and behavior.[46] Output controls include balance sheets, sales data, production data, product-line growth, and performance reviews of personnel. Measures of output are accumulated at regular intervals and forwarded from the foreign locale to headquarters, where they are evaluated and critiqued based on comparisons to the plan or budget. Behavioral controls require the exertion of influence over behavior after—or, ideally, before—it leads to action. Behavioral controls can be achieved through the preparation of manuals on such topics as sales techniques to be made available to subsidiary personnel or through efforts to fit new employees into the corporate culture.

To institute either of these measures, instruments of control have to be decided upon. The general alternatives are either bureaucratic/formalized control or cultural control.[47] Bureaucratic controls consist of a limited and explicit set of regulations and rules that outline the desired levels of performance. Cultural controls, on the other hand, are much less formal and are the result of shared beliefs and expectations among the members of an organization. Table 19.3 provides a schematic explanation of the types of controls and their objectives.

GLOBAL PERSPECTIVE 19.3

International Best Practice Exchange

As growing competitive pressures challenge many global firms, strategies to improve the transfer of best practice across geographically dispersed units and time zones becomes critical. The premise is that a company with the same product range targeting the same markets panregionally should be able to use knowledge gained in one market throughout the organization. The fact is, however, that companies use only 20 percent of their most precious resources—knowledge, in the form of technical information, market data, internal know-how, and processes and procedures. Trying to transfer best practices internationally amplifies the problem even more.

U.K.-based copier maker Rank Xerox, with its 38 operating companies, is working hard to make better use of the knowledge that resides within those companies. A 35-person group identified nine practices that could be applicable throughout the group. These ranged from the way the Australian subsidiary retains customers to Italy's method of gathering competitive intelligence to a procedure for handling new major accounts in Spain. These practices were thought to be easier to "sell" to other operating companies, easy to implement, and would provide a good return on investment.

Three countries were much quicker in introducing new products successfully than others. In the case of France, this was related to the training given to employees. The subsidiary gave its sales staff three days of hands-on practice, including competitive benchmarking. Before they attended the course, salespeople were given reading materials and were tested when they arrived. Those remaining were evaluated again at the end of the course, and performance reports were sent to their managers.

The difficult task is to achieve buy-in from the other country organizations. Six months might be spent in making detailed presentations of the best practices to all the companies and an additional three years helping them implement the needed changes. It is imperative that the country manager is behind the proposal in each subsidiary's case. However, implementation cannot be left to the country organizations after the concept has been presented. This may result in the dilution of both time and urgency and with possible country-specific customization that negates comparisons and jeopardizes the success of the change.

In a similar effort, Procter&Gamble launched an independent venture to develop computer programs to manage and speed up employees' sharing of information. Employees in different offices and different parts of the globe will be able to collaborate on documents, watch commercials under development, or see how a product is marketed elsewhere and coordinate globally.

Sources: "P&G Moves to Set Up a System to Share Employee Know-How," *The Wall Street Journal,* January 23, 2001, B6; Michael McGann, "Chase Harnesses Data with Lotus Notes," *Bank Systems and Technology 34* (May, 1997): 38; "Rank Xerox Aims at Sharing Knowledge," *Crossborder Monitor* (September 18, 1996): 8; "World-wise: Effective Networking Distinguishes These 25 Global Companies," *Computerworld* (August 26, 1996): 7. http://www.rankxerox.co.uk.

Bureaucratic/Formalized Control   The elements of a bureaucratic/formalized control system are: (1) an international budget and planning system; (2) the functional reporting system; and (3) policy manuals used to direct functional performance.

Budgets refers to shorter term guidelines regarding investment, cash, and personnel policies, while *plans* refers to formalized plans with more than a one-year horizon. The budget and planning process is the major control instrument in headquarters-

	TYPE OF CONTROL	
Object of Control	**Pure Bureaucratic/Formalized Control**	**Pure Cultural Control**
Output	Formal performance reports	Shared norms of performance
Behavior	Company policies, manuals	Shared philosophy of management

TABLE 19.3

Comparison of Bureaucratic and Cultural Control Mechanisms

Source: B.R. Baliga and Alfred M. Jaeger, "Multinational Corporations: Control Systems and Delegation Issues," *Journal of International Business Studies* 15 (Fall 1984): 25–40.

subsidiary relationships. Although systems and their execution vary, the objective is to achieve as good a fit as possible with the objectives and characteristics of the firm and its environment.

The budgetary period is typically one year, since it is tied to the accounting systems of the multinational. The budget system is used for four main purposes: (1) allocation of funds among subsidiaries; (2) planning and coordination of global production capacity and supplies; (3) evaluation of subsidiary performance; and (4) communication and information exchange among subsidiaries, product organizations, and corporate headquarters.[48] Long-range plans vary dramatically, ranging from two years to ten years in length, and are more qualitative and judgmental in nature. However, shorter periods such as two years are the norm, considering the added uncertainty of diverse foreign environments.

Although firms strive for uniformity, achieving it may be as difficult as trying to design a suit to fit the average person. The processes themselves are very formalized in terms of the schedules to be followed.

Functional reports are another control instrument used by headquarters in managing subsidiary relations. These vary in number, complexity, and frequency. Table 19.4 summarizes the various types of functional reports used in a total of 117 multinational corporations in the United States, Germany, and Japan. The structure and elements of the reports are typically highly standardized to allow for consolidation in the headquarters level.

Since the frequency of reports required from subsidiaries is likely to increase due to globalization, it is essential that subsidiaries see the rationale for the often time-consuming exercise. Two approaches, used in tandem, can facilitate the process: participation and feedback. The first refers to avoiding the perception at subsidiary levels that reports are "art for art's sake" by involving the preparers in the actual use of the reports. When this is not possible, feedback about their consequences is warranted. Through this process, communication is enhanced as well.

On the behavioral front, headquarters may want to guide the way in which subsidiaries make decisions and implement agreed-upon strategies. U.S.-based multinationals tend to be far more formalized than their Japanese and European counterparts, with a heavy reliance on manuals for all major functions.[49] The manuals discuss such items as recruitment, training, motivation, and dismissal policies. The use of manuals is in direct correlation with the required level of reports from subsidiaries, discussed in the previous section.

TABLE 19.4	Types of Functional Reports in Multinational Corporations		
Type of Report	**U.S. MNCs (33)**	**German MNCs (44)**	**Japanese MNCs (40)**
Balance sheet	97	49	42
Profit and loss statements	91	49	42
Production output	94	50	47
Market share	70	48	31
Cash and credit statement	100	41	39
Inventory levels	88	46	38
Sales per product	88	37	44
Performance review of personnel	9	15	2
Report on local economic and political conditions	33	32	12

Source: Anant R. Negandhi and Martin Welge, *Beyond Theory Z* (Greenwich, CT: JAI, 1984): 18.

Cultural Control   As seen from the country comparisons, less emphasis is placed outside the United States on formal controls, as they are viewed as too rigid and too quantitatively oriented. Rather, MNCs in other countries emphasize corporate values and culture, and evaluations are based on the extent to which an individual or entity fits in with the norms. Cultural controls require an extensive socialization process to which informal, personal interaction is central. Substantial resources have to be spent to train the individual to share the corporate cultures, or "the way things are done at the company."[50] To build common vision and values, managers spend a substantial share of their first months at Matsushita in what the company calls "cultural and spiritual training." They study the company credo, the "Seven Spirits of Matsushita," and the philosophy of the founder, Konosuke Matsushita and learn how to translate the internalized lessons into daily behavior and operational decisions. Although more prevalent in Japanese organizations, many Western entities have similar programs, such as Philips's "organization cohesion training" and Unilever's "indoctrination."[51] This corporate acculturation will be critical to achieve the acceptance of possible transfers of best practice within the organization.[52]

The primary instruments of cultural control are the careful selection and training of corporate personnel and the institution of self-control. The choice of cultural controls can be justified if the company enjoys a low turnover rate; they are thus applied when companies can offer and expect lifetime or long-term employment, as many firms do in Japan.

In selecting home-country nationals and, to some extent, third-country nationals, MNCs are exercising cultural control. The assumption is that the managers have already internalized the norms and values of the company and they tend to run a country organization with a more global view. In some cases, the use of headquarters personnel to ensure uniformity in decision making may be advisable; for example, Volvo uses a home-country national for the position of chief financial officer. Expatriates are used in subsidiaries not only for control purposes but also to effect change processes. Companies control the efforts of management specifically through compensation and promotion policies, as well as through policies concerning replacement.

When the expatriate corps is small, headquarters can still exercise its control through other means. Management training programs for overseas managers as well as time at headquarters will indoctrinate individuals to the company's ways of doing things. Similarly, formal visits by headquarters teams (for example, for a strategy audit) or informal visits (perhaps to launch a new product) will enhance the feeling of belonging to the same corporate family. Some of the innovative global companies assemble temporary teams of their best talent to build local skills. IBM, for example, drafted 50 engineers from its facilities in Italy, Japan, New York, and North Carolina to run three-week to six-month training courses on all operations carried on at its Shenzhen facility in China. After the trainers left the country, they stayed in touch by e-mail, so whenever the Chinese managers have a problem, they know they can reach someone for help. The continuation of the support has been as important as the training itself.[53]

Corporations rarely use one pure control mechanism. Rather, most use both quantitative and qualitative measures. Corporations are likely, however, to place different levels of emphasis on different types of performance measures and on how they are derived.

Exercising Controls

Within most corporations, different functional areas are subject to different guidelines because they are subject to different constraints. For example, the marketing function has traditionally been seen as incorporating many more behavioral dimensions than manufacturing or finance. As a result, many multinational corporations employ control systems that are responsive to the needs of the function. Yet such differentiation is sometimes based less on appropriateness than on personalities. It has been hypothesized that manufacturing subsidiaries are controlled more intensively than sales subsidiaries because production more readily lends itself to centralized direction, and technicians and engineers adhere more firmly to standards and regulations than do salespeople.[54]

In their international operations, U.S.-based multinationals place major emphasis on obtaining quantitative data. Although this allows for good centralized comparisons against standards and benchmarks or cross-comparisons among different corporate units, it entails several drawbacks. In the international environment, new dimensions—such as inflation, differing rates of taxation, and exchange rate fluctuations—may distort the performance evaluation of any given individual or organizational unit. For the global corporation, measurement of whether a business unit in a particular country is earning a superior return on investment relative to risk may be irrelevant to the contribution an investment may make worldwide or to the long-term results of the firm. In the short term, the return may even be negative.[55] Therefore, the control mechanism may quite inappropriately indicate reward or punishment. Standardizing the information received may be difficult if the various environments involved fluctuate and require frequent and major adaptations. Further complicating the issue is the fact that although quantitative information may be collected monthly, or at least quarterly, environmental data may be acquired annually or "now and then," especially when a crisis seems to loom on the horizon. To design a control system that is acceptable not only to headquarters but also to the organization and individuals abroad, great care must be taken to use only relevant data. Major concerns, therefore, are the data collection process and the analysis and utilization of data. Evaluators need management information systems that provide for greater comparability and equity in administering controls. The more behaviorally based and culture-oriented controls are, the more care needs to be taken.[56]

In designing a control system, management must consider the costs of establishing and maintaining it versus the benefits to be gained. Any control system will require investment in a management structure and in systems design. Consider, for example, costs associated with cultural controls: personal interaction, use of expatriates, and training programs are all quite expensive. Yet these expenses may be justified by cost savings through lower employee turnover, an extensive worldwide information system, and an improved control system.[57] Moreover, the impact goes beyond the administrative component. If controls are misguided or too time-consuming, they can slow or undermine the strategy implementation process and thus the overall capability of the firm. The result will be lost opportunities or, worse yet, increased threats. In addition, time spent on reporting takes time from everything else, and if the exercise is seen as mundane, it results in lowered motivation. A parsimonious design is therefore imperative. The control system should collect all the information required and trigger all the intervention necessary; however, it should not lead to the pulling of strings by a puppeteer.

The impact of the environment has to be taken into account, as well, in two ways. First, the control system must measure only those dimensions over which the organization has actual control. Rewards or sanctions make little sense if they are based on dimensions that may be relevant to overall corporate performance but over which no influence can be exerted, such as price controls. Neglecting the factor of individual performance capability would send wrong signals and severely harm motivation. Second, control systems have to be in harmony with local regulations and customs. In some cases, however, corporate behavioral controls have to be exercised against local customs even though overall operations may be affected negatively. This type of situation occurs, for example, when a subsidiary operates in markets in which unauthorized facilitating payments are a common business practice.

Corporations are faced with major challenges in appropriate and adequate control systems in today's business environment. Given increased local government demands for a share in companies established, controls can become tedious, especially if the

MNC is a minority partner. Even if the new entity is a result of two companies' joining forces through a merger—such as the one between Ciba and Sandoz to create Novartis—or two companies joining forces to form a new entity—such as Siecor established by Siemens AG and Corning Incorporated—the backgrounds of the partners may be different enough to cause problems in devising the required controls.

Summary

This chapter discussed the structures and control mechanisms needed to operate in the international business field. The elements define relationships between the entities of the firm and provide the channels through which the relationships develop.

International firms can choose from a variety of organizational structures, ranging from a domestic organization that handles ad hoc export orders to a full-fledged global organization. The choice will depend heavily on the degree of internationalization of the firm, the diversity of international activities, and the relative importance of product, area, function, and customer variables in the process. A determining factor is also the degree to which headquarters wants to decide important issues concerning the whole corporation and the individual subsidiaries. Organizations that function effectively still need to be revisited periodically to ensure that they remain responsive to a changing environment. Some of the responsiveness is showing up not as structural changes, but rather in how the entities conduct their internal business.

In addition to organization, the control function takes on major importance for multinationals, due to the high variability in performance resulting from divergent local environments and the need to reconcile local objectives with the corporate goal of synergism. While it is important to grant autonomy to country organizations so that they can be responsive to local market needs, it is of equal importance to ensure close cooperation among units to optimize corporate effectiveness.

Control can be exercised through bureaucratic means, which emphasize formal reporting and evaluation of benchmark data or through cultural means, in which norms and values are understood by the individuals and entities that make up the corporation. U.S. firms typically rely more on bureaucratic controls, while MNCs from other countries frequently run operations abroad through informal means and rely less on stringent measures.

The implementation of controls requires great sensitivity to behavioral dimensions and the environment. The measurements used must be appropriate and reflective of actual performance rather than marketplace vagaries. Similarly, entities should be judged only on factors over which they have some degree of control.

Key Terms and Concepts

product structure
area structure
functional structure
process structure
customer structure
mixed structure

matrix structure
decentralization
centralization
coordinated
    decentralization

glocal
intranet
virtual team
strategic leader

contributor
implementor
black hole

Questions for Discussion

1. Firms differ, often substantially, in their organizational structures even within the same industry. What accounts for the differences in their approaches?
2. Discuss the benefits gained by adopting a matrix form of organizational structure.
3. What changes in the firm and/or in the environment might cause a firm to abandon the functional approach?
4. Is there more to the not-invented-here syndrome than simply hurt feelings on the part of those who believe they are being dictated to by headquarters?

5. "Implementors are the most important country organizations in terms of buy-in for a global strategy." Comment.
6. One of the most efficient means of control is self-control. What type of program would you prepare for an incoming employee?

Internet Exercises

1. Improving internal communications is an objective for networked global organizations. Using the web site of the Lotus Development Corporation (http://www.lotus.com) and their section on solutions and success stories, outline how companies have used Lotus Notes to help companies interactively share information.

2. Using company and product information available on their web sites, determine why Dow (http://www.dow.com) and Siemens (http://www.siemens.com) have opted for global product/business structures for their organizations.

Recommended Readings

Bartlett, Christopher, and Sumantra Ghoshal. *Managing Across Borders.* Cambridge, MA: Harvard Business Press, 1998.

Bartlett, Christopher, and Sumantra Ghoshal. *Transnational Management: Text, Cases, and Readings in Cross-Border Management.* New York: Irwin, 1995.

Chisholm, Rupert F. *Developing Network Organizations: Learning from Practice and Theory.* Boston: Addison-Wesley, 1997.

Davidson, William H., and José de la Torre. *Managing the Global Corporation.* New York: McGraw-Hill, 1989.

Ghoshal, Sumantra, and Christopher Bartlett. *The Individualized Corporation: A Fundamentally New Approach to Management.* New York: Harper Business, 1999.

Hedlung, Gunar, and Per Aman. *Managing Relationships with Foreign Subsidiaries.* Stockholm, Sweden: Mekan, 1984.

Humes, Samuel. *Managing the Multinational: Confronting the Global-Local Dilemma.* London, England: Prentice-Hall, 1993.

Moran, Robert T., Philip R. Harris, and William G. Strip. *Developing the Global Organization.* Houston, TX: Gulf Publishing Co., 1993.

Negandhi, Anant, and Martin Welge. *Beyond Theory Z.* Greenwich, CT: JAI Press, 1984.

Otterback, Lars, ed. *The Management of Headquarters-Subsidiary Relationships in Multinational Corporations.* Aldershot, England: Gower Publishing Company, 1981.

Pasternak, Bruce A, and Albert J. Viscio. *The Centerless Corporation: A New Model for Transforming Your Organization for Growth and Prosperity.* New York: Simon and Schuster, 1998.

Pfeffer, Jeffrey, and Robert I. Sutton. *The Knowing-Doing Gap: How Smart Companies Turn Knowledge into Action.* Cambridge, MA: Harvard Business School Press, 1999.

Transforming the Global Corporation. New York: The Economist Intelligence Unit, 1994.

Notes

1. Robert J. Flanagan, "Knowledge Management in the Global Organization in the 21st Century," *HR Magazine* 44, 11 (1999): 54–55.
2. Michael Z. Brooke, *International Management: A Review of Strategies and Operations* (London: Hutchinson, 1986); 173–174.
3. Stefan Robock and Kenneth Simmonds, *International Business and Multinational Enterprises* (Homewood, IL: Richard D. Irwin, 1973), 429.
4. Richard D. Robinson, *Internationalization of Business: An Introduction* (Hinsdale, IL: The Dryden Press, 1984).
5. William H. Davidson and Philippe Haspeslagh, "Shaping a Global Product Organization," *Harvard Business Review* 59 (March/April 1982): 69–76.
6. See http://www.loctite.com/about/global_reach.html, and "How Loctite Prospers with 3-Man Global HQ, Strong Country Managers," *Business International,* May 2, 1988, 129–130.
7. See Joan P. Curhan, William H. Davidson, and Suri Rajan, *Tracing the Multinationals* (Cambridge, MA: Ballinger, 1977); M.E. Wicks, *A Comparative Analysis of the Foreign Investment Evaluation Practices of U.S.-based Multinational Corporations* (New York: McKinsey & Co., 1980); and Lawrence G. Franko, "Organizational Structures and Multi-

national Strategies of Continental European Enterprises," in *European Research in International Business.* eds. Michel Ghertman and James Leontiades (Amsterdam, Holland: North Holland Publishing Co., 1977).
8. Davidson and Haspeslagh, "Shaping a Global Product Organization."
9. "How Goodyear Sharpened Organization and Production for a Tough World Market," *Business International* (January 16, 1989): 11–14.
10. "Red Alert at Ford," *Business Week,* December 2, 1996, 38–39.
11. John D. Daniels, "Bridging National and Global Marketing Strategies Through Regional Operations," *International Marketing Review* 4 (autumn 1987): 29–44; and Philippe Lasserre, "Regional Headquarters: The Spearhead for Asia Pacific Markets," *Long Range Planning* 29 (February, 1996): 30–37.
12. Daniel Robey, *Designing Organizations: A Macro Perspective* (Homewood, IL: Richard D. Irwin, 1982), 327.
13. Thomas H. Naylor, "International Strategy Matrix," *Columbia Journal of World Business* 20 (summer 1985): 11–19.
14. "Kodak's Matrix System Focuses on Product Business Units," *Business International* (July 18, 1988): 221–223.

15. See http://www.philips.com/finance/investor/divstruc.html.

16. Thomas J. Peters, "Beyond the Matrix Organization," *Business Horizons* 22 (October 1979): 15–27.

17. See John M. Stopford and Louis T. Wells, *Managing the Multinational Enterprise* (New York: Basic Books, 1972); also A. D. Chandler, *Strategy and Structure* (Cambridge, MA: MIT Press, 1962); and B. R. Scott, *Stages of Corporate Development* (Boston: ICCH, 1971).

18. Stanley M. Davis, "Trends in the Organization of Multinational Corporations," *Columbia Journal of World Business* 11 (summer 1976): 59–71.

19. William Taylor, "The Logic of Global Business," *Harvard Business Review* 68 (March–April 1990): 91–105.

20. Ilkka A. Ronkainen, "Thinking Globally, Implementing Successfuly," *International Marketing Review* 13, 3 (1996): 4–6.

21. Norman Blackwell, Jean-Pierre Bizet, Peter Child, and David Hensley, "Creating European Organizations that Work," *The McKinsey Quarterly* 27, 2 (1991): 376–385.

22. John A. Quelch and Helen Bloom, "The Return of the Country Manager," *International Marketing Review* 13, 3 (1996): 31–43.

23. Rodman Drake and Lee M. Caudill, "Management of the Large Multinational: Trends and Future Challenges," *Business Horizons* 24 (May–June 1981): 83–91.

24. Christopher Bartlett, "MNCs: Get off the Reorganization Merry-Go-Round," *Harvard Business Review* 60 (March/April 1983): 138–146.

25. Thomas Gross, Ernie Turner, and Lars Cederholm, "Building Teams for Global Operations" *Management Review* (June 1987): 32–36.

26. Christopher A. Bartlett and Sumantra Ghoshal, "Matrix Management: Not a Structure, a Frame of Mind," *Harvard Business Review* 68 (July–August 1990): 138–145.

27. "See Jack. See Jack Run Europe," *Fortune,* September 27, 1999, 127–136.

28. Noel Tichy, "The Teachable Point of View: A Primer," *Harvard Business Review* 77 (March–April 1999): 82–83.

29. "GE Mentoring Program Turns Underlings into Teachers of the Web," *The Wall Street Journal,* February 15, 2000, B1, B16.

30. Richard Benson-Armer and Tsun-Yan Hsieh, "Teamwork Across Time and Space." *The McKinsey Quarterly* 33, 4 (1997): 18–27.

31. "Internet Software Poses Big Threat to Notes, IBM's Stake in Lotus," *The Wall Street Journal,* November 7, 1995, A1–5.

32. Ingo Theuerkauf, David Ernst, and Amir Mahini, "Think Local, Organize . . . ." *International Marketing Review* 13, 3 (1996): 7–12.

33. C.K. Prahalad, "Globalization, Digitization, and the Multinational Enterprise," paper presented at the Annual Meetings of the Academy of International Business, November, 1999.

34. James A. Gingrich, "Five Rules for Winning Emerging Market Consumers," *Strategy & Business* (second quarter, 1999): 19–33.

35. Christopher A. Bartlett and Sumantra Ghoshal, "Tap Your Subsidiaries for Global Reach," *Harvard Business Review* 64 (November–December 1986): 87–94.

36. John A. Quelch and Edward J. Hoff, "Customizing Global Marketing," *Harvard Business Review* 64 (May–June 1986): 59–68.

37. "Rebirth of the Z," *Time,* January 15, 2001, 42–44.

38. Richard I. Kirkland, Jr., "Entering a New World of Boundless Competition," *Fortune* (March 14, 1988): 18–22.

39. "Percy Barnevik's Global Crusade," *Business Week Enterprise 1993,* 204–211.

40. David A. Aaker and Erich Joachimsthaler, "The Lure of Global Branding," *Harvard Business Review* 77 (November/December, 1999): 137–144.

41. Louis Kraar, "Your Rivals Can Be Your Allies," *Fortune* (March 27, 1989): 66–76.

42. Julian Birkinshaw and Nick Fry, "Subsidiary Initiatives to Develop New Markets," *Sloan Management Review* 19 (spring 1998): 51–61.

43. Amitai Etzioni, *A Comparative Analysis of Complex Organizations* (Glencoe, England: Free Press, 1961).

44. William G. Egelhoff, "Patterns of Control in U.S., U.K., and European Multinational Corporations," *Journal of International Business Studies* 15 (fall 1984): 73–83.

45. William H. Davidson, "Administrative Orientation and International Performance," *Journal of International Business Studies* 15 (Fall 1984): 11–23.

46. William G. Ouchi, "The Relationship Between Organizational Structure and Organizational Control," *Administrative Science Quarterly* 22 (March 1977): 95–112.

47. B. R. Baliga and Alfred M. Jaeger, "Multinational Corporations: Control Systems and Delegation Issues," *Journal of International Business Studies* 15 (fall 1984): 25–40.

48. Laurent Leksell, *Headquarters-Subsidiary Relationships in Multinational Corporations* (Stockholm, Sweden: Stockholm School of Economics, 1981), Chapter 5.

49. Anant R. Negandhi and Martin Welge, *Beyond Theory Z* (Greenwich, CT: JAI Press, 1984), 16.

50. Richard Pascale, "Fitting New Employees into the Company Culture," *Fortune* (May 28, 1984): 28–40.

51. Bartlett and Ghoshal, "Matrix Management: Not a Structure, a Frame of Mind."

52. Michael R. Czinkota and Ilkka A. Ronkainen, "International Business and Trade in the Next Decade: Report from a Delphi Study," *Journal of International Business Studies* 28, 4 (1997): 676–694.

53. Tsun-Yuan Hsieh, Johanne La Voie, and Robert A. P. Samek, "Think Global, Hire Local," *The McKinsey Quarterly* 35, 4 (1999): 92–101.

54. R. J. Alsegg, *Control Relationships Between American Corporations and Their European Subsidiaries,* AMA Research Study No. 107 (New York: American Management Association, 1971), 7.

55. John J. Dyment, "Strategies and Management Controls for Global Corporations," *Journal of Business Strategy* 7 (spring 1987): 20–26.

56. Hans Schoellhammer, "Decision-Making and Intra-organizational Conflicts in Multinational Companies," presentation at the Symposium on Management of Headquarter-Subsidiary Relationships in Transnational Corporations, Stockholm School of Economics, June 2–4, 1980.

57. Alfred M. Jaeger, "The Transfer of Organizational Culture Overseas: An Approach to Control in the Multinational Corporation," *Journal of International Business Studies* 14 (fall 1983): 91–106.

CHAPTER 20

The Future

LEARNING OBJECTIVES

- To understand the many changing dimensions that shape international business

- To learn about and evaluate the international business forecasts made by a panel of experts

- To be informed about different career opportunities in international business

KEY CONCERNS OF CEOs

Throughout the twentieth century, CEOs ran their firms as mechanical and military models. Today, information technology's emphasis on flexibility, innovation, and a lack of hierarchy and bureaucracy creates new models and new concerns for CEOs around the world. Understanding how people think and work using information technology, and adapting the firm's processes to this understanding, is key to a firm's success in the future.

What keeps CEOs around the world up at night? The importance of information technology—including the Internet, the shortage of skilled information technology workers, and technology's role in keeping the customer satisfied—underlies the results of the CEO Challenge 2001 survey, conducted by Accenture and The Conference Board. The annual survey asks more than 500 CEOs from different parts of the world about the main management and marketplace challenges they face. The results show what CEOs in different parts of the world view as their main concerns and also reveal how their perceptions of the challenges have changed since the previous year.

CEOs around the world see technology—especially the Internet—as crucial to increasing flexibility and speed and to keeping their customer base in the global marketplace. Maintaining and increasing productivity and value to stay ahead of their competition rest on their firms' ability to use technology effectively.

Management concerns: "Fast and flexible" is CEOs' top management challenge around the world. For CEOs in Asia/Pacific and Europe, increasing flexibility and speed weighs in as their top management concern. Reducing costs is ranked second by Asian/Pacific CEOs, while competing for talent is ranked second by European CEOs. North American CEOs rank customer loyalty as their number one concern, and they view increasing flexibility and speed as second—a firm's competitors are only a few mouseclicks away if a customer's needs are not being met to its satisfaction.

Marketplace concerns: Downward pressure on prices, the top marketplace concern of all CEOs in the previous year, fell to fifth in the recent survey. The top marketplace concerns for Asian/Pacific CEOs today? The change in types and level of competition was ranked first, with the impact of the Internet ranked second. European CEOs' top challenge is the impact of the Internet, while North American CEOs are most concerned with a shortage of key skills. CEOs in Europe and in North America both rank industry consolidation second as a marketplace concern.

Not only do the information technology providers and startups continue to view the Internet as a primary challenge, mature enterprises, including trade and services providers, who today use information technology as a way of doing business also see its importance to their success—47.5 percent of CEOs of companies with more than $5 billion in sales ranked the Internet as one of their top concerns, against only 19 percent in the previous year. Customers have come to expect the fast, flexible responses to their needs that effective use of information technology allows. ●

Source: "CEO Challenge Survey Findings," www.accenture.com; www.conference-board-org; *"The Shape of the 21st-Century Corporation,"* www.worldeconomicforum.org.

All international businesses face constantly changing world economic conditions. This is not a new situation or one to be feared, because change provides the opportunity for new market positions to emerge and for managerial talent to improve the competitive position of the firm. Recognizing change and adapting creatively to new situations are the most important tasks of the international business executive, as this chapter's opening vignette shows.

Recently, changes are occurring more frequently, more rapidly, and have a more severe impact. Due to growing real-time access to knowledge about and for customers, suppliers, and competitors, the international business environment is increasingly characterized by high speed bordering on instantaneity.[1] In consequence, the past has lost much of its value as a predictor of the future. What occurs today may not only be altered in short order but be completely overturned or reversed. For example, political stability in a country can be completely disrupted over the course of a few months. A major, sudden decline in world stock markets leaves corporations, investors, and consumers with strong feelings of uncertainty. Overnight currency declines result in an entirely new business climate for international suppliers and their customers. In all, international business managers today face complex and rapidly changing economic and political conditions.

This chapter will discuss possible future developments in the international business environment, highlight the implications of the changes for international business management, and offer suggestions for a creative response to the changes. The chapter also will explore the meaning of strategic changes as they relate to career choice and career path alternatives in international business.

The International Business Environment

This section analyzes the international business environment by looking at political, financial, societal, and technological conditions of change and providing a glimpse of possible future developments as envisioned by an international panel of experts.[2] The impact of these factors on doing business abroad, on international trade relations, and on government policy is of particular interest to the international manager.

The Political Environment

The international political environment is undergoing a substantial transformation characterized by the reshaping of existing political blocks, the formation of new groupings, and the breakup of old coalitions.

Planned versus Market Economies

The second half of the last century was shaped by the political, economic, and military competition between the United States and the Soviet Union which resulted in the creation of two virtually separate economic systems. This key adversarial posture has now largely disappeared, with market-based economic thinking emerging as the front-runner. Virtually all of the former centrally planned economies are undergoing a transition with the goal of becoming market oriented.

International business has made important contributions to this transition process. Trade and investment have offered the populace in these nations a new perspective, new choices, new jobs, and new alternatives for marketing their products and services. At the same time, the bringing together of two separate economic and business systems has resulted in new, and sometimes devastating competition, a loss of government-ordained trade relationships, and substantial dislocations and pain during the adjustment process.

Over the next five years the countries of Eastern and Central Europe will continue to be attractive for international investment due to relatively low labor cost, low-priced input factors, and large unused production capacities. This attractiveness, however, will translate mainly into growing investment from Western Europe for reasons of geographic proximity and attractive outsourcing opportunities.[3] Even these investment flows, however, are likely to take place only selectively, resulting in very unbalanced economic conditions in the region. Firms and governments outside of Western Europe are likely to be much more reluctant to invest in Eastern Europe. This aversion is not so much driven by caution about a potential resurgence of Communism or fear of economic and political instability, but mainly due to attractive investment alternatives elsewhere.

Russia and the other nations of the former Soviet Union are seen as facing great difficulty. The collapse of the ruble and repeated setbacks in economic development have led to a paradox faced by Russia and the world. Russia today is the world's sixth most populous country, a key nuclear power, and the holder of a permanent seat on the UN Security Council. Its economic health and creditworthiness, however, place it in the same tier of global powers as the Sudan and Afghanistan. Economic recovery and participation in world trade are likely to be very gradual. In part, the slowness is a function of self-imposed constraints due to domestic fears of outsiders. In addition, if financial inflows into the region are to make a difference, governments need to find market-oriented ways to reduce the flight of capital abroad.

Overall, many business activities will be subject to regional economic and political instability, increasing the risk of international business partners. Progress toward the institution of market-based economies may be halted or even reversed as large population segments are exposed to growing hardship during the transformation process. It will be important to develop institutions and processes internally which assure domestic and foreign investors that there will be protection from public and private corruption and respect for property rights and contractual arrangements.

The North-South Relationship   The distinction between developed and less-developed countries (LDCs) is unlikely to change. The ongoing disparity between developed and developing nations is likely to be based, in part, on continuing debt burdens and problems with satisfying basic needs. As a result, political uncertainty may well result in increased polarization between the haves and have-nots, with growing potential for political and economic conflict. Demands for political solutions to economic and financial problems are likely to increase particularly in light of the fact that 2.8 billion people live on less than $2 per day.[4] Some countries may consider migration as a key solution to population-growth problems, yet many emigrants may encounter government barriers to their migration. As a result, there may well be more investment flows by firms bringing their labor and skill-intensive manufacturing operations to these countries.[5] In addition, new approaches to international development taken by multilateral institutions may be effective in strengthening the grass roots of developing economies. Global Perspective 20.1 provides an example.

The developing countries of Africa continue as a relatively cool region for international business purposes. Political instability and the resulting inability of many African firms to be consistent trading partners are the key reasons for such a pessimistic view. In light of global competition for investment capital, these drawbacks are instrumental in holding both investment and trade down to a trickle. This starvation for funds is unlikely to be addressed by corporations. Periodic surges in the social conscience of industrialized nations may result in targeted investments by governments, multilateral institutions, and non-governmental organizations (NGOs), but these funds are likely to be insufficient for a transformation of the economic future of the region. Debt forgiveness for the heavily burdened nations helps clean the slate of past mistakes. Special provisions for these nations to have easier access to developed country markets will make a marginal difference in export performance. Most important, however, is

GLOBAL PERSPECTIVE 20.1

Lenders Target Women in the Developing World

The developing world's women are gaining a measure of economic autonomy as perceptions of them and their role in developing economies change. Even the big development agencies and multilateral banks are increasingly funding women-led small businesses and farming projects based on an assumption that women, more than men, are the critical players in the fight to relieve poverty. Agencies such as the World Bank, Agency for International Development, and Inter-American Development Bank say women are usually better at repaying their loans and less prone to waste or loot development money.

The motivation to target women has less to do with sexual politics than with the economic reality that women do much of the work in developing countries. "All over the developing world, in rural areas, the women are the mainstay of the local economy," said Gustave Speth, administrator of the United Nations Development Programme. A recent World Bank study found that women head half the households in sub-Saharan Africa. A study of village life in Cameroon found that women work an average of 64 hours a week, compared with 32 for men. And women's earnings are more likely to be used for the health and education of the next generation.

Microcredit to poor borrowers works because repaying the loans fosters enterprise rather than dependency. The schemes also are self-sustaining. The number of people borrowing from microlenders has grown to 14 million—an 80 percent increase since 1999—and there are between 7,000 and 10,000 microlenders.

The focus on women's economic activities coincides with a growing interest in financing the thousands of tiny businesses that make up the developing world's vast "informal sector." Many of these so-called microenterprises, ranging from food sellers on street corners to one-person apparel makers, are run by women. Though statistics are shaky, it is estimated that informal-sector businesses make up as much as half of all economic activity in many developing countries. Yet, until recently, the international institutions have funneled nearly all development funds to governments and state enterprises for projects that often did little for the poorest population segments.

In the Dominican Republic, the marriage between the large international agencies and grassroots groups is helping to get money into the hands of more poor women running businesses. To some extent, the small Caribbean state is seen as a model for others working on programs to lend to the poor. Within a year, development experts from Botswana, Brazil, Colombia, Jamaica, Mexico, and Senegal visited and studied how Dominican lenders extend credit to the poorest segments of society but still cover costs and stay afloat Pedro Jimenez, the executive director of the largest small-enterprise lender in the Dominican Republic, argued that bankers to the poor have to avoid a "charity window" mentality. To stay in business, he say, lenders must charge real interest rates, usually about 30 percent, that cover the lenders' costs plus any inflation risk. Jimenez's bank grants loans for an average amount of $800 and has a 98.6 percent repayment rate.

In Niger, CARE is helping establish women's savings groups in about 45 villages. "They haven't had access to banking systems anywhere," said Ann Duval, the program's overseer. About 35 women contribute 50 cents per week. Two-week loans are made, with an interest rate of about 10 percent. Periodically the women liquidate their banks and distribute the money for certain needs. But the banks always start up again. Once they have had a bank, the women don't want to go without one.

Microlenders in rural areas encourage poor women in villages to cross-guarantee each others' loans, with the resulting peer pressure keeping default rates to a minimum. In Bangladesh, the Grameen Bank grants a loan to only one member of a group of borrowers at a time; the next borrower is granted a loan only when the outstanding loan is repaid. In urban areas, a stepped lending scheme is more effective at keeping the default rates low. In these schemes, the borrower puts up a little money and the microlender lends her about the same amount. A larger loan can then be granted if she repays the original loan promptly, providing an incentive.

Source: Tim Carrington, "Gender Economics: In Developing World, International Lenders Are Targeting Women," *The Wall Street Journal,* June 22, 1994, A1; "Africa's Women Go to Work," *The Economist,* January 13, 2001, pp. 43–44.

internal reform and the benchmarking of production, so that competitive products and services can be offered. It would appear unlikely that government assistance alone can overcome market reluctance. An emphasis on education and training and the development of a supportive infrastructure are crucial, since that is where the investments and jobs go.[6] It is not enough to expect a rising tide to raise all boats. There must also be significant effort expended to ensure the seaworthiness of the boat, the functioning of its sails, and the capability of its crew. Market-oriented performance will be critical to succeed in the longer run.

The issue of **environmental protection** will also be a major force shaping the relationship between the developed and the developing world. In light of the need and desire to grow their economies, however, there may be much disagreement on the part of the industrializing nations as to what approaches to take. Of key concern will be the answer to the question: Who pays? For example, simply placing large areas of land out of bounds for development will be difficult to accept for nations which intend to pursue all options for further economic progress. Corporations in turn are likely to be more involved in protective measures, since they are aware of their constituents' expectations and the repercussions of not meeting those expectations. Corporations recognize that by being environmentally responsible, a company can build trust and improve its image—therefore becoming more competitive. For example, in the early 1990s the first annual corporate environmental report was published; now over 2,000 companies a year publish such reports.[7]

In light of divergent trends by different groups, three possible scenarios emerge. One scenario is that of continued international cooperation. The developed countries could relinquish part of their economic power to less-developed ones, thus contributing actively to their economic growth through a sharing of resources and technology. Although such cross-subsidization will be useful and necessary for the development of LDCs, it may reduce the rate of growth of the standard of living in the more developed countries. It would, however, increase trade flows between developed and less-developed countries and precipitate the emergence of new international business opportunities.

A second scenario is that of confrontation. Due to an unwillingness to share resources and technology sufficiently (or excessively, depending on the point of view), the developing and the developed areas of the world may become increasingly hostile toward one another. As a result, the volume of international business, both by mandate of governments and by choice of the private sector, could be severely reduced.

A third scenario is that of isolation. Although there may be some cooperation between them, both groups, in order to achieve their domestic and international goals, may choose to remain economically isolated. This alternative may be particularly attractive if each region believes that it faces unique problems and therefore must seek its own solutions.

Emerging Markets   Much of the growth of the global economy will be fueled by the emerging markets of Latin America and the Asia Pacific region. In Latin America, the international business climate will improve due to economic integration, market liberalization, and privatization. In spite of some inefficiencies, Mercosur continues to bring countries closer together and encourages their collaboration. There is also the increasing likelihood of a Free Trade Arrangement of the Americas, which will align the common economic interests of countries in South, Central, and North America. Due to substantial natural resources and relatively low cost of production, an increased flow of foreign direct investment and trade activity is forecast, emanating not only from the United States, but also from Europe and Japan.

The Asia Pacific region is likely to regain its growth in the next decade. For the industrialized nations, this development will offer a significant opportunity for exports and investment, but it will also diminish, in the longer term, the basis for their status and influence in the world economy. While the nations in the region are likely to collaborate, they are not expected to form a bloc of the same type as the European Union or NAFTA. Rather, their relationship is likely to be defined in terms of trade and investment flows (e.g., Japan) and social contacts (e.g., the Chinese business community). A cohesive bloc may only emerge as a reaction to a perceived threat by other major blocs.

China's emergence is likely to be the economic event of the decade. Despite innumerable risks, experts see Chinese pragmatism prevailing. Companies already present in the market and those willing to make significant investments are likely to be the main beneficiaries of growth. Long-term commitment, willingness to transfer technology, and an ability to partner either with local firms through joint ventures or with overseas Chinese-run firms are considered crucial for success. The strategic impact of Chinese trade participation is also likely to change. With membership in the World Trade Organization, the recipients of Chinese goods will be much less able to exclude them with higher tariffs or nontariff barriers. China, in turn, is likely to assume a much higher profile in its trading activities. For example, rather than be the supplier of goods which are then marketed internationally under a Japanese or U.S. label, Chinese firms will increasingly develop their own brand names and fight for their own name recognition, customer loyalty, and market share.[8]

Among the other promising emerging markets are Korea and India. Korea could emerge as a participant in worldwide competition, while India is considered more important for the size of its potential market. Korean firms must still improve their ability to adopt a global mindset. Some experts are also concerned about the chaebols status as the Korean economy becomes democratized. In addition, the possible impact of the reunification of the Korean peninsula on the country's globalization efforts must be taken into account.

With the considerable liberalization that took place in India during the 1990s, many expect it to offer major international marketing opportunities due to its size, its significant natural wealth, and its large, highly educated middle class. While many experts believe that political conflict, both domestic and regional, nationalism, and class structure may temper the ability of Indian companies to emerge as a worldwide competitive force, there is strong agreement that India's disproportionately large and specialized workforce in engineering and computer sciences makes the nation a power to be reckoned with.

Overall, the growth potential of these emerging economies may be threatened by uncertainty in terms of international relations and domestic policies, as well as social and political dimensions, particularly those pertaining to income distribution. Concerns also exist about infrastructural inadequacies, both physical—such as transportation—and societal—such as legal systems. The consensus of experts is, however, that growth in these countries will be significant.

A Divergence of Values   It might well be that different nations or cultures become increasingly disparate in terms of values and priorities. For example, in some countries, the aim for financial progress and an improved quantitative standard of living may well give way to priorities based on religion or the environment. Even if nations share similar values, their priorities among these values may differ strongly. For example, within a market-oriented system, some countries may prioritize profits and efficiency, while others may place social harmony first, even at the cost of maintaining inefficient industries.

Such a divergence of values will require a major readjustment of the activities of the international corporation. A continuous scanning of newly emerging national values thus becomes imperative for the international executive.

The International Financial Environment

Debt constraints and low commodity prices create slow growth prospects for many developing countries. They will be forced to reduce their levels of imports and to exert more pressure on industrialized nations to open up their markets. Even if the markets are opened, however, demand for most primary products will be far lower than supply. Ensuing competition for market share will therefore continue to depress prices.

Developed nations have a strong incentive to help the debtor nations. The incentive consists of the market opportunities that economically healthy developing countries can offer and of national security concerns. As a result, industrialized nations may very well find that funds transfers to debtor nations, accompanied by debt-relief measures such as debt forgiveness, are necessary to achieve economic stimulation at home.

The dollar will remain one of the major international currencies with little probability of gold returning to its former status in the near future. However, some international transaction volume in both trade and finance is increasingly likely to be denominated in nondollar terms, using particularly the euro. The system of floating currencies will likely continue, with occasional attempts by nations to manage exchange rate relationships or at least reduce the volatility of swings in currency values. However, given the vast flows of financial resources across borders, it would appear that market forces rather than government action will be the key determinant of a currency's value. Factors such as investor trust, economic conditions, earnings perceptions, and political stability are therefore likely to have a much greater effect on the international value of currencies than domestic monetary and fiscal experimentation.

Given the close links among financial markets, shocks in one market will quickly translate into rapid shifts in others and easily overpower the financial resources of individual governments. Even if there should be a decision by governments to pursue closely coordinated fiscal and monetary policies, they are unlikely to be able to negate long-term market effects in response to changes in economic fundamentals.

A looming concern in the international financial environment will be the **international debt load** of the United States. Both domestically and internationally, the United States is incurring debt that would have been inconceivable only a few decades ago. For example, in the 1970s the accumulation of financial resources by the Arab nations was of major concern in the United States. Congressional hearings focused on whether Arab money was "buying out America." At that time, however, Arab holdings in the United States were $10 billion to $20 billion. Today the accumulation of foreign dollar holdings inside and outside of the United States consists of much higher levels.

In 1985, the United States became a net negative investor internationally. The United States entered the new century with an international debt burden of more than $2 trillion. This debt level makes the United States the largest debtor nation in the world, owing more to other nations than all the developing nations combined. In light of ongoing trade deficits, it is projected by some that this net negative investment position will grow to $4 trillion by 2005, will be unsustainable, and will lead to a hard landing of the U.S. currency and economy.[9] Others argue against an unsustainable scenario, believing that there are special mitigating circumstances which let the U.S. tolerate this burden, such as the fact that most of the debts are denominated in U.S. dollars and that, even at such a large debt volume, U.S. debt-service requirements are only a relatively small portion of GNP.[10] Yet this accumulation of foreign debt may very well introduce entirely new dimensions into the international business relationships of individuals and nations. Once debt has reached a certain level, the creditor as well as the debtor is hostage to the loans.

Since foreign creditors expect a return on their investment, a substantial portion of future U.S. international trade activity will have to be devoted to generating sufficient funds for such repayment. For example, at an assumed interest rate or rate of return of 10 percent, the international U.S. debt level—without any growth—would require the annual payment of $200 billion, which amounts to almost 20 percent of current U.S. exports. Therefore, it seems highly likely that international business will become a greater priority than it is today and will serve as a source of major economic growth for firms in the United States.

To some degree, foreign holders of dollars may also choose to convert their financial holdings into real property and investments in the United States. This will result in an entirely new pluralism in U.S. society. It will become increasingly difficult and, perhaps, even unnecessary to distinguish between domestic and foreign products—as is already the case with Hondas made in Ohio. Senators and members of Congress, governors, municipalities, and unions will gradually be faced with conflicting concerns in trying to develop a national consensus on international trade and investment.

National security issues may also be raised as major industries become majority owned by foreign firms.

Industrialized countries are likely to attempt to narrow the domestic gap between savings and investments through fiscal policies. Without concurrent restrictions on international capital flows, such policies are likely to meet with only limited success. Lending institutions can be expected to become more conservative in their financing, a move that may hit smaller firms and developing countries the hardest. At the same time, the entire financial sector is likely to face continuous integration, ongoing bank acquisitions, and a reduction in financial intermediaries. Customers will be able to assert their independence by increasingly being able to present their financial needs globally and directly to financial markets, and thus obtaining better access to financial products and providers.

The Effects of Population Shifts

The population discrepancy between less-developed nations and the industrialized countries will continue to increase. In the industrialized world, a **population increase** will become a national priority, given the fact that in many countries, particularly in Western Europe, the population is shrinking. The shrinkage may lead to labor shortages and to major societal difficulties when a shrinking number of workers has to provide for a growing elderly population.

In the developing world, **population stabilization** will continue to be one of the major challenges of governmental policy. In spite of well-intentioned economic planning, continued rapid increases in population will make it more difficult to ensure that the pace of economic development exceeds population growth. If the standard of living of a nation is determined by dividing the GNP by its population, any increase in the denominator will require equal increases in the numerator to maintain the standard of living. With an annual increase in the world population of 100 million people, the task is daunting. It becomes even more complex when one considers that within countries with high population increases, large migration flows take place from rural to urban areas. As a result, by the end of this decade, most of the world's ten largest metropolitan areas will be in the developing world.[11]

The Technological Environment

The concept of the global village is commonly accepted today and indicates the importance of communication. Worldwide, the estimated number of people **online** in March of 2001 was 391 million and expected to grow to more than 774 million by 2003.[12] The United States had the highest number of adults with Internet access, with more than 41 percent of all households having such access and more than 116 million Americans online.[13] However, since the year 2000, the users in the United States and Canada represent less than 50 percent of the global Internet community[14]—which means that the world is catching up. Nonetheless, there is a wide digital gap in the world, where some nations, such as Albania, have only 161 Internet hosts.[15]

For both consumer services and business-to-business relations, the Internet is democratizing global business. It has made it easier for new global retail brands—like **amazon.com** and CDnow—to emerge. The Internet is also helping specialists like Australia's high sensitivity hearing aids manufacturer Cochlear to reach target customers around the world without having to invest in a distribution network in each country. The ability to reach a worldwide audience economically via the Internet spells success for niche marketers who could never make money by just servicing their niches in the domestic market. The Internet also allows customers, especially those in emerging markets, to access global brands at more competitive prices than those offered by exclusive national distributors.[16]

Starting a new business will be much easier, allowing a far greater number of suppliers to enter a market. Small- and medium-sized enterprises, as well as large multi-

GLOBAL PERSPECTIVE 20.2

Direct Importing on the Internet

Can't find a U.S.–made snowboard at your local department store in Japan? Try the new mall on the Internet. A Portland, Oregon, firm is creating what could be described as a Japanese cybermall, an online shopping service that enables U.S. manufacturers and retailers to advertise and sell their products directly to consumers—in Japanese. The Japanese Internet service also teaches customers in Japan how to order products and services directly from the United States.

By setting up shop in local language cybermalls, U.S. firms could target potential customers around the globe without the costly headaches that often scare them away from the international marketplace. TKAI, Inc., has provided Japan-specific e-business web site development, online marketing, strategic consulting, and research services since 1995 to more than forty clients, including Amazon.com, British Telecom, Outpost.com, JCPenney, Nokia, and PeopleSoft.

TKAI's electronic service, called DIYer (for Do-It-Yourself Importer), averages 1,000 unique users per day. More than 5,000 people subscribe to its e-newsletter, according to owner Tim Clark. "We're helping companies enter the Japanese market, companies that want to take a crack without paying for major magazine ads or huge marketing campaigns," he said. The service is for companies "interested in dealing directly with customers in Japan," through catalog sales, for example, he said.

Here's how it works: A U.S. manufacturer or retailer pays TKAI a fee for a display on the Import Center site. The fee varies according to the size and complexity of the display, but runs $350 and up. TKAI, whose staff includes fluent Japanese speakers, translates the copy into Japanese. For the Japanese consumer, the web site is an information resource for customers who want to buy products or services "without going through middlemen or trading companies," said Mr. Clark. Access is free of charge in Japan.

DIYer is not an e-commerce site, however. It provides information about products featured on overseas e-commerce sites that have received positive feedback from Japanese consumers. Japanese consumers visit the site both to learn about featured products and for help with composing English e-mail, interpreting sizes and units of measurement, and understanding different shipping methods.

Mickey Kerbel, president of Xtreme Inc., which makes snowboards, said he paid $345 for a one-year listing with TKAI and has sold about $2,000 worth of merchandise in only a couple of months since going online. The site provides a low-cost way to gain access to some of the world's most affluent customers, said Tim Clark. The Internet growth rate in Japan is outstripping that of the United States: as of June 1999, Japan had approximately 15 million users. "We're happy with the service and the list-building it has helped us with in the Japan market," said Mike Delph, management information systems manager at U.S. Cavalry, a Kentucky retailer of outdoor equipment and survival gear. He said he's amassed a large list of names through electronic mail. "We've had more responses from the (Import Center) than we have on our own English language site," said a system administrator for Blue Tech, a computer products retailer based in La Jolla, California.

 Source: Telephone interview with Tim Clark, June 25, 1999; "Corporate Fact Sheet," TKAI web site, accessed April 25, 2001, **www.tkai.com**; William DiBenedetto, "Home Shopping Internetwork: Buyers Find U.S. Goods at Japanese Cybermall," *The Journal of Commerce* (January 8, 1996): 1A.

national corporations, will now be full participants in the global marketplace. Businesses in developing countries can now overcome many of the obstacles of infrastructure and transport that limited their economic potential in the past. The global services economy will be a knowledge-based economy and its most precious resource will be information and ideas. Unlike the classical factors of production—land, labor, and capital—information and knowledge are not bound to any region or country but are almost infinitely mobile and infinitely capable of expansion.[17] This wide availability, of course, also brings new risks to firms. For example, unlike the past, today one complaint can easily be developed into millions of complaints by e-mail.[18] In consequence, firms are subject to much more scrutiny and customer response on an international level.

Overall, these new technologies, in turn, offer exciting new opportunities to conduct international business, as Global Perspective 20.2 shows.

High technology will also be one of the more volatile and controversial areas of economic activity internationally. Developments in biotechnology are already transforming agriculture, medicine, and chemistry. Chemically engineered foods, patient-specific pharmaceuticals, gene therapy, and even genetically engineered organs are on the horizon. Innovations such as these will change what we eat, how we treat illness, and how we evolve as a civilization.[19] However, skepticism of such technological innovations is rampant. In many instances, people are opposed to such changes due to religious or cultural reasons, or simply because they do not want to be exposed to such "artificial" products. Achieving agreement on what constitutes safe products and procedures, of defining the border between what is natural and what is not, will constitute one of the great areas of debate in the years to come. Firms and their managers must remain keenly aware of popular perceptions and misperceptions and of government regulations in order to remain successful participants in markets.

Even firms and countries that are at the leading edge of technology will find it increasingly difficult to marshal the funds necessary for further advancements. For example, investments in semiconductor technology are measured in billions rather than millions of dollars and do not bring any assurance of success. Not to engage in the race, however, will mean falling behind quickly in all areas of manufacturing when virtually every industrial and consumer product is "smart" due to its chip technology.

Changes in Trade Relations

The formation of the World Trade Organization (WTO) has brought to conclusion a lengthy and sometimes acrimonious round of global trade negotiations. However, key disagreements among major trading partners are likely to persist. Ongoing major imbalances in trade flows will tempt nations to apply their own national trade remedies, particularly in the antidumping field. Even though WTO rules permit for a retaliation against unfair trade practices, such actions would only result in an ever-increasing spiral of adverse trade relations.

A key question will be whether nations are willing to abrogate some of their sovereignty even during difficult economic times. An affirmative answer will strengthen the multilateral trade system and enhance the flow of trade. However, if key trading nations resort to the development of insidious nontariff barriers, unilateral actions, and bilateral negotiations, protectionism will increase on a global scale and the volume of international trade is likely to decline. The danger is real. Popular support for international trade agreements appears to be on the wane. The public demonstrations in Seattle during the WTO meeting there indicate that there is much ambivalence by individuals and non-governmental organizations about trade. It is here where international business academics are, or should be, the guardians who separate fact from fiction in international trade policy discussions. Qualified not by weight of office but by expertise, international business experts are the indirect guarantors of and guides toward free and open markets. Without their input and impact, public apathy and ignorance may well result in missteps in trade policy.[20]

International trade relations also will be shaped by new participants whose market entry will restructure the composition of global trade. For example, new players with exceptionally large productive potential, such as the People's Republic of China and Central Europe will substantially alter world trade flows. And while both governments and firms will be required to change many trading policies and practices as a result, they will also benefit in terms of market opportunities and sourcing alternatives.

Finally, the efforts of governments to achieve self-sufficiency in economic sectors, particularly in agriculture and heavy industries, have ensured the creation of long-term, worldwide oversupply of some commodities and products, many of which historically had been traded widely. As a result, after some period of intense market share competition aided by subsidies and governmental support, a gradual and painful restructuring of these economic sectors will have to take place. This will be particularly true for agricultural cash crops such as wheat, corn, and dairy products and industrial products such as steel, chemicals, and automobiles.

Government Policy

International trade activity now affects domestic policy more than ever. For example, trade flows can cause major structural shifts in employment. Links between industries spread these effects throughout the economy. Fewer domestically produced automobiles will affect the activities of the steel industry. Shifts in the sourcing of textiles will affect the cotton industry. Global productivity gains and competitive pressures will force many industries to restructure their activities. In such circumstances, industries are likely to ask their governments to help in their restructuring efforts. Often, such assistance includes a built-in tendency toward protectionist action.

Such restructuring is not necessarily negative. For example, since 1900, farm employment in the United States has dropped from more than 40 percent of the population to less than 3 percent.[21] Yet today, the farm industry feeds more than 285 million people in the United States and still produces large surpluses. A restructuring of industries can greatly increase productivity and provide the opportunity for resource allocation to emerging sectors of an economy.

Governments cannot be expected, for the sake of the theoretical ideal of "free trade," to sit back and watch the effects of deindustrialization on their countries. The most that can be expected is that they will permit an open-market orientation subject to the needs of domestic policy. Even an open-market orientation will be maintained only if governments can provide reasonable assurances to their own firms and citizens that the openness applies to foreign markets as well. Therefore, unfair trade practices such as governmental subsidization, dumping, and industrial targeting will be examined more closely, and retaliation for such activities is likely to be swift and harsh.

Increasingly, governments will need to coordinate policies that affect the international business environment. The development of international indexes and **trigger mechanisms,** which precipitate government action at predetermined intervention points, will be a useful step in that direction. Yet, for them to be effective, governments will need to muster the political fortitude to implement the policies necessary for cooperation. For example, international monetary cooperation will work in the long term only if domestic fiscal policies are responsive to the achievement of the coordinated goals.

At the same time as the need for collaboration among governments grows, it will become more difficult to achieve a consensus. In the Western world, the time from 1945 through 1990 was characterized by a commonality of purpose. The common defense against the Communist enemy relegated trade relations to second place, and provided a bond that encouraged collaboration. With the common threat gone, however, the bonds have been diminished—if not dissolved—and the priority of economic performance has increased. More often, economic security and national security are seen as competing with each other, rather than as complementary dimensions of national welfare which can operate in parallel and, to some degree, even be traded off against each other. Unless a new key jointness of purpose can be found by governments, collaborative approaches and long-term alliances will become increasingly difficult.[22]

Governmental policymakers must take into account the international repercussions of domestic legislation. For example, in imposing a special surcharge tax on the chemical industry designed to provide for the cleanup of toxic waste products, they need to consider its repercussions on the international competitiveness of the chemical industry. Similarly, current laws such as antitrust legislation need to be reviewed if the laws hinder the international competitiveness of domestic firms.

Policymakers also need a better understanding of the nature of the international trade issues confronting them. Most countries today face both short-term and long-term trade problems. Trade balance issues, for example, are short term in nature, while competitiveness issues are much more long term. All too often, however, short-term issues are attacked with long-term **trade policy measures,** and vice versa. In the United States, for example, the desire to "level the international playing field" with mechanisms such as vigorous implementation of import restrictions or voluntary restraint agreements may serve long-term competitiveness well, but it does little to alleviate the publicly perceived problem of the trade deficit. Similarly, a further opening of Japan's market to foreign corporations will have only a minor immediate effect on that country's trade surplus or the trading partners' deficit. Yet it is the expectation and hope of many in both the public and the private sectors that such instant changes will occur.[23] For the sake of the credibility of policymakers, it therefore becomes imperative to precisely identify the nature of the problem and to design and use policy measures that are appropriate for its resolution.

In the years to come, governments will be faced with an accelerating technological race and with emerging problems that seem insurmountable by individual firms alone, such as pollution of the environment and global warming. As market gaps emerge and time becomes crucial, both governments and the private sector will find that even if the private sector knows that a lighthouse is needed, it may still be difficult, time-consuming, and maybe even impossible to build one with private funds alone. As a result, it becomes increasingly important for government to work closely with the business sector to identify market gaps and to devise market-oriented ways of filling them. The international manager in turn will have to spend more time and effort dealing with governments and with macro rather than micro issues.

The Future of International Business Management

Global change results in an increase in risk. One shortsighted alternative for risk-averse managers would be the termination of international activities altogether. However, businesses will not achieve long-term success by engaging only in risk-free actions. Further, other factors make the pursuit of international business mandatory.

International markets remain a source of high profits, as a quick look at a list of multinational firms would show.[24] International activities help cushion slack in domestic sales resulting from recessionary or adverse domestic conditions and may be crucial to the very survival of the firm. International markets also provide firms with foreign experience that helps them compete more successfully with foreign firms in the domestic market.

International Planning and Research

Firms must continue to serve customers well to be active participants in the international marketplace. One major change that will come about is that the international manager will need to respond to general governmental concerns to a greater degree when planning a business strategy. Further, societal concern about macro problems needs to be taken into account directly and quickly because societies have come to expect more social responsibility from corporations. Taking on a leadership role regarding social causes may also benefit corporations' bottom lines, since consumers appear more willing than ever to act as significant pressure points for policy changes and to pay for their social concerns. Therefore, reputation management, or the art of building reputation as a corporate asset, is likely to gain prominence in the years ahead as the pressure on corporations to be good corporate citizens grows.[25]

Increased competition in international markets will create a need for more niches in which firms can create a distinct international competence. As a result, increased specialization and segmentation will let firms fill very narrow and specific demands or resolve very specific problems for their international customers. Identifying and filling the niches will be easier in the future because of the greater availability of international research tools and information. The key challenge to global firms will be to build and manage decision-making processes that allow quick responses to multiple changing environmental demands. This capability is important since firms face a growing need for worldwide coordination and integration of internal activities, such as logistics and operations, while being confronted with the need for greater national differentiation and responsiveness at the customer level.[26]

In spite of the frequent short-term orientation by corporations and investors, companies will need to learn to prepare for long-term horizons. Particularly in an environment of heated competition and technological battles, of large projects and slow payoffs, companies, their stakeholders, and governments will need to find avenues that not only permit but encourage the development of strategic perspectives. Figure 20.1 provides an example of such a long-term view.

FIGURE 20.1   Long-Term Planning

In our business, it's important to keep an eye on the next quarter. The one that ends midnight, December 31, 2025.

With a lot of hard work and several billion dollars, our 777 jetliner will be delivered, service-ready, in mid-1995.

And, if the market accepts our new airplane as well as it has previous Boeing jetliners, it's reasonable to expect the 777 will be part of the world air transportation system for at least the first half of the next century.

And Boeing will offer service and support for 777s as long as they're in service.

Such long-term expectations and responsibilities are at the very heart of our Company, from jetliners to spacecraft. They are the source of our most important challenges and successes.

And, they're reasons for our continuous investments in research and development, in new plants and equipment, and in talented people capable of mastering rapidly advancing technologies.

Like all businesses, we're subject to the disciplines of financial performance measurements.

But in aviation and aerospace, we have a long horizon.

After 75 years, we've learned that if you aren't in this business for the long term, you aren't likely to be in it for long.

BOEING

Governments both at home and abroad will demand that private business practices not increase public costs and that businesses serve customers equally and nondiscriminately. The concept directly counters the desire to serve first the markets that are most profitable and least costly. International executives will therefore be torn in two directions. To provide results acceptable to governments, customers, and to the societies they serve, they must walk a fine line, balancing the public and the private good.

International Product Policy

One key issue affecting product planning will be environmental concern. Major growth in public attention paid to the natural environment, environmental pollution, and global warming will provide many new product opportunities and affect existing products to a large degree. For example, manufacturers will increasingly be expected to take responsibility for their products from cradle to grave, and be intimately involved in product disposal and recycling.

Firms will therefore have to plan for a final stage in the product life cycle, the "postmortem" stage, during which a firm continues to expend further corporate investment and management attention, even though the product may have been terminated some time ago.[27]

Although some consumers show a growing interest in truly "natural" products, even if they are less convenient, consumers in most industrialized nations will require products that are environmentally friendly but at the same time do not require too much compromise on performance and value.

Worldwide introduction of products will occur much more rapidly in the future. Already, international product life cycles have accelerated substantially. Whereas product introduction could previously be spread out over several years, firms now must prepare for product life cycles that can be measured in months or even weeks.[28] As a result, firms must design products and plan even their domestic marketing strategies with the international product cycle in mind. Product introduction will grow more complex, more expensive, and more risky, yet the rewards to be reaped from a successful product will have to be accumulated more quickly.

Early incorporation of the global dimension into product planning, however, does not point toward increased standardization. On the contrary, companies will have to be ready to deliver more mass customization. Customers are no longer satisfied with simply having a product: They want it to precisely meet their needs and preferences. **Mass customization** requires working with existing product technology, often in modular form, to create specific product bundles for a particular customer, resulting in tailor-made jeans or a customized car.

Factor endowment advantages have a significant impact on the decisions of international executives. Nations with low production costs will be able to replicate products more quickly and cheaply. Countries such as China, India, Israel, and the Philippines offer large pools of skilled people at labor rates much lower than in Europe, Japan, or the United States. All this talent also results in a much wider dissemination of technological creativity, a factor that will affect the innovative capability of firms. For example, in 2000, almost half of all the patents in the United States were granted to foreign entities. Table 20.1 provides an overview of U.S. patents granted to foreign inventors.

This indicates that firms need to make nondomestic know-how part of their production strategies, or they need to develop consistent comparative advantages in production technology in order to stay ahead of the game. Similarly, workers engaged in the productive process must attempt, through training and skill enhancement, to stay ahead of foreign workers who are willing to charge less for their time.

An increase will occur in the trend toward strategic alliances, or partnerings, permitting the formation of collaborative arrangements between firms. These alliances will enable firms to take risks that they could not afford to take alone, facilitate tech-

TABLE 20.1
U.S. Patents Granted to Foreign Inventors in 2000

State/Country	Totals	State/Country	Totals
Arab Emirates	2	Lebanon	4
Argentina	63	Liechtenstein	19
Aruba	2	Lithuania	2
Australia	859	Luxembourg	55
Austria	537	Malaysia	47
Azerbaijan	1	Malta	2
The Bahamas	14	Mexico	100
Bahrain	1	Monaco	15
Belarus	3	Morocco	2
Belgium	756	Namibia	1
Bermuda	2	Neth. Antilles	2
Bolivia	2	Netherlands	1,410
Brazil	113	New Zealand	136
Bulgaria	1	Nigeria	2
Canada	3,923	Norway	266
Cayman Islands	8	Pakistan	5
Chile	16	Panama	2
China, Hong Kong	548	Peru	3
China P. Rep.	163	Philippines	12
Colombia	11	Poland	13
Costa Rica	8	Portugal	12
Croatia	6	Palau	1
Cuba	3	Qatar	1
Cyprus	1	Romania	4
Czech Republic	41	Russian Federation	185
Czechoslovakia	10	Saint Kitts and Nevis	1
Denmark	509	Saudi Arabia	19
Dominica	1	Singapore	242
Dominican Repl.	5	Slovakia	4
Egypt	8	Slovenia	18
Estonia	4	South Africa	124
Finland	649	South Korea	3,472
France	4,173	Spain	318
Germany	10,822	Sri Lanka	5
Gibraltar	1	Sweden	1,738
Greece	18	Switzerland	1,458
Guatemala	2	Syria	4
Guinea	1	Taiwan	5,806
Honduras	1	Thailand	30
Hungary	38	Turkey	6
Iceland	18	Turks and Caicos Islnds	1
India	131	U.S.S.R.	1
Indonesia	14	Ukraine	17
Ireland	139	United Kingdom	4,087
Israel	836	Uruguay	1
Italy	1,967	Uzbekistan	2
Jamaica	2	Venezuela	32
Japan	32,922	Yugoslavia	4
Kazakhstan	4		
Kenya	3	Total patents issued in U.S. 2000	175,983
Kuwait	8	Total patents issued to U.S. inventors	96,920
Kyrgyzstan	1	Total patents issued to foreign inventors	79,063
Latvia	1	Foreign patents as a percentage of total	44.9%

Source: U.S. Patent and Trademark Office/TAF Data Base, 2001; www.pto.gov.

nological advancement, and ensure continued international market access. These partners do not need to be large in order to make a major contribution. Depending on the type of product, even small firms can serve as coordinating subcontractors and collaborate in product and service development, production, and distribution.

International Communications

The advances made in international communications will also have a profound impact on international management. Entire industries are becoming more footloose in their operations; that is, they are less tied to their current location in their interaction with markets. Most affected by communications advances will be members of the services sector. For example, Best Western Hotels in the United States has channeled its entire reservation system through a toll-free number that is being serviced out of the prison system in Utah. Companies could even concentrate their communications activities in other countries. Communications for worldwide operations, for example, could easily be located in Africa or Asia without impairing international corporate activities.

For manufacturers, staff in different countries can not only talk together but can also share pictures and data on their computer screens. These simultaneous interactions with different parts of the world will strengthen research and development efforts. Faster knowledge transfer will allow for the concentration of product expertise, increased division of labor, and a proliferation of global operations.

Distribution Strategies

Advances in telecommunications allow staff in different countries to talk together and share pictures and data on their computer screens. In the state-of-the-art video conference center at Hoffmann-LaRoche's U.S. headquarters in Nutley, NJ, scientists discuss research goals and results with Roche colleagues in Basel, Switzerland.

Source: Courtesy of Hoffmann-LaRoche, Inc.

Innovative distribution approaches will determine new ways of serving markets. For example, television, through QVC, has already created a shopping mall available in more than 60 million homes. The use of the Internet offers new distribution alternatives. For example, self-sustaining consumer distributor relationships emerge through, say, refrigerators that report directly to grocery store computers that they are running low on supplies and require a home delivery billed to the customer's account. Firms that are not part of such a system will simply not be able to have their offer considered for the transaction.

The link to distribution systems will also be crucial to international firms on the business-to-business level. As large retailers develop sophisticated inventory tracking and reordering systems, only the firms able to interact with such systems will remain eligible suppliers. Therefore, firms need to create their own distribution systems that are able to respond to just-in-time (JIT) and direct-order entry requirements around the globe.

More sophisticated distribution systems will, at the same time, introduce new uncertainties and fragilities into corporate planning. For example, the development of just-in-time delivery systems makes firms more efficient yet, on an international basis, also exposes them to more risk due to distribution interruptions. A strike in a faraway country may therefore be newly significant for a company that depends on the timely delivery of supplies.

International Pricing

International price competition will become increasingly heated. As their distribution spreads throughout the world, many products will take on commodity characteristics, as semiconductors did in the 1980s. Therefore, small price differentials per unit may become crucial in making an international sale. However, since many new products and technologies will address completely new needs, **forward pricing,** which distributes development expenses over the planned or anticipated volume of sales, will become increasingly difficult and controversial as demand levels are impossible to predict with any kind of accuracy.

Even for consumer products, price competition will be substantial. Because of the increased dissemination of technology, the firm that introduces a product will no longer be able to justify higher prices for long; domestically produced products will soon be of similar quality. As a result, exchange rate movements may play more significant roles in maintaining the competitiveness of the international firm. Firms can be expected to prevail on their government to manage the country's currency to maintain a favorable exchange rate. Technology also allows much closer interaction on pricing between producer and customer. The success of electronic commerce providers such as e-bay (**www.ebay.com**) or **www.priceline.com** demonstrates how auctioning and bidding, alone or in competition with others, offers new perspectives on the global price mechanism.

Through subsidization, targeting, government contracts, or other hidden forms of support, nations will attempt to stimulate their international competitiveness. Due to the price sensitivity of many products, the international manager will be forced to identify such unfair practices quickly, communicate them to his or her government, and insist on either similar benefits or government action to create an internationally level playing field.

At the same time, many firms will work hard to reduce the price sensitivity of their customers. By developing relationships with their markets rather than just carrying out transactions, other dimensions such as loyalty, consistency, the cost of shifting suppliers, and responsiveness to client needs may become much more important than price in future competition.

Careers in International Business

By studying this book you have learned about the intricacies, complexities, and thrills of international business. Of course, a career in international business is more than jet-set travel between New Delhi, Tokyo, Frankfurt, and New York. It is hard work and requires knowledge and expertise. Yet, in spite of the difficulties, international business expertise may well become a key ingredient for corporate advancement, as Global Perspective 20.3 shows.

To prepare, you should be well versed in a specific functional business area and take summer internships abroad. You should take language courses and travel, not simply for pleasure but to observe business operations abroad and gain a greater appreciation of different peoples and cultures. The following pages provide an overview of further key training and employment opportunities in the international business field.

Further Training

One option for the student on the road to more international involvement is to obtain further in-depth training by enrolling in graduate business school programs that specialize in international business education. A substantial number of universities in the United States and around the world specialize in training international managers. According to the Institute of International Education, the number of U.S. students studying for a degree at universities abroad rose to 130,000 students in 2000. Furthermore, American students increasingly go abroad for business and economics degrees, not just for a semester or two. At the same time, business and management are the most popular fields of study for the 515,000 international students at American universities.[29] A review of college catalogues and of materials from groups such as the Academy of International Business will be useful here.

In addition, as the world becomes more global, more organizations are able to assist students interested in studying abroad or in gathering foreign work experience.

GLOBAL PERSPECTIVE 20.3

Global Experience Leads to the Top

E.V. Goings, president of Tupperware, took part in a total-immersion program in Spanish—his third language—but he hardly stands out on his company's executive committee. The eight other members of the group speak two to four languages each, and all can boast of international work experience.

International exposure has long been trumpeted as essential for middle managers in multinationals, but these days, even chief executives are going global. To keep up with the growing importance of foreign markets, more companies are requiring candidates for top management positions to have strong international resumes. Victor J. Menezes, a native of Puna, India, has worked for Citigroup since 1972—in Hong Kong, China, Brussels, Latin America, and Africa—and is now head of the corporate emerging markets planning group. During a trip to a recent acquisition in Poland, Menezes met with executives: several Poles, three Indians, an Englishman, an Argentinian, a Belgian, an Irishman, and a Chinese-Singaporean—and no Americans.

Executives who climbed the corporate ladder in the past typically ran successively bigger operations of a single product line or specialized in one discipline like finance. Leaving the United States for an overseas post was often perceived as dangerous, taking executives far from the center of power. Today, however, international experience is often a top priority for executive headhunters. Executive-search firms report that major corporations required candidates with in-ternational experience in 28 percent of senior-level searches last year, up from 4 percent in 1990.

"It sends the most powerful signal you can send [to the employees] if the CEO has international experience or has been selected for that reason," says Jean-Pierre Rosso, the president and CEO of Case Corp. Rosso spent 12 years at Honeywell Inc. in France and Belgium. Dana Mead, the CEO of Tenneco Inc. and the person responsible for picking Rosso for the job, says that he "showed he could operate in both [American and French] cultures."

Combining high-profile roles abroad and at home seems to be the formula of success for many top management candidates. The Egyptian-born CEO of Goodyear Tire and Rubber, Samir Gibara, caught the eye of his predecessor Stanley Gault by turning around Goodyear's losses in its European operation in the early 1990s. Then Gibara took on several key U.S. jobs at the tire maker's Akron, Ohio, headquarters before becoming CEO.

Other types of foreign exposure can also offer executives the opportunity for great upward mobility. Expertise in the bigger and more challenging emerging markets such as Brazil, China, and India can often pave the way to success. A key reason why Andrea Jung was elected president of Avon Products Inc. was that she served the firm as president and COO of global marketing, with operating responsibility for all of Avon's global units.

 Source: Joann S. Lublin, "An Overseas Stint Can Be a Ticket to the Top," *The Wall Street Journal,* January 29, 1996, B1; Paul Beckett, "To Fuel Its Growth, Citigroup Depends on Menezes' Work in Emerging Markets," *The Wall Street Journal,* February 21, 2001, p. C1; **www.avon.com.**

 For example **www.iiepassport.org, www.studyabroad.com, www.overseasjobs.com,** or **www.egide.asso.fr** provide rich information about programs and institutions.

For those ready to enter or rejoin the "real world," different employment opportunities need to be evaluated.

Employment with a Large Firm

One career alternative in international business is to work for a large multinational corporation. These firms constantly search for personnel to help them in their international operations. Table 20.2 lists web sites that can be useful in obtaining employment internationally.

Many multinational firms, while seeking specialized knowledge such as languages, expect employees to be firmly grounded in the practice and management of business. Rarely, if ever, will a firm hire a new employee at the starting level and immediately place him or her in a position of international responsibility. Usually, a new employee is expected to become thoroughly familiar with the company's internal operations before being considered for an international position. Reasons a manager is sent abroad include that the company expects him or her to reflect the corporate spirit, to be tightly wed to the corporate culture, and to be able to communicate well with both local and corporate management personnel. In this liaison position, the manager will have to

TABLE 20.2

Web Sites Useful in Gaining International Employment

AVOTEK Headhunters
Nieuwe Markt 54
6511 XL Nijmegen,
NETHERLANDS
Telephone: 31 24 3221367
Fax: 31 24 3240467
E-mail: **avotek@tip.nl**
Lists web sites and addresses of jobs and agencies worldwide. Offers sale publications and other free reference materials.

Council Exchanges
Council on International Educational Exchange
633 3rd Avenue
New York, NY 10017
Telephone: (212) 822-2600
Fax: (212) 822-2649
E-mail: **info@councilexchanges.org**
Paid work and internships overseas for college students and recent graduates. Also offers international volunteer projects, as well as teaching positions.

Datum Online
91 Charlotte Street
London W1P 1LB,
UK
Telephone: 44 171 255 1313/1314/1320
Fax: +44 (0)171 255 1316
E-mail: **admin@datumeurope.com**
Online database providing all the resources to find IT, sales, and accountancy jobs across Europe.

Dialogue with Citizens
Internal Market Directorate General
MARKT A/04, C107 03/52
European Commission
Rue de la Loi, 200
B-1049 Brussels,
BELGIUM
Telephone: (011) 322 299-5804
Fax: (011) 322-295-6695
E-mail: **mail@europe-direct.cec.eu.int**
Factsheets on EU citizens' rights regarding residence, education, working conditions and social security, rights as a consumer, and ways of enforcing these rights, etc. Easy-to-use guides that give a general outline of EU citizens' rights and the possibilities offered by the European Single Market. A Signpost Service for citizens' practical problems.

Ed-U-Link Services
PO Box 2076
Prescott, AZ 86302
Telephone: (520) 778-5581
Fax: (520) 776-0611
E-mail: **info@edulink.com**
Provides listings of and assistance in locating teaching jobs abroad.

80 Days
E-mail: **ken@80days.com**
Links to web sites with job listings worldwide, including volunteer work and teaching English as a foreign language. Has special section on Europe.

(Continued)

TABLE 20.2

Continued

The Employment Guide's CareerWeb
150 West Brambleton Avenue
Norfolk, VA 23510
Telephone: 1-800-871-0800
Fax: (757) 616-1593
E-mail: **support@cweb.com**
Online employment source with international listings, guides, publications, etc.

Escape Artist
EscapeArtist.com Inc.
Suite 832-1245
World Trade Center
Panama,
Republic of PANAMA
Fax: 011-507-317-0139
E-mail: **headquarters@escapeartist.net**
Web site for U.S. expatriates. Contains links on overseas jobs, living abroad, offshore investing, free magazine, etc.

EuroJobs
MediaLinks
London,
UK
Telephone: 44 1903 893 302
E-mail: **medialinks@eurojobs.com**
Lists vacant jobs all over Europe. Also includes the possibility of submitting CV to recruiters; employment tips and other services.

EURopean Employment Services—EURES
Employment and Social Affairs Directorate General
EMPL A/03, BU33 02/24
European Commission
Rue de la Loi, 200
B-1049 Brussels,
BELGIUM
Telephone: (011) 322 299-6106
Fax: (011) 322 299-0508 or 295-7609
E-mail: **empl-info@cec.eu.int**
Aims to facilitate the free movement of workers within the 17 countries of the European Economic Area. Partners in the network include public employment services, trade unions, and employer organisations. The Partnership is coordinated by the European Commission. For citizens of these 17 countries, provides job listings, background information, links to employment services, and other job-related web sites in Europe.

Expat Network
International House
500 Purley Way
Croydon
Surrey CRO 4NZ,
UK
Telephone: 44 20 87605100
Fax: 44 20 8760 0469
E-mail: **expats@expatnetwork.demon.co.uk**
Dedicated to expatriates worldwide, linking to overseas jobs, country profiles, health care, expatriate, gift and bookshop plus in-depth articles and industry reports on issues which affect expatriates. Over 5,000 members. Access is restricted for nonmembers.

(Continued)

TABLE 20.2

Continued

Federation of European Employers (FedEE)
or **http://www.fedee.com**
Superla House
127 Chiltern Drive
Surbiton
Surrey, KT5 8LS,
UK
Telephone: 44 208 339 4134
Fax: 44 1359 269900
E-mail: **fedee@globalnet.co.uk**
FedEE's European Personnel Resource Centre is the most comprehensive and up-to-date source of pan-European national pay, employment law, and collective bargaining data on the web.

FlipDog.com
3210 North Canyon Road
Suite 300
Provo, UT 84604
Telephone: 801-418-7199 or 1-877-887-3547
Fax: 1-801-818-0879
E-mail: **info@flipdog.com**
Constitutes the Internet's largest job collection. In addition to U.S. coverage, includes 82,000 or so vacancies abroad. One of the most comprehensive employment search engines on the Internet.

HotJobs.com
HotJobs.com, Ltd.
406 West 31st Street
New York, NY 10001
Telephone: (212) 699-5300
Fax: (212) 944-8962
E-mail: **hotjobs-support@hotjobs.com**
Contains international job listings, including Europe.

Jobpilot
75 Cannon Street
London C4N 5BN,
UK
Telephone: 44 20 75567044
Fax: 44 20 75567501
E-mail: **info@jobpilot.co.uk**
"Europe's unlimited career market on the Internet."

Monster.com
TMP Worldwide Global Headquarters
1633 Broadway
33rd Floor
New York, NY 10019
Telephone: 1 800 MONSTER or (212) 977-4200
Fax: (212) 956-2142
Global online network for careers and working abroad. Career resources (including message boards and daily chats).

OverseasJobs.com
AboutJobs.com Network
12 Robinson Road
Sagamore Beach, MA 02562
Telephone: (508) 888-6889
E-mail: **info@OverseasJobs.com**

(Continued)

TABLE 20.2

Continued

Job seekers can search the database by keywords or locations and post a resume online for employers to view.

PlanetRecruit.com
PlanetRecruit Ltd.
Alexandria House
Covent Garden
Cambridge CBI 2HR,
UK
Telephone: 44 (870) 321 3 660
Fax: 44 (870) 321 3 661
E-mail: **support@planetrecruit.com**
One of the world's largest UK and international recruitment networks. Features accounting and finance, administrative and clerical, engineering, graduate and trainee, IT, media, new media and sales, marketing and public relations jobs from about 60 countries.

The Riley Guide
Margaret F. Dikel
11218 Ashley Drive
Rockville, MD 20852
Telephone: (301) 984-4229
Fax: (301) 984-6390
E-mail: **webmaster@rileyguide.com**
It is a directory of employment and career information sources and services on the Internet, providing instruction for job seekers and recruiters on how to use the Internet to their best advantage. Includes a section on working abroad, including in Europe.

Russian and International Employment Data Bank Online
420 7th Street, SE
Washington, DC 20003
Telephone: (202) 546-2103
Fax: (202) 546-3275
or
575 Lexington Avenue
Suite 410
New York, NY 10022
Telephone: (212) 572-8357
Fax: (212) 572-8357
E-mail: **webmaster@rusline.com**
Lists job opportunities in Europe.

SCI-IVS USA
814 NE 40th Street
Seattle, WA 98105
Telephone: (206) 545-6585
Fax: (206) 545-6585
E-mail: **scitalk@sci-ivs.org**
Through various noncommercial partner organizations worldwide and through SCI international, national and regional branch development, the U.S. branch of SCI participates in the SCI network which exchanges over 5,000 volunteers each year in short term (2–4 week) international group workcamps and in long term (3–12 months) volunteer postings in over 60 countries.

Tier21
T.I.E.R., abbreviation of "The Internet's Employment Resource," is a comprehensive directory of the Internet's employment sites. Created by Careers International for the purpose of benefiting the worldwide employment effort.

(Continued)

TABLE 20.2	**Transitions Abroad Online: Work Abroad**
Continued	PO Box 1300

Transitions Abroad Online: Work Abroad
PO Box 1300
Amherst, MA 01004-1300
Telephone: (800) 293-0373 or (413) 256-3414
Fax: (413) 256-0373
E-mail: **info@TransitionsAbroad.com**
Contains articles from its bimonthly magazine; a listing of work abroad resources (including links); lists of key employers, internship programs, volunteer programs, and English-teaching openings.

Vacation Work Publications
9 Park End Street
Oxford, OX1 1HJ,
UK
E-mail: **vacationwork@vacationwork.co.uk**
Lists job openings abroad, in addition to publishing many books on the topic. Has an information exchange section and a links section.

Upseek.com
Telephone: 1-877-587-5627
E-mail: **support@upseek.com**
A global search engine that empowers job seekers in the online job search market. Provides job opportunities from the top career and corporate sites with some European listings.

WWOOF International
WWOOF INTERNATIONAL
PO Box 2675
Lewes BN7 1RB,
UK
WWOOF INTERNATIONAL is dedicated to helping those who would like to work as volunteers on organic farms internationally.

Source: European Union, **www.eurunion.org**.

be exceptionally sensitive to both headquarters and local operations. As an intermediary, the expatriate must be empathetic, understanding, and yet fully prepared to implement the goals set by headquarters.

It is very expensive for companies to send an employee overseas. As this chapter's map shows, the annual cost of maintaining a manager overseas is often a multiple of the cost of hiring a local manager. Companies want to be sure that the expenditure is worth the benefit they will receive. Failure not only affects individual careers, but also sets back the business operations of the firm. Therefore, firms increasingly develop training programs for employees destined to go abroad.

Even if a position opens up in international operations, there is some truth in the saying that the best place to be in international business is on the same floor as the chief executive at headquarters. Employees of firms that have taken the international route often come back to headquarters to find only a few positions available for them. After spending time in foreign operations, where independence is often high and authority significant, a return to a regular job at home, which sometimes may not even call on the many skills acquired abroad, may turn out to be a difficult and deflating experience. Such encounters lead to some disenchantment with international activities as well as to financial pressures and family problems, all of which may add up to significant executive stress during reentry.[30] Since family reentry angst is one reason 25 percent of expatriates quit within one year of their return, companies are increasing the attention paid to the spouses and children of employees. For example, about

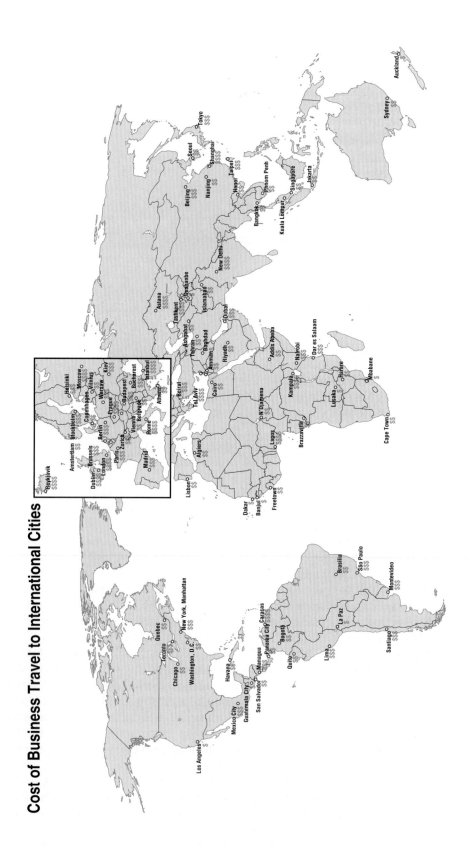

Cost of Business Travel to International Cities

$100 to $150 per diem $
$150 to $200 per diem $$
$200 to $250 per diem $$$
over $250 per diem $$$$

Source: U.S. Department of State

15 percent of Fortune 500 firms offer support for children of employees relocated abroad.[31]

Employment with a Small or Medium-Sized Firm

A second alternative is to begin work in a small or medium-sized firm. Very often, such firms have only recently developed an international outlook, and the new employee will arrive on the "ground floor." Initial involvement will normally be in the export field—evaluating potential foreign customers, preparing quotes, and dealing with activities such as shipping and transportation. With a very limited budget, the export manager will only occasionally visit international markets to discuss business strategies with distributors abroad. Most of the work will be done by mail, by fax, by e-mail, or by telephone. The hours are often long because of the need, for example, to reach a contact during business hours in Hong Kong. Yet the possibilities for implementing creative business transactions are virtually limitless. It is also gratifying and often rewarding that one's successful contribution will be visible directly through the firm's growing export volume.

Alternatively, international work in a small firm may involve importing; that is, finding low-cost sources that can be substituted for domestically sourced products. Decisions often must be based on limited information, and the manager is faced with many uncertainties. Often things do not work out as planned. Shipments are delayed, letters of credit are canceled, and products almost never arrive in exactly the form and shape anticipated. Yet the problems are always new and offer an ongoing challenge.

As a training ground for international activities, there probably is no better starting place than a small or medium-sized firm. Later on, the person with some experience may find work with a trading or export management company, resolving other people's problems and concentrating almost exclusively on the international arena.

Self-Employment

A third alternative is to hang up a consultant's shingle or to establish a trading firm. Many companies are in need of help for their international business efforts and are prepared to part with a portion of their profits in order to receive it. Yet it requires in-depth knowledge and broad experience to make a major contribution from the outside or to successfully run a trading firm.

Specialized services that might be offered by a consultant include international market research, international strategic planning, or, particularly desirable, beginning-to-end assistance for international entry or international negotiations. For an international business expert, the hourly billable rate typically is as high as $400 for principals and $150 for staff. Whenever international travel is required, overseas activities are often billed at the daily rate of $2,000 plus expenses. Even at such high rates, solid groundwork must be completed before all the overhead is paid. The advantage of this career option is the opportunity to become a true international entrepreneur. Consultants and those who conduct their own export-import or foreign direct investment activities work at a higher degree of risk than those who are not self-employed, but they have an opportunity for higher rewards.

Opportunities for Women in Global Management

As firms become more and more involved in global business activities, the need for skilled global managers is growing. Concurrent with this increase in business activity is the ever growing presence and managerial role of women in international business.

Research conducted during the mid-1980s[32] indicated that women held 3.3 percent of the overseas positions in U.S. business firms. Five years prior to that time, almost no women were global managers in either expatriate or professional travel status. Thus,

the 3.3 percent figure represented a significant increase. By 2000, 13 percent of expatriates in U.S. corporations were women.[33] The reason for the low participation of women in global management roles seems to have been the assumption that because of the subservient roles of women in Japan, Latin America, and the Middle East, neither local nor expatriate women would be allowed to succeed as managers. The error is that expatriates are not seen as local women, but rather as "foreigners who happen to be women," thus solving many of the problems that would be encountered by a local woman manager.

There appear to be some distinct advantages for a woman in a management position overseas. Among them are the advantages of added visibility and increased access to clients. Foreign clients tend to assume that "expatriate women must be excellent, or else their companies would not have sent them."

It also appears that companies that are larger in terms of sales, assets, income, and employees send more women overseas than smaller organizations. Further, the number of women expatriates is not evenly distributed among industry groups. Industry groups that utilize greater numbers or percentages of women expatriates include banking, electronics, petroleum, publishing, diversified corporations, pharmaceuticals, and retailing and apparel.

For the future, it is anticipated that the upward trend previously cited reflects increased participation of women in global management roles in the future.

Summary

This final chapter has provided an overview of the environmental changes facing international managers and alternative managerial response to the changes. International business is a complex and difficult activity, yet it affords many opportunities and challenges. Observing changes and analyzing how to best incorporate them in the international business mission is the most important task of the international manager. If the international environment were constant, there would be little challenge to international business. The frequent changes are precisely what make international business so fascinating and often highly profitable for those who are active in the field.

Key Terms and Concepts

environmental protection	population stabilization	trigger mechanisms	mass customization
international debt load	online	trade policy measures	forward pricing
population increase			

Questions for Discussion

1. For many developing countries, debt repayment and trade are closely linked. What does protectionism mean to them?

2. Should one worry about the fact that the United States is a debtor nation?

3. How would our lives and our society change if imports were banned?

Internet Exercises

1. Using the web site of Living Abroad (**www.livingabroad. com**), research several international schools that may interest you. What are the most interesting links to other web sites concerning international issues? Why are you particularly interested in them?

2. The website **www.overseasjobs.com** provides valuable information for those interested in jobs overseas. What skills do international employers seem to value most? Peruse the job listings and find several jobs that you might be interested in. Also take a look at the profiles of several international companies that you might be interested in working for. What characteristics do the international firms listed here possess?

Recommended Readings

Adler, Nancy J., Rob Bloom, and John Szilagyi. *From Boston to Beijing:* Cincinnati, OH: South-Western College Publishing, 2001.

Chandler, Alfred D., Jr., and James W. Cortada, eds. *A Nation Transformed by Information.* Oxford: Oxford University Press, 2001.

Czinkota, Michael R., and Ilkka A. Ronkainen, eds. *Best Practices in International Business.* Fort Worth, TX: Harcourt, 2001.

Friedman, Thomas L. *The Lexus and the Olive Tree: Understanding Globalization.* Wilmington, NC: Anchor Books, 2000.

Giddens, Anthony. *Runaway World: How Globalization Is Reshaping Our Lives.* London, England: Routledge, 2000.

Khosrow, Fatemi, and Katemi Khosrow, eds. *The New World Order.* New York, NY: Elsevier Science Ltd., 2000.

Luttwak, Edward. *Turbo-Capitalism: Winners & Losers in the Global Economy.* Cambridge, MA: MIT Press, 2000.

Micklethwait, John, and Adrian Woolridge. *A Future Perfect: The Challenge and Hidden Promise of Globalization.* New York, NY: Times Books, 2000.

Mittelman, James H. *The Globalization Syndrome,* Princeton, NJ: Princeton University Press, 2000.

Omae, Kenichi. *The Invisible Continent: Four Strategic Imperatives of the New Economy.* New York, NY: Harperbusiness, 2000.

World Investment Prospects. London: Economist Intelligence Unit, 2001.

Yaprak, Attila, and Hülya Tütek. *Globalization, the Multinational Firm, and Emerging Economies: Advances in International Marketing.* New York, NY: JAI Press, 2000.

Notes

1. William Lazer and Eric H. Shaw, "Global Marketing Management: At the Dawn of the New Millennium," *Journal of International Marketing,* 8, 1, (2000): 65–77.

2. The information presented here is based largely on an original Delphi study by Michael R. Czinkota and Ilkka A. Ronkainen utilizing an international panel of experts. More details can be found in: M.R. Czinkota and I. A. Ronkainen, "International Business and Trade in the Next Decade: Report from a Delphi Study," *Journal of International Business Studies* 28, 4 (Fourth Quarter 1997): 827–844.

3. Reiner Springer, and Michael R. Czinkota, "Marketing's Contribution to the Transformation of Central and Eastern Europe," *Thunderbird International Business Review,* 41, 1 (1999): 29–48.

4. James D. Wolfensohn, President, World Bank, Opening Statement at the Annual Meeting of the World Bank, Prague, September 2000.

5. William B. Johnston, "Global Workforce 2000: The New World Labor Market," *Harvard Business Review* (March–April 1991): 115–127.

6. "Business and Political Leaders Discuss Digital Divide," *World Economic Forum,* Davos, www.worldeconomicforum.org, February 2, 2001.

7. "The Corporation and the Public: Open for Inspection," *World Economic Forum,* January 27, 2001, www.worldeconomicforum.org, February 2, 2001.

8. John Pomfret, "Chinese Industry Races to Make Global Name for Itself," *The Washington Post,* April 23, 2000, H1.

9. Robert A. Blecker, "The Ticking Debt Bomb: The U.S. International Financial Position Is Not Sustainable," *Economic Policy Institute,* Washington, DC, June 29, 1999.

10. Catherine L. Mann, "Is the U.S. Trade Deficit Still Sustainable," *Institute for International Economics,* Washington, DC, March 1, 2001.

11. Murray Weidenbaum, "All the World's a Stage," *Management Review,* October 1999. 147–48.

12. www.globalreach.com, March 5, 2001.

13. "Falling Through the Net: Toward Digital Inclusion," U.S. Department of Commerce, Washington, DC, October 2000.

14. "Digital Economy 2000," U.S. Department of Commerce, Washington, DC, 2000.

15. "Bridging the Digital Divide: Internet Access in Central and Eastern Europe," The Center for Democracy and Technology, www.cdt.org, Washington, DC, March 5, 2001.

16. John Ouelch, "Global Village People," *Worldlink Magazine,* January/February 1999, www.worldlink.co.uk.

17. Renato Ruggiero, "The New Frontier," *WorldLink,* January/February 1998, www.worldlink.co.uk.

18. Minoru Makihara, Co-Chairman of the Annual Meeting of the World Economic Forum, Davos 2001, www.worldeconomicforum.org.

19. Polly Campbell, "Trend Watch 2001," *The Edward Lowe Report,* January 2001, 1–3.

20. Michael R. Czinkota, "The Policy Gap in International Marketing," *Journal of International Marketing,* 8, 1 (2000): 99–111.

21. Labour Force Statistics, 1976–2000, Paris, OECD, 2001.

22. Michael R. Czinkota, "Rich Neighbors, Poor Relations," *Marketing Management* (spring 1994): 46–52.

23. Michael R. Czinkota and Masaaki Kotabe, "The Role of Japanese Distribution Strategies," *Japanese Distribution Strategy,* M.R. Czinkota and M. Kotabe, eds. (London: Business Press, 2000): 6–16.

24. *U.S. Manufacturers in the Global Marketplace* (New York: The Conference Board, 1994).

25. "The Corporation and the Public: Open for Inspection," World Economic Forum, www.worldeconomicforum.org, February 2, 2001.

26. Benn R. Konsynski and Jahangir Karimi, "On the Design of Global Information Systems," in *Globalization, Technology, and Competition: The Fusion of Computers and Telecommu-*

nications in the 1990s, ed. S. Bradley, J. Hausman, and R. Nolan (Boston: 1993): 81–108.

27. Michael R. Czinkota and Masaaki Kotabe, *Marketing Management* 2d ed., (Cincinnati: South-Western College Publishing, 2001), 234–235.

28. Michael R. Czinkota and Masaaki Kotabe, "Product Development the Japanese Way," in *Trends in International Business: Critical Perspectives,* ed. M. Czinkota and M. Kotabe (Oxford: Blackwell Publishing 1998), 153–158.

29. Institute of International Education, *Open Doors,* Internet Document, March 5, 2001. **www.iie.org.**

30. Michael G. Harvey, "Repatriation of Corporate Executives: An Empirical Study," *Journal of International Business Studies* 20 (spring 1989): 131–144.

31. Joann S. Lublin, "To Smooth a Transfer Abroad, a New Focus on Kids," *The Wall Street Journal,* January 26, 1999: B1, B14.

32. Nancy J. Adler, "Women in International Management: Where are They?" *California Management Review* 26, 4 (1984): 78–89.

33. "U.S. Woman in Global Business Face Glass Borders," *Catalyst Perspective,* November 2000, **www.catalystwomen.org.**

PART I

IKEA: Furnishing the World

IKEA, the world's largest home furnishings retail chain, was founded in Sweden in 1943 as a mail-order company and opened its first showroom ten years later. From its headquarters in Almhult, IKEA has since expanded to worldwide sales of $8.64 billion from 159 outlets in 30 countries (see Table 1). In fact, the second store that IKEA built was in Oslo, Norway. Today, IKEA operates large warehouse showrooms in Sweden, Norway, Denmark, Holland, France, Belgium, Germany, Switzerland, Austria, Finland, Italy, Canada, the United States, Saudi Arabia, Spain, and the United Kingdom. It has smaller stores in Kuwait, United Arab Emirates, Australia, Hong Kong, Singapore, Malaysia, Taiwan, the Canary Islands, and Iceland. A store near Budapest, Hungary, opened in 1990, followed by outlets in Poland and the Czech Republic in 1991 and Slovakia in 1992. Stores were opened in China in 1998. The first store opened in Russia in 2000, and in Israel in 2001. IKEA first appeared on the Internet in 1997 with the World Wide Living Room web site. The IKEA Group's new organization has three regions: Europe, North America, and Asia-Pacific.

The international expansion of IKEA has progressed in three phases, all of them continuing at the present time: Scandinavian expansion, begun in 1963; West European expansion, begun in 1973; and North American expansion, begun in 1976. Of the individual markets, Germany is the largest, accounting for 21.6, followed by the U.K. at 12.3 percent of company sales. The phases of expansion are detectable in the worldwide sales shares depicted in Figure 1. "We want to bring the IKEA concept to as many people as possible," IKEA officials have said. The company estimates that over 250 million people visit its showrooms annually.

Source: This case, prepared by Ilkka A. Ronkainen, is based on "Oma Tuotanto Vahvistuu," *Kauppalehti*, March 9, 2001, 5; "Furnishing the World," *The Economist* (November 19, 1994): 79; Richard Norman and Rafael Ramirez, "From Value Chain to Value Constellation: Designing Interactive Strategy," *Harvard Business Review* 71 (July/August 1993): 65–77; "IKEA's No-Frills Strategy Extends to Management Style." *Business International* (May 18, 1992): 149–150; Bill Saporito, "IKEA's Got 'Em Lining Up," *Fortune* (March 11, 1991): 72; Rita Martenson, "Is Standardization of Marketing Feasible in Culture-Bound Industries? A European Case Study," *International Marketing Review* 4 (Autumn 1987): 7–17; Eleanor Johnson Tracy, "Shopping Swedish Style Comes to the U.S.," *Fortune*, (January 27, 1986): 63–67; Mary Krienke, "IKEA—Simple Good Taste," *Stores* (April 1986): 58; Jennifer Lin, "IKEA's U.S. Translation," *Stores* (April 1986): 63; "Furniture Chain Has a Global View," *Advertising Age* (October 26, 1987): 58; Bill Kelley, "The New Wave from Europe," *Sales & Marketing Management* (November 1987): 46–48. Updated information available from **http://www.ikea.com.**

The IKEA Concept

Ingvar Kamprad, the founder, formulated as IKEA's mission to "offer a wide variety of home furnishings of good design and function at prices so low that the majority of people can afford to buy them." The principal target market of IKEA, which is similar across countries and regions in which IKEA has a presence, is composed of people who are young, highly educated, liberal in their cultural values, white-collar workers, and not especially concerned with status symbols.

IKEA follows a standardized product strategy with a universally accepted assortment around the world. Today, IKEA carries an assortment of thousands of different home furnishings that range from plants to pots, sofas to soup spoons, and wine glasses to wallpaper. The smaller items are carried to complement the bigger ones. IKEA has very limited manufacturing of its own, but designs all of its furniture. The network of subcontracted manufacturers numbers nearly 1,960 in 53 different countries.

IKEA's strategy is based on cost leadership secured by contract manufacturers, many of which are in low-labor-cost countries and close to raw materials, yet accessible to logistics links. High-volume production of standardized items allows for significant economies of scale. In exchange for long-term contracts, leased equipment, and technical support from IKEA, the suppliers manufacture exclusively at low prices for IKEA. IKEA's designers work with the suppliers to build savings-generating features into the production and products from the outset.

IKEA has some of its production as well, constituting 10 percent of its total sales. While new facilities were opened in 2000 in Latvia, Poland, and Romania to bring the total number to 30, IKEA plans to have its own production not exceed 10 percent, mainly to secure flexibility.

Manufacturers are responsible for shipping the components to large distribution centers, for example, to the central one in Almhult. These twelve distribution centers then supply the various stores, which are in effect mini-warehouses.

IKEA consumers have to become "prosumers"—half producers, half consumers—because most products have to be assembled. The final distribution is the customer's responsibility as well. Although IKEA expects its customers to be active participants in the buy-sell process, they are not rigid about it. There is a "moving boundary" between what consumers do for themselves and what IKEA employees will do for them. Consumers save the most by

			TABLE I	IKEA's International Expansion

Year	Outlets[a]	Countries[a]	Coworkers	Catalog Circulation[b]	Turnover in Swedish Crowns[c]
1954	1	1	15	285,000	3,000,000
1964	2	2	250	1,200,000	79,000,000
1974	10	5	1,500	13,000,000	616,000,000
1984	66	17	8,300	45,000,000	6,770,000,000
1988	75	19	13,400	50,535,000	14,500,000,000
1990	95	23	16,850	n.a.	19,400,000,000
1992	119	24	23,200	n.a.	24,275,000,000
1995	131	27	30,500	n.a.	38,557,000,000
1997	142	28	36,400	n.a.	45,820,000,000
2000	159	30	61,700	n.a.	81,187,000,000

[a]Stores/countries being opened by 2000.

[b]17 languages, 38 editions; exact number no longer made available.

[c]Corresponding to net sales of the IKEA group of companies.

Source: **www.ikea.com**

driving to the warehouses themselves, putting the boxes on the trolley, loading them into their cars, driving home, and assembling the furniture. Yet IKEA can arrange to provide these services at an extra charge. For example, IKEA co-operates with car rental companies to offer vans and small trucks at reasonable rates for customers needing delivery

FIGURE I

IKEA's Worldwide Sales Expressed as Percentages of Turnover by Market Unit

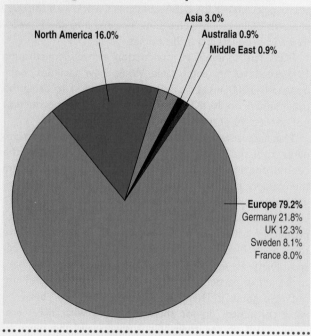

service. Additional economies are reaped from the size of the IKEA outlets; for example, the Philadelphia store is 169,000 square feet (15,700 square meters). IKEA stores include babysitting areas and cafeterias and are therefore intended to provide the value-seeking, car-borne consumer with a complete shopping destination. IKEA managers state that their competitors are not other furniture outlets but all attractions vying for the consumers' free time. By not selling through dealers, the company hears directly from its customers.

Management believes that its designer-to-user relationship affords an unusual degree of adaptive fit. IKEA has "forced both customers and suppliers to think about value in a new way in which customers are also suppliers (of time, labor information, and transportation), suppliers are also customers (of IKEA's business and technical services), and IKEA itself is not so much a retailer as the central star in a constellation of services." Figure 2 provides a presentation of IKEA's value chain.

Although IKEA has concentrated on company-owned, larger-scale outlets, franchising has been used in areas in which the market is relatively small or where uncertainty may exist as to the response to the IKEA concept. These markets include Hong Kong and the United Arab Emirates. IKEA uses mail order in Europe and Canada but has resisted expansion into the United States, mainly because of capacity constraints.

IKEA offers prices that are 30 to 50 percent lower than fully assembled competing products. This is a result of large-quantity purchasing, low-cost logistics, store location in suburban areas, and the do-it-yourself approach to marketing. IKEA's prices do vary from market to market, largely because of fluctuations in exchange rates and differences in

FIGURE 2

IKEA's Value Chain

Source: Richard Norman and Rafael Ramirez, "From Value Chain to Value Constellation: Designing Interactive Strategy," *Harvard Business Review* 71 (July/August 1993): 72.

taxation regimes, but price positioning is kept as standardized as possible.

IKEA's promotion is centered on the catalog. The IKEA catalog is printed in thirteen languages and has a worldwide circulation of well over 50 million copies. The catalogs are uniform in layout except for minor regional differences. The company's advertising goal is to generate word-of-mouth publicity through innovative approaches. The IKEA concept is summarized in Table 2.

IKEA in the Competitive Environment

IKEA's strategy positioning is unique. As Figure 3 illustrates, few furniture retailers anywhere have engaged in long-term planning or achieved scale economies in production. European furniture retailers, especially those in Sweden, Switzerland, Germany, and Austria, are much smaller than IKEA. Even when companies have joined forces as buying groups, their heterogeneous operations have made it diffi-

cult for them to achieve the same degree of coordination and concentration as IKEA. Because customers are usually content to wait for the delivery of furniture, retailers have not been forced to take purchasing risks.

The value-added dimension differentiates IKEA from its competition. IKEA offers limited customer assistance but creates opportunities for consumers to choose (for example, through informational signage), transport, and assemble units of furniture. The best summary of the competitive situation was provided by a manager at another firm: "We can't do what IKEA does, and IKEA doesn't want to do what we do."

IKEA in the United States

After careful study and assessment of its Canadian experience, IKEA decided to enter the U.S. market in 1985 by establishing outlets on the East Coast and, in 1990, one in Burbank, California. In 2000, a total of fifteen stores (seven in the Northeast, six in California, one in Seattle, and one in Texas) generated sales of over $800 million. (10.5 percent of worldwide). The stores employ over 4,000 workers. The overwhelming level of success in 1987 led the company to invest in a warehousing facility near Philadelphia that receives goods from Sweden as well as directly from suppliers around the world. Plans call for two to three additional stores annually over the next twenty-five years, concentrating on the northeastern United States and California.

Success today has not come without compromises. "If you are going to be the world's best furnishing company, you have to show you can succeed in America, because there is so much to learn here," said Goran Carstedt, head of North American operations. Whereas IKEA's universal approach had worked well in Europe, the U.S. market proved to be different. In some cases, European products conflicted with American tastes and preferences. For example, IKEA

TABLE 2   The IKEA Concept

Target market:	"Young people of all ages"
Product:	IKEA offers the same products worldwide. The number of active articles is 12,000. The countries of origin of these products are: Europe (75 percent), Asia (22 percent), and North America (3 percent). Most items have to be assembled by the customer. The furniture design is modern and light.
Distribution:	IKEA has built its own distribution network. Outlets are outside the city limits of major metropolitan areas. Products are not delivered, but IKEA cooperates with car rental companies that offer small trucks. IKEA offers mail order in Europe and Canada.
Pricing:	The IKEA concept is based on low price. The firm tries to keep its price-image constant.
Promotion:	IKEA's promotional efforts are mainly through its catalogs. IKEA has developed a prototype communications model that must be followed by all stores. Its advertising is attention-getting and provocative. Media choices vary by market.

Competition in Furniture Retailing

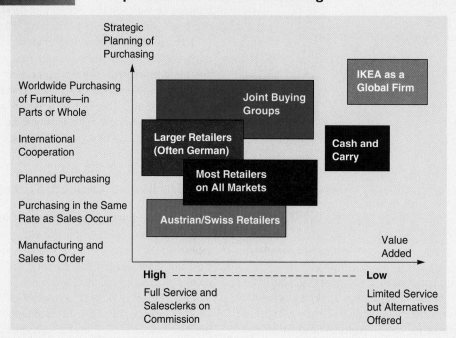

Source: Rita Martenson, "Is Standardization of Marketing Feasible in Culture-Bound Industries? A European Case Study." *International Marketing Review* 4 (Autumn 1987): 14.

did not sell matching bedroom suites that consumers wanted. Kitchen cupboards were too narrow for the large dinner plates needed for pizza. Some Americans were buying IKEA's flower vases for glasses.

Adaptations were made. IKEA managers adjusted chest drawers to be an inch or two deeper because consumers wanted to store sweaters in them. Sales of chests increased immediately by 40 percent. In all, IKEA has redesigned approximately a fifth of its product range in North America. Today, 45 percent of the furniture in the stores in North America is produced locally, up from 15 percent in the early 1990s. In addition to not having to pay expensive freight costs from Europe, this has also helped in cut stock-outs. And because Americans hate standing in lines, store layouts have been changed to accommodate new cash registers. IKEA offers a more generous return policy in North America than in Europe, as well as next-day delivery service.

In hindsight, IKEA executives are saying they "behaved like exporters, which meant not really being in the country. . . . It took us time to learn this." IKEA's adaptation has not meant destroying its original formula. Their approach is still to market the streamlined and contemporary Scandinavian style to North America by carrying a universally accepted product range but with a mind on product lines and features that appeal to local preferences. The North American experience has caused the company to start remixing its formula elsewhere as well. Indeed, now that Europeans are adopting some American furnishing concepts (such as sleeper sofas), IKEA is transferring some American concepts to other markets such as Europe.

Questions for Discussion

1. What has allowed IKEA to be successful with a relatively standardized product and product line in a business with strong cultural influence? Did adaptations to this strategy in the North American market constitute a defeat to their approach?
2. Which features of the "young people of all ages" are universal and can be exploited by a global/regional strategy?
3. Is IKEA destined to succeed everywhere it cares to establish itself?

Substituting U.S. Tobacco Exports for Domestic Consumption

Tobacco and its related products have traditionally played an important role in the U.S. economy. In 1997, tobacco represented the fifth largest cash crop in the United States. Twenty-three U.S. states and Puerto Rico grow tobacco, twenty-one states manufacture tobacco products, thirty-three states export tobacco, and all fifty states are engaged in the marketing of tobacco products.

In 1964, the *Surgeon General's Report* documented the adverse health effects of smoking. Since then, many medical experts have repeatedly warned the public that smoking causes lung cancer, low birth weights, and other health problems. As a result of increased awareness of the consequences of smoking, U.S. cigarette consumption, as well as other forms of tobacco use, have been gradually decreasing. Although health considerations played an important role in discouraging smoking, other factors such as higher cigarette prices, steeper federal and local taxes, and governmental restrictions on smoking in public places also contributed to this decline. Since reaching a peak in 1981, total U.S. cigarette consumption declined by nearly 25 percent, and per capita consumption by 32 percent. In 1999, U.S. cigarette consumption was more than 435 billion cigarettes, accounting for over $68 billion in sales.

The Importance of Tobacco for the U.S. Economy

Taxes on tobacco products contribute significantly to government income and help reduce the budget deficit. As the number of smokers has declined, the government has raised the cigarette tax in order to preserve the level of tax revenues from smoking. The cigarette tax was raised from 8 cents per pack of twenty cigarettes in the period between 1951 and 1982 to 16 cents from 1983 to 1990. By January of 2002, the federal cigarette excise tax will have reached 39 cents per pack. In 1999, the tobacco production and related industries contributed over $34 billion to

Source: This study was prepared by Michael R. Czinkota and Anna Starikovsky, using the following background material: Foreign Agricultural Service statistics; "World Cigarette Situation" by the FAS; "Tobacco Industry Profile 1995" by the Tobacco Institute; Glenn Frankel, "U.S. Aided Cigarette Firms in Conquests Across Asia," *The Washington Post,* November 17, 1996; Saundra Torry and John Schwartz, "Contrite Tobacco Executives Admit Health Risks Before Congress," *Washington Post,* January 30, 1998: A14; Chip Jones, "Cigarette Farmers to Buy Less Leaf," *Richmond Times-Dispatch,* December 3, 1997: A1; John M. Broder, "Cigarette Makers Reach $368 Billion Accord," *New York Times,* June 21, 1997.

government revenues in excise, sales, personal income, and corporate taxes. Of this amount, well over $5 billion was generated by the federal excise tax on tobacco and over $12 billion by state and local taxes. This means that almost 50% of the retail price of tobacco products in the U.S. ends up in the treasuries of the federal and local governments (see Figure 1).

According to a study conducted by Tobacco USA, the tobacco industry, including growers, manufacturers, distributors, and core suppliers, employed over 600,000 people in 1999. In addition, another 759,000 jobs were generated as a result of the tobacco industry's expenditures such as promotion and transportation.

The Importance of Tobacco Exports

In the face of their diminishing domestic market, U.S. tobacco companies are vigorously promoting cigarette exports. Developing countries are the home to most of the world's smokers and are therefore the number one target for cigarette exports (see Table 1). The international cigarette market is dominated by U.S. brands (see Table 2). However, U.S. companies would be able to sell even more cigarettes in developing countries if their products were free of import restrictions.

In the peak year of 1996, the U.S. tobacco industry produced 754 billion pieces of cigarettes. In the same year cigarette exports totaled about 241 billion pieces. The exports of tobacco and trade manufactures resulted in a $5.3 billion surplus in the 1996 trade balance for this group of products, about one-fourth of the surplus in all agricultural products.

In 2000, the tobacco industry has produced 536 billion pieces, exports have fallen by nearly $100 billion cigarettes and the trade surplus has shrunk considerably to $4.1 billion due to lower demand and higher offshore production by domestic manufacturers (see Figure 2). Also, the relatively expensive U.S. leaf tobacco is being replaced in many recessionary countries by lesser-grade tobacco leaf grown abroad. Even though the U.S. is still the third leading exporter of leaf tobacco, countries are demonstrating their willingness to sacrifice quality for lower prices by buying leaf tobacco from Brazil, Zimbabwe, and Malawi. U.S. firms exported to 106 countries in 2000. The leading destinations for these exports were Belgium-Luxembourg (from there, cigarettes are distributed to individual EU countries), Japan, Saudi Arabia, Cyprus, Lebanon, Israel, and Singapore.

FIGURE 1

Federal Excise and Sales Tax Collections on Domestic Tobacco Sales (in Millions of Dollars)

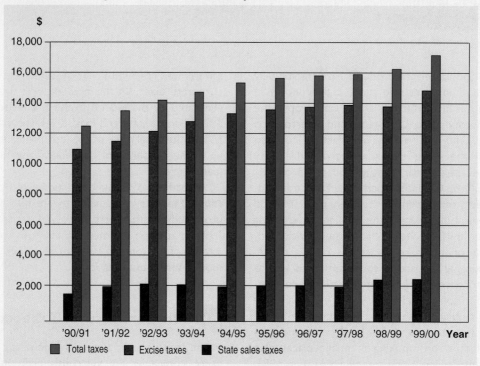

U.S. Trade Policy

Tobacco-related revenue is an important source of income for the governments of many countries. As a result, many nations have traditionally blocked the import of cigarettes by imposing high import tariffs, discriminatory taxes, and restrictive marketing and distribution practices. Japan, China, South Korea, and Thailand even set up state monopolies to produce cigarettes. Throughout the 1980s, the Asian tigers were running huge trade surpluses with the United States. When the U.S. annual trade deficit reached a record high of $123 billion in 1984, the Reagan administration turned to the Office of the U.S. Trade Representative (USTR), a federal agency under the Executive Office of the president. Section 301 of the 1974 Trade Act empowered the USTR to investigate unfair trading practices by foreign countries

toward U.S. exporters and required that the U.S. government impose sanctions if the foreign government found at fault in its trade policy toward U.S. firms does not make changes within one year.

As U.S. tobacco products were among the most restricted goods, the USTR soon turned its attention to this case of foreign trade discrimination. The scrutiny was aided

TABLE 2

Leading International Brands Sold Outside the North American Market (Manufactured in the U.S. and Other Countries)

Brand	Producer
Marlboro	Philip Morris
Mild Seven	Japan Tobacco
Winston	R.J. Reynolds
L&M	Philip Morris
Camel	R.J. Reynolds
Benson & Hedges	PM/BAT/AB
Gaulloise	Gaulloise
Bond Street	Philip Morris
SE555	British American Tobacco
Philip Morris	Philip Morris

TABLE 1

Estimated Number of Smokers (in Millions of Persons)

	Men	Women
Developed Countries	200	100
Developing Countries	700	100

FIGURE 2

U.S. Trade in Tobacco and Tobacco Manufactures (SITC Product Group No. 12) (in Millions of Dollars)

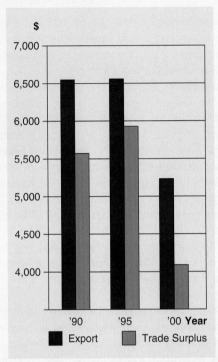

Source: Bureau of the Census, February 2001

by the fact that Japan, South Korea, and Thailand were signatories to the General Agreement on Tariffs and Trade (GATT), and Taiwan was interested in joining as well. By their discriminatory policies toward U.S. cigarette imports, these countries violated the free trade principles they had agreed to respect under the GATT. In September 1985, the White House filed a complaint with the USTR under the Section 301 against Japanese restrictions on the sale of cigarettes. After a long series of negotiations and mounting pressure from the U.S. government, in September 1986, Japan gave in and allowed imports of U.S. cigarettes. Almost immediately, cigarettes rose from the fortieth to the second most-advertised product on Tokyo television. Imported brands currently control 24.7% of the Japanese market with 82.1 billion in annual sales. In 2000, the U.S. share accounted for 94% of the import market.

In January 1988, the U.S. tobacco industry filed a 301 complaint with the USTR against South Korea. The USTR's efforts were supported by members of Congress from tobacco states. In July 1987, even before the USTR initiated its investigation, senators Dole (Kansas), Helms (North Carolina), Gore (Tennessee), and others wrote to the president of South Korea and demanded that U.S. companies be allowed to import and advertise tobacco products. The

pressure on the South Korean government was intensified by a strong lobby in Seoul paid for by R.J. Reynolds and Philip Morris. In May 1988, Seoul agreed to the import of U.S. cigarettes and lifted its ban on cigarette advertising. Within one year, U.S. companies acquired more than 6 percent of the South Korean cigarette market. Taiwan was a similar story. Foreign brands went from 1 percent of the market to 20 percent within two years of the country's opening to cigarette imports in 1986. Thailand liberalized the market for imported cigarettes in August 1991. As a result, imports of foreign brands doubled in 1992 and rose again by 43 percent in 1993.

China is the world's largest cigarette producer and consumer. In 2000 there were 350 million smokers in China who burned up nearly one-third of the annual 5.43 trillion world cigarette consumption. Although per-capita use is slowly declining, overall Chinese consumption is increasing due to the growing population. All Chinese cigarettes are produced by a state monopoly. Because the Chinese government is eager to acquire advanced technology and marketing know-how from the West, it offered limited partnerships to a few foreign cigarette producers, including R.J. Reynolds and Philip Morris. Taxes from cigarette sales raise 12 percent of the Chinese government's annual revenue. As a consequence, the government wants to continue to protect its state monopoly from foreign competition. In 1992, the USTR negotiated an agreement under which China promised to eliminate tariffs and other trade barriers on U.S. cigarette imports within two years. However, the Chinese government has not enforced the agreement.

With the opening of the markets of the former Soviet Union and Eastern Europe at the beginning of the 1990s, U.S. tobacco manufacturers found new opportunities for expansion. With 60 percent of their populations smoking, Hungary, Poland, Bulgaria, the former Yugoslav republics, the Czech Republic, and Slovakia are among the top ten nations in per capita cigarette consumption. Armenia, Georgia, Azerbaijan, Russia, Ukraine, and Moldova rank among the top twenty. Unlike in Asia in the 1980s, U.S. companies are welcomed here as contributors of new technology and scarce investment funds. As part of the privatization process in the formerly communist countries, U.S. cigarette producers were able to buy previously state-owned cigarette factories and are quickly gaining ground in these new markets. Also, these producers are developing infrastructure in these countries with the long-term goal of moving production there due to a more advantageous cost structure and more supportive tax regulations. Some analysts project that over the next decade, Western tobacco manufacturers will gain control over the entire East European cigarette market, which will more than make up for the revenues lost at home.

In addition to these market developments, the conclusion of the Uruguay Round in 1992 and the founding of the World Trade Organization (WTO) brought a number of positive developments for the U.S. tobacco export industry: the European Union agreed to cut export subsidies and reduce tariffs on both unmanufactured and manufactured tobacco, Japan promised to maintain zero duty on cigarettes and to lower duty on cigars, and New Zealand reduced its tariff on cigarettes. Finally, with the protocol on China's participation in the WTO signed in February of 2001, the decrease in tariffs and quotas will allow tobacco exports to enter and penetrate the Chinese cigarette market.

Government Support of the Tobacco Industry

The U.S. Department of Agriculture (USDA) administers laws to stabilize tobacco production and prices. According to the Tobacco Institute, without this regulation, more tobacco would be produced and prices would be lower. In 2000, the Commodity Credit Corporation, an agency established in 1933 to administer commodity stabilization programs for the USDA, made new loans to tobacco farmers of an estimated $395 billion. These loans are to be repaid with interest as collateral tobacco is sold. The only direct cost incurred to the taxpayers is the administrative cost of this program, which is estimated at $15 million for 2001.

Until the late 1980s, the U.S. government was in strong support of the tobacco industry. It funded three export promotion programs: the Foreign Market Development Program (also known as the Cooperator Program), the Targeted Export Assistance Program, and the Export Credit Guarantee programs. The most important of these were the Export Credit Guarantee Programs administered by the Commodity Credit Corporation (CCC) of the Department of Agriculture. Under these programs, the CCC underwrote credit extended by the private banking sector in the United States to approved foreign banks, to pay for tobacco and other agricultural products sold by U.S. firms to foreign buyers. Between October 1985 and September 1989, sixty-six companies received guarantees of credits under these programs for the sale of 127 million pounds of tobacco with a market value of $214 million. The Targeted Export Assistance Program's purpose was to counteract the adverse effects of subsidies, import quotas, or other unfair trade practices on U.S. agricultural products. Under this program, Tobacco Associates, a private organization entrusted to carry out this endeavor, received $5 million in funding in 1990 to provide certain countries with the technical know-how, training, and equipment to manufacture cigarettes that use U.S. tobacco. In addition, Tobacco Associates received funds from the USDA to promote market development activities for U.S. tobacco products.

Currently, the U.S. government no longer funds export promotion programs related to tobacco and tobacco manufactures. All government programs that used to help the U.S. tobacco industry to enter foreign markets have been eliminated since 1990, under the Bush and Clinton administrations. For example, the CCC still supports the income and price of tobacco received by farmers, but it no longer assists in the exports of tobacco.

Conflicting Objectives

The past involvement of the U.S. government in furthering the export of tobacco has generated controversy within the United States. The U.S. government, spearheaded by the Department of Health and Human Services, has been actively discouraging smoking on the domestic scene. In addition, the United States is a strong supporter of the worldwide antismoking movement. The Department of Health and Human Services serves as a collaborating headquarters for the United Nations World Health Organization and maintains close relationships with other health organizations around the world in sharing information on the detrimental health effects of smoking.

During congressional hearings in April 1994, top executives from R.J. Reynolds, Philip Morris, and U.S. Tobacco stated under oath their belief that nicotine was not addictive. In contrast, in 1996, the Food & Drug Administration concluded that nicotine was addictive and should be classified as a drug.

In 1998, the turnaround in the U.S. debate over domestic tobacco policy was evident in the conciliatory testimony of tobacco industry officials admitting before Congress that smoking is hazardous and addictive. Their statements followed four years in which attorneys general and private lawyers in forty-one states mounted lawsuits against the industry, and tobacco industry executives agreed to pay $368.5 billion in a legislative proposal to settle the major lawsuits. Congress approved the proposal, and the industry agreed to restrict marketing, do away with advertising figures like Joe Camel and the Marlboro man, pay fines if youth smoking did not fall to specific levels, and submit to FDA jurisdiction.

Although the Clinton administration has been the most antismoking administration in U.S. history, the government has not initiated any concrete steps to reduce U.S. tobacco exports and U.S. investment in cigarette production abroad. This is partly due to the fact that many in government believe that U.S. tobacco products are merely capturing an existing market share now or previously controlled by state monopolies. In contrast to this claim, the National Bureau of Economic Research estimated that U.S. entry in the 1980s into countries previously closed to cigarette imports pushed up the average per capita cigarette consumption by almost 10 percent in the targeted countries. This occurred due to increased advertising and price competition caused by the entry of U.S. products.

This situation reflects a conflict between morality and economics. Projections show that the declining U.S. cigarette consumption can be easily replaced by foreign markets over the next decade. Thus, by pursuing an antismoking policy only at home, the U.S. government is not risking too much. On the contrary, a smaller number of U.S. smokers will significantly reduce the U.S. health system's expenditures on the treatment of smoking-related illnesses. However, the U.S. policy of permissiveness toward cigarette exports is at odds with government's involvement in the worldwide campaign to reduce smoking for health reasons. Conflicting opinions can be heard from different representatives of the government. While Representative Henry A. Waxman of California and former U.S. Surgeon General C. Everett Koop continue to be staunch supporters of the antismoking campaign and principal opponents of U.S. tobacco exports, Governor Paul E. Patton of Kentucky, who established the Governor's Tobacco Marketing and Export Advisory Council, and Senator Jesse Helms of North Carolina continue to fight against government regulation of tobacco sales and are key supporters of tobacco exports. The dividing force is economics: in 1999, North Carolina (where flue-cured tobacco is grown) was the number one tobacco-growing state with annual cash receipts from tobacco crops of $787 million, and Kentucky (where burley is grown) at a close second with cash receipts of $784 million. Together, North Carolina and Kentucky account for 67 percent of the total U.S. tobacco crop.

Questions for Discussion

1. Should U.S. exports of tobacco products be permitted in light of the domestic campaign against smoking?
2. Should the U.S. government be involved in tearing down foreign trade barriers to U.S. tobacco? Should the personal preference of the president affect U.S. trade policy?
3. Should export promotion support be provided to U.S. tobacco producers? What about such support for the export of U.S. beef, which may cause obesity abroad?
4. To what degree should ethics influence government policy or corporate decision making in the case of tobacco exports?

Sources

"Economic Impact of the United States' Tobacco Industry (AEG)," TMA Tobacco USA Revised 12/1/2000.

"Tobacco Price Support: An Overview of the Program," Congressional Research Service of the Library of Congress, CRS Report for Congress. Updated August 29, 2000.

"World Kicking Cigarette Habit," Worldwatch Issue Alert Data & Graphs, May 9, 2000. www.worldwatch.org/chairman/issue/000509d.html accessed March 16, 2001.

Pete Burr, Tobacco Analyst, FAS/USDA, Interviewed March 23, 2001.

Thomas Capehart, Senior Tobacco Analyst, Economic Research Service, USDA, Interviewed March 21, 2001.

Amelia Trent, Tobacco Analyst, FAS/USDA, Interviewed March 19, 2001.

Nagahama, Masaoki, "Japan Tobacco Annual- Revised 2000." FAS, USDA, May 5, 2000. www.fas.usda.gov/gainfiles/200005/25677628.pdf accessed March 16, 2001.

Commonwealth of Kentucky, Office of the Governor, www.kyagpolicy.com/Start.htm Accessed March 19, 2001.

"Most Frequently Used Tables," ERS/USDA Tobacco Briefing Room, www.ers.usda.gov/Briefing/Tobacco/ accessed March 14, 2001.

"Crop Production," Agricultural Statistics Board, NASS, USDA, May 2000.

PART I

CASE 3

H-1B Visas: A High-Tech Dilemma

Images of immigration typically include border crossings and refugees trying to enter a country illegally. Jobs filled by immigrants are perceived to be low-paying menial ones that cannot find takers among the residents. However, the most heated debate on immigration is being waged in the world of high tech, where industry argues for more freedom to bring in people with "a body of highly specialized knowledge" and where opponents characterize the situation as the present-day version of indentured servitude.

The HI-B is a high-tech visa that allows foreign engineers, computer scientists, and other highly trained technical workers from a variety of countries to work in the United States on a temporary basis for a maximum of six years. The program began in the 1950s to attract individuals with mathematics, engineering, and technical backgrounds during the Cold War. However, the boom of the information-technology sector, which demands 1.6 million workers yearly, has made the H-1B visa a major subject of discussion. In 1999, the full allotment of 115,000 H-1B visas was exhausted by June, and in 2000, by April.

On October 3, 2000, the U.S. Congress overwhelmingly approved legislation in a vote of 96 to 1 that would increase the number of H-1B visas issued from 115,000 to 195,000 each year for the next three years, with the possibility for renewal for another three years. Senator Ernest Hollings, a Democrat from South Carolina, a long-time job protectionist, was the lone dissenter. The bill passed because high-tech lobbyists were successful in positioning the visas as protection for the U.S. competitive edge in technology. In the short term, the United States needs to fill key positions immediately so opportunities are not lost to foreign competitors. The supporters' argued that the survival of U.S. companies is at stake without foreign workers. This view was also taken by Federal Reserve Chief Alan Greenspan, who warned that labor shortages threatened the national economy and who proposed increased immigration as a way to ease labor shortages and reduce inflationary pressure.

Greenspan's comments were only one indication of dramatic changes taking place. Two years earlier, the same legislation had been opposed by anti-immigration Republicans and the labor unions. In 1996, the U.S. Congress focused on deportation, and the U.S. Commission on Immigration Reform (the Jordan Commission) proposed to cut legal immigration by at least a third and eliminate illegal immigration.

Labor's Position

Organized labor has also started to change its traditional stance. While historically opposing immigration on the grounds that it displaces American workers and lowers wages, organized labor abandoned its opposition to the October bill—although they did support the stipulation that U.S. employers must pay the prevailing wage—and announced it would no longer oppose illegal immigration. Union leaders increasingly see immigrants as potential recruits.

While organized labor supported the provision to pay prevailing wages of what a recent college graduate entering the computer science field would typically command, the high-tech industry opposed that provision on the grounds of increased paperwork and administrative costs involved to maintain these statistics. The industry point of view won and the provision that required employers to present tax forms showing how much H-1B holders were paid was dropped from the final version of the legislation.

There is opposition also from non-traditional workers' groups on the issues of wages. According to critics, foreign workers in Silicon Valley earn substantially less than a U.S. citizen with comparable education and experience. For example, newly graduated immigrants with H-1B visas are paid $35,000, while the national average for new computer science graduates is $45,000. Groups of technical workers, such as the Programmers Guild and the American Engineering Association, banded together to fight the bill. Their argument is that U.S. technology businesses rely too heavily on cheaper foreign labor at the expense of older and more expensive U.S. workers. The higher numbers create a market in which employers do not have to cultivate "home grown" talent because there is a constant flow of new people. While some employers may not save on the salaries of programmers of the same age and background, they still save on salaries of employees with H-1B visas whose median age is 28 and who may replace a U.S. citizen over the age of 40.

Source: This case was written by Beverly Reusser and Ilkka Ronkainen. It is based on publicly available materials such as "Visas Bring Labor, But Not for Long," *Fortune*, December 18, 2000, 64–68, "Visas Bill Brings Tech a Manpower Win," *The Washington Post*, October 7, 2000, E2; "Teaching Lessons: Why Should You Subsidise Bill Gates?" *The Statesman*, October 10, 2000, 14; "American Competitiveness in the Twenty-first Century Act of 2000," *Congressional Record–Senate*, Volume 146, No. 117, September 27, 2000; and "High-Tech Cheap Labor," *The Washington Post*, September 12, 2000, A35.

Other groups, such as the Urban League, have demanded that corporations train more U.S. citizens for the jobs that are going to foreign engineers, computer scientists, and other highly trained technicians. Colin Powell stressed the need for increased training of U.S. students at the Republican Convention in 2000. The H-IB visa's filing fee of $500 is supposed to go to programs to increase U.S. student and worker training in science and technology. Since establishing such a program in 1997, the Virginia High Tech Partnership program has placed 140 minority students at 75 firms, including AOL, IBM, and start-ups. However, it is clear that these initiatives will not have any immediate effect on the demand for H-IB visas.

Critics have also argued that, contrary to claims of programmer shortage, U.S. companies such as Cisco, Microsoft, and Qualcomm hire only a small percentage of applicants and reject most without even interviewing them. Cisco, for example, receives 20,000 applications per month but hires only 5 percent of them.

Industry View

The positive vote to increase H-IB visas is seen as further evidence of the clout the high-tech industry has in the United States. In 1999, the U.S. Congress passed a bill that protected Silicon Valley against Y2K litigation. Recent legis-

lation has also eased restrictions on export encryption rules, and high-tech companies are not required to maintain separate tax records on foreign workers. U.S. Congressman Tom Davis, a Republican from Virginia, stated, "This is not a popular bill with the public, it is popular with the CEOs. This is a very important issue for the high-tech executives who give the money."

The industry's argument is straightforward: information technology has dramatically changed the composition of the U.S. workforce by producing an incredible demand for workers. In many sectors, the positions have high complexity and a scarcity of qualified applicants. U.S. companies have been forced to slow their expansion or cancel projects due to the lack of technically qualified individuals. As a result, some have argued for the elimination of H-IB caps altogether.

According to a 2000 report by the General Accounting Office, the average H-IB worker is an Indian male between the ages of 25 and 29 who earns a salary of $45,000. As shown in Figure 1, Indians account for the majority of the new arrivals, with China and Canada as distant followers. In Silicon Valley, immigrants make up one-third of IT workers, and more than 25 percent of them hold senior executive positions. More than 750 Silicon Valley companies worth US$3.5 billion and employing 16,000 workers are owned by Indians.

FIGURE 1   **Percentages of U.S. Immigrants with H-IB Visas from Various Nations**

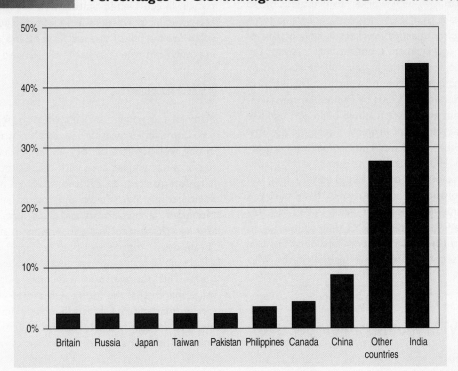

Source: "Alliance Fights Boost in Visas for Tech Workers," *Los Angeles Times*, August 5, 2000, A14.

View from India

The IT industry is growing rapidly in India. The area around Bangalore is known as the Silicon Valley of India. In the past decade, Indian software exports to the United States have grown from $150 million to $3.9 billion. The Indian software industry is expected to grow to $80 billion by 2008. India exports software to 91 countries, with 64 percent going to the United States. In 1998, Microsoft opened a research and development center in Hyderabad. Indian laws were recently liberalized for direct foreign investment and joint ventures. The passage of the visa bill is seen in some parts of Asia—but not all—as having the potential to inspire trading interest in India's frontline software industry.

Exactly one week after passage of the bill, the Indian press (*The Statesman*) issued a broadside that criticized the H-1B program as subsidizing Bill Gates. The argument was that the high-tech industries in Western countries are being fueled with workers trained at Indian institutions at Indian taxpayer expense. The replacement of Indian subsidies with grants and student loans as a way to stem "useless degrees in comparative literature" was urged. However, no mention was made of requiring Indian graduates to work at home, possibly because there are not enough employers in India. Interestingly enough, there is a sector-specific problem. So many technical professionals are leaving for foreign jobs in the United Kingdom, Germany, and Japan that there are already pockets of shortages in the Indian software industry, with projections for a widening and deepening shortage to continue for the foreseeable future.

Why is the Indian high-tech worker so prevalent or so sought after? The fact that there are not enough employers in India to employ qualified workers is only a part of the picture. Their government's educational system has given priority to computer training far longer than many other developing countries. The India Institute of Technology (IIT) was founded in the 1950s by Prime Minister Jawaharlal Nehru to train an elite that could build and manage massive industrial development projects. Today the government runs six institute campuses and accepts only 2 percent of more than 100,000 applicants annually. IIT graduates Vinod Khosla, cofounder of Sun Microsystems, Inc., and Rakesh Gangwal, president of USAirways, have parlayed H-1B visas into lucrative careers. The value added for U.S. companies is three-fold: (1) the pick of the top tier of an educated elite from (2) the largest pool of skilled English-speaking workers second only to the United States, who (3) possess the ability to more easily adapt products for foreign markets.

The Indian Visa Holder's Perspective

The young Indian male between the ages of 25 and 29 who is highly educated, ambitious, and eager to work but unable to find a job in India that will pay enough to attract a wife is happy to go to the United States and earn $45,000 a year, roughly four times what he would earn in India. The October bill offers longer-term attractions, having lifted restrictions that previously hampered career progression. Called the "portability provision," it is now easier for H-1B visa-holders to change jobs without having to wait for the Immigration and Naturalization Service to formally approve the immigrant's application with a new company. This provision facilitates movement up the career ladder, possibly to the level of an officer at an IT firm and the growing of equity in the company and accumulating wealth. In the past, foreign-born workers were often dissuaded from switching jobs because of the fear that they would run into problems in processing of their visa paperwork. Problems could mean that they would have to return home.

Immigrants who have been in the United States for three years on the H-1B visa may have a different perspective. In many cases, the renewal for another three years may come, but not without a lot of work and worry. The initial exhilaration to come to the United States is often followed by homesickness. The spouse, who may also be highly educated, is not necessarily permitted to work in the United States.

With approximately 90,000 Indians arriving every year, and with the strict quota imposed by the Immigration and Naturalization Service of 15,000 green cards per year per country, there is an additional dilemma. The October bill acknowledges this problem; the language in the bill directs the INS to make the unused green card allocations of other countries available to applicants from oversubscribed countries and to extend the amount of time H-1B workers can remain in the United States while waiting for green cards. However, many workers feel discarded at the end of the six years, leaving full of disappointment and delusion and holding much bitterness towards the United States.

The Balance

Many of the young workers who do head abroad will return home and ploy their new wealth into ventures at home. In one well-publicized story, an IIT graduate founded Internet browser Junglee.com with three other Indians, and sold it to Amazon.com in 1998 for US$180 million. He gave $1 million to his alma mater and started another company in Mountain View, California, and Bangalore, India, as well as investing a 25 percent stake in a dot.com startup in India. The "brain drain" may reveal its silver lining as more and more successful Indian entrepreneurs are seeding ventures at home. The dot.com boom in India is seen as one of the mega markets of the future. Instead of sending workers to foreign markets, the Indian IT companies are sending their work to foreign markets via the Internet; "offshore development" is now a viable alternative to onsite workers.

The nascent IT industry in India is becoming more and more attractive to foreign investment. While Indian firms will lobby for more visas and investment, their U.S. counterparts are likely to seek reciprocal concessions. U.S. multinationals interested in establishing a business in India want some improvements in infrastucture, reduction in bureaucratic interference, and quicker responses from the government. New Delhi has taken the first steps aimed at accelerating telecom reform to free long-distance telephone service from their government monopoly and allowing 100 foreign direct investments in Internet service providers.

In the United States, the issue of equitable wages needs to be addressed; currently no reporting and auditing controls are in place to protect both foreign and U.S. workers. The lack of these controls both undercuts the domestic worker and takes advantage of the foreign worker. Many programs have been very successful in training new groups of workers and could work well as a regional model in the industry corridors in the United States. In the long term, the country needs to determine what can be done to make

certain that there are sufficiently trained U.S citizens to fill the demand for high-tech jobs. Perhaps not enough time has passed to judge what effect the retraining of U.S. workers, often older or displaced, has had on the new technologies. Little published data are available at this time, and anecdotal data suggest the retraining may be too little, too late.

Questions for Discussion

1. Comment on the following statement: "The firms of the New Economy seem to be awfully fond of the Old Economy—of 200 years ago, when indentured servitude was in vogue."
2. Will a visa program like the H-1B result in an escalation of brain drain from developing or emerging countries?
3. Should the cap for H-1B visas be eliminated altogether?

Cow Diseases and Trade: The European Epidemics

Background

Bovine spongiform encephalopathy (BSE),[1] or Mad Cow Disease, is a fatal neurological illness found in cattle. It causes afflicted animals to exhibit aggressive behavior, eventually leading to disorientation and death. BSE has overwhelmingly struck herds in Britain, where over 177,500 cases have been confirmed on over 35,000 farms. Though 95 percent of all BSE cases are in Britain, the disease has also been found in native-born cattle throughout Western Europe.

Despite various theories, experts cannot fully explain the cause of Britain's misfortune. One widely held theory points to the parallel incidence in Britain of a related disease found in sheep, known as scrapie. British cow feed processors, in order to provide a more nutritious feed, traditionally "cooked" sheep and other animal remains at unusually low temperatures (100°C, as compared to 130° to 140°C in other countries), perhaps too low to kill the scrapie protein thought to be transmitted to cows. Furthermore, due to the lack of available soybean (the other widely-used cow feed supplement) in Britain, the diets of British herds consist of a greater proportion of sheep and other animal-derived feed than do those of herds in other countries. These and other factors have been linked by experts to Britain's BSE epidemic. Conclusive answers to the most basic of questions regarding BSE, however, remain a mystery. After more than ten years of research, experts cannot even agree on how to dispose of frozen, diseased carcasses.

In the 1980s, concerns over the spread of BSE resulted in most European countries banning all types of animal-derived cow feed. France and Ireland took the further precaution of destroying entire herds that experienced one or more cases of BSE. In the United States, where there has never been a reported case of BSE, an effort to head off an outbreak resulted in a ban on the importation of live British calves and cattle products. Britain responded to the new discovery by making BSE an identifiable disease in 1988. As a means of avoiding a spread of the disease, a ban was instituted within Britain on the use of cow-derived cow feed. Despite these developments, herds of British-born cattle continued to be raised in numerous countries, including France and the Netherlands, which together imported an estimated 400,000 British calves in 1995. Overall, Britain's beef industry remained strong during the first half of the 1990s, generating nearly 1 million metric tons of product in 1995. Since then, however, production has significantly dropped as the effects of the disease, trade restrictions on British beef, and changing consumer behaviors have taken their toll. Production in 2000 was barely 70 percent of what it had been in 1995 (see Figure 1).

A Possible Link to Humans

The possibility that BSE could be transmitted to humans through consumption of beef was always a lingering question. It was not until 1996, however, that the likelihood of such a link was scientifically identified. A British government health commission reported in March of that year that ten recent deaths in the United Kingdom were attributed to a new variant form of Creutzfeldt-Jakob disease (vCJD), a human spongiform encephalopathy. Classical CJD, first identified in the 1920s, is a debilitating disease of the central nervous system that causes degeneration of the brain and ultimately death. The new variant differs from the classical form of the disease in that it affects individuals at a much younger age—an average of 28 versus 63. At about 13 months, the variant takes about twice as long to run its

This case was written by Peter Fitzmaurice, Jesse Nelson, and Professor Michael R. Czinkota. Sources used were "The Costs and Cures," *The Economist*, March 31, 2001; "Divided We Fall?" *The Economist*, January 20, 2001; "A New Type of Farming?" *The Economist*, February 3, 2001; "United States and Europe Deal with Mad Cow Disease," *Food Engineering & Ingredients* March, 2001; "Annihilate or Vaccinate," *New Scientist* March 31, 2001; "Fear on the Hoof: the Evidence Mounts," *Newsweek International Britain*, February 19, 2001; "Holy Cow! It's Bombay Stock Exchange," *The Hindu* December 3, 2000; "Bovine Spongiform Encephalopathy," USDA, www.aphis.usda.gov/oa/bse "All of Europe Seems to Be Shunning Beef," *The Wall Street Journal*, March 29, 1996, A8; "Mad Cows and Englishmen," *The Economist* (March 30, 1996): 25; "Burnt by the Steak," *The Economist* (April 6, 1996): 57; "Burning Steaks," *The Economist* (April 20, 1996): 47; Fred Barbash, "Britain Threatens Trade War," *The Washington Post*, April 23, 1996, A12; Fred Barbash, "Britain Fights Back Over Ban on Beef," *The Washington Post*, May 22, 1996, A27; Warren Hoge, "British Call Halt to Cow Slaughter Demanded by European Union," *The New York Times*, September 20, 1996, A11; Warren Hoge, "For the Farming Life Now, Who'll Give Tuppence?," *The New York Times*, October 23, 1996, A4; Warren Hoge, "Major, Feeling Political Heat, Plans to Step Up Slaughter of Cows," *The New York Times*, December 17, 1996, A15; "Bracing for a Mad Cow Epidemic," *Business Week* (January 27, 1997): 38; Richard Rhodes, "Mad Cows and Americans," *The Washington Post Magazine*, March 9, 1997, 13. Various Issues of the U.S. Department of Agriculture, Foreign Agricultural Service Attache Reports, 3/96–2/97.

[1]BSE is one of several diseases known as spongiform encephalopathies. Most types of diseases are caused by bacteria and viruses that need their own proteins to survive. Such proteins can usually be attacked and destroyed by a host's immune system. Encephalopathies are different in that the infection seems to depend on the infected host's own proteins. Lacking any foreign proteins, encephalopathic infections go unnoticed by the host's immune system.

FIGURE I   **British Beef Production ('000s of metric tons)**

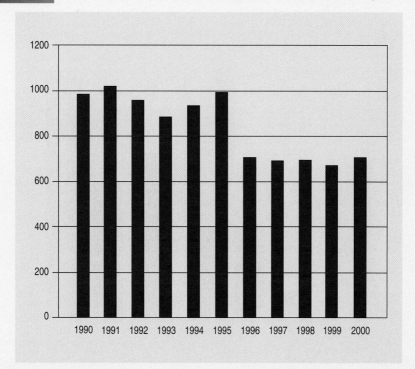

Source: "Table 5.13 Cattle and Calves; Beef and Veal," *Economic and Statistics Group, Ministry of Agriculture, Fisheries and Food,* http://www.maff.gov.uk/ Accessed April 2, 2001.

course. Scientists are also noting that vCJD may have an incubation period of about 30 years before it can be detected in humans.

There have been at least 85 confirmed cases of vCJD in Britain as well as two in France and one in Ireland since 1995 (see Figure 2). Since the 1996 government report, two other high-profile reports in Britain found evidence of a causal relationship between vCJD and BSE. In Britain and throughout most beef-consuming nations, the report caused immediate alarm. Media reaction to the news was "widespread and at times hysterical," according to a U.S. embassy report. Beef consumption and production throughout Europe dropped significantly within days of the commission's announcement, buoying sales of pork, poultry, fish, and vegetarian burgers. The multinational fast-food chains McDonald's and Burger King immediately switched to non-British beef. McDonald's action alone was expected to cost British beef producers $38 million in lost sales for 1996. British consumers were generally unable to differentiate between domestic and imported beef, prompting supermarkets and restaurants to hastily adopt national origin labeling policies in order to maintain sales.

The promises of European butchers and meat merchants not to sell British beef allayed few fears, as consumers questioned the extent of the spread of BSE throughout Europe. In the large German farming state of Bavaria, the market

for beef practically collapsed. A major Munich slaughterhouse reported within days of the announcement that the number of cattle being prepared for slaughter had dropped by 80 percent. In addition to beef, consumers were careful to avoid all sorts of other cattle-derived products. Processed cow fats are sometimes used to make cookies and salty snacks taste rich and to make lipsticks glide smoothly. Cow proteins show up in shampoo. Collagen, extracted from the inner layer of cattle hide, is used to balm wounds and cosmetically puff up lips. Gelatin, refined from cattle hide and bones, is found in such foods as ice cream, gummy candies, and marshmallows—as well as the capsules encasing drugs. While no evidence exists that CJD or BSE can be transmitted through these various products, consumers reacted with extreme caution. Tesco, a large British supermarket chain, pledged to label all of its products to indicate whether they contained any British cattle products.

The Government Reaction

The British government immediately sought to reassure consumers and announced that it was prepared, if necessary, to destroy all 11 million cows in Britain. This drastic solution was soon downplayed, and government officials began a campaign of stressing the "extremely low" risk of contracting an illness from beef. "It isn't the cows that are mad,

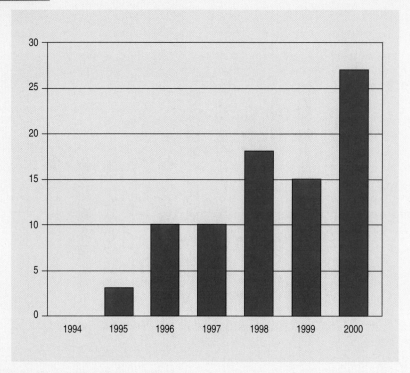

FIGURE 2

The rise of Human vCJD in Britain

Source: UK Department of Health; www.doh.gov.uk/cjd/stats/mar01.htm Accessed April 2, 2001.

it's the people," said Britain's Secretary of State for Health Stephen Dorrell, "I eat beef, and I let my children eat beef." The British Agriculture Minister went so far as to feed a hamburger to his four-year-old daughter on live television.

Despite the British government's pleas for "reasonable" measures, concerned foreign governments immediately imposed various restrictions on British cattle and beef products. Russia and South Africa, which had been key markets for British beef, turned primarily to Australia for shipments. Denmark compiled a blacklist of products made from British beef, ranging from foodstuffs to cosmetics. In the Middle East, fears that Irish herds might also be contaminated led Iran to halt Irish beef imports. Egyptian authorities turned away three shiploads of Irish cattle, stranding the herds offshore for several days. Egypt also banned British leather, while Jordan refused British and Irish dairy products. Hong Kong banned frozen and chilled British beef imports, and Taiwan, which banned most British beef products in 1990, added canned British beef products to the list. In Costa Rica, as in other Latin American countries, customs officers searched tourists' bags for contraband steaks. Ghana and Libya banned imports of all European beef, regardless of origin.

The complete ban on British cattle and beef products instituted by the Commission of the European Union, how-

ever, sent the greatest shockwaves. By April, the EU issued its preliminary conditions for having the ban lifted. Under the plan, all British cattle (the majority of which are dairy cows) over thirty months in age would be slaughtered and incinerated at the end of their useful life. This program, termed the "thirty-month cull," would serve to keep the meat of 4.6 million cows born and raised prior to 1993–1994 (the beginning of Britain's most comprehensive BSE preventive measures), out of the food chain. In addition, under what was designated the "selective cull," Britain was required to slaughter for incineration several tens of thousands of additional younger cattle that were identified as "high risk," including those from herds that had experienced a case of BSE. In recognition of the significant costs to be incurred by British farmers and renderers, the EU agreed to cover 70 percent of related costs, the same level used to compensate Germany during its 1994 outbreak of swine fever.

By mid-April, Britain released its response to the EU proposal, containing most of the details requested by the EU, but falling short in some respects, including the number of cows to be included under the selective cull. Several EU governments were unsatisfied with Britain's proposal, suggesting that the ban remain in place until the next review, six weeks hence. The European Commission conferred, explaining that Britain would have to undertake more drastic measures before a lifting of the ban could be considered. Despite the disagreement, Britain began the culling program.

The "Beef War"

What followed has been described as one of the most serious strains in Britain's historically frayed relationship with the rest of Europe. Repeated attempts by Britain throughout the first half of 1996 to have the costly EU ban lifted failed. Elections in 1997 were fast approaching and the economic impact of the ban was building. British trade unions reported that over 8,000 beef industry workers had lost their jobs in a period of a few weeks. Experts stated that the United Kingdom economy as a whole was poised to lose 1 percent of annual growth and 100,000 jobs, while sustaining nearly 2 percent of added inflation due to higher beef, milk, and related prices. Some suggested that Britain was facing its worst economic catastrophe since the pound had to be bailed out by the IMF in 1976.

After a month, the crisis escalated to threats of a trade war. Advisors to then prime minister John Major let it be known that he was "incandescent" with rage and "fuming" over European leaders' unwillingness to lift the ban. The British government warned that a retaliatory ban on an unspecified list of European imports would be seriously considered. For good measure, Britain brought its case before the European Court of Justice in the hopes of proving the ban illegal. "This is quite a serious crisis," said Kenneth Minogue, a political scientist at the London School of Economics, "(It could) lead to a serious rupture" of British–EU relations.

When many thought the friction could get no worse, the EU's agriculture minister, Franz Fischler, stated in mid-April that the ban was inspired largely by concern for the European beef market, rather than by health fears. He remarked, "(I) wouldn't hesitate to eat beef in England." Other EU officials also conceded that the ban was in response to the health of the market, rather than that of the public. Even McDonald's, in announcing its intentions to halt the use of British beef in its U.K. outlets, stated that British beef is safe, but it could not disregard the growing unease of its customers. The president of McDonald's British operations stated, "This is about public confidence and I have to tell you that people are not feeling confident about British beef right now."

One month after Fischler's admission, in conjunction with additional failed attempts at having the ban lifted, the British government began a strategy of "noncooperation" within the EU governing bodies. Prime Minister Major accused fellow EU members of "willful" behavior and a "breach of faith" in maintaining the two-month-old ban. Addressing the House of Commons, he said Britain "cannot be expected to continue to cooperate normally" in the business of the EU. "We cannot continue business as usual with Europe

when we are faced with this clear disregard by some of our partners of reason, common sense and Britain's national interest." The government's primary targets were EU decisions that required unanimous approval from members countries. The first casualty of this noncooperation was a new set of Europewide bankruptcy rules. After month's time, Britain managed to block more than seventy policy decisions, bog down an intergovernmental conference on the EU's future, and disrupt plans for a June EU summit meeting.

Adding to the British government's frustration was the continuing domestic slump in beef retail sales. For the three-month period ending June 5, 1996, consumption of beef in the United Kingdom was down about 24 percent over the prior-year period. Major supermarkets had begun refusing "clean" beef from slaughterhouses that were also active in the government's new culling program. One supermarket executive said the government was "naive" to believe that material from culled cattle would not find its way into the food chain. In a unique move, Britain's ASDA supermarket chain announced its support of domestic beef by refusing to sell foreign beef. ASDAs CEO stated, "British beef is the best and safest in the world and our shoppers want to buy it."

A Tenuous Compromise

By June of 1996, the British-imposed paralysis of EU decision making and the prospects of a deepening European crisis, finally prompted an agreement between Britain and the EU to have the beef ban gradually lifted in exchange for various measures by Britain, designed to isolate the risks of BSE and assure the global beef market.

Under the agreement, Britain would be required to fully implement corrective measures already underway, as well as to meet several new EU demands. In addition to the complete implementation of the thirty-month cull, the EU imposed an increase of Britain's selective cull, which would now target 147,000 cattle, up from the previous number of 80,000. In addition, the new agreement required Britain to establish a new system to identify cattle and their movements; the removal of meat and bone meal from feed mills and farms; new regulations on farm and equipment cleaning; and tighter controls on the British rendering industry. Despite predictions by John Major that conditions would be met and the ban would be lifted by early 1997, no firm dates or time frames were specified in the agreement.

Though EU decision making was restored with Britain's suspension of its nonparticipation tactics, relations remained strained between European partners. With the announcement of the June agreement, French farmers set fires, blocked roads, and prevented British ships from docking. Throughout Europe, farmers and others registered their anger, blaming Britain for the crisis and claiming that the risk to health and jobs remained. One French cattle breeder explained, "You have animals, you keep feeding them, and no one comes to buy them. This is a living product. We are very worried today because there is no market for our product." Strong criticism came not only from other Europeans—then-British opposition leader Tony Blair voiced these harsh words: "There is a humiliation in this deal. There is ignominy in this deal. In fact, it is not a deal at all, it is a rout."

The British government was initially hopeful that the repeal of the ban would begin by autumn of 1996, despite a July setback by the EU's High Court, which found that the EU was justified in imposing the restriction. It soon became apparent, however, that fellow EU governments were in no hurry to have the ban lifted and that it could be many months, if not years, before most British beef would be eligible for import. This realization, coupled with new findings by Oxford University scientists that BSE would run its course by the year 2001 even without the proposed wholesale slaughter, resulted in the decision by Britain in September to amend its commitment under the June agreement. It would now be willing to slaughter 22,000 cattle under the selective cull, as opposed to the agreed upon 147,000. The British government stated, "For the present, (we) are not proceeding with the selective cull, but will return to cull options in the light of the developing science." An EU spokesman responded, "There are some perplexing

thoughts in Brussels about what is actually happening in the UK. We don't actually understand why it appears from time to time that the Government of the U.K. appears to want to go it alone."

It was December before Britain had a change of heart and decided to restart the selective cull of thousands of cows from BSE-infected herds. In a reversal of attitudes, the Agriculture Minister stated, "Unless we commit ourselves to the selective cull, the entire ban will remain in place for the foreseeable future." The change of heart was largely rooted in domestic politics. The region of the U.K. to benefit first from an initial lifting of the ban would most likely be Northern Ireland, which has the most grass-fed herds and has suffered the fewest cases of BSE. Interestingly, the Prime Minister had just lost his majority in the House of Commons, and his Government's survival depended on the nine votes of the Ulster (Northern Ireland) Unionist Party.

A Midterm Assessment

By the end of 1996, Britain had slaughtered 1.5 million cattle under the culling programs. British beef production and consumption for 1996 alone had declined 27 and 16 percent, respectively. British beef exports had dropped by over 80 percent from 1995 levels. Other EU beef producers were also caught in the downturn. Reduced world demand forced

---

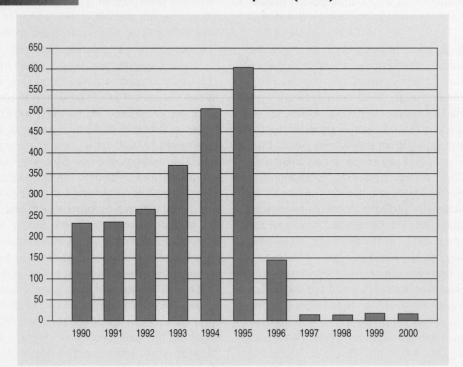

FIGURE 3   **Value of British Beef Exports (£000)**

Source: "UK Trade in Food, Feed, and Drink, Including Indigeneity and Degree of Processing," *Economic and Statistics Group, Ministry of Agriculture, Fisheries and Food,* http://www.maff.gov.uk/ Accessed April 2, 2001.

FIGURE 4   Beef Reference Prices in the European Union, 1996; Week Ending August 15, 1996

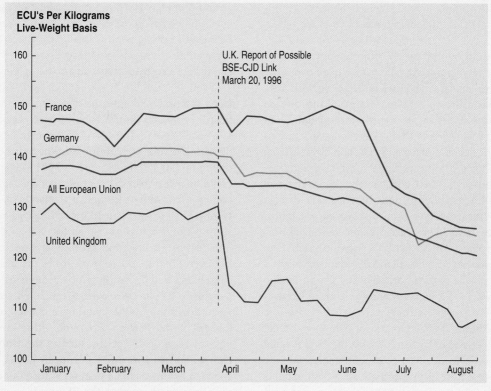

ECU's Per Kilograms
Live-Weight Basis

U.K. Report of Possible
BSE-CJD Link
March 20, 1996

France

Germany

All European Union

United Kingdom

 Source: http://ffas.usda.gov/fasprograms/f...mmodity/dip/nov96circular/bsel.gif.

EU producers to store beef. Beef inventories increased from 8,810 tons at the beginning of 1996 to 417,932 tons by year's end. Beef consumption for the year was down 8 percent in France, 10 percent in Germany, and 25 percent in Italy. Market returns for EU beef deteriorated precipitously, despite expanded intervention and slaughter programs. Reference prices for beef in Europe's major markets dropped significantly for the period of March to August 1996 (see Figures 3 and 4).

British farmers were growing increasingly wary as the new year passed and a lifting of the ban was not in sight. "The farmer finds it depressing to have a herd and not be able to have any control over it. It gets under people's agricultural skin," according to one British auctioneer: Property listings in farming areas throughout Britain became full of notices of farm and herd sales. "There already was a move off the small family farm, but this thing has turbocharged it," said one industry expert.

Slaughterhouses quickly became overloaded throughout 1996, requiring cattle farmers and dairymen to feed and house condemned cows through the winter and into the spring, creating shortages for younger, productive cattle.

Though most expenses were being covered with public funds, the British government proposed in February 1997 that the subsidies paid to renderers be withdrawn by March 1998. The Agriculture Ministry assumed in the proposal that a substantial portion of the extra costs would be passed back to producers, resulting in a drop in gross margins for beef farmers of between 5 and 25 percent. The proposal stated that it is not the government's objective to provide support to avoid business closures or rationalization as support is removed, but rather to aid the transition back to a market-driven system.

Through mid-1997, there had been practically no easing of the global ban. The agreed-upon slaughter program continued, as did consultations between London and Brussels. Although Britain ultimately agreed to the EU conditions, most observers believe it unlikely that the ban will be lifted swiftly. It is more likely that exports of live calves and beef from certified BSE-free herds will be permitted first, followed by a gradual lifting of the overall ban. Consumer resistance in importing countries and newly imposed EU-wide country-of-origin labeling requirements will likely constrain any large-scale resumption of exports.

The New Millennium

Between 1998 and 2000 there were only slight improvements for the British beef industry. While there was an increase in the total value of beef exports of over £6 million between 1998 and 2000, the industry began the new millennium with export values still 97 percent lower than in 1995. Britain had spent about $6 billion and culled over four million cattle over the past 15 years in its battle with BSE.

BSE is not just a British problem. Cases of the disease are now reported in native-born cattle in Belgium, Denmark, France, Germany, Ireland, Italy, Liechtenstein, Luxembourg, the Netherlands, Portugal, Spain, and Switzerland. Table 1 shows where there have been substantial numbers of cases reported since 2000. BSE has also been found in British cattle in Canada, Oman, and the Falklands, though no native-born cases have yet been discovered outside of Europe. All cases have been traced either to the importation of British cattle or to British ruminant-based feed that was still imported by more than 100 countries around the world after it was banned for domestic use in Britain in 1986. The United Nations Food and Agriculture Organization in early 2001 issued strong warnings that BSE is a threat in each country that imported British animal feed, especially in the regions of Eastern Europe, the Mideast, and Asia, where large herds of cattle could be infected but the disease not yet detected. Many international health experts have concerns for developing countries that may not have the resources to detect, prevent and manage an outbreak of BSE.

BSE has direct consumer effects across Europe as new cases are found in many countries. Its discovery in Germany in November 2000 produced a national crisis. Beef consumption immediately declined by 50 percent and prices by over 30 percent. Polls show that one in three Germans has given up beef, while three out of four express strong concern. The discovery has also shaken up Chancellor Gerhard Schröder's government as the ministers of health and food resigned. Schröder is now directing an overhaul of the agriculture system to put an end to the epidemic.

The European Union Council of Agricultural Ministers is faced with many important decisions, such as how to dispose of 500,000 metric tons of beef recently slaughtered as a result of BSE. There are also questions of how to handle rising stocks of stored beef, which are expected to increase to 750,000 metric tons in 2001 alone. By 2003 stocks could be more than the current storage capacity of 1.2 million metric tons. The European Commission is requiring the testing of all cattle over 30 months of age for BSE. There is also a Pan-European ban on all animal-based feed. The commission has plans to compensate farmers for the slaughter of infected herds. EU control of the situation, however, has been hampered by many member countries' nationalist tendencies to handle their own crises. Some countries, such as Austria and the Netherlands, have chosen not to take part in cattle compensation programs. Other countries are taking unilateral trade actions, such as the German and Italian ban on French meat. The European Union is expected to spend about $1 billion a year, separate from individual country spending, to combat the BSE crisis.

The final outcome of BSE and its full impact on the European beef industry will be unknown for years. Many adjustments are continually being made by the EU and individual member states to their herds of BSE and its disabling

TABLE 1   Number of Reported Cases of BSE in Native-born Cattle

	Britain	Belgium	Denmark	France	Germany	Ireland	Netherlands	Portugal	Spain	Switzerland
1987	446	0	0	0	0	0	0	0	0	0
1988	2,514	0	0	0	0	0	0	0	0	0
1989	7,228	0	0	0	0	10	0	0	0	0
1990	14,407	0	0	0	0	13	0	0	0	2
1991	25,359	0	0	5	0	15	0	0	0	8
1992	37,280	0	0	0	0	16	0	0	0	15
1993	35,090	0	0	1	0	16	0	0	0	29
1994	24,436	0	0	4	0	18	0	12	0	64
1995	14,562	0	0	3	0	15	0	14	0	68
1996	8,149	0	0	12	0	73	0	29	0	45
1997	4,393	1	0	6	0	80	2	30	0	38
1998	3,235	6	0	18	0	83	2	106	0	14
1999	2,301	3	0	30	0	91	2	170	0	50
2000	1,101	9	1	161	40	145	2	141	2	33

 BSE not found in Italy until 2001. Luxembourg reported one isolated case in 1997.

Source: Office International des Epizooties; www.oie.int/eng/info/en_esbmonde.htm. Accessed April 2, 2001.

effects. Expectations for a sizable jump in consumer confidence and beef consumption are dependent upon the measures put forward by the various governments. The reality is that the European beef market will remain highly susceptible to BSE scares in the future. Europe is not alone, however. Consumers in Malaysia became hysterical in early 2001 when reporters quoted a doctor as saying that two men in neighboring Thailand were diagnosed with vCJD. It later became clear that the doctor had been misquoted, but not before consumption and prices of beef plummeted.

Several studies in recent years have provided strong evidence that people can and have been infected by eating BSE-tainted beef. Even if transmission is extremely difficult, millions of Britons may have been exposed to bad beef before the government introduced measures to eradicate the disease in 1988. Given that the disease can take 30 years or more to manifest itself in those infected, slight increases in cases may signal an epidemic that could eventually affect hundreds of thousands of Britons.

A Second Epidemic: Foot and Mouth Disease

On February 20, 2001, the British agriculture industry was rocked by the confirmation of a second epidemic: foot and mouth disease (FMD). Within two months over a million cattle, sheep, and pigs had been slaughtered and a halt had been put on all animal movements as the British government desperately attempted to control the FMD threat to an already devastated agricultural industry.

FMD is a highly contagious disease that can kill young animals and render adult animals useless by producing lesions on hooves and in mouths as well as reducing both body weight and milk production. Unlike BSE, there is no evidence that FMD is transmittable to humans. What makes FMD so contagious is that the virus is airborne and remains present in the carcasses of dead animals. It has the potential to easily infect large numbers of animals very quickly, as happened in Britain. Carcasses must be entirely destroyed and disposed to prevent further spread of the virus.

In late March 2001, the British agriculture minister offered the official theory of how the epidemic began: infected meat was illegally imported from a region of East Asia, where the disease is known to exist, and fed to pigs in northeast England in early 2001. The disease spread as animals from that region were moved to markets around Britain. One shipment of infected sheep was sent to France. At a holding farm en route, other sheep bound for the Netherlands were also infected. By the end of March 2001, there were more than 700 cases of FMD in Britain, seven in the Netherlands, two in France, and one in Ireland.

The highly contagious nature of the disease implies that all animals in the vicinity of reported cases are at risk of contracting FMD. There are two methods of preventing further spread of the disease: slaughter and vaccination. Due to the reluctance on the part of the European Union to allow the use of vaccines for FMD, all threats were contained through the systematic slaughtering of millions of animals. The use of vaccines is avoided because most countries around the world will not import meat from countries unless they are certified to be FMD disease free by the Office International des Epizooties in Paris. Because it is very difficult to distinguish biologically between animals that are infected and those that have been vaccinated for FMD, a country cannot vaccinate and claim to be disease free. The European Union would like to avoid vaccination and eradicate the disease through slaughter in order to quickly regain the disease-free certification. The Dutch, however, have won approval from the EU to use vaccines should the situation get any worse because, they argue, there is not enough room to burn and bury large numbers of animal carcasses.

Exporting and barring cheap imports are both compelling reasons for the EU to maintain the policy of not vaccinating. Without vaccinations the EU is able to sell meat to North America and Japan, which together will account for about 5 percent of the EU's meat sales once FMD is again eradicated. If the EU were to begin using vaccines for FMD, it would lose its ability to reject low-cost meat from Russia, Africa, and South America, where vaccines are currently used.

From FMD alone, the British agriculture industry is expected to lose between £500 million and £1.6 billion in 2001. FMD has had quite an impact on British tourism, which is expected to lose as much as £3.4 billion. All told, total costs of the FMD outbreak in Britain could approach £8 billion. In light of this, some experts are calling for the use of vaccinations to save the British economy. The argument goes that the use of vaccinations will result in a loss of only about £310 million in meat exports, a small amount when considering how much other industries, such as tourism, are suffering with the virus on the loose. The implications of FMD on the British economy are dependent on many variables, including what policy decisions the government makes concerning the use of vaccinations. The European Union can only hope that this epidemic can quickly be contained and not spread as widely as BSE.

Questions for Discussion

1. Was the EU justified in banning British cattle products? Was the immediate intent of the ban to prevent a market collapse, rather than to protect the public from BSE?
2. Evaluate the British government's strategy of non-cooperation within the EU.
3. How might this case have been different had the EU not existed?
4. What lessons for globalization advocates does this case raise?
5. Should the UK and the rest of the EU vaccinate for FMD?

Harley-Davidson (A): Protecting Hogs

On September 1, 1982, Harley-Davidson Motor Company and Harley-Davidson York, Inc., filed a petition for "relief," or protection, with the U.S. International Trade Commission (ITC). The filing, a request under Section 201 of the U.S. Trade Act of 1974, was a request for escape clause relief from the damaging imports of heavyweight motorcycles into the United States. Harley-Davidson Motor Company, and more specifically its traditional large engine motorcycle, the hog,[1] was facing dwindling domestic market share. This was a last desperate act for survival.

Import Penetration

Throughout most of the first half of the twentieth century, there were more than 150 different manufacturers of motorcycles in the United States. By 1978, however, there were only three, and only one, Harley-Davidson, was U.S.–owned. The other two U.S. manufacturers were Japanese-owned, Kawasaki and Honda America.

By the early 1980s, Harley-Davidson was in trouble. Imports held a 60 percent share of the total heavyweight motorcycle market by 1980, and they continued to grow. Harley's difficulties worsened as its products suffered increasing quality problems, with labor and management facing off against one another instead of against the competition. By the end of 1982, in a total domestic market that had seen no growth in three years, import market share rose to 69 percent.

The declining market share of domestic producers in a flat market translated into a fight of Harley against all competitors, because Harley was up against two domestic competitors who were really not domestic. Kawasaki and Honda America were producing in the United States essentially the same products as those being imported. In fact, Harley argued that the two domestic competitors were only assembling foreign-made parts in the United States and were therefore not domestic producers at all.

Source: This case was written by Michael H. Moffett. This case is intended for class discussion purposes only and does not represent either efficient or inefficient management practices.

[1]The motorcycles produced and sold by Harley-Davidson have traditionally been known as *hogs*. The nickname is primarily in reference to their traditional large size, weight, and power. See **http://www.harley-davidson.com**.

The Harley Law

What has become known as the "Harley Law" was the resulting finding of the ITC that imports were a contributing cause of injury to the domestic heavyweight motorcycle industry. The ITC recommended to then–President Ronald Reagan that import duties be increased for a period of five years. Duties were to be raised to 45 percent the first year (1983), with the duty declining steadily over each following year until reaching 10 percent in the fifth and final year of protection (1988).

The president and his staff agreed with the finding but wanted a tariff rate quota (TRQ) instead of a straight tariff increase. A TRQ is a combination of tariffs and quotas; in this case, the increased tariff rates would be imposed only on imports (by volume) above a specific number per year. This was intended to allow specific small foreign producers to have continued access to the U.S. markets, while still providing Harley with protection from the large-volume importers who were rapidly gaining domestic market share. Table 1 provides a listing of the major tariff rate quotas as specified by the ITC.

The domestic industry that was to be protected was defined as those motorcycles "with a total piston displacement of over 700 cc."[2] This was strategic success for Harley, in that most of its motorcycle sales were actually 1000 cc and higher. This meant Harley was able to hinder competitor sales in product categories other than those reflecting the head-to-head competition. Harley had also requested that the imported parts that were being used by its two domestic competitors also be subject to tariff restrictions. Harley argued that the lower-cost product that was damaging the domestic industry was composed of the same parts, whether assembled in Japan or in the United States by Kawasaki and Honda America. On this last point, however, they were unsuccessful. Domestic producers would be protected against final product sales only, and no restrictions would be placed on imported parts.

Competitive Response: Competitors

TRQs were implemented for the 1983 through 1988 period. As seen in Table 2, the first two years of protection did have the desired result: import market share fell precipitously. Imports fell from a high of 69 percent in 1982

[2]Hufbauer, 1986, 263.

TABLE 1 — Tariff Rate Quotas for Heavyweight Motorcycles

Country	Pre-1983 Share[1]	1983 Quota[2]	1983 Share	1988 Quota[3]
West Germany	.4%	5,000	33.3%	10,000
Japan	93.0%	6,000	40.0%	11,000
Others	6.6%	4,000	26.7%	9,000

[1]Pre-1983 shares are percentage of total imports into the United States originating from that country.

[2]These quotas and tariff schedules applicable to motorcycles with engine displacement of 700 cubic centimeters and greater, only. Volume quotas are per engine.

[3]All quota shares rise 1,000 units per year after 1983, with the terminal quotas of 1988 being effective only for that final year (after which there would be no further Tariff Rate Quotas).

Source: Adapted from Trade Protection in the United States: 31 Case Studies (Washington, D.C.: Institute for International Economics, 1986), 263–264.

to just 24 percent in 1984. It is also interesting to note, however, that total market sales fell dramatically over this same period. After two years of significant protection, domestic production had increased only 20 percent (from 100,000 to 121,000 units per year), although the total market had fallen by 130,000 from 1982 to 1983 alone (and 1983 was a year of rapid economic growth in the United States following the severe recession of 1981–1982).

The response of Harley's major competitors to the TRQs was rapid and predictable. First, the two major domestic producers, Kawasaki and Honda America, immediately stepped up production of heavyweight motorcycles within the United States. The ITC estimates that imports of parts other than engines increased 82 percent in the first year of protection (1983) and more than 200 percent in the second year (1984). The ITC also estimates that between 50 and 70 percent of the final value of the domestically produced Kawasaki and Honda America motorcycles was imported as parts. Second, the same Japanese-owned producers altered the product manufactured outside the United States, primarily in Japan, to reduce engine dis-

placement from the designed 750 cc to between 690 and 700 cc in order to fall below the TRQ coverage. Third, the Japanese government, on behalf of its own producers, filed a complaint under Article XIII of the General Agreement on Tariffs and Trade (GATT) that the European competitors (Germany) were receiving discriminatory treatment (although filed, there were no formal findings ever made on this complaint).

Competitive Response: Harley

Harley-Davidson used the period of import relief to restructure, retool, and retrain. Two specific actions were taken to strengthen Harley to once again be a competitive firm.

1. **A Rededication to Quality**—Although Harley had instituted *quality circles* in manufacturing as early as 1976, renewed efforts in quality monitoring and labor involvement dramatically improved the quality of

TABLE 2 — Import and Domestic Heavyweight Motorcycle Market Shares (thousands of units)

Year	Total Sales[1]	Domestic Share (%)	Import Share (%)
1980	326 (100%)	130 (40%)	196 (60%)
1981	327 (100%)	125 (38%)	202 (62%)
1982	324 (100%)	100 (31%)	224 (69%)
1983 (TRQ)	194 (100%)	100 (52%)	94 (48%)
1984 (TRQ)	159 (100%)	121 (76%)	38 (24%)

[1]Total sales is the sum of domestic production and imports; exports were negligible over the subject period.

Source: Adapted from Trade Protection in the United States: 31 Case Studies (Washington, D.C.: Institute for International Economics, 1986, and various publications of the U.S. International Trade Commission)

the product.[3] By 1988, Harley had 117 quality circles in operation with more than 50 percent of all employees involved in the improvement of their own product. The implementation of a just-in-time materials-management program, which Harley termed "materials as needed," also aided greatly in reducing costs of production.

2. **Diversification of Earnings**—In 1986, Harley purchased Holiday Rambler Corporation of Wakarusa, Indiana. Holiday Rambler is a recreational vehicle manufacturer that was expected to provide Harley with broadened earnings flows as the domestic motorcycle industry was increasingly stagnant in growth. Harley has also continued to increase production and sales of other products, such as metal bomb casings and liquid-fuel rocket engines for the U.S. Department of Defense.

Harley's measures were indeed effective in returning the company to profitability and competitiveness. In 1987, a year ahead of schedule, Harley requested that the tariff rate quotas be removed from imported motorcycles.

Questions for Discussion

1. Were the tariff rate quotas (TRQs) really effective in protecting Harley-Davidson against Japanese manufacturers' import penetration? What was the role of imported parts in this effectiveness of protection?

2. Did Harley-Davidson "adjust" to changing market conditions during the period in which the U.S. government afforded it protection from foreign competition? Do you

believe it responded to the expectations of public policymakers to reclaim competitiveness on world markets?

References

Beals, Vaughn. "Harley-Davidson: An American Success Story." *Journal for Quality & Participation* 11, 2 (June 1988): A19–A23.

Gelb, Thomas. "Overhauling Corporate Engine Drives Winning Strategy." *Journal of Business Strategy* 10, 6 (November/December 1989): 8–12.

Grant, Robert M., R. Krishnan, Abraham B. Shani, and Ron Baer. "Appropriate Manufacturing Technology: A Strategic Approach." *Sloan Management Review* 33, 1 (Fall 1991): 43–54.

Hackney, Holt. "Easy Rider." *Financial World* 159, 18 (September 4, 1990): 48–49.

"How Harley Beat Back the Japanese." *Fortune* (September 25, 1989): 155–164.

Hufbauer, Gary Clyde, Diane T. Berliner, and Kimberly Ann Elliot. *Trade Protection in the United States: 31 Case Studies.* Washington, D.C.: The Institute for International Economics, 1986.

"Mounting the Drive for Quality." *Manufacturing Engineering* 108, 1 (January 1992): 92, 94.

Muller, E. J. "Harley's Got the Handle on Inbound." *Distribution* 88, 3 (March 1989): 70, 74.

Pruzin, Daniel R. "Born to be Verrucht." *World Trade* 5, 4 (May 1992): 112–117.

Reid, Peter C. *Well-Made in America.* New York: McGraw-Hill, 1989.

Rudin, Brad. "Harley Revs Up Image Through Diversifying." *Pensions & Investment Age* 15, 3 (February 9, 1987): 21–23.

Sepehri, Mehran. "Manufacturing Revitalization at Harley-Davidson Motor Co." *Industrial Engineering* 19, 8 (August 1987): 86–93.

---

[3]When the first quality circles were created in 1976, it was estimated that the first 100 motorcycles off the production line were costing an additional $100,000 to "repair" before they were up to standards for sale. This had to change.

Gabriel Benguela had just walked into his office from attending an operations review when the telephone rang. Gabriel guessed that a call late in the day must be from one of his marketing managers based in the Far East. It was indeed; Peter Mai was calling from Avicular's Singapore office. Peter was the lead negotiator on a deal under negotiation with Pakistan International Airlines (PIA). It was July 6, 1997.

Peter: Gabriel, we have a problem with the PIA proposal. Although our local agent keeps assuring me that we have won this competition and we will get the deal, I'm not so sure. Pakistan's negotiations with the International Monetary Fund (IMF) to secure yet another loan to finance their current account deficit are causing more problems for this deal. Recent economic data for the country is also not very good, with low economic growth and continuing employment problems. There have been more demonstrations in Lahore because of the European Union's recent antidumping ruling imposing high tariffs against several cotton exporting countries, including Pakistan. The export of cotton is not only a major source of employment but also a source of badly needed hard currency. All this on the heels of the IMF's austerity program.

Gabriel: What does PIA want now? How long have we been trying to finalize this deal?

Peter: Seven months. PIA has asked that we accept local currency.

Gabriel: "That's just great! Peter, you know our division never accepts payment in local currency. Although nearly 50 percent of our business is international, we are just not set up to accept the risk that denominating sales in other currencies would bring. In fact, the whole aerospace business is conducted in U.S. dollars."

Peter: Hey, blame the IMF. They should be charged for inciting riots and billed for our expenses.

Gabriel: We need this program badly. These large cockpit retrofit opportunities are hard to find, and it seems that our division's management has already committed this $23.7 million sale to corporate on our latest stretch goal.

THUNDERBIRD

THE AMERICAN GRADUATE SCHOOL
OF INTERNATIONAL MANAGEMENT

Source: Copyright © 2000 Thunderbird, The American Graduate School of International Management. All rights reserved. This case was prepared by Teak Macedo under the direction of Professor Michael H. Moffett for the purpose of classroom discussion only, and not to indicate either effective or ineffective management.

Peter: There is an alternative. Our agent, Makran, advised me that PIA can buy the receivable from us at a 5 percent discount and take all of the currency risk. Their Los Angeles subsidiary would pay us 30 days after our invoice.

Gabriel: But we can't take another hit to the return on sales on this deal. As the deal stands, we had to go to Group Level for approval on this one. This isn't good. I'll speak with the finance people and call you back within 24 hours.

Avicular Controls

Avicular Controls, Inc. (ACI), based in Chicago, had dominated the field of automatic controls since its founding in 1903. Beginning with furnace controls for the steel and power industries in 1903, it continued to grow for over 90 years. By 1996, Avicular employed 13,000 people and conducted business in 52 countries. ACI was composed of two major business units: Industrial Process Controls (AvIPC, with 1996 sales of $1.75 billion), and Aviation Control (AvAC, with 1996 sales of $1.21 billion). In the summer of 1997 ACI was positioned to achieve its sales growth goal of $4 billion by the year 2000.

AvAC was once again on a growth path after several tough years. Avicular was recognized as the dominant force in the avionics market; market share had grown to a hefty 53 percent by 1996. But the industry had suffered a severe downturn beginning in 1992, and was only now reaching the sales levels last achieved in 1991. In fact, AvAC sales had been $1.6 billion in 1991, and would hopefully once again break $1.5 billion in 1997. The commercial aircraft industry returned to a healthy growth path in 1996 and early 1997, and growth was expected to stay robust through the year 2000.

ACI, specifically the Air Transport Systems division of the Space and Aviation Control business unit, had recorded a number of major wins in 1996. These wins included the contract for the cockpit retrofits for a major overnight package delivery firm's fleet of DC-10s, and numerous orders for the firm's new enhanced airborne collision avoidance system. Although U.S. government spending for electronic components was leveling off, international opportunities for military avionics retrofits and space systems were on the rise. Commercial space programs were also projected to grow rapidly, and ACI had landed key initial contracts with NASA and Lockheed Martin.

ACI was not new to international business, establishing its first foreign subsidiaries in 1936. Global treasury was headquartered (along with corporate) near O'Hare International Airport outside Chicago. Corporate treasury was a profit center, and charged 1 percent commission on all sales. Treasury, however, passed on the currency risk to the business unit. If a local affiliate, joint venture, or subsidiary required local currency, then treasury would try and match those requirements by accepting the A/R in the local currency. For many developing countries where ACI had little or no activities (such as Pakistan), this was only done on an exception basis. Treasury did agree that Aviation Controls could use their local affiliates to manage the sale of aviation products, but would have to pay between 3 percent and 8 percent for currency cover (the final fee would have to be negotiated between treasury and Aviation Controls). This was something that the division had an unwritten policy of not doing; the standard transfer charge imposed by treasury cut into sales margins.

Pakistan International Airlines (PIA)

Pakistan International Airlines Corporation (PIA) was the national carrier of the Islamic Republic of Pakistan. Founded in 1954, PIA operated both scheduled passenger and cargo services. The firm was 57 percent state-owned, with the remaining 43 percent held by private investors internal to Pakistan. PIA had been Pakistan's only airline for over 40 years, but in 1993 Aero Asia International Ltd. was born. By 1996, however, it had captured little of the domestic or Pakistan international market (only 5 percent of Aero Asia's sales were international). Two other recent entrants into the domestic market, Bhoja Airlines Pvt. LTD and Shaheen Air, had captured little of the market.

The latest projections of the International Air Transport Association (IATA) indicated that passenger and cargo traffic would double in Asia by the year 2010. Asia was expected to surpass Europe and North America in both size of fleets and passenger/cargo hauled. PIA was experiencing some of this growth, but its aging fleet was resulting in losses. Increasing numbers of flights were either delayed or canceled as a result of maintenance problems. Although a larger and larger proportion of the population was traveling by air, given the choice of taking a PIA or foreign carrier, passenger traffic was opting for the latter. It was imperative that PIA modernize its fleet.

In addition to PIA's traditional passenger and cargo services, a growing proportion of sales was arising from the yearly Islamic Haj (pilgrimage) traffic to Mecca and Medina in Saudia Arabia. Demand had always been strong, but increasing numbers of Pakistani citizens were obtaining visas for the pilgrimage, as Saudi Arabia had recently shuffled the allocation of Haj visas among nations and Pakistan had benefited. PIA was a direct beneficiary of the increased visa allocation.

PIA had originally planned to purchase new commercial aircraft to replace and add to their existing fleet. The fleet modernization program, however, was put on hold due to higher priorities within the Pakistan government in Islamabad. These priorities were established after a review by the IMF of the government's spending plan. Much to PIA's discomfort, the austerity plan proposed by the IMF did not include funds for modernization. PIA had been counting on this fleet modernization and had postponed the incorporation of some Federal Aviation Administration (FAA) safety directives. With the cancellation of the fleet modernization program, PIA now had to move fast to ensure compliance with FAA safety mandates, or face being locked out of some of its most profitable gates. If PIA did not have some of these safety systems and quieter engines installed on their aircraft by June 30, 1998, they would be barred from U.S. airspace.

PIA was in a predicament. It knew exactly what should be done, but government control—especially in these times of crisis—left it no choice. Once PIA agreed to putting the fleet *modernization program* on hold, the managing board decided to pursue a fleet *renovation program* which would require much less hard currency. This plan called for extensively refurbishing PIA's existing aircraft at their new heavy maintenance facility in Karachi. For example, instead of the new quieter engines which new aircraft possessed, PIA would have to make do with the use of *hush kits* for the older engines. It would also require completely new cockpit avionics to take advantage of not only FAA mandates, but recent improvements in the Air Traffic Network (ATN) infrastructure. The first aircraft to be modified would be those utilized on their long-haul flights to the United States, primarily the *B747 classics* (Boeing). Aircraft engine suppliers were approached first and negotiations concluded.

What remained on the table was the cockpit avionics integration supplier. A cockpit retrofit program would require contracts both with the appropriate original equipment manufacturer (OEM), in this case Boeing, and a systems integrator, such as Avicular. Prior to the adoption of the economic austerity plan, Karachi had been the sight of an intense competition between the largest OEMs, Boeing, McDonnell Douglas, and Airbus, for new aircraft sales. It was only after the adoption of the austerity plan that Boeing was willing to discuss cockpit retrofits instead. Due to ACI's extensive experience with a variety of control systems for Boeing, its history with PIA, and its recent work on cockpit retrofit for McDonnell Douglas aircraft, ACI felt it was truly the preferred supplier for PIA. ACI believed that if any other vendor were selected, the added regulatory certification costs and delays would be prohibitively expensive. However, ACI had not undertaken Boeing cockpit retrofits to date (no one had), and looked to the PIA deal as an opportunity to build a new competitive base. But ACI's best and final bid had been too high. PIA's insistence on payment in local currency terms was now thought to be a tactic to extract better concessions from ACI and their agent, Makran.

The Pakistani Economy

Pakistan was divided from India in 1947 as a homeland for Muslims. Pakistan's relationship with India had, however, been under continuous strain since that time for a variety of reasons. The sources of friction included overlapping claims to Kashmir, India's involvement in the demise of East Pakistan, and the birth of Bangladesh in 1971, to name but a few. Because of these conflicts the military had always loomed large over politics in Pakistan. The country's persistence in continuing a nuclear rivalry with India, when neither nation was thought to be able to afford such a *luxury,* was one indication of this. The United States is frequently at odds with Pakistan regarding its nuclear weapons program and had suspended military aid on several occasions, including a large F16 purchase in the early 1990s. However, Pakistan's proximity to Afghanistan and India make it strategically important to U.S. interests.

Pakistan practices Islamic Banking, which is based on the *shariah.* This code prohibits the payment of interest, and the suppliers of funds find themselves becoming investors, rather than creditors. Although financial profit in most forms was looked down upon under Islamic rule, there were 28 publicly traded equities in Pakistan in 1996. The trading of equity shares for profit was also somewhat inconsistent with the *shariah.*

Pakistan has relied upon the World Bank (WB), the IMF, and other multinational lenders (in addition to specific national foreign aid and investment providers) for much of its capital. The country's deteriorating trade gap in the mid-1990s had caused a sudden and significant drop in foreign currency reserves, from US$3 billion to less than US$1.5 billion in September of 1996. The IMF immediately interceded in the economy, imposing an austerity program in October. The government submitted to this austerity plan as a precondition of receiving a $600 million standby loan extended to cover balance of payments shortfalls. The political repercussions were swift and severe: the fall of the Benazir Bhutto administration.[1]

A central part of the IMF's austerity program was a devaluation of the Pakistan rupee by 7.86 percent against the U.S. dollar on October 22, 1996. Roughly six months later, there was renewed speculation that another devaluation was imminent in order to limit imports and help the export sector earn badly needed hard currency. Another recent economic setback had been the ruling by the European Union that Pakistan was guilty of dumping cotton, and had imposed anti-dumping fines of between 13.0 percent and 22.9 percent on Pakistani cotton. It was a painful blow to the export sector. The current exchange rate of 40.4795 Pakistan rupee (Rp) per dollar was maintained by the Pakistani Central Bank; all currency transactions were controlled by the Pakistani government, and were conducted at the official rate. The *black market rate* was approaching Rp50/US$, and as the spread between the black market rate and official rate increased, the probability of devaluation increased. There was no forward market for the Pakistani rupee.[2] Exhibit 1 illustrates the recent travails of the rupee.

The Avicular/PIA Relationship

ACI had been the preferred avionics supplier to PIA for many years, and the retrofit segment of the business was thought to fit well with the overall strategy of the division. The group president was personally involved with the PIA proposal since this new retrofit market niche was central to the division's growth plan.

The avionics business was divided into two segments: Standard Furnished Equipment (SFE) and Buyer Furnished Equipment (BFE). OEMs such as Boeing, McDonnell Douglas, and Airbus purchased avionics equipment to be installed on new aircraft as SFE. The margins in selling to this segment were traditionally very low due to the competitive necessity of keeping competitors "off the aircraft." The low margins on OEM sales, however, were made up by higher margins in the sales of spare avionics packages to the same airlines. The purchase of BFE (also called *freedom of choice*) by the airlines is optional, and usually bid among three suppliers. BFE was purchased directly by the airline and installed by either the airline itself or the OEM. Each time an airline made a new aircraft purchase, a BFE proposal would be presented to the airline. The PIA B747 classic fleet retrofit fell into this category.

The major players in the global avionics business in 1996, in addition to Avicular (U.S.), were Honeywell Incorporated (U.S.), Rockwell Collins (U.S.), Allied-Signal (U.S.), and Sextant Avionique (France). To a lesser extent, Litton Industries (U.S.) and Smiths Industries (UK) competed in small specialized segments. Of this competition, however, only Rockwell Collins and Honeywell had the capability to take on such a large cockpit retrofit job. Rockwell Collins was considered very competitive, and had extensive experience in dealing with the Pakistani government on several large military contracts completed under the U.S. Foreign Military Assistance program.

The global aerospace industry was historically a U.S. dollar business; a dollar-denominated industry. The large air-

---

[1] Benazir Bhutto is the daughter of the assassinated former Prime Minister Ali Bhutto and the first woman elected to lead a Muslim nation.

[2] Forward markets for currencies are contracts offered by financial institutions for exchanges of currency at future dates at predetermined exchange rates. These forward contracts are an extremely common and efficient method of managing currency risk on short-to-medium-term transactions. Unfortunately, forward contracts have in the past been typically limited in availability to the 10 or 15 most widely traded world currencies.

EXHIBIT I   Daily Exchange Rates: Pakistani Rupees per U.S. Dollar

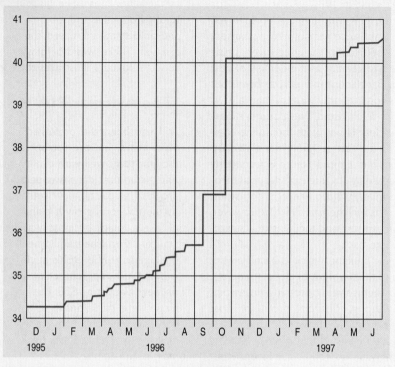

Source: © 1999 by Prof. Werner Antweiler, University of British Columbia, Vancouver BC, Canada. Time period shown in diagram: 1/Dec/1995 - 30/Jun/1997.
http://www.pacific.commerce.ubc.ca/xr.

frame manufacturers like Boeing had long taken the lead with the sheer size of their purchase deals. Recently, however, cracks were appearing in this business practice. Competition now focused on more than price. Other competitive elements included credit terms, credit risk, as well as currency of contract denomination.

Ibrahim Makran Pvt. LTD

In countries like Pakistan, the use of an agent is often considered a necessary evil. The agent can oftentimes help to bridge the two business cultures and provide invaluable information—at a cost. ACI's agent, Ibrahim Makran Pvt. LTD., based in Hyderabad, was considered one of the most reliable and well connected in Pakistan. Makran was also one of the largest import/export trading houses in Pakistan, giving it access to hard currency. It was 100 percent family-owned and managed.

Standard practice in the avionics business was to provide the agent with a 10 percent commission (10 percent of the total final sales price paid after payment is received). Typically, it was the agent who identified the business opportunity and submitted a Business Opportunity Request (BOR) to ACI Marketing. Sometimes this commission was negotiated, but due to the size and importance of this proposal, the commission was accepted without debate.

After PIA contacted ACI and Makran with their latest demand, Makran knew that ACI would want to maintain the deal in U.S. dollars. Makran had immediately inquired as to the availability of dollar funds from its own finance department for a deal of this size. The finance department confirmed that they had the necessary U.S. dollar funds to pay ACI, but noted that the standard fee was 5 percent of the invoiced amount.

Makran then advised ACI that it would be willing to purchase the receivable for the additional 5 percent (in addition to the 10 percent commission). The company's U.S. subsidiary based in Los Angeles would credit ACI within 30 days of ACI invoicing Makran. PIA advised Makran that if ACI accepted payment in Pakistan rupees, then local (Pakistan) payment terms would apply. This meant 180 days in principle, but often was much longer in practice. The agent also advised ACI that the Pakistan rupee was due for another devaluation soon. When pressed for more information, Makran simply replied that the company president, the elder Ibrahim Makran, had "good connections."

The ATS Finance Department

Philip Costa, the finance director for AvAC, had always wanted to be an engineer. His passion for exactness and numbers had, however, included the dollar sign, and he had moved up through the ranks at ACI quickly. The finance department he led was now in the midst of redesigning most of their processes and systems to reduce net working capital (NWC). One of these initiatives included a thorough review of existing payment terms and worldwide days sales receivable (DSR) rates. The department had a goal of reducing the worldwide DSR rate from 55 to 45 days in the current fiscal year. The Pay for Performance target for the current year (the annual performance bonus system at ACI) included NWC goals, and there was concern in the organization that the NWC goal might prove the obstacle to achieving a payout bonus despite excellent sales growth. And all cash flows, in and out, were to be evaluated in present value terms using a 12 percent discount rate. Philip started his assessment by reviewing the latest DSR report shown in Exhibit 2.

ACI payment terms were net 30 from date of invoice. However, payment terms and practices varied dramatically across country and region. ACI had not in the past enforced stringent credit terms on many customers; for example, neither contracts nor invoices stated any penalties for late payment. Many airlines did pay on time, but others availed themselves of ACI's low-cost financing.

A review of PIA's accounts receivable history indicated they consistently paid their invoices late. The current average DSR was 264 days. PIA had been repeatedly put on hold by the collections department, forcing marketing staff representatives to press the agent who in turn pressed PIA for payment. Philip's concern over the collection had driven him to search for guarantees of prompt payment. In the end, he had required the inclusion of a 20 percent advance payment clause in the contract as a means of self-insuring. Although marketing took the high DSR rate up with PIA and the agent, this deal was expected to be the same if not worse. One positive attribute of the contract was the fact that deliveries would not commence until one year after project start. If the expected improvements to the DSR were made in the meantime, maybe the high DSR rate on the PIA deal could be averaged with the rest of Asia. The 20 percent advance payment would be used to fund the front-end engineering work. Philip also insisted that it was the responsibility of his department to assess credit risk for the project. This typically required a detailed review of the buyer's financials. Unfortunately, the most recent published financial data for PIA was extremely sparse, and out of date (1990).

Meeting with Finance

Gabriel: Good morning, Philip. I am sorry to trouble you yet again with this PIA deal, but we have a problem. Peter called me last night and advised me that PIA wanted to pay in local currency. If we don't agree, we risk losing the deal. I think it's fallout from the 20 percent advance payment clause. Our agent, Makran, said they could accept the risk and net 30 payment terms for 5 percent of the sales price. Although we're confident that we are the only competing

---

EXHIBIT 2	Average Days Sales Receivables by Region and OEM, Aviation Systems Division

Region	Actual	Target	Amount
North America	44	40	$31 million
South America	129	70	$2.1 million
Europe	55	45	$5.7 million
Middle East	93	60	$3.2 million
Asia	75	55	$11 million
Firm			
PIA	264	180	$0.7 million
Boeing		3930	$41 million
McDonnell Douglas	35	30	$18 million
Airbus Industrie	70	45	$13 million
Worldwide	55	45	

1. Many foreign carriers make purchases through U.S.-based trading companies, distorting the actual DSR practices by country.

2. The spread between individual customers within regions can be extremely large.

3. Disputed invoices are included. Amount is for all products, services, and exchanges.

4. Firms consistently meeting ACI's net 30-day terms were eligible for participation in ACI's preferred supplier program which entitled them to a 10 percent discount on future purchases. Only the largest customers had, to date, taken advantage of this discount.

company that can meet PIA's requirements, should this requirement be real and we refuse, it could derail the whole PIA project.

Philip: Five percent is too steep! We simply cannot accept that. This is already one of the riskiest projects we have undertaken. The 20 percent advance payment is to help with the DSR since it is one of our primary goals. The DSR is being watched on a daily basis by division management. We already had to secure Group Level approval for this deal because it fell below our minimum 20 percent ROS [return on sales] target. Whose side is this agent on?

Gabriel: Why don't we accept the forex risk? After all, the rupee is fixed by the government.

Philip: Gabriel, fixed exchanged rates are actually less stable than floating rates. If you consider the IMF and World Bank part of the Pakistani government, then you are right. However, the IMF and World Bank have far more influence over Pakistan's exchange rate than the Pakistani government. The recent currency devaluations in many emerging markets could keep spreading. In the last few days the Thai baht and Philippine peso were devalued, and this is likely to spill over to other Asian export-based countries. The Pakistan rupee was devalued late last year, and I would expect another late this year or early next year.

Gabriel: I agree we would prefer not to accept this risk, but we need to make the sale so we don't create a hole in our strategic plan. If PIA certifies our latest B777 cockpit technology in their B747 classics, we have a tremendous opportunity worldwide with that workhorse jumbo. What about our other unit, the local Industrial Process Controls (AvIPC) unit in Pakistan? Didn't they recently score a big contract with the national Pakistani petrochemical company? Don't they need rupees?

Philip: True, they must. Unfortunately, the CMS system charges 1 percent transaction cost but still passes on the currency risk to us. Unless we pay substantially more. If we were to receive the rupee receivable in the next few weeks, I might be willing to pay the 1 percent and take the risk, but that's not the case here. The dollar is continuing to climb, and it looks like a lot of Asia is starting to fall.

Gabriel: I need to get back to Peter. What should we do?

The Global Car Market: The European Battleground

Cars are as essential to people as the clothes they wear; after a home, a car is the second-largest purchase for many. The car provides more than just instant and convenient personal transportation: it can be a revered design or a sign of success. Developers estimate that 200 yards is the maximum distance an American is prepared to walk before getting into a car. When the Berlin Wall came down, one of the first exercises of a newfound freedom for the former East Germans was to exchange their Trabants and Wartburgs for Volkswagens and Opels.

Western Europe is the largest car market in the world (see Figure 1). But while the car markets of Western Europe, North America, and Japan account for 90 percent of the vehicles sold, these markets are quite saturated. By the early part of the 21st century, for example, there will probably be one car per person aged 20–64 in North America.

Two general approaches will become evident. First, car manufacturers need to sell fewer cars, but more profitably. Secondly, they need to look for new markets. In the coming decades market growth will come from Asia, Eastern and Central Europe, and Latin America. China and India will eventually provide millions of new drivers. These new realities will have a profound impact on the car market and its players in the future.

In 1986, the Massachusetts Institute of Technology started a study that was published in a book, *The Machine that Changed the World*. The results showed that the Japanese took less time to make a car with fewer defects than the Americans or the Europeans. The main differences were due to the way factories were organized, as shown in Figure 2. The higher productivity of the Japanese has given them an overwhelming advantage: though they have not used it to cut prices, it has given them more profit per car than competitors get. As earnings mount, they can spend more to develop better cars or build the sales networks they need to expand sales. With huge overcapacity in the European car market, inefficiencies and redundancies have been inevitable with devastating results; for example, Renault lost $850 million in 1996.

The European Car Market

The "1992" process was to have opened up the European car market to competition by December 31, 1992. However, largely due to the performance gap between the Europeans and the Japanese producers, the European Commission pushed the dismantling of trade barriers to the end of 1999. This took the form of voluntary quotas, which were at the level of 993,000 cars throughout the 1990s. The Europeans have traditionally feared that while the Japanese car makers jointly match the share of number two General Motors, things could change rapidly in a market where no one company has even 20 percent market share (see Figure 3).

Japanese car manufacturers are also hindered in Europe due to exclusive dealerships; that is, dealers are not allowed to sell competing brands. Car manufacturers argue that such arrangements are critical in protecting the character, quality, and service of their cars. In practice, this means that outsiders would have to develop distribution systems from scratch. The European Commission has granted a block exemption for this practice from the antitrust provisions of the Treaty of Rome.

Behind the protectionism is that European carmakers want to avoid the fate of their American counterparts a decade earlier, when Japanese market share jumped from 20 percent to 32 percent in the United States. By the early part of the 21st century, the Japanese could be producing more than 1.5 million cars in Europe. Added to growing imports from Japan, Japanese market share could grow from 12 percent to 18 percent of the market. The prospect has stirred both protectionist impulses, especially in France and Italy, and new competitiveness by the European producers.

Both in France and in Italy, the car industry is one of the national champions that have fared well in protected markets but are relative weaklings in the global marketplace. Italy's Fiat, for example, produces about 4 percent of the country's GNP, which makes it impossible for the government to let it go down. In France, Jacques Calvet, the chairman of PSA (producer of Peugeot and Citron) has repeatedly called for prohibiting new Japanese transplant factories in Europe, strict quotas, and freezing Japanese market share within the European Union.

Sources: This case was prepared by Ilkka A. Ronkainen. It is largely based on "The Endless Road," *The Economist* (October 17, 1992): 1–18; "On Guard, Europe," *Business Week* (December 14, 1992): 54–55; Carla Rapoport, "Europe Takes on the Japanese," *Fortune* (January 11, 1993): 14–18; "Back to the Way We Were," *The Economist* (November 6, 1993): 83–84; and Louis Kraar, "Korea's Automakers," *Fortune* (March 6, 1995): 152–164.

FIGURE 1   **World Car Sales by Region, 1992–2002 (in Millions of Cars)**

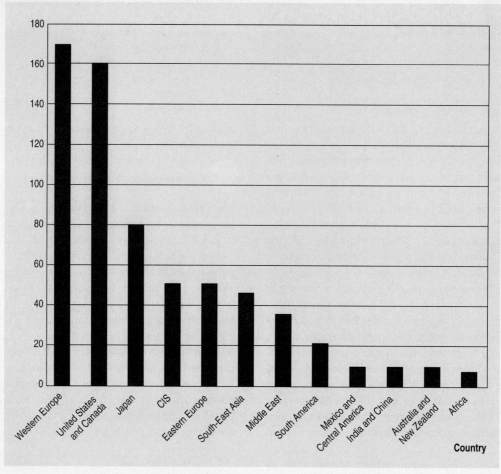

Source: "The Car Industry: In Trouble Again," *The Economist* (October 17, 1992): 4.

More alarming for the Europeans is their loss of share outside of Europe. France's Renault and PSA have completely written off the U.S. market, believing that they can prosper with a strong European base while holding off the Japanese. Even some of the European specialists, such as Mercedes Benz and Volvo, have been steadily losing share in the growing luxury segment of the U.S. market. Some have faith in their own markets. One auto executive forecast by saying: "The French are, well, so French. I don't think foreign cars, especially Japanese cars will do well in France. Not in our lifetime."

Globalization and Realignment in the Auto Industry

Globalization has become a central reality for car makers and suppliers. Acquisition is now the name of the game for the biggest players in the industry, who wish to spread costs across increasingly global operations. In 1998, there were 320 mergers and acquisitions in the industry at a disclosed value of $30.4 billion, almost twice as many as in 1997 After Daimler-Benz and Chrysler merged in 1998, others followed suit. Ford bought Volvo and Land Rover, General Motors bought all of Saab and part of Subaru, and Volkswagen acquired Lamborghini, Rolls Royce, Bentley, and Bugatti. The Korean car makers are expected to be acquired by either U.S. or European players. Even well-established manufacturers, such as BMW, may not be safe—their smaller size may not allow them to survive in the competitive environment of the twenty-first century. While luxury cars are among the most profitable segments in the industry, dominant players acquire them to run as independent subsidiaries, while helping them procure parts as part of the larger entity.

FIGURE 2 — Differences in Car Manufacturing

	AVERAGE* FOR CAR PLANTS IN:		
	Japan	United States	Europe
Performance			
Productivity (hours per car)	16.8	25.1	36.2
Quality (defects per 100 cars)	60	82	97
Layout			
Factory space (per sq ft per car per year)	5.7	7.8	7.8
Size of repair area (as % of assembly space)	4.1	12.9	14.4
Stocks**	0.2	2.9	2
Employees			
Workforce in teams (%)	69.3	17.3	0.6
Suggestions (per employee per year)	61.6	0.4	0.4
Number of job classifications	12	67	15
Training of new workers (hours)	380	46	173
Automation (% of process automated)			
Welding	86	76	77
Painting	55	34	38
Assembly	2	1	3

*1989

**For eight sample parts

Source: "The Secrets of the Production Line," The Economist, October 17, 1992, 6.

FIGURE 3 — Europe's Fiercely Contested Car Market

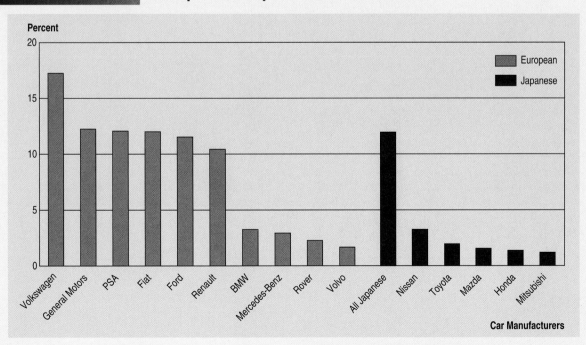

Source: Carla Rapoport, "Europe Takes on the Japanese," Fortune (January 11, 1993): 14.

Questions for Discussion

1. The CEO of BMW, Eberhard von Kuenheim, commented on the Japanese threat by saying: "Where is the rule that the Japanese must win? The story of their endless success just may be ending." Is he realistic?

2. What must the European car manufacturers do to face the global realities of their industry to survive and succeed?

3. Two of the largest car manufacturers in Europe are General Motors and Ford. Neither has been targeted by European Commission moves and are not generally seen as a threat. Why?

PART 3
CASE 8

General Motors and AvtoVAZ of Russia

*T*ogliatti, Russia, February 28, 2001. The General Motors team is arriving for a potentially final series of discussions on the establishment of a Memorandum of Understanding (MOU) with representatives of OAO AvtoVAZ, the largest domestic automobile producer in Russia, and representatives of the Russian Ministry of Economic Development and Foreign Investment. The MOU would commit all parties to the development of a GM joint venture with AvtoVAZ to produce and sell the *Chevrolet Niva,* a low-priced Russian-engineered sport utility vehicle (SUV).

The present negotiations have been continuing for over two years, and David Herman of GM hopes that final details can now be concluded in order to do the deal. Herman is afraid if the process drags on much longer, not only could he lose the support of General Motors itself, but competitive Western producers could move in before GM, eliminating the market opportunity.

The problems, inside and outside of Russia, were numerous and pointed for GM. The Russian marketplace continued to be in disarray. The second largest automobile producer had been the victim of a hostile takeover in the previous month (November 2000), and there was now increasing uncertainty over the actual ownership of AvtoVAZ itself. This was in addition to the fact that AvtoVAZ had been the subject of an aggressive income tax evasion case by Russian tax authorities in the summer of 2000. Not to mention that it took AvtoVAZ 320 hours to build a car compared to the 28 hours typical in Western Europe, or 17 hours in Japan.

GM International, headquartered in Zurich, Switzerland, had been against the Russian joint venture from the very beginning. The GM group in many ways closest to the potential joint venture, GM Opel (Germany), was 'cautiously optimistic' about the venture assuming that Opel-engineering could be introduced to assure a quality product. Meanwhile Ford was proceeding with a substantial joint venture of its own in Russia, and was scheduled to begin producing the Ford Focus in late 2001. Herman was increasingly convinced that if GM did not move decisively and soon, the market opportunity would be lost.

General Motors Corporation

General Motors (GM) was the largest automobile manufacturer in the world. But its market share was slipping. By the end of 2000, GM's global market share was 13.6 percent, with the Ford/Mazda/Volvo group closing quickly with a 11.9 percent share, and Volkswagen of Germany a very close third at 11.5 percent. There were three remaining automotive frontiers in the world: China, India, and Russia. Each of the three posed unique challenges for Western automobile manufacturers.

GM had little to show for over a decade of relationship-building in Russia. GM did have a standing agreement with the Russian government to import semi-knockdown kits (SKDs) of Chevrolet Blazers and Opel Vectras, which were assembled in cooperation with Yelaz of Russia. The JV had suspended operations temporarily in 1998, then permanently after a short restart in 1999.

The Russian Automobile Industry

The Russian auto industry was far behind that of the Western European, North American, or Japanese industries. Plagued by inadequate capital, a dysfunctional infrastructure, and deeply-seated mismanagement and corruption, the domestic auto industry continued to produce out-dated, unreliable, and unsafe automobiles. The Russian government had made it a clear priority to aid in the industry's modernization and development.

Despite this, the industry was considered healthy and promising because of the continuing gap between what the Russian market demanded and what was supplied. Between 1991 and 1994 the Russian auto market—purchases within Russia—had grown dramatically. But this growth had been at the expense of domestic producers, as imports had garnered all the increase in sales. Domestic producers increasingly focused on export sales, largely to former CIS countries. (Exports ranged between 18 percent and 56 percent of all production during the 1991–1995 period.) The Russian marketplace hit something of a watershed in 1993–1994 as imports made up 49 percent of domestic sales, and Russian production hit the lowest level of the decade. This was a direct result of a reduction on import duties on automobiles from the West.

With the reimposition of import duties in 1994, the import share of the Russian marketplace returned to a still-steady level of about 7 to 10 percent. Domestic production began growing again, and fewer Russian-made autos were

EXHIBIT 1   The Russian Automobile Industry, 1991–2000 (units)

	1991	1992	1993	1994	1995	1996	1997	1998	1999
Russian Production									
AvtoVAZ	677,280	676,857	660,275	530,876	609,025	684,241	748,826	605,728	717,660
GAZ	69,000	69,001	105,654	118,159	118,673	124,284	124,339	125,398	125,486
AvtoUAZ	52,491	54,317	57,604	53,178	44,880	33,701	51,411	37,932	38,686
Moskovich	104,801	101,870	95,801	67,868	40,600	2,929	20,599	38,320	30,112
KamAZ	3,114	4,483	5,190	6,118	8,638	8,935	19,933	19,102	28,004
IzhMash	123,100	56,500	31,314	21,718	12,778	9,146	5,544	5,079	4,756
DonInvest	0	0	0	0	321	4,062	13,225	4,988	9,395
Other	14	14	6	7	1	41	3,932	3,061	1,307
Total	1,029,800	963,042	955,844	797,924	834,916	867,339	985,809	839,608	955,406
Percent change	−6.6%	−6.5%	−0.7%	−16.5%	4.6%	3.9%	13.7%	−14.8%	13.8%
Russian Exports	411,172	248,032	533,452	143,814	181,487	144,774	120,551	67,913	107,701
Percent of production	39.9%	25.8%	55.8%	18.0%	21.7%	16.7%	12.2%	8.1%	11.3%
Imports into Russia	26,649	43,477	405,061	97,400	69,214	54,625	42,974	62,718	55,701
Percent of sales	4.1%	5.7%	49.0%	13.0%	9.6%	7.0%	4.7%	7.5%	6.2%
Auto Sales in Russia	645,277	758,487	827,453	751,510	722,643	777,190	908,232	834,413	903,406
Percent growth		17.5%	9.1%	−9.2%	−3.8%	7.5%	16.9%	−8.1%	8.3%

re-directed to the export market. Unfortunately, about the time the domestic producers were nearly back to early 1990s production levels, the 1998 financial crisis sent the Russian economy into a tailspin. Domestic production of automobiles fell nearly 15 percent in 1998. Auto sales in Russia as a whole fell 8 percent. Although there was a relatively strong resurgence in 1999, preliminary results for 2000 indicated rather anemic production and sales levels. See Exhibit 1.

Russian auto manufacturing was highly concentrated, with AvtoVAZ holding a 65 percent market share in 2000, followed by GAZ with 13 percent, and an assorted collection of what could be called "boutique producers" and assemblers totaling an additional 20 percent.[1] Foreign producers accounted for less than 2 percent of all auto manufacturing in Russia in the year 2000.

GM had already stumbled once in the Russian marketplace. In December 1996 GM had opened a plant in Elabuga to produce Chevrolet Blazers and Opel Vectras from imported kits. The original plan had been to ramp-up production volumes rapidly to 50,000 units a year. Operations, however, were suspended in less than two years—in late 1998 following the financial crisis—after only limited assembly (3600 units total). An attempt was made to restart assembly operations in July 1999, but that too was closed quickly when it became apparent that the market for a

vehicle costing $20,000 would not succeed in the needed volumes.[2]

The primary driver of auto sales in Russia was price. The average income levels of the Russian people prevented pricing at anything approaching Western levels. As illustrated by Exhibit 2, the already low relative market shares by price had dropped even further as a result of the 1998 financial crisis. General Motors now estimated that nearly the entire volume market for auto sales in Russia was below $10,000 in price. Given that the average Russian's salary (officially) was $100/month, or $1200 annually, this was still exorbitantly expensive for the average Russian.

In a September 2000 interview, Herman, the impetus behind GM's Russian initiatives, summarized GM's viewpoint on pricing and positioning:

> We could not make an interesting volume with a base price above $10,000. Such a vehicle would feature few specifications—ABS and airbags plus a 1.6-liter 16-valve engine. But, if the car costs $12,000, it is only $2,000 less than certain foreign imports, and this gap may be too small to generate enough sales to justify a factory. We knew we could make a vehicle cheaper with AvtoVAZ, but we need to ensure the price advantage of T3000 imports over competitive models is closer to $7,000 than $2,000.[3]

[1]Other significant Russian automobile manufacturers included AutoUAZ, AZLK, KAMAZ, Roslada, SeAZ, IzhMash, and DonInvest.

[2]Although GM never fully explained its original optimism about the Russian marketplace, at the time the original project was conceived, in 1994 and 1995, the outlook for the Russian economy had been much more bullish, and the financial crisis of 1998 was not on the horizon.

[3]"Exclusive Interview: David Herman on GM's Strategy for Russia," just-auto.com, September 2000.

EXHIBIT 2

Russian Auto Market Shares by Price

Price Range	1998		1999	
	Seg	Cum	Seg	Cum
Below $5,000	3%	3%	85%	85%
$5,001–$10,000	65%	68%	12%	97%
$10,001–$15,000	15%	83%	1%	98%
Above $15,000	17%	100%	2%	100%

Seg=segment

Cum=cumulative.

Source: General Motors.

But price was not the only factor. GM had originally considered the traditional emerging market approach of building complete cars in existing plants, for example the Opel in Germany. The completed car would then be disassembled—removing bumpers, wheels, and other separable parts, shipping the disassembled "kit" into Russia, and reassembling with local labor. The disassembly/assembly process was in order to have the automobile considered domestically produced by Russian authorities, thereby avoiding prohibitive import duties. The market assessment group at GM, however, believed that Russian buyers (as opposed to customs officials) would see through the ruse and consider the cars high-quality imports. But marketing studies indicated the opposite: Russians did not want to buy cars assembled or reassembled by Russians. The only way they would purchase a Russian-made automobile was if it was extremely cheap, like the majority of the existing AvtoVAZ and GAZ product lines, which retailed for roughly $3,000 per car. GM, realizing that it could not deliver the reassembled Opel to the Russian marketplace for less than $15,000 per car, dropped the proposal. An additional critical element, however, was unveiled in the marketing study: Russians would gladly pay an additional $1,000 to $1,500 per car if it had a Chevrolet label or badge on it.

This had led to the original proposal which David Herman and his staff had been pursuing since early 1999: a two-stage joint venture investment with AvtoVAZ which would allow GM to both reach price targets and position the firm for expected market growth. In the first stage, GM would coproduce a four-wheel-drive sport utility vehicle (SUV) named the Lada Niva II (VAZ-2123). The target price was $7500, and plant capacity was to be 90,000 cars. The Niva II would be largely Russian-engineered, therefore saving a significant component of the costs associated with the introduction of a totally new vehicle. The Lada Niva I had originally been introduced in 1977, and updated in new models in 1990 and again in 1996. It had been a successful line for AvtoVAZ, averaging 70,000 units per year through-

out the 1990s.[4] Since the Niva II was largely Russian-engineered, GM would primarily be bringing capital and name to the venture.

The second stage of the project would be the construction of a new factory to produce 30,000 Opel Astras (T3000) for the Russian market. Herman's proposal was for AvtoVAZ to use a basic Opel AG vehicle platform as a preengineering starting point. This represented roughly 30 percent of the content of a vehicle. The remaining 70 percent would then be developed by AvtoVAZ's 10,000 engineers and technicians—who obviously worked at a much lower cost than Opel's engineers in Germany. Herman's Russian Group estimated that even if GM and AvtoVAZ used AvtoVAZ's factory to build the existing Opel Astra from mostly imported parts and kits from Germany, the resulting price tag would have to fall between $12,500 and $14,000 per car. This was still thought too expensive for substantial economic volumes. Using the Russian engineering approach, the car would be cheaper, but still fall at the higher end of the spectrum, retailing at about $10,000 per car. As seen in Exhibit 3, this would still put the higher-priced Chevrolet in the lower end of the foreign-made market.

Others inside of GM and Adam Opel, however, disagreed with elements of the two-stage approach. For example, as a result of the cash-shortage at AvtoVAZ and the slow rate of negotiation progress, in order to build test-models of the new Niva AvtoVAZ had to use 60 percent of the old Niva's parts. Although many of the consumers at the research event at which the Niva II was tested ranked it above all

EXHIBIT 3

Projected Foreign-Made Model Prices for the Russian Market

Manufacturer Brand	Model	Price
Chevrolet	Niva	$7,500
Renault	Clio Symbol	$8,500
Skoda	Fabia	$8,500
Fiat	Palio	$9,000
Chevrolet	Astra T3000	$10,000
Fiat	Siena	$10,000
Ford	Focus	$13,000
Renault	Megane	$13,500

 Source: **www.just-auto.com**. December 2000.

[4]One of the primary reasons for the success of the Niva was the sorry state of Russian roads. The four-wheel-drive Niva handled the pot-holed road infrastructure with relative ease. Although considered an "off-road" vehicle design in the West, it was considered "on-road necessary" in Russia.

other Russian-built cars, the car was still rough-riding and noisy by Western standards. One Opel engineer from Germany who safety-tested the Niva II and evaluated its performance declared it "a real car, if primitive." Heidi-McCormack, finance chief for GM's Russian operations believed that with some minor engineering adjustments, better materials for the interior construction, and a new factory built and operated by GM, the quality of the Niva II would be "acceptable."

It had, in fact, taken quite a bit of prodding by GM to get AvtoVAZ to give up the revived Niva to the joint venture. "That's their brand new baby," said McCormack. "It's been shown in auto shows. And here's GM, typical big multinational, saying, 'Just give us your best product,'" But in the end, AvtoVAZ's limited access to capital was the driver. Without GM, AvtoVAZ would probably take five years to get the Niva II to market; with GM, the time could be cut in half.

AvtoVAZ

AvtoVAZ, originally called "VAZ" for Volzhsky Avtomobilny Zavod (Volga Auto Factory), was headquartered approximately 1,000 kilometers southeast of Moscow in Tolyatti. The original auto manufacturing facility was a joint venture (in effect a pure turn-key operation) with Fiat SpA of Italy. The original contract, signed in 1966, resulted in the first autos rolling off the production lines in May of 1970. The cars produced at the factory were distributed under the Lada and Zhiguli brands. For the following 20 years the average Russian dreamed of owning a VAZ.

In the early 1990s, following the era of Perestroika and the introduction of economic reforms, AvtoVAZ embarked upon additional technological development—and auto price increases. As prices skyrocketed, Russians quickly switched to comparably-priced imports of higher quality. AvtoVAZ suffered continual decreases in market share throughout the 1990s (see Exhibit 1). The financial crisis of August 1998—in a perverse way—served to bolster AvtoVAZ's market position. The 1998 crisis saw the Russian rouble fall from roughly Rb1 11/$ to over Rb1 25/$, effectively pricing-out imports from Russian buyers. AvtoVAZ gained what foreign imports lost.

> It's cynical to say, but in the case of a devaluation, the situation at AvtoVAZ would be better. There would be a different effectiveness of export sales, and demand would be different. Seeing that money is losing value, people would buy durable goods in the hopes of saving at least something.
> Vladimir Kadannikov, CEO of AvtoVAZ, May 1998

AvtoVAZ had also been something of what the Russian press called a "tax deadbeat." On July 13, 2000, the Russian Tax Police had accused AvtoVAZ of tax fraud. The accusations centered on reported under-reporting of automobile

production by falsifying vehicle identification numbers. The opening of the criminal case coincided with warnings from the Kremlin that the new administration of President Vladimir Putin would not tolerate continued industry profiteering and manipulation from the country's *Oligarchs*, individuals who had profited greatly from Russia's difficult transition to market capitalism. AvtoVAZ had denied the charges, and less than one month later, the case was thrown out by the chief prosecutor for tax evasion. A spokesman for the prosecutor's office stated that investigators had found no basis for the allegations against AvtoVAZ executives.

For all its problems, AvtoVAZ still employed more than 250,000 people in 1999 (who were paid an average of $333 per month), produced 677,700 cars, $1.9 billion in sales, and $458 million in gross profits (a loss of $123 million, however, in pre-tax profits). The plant, with an estimated capacity of 750,000 vehicles per year, was expected to approach or surpass capacity in 2000–2001.

AvtoVAZ enjoyed little vertical integration, depending on a variety of suppliers for components and subassemblies, and an assortment of retail distributors to get to market. AvtoVAZ's supplier base had also been continually reduced through acquisition and concentration. The three biggest suppliers to AvtoVAZ were DAAZ (headlamps and lights), Plastik (plastic parts), and Avtopribor (clusters of gauges and instrument panels), all of which had been purchased by the Samara Window Company (abbreviated as "SOK" from the Russian name) in the preceding years.[5]

Starting from a relatively small base, SOK had grown from a small glass window factory to a diversified enterprise of roughly $2 billion in 1999, with business-lines including bottled water, building construction, medical equipment manufacturing, plastic parts and windows, and most recently, AvtoVAZ's largest supplier and retailer. Although SOK officially purchased only 8,000 cars per year for distribution from AvtoVAZ, it was purportedly selling over 40,000 cars per year. The difference was rumored to be composed of car units assembled by SOK from kits purchased or "exchanged" with AvtoVAZ. AvtoVAZ, often short of cash, frequently paid taxes, suppliers, and management in cars.

Russian Corporate Governance

One of the primary deterrents to foreign investment in Russia had been the relatively lax legal and regulatory structure for corporate governance. Identifying who actually owned most major Russian companies was extremely difficult. This had become very apparent in November 2000

---

[5]Sok in Russian means "juice," but in the auto sector in Russia, the English-language joke was that SOK was SOKing-up the supplier industry.

when the second largest automobile manufacturer in Russia, GAZ, had been the victim of a hostile takeover.

Beginning in August of 2000, Sibirsky Alyuminiy (SibAl) started accumulating shares in GAZ until reaching the 25 percent plus one threshold necessary for veto power under Russian law. The exact amount of SibAl's ownership in GAZ, however, was unknown, even to GAZ. Current regulations required only the disclosure of the identity and stake of stockholders of 5 percent equity stake or more. Only direct investors were actually named, and those named were frequently only agents operating on behalf of the true owners. Adding to the confusion was the fact that frequently the "nominees" named represent multiple groups of ultimate owners.[6]

Rumors surfaced immediately that AvtoVAZ could be next. Although publicly traded on the Moscow Stock Exchange, the actual number of shares freely floating on the exchange of the total number of shares outstanding, was unknown (estimates varied between 5 percent and 40 percent of total shares). AvtoVAZ was, however, very thinly traded and currently trading at a very low price. Any major movement by an investor to acquire a significant amount of shares in such a thinly-traded security would quickly send its price skyward.[7]

But the question remained of who actually controlled AvtoVAZ?[8] It was believed that management, including the CEO Vladimir Kadannikov, held over half the shares in the firm. AvtoVAZ itself held 80.8% interest in the AVVA Group, an investment fund. AVVA, in turn, held a 33.2 percent interest in AvtoVAZ (see Exhibit 4). AVVA itself was in some way influenced, controlled, or owned in part, by one of the most high-profile oligarchs in Russia, Boris Berezovsky.

In 1989, prior to the implementation of President Yeltsin's economic reforms, Berezovsky, a mathematician and management-systems consultant to AvtoVAZ, persuaded the CEO of AvtoVAZ, Vladimir Kadannikov, to cooperate in a new car distribution system. Berezovsky formed an automobile

dealer network, Logo VAZ, which was supplied with AvtoVAZ vehicles on consignment. LogoVAZ did not pay AvtoVAZ for the cars it distributed (termed "re-export" by Berezovsky) until a date significantly after his dealer network sold the cars and received payment themselves. The arrangement proved disastrous for AvtoVAZ, and incredibly profitable for Berezovsky. In the years that followed, hyperinflation raged in Russia, and Berezovsky was able to run his expanding network of businesses with AvtoVAZ's cash flow.[9] LogoVAZ was also one of the largest auto importers in Russia.

In 1994, the Russian government began privatizing many state-owned companies, including AvtoVAZ. Berezovsky, Kadannikov, the CEO of AvtoVAZ, and Alexander Voloshin, recently appointed chief of staff for Russian President Vladimir Putin, formed the All-Russian Automobile Alliance (AVVA). The stated purpose of AVVA was to begin building a strong dealer network for the automobile industry in Russia. AVVA quickly acquired a 33.2 percent shareholding in AvtoVAZ, in addition to many other enterprises. Exhibit 4 provides an overview of what was known regarding AvtoVAZ's ownership structure.

By 2000 Berezovsky purportedly no longer had formal relations with AVVA, but many observers believed he continued to have a number of informal lines of influence. On December 2, 2000, AVVA surprised many analysts by announcing that it was amending its charter to change its status from an investment fund to a holding company. Auto analysts speculated that AVVA was positioning itself to command a reorganized AvtoVAZ, one in which the different parts of the traditional business were organized into divisions (car production, marketing and sales, research and development).

The success of AVVA was only the beginning of AvtoVAZ's distribution problems. In the early 1990s hundreds of trading companies were formed around the company. Most trading companies would exchange parts and inputs for cars, straight from the factory, at prices 20 percent to 30 percent below market value. The trading companies then sold the cars themselves, capturing significant profit, while AvtoVAZ waited months for payment of any kind from the trading companies. The practice continued unabated in 1996 and 1997 because most of the trading companies were owned and operated by AvtoVAZ managers. Russian law did not prevent management from pursuing private interests related to their own enterprises. Many of the trading companies became simple facades for organized crime.[10] By the

---

[6]The inadequacy of information about ownership was demonstrated by GAZ's inability to actually confirm whether SibAl did indeed have a 25 percent ownership position. It did not know, and had to take the group's word for it.

[7]Management of AvtoVAZ also felt they had an additional takeover defense, which strangely enough, arose from their history of not paying corporate taxes. In 1997, as part of a settlement with Russian tax authorities on $2.4 billion in back-taxes, AvtoVAZ gave the Russian tax authorities the right to 50 percent plus one share of AvtoVAZ if the firm failed—in the future—to make its tax payments. AvtoVAZ management now viewed this as their own version of a "poison pill." If the target of a hostile takeover, management could stop paying taxes and the Russian government would take management control, defeating the hostile takeover.

[8]AvtoVAZ had actually approached Adam Opel AG, the German unit of General Motors Corporation, in February of 1997—prior to the Russian financial crisis—to inquire as to GM's interest in buying controlling interest in AvtoVAZ. A spokesman for GM's European Operations was quoted as saying "We have told AvtoVAZ in the past we aren't really interested."

[9]Berezovsky has admitted to the arrangement and its financial benefits to him. He has also pointed out, correctly, that under Russian law he has not broken any laws.

[10]After AvtoVAZ's privatization, there were reported instances in which "mobsters" would enter the AvtoVAZ factory and take cars directly from the production lines at gunpoint. Buyers or distributors were charged $100 for "protection" at the AvtoVAZ factory gates. To quote one automobile distributor, "They were bandits. Nevertheless, they provided a service."

EXHIBIT 4   AvtoVAZ's Web of Influence

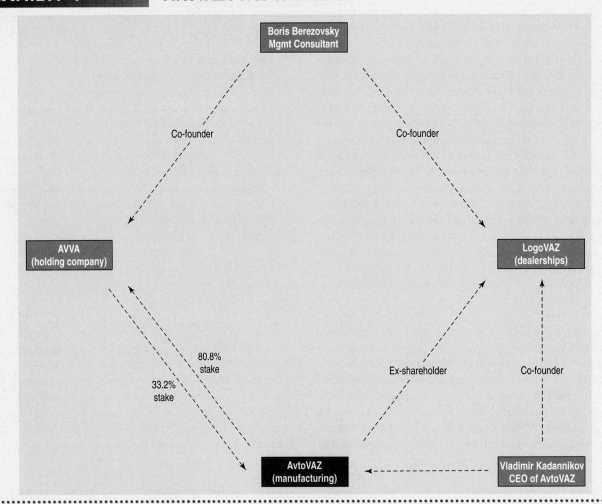

fall of 1997 the intrusion of organized crime became so rampant within AvtoVAZ that Vladimir Kadannikov requested Russian troops to enter and clear the plant of thugs, which they did.

Joint Venture Negotiations

Negotiations between AvtoVAZ and GM had taken a number of twists and turns over the years, but always with Herman in the center of the process. Beginning in 1996, the joint venture proposal had always seemingly been supported more strongly by AvtoVAZ than GM.

Herman had been appointed vice president of General Motors Corporation for the former Soviet Union in 1998. Starting with General Motor's Treasury as an attorney in 1973, Herman had extensive international experience, including three years as GM's manager of sales development in the USSR (1976–79), and other managing director positions in Spain (1979–1982), Chile (1982–1984), and Belgium (1986–1988). These were followed by chief executive positions for GM (Europe) in Switzerland and Saab Automobile.

From 1992 to 1998, Herman had been chairman and managing director of Adam Opel AG in Germany.

Herman's departure from Opel in Germany was purportedly the result of losing a highly publicized internal battle over the future strategic direction of Opel. Herman had argued that Opel should focus on developing product for the domestic market, while others in the organization argued that Opel should focus on "filling the pipeline for GM's ambitions in emerging markets." Many have characterized his new appointment as head of GM's market initiatives in Russia as a Siberian exile. Herman was fluent in Russian.

As early as the summer of 1999, AvtoVAZ had formally announced to the press the creation of a joint venture with General Motors to produce Opel Astras and the Chevrolet Niva. This was not confirmed by GM. Later in the same year, GM's European Management, primarily the Opel Unit, lobbied heavily within GM to postpone the proposed Chevrolet Niva launch until 2004 to allow a longer period of economic recovery in Russia. Upon learning of this, the CEO of AvtoVAZ, Vladimir Kadannikov, reportedly told GM to "keep its money," that AvtoVAZ would launch the new

Niva on its own. David Herman calmed Mr. Kadannikov and the two parties compromised on a 2003 launch date.

David Herman brought AvtoVAZ senior management to the Detroit auto show in the spring of 2000 to meet with GM president Rick Wagoner and vice chairman Harry Pearce. The meetings went well, and the vodka was passed. Weeks later, however, GM announced a new global alliance with Fiat of Italy. Fiat also had Russian ambitions. Herman returned to Russia, once again slowing negotiations until any possible overlap between GM and Fiat ambitions in Russia were resolved.[11]

As a result of the 1998 financial crisis, a number of people inside both GM and AvtoVAZ pushed for a joint venture which would produce a car designed for both Russian sales and export sales. The Russian domestic market continued to be protected with a 30 percent import duty. The new weaker Russian rouble assured Russian exports of being relatively cheap, if the product quality was competitive for the targeted markets. David Herman expanded his activities to include export market development. The working proposal now assumed that a one-third of all the Chevrolet Nivas produced would be exported.

In May 2000 Herman's presentation of the JV proposal to Wagoner and Pearce in Detroit hit another roadblock: the proposed $250 million investment was considered "too large and too risky for a market as risky as Russia—with a partner as slippery as AvtoVAZ." Mr. Wagoner instructed David Herman to find a third party to share the capital investment and the risk. Within three months Herman found his third party—the European Bank for Reconstruction and Development (EBRD). (See Exhibit 5.) EBRD was willing to provide debt and equity. It would lend $93 million to the venture and invest an additional $40 million for an equity stake of 17 percent.[12]

---

[11]GM owns 20 percent of Fiat of Italy; Fiat, in turn, owns 5 percent of General Motors.

[12]The willingness of EBRD to invest was a bit surprising given that two of its previous investments with Russian automakers, GAZ and KamAZ, had resulted in defaults on EBRD credits. A third venture in which EBRD was still a partner (20 percent equity), Nizhegorod Motors, a joint venture between Fiat and GAZ, had delayed its car launch from late 1998 to the first half of 2002.

EXHIBIT 5

EBRD to Back AvtoVAZ-GM Venture

August 31, 2000. The European Bank for Reconstruction and Development is expected to offer roughly $175 million in support for a $500—$600 million car-making venture planned in Russia by domestic producer AO AvtoVAZ and US auto giant General Motors Corp—one of the EBRD's largest undertakings in the former USSR. Some details of the bank's involvement remain unfixed, but the EBRD would offer credit and take a 14 percent stake in the venture. AvtoVAZ and GM each would hold 43 percent.

Back in Detroit, the JV proposal once again ran into renewed opposition. GM's president Wagoner continued to question whether the Russian market could actually afford the Opel-based second car, the Opel T3000. Wagoner ordered the second phase cut from the JV, making the Niva the single product which the joint venture would produce. This reduced GM's proposed investment to $100 million.

Throughout the fall, however, complexities continued to rise. Just prior to the venture's going before the GM Board, AvtoVAZ made new surprising demands that GM increase the price the JV would pay AvtoVAZ for Niva parts by 25 percent. When Herman warned them this would scuttle the deal, AvtoVAZ backed off. Again, primarily out of frustration with the pace of negotiations, AvtoVAZ announced in January 2001 that it would begin small scale production of an SUV under its own Lada brand. Herman once again provided damage control. Herman promised GM's Board that AvtoVAZ would actually build no more than a few dozen of the SUVs "for show."

Finally, on February 6, 2001, Herman presented the current proposal to GM's board in Detroit (see Exhibit 6). After heated debate, the board approved the proposal. The possibility of entering a large and developing market, with shared risk and investment of EBRD, was a rare opportunity to get in on the ground and develop a new local market. According to GM president Wagoner, "Russia's going to be a very big market."

EXHIBIT 6   Evolving GM/AvtoVAZ Joint Venture Structure

Party	NIVA II ALONE			NIVA II + OPEL T3000	
	Ownership	Equity	Debt	Equity	Capital
AvtoVAZ	41.5%	$100m		43.0%	$200m
General Motors	41.5%	100m		43.0%	175m
EBRD	17.0%	40m	93m	14.0%	175m
Total	100.0%	$250m		100.0%	$550m

Over 200,000 pieces of stainless steel flatware are just sitting in a Pier 1 Imports warehouse. Where did these come from? Most recently they were stocked in Pier 1 stores—that is until a couple of customers informed store managers that the stainless steel pieces rusted. The company response? After a very rapid testing process that confirmed the customers' observations, the offending product was pulled from all stores and sent to its "resting place" —all within a two-week period.

The people in merchandising at company headquarters in Fort Worth, Texas, and the local Pier 1 agent in China now have ascertained that while there are 47 different types of stainless steel, only one—referred to as 18-8—can be used to make serviceable flatware that won't rust. This newly recognized quality specification has been quickly communicated to all other company agents who purchase flatware assuring that this product quality issue will not arise again.

It is John Baker's responsibility to oversee the network of corporate buyers and on-site agents who are directly responsible for finding, choosing, and assuring the quality of merchandise imported from around the world. Baker, the Senior Manager of Merchandise Compliance, accepted a position at Pier 1 Imports over twenty years ago after working for various department stores purchasing tabletop and kitchen wares. When he first came on board as a buyer, he spent nearly six months of the year on the road, working with the agent network and finding new vendors for Pier 1 merchandise. Today, Baker also handles the increasingly complex area of government regulations of merchandise.

Because such a high percentage of Pier 1 Imports' merchandise is imported (over 85 percent), it is especially critical that U.S. government regulations regarding various product categories be studied and communicated to the manufacturers in other countries. These government regulations form one of the two measures of quality assurance for Pier 1 products. The second is that the products must conform to aesthetic standards that guarantee that the product fits the Pier 1 image and Pier 1 customer desires. It is in large part the buyer's expertise that assures that these standards are met.

What is the process for finding and selecting vendors in countries other than the United States? First of all, Pier 1 depends upon a well- and long-established network of agents in every country from which they import. In some lesser-developed regions, Pier 1 agents work with governments to help locate professional exporters. Some exporters are found at international trade fairs as well. The bulk of Pier 1 agents are native to the country in which they work, and some have been in place for as long as thirty years with their children now taking over the local positions.

The agents' jobs include finding local producers of handcrafted items that fit the Pier 1 customer needs. Buyers look for new sources of products at local craft fairs and even flea markets. Right now, for example, local agents in several countries are looking for sources of wooden furniture— primarily chests and tables—because Pier 1 would like to add to this in-store category. Based upon the location of raw materials, in this case in Italy, South America, Indonesia, and Thailand, agents are searching for just the right manufacturers to be brought to the buyers' attention.

Because it is the agents based within the various exporting countries who must enforce quality requirements, it is critical that John Baker and his colleagues carefully communicate both governmental and aesthetic product requirements to the agents. The agents can then "sit down at the table" with the manufacturers and work out the quality issues. If misunderstandings occur, Pier 1 is always ready to accept some of the responsibility because they view their manufacturers and agents as their partners in this business.

Because Pier 1 Imports has carefully carved out a unique niche in the specialty retail store industry, buyers are hard to hire from outside the company. As Baker noted, "The bulk of our staff has come out of our stores. It is easy for a buyer to move from Macy's to Hudson's—the products are the same as are most of the vendors. The Pier 1 buyer, however, must understand the Pier 1 store in order to be able to effectively and efficiently buy for it." These Pier 1 buyers, along with their agents onsite around the globe, serve as the company's primary link to product quality.

Questions for Discussion

1. What are the implications for sales, customer satisfaction, and profits for companies like Pier 1 (http://www.pier1.com) when low quality merchandise is not identified early in the purchasing process?

2. Do you think that Pier 1 might have avoided this problem if it had a very aggressive quality assurance program, i.e., ISO 9000, in place?

PART 4

CASE 10

Water from Iceland

Stan Otis was in a contemplative mood. He had just hung up the phone after talking with Roger Morey, vice president of Citicorp. Morey had made him a job offer in the investment banking sector of the firm. The interviews had gone well, and Citicorp management was impressed with Stan's credentials from a major northeastern private university. "I think you can do well here, Stan. Let us know within a week whether you accept the job," Morey had said.

The three-month search had paid off well, Stan thought. However, an alternative plan complicated the decision to accept the position.

Stan had returned several months before from an extended trip throughout Europe, a delayed graduation present from his parents. Among other places, he had visited Reykjavik, Iceland. Even though he could not communicate well, he found the island enchanting. What particularly fascinated him was the lack of industry and the purity of the

Source: This study was prepared by Michael R. Czinkota and Jesse Nelson, using the following background material: International Bottled Water Association statistics: "Top 10 Bottled Water Companies: 1994," *Beverage World* (2001); Beverage Marketing Corporation, 2001.

natural landscape. In particular, he felt the water tasted extremely good. Returning home, he began to consider making this water available in the United States.

The Water Market in the United States

In order to consider the possibilities of importing Icelandic water, Stan knew that he first had to learn more about the general water market in the United States. Fortunately, some former college friends were working in a market research firm. Owing Stan some favors, these friends furnished him with a consulting report on the water market.

The Consulting Report

Bottled water has more than a 12 percent market share of total beverage consumption in the United States. The overall distribution of market share is shown in Figure 1. Primary types of water available for human consumption in the United States are treated or processed water, mineral water, sparkling or effervescent water, and spring well water.

FIGURE 1   **Retail Market Shares of Beverage Products in 1999**

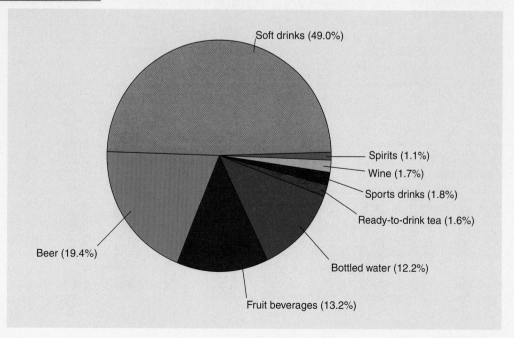

Soft drinks (49.0%)
Spirits (1.1%)
Wine (1.7%)
Sports drinks (1.8%)
Ready-to-drink tea (1.6%)
Bottled water (12.2%)
Fruit beverages (13.2%)
Beer (19.4%)

Source: Beverage World, 2000

TABLE I	U.S. Beverage Consumption 1999	
	Retail Receipts in Billions of Dollars	Per Capita Consumption in Gallons
Soft drinks	54.84	55.9
Beer	55.05	22.4
Spirits	34.8	1.2
Fruit beverages	18.57	15.2
Wine	17.91	1.9
Bottled water	5.92	15.5
Ready-to-drink tea	2.67	1.9
Sports drinks	2.91	2.3

Source: *Beverage World*, 2000

Treated or processed water comes from a well stream or central reservoir supply. This water usually flows as tap water and has been purified and fluoridated.

Mineral water is spring water that contains a substantial amount of minerals, which may be injected or occur naturally. Natural mineral water is obtained from underground water strata or a natural spring. The composition of the water at its source is constant, and the source discharge and temperature remain stable. The natural content of the water at the source is not modified by an artificial process.

Sparkling or effervescent water is water with natural or artificial carbonation. Some mineral waters come to the surface naturally carbonated through underground gases but lose their fizz on the surface with normal pressure. Many of these waters are injected with carbon dioxide later on.

Minerals are important to the taste and quality of water. The type and variety of minerals present in the water can make it a very healthy and enjoyable drink. The combination of minerals present in the water determines its relative degree of acidity. The level of acidity is measured by the pH factor. A pH 7 rating indicates a neutral water. A higher rating indicates that the water contains more solids, such as manganese calcium, and is said to be "hard." Conversely, water with a lower rating is classified as "soft." Most tap water is soft, whereas the majority of commercially sold waters tend to be hard.

FIGURE 2	U.S. Bottled Water Market, 1990–1999

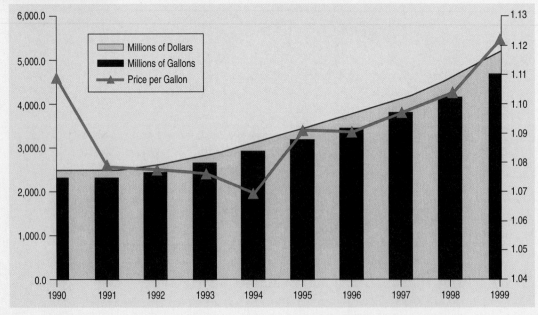

Source: Beverage Marketing Corporation

TABLE 2

Projected U.S. Bottled Water Market Volume, 1976–2004

Year	Millions of Gallons	Year	Millions of Gallons
1976	354.3	1992	2,422.0
1980	605.0	1993	2,623.9
1985	1,214.2	1994	2,901.9
1986	1,365.7	1995	3,167.5
1987	1,554.0	1996	3,449.3
1988	1,777.2	1997	3,775.8
1989	2,029.4	1998	4,146.0
1990	2,237.6	1999	4,646.1
1991	2,286.5	2004	6,783.9

Source: Beverage Marketing Corporation, 2000

Water Consumption in the United States

Tap water has generally been inexpensive, relatively pure, and plentiful in the United States. Traditionally, bottled water has been consumed in the United States by the very wealthy. In the past several years, however, bottled water has begun to appeal to a wider market. The four main reasons for this change are:

1. An increasing awareness among consumers of the impurity of city water supplies
2. Increasing dissatisfaction with the taste and odor of city tap water
3. Rising affluence in society
4. An increasing desire to avoid excess consumption of caffeine, sugar, and other substances present in coffee and soft drinks.

Bottled water consumers are found chiefly in the states of California, Texas, Florida, New York and Arizona. Combined, these states represent 53 percent of nationwide bottled water sales. California alone represents over 24 percent of industry consumption. Nationwide, per capita consumption is estimated to be over 15 gallons—far ahead of per capita consumption of spirits, wine, ready-to-drink tea and sports drinks. For comparison of per capita consumption of bottled water and other beverages, see Table 1.

Before 1976, bottled water was considered primarily a gourmet specialty, a luxury item consumed by the rich. Today, there are over 700 brands of bottled water available on the U.S. market. Since the entry of Perrier Group into the U.S. market, bottled water consumption has shown exceptional growth.

The volume of bottled water sold rose from only 354.3 million gallons in 1976 to nearly 5 billion gallons in 2000—almost a fourteen-fold increase (see Figure 2). Since 1995 there has been growth of 50 percent, taking market share from soft drinks, ready-to-drink tea, beer, and spirits. Volume is expected to increase to 6.8 billion gallons in 2004, a 35 percent increase over 2000 levels (see Table 2).

In 1999, the industry's receipts totaled $4.94 billion on the wholesale and $5.92 billion on the retail level, a 14 percent increase from 1998. Nonsparkling water accounts for 93.6 percent of total bottled water gallonage (see Figure 3).

FIGURE 3   Market Share of Bottled Water by Segment in 1999 (Based on Volume)

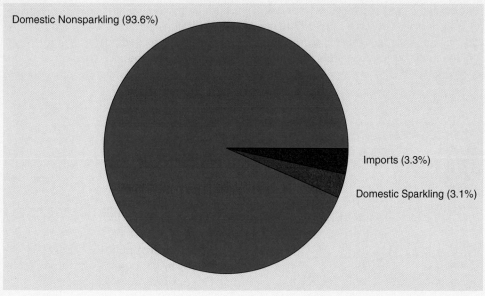

Source: Beverage Marketing Corporation

FIGURE 4　**Bottled Water Imports by Country**

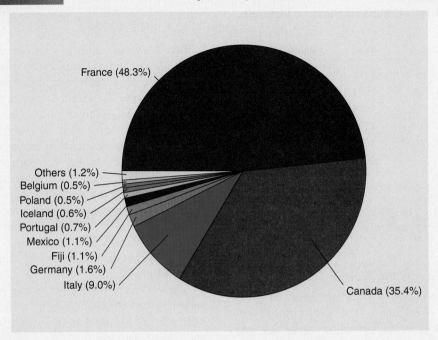

France (48.3%)

Others (1.2%)
Belgium (0.5%)
Poland (0.5%)
Iceland (0.6%)
Portugal (0.7%)
Mexico (1.1%)
Fiji (1.1%)
Germany (1.6%)
Italy (9.0%)

Canada (35.4%)

Source: Beverage Marketing Corporation, 2000

While the volume of total bottled water more than doubled between 1990 and 1999, consumption of nonsparkling bottled water increased 119 percent as consumption of sparkling water declined by 17 percent.

As Figure 4 shows, by 1999 imported water held a 3.3 percent share of the domestic market in terms of volume but over a 20 percent share in terms of wholesale prices (see Table 3). Though between 1998 and 1999 the volume of imported bottled water decreased 6.1 percent, imports have risen well over 100 percent since 1990 (see Table 4). The leading country importing water to the U.S. is France, with a 48.3 percent share of total bottled water imports. Canada is second with 35.4 percent market share.

Ranked eighth, bottled water from Iceland holds 0.6 percent market share (see Figure 4).

Among producers, Perrier is a strong leader with a 30.5 percent market share. The Perrier Group's top four selling bottled water brands are Arrowhead, Poland Spring, Ozarka and Zephyrhills—all among the top ten selling brands in the United States. Suntory Water Group has 9.7 percent and McKesson has 8.0 percent of the market share, with both companies comprised of many relatively small brands.

Overall, a cursory analysis indicates good potential for success for a new importer of bottled water in the United States. This is especially true if the water is exceptionally pure and can be classified as mineral water.

Additional Research

Further exploring his import idea, Stan Otis gathered information on various other marketing facets. One of his main concerns was government regulations.

Bottled Water Regulations in the United States

The bottled water industry in the United States is regulated and controlled at two levels—by the federal government and by various state governments. Some states, such as California and Florida, impose even stricter regulations on bottled water than they are required to follow under the federal regulations. Others, such as Arizona, do not reg-

TABLE 3

Share of Imports in U.S. Bottled Water Market

	Estimated Wholesale Dollars	Gallonage
1985	11.7%	2.8%
1990	13%	3.7%
1995	14.4%	3.6%
1999	21.2%	3.3%

Source: International Bottled Water Association; Beverage Marketing Corporation

TABLE 4 — U.S. Bottled Water Market by Segments 1990–1999

Year	Non-Sparkling Volume*	Non-Sparkling Change	Sparkling Volume*	Sparkling Change	Imports Volume*	Imports Change	Total Volume*	Total Change
1990	1,987.7	8.2%	176.0	28.4%	73.9	32.9%	2,237.6	10.3%
1991	2,042.8	2.8%	172.3	−2.1%	71.4	−3.4%	2,286.5	2.2%
1992	2,163.4	5.9%	172.3	0.0%	86.3	20.9%	2,422.0	5.9%
1993	2,356.7	8.9%	174.7	1.4%	92.5	7.2%	2,623.9	8.3%
1994	2,623.1	11.3%	174.8	0.1%	104.0	12.4%	2,901.9	10.6%
1995	2,906.2	10.8%	164.2	−6.1%	97.1	−6.7%	3,167.5	9.2%
1996	3,178.5	9.4%	159.0	−3.2%	111.8	15.2%	3,449.3	8.9%
1997	3,472.9	9.3%	153.8	−3.3%	149.1	33.4%	3,775.8	9.5%
1998	3,839.1	10.5%	146.1	−5.0%	160.8	7.9%	4,146.0	9.8%
1999	4,349.0	13.3%	146.0	−0.1%	151.1	−6.1%	4,646.1	12.1%

*Millions of gallons

Source: Beverage Marketing Corporation, 2000

ulate the bottled water industry beyond the federal requirements. About 75 percent of bottled water is obtained from springs, artesian wells, and drilled wells. The other 25 percent comes from municipal water systems, which are regulated by the Environmental Protection Agency (EPA). All bottled water is considered food and is thus regulated by the Food and Drug Administration (FDA). Under the 1974 Safe Drinking Water Act, the FDA adopted bottled water standards compatible with EPA's standards for water from public water systems. As the EPA revises its drinking water regulations, the FDA is required to revise its standards for bottled water or explain in the Federal Register why it decided not to do so. The FDA requires bottled water products to be clean and safe for human consumption, processed and distributed under sanitary conditions, and produced in compliance with FDA good manufacturing practices. In addition, domestic bottled water producers engaged in interstate commerce are subject to periodic, unannounced FDA inspections.

In 1991, an investigation by the U.S. House Energy and Commerce Committee found that 25 percent of the higher-priced bottled water comes from the same sources as ordinary tap water, another 25 percent of producers were unable to document their sources of water, and 31 percent exceeded limits of microbiological contamination. The Committee faulted the FDA with negligent oversight. In response, the FDA established, in November of 1995, definitions for artesian water, groundwater, mineral water, purified water, sparkling bottled water, sterile water, and well water in order to ensure fair advertising by the industry. These results went into effect in May 1996. They include specification of the mineral content of water that can be sold as mineral water. Previously, mineral water was not regulated by the FDA, which resulted in varying standards for mineral water across states. In addition, under these rules, if bottled water comes from a municipal source, it must be labeled to indicate its origin.

The Icelandic Scenario

Iceland is highly import-dependent. In terms of products exported, it has little diversity and is dangerously dependent on its fish crop and world fish prices. The government, troubled by high inflation rates and low financial reserves, is very interested in diversifying its export base. An Icelandic Export Board has been created and charged with developing new products for export and aggressively promoting them abroad.

The Ministry of Commerce, after consulting the Central Bank, has the ultimate responsibility in matters concerning import and export licensing. The Central Bank is responsible for the regulation of foreign exchange transactions and exchange controls, including capital controls. It is also responsible for ensuring that all foreign exchange due to residents is surrendered to authorized banks. All commercial exports require licenses. The shipping documents must be lodged with an authorized bank. Receipts exchanged for exports must be surrendered to the Central Bank.

All investments by nonresidents in Iceland are subject to individual approval. The participation of nonresidents in Icelandic joint venture companies may not exceed 49 percent. Nonresident-owned foreign capital entering in the form of foreign exchange must be surrendered.

Iceland is a member of the United Nations, the European Free Trade Association, and the World Trade Organization. Iceland enjoys "most favored nation" status with the United States. Under this designation, mineral and carbonated water from Iceland is subject to a tariff of 0.33 cents per liter, and natural (still) water is tariff-free.

Questions for Discussion

1. Is there sufficient information to determine whether importing water from Iceland would be a profitable business? If not, what additional information is needed to make a determination?
2. Is the market climate in the United States conducive to water imports from Iceland?
3. What are some possible reasons for the fluctuation in the market share held by imports over the past ten years?
4. Should the U.S. government be involved in regulating bottled water products?

VIDEO CASE
Whirlpool and the Global Appliance Industry

Within a few months after becoming CEO of Whirlpool Corp. in 1987, David Whitwam met with his senior managers to plot a strategy for securing future company growth. At the time, Whirlpool was the market leader among U.S. appliance makers, but it generated only weak sales outside North America. Operating in a mature market, it faced the same low profit margins as major competitors like General Electric and Maytag. In addition to price wars, especially in mature markets, the industry had started to consolidate, and consumers were demanding more environmentally friendly products.

Whirlpool and Its Options

Whitwam and his management team explored several growth options, including diversifying into other industries experiencing more rapid growth, such as furniture or garden products; restructuring the company financially; and expanding vertically and horizontally. The group sharpened its focus to consider opportunities for expanding the appliance business beyond North American markets. After all, the basics of managing the appliance business and the product technologies are similar in Europe, North America, Asia, and Latin America. As Whitwam put it, "We were very good at what we did. What we needed was to enter appliance markets in other parts of the world and learn how to satisfy different kinds of customers."

Whirlpool industry data predicted that, over time, appliance manufacturing would become a global industry. As Whitwam saw it, his company had three options: "We could ignore the inevitable—a decision that would have condemned Whirlpool to a slow death. We could wait for globalization to begin and then try to react, which would have put us in a catch-up mode, technologically and organizationally. Or we could control our own destiny and try to shape the very nature of globalization in our industry. In short, we could force our competitors to respond to us."

Sources: Portions of this case were researched from material available at **http://www.whirlpool.com.** The Global Success Factors section is derived from a report on the global appliance industry by John Bonds, German Estrada, Peter Jacobs, Jorge Harb-Kallab, Paul Kunzer, and Karin Toth at Georgetown University, March 2000. See also Ilkka A. Ronkainen and Ivan Menezes, "Implementing Global Marketing Strategy," *International Marketing Review* 13 (Number 3, 1996): 56–63; "The Right Way to Go Global: An Interview with Whirlpool CEO David Whitwam," *Harvard Business Review* 72 (March–April 1994): 134–145; and "Chinese Industry Races to Make a Global Name for Itself," *Washington Post,* April 23, 2000, H1, H5.

Whitwam and his team chose the third option and set out on a mission to make Whirlpool "one company worldwide." They aimed much higher than simply marketing products or operating around the globe. For decades, Whirlpool had sold some appliances in other countries to buyers who could afford them. Whitwam wanted to expand this reach by establishing a vision of a company that could leverage global resources to gain a long-term competitive advantage. In his words, this effort meant "having the best technologies and processes for designing, manufacturing, selling, and servicing your products at the lowest possible costs. Our vision at Whirlpool is to integrate our geographical businesses wherever possible, so that our most advanced expertise in any given area—whether it's refrigeration technology or distribution strategy—isn't confined to one location or one division. We want to be able to take the best capabilities we have and leverage them in all of our operations worldwide."

As its first step in transforming a largely domestic operation into a global powerhouse, Whirlpool purchased the European appliance business of Dutch consumer goods giant, Philips Electronics. Philips had been losing market share for years, running its European operations as independent regional companies that made different appliances for individual markets. "When we bought this business," Whitwam recalls, "we had two automatic washer designs, one built in Italy and one built in Germany. If you as a consumer looked at them, they were basically the same machines. But there wasn't anything common about those two machines. There wasn't even a common screw."

The Whirlpool strategy called for reversing the decline in European market share and improving profitability by changing product designs and manufacturing processes and by switching to centralized purchasing. The change reorganized the national design and research staffs inherited from Philips into European product teams that worked closely with Whirlpool's U.S. designers. Redesigned models shared more parts, and inventory costs fell when Whirlpool consolidated warehouses from 36 to 8. The transformation trimmed Philips's list of 1,600 suppliers by 50 percent, and it converted the national operations to regional companies.

Whitwam believed that the drive to become one company worldwide required making Whirlpool a global brand—a formidable task in Europe, where the name was not well-known. The company rebranded the Philips product lines, supported by a $135 million pan-European advertising campaign that initially presented both the Philips and

Whirlpool names and eventually converted to Whirlpool alone.

Another important component of the Whirlpool global strategy—product innovation—sought to develop superior products based on consumer needs and wants. "We have to provide a compelling reason other than price for consumers to buy Whirlpool-built products," says Whitwam. "We can do that only by understanding the consumer better than anyone else does and then translating our understanding into clearly superior product designs, features, and after-sales support. Our goal is for consumers to prefer the Whirlpool brand because it offers greater overall value than competing products."

One successful product innovation led to the Whirlpool Crispwave microwave oven. Extensive research with European consumers revealed a desire for a microwave that could brown and crisp food. In response, Whirlpool engineers designed the VIP Crispwave, which can fry crispy bacon and cook a pizza with a crisp crust. The new microwave proved successful in Europe, and Whirlpool later introduced it in the United States.

Whirlpool's global strategy includes a goal to become the market leader in Asia, which will be the world's largest appliance market in the 21st century. In 1988, it began setting up sales and distribution systems in Asia to help it serve Asian markets and to make the firm more familiar with those markets and potential customers. The company established three regional offices: one in Singapore to serve Southeast Asia, a second in Hong Kong to handle the Chinese market, and a Tokyo office for Japan. Through careful analysis, Whirlpool marketers sought to match specific current products with Asian consumers. They studied existing and emerging trade channels and assessed the relative strengths and weaknesses of competitors in the Asian markets. The company set up joint ventures with five Asian manufacturers for four appliance lines with the highest market potential: refrigerators, washers, air conditioners, and microwave ovens. With a controlling interest in each of the joint ventures, the newly global company confidently expects to excel in the world's fastest-growing market.

Whirlpool has come a long way since embarking on its global strategy. By 2000, revenues had doubled to more than $10 billion. The company now reaches markets in more than 170 countries, leading the markets in both North America and Latin America. Whirlpool is number three in Europe and the largest Western appliance company in Asia. For building its integrated global network, "Whirlpool gets very high marks," says an industry analyst. "They are outpacing the industry dramatically."

Global Success Factors

From a global perspective, there are three success factors that affect all of the different geographic regions. The first key success factor on a global scale is successful branding.

Each of the large global manufacturers has been very successful in developing a branding strategy. Most of these players sell a variety of brands, where each is targeted to certain quality and price levels. In addition, the strong brand reputation has been necessary for the major manufacturers either to expand operations into new regions or to launch new product lines. For example, Maytag did not have a line of products in the dishwasher category but had a large brand presence in the washer/dryer category. To expand its product line, Maytag decided to launch a new line of products in the dishwasher segment. Through a successful branding campaign, in less than two years Maytag captured the second largest market share in the segment. It leveraged its successful brand image in one segment to quickly steal share from less successful competitors.

The second key success factor on a global scale is price sensitivity. Given the large cost of these goods, large-scale manufacturers have been able to lower prices to meet the demand of customers. While there is little price elasticity, some manufacturers have been able to raise prices on their high-end goods, but for the most part, most manufacturers have lowered prices, and thus margins, to stay competitive with other brands. With razor-thin margins across each segment, only manufacturers that have the size to realize economies of scale have been able to remain competitive and lower prices to meet demands of their customers. This price sensitivity and the need to continually lower prices made up one of the major forces driving the consolidation within the industry. Many smaller brands were not able to compete and therefore were sold to the larger appliance brands.

The third success factor is presence in the major markets of the world. Not only does this provide the necessary scale to compete but also the opportunity to learn and cross-subsidize resources across borders. Chinese appliance makers, such as Haier and Kelon, are both expanding globally. Beyond the goal of expanded sales, one of the most significant drivers in establishing operations in India, Malaysia, and the United States, is to remain competitive at home. Joining the WTO means that China's trade barriers will fall, bringing the best foreign products to China.

China and Asia

Aside from the global key success factors, two key success factors within China and Asia are very important. First, appliance manufacturers must have access to distribution channels and therefore the ability to provide the products across several different Chinese regions. The access to Chinese distribution channels can be very limiting for international corporations whereas China-based companies, such as Kelon and Haier, have a definite competitive advantage.

Second, large appliance manufacturers must have a large scope of products for success. Specifically, it is the number of different segments in which a company sells products that will lead to success in China, not the scope of products within a given segment. Kelon manufactures 112 different types of air conditioners, but it is not a full-line supplier of appliances to its customers. Contrarily, Haier is a full-line supplier that manufactures products in each product segment and so provides its customers with a variety of appliances under one brand name.

The Japanese market has a different set of criteria for success than China and the rest of Asia. Instead, the Japanese market closely resembles certain aspects of the European and U.S. markets. Aside from the global success factors, success in the Japanese market is based on two key factors. First, due to the size of dwellings in Japan, innovation with regard to product size is very important. Japanese customers are looking for product innovations that will fit into smaller spaces while providing the most use of cabinet space. Second, to be successful in Japan, a manufacturer must sell a product that is very high in quality. Japanese customers are very demanding in regard to product quality, and they expect their products to last decades. Therefore, manufacturers selling products that are very high in quality will have a competitive advantage.

United States

Within the United States, two key success factors outside of the global factors are necessary for a company's success. First, a company must develop innovative products that incorporate new features while still operating efficiently. U.S. customers are very aware that energy consumption of a product will have a long-term effect on their utility bills, so they look for products that operate more efficiently. In addition, customers are willing to pay a premium for innovative features on a high-end product. Many manufacturers were surprised that Maytag was able to raise its prices for its front-loading washer not once, but twice. Customers were not as concerned with the price as they were concerned with the convenience of the product.

The second key success factor within the U.S. market is product quality, in respect to durability. U.S. consumers are willing to pay more for a product, but they expect it to operate for well over a decade with little to no maintenance. Therefore, for an appliance manufacturer to succeed in the United States, it must deliver products that are of high quality and of innovative design.

Europe

Outside of the two global success factors, the European market has two distinct factors that are required for suc-

cess. First, to succeed in Europe, manufacturers must develop innovative products. In this context, innovative products are defined as products that are efficient and environmentally friendly. The "green" movement within Europe is very strong, and therefore a manufacturer that does not sell "eco-products" will not succeed when compared to a company that offers that type of product.

Second, quality is a key success factor for Europe. Similar to other markets, in this context quality refers to durability. European consumers are looking for products that are durable and will last over a long period of time. In this regard, the European market is very similar to the U.S., Japanese, and Latin American markets.

Latin America

Within Latin America, there are two additional success factors for a manufacturer to consider outside the global success factors. First, Latin American companies that provide excellent service to customers will have an advantage over the competition. The amount of time that the average consumer owns an appliance in Latin America is somewhat longer than in other global regions, so consumers are looking for excellent service. The economy in Latin America has had several challenges in recent history, and so consumers would much rather repair an existing product than buy a new appliance.

Second, quality is another success factor for Latin America. This key success factor ties directly into the service success factor. Initially, Latin Americans are looking for a durable product that will last for over a decade; then through customer service, the product will be repaired to extend its life for several more years.

Questions for Discussion

1. Whirlpool's marketing goal is to leverage resources across borders. How is this evident in its marketing approach? Consult **www.whirlpool.com** for additional information.

2. The challenge facing Whirlpool is not only external in catering to local customers' needs worldwide, but also internal—all the regional and local units have to "buy in" to the global vision. What types of particular issues (such as product or technology transfers) may arise, and how should they be dealt with?

3. Visit the web site of the Association of Home Appliance Manufacturers, **www.aham.org,** and suggest some of the global trends among the major manufacturers of household appliances.

Amazon.com opened its virtual doors in July 1995 with a mission "to use the Internet to offer products that educate, inform, and inspire." By 2000, Amazon.com was the largest Internet-based seller of books and music and operated one of the most frequently used Web sites on the Internet, offering over 4.7 million discounted books as well as CDs, DVDs, computer games, audio books, and videotapes. The company had an 85 percent share of online book sales, with over 20 million customers in more than 160 countries.

Customers use Amazon.com's interactive Web site both to select and to purchase products. Specifically, customers are able to use the site to search for titles, browse selections, read and post reviews, register for personalized services, make a credit card purchase, and check order status. Most orders are shipped to customers directly from Amazon.com's warehouses, usually within 24 to 72 hours. If a customer needs to return a product, complimentary return postage is provided to the customer.

Amazon.com communicates with its customers electronically throughout the order process. A confirmation e-mail is sent to the customer when the order is received, and another when the order has been processed. Customers can then track the delivery status of orders online by using a key code number. Customers who prefer not to use a credit card on the Internet may fax or telephone in the credit card number using Amazon.com's toll-free numbers.

Amazon.com's headquarters are located in Seattle, Washington, with distribution facilities in Seattle, Delaware, Nevada, the United Kingdom, and Germany. In 1999, the firm had over 2,100 employees and was expanding rapidly. Since May 1997, Amazon.com has been publicly owned, with common stock shares traded on the NASDAQ National Market exchange in the United States. Amazon.com's stock is volatile—after its initial offering price of $9 per share in 1997 it has ranged from $209 per share to $14.88 in the fourth quarter of 2000.

Source: Georgetown MBA candidates Sarah Knight, Harry Kobrak, and Paul Lewis prepared this case study under the direction of Professor Michael R. Czinkota; © Michael R. Czinkota. In addition to interviews with Amazon.com personnel, use was made of company sports and media coverage of Amazon.com.

Major Events and Players in Its Development

The most significant player in Amazon.com's short history is its founder and chief executive officer, Jeff Bezos. With a background in computer science and finance, including fund management at Bankers Trust, Bezos decided in 1994 that the Internet could provide customers with services unavailable through traditional retailers, including discounted prices, wider selection, and greater product information.

In a November 1998 interview with *The Washington Post*, Bezos explained that he sees the success of electronic retailers as depending on their ability to analyze each customer's tastes. "If we have 4.5 million customers, we shouldn't have one store," he said. "We should have 4.5 million stores." Using its proprietary personalization technology, the Amazon.com Web page greets customers by name and, through mathematical formulas that analyze a customer's purchase history, provides instant recommendations for other products to consider for purchase.

Bezos oversees six senior vice presidents, including a chief financial officer and a chief information officer. The longest tenure with the firm of these executive officers is three years.

Since its founding, Amazon.com has undergone frequent and significant changes to maintain its leadership position as an Internet firm. Among the most notable developments are:

- *May 1997* **Initial public offering** of 3 million shares of common stock. The capital generated from going public was used to pay existing debts and make future systems investments.
- *June 1998* **Expanded product line** to include music. Amazon.com now offers more than 125,000 CD titles. Through its Web site, Amazon.com's customers can listen to song samples before purchasing. As of December 1998, Amazon.com stood as the Internet's largest music retailer.
- *September 1998* Amazon.com **established local Internet presence in Germany and the United Kingdom** by purchasing two existing online book companies. In just three months, Amazon.com became the leading online bookseller in these markets.

- *October 1999* Amazon launches **wireless shopping** from handheld devices.
- *August 2000* A strategic alliance with **ToysRUS** is formed, with Amazon managing online sales.

Sales and Profit Record

In its four-year existence, Amazon.com has experienced explosive sales. In 2000, sales jumped to $2,761 million, a fourfold increase from 1998 sales of $610 million (see Table 1 for details). Amazon.com's customer base has been building at a similar rate. In 1998 customer accounts stood at 20 million, a 300 percent increase from 6,700,000 in 1998.

Despite rapidly growing sales, Amazon.com continues to generate multimillion–dollar operating losses ($1,411,273 in 2000, compared with $111.9 million in 1998). According to the company's 1998 10-K: "the company will continue to incur substantial operating losses for the foreseeable future and these losses may be significantly higher than our current losses." These persistent losses are due primarily to low product gross margins. The company is also making significant investments in its technological and distribution infrastructure, as well as on building brand recognition.

The Amazon.com Business Model

The Amazon.com business model creates value for customers by offering:

1. Shopping convenience (from home or office)
2. Decision-enabling information
3. Discounted pricing
4. Ease of purchase
5. A wide selection
6. Speed, and
7. Reliability of order fulfillment

No single aspect of Amazon.com's business model is sufficient to create a competitive advantage. Locational shopping convenience, ease of purchase, and wide selection are clearly not sources of sustainable competitive advantage. Customers have long been able to order books from wide selections through catalogs or by telephone. Furthermore, decision-enabling information is available at a plethora of online sites and most public libraries. Finally, speed and reliability are clearly superior at a "real" bookstore, where one can receive the product immediately (as long as it is in stock). Thus, it is the combination of some or all of these characteristics that comprise Amazon.com's competitive advantage. As a pure retailer, which does not engage in the physical customization of the products it sells, Amazon.com

TABLE 1   Amazon.com Financial History

	2000	1998	1996
Net Sales	$2,761,983	$609,996	$15,746
Cost of Sales	2,106,206	476,155	12,287
Gross Profit	**655,777**	**133,841**	**3,459**
Operating Expenses:			
Marketing & Sales	594,489	133,023	6,090
Product Development	269,326	46,807	2,401
General & Administrative	108,962	15,799	1,411
Stock-based compensation	24,797		
Amortization of goodwill and other intangibles	321,772		
Impairment-related and other	200,311		
Merger & Acquisition-Related Costs	50,172		
Total Operating Expenses	1,519,657	245,801	9,902
Loss from Operations	**(863,880)**	**(111,960)**	**(6,443)**
Interest Income	40,821	14,053	202
Interest Expense	(130,921)	(26,639)	(5)
Other income (expense), net	(10,058)		
Non-cash gains and losses, net	(142,639)		
Net interest expense and other	(242,797)	(12,586)	197
Loss before equity in losses of equity-method investees, net	(1,106,677)		
Equity in losses of equity-method investees, net	(304,596)		
Net Loss	**(1,411,273)**	**(124,546)**	**(6,246)**

Figures in thousands of U.S. dollars.

Source: Amazon.com 2000 10-K report.

creates value for customers through a series of information services and logistical processes.

Logistical Processes as a Source of Competitive Advantage

Maintaining and improving operational efficiencies is absolutely essential for Amazon.com. The ability to offer a wide selection, discounted prices, speed and reliability are all tied directly to the company's logistical competencies.

In a bid to simultaneously improve its margins and increase price discounts, Amazon.com is attempting to purchase more product directly from publishers. The firm hopes to increase the mid-40 percent discounts received from wholesalers to the mid-50 percent rates available from publishers. Circumventing wholesalers would also enable the company to shorten shipping times.

Between 1996 and 1998, Amazon.com increased its Seattle warehouse space by 70 percent and built a new warehouse in Delaware. It also began leasing a highly mechanized distribution facility in Fernley, Nevada. These recent investments in material handling systems, together with the increases in warehouse capacity, are expected to result in a six to eightfold improvement in throughput within one year. Currently, Amazon.com ships 20 percent of books on the day they are ordered and aims to raise that rate to 95 percent. This is a staggering logistical challenge as the company stocks over 700,000 copies of approximately 200,000 titles.

Despite Amazon.com's focus on improving operational efficiencies, industry analysts are sharply divided on whether the company's logistical processes are truly competitive. J. Cohen at Merrill Lynch Capital Markets observed that:

> [Amazon.com] is not large enough (in terms of order volumes and distribution infrastructure) to generate the economies of scale necessary to compete effectively with large physical-world retail chains. At the same time, Amazon.com is far too large in terms of the cost structure (associated with its proprietary inventory and distribution systems) to compete effectively with companies that forego that structure and provide a linkage with existing distributors.

Amazon.com's disadvantages in scale relative to traditional booksellers, such as Barnes and Noble, are apparent. It is important to note that in 1998, Internet book sales accounted for approximately $300 million, slightly less than 1 percent of the U.S. market. Despite the expectation that Internet book sales will double in 1999, national retailers will retain massive scale economies. Furthermore, both Borders and Barnes and Noble have Web sites, which are expected to grow with the market (or faster). Barnes and Noble, which formed a strategic alliance with the German media conglomerate Bertelsmann, has direct relationships with some 20,000 publishers and distributors. In addition, Barnes and Noble's state-of-the-art distribution center has roughly 750,000 titles available for sameday shipping.

Building Brand Equity

Amazon.com has steadily increased its spending on advertising and promotion both in absolute terms and as a percentage of revenue. Between 1996 and 1998, Amazon.com spent roughly one-quarter of its sales on advertising and promotion. The company invested in promotional relationships with both the domestic and international sites of America Online, Excite, and Yahoo!.

Amazon.com's efforts to build brand equity through its extensive advertising and promotion have received mixed reviews from industry analysts. One Merrill Lynch analyst criticized Amazon.com's attempt to develop brand equity, questioning its value for the distributor of commodity products, such as books:

> We do not believe that online commodity product sales produce the sort of brand equity generated by the distribution of proprietary information or media products. The implication here is that while it may make economic sense for Yahoo! to lose money while building a user population, it probably does not make sense for Amazon.com to follow the same path.

Although advertising and promotion are extremely important to a growing business, it is doubtful brand equity alone will be enough to gain new customers and retain old ones if competitors with superior logistical systems and identical products enter the market. This increases the importance of Amazon.com's value-added information services to customers.

Value-Added Information Services

Amazon.com is strongly focused on achieving value-added differentiation through customer-oriented information services. Perhaps the most important information service Amazon.com provides is a comprehensive online catalog, which enables customers to search for books or CDs. Amazon.com's proprietary software will also track individual customer orders and subsequently recommend titles of a similar genre or related subject matter. Thus, Amazon.com's site provides automated customization for users. Jeff Bezos, the founder and CEO, has a vivid vision for how this technology will be used:

> Personalization is like retreating to the time when you have small-town merchants who got to know you, and they could help you get the right products. The right products can improve your life, and the wrong products detract from it. Before the era of mass merchandising, it used to be that most things were personalized. The promise of . . . customization is . . . you get the economies of mass merchandising and the individuality of 100-years-ago merchandising.

In addition to retaining customer preferences, the system retains customer purchase information, eliminating the need for repeat customers to reenter the same address and billing information. This is an extremely powerful tool and may represent a strong incumbency advantage. For example, in the fourth quarter of 1997, Amazon.com's automated system captured information for over 1.5 million customers, including e-mail address, mailing address, credit card number, and the products they purchased (including various classifications such as genre or topic). Unless a customer objects, Amazon.com reserves the right to utilize—or even possibly sell—this information.

Repeat customers account for approximately 60 percent of Amazon.com's orders, and this proportion appears to be growing. This statistic *may* indicate a high level of customer satisfaction. However, it could merely indicate customers' lack of awareness of Amazon.com's new online competitors, such as barnesandnoble.com. In the Barnes and Noble and Bertlesmann joint venture announced in late 1998, both companies pledged to invest $100 million in expanding barnesandnoble.com's U.S. sales (compared to $20 million for the Barnes and Noble superstores). This will lessen the incumbency advantage of brand awareness. Amazon.com will be under pressure to provide a higher level of value-added differentiation in customer service. Ultimately, Amazon.com's market success depends on its ability to maintain and grow its customer base by knowing and serving its customers better than its competitors.

International Activities

Amazon.com began direct exporting almost immediately after its inception in 1995. Preliminary exports could be described as reactive, as the company's first international customers sought out Amazon.com rather than vice versa. Early on, international orders were more concentrated in nonfiction technological and computer-oriented publications, although that customer base soon diversified. Amazon.com's international orders now follow a similar pattern to domestic orders, with customer interest in a wide range of subject matter.

Amazon.com currently sells to over 160 countries and is aggressively pursuing international sales through direct exporting as well as local overseas presence. In 1998 Amazon.com established a local presence in the United Kingdom and Germany by purchasing two existing online book companies, Telebook and BookPages. Amazon.com is currently the largest online retailer in these markets. The European subsidiaries have been set up to serve the entire EU market and have currency and shipping procedures in place. These efforts, as part of Amazon.com's international strategy, appear to be paying off; in 1998, about 20 percent of Amazon.com's sales were from international customers.

Despite the fact that Amazon.com exports to such a high number of countries, the company is still in the process of establishing an international presence. Amazon.com is continually increasing its efforts to reach out to international customers. As the company explained in its 1997 annual report:

> [Amazon.com] has only limited experience in sourcing, marketing, and distributing products on an international basis and in developing localized versions of its Web site and other systems. The Company expects to incur significant costs in establishing international facilities and operations, in promoting its brand internationally, in developing localized versions of its Web site and other systems, and in sourcing, marketing, and distributing products in foreign markets.

Amazon.com's use of regional interfaces adds a third layer to its international business activities. The cornerstone of Amazon.com's approach to international business is to leverage its existing systems and routines to serve all of its customers, regardless of location. The regional interfaces allow most of Amazon.com's customers to use their own language. Standardized algorithms and routines provide the same automated personalized services to international customers.

Continuing to expand local overseas operations, according to CEO Jeff Bezos, is the only way Amazon.com can stay competitive in the face of growing international competition. As in the U.S. market, Amazon.com has strong, albeit relatively new, competitors in the international marketplace. This competition increased considerably when in the fall of 1998, Bertelsmann agreed to purchase half of the interest in barnsandnoble.com for $200 million. Both Bertelsmann and Barnes and Noble plan to invest heavily in expanding barnesandnoble.com's international business.

The partnership between Bertelsmann and Barnes and Noble thus far does not appear to be hurting Amazon.com's international or domestic sales. Nonetheless, Media Metrix, a company that measures traffic on the Internet, calculates that the number of people visiting barnesandnoble.com's site is skyrocketing. As research shows that online customers like to browse for six months or longer before buying, Barnes and Noble is hoping that its domestic and international sales will soon pick up.

Amazon.com uses global merchant agreements with other Internet-based companies to promote the company internationally. In September 1998, Yahoo! Inc. agreed to place Amazon.com merchant links on its international sites, including those in Asia, UK and Ireland, France, Germany, Denmark, Sweden, Norway, Canada, Australia and New Zealand, Japan, and Korea. According to David Risher, senior vice president at Amazon.com: "This agreement with Yahoo!, combined with our local presence in Germany and the United Kingdom, strengthens our position around the world as a leading global book merchant." Similar agreements have been established with other popular Internet websites including Netscape, @Home, GeoCities, and AltaVista.

Like its domestic customers, Amazon.com's international customers select and purchase products through the company's U.S. or European Web pages. There are several foreign language versions, including Japanese, Dutch, French, Italian, Portuguese, German, and Spanish. The majority of Amazon.com's international customers pay with a credit card, such as Visa, MasterCard, and JB. International customers are required to bear all customs and duty charges.

For shipping, Amazon.com gives its customers a choice of international mail (estimated time of 7–21 business days with a minimum shipping and handling charge of $12.95) or DHL Worldwide Express International (1–4 business days with a minimum charge of $35.95). Amazon.com has been actively working to reduce the delivery times and shipping costs for its international (as well as its domestic) customers. The establishment of local distribution centers in Germany and the UK significantly reduces both delivery lead times and shipping costs for customers, and thus brings Amazon.com closer to its customers, both physically and psychologically.

Export Complaint Management

Amazon.com prides itself on superior service for both its international and domestic customers. The company has seen superior customer service and in particular complaint management as a key point of differentiation and therefore a source of competitive advantage. Amazon.com believes its international customers are "quite happy" with the level of service they have received.

One key to the quality of service is a high degree of responsiveness from Amazon.com's customer service department. Customer service representatives in the Seattle, Washington headquarters handle complaints from both domestic and international customers. These representatives are given a great deal of authority to resolve customer complaints. As Amazon.com's Customer Service Manager explained, complaints are rarely elevated to higher level managers:

> Most things are caught on the first shot. Escalations occur if a customer is not satisfied with a response, or if there is a complex issue such as large quantities or a complex billing issue like suspected fraud. Non-English phone or e-mail messages are escalated—e-mail is escalated mostly for tracking purposes since [it is usually] obvious what the customer needs from the e-mail message. Obviously, phone calls are more difficult if English is not spoken at all.

Training for Customer Satisfaction

Training is vital to ensure Amazon.com can run a highly responsive customer service program. Founder and CEO Bezos emphasizes the importance of developing people with the term "people bandwidth." Bezos describes people bandwidth as "smart people, working hard, passionately and

smartly." With huge numbers of investors eager to purchase a stake in Amazon.com, Bezos claims that the real constraint on the company's growth is not capital, but people. The CEO's comments provide insight into the strategic importance the company places on training. Amazon.com's Customer Service Manager described how the training process certifies representatives at different levels on an ongoing basis to respond quickly to customer needs:

> Classroom and on-the-job training and mentoring are all utilized. There is follow-up training to advance to the next skill/task level and review training on any new products or business processes. We also keep a pretty extensive intranet for reference.

Within the standard training curriculum, Amazon.com's customer service representatives also receive special training in how to correspond with international customers.

Communicating with Overseas Customers

As its business is based on the Internet, the majority of Amazon.com's international customers communicate via e-mail. Some customers choose to complain by telephone, although toll-free numbers are offered only domestically. The benchmark for answering e-mails is 100 percent within 24 hours or less. Customer service response routines are designed to be predictive, automated, and efficient.

Most international customers complain in English or Spanish, but customer service representatives are equipped to handle complaints in other languages. In fact, Amazon.com claims to have representatives conversant in nineteen languages. These include all the major European languages, as well as Japanese, Chinese, Korean, Vietnamese, Thai, Hebrew, Zulu, Swazi, and Hausa.

Export Complaints and Resolution Policies

The most frequent complaints from international customers center on distribution problems. This is not surprising, given the long lead times and high shipping costs Amazon.com's international customers must endure. As a result, customers are dissatisfied if their purchases arrive later than expected, or if their order is never received. According to Amazon.com's customer service department, the quantity of complaints are similar for domestic and overseas customers.

There is no separate department at Amazon.com to deal with overseas complaints. Within this organizational structure, customer service representatives must rely largely on standardized routines and protocol for interacting with customers. As a heuristic, customer service representatives are taught to mirror the tone and formality of their e-mail to the complaint they receive. Amazon.com's standard methods for placating dissatisfied international customers include a range of remedies that are designed to cost effectively maintain customer goodwill. These remedies include:

1. Upgraded or complementary shipping
2. Free replacements for lost or damaged items
3. Allowing customers to donate to charity a book delivered late or incorrectly where return shipping is not cost effective

Amazon.com tracks customer complaints through regular internal management reports. Complaints are routinely used to make continuous improvements to the shipping, billing, and order taking processes. Also, other departments, including Website Software, Product Development, and Marketing use customer service reports to make continuous improvements to their operating processes.

Questions for Discussion

1. Approximately a quarter of Amazon.com's sales are to overseas customers. How could Amazon.com structure its customer service department to better serve an increasingly international and culturally and linguistically diverse customer base? Should Amazon.com have "country specialists" for markets where it lacks an overseas presence?

2. How should Amazon.com address the two key areas of export complaints—long distribution times and high shipping costs? Although Amazon.com's existing international expansion strategy has emphasized inhouse ownership of warehousing and inventory, potential arrangements with specialized third parties are an alternative model. Is the outsourcing of warehousing and inventory management consistent with their existing business model?

3. How could Amazon.com better measure customer service? How could the customer service manager implement a continuous improvement process? What companies would you benchmark and how?

Company Background

In 1983, Ian J. Ward was an export merchant in difficulty. Throughout the 1970s his company, Ward, Bedas Canadian Ltd., had successfully sold Canadian lumber and salmon to countries in the Persian Gulf. Over time, the company had opened four offices worldwide. However, when the Iran–Iraq war erupted, most of Ward's long-term trading relationships disappeared within a matter of months. In addition, the international lumber market began to collapse. As a result, Ward, Bedas Canadian Ltd. went into a survivalist mode and sent employees all over the world to look for new markets and business opportunities. Late that year, the company received an interesting order. A firm in Korea urgently needed to purchase lumber for the production of chopsticks.

Learning about the Chopstick Market

In discussing the wood deal with the Koreans, Ward learned that in order to produce good chopsticks more than 60 percent of the wood fiber would be wasted. Given the high transportation cost involved, the large degree of wasted materials, and his need for new business, Ward decided to explore the Korean and Japanese chopstick industry in more detail.

He quickly determined that chopstick making in the Far East is a fragmented industry, working with old technology and suffering from a lack of natural resources. In Asia, chopsticks are produced in very small quantities, often by family organizations. Even the largest of the 450 chopstick factories in Japan turns out only 5 million chopsticks a month. This compares to an overall market size of 130 million pairs of disposable chopsticks a day. In addition, chopsticks represent a growing market. With increased wealth in Asia, people eat out more often and therefore have a greater demand for disposable chopsticks. The fear of communicable diseases has greatly reduced the use of reusable chopsticks. Renewable plastic chopsticks have been attacked by many groups as too newfangled and as causing future ecological problems.

Source: This case was written by Michael R. Czinkota based on the following sources: Mark Clayton, "Minnesota Chopstick Maker Finds Japanese Eager to Import His Quality Waribashi," *The Christian Science Monitor,* October 16, 1987, 11; Roger Worthington, "Improbable Chopstick Capitol of the World," *Chicago Tribune,* June 5, 1988, 39; Mark Gill, "The Great American Chopstick Master," *American Way,* August 1, 1987, 34, 78–79; "Perpich of Croatia," *The Economist,* April 20, 1991, 27; and personal interview with Ian J. Ward, president, Lakewood Forest Products.

From his research, Ward concluded that a competitive niche existed in the world chopstick market. He believed that, if he could use low-cost raw materials and ensure that the labor cost component would remain small, he could successfully compete in the world market.

The Founding of Lakewood Forest Products

In exploring opportunities afforded by the newly identified international marketing niche for chopsticks, Ward set four criteria for plant location:

1. Access to suitable raw materials
2. Proximity of other wood product users who could make use of the 60 percent waste for their production purposes
3. Proximity to a port that would facilitate shipment to the Far East
4. Availability of labor

In addition, Ward was aware of the importance of product quality. People use chopsticks on a daily basis and are accustomed to products that are visually inspected one by one, so he would have to live up to high quality expectations to compete successfully. Chopsticks could not be bowed or misshapen, have blemishes in the wood, or splinter.

Ward needed financing to implement his plan. Private lenders were skeptical and slow to provide funds. The skepticism resulted from the unusual direction of Ward's proposal. Far Eastern companies have generally held the cost advantage in a variety of industries, especially those as labor intensive as chopstick manufacturing. U.S. companies rarely have an advantage in producing low-cost items. Further, only a very small domestic market exists for chopsticks.

However, Ward found that the state of Minnesota was willing to participate in his new venture. Since the decline of the mining industry, regional unemployment had been rising rapidly in the state. In 1983, unemployment in Minnesota's Iron Range peaked at 22 percent. Therefore, state and local officials were anxious to attract new industries that would be independent of mining activities. Of particular help was the enthusiasm of Governor Rudy Perpich. The governor had been boosting Minnesota business on the international scene by traveling abroad and receiving many foreign visitors. He was excited about Ward's plans, which called for the creation of more than 100 new jobs within a year.

Hibbing, Minnesota, turned out to be an ideal location for Ward's project. The area had an abundant supply of aspen wood, which, because it grows in clay soil, tends to be unmarred. The fact that Hibbing was the hometown of the governor also did not hurt. In addition, Hibbing boasted an excellent labor pool, and both the city and the state were willing to make loans totaling $500,000. Further, the Iron Range Resources Rehabilitation Board was willing to sell $3.4 million in industrial revenue bonds for the project. Together with jobs and training wage subsidies, enterprise zone credits, and tax increment financing benefits, the initial public support of the project added up to about 30 percent of its start-up costs. The potential benefit of the new venture to the region was quite clear. When Lakewood Forest Products advertised its first 30 jobs, more than 3,000 people showed up to apply.

The Production and Sale of Chopsticks

Ward insisted that to truly penetrate the international market, he would need to keep his labor cost low. As a result, he decided to automate as much of the production as possible. However, no equipment was readily available to produce chopsticks, because no one had automated the process before.

After much searching, Ward identified a European equipment manufacturer who produced machinery for making popsicle sticks. He purchased equipment from the Danish firm to better carry out the sorting and finishing processes. However, because aspen wood was quite different from the wood for which the machine was designed, as was the final product, substantial design adjustments had to be made. Sophisticated equipment was also purchased to strip the bark from the wood and peel it into long, thin sheets. Finally, a computer vision system was acquired to detect defects in the chopsticks. The system rejected more than 20 percent of the production, and yet some of the chopsticks that passed inspection were splintering. However, Ward firmly believed that further fine-tuning of the equipment and training of the new work force would gradually take care of the problem.

Given this fully automated process, Lakewood Forest Products was able to develop capacity for up to 7 million chopsticks a day. With a unit manufacturing cost of $0.03 and an anticipated unit selling price of $0.057, Ward expected to earn a pretax profit of $4.7 million in 1988.

Due to intense marketing efforts in Japan and the fact that Japanese customers were struggling to obtain sufficient supplies of disposable chopsticks, Ward was able to presell the first five years of production quite quickly. By late 1987, Lakewood Forest Products was ready to enter the international market. With an ample supply of raw materials and an almost totally automated plant, Lakewood was positioned as the world's largest and least labor-intensive manufacturer of chopsticks. The first shipment of six containers with a load of 12 million pairs of chopsticks to Japan was made in October 1987.

Questions for Discussion

1. Is Lakewood Forest Products ready for exports? Using the export-readiness framework developed by the U.S. Department of Commerce and available through various sites such as **www.tradeport.org** (from "Trade Expert" go to "Getting Started" and finally to "Assess Your Export Readiness"), determine whether Lakewood's commitment, resources, and product warrant the action they have undertaken.

2. What are the environmental factors that are working for and against Lakewood Forest Products both at home in the United States and in the target market, Japan?

3. New-product success is a function of trial and repurchase. How do Lakewood's chances look along these two dimensions?

Customer Service Online: The HP DesignJet

At the beginning of September 1997, Ignacio Fonts, marketing director of the Barcelona Division of Hewlett-Packard Española, S.A., had a number of decisions to make regarding the start-up of the **www.designjet-online.hp.com** project, a relationship-marketing program that would allow HP to communicate on an interactive basis with the users of its large-format printers.

Hewlett-Packard (HP) was a multinational company with a presence in more than 120 countries worldwide whose activities included the manufacture and sale of personal and business computing products. In Europe it had 11 manufacturing sites, including one in the town of Sant Cugat del Vallés, near Barcelona (Spain), where it designed and manufactured large-format printers for the world market. HP was the undisputed world leader in this product category, with a market share of over 50 percent.

The Barcelona Division (HP-BCD) already had a Web presence at **www.hp.com/go/designjet,** but the new proposal Fonts was considering would entail major changes. Fonts had to carefully consider all the implications. The target visitors of the new web site would not be the general public, or even potential customers; rather, the site would be very specifically aimed at existing users of the approximately 500,000 HP large-format printers in use around the world. The problem, however, was that only around 50,000 of these users had been identified and registered.

For the first time, HP-BCD would try to interact directly with the end users of its large-format printers scattered around the world, and at the same time offer them new technical support tools. As the project advanced, the situation turned out to be considerably more complicated than expected.

One of Fonts's concerns was that, for the project to succeed, it was vital to get the Technical Support Organization and the Territorial Sales Organization involved (both operated at a global level and with total independence within HP). It was vital that they accepted the new web site as a useful marketing tool that also served their interests and not as an intrusion into their respective areas of responsibility.

Fonts had just returned from his summer holiday and had a meeting with his team planned for the coming Monday. At that meeting they would have to decide whether or not to go ahead and set up the new site. If they chose to go ahead, they would have to decide on the definitive content of the site, what measures would have to be taken to ensure its smooth operation, and which team member should be appointed as manager of the new web site. If the new web site were set up, it would be possible for any end user of large-format printers to start talking directly to "the manufacturer." Various departments within the HP organization, both within Fonts's direct area of responsibility and beyond it, therefore would have to respond effectively for the service to generate added value for the customer. Fonts thought that if any part of the HP organization was not properly prepared to communicate appropriately with the end users, it might be better to postpone the project or limit its scope so as not to harm the current excellent image of both HP Barcelona Division and its products in the world market.

Large-Format Printers

By 1997 there had been, for several years, a number of computer programs capable of creating and manipulating images by computer. CAD (Computer Assisted Design) and similar applications were regularly used by architects, engineers, and graphic designers to create two- and three-dimensional drawings. Large-format printers were a type of computer peripheral capable of printing the on-screen designs onto paper or other similar media more than one meter wide and almost unlimited length.

The earliest users of large-format printers were the pioneers of CAD in the fields of engineering and architecture. Later, graphic designers started to experiment, generating and printing large poster-size images. The CAD market initially used plotters, which could print large formats but were limited to line drawings and could not print large shaded areas (patterns or halftones) or solid color, which were often needed in graphic design. By 1997, most manufacturers had stopped using the term "plotter" for their machines, using the term "printer" instead. The performance of the machines had improved considerably and some models were capable of producing photo-quality prints. There were different types of large-format printers, using different printing technologies. All of HP's large-format printers used the inkjet printing system.

The purchasing process of large-format inkjet printers differed in important respects from that of the usual small desktop printers, which were regarded as consumer items.

Source: Case of the Research Department at IESE. Prepared by Professors Lluís G. Renart and José Antonio Segarra, and Lecturer Francisco Parés, October 1999. Copyright © 1999, IESE. This is a condensed version of the case "Hewlett-Packard: DesignJet Online." The complete version is available from IESE. Most IESE cases are available from either ECCH or Harvard.

FIGURE I

A Large-Format Hewlett-Packard Printer

Large-format printers required an investment of between $2,000 and $12,000, depending on the model and the features. The decisive purchasing factors were quality and printing speed, based above all on reliability and robustness. For the end users it was particularly important that the printer worked smoothly, without unevenness between one print and another, making as little noise as possible, and if necessary for many hours at a stretch. Printing jobs often had to be done in a rush, just before the deadline for delivery of a project. If a printer broke down, a technician had to go to the user's premises to repair it. Only very rarely did the printer have to be transported to a repair shop.

Large-format printers had a useful life of over ten years, but in practice they became outdated within five years due to technological obsolescence resulting from the rapid pace of innovation. They were sold with a one-year warranty. When customers needed a large-format printer, they tended to go to their regular computer equipment supplier and to think the decision over much more carefully than they would normally do in the case of conventional office computing equipment. Most HP distributors were multibrand and sold to all types of customers. If a particular market warranted it, HP would have one or two large-format printer specialists in that country's sales organization, who would visit the distributors and respond to any requests for help from end users.

Figure I shows a model of one of the large-format inkjet printers developed and manufactured by HP Barcelona Division for the world market. The different models were sold under names that consisted of the expression "HP DesignJet," which was common to all, followed by a number or combination of numbers and letters, such as "HP DesignJet 450" and "HP DesignJet 750C Plus."

The World Market for Large-Format Printers

Almost all architectural and engineering firms already had one or more large-format printers, or at least a plotter, and the number of new firms needing CAD equipment was growing very slowly. Also, the motivation to buy a new high-quality graphic printer was low, as there was no demand for spectacular improvements in performance or print quality in this sector. This was, therefore, basically a replacement market segment.

In contrast, the graphic design segment of large-format printer users continued to grow rapidly. Customers in this segment appreciated the cost reductions and the enhanced print quality and performance offered by large-format inkjet printers. Higher printing speeds and a more robust design had stimulated the demand for this type of printer by such users as advertising agencies, poster producers, industrial designers, interior designers, printers, design schools, and design departments in companies.

The graphic design market segment had two types of purchasers: (1) companies that used the printers in house and (2) print shop service providers—shops where anyone who had created an on-screen graphic design could get it printed, paying a price per copy. The main suppliers of large-format printers in 1997 in the world are as shown in Table 1.

HP was the undisputed leader in large-format printers, with a market penetration in 1996 of more than 50 percent of the installed base. None of its competitors had as much as 20 percent of the world market, which was estimated at some $1 billion per year at manufacturers' selling prices. HP's competitors in the large-format printer market were generally companies with more specific products for specialist uses, such as large-format printers for printing on fabric to be used as weather protection to cover scaffolding during renovation work on buildings in large cities, which

TABLE I

Key Suppliers of Large-Format Printers

Name	Graphic Applications Focus	Graphic and CAD Application Focus
Hewlett-Packard	XXX	
Encad	XXX	
Calcomp		XXX
Xerox		XXX
Scitex	XXX	
Epson	XXX	
Mutoh	XXX	
Roland	XXX	
SELEX		XXX

was also used as a gigantic advertising medium. HP maintained one entry barrier that gave it a competitive advantage in the sector: its constant investment in research and development aimed at continuous improvement, which could be justified economically only by having a high market share.

Hewlett-Packard (HP)

In 1997, HP was a multinational company present in some 120 countries, with more than 120,000 employees and net revenue of more than $40 billion. It specialized in the manufacture and sale of personal and business computing products, peripherals, products for the world of electronics, test and measurement products, networking products, medical electronic equipment, chemical analysis, handheld calculators, and electronic components. It had 141 sales and support offices spread across 27 countries, which, together with 95 national distributors, supported a network of more than 600 retail distributors. HP had 111 manufacturing centers in Europe, including the facility in Sant Cugat del Vallés in the province of Barcelona (Spain).

HP's Operations in Spain

Under a single legal identity (HP Española, S.A.), three different and separate operational organizations each had a different functional relationship to the parent company shown in Table 2.

The *Territorial Sales Organization* was responsible for selling Hewlett-Packard's product lines in Spain, with its head office in Madrid. Its global headquarters was located in Geneva, Switzerland. The Territorial Sales Organization was responsible for developing and strengthening the network of local distributors and agents, some of which were exclusive HP agents who sold to large companies or specialists, although most were shops selling computer equipment for office use. HP provided specialized area managers and sales engineers for particular products if the market warranted it. In Spain two specialist sales representatives for large-format printers visited the agents and called on potential customers with them. In addition to maintaining the network of distributors and agents, the Territorial Sales Organization was responsible for implementing the entire marketing plan for Spain, following general guidelines laid down by each product division while adapting them to the domestic market. Thus, the Territorial Sales Organization decided on prices, promotional and advertising campaigns, and so on, and kept in touch with the local market. Each product division's marketing department would suggest marketing campaigns and plans, even prices, but ultimately each country was responsible for its own decisions and for the results of HP's general sales plan.

The *Technical Support Organization* also had its head office in Madrid, but reported to its own headquarters in Boise, Idaho. It was responsible for providing technical assistance for all the products and equipment of all of HP's product divisions established in Spain. It had technicians and specialized workshops to attend to the needs of the users of the equipment. It also organized the official technical assistance services through associated technical service centers. Besides carrying out repairs under warranty, which were charged to the corresponding product division, it offered its customers maintenance plans and charged for all its services, including those provided by telephone, when the products and equipment were out of warranty.

The Territorial Sales Organization and the Technical Support Organization coexisted in all those countries in which HP had a direct market presence. In other countries, or in smaller or less developed territories, their functions were performed by one or more independent importer-distributors.

The third operational organization in Spain was *HP Barcelona Division* (HP-BCD). Located in Sant Cugat del Vallés, near Barcelona, HP-BCD designed and manufactured large-format printers, reporting to HP Inkjet Products Group, with its headquarters in San Diego, California.

HP Barcelona Division (HP-BCD)

Founded in 1985, HP-BCD was responsible for performing the research and development (R&D), marketing, and manufacturing functions for the entire range of HP large-format printers for the entire world market. It also manufactured a range of HP inkjet products for Europe. In 1997, HP-BCD had about 1,250 employees. Most of them were directly involved in the production processes, which for most of the

---

TABLE 2   **Organizations Legally Integrated in Hewlett-Packard Española, S.A.**

Name	Deployment	Description	Headquarters
Territorial Sales Organization	Territorial lines	Multiproduct	Geneva, Switzerland
Technical Support Organization	Territorial lines	Territorial lines	Boise, Idaho
Barcelona Division	Worldwide	Design and manufacture of large-format printers for the world market	San Diego, California

year were carried out in four shifts (three shifts per day plus Saturdays and Sundays). The General Management of HP-BCD oversaw six departments:

- Research and Development
- Marketing
- Finance
- Human Resources
- Production
- Internal Services

With exports of more than 90 billion pesestas, HP-BCD was one of Spain's largest exporters of computer products.

Under Ignacio Fonts's management, the marketing department at HP-BCD designed and monitored the global marketing strategy for the products manufactured by the division. It employed around 70 people. It was responsible for applying the funds corresponding to the total marketing campaign budget for large-format printers, and it negotiated with each country the specific campaigns each wanted to run. The marketing department was organized into four sections:

1. *Product marketing.* This section had two main functions: (1) To propose new products, which involved visiting customers and distributors to detect new needs, adding whatever qualitative data were needed, and (2) to work closely with the R&D department to ensure that products under development matched the established specifications.
2. *Market development.* This section developed the market for HP-BCD's products. It gave each Territorial Sales Organization guidelines on
   a. Communication (advertising, publications, public relations campaigns, etc.)
   b. Prices (a price level for each country—normally a price band)
   c. Promotions (for example, the Renewal Plan, whereby an old large-format printer would be accepted as a partial exchange for a new one with a variable discount depending on the age of the machine to be replaced, whether it was an HP machine or not, and so on. This plan had recently been accepted by a large number of countries with great success.)
   d. Product (which accessories should be included as standard)
3. *Technical support.* This third section of the marketing department was responsible for developing easy and effective technical support or assistance systems to be used by the Technical Support Organization in each country. The local Technical Support Organization in each country (reporting to Boise, Idaho) provided on-site technical assistance for all types of HP equipment. The technical support section of the marketing department at HP-BCD, however, dealt ex-

clusively with large-format printers and acted only through the Technical Support Organization of each country.

The technical support section of the marketing department at HP-BCD also trained repair technicians (support engineers), both those employed by HP and those employed by the distributors; monitored warranties; and even resolved technical problems that were too complex for the Technical Support Organizations to handle. For example, when a customer used a printer in very special conditions (such as an unusual software environment or special print media), the Technical Support Organization might not be able to respond appropriately and the limitations of the product under extreme conditions of use might be brought to light. By studying and classifying the technical problems that emerged, the technical support section could help design and propose improvement plans for the development of future generations of printers.
4. *Strategic planning.* The main task of this section was to supply the marketing management with information and data relating to sales and marketing. To do this it closely monitored data on sales, installed customer base, reasons for purchasing HP products, and competition at world level. It was also responsible for planning sales and negotiating targets with the Territorial Sales Organizations.

The Origins of the New Web Site Project

In January 1997, a group of managers from the marketing department at HP-BCD discussed the possibility of communicating directly with the end users of HP's large-format printers. There was an installed base of some 500,000 of these printers scattered around the world. Very frequently, these end users were working in very diverse computing environments, often unlike those of typical users of HP products. The idea of offering this group of users a tool to communicate directly and at any time with HP-BCD seemed an excellent marketing opportunity. The initial idea was to publish a printed newsletter, in various languages, that would be mailed to all end users of HP large-format printers. This new channel of communication would complement the messages that were already being sent through HP distributors and the sales and technical support organizations. It would also complement the advertising messages and news that the end users of large-format printers received through the traditional mass media. The problem was that of the 500,000 printers sold, only 50,000 end users had registered when they purchased their large-format printer. HP-BCD did not have a complete and unified database with the names and addresses of the end users of the printers.

The Focus Groups

Before proceeding with the newsletter idea, six focus groups were organized with end users (two in Germany, two in the United States, and two in the United Kingdom), and the project was explained to them. The reaction of the participants in the focus groups was unanimous: what most concerned them was technical assistance.

The Web Site Project

From the outset, the possibility of using the World Wide Web as the channel for communicating directly with end users had been considered. This idea had been discarded on the grounds that many end users did not have Internet access and so would effectively be excluded. The pros and cons of using electronic media rather than print were now reconsidered. In the United States in 1996, around 70 percent of the users of large-format printers of any brand had Internet access; in 1997 in the world as a whole, the figure was 55 percent. In light of these findings, the idea of using paper was abandoned and the development of a new web site was seen as the best alternative. After a number of brainstorming sessions involving various departments at Sant Cugat, the project began to take shape. It was assigned to Joan[1] Miró from strategic planning, who in a report dated July 1997 summed up the conclusions reached so far.

Description of The Designjet Online Project

Target of the program: Users of HP Designjet printers (not retailers or potential customers). Definition of the program's main objectives:

- Stimulate and speed up renewal of the installed base.
- Increase HP's involvement in the sale of consumables.
- Strengthen and increase the loyalty of our customers.
- Increase our knowledge of the market.

The main criterion for including services in this web site will be whether they offer anything that may be considered to be "of added value" to the end user. Another important feature of the program is its interactive nature: We must allow the users of our printers to talk to us and ask us questions, and we must talk to them, proactively and continuously, whenever possible.

Services Included in the Program

For Your Eyes Only. This service will inform users directly of the appearance of any new HP product. Registered users will receive an e-mail on the date of the launch of a new product and will be able to visit the web site if they want more information.
HP DesignJet Speaking! Online discussion forum for users. HP will not take part in the discussion. The messages will be 100 percent from users. In the future, when the necessary internal resources are available, we will have to try to reply to all the messages.

Feedback. Users will send in messages about the products and the solutions that HP offers. HP will reply, thanking each user for the message, but it will not give a personalized reply. In the future, if the volume of messages allows it, we should try to develop a team capable of answering them.

Quarterly Newsletter: *Big Impressions*. Quarterly publication by HP to keep its customers informed of important events in their business or field of activity. Registered users will receive an e-mail containing a list of the subjects covered in each newsletter as it is published and will be able to visit the web site if they want to read the full text of the articles.

Success Stories. Users will be able to share their positive experiences with their DesignJets. Each month, the best story will be rewarded with an HP polo shirt.

Warranty Status. Information on the coverage provided by the HP warranty.

Technical Assistance Information. List of Technical Assistance services available at HP. Contact addresses and telephone numbers for all countries.

Diagnostics for DesignJets. Online tool for breakdowns. (An interactive tool enabling users to resolve some technical problems affecting their printers themselves.)

Pass the word on! Users invite a colleague to visit the web site. (Positive word-of-mouth advertising, "member invites member.")

Driver Upgrades. Users will be able to download the latest versions of the drivers for HP DesignJets.

Besides all the above-mentioned services, HP will at regular intervals send users an e-mail containing:

- Information on new products and drivers
- Update on the content of the web site
- Newsletter: list of articles
- General news: Y2K effect, printing the new Euro symbol, etc.

Under the plan, it is estimated that each user will receive around 10 e-mails per year.

The Budget

The preliminary budget for printing the newsletter on paper had been put at $1 million per year. The same budget was maintained for the web site project. More than 50 percent of this amount was earmarked for the development and subsequent maintenance of the computer program. The rest would be devoted to promotional material and other derivative costs. The figure of $1 million, though large, was acceptable within HP-BCD's general marketing budget.

How to Get the Rest of the HP Organization Involved?

Although HP-BCD had assigned two people full-time to the project and planned to continue to do so, other people in HP outside the Barcelona Division needed to be actively involved. Joan Miró explained:

---

[1]Joan is the male name equivalent to John in the local Catalan language spoken in Barcelona and its surroundings.

Initially, there was no plan to reply to the e-mails from users. But we'd like the Technical Support Organization to e-mail a reply to all the messages that come in via the web site. And we'd like the Territorial Sales Organizations throughout the world to publicize the web site and inform people about it in all their publications. Also, we'd like them to pass on to us any recent information that may be of interest to their users, so that we can keep the site up-to-date and attractive.

What all these ideas that emerged during the various stages of project development amounted to was an organizational challenge. The project would require the collaboration of a large part of the structure of HP. It went beyond the scope of responsibility of the marketing department of HP-BCD.

The Reaction of HP's Other Organizational Units

The Technical Support Organization, which was responsible for Technical Assistance, had its headquarters in the United States. It was totally independent and had its own budgets. The collaboration of the Technical Support Organization was vital. The web site was supposed to improve customer satisfaction, so what was needed was not just an attractive array of pull information on the web site, such as self-solve tools, a driver library, Frequently Asked Questions (FAQ), and so on, but also giving the customers professional expertise in e-mails that provided tailored solutions to specific problems. "The web site had to be connected to specific support groups that would answer the customers' e-mails in 24 hours and free of charge," said Joan Miró. "All of this had to be done in a variety of languages. Initially, we thought of using six languages: English, German, French, Italian, Portuguese, and Spanish. We at HP-BCD said that our program had to be free of charge; we argued that the Internet had created a low-cost standard, and we couldn't charge customers for the service."

One thing was clear: large-format printers accounted for only 3.5 percent of the Technical Support Organization's revenue. Their overall financial results were not going to be seriously affected if they did not charge for the assistance they provided over the Internet. But they could not allow this practice to set a precedent for other HP products, to stop charging for all of their services. It was also important to bear in mind that some distributors had their own profitable technical assistance organizations, whose interests the web site could conceivably damage.

With the Territorial Sales Organization the problem was even more complicated. Being close to the customer in each territory, it welcomed the idea of giving better service. But who would decide the content of the marketing messages to be sent to end users—HP-BCD? Would HP-BCD tell the users what they wanted when they wanted? For the Territorial Sales Organization it was very important that its permission be sought first, but how? How could they impose territorial limits on the web site? How could the new channel of communication be coordinated with the marketing and sales campaigns in each individual country? And what about distributors? How would the distributors react to the project? Should they be consulted? Would they feel threatened?

The Decision

Ignacio Fonts had no doubt that it would be difficult to secure the formal approval of all the organizations affected. He also fully realized that, to work well, the project would require sufficient financial and human resources and a great effort of coordination and communication, both internal and external. He was convinced that HP-BCD and he himself as marketing director had the power and the resources to set up the new web site. But the risks, both internal and external, were not to be underestimated.

Was it worth the effort? HP-BCD's marketing department already issued guidelines for large-format printers to all the Territorial Sales and Technical Support Organizations, and they adapted the guidelines to the circumstances in their countries. But the marketing department had never been directly in touch with HP customers before, which prompted some reservations.

Within the marketing department, Fonts was not even sure who should develop and maintain the web site. Initially, the project had been assigned to strategic planning, but should that section continue to be in charge of the development or start-up of the new project? All the heads of the four sections of the marketing department agreed that the new project should go ahead, but their opinions did not coincide exactly, as can be seen from the following comments:

- *Product marketing:* "There's no doubt that it may be a very effective tool for our work. It is essential for us to know our customers' future needs, and this project will help us achieve that. Even before we launch a new project, when we do the beta test it will be easy for us to identify the users who we want to test out prototypes. Right now, it is difficult for us to find the most appropriate users for our tests."
- *Market development:* "Essentially, it is a tool for developing the market and our department. The culture of horizontal and vertical communication is very well established in HP. Deciding what relationship we should have with other departments and divisions is a challenge for us; although we don't have the means or the experience of communicating as intensely as this, communication has always been part of our job."
- *Technical support:* "It is very clearly a question of improving the satisfaction of the users of our printers, and we've always played a key role in that. We need to ensure that the support units get involved at an international level. It may not depend on us alone, but

judging by the results of the focus groups, we are undoubtedly one of the keys to success."

- *Strategic planning:* "The web site is a window through which users will be able to make contact with HP, and they won't be familiar with our internal organization. They'll want answers, and we'll try to ensure that the messages we receive are answered by those in our organization responsible for doing so, whatever department or division they belong to. Coordinating between the different departments is part of my regular job."

Creating ideas is easy up to a point, but making them work is more difficult, thought Fonts. Are we about to jeopardize the prestige of HP-BCD? Are there any changes we ought to make? Would the users even appreciate the new web site? Would they value all the services offered? If the services were not well received, would HP be able to change its mind and back out, once the site had been launched and publicized?

All these doubts crowded into Fonts's mind as he prepared for the meeting with the heads of his department and drew up the following list of the subjects that would have to be discussed before deciding whether or not to give the project his final approval.

HP-BCD Marketing Department Meeting
Monday, September 8, 1997
Room GD 124, 9:30 A.M.

- Analysis of costs, risks, and benefits of this new Web project
- Key success factors; ways to measure and to ensure success

- Internal marketing plan: How to secure the collaboration of the territorial organizations
- Approval or suggestions for change of the new web site contents
- Budget and organizational matters
- Appointment of Web manager responsible for site launch, development and upkeep.

Questions for Discussion

1. What is your evaluation of the costs and benefits of this project?
2. How could the HP-BCD marketing team measure the level of success of the new web site?
3. What action plans could the marketing team design and implement in order to increase the web site's success?
4. What could be done to further involve and commit the HP Sales and Technical Support Organizations?
5. Would you suggest any changes in the specific contents of the new web pages? Which ones? Why?
6. In your opinion, will the new Web project generate further changes in the HP organization?
7. Who should be designated as Web master, to be in charge of the new web site? What should be the new job description?

Harley-Davidson (B) Hedging Hogs

Harley-Davidson's competitive comeback in the late 1980s is one of the few protectionist success stories. It is the story of a firm that used government protection to adjust to a changing competitive global market. But Harley's success in the late 1980s brought along new problems that threatened to undermine much of the progress already attained. Harley's primary problem was the same problem faced by many undiversified international firms: it produced its motorcycles, hogs,[1] in only one country and exported its product to all foreign markets. But exchange rates change, and prices and earnings originally denominated in foreign currencies end up being worth very different amounts when finding their way back home to the dollar.[2]

Exporting Hogs

Harley's sales in 1990 were more than $864 million. Of total sales, $268 million, or 31 percent, were international sales. Harley had been exporting for a very long time: for 50 years to Japan and more than 80 years to Germany. New markets were growing in countries such as Greece, Argentina, Brazil, and even the Virgin Islands. Although international sales were obviously very important to Harley's present profitability, they also represented its future. The domestic market in the United States for motorcycles—any firm's motorcycles—was beginning to decline. This was generally thought to be a result of changing consumer profiles and tastes. International market potential for Harley looked quite promising, but Harley had only 15 percent of the world market. It needed to do better, much better.

Harley's problem was that foreign distributors and dealers needed two things for continued growth and market share expansion: (1) local currency prices and (2) stable prices. First, local currency pricing, whether it be Japanese yen, German marks, Australian dollars, or Canadian dollars, would allow the foreign dealers to compete on price in same currency terms with all competitors. And this competition would not be hindered by the dealers and distributors adding currency surcharges to sticker prices as a result of their own need to cover currency exposure.[3] Harley needed to sell its hogs to foreign dealers and distributorships in local currency, but that would not really solve the problems. First, Harley itself would now be responsible for managing the currency exposure. Second, it still did not assure the foreign dealers of stable prices, not unless Harley intended to absorb all exchange rate changes itself.

Figure 1 illustrates the foreign currency pricing issue for sales of Harleys in Australia and Japan. Australian consumers shop, compare, and purchase in Australian dollars. Starting at the opposite end, however, is the fact that Harley hogs are produced and initially priced in U.S. dollars. Someone must bear the risk of currency exchange, either the parent, the distributor, or the consumer; it rarely will be the consumer.

Currency Risk Sharing at Harley

John Hevey, manager of international finance, instituted a system that Harley calls "risk sharing." The idea is not new, but it has not been fashionable for some time. The idea is fairly simple: as long as the spot exchange rate does not move a great distance from the rate in effect when Harley quotes foreign currency prices to its foreign dealers, Harley will maintain that single price. This allows the foreign dealers and distributors, both those owned and not owned by Harley, to be assured of predictable and stable prices. The stable prices needed to be denominated in the currency of the foreign dealer and distributor's operations. Harley would then be responsible for managing the currency exposures.

A typical currency risk-sharing arrangement specifies three bands or zones of exchanges: (1) neutral zone, (2) sharing

Source: This case was written by Michael H. Moffett, the University of Michigan, March 1993. The case is intended for class discussion purposes only and does not represent either efficient or inefficient financial management practices. Do not quote without prior permission.

[1]The motorcycles produced and sold by Harley-Davidson have traditionally been known as hogs. The nickname is primarily in reference to their traditional large size, weight, and power.

[2]This case draws upon several articles including "Harley Uses 'Risk Sharing' To Hedge Foreign Currencies," by Lawrence R. Quinn, *Business International Money Report* (March 16, 1992): 105–106; and "Harley: Wheeling and Dealing," by Lawrence Quinn, *Corporate Finance* (April 1992): 29–30.

[3]For example, an independent Australian dealer who sells and earns Australian dollar revenues but must pay for the Harley hogs shipped from the United States in U.S. dollars will be accepting currency risk. If the Australian dealer then adds a margin to the hog price to cover currency-hedging costs, the product is less competitive.

FIGURE 1   Harley-Davidson's Foreign Pricing Flow

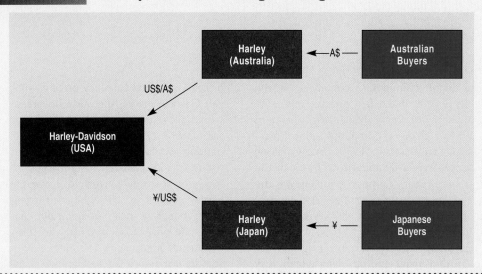

zone, and (3) renegotiation zone. Figure 2 provides an example of how the currency zones may be constructed between a U.S. parent firm and its Japanese dealers or distributors. The neutral zone in Figure 2 is constructed as a band of +/−5 percent change about the central rate specified in the contract, ¥130.00/$. The central rate can be determined a number of ways, for example, the spot rate in effect on the date of the contract's consummation, the average rate for the past three-month period, or a moving average of monthly rates. In this case, the neutral zone's boundaries are ¥136.84/$ and ¥123.81/$.[4] As long as the spot exchange rate between the yen and dollar remains within this neutral zone, the U.S. parent assures the Japanese dealers of a constant price in yen. If a particular product line was priced in the United States at $4,000, the yen-denominated price would be ¥520,000. This assures the Japanese dealers a constant supply price in their own currency terms. The predictability of costs reduces the currency risks of the Japanese dealers and allows them to pass on the more predictable local currency prices to their customers.

If, however, the spot rate moves out of the neutral zone into the sharing zone, the U.S. parent and the Japanese dealer will share the costs or benefits of the margin beyond the neutral zone rate. For example, if the Japanese yen depreciated against the dollar to ¥140.00/$, the spot rate will

have moved into the upper sharing zone. If the contract specified that the sharing would be a 50/50 split, the new price to the Japanese dealer would be

$$\$4,000 \times \left[¥130.00/\$ + \frac{¥140.00/\$ - ¥136.84/\$}{2} \right]$$
$$= \$4,000 \times ¥131.58/\$ = ¥526,320.$$

Although the supply costs have indeed risen to the Japanese dealers, from ¥520,000 to ¥526,320, the percentage increase is significantly less than the percentage change in the exchange rate.[5] The Japanese dealer is insulated against the constant fluctuations of the exchange rate and subsequent fluctuations on supply costs.

Finally, if the spot rate were to move drastically from the neutral zone into the renegotiation zone, the risk-sharing agreement calls for a renegotiation of the price to bring it more in line with current exchange rates and the economic and competitive realities of the market.

Currency Management at Harley

Harley's risk-sharing program has allowed the firm to increase the stability of prices in foreign markets. But this stability has come about by the parent firm's accepting a larger proportion of the exchange rate risk. Harley's approach to currency management is conservative, both in what it hedges and how it hedges.

The "what," the exposures that Harley actually manages, are primarily its sales, which are denominated in for-

[4]The upper and lower exchange rates of the band are calculated as:

$$\frac{¥130.00/\$ - ¥136.84/\$}{¥136.84/\$} \times 100 = -5.0\%.$$

and

$$\frac{¥130.00/\$ - ¥123.81/\$}{¥123.81/\$} \times 100 = +5.0\%.$$

[5]The yen price has risen only 1.22 percent while the Japanese yen has depreciated 7.14 percent versus the U.S. dollar.

FIGURE 2   Currency Risk Sharing

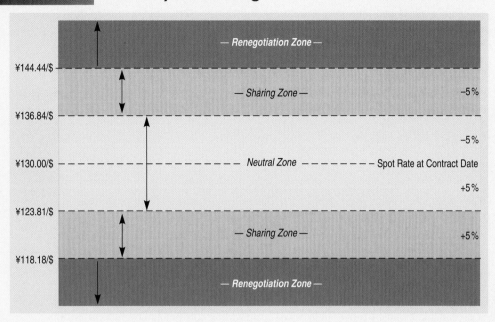

Note: Percentage changes are in the value of the Japanese yen versus U.S. dollar. For example, a "+5%" is a 5 percent appreciation in the value of the yen, from ¥130.00/$ to ¥123.81/$.

eign currencies. Although Harley does import some inputs, the volume of imports denominated in foreign currencies (accounts payable) are relatively small compared to the export sales (the accounts receivable). Harley is a bit more aggressive in its exposure time frame than many other firms, however. Harley will hedge sales that will be made in the near future, anticipated sales, extending about twelve months out. The ability of the firm to hedge sales that have not yet been "booked" is a result of the firm's consistency and predictability of sales in the various markets. Like most firms that hedge future sales, however, Harley will intentionally leave itself a margin of error, therefore hedging less than 100 percent of the expected exposures.

Presently Harley is rather conservative in the "how," the instruments and methods used for currency hedging. Harley uses currency forward contracts for all hedging. Harley will estimate the amount of the various foreign currency payments to be received per period and sell those foreign currency quantities forward (less the percentage margin for error). Like many other firms expanding international operations, Harley is now studying the use of additional currency management approaches, such as the use of foreign currency options. At present, however, Harley executives are satisfied with their currency management program.

Financial Management's Growing Responsibilities

A third dimension of the new financial/currency management program at Harley is the increased role of financial management with sales. The finance staff keeps in touch with the sales and marketing staffs to work toward the most competitive combinations and packages of pricing. Financial staff also attempts to keep information lines open between its foreign dealers and distributors to help them maintain price competitiveness.

Harley-Davidson is a firm that continues to be unique in many ways. Not only is it one of the true "success stories" for American protectionism, but it has continued to work to improve its international competitiveness by responding to the needs of not only its customers, but also its distributors and dealers.

Questions for Discussion

1. Why is it so important for Harley-Davidson to both price in foreign currencies in foreign markets and provide stable prices?
2. How effective will "risk sharing" be in actually achieving Harley's stated goals? Is there a better solution?
3. Who is bearing the brunt of the costs of the financial risk management program?

References

Hufbauer, Gary Clyde, Diane T. Berliner, and Kimberly Ann Elliot. *Trade Protection in the United States: 31 Case Studies.* Washington, D.C.: The Institute for International Economics, 1986.

Pruzin, Daniel R. "Born to be Verrucht." *World Trade* 5, Issue 4 (May 1992): 112–117.

Quinn, Lawrence R. "Harley Uses 'Risk Sharing' to Hedge Foreign Currencies." *Business International Money Report,* March 16, 1992, 105–106.

———, "Harley: Wheeling and Dealing." *Corporate Finance* (April 1992): 29–30.

An Expatriate Tour in El Salvador

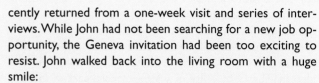

December 10, 1998: The Job Offer

John and Joanna Lafferty had just opened a bottle of wine to share with friends who had come to see their new apartment in Toronto when the telephone rang. John, a lanky, easygoing development economist, excused himself to answer the phone in the kitchen.

Recently married, John and Joanna were excited to be building a life together in the same city at last. As a development economist specializing in Latin America, John Lafferty's work had taken him to Peru, Bolivia, and Guatemala on a series of three- to four-month assignments over the previous three years. While he loved the challenge and adventure of this fieldwork and had come to love the people and culture, he also wanted a home base and steady presence in Toronto, where Joanna worked as a human resource management consultant. Just before their wedding six months earlier, John accepted a position with a Toronto-based NGO (non-governmental organization) focused on research, fund-raising and government lobbying on issues related to Central American political refugees. Throughout the 1980s, tens of thousands of refugees had fled political persecution and human rights abuse in war-torn Central America to seek political asylum in Canada; John's field experience in Guatemala and his natural diplomacy were invaluable to the Canadian organization. He was passionate about his work and quickly gained a reputation for being a savvy and politically astute advocate of refugees' cases.

As Joanna went to get some wineglasses from the kitchen, she could overhear her husband speaking in Spanish on the phone. Joanna had studied Spanish in college but had difficulty following the rapid, one-sided conversation. However, one phrase, "Me allegre mucho" and John's broad grin as he said it, was impossible to misinterpret. Joanna returned to her guests in the living room:

"It sounds like good news."

John's work with refugees in the Canadian NGO had caught the attention of the United Nations High Commission for Refugees, headquartered in Geneva, and he had re-

cently returned from a one-week visit and series of interviews. While John had not been searching for a new job opportunity, the Geneva invitation had been too exciting to resist. John walked back into the living room with a huge smile:

"Forget the wine, I think we should open some champagne. The U.N. has just offered me the most incredible job."

"In Geneva?" Joanna asked excitedly.

John's smile grew even broader. *"No. In El Salvador."*

December 17, 1998: The Decision

The El Salvador assignment would be for two years, as a Program Officer responsible for organizing the repatriation of Salvadoran refugees from various refugee camps back to El Salvador and developing programs to ensure the protection and well-being of such refugees in their return to Salvadoran communities. The position would report to the Charge de Mission of the El Salvador office. While this office was based in the capital city, San Salvador, the job would also require frequent travel to various field offices and refugee camps throughout El Salvador, Nicaragua, Guatemala, and Honduras. The challenge of the assignment excited John tremendously; he also believed that this was an exceptional opportunity for him to make a real difference in the lives of the refugees of Central America. He certainly wanted to accept the job; however, he would only go if Joanna would be willing and happy to go with him.

Two questions would weigh heavily on Joanna's mind:

1. *"What about the political instability of the area?"*

The politics of El Salvador were complicated and difficult to understand, and the story seemed to vary depending on the source. As Joanna gathered, the civil war in El Salvador had come to an end in 1992 with a U.N.–brokered peace treaty between the conservative government of the Republican Nationalist Alliance (Arena) and the Marxist-led Farabundo Marti National Liberation Front (FMLN). Throughout the war, the U.S. had apparently spent more than $4 billion to support the government and military, while the Soviet Bloc supported the FMLN. Human-rights groups alleged that right-wing death squads had murdered 40,000 of the 70,000 people killed during the twelve-year war. However, the peace agreement had significantly reduced the size of the army, disbanded corrupt police forces, purged the country of the most notorious human-rights abusers, and disarmed the FMLN, allowing it to become a legal political

Source: This case was written by Susan Bartholomew based on personal interviews. Names, dates, and details of situations have been modified for illustrative purposes. The various economic, political, and cultural conditions described are presented as perceptions of the individuals in the case; they do not necessarily reflect the actual conditions in the region. The events described are presented as a basis for classroom discussion rather than to illustrate effective or ineffective handling of a cross-cultural situation. For more information on El Salvador, see **http://www.yahoo.com/Regional/Countries/El_Salvador.**

party. The country appeared to have made substantial progress towards peace and democracy. The information and briefings they received from Salvadorans and other ex-patriates who had recently returned from the country suggested that life in the capital San Salvador was quite safe. Economically, the country was becoming more internationally open, with establishment of large export factories, increasing privatization, and reforms aimed at stimulating foreign investment. While certain precautions were required, and the area was still heavily patrolled by armed forces, Joanna was told she could expect a relatively normal lifestyle. They would live in a highly secure part of the city, in the area populated by all the foreign embassies. They would also be living and traveling on a U.N. diplomatic passport ("Laissez-passer"), which would afford them excellent protection.

2. *"What about my career?"*

Moving to El Salvador was the last thing Joanna had imagined when she married John Lafferty six months earlier. Joanna had worked in Toronto for three years as a human resource consultant after graduating with an MBA. She was bright and ambitious, and her career was advancing well. While she was very happy to be married, she also enjoyed her professional and financial independence. Besides, Toronto was not only professionally rewarding, it was also home, friends, and family. However, Joanna was also ready for a change; secretly, she had always envied John the sense of adventure that accompanied his work. Maybe this was an opportunity for her to develop her human resource consulting skills in an international context.

After much discussion, they decided that John would accept the assignment.

January–March, 1999: Predeparture Arrangements

When John confirmed with the Geneva office that he would take the assignment, it was arranged for him to move to San Salvador at the end of March and for Joanna to follow one month later. It was often recommended in assignments of this kind to send married staff ahead of time to get settled into the job before their spouse and/or family arrived. This option made sense to the Laffertys and had several advantages. First, it would give Joanna more time to finish off her current consulting projects in Toronto and make a graceful exit from her present firm. She had a strong professional reputation and wanted to ensure she was remembered favourably by her corporate clients when she returned to Toronto two years later.

Second, John would be able to get the housing arrangements settled before Joanna's arrival. John's employer would provide ample financial and logistical support to staff in

finding housing; however, John also knew from past experience that dealing with local realtors and utility companies in Central America could be highly frustrating. Tasks that were quite simple in Toronto, such as having a lease drawn up and getting a telephone installed, just didn't seem to follow any system or set of procedures. "Tomorrow" could mean next week or even next month. Patience, flexibility, and a good deal of charm were usually required; getting angry rarely helped. While John was used to the inconvenience and unpredictability of local services in Central America, he was uncertain how Joanna would react initially. John held a deep affection for the Central American people and felt hopeful that Joanna would develop an affinity for the culture as well. However, he hoped to at least have the majority of the living arrangements worked out before she arrived to make her transition to El Salvador as smooth as possible.

Finally, the extra time gave Joanna more opportunity to prepare herself for the transition. Joanna had taken a course on International Human Resource Management as an MBA and was familiar with the phenomenon of culture shock in international assignments. She recalled from her course that predeparture preparation and cultural orientation made a significant difference in helping employees and their families adapt to the foreign environment. Joanna was determined to read and learn as much about Salvadoran history and politics as she could. She was also keen to improve her Spanish before she arrived, and as soon as the decision was made that they would be going to El Salvador, she enrolled in night courses for six hours a week.

As Joanna walked home from her Spanish class one evening, pleased with her results on her comprehension test, she recalled with amusement a conversation she had had with Joan Taylor. Joan was the wife of a senior executive with Altron, a Canadian firm with offices throughout Latin America. The Taylors had just returned from a two-year assignment in Guatemala City, and Joanna had contacted Joan to get some insight on the practicalities of living in the region.

"My dear Joanna," Joan began, *"you will have a very fine life in Central America, or in most developing countries your husband will be sent to, for that matter. You will live better than you ever could anywhere else."* Joan gave Joanna a playful nudge *"Just watch out for the 'gilded cage syndrome'."*

"The what?" Joanna had asked.

"As corporate executives or diplomats in third-world postings, we live a pretty high life, certainly a standard of living far beyond what we could have in our own countries. Everything is there for you and everything is done for you. It's like living in a gilded cage. Some people love it, and get pretty spoiled; after a while you can't imagine even making a sandwich for yourself...."

Humph, Joanna thought to herself at the time. *That would certainly never happen to me. I am a professional. This is an in-*

credible learning opportunity, and I am going to make the most of it!

May, 1999: Joanna's Arrival in El Salvador

Joanna arrived on a balmy afternoon, grateful for the warm breeze after a cold Toronto winter. She was excited to see John and only slightly disappointed that their first drive into San Salvador would not be alone, but accompanied by a young Salvadoran named Julio Cesar, who had been assigned as their driver. On the drive from the airport, Joanna tried hard to follow his rapid banter as he pointed out the sights to her. She had felt confident in her Spanish in the classroom in Toronto, but now she could barely understand a word Julio Cesar said. John, sensing her frustration, began to translate, and by the time they reached the house, Joanna was exhausted and discouraged.

John was proud of the house he had found, next door to the Mexican embassy and only a block from a tennis club where most of the members were expatriates. He thought this might provide a good social base for Joanna if she got homesick for North American lifestyle. The large twelve-room house was certainly impressive, with its shining terazzo floors and two large gardens. Joanna wondered what to do with all the space. It was also quite secure, with metal bars on all the windows, and surrounded by twelve-foot walls.

"This isn't a house, John, it's a fortress," Joanna said in amazement.

"Yeah . . . I know it's a bit much," said John. "But this is the one area of the city we are strongly advised to live in, for security reasons. Smaller homes or apartments just don't exist. Most of the families living here are either expats or very wealthy Salvadorans. Most have live-in help and need the space."

"But I don't want anyone else living with us. . . ."

"Come . . . I want you to meet Maria." Joanna followed John out to the back of the house, and was introduced to a small, brown woman, vigorously scrubbing clothes. "Maria worked for the family who lived here before; it only seemed right that she should stay. She only lives a few blocks away, though, so she will go home each evening."

After a week, Joanna soon learned Maria's work patterns. Maria would hand wash all their clothes in the cement tub and hang them to dry outside, a chore that would take all day long, as Maria would often wash things three times. The following day she would return to do the ironing, which would take another full day. As Joanna sat in her study upstairs, reading her books and newspapers, she felt an overwhelming sense of guilt thinking of Maria, hand washing every last item of their clothing in the cement tub. Some days Joanna longed to just walk into an empty house and put her own clothes in a washing machine. Then, when Joanna found out that John paid Maria $6.00 per day, she was furious. John explained to Joanna that this was the customary wage for the women from the "barrios marginales" who worked as domestic help for wealthy Salvadorans and expatriates. These "marginal communities" were small groupings of tin shacks located in the ravines that surrounded the city. A few had electricity, but many of the communities, including Maria's, still cooked their meals over fires and lit their homes with candles. Joanna began to slip more money into Maria's pay envelope.

Joanna hoped to make a friend of Maria and looked forward to having lunch each day with her and learning more of the local way of speaking. Joanna realized now that the formal Spanish she had learned in school was vastly different from the language she heard each day on the streets of San Salvador. However, Maria refused to eat at the same table as Joanna and insisted on serving Joanna first in the dining room, and then eating her own lunch on the stone steps in the back room. Joanna was deeply uncomfortable with this and began to eat lunch at the restaurant in her nearby tennis club instead.

Other things began to irritate Joanna as well. For example, one day, she started to wash the car in the driveway. Suddenly, Maria's son appeared and insisted that he do the job for her, horrified that "la Senora" would undertake such a task herself. Another time, Joanna began to dig up some of the plants in the garden for replanting; the following morning, a gardener appeared at the door, saying that he was a cousin of Maria's and would be pleased to take on additional gardening work.

Joanna resented this intrusion into her daily life. If she was going to be spending so much time at home, she wanted privacy to read and study. It was going to be a while, she realized, before she found a job. Joanna was disappointed with the job prospects among local and even international companies. Most available positions were clerical, for which she was vastly overqualified. "I didn't get an MBA to work as a file clerk!" she would think to herself angrily. Then, she would think sadly, "My Spanish probably isn't even good enough to get a job as a file clerk."

One day, in frustration, Joanna called her two closest friends in Toronto, colleagues from her old firm.

"I can't win!" Joanna complained. "I feel guilty all the time. I feel guilty because I don't do anything myself. And I feel guilty if I don't hire local people to do the housework. They need the money so much. Then I feel guilty that we pay them six dollars a day. We can afford so much more. I feel guilty that I have a maid, and she lives in a tin shack in a ravine two blocks from my house. But John says we can't pay her more than the going rate because it would upset the whole balance of her community. He says they have their own economic structure and norms and we have to respect that. My Salvadoran neighbors tell me that if I pay Maria or the gardener more they won't respect me. But I do anyway, and then I feel guilty because I don't tell John. And then our driver, Julio Cesar. . . ."

The sarcastic response was the same from both. *"Gee, Joanna, sounds tough. Beautiful house, a maid, gardener, and driver, afternoons at the tennis club . . . no wonder you're so miserable?"*

Joanna got off the phone, feeling worse than ever. Had accepting this assignment been a big mistake? She knew how much this job meant to John, and it was a great step forward for his career. But what about her career and her own happiness? This had been a mutual decision. Something was going to have to change or they would be on a plane back to Toronto very soon. The question was . . . what?

Questions for Discussion

1. Is Joanna suffering from culture shock? What elements of the Salvadoran culture seem most difficult for her to adapt to?

2. Should Joanna have done anything differently in terms of her preparation for moving to El Salvador? What do you think she should do now?

3. How could Joanna further her career as a human resource consultant while living in El Salvador? What skills could she develop? Would these skills be transferrable if she moved back to Toronto? To another country?

4. If you were John, would you have taken the job in El Salvador? If you were Joanna, would you have agreed to go?

5. Do you think international careers are feasible for dual-career couples? What issues are important to consider for the individuals involved?

6. What can companies do to make foreign assignments more successful for couples and families? Is the happiness of the employee's spouse the responsibility of the company?

7. What recommendations would you make to international organizations and companies sending employees to politically unstable regions? Do companies have a responsibility for the physical safety of expatriate employees? Does this responsibility extend to locally hired staff as well?

8. Do you think Joanna should pay her cleaning lady and gardener more than the standard $6.00 per day? Why or why not?

GLOSSARY

abandoned product ranges The outcome of a firm narrowing its range of products to obtain economies of scale, which provides opportunities for other firms to enter the markets for the abandoned products.

absolute advantage The ability to produce a good or service more cheaply than it can be produced elsewhere.

accounting diversity The range of differences in national accounting practices.

acculturation The process of adjusting and adapting to a specific culture other than one's own.

adaptability screening A selection procedure that usually involves interviewing both the candidate for an overseas assignment and his or her family members to determine how well they are likely to adapt to another culture.

agent A representative or intermediary for the firm that works to develop business and sales strategies and that develops contacts.

airfreight Transport of goods by air; accounts for less than one percent of the total volume of international shipments, but more than 20 percent of value.

allocation mentality The tradition of acquiring resources based not on what is needed but on what is available.

American terms Quoting a currency rate as the U.S. dollar against a country's currency (e.g., U.S. dollars/yen).

analogy A method for estimating market potential when data for the particular market do not exist.

antidumping Laws that many countries use to impose tariffs on foreign imports. They are designed to help domestic industries that are injured by unfair competition from abroad due to imported products being sold at less than fair market value.

antitrust laws Laws that prohibit monopolies, restraint of trade, and conspiracies to inhibit competition.

arbitration The procedure for settling a dispute in which an objective third party hears both sides and makes a decision; a procedure for resolving conflict in the international business arena through the use of intermediaries such as representatives of chambers of commerce, trade associations, or third-country institutions.

area expertise A knowledge of the basic systems in a particular region or market.

area structure An organizational structure in which geographic divisions are responsible for all manufacturing and marketing in their respective areas.

area studies Training programs that provide factual preparation prior to an overseas assignment.

arm's length price A price that unrelated parties would have reached.

autarky Self-sufficiency: a country that is not participating in international trade.

average cost method An accounting principle by which the value of inventory is estimated as the average cost of the items in inventory.

---

backtranslation The retranslation of text to the original language by a different person than the one who made the first translation. Useful to find translation errors.

backward innovation The development of a drastically simplified version of a product.

balance of payments (BOP) A statement of all transactions between one country and the rest of the world during a given period; a record of flows of goods, services, and investments across borders.

bank draft A financial withdrawal document drawn against a bank.

barter A direct exchange of goods of approximately equal value, with no money involved.

base salary Salary not including special payments such as allowances paid during overseas assignments.

bearer bond A bond owned officially by whoever is holding it.

bilateral negotiations Negotiations carried out between two nations focusing only on their interests.

bill of lading A contract between an exporter and a carrier indicating that the carrier has accepted responsibility for the goods and will provide transportation in return for payment.

---

black hole The situation that arises when an international marketer has a low-competence subsidiary—or none at all—in a highly strategic market.

boycott An organized effort to refrain from conducting business with a particular seller of goods or services; used in the international arena for political or economic reasons.

brain drain A migration of professional people from one country to another, usually for the purpose of improving their incomes or living conditions.

Bretton Woods Agreement An agreement reached in 1944 among finance ministers of 45 Western nations to establish a system of fixed exchange rates.

bribery The use of payments or favors to obtain some right or benefit to which the briber has no legal right; a criminal offense in the United States but a way of life in many countries.

Buddhism A religion that extends through Asia from Sri Lanka to Japan and has 334 million followers, emphasizing spiritual attainment rather than worldly goods.

buffer stock Stock of a commodity kept on hand to prevent a shortage in times of unexpectedly great demand; under international commodity and price agreements, the stock controlled by an elected or appointed manager for the purpose of managing the price of the commodity.

bulk service Ocean shipping provided on contract either for individual voyages or for prolonged periods of time.

buy-back A refinement of simple barter with one party supplying technology or equipment that enables the other party to produce goods, which are then used to pay for the technology or equipment that was supplied.

---

capital account An account in the BOP statement that records transactions involving borrowing, lending, and investing across borders.

capital budget The financial evaluation of a proposed investment to determine whether the expected returns are sufficient to justify the investment expenses.

capital flight The flow of private funds abroad because investors believe that the return on investment or the safety of capital is not sufficiently ensured in their own countries.

Caribbean Basin Initiative (CBI) Extended trade preferences to Caribbean countries and granted them special access to the markets of the United States.

carriage and insurance paid to (CIP) The price quoted by an exporter for shipments not involving waterway transport, including insurance.

carriage paid to (CPT) The price quoted by an exporter for shipments not involving waterway transport, not including insurance.

cartel An association of producers of a particular good, consisting either of private firms or of nations, formed for the purpose of suppressing the market forces affecting prices.

cash pooling Used by multinational firms to centralize individual units' cash flows, resulting in less spending or foregone interest unnecessary cash balances.

center of excellence The location of product development outside the home country because of an advantage of skills.

central plan The economic plan for the nation devised by the government of a socialist state; often a five-year plan that stipulated the quantities of industrial goods to be produced.

centralization The concentrating of control and strategic decision making at headquarters.

change agent A person or institution who facilitates change in a firm or in a host country.

channel design The length and width of the distribution channel.

Christianity The largest world religion with 1.8 billion followers; Protestantism encourages work and accumulation of wealth.

code law Law based on a comprehensive set of written statutes.

codetermination A management approach in which employees are represented on supervisory boards to facilitate communication and collaboration between management and labor.

commercial invoice A bill for transported goods that describes the merchandise and its total cost and lists the addresses of the shipper and seller and delivery and payment terms.

Commercial Service A department of the U.S. Department of Commerce that gathers information and assists business executives in business abroad.

Committee on Foreign Investments in the United States (CFIUS) A federal committee, chaired by the U.S. Treasury, with the responsibility to review major foreign investments to determine whether national security or related concerns are at stake.

commodity price agreement An agreement involving both buyers and sellers to manage the price of a particular commodity, but often only when the price moves outside a predetermined range.

common agricultural policy (CAP) An integrated system of subsidies and rebates applied to agricultural interests in the European Union.

common law Law based on tradition and depending less on written statutes and codes than on precedent and custom—used in the United States.

common market A group of countries that agree to remove all barriers to trade among members, to establish a common trade policy with respect to nonmembers, and also to allow mobility for factors of production—labor, capital, and technology.

communication services Services that are provided in the areas of videotext, home banking, and home shopping, among others.

comparative advantage The ability to produce a good or service more cheaply, relative to other goods and services, than is possible in other countries.

competitive advantage The ability to produce a good or service more cheaply than other countries due to favorable factor conditions and demand conditions, strong related and supporting industries, and favorable firm strategy, structure, and rivalry conditions.

competitive assessment A research process that consists of matching markets to corporate strengths and providing an analysis of the best potential for specific offerings.

composition of trade The ratio of primary commodities to manufactured goods in a country's trade.

concentration strategy The market expansion policy that involves concentrating on a small number of markets.

confiscation The forceful government seizure of a company without compensation for the assets seized.

Confucianism A code of conduct with 150 million followers throughout Asia, stressing loyalty and relationships.

consulting services Services that are provided in the areas of management expertise on such issues as transportation and logistics.

container ships Ships designed to carry standardized containers, which greatly facilitate loading and unloading as well as intermodal transfers.

contract manufacturing Outsourcing the actual production of goods so that the corporation can focus on research, development, and marketing.

contractual hedging A multinational firm's use of contracts to minimize its transaction exposure.

contributor A national subsidiary with a distinctive competence, such as product development.

control Refers to restrictions on what a foreign investor may own or control in another country.

coordinated decentralization The providing of overall corporate strategy by headquarters while granting subsidiaries the freedom to implement it within established ranges.

coordinated intervention A currency value management method whereby the central banks of the major nations simultaneously intervene in the currency markets, hoping to change a currency's value.

corporate income tax A tax applied to all residual earnings, regardless of what is retained or what is distributed as dividends.

corruption Payments or favors made to officials in return for services.

correspondent banks Banks located in different countries and unrelated by ownership that have a reciprocal agreement to provide services to each other's customers.

cost and freight (CFR) Seller quotes a price for the goods, including the cost of transportation to the named port of debarkation. Cost and choice of insurance are left to the buyer.

cost, insurance, and freight (CIF) Seller quotes a price including insurance, all transportation, and miscellaneous charges to the point of debarkation from the vessel or aircraft.

cost leadership A pricing tactic where a company offers an identical product or service at a lower cost than the competition.

cost of communication The cost of communicating electronically or by telephone with other locations. These costs have been drastically reduced through the use of fiber-optic cables.

cost of living allowance (COLA) An allowance paid during assignment overseas to enable the employee to maintain the same standard of living as at home.

cost-plus method A pricing policy in which there is a full allocation of foreign and domestic costs to the product.

counterpurchase A refinement of simple barter that unlinks the timing of the two transactions.

coups d'etat A forced change in a country's government, often resulting in attacks of foreign firms and policy changes by the new government.

critical commodities list A U.S. Department of Commerce file containing information about products that are either particularly sensitive to national security or controlled for other purposes.

cross-marketing activities A reciprocal arrangement whereby each partner provides the other access to its markets for a product.

cross rates Exchange rate quotations which do not include the U.S. dollar as one of the two currencies quoted.

cross-subsidization The use of resources accumulated in one part of the world to fight a competitive battle in another.

cultural assimilator A program in which trainees for overseas assignments must respond to scenarios of specific situations in a particular country.

cultural convergence Increasing similarity among cultures accelerated by technological advances.

cultural risk The risk of business blunders, poor customer relations, and wasted negotiations that results when firms fail to understand and adapt to the differences between their own and host countries' cultures.

cultural universals Manifestations of the total way of life of any group of people.

culture shock The more pronounced reactions to the psychological disorientation that most people feel when they move for an extended period of time in to a markedly different culture.

cumulative transaction adjustment (CTA) A balance sheet account created to maintain a balanced translation for the purchase of a subsidiary; the CTA has no effect on the firm until the subsidiary is either sold or liquidated.

currency flows The movement of currency from nation to nation, which in turn determine exchange rates.

currency swap An agreement by which a firm exchanges or swaps its debt service payments in one currency for debt service payments in a different currency. The equivalent of the interest rate swap, only the currency of denomination of the debt is different.

current account An account in the BOP statement that records the results of transactions involving merchandise, services, and unilateral transfers between countries.

current transfer A current account on the Balance of Payments statement that records gifts from the residents of one country to the residents of another.

customer involvement The active participation of customers; a characteristic of services in that customers often are actively involved in the provision of services they consume.

customer service A total corporate effort aimed at customer satisfaction; customer service levels in terms of responsiveness that inventory policies permit for a given situation.

customer structure An organizational structure in which divisions are formed on the basis of customer groups.

customs union Collaboration among trading countries in which members dismantle barriers to trade in goods and services and also establish a common trade policy with respect to nonmembers.

data privacy Electronic information security that restricts secondary use of data according to laws and preferences of the subjects.

decentralization The granting of a high degree of autonomy to subsidiaries.

deemed exports Addresses people rather than products where knowledge transfer could lead to a breach of export restrictions.

delivery duty paid (DDP) Seller delivers the goods, with import duties paid, including inland transportation from import point to the buyer's premises.

delivery duty unpaid (DDU) Only the destination customs duty and taxes are paid by the consignee.

Delphi studies A research tool using a group of participants with expertise in the area of concern to state and rank major future developments.

density Weight-to-volume ratio; often used to determine shipping rates.

deregulation Removal of government regulation.

differentiation Takes advantage of the company's real or perceived uniqueness on elements such as design or after-sales service.

direct intervention The process governments used in the 1970s if they wished to alter the current value of their currency. It was done by simply buying or selling their own currency in the market using their reserves of other major currencies.

direct investment account An account in the BOP statement that records investments with an expected maturity of more than one year and an investor's ownership position of at least 10 percent.

direct involvement Participation by a firm in international business in which the firm works with foreign customers or markets to establish a relationship.

direct quotation A foreign exchange quotation that specifies the amount of home country currency needed to purchase one unit of foreign currency.

direct taxes Taxes applied directly to income.

discriminatory regulations Regulations that impose larger operating costs on foreign service providers than on local competitors, that provide subsidies to local firms only, or that deny competitive opportunities to foreign suppliers.

distributed earnings The proportion of a firm's net income after taxes which is paid out or distributed to the stockholders of the firm.

distributor   A representative or intermediary for the firm that purchases products from the firm, takes title, and assumes the selling risk.

diversification   A market expansion policy characterized by growth in a relatively large number of markets or market segments.

division of labor   The premise of modern industrial production where each stage in the production of a good is performed by one individual separately, rather than one individual being responsible for the entire production of the good.

domestication   Government demand for partial transfer of ownership and management responsibility from a foreign company to local entities, with or without compensation.

double-entry bookkeeping   Accounting methodology where each transaction gives rise to both a debit and a credit of the same currency amount. It is used in the construction of the Balance of Payments.

dual pricing   Price-setting strategy in which the export price may be based on marginal cost pricing, resulting in a lower export price than domestic price; may open the company to dumping charges.

dual use items   Goods and services that are useful for both military and civilian purposes.

dumping   Selling goods overseas at a price lower than in the exporter's home market, or at a price below the cost of production, or both.

....

e-commerce   The ability to offer goods and services over the Web.

economic and monetary union (EMU)   The ideal among European leaders that economic integration should move beyond the four freedoms; specifically, it entails (1) closer coordination of economic policies to promote exchange rate stability and convergence of inflation rates and growth rates, (2) creation of a European central bank, and (3) replacement of national monetary authorities by the European Central Bank and adoption of the euro as the European currency.

economic exposure   The potential for long-term effects on a firm's value as the result of changing currency values.

economic infrastructure   The transportation, energy, and communication systems in a country.

economic security   Perception of a business activity as having an effect on a country's financial resources, often used to restrict competition from firms outside the country.

economic union   A union among trading countries that has the characteristics of a common market and also harmonizes monetary policies, taxation, and government spending and uses a common currency.

economies of scale   Production economies made possible by the output of larger quantities.

education allowance   Reimbursement by company for dependent educational expenses incurred while a parent is assigned overseas.

effective tax rate   Actual total tax burden after including all applicable tax liabilities and credits.

embargo   A governmental action, usually prohibiting trade entirely, for a decidedly adversarial or political rather than economic purpose.

engineering services   Services that are provided in the areas of construction, design, and engineering.

environmental protection   Actions taken by governments to protect the environment and resources of a country.

environmental scanning   Obtaining ongoing data about a country.

ethnocentric   Tending to regard one's own culture as superior; tending to be home-market oriented.

ethnocentrism   The regarding of one's own culture as superior to others'.

euro   A single currency proposed for use by the European Union that will eventually replace all the individual currencies of the participating member states.

Eurobond   A bond that is denominated in a currency other than the currency of the country in which the bond is sold.

Eurocurrency   A bank deposit in a currency other than the currency of the country where the bank is located; not confined to banks in Europe.

Eurodollars   U.S. dollars deposited in banks outside the United States; not confined to banks in Europe.

Euromarkets   Money and capital markets in which transactions are denominated in a currency other than that of the place of the transaction; not confined to Europe.

European Monetary System (EMS)   An organization formed in 1979 by eight EC members committed to maintaining the values of their currencies within a 2 1/4 percent of each other's.

European terms   Quoting a currency rate as a country's currency against the U.S. dollar (e.g., yen/U.S. dollars).

European Union   The January 1, 1994, organization created by the 12 member countries of the European Community (now 15 members).

exchange controls   Controls on the movement of capital in and out of a country, sometimes imposed when the country faces a shortage of foreign currency.

exchange rate mechanism (ERM)   The acceptance of responsibility by a European Monetary System member to actively maintain its own currency within agreed-upon limits versus other member currencies established by the European Monetary System.

expatriate   One living in a foreign land; a corporate manager assigned to an overseas location.

experiential knowledge   Knowledge acquired through involvement (as opposed to information, which is obtained through communication, research, and education).

experimentation   A research tool to determine the effects of a variable on an operation.

export complaint systems   Allow customers to contact the original supplier of a product in order to inquire about products, make suggestions, or present complaints.

export-control system   A system designed to deny or at least delay the acquisition of strategically important goods to adversaries; in the United States, based on the Export Administration Act and the Munitions Control Act.

export license   A license obtainable from the U.S. Department of Commerce Bureau of Export Administration, which is responsible for administering the Export Administration Act.

export management companies (EMCs) Domestic firms that specialize in performing international business services as commission representatives or as distributors.

export trading company (ETC) The result of 1982 legislation to improve the export performance of small and medium-sized firms, the export trading company allows businesses to band together to export or offer export services. Additionally, the law permits bank participation in trading companies and relaxes antitrust provisions.

expropriation The government takeover of a company with compensation frequently at a level lower than the investment value of the company's assets.

external economies of scale Lower production costs resulting from the free mobility of factors of production in a common market.

extraterritoriality An exemption from rules and regulations of one country that may challenge the national sovereignty of another. The application of one country's rules and regulations abroad.

ex-works (EXW) Price quotes that apply only at the point of origin; the seller agrees to place the goods at the disposal of the buyer at the specified place on a date or within a fixed period.

. . . .

factor intensities The proportion of capital input to labor input used in the production of a good.

factor mobility The ability to freely move factors of production across borders, as among common market countries.

factor proportions theory Systematic explanation of the source of comparative advantage.

factors of production All inputs into the production process, including capital, labor, land, and technology.

factual cultural knowledge Knowledge obtainable from specific country studies published by governments, private companies, and universities and also available in the form of background information from facilitating agencies such as banks, advertising agencies, and transportation companies.

field experience Experience acquired in actual rather than laboratory settings; training that exposes a corporate manager to a different cultural environment for a limited amount of time.

FIFO Method of valuation of inventories for accounting purposes, meaning First-In-First-Out. The principle rests on the assumption that costs should be charged against revenue in the order in which they occur.

financial incentives Monetary offers intended to motivate; special funding designed to attract foreign direct investors that may take the form of land or building, loans, or loan guarantees.

financial infrastructure Facilitating financial agencies in a country; for example, banks.

financing cash flows The cash flows arising from the firms funding activities.

fiscal incentives Incentives used to attract foreign direct investment that provide specific tax measures to attract the investor.

fixed exchange rate The government of a country officially declares that its currency is convertible into a fixed amount of some other currency.

flextime A modification of work scheduling that allows workers to determine their own starting and ending times within a broad range of available hours.

floating exchange rate Under this system, the government possesses no responsibility to declare that its currency is convertible into a fixed amount of some other currency; this diminishes the role of official reserves.

focus group A research technique in which representatives of a proposed target audience contribute to market research by participating in an unstructured discussion.

foreign availability The ability of a firm's products to be obtained in markets outside the firm's home country.

foreign bond Bonds that are issued by a country's borrowers in other countries, subject to the same restrictions as bonds issued by domestic borrowers.

Foreign Corrupt Practices Act A 1977 act making it a crime for U.S. executives of publicly traded firms to bribe a foreign official in order to obtain business.

foreign direct investment The establishment or expansion of operations of a firm in a foreign country. Like all investments, it assumes a transfer of capital.

foreign market opportunity analysis Broad-based research to obtain information about the general variables of a target market outside a firm's home country.

foreign policy The area of public policy concerned with relationships with other countries.

foreign service premium A financial incentive to accept an assignment overseas, usually paid as a percentage of the base salary.

foreign tax credit Credit applied to home-country tax payments due for taxes paid abroad.

foreign trade zones Special areas where foreign goods may be held or processed without incurring duties and taxes.

Fortress Europe Suspicion raised by trading partners of Western Europe, claiming that the integration of the European Union may result in increased restrictions on trade and investment by outsiders.

forward contracts Agreements between firms and banks which permit the firm to either sell or buy a specific foreign currency at a future date at a known price.

forward pricing Setting the price of a product based on its anticipated demand before it has been introduced to the market.

forward rates Contracts that provide for two parties to exchange currencies on a future date at an agreed-upon exchange rate.

franchising A form of licensing that allows a distributor or retailer exclusive rights to sell a product or service in a specified area.

free alongside ship (FAS) Exporter quotes a price for the goods, including charges for delivery of the goods alongside a vessel at a port. Seller handles cost of unloading and wharfage; loading, ocean transportation, and insurance are left to the buyer.

free carrier (FCA) Applies only at a designated inland shipping point. Seller is responsible for loading goods into the means of transportation; buyer is responsible for all subsequent expenses.

free on board (FOB) Applies only to vessel shipments. Seller quotes a price covering all expenses up to and including delivery of goods on an overseas vessel provided by or for the buyer.

free trade area An area in which all barriers to trade among member countries are removed, although sometimes only for certain goods or services.

Free Trade Area of the Americas (FTAA) A hemispheric trade zone covering all of the Americas. Organizers hope for it to be operational by 2005.

freight forwarders Specialists in handling international transportation by contracting with carriers on behalf of shippers.

functional structure An organizational structure in which departments are formed on the basis of functional areas such as production, marketing, and finance.

gap analysis Analysis of the difference between market potential and actual sales.

General Agreement on Tariffs and Trade (GATT) An international code of tariffs and trade rules signed by 23 nations in 1947; headquartered in Geneva, Switzerland; 132 members currently; now part of the World Trade Organization.

General Agreement on Trade in Services (GATS) A legally enforceable pact among GATT participants that covers trade and investments in the services sector.

glasnost The Soviet policy of encouraging the free exchange of ideas and discussion of problems, pluralistic participation in decision making, and increased availability of information.

global account management Global customers of a company may be provided with special services including a single point of contact for domestic and international operations and consistent worldwide service.

global Worldwide interdependencies of financial markets, technology, and living standards.

globalization Awareness, understanding, and response to global developments as they affect a company.

glocalization A term coined to describe the networked global organization approach to an organizational structure.

gold standard A standard for international currencies in which currency values were stated in terms of gold.

goods trade An account of the BOP statement that records funds used for merchandise imports and funds obtained from merchandise exports.

government regulation Interference in the marketplace by governments.

gray market A market entered in a way not intended by the manufacturer of the goods.

hardship allowance An allowance paid during an assignment to an overseas area that requires major adaptation.

hedge To counterbalance a present sale or purchase with a sale or purchase for future delivery as a way to minimize loss due to price fluctuations; to make counterbalancing sales or purchases in the international market as protection against adverse movements in the exchange rate.

high-context cultures Cultures in which behavioral and environmental nuances are an important means of conveying information.

Hinduism With 750 million followers, a way of life rather than a religion, with economic and other attainment dictated by the caste into which its followers are born.

housing allowance An allowance paid during assignment overseas to provide living quarters.

implementor The typical subsidiary role, which involves implementing strategy that originates with headquarters.

import substitution A policy for economic growth adopted by many developing countries that involves the systematic encouragement of domestic production of goods formerly imported.

income elasticity of demand A means of describing change in demand in relative response to a change in income.

incoterms International Commerce Terms. Widely accepted terms used in quoting export prices.

indirect involvement Participation by a firm in international business through an intermediary, in which the firm does not deal with foreign customers or firms.

indirect quotation Foreign exchange quotation that specifies the units of foreign currency that could be purchased with one unit of the home currency.

indirect taxes Taxes applied to non-income items, such as value-added taxes, excise taxes, tariffs, and so on.

information system Can provide the decision maker with basic data for most ongoing decisions.

infrastructure shortages Problems in a country's underlying physical structure, such as transportation, utilities, and so on.

input-output analysis A method for estimating market activities and potential that measures the factor inflows into production and the resultant outflow of products.

insurance services Services that are provided in underwriting, risk evaluation, and operations.

intangibility The inability to be seen, tasted, or touched in a conventional sense; the characteristic of services that most strongly differentiates them from products.

interbank interest rates The interest rate charged by banks to banks in the major international financial centers.

interest rate swap A firm uses its credit standing to borrow capital at low fixed rates and exchange its interest payments with a slightly lower credit-rated borrower who has debt service payments at floating rates.

intermodal movements The transfer of freight from one mode or type of transportation to another.

internal bank A multinational firm's financial management tool that actually acts as a bank to coordinate finances among its units.

internal economies of scale Lower production costs resulting from greater production for an enlarged market.

internalization Occurs when a firm establishes its own multinational operation, keeping information that is at the core of its competitiveness within the firm.

international bond Bond issued in domestic capital markets by foreign borrowers (foreign bonds) or issued in the Eurocurrency markets in currency different from that of the home currency of the borrower (Eurobonds).

international competitiveness The ability of a firm, an industry, or a country to compete in the international marketplace at a stable or rising standard of living.

international debt load Total accumulated negative net investment of a nation.

international law The body of rules governing relationships between sovereign states; also certain treaties and agreements respected by a number of countries.

International Monetary Fund (IMF) A specialized agency of the United Nations established in 1944. An international financial institution for dealing with Balance of Payment problems; the first international monetary authority with at least some degree of power over national authorities.

International Trade Organization (ITO) A forwardlooking approach to international trade and investment embodied in the 1948 Havana Charter; due to disagreements among sponsoring nations, its provisions were never ratified.

interpretive knowledge An acquired ability to understand and appreciate the nuances of foreign cultural traits and patterns.

interviews A face-to-face research tool to obtain in-depth information.

intra-industry trade The simultaneous export and import of the same good by a country. It is of interest due to the traditional theory that a country will either export or import a good, but not do both at the same time.

intranet A process that integrates a company's information assets into a single accessible system using Internet-based technologies such as e-mail, news groups, and the World Wide Web.

inventory Materials on hand for use in the production process; also finished goods on hand.

inventory carrying costs The expense of maintaining inventories.

investment income The proportion of net income that is paid back to a parent company.

Islam A religion that has over 1 billion followers from the west coast of Africa to the Philippines, as well as in the rest of the world and is supportive of entrepreneurism but not of exploitation.

joint occurrence Occurrence of a phenomenon affecting the business environment in several locations simultaneously.

Joint Research and Development Act A 1984 act that allows both domestic and foreign firms to participate in joint basic-research efforts without fear of U.S. antitrust action.

just-in-time inventory Materials scheduled to arrive precisely when they are needed on a production line.

lags Paying a debt late to take advantage of exchange rates.

land bridge Transfer of ocean freight on land among various modes of transportation.

Law of One Price The theory that the relative prices of any single good between countries, expressed in each country's currency, is representative of the proper or appropriate exchange rate value.

leads Paying a debt early to take advantage of exchange rates.

Leontief Paradox Wassily Leontief's studies of U.S. trade indicated that the United States was a labor-abundant country, exporting labor-intensive products. This was a paradox because of the general belief that the United States was a capital-abundant country which should be exporting capital-intensive products.

LIBOR The London InterBank Offer Rate. The rate of interest charged by top-quality international banks on loans to similar quality banks in London. This interest rate is often used in both domestic and international markets as the rate of interest on loans and other financial agreements.

licensing A firm gives a license to another firm to produce or package its product.

licensing agreement An agreement in which one firm permits another to use its intellectual property in exchange for compensation.

LIFO Method of valuation of inventories for accounting purposes, meaning Last-In-First-Out. The principle rests on the practice of recording inventory by "layer" of the cost at which it was incurred.

liner service Ocean shipping characterized by regularly scheduled passage on established routes.

lingua franca The language habitually used among people of diverse speech to facilitate communication.

lobbyist Typically, a well-connected person or firm that is hired by a business to influence the decision making of policymakers and legislators.

local content Regulations to gain control over foreign investment by ensuring that a large share of the product is locally produced or a larger share of the profit is retained in the country.

location decision A decision concerning the number of facilities to establish and where they should be situated.

logistics platform Vital to a firm's competitive position, it is determined by a location's ease and convenience of market reach under favorable cost circumstances.

longitudinal analysis A method of estimating market demand by factoring in the time lag of demand patterns.

low-context cultures Cultures in which most information is conveyed explicitly rather than through behavioral and environmental nuances.

Maastricht Treaty The agreement signed in December 1991 in Maastricht, the Netherlands, in which European Community members agreed to a specific timetable and set of necessary conditions to create a single currency for the EU countries.

macroeconomic level Level at which trading relationships affect individual markets.

management contract An international business alternative in which the firm sells its expertise in running a company while avoiding the risk or benefit of ownership.

managerial commitment The desire and drive on the part of management to act on an idea and to support it in the long run.

maquiladoras Mexican border plants that make goods and parts or process food for export back to the United States. They benefit from lower labor costs.

marginal cost method This method considers the direct costs of producing and selling goods for export as the floor beneath which prices cannot be set.

market audit A method of estimating market size by adding together local production and imports, with exports subtracted from the total.

market-differentiated pricing Price-setting strategy based on demand rather than cost.

market segment Overlapping ranges of trade targets with common ground and levels of sophistication.

market transparency Availability of full disclosure and information about key market factors such as supply, demand, quality, service, and prices.

marketing infrastructure Facilitating marketing agencies in a country; for example, market research firms, channel members.

mass customization Working with existing product technology to create specific product bundles, resulting in a customized product for a particular customer.

materials management The timely movement of raw materials, parts, and supplies into and through the firm.

matrix structure An organizational structure that uses functional and divisional structures simultaneously.

maximization of shareholder value The ultimate goal of the management of a multinational firm is to increase the value of the shareholder's investment as much as possible.

media strategy Strategy applied to the selection of media vehicles and the development of a media schedule.

mercantilism Political and economic policy in the seventeenth and early eighteenth centuries aimed at increasing a nation's wealth and power by encouraging the export of goods in return for gold.

microeconomic level Level of business concerns that affect an individual firm or industry.

mininationals Newer companies with sales between $200 million and $1 billion that are able to serve the world from a handful of manufacturing bases.

minority participation Participation by a group having less than the number of votes necessary for control.

mixed aid credits Credits at rates composed partially of commercial interest rates and partially of highly subsidized developmental aid interest rates.

mixed structure An organizational structure that combines two or more organizational dimensions; for example, products, areas, or functions.

Most Favored Nation (MFN) A term describing a GATT clause that calls for

member countries to grant other member countries the same most favorable treatment they accord any country concerning imports and exports.

multidomestic strategy A business strategy where each individual country organization is operated as a profit center.

multilateral trade negotiations Trade negotiations among more than two parties; the intricate relationships among trading countries.

multinational corporations Companies that invest in countries around the globe.

national security The ability of a nation to protect its internal values from external threats.

national sovereignty The supreme right of nations to determine national policies; freedom from external control.

natural hedging The structuring of a firm's operations so that cash flows by currency, inflows against outflows, are matched.

net errors and omissions account Makes sure the balance of payments (BOP) actually balances.

net present value (NPV) The sum of the present values of all cash inflows and outflows from an investment project discounted at the cost of capital.

netting Cash flow coordination between a corporation's global units so that only one smaller cash transfer must be made.

1992 White Paper A key document developed by the EC Commission to outline the further requirements necessary for a successful integration of the European Union.

nonfinancial incentives Nonmonetary offers intended to motivate; special offers designed to attract foreign direct investors that may take the form of guaranteed government purchases, special protection from competition, or improved infrastructure facilities.

nontariff barriers Barriers to trade, other than tariffs. Examples include buy-domestic campaigns, preferential treatment for domestic bidders, and restrictions on market entry of foreign products such as involved inspection procedures.

not-invented-here syndrome A defensive, territorial attitude that, if held by managers, can frustrate effective implementation of global strategies.

observation A research tool where the subjects' activity and behavior are observed.

ocean shipping The forwarding of freight by ocean carrier.

official reserves account An account in the BOP statement that shows (1) the change in the amount of funds immediately available to a country for making international payments and (2) the borrowing and lending that has taken place between the monetary authorities of different countries either directly or through the International Monetary Fund.

offshore banking The use of banks or bank branches located in low-tax countries, often Caribbean islands, to raise and hold capital for multinational operations.

one-stop logistics Allows shippers to buy all the transportation modes and functional services from a single carrier.

operating cash flows The cash flows arising from the firm's everyday business activities.

operating or service lease A lease that transfers most but not all benefits and costs inherent in the ownership of the property to the lessee. Payments do not fully cover the cost of purchasing the asset or incurring the liability.

operating risk The danger of interference by governments or other groups in one's corporate operations abroad.

opportunity cost Cost incurred by a firm as the result of foreclosure of other sources of profit; for example, for the licenser in a licensing agreement, the cost of forgoing alternatives such as exports or direct investment.

order cycle time The total time that passes between the placement of an order and the receipt of the merchandise.

orientation program A program that familiarizes new workers with their roles; the preparation of employees for assignment overseas.

ownership risk The risk inherent in maintaining ownership of property abroad. The exposure of foreign owned assets to governmental intervention.

Patent Cooperations Treaty (PCT) An agreement that outlines procedures for filing one international patent application rather than individual national applications.

pax Americana An American peace between 1945 through 1990 that led to increased international business transactions.

pax Romana Two relatively peaceful centuries in the Roman Empire.

pension liabilities The accumulating obligations of employers to fund the retirement or pension plans of employees.

perestroika A movement to fundamentally reform the Soviet economy by improving the overall technological and industrial base and the quality of life for Soviet citizens through increased availability of food, housing, and consumer goods.

perishability Susceptibility to deterioration; the characteristic of services that makes them difficult to store.

physical distribution The movement of finished products from suppliers to customers.

Plaza Agreement An accord reached in 1985 by the Group of Five that held that the major nations should join in a coordinated effort to bring down the value of the U.S. dollar.

political risk The risk of loss by an international corporation of assets, earning power, or managerial control as a result of political actions by the host country.

political union A group of countries that have common foreign policy and security policy and that share judicial cooperation.

population increase The effect of changes in countries' populations on economic matters.

population stabilization An attempt to control rapid increases in population and ensure that economic development exceeds population growth.

portfolio investment account An account in the BOP statement that records investments in assets with an original maturity of more than one year and where an investor's ownership position is less than 10 percent.

portfolio models Tools that have been proposed for use in market and competitive analysis. They typically involve two measures—internal strength and external attractiveness.

ports Harbor towns or cities where ships may take on or discharge cargo; the lack of ports and port services is the greatest constraint in ocean shipping.

positioning The perception by consumers of a firm's product in relation to competitors' products.

preferential policies Government policies that favor certain (usually domestic) firms; for example, the use of national carriers for the transport of government freight even when more economical alternatives exist.

price controls Government regulation of the prices of goods and services; control of the prices of imported goods or services as a result of domestic political pressures.

price escalation The establishing of export prices far in excess of domestic prices—often due to a long distribution channel and frequent markups.

primary data Data obtained directly for a specific research purpose through interviews, focus groups, surveys, observation, or experimentation.

private placement The sale of debt securities to private or institutional investors without going through a public issuance like that of a bond issue or equity issue.

privatization A policy of shifting government operations to privately owned enterprises to cut budget costs and ensure more efficient services.

process structure A variation of the functional structure in which departments are formed on the basis of production processes.

product cycle theory A theory that views products as passing through four stages: introduction, growth, maturity, decline; during which the location of production moves from industrialized to lower-cost developing nations.

product differentiation The effort to build unique differences or improvements into products.

product structure An organizational structure in which product divisions are responsible for all manufacturing and marketing.

production possibilities frontier A theoretical method of representing the total productive capabilities of a nation used in the formulation of classical and modern trade theory.

promotional message The content of an advertisement or a publicity release.

protectionistic legislation A trade policy that restricts trade to or from one country to another country.

proxy information Data used as a substitute for more desirable data that are unobtainable.

punitive tariff A tax on an imported good or service intended to punish a trading partner.

purchasing power parity (PPP) A theory that the prices of tradable goods will tend to equalize across countries.

qualitative information Data that have been analyzed to provide a better understanding, description, or prediction of given situations, behavioral patterns, or underlying dimensions.

quality circles Groups of workers who meet regularly to discuss issues related to productivity.

quality of life The standard of living combined with environmental factors, it determines the level of well-being of individuals.

quality of work life Various corporate efforts in the areas of personal and professional development undertaken with the objectives of increasing employee satisfaction and increasing productivity.

quotas Legal restrictions on the import quantity of particular goods, imposed by governments as barriers to trade.

reference groups Groups such as the family, co-workers, and professional and trade associations that provide the values and attitudes that influence and shape behavior, including consumer behavior.

reinvoicing The policy of buying goods from one unit and selling them to a second unit and reinvoicing the sale to the next unit, to take advantage of favorable exchange rates.

reliability Dependability; the predictability of the outcome of an action. For example, the reliability of arrival time for ocean freight or airfreight.

representative office An office of an international bank established in a foreign country to serve the bank's customers in the area in an advisory capacity; does not take deposits or make loans.

reverse distribution A system responding to environmental concerns that ensures a firm can retrieve a product from the market for subsequent use, recycling, or disposal.

roll-on-roll-off (RORO) Transportation vessels built to accommodate trucks, which can drive on in one port and drive off at their destinations.

royalty The compensation paid by one firm to another under an agreement.

....

sanction A governmental action, usually consisting of a specific coercive trade measure, that distorts the free flow of trade for an adversarial or political purpose rather than an economic one.

scenario building The identification of crucial variables and determining their effects on different cases or approaches.

sea bridge The transfer of freight among various modes of transportation at sea.

secondary data Data originally collected to serve another purpose than the one in which the researcher is currently interested.

self-management Independent decision making; a high degree of worker involvement in corporate decision making.

self-reference criterion The unconscious reference to one's own cultural values.

selling forward A market transaction in which the seller promises to sell currency at a certain future date at a prespecified price.

sensitivity training Training in human relations that focuses on personal and interpersonal interactions; training that focuses on enhancing an expatriate's flexibility in situations quite different from those at home.

service capacity The maximum level at which a service provider is able to provide services to customers.

service consistency Uniform quality of service.

service heterogeneity The difference from one delivery of a product to another delivery of the same product as a result of the inability to control the production and quality of the process.

services trade The international exchange of personal or professional services, such as financial and banking services, construction, and tourism.

shipper's order A negotiable bill of lading that can be bought, sold, or traded while the subject goods are still in transit and that is used for letter of credit transactions.

Single Europe Act The legislative basis for the European Integration.

Smoot-Hawley Act A 1930 act that raised import duties to the highest rates ever imposed by the United States; designed to promote domestic production, it resulted in the downfall of the world trading system.

social infrastructure The housing, health, educational, and other social systems in a country.

social stratification The division of a particular population into classes.

sogoshosha A large Japanese general trading company.

special economic zones Areas created by a country to attract foreign investors, in which there are no tariffs, substantial tax incentives, and low prices for land and labor.

specie Gold and silver.

spot rates Contracts that provide for two parties to exchange currencies with delivery in two business days.

standard of living The level of material affluence of a group or nation, measured as a composite of quantities and qualities of goods.

standard worldwide pricing Price-setting strategy based on average unit costs of fixed, variable, and export-related costs.

state-owned enterprise A corporate form that has emerged in non-Communist countries, primarily for reasons of national security and economic security.

straight bill of lading A nonnegotiable bill of lading usually used in prepaid transactions in which the transported goods involved are delivered to a specific individual or company.

strategic alliances A new term for collaboration among firms, often similar to joint ventures.

strategic leader A highly competent firm located in a strategically critical market.

supply-chain management Results where a series of value-adding activities connect a company's supply side with its demand side.

surveys Typically, the use of questionnaires to obtain quantifiable research information.

systems concept A concept of logistics based on the notion that materials-flow activities are so complex that they can be considered only in the context of their interaction.

....

tariffs Taxes on imported goods and services, instituted by governments as a means to raise revenue and as barriers to trade.

tax equalization Reimbursement by the company when an employee in an overseas assignment pays taxes at a higher rate than if he or she were at home.

tax policy A means by which countries may control foreign investors.

teaching services Services that are provided in the areas of training and motivating as well as in teaching of operational, managerial, and theoretical issues.

team building A process that enhances the cohesiveness of a department or group by helping members learn how to organize their work and assume responsibility for it.

technology transfer The transfer of systematic knowledge for the manufacture of a product, the application of a process, or the rendering of a service.

"tentative U.S. tax" The calculation of U.S. taxes on foreign source incomes to estimate U.S. tax payments.

terrorism Illegal and violent acts toward property and people.

theocracy A legal perspective based on religious practices and interpretations.

total cost concept A decision concept that uses cost as a basis for measurement in order to evaluate and optimize logistical activities.

tourism The economic benefit of money spent in a country or region by travelers from outside the area.

tracking The capability of a shipper to track goods at any point during the shipment.

trade creation A benefit of economic integration; the benefit to a particular country when a group of countries trade a product freely among themselves but maintain common barriers to trade with nonmembers.

trade diversion   A cost of economic integration; the cost to a particular country when a group of countries trade a product freely among themselves but maintain common barriers to trade with nonmembers.

trade draft   A withdrawal document drawn against a company.

trade-off concept   A decision concept that recognizes linkages within the decision system.

trade policy measures   Mechanisms used to influence and alter trade relationships.

trade promotion authority   The right to negotiate, accept, or reject trade treaties and agreements with minimal amendments by other parties.

trading blocs   Formed by agreements among countries to establish links through movement of goods, services, capital, and labor across borders.

tramp service   Ocean shipping via irregular routes, scheduled only on demand.

transaction exposure   The potential for losses or gains when a firm is engaged in a transaction denominated in a foreign currency.

transfer prices   The prices at which a firm sells its products to its own subsidiaries and affiliates.

transfer risk   The danger of having one's ability to transfer profits or products in and out of a country inhibited by governmental rules and regulations.

transit time   The period between departure and arrival of a carrier.

translation exposure   The potential effect on a firm's financial statements of a change in currency values.

Treaty of Rome   The original agreement that established the foundation for the formation of the European Economic Community.

triangular arbitrage   The exchange of one currency for a second currency, the second for a third, and the third for the first in order to make a profit.

trigger mechanisms   Specific acts or stimuli that set off reactions.

turnkey operation   A specialized form of management contract between a customer and an organization to provide a complete operational system together with the skills needed for unassisted maintenance and operation.

undistributed earnings   The proportion of a firm's net income after taxes which is retained within the firm for internal purposes.

unsolicited order   An unplanned business opportunity that arises as a result of other activities.

unstructured data   Information collected for analysis with open-ended questions.

value-added tax (VAT)   A tax on the value added at each stage of the production and distribution process; a tax assessed in most European countries and also common among Latin American countries.

virtual team   A team of people who are based at various locations around the world and communicate through intranet and other electronic means to achieve a common goal.

voluntary restraint agreements   Trade-restraint agreements resulting in self-imposed restrictions not covered by the GATT rules; used to manage or distort trade flows. For example, Japanese restraints on the export of cars to the United States.

Webb-Pomerene Act   A 1918 statute that excludes from antitrust prosecution U.S. firms cooperating to develop foreign markets.

withholding taxes   Taxes applied to the payment of dividends, interest, or royalties by firms.

works council   Councils that provide labor a say in corporate decision making through a representative body that may consist entirely of workers or of a combination of managers and workers.

work redesign programs   Programs that alter jobs to increase both the quality of the work experience and productivity.

work scheduling   Preparing schedules of when and how long workers are at the workplace.

working capital management   The management of a firm's current assets (cash, accounts receivable, inventories) and current liabilities (accounts payable, short-term debt).

World Bank   An international financial institution created to facilitate trade.

world-class competitors   Multinational firms that can compete globally with domestic products.

World Trade Organization   The institution that supplanted GATT in 1995 to administer international trade and investment accords.

NAME INDEX

Aaker, David A., 531n40
ABB Strömberg, 523
Abdel-Latif, Abla M., 450n10
Abouzeid, Kamal M., xii
Accenture, 357
Adams, Patrick, 60n44
Adams, Roger, 461
Adler, Nancy J., 485n, 500, 501n35, 501n42, 559, 560n32
Agenor, Pierre-Richard, 163
Aggarwai, Raj, 472
Agnew, Joe, 60n39
Aheran, Raymond, 222n21
Aheroni, Yaur, xii
Ahmed, Zafar U., xii
Ajami, Riad, xii, 19n7
Akhter, Syed H., 364n34
Alam, Pervaiz, 364n34
Alber, Antone, 502n61
Aldi Group, 206
Al-Eryani, Mohammad F., 364n34
Alhashim, Dhia D., 472
Allied-Lyons, 436
Allied-Signal, 587
Alsegg, R. J., 531n54
Aman, Per, 530
Ambler, Tim, 59n–60n59, 60n43
America Online, 340
Andelman, David A., 264n14
Anderson, Erin, 450n8
Anderson, Joe, xii
Anderson, Larry, 192
Anderson, Sallie, 388
Anderson Consulting: as Accenture, 357
Anheuser-Busch: channel design and, 350
Antweiler, Werner, 160n, 182n, 588n
ARCO Chemical Co.: supply chain of, 388
Arend, Anthony Clark, 115
Arpan, Jeffery S., 472
Asea: and Brown Boveri, 496–497
AT&T: breakup of, 67; deregulation and, 376; globalization by, 523
Atari: Pong of, 11
Aubey, Robert, xii
Aurik, Johan C., 417n29
Austin, James, 500
Avicular Controls, Inc. (ACI): Pakistan International Airlines and, 585–590
Aviel, David, xii
AvtoVAZ of Russia, 598; General Motors and, 595–601; influence of, 600
Axtell, Roger, 59, 60n34
Ayal, Igal, 339n, 364n10
Aydin, Nizamettin, 302n27

Baalbaki, Imad B., 319n, 328n36
Bache, Ellyn, 59
Bachman, Vanessa, 302n24
Baerwald, Thomas J., 20n1
Baker, James C., 364n28
Baker, John, 602
Baker, Marilynn, xii

Balassa, Bela, 221n1
Baldwin, Richard, 221, 222n15
Baliga, B. R., 525n, 531n47
Ball, Jeffrey, 257n
Ballon, Marc, 375n
Ballou, Ronald H., 399n
Banco do Brasil, 110
Banks, Gary, 222n32
Bannister, Rebecca R., 221
Banyu Pharmaceutical, Ltd., 482
Barbash, Fred, 574n
Barber, Edwin L., III, 89n3
Barnard, Bruce, 84n
Barnes and Noble, 615
Barnett, Carole K., 500
Bartels, Robert, 364n2
Bartholomew, Susan, 631n
Bartlett, Christopher A., 500n6, 515n, 522n, 530, 531n24, 531n26, 531n35, 531n51
Basanes, Federico, 240
Bateson, John E. G., 386
Bathon, Greg, 60n40
Bäuerle, Iris, 301n6, 301n7
Bay, The (Quebec), 37
Beamish, Paul W., 302n46
Bean, L.L., 401
Becker, Tom, 302n16
Beckett, Paul, 550n
Behrman, Jack N., 80n
Bell companies, 67
BenDaniel, David J., 472
Benetton, 357
Benguela, Gabriel, 585, 589–590
Bennett, Peter D., 51n, 60n45
Benson-Armer, Richard, 531n30
Berezovsky, Boris, 599
Bergsten, C. Fred, 163
Berry, Leonard L., 386n1
Berthon, Jean Paul, 386n5
Berthon, Pierre, 386n5
Bertlesmann, 615
Bestor, Theodore C., 67n
Best Western Hotel, 548
Bezos, Jeff, 612, 614, 615, 616
Bhagwati, Jagdish, 142
Bhalla, Bharat B., xii
Bhandari, Jagdeep S., 163
Bhutto, Benazir, 587
Birkinshaw, Julian, 531n42
Birtwistle, Jannine, 462
Bizet, Jean-Pierre, 516n, 531n21
Black, J. Stewart, 56n, 476n, 500
Black & Decker, 510
Blackwell, Norman, 516n, 531n21
Blackwell, Roger D., 59n28
Blair, Tony, 578
Bleakley, Fred R., 16n
Blecker, Robert A., 559n9
Bleeke, Joel, 292n, 302n33, 501n28
Bloom, Helen, 480n, 501n8, 531n22
Bloom, Rob, 559
Bloomgarden, Kirk, 290n
Blustein, Paul, 3n, 114n22

Bodner, Paul M., 472
Body Shop, The, 413–414
Boeing: builders of 777, 69; international team at, 520; Lufthansa and, 436–438
Boliden Intertrade Inc., 498
Bond, Michael H., 60n47
Bonds, John, 609n
Borden, George A., 18
Boston Consulting Group, 279
Botafogo Jose, 210
Boutros, Mourad, 37n
Bowen, Margareta, 59n20
Bowersox, Donald J., 416
Bradley, S., 559n–560n26
Brand, Joseph L., 195n
Brealey, Richard A., 449
Bright, Christopher, 127n
Brislin, R. W., 59
British Airways, 357
British Coal, 461
Broadman, Harry G., 240n7
Broder, John M., 565n
Brooke, Michael Z., 302n39, 530n2
Brown, Dale, 382
Brown, Eryn, 364n41
Brown Boveri: Asea and, 496–497
Browning, Sharon, xii
Brownstein, Vivian, 89n19
Bryan, Anthony T., 88
BSO/Origin, 461
Buckley, Peter J., 140, 142
Burghardt, Guenther, 222n14
Burgi, Peter T., 57n
Burstein, Daniel, 240
Business Software Alliance, 346
Butscher, Stephen A., 364n30
Buxbaum, Peter, 416n18
Byrne, Patrick M., 416n2, 417n29

Callaghan, James, 79
Calvet, Jacques, 591
Campbell, 45
Campbell, Joan, 498n
Campbell, Polly, 559n19
Canna, Elizabeth, 417n34
CareNetInc, 286
Carlton, Jim, 222n28
Carrington, Tim, 536n
Caspar, Christian, 222n45
Casse, Pierre, 500
Casson, Mark, 89n18, 140, 142
Castaldi, Richard M., 283n
Caterpillar, 311, 350
Catlin, Linda, 59
Caudill, Lee M., 531n23
Caudron, Shari, 476n
Caves, Richard E., 139, 142
Cavusgil, S. Tamer, 88, 249n, 301n4, 301n9, 364n26
Cederholm, Lars, 518n, 531n25
Chandler, A. D., 531n17, 559
Chandler, Clay, 234n